42 95

508-67

Ch. 12
715-752

BUSINESS ASSOCIATIONS, AGENCY, PARTNERSHIPS, AND CORPORATIONS (1991)

William A. Klein, Professor of Law, University of California, Los Angeles.
Mark Ramseyer, Professor of Law, University of California, Los Angeles.

BUSINESS CRIME (1990)

Harry First, Professor of Law, New York University.

BUSINESS ORGANIZATION, see also Enterprise Organization

BUSINESS PLANNING (1991)

Franklin Gevurtz, Professor of Law, McGeorge School of Law.

BUSINESS PLANNING, Temporary Second Edition (1984)

David R. Herwitz, Professor of Law, Harvard University.

BUSINESS TORTS (1972)

Milton Handler, Professor of Law Emeritus, Columbia University.

CHILDREN IN THE LEGAL SYSTEM (1983) with 1990 Supplement (Supplement edited in association with Elizabeth S. Scott, Professor of Law, University of Virginia)

Walter Wadlington, Professor of Law, University of Virginia.
Charles H. Whitebread, Professor of Law, University of Southern California.
Samuel Davis, Professor of Law, University of Georgia.

CIVIL PROCEDURE, see Procedure

CIVIL RIGHTS ACTIONS (1988), with 1990 Supplement

Peter W. Low, Professor of Law, University of Virginia.
John C. Jeffries, Jr., Professor of Law, University of Virginia.

CLINIC, see also Lawyering Process

COMMERCIAL AND DEBTOR–CREDITOR LAW: SELECTED STATUTES, 1990 EDITION

COMMERCIAL LAW, Second Edition (1987)

Robert L. Jordan, Professor of Law, University of California, Los Angeles.
William D. Warren, Professor of Law, University of California, Los Angeles.

COMMERCIAL LAW, Fourth Edition (1985), with 1991 Case Supplement

E. Allan Farnsworth, Professor of Law, Columbia University.
John Honnold, Professor of Law, University of Pennsylvania.

COMMERCIAL PAPER, Third Edition (1984), with 1991 Case Supplement

E. Allan Farnsworth, Professor of Law, Columbia University.

COMMERCIAL PAPER, Second Edition (1987) (Reprinted from COMMERCIAL LAW, Second Edition (1987))

Robert L. Jordan, Professor of Law, University of California, Los Angeles.
William D. Warren, Professor of Law, University of California, Los Angeles.

COMMERCIAL PAPER AND BANK DEPOSITS AND COLLECTIONS (1967), with Statutory Supplement

William D. Hawkland, Professor of Law, University of Illinois.

University Casebook Series

June, 1991

ACCOUNTING AND THE LAW, Fourth Edition (1978), with Problems Pamphlet (Successor to Dohr, Phillips, Thompson & Warren)

George C. Thompson, Professor, Columbia University Graduate School of Business.

Robert Whitman, Professor of Law, University of Connecticut.

Ellis L. Phillips, Jr., Member of the New York Bar.

William C. Warren, Professor of Law Emeritus, Columbia University.

ACCOUNTING FOR LAWYERS, MATERIALS ON (1980)

David R. Herwitz, Professor of Law, Harvard University.

ADMINISTRATIVE LAW, Eighth Edition (1987), with 1989 Case Supplement and 1983 Problems Supplement (Supplement edited in association with Paul R. Verkuil, Dean and Professor of Law, Tulane University)

Walter Gellhorn, University Professor Emeritus, Columbia University.

Clark Byse, Professor of Law, Harvard University.

Peter L. Strauss, Professor of Law, Columbia University.

Todd D. Rakoff, Professor of Law, Harvard University.

Roy A. Schotland, Professor of Law, Georgetown University.

ADMIRALTY, Third Edition (1987), with Statute and Rule Supplement

Jo Desha Lucas, Professor of Law, University of Chicago.

ADVOCACY, see also Lawyering Process

AGENCY, see also Enterprise Organization

AGENCY—PARTNERSHIPS, Fourth Edition (1987)

Abridgement from Conard, Knauss & Siegel's Enterprise Organization, Fourth Edition.

AGENCY AND PARTNERSHIPS (1987)

Melvin A. Eisenberg, Professor of Law, University of California, Berkeley.

ANTITRUST: FREE ENTERPRISE AND ECONOMIC ORGANIZATION, Sixth Edition (1983), with 1983 Problems in Antitrust Supplement and 1990 Case Supplement

Louis B. Schwartz, Professor of Law, University of Pennsylvania.

John J. Flynn, Professor of Law, University of Utah.

Harry First, Professor of Law, New York University.

BANKRUPTCY, Second Edition (1989), with 1990 Case Supplement

Robert L. Jordan, Professor of Law, University of California, Los Angeles.

William D. Warren, Professor of Law, University of California, Los Angeles.

BANKRUPTCY AND DEBTOR–CREDITOR LAW, Second Edition (1988)

Theodore Eisenberg, Professor of Law, Cornell University.

i

COMMERCIAL TRANSACTIONS—Principles and Policies, Second Edition (1991)

Alan Schwartz, Professor of Law, Yale University.
Robert E. Scott, Professor of Law, University of Virginia.

COMPARATIVE LAW, Fifth Edition (1988)

Rudolf B. Schlesinger, Professor of Law, Hastings College of the Law.
Hans W. Baade, Professor of Law, University of Texas.
Mirjan P. Damaska, Professor of Law, Yale Law School.
Peter E. Herzog, Professor of Law, Syracuse University.

COMPETITIVE PROCESS, LEGAL REGULATION OF THE, Revised Fourth Edition (1991), with 1989 Selected Statutes Supplement

Edmund W. Kitch, Professor of Law, University of Virginia.
Harvey S. Perlman, Dean of the Law School, University of Nebraska.

CONFLICT OF LAWS, Ninth Edition (1990)

Willis L. M. Reese, Professor of Law, Columbia University.
Maurice Rosenberg, Professor of Law, Columbia University.
Peter Hay, Professor of Law, University of Illinois.

CONSTITUTIONAL LAW, Eighth Edition (1989), with 1990 Case Supplement

Edward L. Barrett, Jr., Professor of Law, University of California, Davis.
William Cohen, Professor of Law, Stanford University.
Jonathan D. Varat, Professor of Law, University of California, Los Angeles.

CONSTITUTIONAL LAW, CIVIL LIBERTY AND INDIVIDUAL RIGHTS, Second Edition (1982), with 1989 Supplement

William Cohen, Professor of Law, Stanford University.
John Kaplan, Professor of Law, Stanford University.

CONSTITUTIONAL LAW, Eleventh Edition (1985), with 1990 Supplement (Supplement edited in association with Frederick F. Schauer, Professor, Harvard University)

Gerald Gunther, Professor of Law, Stanford University.

CONSTITUTIONAL LAW, INDIVIDUAL RIGHTS IN, Fourth Edition (1986), (Reprinted from CONSTITUTIONAL LAW, Eleventh Edition), with 1990 Supplement (Supplement edited in association with Frederick F. Schauer, Professor, Harvard University)

Gerald Gunther, Professor of Law, Stanford University.

CONSUMER TRANSACTIONS, Second Edition (1991), with Selected Statutes and Regulations Supplement

Michael M. Greenfield, Professor of Law, Washington University.

CONTRACT LAW AND ITS APPLICATION, Fourth Edition (1988)

Arthur Rosett, Professor of Law, University of California, Los Angeles.

CONTRACT LAW, STUDIES IN, Fourth Edition (1991)

Edward J. Murphy, Professor of Law, University of Notre Dame.
Richard E. Speidel, Professor of Law, Northwestern University.

CONTRACTS, Fifth Edition (1987)

John P. Dawson, late Professor of Law, Harvard University.
William Burnett Harvey, Professor of Law and Political Science, Boston University.
Stanley D. Henderson, Professor of Law, University of Virginia.

CONTRACTS, Fourth Edition (1988)

> E. Allan Farnsworth, Professor of Law, Columbia University.
> William F. Young, Professor of Law, Columbia University.

CONTRACTS, Selections on (statutory materials) (1988)

CONTRACTS, Second Edition (1978), with Statutory and Administrative Law Supplement (1978)

> Ian R. Macneil, Professor of Law, Cornell University.

COPYRIGHT, PATENTS AND TRADEMARKS, see also Competitive Process; see also Selected Statutes and International Agreements

COPYRIGHT, PATENT, TRADEMARK AND RELATED STATE DOCTRINES, Third Edition (1990), with 1989 Selected Statutes Supplement and 1981 Problem Supplement

> Paul Goldstein, Professor of Law, Stanford University.

COPYRIGHT, Unfair Competition, and Other Topics Bearing on the Protection of Literary, Musical, and Artistic Works, Fifth Edition (1990), with 1991 Statutory and Case Supplement

> Ralph S. Brown, Jr., Professor of Law, Yale University.
> Robert C. Denicola, Professor of Law, University of Nebraska.

CORPORATE ACQUISITIONS, The Law and Finance of (1986), with 1990 Supplement

> Ronald J. Gilson, Professor of Law, Stanford University.

CORPORATE FINANCE, Third Edition (1987)

> Victor Brudney, Professor of Law, Harvard University.
> Marvin A. Chirelstein, Professor of Law, Columbia University.

CORPORATION LAW, BASIC, Third Edition (1989), with Documentary Supplement

> Detlev F. Vagts, Professor of Law, Harvard University.

CORPORATIONS, see also Enterprise Organization and Business Organization

CORPORATIONS, Sixth Edition—Concise (1988), with 1990 Case Supplement and 1990 Statutory Supplement

> William L. Cary, late Professor of Law, Columbia University.
> Melvin Aron Eisenberg, Professor of Law, University of California, Berkeley.

CORPORATIONS, Sixth Edition—Unabridged (1988), with 1990 Case Supplement and 1990 Statutory Supplement

> William L. Cary, late Professor of Law, Columbia University.
> Melvin Aron Eisenberg, Professor of Law, University of California, Berkeley.

CORPORATIONS AND BUSINESS ASSOCIATIONS—STATUTES, RULES, AND FORMS (1990)

CORRECTIONS, SEE SENTENCING

CREDITORS' RIGHTS, see also Debtor-Creditor Law

UNIVERSITY CASEBOOK SERIES—Continued

GOVERNMENT CONTRACTS, FEDERAL, Successor Edition (1985), with 1989 Supplement

John W. Whelan, Professor of Law, Hastings College of the Law.

GOVERNMENT REGULATION: FREE ENTERPRISE AND ECONOMIC ORGANI-ZATION, Sixth Edition (1985)

Louis B. Schwartz, Professor of Law, Hastings College of the Law.
John J. Flynn, Professor of Law, University of Utah.
Harry First, Professor of Law, New York University.

HEALTH CARE LAW AND POLICY (1988)

Clark C. Havighurst, Professor of Law, Duke University.

HINCKLEY, JOHN W., JR., TRIAL OF: A Case Study of the Insanity Defense (1986)

Peter W. Low, Professor of Law, University of Virginia.
John C. Jeffries, Jr., Professor of Law, University of Virginia.
Richard C. Bonnie, Professor of Law, University of Virginia.

INJUNCTIONS, Second Edition (1984)

Owen M. Fiss, Professor of Law, Yale University.
Doug Rendleman, Professor of Law, College of William and Mary.

INSTITUTIONAL INVESTORS, (1978)

David L. Ratner, Professor of Law, Cornell University.

INSURANCE, Second Edition (1985)

William F. Young, Professor of Law, Columbia University.
Eric M. Holmes, Professor of Law, University of Georgia.

INSURANCE LAW AND REGULATION (1990)

Kenneth S. Abraham, University of Virginia.

INTERNATIONAL LAW, see also Transnational Legal Problems, Transnational Business Problems, and United Nations Law

INTERNATIONAL LAW IN CONTEMPORARY PERSPECTIVE (1981), with Essay Supplement

Myres S. McDougal, Professor of Law, Yale University.
W. Michael Reisman, Professor of Law, Yale University.

INTERNATIONAL LEGAL SYSTEM, Third Edition (1988), with Documentary Supplement

Joseph Modeste Sweeney, Professor of Law, University of California, Hastings.
Covey T. Oliver, Professor of Law, University of Pennsylvania.
Noyes E. Leech, Professor of Law Emeritus, University of Pennsylvania.

INTRODUCTION TO LAW, see also Legal Method, On Law in Courts, and Dynamics of American Law

INTRODUCTION TO THE STUDY OF LAW (1970)

E. Wayne Thode, late Professor of Law, University of Utah.
Leon Lebowitz, Professor of Law, University of Texas.
Lester J. Mazor, Professor of Law, University of Utah.

JUDICIAL CODE and Rules of Procedure in the Federal Courts, Students' Edition, 1989 Revision

Daniel J. Meltzer, Professor of Law, Harvard University.
David L. Shapiro, Professor of Law, Harvard University.

JURISPRUDENCE (Temporary Edition Hardbound) (1949)

Lon L. Fuller, late Professor of Law, Harvard University.

JUVENILE, see also Children

JUVENILE JUSTICE PROCESS, Third Edition (1985)

Frank W. Miller, Professor of Law, Washington University.
Robert O. Dawson, Professor of Law, University of Texas.
George E. Dix, Professor of Law, University of Texas.
Raymond I. Parnas, Professor of Law, University of California, Davis.

LABOR LAW, Eleventh Edition (1991), with 1991 Statutory Supplement

Archibald Cox, Professor of Law, Harvard University.
Derek C. Bok, President, Harvard University.
Robert A. Gorman, Professor of Law, University of Pennsylvania.
Matthew W. Finkin, Professor of Law, University of Illinois.

LABOR LAW, Second Edition (1982), with Statutory Supplement

Clyde W. Summers, Professor of Law, University of Pennsylvania.
Harry H. Wellington, Dean of the Law School, Yale University.
Alan Hyde, Professor of Law, Rutgers University.

LAND FINANCING, Third Edition (1985)

The late Norman Penney, Professor of Law, Cornell University.
Richard F. Broude, Member of the California Bar.
Roger Cunningham, Professor of Law, University of Michigan.

LAW AND MEDICINE (1980)

Walter Wadlington, Professor of Law and Professor of Legal Medicine, University of Virginia.
Jon R. Waltz, Professor of Law, Northwestern University.
Roger B. Dworkin, Professor of Law, Indiana University, and Professor of Biomedical History, University of Washington.

LAW, LANGUAGE AND ETHICS (1972)

William R. Bishin, Professor of Law, University of Southern California.
Christopher D. Stone, Professor of Law, University of Southern California.

LAW, SCIENCE AND MEDICINE (1984), with 1989 Supplement

Judith C. Areen, Professor of Law, Georgetown University.
Patricia A. King, Professor of Law, Georgetown University.
Steven P. Goldberg, Professor of Law, Georgetown University.
Alexander M. Capron, Professor of Law, University of Southern California.

LAWYERING PROCESS (1978), with Civil Problem Supplement and Criminal Problem Supplement

Gary Bellow, Professor of Law, Harvard University.
Bea Moulton, Professor of Law, Arizona State University.

LEGAL METHOD (1980)

Harry W. Jones, Professor of Law Emeritus, Columbia University.
John M. Kernochan, Professor of Law, Columbia University.
Arthur W. Murphy, Professor of Law, Columbia University.

LEGAL METHODS (1969)

Robert N. Covington, Professor of Law, Vanderbilt University.
E. Blythe Stason, late Professor of Law, Vanderbilt University.
John W. Wade, Professor of Law, Vanderbilt University.
Elliott E. Cheatham, late Professor of Law, Vanderbilt University.
Theodore A. Smedley, Professor of Law, Vanderbilt University.

LEGAL PROFESSION, THE, Responsibility and Regulation, Second Edition (1988)

Geoffrey C. Hazard, Jr., Professor of Law, Yale University.
Deborah L. Rhode, Professor of Law, Stanford University.

LEGISLATION, Fourth Edition (1982) (by Fordham)

Horace E. Read, late Vice President, Dalhousie University.
John W. MacDonald, Professor of Law Emeritus, Cornell Law School.
Jefferson B. Fordham, Professor of Law, University of Utah.
William J. Pierce, Professor of Law, University of Michigan.

LEGISLATIVE AND ADMINISTRATIVE PROCESSES, Second Edition (1981)

Hans A. Linde, Judge, Supreme Court of Oregon.
George Bunn, Professor of Law, University of Wisconsin.
Fredericka Paff, Professor of Law, University of Wisconsin.
W. Lawrence Church, Professor of Law, University of Wisconsin.

LOCAL GOVERNMENT LAW, Second Revised Edition (1986)

Jefferson B. Fordham, Professor of Law, University of Utah.

MASS MEDIA LAW, Fourth Edition (1990)

Marc A. Franklin, Professor of Law, Stanford University.
David A. Anderson, Professor of Law, University of Texas.

MUNICIPAL CORPORATIONS, see Local Government Law

NEGOTIABLE INSTRUMENTS, see Commercial Paper

NEGOTIATION (1981) (Reprinted from THE LAWYERING PROCESS)

Gary Bellow, Professor of Law, Harvard Law School.
Bea Moulton, Legal Services Corporation.

NEW YORK PRACTICE, Fourth Edition (1978)

Herbert Peterfreund, Professor of Law, New York University.
Joseph M. McLaughlin, Dean of the Law School, Fordham University.

OIL AND GAS, Fifth Edition (1987)

Howard R. Williams, Professor of Law, Stanford University.
Richard C. Maxwell, Professor of Law, University of California, Los Angeles.
Charles J. Meyers, late Dean of the Law School, Stanford University.
Stephen F. Williams, Judge of the United States Court of Appeals.

ON LAW IN COURTS (1965)

Paul J. Mishkin, Professor of Law, University of California, Berkeley.
Clarence Morris, Professor of Law Emeritus, University of Pennsylvania.

PENSION AND EMPLOYEE BENEFIT LAW (1990)

John H. Langbein, Professor of Law, University of Chicago.
Bruce A. Wolk, Professor of Law, University of California, Davis.

PLEADING AND PROCEDURE, see Procedure, Civil

POLICE FUNCTION, Fifth Edition (1991)

> Reprint of Chapters 1–10 of Miller, Dawson, Dix and Parnas's CRIMINAL JUSTICE ADMINISTRATION, Fourth Edition.

PREPARING AND PRESENTING THE CASE (1981) (Reprinted from THE LAWYERING PROCESS)

> Gary Bellow, Professor of Law, Harvard Law School.
> Bea Moulton, Legal Services Corporation.

PROCEDURE (1988), with Procedure Supplement (1991)

> Robert M. Cover, late Professor of Law, Yale Law School.
> Owen M. Fiss, Professor of Law, Yale Law School.
> Judith Resnik, Professor of Law, University of Southern California Law Center.

PROCEDURE—CIVIL PROCEDURE, Sixth Edition (1990), with 1991 Supplement

> Richard H. Field, late Professor of Law, Harvard University.
> Benjamin Kaplan, Professor of Law Emeritus, Harvard University.
> Kevin M. Clermont, Professor of Law, Cornell University.

PROCEDURE—CIVIL PROCEDURE, Fifth Edition (1990)

> Maurice Rosenberg, Professor of Law, Columbia University.
> Hans Smit, Professor of Law, Columbia University.
> Rochelle C. Dreyfuss, Professor of Law, New York University.

PROCEDURE—PLEADING AND PROCEDURE: State and Federal, Sixth Edition (1989), with 1990 Case Supplement

> David W. Louisell, late Professor of Law, University of California, Berkeley.
> Geoffrey C. Hazard, Jr., Professor of Law, Yale University.
> Colin C. Tait, Professor of Law, University of Connecticut.

PROCEDURE—FEDERAL RULES OF CIVIL PROCEDURE, 1991 Edition

PRODUCTS LIABILITY AND SAFETY, Second Edition, (1989), with 1989 Statutory Supplement

> W. Page Keeton, Professor of Law, University of Texas.
> David G. Owen, Professor of Law, University of South Carolina.
> John E. Montgomery, Professor of Law, University of South Carolina.
> Michael D. Green, Professor of Law, University of Iowa

PROFESSIONAL RESPONSIBILITY, Fifth Edition (1991), with 1991 Selected Standards on Professional Responsibility Supplement

> Thomas D. Morgan, Professor of Law, George Washington University.
> Ronald D. Rotunda, Professor of Law, University of Illinois.

PROPERTY, Sixth Edition (1990)

> John E. Cribbet, Professor of Law, University of Illinois.
> Corwin W. Johnson, Professor of Law, University of Texas.
> Roger W. Findley, Professor of Law, University of Illinois.
> Ernest E. Smith, Professor of Law, University of Texas.

PROPERTY—PERSONAL (1953)

> S. Kenneth Skolfield, late Professor of Law Emeritus, Boston University.

PROPERTY—PERSONAL, Third Edition (1954)

> Everett Fraser, late Dean of the Law School Emeritus, University of Minnesota.
> Third Edition by Charles W. Taintor, late Professor of Law, University of Pittsburgh.

PROPERTY—INTRODUCTION, TO REAL PROPERTY, Third Edition (1954)

Everett Fraser, late Dean of the Law School Emeritus, University of Minnesota.

PROPERTY—FUNDAMENTALS OF MODERN REAL PROPERTY, Second Edition (1982), with 1985 Supplement

Edward H. Rabin, Professor of Law, University of California, Davis.

PROPERTY, REAL (1984), with 1988 Supplement

Paul Goldstein, Professor of Law, Stanford University.

PROSECUTION AND ADJUDICATION, Fourth Edition (1991)

Reprint of Chapters 11–26 of Miller, Dawson, Dix and Parnas's CRIMINAL JUSTICE ADMINISTRATION, Fourth Edition.

PSYCHIATRY AND LAW, see Mental Health, see also Hinckley, Trial of

PUBLIC UTILITY LAW, see Free Enterprise, also Regulated Industries

REAL ESTATE PLANNING, Third Edition (1989), with Revised Problem and Statutory Supplement (1991)

Norton L. Steuben, Professor of Law, University of Colorado.

REAL ESTATE TRANSACTIONS, Revised Second Edition (1988), with Statute, Form and Problem Supplement (1988)

Paul Goldstein, Professor of Law, Stanford University.

RECEIVERSHIP AND CORPORATE REORGANIZATION, see Creditors' Rights

REGULATED INDUSTRIES, Second Edition, (1976)

William K. Jones, Professor of Law, Columbia University.

REMEDIES, Second Edition (1987)

Edward D. Re, Chief Judge, U. S. Court of International Trade.

REMEDIES, (1989)

Elaine W. Shoben, Professor of Law, University of Illinois.
Wm. Murray Tabb, Professor of Law, Baylor University.

SALES, Second Edition (1986)

Marion W. Benfield, Jr., Professor of Law, University of Illinois.
William D. Hawkland, Chancellor, Louisiana State Law Center.

SALES AND SALES FINANCING, Fifth Edition (1984)

John Honnold, Professor of Law, University of Pennsylvania.

SALES LAW AND THE CONTRACTING PROCESS, Second Edition (1991)

(Reprinted from Commercial Transactions, Second Edition (1991)
Alan Schwartz, Professor of Law, Yale University.
Robert E. Scott, Professor of Law, University of Virginia.

SECURED TRANSACTIONS IN PERSONAL PROPERTY, Second Edition (1987) (Reprinted from COMMERCIAL LAW, Second Edition (1987))

Robert L. Jordan, Professor of Law, University of California, Los Angeles.
William D. Warren, Professor of Law, University of California, Los Angeles.

UNIVERSITY CASEBOOK SERIES—Continued

SECURITIES REGULATION, Sixth Edition (1987), with 1990 Selected Statutes, Rules and Forms Supplement and 1990 Cases and Releases Supplement

Richard W. Jennings, Professor of Law, University of California, Berkeley.
Harold Marsh, Jr., Member of California Bar.

SECURITIES REGULATION, Second Edition (1988), with Statute, Rule and Form Supplement (1988)

Larry D. Soderquist, Professor of Law, Vanderbilt University.

SECURITY INTERESTS IN PERSONAL PROPERTY, Second Edition (1987)

Douglas G. Baird, Professor of Law, University of Chicago.
Thomas H. Jackson, Dean of the Law School, University of Virginia.

SECURITY INTERESTS IN PERSONAL PROPERTY (1985) (Reprinted from Sales and Sales Financing, Fifth Edition)

John Honnold, Professor of Law, University of Pennsylvania.

SELECTED STANDARDS ON PROFESSIONAL RESPONSIBILITY, 1991 Edition

SELECTED STATUTES AND INTERNATIONAL AGREEMENTS ON UNFAIR COMPETITION, TRADEMARK, COPYRIGHT AND PATENT, 1989 Edition

SELECTED STATUTES ON TRUSTS AND ESTATES, 1991 Edition

SOCIAL RESPONSIBILITIES OF LAWYERS, Case Studies (1988)

Philip B. Heymann, Professor of Law, Harvard University.
Lance Liebman, Professor of Law, Harvard University.

SOCIAL SCIENCE IN LAW, Second Edition (1990)

John Monahan, Professor of Law, University of Virginia.
Laurens Walker, Professor of Law, University of Virginia.

TAXATION, FEDERAL INCOME (1989)

Stephen B. Cohen, Professor of Law, Georgetown University

TAXATION, FEDERAL INCOME, Second Edition (1988), with 1990 Supplement (Supplement edited in association with Deborah H. Schenk, Professor of Law, New York University)

Michael J. Graetz, Professor of Law, Yale University.

TAXATION, FEDERAL INCOME, Seventh Edition (1991)

James J. Freeland, Professor of Law, University of Florida.
Stephen A. Lind, Professor of Law, University of Florida and University of California, Hastings.
Richard B. Stephens, late Professor of Law Emeritus, University of Florida.

TAXATION, FEDERAL INCOME, Successor Edition (1986), with 1991 Legislative Supplement

Stanley S. Surrey, late Professor of Law, Harvard University.
Paul R. McDaniel, Professor of Law, Boston College.
Hugh J. Ault, Professor of Law, Boston College.
Stanley A. Koppelman, Professor of Law, Boston University.

TAXATION, FEDERAL INCOME, OF BUSINESS ORGANIZATIONS (1991)

Paul R. McDaniel, Professor of Law, Boston College.
Hugh J. Ault, Professor of Law, Boston College.
Martin J. McMahon, Jr., Professor of Law, University of Kentucky.
Daniel L. Simmons, Professor of Law, University of California, Davis.

TAXATION, FEDERAL INCOME, OF PARTNERSHIPS AND S CORPORATIONS (1991)

Paul R. McDaniel, Professor of Law, Boston College.
Hugh J. Ault, Professor of Law, Boston College.
Martin J. McMahon, Jr., Professor of Law, University of Kentucky.
Daniel L. Simmons, Professor of Law, University of California, Davis.

TAXATION, FEDERAL INCOME, OIL AND GAS, NATURAL RESOURCES TRANSACTIONS (1990)

Peter C. Maxfield, Professor of Law, University of Wyoming.
James L. Houghton, CPA, Partner, Ernst and Young.
James R. Gaar, CPA, Partner, Ernst and Young.

TAXATION, FEDERAL WEALTH TRANSFER, Successor Edition (1987)

Stanley S. Surrey, late Professor of Law, Harvard University.
Paul R. McDaniel, Professor of Law, Boston College.
Harry L. Gutman, Professor of Law, University of Pennsylvania.

TAXATION, FUNDAMENTALS OF CORPORATE, Third Edition (1991)

Stephen A. Lind, Professor of Law, University of Florida and University of California, Hastings.
Stephen Schwarz, Professor of Law, University of California, Hastings.
Daniel J. Lathrope, Professor of Law, University of California, Hastings.
Joshua Rosenberg, Professor of Law, University of San Francisco.

TAXATION, FUNDAMENTALS OF PARTNERSHIP, Second Edition (1988)

Stephen A. Lind, Professor of Law, University of Florida and University of California, Hastings.
Stephen Schwarz, Professor of Law, University of California, Hastings.
Daniel J. Lathrope, Professor of Law, University of California, Hastings.
Joshua Rosenberg, Professor of Law, University of San Francisco.

TAXATION OF CORPORATIONS AND THEIR SHAREHOLDERS (1991)

David J. Shakow, Professor of Law, University of Pennsylvania.

TAXATION, PROBLEMS IN THE FEDERAL INCOME TAXATION OF PARTNER-SHIPS AND CORPORATIONS, Second Edition (1986)

Norton L. Steuben, Professor of Law, University of Colorado.
William J. Turnier, Professor of Law, University of North Carolina.

TAXATION, PROBLEMS IN THE FUNDAMENTALS OF FEDERAL INCOME, Second Edition (1985)

Norton L. Steuben, Professor of Law, University of Colorado.
William J. Turnier, Professor of Law, University of North Carolina.

TORT LAW AND ALTERNATIVES, Fourth Edition (1987)

Marc A. Franklin, Professor of Law, Stanford University.
Robert L. Rabin, Professor of Law, Stanford University.

TORTS, Eighth Edition (1988)

William L. Prosser, late Professor of Law, University of California, Hastings.
John W. Wade, Professor of Law, Vanderbilt University.
Victor E. Schwartz, Adjunct Professor of Law, Georgetown University.

TORTS, Third Edition (1976)

Harry Shulman, late Dean of the Law School, Yale University.
Fleming James, Jr., Professor of Law Emeritus, Yale University.
Oscar S. Gray, Professor of Law, University of Maryland.

TRADE REGULATION, Third Edition (1990)

Milton Handler, Professor of Law Emeritus, Columbia University.
Harlan M. Blake, Professor of Law, Columbia University.
Robert Pitofsky, Professor of Law, Georgetown University.
Harvey J. Goldschmid, Professor of Law, Columbia University.

TRADE REGULATION, see Antitrust

TRANSNATIONAL BUSINESS PROBLEMS (1986)

Detlev F. Vagts, Professor of Law, Harvard University.

TRANSNATIONAL LEGAL PROBLEMS, Third Edition (1986) with 1991 Revised Edition of Documentary Supplement

Henry J. Steiner, Professor of Law, Harvard University.
Detlev F. Vagts, Professor of Law, Harvard University.

TRIAL, see also Evidence, Making the Record, Lawyering Process and Preparing and Presenting the Case

TRUSTS, Sixth Edition (1991)

George G. Bogert, late Professor of Law Emeritus, University of Chicago.
Dallin H. Oaks, President, Brigham Young University.
H. Reese Hansen, Dean and Professor of Law, Brigham Young University.
Claralyn Martin Hill, J.D. Brigham Young University.

TRUSTS AND ESTATES, SELECTED STATUTES ON, 1991 Edition

TRUSTS AND WILLS, See also Decedents' Estates and Trusts, and Family Property Law

UNFAIR COMPETITION, see Competitive Process and Business Torts

WATER RESOURCE MANAGEMENT, Third Edition (1988)

The late Charles J. Meyers, formerly Dean, Stanford University Law School.
A. Dan Tarlock, Professor of Law, IIT Chicago-Kent College of Law.
James N. Corbridge, Jr., Chancellor, University of Colorado at Boulder, and
    Professor of Law, University of Colorado.
David H. Getches, Professor of Law, University of Colorado.

WILLS AND ADMINISTRATION, Fifth Edition (1961)

Philip Mechem, late Professor of Law, University of Pennsylvania.
Thomas E. Atkinson, late Professor of Law, New York University.

WRITING AND ANALYSIS IN THE LAW, Second Edition (1991)

Helene S. Shapo, Professor of Law, Northwestern University
Marilyn R. Walter, Professor of Law, Brooklyn Law School
Elizabeth Fajans, Writing Specialist, Brooklyn Law School

CASES AND MATERIALS

ON

EVIDENCE

SEVENTH EDITION

By

JOHN KAPLAN
Late Jackson Eli Reynolds Professor of Law,
Stanford University

JON R. WALTZ
Edna B. and Ednyfed H. Williams Professor of Law
and Lecturer in Medical Jurisprudence,
Northwestern University

ROGER C. PARK
Fredrikson & Byron Professor of Law
University of Minnesota

Westbury, New York
THE FOUNDATION PRESS, INC.
1992

Library of Congress Cataloging-in-Publication Data

Kaplan, John.
   Cases and materials on evidence / by John Kaplan, Jon R. Waltz,
Roger C. Park.
     p.   cm. — (University casebook series)
   Includes index.
   ISBN 0–88277–952–4
   1. Evidence (Law)—United States—Cases. I. Waltz, Jon R.
II. Park, Roger. III. Title. IV. Series.
KF8934.K37 1992
347.73'6—dc20
[347.3076]   91–30162

Kaplan, Waltz & Park Cs.Evid. 7th Ed. UCB

For
JOHN KAPLAN
One of the Great Ones

*

PREFACE TO THE SEVENTH EDITION

From its start, this casebook has benefited from the singular gifts of John Kaplan. His untimely death in 1989 prevented him from completing his contribution to this edition, but his earlier work is evident throughout the book. With admiration and affection, we dedicate it to him.

We have tried to be faithful to the original conception of the book. We selected new cases because we thought that they would teach well. When we thought a case or excerpt was not working, we replaced it.

Of course, there are some cases that simply cannot be ignored. The Supreme Court's sprouting interest in evidence law has dictated some of our choices. In this volume the reader will find new Supreme Court cases on the hearsay rule, the right to confrontation, the attorney-client privilege, the admission of uncharged misconduct evidence, the testimony of jurors, and the right to produce evidence. One of the principal purposes of this edition was to bring the book up to date by including these important cases.

Another goal was to revise and extend the materials on expert and opinion testimony. We have included several new cases on the form and bases of expert testimony. We have also expanded the related section on scientific evidence.

One of the hardest challenges in preparing a casebook is deciding what should be taken out to make way for new material. We have made major deletions in three areas. We have limited our confrontation clause coverage to the most recent cases. We have eliminated the ethics and loyalty section from the attorney-client privilege material, believing that this subject is adequately covered in mandatory courses on legal ethics or professional responsibility. We have also shortened the chapter on the right against self-incrimination, on grounds that relatively few teachers reach this topic, and that the topic is partly covered in courses on criminal law or procedure.

In general, we have preferred to leave the creation of hypotheticals and questions to the discretion and ingenuity of the individual teacher. However, we have continued the practice of including selected hypotheticals from Judge Bernard Jefferson's remarkable *California Evidence Benchbook*.

As usual, we have profited from the comments and suggestions of numerous users of this casebook—students and instructors alike. We will continue to be grateful for their communications.

JON R. WALTZ
ROGER C. PARK

July, 1991

*

xxi

SUMMARY OF CONTENTS

CHAPTER I. MAKING THE RECORD [page 1]

CHAPTER II. AN INTRODUCTION TO RELEVANCE

CHAPTER III. THE HEARSAY RULE

CHAPTER IV. A RETURN TO RELEVANCE

CHAPTER V. IMPEACHMENT AND CROSS EXAMINATION

CHAPTER VI. CONFIDENTIALITY AND CONFIDENTIAL COMMUNICATION

CHAPTER VII. THE PRIVILEGE AGAINST COMPULSORY SELF–INCRIMINATION

CHAPTER VIII. GOVERNMENTAL PRIVILEGES [page 608]

CHAPTER IX. WRITINGS

CHAPTER X. COMPETENCY OF WITNESSES [page 654]

CHAPTER XI. JUDICIAL NOTICE

CHAPTER XII. THE BURDEN OF PROOF AND PRESUMPTIONS

CHAPTER XIII. OPINION, EXPERTISE AND EXPERTS; SCIENTIFIC AND DEMONSTRATIVE EVIDENCE

APPENDICES

*

TABLE OF CONTENTS

CHAPTER V. IMPEACHMENT AND CROSS EXAMINATION

CHAPTER VI. CONFIDENTIALITY AND CONFIDENTIAL COMMUNICATION

CHAPTER X.   COMPETENCY OF WITNESSES

CHAPTER XI.   JUDICIAL NOTICE

CHAPTER XII.   THE BURDEN OF PROOF AND PRESUMPTIONS

CHAPTER XIII. OPINION, EXPERTISE AND EXPERTS; SCIENTIFIC AND DEMONSTRATIVE EVIDENCE

APPENDICES

*

TABLE OF CASES

Principal cases are in italic type. Non-principal cases are in roman type. References are to Pages.

TABLE OF FEDERAL EVIDENCE RULES

*

TABLE OF CALIFORNIA EVIDENCE CODE SECTIONS

*

CASES AND MATERIALS

ON

EVIDENCE

*

Chapter I

MAKING THE RECORD *

I.

"THE RECORD": WHAT IT MEANS AND HOW IT IS "MADE"

A.

The Meaning and Purpose of the Trial Record

Every experienced trial lawyer realizes as he or she goes into a litigation that his or her cause may not prevail at the trial level and that his/her client may wish to appeal to a higher court if, in counsel's opinion, errors occurring at trial contributed significantly to the unhappy outcome. An experienced trial lawyer knows, therefore, that she must be in a position to show a reviewing court precisely what happened during the trial (and perhaps also at any important pre-trial and out-of-court hearings or conferences). It follows that a lawyer must do two things at once—she must operate at two quite different levels—as she goes about the trial of her case. First, she must bend every proper effort to the winning of her client's case at the trial level, which means, essentially, that she must persuade the factfinder—judge or jury—of the rightness of her cause. Second, because counsel can never be absolutely certain of victory at the trial level, she must do everything she can to generate a record of the trial that will serve to convince a reviewing court that justice did not prevail in the court below.

An appellate court can neither speculate about what occurred at trial nor take on faith counsel's uncorroborated description of events in the lower court. A reviewing court can act only on the formal record of the trial that has been officially transmitted to it by the clerk of the trial court.

That record, assembled and bound into one or more volumes after the trial is over, is made up of all the "suit papers": the pleadings in the case (Complaint, Answer, possibly a Reply and perhaps Cross-Complaints, Counterclaims, and Third-Party Complaints and the Answers or Replies to them). It will include every other piece of paper that was filed during the course of the litigation: motions, supporting briefs, orders of the trial court, written stipulations of the parties, proposed jury instructions, journal entries, everything. The record also contains what in some jurisdictions is called the "Report of Proceedings." This is the verbatim transcript of any on-the-record proceedings in the case. There will be the actual trial transcript—the recordation of all the words that were spoken by the trial's participants (judge, jurors, lawyers, witnesses, and perhaps others)—and there will be transcript from any on-the-record pre-trial or out-of-court hearings and

* Prepared by Professor Jon R. Waltz.

conferences. Attached to the back of the trial transcript, or in the final
volumes of a bulky record, will be the exhibits, received and unreceived,
that were identified and offered at trial. The record, then, in all but
the most minor of litigations, has three basic parts: (1.) the litigation's
paperwork, (2.) the verbatim transcript of hearings, conferences, and
trial testimony, and (3.) the tangible exhibits that the parties offered
into evidence. It will ordinarily contain less only if counsel have
agreed to a "short" record, as when only designated portions of the
record are needed for the effective presentation of an appeal.

B.

How the Record is Made

The active participants in a trial, which means the judge and the
lawyers, literally "make" the trial record. They go about it almost as
though they were dictating a non-fiction book, or the scenario for a
documentary film, to an especially capable secretary. They create the
record, in other words, with the assistance of that most important of
courtroom functionaries, the court reporter. The reporter has a number of responsibilities during a trial but the most crucial one is the
accurate taking down, with high-speed shorthand or by mechanical
means, of everything that is said by the participants. The reporter will
take down not only the testimony of the witnesses but the evidentiary
objections and arguments of counsel and the comments, rulings, and
instructions of the judge. The reporter will ordinarily also be assigned
the job of placing identifying markings on tangible exhibits at offering
counsel's request and will have the practical responsibility for taking
care of the exhibits when they are not in use during the trial.

The proficiency displayed by court reporters under even the most
difficult heat-of-trial circumstances is almost invariably impressive.
The confidence of courts and lawyers in the trial records produced by
court reporters is reflected in statutes providing that these records are
to be deemed *prima facie* correct (28 U.S.C. § 753(b) (1976)), and in such
rules as Federal Rule of Civil Procedure 80(c) which provide that
whenever the stenographically recorded testimony of a witness at a
trial or hearing is admissible at a later trial, it may be proved by the
court reporter's certified transcript of it. Perhaps the ultimate affirmation of the importance of the court reporter's product, the transcript,
lies in those rulings—dating from the days when reporting by shorthand rather than mechanical means was the usual practice—that the
plaintiff who lost in the trial court is entitled to a new trial if he is
unable, because of the inability for any reason of the court reporter, or
of a substitute for him, to make a transcript from the reporter's notes.

Furthermore, the court reporter's transcript is an almost sacred
thing. Although it is true in a general way that the reporter is subject
to the trial court's direction, the court cannot curtail the performance
of the reporter's essential duties. In other words, the parties' right to
have a word-for-word record of everything said cannot be negated by a
trial judge, no matter how much the judge might wish to interfere—
possibly to excise his own errors or inappropriate language. Appellate

courts have repeatedly held that a trial judge has no authority to order the court reporter to disregard his sworn obligation to make a complete transcript and some statutes specifically provide that a judge's overreaching in this regard is, in and of itself, prejudicial error.

It thus is no exaggeration to say that during a trial the judge and the lawyers are working with the court reporter in a joint effort that culminates in a complete record of the trial. Competent judges and attorneys are therefore continuously aware of the court reporter and his (or her) importance as the trial process unfolds. It may even be that verbatim court reporting sometimes promotes an attitude of stiffness, of undue formality, on counsel's part. On the whole, however, the influence of verbatim reporting, on all but those lawyers who are already gripped by a form of stage fright, is benign. Verbatim reporting tends to induce lawyers to be precise in their language, thorough and careful in their examinations. It tends to restrain the impetuous and the flamboyant. In short, it casts over all the trial participants a sense of the high responsibility engendered by the psychology of "making the record."

The trial record is so important that, in "big" cases that will bear the considerable expense involved, the parties often order daily transcript. Relays of court reporters will take down the testimony and immediately type it up, so that by the day's end court and counsel will be provided with the typed transcript of that day's proceedings. They will burn the midnight oil reading the transcript and indexing it in preparation for the days ahead. Otherwise, typed transcript is provided only as specifically ordered by court or counsel. If neither court nor counsel have any need for designated blocks of transcript during the trial, or if there is no appeal from verdict and judgment, the court reporter's notes may never be transcribed at all and a potentially taxable cost item of sizeable magnitude will be avoided.

Consciousness of the record and of the court reporter's part in the making of it has a discernible effect on the way the judge and counsel go about their work. In the first place, it is vital that the court reporter be able to hear and understand everything that is said by the participants in a trial or hearing. It has been said, correctly, that it may even be more important that the reporter hear than the judge, the jurors, and the lawyers, since the reporter can then repeat from his notes any remarks unheard by them.

C.

Conduct of Lawyers that Hampers Court Reporters

Some years ago the National Shorthand Reporters Association catalogued some common practices of trial lawyers that create problems for court reporters. The most frustrating of them are paraphrased below.

1. *"Echoing."* A nervous trial lawyer, or one who is seeking an extra moment of time in which to frame his next question, sometimes

engages in the practice known to court reporters as "echoing." That is, he constantly repeats the witness' response to a question.

> Q. What is your name, sir?
>
> A. Clyde Bushmat.
>
> Q. Clyde Bushmat. Where do your reside?
>
> A. At 3730 North Lake Shore Drive in Chicago, Illinois.
>
> Q. 3730 North Lake Shore Drive, Chicago. And how old are you, sir?
>
> A. I'll be forty-two next October 11.
>
> Q. Forty-two in October. What is your present occupation?

Since he must take down everything that is said by the participants in a trial, this unnecessary repetition is distracting to the reporter, wasteful of trial time, and costly to the litigants.

2. *"Overlapping."* It is difficult for a court reporter, no matter how competent, to make an accurate and readable record when more than one person talks at the same time. The reporter may be unable to hear everything that is said or he may be unable to remember all of the overlapping statements long enough to sort out and record them while trying to keep up with the continuing testimony or argument. Counsel, although occasionally forced to prevent a witness from forging ahead with objectionable testimony, generally should avoid interruptions that result in broken sentences and garbled transcripts.

3. *Numbers.* What does a court reporter do when a trial lawyer says "twenty-one-O-two"? Does the lawyer mean 21.02, 2,102.00, or 20,102? Does he mean dollars or something else? He should say, "Twenty-one dollars and two cents" if that is what he means. If he is dealing with a long number, such as the number of an insurance policy, counsel should avoid trying to give the millions, thousands, hundreds, and digits; he is likely to mix up not only himself, the judge, and the jury, but also the court reporter. It is simple enough to say, "Policy Number one-nine-four-seven-nine-six-three." References to dates can also be confusing. Counsel's reference to "October 31" can mean either October the 31st or October, 1931.

4. *Proper Names.* Many proper names have a similar sound. "White, Weit, Whyte, Wight, Wite, Wyatt." Counsel should be particularly careful to enunciate proper names slowly and clearly, in some instances spelling out the name or requesting the witness to do so. Indeed, counsel who is not known to the court reporter would do well to provide the correct spelling of her *own* name at the outset of the trial.

5. *Exhibits.* The Shorthand Reporters Association has observed that trial lawyers are often careless in the way they refer to exhibits. We shall be discussing the correct ways of marking and referring to exhibits. It is enough to mention here that court reporters do not appreciate the lawyer who gets his exhibit properly marked and then fails to make the intended use of the exhibit's number or letter. References to "this photograph" or "that letter" result in an incompre-

hensible record. Exhibits are marked *for identification.* Counsel's reference should be complete: "I hand you what has been marked Defendant's Exhibit Number 2 for Identification."

6. *Indications and Gestures.* Unclarified statements such as "About this long," "Approximately that far away," and "He had a jagged scar right here" may be comprehensible enough to those who were present in the trial court to see the witness' physical gestures but they become meaningless on the typed record. Either the witness will have to be asked to give an explicit oral response or, as we shall discuss later, counsel or the court will have to make a clarifying statement for the record.

7. *"Off the Record."* The practice of lawyers during depositions, pre-trial hearings and even occasionally in the midst of trial of directing the court reporter to go "off the record" is often confusing to the reporter. In some instances she may be unclear as to her authority to halt her note-taking, as when neither the trial judge nor opposing counsel has indicated his agreement that recordation can be interrupted; in others she may be uncertain as to precisely when recordation should recommence. If she is unclear of her authority, an experienced court reporter will simply continue to record. And whenever she halts recordation she will protect herself by making a notation in the transcript: "Whereupon discussion off the record was had."

Any confusion about when to resume note-taking can be far more embarrassing to counsel than it is to the reporter where counsel discovers later that an important concession or stipulation did not get on the record or got on it in such a truncated form that it is impossible to determine what it related to. Counsel should give a clear indication when they want to "go back on the record." It is easy to do. A hand signal may be all that is needed, or a statement by counsel such as "Let's go back on now. I want to put our stipulation on the record."

8. *Sidebar Conferences.* A variation on the off-the-record problem arises when counsel engage in whispered "sidebar" conferences—conferences occurring at the bench. These conferences, usually held in connection with an evidentiary objection, are calculated to be outside the jury's hearing but they may prove to be beyond the court reporter's hearing as well. If anything significant occurs during such a conference, such as a ruling by the judge or a stipulation between the parties, counsel should make certain that the reporter has been able to get it on the record.

9. *Abstruse Terminology.* In lawsuits that will involve substantial amounts of esoteric terminology, such as patent cases, counsel can contribute to the record's accuracy by supplying the reporter with a glossary of the specialized terms that are likely to come up.

10. *Reading Testimony into the Record.* In reading deposition testimony or previous trial testimony into the record, counsel should read slowly enough, and enunciate sharply enough, that the court reporter can follow. It helps the reporter if counsel always reads the words "Question" and "Answer" at the appropriate points. Later, counsel should supply to the reporter the deposition or transcript from

which she read. This will permit the reporter to check the accuracy of
his notes against the written exhibit.

D.

Requesting the Making of a Record

It has already at least been implied that now and then a lawyer's
making of the trial record involves little more than remembering to see
to it that particular proceedings are "on the record"; that is, that they
are being recorded by a court reporter. Many aspects of a litigated
matter will not become part of the record unless counsel see to it, first,
that there is a court reporter present and, second, that he is recording
the proceedings. For example, there often will not be a reporter
present at a pre-trial conference of the sort described in Rule 16 of the
Federal Rules of Civil Procedure, or at conferences with the trial judge
in his or her chambers, unless counsel requests that one be brought in
when needed. Important matters, of both a procedural and an evidentiary nature, are frequently resolved at such sessions and a court
reporter should be summoned in order that these stipulations can be
put in the record.

In a few jurisdictions the court reporter will not record the examination of prospective jurors—the *voir dire*—or counsel's opening statements or closing arguments to the jury unless specifically instructed by
court or counsel to do so. Since error can occur during any of these
trial phases (although it rarely does), counsel will request recordation
in cases that can support the added expense. (He may also want the
opening statements transcribed so that he can refer to them—his own
or his adversary's—during his closing argument to the jury.)

Some courts, usually those of less than general jurisdiction (municipal courts, "small claims" courts, traffic courts, and the like), have no
official court reporters regularly attached to them. Here the litigants
have the obligation to provide and pay for the services of a qualified
reporter. Often the parties agree to share the cost. Court reporters
can be obtained from the same organizations that supply them for the
taking of depositions. The Yellow Pages of the Chicago Telephone
Directory list 154 individuals and partnerships under the heading,
"Reporters—Court and Convention."

E.

Requiring Audible Responses from Witnesses

The principal task of a court reporter, and it is a formidable one, is
to take down testimony completely and accurately. The reporter
ordinarily cannot take down an answer unless there has been an
audible one; it is not the reporter's job to invent words which the
witness did not speak. An alert court reporter may have time to insert
in the record a bracketed statement of what the witness did—for
example, "A: [Witness nodded in the affirmative.]"—but often the pace
of the trial leaves no time for this. It is counsel's duty to obtain audible
oral answers from witnesses or else, as will be described, he must

himself insert an oral statement in the record.　When a witness nods or gestures instead of answering audibly, counsel ordinarily should advise him that "The court reporter cannot get your answer unless you say it in words, sir."

F.

Statements for the Record

There are all manner of situations in which counsel or the court find it necessary to make a statement for the record.　This means, in effect, that counsel or the trial judge is dictating a statement into the trial record; they, not a witness on the stand, speak and the court reporter takes down what they say as an integral part of the trial record.

Statements for the record are commonly employed to fill in testimonial gaps created by the witness, mentioned above, who provides inaudible or nonverbal responses.　Instead of reminding the witness to give audible oral answers, assuming that such an answer was the appropriate mode of response to the question, examining counsel may turn to the court reporter and say, "Let the record show that the witness, in response to the question, nodded his head in the affirmative."

Sometimes witnesses, whether directed to do so or not, will respond to questions with their hands rather than vocally.　Counsel inquires, "How long was the blade of the knife?" and the witness, instead of saying "About four inches," indicates the length with the thumb and index finger of one hand.　In this situation counsel may make a statement for the record rather than insist on an oral response.　"Let the record reflect that in answer to the question the witness, using the thumb and index finger of his right hand, indicated a length of approximately four inches."　If opposing counsel objects to the statement, saying it looked more like three inches to her, counsel may have to call for an oral response.　If opposing counsel remains silent, the statement for the record stands.　If examining counsel inquires of opposing counsel, as out of courtesy he might, whether his statement for the record is satisfactory and gets an affirmative reply, the statement for the record rises to the level of a stipulation between counsel.

Whenever counsel expressly requests a witness to communicate information by means other than oral testimony, a statement for the record will be essential in order to avoid later confusion.　Here a typical example involves the drama-conscious prosecutor who asks the witness,

　　Q.　Do you see the man you have described anywhere in the courtroom?

　　A.　I do.

　　Q.　Please come down off the witness stand and place your hand on the shoulder of the man whom you have described as the one who assaulted the little girl.　[Witness complies.]

BY THE PROSECUTOR: Let the record show that the
witness crossed directly to the accused, Clyde Bushmat, and
placed her hand on his right shoulder. [Or he may simply say,
'Let the record show that the witness identified the accused.']

Sometimes a witness will give a response which, although oral and
audible, nonetheless calls for a clarifying statement for the record.

Q. How far from the automobile were you when this
happened?

A. Oh, about from here to the back wall of the courtroom.

BY EXAMINING COUNSEL: Let the record show that
the witness has indicated a distance of approximately fifty feet.
Does that meet with your approval, counsel?

BY OPPOSING COUNSEL: Yes, that seems about right.

A statement for the record can be used to place in the trial record
pertinent matter that is not in dispute and which would not be
expected to come from a witness on the stand; matter which, in a
sense, is non-evidentiary. For example, it may from time to time be
prudent to make a statement for the record to the effect that described
proceedings or events took place while the jury was out, lest it later be
suggested that comments, legal arguments, or events such as disrup-
tions by defendants or spectators occurring during the period in question may have prejudiced the jury.

G.

Stipulations

Stipulations by counsel are a near relative of the sort of statements
for the record that were discussed in the preceding section. As was
suggested there, a statement for the record which opposing counsel
affirmatively accepts as accurate rises to the level of a stipulation. An
unchallenged statement for the record—one that is not objected to by
the opposite side—probably qualifies as an implied stipulation. Stipulations can be extremely important in litigation. They are in the
nature of contracts entered into by lawyers acting as special agents of
their clients. These agreements between counsel can simplify and
expedite trial and fill evidentiary gaps. But they are worse than
useless unless they have been clearly made a part of the trial record.

A stipulation is simply a voluntary agreement entered into between counsel for the parties to a litigation respecting some matter that
is before the trial court. In the absence of special circumstances that
might induce a court to vacate it, a stipulation by counsel binds their
principals, the clients. (Courts will usually vacate stipulations that
were entered into by mistake, and they will always vacate those that
were obtained by fraud or deceit.)

Stipulations can relate either to procedure or to evidence. Typical
examples of procedural stipulations can be found in Rule 29 of the
Federal Rules of Civil Procedure, which treats of "Stipulations Regarding Discovery Procedure." In order that any such stipulations shall be

a discernible part of the record, Rule 29 provides that they must be in writing. (See also FRCP 15, which provides that a party, after the filing of a responsive pleading by the opposing side, can amend his or her pleading either with the trial court's permission "or by written consent of the adverse party.")

An evidentiary stipulation acts to admit or concede specified facts, relieving a party of the burden of making full-scale proof. Such an evidentiary stipulation constitutes a formal judicial admission—an abandonment of any contention to the contrary—and, unless vacated by the trial court, prevents those who enter into it from offering evidence to dispute it. It is identical in force to an admission contained in a pleading.

Complicated stipulations, like complex hypothetical questions to be posed to an expert witness, are usually written out by counsel and then edited. The final written product can then be filed in the case or read into the record. Simple, single-subject stipulations are stated for the record extemporaneously. Here the only problems involve (1.) remembering to state the stipulation, (2.) making certain that the court reporter is recording it, (3.) making certain that the terms of the stipulation are clear and unambiguous, and (4.) getting on the record opposing counsel's unqualified acquiescence in the stipulation.

Stipulations, whether entered into during a deposition, a pre-trial conference, or in the midst of trial, may evolve in a most informal way.

PLAINTIFF'S COUNSEL [speaking to defense counsel at a pre-trial conference]: Susan, will you agree to our photographs?

DEFENSE COUNSEL: What have you got, Charlie? I'll be glad to look at them. They're all in living color, I suppose?

PLAINTIFF'S COUNSEL: We're not using photos of the injuries, just some pictures of the accident site, the intersection. And they're black-and-white. We've got a group of four shots, taken about a month after the accident. There haven't been any changes out there and there's nothing staged. Just four shots of the intersection, East, West, North, South. Take a look.

DEFENSE COUNSEL: Well, these are all O.K., I think. Let's put it this way. I'll agree to yours if you'll agree to ours.

PLAINTIFF'S COUNSEL: I've seen yours and they're all right. Now these photos were all used in the depositions we took in this case and each one has an identifying mark put on it by the reporter at those depositions. We can use those numbers for now, and then change them at trial. Can we go on the record for this, Miss Nixon?

THE COURT REPORTER: Yes, I'm ready.

PLAINTIFF'S COUNSEL: Let the record show that it is hereby stipulated by and between the parties to this action, through their counsel, that Plaintiff's Bushmat Deposition Exhibits Numbers 4, 5, 6, and 7 for Identification will be admissible in evidence at the trial of this case, without further foundation or proof, as being true and fair representations of what they purport to show. The same stipulation pertains to Defendant's Bushmat Deposition Exhibits C, D, E, F, and G for Identification. Is that satisfactory, Charlie?

DEFENSE COUNSEL: Yes, that'll do it.

At trial, counsel will have the court reporter mark the deposition exhibits with new identifying numbers and letters with which the exhibits will be identified from then on. Each lawyer, when offering the exhibits, will inform the court that their admissibility has been stipulated by counsel. Each lawyer will repeat the full stipulation for the record and within the jury's hearing, thus making the record in an orderly and sequential manner. The exhibits will be received by the trial court without further foundation proof, although witnesses may make use of them as adjuncts to their testimony.

Stipulations are often entered into for the first time in the midst of trial. As one lawyer sets about laying the proper foundation for the introduction of a writing opposing counsel, seeing no reason not to spare his adversary from these laborious preliminaries, may interrupt to say, "We will stipulate that Plaintiff's Exhibit 10 for Identification is what it purports to be." The proposed stipulation, if accepted by offering counsel, serves to authenticate the document. Alert offering counsel will realize, however, that the proposed stipulation goes no further than that; by agreeing only that the writing "is what it purports to be," opposing counsel has reserved the right to assert objections based on evidentiary rules other than those governing authentication. It may go this way:

Q. Handing you what has been marked Plaintiff's Exhibit Number 10 for Identification, Mrs. Stitz, I'll ask you what it is, if you know?

A. This appears to be a letter dictated by my former employer, Mr. Morton P. Lishniss.

BY OPPOSING COUNSEL: Pardon me, counsel. We will stipulate that your Exhibit 10 is what it purports to be.

BY OFFERING COUNSEL: In that case, your Honor, we now offer in evidence what has been marked Plaintiff's Exhibit 10 for Identification.

BY OPPOSING COUNSEL: Well, now, just a moment. We object to it, your Honor. We agree that it is what it appears to be on its face, a letter from Lishniss to Bushmat dated April 1, 1991, but we don't think it has any relevance to this case. Furthermore, its receipt would violate the hearsay rule.

THE COURT: We'll take a brief recess while I hear argument from both sides on this.

Counsel will ordinarily be required by the trial court to accept any stipulation offered by the opposing side which unequivocally concedes everything that counsel would be entitled to show by making full proof.

In such a situation the making of complete proof, the laying of every brick in the evidentiary foundation, would be a needless waste of time. On the other hand, offered stipulations do not always supply everything to which counsel is entitled. In that situation she will be free to make a complete record on the matter in question. A common example has to do with the qualifications of an expert witness. Opposing counsel, desiring to keep the jury from hearing all of the witness' impressive credentials, may interrupt the preliminary examination to say, "We'll stipulate that Doctor Faust is a qualified orthopedist, your Honor." But such a stipulation does not give examining counsel everything to which she is entitled in a case that may involve a so-called battle of experts. In order to assign comparative weight to the opinions of opposing experts appearing in the case, the jurors are entitled to hear and assess the qualifications of each of them. And examining counsel is therefore entitled to make full proof of those qualifications, thus:

Q. Doctor, will you please give the court and jury your full name?

A. Myron L. Faust.

Q. Where do you reside?

A. 1000 Astor Place, Chicago, Illinois.

Q. What is your profession?

A. Physician and surgeon.

Q. Are you duly licensed to practice as a physician and surgeon in Illinois?

A. I am.

Q. What specialty, if any, have you made in your medical practice?

A. I specialize in orthopedic surgery.

Q. We will come back to that, Doctor. How long have you practiced medicine?

A. Twenty-six years this coming June.

Q. Of what medical school are you a graduate, Doctor Faust?

A. The Northwestern University Medical School in Chicago.

BY OPPOSING COUNSEL: Excuse me a moment. We're willing to stipulate that Doctor Faust is a qualified orthopedic surgeon and can testify here.

BY EXAMINING COUNSEL: We would prefer to make our proof on this, your Honor. The jury is entitled to hear his training and experience. The jurors have got to decide what weight to give his testimony and they can't very well do that without hearing his qualifications.

THE COURT: It would speed things up if you accepted the stipulation, counsel, but you can't be required to do so. You may proceed to establish the witness' qualifications.

Q. Very well, your Honor. Doctor Faust, what other
training or study have you had?

BY OPPOSING COUNSEL: In view of our offer to stipulate, we object to this, your Honor.

THE COURT: Overruled.

II.

OFFERING EVIDENCE

Obviously, the making of a trial record consists in large part of
offering evidence for the factfinder's consideration. The evidence will
be in the form of oral testimony and tangible exhibits. The usual
method for offering oral testimony into evidence is by engaging in the
direct examination or cross-examination of a witness who has been
called to the stand to testify under oath. (Sometimes oral testimony
can also be offered by way of a deposition or a transcript of previously
recorded testimony.) A tangible exhibit is ordinarily presented through
a "sponsoring" witness who can identify or authenticate the item and
reveal its relevance to some material issue in the case. After laying
the necessary foundation, counsel will say something like "Your Honor,
we now offer into evidence what has previously been marked Plaintiff's
Exhibit Number 6 for Identification," at which point the trial court will
rule on the offer, either receiving or rejecting it.

A.

Direct Examination of Witnesses

Unlike the practice in most European countries, where the witness
merely stands up and delivers a long and sometimes rambling narrative
concerning what he or she knows about the case, in Anglo-American
law the witnesses relate their stories through the question-and-answer
method. We require the witness to give his answers in response to
relatively pointed questions so that the opposing counsel, forewarned by
the question that the jury may be about to hear inadmissible material,
can object in time to prevent receipt of the damaging answer.

In Anglo-American law not only must the parties proceed by
question and answer, but they must adhere to certain forms of questions. And the restrictions are far more severe on the side calling the
witness to the stand. The examination of one's own witness—direct
examination as distinguished from cross-examination—is hedged about
by a number of rules, the most familiar one being the rule against
"leading" questions.

1. *Leading Questions.* A leading question is one that suggests its
own answer. A typical leading question is, "You were driving your
automobile well under the posted speed limit, isn't that so?" The
witness may answer "Yes" but it is the attorney's version of the story
that the jury hears. This type of question, at least when it goes to
matters at the very heart of the case, is, with some exceptions that we
will discuss, objectionable on direct examination. For example, Rule

611(c) of the Federal Rules of Evidence provides that "Leading questions should not be used on the direct examination of a witness except as may be necessary to develop the witness' testimony."

The notion has caught on that any question that can be answered "Yes" or "No" is automatically a leading one. This has led some lawyers to believe that they have only to preface their direct questions with "Did you or did you not * * *?" or "What is the fact as to whether or not * * *?" in order to avoid a successful objection. In fact, a question that is susceptible of a "Yes" or "No" response may be essentially non-leading, while the question with the seemingly neutral preface may strongly suggest the desired answer. The point is simply that although questions on direct examination can properly point the witness to a particular subject of inquiry, they should be reasonably balanced and neutral.

"Did you or did you not hear the man say, 'I just killed my wife'?" is a leading question, despite the seemingly neutral alternatives offered in the prefatory "Did you or did you not * * *?" "And then did you hear the man say anything?" is technically leading but probably is permissible to suggest the desired topic of inquiry: what was *said* rather than what was *done* next. The wholly non-leading approach would be,

> Q. What, if anything, happened next?

> A. The man blurted out, "I just killed my wife!"

And everyone knows the all-time favorite non-leading question, "Directing your attention to April 1, 1991, I'll ask you whether anything unusual occurred?"—which may occasionally leave the witness totally baffled.

There are a number of situations in which leading questions are permitted even on direct examination.

(a.) Leading questions are allowed on preliminary matters that do not go to the heart of the case, and they are permitted to provide a transition from one subject of inquiry to another.

> Q. And you are employed by the Acme Tool Company, I believe?

> A. Yes.

> Q. And have been for about ten years?

> A. That's true.

> * * *

> Q. Now, Mr. Bushmat, turning to the day in question, were you and your family out driving in the country?

> A. Yes, we were.

(b.) Leading questions are permitted with respect to undisputed matters where the question is used as a connective.

> Q. You testified earlier, I believe, that you were driving at about thirty miles an hour, is that right?

> A. Yes.

Q. Very well, then let me ask you this, * * *

(c.) An adverse or hostile witness can be asked leading questions. There is very little danger that such a witness would accept a false suggestion contained in a leading question. In the federal practice, leading questions can be put to "a witness identified with an adverse party." (Fed.R.Evid. 611(c).)

(d.) Leading questions are allowed during direct examination when a witness gives "surprise" answers. Surprise is most commonly demonstrated where the witness' direct testimony is sharply at odds with his or her deposition testimony or with a previous statement. Of course, some courts suggest that examining counsel is not free to call a potentially adverse witness in the blind hope that his testimony will be helpful and then when it proves not to be, commence to lead and impeach him.

(e.) Leading questions may be allowed in connection with a witness of limited understanding, such as a child, an adult of diminished intelligence, or a person who is experiencing some language difficulty.

(f.) Leading questions can be put to a witness whose recollection has been exhausted but who apparently possesses additional information of a relevant sort. In other words, it is sometimes proper to refresh a witness' recollection by means of a leading question, thus—

Q. Can you remember the names of any other people who attended this meeting?

A. No, I can't. I know there were others but I just can't seem to come up with their names now.

Q. You have exhausted your recollection of those persons who were present?

A. I'm afraid so.

Q. Would it ring any bells if I suggested to you that Mr. Clyde Bushmat also attended that meeting?

A. You're right! Now I remember. Bushmat was there, too.

Some courts would require that counsel request permission before posing a leading question of this type. Immediately after receiving the response "I'm afraid so," counsel would inquire of the trial court, "Your Honor, may I ask the witness a leading question? His recollection is exhausted and yet he has indicated that he has additional knowledge." Under the circumstances indicated above, this request would undoubtedly be granted.

(g.) Hypothetical questions of the sort once commonly put to expert witnesses are intensely leading, up to a point, but they are permissible as a means of providing a factual basis for the expert's opinion.

Q. Doctor, I am going to ask you to assume that all of the following facts are true and then I will ask you for your opinion with respect to them. First, please assume that the plaintiff is a woman who on April 1, 1991, was thirty-five years of age. Assume that on that day she * * * [Counsel provides additional data, the truth of which is to be assumed by the witness.]

Now, assuming all of these facts to be true, do you have an opinion, based on a reasonable degree of medical certainty, as to whether the plaintiff's current condition was caused by the accident that she had on April 1, 1991?

A. I do.

Q. What is that opinion?

2. *Compound and Otherwise Confusing Questions.* In making the testimonial record, counsel should avoid the use of questions that will confuse or mislead the witness. The principal offender is the double or compound question, which may leave everyone in the courtroom baffled. Such questions result in ambiguous or incomplete responses.

Q. State where you were and whether at that time you had a conversation with Clyde Bushmat—was that his first name?—and, if so, what it was.

A. That's right, he said his first name was Clyde, and * * * What was the rest of your question?

BY EXAMINING COUNSEL: Would the court reporter please read the question back?

THE COURT: Maybe it would be better to ask him one question at a time, counsel. Put another question.

Questions should be brief, clear, and cast in reasonably simple terms. The use of negatives in questions is worth avoiding because they generate confusion.

Q. Actually, you don't know whether Bushmat was there, do you?

A. Yes.

THE COURT: Just one moment. Does the witness mean 'Yes, I know,' 'Yes, it is true that I don't know,' or 'Yes, Bushmat was there'?

3. *Questions Assuming Unproved Facts.* The record cannot effectively be made by means of questions that assume the existence of facts that have neither been proved nor conceded. The classic example under this heading is "when did you stop beating your wife?" Nonexistent evidence cannot be supplied by means of "loaded" questions, since counsel is not testifying, and such questions only confuse the witness and the jury.

Expert Witnesses. The direct examination of an expert witness will differ somewhat from that of ordinary witnesses. This is true because of the operation of the so-called opinion rule. Generally speaking, witnesses are required to testify only about facts of which they have direct knowledge and they are not free to unburden themselves of opinions and beliefs about subjects on which any reasonably knowledgeable lay juror could form a conclusion. On the other hand, experts of one sort and another are allowed to express their opinions on relevant matters so long as a proper foundation has been laid.

An expert witness can state an opinion or conclusion if four conditions are satisfied:

1. The validity of the opinion or conclusion depends on special knowledge, experience, skill, or training not ordinarily found in lay jurors;

2. The witness must be qualified as an expert in the pertinent field;

3. She must possess a reasonable degree of certainty (probability) about her opinion or conclusion; and

4. Generally, in common law jurisdictions an expert witness must first describe the data on which his or her conclusion is based, or he/she must testify in response to a hypothetical question that sets forth such data. This means that three approaches are open to the expert witness. (a.) He can express an opinion based on facts personally observed, also perhaps taking into account facts communicated to him by another expert—as when a physician bases his opinion in part on the report of a radiologist. (b.) The expert who has been present in the courtroom can base her opinion on the evidence if it is not in conflict (the expert will not be permitted to weigh conflicting evidence). (c.) The expert can base an opinion on a hypothetical question embracing evidence of record.

Making the necessary record in connection with an expert witness involves two basic steps. First, he must be "qualified," that is, he must be asked a series of questions that will bring out his qualifications as an expert. Second, in many state jurisdictions the record must show the data on which the witness' opinion is to be based.

"Qualifying" an Expert Witness. Needless to say, the qualifying questions will vary depending on the field of expertise that is involved.

There follows a typical sequence of direct questions aimed at qualifying a witness as a medical expert:

> Q: Doctor, would you please state your full name and address for the court and jury?
>
> A: Lenore T. Walsh, and I reside at 1213 North Lake Shore Drive, Chicago.
>
> Q: What is your occupation or profession?
>
> A: Physician.
>
> Q: Are you licensed to practice as a physician in Illinois?
>
> A: I am.
>
> Q: Of what medical school are you a graduate?
>
> A: Northwestern University Medical School, here in the city. I graduated in 1949.
>
> Q: Are you in general practice or do you specialize?
>
> A: I specialize.
>
> Q: What is your specialty, Doctor?
>
> A: Basically I'm a neurologist but my specialty is a narrow one, epilepsy and electroencephalography.

Q: Did you undergo special training for your specialty?

A: Yes, I did.

Q: Would tell us about it, please?

A: After graduating from medical school I went to Boston, to the Harvard Medical School, where I was an assistant in neuropathology. That's the study of manifestation of disease in nervous systems. I remained there one year and then I went to Johnson's Foundation for Medical Physics at the University of Pennsylvania, where I did research designed to provide us with improved diagnostic techniques for discovery and treatment of nervous diseases.

Q: What did you develop at Pennsylvania?

A: I developed a blood flow recording in the form of a needle that could be inserted in the large vein that drains blood from the brain, and I learned the technique for recording electroencephalograms from the body. I later applied this to recording the electric activity of the brain.

Q: That's what is called the electroencephalograph, right?

A: That's right.

Q: Can you describe to us, just in ordinary layman's language that we can all understand, how an electroencephalograph works?

A: [Witness complies.]

Q: And how long have you been taking electroencephalograms?

A: Since 1951.

Q: And have you read tracings since 1951?

A: Yes.

Q: Would you tell us approximately how many EEG's you have taken and interpreted?

A: I now have over 300 in my cross-index file, filed for diagnosis and for types of electroencephalogram abnormalities.

Q: Have you ever held a medical teaching position, Doctor Walsh?

A: Yes, I am professor of neurology at Northwestern.

Q: Are you a member of any learned medical societies?

A: Yes, quite a few. Besides the Illinois Medical Association, Chicago Medical Association, and American Medical Association, I am a member of the American Neurological Association, the American Academy of Neurologists, the American Epilepsy Society, the American Cerebral Society, and the American Electroencephalographic Association.

Q: Now, you indicated that you hold a teaching position at Northwestern's Medical School. Have you done teaching there concerning neurology and electroencephalograms?

A: Yes, those are my subject areas.

Q: You lecture to students on these subjects?

A: Yes, and to doctors.

Q: Have you ever written articles for medical journals on your specialty?

A: Yes, quite often.

Q: Would you give us some of the titles of your publications in learned journals?

A: [Witness complies.]

(At this point the witness would be tendered as an expert and opposing counsel would be permitted to engage in a *voir dire* examination, described hereafter, further to test the witness' level of expertise.)

Of course, the list of trained experts includes a broad range of persons who function in fields other than medicine but the mode of questioning to get their qualifications on the record is pretty much the same. Here is an example involving a trained expert from a field other than medicine:

Q: What is your name, please?

A: Milton F. Pine.

Q: And where do you live?

A: 630 North Beechwood Avenue, in Urbana, Illinois.

Q: What is your occupation?

A: I am on the faculty of the University of Illinois, Department of Forestry.

Q: Could you give us some notion of your background, sir?

A: Well, I had my undergraduate work at Purdue University in forestry. My Masters is from the New York State College of Forestry, and my Doctorate is from Yale University. At Yale I specialized in the field of wood properties, wood technology, and wood science.

Q: These are your specialties?

A: That's correct.

Q: Do you teach?

A: Yes, at Illinois, as I say. I teach those courses that have to do with the chemical, physical, and mechanical properties of wood.

Q: And when you speak of the properties of wood, what do you mean, just in everyday language?

A: [Witness explains his field in layman's terms.]

Q: Do you belong to any learned societies in your field of specialization?

A: Yes, I'm a member of the American Society for Testing and Materials. I am on two committees of the Society. I belong to the Forest Product Research Society and the American Wood Preservers Association.

Q: Have you had any experience with ladders, including the testing of them?

A: Yes, for the past twenty years or so. I have looked at a good many ladders, I can tell you, trying to find out why some of them failed. I have tested ladders, and I have tested components of ladders. I'm the author of an article, a technical report, on how one might use the weight of a ladder as a predictor of its bending strength and its service design.

Q: Could you tell us, Mr. Pine, if there are any standards that are used in the ladder industry?

A: Two main ones. The United States of America Standards Institute puts one out, Number A14.1. And the Underwriter's Laboratory has a standard on ladders.

Q: What is the purpose of publishing these standards for ladders?

A: [Witness explains that the standards are aimed at promoting the manufacture of safe, serviceable ladders.]

Q: And are you thoroughly familiar with these two standards?

A: Yes, indeed.

Q: Now, Mr. Pine, have you had occasion to examine Plaintiff's Exhibit 1 in this case, which is the ladder involved in the plaintiff's lawsuit?

A: Yes, at your request.

Q: Tell us what your examination consisted of.

A: [Witness complies.]

Q: Was your visual examination of Plaintiff's 1 sufficient for you to determine the cause of the collapse or breaking of this ladder?

A: Yes, it was.

Q: And you have an opinion about the cause?

A: Yes.

Q: What is that opinion?

A: The failure was a result of the cross-grain. The ladder's rails had less than 100 percent of their bending strength. It was a defect in the wood and it failed because of the defective wood.

There are those who have the mistaken belief that the title of "expert" can only be bestowed on a few members of professional groups

who have a string of advanced degrees after their name. Some people
think that only a scientist of one sort or another and perhaps a few
engineers can rightly be called experts. But the term "expert" is far
broader in meaning than this. Anyone who has ever tried to repair his
own television set or automobile knows that some people are experts at
these kinds of work and some are not. The proficient television
repairer is an expert in his field even though a Ph.D. may be the last
thing he ever hoped to acquire; the trained and experienced garage
mechanic or plumber or brick mason is just as surely an expert as the
most renowned neurosurgeon. The label "expert" applies to the sheet
metal worker, the carpenter, the electrician, the candlestick maker. It
applies to the firearms identification technician and those who are
adept at handwriting or fingerprint comparison. It applies to the
police officer who knows how to use, interpret, and explain special
equipment, such as radar vehicular speed measuring devices and equipment for measuring blood-alcohol ratios. As Rule 702 of the Federal
Rules of Evidence points out, a witness may be qualified as an expert
"by knowledge, skill, experience, training, or education."

And so counsel's qualifying questions sometimes focus on skill,
knowledge, and experience rather than on educational background and
memberships in learned societies. One short, somewhat unusual example will suffice. It combines expertise and personal knowledge.

Q: What is your name, young man?

A: Billy Walsh.

Q: Where do you live?

A: Here in Toledo.

Q: How old are you, Billy?

A: Eleven, pretty soon.

Q: How soon?

A: In two months, July.

Q: Do you have any hobbies, Billy; things you do for fun?

A: Yes.

Q: Name some of them, will you?

A: Baseball, swimming. I've got a little stamp collection.
And I collect bugs.

Q: By that you mean insects?

A: That's the fancy name for them. I call 'em bugs.

Q: Good enough. How long have you been collecting
bugs or insects?

A: For about four years.

Q: You collect them around here, around Toledo?

A: Yes, all around here, and out in the country, too.

Q: In the country around Toledo?

A: Yes, sir.

Q: Now, Billy, we have a question here as to whether a
certain type of bug or insect is ever found around or in Toledo.
In other words, in this part of the country. I want you to take
a look at this bottle, which is marked Plaintiff's Exhibit
Number 2. You'll see that there's a bug in the bottle. Turn
the bottle all around and look at the bug and then tell us
whether you have ever seen that kind of bug in or around
Toledo, Ohio.

A: Sure, I have. I've got a whole box full of them in my
room.

Q: Your witness, counsel.

At the conclusion of the direct questions aimed at qualifying a
witness as an expert, and before examining counsel gets into substantive questions, opposing counsel is entitled to interrupt and engage in
cross-examination as to the witness' expertise. This, somewhat confus-
ingly, is often referred to as a *voir dire* of the witness. At this time the
cross-examiner, believing the witness to be unqualified to express an
"expert" opinion, makes his record. His cross-questions will be limited
strictly to the matter of the witness' qualifications.

Hypothetical Questions to Experts. The medium of the hypothetical question is employed where the expert witness does not have direct
knowledge of the facts, or the evidence, on which an opinion is desired.
Careful trial counsel will usually draft the hypothetical question well in
advance of its use at trial. In doing this she will usually be assisted by
the expert, thus making sure that all the essential facts are included in
the question in a sensible sequence. At the beginning of a hypothetical
question the witness is called upon to assume as true all of the facts
that will be asserted by counsel in the body of the question. The body
of the question then sets forth, in hypothetical form, the material facts
as to which the expert's opinion is sought. (In the federal practice, as
will be further explained later, it is not necessary to lay out *all* of the
underlying facts, however. See Fed.R.Evid. 705: "The expert may
testify in terms of opinion or inference and give reasons therefor
without prior disclosure of the underlying facts or data, unless the
judge requires otherwise.") A hypothetical question's conclusion inquires whether the witness has an opinion, based upon a reasonable
degree of certainty, regarding the assumed facts. Thus a hypothetical
question may end this way:

Q: Doctor Faust, assuming all of these facts to be true,
have you an opinion, based on a reasonable degree of certainty
from a surgical point of view, whether the facts assumed in the
question and the injury assumed, namely, the dislocation of the
vertebrae, and the fracture of the lamina of the fifth cervical
vertebra, are sufficient to cause the symptoms and the conditions assumed in my hypothetical question?

A: I do have an opinion.

Q: What is that opinion, doctor? [At this point any
objection to the question will be made and ruled upon.]

Hypothetical Questions Under the Federal Rules of Evidence. The approach to expert testimony taken by the Federal Rules of Evidence is less limiting than the typical common law approach outlined above.

In the first place, Rule 703 provides that an expert witness can base his opinion testimony on facts or data "perceived by or made known to the expert at or *before* the hearing" (emphasis added). This means that underlying facts or data can be gleaned not only from firsthand observation or from listening to testimony or a fullblown hypothetical question but also from a presentation made to the witness outside the courtroom. For example, this presentation might consist of showing an expert medical witness the pertinent medical records of the person about whose mental or physical condition the witness is to testify.

> Q: Doctor Faust, prior to this trial did you, at my request, review all of the medical records of the plaintiff Clyde Bushmat, including his medical history?

> A: I did, very thoroughly.

> Q: And did you have occasion to examine Mr. Bushmat in your office?

> A: Yes, I conducted a complete neurological examination.

> Q: I will ask you whether, on the basis of your review of all his records and your clinical examination, you have formed an opinion, to a reasonable degree of medical certainty, regarding the cause of his reported back pain?

> A: I have, yes.

> Q: Would you please tell the court and jury what your opinion is, and your reasons for arriving at that opinion?

> A: [Witness states his opinion and describes his reasons for reaching it, but does not describe—at least not in complete detail—the specific facts of the plaintiff's case.]

The expert's omission of all the facts underlying his or her opinion is explicitly authorized by the Federal Rules of Evidence. Rule 705 provides that an expert can testify to his/her conclusions and explain the reasons for them without prior in-court disclosure of the underlying facts or data, unless the trial judge requires disclosure.

This provision eliminates the necessity for lengthy and often tedious hypothetical questions, used as a vehicle for revealing the data on which an expert's opinion builds. However, Rule 705 does not do away with the hypothetical question absolutely; it simply does away with any absolute requirement that a hypothetical question, or a complete one, be used. The putting of a hypothetical question sometimes has its advantages as an educational device (or, to put it on a tactical plane, it permits counsel to summarize some of the evidence long before the time for his or her closing argument or summation) and it is safe to predict that trial lawyers will not invariably accept the rule's invitation to forego their use altogether. What Rule 705 does do is permit some streamlining of expert testimony, either by omission of the hypothetical question or its abbreviation. The rule forecloses successful assignments of error based on a claim that opposing counsel's hypothetical was incomplete, that is, did not include every scrap of underlying data. Thus the rule should make counsel less nervous about the use of hypotheticals. In effect, Rule 705 places on the cross-examiner the burden of eliciting any weak, unreliable, or missing data. This strongly suggests that opposing counsel will be at a distinct disadvantage unless she has engaged in adequate pre-trial discovery. (Consult Federal Rule of Civil Procedure 26(b)(4), as revised.)

Laying the Foundation for Admission of Evidence. Before plunging into testimony on the merits the direct examiner of a witness usually finds it necessary to lay a preliminary foundation for the witness' testimony or for the admission of an exhibit that the witness is "sponsoring". For example, some foundation questions will be required to demonstrate that the witness is a percipient one; that is, that he or she was in a spatial and temporal position to obtain personal knowledge of the matters about which he/she is to testify. (Fed.R.Evid. 602 reads: "A witness may not testify to a matter unless evidence is introduced sufficient to support a finding that the witness has personal knowledge of the matter. Evidence to prove personal knowledge may, but need not, consist of the witness' own testimony.") This involves putting questions aimed at showing that the witness was in a position to see, hear, etc., the matters about which he or she is going to testify. It may not be much more complicated than inquiring, "About how far away were you from the two vehicles when you saw them collide?"

A foundation attesting relevance is also essential, although this is often self-evident from the natural flow of the witness' descriptive testimony. Still, careless trial counsel sometimes neglect it. It is not enough, in connection with a railroad grade crossing accident that occurred on April 1, 1991, to ask a witness who has been handed a photograph, "Is Plaintiff's Exhibit 9 for Identification a true and fair representation of the Madison Street grade crossing of the Illinois Central Railroad?" Time is frequently an indispensable ingredient of relevance; perhaps the characteristics of the grade crossing have changed significantly since April 1, 1991. A vital component of the relevance foundation for plaintiff's photograph is the time factor, since the factfinder requires assurance that the photograph accurately depicts the crossing's appearance at the *pertinent* time. Thus the proper sequence of examination would run something like this:

Q: As a result of your daily route to work, about which you have previously testified, were you familiar with the appearance of the Madison Street grade crossing of the Illinois Central Railroad as of April 1, 1991?

A: Yes, I had been over it, both ways, almost every day during both March and April of that year.

Q: Then I want you to cast your mind back to that time, April 1, 1991. I hand you what has been marked Plaintiff's Exhibit 9 for Identification and I'll ask you whether or not it is a true and fair representation of the Illinois Central's Madison Street grade crossing as it existed on April 1, 1991?

A: Yep, that's the way it looked back then.

Obviously, counsel often must lay a foundation—make a record—that demonstrates the existence of the essential elements of some evidentiary principle on which she intends to rely. Here a list of examples could be extended to cover every rule of admissibility. We can content ourselves with two examples that illustrate the meticulous making of the record preliminary to the offering of an item of evidence through an exception to the rule against hearsay. First, an example involving an item of past recollection recorded; then one involving a business record.

The past recollection recorded example (see Fed.R.Evid. 803(5)) comes from an insurance case. Counsel is trying to establish that a stolen Chinese painting had, at the pertinent time, been in the possession of her client, plaintiff Edman. The witness on the stand is an art dealer.

Q: As I understand it, then, you were in Mr. Edman's hotel room in London. He unwrapped the package, which was a sort of cylinder about a foot and a half long and as big around as your wrist, is that right?

A: That's correct, took the paper off of it.

Q: Can you describe what was in the package or tube?

A: Yes, I can. It was a Chinese scroll painting.

Q: A scroll, rolled up?

A: Yes, but Mr. Edman unrolled it on the table so I could examine it.

Q: What was it of, a landscape or figure or what?

A: Typical Chinese landscape.

Q: Did it bear any identifying markings of any kind?

A: It did.

Q: Please describe any identifying markings you saw on the Edman painting.

A: Well, I don't read old Chinese but there was a single Chinese character at the top of the painting, in the margin.

Q: You observed this marking on the painting?

A: Yes, but I couldn't read it, if that's what you're asking.

Q: I understand. But can you describe the mark to us? Do you recall what it looked like?

A: Vaguely. It had dots in it. Little circles. I can't give you a much better description. I don't remember it that well. It was just a Chinese character. Most Chinese pictures have a number of characters on them. The big one may be the artist's signature. The little ones along the side, made with a seal, are often collectors' marks.

Q: This painting had just one big character on it?

A: Yes.

Q: And you knew what that character looked like while you were there in Mr. Edman's hotel room?

A: Of course, I was looking right at it.

Q: Thank you. After you looked at the picture, what did you do?

* * *

Q: When you got back to your hotel room, what time was it, if you know?

A: It was 9:30.

Q: And you think you left Mr. Edman's room at about 9:15?

A: Yes. It was on the sixteenth floor and I was on the twenty-second. I'm being conservative but it took me a few minutes to get an elevator.

Q: When you got back to your own room, what did you do?

A: I sat down at the desk and made a memorandum of our meeting.

Q: The meeting with Mr. Edman?

A: Yes.

Q: What, in general, did you include in this memo?

A: There wasn't anything general about it. I put down everything that happened, what was said, the whole thing. I wanted some future protection.

Q: How would you characterize your memory of that meeting at the time you prepared your memo?

A: Perfect, excellent. I could remember everything that went on.

Q: Did you describe the Chinese character in your memo?

A: Not in words.

Q: Did you describe it at all?

A: Yes, I drew a sketch of it.

Q: You still remembered what it looked like?

A: Then, I did.

Q: But you don't now?

A: Not well enough to draw it again accurately, no. I see a lot of characters in my business.

Q: Don't we all? When you drew the sketch of the character that night, did you draw it accurately?

A: Yes.

Q: On what sort of paper did you draw it?

A: On the hotel stationery. Claridge's.

[To the court reporter]: I will ask the court reporter to mark this for identification as Plaintiff's Exhibit 6. [Reporter does so; counsel shows the exhibit to the judge and opposing counsel.]

Q: Handing you what has been marked Plaintiff's Exhibit 6 for Identification, I'll ask you if you know what it is?

A: Yes, this is my memo.

Q: In your longhand?

A: Yes.

Q: Made about 9:30 on the night of January 14, 1982?

A: That's right.

Q: Does Exhibit 6 contain the drawing or sketch about which you have just testified; the drawing or sketch you made of the Chinese character that was on the painting that Mr. Edman showed you that night?

A: Yes. Do you want me to point it out to you?

Q: Better yet, take this pencil and draw a circle around the sketch as it appears on Plaintiff's Exhibit 6 for Identification.

The foundation for a business record offered, for example, under Federal Rule of Evidence 803(6), will involve this sort of questioning:

Q: What is your name, sir?

A: Arthur L. Jackson, of 1300 Terrace Road, East Cleveland.

Q: What is your business or occupation, Mr. Jackson?

A: I'm a bookkeeper.

Q: Employed by whom?

A: Flashner Furniture Company, here in Cleveland.

Q: Were you employed by Flashner Furniture on March 17, 1982?

A: Yes.

Q: Who was in charge of the bookkeeping department there at that time?

A: I was, and I still am.

Q: Very good, sir. Were all the entries in the books and records of the Flashner Furniture Company kept and maintained by you?

A: Yes, and they were made under my supervision.

Q: What books of account did you use in 1982?

A: Same as now. A ledger, cash book, journal, and the invoice or sales book.

Q: Will you describe the method you followed in 1982 in keeping your books?

A: Sales tickets are made for all sales and from there, posted to the general ledger. The sales tickets are bound together in what we call a sales book. All cash received is entered in the cash book and then posted to the ledger. The journal is used for general entries.

Q: I show you what has been marked Plaintiff's Exhibit 1 for Identification and ask you what it is, if you know?

A: It is a ledger sheet account of Mr. Robert H. Watkins.

Q: How do you know that?

A: In the first place, I brought it to court this morning in response to a subpoena you issued to me. I brought it from my office. And it is in the handwriting of my assistant.

Q: Was Plaintiff's Exhibit 1 made in the usual and ordinary course of your business, if you know?

A: It was.

Q: I show you Plaintiff's Exhibits 2 and 3 for Identification. Well, take 2 first. Do you know what 2 is?

A: Yes, it is the sales book that I referred to earlier.

Q: What is Exhibit 3, if you know?

A: The cash book.

Q: Were Exhibits 2 and 3 prepared and kept under your supervision?

A: Yes, sir.

Q: In the usual course of business?

A: Certainly.

Q: In whose handwriting are Exhibits 2 and 3?

A: My assistant's.

Q: Who provided the information contained in Exhibits 2 and 3? Who transmitted that information to your assistant?

A: Our sales personnel.

Q: They are required to do that?

A: Yes, that's one of their duties.

Q: Did you bring Exhibits 2 and 3 here in response to my subpoena?

A: Yes. I would have brought them anyway, with or without.

Q: Thank you very much. It's just a formality. Did you bring them from your office at Flashner's?

A: I did. From the files.

Q: Who would have posted the items shown on Plaintiff's Exhibit 2, the sales book, to Exhibit 1, the ledger sheet?

A: My assistant.

Q: Would his doing this have been in accordance with regular practice in your business?

A: Yes, sir.   1

Q: Who would have posted items from the cash book,   2
which is Exhibit 3, to Exhibit 1, the ledger sheet?   3
                                                                            4
A: Again, my assistant.   5

Q: All in the usual and regular course of your business?   6

A: Yes.   7
                                                                            8
BY OFFERING COUNSEL: Your Honor, we now offer   9
into evidence what have been marked Plaintiff's Exhibits 1, 2,   10
and 3.   11

THE COURT: They will be received.   12
                                                                           13
Using an Interpreter. When a witness has a serious language   14
barrier—when he or she speaks no English or very little—the testimo-   15
nial record will have to be made with the assistance of a qualified   16
interpreter. The interpreter must be shown to be disinterested and   17
will be required to swear or affirm that he "will truly and correctly   18
translate the questions of counsel from English to [German, Spanish,   19
whatever the witness' language may be] and the answers of the witness   20
from [German, Spanish] to English, so help me God." He must trans-   21
late the questions and the answers verbatim. Counsel will frame her   22
questions just as though she were questioning the witness directly in   23
English. That is, counsel, looking at the witness on the stand and not   24
at the interpreter, will inquire, "What happened next?"; she will not   25
address her question to the interpreter, saying, "Now ask him what   26
happened next." A useful precaution involves the making of an audi-   27
otape of any translated examination.   28
                                                                           29
                                                                           30
                          B.   31
                                                                           32
             Cross-Examination of Witnesses   33

As was suggested earlier, cross-examination is a much more flexi-   34
ble instrument than direct examination. It is hedged about by far   35
fewer restrictive rules. Relevance is the principal test of a cross-   36
question's propriety; relevance, and whether the cross-questions are   37
ranging too far beyond the contours of opposing counsel's direct exami-   38
nation of the witness.   39

The proper purposes of cross-examination are numerous. At its   40
most innocuous, cross-examination may do no more than clarify, sup-   41
plement, or qualify the direct testimony of a not very damaging   42
witness. However, cross-examination is usually used in a much more   43
aggressive fashion. In an effort to weaken the witness' direct evidence, 44
the cross-examiner's questions may challenge the sources of the wit-   45
ness' knowledge, together with his perception and his memory. The   46
examiner may also try to demonstrate the witness' inability to describe   47
events consistently and accurately. Cross-examination can be em-   48
ployed to extract admissions of fact that undermine the witness' direct   49
testimony. And cross-examination can be used to impeach the witness'   50
veracity, to cast a cloud on his truthfulness.   51

On one level a witness' veracity can be put in doubt by inquiries revealing an interest or partisanship, the existence of a bias or prejudice, which might lead him to misrepresent the facts or to twist them. That he is related to or friendly with the opposite party, or hostile to the examining side, can be developed, and any direct or indirect pecuniary interest in the outcome of the lawsuit can be gone into.

A witness can be impeached, on a somewhat different level, by cross-questions revealing that he has made prior out-of-court statements that are inconsistent with the answers he gave on his in-court direct examination. Occasionally a witness can also be impeached, on yet another level, by evidence of serious criminal convictions or prior "bad acts" tending to cast doubt on his current reliability.

It follows from what has just been said that counsel is free to use leading questions to make his or her record on cross-examination. (See, e.g., Fed.R.Evid. 611 (c): "Ordinarily leading questions should be permitted on cross-examination.") It is virtually impossible to conduct an impeaching cross-examination without asking leading questions. This does not mean, however, that excessively argumentative cross-questions will be countenanced by a trial court. It is one thing to inquire, in altogether leading fashion, "Isn't it a fact that on the night in question you could see only about ten or twelve feet ahead of you?" It is quite another thing, upon being given an unsatisfying response, heatedly to inquire, "Do you really expect the jury to believe that?" The first question is proper on cross-examination, there being scant risk that the opposing party's witness will accept the suggestion built into a leading question and supply the cross-examining party with a favorable but false answer. The second question is improper on either direct or cross-examination; it is unduly argumentative and contributes nothing of value to the trial record.

Questions assuming unproved facts ("loaded" questions), compound and otherwise confusing questions are no more allowable on cross-examination than they are on direct.

C.

Tangible Evidence

Standing in contrast to testimonial evidence is tangible evidence. Tangible evidence may be a writing, a murder weapon, the seized marijuana, a rusted metal container, the scar on a tort plaintiff's face. Putting writings to one side for a moment, because special rules have clustered around them, we can say that there are two basic types of tangible evidence: (1.) real evidence, and (2.) demonstrative evidence. And just as one must qualify oral testimony for admission into evidence by showing, for example, that the witness has personal knowledge of relevant facts, one must also qualify items of tangible evidence for receipt into evidence.

Tangible exhibits should be offered during the direct or re-direct examination of a party's witnesses and not during the cross-examination of the adverse party's witnesses. To put it a different way, *your* exhibits should be offered during *your* direct case, not opposing counsel's. It is not reversible error, however, to receive exhibits during cross-examination; the trial court can permit it and the parties can agree to it, expressly or by implication (as when no objection is interposed).

Real Evidence. This is "the real thing"—the actual murder weapon, not a mere example of a weapon of the type said to have been used in the alleged crime. Real evidence can be direct evidence, offered to establish facts about the tangible thing itself, such as the extent of plaintiff's disfigurement as a consequence of the observable facial scar. Real evidence can also be circumstantial, as when facts about an object are offered as the basis for an inference that some other fact is true; for example, rust inside a metal container implies the prior presence of moisture in the container.

The procedure for making the record in connection with real evidence is sometimes quite elaborate, depending on the nature of the particular exhibit. (It is usually easier to get a single letter into evidence than a patient's complete medical record, consisting of numerous separate records made by different authors at different times in different places for different reasons.) In general, there are six steps, all of them important:

1. *Marking for Identification.* In order to build a trial record that will be understandable and efficient to work with later on, counsel will cause real evidence to be marked or tagged for identification, usually by the court reporter. Thereafter, during her examination of witnesses, counsel will refer to the item by its identifying number or letter. Still later, when someone reads the typewritten trial record, she can readily associate the witness' testimony with the marked exhibits that are bound into the record either at the end of the transcribed testimony or, if the record is a lengthy one, in one or more separate volumes.

With experienced trial counsel the matter of marking exhibits for identification becomes almost automatic: when a trial lawyer picks something up with the intention of introducing it in evidence, he or she will first proceed to the court reporter and ask him to mark it in numerical or alphabetical sequence. Counsel will then subside into silence, since the reporter cannot record counsel's comments or continued questions to a witness while at the same time marking or tagging the exhibit. After the exhibit has been marked, counsel will as a matter of courtesy show the exhibit to the trial judge and opposing counsel unless they have already seen it or, in the case of a writing, diagram, chart, map, or the like, been provided by counsel with copies.

Step No. 1 goes this way, then:

> OFFERING COUNSEL [having picked up a letter from the counsel table]: I will ask the court reporter to mark this for identification. If I recall correctly, this would be Plaintiff's 9.

> COURT REPORTER [marking the exhibit]: Yes, this will be Plaintiff's 9.

OFFERING COUNSEL: Your Honor, I believe we gave you a Xerox copy of this letter. It is dated April 1, 1991, on the defendant's letterhead.

THE COURT: Yes, I have it.

OFFERING COUNSEL [addressing opposing counsel]: And we supplied you with a copy, too, did we not?

OPPOSING COUNSEL: Yes, we have our copy, although of course we reserve our right to object to it at the appropriate time.

OFFERING COUNSEL: Of course.

In complex litigations, counsel may have caused all or most of the tangible exhibits, especially writings, to be marked for identification prior to the onset of trial, often at a judicially supervised pre-trial conference at which objections to the exhibits were considered and ruled upon. (See III., Objections to Evidence, infra.)

2. *Laying the Necessary Foundation.* In the absence of a pretrial ruling or an agreement (stipulation) with opposing counsel that the exhibit is receivable, it will next be necessary to lay the foundation for admission of the item of real evidence. (See, e.g., Fed.R.Evid. 901.) This is usually accomplished through one or more witnesses who "sponsor" the exhibit, identifying (authenticating) it and illuminating its relevance to the issues in the case. Basically, this involves testifying that the exhibit is "the genuine article," "the real thing." Sometimes it involves testimony that the exhibit is a legitimate form of demonstrative evidence. Examination under Step No. 2 may proceed in this way:

BY OFFERING COUNSEL: Officer, I hand you what has been marked Prosecution Exhibit Number 1 for Identification and ask you if you know what it is?

A. Yes, I recognize it.

Q. What is it?

A. This is the knife that I found next to the victim's body that night.

Q. And by 'this' you mean Prosecution Exhibit Number 1?

A. Yes, sir.

Q. How do you know that Prosecution Exhibit Number 1 is the same knife that you saw that night?

A. At that time I scratched the date and my initials on the handle of the knife, right here. [Indicating.]

If the witness, unlike the one in the preceding example, is unable to identify the exhibit to the exclusion of all similar objects, the chain of custody, without any hearsay links, must be traced in order to establish that the exhibit is "the real thing." This means that there will be a whole series of witnesses called to the stand, each one accounting for the period during which the exhibit was in his or her custody. In this manner each link in the chain of custody is forged and it is demonstrated that the exhibit is in fact "the genuine article."

If the condition of the object is significant, the sponsoring witness must be prepared to testify that its condition has not changed in any important way since the pertinent time, thus—

BY OFFERING COUNSEL: Mrs. Stitz, I show you Plaintiff's Exhibit Number 3 for Identification. Do you know what that is?

A. Yes, that's the tin can that I cut my hand on.

Q. How do you happen to know that?

A. It's been on a shelf in my kitchen ever since that day, except for the time I brought it to your office to show to you, and I brought it to court today myself.

Q. Can you tell us whether the condition of Exhibit Number 3 has changed since the day of your accident?

A. Just that there aren't any green beans in it any more. I cleaned it out.

Q. Otherwise it looks the same?

A. Yes, sir. You can still see the jagged metal protrusion that cut my hand. [Indicating.]

Finally, it should be mentioned that the record has not been satisfactorily made where the instrumentality of an alleged crime has not been linked to the crime and to the accused.

3. *Offering the Exhibit into Evidence.* The third step involves offering the exhibit into evidence once the proper foundation has been laid. Step No. 3, although sometimes forgotten by inexperienced trial counsel, is a mechanical one:

BY OFFERING COUNSEL: Your Honor, we now offer into evidence, as Plaintiff's Exhibit Number 1, what has previously been marked as Plaintiff's Exhibit Number 1 for Identification.

THE COURT: There being no objection, it will be received.

4. *Securing an Express Ruling on the Record.* In the preceding example the trial court made a prompt and explicit ruling on counsel's offer. Occasionally, however, counsel may find it necessary to request the court to make an unequivocal ruling. The trial court's silence in the face of an offer will not necessarily be taken, on review, as an acceptance of the offered evidence.

5. *A Precautionary Measure.* Cautious counsel, having obtained a ruling admitting his exhibit into evidence, may foreclose any possible future confusion by requesting the court reporter to scratch out the words "for Identification" in the exhibit-mark, thereby making it doubly clear that the exhibit was received in evidence.

6. *Showing or Reading the Exhibit to the Jury.* Now, for the first time, offering counsel is free to show the exhibit to the jurors or, in the case of written material, read it to them or direct the witness to read it

to them. As a matter of courtesy, however, express permission to do so is usually requested of the trial judge.

> BY OFFERING COUNSEL: Your Honor, may we now pass the exhibit, Plaintiff's Number 1, to the members of the jury for their examination?

> THE COURT: You may.

Counsel will put no new questions to the witness on the stand until the jurors have had an opportunity to inspect the exhibit that has been handed to them.

So-called "testimonial exhibits," such as a deposition that has been placed in evidence or a learned treatise offered under Fed.R.Evid. 803(18), usually must be read into the record (in the fact-finders' hearing, of course) since most jurisdictions will not permit this sort of exhibit to be taken by the jurors to their deliberation room for examination along with the other exhibits in the case. (It is thought that giving the testimonial exhibit to the jurors might unduly highlight an isolated block of testimony.) Counsel can read the exhibit into the record herself or, in the case of a deposition or prior recorded testimony, she can put someone in the witness chair—another lawyer with whom she is associated, even a moonlighting actor hired as a deposition reader—to read the deponent's or witness' answers in response to counsel's reading of the questions contained in the deposition or transcript.

Demonstrative Evidence. This is *not* "the real thing." It is tangible material used for explanatory or illustrative purposes only: it is a visual aid, such as an anatomical model, a chart, a diagram, a map, a film, and the like. Evidence that is demonstrative only—that does not qualify as substantive evidence—is not ordinarily offered into evidence in the way real evidence is and it thus does not go to the jury's deliberation room. However, this does not mean that there is no foundational procedure, no record to be made, in connection with demonstrative material.

There are two basic types of demonstrative evidence. First there is "selected" demonstrative evidence, such as handwriting exemplars (specimens) used as standards of comparison by a handwriting expert. Then there is "prepared" or "reproduced" demonstrative evidence, such as the model or the diagram.

It is in connection with prepared or reproduced demonstrative material that there is the greatest risk of fabrication or distortion. The law seeks to minimize these risks by requiring certain testimonial assurances. These assurances are a part of the foundation, part of the record that must be made, as a precondition to the use of demonstrative materials in the courtroom.

In the first place, it is again true, as it usually is with real evidence, that conditions shown by the exhibit must not be significantly different from those that existed at the time of the events in question. If conceded changes are irrelevant, they must at least be accounted for, as, for example, in connection with a photograph of the accident site that reveals buildings constructed since the incident in question.

Secondly, there must be testimony that a particular demonstrative exhibit is a "true and fair representation" of what it purports to show. Thus a person familiar with the scene depicted in a photograph (it need not necessarily be the photographer) can lay the foundation for the photograph's use as an item of demonstrative material. In connection with motion picture film and tapes, there must be testimony from a knowledgeable witness that they have not been improperly edited by means of splicing, erasing and the like.

Writings. The evidentiary significance of writings frequently depends on their authorship. If the asserted letter of acceptance was dictated and signed by the defendant corporation's president, it will be a crucial item of evidence in a contract case; if it was signed by someone lacking any authority, real or apparent, to do so, it will be of no legal consequence. Accordingly, it often is necessary to make a record on the question of authorship. Is the writing truly what it purports to be on its face, a letter composed and signed by the defendant's president? A writing, in other words, is not receivable in evidence until it has been authenticated. (See e.g., Fed.R.Evid., Arts. IX–X.) Its genuineness must be demonstrated to the trial judge, as a preliminary matter, before the jury can consider it. It cannot be read or shown to the jury until the record has been made and the writing has been formally admitted into evidence by the judge.

A writing can be authenticated in a variety of ways:

    1. By a notice or request to admit genuineness, as under Rule 36 of the Federal Rules of Civil Procedure.

    2. By *direct* evidence that proves the handwriting in question. This can be either the identifying testimony of the writing's author, or the testimony of anyone who observed the writing being made.

    3. By proving the handwriting *circumstantially,* which can be accomplished—

        a. By the identifying testimony of someone who is familiar with the handwriting of the person in question;

        b. By the testimony of a handwriting expert who compares the questioned handwriting with one or more genuine specimens; or

        c. By letting the jurors themselves compare the questioned handwriting with genuine specimens (an approach which appeals to very few trial lawyers).

    4. By reliance on common law, statutory or rules provisions that render some writings self-authenticating or that set up presumptions of authenticity. (A good example is the so-called ancient documents rule (see generally, Fed.R.Evid., Art. IX).)

    The following is a simple example of direct authenticating testimony:

Q. Give your full name to the jury, please.

A. Clyde Bushmat.

Q. Your address?

A. 1313 Euclid Avenue, Cleveland, Ohio.

Q. What is your occupation?

A. I'm a deliveryman for C.D. Pigeon, a jewelry company here in the city.

Q. Do you know Morton P. Lishniss, the defendant in this case?

A. I do.

Q. How do you happen to know him?

A. I have delivered merchandise to him from time to time.

BY EXAMINING COUNSEL [to court reporter]: Please mark this Plaintiff's Exhibit Number 1 for Identification.

Q. Showing you what has just been marked Plaintiff's Exhibit Number 1 for Identification, Mr. Bushmat, I will ask you whether you have ever seen it before?

A. I've seen it before, yes.

Q. When, sir?

A. When I delivered the merchandise that's listed on it.

Q. On the occasion of that delivery did you see Morton P. Lishniss?

A. Sure I did.

Q. Tell us what happened.

A. I delivered the diamond necklace to Mr. Lishniss myself and I requested that he sign the receipt for it.

Q. Did he do so?

A. Yes, sir.

Q. How do you know he did?

A. I saw him do it.

Q. You saw him?

A. Yes I did. He signed it right there while I was watching him.

Q. Whose signature is this on Plaintiff's Exhibit Number 1 for Identification, Mr. Bushmat?

A. That's the signature that Mr. Lishniss made in my presence.

BY EXAMINING COUNSEL: We offer Plaintiff's Exhibit Number 1 for Identification as Plaintiff's Exhibit Number 1, your Honor.

THE COURT: It will be received.

If counsel is offering something other than the original of a writing his making of the record will include an indication of compliance with the "best evidence" rule. (See Fed.R.Evid., Art. X.) The following example begins in midstream:

Q. How many copies of the contract were signed, Ms. McLaren?

A. Just one.

Q. Who retained that? Who kept it?

A. I did.

Q. Do you have that original agreement that was executed by you and Mr. Bushmat?

A. No, I don't.

Q. Do you know where it is?

A. No, I do not. I can't find it.

Q. When did you last see it, Ms. McLaren?

A. The day we signed it.

Q. What did you do with it?

A. I put it in one of my desk drawers right after we executed it.

Q. Have you seen it since then?

A. No.

Q. When did you first look for it again?

A. About ten days ago, but I couldn't find it anywhere.

Q. Where did you search?

A. In my desk drawers, on top of the desk, all around my office, at home. Everywhere that I ordinarily keep papers. I looked everywhere.

Q. Have you tried to find it since then?

A. Yes. No luck.

Q. What do you think has happened to the original of the agreement?

A. Well, it's lost, that's all.

Q. Did you intentionally lose it or destroy it?

A. Of course not.

BY EXAMINING COUNSEL: Mark this Plaintiff's Exhibit Number 1 for Identification, if you please.

Q. Handing you what has been marked Plaintiff's Exhibit Number 1 for Identification, Ms. McLaren, I will inquire whether you have ever seen it before?

A. Oh, yes.

Q. Where and when?

A. In my office. I saw it there at the same time that the original agreement was executed. This is a Xerox copy of the original.

Q. Can you tell by looking at it whether or not it's a true and correct copy of the original?

A. Yes.

Q. Is it, or not?

A. Yes, it is. It was made that day, off the original. The Xerox shows the signatures, everything.

BY EXAMINING COUNSEL: We offer in evidence Plaintiff's Exhibit Number 1 for Identification.

THE COURT: It will be admitted as Plaintiff's Exhibit Number 1.

D.

Judicial Notice

Counsel who wish to take advantage of the time- and effort-saving judicial notice procedure should take care to make a proper record. Judicial notice is a form of evidence, substituting for more elaborate proof of facts that are (1.) subject to common knowledge among reasonably informed persons in the jurisdiction or (2.) capable of accurate and ready determination by resort to sources whose accuracy cannot reasonably be disputed.

If one or the other of these two bases for judicial notice is present, the taking of notice by a trial judge is mandatory if a proper record is made. This involves (1.) an on-the-record request for the taking of judicial notice and for the giving of an appropriate jury instruction— "We ask the court to take judicial notice, and so instruct the jury, that the Chicago River runs backwards, away from and not into Lake Michigan"—and (2.) presentation to the court, on the record, of any necessary back-up information such as an authoritative source of the sort mentioned in Federal Rule of Evidence 201(b)(2). The procedure might sound like this:

BY REQUESTING COUNSEL: Your Honor, we request the court to take judicial notice, and so instruct the jury, that October 11, 1990, fell on a Thursday.

THE COURT: Well, counsel, I don't know that as a fact and I doubt if it's common knowledge.

BY REQUESTING COUNSEL: Your Honor, I was just going to hand up to you a 1990 calendar published and distributed to lawyers by the Chicago Title & Trust Company.

THE COURT: All right, I see that October 11 was a Thursday. I don't suppose opposing counsel wants a hearing on the accuracy of this calendar?

BY OPPOSING COUNSEL: That won't be necessary, your Honor.

THE COURT: Ladies and gentlemen of the jury, you are
instructed to take it as established in this case, without further
proof, that October 11, 1990, was a Thursday.

III.

OBJECTIONS TO EVIDENCE

A.

Party Responsibility for Making Objections

The rules of evidence can be made to work only if a party who
contends that opposing counsel's question is improper or that certain
evidence should be excluded promptly advises the trial judge, who is the
umpire of the litigation, of the contention and the reasons for it. The
initiative with respect to evidentiary objections lies with the parties,
acting through their counsel, and not with the trial judge. This is
simply another example of party responsibility in the adversary trial
process. (See, e.g., Fed.R.Evid. 103.)

It is a responsibility gladly assumed by competent trial counsel,
who dislike few things more than a trial judge's usurpation of the
litigator's obligation to decide which objections, perhaps for purely
tactical or strategic reasons, he will forego. Thus it is unusual, although it would not be without precedent, to hear a judge exclude
evidence to which counsel has not objected; a competent judge will do
this only where the offered evidence is not only incompetent but also
irrelevant or potentially unfairly prejudicial or where she is preserving
the rights of an absent holder of some testimonial privilege. Occasionally, however, one encounters, the sort of judge who, possibly because
he is himself a frustrated trial lawyer, will interrupt testimony to
inquire of one silent side, "Do I hear an objection?" With almost equal
frequency one will hear the lawyer for that side respond, "You do not,
your Honor." Counsel, for reasons of her own, has made a deliberate
decision to dispense with any objection.

B.

Reasons for Foregoing Available Objections

No trial lawyer makes every evidentiary objection that may be
open to him. There are a variety of reasons for this. (1.) Trial counsel
has no need or wish to complain about every innocuous leading question put by opposing counsel since the use of leading questions as to
preliminary matters expedites the examination of witnesses, which is
usually advantageous to all concerned and poses no real risk of
prejudice. (2.) Counsel may let a questionable objection go by the board
because he does not want to run the risk that he will only underscore
hurtful testimony. (3.) He may abandon an available objection because
he does not want to give the jurors the impression that he is excessively
obstructive or that he distrusts them. (4.) Often counsel foregoes
objection because the evidence, although arguably inadmissible, actually in some way favors her client's cause. (5.) And sometimes counsel

remains silent because the opposing lawyer's offer of objectionable evidence "opens the door" for more important evidence that the silent lawyer hopes to offer later.

C.

Objections Made for Effect

The truth is that objections that go to nothing more important than the form of the question (e.g., leading) are as often made for jury-effect as they are for any weightier purpose. ("We've been very patient, your Honor, but the jurors might like to have a little more testimony from the witness and a little less from opposing counsel. This is all leading, your Honor, and we have to object to it.") Of course, the use of objections as an excuse to make speeches for the jurors' benefit is ethically questionable, as is their use solely to interrupt a damaging examination or to coach a witness who is undergoing effective cross-examination. The making of objections for improper purposes can bring an embarrassing admonition from the bench. It is the practice of an increasing number of trial judges to require that any argumentation in support of an objection be made at the bench, out of the jurors' hearing. Objecting counsel inquires, "May we approach the bench?" If the trial judge is receptive to argument on the objection, he or she will permit counsel to engage in a whispered sidebar presentation and may even adjourn to chambers if the arguments are likely to be extensive. Since jurors probably resent these mystifying huddles between the judge and the lawyers, there is all the more reason to forego needless objections.

D.

Time for Objecting to Testimony: Waiver

Because the burden of interposing legitimate objections, to "protect the record," is lodged with counsel and not the trial court, the failure to make a timely objection, in proper form, to an offer of evidence will usually operate to waive any possible basis of complaint about its receipt. "Let him speak now or forever hold his peace" is as applicable at trials as it is at weddings.

An objection must be made as soon as the basis for it becomes apparent. Counsel is not free to sit back, gambling that the witness will give a harmless or even a favorable answer, and then object when the answer proves to be damaging. The trial court is likely to respond to the belated objection with a terse, "Asked and answered, counsel." Ordinarily examining counsel's question will by its own terms reveal that it calls for inadmissible testimony. Opposing counsel must make an effort to interpose his objection before the witness answers.

> Q.　What did your sister tell you about the incident that she had observed?

> BY OPPOSING COUNSEL: Just one moment, please. We object, your Honor. It calls for hearsay and we ask that the witness not be permitted to answer.

THE COURT: The objection is sustained.

If the objection to a question is sustained before any answer is given but the terms of the question disclosed the expected answer, counsel can obtain an instruction to the jury that the question itself is not evidence in the case and should be wholly disregarded.

Q. Officer, did you issue a traffic ticket to the plaintiff?

PLAINTIFF'S COUNSEL: Now, we object to that question. Irrelevant.

THE COURT: Sustained.

PLAINTIFF'S COUNSEL: We ask that your Honor instruct the jury to disregard the implication contained in defense counsel's question.

THE COURT: Yes, the jurors are instructed to disregard the question completely. It is not evidence in this case and an objection to it has been sustained.

Of course, it is not always feasible neatly to insert one's objection between the question and the answer. For one thing, the witness may respond too quickly. All that opposing counsel can do in this situation is state her objection as soon as she can, adding a two-part request that the witness' answer be stricken and that the trial court instruct the jurors to disregard it. Sometimes an apparently unobjectionable question brings out an inadmissible answer. Here, obviously, counsel, be it examining counsel or opposing counsel, cannot phrase her objection until the infirmity in the witness' response emerges. Perhaps the answer is unresponsive, with the result that examining counsel is entitled to object. She will make what is sometimes referred to as an "after-objection":

Q. Did you observe the plaintiff enter the crosswalk?

A. Yes, and he appeared to be looking down at his feet instead of watching where he was going.

BY EXAMINING COUNSEL: Object to everything after the word 'Yes' and ask that it go out, your Honor. We also ask that you instruct the jury to disregard everything except the answer 'Yes' as being unresponsive to the question.

THE COURT: Your objection is sustained, and the jury is so instructed.

It is generally said that only examining counsel is entitled to object to an answer whose only infirmity is its lack of responsiveness. In other words, examining counsel is free to "adopt" an unresponsive but favorable answer, which he does either by expressly saying so or by the simple expedient of foregoing any objection to it. Opposing counsel, not being the author of the question, lacks standing to object to any unresponsive answer unless it is excludable on some evidentiary ground over and beyond unresponsiveness; for example, the witness' answer is not only unresponsive but also violative of the hearsay rule. Here are two examples of correct rulings:

> BY PLAINTIFF'S COUNSEL: Did you observe the plaintiff enter the crosswalk?
>
> A. Yes, and he looked in both directions first.
>
> BY DEFENSE COUNSEL: Object, unresponsive.
>
> BY PLAINTIFF'S COUNSEL: We adopt the entire answer, your Honor.
>
> THE COURT: The objection will be overruled.

The result will be different if the witness' answer is varied somewhat.

> BY PLAINTIFF'S COUNSEL: Did you observe the plaintiff enter the crosswalk?
>
> A. No, I didn't, but my sister did and she said that the man looked both ways first.
>
> BY DEFENSE COUNSEL: Object, unresponsive and hearsay, your Honor.
>
> BY PLAINTIFF'S COUNSEL: We adopt the entire answer, your Honor.
>
> THE COURT: The objection is sustained on the ground of hearsay.

Occasionally the inadmissibility of testimony does not emerge clearly until long after it has been received in evidence. This happens where it is revealed only after searching cross-examination that a witness' responses to direct examination were based on hearsay rather than personal knowledge, in which case opposing counsel will move to strike all of the witness' testimony and ask that the jurors be instructed to disregard it. It can also be said to happen in instances of so-called conditional relevance. When one side fails to "tie up" or "connect up" conditionally relevant evidence with other evidence that renders the earlier evidence relevant, a renewed objection to the earlier evidence will be sustained, it will be stricken, and the jury, upon request, will be ordered to disregard it in their deliberations.

Sometimes evidence is admissible only for a limited purpose. It may be admissible as to one party or for one purpose but not admissible as to another party or for some other purpose. For example, a witness' unsworn prior inconsistent statement may be admissible to impeach his credibility but not as substantive evidence of the truth of its contents. A prior criminal conviction may be receivable to impeach but not to prove that the accused is guilty of the current charge against him. Here counsel may wish to obtain an instruction that limits the evidence to its permissible scope. (This process is described in Fed.R.Evid. 105.)

E.

Objecting to Exhibits

Objections to an exhibit that constitutes real evidence will normally be made at the time the exhibit is formally offered in evidence.

Offering counsel is entitled to accomplish the laying of the necessary
evidentiary foundation for receipt of the exhibit. This he will do, as we
have seen, through one or more "sponsoring" witnesses who are capable
of identifying and otherwise authenticating the exhibit. Objections
interjected before offering counsel has had a chance to lay the foundation for the exhibit would ordinarily be premature. Certainly an
objection made at the juncture at which an exhibit is marked by the
court reporter for identification would be premature in all but the most
exceptional circumstances.

Q. Would you give the court and jury your full name,
please?

A. Mrs. Irene Stitz.

Q. And where do you reside, Mrs. Stitz?

A. At 3730 North Lake Shore Drive, in Chicago, Illinois.

Q. What is your present occupation, Mrs. Stitz?

A. I am the Records Librarian at Jefferson Memorial
Hospital here in the city.

Q. Would you describe your duties as a records librarian?

A. [Witness details her duties.]

Q. In response to a subpoena which I caused to be issued
to you, Mrs. Stitz, have you brought anything with you to court
today?

A. I have.

Q. What have you brought?

A. The records of Jefferson Memorial Hospital pertaining
to a patient named Clyde Bushmat.

BY OPPOSING COUNSEL: Object, your Honor.

THE COURT: Overruled. Proceed.

Q. Would you hand that folder to me, please? [Witness
hands folder to examining counsel.]

BY OFFERING COUNSEL: There appear to be nineteen
pages or pieces of paper in the folder that the witness has
handed to me. I will ask the court reporter to mark each
separate page, front and back. What number have we reached
with our exhibits at this point?

BY THE COURT REPORTER: This would be number 8.

BY OFFERING COUNSEL: Then we can begin with 8–A.

[Court reporter marks the group exhibit.]

Q. Mrs. Stitz, handing you what has been marked Plaintiff's Group Exhibit 8–A on the front and 8–B on the back, I'll
ask you what it is.

BY OPPOSING COUNSEL: Objection, your Honor.

BY OFFERING COUNSEL: Your Honor, I haven't offered
the exhibit yet. I've just barely gotten it marked for identification. May I have an opportunity to lay the proper foundation

for its admission? I believe I can do that through this witness.
Then I'll offer it and opposing counsel can then interpose any
objection he may have.

THE COURT: The objection is overruled. You're jumping
the gun, counsel. Wait until the exhibit is offered.

Q. Read the last question back, please.

Of course, an early objection, in advance of the offer, is appropriate
if improper use of an exhibit is being made. If, for example, examining
counsel displays the exhibit, such as a photograph or diagram, to the
jury in advance of its receipt in evidence, or if he asks the sponsoring
witness to read a written exhibit to the jury prior to its receipt in
evidence, an objection will be sustained.

BY THE COURT REPORTER [reading the last question to
the witness]: 'Mrs. Stitz, handing you what has been marked
Plaintiff's Group Exhibit 8–A on the front and 8–B on the back,
I'll ask you what it is.'

A. It is the admission sheet pertaining to Mr. Clyde
Bushmat's admission to Jefferson Memorial Hospital.

Q. Would you just read the first seven lines of that to the
jury, please?

BY OPPOSING COUNSEL: Now, I object to any reading
of this exhibit, your Honor. He's not doing what he said he
would. He hasn't laid an adequate foundation for its admission and he hasn't offered it. It can't be read to the jury yet.

THE COURT: Sustained. Lay your foundation, counsel.
Then we'll see whether this exhibit can be read to the jury.

Pre-Trial Objections to Exhibits in Complex Cases. In complex
litigations, or where particularly sensitive evidentiary questions are
involved, counsel will seek pre-trial rulings on proposed items of evidence. For example, in the federal practice the trial judge, by pre-trial
order, may fix a time for listing and marking the documents to be
offered by the parties and for inspection of the documents by the
opposing parties for the purposes of (1.) waiving formal authentication,
(2.) waiving objections on other grounds, and (3.) filing written objections. At the final pre-trial conference the judge will often make
unconditional rulings on counsel's objections. Documents admitted in
evidence unconditionally by pre-trial orders or rulings can then be used
at trial without further order or ruling.

Occasionally the trial judge will make conditional pre-trial evidentiary rulings for the guidance of counsel. Documents admitted conditionally are reoffered during trial, at which time a further ruling, now
unconditional, will be obtained.

Documents which have been unconditionally excluded at a pre-trial
conference need not be reoffered during trial; indeed, to do so would
ordinarily be improper.

In some jurisdictions lawyers who love the Latin speak of filing a
motion *in limine* (literally, "at the threshold") to obtain an advance-of-

trial ruling on a controversial item of evidence. A pre-trial exclusionary ruling will prevent the embarrassing in-court offering of improper
evidence. The process might go this way:

> BY OBJECTING COUNSEL: Your Honor, there's a police
> accident report floating around in this case and it's full of
> typical bystander statements picked up by the investigating
> officer. I'll show it to you. You can see that it is the sort of
> report that is inadmissible under *Johnson v. Lutz* and under
> the Federal Rules, specifically, 803(8). We don't want this
> report to be offered at trial, in the presence of the jury, and
> we're making a motion *in limine* at this time that it be kept
> out.

> THE COURT: This police report is plainly inadmissible. I
> am ruling that it will be excluded.

> BY OPPOSING COUNSEL: Well, your Honor, can we at
> least make our offer of it at trial, so we can make a record on
> it?

> THE COURT: No, you can't. You're making your record
> right now. Any reference during trial to this report and you'll
> have a mistrial. And I know I don't need to discuss contempt
> of court, counsel.

F.

Specificity of Objections

The question naturally comes up, how specific must an objection
be? Is it enough simply to stand up and say, "Object, your Honor"? Is
something more accomplished where counsel, after the fashion of Perry
Mason and other lawyers whose practice is limited to television serials,
intones, "Object, your Honor. Irrelevant, incompetent, and immaterial"? Or should a trial lawyer be quite specific: "Object, your Honor.
Hearsay"? Or: "Object, the best evidence rule hasn't been satisfied"?

A reading of the countless cases dealing with specificity *versus*
generality in the phrasing of objections would lead one to believe that
the bare announcement that "I object" is insufficient and that even the
somewhat more elaborate "Three I's," "Irrelevant, incompetent, and
immaterial," which McCormick called a "meaningless ritual," are unavailing except perhaps to preserve the question of relevance. The
codes and cases recommend that any objection be accompanied by a
reasonably specific statement of the ground(s) for it. (See, e.g., Fed.R.
Evid. 103(a)(1)). The idea is that a trial judge cannot be expected to
recognize instantly the particular evidentiary rules applicable to the
testimony and exhibits being offered in a given case. It may be asked,
why should a judge be any less equipped to detect the applicable rules
than the lawyers appearing before her? The answer is that the lawyers
have had the case for many months, even years, analyzing it and
preparing it for trial; they have had plenty of time to get a firm grip on
the evidentiary questions. Of course, the concept of adversariness is at

work here. It is up to the contending lawyers, and not the judge, not only to make objections but to support them with reasons.

In making objections the trial lawyer will have three aims in mind, two of which are directly concerned with the "making" of the record. First, counsel is seeking to educate the trial judge on the rule or rules of evidence that authorize the objection and the exclusion of the challenged evidence. Counsel is being an advocate. Second, by being reasonably explicit, counsel is preserving a record for possible appeal in case the judge overrules his objection. Thirdly, and this is nothing more than the reverse of the same coin, he is making a record that will support the trial judge on appeal in the event that she sustains counsel's objection.

An exhaustive catalog of instances in which a specific objection is essential to preserve error would be very lengthy. The following examples are of recurring bases for specific objections in many jurisdictions, although some of them do not come up with much frequency:

Argumentative question	Narrative answer called for by the question
Best evidence rule violated	Parol evidence rule violated
Compound question	Privileged communication
Conclusion of law or fact improperly called for by the question	Unresponsive answer
Cross-examination exceeding scope of the direct examination	Witness incompetent to testify
Dead Man's Act renders witness incompetent to testify	Hypothetical question is misleading or unfairly prejudicial
Facts not in evidence assumed in the question	Improper impeachment
Foundation for introduction of real or demonstrative evidence inadequate (chain of custody, etc.)	Counsel is misstating the testimony
Foundation for introduction of writing inadequate to authenticate	Irrelevant
Hearsay	No personal knowledge
Instructions of trial court incorrect	Unfairly prejudicial—Rule 403
Leading question on direct examination	

(For a comprehensive catalog of objections, see R. Park, Trial Objections Handbook (Shepard's McGraw-Hill 1991).)

The rules regarding the required form of objections are heavily weighted in favor of the trial judge. If a generalized objection is made and overruled, appellate courts will not reverse unless a valid basis for the objection is perfectly clear. Obviously, in many situations of a recurring sort it would be a waste of time to require a recitation of reasons for a self-evident objection and the trial court is likely to rule before counsel can do more than say "I object." A common example would be the question that by its terms plainly seeks to elicit hearsay testimony. A simple "I object" should suffice to make the record here.

Occasionally it is also said that a general objection is enough where receipt of the offered evidence cannot be justified on any legal basis at all. However, it would be dangerous to gamble on the availability of this argument, which is often grounded on a lawyer's 20–20 hindsight. The rationale behind appellate courts' unwillingness to reverse on the basis of a trial judge's overruling of a general objection is that counsel should not be free to shift to the judge the burden of searching for an applicable exclusionary rule.

The rules also aid the trial judge when he or she has sustained a general objection—and here they redound to objecting counsel's benefit, too. On appeal the trial court will be upheld if there was any ground on which the evidence could properly have been excluded. It is assumed that the trial judge had the right reason in mind when he or she rejected the evidence. To sum up, then, a trial court will ordinarily be upheld on appeal whether it has sustained or overruled a general objection.

Where a specific objection ("Object, hearsay") is erroneously overruled, the record thus made will support a reversal if the evidence is unfairly prejudicial. If a specific objection is properly sustained, there obviously has been no reversible error. But what if the ground specified by court and counsel is invalid but there existed another and valid but unstated basis for the objection? Again, for common-sense reasons, the rule favors the trial judge and, indirectly, the objecting counsel. It is sometimes said that rejection of the evidence was not prejudicial since there was a good, albeit unmentioned, ground for its exclusion. A more sensible approach is to recognize how futile it would be to reverse the trial court, and remand the case for a new trial, for having rejected the evidence on the wrong ground, only to have the trial court exclude it for the right reason the second time around.

We have seen that an objector should be explicit about his or her legal grounds. The precise target at which the objection is aimed should also be made clear. An offer of evidence frequently consists of several statements or parts which make up a whole; for example, an entire deposition, a set of hospital records, or a transcript of previously recorded testimony may be tendered. If only portions of the offer are objectionable, counsel must point them out for the trial judge, who will not himself be required to sift the admissible from the inadmissible. Of course, the real fault may lie with the side offering the evidence as a unit. Where admissibility as a unit is questionable, counsel for the offering party probably should break down the evidence into its component parts, marking and offering those parts separately so that objections can be made and rulings secured in an efficient way. If this is inordinately time-consuming (it probably should have been done at a pre-trial conference), another approach is for offering counsel to see to it that each page of a voluminous exhibit bears a separate, sequential identifying number so that opposing counsel and the court can make convenient references to any portions objected to, thus:

> BY OFFERING COUNSEL: Your Honor, we will ask the court reporter to mark the pages of this group exhibit [a group of medical records, for example] separately. There are twenty-three pages in the group, so they can be marked Plaintiff's Group Exhibit 3–A through 3–X for identification.

> THE COURT: We'll just relax for a minute while the reporter marks the exhibits.

> BY OPPOSING COUNSEL: Your Honor, we have an objection to 3–B and the reverse side of it, 3–C. That is the history sheet and it contains some inadmissible hearsay.

> [Whereupon discussion out of the hearing of the jury is had.]

> THE COURT: Certain deletions from exhibits 3–B and 3–C having been made, the objection will be overruled and Plaintiff's Group Exhibit 3–A through 3–X for Identification will be received in evidence as Plaintiff's Group Exhibit 3–A through 3–X.

A general objection is also unavailing where offered evidence is admissible against some parties, although not against all of them, or on a particular issue, although it is not admissible as to some other issue in the case. As was indicated earlier, it is objecting counsel's duty to couple with his or her objection a request that the evidence be restricted to the particular issue or party. This will be accomplished by means of a brief jury instruction.

> BY OPPOSING COUNSEL: On behalf of the defendant Freightco, we object to the witness' testimony concerning what the defendant truck driver, Mr. Bushmat, may have said to plaintiff after the accident. It may be receivable against Bushmat under some exception to the hearsay rule but it certainly isn't binding on us, your Honor. He was not our authorized agent for the making of such statements.

> THE COURT: The objection is well taken. The jury is instructed that the testimony they have just heard is received in evidence as against the defendant Bushmat only and is not to be considered by the jury in determining the liability, if any, of the defendant Freightco.

G.

Necessity for Repeating Objections

Where one side, through one or more witnesses, repeatedly offers similar evidence that opposing counsel considers inadmissible, an objection must be interposed each time the evidence is offered unless the trial court permits a single statement of the objection to stand as a "continuing" objection to the entire line of questioning or class of

evidence. If opposing counsel's objection to the first of a string of offers
of similar evidence is sustained, she will ordinarily find it necessary to
object to each subsequent offer. If her initial objection is overruled,
however, the trial court may allow a continuing objection in order to
conserve time and save opposing counsel from seeming unduly obstructive in the eyes of the jurors.

BY EXAMINING COUNSEL: Had you received any previous complaints about bottles of Dispepsia Cola exploding?

BY OPPOSING COUNSEL: We object, your Honor. Irrelevant and immaterial, since notice is not an issue in this case.

THE COURT: Overruled, counsel. I'm inclined to let it in
on the issue of punitive damages.

BY OPPOSING COUNSEL: Can the record show that our
objection goes to all similar evidence that plaintiff's counsel
may offer? May we have a standing objection, in other words?

THE COURT: You may. The record will show it.

To avoid any possibility of confusion, when additional evidence of the
same type is later offered, opposing counsel should point out at least
once that her earlier objection is applicable.

The failure to object to an inadmissible item of evidence may not
preclude counsel from objecting successfully to subsequent efforts to
offer more of the same. Some lawyers, not wishing to object excessively, will wait until it becomes unvoidably apparent that a type of
evidence is potentially damaging before objecting to it. The deliberate
waiver of objection as to the earlier evidence probably does not work a
waiver as to later offers of similar evidence. For example, the fact that
counsel permitted some hearsay to come in on a particular subject
matter does not foreclose him from objecting to subsequent offers of
additional hearsay on the same subject.

H.

Necessity for Obtaining a Ruling

The record in connection with an evidentiary objection has not
been effectively made where no ruling from the trial judge has been
obtained. It is the objector's burden to secure an express ruling on his
objection. This is essential to appellate review since a trial judge's
silence is not considered tantamount to an overruling of the objection.
In the heat of trial the judge may neglect to make an explicit, audible
ruling. If the matter is of any importance, objecting counsel can
interrupt to forestall the witness from responding to the challenged
question and can respectfully request an on-the-record ruling from the
trial judge.

Q. What did your friend tell you about the incident?

BY OPPOSING COUNSEL: Object, your Honor, calls for
hearsay.

BY EXAMINING COUNSEL: Well, it's perfectly relevant.

BY OPPOSING COUNSEL: It's still hearsay.

BY THE WITNESS: He told me * * *

BY OPPOSING COUNSEL: Just one moment, sir. Your Honor, we would appreciate your instructing the witness not to answer the question until your Honor has ruled. And we would like very much to have a ruling from your Honor on our hearsay objection.

THE COURT: Let me ponder this for a minute. The witness will not answer. Yes, the objection will be sustained. The question clearly calls for a hearsay response.

I.

Exceptions

At one time it was necessary, in many jurisdictions, for counsel to record an express exception to those evidentiary rulings of the trial court that counsel considered erroneous. Today this is rarely required. No longer does one hear the following exchange: "Object, your Honor, irrelevant." "Overruled, counsel." "Please note our exception." Instead, one encounters rules such as Federal Rule of Civil Procedure 46: "Formal exception to rulings or orders of the court are unnecessary; but for all purposes for which an exception has heretofore been necessary it is sufficient that a party, at the time the ruling or order of the court is made or sought, makes known to the court the action which the party desires the court to take or the party's objection to the action of the court and the grounds therefor. * * *" Of course, it will subsequently be necessary to set up in a specific and detailed motion for new trial any assignments of error that are based on objections made during trial.

IV.

OFFER OF PROOF

A.

Offer of Evidence as Distinguished from Offer of Proof

In the trial practice the phrase "offer of proof" is something of a term of art. It is a somewhat confusing one because in litigation the word "offer", taken alone, has a common meaning all its own. The two terms need to be distinguished.

The "offer" is the last step, other than possible supportive argumentation, in the introduction of evidence. (We discussed the offering of evidence in section II., above.) The meaning of the word "offer" and of the synonymous phrase "offer of evidence" is perhaps most readily grasped when one thinks in terms of tangible evidence: writings, photographs, murder weapons, and the like. The proponent of a writing, for example, will cause it to be marked for identification and then will do the trial judge and opposing counsel the courtesy of letting them examine the exhibit preliminarily, if they are not already familiar with it as a consequence of pre-trial discovery. Counsel will then hand the exhibit to its "sponsoring" witness on the stand and pose

questions aimed at authenticating the writing. When this process has
been accomplished to the proponent's satisfaction, he will hand the
exhibit to the judge and say, "Your Honor, we now offer in evidence
what has been marked Plaintiff's Exhibit Number 1 for Identification."

As we have seen, one "offers" testimonial evidence, too, although
there will be no need to say the word "offer" out loud. Counsel offers
oral testimony simply by engaging in the direct examination or cross-
examination of a witness on the stand.

The so-called offer of proof is something quite apart from the
typical offer of evidence described above and in section II. The offer of
proof can come into play before or during an offer of evidence. It can
come into play when an objection is made, during the examination of a
witness, to the offer either of tangible or testimonial evidence. The
offer of proof also comes into play when counsel, with no objection
pending and perhaps with no witness as yet on the stand, makes an
offer to prove specified matters in order to induce a ruling by the trial
court as to the relevance and competence of those matters. We
consider first the offer of proof as it is made during the course of
examination of a witness on the stand.

B.

Offer of Proof Made During the Examination of a Witness

The necessity for an offer of proof is most commonly encountered
during the examination of a witness on the stand. Counsel poses a
question to the witness in an effort to elicit testimony; she may value
the anticipated testimony for its own sake or because it lays the
authenticating or identifying foundation for the introduction of tangible evidence, such as a writing. Opposing counsel, for some stated
reason rooted in the rules of evidence, makes a timely objection to
counsel's question. Counsel for the introducing party (the "offering"
party), either before or after the trial court's ruling on the objection,
must make an offer of proof unless she is prepared to concede the merit
of her opponent's objection.

The offer of proof has two legitimate purposes: (1.) if properly
made, it will permit the trial court to make a fully informed and,
hopefully, correct ruling on the objection; (2.) if the ruling is adverse to
the introducing party and arguably erroneous, an adequate offer of
proof is ordinarily essential to preserve the point for post-trial review.

Harold W. Huff, a Chicago trial lawyer of extensive experience,
focused on appellate review when he described the purpose of an offer
of proof:

> *   *   * sooner or later you can anticipate that you will be
> placed in a position in which you see your case disintegrating
> because the man [or woman] in the black robe will not receive
> your evidence.

What do you do in that situation? You make a record of
what it was that you were not permitted to prove. The record
is made, essentially, for the benefit of an appellate court.*

The offer of proof, as Huff indicates, is another aspect of "making
the record" or "perfecting the record" for appeal. In the absence of an
explicit offer of proof an appellate court often will have no sure way of
knowing whether the trial court's evidentiary ruling was correct.
Equally important, the reviewing court will have no sure way of
knowing whether the loss of the excluded evidence was unfairly prejudicial to the introducing party's case; it can hardly weigh the importance of rejected evidence without knowing what that evidence would
have been.

It has occasionally been suggested that the failure to make an offer
of proof is excusable where the trial court has indicated to counsel in no
uncertain terms that an offer would be useless. And a full offer of
proof is unnecessary where described evidence has been rejected as a
class by the trial court. Here in a very real sense the trial judge has
made (and rejected) the offer of proof, as when he or she announces,
"I'm not going to allow any evidence of previous reported explosions
involving this type of glass container because I don't think any such
reports could possibly be relevant to the present case."

It is ordinarily reversible error to refuse counsel an opportunity to
make a proper offer of proof. A trial court's refusal to entertain an
offer of proof is unjustifiable even where it is based on the court's
knowledge of the witness' earlier testimony in the case since the
current offer may embrace new matter. So important is counsel's
freedom to make his or her record that it has been stated that any
judicial discouraging of offers of proof is improper. However, a trial
court need not hear lengthy offers where it is evident that the proposed
evidence would not be admissible on any ground.

The necessity of an offer of proof after a sustained objection is
generally limited to direct examination, the thought being that while
counsel should experience no difficulty describing what his own witness
would say in response to a question, he may not be equipped to predict
precisely the response of an adverse witness. Certainly it would
ordinarily be unfair for a trial court to require an offer of proof during
cross-examination. However, enough must be done to show that the
sustaining of an objection to a cross-question was error. The cross-
question must on its face be proper. Counsel may have to elaborate
somewhat to reveal what benefit he expects from his cross-question or
line of cross-examination; in other words, it is as incumbent upon
counsel during cross-examination as it is during direct examination to
make clear the purpose, the materiality, of the anticipated response.

While it may be reasonably accurate to say that no offer of proof—
certainly no very explicit or detailed one—is essential during cross-
examination, it is also true that counsel is entirely free to make an

* H. Huff, Offers of Proof in Proceedings,
Fifth Annual Trial Evidence Seminar (Ill.
Inst. for Cont.Legal Ed.) 4 (1971).

offer during cross-examination if she can, and, in the absence of
effective contradiction, the trial court can rely on it. If counsel has any
reason to suspect that the point of her cross-examination is escaping
the trial judge (and the sustaining of objections to it is an observable
straw in the wind), she will be at pains to give at least some intimation
of its purpose.

The required elements of an offer of proof made during the interrogation of a witness can rarely be found in procedural or evidentiary
codes. At one time Rule 43(c) of the Federal Rules of Civil Procedure
made at least a minimal effort to describe the mechanics of an offer of
proof. It read in its entirety as follows:

Rule 43.

EVIDENCE

* * *

(c) Record of Excluded Evidence. In an action tried by a
jury, if an objection to a question propounded to a witness is
sustained by the court, the examining attorney may make a
specific offer of what he expects to prove by the answer of the
witness. The court may require the offer to be made out of the
hearing of the jury. The court may add such other or further
statement as clearly shows the character of the evidence, the
form in which it was offered, the objection made, and the
ruling thereon. In actions tried without a jury the same
procedure may be followed, except that the court upon request
shall take and report the evidence in full, unless it clearly
appears that the evidence is not admissible on any ground or
that the witness is privileged.

Rules such as FRCP 43(c) are never especially helpful to the
practitioner because they are couched in general terms and leave so
much to unwritten local practice. In one respect Rule 43 (c) may even
have been potentially misleading. The rule suggested that a lawyer
whose evidence has been excluded "may" make an offer of proof. The
word "may" could be read in the sense of "might." As we have said,
the lawyer *can* make an offer of proof—it would ordinarily be reversible
error to refuse him the opportunity to make a proper one—and usually
he *must* make one if he is to preserve for review the propriety of the
trial court's exclusionary ruling.

FRCP 43(c) has now been superseded by an equally brief Federal
Rule of Evidence. Rule 103 of the Federal Rules of Evidence reads in
relevant part as follows:

Rule 103.

RULINGS ON EVIDENCE

(a) Effect of erroneous ruling. Error may not be predicated upon a ruling which admits or excludes evidence unless a
substantial right of the party is affected, and * * *

(2) Offer of proof. In case the ruling is one excluding evidence, the substance of the evidence was made known to the judge by offer or was apparent from the context within which questions were asked.

(b) Record of offer and ruling. The court may add any other or further statement which shows the character of the evidence, the form in which it was offered, the objection made, and the ruling thereon. It may direct the making of an offer in question and answer form.

(c) Hearing of jury. In jury cases, proceedings shall be conducted, to the extent practicable, so as to prevent inadmissible evidence from being suggested to the jury by any means, such as making statements or offers of proof or asking questions in the hearing of the jury.

Because Rule 103(a) has to do with the preservation for appeal of claimed trial level error in rulings on evidence, subdivision (a)(2) in no way relates to the sort of offer of proof that is sometimes made by counsel prior to any in-court testimony and thus obviously prior to any objection and ruling.

What subdivision (a)(2) does do is require that where the trial court's ruling is one *excluding* evidence, the substance of the evidence must be made known by offer *unless* its substance was evident from the context.

Subdivision (b) of the Rule provides that the trial judge "may" direct that the offer of proof be made in question-and-answer form. This means that questions will be put to the witness by examining counsel and his or her responses will then constitute the offer; otherwise, examining counsel himself simply makes a narrative offer in his own words.

In the Advisory Committee's Preliminary Draft of the Federal Rules of Evidence the question-and-answer method was *required* in non-jury cases, presumably so that a reviewing court would have before it the precise evidentiary basis for possible final disposition of the case in the event of reversal for erroneous exclusion of evidence. This absolute requirement was thought to be an unnecessary intrusion upon judicial discretion and, on revision, it was dropped. It was realized that this requirement would foreclose the sort of offer of proof that is occasionally made with no witness on the stand.

There are three basic ways of making an offer of proof during the course of a witness' oral examination. These three methods can be labelled (1.) the tangible offer, (2.) the witness offer, and (3.) the lawyer offer.

1. *Tangible Offer.* The tangible offer is easy enough. Any lawyer who knows how to mark, authenticate or identify, and offer into evidence an item of tangible evidence knows, almost *ipso facto*, how to make an offer of proof of the exhibit's contents if her offer of it is successfully objected to by opposing counsel. The proponent of the rejected exhibit need only hand it to the court reporter for inclusion in

the trial record. (Or, if the exhibit happens to be a writing, such as a
deposition, she might also, out of the jury's hearing, read it into the
record at the time of its rejection, thereby ensuring its consideration in
context.) Unlike received exhibits, the rejected item will not be handed
to the jurors and will not go with them to their deliberation room. It
will, however, find its way into the record on appeal, along with all
other offered exhibits whether received or rejected. Counsel's only
additional task may be to state for the record the evidential purpose of
the evidence, if there exists any possibility that its function is unclear.
She may also wish to be certain that the record reflects the trial judge's
reasons for rejecting the exhibit since the judge may be focusing on a
ground for rejection while erroneously disregarding a legitimate alternative basis for admission.

An offer of tangible proof that commingles admissible matter with
inadmissible is not a good offer and its rejection *in toto* will not be
reversible error. This is not to say that admissible portions of an offer
are properly excludable merely because other portions are inadmissible.
For example, the competency of a writing in its entirety is not essential
to the receipt of unobjectionable parts. It simply means that the
inadmissible portions must be omitted from the offer. More than this,
it means that the obligation to screen out inadmissible matters belongs
to counsel for the offering party; neither the trial court nor the
objecting party is obliged to separate the admissible from the inadmissible.

The risk of rejection *in toto* is at its greatest in connection with
"omnibus" offers or offers "in bulk." An unsegregated offer of all the
hospital records pertaining to the plaintiff in a personal injury action
would be a typical example of an omnibus or in bulk offer. Counsel
cannot hope to produce error—to provide himself with an ace in the
hole, so to speak—by offering, in bulk, a tall stack of pages comprising a
patient's entire medical record, which may begin with an admission
history, include laboratory and radiology reports, a report of operation,
anesthesia record, progress notes, nurses' notes, and end with a discharge summary. The trial court's rejection of this offer is not improper where counsel has been accorded an opportunity to designate the
admissible parts, even though buried in the pile are records which by
themselves would be perfectly admissible. Counsel must offer only the
admissible portions of his client's medical record or of any other writing
or group of writings. Before making his offer he can pull out inadmissible items or mask or cut out inadmissible passages. (In one recent
case it was suggested that a piece of paper might be pasted over the
inadmissible part of a writing. However, experience teaches that
jurors are inclined to peek. A better approach involves masking out
the objectionable portion on the original of the exhibit and making a
photographic copy for the jury, or using scissors to cut objectionable
portions from a photographic copy of the exhibit.)

Counsel must be specific as to what parts of a writing or group of
writings are included in his offer of proof. It is not ordinarily enough
to make a general representation that all objectionable parts will be
deleted. Where an offer of a writing has been rejected, counsel cannot

later insist that he offered only its receivable portions unless he in fact designated them explicitly at the trial level. When a writing is offered without such designations it is presumed that the entire exhibit is offered.

When a writing is offered as being impeaching, it is incumbent upon the proponent to isolate those portions thought to be receivable on this ground.

2. *Witness Offer.* The witness offer is an even more simple procedure than the tangible offer. When an objection has been made to a question put to a witness on the stand and an exclusionary ruling is made by the trial judge, examining counsel can make his or her offer of proof through the witness. Counsel simply proceeds with the examination of the witness, employing the usual question-and-answer method, and the witness' recorded responses, usually taken outside the jurors' hearing, constitute the offer of proof. This is the method adverted to in Rule 103(b) of the Federal Rules of Evidence, discussed above.

As in the case of tangible offers, counsel's only remaining task may be to explain the relevance of the offered testimony more fully than he or she did at the point of opposing counsel's successful objection to it. Again, offering counsel may want to be sure that the record accurately reflects the judge's reasons for excluding the testimony.

Normally, counsel should state for the record not only the purport (synopsized meaning) but the purpose (relevance, intended function) of the anticipated response. It is sometimes said that a formal offer of proof is unnecessary where counsel's question to a witness clearly calls for admissible evidence. The Illinois Supreme Court has made the broadest generalization on this point:

> It is not necessary that offer of proof be made where the question shows the purpose and materiality of the evidence. It is not necessary that counsel state what the answer would be. If a question is in proper form and clearly admits of an answer relative [*sic.* relevant?] to the issues, the party by whom the question is propounded is not bound to state facts proposed to be proved by the answer unless the court requires him to do so.*

This sweeping language seems to disregard the circumstance that a question that quite plainly calls for an admissible answer may be little more than an exercise in optimism in the absence of some discernible assurance that the witness is not only able to answer counsel's question but to answer it favorably to his client's position. In most of the cases suggesting that a formal statement of the expected answer can safely be omitted, the record, in one way or another, showed unmistakably what counsel was after and what he or she was likely to have gotten had the witness been permitted to answer. Since appellate courts will not invariably presume that an unstated answer would be forthcoming and that it would be both relevant and favorable to the side represented by

---

* Creighton v. Elgin, 387 Ill. 592, 606, 56 N.E.2d 825, 831 (1944).

examining counsel, prudence will ordinarily dictate the making of a reasonably detailed offer of proof following an exclusionary ruling.

If rejection of the offered testimony was based on an exclusionary rule of evidence, such as the hearsay rule or some testimonial privilege, the offer of proof should include any information suggesting the inapplicability of the rule. (A collateral but obviously important possible advantage of a comprehensive and comprehensible offer of proof is that it may cause the trial judge to change his or her ruling.)

3. *Lawyer Offer.* Where it appears that a question in proper form was posed during the direct examination of a witness on the stand and that, upon objection by opposing counsel, the trial court ruled out the answer, examining counsel's offer of proof may consist of a statement to the court at the time of its ruling, and on the record, showing what the witness' answer would have been. Counsel's statement will include any additional matters essential to demonstrate that the described response would be relevant and otherwise admissible in evidence. Counsel's statement will also show that the response would benefit his client; that is, that it would be of such a character as could reasonably be expected to affect the finding of the jury in his client's favor.

This so-called lawyer offer will begin this way: the examining counsel poses a question to a witness on the stand, opposing counsel's objection to the question is sustained by the trial judge, and the examining counsel, to make the record for possible appeal, states to the judge, "Your Honor, through this witness we offer to prove [such-and-such]". Of course, there is no magic in the form of words employed in an offer of proof; examining counsel may say, "The witness, were he permitted to answer the last question, would have testified [to such-and-such]."

Ordinarily, the offer of proof should be made immediately after the adverse ruling that cut off the witness' response. Usually it is made out of the jury's presence, as is specifically suggested in Rule 103(c) of the Federal Rules of Evidence, quoted previously. Certainly the time for an offer has arrived when the trial court indicates unequivocally that it will permit no further inquiry along a particular line.

It has repeatedly been held that a lawyer offer is ineffective where the lawyer's statement of the anticipated answer goes beyond or is unresponsive to the question put to the witness. This rule seems as much an artificial device to avoid reversal as anything else, since counsel presumably could readily have put any number of additional questions to his witness. Furthermore, as will be discussed later, there is no pending question at all in the case of lawyer offers made prior to the calling of a witness to the stand. It is true, of course, that a methodical question and answer approach makes it easier for the opposing counsel to frame specific objections and this may be one reason for the rule. Perhaps this rule simply reflects persistent distrust of the lawyer offer. Although an unethical lawyer could as easily fabricate "anticipated" responsive answers as he could unresponsive ones, the better practice is to proceed by means of questions of limited scope, followed by the statement of an expected answer corresponding to the question.

A possible safeguard against a fabricated lawyer offer lies in the witness' ability—especially upon inquiry by a skeptical trial judge or opposing counsel—to contradict the offer, pointing out that in fact the stated answer would not be his response to the question asked. This, of course, assumes a witness who is sufficiently alert, sufficiently honest, and sufficiently brave to take exception to counsel's narrative.

C.

Offer of Proof Made With No Witness on the Stand

Few commentators on the making of the trial record have considered a special and sometimes difficult type of offer of proof, the type of offer that is made prior to any in-court testimony by a witness and thus obviously prior to any explicit objection and ruling. This is the second principal type of offer. It may be made because offering counsel has a number of witnesses, who are readily available but not presently in court, to establish a line of facts but the trial judge's rulings have strongly suggested that he would exclude their testimony. Such an offer can also be made to induce a ruling with respect to a line of facts. Counsel will make an offer when he is doubtful of the reception that his proposed evidence will receive from the trial judge and wishes to obtain a ruling, and make his record, without first going to the expense and inconvenience of calling and examining the witnesses involved. This approach permits a trial court, out of the jurors' hearings, to pre-test proposed evidence and avoid possible prejudicing of the jurors.

An offer of this second type will sound something like this in a simple case:

> BY PLAINTIFF'S COUNSEL: Your Honor, we offer to prove in this case that the defendant had notice, repeated notice, that metal cans containing its product had exploded without warning, causing serious bodily injury. We can call to the stand six eye-witnesses to six separate incidents of this sort, all antedating the incident involving this plaintiff. Those witnesses are readily available on short notice.

> COUNSEL FOR DEFENDANT: Well, we would object to that, your Honor. We don't think notice is an element in a strict liability case of this kind. Counsel is just trying to put in some inflammatory evidence.

> COUNSEL FOR PLAINTIFF: If nothing else, your Honor, the proposed evidence would be relevant to our prayer for punitive damages.

> THE COURT: The offer of proof will be denied. [Or, 'The offer is sustained. You can have until tomorrow morning to get your witnesses here.']

When a trial court rejects an offer of proof of this second type it is taken to have conceded that counsel could have made the described proof if he had been permitted to proceed. The only open question is whether the facts embodied in the offer are properly admissible.

It is the burden of the offering party to include in his or her offer everything necessary to support the admissibility of the proposed evidence. This must be shown to the trial judge at the time of the making of the offer; if for some reason admissibility cannot be shown until a subsequent time during the trial, the offer, as will be more fully discussed later, should then be renewed. Where the facts supporting admissibility are unclear, no amount of hindsight at the appellate level will put the trial court in error for having rejected the offer.

For instance, an offer must be definite as to the time of events in order that the admissibility of the offer will be apparent. Thus the relevance of prior complaints concerning the condition of a stairway will depend in part on their nearness in point of time to the accident of which the plaintiff complains. Similarly, testimony regarding a post-accident inspection will be rejected where the offer fails to reveal its date.

Often it may also be essential to indicate other facets of relevance, such as similarity of conditions in connection with evidence of prior accidents and the like.

Furthermore, offering counsel may find it necessary to show that the offered evidence would not merely be cumulative to evidence already received in the case.

It will frequently be vital to include foundational elements in an offer of proof. These foundational elements are themselves to be found in the law of evidence. It may, for example, be necessary to state that offered out-of-court declarations would be admissible because they constituted excited utterances. To cite a much more common example, it may be crucial to include in the offer a clear indication that the witness whose testimony is being offered is qualified as an expert of some sort. Obviously, there is a serious flaw in an offer "to prove through Clyde Bushmat that cancer can be induced by trauma"; it will be necessary to include in the offer the fact that this is *Doctor* Clyde Bushmat, whose training, licensure, and experience equip him, in terms of the conventional wisdom respecting opinion evidence, to express a complex medical conclusion.

Much of this is simply one way or another of saying that an offer of proof must descend into specifics; it is not permissible to couch an offer in vague generalities. For instance, it is insufficient to announce that evidence will be adduced "to show bad faith," to show "insolvency," to show that goods for which a note was given "were not as represented," to show "bias and prejudice," or to show "surrounding circumstances and conditions." It is, in other words, not sufficient in an offer of proof to state ultimate facts that might be more appropriate to a pleading; thus reading the allegations of a pleading into the record will not result in an effective offer of proof. And if "ultimate" facts are not good enough it is doubly clear that broad-gauge conclusions are unavailing in an offer. An offer can be a summarization of proposed evidence but it must be cast in terms of evidentiary facts—what the proposed witnesses said, saw, heard, touched, or smelled; what the proposed items of tangible evidence reveal.

Needless to say, an offer that is based on nothing more than counsel's sense of hope and optimism is doomed. Thus the denial of an omnibus or "in bulk" offer is proper where the offering party, having neglected to employ pre-trial discovery devices to secure and examine the opposing party's records, bases his offer on nothing more than his unsubstantiated hope that those records might contain something helpful to his client. An offer of proof, in other words, must be made in good faith on the basis of evidence that is known to be available and beneficial.

As an offshoot of the basic premise that the offer must be in good faith, it is frequently asserted that the offering party must identify the witnesses who are in a position to testify to the matters described in the offer. From time to time this requirement has been pushed one long step farther, to demand a showing that the witness is presently in court and ready to testify. It is even occasionally suggested that a witness must be placed on the stand and the offer made through him. Any such requirement would effectively eliminate the second type of offer of proof and restrict counsel to the traditional post-objection witness offer.

It is clear enough, nonetheless, that an offer upon which counsel cannot possibly make good, because the necessary witnesses are unavailable to him, is properly rejected. This situation arises most commonly where witnesses, not previously subpoenaed by offering counsel, are shown to be beyond the trial court's subpoena power at the time of the offer of proof involving them. It is also plain that a trial judge, entertaining doubts about counsel's ability to make good on his offer, can insist on an offer made through one or more witnesses called to the stand (or to a pre-trial conference) in an out-of-court session. However, the weight of authority, which includes a decision of the United States Supreme Court, is to the effect that a lawyer offer, with no witness on the stand, is sufficient if an adequate demonstration of good faith is made. In Scotland County v. Hill * the Court said, "[I]f the trial court has doubts about the good faith of an offer of testimony, it can insist on the production of the witness, and upon some attempt to make the proof before it rejects the offer; but if it does reject it * * * and there is nothing else in the record to indicate bad faith, an appellate court must assume that the proof could have been made, and govern itself accordingly."

Offers of proof in more complex cases, and objections to such offers, are usually required to be in writing. As has been pointed out in the *Manual for Complex Litigation* followed by federal trial judges, this process is especially helpful in cases in which the parties expect to offer opinion evidence on complicated scientific, technical, or economic issues.

A typical written offer of proof in a complex case involving expertise will include (1.) an identification of the expert, (2.) a summary of

* 112 U.S. 183, 186, 5 S.Ct. 93, 28 L.Ed. 692 (1884).

his or her qualifications, (3.) a detailed disclosure of the factual data
and scientific, technical, or economic authorities and other material
relied on by the expert in arriving at his or her opinion, (4.) a clear
statement of the expert's opinion, and (5.) a summary of the reasons for
the opinion.

In "big" cases it is also essential that there be pre-trial offers of
deposition evidence, an opportunity to require the offeror to introduce
additional portions of the deposition as provided in Federal Rules of
Civil Procedure 32(a)(4), an opportunity to object to the offered deposition evidence, and rulings on any such objections.

Federal judges are accustomed to scheduling pre-trial offers of
deposition evidence and the filing of objections, counter-offers, and
suggested requirements under 32(a)(4), supra. A useful technique is for
the deposition material offered by each party to be enclosed in brackets
in a distinctive color on the outer margin of the deposition pages.
Opposite these colored brackets the opposing counsel can mark his or
her objections in abbreviated language such as "D Acme obj. hearsay."
The trial court's ruling on designated deposition offers can be indicated
in similar fashion so that the admitted portion of the deposition can
easily be read into evidence from the original deposition.

D.

Renewing Offers of Proof

Occasionally a particular offer of proof must be made more than
once or, more precisely, it must be renewed. This happens when an
offer, defective when first made, is thereafter perfected. Sometimes an
offer will be ruled premature because, for example, some element of its
foundation is missing or because it has been made during the wrong
stage of the trial. It is vital that counsel renew his or her offer after
having adduced additional evidence by way of essential predicate;
otherwise, the trial court is free to treat the earlier offer as having been
abandoned.

A renewed offer may be necessary after counsel has put on proof
rendering inapplicable some exclusionary rule of evidence, such as the
best evidence rule. Where an offer of proof has been rebuffed because
it was made during cross-examination of an adverse party's witness
rather than in the offering party's own case, counsel usually must
renew the offer at the appropriate juncture. Of course, express withdrawal of a question waives any error with respect to the treatment
accorded an objection to it. There is, however, no need to make
repeated offers of proof where the court has indicated that it will under
no circumstances receive the indicated evidence or where the court has
sustained an objection to an entire line of questioning. There need be
no renewal of an offer where the trial court has not made it clear to
counsel that it was excluding evidence only temporarily, as where a
witness—usually a medical witness—has been put on the stand out of
the regular order.

The need to renew an offer of proof after the taking of additional evidence can be avoided if in the original offer counsel expresses a willingness to connect up the offered evidence with other testimony that will render the offered evidence material. This is simply another way of saying that an offer of proof must be reasonably complete.

E.

Making Offers of Proof Outside the Jurors' Hearing

The trial court, for a fairly self-evident reason that we will come to shortly, will usually require that counsel present his or her offer of proof in such a way that although the court, opposing counsel, the witness (if any), and the court reporter can hear it, the jury cannot. (See Fed.R.Evid. 103(c), quoted above.) A court has the right to insist that it be made out of the jury's hearing. Some judicial hints to the contrary notwithstanding, a court is not invariably required to exercise this power, however. Whether an offer of proof shall be presented outside the jury's hearing is a question addressed to the trial judge's discretion.

It would be both disruptive and wasteful of time were a trial court to send the jury out for every offer of proof made during a trial, having in mind that many lawyer offers following objection are one brief sentence in length. Moreover, the content of many offers of proof is quite harmless. If the trial judge believes that an offer is of innocuous material she can properly permit it to be made in the jury's hearing, especially if there is no objection and if she instructs the jurors to disregard the procedure. If opposing counsel disputes the propriety of an offer made in the jury's hearing, he should indicate for the record the jury's presence since this circumstance may not otherwise be apparent unless the trial judge or the court reporter notes it.

Despite what has been said of the trial court's discretion, it is advisable, because of the potential for prejudice, that all but the most neutral and routine offers of proof be presented outside the juror's hearing. The trial judge can send the jury out of the courtroom or she can retire to chambers if the offer is likely to be a lengthy one or if the risk of prejudice would be great were any juror to overhear it; otherwise, the judge can direct that the offer be made at a whispered sidebar conference. Of course, all of this suggests the wisdom of making important offers of proof at a pre-trial conference.

V.

THE INSTRUCTIONS TO THE JURY

A.

Making the Record on Instructions Given and Refused

In almost all jurisdictions, including those using court-approved "pattern" instructions, the trial judge will either require or at least permit participation by counsel in the preparation of the court's charge to the jury. In some jurisdictions counsel for each side prepares a complete proposed charge; in others counsel prepares only those instructions that apply, at least arguably, to his client's claims or affirmative defenses. Often counsel will have researched and briefed the underlying law and drafted the proposed instructions prior to the commencement of the trial. (Some jurisdictions require that proposed instructions be submitted to the trial judge at the beginning of the trial, although obviously they remain subject to modification as the trial unfolds.)

A conference on the charge is usually conducted in the trial judge's chambers after the parties have rested their cases and before their closing arguments commence. (Counsel prefer to have this conference before rather than after their closing arguments so that they can, with accuracy, make some reference in their arguments to the court's impending instructions.) At this conference the judge, after discussion with counsel, announces what instructions he or she will give to the jury. It is prudent to have a court reporter present to record the conference although some trial lawyers are content to have the words "Given _____" and "Refused _____" typed at the bottom of each of their requested instructions, the blank lines being for check-marks. Counsel, having submitted his requested instructions separately ("Plaintiff's Requested Instruction No. 1," "Plaintiff's Requested Instruction No. 2," etc.), will place a check-mark after the appropriate term and deliver his set of requested instructions to the court reporter for inclusion in the record.

B.

Objecting to the Court's Instructions

If counsel has any objections to the jury instructions as given in open court, over and beyond those recorded during the aforementioned conference, she must make them out of the jury's hearing immediately after the trial judge has concluded the giving of the charge; otherwise, they are waived. (Grounds for objection may arise for the first time during the giving of the charge either because the judge was not explicit in describing some portion of the instructions during the pre-charge conference or because he or she has undertaken extemporaneous amendments to the charge that was agreed upon in that conference.) A general exception to the instructions is insufficient to preserve error for appellate review. Counsel's objections must be specific, thus affording the judge an opportunity to correct any errors that he can be convinced he made. In other words, it is futile to approach the bench after the charge and say, "We object [or 'except'] to the charge in its entirety." Counsel must say something like "Your Honor, we object to your use of the word 'possible,' instead of the word 'probable,' in that portion of your instructions that dealt with the question of proximate cause."

VI.

VERDICTS

A.

General and Special Verdicts in Civil Cases

A jury's verdict in typical civil cases is usually a "general" verdict; that is, the jurors simply find for the plaintiff, stating the amount of damages they have decided to award to the plaintiff, or they find the defendant not liable. The jury's foreperson enters its findings on printed verdict forms that are supplied to the jury by the trial court. These forms become a part of the trial record.

Many jurisdictions, including the federal, also provide for "special" verdicts. With this type of verdict, usually called for only in quite complicated lawsuits, the trial court directs the jury to make a specific written finding on each fact-issue in the case. The court either submits to the jurors written questions that are susceptible of categorical (Yes or No) or other brief answers, or it supplies them with written forms that embody the special findings that they could make under the pleadings and the evidence. These questions or special findings are submitted to the court by counsel for the side requesting them and the record regarding the court's giving or rejection of them is made in much the same way as it is with requested instructions, discussed in section V., above.

B.

Demand for Submission of Fact Issues

It is incumbent upon counsel to make a specific demand, on the record, that the trial court submit particular fact-issues to the jury under the special verdict procedure just described. The practice under Federal Rule of Civil Procedure 49 is typical and underscores this point. If in providing the jury with questions or special finding forms the federal court omits any issue of fact, each party is taken to waive its right to jury trial on that issue unless a specific, on-the-record demand is made before the jurors retire to deliberate. The trial judge can make his or her own finding as to any fact issue that was omitted without objection, just as though the court were sitting without a jury.

VII.

POLLING THE JURY

In litigation the moment of truth arrives with the reading of the jury's verdict. A buzzer has sounded; the word is that the jury is coming back. Court is reconvened. The jurors file into their places.

THE COURT: Have you reached a verdict?

THE FOREPERSON: We have, your Honor.

THE COURT: How do you find the defendant, guilty or not guilty?

THE FOREPERSON: Guilty, your Honor.

But perhaps this is not the moment of truth, after all. In many jurisdictions the losing side in either a criminal or a civil case is permitted to have the jurors polled with respect to the announced verdict. Upon request the judge will have the clerk or bailiff inquire of each juror, "Is this your true verdict?" Occasionally this polling process turns up improprieties that occurred during the jury's deliberations and which will require either further deliberations or perhaps even the declaring of a mistrial. (But see Fed.R.Evid. 606(b), restricting jurors to a description of "extraneous prejudicial information" and "outside influence.") The polling of the jury, and any comments made by the jurors during their interrogation, should be on the record.

VIII.

CONCLUSION

We have discussed the most important situations in which trial counsel must "make the record." Consciousness of the record and its significance can have a beneficial influence on a lawyer's effectiveness at the trial level. Awareness of the record induces counsel to make an orderly, logical presentation of evidence and argument. It also tends to inspire clarity of thought and speech. But sometimes counsel's ultimate reward, the real moment of truth, is found in the appellate courts, where the difference between affirmance and reversal may depend on his or her ability at perfecting the record.

Chapter II

AN INTRODUCTION TO RELEVANCE

PART A. RELEVANCE TO WHAT?

THE JUDGMENT OF SOLOMON
1 Kings 3:16–28 (King James) (c. 960 B.C.).*

Then came there two women, unto the king, and stood before him. And the one woman said, "O my lord, I and this woman dwell in one house; and I was delivered of a child with her in the house. And it came to pass the third day after that I was delivered, that this woman was delivered also: and we were together; there was no stranger with us in the house, save we two in the house. And this woman's child died in the night; because she overlaid it. And she arose at midnight, and took my son from beside me, while thine handmaid slept, and laid it in her bosom, and laid her dead child in my bosom. And when I rose in the morning to give my child suck, behold, it was dead: but when I had considered it in the morning, behold it was not my son, which I did bear." And the other woman said, "Nay; but the living is my son, and the dead is thy son." And this said, "No; but the dead is thy son, and the living is my son." Thus they spoke before the king. Then said the king, "The one saith, 'This is my son that liveth, and thy son is the dead': and the other saith, 'Nay; but thy son is the dead, and my son is the living.'" And the king said, "Bring me a sword." And they brought a sword before the king. And the king said, "Divide the living child in two, and give half to the one, and half to the other." Then spoke the woman whose the living child was unto the king, for her bowels yearned upon her son, and she said "O my lord, give her the living child, and in no wise slay it." But the other said, "Let it be neither mine nor thine, but divide it." Then the king answered and said, "Give her the living child, and in no wise slay it: she is the mother thereof." And all Israel heard of the judgment which the king had judged; and they feared the king: for they saw that the wisdom of God was in him, to do judgment.

HART AND McNAUGHTON, EVIDENCE AND INFERENCE IN THE LAW
51–56 (1958).**

It will be noticed in the first place that, while the issue to be decided is formally one of fact only, the rule of law is nevertheless

* 3 Kings 3:16–28 (Douay).

** The Hayden Colloquium on Scientific Concept and Method edited by Daniel Lerner. Copyright, 1958 by American Academy of Arts & Sciences, copyright, 1959 by The Free Press, Excerpts from material by Henry M. Hart, Jr., and John McNaughton.

functioning importantly. For it is the rule which makes the fact significant. If, for example, a child could not inherit, the question of the claimant's parentage could be left to his biographer or to the genealogists.

The kinds of evidence used by the law in making determinations of adjudicative fact are unlike those used by other disciplines in pursuance of their objectives.

The adjudicative facts of interest to the law, being historical facts, will rarely be triable by the experimental methods of the natural sciences. To be sure, ballistics tests in the murder case may prove beyond rational dispute that the bullet which killed the victim came from the defendant's gun. Laboratory tests in the breach-of-warranty case may settle beyond question the quality of the goods. And blood tests in the inheritance controversy may show that it is virtually impossible that the claimant was the child of the deceased. But these instances will be exceptional. For the most part the law must settle disputed questions of adjudicative fact by reliance upon the ambiguous implications of non-fungible "traces"—traces on human brains and on pieces of paper and traces in the form of unique arrangements of physical objects.

Type of facts used

Furthermore, the law uses different evidence and uses it in a different way than other disciplines do even when those disciplines are similarly interested in the determination of historical facts. These differences result from the fact that what is involved, when the most distinctive practices of the law in the handling of evidence come into play, is the formal and official settlement of a controversy.

To understand the law's peculiar ways of treating evidence it is necessary to have some appreciation of the role which formal adjudication plays in the total functioning of the legal system.

A contested lawsuit is society's last line of defense in the indispensable effort to secure the peaceful settlement of social conflicts. In the overwhelming majority of instances, the general directions of the law function smoothly with no controversy whatever. When controversies do arise, the overwhelming majority of them are settled informally or, if formally, without a contest, as by plea of guilty in a criminal case. In almost all these situations lawyers are likely to handle evidence in the same common-sense fashion that anybody else would, unless special calculations are called for by a real possibility of formal litigation.

Evidence in contested suits

When a question has reached the point of a contested trial, however, its whole context is changed. Victory, and not accommodation, is the objective of the parties. The adversary atmosphere and the delays of litigation naturally repel evidence, especially testimony and things under the control of disinterested persons, so that the litigants have available for use only the partisan and coerced residue after people with ingenuity have made themselves anonymous. That residue is culled by the parties with a view not so much to establishing the whole truth as to winning the case. And the evidence which survives this attrition (and the exclusionary rules of evidence described below) is communicated to the trier of fact in an emotion-charged setting.

In judging the law's handling of its task of fact-finding in this setting, it is necessary always to bear in mind that this is a last-ditch process in which something more is at stake than the truth only of the specific matter in contest. There is at stake also that confidence of the public generally in the impartiality and fairness of public settlement of disputes which is essential if the ditch is to be held and the settlements accepted peaceably.

The law does not require absolute assurance of the perfect correctness of particular decisions. While it is of course important that the court be right in its determinations of fact, it is also important that the court decide the case when the parties ask for the decision and on the basis of the evidence presented by the parties. A decision must be made now, one way or the other. To require certainty or even near-certainty in such a context would be impracticable and undesirable. The law thus compromises.

[margin note: Evid. doesn't have to be perfect]

The compromise is expressed in the formulas used to guide decision of questions of adjudicative fact. In a criminal case, guilt need not be found beyond all doubt; the trier of the fact must be satisfied of the defendant's guilt only "beyond a reasonable doubt." In a civil case, the facts are ordinarily to be found on the basis of "a preponderance of the evidence"; this phrase is generally defined as meaning simply "more likely than not." The formula for determining whether a case should even be submitted to a jury assumes a wide leeway for differing judgments. The question for the trial judge is whether a "reasonable jury" on the evidence submitted could find that the facts have been proved by a preponderance of the evidence. The judge uses a similar formula in determining whether a verdict already rendered by the jury may stand, and so does the reviewing court in deciding whether to upset either the jury's verdict or the trial judge's own finding if the trial judge sat without a jury. * * *

[margin notes: crim case / civ case / case to be submitted / judge on app crt review]

The most conspicuous difference between the law's problems in determining historical facts and those of other disciplines lies in the procedure of decision. Other disciplines rely primarily on the method of inquiry, reflection, and report by trained investigators. In other disciplines the final conclusions as to key facts are drawn by experts, and the conclusions may be changed if they are found later—after further inquiry and reflection—to be wrong. The law, in contrast, depends in most formal proceedings upon presentation by the disputants in public hearing before an impartial tribunal, a tribunal previously uninformed about the matters in dispute. And findings of fact by the tribunal are usually final so far as the law is concerned.

[margin note: Other disciplines vs. Legal field]

Typical of such formal proceedings is the trial in court. A trial suffers from immobility. It suffers from shortage and inflexibility of time. It is dependent largely upon non-expert sources of information and upon non-expert evaluators of information (the jury). In addition, proof at a trial is rather strictly governed by procedural rules called rules of evidence.

JAMES, RELEVANCY, PROBABILITY AND THE LAW

29 Calif.L.Rev. 689 (1941).
[Most footnotes omitted.]

Since scholars first attempted to treat the common law of evidence as a rational system, relevancy has been recognized as a basic concept underlying all further discussion. Thayer gave this recognition its classic form:

"There is a principle—not so much a rule of evidence as a presupposition involved in the very conception of a rational system of evidence, as contrasted with the old formal and mechanical systems—which forbids receiving anything irrelevant, not logically probative."

"The two leading principles should be brought into conspicuous relief, (1) that nothing is to be received which is not logically probative of some matter requiring to be proved; and (2) that everything which is thus probative should come in, unless a clear ground of policy or law excludes it."

* * * Relevancy, as the word itself indicates, is not an inherent characteristic of any item of evidence but exists as a relation between an item of evidence and a proposition sought to be proved. If an item of evidence tends to prove or to disprove any proposition, it is relevant to that proposition. If the proposition itself is one provable in the case at bar, or if it in turn forms a further link in a chain of proof the final proposition of which is provable in the case at bar, then the offered item of evidence has probative value in the case. Whether the immediate or ultimate proposition sought to be proved is provable in the case at bar is determined by the pleadings, by the procedural rules applicable thereto, and by the substantive law governing the case. Whether the offered item of evidence tends to prove the proposition at which it is ultimately aimed depends upon other factors, shortly to be considered. But because relevancy, as used by Thayer and in the Code, means tendency to prove a proposition properly provable in the case, an offered item of evidence may be excluded as "irrelevant" for either of these two quite distinct reasons: because it is not probative of the proposition at which it is directed, or because that proposition is not provable in the case.

* * * Let us analyze a single interesting case, Union Paint & Varnish Co. v. Dean,* an action of assumpsit to recover the purchase price of waterproof roof paint. The defendant relied upon the plaintiff's warranty that the paint would wear for ten years, breach of which he sought to show by proof that another drum of paint of the same brand, which he had purchased six months earlier, not only had failed to prevent leaks but had ruined the shingles to which it had been applied. The drum of paint in issue, purchased just before leaks developed in the first roof painted, had never been opened. Reversing the trial court, the Supreme Court of Rhode Island held that the

* 48 R.I. 288, 137 A. 469 (1927) [Ed.].

defendant's offer of proof (apparently almost the only evidence offered in defense) should have been received, saying:

> "If paint of the same brand, sold by the same concern under the same warranty within six months, had proved within that time to be not in conformity with the warranty, in that it was not only not suitable for stopping and preventing leaks but was actually injurious to a roof, a person might well hesitate before using more paint of the same brand when he had no reason to expect the second lot to be any better than the first."

Considered as evidence of the condition of the second drum of paint, proof of the results of use of the first is not very impressive. Waiving any doubts whether the leaks in the first roof were traceable to defects in paint in the first drum, there is no showing whether the defects in the first drum of paint were due to poor ingredients, to a poor formula, or to some error in preparation. If poor ingredients had been used, there is no showing that use of poor ingredients was a policy of, rather than an error of, the plaintiff company. It is easier to believe that one lot of defective paint went out than it is to believe that plaintiff customarily sold, under a ten-year guaranty, waterproof roof paint which would rot out shingles and cause leaks in six months. And the two drums of paint were probably not out of one lot; certainly there was no showing that they were. Proof of the condition of the paint in the first drum was of negligible value in judging the probable character of the paint in the second, unopened drum. It merely showed that plaintiff company sometimes sold bad paint. If the issue was whether the paint in the second drum *was* bad, an issue on which the defendant had the burden, the trial judge's ruling seems sound. At worst, the issue is close enough so that an appellate court should not reverse. Yet there is still a ring of reason to the supreme court's statement that "a person might well hesitate before using more paint of the same brand". He would hesitate to risk ruining a second roof even if he only feared that the second drum of paint might be no better than the first. And if he was reasonable in his hesitation, should the plaintiff be allowed to recover even if it could show at trial that the paint in the second drum was perfectly good? The defendant, reasonably hesitant to use the doubtful paint, by now has probably painted all of his roofs with some other paint and has no further use for the drum which he is tendering back to the vendor. If the customer is to be protected, even against proof that the second drum of paint was in fact satisfactory (as the writer should like to do in such a case), a novel rule of substantive law stands revealed behind a somewhat doubtful ruling on evidence.

But after excluding all cases which turn upon the materiality or immateriality under the pleadings and substantive law of ultimate propositions sought to be proved, there remain many cases in which there is no question of the materiality of the proposition sought to be proved and the probative value of the offered evidence is the real issue. These cases, and these alone, raise the problem of relevancy as a problem in the law of evidence. How should they be handled?

Crux of Thayer's principle

Thayer, after stating the principle which forbids receiving anything not "logically probative", excluded legal criteria from further operation, saying:

> "How are we to know what these forbidden things are? Not by any rule of law. The law furnishes no test of relevancy. For this, it tacitly refers to logical and general experience,— assuming that the principles of reasoning are known to its judges and ministers, just as a vast multitude of other things are assumed as already sufficiently known to them." * * *

PART B. RELEVANCE AND INFERENCE

MORGAN, BASIC PROBLEMS OF EVIDENCE
185–188 (1961).*

* * * Assume that X has met his death by violence; the proposition to be proved is that Y killed him; the offered item of evidence is a love letter written by Y to X's wife. The series of inferences is about as follows: From Y's letter, (A), to Y's love of X's wife, (B), to Y's desire for the exclusive possession of X's wife, (C), to Y's desire to get rid of X, (D), to Y's plan to get rid of X, (E), to Y's execution of the plan by killing X, (F). The unarticulated premise, (M), conjoined with (A) is, "A man who writes a love letter to a woman is probably in love with her"; that, (N), conjoined with (B) is, "A man who loves a woman probably desires her for himself alone"; that, (O), conjoined with (C) is, "A man who loves a married woman and desired her for himself alone desired to get rid of her husband"; that, (P), conjoined with (D) is, "A man who desires to get rid of the husband of the woman he loves probably plans to do so"; and that, (Q), conjoined with (E) is, "A man who plans to get rid of the husband of the woman he loves is probably the man who killed him." If an arrow represents the drawing of an inference, the series may be represented thus:

```
A)
+)⟫⟶ B)
M)        +)⟫⟶ C)
      N)        +)⟫⟶ D)
            O)        +)⟫⟶ E)
                  P)        +)⟫⟶ F
                        Q)
```
[C1912]

Now it must be obvious that the value of item A as probative of F varies with the degree of probability of the existence of each presumed fact and inversely with the number of inferences between A and F. As A + M cannot possibly equal B but necessarily represent only a fraction of B, and B + N likewise but a fraction of C, and so on through the series it might well be said that the strength of item A as evidence of the existence of F is represented by a fraction which is the product of a series of fractions, each of which represents the portion of certainty of

* Joint Committee on Continuing Legal Education of The American Law Institute and The American Bar Association, Philadelphia, 1961.

the respective inferences. For in this lawsuit, it must be remembered that the court will begin with the assumption of the nonexistence of A, B, C, D, E and F.

Next, a distinction must be made between the relevance of A as evidence of F on the one hand and its weight on the other. Obviously A standing by itself would not justify the inference F; indeed, it might not justify even D or E. But the proponent of A may offer another item or several other items, each of which will begin a series of inferences leading to F. Thus, suppose that he introduces evidence (1) that two months before X's death Y threatened to kill X; (2) that Y held a pistol pointed toward X, that the pistol fired and X fell over dead; (3) that (a) Y one month before X's death bought a pistol bearing a specified number, (b) that a pistol, Exhibit M, bearing that number was found two weeks after X's death in a near-by abandoned well, (c) that a bullet, Exhibit N, found in X's heart, caused X's death, and (d) that test bullets O and Q fired from Exhibit M bore rifling marks and other surface marks identical with those on Exhibit N. The series of inferences as to the first of these items is from Y's threat to Y's then existing intent, thence to continuance of the intent to the instant of the shooting, thence to the shooting and killing; as to the second item, from the holding of the pistol to the firing of the pistol, thence to the impact of the bullet upon X; as to the third item from the purchase of the pistol to its possession at the time of the shooting, from the identity of the marks on the bullets to the firing of all three from Exhibit M; and from the combination of (a), (b), (c) and (d) to the firing of the bullet N from Exhibit M by Y. Here again the persuasive value of each of these items will depend upon the number of inferences required and the degree of probability of the coexistence of the basic fact of each inference and the fact inferred. But when all the items are considered, the greater the number of items, the stronger will be the foundation for the ultimate inference. Nevertheless, no matter how numerous the items or how short the series of inferences required for each of them, they will never produce certainty. If one witness testified that he saw Y shoot X, the trier may be persuaded that the chances are three out of four that Y did shoot X; but if three others testified to the same effect with equal persuasiveness, the sum of the testimony of all four would not equal three times certainty. On the other hand, no matter how great the number of items established, they will never make the existence of the ultimate fact a question for the trier unless the total would justify reasonable men in concluding that the existence of the ultimate fact is more probable than its nonexistence.

McCORMICK'S HANDBOOK ON THE LAW OF EVIDENCE

316–17 (1954) *

Under our system, molded by the tradition of jury-trial and of predominantly oral proof, a party offers his evidence not in mass, but item by item. The problem of relevancy may arise as to each fact proposed to be elicited by successive questions of counsel, or by succes-

sive offers of writings or other objects. Such items are normally offered
and admitted or rejected as units, though of course the judge will
consider any proof already made by the proponent as indicating the
bearing of the item offered, and may in his discretion ask the proponent
what additional circumstances he expects to prove. But when it is
offered and judged singly and in isolation, as it frequently is, it cannot
be expected by itself to furnish conclusive proof of the ultimate fact to
be inferred. Thus the common argument of the objector that the
inference for which the fact is offered "does not necessarily follow" is
untenable, as it supposes a standard of conclusiveness which probably
no aggregation of circumstantial evidence, and certainly no single item
thereof, could ever meet. This same practice of determining the
admissibility of items of evidence singly as they are offered leads to
another distinction, often stressed in judicial opinions. This is the
distinction between relevancy and sufficiency. The test of relevancy,
which is to be applied by the trial judge in determining whether a
particular item or group of items of evidence is to be admitted, is a
different and less stringent one than the standard used at a later stage
in deciding whether all the evidence of the party on an issue is
sufficient to permit the issue to go to the jury. A brick is not a wall.

KNAPP v. STATE

Supreme Court of Indiana, 1907.
168 Ind. 153, 79 N.E. 1076.

GILLETT, J. Appellant appeals from a judgment in the above-
entitled cause, under, which he stands convicted of murder in the first
degree. Error is assigned on the overruling of a motion for new trial.

Appellant, as a witness in his own behalf, offered testimony tending to show a killing in self-defense. He afterwards testified, presumably for the purpose of showing that he had reason to fear the deceased,
that before the killing he had heard that the deceased, who was the
marshal of Hagerstown, had clubbed and seriously injured an old man
in arresting him, and that he died a short time afterwards. On
appellant being asked, on cross-examination, who told him this, he
answered: "Some people around Hagerstown there. I can't say as to
who it was now." The state was permitted, on rebuttal, to prove by a
physician, over the objection and exception of the defense, that the old
man died of senility and alcoholism, and that there were no bruises or
marks on his person. Counsel for appellant contend that it was error
to admit this testimony; that the question was as to whether he had, in
fact, heard the story, and not as to its truth or falsity. While it is laid
down in the books that there must be an open and visible connection
between the fact under inquiry and the evidence by which it is sought
to be established, yet the connection thus required is in the logical
processes only, for to require an actual connection between the two
facts would be to exclude all presumptive evidence. Best on Evidence
(Morgan's Ed.) § 90. Within settled rules, the competency of testimony
depends largely upon its tendency to persuade the judgment. As said
by Wharton: "Relevancy is that which conduces to the proof of a
pertinent hypothesis." 1 Wharton, Ev. § 20. In Stevenson v. Stuart,

[handwritten margin note at top: If fact would reasonably help to resolve primary issue on trial = ok as far as relevency]

11 Pa. 307, it was said: "The competency of a collateral fact to be used as the basis of legitimate argument is not to be determined by the conclusiveness of the inferences it may afford in reference to the litigated fact. It is enough if these may tend in a slight degree to elucidate the inquiry, or to assist, though remotely, to a determination probably founded in truth."

We are of opinion that the testimony referred to was competent. While appellant's counsel are correct in their assertion that the question was whether appellant had heard a story to the effect that the deceased had offered serious violence to the old man, yet it does not follow that the testimony complained of did not tend to negative the claim of appellant as to what he had heard. One of the first principles of human nature is the impulse to speak the truth. "This principle," says Dr. Reid, whom Professor Greenleaf quotes at length in his work on Evidence (volume 1, § 7n), "has a powerful operation, even in the greatest liars, for where they lie once they speak truth 100 times." Truth speaking preponderating, it follows that to show that there was no basis in fact for the statement appellant claims to have heard had a tendency to make it less probable that his testimony on this point was true. Indeed, since this court has not, in cases where self-defense is asserted as a justification for homicide, confined the evidence concerning the deceased to character evidence, we do not perceive how, without the possibility of a gross perversion of right, the state could be denied the opportunity to meet in the manner indicated the evidence of the defendant as to what he had heard, where he, cunningly perhaps, denies that he can remember who gave him the information. The fact proved by the state tended to discredit appellant, since it showed that somewhere between the fact and the testimony there was a person who was not a truth speaker, and, appellant being unable to point to his informant, it must at least be said that the testimony complained of had a tendency to render his claim as to what he had heard less probable.

Judgment affirmed.

FISCH ON NEW YORK EVIDENCE

123–24, 133–38 (1959). *

[Footnotes omitted.]

§ 231. Ability and Opportunity

Proof of physical or mental capacity, or the presence or lack of knowledge, skill, means or opportunity to execute an act is admissible to raise or negative an inference as to its performance by the person charged with its commission. When relevant, however, evidence of financial condition may be introduced, and is frequently used to establish a motive or to show sudden enrichment. It is also commonly received in contested probate proceedings to demonstrate that the testator disregarded the needs, or recognized the good financial condition of those having a claim on his bounty, as these circumstances are

* Copyright 1959 Edith L. Fisch, Lond Publications, N.Y., 1959.

[handwritten margin notes: Collateral facts can be proven if. / Cmt say people tell the truth / Therefore the (D) didn't probably hear the story / Also since (D) couldn't I.D. his source fact of story is less probable / Whats admissible]

indicative of the presence or absence of undue influence, overreaching
or testamentary capacity.

A defense of payment or claim of a loan may be negatived by
pecuniary inability, and, although financial ability may generally not
be introduced to establish the *making* of a loan or the *payment* of a
debt, possession by the adversary of sufficient means to have made
payment may be proved to rebut evidence of his pecuniary inability to
have done so.

On the issue of whether credit was given to A or B, it is improper
to receive evidence of financial condition as "(n)o fair inference can be
drawn that one person received credit instead of another, because he
happened to have the most property. Men are often trusted on account
of their good character and strict integrity, and sometimes upon their
business capacity, and sometimes upon their future prospects. There
are too many circumstances which may exist to cause a credit to be
given, to permit the amount of a person's property, to be thrown in the
scale upon such a question."

The financial responsibility of the defendant is a factor that may be
considered by the jury in awarding exemplary damages as these damages are based on the theory of punishment and deterrence and the
sum effective for such purposes depends upon the financial resources of
the defendant.

§ 240. Motive

Motive is the inducement by which a person is impelled to act in
order to achieve a preconceived goal. Never an essential element of a
crime, it is often of probative value in determining whether the accused
committed the act charged, since a person who possesses a motive to act
or not to act in a certain manner is more likely to do so than one in
whom such an impetus is lacking. For this reason lack of motive is
also relevant as a circumstance tending towards exoneration of the
accused. Evidence of motive is used principally to prove the doing of
an act, but even when performance of the act in question by defendant
is not disputed, motive may be relevant, and hence admissible, for such
other purposes as establishing intent or negativing a defense of accident
or mistake.

* * *

The factual situations capable of giving rise to an inference of
motive are innumerable and run the entire gamut of human emotions.
Because "frequently obscure, often trivial, and never adequate," considerable latitude in proof is allowed, and generally any fact that can
possibly tend to establish a motive may be introduced. Proof of the
awareness by the defendant of these facts is the only condition of
admissibility.

§ 241. Design, Plan or Scheme

It is to some extent probable that a person will act in accordance
with a plan, design or scheme devised by him. Thus, the existence of
these factors has probative value in determining whether he did or did

scheme
p & D
have proba... relie...

1 not do a particular act. While the variety of acts that may be
2 evidenced by proof of a design, plan or scheme are limitless, such proof
3 most frequently appears in cases involving suicide, the making of a gift
4 or contract, the execution or revocation of a will, or the commission of a
5 criminal act.

How these established

6   Design, plan or scheme may be established by declarations as well
7 as acts, and any act or declaration that according to common sense and
8 experience, would indicate the existence of a design, plan or scheme is
9 admissible. Such circumstances as the possession by the accused of
10 tools or instruments ordinarily used for performing the act in question,
11 other similar acts, prior attempts and threats, whether of a general and
12 specific nature, have been received. However, a defendant, claiming to
13 have killed in self-defense, may introduce the threats of his victim on
14 the theory that they are probative of a plan or design to commit the
15 acts threatened. This inference in turn is used as the basis for
16 concluding that the victim attempted to carry out his plan and was
17 thus the aggressor on the occasion in question. As the circumstances of
18 evidentiary importance is the plan or design to do the act, the fact that
19 the threat was never communicated to the defendant is without legal
20 significance.

Threats made by 3rd persons have never been used

21
22   The admissibility of threats made by third persons against the
23 victim of a crime, to be used for the purpose of exonerating the accused,
24 has apparently never been adjudicated in this state. While some
25 jurisdictions have refused to admit these statements there appears to be
26 no valid reason for an exclusionary ruling.

27
28 ## § 242. Intent

when it needs to be shown is admitted

29   Whenever intent, by which is meant the state of mind that accom-
30 panies an act, is a necessary element of the crime charged and the act
31 is one that could have been performed by mistake or accident or with a
32 lawful intent, evidence probative of intent, including proof of emotions
33 that affect the quality or persistence of the intent, may generally be
34 received.

How to establish

35   As the defendant is entitled to testify to his lawful intent or lack of
36 guilty knowledge, direct proof of these facts is more readily obtainable
37 than direct evidence of unlawful intent. Consequently, the latter is
38 seldom provable except by circumstantial evidence. Such events as
39 similar offenses, prior attempts to commit the same crime, preparations
40 for the act, threats, quarrels, or other indications of malice or ill-will
41 are often utilized as the basis for inferring unlawful intent. As is true
42 of motive, evidence indicative of intent is not rendered inadmissible
43 because it also tends to prove the commission of another crime.

44
45   Intent is often material in civil as well as criminal proceedings, for
46 the legal character of many non-criminal acts is determined by the
47 state of mind with which they were performed. For example, the
48 transfer of property from one person to another is equivocal in that its
49 legal significance can not be determined by the physical act alone. The
50 transfer may have been made in pursuance of an agency, to defraud
51 creditors, for the convenience of the original owner or as a loan or gift.

Hence, if it is contended that the transfer was a gift, it becomes necessary to establish a donative intent. This may be accomplished by direct evidence. It may also be established circumstantially by inferring the intent from the declarations of the alleged donor by donee, or from such circumstances as the fact that the alleged donor entirely divested himself of possession and dominion over the property, registered stock on the corporate books in the name of the alleged donee, or owed a moral obligation to the person claiming that a gift was made.

Intent to defraud and fraud in fact are also frequently evidenced circumstantially. Knowledge, or at least the belief, of the person charged that his statement is false, is the usual basis for an inference of intent in fraud actions based upon misrepresentations. Such an inference, however, may be predicated on other circumstances that amount to the same thing, such as the reckless making of the statement, termed "reckless indifference," or from a pretense of exact knowledge. The fact that other acts of the same character have been committed may also give rise to an inference of fraudulent intent.

§ 243. Mental and Physical Condition

An almost endless variety of facts may be admitted to circumstantially establish mental condition. The necessity for this type of proof is most often encountered when the defense of insanity is raised in a criminal case or when probate of a will is opposed on the ground of lack of testamentary capacity.

In determining testamentary capacity the life, surroundings, relationships and friendships of the testator can properly be considered. Where insanity is relied upon as a defense to a criminal act, the whole previous career of the accused may be relevant to his mental condition at the time of the alleged offense.

The oral and written declarations of the person whose mental condition is in question are admissible as the basis for an inference thereto, and declarations made to him, when introduced to establish that they affected his mind to such an extent as to render him insane, may also be received. Conduct and behavior such as the fact that until his death an individual wisely and prudently supervised a large estate, made an unnatural disposition of his property by disinheriting his expected beneficiaries or suffered from delusions, may be considered in determining mental soundness.

Head injuries, confinement in a mental institution, or the appointment of a committee are also probative of this issue. It may also be proved that other members of the family were afflicted with a hereditary or transmissible disease, provided evidence has been introduced to show that the person in question is similarly afflicted. Consequently, it was held error to exclude hospital records tending to show that an ancestor of the accused suffered from dementia praecox when evidence was introduced in support of the claim of defendant that he too was suffering from this illness, and that it was hereditary. But absent evidence indicating that the person in question is afflicted with the claimed hereditary or transmissible disturbance, its existence may not be inferred solely from the fact that it was present in other members of his family.

That a testator was not intoxicated at the time he executed his will may be shown by the fact that immediately prior thereto he had operated a trolley car and placed it in the car barn without any difficulty.

It is often declared that the circumstances used as the basis for an inference as to mental or physical condition must not be too remote in point of time, but whether the time interval is too long necessarily depends upon the condition to be proved. Thus, if it is sought to prove intoxication, evidence of drinking will not be admitted unless it concerns a period shortly before the event in question. If, on the other hand, mental condition is to be shown, events that occurred in infancy or early childhood may be probative and therefore admissible. Evidence of condition both subsequent as well as prior to the period in question will be received when relevant to establish condition at the time in question.

[handwritten margin note: circumstance showing mental condition must be after a reasonable time]

JONES, THE LAW OF EVIDENCE

§ 155 (1958). *
[Most footnotes omitted.]

What is Irrelevant.—The following examples of what the courts have held to be irrelevant may serve to illustrate further the theory of relevancy: The reason or motive impelling a party to retain a particular attorney to represent him in the case; a witness' reasons for believing certain facts; a party's personal opinions and prejudices as to matters wholly unrelated to the subject matter of the suit; and, on the issue as to desertion in a divorce suit between persons long married, evidence as to the place where they first lived after marriage.

The success of a discharged employee in similar positions after her discharge is irrelevant to the issue as to the propriety of her discharge from the position in suit for incompetency. And the personal practices of students and faculty members of a state university in another community are irrelevant to the issue as to the propriety of the expulsion from a state normal school of a female student for indulgence in such practices.

The identity of the handwriting of the portion of a writing which contained the defamatory charge with that of other portions of the same writing is irrelevant to the issue as to the truth or falsity of the alleged libel; a rejected bid for public work, which stipulated the damages for delay, is irrelevant to the issue of damages for delay under the accepted bid which contained no such stipulation, and, in an action against a broker for damages for breach of an oral contract, it is irrelevant to show a written contract between the parties relating to an entirely different subject matter.

Likewise, evidence of value or usual price is irrelevant in an action on a contract to pay a fixed sum; proof that a low price was paid for goods is irrelevant to disprove a claim of warranty of quality; and evidence as to the amount of wages paid in a certain employment in towns in another state is too remote to be relevant to the issue of the proper amount of wages for such work in the place of suit.

PART C.   PROBATIVE VALUE VERSUS PREJUDICIAL EFFECT

BALLOU v. HENRI STUDIOS, INC.

United States Court of Appeals, Fifth Circuit, 1981.
656 F.2d 1147.

JERRE S. WILLIAMS, Circuit Judge: The plaintiffs filed this diversity suit in Texas federal district court against Appellant Henri Studios, Inc., alleging that the death of Jesse Ballou [was] proximately caused by the negligence of Henri Studios' employee, John Woelfel, the driver of the truck.

Prior to trial, the plaintiffs filed a motion in limine seeking to prevent the introduction at trial of any evidence that Jesse Ballou was intoxicated at the time of the collision.   Specifically, the motion in limine sought to exclude the results of a blood alcohol test performed by the Beaumont Regional Crime Laboratory upon a blood sample allegedly taken from the body of Ballou which reflected that his blood contained 0.24% alcohol by weight at the time of his death.   On the day the trial of the case began, the district court held a hearing outside the presence of the jury on the issue whether the results of the blood alcohol test should be excluded from evidence at trial.   After hearing argument and testimony, the district court sustained the motion in limine and ruled the results of the blood test inadmissible.

* * *

At the hearing, the plaintiffs sought to refute the results of the blood test through proof that Ballou was not intoxicated at the time of the collision.

To support their claim that Ballou was not intoxicated, the plaintiffs called to the stand Mrs. Eula Eisenhower, a registered nurse [who] testified that on the afternoon of June 14, 1977, Jesse Ballou came to Dr. Washburn's office to have some stitches removed from his hand. She testified that in removing the stitches she was eighteen inches from Ballou's face, and that Ballou did not have alcohol on his breath and that she was positive that he was not intoxicated.

In response to the plaintiffs' arguments, Henri Studios outlined the chain of events leading from the removal of Ballou's body from his automobile through the chemists' analysis of one of the samples of his blood.   [T]he defendant noted the chemists' deposition testimony that the test results indicated Ballou was grossly intoxicated at the time of the collision.

After hearing the foregoing arguments and testimony, the district judge sustained the motion in limine. The court gave the following reasons for granting the motion:

> The Court does not feel that the tests [sic] were made with sufficient reliability, that it can be offered ∗ ∗ ∗.
>
> The Court will sustain the Plaintiffs' Motion in Limine because of the lack of credibility of the tests of alcoholism at the time of the wreck, especially in view of the testimony of Mrs. Eisenhower and the time which the accident occurred. Further, the Court feels to permit it would be prejudicial to the Plaintiffs because it is never possible to judge the attitude of a Jury and how they are affected by the subject of alcohol. Now if it was tried before the Court, it would be a different question, but trying it before the Jury, the Court feels that it would be too harmful and would be extremely prejudicial to the Plaintiff.

∗ ∗ ∗

In reviewing the district court's exclusion of the results of the blood alcohol test, it is important to note at the outset that even though this is a diversity case, the Federal Rules of Evidence govern the admissibility of evidence.

Under Rule 403 of the Federal Rules of Evidence, a district court may exclude evidence, even if relevant, "if its probative value is substantially outweighed by the danger of unfair prejudice." A trial court's ruling on admissibility under Rule 403's balancing test will not be overturned on appeal absent a clear abuse of discretion.

Although the district court neither stated with precision the grounds for its decision to exclude the results of the blood alcohol test nor specifically invoked Rule 403, the record clearly reveals that the court excluded the evidence because it believed that its prejudicial potential substantially outweighed its probative value. The court explicitly found that the evidence of Ballou's intoxication "would be too harmful" and "would be extremely prejudicial to the Plaintiff" because "it is never possible to judge the attitude of a Jury and how they are affected by the subject of alcohol." The court's comments also reveal that the court believed that the results of the blood alcohol test lacked "credibility." According to the court, its primary reason for determining that the test results lacked credibility was the testimony of Mrs. Eisenhower that Ballou was not intoxicated just a few minutes before the collision and Jim Middleton's testimony that it would probably take at least one hour of alcohol consumption to reach a blood alcohol level of 0.24%.

In challenging the district court's exclusion of the results of the blood alcohol test, Henri Studios argues, inter alia, (1) that the court's decision to believe Mrs. Eisenhower's testimony rather than the results of the blood alcohol test constituted a credibility choice which should properly have been reserved for the jury; and (2) that an adequate showing was made with respect to the chain of custody and lack of contamination of Ballou's body and blood samples, and that therefore any evidence concerning possible breaks in the chain of custody or contamination go to the weight and not the admissibility of the evidence. Because we agree with both of these contentions, and in addition conclude as a matter of law that the potential for unfair prejudice of the blood alcohol test did not substantially outweigh its probative value, we hold that the exclusion of the results of the test was an abuse of discretion requiring a reversal of the judgment and a new trial.

Henri Studios' argument that the district court made an impermissible credibility choice in deciding to believe Mrs. Eisenhower's testimony rather than the results of the blood alcohol test is well taken. It is clear that the district court credited Mrs. Eisenhower's testimony, and that her statement that Ballou was not intoxicated a few minutes before the collision was the primary basis for the court's decision that the results of the blood alcohol test were not worthy of belief. Of course, since the court found that the test results lacked credibility, they were assigned little or no probative value in the Rule 403 balancing test, which ultimately led to their exclusion from evidence.

Although we find the court's skepticism about the test results understandable in light of Mrs. Eisenhower's testimony, we cannot sanction the type of credibility choice made by the district court here. Under Fed.R.Evid. 104, a district court is authorized to conduct the balancing test required by Rule 403 outside the presence of the jury, in deciding the preliminary question of the admissibility of evidence. However, we have recently held that "Rule 403 does not permit exclusion of evidence because the judge does not find it credible." "Weighing probative value against unfair prejudice under [Rule] 403 means probative value with respect to a material fact *if the evidence is believed, not the degree the court finds it believable.*" Rather than discounting the probative value of the test results on the basis of its perception of the degree to which the evidence was worthy of belief, the district court should have determined the probative value of the test results *if true*, and weighed that probative value against the danger of unfair prejudice, leaving to the jury the difficult choice of whether to credit the evidence.

*   *   *

The question remains whether the test results, when properly taken as true, have a potential for unfair prejudice that substantially outweighs their probative value. We hold as a matter of law that the potential for unfair prejudice of the test results does not substantially outweigh their probative value.

The results of the blood alcohol test indicate that Ballou was intoxicated at the time of the collision. Proof of Ballou's intoxication is, of course, highly relevant to and probative of one of the ultimate questions before the jury—Ballou's contributory negligence—and would doubtless have a major effect on the jury's apportionment of fault. On the other hand, in our view the potential prejudice of the test results is comparatively slight. As this court has consistently held, " 'unfair prejudice' as used in Rule 403 is not to be equated with testimony simply adverse to the opposing party. Virtually all evidence is prejudicial or it isn't material. The prejudice must be 'unfair.'" Unfair prejudice within the context of Rule 403 "means an undue tendency to suggest [a] decision on an improper basis, commonly, though not necessarily, an emotional one." Notes of the Advisory Committee on Proposed Federal Rules of Evidence, Rule 403. Although evidence of Ballou's intoxication would surely have an adverse effect on the plaintiffs' case, most of the potential prejudice flowing from the evidence cannot be considered to be unfair since Ballou's intoxication is unquestionably a legitimate ground for a finding of contributory negligence. While there is a slight possibility that evidence of Ballou's intoxication might adversely affect the jury's deliberation on issues other than Ballou's contributory negligence, this slight potential for unfair prejudice is virtually insignificant when compared with the high relevance and probative value of the evidence. We therefore conclude that the district court committed reversible error in excluding the results of the blood test under Rule 403 and that the judgment in favor of Yolanda and Terrence Ballou must be reversed and the cause remanded for a new trial.

See Federal Rules of Evidence 401, 402, 403; California Evidence Code §§ 210, 350, 351, 352. See also Waltz, *Judicial Discretion in the Admission of Evidence Under the Federal Rules of Evidence,* 79 Nw.U.L.Rev. 1097 (1984–1985).

Hypotheticals

(1) A, a surviving widow, sues X for the wrongful death of B, A's husband. B, a pedestrian, was struck and killed by X's car. X's answer admits liability. A offers evidence that X was driving while intoxicated, and that B was thrown 80 feet by the force of the impact. X objects to this evidence as irrelevant. Is X's objection proper?

(2) P sues D for damages for personal injuries to himself and for the wrongful death of P's wife arising out of D's rear-ending of P's car. P was in his car parked at a curb and his wife was at the car door, starting to get in. P also seeks damages for emotional trauma resulting from his presence at the scene of the accident. P testifies that he did not see his wife after the impact because he was rendered unconscious. D admits liability. P proffers photographs of his wife's body at the accident site to show the condition of her body as a result of the collision, the autopsy report, and testimony of the autopsy surgeon and a friend regarding the reconstruction of the wife's body required to permit an open coffin funeral. D makes an irrelevancy objection to P's proffered evidence. What result?

(3) D is charged with the sale of marijuana. The prosecutor introduces evidence that in the company of I, an informer, PO, a police officer, made a purchase of marijuana from D at D's residence. D's defense is a "frame-up"— that PO had the informer plant the marijuana in D's residence. D seeks to introduce evidence that before the alleged sale, D had filed a false arrest suit against the police department growing out of an arrest of D made nine months before the alleged sale. The prosecutor makes an irrelevancy objection to D's proffered evidence. What result?

(4) X is charged with the sale of heroin. A, an undercover police officer, testifies that she purchased heroin from X at approximately 8:00 p.m. on January 30, which was six months before X's arrest. X's defense is an alibi. He testifies that on January 30 he and his wife went to the Movie Theater and saw the movie "Airport," and that it was raining that night. X's wife corroborates his testimony. X calls the theater manager, who testifies that "Airport" was shown at the Movie Theater for seven days, from January 25 to January 31. X then calls B, a meteorologist to testify that between January 25 and January 31 it rained on January 30 from 6:00 to 10:00 p.m., but not on any other day or night during that period. The prosecution makes an irrelevancy objection to B's testimony. What result?

(5) D is charged with forgery of a check and of using it to obtain cash from V, a grocer. D offers evidence that he made restitution to V a week after the incident. Should the prosecution's irrelevancy objection to D's proferred evidence be sustained?

Chapter III

THE HEARSAY RULE

PART A. RATIONALE AND MEANING: DEFINITIONS

The general rule excluding hearsay statements did not become firmly fixed in England until the latter part of the 17th Century. Thus Sir Walter Raleigh had his problems with hearsay earlier in that century.

Sir Walter Raleigh's Case (J.G. Phillimore, "History and Principles of the Law of Evidence," 1850, p. 157). (1603. Raleigh was tried for a conspiracy of treason to dethrone Elizabeth and to put Arbella Stuart in her place, by the aid of Spanish money and intrigue. Sir Edward Coke, attorney-general, conducted the prosecution. The principal evidence against him was the assertion of Lord Cobham, a supposed fellow-conspirator, who had betrayed Raleigh in a sworn statement made before trial. Cobham himself was in prison, and was not produced on the trial.) * * *

Raleigh. "But it is strange to see how you press me still with my Lord Cobham, and yet will not produce him; it is not for gaining of time or prolonging my life that I urge this; he is in the house hard by, and may soon be brought hither; let him be produced, and if he will yet accuse me or avow this confession of his, it shall convict me and ease you of further proof."

Lord Cecil. "Sir Walter Raleigh presseth often that my Lord Cobham should be brought face to face; if he ask a thing of grace and favour, they must come from him only who can give them; but if he ask a matter of law, then, in order that we, who sit here as commissioners, may be satisfied, I desire to hear the opinions of my Lords, the judges, whether it may be done by law."

The Judges all answered, "that in respect it might be a mean to cover many with treasons, and might be prejudicial to the King, therefore, by the law, it was not sufferable."

Popham, C.J. "There must not such a gap be opened for the destruction of the King as would be if we should grant this; you plead hard for yourself, but the laws plead as hard for the King. Where no circumstances do concur to make a matter probable, then an accuser may be heard; but so many circumstances agreeing and confirming the accusation in this case, the accuser is not to be produced; for, having first confessed against himself voluntarily, and so charged another person, if we shall now hear him again in person, he may, for favour or fear, retract what formerly he hath said, and the jury may, by that means, be inveigled." * * *

Raleigh.—"I never had intelligence with Cobham since I came to the Tower."

Lord Cecil.—"Sir Walter Raleigh, if my Lord Cobham will now affirm, that you were acquainted with his dealings with Count Aremberg, that you knew of the letter he received, that you were the chief instigator of him, will you then be concluded by it?"

Raleigh.—"Let my Lord Cobham speak before God and the King, and deny God and the King if he speak not truly, and will then say that ever I knew of Arabella's matter, or the money out of Spain, or the Surprising Treason, I will put myself upon it."

Lord Henry Howard.—"But what if my Lord Cobham affirm anything equivalent to this; what then?"

Raleigh.—"My Lord, I put myself upon it."

Attorney-General.—"I shall now produce a witness viva voce:"

He then produced one *Dyer*, a pilot, who, being sworn, said, "Being at Lisbon, there came to me a Portuguese gentleman, who asked me how the King of England did, and whether he was crowned? I answered him, that I hoped our noble king was well, and crowned by this; but the time was not come when I came from the coast of Spain. 'Nay,' said he 'your king shall never be crowned, for Don Cobham and Don Raleigh will cut his throat before he come to be crowned.' And this, in time, was found to be spoken in mid July."

Raleigh.—"This is the saying of some wild Jesuit or beggarly priest; but what proof is it against me?"

Attorney-General.—"It must perforce arise out of some preceding intelligence, and shews that your treason had wings." * * *

Thus on the single evidence of Cobham, never confronted with Raleigh, who retracted his confession, and then (according to the advocates of the Crown) recalled his retraction, did an English jury, to the amazement and horror of the bystanders, and the perpetual disgrace of the English name, find the most illustrious of their fellow subjects guilty of high treason.

STATE v. ENGLISH

Supreme Court of North Carolina, 1931.
201 N.C. 295, 159 S.E. 318.

Stephen English was convicted of murder in the second degree, and he appeals. * * *

The defendant offered evidence tending to show that on Sunday, the day after the murder, a Negro by the name of Dave Locke, was arrested in Wilmington, and this Negro, in the presence of three Wilmington officers, admitted that he killed Berta English "and described the house, the conditions of the body and the entire condition of the woman" as she was afterwards found. This Negro also stated that he killed Mrs. English with a fire poker and tore her bloomers off, and stated that the fire poker was bent at one end, and that in the struggle with Mrs. English he lost two buttons from his overalls, and that he produced these buttons and showed them to the officers at the time of the confession. The statement of the suspect gave "a pretty good description of the house and of the roads about the premises."

Thereafter, on January 19, 1930, a warrant was issued for Locke, charging him with the murder of Mrs. English. This warrant was returnable before a magistrate. The record is not clear, but apparently the Negro was discharged and has since not been seen about that part of the country. All of the foregoing evidence was excluded by the court.

* * *

Subsequently, on March 5, 1930, the defendant, Stephen English, husband of the deceased woman, was arrested and charged with the murder of his wife. * * *

The jury convicted the defendant of murder in the second degree, "asking the mercy of the court." Upon the verdict the court pronounced judgment that the defendant be confined in the state's prison for a term of not less than twenty years nor more than thirty years.

From the foregoing judgment defendant appealed.

BROGDEN, J.

Is the voluntary confession of a third party, made to officers of the law, that he killed the deceased, detailing the circumstances, competent evidence in behalf of the defendant charged with the murder?

The admissibility of confessions of a third party in criminal actions has been bitterly assailed and warmly defended by courts and text-writers. The numerical weight of authority excludes such testimony. About one hundred years ago it appears in State v. May, 15 N.C. 328, that a defendant was charged with stealing a slave. At that time this was a capital felony in North Carolina, and the defendant having been convicted, the judgment of death was pronounced against him. In that case the defendant offered testimony that another man had confessed to stealing the slave and had made compensations therefor. The testimony was rejected. The court said: "Except the facts of the respective residences of the parties, which of themselves, do not tend to establish guilt in either of the parties, it is obvious, that all the evidence, as well that received as that rejected, consists of the acts and declarations of other persons, to which neither the State nor the prisoner is privy. I think the whole of it was inadmissible. The confession is plainly so. It is mere hearsay. It may seem absurd to one not accustomed to compare proofs, and estimate the weight of testimony according to the tests of veracity within our power, that an unbiased confession of one man that he is guilty of an offense with which another is charged, should not establish the guilt of him who confesses it, and by consequence, the innocence of the other, but the law must proceed on general principles; and it excludes such a confession upon the ground, that it is hearsay evidence—the words of a stranger to the parties, and not spoken on oath. Indeed, all hearsay might have more or less effect, and from some persons of good character, well known to the jury, it might avail much. Yet it is all rejected, with very few exceptions; which do not in terms or principle extend to this case. Even a judgment upon the plea of guilty could not be offered in evidence for or against another; much less a bare confession. As a declaration of another establishing his own guilt, the confession of a slave might be used upon the same principle."

The May Case is the original legal patriarch of an increasing line of legal descendants in this state. The states holding the same interpretation of the law are assembled in a note in the decision of Donnelly v. U.S., 228 U.S. 243, 33 S.Ct. 449, 461, 57 L.Ed. 820, Ann.Cas. 1913E, 710. The minority view is clearly and concisely stated by Mr. Justice Holmes who wrote a dissenting opinion in the Donnelly Case, supra, in which Justices Lurton and Hughes concurred. Justice Holmes said: "The confession of Joe Dick, since deceased, that he committed the murder for which the plaintiff in error was tried, coupled with circumstances pointing to its truth, would have a very strong tendency to make anyone outside of a court of justice believe that Donnelly did not commit the crime. I say this, of course, on the supposition that it should be proved that the confession really was made, and that there was no ground for connecting Donnelly with Dick. The rules of evidence in the main are based on experience, logic, and common sense, less hampered by history than some parts of the substantive law. There is no decision by this court against the admissibility of such a confession; the English cases since the separation of the two countries do not bind us; the exception to the hearsay rule in the case of declarations against interest is well known; no other statement is so much against interest as a confession of murder; it is far more calculated to convince than dying declarations, which would be let in to hang a man; * * * and when we surround the accused with so many safeguards, some of which seem to me excessive I think we ought to give him the benefit of a fact that, if proved, commonly would have such weight. The history of the law and the arguments against the English doctrine are so well and fully stated by Mr. Wigmore that there is no need to set them forth at greater length. 2 Wigmore, Ev. §§ 1476, 1477."

* * *

The great jurist who wrote the May Case, confesses that the holding might seem absurd to a layman, "but the law must proceed on general principles," and hence if proffered testimony is technically and legalistically hearsay, then the technical interpretation must prevail. Furthermore, the suggested possibility that some man accused of crime would procure a confession of guilt by a slave and thus escape punishment, might have been a consequence which law-writers of a hundred years ago were seeking to avoid.

The writer of this opinion, speaking for himself, strings with the minority, but it was the duty of the trial judge to apply the law as written, and the exceptions of the defendant are not sustained. * * *

No error.

LILLY, AN INTRODUCTION TO THE LAW OF EVIDENCE
213–14 (2d ed. 1987).*

Suppose that a child is taken to the defendant's house and molested. The victim subsequently describes to her mother what the house looked like and includes additional details about the appearance of the interior. At trial, the prosecutor introduces evidence describing the exterior and interior of the defendant's home. May the mother now testify as to her daughter's prior statements in which the child accurately recited what her captor's house looked like? If the prosecutor also supplied evidence that it was highly unlikely that the victim could have gained knowledge of these surroundings except by having been transported there on the occasion in question, the little girl's prior statements ought to be admissible to show her knowledge. Her statements would not be offered to prove the appearance of the defendant's house—this having been established by other evidence. Nor are they offered to prove the appearance of the house in which she was molested, although of course she could repeat her description of the surroundings from the witness stand. Her out-of-court description, congruent with the *actual physical* appearance of the defendant's home, constitutes convincing circumstantial evidence that she once saw it, at least if there is sufficient detail in her account to distinguish the house in question from other houses. See Bridges v. State, 247 Wis. 350, 19 N.W.2d 529 (1945), rehearing denied, 247 Wis. 350, 19 N.W.2d 862 (1945).

For a modern application of the *Bridges* principle, see United States v. Muscato, 534 F.Supp. 969 (E.D.N.Y.1982). There W gave an accurate extra-judicial description of a gun having unique features. The opportunities for gaining this knowledge, other than by actually seeing the weapon in the circumstances claimed by W, were limited. The fact that W also identified the gun in the courtroom and was subject to cross-examination concerning other ways in which he might have gained knowledge of its appearance buttressed the prosecution's case for admissibility.

The trial judge in *Muscato* (Judge Jack Weinstein), after discussing *Bridges* and similar cases, allowed the previous description into evidence. He characterized the evidence, used not to prove the fact asserted but to prove the declarant's knowledge of the fact, as nonhearsay. Judge Weinstein acknowledged, however, that this kind of evidence might be highly influential to the jury, an influence that would be unwarranted if the witness might have gained his knowledge by more than one means. Nonetheless, in the case before him, not only was it unlikely that the witness gained the knowledge other than by seeing the gun (as claimed), but the witness also testified, identified the weapon again, and was subject to a full cross-examination about the source of his knowledge. Thus, applying Rule 403, the court ruled that the probative value of the nonhearsay, out-of-court declaration was not outweighed by the risk of jury misuse.

TRIBE, TRIANGULATING HEARSAY

87 Harvard Law Review 957, 958–61 (1974).*

[Some footnotes omitted.]

I. THE TESTIMONIAL TRIANGLE

The basic hearsay problem is that of forging a reliable chain of inferences, from an act or utterance of a person not subject to contemporaneous in-court cross-examination about that act or utterance, to an event that the act or utterance is supposed to reflect. Typically, the first link in the required chain of inferences is the link from the act or utterance to the belief it is thought to express or indicate. It is helpful to think of this link as involving a "trip" into the head of the person responsible for the act or utterance (the declarant) to see what he or she was really thinking when the act occurred. The second link is the one from the declarant's assumed belief to a conclusion about some external event that is supposed to have triggered the belief, or that is linked to the belief in some other way. This link involves a trip out of the head of the declarant, in order to match the declarant's assumed belief with the external reality sought to be demonstrated.

The trier must obviously employ such a chain of inferences whenever a witness testifies in court. But the process has long been regarded as particularly suspect when the act or utterance is not one made in court, under oath, by a person whose demeanor at the time is witnessed by the trier, and under circumstances permitting immediate cross-examination by counsel in order to probe possible inaccuracies in the inferential chain. These inaccuracies are usually attributed to the four testimonial infirmities of ambiguity, insincerity, faulty perception, and erroneous memory. In the absence of special reasons, the perceived untrustworthiness of such an out-of-court act or utterance has lead the Anglo-Saxon legal system to exclude it as hearsay despite its potentially probative value.

There exists a rather simple way of schematizing all of this in terms of an elementary geometric construct that serves to structure its several related elements. The construct might be called the Testimonial Triangle. By making graphic the path of inferences, and by functionally grouping the problems encountered along the path, the triangle makes it easier both to identify when a hearsay problem exists and to structure consideration of the appropriateness of exceptions to the rule that bars hearsay inferences.

The diagram is as follows:

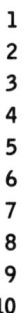

B   (belief of actor
    responsible for A)¹

(1) ambiguity   (3) erroneous
(2) insincerity   memory
                                           (4) faulty
                                               perception

A   C
(action or utterance)   (conclusion to which B points)

[C1913]

If we use the diagram to trace the inferential path the trier must follow, we begin at the lower left vertex of the triangle (A), which represents the declarant's (X's) act or assertion. The path first takes us to the upper vertex (B), representing X's belief in what his or her act or assertion suggests, and then takes us to the lower right vertex (C), representing the external reality suggested by X's belief. When "A" is used to prove "C" along the path through "B," a traditional hearsay problem exists and the use of the act or assertion as evidence is disallowed upon proper objection in the absence of some special reason to permit it.

It is of course a simple matter to locate the four testimonial infirmities on the triangle to show where and how they might impede the process of inference. To go from "A" to "B," the declarant's belief, one must remove the obstacles of (1) ambiguity and (2) insincerity. To go from "B" to "C," the external fact, one must further remove the obstacles of (3) erroneous memory and (4) faulty perception.

When it is possible to go directly from "A" to "C" with no detour through "B," there is no hearsay problem unless the validity of the trier's conclusion depends upon an implicit path through "B."¹ Suppose, for example, that the issue in a lawsuit is whether the Government took adequate safety precautions in connection with the nuclear test at Amchitka in 1971. James Schlesinger, then Chairman of the Atomic Energy Commission, "told reporters at Elmendorf Air Force Base outside Anchorage that he was taking his wife * * * and daughters * * * with him [to the site of the Amchitka blast] in response to Alaska Gov. William E. Egan's invitation. Egan strongly

---

1. An uncompromising behaviorist might insist that no detour through mental states is ever necessary because every trip from an act or utterance "A" to a conclusion "C" is reducible to a circumstantial inference about the statistical frequency with which "C" is present when "A" is present. There are difficulties with accepting the behaviorist perspective as a coherent one. See Chomsky, A Review of B.F. Skinner's Verbal Behavior, 35 Language 26 (1959); Chomsky, The Case Against B.F. Skinner, New York Review of Books, Dec. 30, 1971, at 18. But even if one does adopt such a perspective, it does not follow that the trier's way of using the evidence "A" will in fact mirror that perspective, for the trier is likely to reason about states of mind even if it is in some sense incorrect or unnecessary to do so. Moreover, the connection between "A" and "C" may well be such that the frequency with which the latter accompanies the former depends upon the actor's testimonial capacities so that, even from a behaviorist perspective, information about a declarant's use of language, tendency to lie, eyesight, and so forth, may increase or decrease the statistical correlation between the utterance and the fact reported.

disapprove[d] of the test." [2]   In these circumstances, the trip from "A,"
the Chairman's proposed travel with his family to the site of the blast,
to "C," the conclusion that the blast was reasonably safe, may appear at
first to be purely "circumstantial," but in fact that trip requires a
journey into the Chairman's head and out again—a journey through
the belief "B" suggested by his willingness to be near the blast with his
family.   The journey from "A" to "B" involves problems of possible
ambiguity and of insincerity in that the Chairman was apparently
seeking to dispel fears of danger, so that his act may not bespeak an
actual belief in the test's safety.   And the journey from "B" to "C"
involves problems of memory and perception in that he may not have
recalled all the relevant data and may have misperceived such data in
the first instance, so that his belief in the test's safety, even if we
assume the journey from "A" to "B" safely completed, may not correspond to the facts sought to be demonstrated.   On both legs of the
triangle, therefore, there are testimonial infirmities that cross-examination contemporaneous with the act "A" could help to expose.

By contrast, when the trier's inference can proceed from "A"
directly to "C," the infirmities of hearsay do not arise.   For example,
the out-of-court statement "I can speak" would be admissible as
nonhearsay to prove that the declarant was capable of speech, for it is
the fact of his speaking rather than the content of the statement which
permits the inference, and that involves no problems of the statement's
ambiguity, or of sincerity, memory, or perception.

PARK, TWO DEFINITIONS OF HEARSAY [1]

Definitions of hearsay are usually either assertion-centered or
declarant-centered.   Under an assertion-centered definition, an out-of-
court statement is hearsay when it is offered in evidence to prove the
truth of the matter asserted.   Under a declarant-centered definition, an
out-of-court statement is hearsay when it depends for value upon the
credibility of the declarant.   The term "credibility" refers to the testimonial qualities of sincerity, narrative ability, memory, and perception.

Over much hearsay territory, the difference between the two definitions has no effect.   Most utterances that are not hearsay under an
assertion-centered definition would not be hearsay under a declarant-
centered definition.   However, the two definitions can produce different
results in some cases.   For example, suppose that a criminal defendant
is charged with committing a crime in Miami.   After the crime, the
police questioned the defendant's wife, who told them that the defendant was with her in Honolulu on the evening of the crime.   The wife's
statement is demonstrably false, and the prosecution seeks to use her
statement against the defendant for the inference that the wife lied

2. Boston Globe, Nov. 5, 1971, at 16.
The fact pattern of the Amchitka example
is remarkably similar to a hypothetical
presented by Baron Parke in his opinion in
Wright v. Doe dem. Tatham (experienced
ship captain inspecting and setting sail on
a ship).

1. Adapted from Park, "I Didn't Tell
Them Anything About You": Implied Assertions as Hearsay Under the Federal
Rules of Evidence, 74 Minn.L.Rev. 783, 783
(1990).

because she knew the defendant to be guilty. Under an assertion-centered definition, the wife's statement is not hearsay because it is not offered to prove the truth of the matter asserted. Under a declarant-centered definition, her statement would be hearsay because the trier's use of it would require reliance on her powers of memory, perception, and narration. She might have been mistaken about the date on which her husband was in Honolulu or she might have misspoken the date. Even if she was trying to cover up for her husband because she believed him to be guilty, her belief might have been based upon misperception or misinterpretation.

———

See Federal Rules of Evidence 801(b), (c), 802; California Evidence Code § 1200.

ESTATE OF MURDOCK
32 Muc. 352 (1983).*

This is a dispute that could easily have been avoided by competent estate planning. But, unfortunately, what a lawyer could have done in two minutes in his office has required two years of expensive litigation. The case involves a contest between the children of Sarah Hayes Murdock by her first marriage (called hereinafter the Hayes children) and the children of Arthur G. Murdock by his first marriage (called hereinafter the Murdock children.)

Arthur G. Murdock had executed a will, leaving his entire estate to Sarah, his second wife, if she should survive him, but if she did not, then to his children by his first marriage (the Murdock children) in equal shares. Sarah Hayes Murdock, on the other hand, had made a substantially similar will, leaving her entire estate to Arthur G. Murdock, if he should survive her, and to her children by her first marriage (the Hayes children) if she survived him.

The problem, of course, comes from the fact that Sarah and Arthur were in their private airplane when it crashed, resulting in their deaths. Since this state has not adopted the Uniform Simultaneous Death Act, that becomes extremely important which would otherwise not have been a very significant issue—who died first?

Expert medical testimony was presented on both sides as to how long both Sarah and Arthur Murdock had lived after the crash. The crucial testimony at issue in this appeal was that of Deputy Sheriff Alfred Linden, who arrived at the scene of the crash some ten minutes after the crash. Linden testified that he saw immediately upon his arrival that Sarah was dead (in the interest of good taste, we will leave out his extremely graphic description of how he was able to determine that this was the case) and thereafter passed close to the other passenger, Arthur G. Murdock. The precise evidentiary ruling at issue here

* Unfortunately, the editors have been unable in their search of the appellate reports to find a truly good case with which to begin the study of hearsay. As a result, Muc., the citation here, stands for made-up cases.

arose when Deputy Linden wished to testify that he heard Mr. Murdock whisper, "I'm still alive."

On objection, this evidence was excluded by the trial judge on the grounds that it was hearsay. Nor would the judge listen to any argument on this, saying:

> "The hearsay rule says you are not permitted to introduce an out-of-court statement, which this indubitably is, to show the truth of that statement which is exactly what you are trying to do here, counsel.

Unfortunately, the learned trial judge was wrong. Although the definition of hearsay, as given by the statutes and the common law, seems, by its words, to require the exclusion of the evidence at issue here, hearsay is really a type of reasoning not easily capturable in a few simple words. In essence, the hearsay rule precludes reliance on the credibility of an out-of-court declarant. By excluding hearsay, the law seeks to guarantee to the party against whom such evidence is sought to be introduced the right meaningfully to cross-examine the out-of-court declarant who is in substance, though not in form, the real witness against him. The opponent of the out-of-court hearsay statement sought to be related by the witness is denied the right to cross-examine the declarant on his perception, memory, sincerity and ability to communicate what he remembers.

In the case at bar, the forbidden hearsay reasoning would be as follows:

> "Arthur Murdock said he was alive; he was a man of principle, alert, and of sound faculties. He would never get something like that wrong, or lie about it."

The reasoning properly used here is not hearsay reasoning at all, it does not rely for its probative value on Arthur Murdock's perception, memory, sincerity and ability to communicate at the time he said the words. Rather we reason here from the converse. People who are dead do not say, "I am still alive"—or anything else. (Obviously for this purpose it would have made no difference whether Murdock had said, "I am dead.") If Arthur Murdock had said this—and the jury could so believe by weighing the testimony of Deputy Linden, who was subject to cross examination—then he was alive at the time.

Nor can we affirm the exclusion of the evidence on the principle that where a piece of evidence is admissible for one purpose (its non-hearsay purpose) and inadmissible for another (its hearsay purpose), the judge would have a discretion to exclude it on the ground that its prejudicial effect outweighed its probative value. Assuming this evidence could conceivably be used for a hearsay purpose, the non-hearsay purpose was so much more obvious and so clearly drowned out any hearsay reasoning (if indeed there were such) that any action of the trial judge in excluding it would be clear abuse of discretion.

Judgment reversed.

SUBRAMANIAM v. PUBLIC PROSECUTOR

Judicial Committee of the Privy Council, 1956.
100 Solicitor's Journal 566.

This was an appeal, by special leave, by Subramaniam, a rubber tapper, from an order of the Supreme Court of the Federation of Malaya (Court of Appeal at Kuala Lumpur), dated 12th September, 1955, dismissing his appeal against a judgment and order of the High Court of Johore Bahru, whereby he was found guilty on a charge of being in possession of twenty rounds of ammunition without lawful authority, contrary to reg. 4(1)(b) of the Emergency Regulations, 1951, and sentenced to death. It was common ground that on 29th April, 1955, at a place in the Rengam District in the State of Johore, the appellant was found in a wounded condition by certain members of the security forces; that when he was searched there was found around his waist a leather belt with three pouches containing twenty live rounds of ammunition. The defense put forward was that he had been captured by terrorists, that at all material times he was acting under duress, and that at the time of his capture by the security forces he had formed the intention to surrender, with which intention he had come to the place where he was found. He gave evidence describing his capture and sought to give evidence of what the terrorists said to him, but the trial judge ruled that evidence of the conversation with the terrorists was not admissible unless they were called. The judge said that he could find no evidence of duress, and in the result the appellant, as stated, was convicted.

Mr. L. M. D. De Silva, giving the judgment said that the trial judge was in error in ruling out peremptorily the evidence of conversation between the terrorists and the appellant. Evidence of a statement made to a witness by a person who was not himself called as a witness might or might not be hearsay. It was hearsay and inadmissible when the object of the evidence was to establish the truth of what was contained in the statement. It was not hearsay and was admissible when it was proposed to establish by the evidence, not the truth of the statement, but the fact that it was made. Statements could have been made to the appellant by the terrorists which, whether true or not, if they had been believed by the appellant, might, within the meaning of s. 94 of the Penal Code of the Federated Malay States, reasonably have induced in him an apprehension of instant death if he failed to conform to their wishes. Thus a complete, or substantially complete, version according to the appellant of what was said to him by the terrorists and by him to them had been shut out, and their lordships had to consider whether, in the circumstances of this case, that exclusion of admissible evidence afforded sufficient reason for allowing the appeal. In Muhammad Nawaz v. King-Emperor, it was said: "Broadly speaking, the Judicial Committee will only interfere where there has been an infringement of the essential principles of justice. An obvious example would be * * * where [the accused] was not allowed to call relevant witnesses." In the present case the appellant had not been allowed to give relevant and admissible evidence, which was a circumstance very similar in its consequence to not being allowed "to call relevant witnesses." The appellant's version, if believed, could and might have afforded cogent evidence of duress brought to bear on him. He had not been allowed to give relevant and admissible evidence, and it could not be held with any confidence that had the excluded evidence, which went to the very root of the defense of duress, been admitted, the result of the trial would probably have been the same. Their lordships, for those reasons, had humbly advised Her Majesty that the appeal should be allowed.

VINYARD v. VINYARD FUNERAL HOME, INC.

St. Louis Court of Appeals, Missouri, 1968.
435 S.W.2d 392.

CLEMENS, Commissioner.

Plaintiff got a verdict and $13,000 judgment for injuries from a fall on defendant's parking lot. (Plaintiff was the daughter-in-law of the corporate defendant's president.) Defendant appeals. * * *

[O]ne rainy night plaintiff slipped and fell when she stepped from a roughly paved surface onto a smoothly paved surface of a ramp in defendant's dimly lighted parking lot. * * *

* * *

Defendant's [appeals] the admission of evidence that people complained to its officers and employees that the sealed surface was slippery when wet. Plaintiff offered this evidence to show that defendant knew its parking lot was slippery when wet. Witness Keith Vinyard was defendant's vice-president and plaintiff's husband. Testifying for plaintiff he was asked: "Now, Keith, after this sealer was put on did you receive any complaints from anyone visiting the funeral home?" Over defense objection that the question was hearsay unless limited to the same conditions as plaintiff's fall, the witness answered: "Yes, several people said it was slick." Later, witness Leroy Lucas, one of defendant's regular employees, was asked: "Did you yourself hear complaints of people that would come in and complain about it being slick when it was wet?" Over the defendant's hearsay objection Mr. Lucas answered: "I had heard different people comment on it that it was slick when it was wet."

These questions and answers were improper as hearsay if offered only to prove the fact that the sealed area was slick. But aside from the *fact* of slickness there was the issue of defendant's *knowledge* of slickness. Evidence of *complaints* of slickness made to defendant was relevant to the material issue of defendant's knowledge. As said in Miller v. Brunson Const. Co., Mo., 250 S.W.2d 958[9]: "Where, regardless of the truth or the falsity of a statement, the fact that it has been made is relevant, the hearsay rule does not apply, but the statement may be shown. Evidence as to the making of such statement is not secondary but primary, for the statement itself may constitute a fact in issue, or be circumstantially relevant as to the existence of such a fact."

The defendant's own witnesses later testified that the parking lot was slick when wet, and that the sealed upper area was slicker than the unsealed lower area. But to make her case the plaintiff was obliged to show that defendant's officers knew about the slickness. Under the circumstances of this case the trial court properly admitted evidence that this knowledge had come to them through complaints of patrons that the parking lot's sealed area was slick when wet.

Affirmed.

JOHNSON v. MISERICORDIA COMMUNITY HOSPITAL

Court of Appeals of Wisconsin, 1980.
97 Wis.2d 521, 294 N.W.2d 501.

[Plaintiff sued hospital for negligence in hiring one Dr. Salinsky and in allowing him to perform surgery on plaintiff's hip].

* * *

* * * [F]or Misericordia to be liable here, it must have failed to exercise that degree of care and skill usually exercised or maintained by other reputable hospitals in similar situations.

There was abundant expert testimony in this case regarding the procedures utilized by hospital committees to check a physician's references upon application for staff privileges, and the ease with which Misericordia could have had access to Dr. Salinsky's records. Once having obtained such records, Dr. Salinsky's incompetence would have been apparent to the executive committee of Misericordia Hospital.

* * *

Misericordia objects to the introduction of testimony regarding the restrictions imposed on Dr. Salinsky's practice at Doctors Hospital and to the introduction of Doctors Hospital medical executive committee reports dealing with the investigation and suspension of Dr. Salinsky's privileges. Misericordia similarly objects to the admission of testimony by the attorney for St. Anthony Hospital regarding the hospital's refusal to allow Dr. Salinsky on the staff. Finally, defendant objects to the introduction of documents concerning the action of the credentials committee of St. Anthony Hospital in regard to Dr. Salinsky's application.

The objections to the introduction of the minutes and records are based on hearsay. The trial court received the documents into evidence under the hearsay exception for records of regularly conducted activities. The trial court also noted that even if such records constituted medical opinions, they were not admitted to establish the truth of the opinions, but to show that such opinions did exist and should have been considered by those investigating Dr. Salinsky's application. We affirm the trial court.

Hearsay evidence is generally excluded as untrustworthy; lacking the traditional guarantees of oath, confrontation and cross-examination for the credibility of the out-of-court declarant. Thus hearsay rests its value upon the credibility of the out-of-court declarant. Misericordia claims that for these reasons, the individuals who comprised the committees and conducted the investigation leading to restriction and denial of staff privileges should have been present to testify. Nevertheless, Misericordia made no effort to prove the untruthfulness of the reports or to challenge the trustworthiness of physicians involved.

* * *

Based upon the facts as incorporated in this record, we affirm the trial court's receipt into evidence of the committee reports regarding Dr. Salinsky's professional competence. The reports were properly considered by the jury as evidence of the type of information available to Misericordia at the time of Dr. Salinsky's application for staff privileges.

The evidence concerning the "credentials process" was admissible to show the existence of information regarding Dr. Salinsky's professional qualifications and the availability of such knowledge to Misericordia's medical executive committee. Thus Misericordia should have known of the restrictions placed on Dr. Salinsky's practice by other Milwaukee hospitals and that one hospital had denied him staff privileges. Once admissible for the purpose of showing the existence and availability of information, Misericordia's remedy at trial was to ask for a limiting instruction if it believed that the evidence was to be used to establish Dr. Salinsky's incompetence. * * *

Misericordia also objects to the introduction into evidence of the testimony of Dr. Nesemann that between the years of 1967 and 1975, he had heard other physicians state that "Dr. Salinsky was incompetent as an orthopedic surgeon."

Again, as above, this evidence was admissible for the purpose of showing the availability of knowledge concerning Dr. Salinsky's competence. If counsel for Misericordia thought this evidence might be used for an improper purpose, a limiting instruction should have been requested.

Judgment affirmed.

RIES BIOLOGICALS, INC. v. THE BANK OF SANTA FE

United States Court of Appeals, Tenth Circuit, 1986.
780 F.2d 888.

CROW, District Judge.

This is an appeal by the defendant, the Bank of Santa Fe, from a judgment for the plaintiff, Ries Biologicals, Inc., based upon the bank's alleged oral guarantee of payment for supplies delivered by Ries to Dialysis Management Systems, Inc. The trial court awarded the plaintiff $20,276.69 plus interest in the amount of $6,632.96, and costs including attorneys fees.

Ries Biologicals is a distributor of medical supplies. In 1979, Ries began selling supplies to Dialysis Management Systems, Inc. (DMS) a health care provider specializing in kidney dialysis, operating in New Mexico and adjacent states. DMS was experiencing financial problems quickly accumulating a debt to Ries Biologicals in the approximate amount of $42,000. Because of the size of this debt, in January of 1980 Ries refused to make further shipments to DMS except for cash on delivery. Sometime in the first quarter of 1980, Ries resumed shipments to DMS on credit. The trial court found that resumption of credit shipments resulted from Ries' reliance on the Bank's oral agreement to guarantee payment for orders which were approved in advance. From the time of the agreement until July 30, 1980, Ries made regular shipments to DMS based upon prior approval of the senior vice-president of the bank, Philip Levitt. * * *

Despite obtaining advance approval from the bank, Ries was not paid the full amount due for materials shipped under this arrangement. The trial court entered judgment in favor of Ries for the balance due.

* * *

The defendants contend that the trial court erroneously admitted testimony concerning Philip Levitt's oral, out-of-court statements guaranteeing payment for approved shipments. * * *

The oral statements of Philip Levitt were expressly offered for a nonhearsay purpose. The relevance of Levitt's statements is not their truth or falsity, rather it is the fact the statements were made. The relevance of the statements depends, therefore, not on the credibility of the out-of-court declarant, Philip Levitt, but on that of the testifying witness. See J. Weinstein & M. Berger, Weinstein's Evidence ¶ 801(c)[01]. There was no manifest error in the admission of testimony concerning the oral statements of Philip Levitt.

[Affirmed].

STRAHORN, A RECONSIDERATION OF THE HEARSAY RULE AND ADMISSIONS

85 U.Pa.L.Rev. 484, 490 (1937).*

Utterances as operative conduct

If the making of the utterance is the ultimate thing sought to be proven in the case, rather than a device for proving that thing, the suspicion of hearsay attaches the least. So it is that the topic of utterances as operative conduct is the one of simplest application under the hearsay rule. No question of possible testimonial or narrative use can arise when the speaking of the words determines the rights being litigated. Thus it is that such typical examples as the making of a promise, the speaking of a slander, the printing of a libel, the speaking of marriage vows are all species of extra-judicial utterances provable despite the hearsay rule because they are the operative conduct of the speaker. For them there is no possible question of the trustworthiness of the utterance. * * *

UNITED STATES v. HERNANDEZ

United States Court of Appeals, Fifth Circuit, 1985.
750 F.2d 1256.

ALVIN B. RUBIN, Circuit Judge:

We reverse the conviction of Herminio Hernandez on two counts relating to possession and distribution of cocaine because the prosecut-

* Copyright, 1936–1937 by The University of Pennsylvania.

ing attorney elicited inadmissible testimony from a government witness, a Drug Enforcement Administration (DEA) special agent, that
U.S. Customs had identified Hernandez as a drug smuggler. The
district judge overruled an objection to the testimony, and the prosecutor, in her closing argument to the jury, later emphasized this evidence,
embellishing it to go even beyond the actual testimony.

Viewing the facts in the light most favorable to the government,
the evidence showed that an informant, Gholson, accompanied by
special agent Ana Saulnier, who posed as Gholson's wife, met Hernandez by prearrangement in a coffee shop. Hernandez offered to sell
them a kilo of cocaine for $52,000. Hernandez, who took the stand,
denies that the conversation at the coffee shop involved controlled
substances. Later Gholson and agent Saulnier, the ostensible Mrs.
Gholson, driving in an automobile, met Hernandez at a service station
and followed Hernandez's car to his tire shop. There, in a back room,
two packages of cocaine wrapped in newspaper lay atop a television
tray table. Hernandez said he did not want to transact business in the
presence of [Saulnier], so Saulnier left the room. Gholson then accepted the cocaine. As Gholson and Hernandez were proceeding to the
place where payment was to be made, Hernandez was arrested.

Hernandez testified that he had been "set up" by Gholson. The
conversation in the coffee shop, he said, concerned leasing a room at his
tire shop to Gholson to be used to make pornographic films. He had
led Gholson and Saulnier to his shop and had merely shown the room
to Gholson, but he had not entered it. Hernandez, by cross-examination and other evidence, attacked Gholson's credibility. Gholson had
been charged on numerous occasions with felony charges stemming
from his involvement in the pornography business. He also had made
his living as an informant for thirteen years, and was paid by the
arrest, not the conviction. An officer of the Houston Police Department testified that his department had stopped using Gholson as an
informant because they suspected him of making cases against innocent
people. Thus, the case boiled down to the jury's acceptance of the
version of the facts testified to by Gholson and Saulnier or Hernandez's
version. Both sides, in oral argument, correctly referred to the testimony as a "swearing match."

Near the beginning of Saulnier's testimony, the following occurred:

Q. (Prosecutor) Now, Special Agent Saulnier, what first
brought the attention of the Drug Enforcement Administration
to Herminio Hernandez?

A. We received a referral by the U.S. Customs as Hernandez
being a drug smuggler.

Mr. Suarez: Judge, may I object to this testimony * * *.

The Court: I'm going to overrule the objection.

The government's argument that this testimony was not hearsay
and was relevant to show Saulnier's state of mind lacks merit.
Saulnier's state of mind was not at issue. The testimony was, therefore, clearly hearsay. The referral was a "statement" other than one

made by Saulnier * * * while testifying at trial, offered to prove the truth of the matter asserted (that Hernandez was a drug smuggler). The government's protestation that the evidence was not elicited to prove Hernandez was a drug smuggler, but merely to explain the motivation behind DEA's investigation is unconvincing from both a common sense perspective, and from the government's subsequent use of that testimony. * * *

The prosecuting attorney (who was not the Assistant U.S. Attorney who presented the case on appeal) was not content to leave bad enough alone. In her closing argument, she told the jury:

> What kind of case has the government brought to you today? You heard testimony that this case, this defendant, was brought to the attention of the Drug Enforcement Administration through a referral from another law enforcement agency, United States Customs. And what was the nature of that referral? The nature of that referral was that this individual was a *known cocaine trafficer* [sic] * * *. (Emphasis added.)

* * * The government thus relied on the evidence not as proof of Saulnier's state of mind at the inception of the investigation, but as evidence of Hernandez's guilt. This type of evidence is inadmissible under Fed.R.Evid. 802.

The state of mind of the DEA agent for beginning an investigation of the defendant, was not relevant. * * *

Reversed.

Hypotheticals

(1) X is prosecuted for assault with a deadly weapon on A by use of a billiard cue. X's defense is self-defense. In rebuttal the prosecution calls B, who proposes to testify that a week before the fight A told him that X had struck him several times with a baseball bat a month before in a sudden fit of temper. X makes a hearsay objection to B's testimony.

(2) X is prosecuted for murder of A. A died from a bullet wound received while in X's apartment. X's defense is that X was showing a pistol to A at A's request and that it accidentally went off as A was handling it. The prosecution calls B who proposes to testify that a week before A's death, A told him that X had threatened to kill A. X objects to B's testimony as hearsay.

(3) X is prosecuted for the murder of A, his wife. It is undisputed that while A was seated in a chair watching television, X pulled a pistol from his pocket and fired three shots into A, killing her instantly. In order to negate the intent requisite for first degree murder, X testifies to a history of marital difficulties, which he claims impaired his mental condition. In rebuttal, to prove A's state of mind shortly before her death, the prosecution calls B, who proposes to testify that in a telephone conversation with A on the day before her death, A said, "I know X is going to kill me. I wish he would hurry up and get it over with, because he will never let me leave him." X objects to B's proposed testimony on the grounds of hearsay.

UNITED STATES v. ZENNI

United States District Court, Eastern District of Kentucky, 1980.
492 F.Supp. 464.

BERTELSMAN, District Judge.

This prosecution for illegal bookmaking activities presents a classic problem in the law of evidence, namely, whether implied assertions are hearsay. The problem was a controversial one at common law, the discussion of which has filled many pages in the treatises and learned journals. Although the answer to the problem is clear under the Federal Rules of Evidence, there has been little judicial treatment of the matter, and many members of the bar are unfamiliar with the marked departure from the common law the Federal Rules have effected on this issue.

FACTS

The relevant facts are simply stated. While conducting a search of the premises of the defendant, Ruby Humphrey, pursuant to a lawful search warrant which authorized a search for evidence of bookmaking activity, government agents answered the telephone several times. The unknown callers stated directions for the placing of bets on various sporting events. The government proposes to introduce this evidence to show that the callers believed that the premises were used in betting operations. The existence of such belief tends to prove that they were so used. The defendants object on the ground of hearsay.

COMMON LAW BACKGROUND

At common law, the hearsay rule applied "only to evidence of out-of-court statements offered for the purpose of proving that the facts are as asserted in the statement."

On the other hand, not all out-of-court expression is common law hearsay. For instance, an utterance offered to show the publication of a slander, or that a person was given notice of a fact, or orally entered into a contract, is not hearsay.

In the instant case, the utterances of the absent declarants are not offered for the truth of the words,[7] and the mere fact that the words were uttered has no relevance of itself. Rather they are offered to show the declarants' belief in a fact sought to be proved. At common law this situation occupied a controversial no-man's land. It was argued on the one hand that the out-of-court utterance was not hearsay, because the evidence was not offered for any truth stated in it, but for the truth of some other proposition inferred from it. On the other hand, it was also argued that the reasons for excluding hearsay applied, in that the evidence was being offered to show declarant's belief in the implied proposition, and he was not available to be cross-examined.

7. That is, the utterance, "Put $2 to win on Paul Revere in the third at Pimlico," is a direction and not an assertion of any kind, and therefore can be neither true nor false.

Thus, the latter argument was that there existed strong policy reasons for ruling that such utterances were hearsay.

The classic case, which is discussed in virtually every textbook on evidence, is Wright v. Tatham, 7 Adolph. & E. 313, 386, 112 Eng.Rep. 488 (Exch. Ch. 1837), and 5 Cl. & F. 670, 739, 47 Rev.Rep. 136 (H.L. 1838). Described as a "celebrated and hard-fought cause," Wright v. Tatham was a will contest, in which the will was sought to be set aside on the grounds of the incompetency of the testator at the time of its execution. The proponents of the will offered to introduce into evidence letters to the testator from certain absent individuals on various business and social matters. The purpose of the offer was to show that the writers of the letters believed the testator was able to make intelligent decisions concerning such matters, and thus was competent.

One of the illustrations advanced in the judicial opinions in Wright v. Tatham is perhaps even more famous than the case itself. This is Baron Parke's famous sea captain example. Is it hearsay to offer as proof of the seaworthiness of a vessel that its captain, after thoroughly inspecting it, embarked on an ocean voyage upon it with his family?

The court in Wright v. Tatham held that implied assertions of this kind were hearsay. The rationale, as stated by Baron Parke, was as follows:

> "The conclusion at which I have arrived is, that proof of a particular fact which is not of itself a matter in issue, but which is relevant only as implying a statement or opinion of a third person on the matter in issue, is inadmissible in all cases where such a statement or opinion not on oath would be of itself inadmissible; and, therefore, in this case the letters which are offered only to prove the competence of the testator, that is the truth of the implied statements therein contained, were properly rejected, as the mere statement or opinion of the writer would certainly have been inadmissible."

This was the prevailing common law view, where the hearsay issue was recognized. But frequently, it was not recognized. Thus, two federal appellate cases involving facts virtually identical to those in the case at bar did not even discuss the hearsay issue, although the evidence admitted in them would have been objectionable hearsay under the common law view.

THE FEDERAL RULES OF EVIDENCE

The common law rule that implied assertions were subject to hearsay treatment was criticized by respected commentators for several reasons. A leading work on the Federal Rules of Evidence, referring to the hotly debated question whether an implied assertion stands on better ground with respect to the hearsay rule than an express assertion, states:

> "By the time the federal rules were drafted, a number of eminent scholars and revisers had concluded that it does. Two principal arguments were usually expressed for removing im-

plied assertions from the scope of the hearsay rule. First, when a person acts in a way consistent with a belief but without intending by his act to communicate that belief, one of the principal reasons for the hearsay rule—to exclude declarations whose veracity cannot be tested by cross-examination—does not apply, because the declarant's sincerity is not then involved. In the second place, the underlying belief is in some cases self-verifying:

> 'There is frequently a guarantee of the trustworthiness of the inference to be drawn * * * because the actor has based his actions on the correctness of his belief, i.e., his actions speak louder than words.' "

In a frequently cited article the following analysis appears:

> "But ought the hearsay rule be deemed applicable to evidence of conduct? As McCormick has observed, the problem 'has only once received any adequate discussion in any decided case,' i.e., in Wright v. Tatham, already referred to. And even in that case the court did not pursue its inquiry beyond the point of concluding that evidence of an 'implied' assertion must necessarily be excluded wherever evidence of an 'express' assertion would be inadmissible. But as has been pointed out more than once (although I find no *judicial* recognition of the difference), the 'implied' assertion is, from the hearsay standpoint, not nearly as vulnerable as an express assertion of the fact which the evidence is offered to establish.

> "This is on the assumption that the conduct was 'nonassertive;' that the passers-by had their umbrellas up for the sake of keeping dry, not for the purpose of telling anyone it was raining; that the truck driver started up for the sake of resuming his journey, not for the purpose of telling anyone that the light had changed; that the vicar wrote the letter to the testator for the purpose of settling the dispute with the latter, rather than with any idea of expressing his opinion of the testator's sanity. And in the typical 'conduct as hearsay' case this assumption will be quite justifiable.

> "On this assumption, it is clear that evidence of conduct must be taken as freed from at least one of the hearsay dangers, i.e., mendacity. A man does not lie to himself. Put otherwise, if in doing what he does a man has no intention of asserting the existence or non-existence of a fact, it would appear that the trustworthiness of evidence of this conduct is the same whether he is an egregious liar or a paragon of veracity. Accordingly, the lack of opportunity for cross-examination in relation to his veracity or lack of it, would seem to be of no substantial importance. Accordingly, the usual judicial disposition to equate the 'implied' to the 'express' assertion is very questionable."

The drafters of the Federal Rules agreed with the criticisms of the common law rule that implied assertions should be treated as hearsay and expressly abolished it. They did this by providing that no oral or written expression was to be considered as hearsay, unless it was an "assertion" concerning the matter sought to be proved and that no nonverbal conduct should be considered as hearsay, unless it was intended to be an "assertion" concerning said matter.[18] The relevant provisions are:

> **Rule 801.** "(a) Statement.—A *'statement'* is (1) an oral or written *assertion* or (2) nonverbal conduct of a person, if it is *intended by him as an assertion.*
>
>   *   *   *
>
> (c) Hearsay. 'Hearsay' is a statement, other than one made by the declarant while testifying at the trial or hearing, offered in evidence to prove the truth of the matter asserted."

"Assertion" is not defined in the rules, but has the connotation of a forceful or positive declaration.

The Advisory Committee note concerning this problem states:

> "The definition of 'statement' assumes importance because the term is used in the definition of hearsay in subdivision (c). *The effect of the definition of 'statement' is to exclude from the operation of the hearsay rule all evidence of conduct, verbal or nonverbal, not intended as an assertion. The key to the definition is that nothing is an assertion unless intended to be one.*
>
> "It can scarcely be doubted that an assertion made in words is intended by the declarant to be an assertion. Hence verbal assertions readily fall into the category of 'statement.' Whether nonverbal conduct should be regarded as a statement for purposes of defining hearsay requires further consideration. Some nonverbal conduct, such as the act of pointing to identify a suspect in a lineup, is clearly the equivalent of words, assertive in nature, and to be regarded as a statement. Other nonverbal conduct, however, may be offered as evidence that the person acted as he did because of his belief in the existence of the condition sought to be proved, from which belief the existence of the condition may be inferred. This sequence is, arguably, in effect an assertion of the existence of the condition and hence properly includable within the hearsay concept. Admittedly evidence of this character is untested with respect to the perception, memory, and narration (or their equivalents) of the actor, *but the Advisory Committee is of the view that these dangers are minimal in the absence of an intent to assert*

---

18. *See* the sea captain illustration discussed, supra. In an unpublished ruling this court recently held admissible as nonhearsay the fact that a U.S. mining inspector ate his lunch in an area in a coal mine now alleged to have been unsafe, and that other inspectors who observed operations prior to a disastrous explosion issued no citations, when it would have been their duty to do so, if there had been safety violations. These non-assertive acts would have been hearsay under the rule of *Wright v. Tatham* but are not hearsay under Rule 801 of the Federal Rules of Evidence, because the inspectors did not intend to make assertions under the circumstances. *Boggs v. Blue Diamond Coal Company* (E.D.Ky. No. 77–69, Pikeville Division).

and do not justify the loss of the evidence on hearsay grounds.
No class of evidence is free of the possibility of fabrication, but
the likelihood is less with nonverbal than with assertive verbal
conduct. The situations giving rise to the nonverbal conduct
are such as virtually to eliminate questions of sincerity. Motivation, the nature of the conduct, and the presence or absence
of reliance will bear heavily upon the weight to be given the
evidence. *Similar considerations govern nonassertive verbal
conduct and verbal conduct which is assertive but offered as a
basis for inferring something other than the matter asserted,*
also excluded from the definition of hearsay by the language of
subdivision (c)." (Emphasis added).

This court, therefore, holds that, "Subdivision (a)(2) of Rule 801
removes implied assertions from the definition of statement and consequently from the operation of the hearsay rule."

Applying the principles discussed above to the case at bar, this
court holds that the utterances of the betters telephoning in their bets
were nonassertive verbal conduct, offered as relevant for an implied
assertion to be inferred from them, namely that bets could be placed at
the premises being telephoned. The language is not an assertion on its
face, and it is obvious these persons did not intend to make an assertion
about the fact sought to be proved or anything else.[19]

As an implied assertion, the proffered evidence is expressly excluded from the operation of the hearsay rule by Rule 801 of the Federal
Rules of Evidence, and the objection thereto must be overruled. An
order to that effect has previously been entered.

COMMONWEALTH v. KNAPP

Supreme Judicial Court of Massachusetts, 1830.
VII American State Trials 395, 515–516.

[John Francis Knapp was tried in 1830 for the murder of one
Joseph White. The prosecution, headed by Daniel Webster, claimed
that Knapp aided and abetted one Crowninshield, who actually struck
the fatal blows. It was therefore crucial to the prosecution to show
Crowninshield's guilt—even though Crowninshield himself had committed suicide before the trial. In his closing argument, Daniel Webster
discussed the probative value of the suicide on the issue of Crowninshield's guilt—Ed.]

19. A somewhat different type of analysis would be required by words non-assertive in form, but which under the circumstances might be intended as an assertion.
For example, an inspector at an airport
security station might run a metal detector
over a passenger and say "go on through."
In the absence of the inspector, would testimony of this event be objectionable hearsay, if offered for the proposition that the
passenger did not have a gun on him at
that time? Although Rule 801(a) does not
seem to require a preliminary determination by the trial court whether verbal conduct is intended as an assertion, it is submitted that such a determination would be
required in the example given. If an assertion were intended the evidence would be
excluded. If not, it would be admissible.
This result is implicit in the policy of the
drafters of the Federal Rules of Evidence
that the touchstone for hearsay is the intention to make an assertion.

1   The fatal blow is given! and the victim passes, without a struggle or
2 a motion, from the repose of sleep to the repose of death! It is the
3 assassin's purpose to make sure work, and he yet plies the dagger,
4 though it was obvious that life had been destroyed by the blow of the
5 bludgeon. He even raises the aged arm, that he may not fail in his aim
6 at the heart, and replaces it again over the wounds of the poignard! To
7 finish the picture, he explores the wrist for the pulse! he feels it, and
8 ascertains that it beats no longer! It is accomplished. The deed is
9 done. He retreats, retraces his steps to the window, passes out through
10 it, as he came in, and escapes. He has done the murder—no eye has
11 seen him, no ear has heard him. The secret is his own, and it is safe!

12   Ah! gentlemen, that was a dreadful mistake. Such a secret can be
13 safe nowhere. The whole creation of God has neither nook nor corner,
14 where the guilty can bestow it, and say it is safe. Not to speak of that
15 eye which glances through all disguises, and beholds everything, as in
16 the splendor of noon, such secrets of guilt are never safe from detection,
17 even by men. True it is, generally speaking, that "murder will out."
18 True it is, that Providence hath so ordained, and doth so govern things,
19 that those who break the great law of heaven, by shedding man's blood,
20 seldom succeed in avoiding discovery. Especially, in a case exciting so
21 much attention as this, discovery must come, and will come, sooner or
22 later. A thousand eyes turn at once to explore every man, every thing,
23 every circumstance, connected with the time and place; a thousand
24 ears catch every whisper; a thousand excited minds intensely dwell on
25 the scene, shedding all their light, and ready to kindle the slightest
26 circumstance into a blaze of discovery. Meantime the guilty soul
27 cannot keep its own secret. It is false to itself; or rather it feels an
28 irresistible impulse of conscience to be true to itself. It labors under its
29 guilty possession, and knows not what to do with it. The human heart
30 was not made for the residence of such an inhabitant. It finds itself
31 preyed on by a torment which it does not acknowledge to God nor man.
32 A vulture is devouring it, and it can ask no sympathy or assistance,
33 either from heaven or earth. The secret which the murderer possesses
34 soon comes to possess him; and, like the evil spirits of which we read, it
35 overcomes him, and leads him whithersoever it will. He feels it
36 beating at his heart, rising to his throat, and demanding disclosure. He
37 thinks the whole world sees it in his face, reads it in his eyes, and
38 almost hears its workings in the very silence of his thoughts. It has
39 become his master. It betrays his discretion, it breaks down his
40 courage, it conquers his prudence. When suspicions, from without,
41 begin to embarrass him, and the net of circumstance to entangle him,
42 the fatal secret struggles with still greater violence to burst forth. It
43 must be confessed, it will be confessed; there is no refuge from
44 confession but suicide, and suicide is confession.

MORTON, THE ROTHSCHILDS *
49–50 (1962).

And there was no news more precious than the outcome of Waterloo. For days the London 'Change [1] had strained its ears. If Napoleon won, English consols [2] were bound to drop. If he lost, the enemy empire would shatter and consols rise.

For thirty hours the fate of Europe hung veiled in cannon smoke. On June 19, 1815, late in the afternoon a Rothschild agent named Rothworth jumped into a boat at Ostend. In his hand he held a Dutch gazette still damp from the printer. By the dawn light of June 20 Nathan Rothschild stood at Folkstone harbor and let his eye fly over the lead paragraphs. A moment later he was on his way to London (beating Wellington's envoy by many hours) to tell the government that Napoleon had been crushed. Then he proceeded to the stock exchange.

Another man in his position would have sunk his worth into consols. But this was Nathan Rothschild. He leaned against "his" pillar. He did not invest. He sold. He dumped consols.

His name was already such that a single substantial move on his part sufficed to bear or bull an issue. Consols fell. Nathan leaned and leaned, and sold and sold. Consols dropped still more. "Rothschild knows," the whisper rippled through the 'Change. "Waterloo is lost."

Nathan kept on selling, his round face motionless and stern, his pudgy fingers depressing the market by tens of thousands of pounds with each sell signal. Consols dived, consols plummented—until, a split second before it was too late, Nathan suddenly bought a giant parcel for a song. Moments afterwards the great news broke, to send consols soaring.

We cannot guess the number of hopes and savings wiped out by this engineered panic. We cannot estimate how many liveried servants, how many Watteaus and Rembrandts, how many thoroughbreds in his descendants' stables, the man by the pillar won that single day.

See Federal Rules of Evidence § 801(a); Cal. Evidence Code § 225.

UNITED STATES v. RHODES
Trial by General Court Martial, Fort McNair, District of Columbia, 1958.

[During February, 1958, Master Sergeant Roy A. Rhodes, United States Army, was tried by General Court Martial for having conspired with certain named and unnamed persons to violate the espionage laws of the United States by, among things, communicating information concerning the national defense to agents of the Union of Soviet Socialist Republics. Two of the accused's co-conspirators were alleged

* Copyright 1961 by The Curtis Publishing Co.

1. The international currency exchange—Ed.

2. Pounds—Ed.

to be Col. Rudolph Ivanovich Abel and Lt. Col. Reino Hayhanen of the Soviet Secret Police. The evidence showed that in July, 1956, Abel had transmitted to Hayhanen some written information regarding the accused—whose code name was "Quebec"—which Abel had received from Moscow. The information was on "hard" film; Hayhanen had made "soft" film of it and hidden it in a hollowed-out bolt at his home in Peekskill, New York. The bolt and its contents were retrieved by agents of the Federal Bureau of Investigation and a copy of the piece of "soft" film was offered, over objection, and received at Rhodes' trial. The message on the piece of film is reproduced below. Counsel for the accused objected to receipt of this message on grounds of hearsay. On what basis was the exhibit received? Do you agree that it was properly admissible?—Ed.]

PROSECUTION EXHIBIT NO. 7.

QUEBEC, Roy A. Rhodes, born 1917 in Oilton, Oklahoma, U.S., senior sergeant of the War Ministry, former employee of the U.S. Military Attache Staff in our country. He was a chief of the garage of the Embassy.

He was recruited to our service in January 1952 in our country which he left in June 1953; recruited on the basis of compromising materials, but he is tied up to us with his receipts and information he had given in his own handwriting.

He had been trained in code work at the Ministry before he went to work at the Embassy, but as a code worker he was not used by the Embassy.

After he left our country he was to be sent to the school of communications of the Army C-I Service which is at the city of San Luis, California. He was to be trained there as a mechanic of the coding machines.

He fully agreed to continue to cooperate with us in the States or any other country. It was agreed that he was to have written to our Embassy here special letters, but we had received none during the last year.

It has been recently learned that Quebec is living in Red Bank, N.J. where he owns three garages. The garage job is being done by his wife. His own occupation at present is not known.

His father—Mr. W.A. Rhodes resides in the U.S. His brother is also in the States where he works as an engineer at an atomic plant in Camp, Georgia with a brother-in-law of his father.

McCORMICK, THE BORDERLAND OF HEARSAY

39 Yale L.J. 489, 502–4 (1930).*
[Footnotes omitted.]

[The author, after discussing a number of cases including Wright v. Tatham, see p. 101, supra, concludes:]

Probably the foregoing presents a fair sampling of the cases and comments pro and con on the question. From the data given it seems apparent, first, that Wright v. Tatham expresses the more generally accepted view in holding that conduct, even when not intended as assertive, is hearsay when offered to show the actor's belief and hence the truth of the belief, and second, that this view has, since the leading case, received such slight consideration in subsequent decisions which follow it, and has evoked such contrariety of opinion among the commentators (as well as a sprinkling of contrary decisions) that it is open for re-examination in the light of general policy.

It is only the technique of that general reconsideration that is of any real importance, and the assembling of the foregoing chance driftwood from the decisions is of value only so far as it clears the way for such a reconsideration. These decisions, though casual and inharmonious, serve chiefly to show the situations in real life which call for the application of such theory as we may adopt. And it is just here that the reader may ask, "Why assume that any one solution is likely to work for all the types of cases which seem to occur?" It will have been observed, certainly, that the cases fall into three groups. The first and simplest, for present purposes, are the cases of stark action with no element of communication at all. Such is the ship-captain example, [see p. 109] and most of Parke's other illustrations. But in real life, as the cases show, the element of words enters in. Thus we may distinguish a second group where acts and words explaining them are offered together. Of this type is the evidence of the guest who refuses the hotel-room, objecting that it is too dark, offered to show the undesirability of the room, and the evidence of the rejection of similar goods as defective by other customers, to show breach of warranty. Finally, the third group comprises those cases where the conduct consists of words solely, but words not of *assertion,* but of *action,* such as an offer of a position (to show the *offeree's* skill) or the letters in Wright v. Tatham itself. It seems, however, that to base any difference in results on the mere circumstance that the conduct is verbal or non-verbal would be an undesirable rule of thumb not corresponding to any difference in probable trustworthiness.

If all three types, then, are to be treated alike, what shall that treatment be? The problem is one that will eventually be solved according as the profession adopts one or another general attitude toward the rules of proof. Possible attitudes might favor the admission of any and all offered items of proof, as seems to be the method in French criminal trials, or might lean toward vesting a large discretion in the trial judge to admit or exclude, guided only by certain general canons and standards, as seems to be the present English tendency, or, on the other hand, the attitude may remain one of adherence to the present system in vogue in the United States, of sharply defined rules prohibiting the admission of many rigidly classified types of evidence.

The advocates of entire exclusion of evidence of conduct to show belief, to show the truth of the fact believed, as being hearsay, hark back to the traditional technique of jury trial administration as it hardened in the eighteenth century. Judges then, to paraphrase a

well-worn epigram, were surer about everything than judges today are
about anything. That technique consisted of creating large, simple, but
definite categories under which offered items of proof could be classified
accurately and, above all, quickly. All the contents of each of these
classes were either black or white, admissible or inadmissible. The
largest of these categories of inadmissible evidence (though its recognition as such was later than we usually supposed) is that of hearsay.
The advantages of these clear-cut rules of exclusion are obvious. They
enable the lawyer preparing his case to know in advance with fair
certainty what he can get in, and what he cannot. If a question as to
admissibility does arise, the judge who has no time for subtle discrimination in the heat of trial can make a decision in his stride, as it were.
This is splendid, and the only difficulty is that it does not work. The
rule excluding all hearsay, clear and simple in its original form, when
it was tested by the offer of particular hearsay evidence of a peculiarly
indispensable or reliable kind cracked under the strain. To relieve the
pressure, exception after exception was recognized until today the rule
is riddled with thirteen or more exceptions. The exceptions are in
some instances quite as rigidly defined as the rule itself.

To be contrasted with this sort of progress through the mitigation
of a rigid rule by numerous rigid exceptions, is the different technique
of development of such rules as, for example, those which provide for
the order of presenting proof. These have from the outset been merely
guides and not limits to the judge's discretion and consequently have
never had to be complicated by exceptions. Would it not have been
wiser to set up the hearsay rule also in some similar form, as for
example: "Hearsay is inadmissible except where the judge in his
discretion finds it needed and trustworthy"? The astonishing conserva-
tism of most lawyers and of most judges drawn from their ranks, and
their almost religious reverence for these mere procedural rules, will
make progress towards such a result slow, but doubtless such a change
is on the cards. At all events, newly evolved evidence rules are likely
to be of that discretionary type.

Focusing these considerations upon our present problem, we find
the orthodox, but not wholly settled or established, view to be that
conduct to show belief, to show the fact believed, is invariably to be put
in the "hearsay" category and banned as such. The result is that
evidence which has the strongest circumstantial guaranties of reliability may be banned. Evidence that a doctor, since deceased, has operated
upon a man for appendicitis, would be inadmissible as evidence that the
patient actually had that disease. It is true, on the other hand, that
very much of such conduct-evidence if admitted would be of trivial
value and probably a general inclusionary rule, that all such evidence
is admissible wherever the actor's testimony on the stand would be,
would be only one degree better than wholesale exclusion. It would
seem sensible to conclude that conduct (other than assertions) when
offered to show the actor's beliefs and hence the truth of the facts so
believed, being merely analogous to and not identical with typical
hearsay, ought to be admissible whenever the trial judge in his discre-

tion finds that the action so vouched the belief as to give reasonable assurance of trustworthiness.

SILVER v. NEW YORK CENTRAL RAILROAD

Supreme Judicial Court of Massachusetts, Suffolk, 1952.
329 Mass. 14, 105 N.E.2d 923.

WILKINS, J. On January 14, 1948, Frances Silver became a passenger, bound from Boston to Cincinnati, on a train operated by the defendant railroad. The following morning the Pullman car in which she had a berth was detached at Cleveland and stood for nearly four hours in the yard to await connection with the next train to Cincinnati. She was suffering from a circulatory ailment known as Raynaud's disease. The temperature in the car became too cold for her, and she experienced ill effects. Mrs. Silver, who will be referred to as the plaintiff, brought this action against the defendant railroad and The Pullman Company.

* * *

The porter in the plaintiff's car was rightly allowed to testify as to the temperature conditions in that car. He was giving at first hand his experience with the same conditions which confronted the plaintiff. But he was not permitted to give evidence that eleven other passengers in that car made no complaint to him as to the temperature while at Cleveland. This is a somewhat different proposition, as it was sought to draw from the silence of those passengers a deduction that the car was not too cold, otherwise they would have spoken. In certain courts evidence of absence of complaints by customers has been excluded on the issue of defective quality of goods sold, and the hearsay rule has been relied upon or referred to. In Menard v. Cashman,—which was an action of tort arising out of a fall on a defective stairway in a business block, it was held proper to exclude testimony of a tenant that none of her customers had ever complained of any defects, the court saying that the testimony had the characteristics of hearsay, and that if it was not hearsay, it was only evidence of inclusive silence, which might be excluded in the discretion of the trial judge.

Evidence as to absence of complaints from customers other than the plaintiff has been admitted in four cases, all relating to breach of warranty in the sale of food, in this Commonwealth. In three of them the testimony was apparently received without objection. In Landfield v. Albiani Lunch Co. the plaintiff alleged that he had been made ill by eating beans purchased at the defendant's restaurant. Subject to his exception, evidence was admitted that on that day and on the day preceding no complaint as to the beans was made by any other customer. In upholding the ruling on evidence, it was said, "The fact that others than the plaintiff ate of the food complained of without ill effects is competent evidence that it was not unwholesome. * * * There is a reasonable inference based on common experience that one who ate and suffered as he believed in consequence would make complaint. There is a further reasonable inference, based on logic, that if no one complained no one suffered. Obviously, the latter conclusion is not convincing that the food was wholesome, unless one is satisfied that both plaintiff and others ate of it. Evidence of no complaint is too remote and should not be admitted unless, in addition to the fact that no complaints were made, there is evidence of circumstances indicating that others similarly situated ate and had opportunity for complaining."

It has often been said that where collateral issues may be opened, much must rest in the discretion of the trial judge. In the case at bar, should the circumstances of the plaintiff and of the other passengers as to exposure to the cold be shown to be substantially the same, the negative evidence that none of the others spoke of it to the porter might properly be admitted. The evidence would not be equivocal, and would then be offered on the basis of a common condition which all in the car encountered. The porter's duties should be shown to include the receipt of that sort of complaints from those passengers. It should appear that he was present and available to be spoken to, and that it was not likely that complaints were made by these passengers to other employees of the railroad or the sleeping car company. This would not seem to be a situation where one might prefer to remain silent rather than to make any statement. Indeed, if the car was too cold, ordinary prudence might seem to require that one speak out. There would be no ambiguity of inference. There would be at least as strong a case for admissibility as in the food cases, and a far stronger one than those relating to the sale of allegedly defective goods in which little may be known of the terms of sale to the noncomplaining buyers. Unlike the unknown users of a stairway in a business block, the uniform result of silence in the cases of a large number of passengers, here apparently eleven, would not be inconclusive.

Exceptions sustained.

MORGAN, BASIC PROBLEMS OF EVIDENCE
248–50 (1961) *
[Footnotes omitted.]

C. Where the evidence of declarant's conduct is offered to prove that it truly reflected his then existing state of mind, his sincerity is necessarily involved. Thus where evidence of his abnormal objective conduct is offered as tending to prove his insanity, it has no value if it was feigned. His sincerity is a peculiarly important element where his conduct is a positive assertion and the issue is whether he was suffering an insane delusion that the assertion was true. Thus if a woman asserted "I am the Pope," and the issue is whether she had an insane delusion that she held that high office, her belief in the truth of the statement is determinative. And yet, the courts rarely, if ever, treat such evidence as hearsay, and Wigmore agrees, though Hinton dissented. Speaking generally, where evidence of the declarant's conduct, other than a direct assertion that he has a specified state of mind, is offered as tending to prove his state of mind at the time, and the state of mind at that time or at a later time only is in issue, the evidence is

* Joint Committee on Continuing Legal Education of The American Law Institute and The American Bar Association, Philadelphia, 1961.

not classed as hearsay. This is difficult to harmonize with the theory of
courts and commentators that one of the chief functions of cross-
examination is to expose defects in sincerity, and with the accepted
justification for most of the recognized exceptions to the hearsay rule
on the ground that the circumstances of the utterance furnish a
guaranty of sincerity.

UNITED STATES v. BROWN

United States Court of Appeals, Fifth Circuit, 1977.
548 F.2d 1194.

JOHN R. BROWN, Chief Judge:

This case, one of the very few in the recorded annals of the 85 year
history of the Fifth Circuit, involves not the trials and tribulations,
attempted frauds and other derelictions of taxpayers, which are common grist for our mill. Rather, it involves fraud by a tax preparer, one
whose Twentieth Century occupation is now almost indispensable to all
save those taxpayers who can use, or risk the use of, a short form with
standard deductions. In this Bicentennial foray we see the hazards
both to the system and to the protection of rights of the public and the
individuals concerned. To be remembered is that it is the fraud or false
misstatement of the preparer, not the taxpayer, which counts. Indeed,
the tax properly due may be of no, or only secondary, significance.

Defendant-Appellant Amos P. Brown, Sr., a part-time income tax
preparer, was convicted by a jury on 12 counts of counseling, procuring
and advising the preparation and presentation of fraudulent and false
United States Individual Income Tax Returns for others in violation of
26 U.S.C.A. § 7206(2), Internal Revenue Code. * * * We find that
the Trial Judge committed plain error by improperly admitting certain
evidence which was highly prejudicial to the defendant. Accordingly,
we reverse and remand for a new trial.

* * *

The Peacock's Tale

Among other evidence the Government also introduced the testimony of IRS agent Adrienne Peacock, who testified that between 90% and
95% of about 160 returns prepared by defendant contained overstated
itemized deductions.

* * *

Hearsay

* * *

In this case, Peacock's testimony that between 90% and 95% of the
returns she audited contained substantially overstated itemized deductions was introduced for the sole purpose of proving, circumstantially,
the "willfulness" requirement of § 7206(2). In order to arrive at the
conclusion that the deductions in these returns were overstated, Peacock's perusal of the 160 tax returns was not sufficient, since the
returns obviously do not show on their face which deductions are
overstated. The record shows that Peacock must have gotten her
"proof" of the overstatements through conversations with each of the

taxpayers audited. Presumably, the proof consisted either of statements by these taxpayers to Peacock that they all gave different information to the defendant tax preparer than defendant put down on their returns, or that they were unable to substantiate their deductions, because they did not have any (or had inadequate) supporting records. The proof might also have consisted of the fact that the IRS had legitimate disagreements with all or some of the deductions claimed. However, a prerequisite to this form of proof would be the initial conversation between Peacock and each taxpayer, so that Peacock could determine the bases for the deductions claimed.

The point to be emphasized, therefore, is that the information obtained by Peacock from the out-of-court statements made by the 160 taxpayers whose returns she audited, was absolutely vital to her ultimate in-court conclusion that between 90% and 95% of the 160 returns she audited contained substantially overstated itemized deductions. Because her testimony had to have been based directly on the out-of-court statements of these taxpayers, defendant had no opportunity to test their ultimate assumptions through cross-examination. He obviously could not cross-examine the taxpayers concerned, because they were not in court. He could not even cross-examine Peacock adequately, because she did not have with her any of the records of conversations she had had with these taxpayers, but was testifying solely from memory, in the most general, amorphous terms. Thus, the jury had no way to examine the trustworthiness of Peacock's testimony, because it could not examine the statements of the declarant taxpayers or others on which Peacock's testimony was directly and substantially founded. Given the rationale of the hearsay rule, a clearer case of hearsay testimony would be difficult to imagine.[1]

* * *

The judgement of conviction against defendant is reversed, and the case remanded for new trial on all counts.

Reversed and remanded.

GEE, Circuit Judge, dissenting:

The majority's characterization of Agent Peacock's testimony as "hearsay" represents an unprecedented departure from usual hearsay concepts * * * Agent Peacock's statements at trial were (1) that she personally audited all but two or three of the 163 tax returns prepared by appellant and audited by IRS, and (2) that her audit had determined that 90 to 95 percent of those returns contained overstated itemized deductions disallowed under IRS standards. Agent Peacock obviously testified from her own personal knowledge about the results of tax audits she conducted. In her testimony she neither related nor relied upon out-of-court statements by other persons.

---

1. Peacock's testimony also inescapably presented by implication the facts leading to her conclusion which she got from other nontestifying declarants, such as the taxpayers concerned. The implication was strong that she satisfied herself from talking to others that what the preparer entered was not what the taxpayer told him. It was an implied assertion that the defendant was responsible for the repetitious acts or practices from which the jury could infer the requisite willfulness. It was an assertion, in other words, of the ultimate fact that these faulty returns were due to defendant's acts.

It is too plain for argument that Peacock's testimony as to what she knew herself from the returns she individually audited does not fall within Rule 801's hearsay definition. An examination of the record reveals that *all* of Peacock's testimony was based on knowledge she personally acquired while auditing the tax returns prepared by Brown. In fact, the majority points to no *statement* whatever by Agent Peacock which it claims contains hearsay; she mentioned no statements others had made to her during the course of her audit. The majority objects, however, that Agent Peacock's audit necessarily rested on " 'proof' of the overstatements through conversations with each of the taxpayers audited." Since her testimony had to have been based directly on the out-of-court statements of these taxpayers who could not be cross-examined, it is said that "a clearer case of hearsay testimony would be difficult to imagine." I find little difficulty in doing so.

See Federal Rules of Evidence 602; California Evidence Code § 702.

MORGAN, HEARSAY DANGERS AND THE APPLICATION OF THE HEARSAY CONCEPT

62 Harv.L.Rev. 177, 192–93 (1948), * in Selected Writings on Evidence and Trial, 764, 774–75 (1957). **

[Footnotes omitted.]

Prior Declarations of Witness.—

* * * But there is one situation where the courts are prone to call hearsay what does not in fact involve in any substantial degree any of the hearsay risks. When the Declarant is also a witness, it is difficult to justify classifying as hearsay evidence of his own prior statements. This is especially true where Declarant as a witness is giving as part of his testimony his own prior statement. Although there are numerous dicta accepting Greenleaf's statement that hearsay is "that kind of evidence which does not derive its value solely from the credit to be given to the witness himself, but rests also, in part, on the veracity and competency of some other person," the dictum rarely becomes decision. The courts declare the prior statement to be hearsay because it was not made under oath, subject to the penalty for perjury or to the test of cross-examination. To which the answer might well be: "The declarant as a witness is now under oath and now purports to remember and narrate accurately. The adversary can now expose every element that may carry a danger of misleading the trier of fact both in the previous statement and in the present testimony, and the trier can judge whether both the previous declaration and the present testimony are reliable in whole or in part." To this Mr. Justice Stone of the Minnesota Supreme Court, speaking of evidence of prior contradictory statements, has framed this reply:

> The chief merit of cross-examination is not that at some
> future time it gives the party opponent the right to dissect

adverse testimony. Its principal virtue is in its immediate application of the testing process. Its strokes fall while the iron is hot. False testimony is apt to harden and become unyielding to the blows of truth in proportion as the witness has opportunity for reconsideration and influence by the suggestions of others, whose interest may be, and often is, to maintain falsehood rather than truth.

He adds "practical reasons" that receipt of such evidence would create temptation and opportunity to manufacture evidence and entrap witnesses, and would require admission of prior consistent statements. Why does falsehood harden any more quickly or unyieldingly than truth? What has become of the idea that truth is eternal and, though crushed to earth, will rise again? Isn't the opportunity for reconsideration and for baneful influence by others even more likely to color the later testimony than the prior statement? Furthermore, it must be remembered that the trier of fact is often permitted to hear these prior statements to impeach or rehabilitate the declarant-witness. In such event, of course, the trier will be told that he must not treat the statement as evidence of the truth of the matter stated. But to what practical effect? Wasn't Judge Swan right in saying, "Practically, men will often believe that if a witness has earlier sworn to the opposite of what he now swears to, he was speaking the truth when he first testified"? Do the judges deceive themselves or do they realize that they are indulging in a pious fraud? * * *

BUCK v. STATE

Criminal Court of Appeals of Oklahoma, 1943.
77 Okl.Cr. 17, 138 P.2d 115.

BAREFOOT, Judge. Defendant, G.R. Buck, was charged in the District Court of Okmulgee County with the crime of arson, was tried, convicted and sentenced to serve a term of two years in the State Penitentiary, and has appealed.

The only contention presented in the brief of defendant is that the evidence is insufficient to sustain the judgment and sentence, and that the court erred in refusing to direct a verdict of not guilty.

This case may be said to rest almost wholly upon circumstantial evidence. It presents to this Court for the first time the question of the admissibility in evidence of the trailing of one by bloodhounds. We find that this question has heretofore been presented to the highest appellate courts of many states, and that some consideration has been given thereto by textbook writers. However, this Court has never been called upon to consider the question, although the use of bloodhounds at the State Penitentiary has been in vogue for many years.

In the early case of State v. Thomas Hall, a history of the bloodhound is given as follows:

"It is a matter of common knowledge, and therefore a matter of which courts will take notice, that the breed of dogs known as bloodhounds is possessed of a high degree of intelligence, and acuteness of scent, and may be trained to follow

human tracks with considerable certainty and success, if put
upon a recent trail.   In Chambers' Encyc., under the title
'Bloodhound,' it is said of this dog, that 'it is remarkable for its
exquisite scent and for its great sagacity and perseverance in
tracking any object to the pursuit of which it has been trained;'
that 'it has been frequently used for the pursuit of felons and
deerslayers, and, in America, for the capture of fugitive slaves;'
and the writer refers to the use of these dogs in border warfare,
and to their importation 'into Jamaica in 1796 to be used in
suppressing the Maroon insurrection, but the terror occasioned
by their arrival produced the effect without their actual employment.'   The Encyc. Britannica (9th Ed.) under the title
'Dog,' bears this testimony to the well known traits of this
animal: 'The bloodhound is remarkable for its acuteness of
scent, its discrimination in keeping to the particular scent on
which it is first laid, and the intelligence and pertinacity with
which it pursues its object to a successful issue.   These qualities have been taken advantage of not only in the chase, but
also in the pursuit of felons and fugitives of every kind.
According to Strabo, these dogs were used in an attack upon
the Gauls.   In the clan feuds of the Scottish Highlands, and in
the frequent wars between England and Scotland, they were
regularly employed in tracking fugitive warriors, and were
thus employed, according to early chroniclers, in pursuit of
Wallace and Bruce.   The former is said to have put the hound
off the scent by killing a suspected follower, on whose corpse
the hound stood.   For a similar purpose captives were often
killed.   Bruce is said to have baffled his dogged pursuer as
effectually, though less cruelly, by wading some distance down
stream, and then ascending a tree by a branch which overhung
the water and thus breaking the scent.   In the histories of
border feuds these dogs constantly appear as employed in the
pursuit of enemies, and the renown of the warrier was great,
who,

" 'By wily turns and desperate bounds, had baffled Percy's
best bloodhounds.'

"In suppressing the Irish rebellion in the time of Queen
Elizabeth, the Earl of Essex had, it is said, 800 of these animals
accompanying the army.   *   *   *

"Both history, therefore, and natural history testify to the
exceptional keenness of scent and capacity for training of this
variety of hound.   Whatever may be said of the wisdom or
humanity of resorting to this means of detecting and securing
the apprehension of criminals, there can be no doubt, that,
where a well trained dog is set upon a recent track and follows
it, in the usual manner of such dogs in following a trail, up to
the person or home of the accused, these facts may, on the
plain principles governing circumstantial evidence, be shown
as tending to connect him with the crime charged.   It was so

held in the case of Hodge v. State, supra, which is the only case I have found directly in point.

"Of course in such cases full opportunity should be given to inquire into the breeding, training and testing of the dog, and to all the circumstances attending the trailing in the case on trial, and to the manner in which the dog then acted and was handled by the person having it in charge. The weight to be given to the tracking as evidence against the accused will depend largely upon these matters."

Also in the case of Blair v. Commonwealth, in which a beautiful tribute is paid to the dog, where it is said:

"If we may credit Sir Walter Scott, such evidence was looked upon with favor as early as the twelfth century. In the Talisman it is related that in the joint crusade of Richard I of England and Phillip II of France, Roswell, the hound, pulled from the saddle Conrade, Marquis of Montserrat, thus mutely accusing him of the theft of the banner of England. Phillip defended the Marquis with the remark:

" 'Surely the word of a knight and a prince should bear him out against the barking of a cur,'

"To which Richard replied:

" 'Royal brother, recollect that the Almighty who gave the dog to be companion of our pleasures and our toils, both invested him with a nature noble and incapable of deceit. He forgets neither friend nor foe; remembers, and with accuracy, both benefit and injury. He hath a share of man's intelligence, but no share of man's falsehood. You may bribe a soldier to slay a man with his sword, or a witness to take life by false accusation; but you cannot make a hound tear his benefactor; he is the friend of man save when man justly incurs his enmity. Dress younder Marquis in what peacock robes you will, disguise his appearance, alter his complexion with drugs and washes, hide himself amidst a hundred men; I will yet pawn my scepter that the hound detects him, and expresses his resentment, as you have this day beheld.'

"The doctrine of the admissibility of bloodhound evidence in criminal prosecutions has been slowly gaining ground during the past 20 years.

* * * "The general rules deductible from these decisions are as follows:

"(1) The bloodhound in question must be shown to have been trained to follow human beings by their tracks and to have been tested as to its accuracy in trailing upon one or more occasions; and,

"(2) The evidence of the acts of bloodhounds in following a trail may be received merely as circumstantial of corroborative evidence against a person towards whom other circumstances point as being guilty of the commission of the crime charged.

"The admission of this class of evidence is therefore hedged about with abundant safeguards in the way of other and human testimony; and as long as these rules are adhered to bloodhound evidence is no more dangerous than any other class of circumstantial evidence.

"In Kentucky it is settled that testimony as to trailing by bloodhounds of one charged with crime may be permitted to go to the jury for what it is worth, as one of the circumstances which may tend to connect the defendant with the crime only after it has been shown by some one having personal knowledge of the facts: (a) That the dog in question is of pure blood and of a stock characterized by acuteness of scent and power of discrimination; (b) is itself possessed of these qualities and has been trained or tested in the tracking of human beings; and (c) that the dog so trained and tested was laid on the trail, whether visible or not, concerning which testimony has been admitted, at the point where the circumstances tend clearly to show that the guilty party had been, or upon a track which such circumstances indicated had been made by him."

* * * The evidence with reference to the history, qualification and experience of the dogs was given by the witness M.I. Stokes. He testified that he was employed by the State of Oklahoma at the State Penitentiary at McAlester. That he had charge of the dogs, about fifteen or twenty in number. That the witness Hubert Wilson was a trusty at the penitentiary who had been appointed to assist him in handling the dogs. That the witness had had fifteen or twenty years' experience in the handling of dogs. That he had been at the State Penitentiary at McAlester in this capacity for about three years, and that the two dogs which he brought to Okmulgee on the 22nd of August, 1938, were "Old Boston," and "Diana." That he selected them as his two best dogs from a pack of fifteen or twenty. "Old Boston" was nine years old and "Diana" a younger dog. He testified at length as to the experience and training which these dogs had received, and especially "Old Boston," and gave individual instances of performances by him in the trailing of human beings. He testified:

"Q. And they can distinguish between the smells of human beings? A. I will answer that question like this, it has been my experience with bloodhounds, with a trained bloodhound, they have an instinct, we call it, I call it a sense to trail a man better than any other dog would trail anything else, and apparently they have an instinct that will enable them to carry a trail through places that apparently other dogs couldn't carry it at all, and they always know one track from the other. It is impossible for you to cause them to change tracks, they won't do that.

"Q. You mean, if he is a well trained and experienced bloodhound, if he starts on the track of one human being, he will stay with that particular track? A. He will trail no other track than that. It is impossible to get him to change tracks."

* * *

"Q. Does it make a difference whether the trail is fresh or cold? A. Those two dogs I had there would trail a twenty-four hour track. I have known them to do that. They wouldn't trail as fast as one we call warmer, fresher track, you understand, but those dogs would trail a ten or twelve hour track and move right along with it; but a four or five hour track is nothing at all for them.

"Q. Would that be considered a comparatively fresh trail? A. It certainly would.

"Q. Now then, you used Old Boston as the lead dog, did you? A. Yes sir. However, we had this Diana there, one of the greatest dogs I ever knew and one of the most accurate dogs.

"Q. Did you select these two dogs out of a kennel of how many dogs? A. We had fifteen or twenty dogs, but on all special occasions I used those two dogs because they were the best I had and the best I ever saw.

"Q. Let's take, for instance, Old Boston, I understand he has since died, since the trailing of this track up there? A. Yes, sir.

"Q. When did she die? A. Boston died, I think, about a month after I left down there.

"Q. To refresh your memory, was it sometime in March, 1939? A. Right along then, yes sir.

"Q. And what age dog was she? A. Boston was about nine years of age.

"Q. Was that dog owned by the state of Oklahoma? A. Yes sir. Yes, she was owned by the State.

"Q. How long were you its keeper or trainer? A. Boston individually?

"Q. Yes. A. I only ran Boston about two and a half years. I used him some several years before that when they first got him from Texas. That was before I went to Granite.

"Q. What age dog was he, if you know, when he was brought to Oklahoma? A. He was said to be about three years of age.

"Q. Have you ever seen him on a man's trail? A. Yes, several hundred."

* * *

"Q. Did you ever know Old Boston to lie on any trail? A. I never knew him to make a mistake."

* * *

"A. I would have to answer that question like this, that this Master Mind dog of Pennsylvania has greater reputation

than Boston.   Boston was considered the second dog in the
United States at that time."

He then testified to the individual work of these dogs in many cases
that came under his personal observation, and where they had successfully tracked human beings, and then testified as to the instant case as
above related.   On cross examination he was asked:

"Q. There hasn't been any monument or any money or
anything appropriated to build a monument to Boston since he
died? A. I don't know. There ought to be."

In view of this testimony, we have decided that the tribute to the
hound by Richard I of England, as above quoted, shall be a monument
or tribute to "Old Boston," and for this reason we perpetuate his name
in the law books of this State.   Though the State has not erected a
monument to his memory, his services will ever be remembered, not
only in the instant case but others.

As above stated, the evidence in this case is almost wholly based
upon circumstantial evidence, and while we recognize the rule announced in the decisions which have been cited, that a conviction will
not be upheld upon the evidence alone of trailing by bloodhounds, yet
that evidence being competent as a circumstance, together with the
other evidence in the case, where competent proof has been given as to
the qualifications, training and experience of the bloodhounds used, as
in the instant case, this testimony together with the other evidence in
the case presented a question of fact for the jury to pass upon as to the
guilt or innocence of the defendant.

There can be no question but that the evidence as to the training
and experience of the two dogs, and especially "Old Boston," was such
that it entitled the court to submit it to the jury for their consideration,
together with the other facts and circumstances and under the law we
can not say that the verdict of the jury should be set aside.

We have, therefore, reached the conclusion that the judgment and
sentence of the District Court of Okmulgee County should be affirmed.

Jones, P.J., and Doyle, J., concur.

CONVERSATIONS WITH A GORILLA
By Francine Patterson
154 National Geographic 438, 438, 459, 461 (1978).*

KOKO is a 7-year-old "talking" gorilla.   She is the focus of my
career as a developmental psychologist, and also has become a dear
friend.

Through mastery of sign language—the familiar hand speech of the
deaf—Koko has made us, her human companions, aware not only that
her breed is bright, but also that it shares sensitivities commonly held
to be the prerogative of people.

Remembrance of Events and Emotions

A cardinal characteristic of human language is displacement, the ability to refer to events removed in time and place from the act of communication. To learn whether another animal has this ability, we try to find out if the animal uses its sign vocabulary merely to label the events of its world, or if it is framing propositions that re-create a particular event. Does the animal use its symbols to refer to events earlier or later in time?

Koko and I had a revealing conversation about a biting incident. My try at cross-examination—three days after the event—went much as follows:

> Me: "What did you do to Penny?"
>
> Koko: "Bite". (Koko, at the time of the incident, called it a scratch.)
>
> Me: "You admit it?"
>
> Koko: "Sorry bite scratch."
>
> (At this point I showed Koko the mark on my hand—it really did look like a scratch.)
>
> Koko: "Wrong bite."
>
> Me: "Why bite?"
>
> Koko: "Because mad."
>
> Me: "Why mad?"
>
> Koko: "Don't know."

The entire conversation concerns a past event and, equally significant, a past emotional state. It is not a discussion one would expect to have with an animal whose memories were dim, unsorted recollections of pain and pleasure. Of striking import to me was that Koko knew she could not remember or express whatever it was that had prompted the bite.

Koko Learns to Lie

Perhaps the most telling, yet elusive, evidence that a creature can displace events is lying. When someone tells a lie, he is using language to distort the listener's perception of reality. He is using symbols to describe something that never happened, or won't happen. Evidence I have been accumulating strongly suggests that Koko expresses a make-believe capacity similar to humans'.

At about the age of 5 Koko discovered the value of the lie to get herself out of a jam. After numerous repeat performances I'm convinced that Koko really is lying in these circumstances and not merely making mistakes. One of her first lies also involved the reconstruction of an earlier happening. My assistant Kate Mann was with Koko, then tipping the scales at 90 pounds, when the gorilla plumped down on the kitchen sink in the trailer and it separated from its frame and dropped out of alignment. Later, when I asked Koko if she broke the sink, she signed, "Kate there bad," pointing to the sink. Koko couldn't know, of course, that I would never accept the idea that Kate would go around breaking sinks.

Some of Koko's lies are startlingly ingenious. Once, while I was busy writing, she snatched up a red crayon and began chewing on it. A moment later I noticed and said, "You're not eating that crayon are you?" Koko signed, "Lip," and began moving the crayon first across her upper, then her lower lip as if applying lipstick.

CITY OF WEBSTER GROVES v. QUICK

St. Louis Court of Appeals, Missouri, 1959.
323 S.W.2d 386.

ANDERSON, Judge. This case arose upon the filing of a complaint against defendant in the City Court of Webster Groves, Missouri, for the violation of a speed ordinance of said city. Defendant was found guilty in said court and thereafter appealed to the Circuit Court of St. Louis County. A trial was had in the Circuit Court resulting in a verdict and judgment finding defendant guilty as charged and assessing as punishment a fine of $10. From this judgment, defendant appealed to the Supreme Court on the theory that because he was convicted on the readings of an electric timer his constitutional rights had been invaded, contrary to Article 1, Sections 10 and 18(a) of the Missouri Constitution, V.A.M.S.; the Fifth Amendment of the Constitution of the United States; and the Sixth Amendment of the Constitution of the United States. The Supreme Court, in an opinion, 319 S.W.2d 543, held that appellant's purported constitutional issues were without substance and colorable only, and transferred said cause to this court.

On March 4, 1957, about 8:00 o'clock a.m., appellant was driving westwardly on Kirkham Boulevard in Webster Groves. As he proceeded westwardly he was driving toward a parked police car which was headed eastward. When appellant reached a point about opposite the police car he was stopped by a police officer and informed he was driving 40 miles per hour in a 30 mile an hour zone. Appellant was advised that an electric timer which was operated by the police showed he was driving at that speed.

The electric timer consists of a control panel which contains a stop watch, a switch and a reset button. In addition, there is a cable, 500 feet long, that plugs into the box. There are two rubber tubes which stretch the width of the street. There are two mercury switches to which the tubes are connected and which are in turn connected to the electric cable, and four weights to anchor the tubes across the street. In the middle of these rubber tubes is a plug to prevent eastbound traffic from having any effect on the unit when the mechanism is set for timing westbound traffic. When laid out for operation the rubber tubes are placed across the street 132 feet apart. The mercury switches to which the tubes are connected are in turn connected to the electric cable which runs from the first tube to the control box on the police car. The first tube is located 500 feet east of the parked police car, and the second tube 368 feet east of said automobile. The police car in the instant case was placed at a point where both tubes could be observed by the occupant of the police car. As the officer sitting in the car observes a car approaching which he wishes to clock he sets the switch on the control panel which opens the first tube. When the tires of the approaching car pass over that tube it activates the mercury switch, which starts a stop watch located in the police car. The switch is then closed to the neutral position, and any automobiles following the car which crossed the first tube have no effect on the unit. Then, as the clocked automobile approaches the second tube, the switch is thrown to the right, which is the control on the second tube, and when the tires of the automobile being clocked run over the second tube it stops the clock. Around the outside of the clock is a calibrated scale laid out in miles which indicates the miles per hour the automobile being observed is traveling. From the point at which the speed of the automobile is indicated on the clock to the police car there is a distance of 368 feet.

A certified steel tape is used to measure the distance between the two tubes to insure that they are laid out exactly 132 feet.

The speed watch device, which had been in use in the city regularly during the two and one-half years before the date of the trial, is checked each day when it is put out by driving a police department vehicle through it at varying speeds. The speedometer reading of the vehicle is checked with the reading of the speed watch. This was done on the day of defendant's arrest. The arresting officer testified he saw no reason why atmospheric disturbances could effect the accurate operation of the machine.

The clock, which is a unit itself, the size of a pocket watch, is checked for accuracy the first week of each month by a watchmaker and jeweler of twelve years' experience. It is the same type of watch used in timing sports, and is tested against the standard of the National Bureau of Standards. The watch is started on a tone put out by the National Bureau of Standards, and is stopped on the tone. The watchmaker checks to see if the watch has the required number of seconds in those tones. The signals of the National Bureau are accurate to one fifty thousandth of a second each twenty-four hours. The watchmaker who testified in this case had never heard of any of the relays of this current or beam being wrong. That is the time used by the Government, and all our ships at sea, and the Air Force, set their watches by it. * * *

The arresting officer, Maurice Paillou, who was sitting in the police car, observed defendant's car approaching from the east. He decided to clock the speed of defendant's car. The officer activated the first tube shortly before defendant crossed it. He saw defendant's car cross the first tube and saw the stop watch start to operate. He then activated the second tube and as defendant crossed the latter the officer observed the stop watch come to a stop. A reading of 40 miles per hour was indicated on the stop watch. The officer then stepped out of the car, flagged down defendant and invited him over to the police car where he showed defendant the reading on the dial and explained to him how the machine worked.

On cross-examination, the police officer testified that there were no other cars on either the eastbound lane or the westbound lane when defendant came through the unit. He could see eastward approximately six to seven hundred feet. He was visually aware of the fact that defendant was traveling at a speed in excess of 30 miles per hour.

Meryle Mikel, a jeweler, testified he checked the watch mechanism during the first week in March, 1957, and found it to be accurate. He also testified he had checked the watch mechanism during the first week of February, 1957, and found it accurate.

Del Reinemer, a Webster Groves Police Sergeant, testified he had taken the stop watch to Mr. Mikel in the first week of February, 1957, the first week of March, 1957, and again in the first week of April, 1957.

Defendant denied he was going over 28 to 30 miles per hour, stating that his recently tested speedometer showed a reading between those figures.

Appellant's first point is that the court erred in permitting Police Officer Paillou to testify as to the readings of the electric timer showing defendant's speed at 40 miles per hour, for the reason that it constituted hearsay evidence.

There is no merit to the point made. The officer himself testified to the reading of the mechanism in question and not to what someone else had told him; thus, the hearsay rule does not apply. The witness when testifying was under oath, and was thoroughly cross-examined, thus satisfying the principal requirements of the hearsay rule. Evidence is called hearsay when its probative force depends, in whole or in part, on the competency and credibility of some person other than the witness by whom it is sought to be produced. It is an extrajudicial utterance, including both oral statements and writings. The hearsay rule cannot be applied to what the witness, on the stand and subject to cross-examination, observed, either through his own senses or through the use of scientific instruments. If appellant's contention were sound then results of the use of a measuring device on some object to ascertain its length would be inadmissible; a doctor could not testify to what a fluoroscope revealed concerning the condition of his patient, and, likewise, he would not be permitted to testify as to the results heard through a stethoscope. Many other examples of the absurdity of such a rule could be cited. In such cases, as in the case at bar, the evidence as to the results obtained by the witness is not dependent on the perception, memory, and sincerity of an absent declarant. The circumstantial guarantee of trustworthiness is satisfied by the exercise of the right of cross-examination of the witness on the stand, both as to the results obtained and his testimony as to the reliability and accuracy of the device used. As to the latter, there was sufficient evidence in the case at bar. A police vehicle was operated through the device the morning defendant was arrested, and the device was found to be operating properly. In addition, the stop watch was tested during that week and the first week of the preceding and subsequent months. The witnesses to those facts were produced and were subjected to rigorous cross-examination. We rule there was no error in the court's ruling on the admission of the evidence in question. ✳ ✳ ✳

[Affirmed]

MORGAN, HEARSAY AND NON–HEARSAY

48 Harv.L.Rev. 1138, 1145–6 (1935).✳
[Footnotes omitted.]

✳ ✳ ✳ The courts constantly and correctly receive as reliable evidence what careful analysis discloses to be hearsay. They sometimes obscure the question by a resort to the doctrine of judicial notice. Where a court receives an almanac as evidence of an astronomical fact, it is not taking judicial notice of the fact: it is admitting anonymous hearsay and taking judicial notice of the reliability of the almanac as a source of authentic information. Again, nothing is more common than to allow a witness to rely upon a timepiece in stating the time of day when an event happened. If he should testify that he looked at a Western Union clock and noted the time, he would be considered as giving particularly accurate testimony, but would it not be anonymous hearsay upon anonymous hearsay? Certainly the person in charge of the master mechanism which regulated the clock consulted by the witness did not make the astronomical observations in accordance with which that clock was made to indicate the hour and minute of the day. Yet just as certainly an objection upon the ground of hearsay would receive scant attention. Only a little less easy is a demonstration of the hearsay element in the indication of time upon a sundial unless preceded by the testimony of a witness who checked it against his own astronomical observations. Much the same may be said of the automatic weighing machines which in return for a coin furnish a printed assertion of a person's weight, and of non-automatic scales where the position of the marker which produces a balance of the beam announces the weight of the object upon the platform. In each of these cases, the anonymous maker or regulator of the machine intended that the reaction of the machine should operate as an assertion. In each of them he may have fixed the instrument so as to produce a false declaration, as where the faker who gambles upon his pretended ability to guess his victim's weight controls the balance by a hidden mechanism, or a practical joker sets a series of timepieces so as to cause another to miss an appointment. Generally speaking, however, the court regards these mechanisms as sufficiently accurate to justify a trier of fact in relying upon their reactions for most purposes, at least after a preliminary showing of reasonable accuracy. In other words, it takes judicial notice of the reliability of these sources of information under ordinary circumstances notwithstanding their hearsay character.

Somewhat the same process is used when expert witnesses are permitted to base their opinions upon data as to which they have not the slightest personal knowledge. Though no witness gives first-hand evidence of the truth expressed or implied in these data, the expert is permitted to draw deductions therefrom which the jury may hear and consider.

MORGAN, EVIDENCE EXAM, SUMMER TERM, 1946, HARVARD LAW SCHOOL

Which of the following items is hearsay?

N   1. On the issue whether X and D * were engaged to be married, D's statement to X, "I promise to marry you on June 1, 1931."

N   2. On the issue of the sanity of D, a woman, D's public statement, "I am the Pope."

N   3. On the issue of D's adverse possession of Blackacre, D's assertion "I am the owner of this farm."

N   4. On the issue of X's provocation for assaulting Y, D's statement to X, her husband, "Y ravished me."

N   5. On the issue of D's consciousness after the attack, D's statement, "X shot me, as he often threatened to do."

Y   6. On the issue of identity of the shooter, D's statement in 5.

Y   7. On the issue whether X made threats to shoot D, D's statement in 5.

N   8. On the issue of X's knowledge of speedily impending death, D's statement to X, "You have only a few minutes to live."

Y   9. In 8, X's out of court statement, "I realize that I am dying."

N   10. On the issue whether a transfer of a chattel from D to X was a sale or gift, D's statement accompanying the transfer, "I am giving you this chattel as a birthday present."

Y   11. On the issue in 10, D's statement the day following the transfer, "I gave you the chattel as a birthday present."

* * *

Y   14. On the issue of damages to the family reputation in an action for the seduction of P's daughter, her reputation for chastity.

N   15. On the issue of D's ill-feeling toward X, D's statement, "X is a liar and a hypocrite."

N   16. On the issue of reasonableness of X's conduct, in the shooting of Y by X, D's statement to X, "Y has threatened to kill you on sight."

N   17. On the issue in 16, Y's reputation, known to X, as a violent, quarrelsome man.

N   18. Action for malicious prosecution of P by X on the charge of murdering Y. On the issue of probable cause, P's reputation as a gangster, known to X.

N   19. In 18, Y's reputation, known to X, as a quiet, peace-loving citizen.

---

* In each of the following questions concerning a statement made by D, that statement is of course, made out of court.

NOT BEING OFFERED FOR TRUTH of statement

N 20. On the issue of the terms of a contract with T negotiated by D, D's statement "I am making this offer to you, as the agent of P."

Y 21. On the issue whether D was the agent of P, the statement in 20.

N 22. As tending to prove that X was suffering from tuberculosis, the fact that D, a physician, ordered X to a tuberculosis sanitarium for six months, concealing from X and X's relatives the character of the hospital.

N 23. As tending to prove X's honesty, the mere fact that D, X's employer, promoted him from the position of order clerk to cashier.

— 24. As tending to prove D's guilt of the crime of killing X, the fact that D fled under suspicious circumstances immediately after X's murder, in order to draw suspicion upon himself.

N 25. As tending to prove X's insanity, the fact that he was confined in an insane asylum.

Y 26. As tending to prove forgery of a will by X, D's angry statement to X, "Well, I never forged a will, anyway!"

N 27. As tending to prove D's guilt of a particular criminal act, the fact that D fled under suspicious circumstances immediately after the criminal act was committed, solely in order to escape.

— 28. On the issue whether a transfer of a chattel from D to X was a sale or a gift, D's statement accompanying the transfer, "Here is your birthday gift."

N 29. As tending to prove that X was suffering from disease T, the mere fact that D, a physician, treated him for disease T.

N 30. On the issue of D's adverse possession of Blackacre, D's statement, "I paid X $5000 for this farm."

Y 31. To show that X was ill, W offers to testify that X complained of pain in his chest.

N 32. In a contest of a will on ground of forgery, to show testator's feelings toward X, the sole legatee, W offers to testify that testator had X arrested for forgery.

N 33. In 32, for the same purpose, W offers to testify that testator ordered his superintendent to discharge X from testator's employ.

N 34. In 32, for the same purpose, W offers to testify that testator falsely charged X with the crime of bigamy under such circumstances that testator must have known the charge to be false.

N 35. Action for $500, the price of an automobile. Plea, payment. On the issue of payment, W offers to testify that he saw defendant hand plaintiff a $500 bill, and say: "This is the payment for that car."

36. In 35, on the issue of payment, W offers to testify that on the following day [defendant] said to [plaintiff]: "I was glad to be able to pay you cash for that car."

37. Action for conversion of an automobile. To prove value, plaintiff offers a receipt for the purchase price, $5000, signed by the dealer from whom he bought it.

38. Action for personal injuries by a guest in an automobile against the owner. Defense, contributory negligence and assumption of risk. W offers to testify that an hour before the accident, in the presence of plaintiff, defendant, a mechanic said: "The spindle on that front wheel may break at any moment." If offered to show the spindle defective.

39. The testimony is 38 offered as tending to show assumption of risk.

40. As tending to show that D had never repaid a loan, W offers to testify that P hired W to collect the sum from D.

44. As tending to show that D had a revolver at an affray, W offers to testify that as D passed W's house, W called his wife's attention to a revolver sticking out of D's pocket.

* * *

48. W testified that he saw D do act X, and offers to testify: "I told M within one hour after the event that I had seen D do act X." Offered to show D's conduct.

* * *

50. W testified that he saw D do act X, could not remember the date, but within an hour thereafter reported to M. M offers to testify that at 3:30 p.m. of June 1, 1944, W told M that he had just seen D do act X. M's testimony is offered to fix the time.

51. To prove that the defendant committed the crime, the prosecution offers a confession made to police officers.

52. To prove that the defendant committed the crime, the prosecution offers evidence that the defendant remained silent after being arrested for the crime.

53. To prove that the defendant committed the crime, the prosecution offers into evidence a certified copy of a prior judgment of conviction for the same offense.

54. To prove that the defendant committed the crime, the prosecution offers a witness to testify that he was present and observed the jury return a verdict of guilty in a prosecution of the defendant for a similar prior offense.

55. To prove that her husband was insane, a wife offers evidence that he lived in a nest in the top of a tree for the last five years.

56. In an action for breach of contract, the plaintiff offers into evidence an advertisement conceded to be that of the defen-

dant offering a reward for certain information which the plaintiff claims to have provided.

57. To prove that the defendant committed a crime, the prosecution offers evidence that the F.B.I. offered a reward for his capture.

58. In an heirship proceeding, the claimant testifies that the deceased was his father.

59. To prove paternity, the plaintiff offers evidence that the defendant referred to the child as "my son."

60. To fix the time of a murder, the prosecution offers a witness who testifies that minutes after he heard the shot, he heard a clock chime three times.

61. To prove adultery, the husband offers proof that a house guest after a visit had described to one of his cronies a birthmark that the accused wife has on an intimate part of her anatomy. The existence of the mark has previously been testified to by the husband while the wife has testified that only her parents and her husband knew of the mark.

62. To prove that a couple is married, a witness is offered to testify that he heard the exchange of nuptial vows.

63. To prove notice of a defect in the defendant's car in a personal injury suit, the plaintiff introduces evidence of the defendant's past attempts to repair his car.

64. In a common disaster case, in order to establish survivorship, evidence is offered that after the accident one of the victims was heard to cry: "I'm alive."

65. In a prosecution for the theft of valuable homing pigeons, evidence is offered that when the defendant's pigeon coop was opened, all of the birds flew to the home of the victim.

66. In a prosecution for sale of pornography, the prosecution offers one hundred letters sent to the defendant's post office box, each of which says, in substance: "Send me some of those dirty books."

67. Personal injury case. To show pain and suffering, plaintiff calls a nurse who testifies that the plaintiff was screaming when he was brought to the hospital.

68. In a divorce case, after the husband has testified that his wife was always nagging him at the top of her voice, the wife calls a neighbor to testify that she never heard any nagging.

69. In a paternity suit, the mother takes the stand and when asked to identify the father of her child, she points to the defendant.

70. To prove that defendant is the father of her child, the mother offers a letter in evidence from defendant's attorney in which the attorney states that his client has admitted he is the father of the child.

N̲ 71. Personal injury litigation. Plaintiff testifies that there was a
      sign facing the intersection toward the direction that the
      defendant had come from without stopping and that sign
      said: "STOP".

Y̲ 72. To prove that the insured under a life policy is dead, his wife
      offers a death certificate.

N̲ 73. In a plagiarism suit, the plaintiff testifies that he caught the
      defendant in his apartment copying portions of the plaintiff's
      typed manuscript in longhand on a sheet of paper.

cant assent / state of mind 74. Murder prosecution. To support a self-defense claim, defen-
      dant introduces witnesses who testify that before the killing
      defendant told them he was afraid of the victim.

Y̲ 75. To show that defendant was home and thus could have killed
      his wife the prosecution calls her paramour who testifies that
      when hubby was gone and the coast was clear, the wife
      always pulled down a shade on a particular window but when
      he was home the shade was always open. The prosecution
      calls a neighbor who testifies that on the night of the murder
      the shade was open. = *husband home*

PART B. EXCEPTIONS TO THE HEARSAY RULE

---

1. DYING DECLARATIONS

CAIRNS, LAW AND THE SOCIAL SCIENCES
173–74 (1935).*
[Footnotes omitted.]

* * * A large part of the business of psychology is to ascertain
how people generally conduct themselves in certain situations; this is
also, but to a much lesser extent, the concern of the law. If, for
example, the courts decide that a dying declaration made by an individual, the manner of whose death is being investigated in a criminal
proceeding, is admissible because the solemnity of the occasion is likely
to impel truthfulness, they are making an assumption more properly
describable as psychological than legal. In the establishing of the rule,
which is perhaps rooted in a custom which goes back at least to the
twelfth century, theological beliefs were perhaps a dominant factor.
Psychology may or may not confirm the law's assumption but at least it
would be wise for the courts to inquire what it has to offer. * * *

* New York, Harcourt, Brace and Company, 1935.

KING JOHN *
Act V, iv, 10–61

SALISBURY

May this be possible? may this be true?

MELUN

Have I not hideous death within my view,

Retaining but a quantity of life,

Which bleeds away, even as a form of wax

Resolveth from his figure 'gainst the fire?

What in the world should make me now deceive,

Since I must lose the use of all deceit?

Why should I then be false, since it is true

That I must die here and live hence by truth?

I say again, * * *

COMMENTARY, THE IMPACT OF PROFANITY ON HEARSAY EVIDENCE
Ralph Slovenko.

* * * In 1635, Lope de Vega, the Spanish dramatist, earnestly asked those gathered at his bedside, "Am I really dying?" When they assured him that he was going fast, he explained, "All right then, I'll say it—Dante makes me sick".

Dying Declarations in the Punjab **

The rule [admitting dying declarations] is in many ways remarkable. It has worked, I am informed, ill in India, into which country it has been introduced together with many other parts of the English law of evidence. I have heard that in the Punjab the effect of it is that a person mortally wounded frequently makes a statement bringing all his hereditary enemies on to the scene at the time of his receiving his wound, thus using his last opportunity to do them an injury. A remark made on the policy of the rule by a native of Madras shows how differently such matters are viewed in different parts of the world. "Such evidence," he said, "ought never to be admitted in any case. What motive for telling the truth can any man possibly have when he is at the point of death?"

* * *

* *The Complete Works of Shakespeare,* The Cambridge Edition Text, as edited by W. A. Wright (Rockwell Kent).

** 1 Sir James Fitzjames STEPHEN, A History of the Criminal Law of England (1883).

SOLES v. STATE

Supreme Court of Florida, 1929.
97 Fla. 61, 119 So. 791.

BROWN, J. Carl Soles was convicted of manslaughter on an indictment charging him with the murder of Clifford Long in May, 1928. The weapon which was alleged to have been used was a 22-caliber rifle.

The judgment is attacked because it is said that the court erred in admitting in evidence the dying declaration of Clifford Long; that it erred in refusing an instruction requested by the defendant upon the subject of dying declaration which embodied the proposition that, if the jury should find from the evidence that the statement admitted as a dying declaration was made "without consciousness on the part of the deceased of impending death," then the jury should not consider it as a dying declaration; and that the evidence was not sufficient to support the verdict.

Arthur Robinson, a witness for the state, was driving the automobile in which the boy, Clifford Long, was sitting when the latter was shot. They had been trying to obtain some whisky for Robinson. While searching for it, or pretending to do so, they were frightened away by what they supposed to be a rifle shot. The two, with one Jesse Jackson, who was also a member of the party, returned to the automobile and drove away. As they proceeded along the road, another shot was fired from a point down the road to their rear, and Clifford Long was wounded in the back of the head. He died as the result of that wound.

About an hour before he died, according to the testimony of his father, who asked who had hurt him, he replied: "Oh Daddy! Carl Soles shot me with a 22 rifle. I have got to die." The statement was made about 20 or 25 minutes after he was shot. The defendant objected to the question propounded to the father of the boy which elicited the above statement from him. The objection was overruled and exception was noted. No motion was made to exclude the answer.

The sister of deceased, a girl about 14 years old, testified to the same fact, and added that about 15 minutes after the deceased was brought to the place where the statement was made the defendant came on the scene driving a truck. No one was with him and he had a "22 rifle." She was permitted to repeat the "conversation," as it was called, which occurred between the boy who had been shot and his father over defendant's objection. The conversation consisted of a question by the father, addressed to no one in particular, as follows: " 'Who has hurt my darling boy?' " and Clifford replied, according to the father: " 'Oh, Daddy! Carl Soles shot me with a 22 rifle. I have got to die.' " According to the girl, the boy replied as follows: " 'Papa, Carl Soles shot me with a 22 rifle and I have got to die.' "

The admission of this evidence constituted the basis of the first and second assignments of error.

It is argued that the statement was inadmissible, not only because the court did not inquire of others present whether the deceased said he had to die, and that one other witness who was present said he did not hear such statement, but that the statement contained no evidence that the declarant made it in the belief that death was impending.

The boy had gone with two negroes in an automobile a short distance from where he lived and was returning when he was shot. After riding a short distance he left the automobile, transferred to a truck, which was about to pass, and was driven to Sammy Long's store, where his father assisted him in getting out of the truck. He soon became unconscious, but before passing into unconsciousness he made the statement.

The defendant's counsel requested the court to give the following instruction to the jury: "The court has admitted in evidence for your consideration an alleged dying declaration of the deceased. In so admitting said dying declaration the Court has only passed upon its admissibility. In order that a statement of the deceased may properly be considered as a dying declaration it must have been made by the deceased with a consciousness of impending death, and if you find from the evidence that such statement by the deceased, if made, was without consciousness on the part of the deceased of impending death you should not further consider it as a dying declaration."

There was no error in admitting the testimony of the two witnesses above referred to.

We are inclined to the opinion that the court below was correct in refusing to give the quoted instruction requested by the defendant, and that the judgment of conviction should be affirmed. While there is some conflict of authority on the question, it appears to us from a careful review of the cases in the notes under section 1451 of Wigmore on Evidence (2d Ed.), that the weight of authority and the trend of our own former decisions is to the effect that such an instruction should not be given. In the text of said section 1451, Dean Wigmore in discussing the question in part says:

Section 1451. "That the judge is to pass on the preliminary condition necessary to the admissibility of evidence is unquestioned (post Sec. 2550). It follows, as of course, that, since a consciousness of impending death is according to the foregoing principles legally essential to admissibility, the *judge must determine* whether that condition exists before the declaration is admitted.

"After a dying declaration, or any other evidence has been admitted, the *weight* to be given to it is a matter exclusively for the jury. They may believe it or may not believe it; but, so far as they do or do not, their judgment is not controlled by rules of law. Therefore, though they themselves do not suppose the declarant to have been conscious of death, they may still believe the statement; conversely, though they do suppose him to have been thus conscious, they may still not believe the statement to be true. In other words, their canons of ultimate belief are not necessarily the same as the preliminary legal conditions of admissibility, whose purpose is an entirely different one (ante, Sec. 29). It is, therefore, erroneous for the judge, after once admitting the declaration, to instruct the jury that they must reject the declaration, or exclude it from consideration, if the legal requirement as to consciousness of death does not in their opinion exist. No doubt they *may* reject it, on this ground or on any other; but they are not to be expected to follow a definition of law intended for the Judge."

To much the same effect is the treatment of the point by Greenleaf, in vol. 1 (16th Ed.) § 161–b. After laying down the general rule as to the court's determination of the admissibility of the declaration, he adds: "But, after the evidence is admitted, its credibility is entirely within the province of the jury, who of course are at liberty to weigh all the circumstances under which the declaration were made, including those already proved to the judge, and to give the testimony only such credit as upon the whole they may think it deserves."

In the note to section 1451 of Wigmore on Evidence it is said that a contrary ruling was made in R.V. Woodcock, Leach, an English case decided in 1790, but that this was subsequently repudiated in England, and that the principle as stated above does not appear to have since been doubted. He quotes Starkie as having observed: "It might as well be left to a jury to say whether a witness ought to be sworn, or whether he is not incapacitated by ignorance or infamy or other cause from giving evidence upon oath."

In Holland v. State, this court held that: "The court determines the admissibility, and the jury the credibility, of confessions. It is not error, therefore, for the court to refuse to charge the jury that if they believe from all the evidence that defendant's confession was procured from fear or terror, or hope of reward, they should disregard the confession in making up their verdict." This appears to be the orthodox rule, in regard to confessions. The analogy to dying declarations is, in this respect, quite complete. In Roten v. State, it was held that the question of the admissibility of a dying declaration was exclusively one for the court to decide.

Affirmed.

Terrell, C.J., and Whitfield, Strum, and Buford, JJ., concur.

———

See Federal Rules of Evidence 804(b)(2); California Evidence Code § 1242.

KAPLAN, OF MABRUS AND ZORGS—AN ESSAY IN HONOR OF DAVID LOUISELL
66 Cal.L.Rev. 987 (1978).*

[Editor's Note: This article has been edited and adapted somewhat for publication in this casebook].

* * * [A]n infrequently thought about—or at least infrequently written about—area is the distribution of functions between the judge and the jury in determining what are called preliminary questions of fact. In general, we have two rules to cover two different questions

that come up in the trial of cases. The first question occurs when the issue is whether a proffered piece of evidence is admissible. Here the elementary rule is that the judge, not the jury, must decide the issue. The second question occurs when an issue of fact arises and the evidence bearing on it is such that a reasonable person could find either way. There, the equally elementary rule is that the jury, not the judge, is to resolve the question.

In large numbers of cases, we have no trouble telling the two situations apart and the two rules peacefully coexist. Virtually no one would suggest that the jury should determine whether an item of evidence is or is not hearsay, or whether an accountant has or does not have a privilege not to testify against his client. Similarly, most judges would not dream of directing a verdict on the issue of who went through the red light where the usual crowds of drivers, passengers, and bystanders fell to disputing whether the plaintiff or the defendant was the guilty party. It is elementary, however, that we often come across questions that seem to fall within both categories—cases in which the admissibility of a piece of evidence turns on the resolution of a question of fact.

Before examining the conventional wisdom about distinguishing the two rules, let us examine a hypothetical and ask ourselves how a rational legal system—assuming that any legal system which makes use of a two-headed problem solving institution such as a judge and a jury could properly be called rational—should allocate the preliminary factfinding task.

> (1) Prosecution of D for the murder of A. W testifies that while A lay in the hospital, two days after suffering a gunshot wound in the stomach, A said, "I saw D shoot me," and, without commenting further on the subject, died shortly thereafter.

Clearly, A's out-of-court declaration is hearsay. Arguably, however, it is within the dying declaration exception to the hearsay rule which provides that in a homicide prosecution a statement of the deceased as to the cause of his death, made on personal knowledge and under a sense of impending death, is admissible to show the truth of the facts asserted.

Let us assume that there is no dispute about A's personal knowledge and that the only real issue as to admissibility is whether the statement was made under a sense of impending death—an issue as to which there is conflicting evidence. One witness testifies that he, a physician, told A, just before A made the statement at issue, that his condition was hopeless and that he would die very shortly. Another witness, a nurse of somewhat dubious credibility because she turns out to have been a girlfriend of D, testifies that, a moment after the statement, the deceased whispered to her that doctors are often wrong and that he felt much better than he had the day before.

Is this question one which the judge should decide on the principle that the court must rule on the admissibility of evidence? Or is it one

which the jury should decide (under proper instructions, of course) on
the theory that it is the proper trier of the facts? * * *

There are several ways of handling the problem of hypothetical 1.
In theory, we could interrupt the trial and empanel a separate jury to
listen to the evidence about A's death and decide the sole issue of
whether A's statement was made under a sense of impending death.
Thus, the question of fact would be decided by a jury, and the judge,
bound by this factual finding, could decide the question of admissibility
or what was left of it. We would then have two separate questions
decided at different times, and our two rules could lie down like the
proverbial lion and lamb.[1] If the specially empaneled jury were to
decide that A's statement was not made under a sense of impending
death, the trial judge would exclude the evidence, and the jury trying
the prosecution itself would not hear her testimony. Alternatively, if
the specially empaneled jury were to find that A's statement was made
under a sense of impending death, would allow the evidence in and the
trial jury would then listen to what W had to say.

If questions of preliminary fact were relatively rare, we might
seriously consider this course. Such questions, however, are very
common and a given trial may raise dozens of them. We have enough
difficulty disposing of our litigation with one jury per case. Obviously,
it would be that much more time-consuming and expensive to empanel
in each case additional juries—or even just one additional jury—to
decide all the questions of preliminary fact.

A somewhat less taxing proposal would be to use the trial jury
itself to decide each preliminary fact question, but require it to do so
before the judge could decide the admissibility of the questioned evidence. Thus, in hypothetical 1, the jurors would first hear all the
evidence bearing on the circumstances surrounding A's statement and
then, under proper instructions from the judge, retire for their deliberations on this issue. If the jurors were to decide that A's statement was
not made under a sense of impending death, they would so inform the
judge who would excuse W from the witness stand. If the jurors were
to decide the opposite then, on their return, the judge would permit
them to hear W's testimony.

Although it is not quite so impractical as the first possibility, this
proposal also poses overwhelming problems. First, it would be enor-
mously expensive in terms of time and effort to require many interruptions of the trial while the jury deliberated the numerous preliminary
fact questions that arise in the trial of any lawsuit. And this waste of
lawyers' and witnesses' time would not be the only problem. We would
also have to determine what to do when the jury could not reach
unanimous agreement on the preliminary fact issue. Most important,
however, we would be unable to cope with the natural inclination of
jurors routinely to find the existence of the preliminary facts necessary

1. *Isaiah* 11:6. It has been pointed out,
by the way, that in such a situation, the
lamb—at best—gets very little sleep.

to the admissibility of evidence so that they could better perform their factfinding duties and satisfy their own curiosities as well.

The next possibility is considerably more administrable than either of the aforementioned, but is itself fatally defective. Why not, one might suggest, simply let the jurors hear both the evidence bearing on the preliminary facts concerning the circumstances surrounding A's statement and W's testimony as to A's statement itself, but instruct them to consider W's testimony as evidence only if they first find that A made his statement under a sense of impending death.

The problem with this course stems from the jury's role being basically quite different from the judge's. A judge's duty is to apply the rules of a legal system which is, one would hope, designed to reach the appropriate factual resolution in the largest possible number of cases, giving appropriate weight as well to other societal values. These other values which shape many of our rules of evidence but which are often unrelated to the fact determining role, include privacy, encouragement of certain confidential relations, convenience in administering a complex body of evidence law, and notions of fairness. A jury, on the other hand, focuses on the determination of the facts of one particular case and in doing so frequently is far less interested than a judge in the societal values underlying our rules of evidence or anything else which might get in the way of their determining the facts of the case at hand.

Obviously the jury will not be prepared to enforce the policy of the law to exclude such statements that were not made under a sense of impending death. The jury will be much more interested in whether A had had a grudge against D, whether A wished to shield someone else, and whether his memory and perception of the shooting were good. [T]he jurors might be somewhat interested in the preliminary fact at issue because if A had spoken under a sense of impending death and had been a religious man, that might be an extra guarantee of his sincerity. In most cases, however, they would be much more interested in other facts about the statement. As a result, if anyone is going to enforce the policy of the hearsay exception, it will have to be the judge.

Can we then conclude that in all cases the judge should decide the factual questions which determine the admissibility of evidence and let the jury hear the evidence only if he finds those facts in favor of admissibility? The conventional wisdom is to the contrary, and for good reason. Let us consider another hypothetical:

> (2) Plaintiff, P, injured in an automobile accident, alleges that the defendant, D, was driving at an excessive speed. To help show this, he produces a witness, W, to testify that about a minute before the accident and one mile from the scene he (W) saw D's car travelling at an excessive speed on the road toward the place of impact. D, however, produces evidence that indicates it was another car that W saw, not D's.

Presumably no one would argue that W's testimony is sufficiently relevant to show D's speed if the car W saw was not D's car. Assuming, then, that one mile is close enough to the accident, the relevance of this evidence depends on a question of fact: whether the car observed by W

was the defendant's. Is there any reason why this question must be
decided by the judge as was the case in the dying declaration hypothetical hypotheticals? Obviously not. The judge can let the jury hear all
the evidence on the issue of which car W saw, confident that if the
jurors decide that W saw another car and not the defendant's, they will
ignore W's testimony as to its speed and decide the case on other
evidence.

Similarly, let us examine another hypothetical, illustrating the
same point:

> (3) A sues B on a note that purportedly carries B's signa-
> ture. B's defense is that the note is a forgery, and there is
> evidence both ways on the question of genuineness. Under the
> facts of the case, a forged note would bear no relation to the
> rights and liabilities of the parties.[8] For this reason, when A
> attempts to introduce the purported note into evidence, B
> objects on the ground of relevance.

Here again we have a question to be decided by the jury. If the
jurors are at all rational in attempting to perform their job, we would
certainly expect them to ignore a forged note in determining the rights
and liabilities of A and B.

Even where a preliminary fact question is to be decided by the jury,
the judge still retains his function of making sure there is sufficient
evidence from which a rational jury could find the preliminary fact. If
not, the evidence must be kept from the jury—but not because the
judge had decided the preliminary fact question. Rather, the judge
would simply be holding that there was, in contemplation of the law, no
question to be decided. In our legal system, all jury questions presup-
pose a situation in which the evidence is sufficient to support a jury
finding.

————

See Federal Rules of Evidence 104; California Evidence Code
§§ 403, 405.

Hypotheticals

(1) X is prosecuted for murder in shooting A to death in a barroom brawl.
In defense, X calls B and makes an offer of proof that B will testify that she
talked with A in the hospital the day before his death, that A had difficulty in
breathing, and said: "I don't think I can make it. It was not X's fault. C was
going after X with a knife before X drew his gun. C ducked when X fired and
that's how I got shot." The prosecutor makes a hearsay objection to B's
testimony and offers to prove by Y, a nurse, that five minutes before B talked
with A, A told her that he was feeling fine and expected to be able to leave the
hospital within a few days. The judge listens to the testimony of B and Y out
of the presence of the jury and believes that both witnesses are telling the
truth. Must she then admit A's statement in evidence? Must she then keep it
out?

8. This is not to say that the note would
be inadmissible for all purposes. For example, the very fact that A was desperate
enough to forge a note might show that he
was liable, let us say, on a counterclaim.

(2) Assume the same facts as given in Illustration (1), except that the judge admits in evidence A's statement to B upon finding that the requirements of the dying declaration exception are satisfied. The prosecutor calls Y, the nurse, to testify before the jury to A's statement made to her. X objects that Y's testimony is inadmissible in view of the court's ruling admitting A's statement to B. What result?

2. SPONTANEOUS AND CONTEMPORANEOUS EXCLAMATIONS

HUTCHINS & SLESINGER, SOME OBSERVATIONS ON THE LAW OF EVIDENCE

28 Colum.L.Rev. 432 (1928).*

[Footnotes omitted.]

I. SPONTANEOUS EXCLAMATIONS

Spontaneous utterances, exclamations or declarations are, under certain conditions, admissible in evidence though the party who made them does not take the stand. According to most courts the occasion must be startling enough to cause shock, which in turn creates an emotional state. The utterance must be made under stress of that emotion; it must be "spontaneous and natural; impulsive and instinctive"; it should be immediate, or "so clearly connected (with the occasion) that the declaration may be said to be the spontaneous explanation of the real cause." Although in some jurisdictions there is insistence that the declaration be "contemporaneous" with the act, or "while the act is going on," the progressive view seems to be that the time interval, beyond which a declaration would no longer be spontaneous, is in the sound discretion of the trial court * * *.

Apparently the type of utterance toward which the courts are most favorably inclined is that which follows a severe shock to the declarant. A startling invasion of the declarant's repose is assumed to lead to a trustworthy statement, whether the declarant be a congenital liar, an infant, a murderer, or a minister of the gospel. Whereas an identical blow on the head might conceivably produce different emotions in a boxer and a bookkeeper, it is likely that statements made by each would, by many courts, be admitted in evidence as spontaneous exclamations.

Since the shock is what guarantees the truth of these declarations, some courts rule that it alone must produce them. Although dying in agony, if, in response to an inquiry as to the identity of his assailant, the declarant says that the defendant shot him, the statement must be excluded. As a result of the interpolation of the question, what would otherwise be admissible becomes "not the natural and spontaneous outgrowth of the murderous assault on him, but a mere narrative of a past transaction, and hence not a part of the *res gestae*."

* Copyright, 1928 By the Trustees of The Columbia Law Review.

Where no questions have been asked, the courts are willing to concede that physical shock to the declarant is likely to produce the truth if the utterance comes before time to misrepresent has been afforded him. They are willing to go a step further and concede that a speaker who has received no injury, but who is involved in the startling occurrence will, if sufficiently excited, be honest, too. A motorman, a brakeman, or an engineer, although he escapes unscathed from the wreckage of his train, will not lie about the cause of the catastrophe until he has regained his equilibrium. But the casual bystander who has no interest in later suits against the railroad, but who is much affected by the sad spectacle, is by no means so reliable. Some courts exclude what he has said because he is disinterested. He is not an actor, however much he was moved by the action. The fact that his statement appears to be made without premeditation or design cannot save it. The reason given for admitting an actor's statement is sufficient to exclude his. As the Kentucky court has put it, the admission of the utterances of excited bystanders would open the door to "reckless, thoughtless and ill-considered exclamations," which are precisely the kind, and the only kind that are admitted under the rule as to spontaneous declarations made by injured persons or actors.

Even though most courts do admit the statements of excited bystanders, where there is a stimulus which is not sufficient to produce excitement, they do not ordinarily attribute to it the truth-evoking qualities ascribed to shock. This is so even though there is no conceivable motive to misrepresent, and the person who heard the exclamation is on the stand, subject to cross-examination as to all the circumstances of its making. Thus, if just before an automobile runs down a pedestrian, a witness watching it from a trolley car remarks on its high speed, the statement is inadmissible. If, where the plaintiff's contention is that death was caused by the unnecessary blowing of a whistle which resulted in the frightening of the deceased's horse, he offers a woman's statement, made a block and a half away, that "it was brutish the way they whistled," the evidence cannot come in because the declarant was sitting calmly in her home. The declarant's report that, at the time of the shot, which he heard three-quarters of a mile off, he said someone was trying his pistol, is not admitted as a spontaneous exclamation.

The general theory under which these declarations are admissible has been well stated by Mr. Wigmore. "Under certain external circumstances of physical shock a state of nervous excitement may be produced which stills the reflective faculties and removes their control, so that the utterance which occurs is a spontaneous and sincere response to the actual sensations and perceptions already produced by the external shock." And "since this utterance is made under the immediate and controlled domination of the senses, and during the brief period when considerations of self-interest could not have been fully brought to bear by reasoned reflection, the utterances may be taken to be particularly trustworthy."

This reflective self-interest is a curious doctrine, dating back to a mentalist psychology, and the utilitarian philosophy that made use of it. Man's conduct, according to this theory of behavior, was always personally motivated, his acts being planned by an elaborate calculus of interests, immediate and remote. Since that calculus involved reflection, it clearly followed that by eliminating reflection, self-interested conduct became impossible. The entrance of instinct into psychology shifted the emphasis, without changing the fundamental idea, by putting self-interest on an instinctive basis. The modern tendency is to substitute groups of habits or habit patterns for such general concepts as self-interest. These, if they serve the self, may afterward be called self-interested. That they are not, in fact, due to a force or instinct of self-interest, is shown by their persistence beyond the point of general efficiency. The habit of saving money, for example, is, in certain circumstances, self-interested. But a person having the habit will tend to continue to save even when it is directly against his interest. Reflection plays a part, both in the formation of habits, and in resolving conflicts between them. But once formed, they continue, on their own inertia, creating the illusion of a definite force.

To still, or circumvent this "force," the law relies in part on immediacy. The veracity of a response, according to the courts, varies directly with its speed. The desire to lie requires time and reflection to develop. And the intervention of reflection may be avoided by giving it no time to occur, thus rendering lying difficult, if not impossible.

In order to estimate the time required for reflection, it is necessary to know something of the difficulty of the task reflection is to perform. Ordinarily the choices are very simple ones, involving few alternatives. "John did it!" or "John did not do it!" The gentleman of after-dinner fame who, on being informed that his train had fallen over an embankment while he slept, cried, "Oh, my shoulder" in all probability did not take many moments to respond to the situation. If his general character is pointed to by way of explanation, the answer is simply that it is precisely that sort of character that the courts are guarding against.

A number of laboratory psychological experiments have been performed which throw some light on the problem under consideration. A subject is asked to disobey one of several orders, concealing from the examiner which order he has disobeyed. Or two subjects are sent out of the room, one to perform a series of acts, the other to do nothing, the actor trying to conceal his "crime." To each subject, then, is read a series of words, some of which are directly associated with the crimes in question, with the request that he respond as quickly as possible with the first word that comes to his mind, taking care, however, to avoid giving away his crime. All observers report a delay in reaction time to key words where deception is attempted, although Marston discovered a small group, which he called good liars, whose reaction time to significant words was actually faster than to the rest of the list. It seems, then, that the courts are on the right track in demanding speed as a guarantee of truth, or, at least of the absence of attempted falsehood. The difficulty comes when the speed is considered, not as a general idea, but quantitatively. Here we find that the difference in time between the ordinary reaction and the deception reaction to significant words is so slight, from .83 seconds to 3½ minutes, that it cannot be measured without the aid of instruments. The sound discretion of the trial judge, with the best of intention in these cases, is likely to be fallible.

But it will be remembered that speed is not the only guarantee of truthful response. In order more fully to guard against deceit, a good deal of reliance is placed on shock, and the emotion generated thereby, provided it is severe enough to still the reflective faculties. There is every reason to suppose that such an emotion would render difficult a consciously planned lie. As Mr. Watson inelegantly puts it, emotion is an affair of the guts, beyond control of the intellect, and pretty well running it during its active phase. It halts digestion, speeds up heart rate, increases blood pressure, creates general muscular tension throughout the body, pours sugar and adrenalin into the blood stream. These bodily changes are certainly discomforting to intellectual activity. They paralyze and distort it all along the line; unfortunately, while they make thinking difficult, they render observation and judgment all but impossible.

One need not be a psychologist to distrust an observation made under emotional stress; everybody accepts such statements with mental reservation. M. Gorphe cites the case of an excited witness to a horrible accident who erroneously declared that the coachman deliberately and vindictively ran down a helpless woman. Fiore tells of an emotionally upset man who testified that hundreds were killed in an accident; that he had seen their heads rolling from their bodies. In reality only one man was killed, and five others injured. Another excited gentleman took a pipe for a pistol. Besides these stories from real life, there are psychological experiments which point to the same conclusion. After a battle in a classroom, prearranged by the experimenter but a surprise to the students, each one was asked to write an account of the incident. The testimony of the most upset students was practically worthless, while those who were only slightly stimulated emotionally scored better than those left cold by the incident. Miss Hyde of Nebraska tells of an unpublished experiment, the results of which differed only in the general inaccuracy of all accounts, regardless of the amount of emotion generated. The conclusion drawn from these, and other similar experiments, is that "emotion may virtually hold connected perception in abeyance so that the subject has only isolated sensations to remember instead of a logically connected unit perception."

That participants, as well as bystanders, have their perceptions clouded by strong emotions will not be doubted. When a carriage containing the inevitable psychologist upset, that worthy gentleman amused himself and his companions by taking depositions while they awaited assistance. He had no known reality to check their stories against, but it was obvious that if any one was right, all the rest were wrong. That even trained observers are fallible is well brought out in an editorial in the *New York World* in which several accounts of newspaper reports of the striking of Kerensky on his recent visit to America are printed. Though the reporters were all experts, and sitting close to the platform, each one told a different story of what must have been a fairly simple event.

The result of these observations is a dilemma. From the point of view of subjective veracity, the speed the courts demand does not necessarily guarantee truth. And from the standpoint of objective accuracy, emotion is little better. If a speedy reaction means nothing without the aid of a stopwatch, an emotional reaction means nothing without eliminating the emotion. What the emotion gains by way of overcoming the desire to lie, it loses by impairing the declarant's power of observation. On the one hand, if reflective self-interest has not had a chance to operate because of emotional stress, then the statement should be excluded because of the probable inaccuracy of observation. On the other, if little emotion is involved, clearly a very short time is sufficient to allow reflected self-interest to assume full sway. On that basis there would seem to be no reason for this hearsay exception. In fact, the emphasis should be all the other way. On psychological grounds, the rule might very well read: Hearsay is inadmissible, especially (not except) if it is by a spontaneous exclamation.

Of course, such a result would be preposterous. The evidence is relevant and should be admitted unless it is so worthless as to mislead the tribunal or waste its time. It would do neither to a tribunal trained to decide the weight to be given to evidence in the light thrown by a knowledge of the background of the declarant, and the circumstances in which an exclamation was made. To this tribunal statements now viewed with suspicion because they are not made under emotional stress, would seem to represent more accurate observation for that very reason. Since an injured person is the one most affected by his injury, his observations would be considered less reliable than those of an uninjured motorman, brakeman, or engineer, and *a fortiori* less than those of a casual, unexcited bystander. And, according to this view, the best evidence of all is a statement made in immediate response to an external stimulus which produces no shock or nervous excitement whatever.

Professor Morgan's insistence on the admissibility of declarations closely connected in time with such a stimulus seems entirely justified. With emotion absent, speed present, and the person who heard the declaration on hand to be cross-examined, we appear to have an ideal exception to the hearsay rule. Statements by passengers before any damage has been done about the roughness of the train ride; observations as to the speed of a train as it is going by; remarks made on hearing a fight in progress some distance away; "why don't the train whistle?", spoken as the declarant saw it approaching the crossing;—all these are exclamations the value of which is indicated by the opportunity to cross-examine the hearer as to the surrounding circumstances, by the speed of the reaction, and the unemotional condition of the speaker.

Thus it appears that the spontaneous declarations regarded with least favor by the courts are more trustworthy than those which most of them admit without question: those where the trial judge rules that the statement was made under the influence of severe physical shock. It is by no means suggested, however, that these last should be excluded simply because other types of evidence assumed to be less reliable turn out, on investigation, to be more reliable. It is suggested, on the contrary, that all these varieties of declarations be admitted. If relevant they should go to the jury; for some are demonstrably more accurate than we have hitherto supposed, and those now admitted are not so inaccurate as to be arbitrarily excluded. To exclude any because they are not the immediate outpourings of an injured person is to insist on requirements shown to be artificial, if not mistaken.

TRUCK INSURANCE EXCHANGE v. MICHLING

Supreme Court of Texas, 1963.
364 S.W.2d 172.

CULVER, Justice.

This suit was brought by Mrs. Martha Michling and other statutory beneficiaries to recover death benefits provided by the Texas Workmen's Compensation Act. Judgment was rendered in favor of these beneficiaries by the trial court and the Court of Civil Appeals has affirmed.

The only evidence offered to prove that the deceased, Hugo Michling, sustained an accidental injury in the scope of his employment was that given by his wife, Mrs. Michling. She related that her husband left home to go to his place of work about 30 miles away on the morning of April 12, 1958, and at that time was apparently in good health; that she saw him when he got out of his car on his return home about 3:30 that afternoon and that "he sort of stumbled and caught himself and walked on up to the house and he said his head was hurting him terribly; he was batting his eyes and was very pale." She quoted him as saying that "he had hit his head on the bulldozer, the iron bar across the seat. It slipped off the hill and he hit his head." She also testified that he said "his head hurt so bad that he couldn't do anything else but had to put up the bulldozer and come home." Michling died at the hospital on May 11, 1958.

This case turns on the question of whether or not the foregoing testimony given by Mrs. Michling is admissible under the rule which admits res gestae * utterances as an exception to the hearsay rule.

* * *

This then brings us to the question of what are the general rules governing the admission of hearsay statements as res gestae. Wigmore in his work on Evidence, 3rd Edition, § 1747, has the following to say:

> "This general principle is based on the experience that, under certain external circumstances of physical shock, a stress of nervous excitement may be produced which stills the reflective faculties and removes their control, so that the utterance which then occurs is a spontaneous and sincere response to the actual sensations and perceptions already produced by the external shock. Since this utterance is made under the immediate and uncontrolled domination of the senses, and during the brief period when considerations of self-interest could not have been brought fully to bear by reasoned

---

* "res gestae" in many jurisdictions was the old fashioned name for what we now call "excited utterances" or "spontaneous exclamations." See pp. 140–145.

reflection, the utterance may be taken as particularly trustworthy (or, at least, as lacking the usual grounds of untrustworthiness), and thus as expressing the real tenor of the speaker's belief as to the facts just observed by him; and may therefore be received as testimony to those facts. * * *."

In § 1750 he sets out the requirements as follows:

"(a) Nature of the Occasion. There must be some *occurrence, startling enough* to produce this nervous excitement and render the utterance spontaneous and unreflecting. * * *."

"(b) Time of the Utterance. The utterance must have been *before there has been time to contrive and misrepresent, i.e.,* while the nervous excitement may be supposed still to dominate and the reflective powers to be yet in abeyance. This limitation is in practice the subject of most of the rulings.

"It is to be observed that the statements *need not be strictly contemporaneous* with the exciting cause; they may be subsequent to it, provided there has not been time for the exciting influence to lose its sway and to be dissipated. · * * *

"Furthermore, there can be *no definite and fixed limit* of time. Each case must depend upon its own circumstances.

"(c) Subject of the Utterance. The utterance must *relate to the circumstances of the occurrence preceding it.* * * *."

The very unusual circumstance in this case is that the hearsay statement of Mrs. Michling is the only evidence of the event which gives rise to the statement. A hearsay statement, as res gestae, is admitted as an exception to the hearsay rule because it is made under circumstances which raise a reasonable presumption that it is the spontaneous utterance of thought created by or springing out of the occurrence itself and, so to speak, becomes a part of the occurrence. But in this case the only evidence of the occurrence is the hearsay statement. Thus the Court of Civil Appeals is conceding credit to a narrative to prove the very circumstances from which it is said to derive its credit. Its trustworthiness, as to the happening of an accident, is presumed from the influence of the accident which its trustworthiness is taken to prove. Thus this proof, to use a trite expression, is attempting to lift itself by its own bootstraps. There is not any independent proof that Hugo Michling suffered any injury at approximately the time and place alleged.

* * *

The medical testimony is that Michling died of a cerebral hemorrhage resulting from a congenital weakness in one of the blood vessels in the brain and that such a hemorrhage may be precipitated by a cough, a strain, a blow to the head or may occur spontaneously. The fact that Michling died from a cerebral hemorrhage does not necessarily indicate any accidental injury. There was no visible mark of any injury upon his head.

* * *

For declarations to be admissible in evidence as part of the res gestae they must be made in connection with an act proven. In other words there must be evidence of an act itself admissible in the case independently of the declaration that accompanies it.

As aptly said in 32 C.J.S. Evidence § 405:

> " * * * It is proceeding in a circle to use the declarations as proof of facts necessary to constitute declarations part of the res gestae."

* * *

Our holding in Wade v. Texas Employers' Ins. Ass'n, 150 Tex. 557, 244 S.W.2d 197 (1951) cited by the Court of Civil Appeals, is not an authority for the proposition that the statement made by Michling to his wife is admissible as evidence. In that case the deceased employee was at work when he made the statement that "this gas is about to get me," which was admitted as a res gestae utterance. But two of his fellow employees testified that there was an unusual amount of chlorine gas present when they were at work which was produced from nearby operations in a chemical plant. The proof of the occurrence, namely, the presence of chlorine gas, which gave rise to the statement, did not depend upon the statement of the deceased.

For the foregoing reasons the judgments of the trial court and of the Court of Civil Appeals are reversed and judgment here rendered in favor of petitioner, Truck Insurance Exchange.

BOOTH v. STATE

Maryland Court of Appeals, 1986.
306 Md. 313, 508 A.2d 976.

McAULIFFE, Judge.

John E. Booth was convicted in the Circuit Court for Baltimore City of the premeditated murder and armed robbery of James Edward ("Pie") Ross, and was sentenced by Judge Martin Greenfeld to consecutive terms of life and twenty years imprisonment. Booth appealed to the Court of Special Appeals, contending that the trial judge erred in admitting hearsay evidence, * * * The Court of Special Appeals affirmed, and we granted certiorari to consider the question of the admissibility of evidence under the present sense impression exception to the hearsay rule.

At trial, the State proffered evidence that Regina Harrison telephoned Ross between 5:30 and 6:00 p.m. on the day of his murder. Harrison testified that Ross said he was getting ready to prepare dinner and was going to ask his company, a girl named Brenda, to leave. Harrison said she then heard the door at Ross' home open and questioned Ross as to who was there. Ross told Harrison that Brenda was talking to "some guy" behind the door.[a] According to Harrison, the

---

a. Editors' Note: Other evidence in the case linked the defendant to the murder and indicated that he was the person behind the door. One prosecution witness testified that, later in the same evening, defendant told of having gone to the house of someone Brenda knew, gaining entrance, and then stabbing the occupant and stealing his money. See Booth v. State, 62

general tone of the conversation was normal and Ross did not sound nervous or anxious.

Booth objected to the testimony of Harrison on the ground that it was impermissible hearsay. The trial judge admitted the testimony, concluding that it fell within the present sense impression exception to the hearsay rule.[1] Judge Greenfeld said in his well considered oral opinion:

> It seems to me that the present sense impression has as much reliability as the excited utterance exception or res gestae exception as it is sometimes called, and may even be more accurate, since the Maryland Court of Appeals permits excited utterances to be admitted under the proper circumstances as an exception to the hearsay rule. I see no reason why present sense impression should not also be admitted if reliability exists. So in the general sense I find that reliability does exist here because there would be no reason for Mr. Ross to inaccurately state to Miss Harrison over the telephone that Brenda was there or that she was talking to somebody at the door. And, of course, the jury can evaluate her demeanor and the accuracy of, and reliability, and trustworthiness of the statement themselves.

Booth argues that Maryland should not adopt the present sense impression exception because the mere contemporaneity of a statement and an allegedly perceived event does not establish trustworthiness. Alternatively, Booth contends that even if the exception is adopted this testimony should not be admitted because there was no corroboration by an "equally percipient witness."

The present sense impression exception has its origins in what was known as the "res gestae" exception to the hearsay rule.[2] The term "res gestae" came into usage in discussion of admissibility of declarations in the early 1800's. As Professor McCormick points out, the term is more generic than particular and includes within its definition four distinct exceptions: declarations of present bodily condition; declarations of present mental states and emotions; excited utterances; and declarations of present sense impressions. Although the term res gestae is now condemned in academic circles, the exceptions included within its definition are recognized by most scholars.[3]

Md.App. 26, 30, 488 A.2d 195, 197 (Md.Ct. Spec.App.1985).

1. Judge Greenfeld carefully distinguished between that part of the conversation which was a contemporaneous account of the occurrence, and that which was a report of a statement made by Brenda at an undisclosed earlier time. The latter statement, to the effect that Brenda had told Ross she wanted $2.50 for "a bag of reefer," was excluded.

2. Res gestae is a Latin phrase meaning "things done." Black's Law Dictionary 1173 (5th ed. 1979).

3. See, e.g., 6 J. Wigmore, Evidence § 1767, at 255 (Chadbourn Rev.1976) ("The phrase 'res gestae' has long been not only entirely useless, but even positively harmful."); Morgan, A Suggested Classification of Utterances Admissible as Res Gestae, 31 Yale L.J. 229 (1923) ("The marvelous capacity of a Latin phrase to serve as a substitute for reasoning and the confusion of thought inevitably accompanying the use of inaccurate terminology, are nowhere better illustrated than in the decisions dealing with the admissibility of evidence as 'res gestae.' It is probable that this

The present sense impression exception was first defined by the evidence scholar, James Bradley Thayer, when he reviewed res gestae cases in 1881.[4] Thayer reported what he considered to be a longstanding rule of admissibility which grew out of the res gestae concept:

> The exception to the hearsay rule which is now mentioned takes notice of one of these strong elements of authenticity, contemporaneousness; it deals, however, not with memoranda signed by the parties, but with statements, oral or written, made by those present when a thing took place, made about it, and importing what is present at the very time,—present, either in itself or in some fresh indications of it, to the faculties of the witness as well as of the declarant.
>
>   *   *   *
>
> The leading notion in the doctrine * * * seems to have been that of withdrawing from the operation of the hearsay rule declarations of fact which were very near in time to that which they tended to prove, fill out, or illustrate,—being at the same time not narrative, but importing what was then present or but just gone by, and so was open, either immediately or in the indications of it, to the observation of the witness who testifies to the declaration, and who can be cross-examined as to these indications. Thayer, Bedingfield's Case—Declarations as a Part of the Res Gesta, (Part III) 15 Am.L.Rev. 71, 83, 107 (1881).[5]

However, one of Thayer's most influential students, Dean Wigmore, in his 1904 evidence treatise refused to recognize the present sense impression exception, claiming that contemporaneousness of event and

troublesome expression owes its existence and persistence in our law of evidence to an inclination of judges and lawyers to avoid the toilsome exertion of exact analysis and precise thinking."); Thayer, Bedingfield's Case—Declarations as a Part of the Res Gesta, (Part II) 15 Am.L.Rev. 1, 10 (1881) ("[P]hrase did * * * what a 'catch-all' does for a busy housekeeper or an untidy one—some things belonged there, other things might, for purposes of present convenience, be put there."); United States v. Matot, 146 F.2d 197, 198 (2d Cir.1944) ("[A]s for 'res gestae' * * * if it means anything but an unwillingness to think at all, what it covers cannot be put in less intelligible terms.") (L. Hand, J.).

4. The case most commonly cited to illustrate the recognition of the exception is Houston Oxygen Co. v. Davis, 139 Tex. 1, 161 S.W.2d 474 (Tex.Comm'n App.1942, Op.Adopted). See McCormick on Evidence § 298, at 861 (3d ed. E. Cleary 1984). In *Houston Oxygen*, the Texas Supreme Court held it was error to exclude testimony of a witness that when plaintiff's car passed her about four miles before the traffic accident, the witness said that "they must have been drunk, that we would find them somewhere on the road wrecked if they kept that rate of speed up."

5. In response to the furor in the English press to the case of *Regina v. Bedingfield,* [no official cite], Thayer wrote his article in order to place the doctrine of res gesta or res gestae "in a more intelligible shape." Thayer, Bedingfield's Case—Declarations as a Part of the Res Gesta, (Part I) 14 Am.L.Rev. 817 (1880). In the Bedingfield case, the defendant was charged with the murder of his mistress. As reported in The London Times, Bedingfield had gone into a room where the victim was, and "in a minute or two," the victim emerged from the room with her throat slashed. The victim, "bleeding very much, and seeming very much frightened," said to a witness, "Oh, aunt, see what Bedingfield has done to me." Lord Chief Justice Cockburn refused to admit the evidence at trial, stating it was not part of the res gestae, "for it was not part of anything done, or something said while something was being done, but something said after something done." The defendant was nevertheless convicted of the murder without the evidence, but the Justice's ruling precipitated a controversy that was to assist in the development in this area of the law of evidence.

descriptive statement, without more, did not guarantee the statement's trustworthiness.

Thayer's formulation of the present sense impression exception was revived by Edmund Morgan. Professor Morgan pointed out:

> A statement by a person as to external events then and there being perceived by his senses is worthy of credence for two reasons. First, it is in essence a declaration of a presently existing state of mind, for it is nothing more than an assertion of his presently existing sense impressions. As such it has the quality of spontaneity * * *. Second, since the statement is contemporaneous with the event, it is made at the place of the event. Consequently the event is open to perception by the senses of the person to whom the declaration is made and by whom it is usually reported on the witness stand. The witness is subject to cross-examination concerning that event as well as the fact and content of the utterance, so that the extra-judicial statement does not depend solely upon the credit of the declarant.

Currently, a present sense impression is excepted from the operation of the hearsay rule by the Federal Rules of Evidence, and by a majority of states. Additionally, this exception is recognized by the Model Code of Evidence, Rule 512(a), and by the Uniform Rules of Evidence (1974), Rule 803(1). Fed.R.Evid. 803(1) provides:

> The following are not excluded by the hearsay rule, even though the declarant is available as a witness:
>
> (1) *Present sense impression.* A statement describing or explaining an event or condition made while the declarant was perceiving the event or condition, or immediately thereafter.

The underlying theory of this exception is that "substantial contemporaneity of event and statement negative the likelihood of deliberate or conscious misrepresentation." Advisory Committee Note, Fed.R. Evid. 803(1). The Note further states that "in many, if not most, instances precise contemporaneity is not possible, and hence a slight lapse is allowable." Although the Note does not state that the witness must be the declarant, it indicates that "if the witness is not the declarant, he may be examined as to the circumstances as an aid in evaluating the statement." Finally, the Note limits the permissible subject matter under the exception to a "description or explanation of the event or condition, the assumption being that spontaneity, in the absence of a startling event, may extend no farther."

At least twenty-eight states recognize this exception to the hearsay rule in their codified evidence codes, most of which have been patterned after the Federal Rules of Evidence. Colorado's rule requires precise contemporaneity and deletes the words "or immediately thereafter" found in the Federal Rule. Florida and Ohio add language that a present sense impression is admissible unless the statement is made under circumstances that indicate its lack of trustworthiness. The Ohio Staff Note explains that the additional language serves to narrow the availability of the exception by vesting discretion in the trial judge.

Most commentators, with the notable exception of Dean Wigmore, recognize the present sense impression exception. The exception was approved in McCormick on Evidence § 298, at 860 (3d ed. E. Cleary 1984):

> Although [present sense impression] statements lack whatever assurance of reliability there is in the effect of an exciting event, other factors offer safeguards. First, since the report concerns observations being made at the time of the statement it is safe from any error caused by a defect of the declarant's memory. Second, a requirement that the statement be made contemporaneously with the observation means that there will be little or no time for calculated misstatement. Third, the statement will usually have been made to a third person (the witness who subsequently testifies to it) who, being present at the time and scene of the observation, will probably have an opportunity to observe the situation himself and thus provide a check on the accuracy of the declarant's statement, i.e. furnish corroboration. Moreover, since the declarant himself will often be available for cross-examination, his credibility will be subject to substantial verification before the trier of fact. (Footnotes omitted.)

In J. Weinstein & M. Berger, Weinstein's Evidence paragraph 803(1)[01] (1985), the Federal Rule was explained as follows:

> Underlying Rule 803(1) is the assumption that statements of perception substantially contemporaneous with an event are highly trustworthy because:
>
>> (1) the statement being simultaneous with the event, there is no memory problem; (2) there is little or no time for calculated misstatement, and (3) the statement is usually made to one who has equal opportunity to observe and check misstatements.
>
> This exception has been viewed with favor by those who fear that excitement—such as that required by the excited utterance exception—operates to impair the accuracy of perception. The exception is useful in admitting statements uttered minutes before the event in question and before the declarant was aware that something startling was about to happen. (Footnotes omitted.)

* * *

As observed by the Advisory Committee to the Federal Rules, the "excited utterance" and "present sense impression" exceptions "overlap, though based on somewhat different theories." Advisory Committee Note, Fed.R.Evid. 803(1). The underlying rationale of the two exceptions are similar, i.e., both preserve the benefit of spontaneity in the narrow span of time before a declarant has an opportunity to reflect and fabricate. We conclude that the "present sense impression" exception to the hearsay rule rests upon a firm foundation of trustworthiness, and we adopt it in the form in which it appears at Fed.R.Evid. 803(1).

We turn to a consideration of practical problems that may be encountered in the application of this exception. Initially, we consider the question of requisite spontaneity. Although statements offered under this exception will usually be those made at the time an event is being perceived, we recognize that precise contemporaneity is not always possible, and at times there may be a slight delay in converting observations into speech. However, because the presumed reliability of a statement of present sense impression flows from the fact of spontaneity, the time interval between observation and utterance must be very short. The appropriate inquiry is whether, considering the surrounding circumstances, sufficient time elapsed to have permitted reflective thought. In the words of Professor Jon Waltz, "absent some special corroborative circumstance, there should be no delay beyond an acceptable hiatus between perception and the cerebellum's construction of an uncalculated verbal description." Waltz, The Present Sense Impression Exception to the Rule Against Hearsay: Origins and Attributes, 66 Iowa L.Rev. 869, 880 (1981).

Next, we consider the extent to which there must be proof that the declarant is speaking from personal knowledge before the statement may be admitted. Although the declarant need not have been a participant in the perceived event, it is clear that the declarant must speak from personal knowledge, i.e., the declarant's own sensory perceptions. The more difficult question involves the quantity and quality of evidence required to demonstrate the existence of the requisite personal knowledge. We conclude that in some instances the content of the statement may itself be sufficient to demonstrate that it is more likely than not the product of personal perception, and in other instances extrinsic evidence may be required to satisfy this threshold requirement of admissibility.[6] Identification of the declarant, while often helpful in establishing that he or she was a percipient witness, is not a condition of admissibility. When the statement itself, or other circumstantial evidence demonstrates the percipiency of a declarant, whether identified or unidentified, this condition of competency is met.

An additional problem often encountered in the consideration of this exception to the hearsay rule is the tendency of a spontaneous declarant to characterize that which is being observed in language that involves, or often appears to involve, the opinion of the speaker.
*   *   *

We concur generally with the views expressed by Professor Jon Waltz:

> The indiscriminate generalization is often made that spontaneous utterances, excited or otherwise, in the form of an opinion or conclusion are inadmissible. This generalization has been branded "absurd" by Morgan and it assuredly wants more careful analysis than it has gotten in the past.

6. Because the question of admissibility is solely for the court, testimony otherwise inadmissible, including reasonably reliable hearsay, may be received out of the presence of the jury for the purpose of determining whether the declarant spoke from personal knowledge.

It is useful to contrast, on one hand, contemporaneous declarations cast in the form of a conclusion and, on the other, later direct in-court testimony that is conclusory in form. In-court opinion testimony has been disfavored, although less so under the Federal Rules of Evidence than before, because it is often the speculative hindsight of one who, having been summoned as a witness in a litigated dispute, is obviously aware of the existence of the litigation and who has had ample time and perhaps identifiable motive to reflect and concoct. Except when backward-looking narrations of in-court witnesses are the inescapable shorthand of one who is attempting, as best he can, to reconstruct and articulate observed facts, they represent a choosing of sides by the witness and are to be excluded from evidence not so much because they "invade the province of the jury," as once was the standard judicial response, as because they simply are not helpful to the factfinder and may be positively confusing. The situation is similar, and induces a like judicial response, when an out-of-court declarant has made a backward-looking characterization of events, especially when it has not been demonstrated that he was himself an observer of those events.

However, these situations are markedly different from the situation in which a percipient observer has made a contemporaneous statement in conclusory form * * * If the out-of-court declaration is not the sort of conscious deduction which the conditions attaching to the present sense impression exception would themselves prohibit, it should be receivable as a shorthand fact description. Waltz, supra, 66 Iowa L.Rev. at 881–82 (footnotes omitted).

Finally, there is the difficult question of whether a present sense impression must be corroborated by an independent and equally percipient observer. Examination of the Federal Rule reveals that nothing in the language of the rule purports to require corroboration. Furthermore, as pointed out by several commentators, the drafters of the Federal Rules knew how to word a requirement of corroboration, and did not do so.

The federal and state courts are not in accord as to whether corroboration is required for admission of a statement. In the case most often cited on this question, Houston Oxygen Co. v. Davis, 139 Tex. 1, reliance was placed on the fact that "the statement will usually be made to another (the witness who reports it) who would have equal opportunities to observe and hence to check a misstatement."

Since *Houston Oxygen*, some courts have rejected the contention that there must be corroboration by witnesses who were in the same position to observe the described event. Others have considered corroboration of an equally percipient witness a factor in guaranteeing the trustworthiness of a statement. At least two courts have refused to admit statements of present sense impression that were not corroborated.

Professor Waltz, in tracing the development of the present sense impression exception from Thayer's article to the present, concluded:

> [I]t will be recognized that Thayer never insisted on corroboration by an equally percipient witness. He certainly did not insist on it when the declarant was the in-court narrator of his own out-of-court declaration and, although Thayer did not address the point, he might not have insisted on it in those uncommon instances in which the out-of-court declarant is available but is not produced in court by the proponent of his declaration. And Thayer did not insist that an in-court witness serving as a testimonial conduit for an out-of-court sense impression declaration must have perceived everything which was apparently open to the declarant's faculties. Thayer believed in the pebble-in-the-pond principle. Every consequential act, like the stone thrown into water, produces ripples which extend outward after the stone has sunk from sight. These are the "fresh indications" of the event to which Thayer repeatedly referred in sketching the content of anticipated corroboration. * * * [T]estimony attesting the existence of the corroborating ripples generated by the event, of that event's surrounding circumstances, may occasionally be adequately supplied by someone other than the witness who heard and transmits to the factfinder the sense impression which described the event.

Waltz, supra, 66 Iowa L.Rev. at 898 (footnotes omitted).

* * *

We reject the contention that corroboration by an equally percipient witness is required as a condition to the admissibility of a statement of present sense impression. As we have noted, extrinsic evidence may sometimes be required to demonstrate the contemporaneity of the statement, or to show that it is the product of personal perception by the declarant. Accordingly, it may be correct in a particular case to say that "corroboration" is required, but this does not mean that corroboration is required in every instance, or that the corroboration must be that of an equally percipient witness. Even when not required for admissibility, corroboration (or the lack thereof) may be important in determining the weight to be given the statement.

* * *

The content of the statement with which we are concerned in this case, at least when coupled with the evidence of what Harrison heard in the background, offered sufficient evidence that Ross was describing events he was personally witnessing, and that his description of those events was being given contemporaneously with their occurrence. There were no extrinsic circumstances indicating to the contrary. After directing the excision of that part of the statement which apparently represented a recitation of earlier events, the trial judge properly admitted the balance of the statement pursuant to the present sense impression exception to the hearsay rule.

Affirmed.

LIRA v. ALBERT EINSTEIN MEDICAL CENTER

Superior Court of Pennsylvania, 1989.
384 Pa.Super. 503, 559 A.2d 550.

WIEAND, Judge:

In this medical malpractice action, the trial court awarded a new trial on motion of the defendant-health care providers because of an erroneous evidentiary ruling which permitted a witness to testify that when the plaintiff-patient was examined by a non-testifying physician, the physician asked, "Who's the butcher who [did] this?" On appeal, the plaintiffs argue that the physician's declaration was properly received and did not warrant a new trial. * * * We affirm the order awarding a new trial.

[Plaintiffs Jose and Bonnie Lira alleged that plaintiff Bonnie Lira was injured while one of the defendants was inserting a nasogastric tube into her throat. The jury returned a verdict for the plaintiffs. Dr. Silberman, whose out-of-court statement is described in the following excerpt, was not a party to the lawsuit.]

When Jose Lira was called as a witness, he testified as follows:

[MR. LIRA]: I remember the day I take my wife to see [Dr. Silberman], and we wait like everybody else; and as our turn to sit there and see what's wrong, he put my wife in the chair—

[PLAINTIFF'S COUNSEL]: Were you in the room with your wife with the doctor?

[MR. LIRA]: I was with my wife in the room, yes, I was.

[PLAINTIFF'S COUNSEL]: And tell us what you observed.

[MR. LIRA]: My wife was following the instructions from the doctor, open your mouth, and the doctor is looking inside with some kind of instruments and lights, and he said: Who's the butcher who do this!

[DEFENSE COUNSEL]: Objection, Your Honor. In fact, I move for a mistrial with that statement, Your Honor.

THE COURT: Overruled.

Dr. Silberman was not present in court and did not testify. During closing argument to the jury, plaintiff's counsel referred to Lira's testimony, saying: "You will remember that Dr. Silberman examined her throat and asked Bonnie Lira, 'Who butchered you?'" A defense objection to the argument by plaintiff's counsel was sustained, and the jury was told that the testimony "was not proper testimony for you to consider." A motion for mistrial, however, was denied. In response to a defense motion for new trial, the trial court, with commendable candor, determined that its evidentiary ruling had been erroneous and, despite the subsequent sustaining of a defense objection to a reference to the testimony by plaintiff's counsel, may have contributed to the verdict. Therefore, a new trial was awarded. Plaintiffs argue on appeal that the physician's declaration was admissible as an excited utterance or present sense impression exception to the hearsay rule. We disagree.

Dr. Silberman's statement was clearly hearsay. It was an extrajudicial statement offered to prove the truth of the matter asserted, i.e., that Mrs. Lira had been "butchered." Hearsay evidence is inadmissible unless it falls within a recognized exception to the exclusionary rule. Even if it falls within an exception to the rule, however, hearsay evidence may not be received unless it is relevant and not excluded under another rule of evidence.

Appellants contend that Dr. Silberman's declaration was admissible under the "res gestae" exception. More specifically, they argue that it was admissible as an excited utterance or a present sense impression. An excited utterance is a spontaneous declaration by a person whose mind has been suddenly made subject to an overpowering emotion caused by some unexpected and shocking occurrence. When Dr. Silberman, an ear, nose and throat specialist, examined a patient who was complaining of a sore throat and difficulty in breathing, it cannot be said that his discovery of a throat abnormality was a shocking occurrence causing the specialist to be overcome with emotion. Dr. Silberman's declaration in this case simply was not an excited utterance.

Similarly, Dr. Silberman's extrajudicial declaration was not admissible as a present sense impression.

> Under this exception the necessity for the presence of a startling occurrence or accident to serve as a source of reliability is not required. The truthfulness of the utterance is dependent upon its spontaneity. It must be certain from the circumstances that the utterance is a reflex product of immediate sensual impressions, unaided by retrospective mental processes. Restated, the utterance must be "instinctive, rather than deliberate."

Commonwealth v. Farquharson, 467 Pa. 50, 68, 354 A.2d 545, 554 (1976), citing Commonwealth v. Coleman, 458 Pa. 112, 117, 326 A.2d 387, 389 (1974). Here, the evidence failed to establish that the declaration of Dr. Silberman, a throat specialist, was "instinctive, rather than deliberative—in short, the reflex product of immediate sensual impressions, unaided by retrospective mental action." Commonwealth v. Coleman, supra. It was, rather, an expression of opinion based on medical training and experience.

To permit a physician's extrajudicial statement of medical opinion, made upon examination of a patient, to be received in evidence as an excited utterance or under the present sense impression exception to the hearsay rule would run afoul not only of the hearsay exclusion but also of the rule which holds that expressions of medical opinion are generally inadmissible unless the physician expressing the opinion is available for cross-examination. In Ganster v. Western Pennsylvania Water Co., 349 Pa.Super. 561, 504 A.2d 186 (1985), the Superior Court said, in holding that the business records exception to the hearsay rule did not encompass opinion testimony:

"Cross-examination," it has been said, "is a vital and fundamental part of a fair trial." Commonwealth v. Shirey, 333 Pa.
Super. 85, 151, 481 A.2d 1314, 1350 (1984). Although the right
of cross-examination is not absolute and although hearsay
evidence may be received upon proof of exceptional circumstances, including factual evidence received under the business
records in evidence exception, cross-examination is particularly
important where it is the only means for testing the reliability
of an opinion regarding disputed facts.

Id. 349 Pa.Super. at 573, 504 A.2d at 192.

Affirmed.

STATE v. JONES

Court of Appeals of Maryland, 1987.
311 Md. 23, 532 A.2d 169.

McAULIFFE, Judge.

A motorist testified that she had been sexually assaulted by a state
trooper who stopped her for operating a vehicle without a tail light.
The state trooper adamantly denied the charge. The deciding factor in
the resolution of this dispute may well have been the hearsay statements of two unknown individuals heard over channel 19 of a citizens
band radio. Our task is to decide whether the trial judge erred in
admitting evidence of the statements.

At about 11 p.m. on October 15, 1983, Trooper First Class Jeffrey
Jones of the Maryland State Police stopped a southbound 1972 Ford
Pinto on Interstate Route 95, north of the Maryland House rest stop in
Harford County. The stop was made because Trooper Jones could not
determine whether the vehicle was displaying a rear license plate—a
condition, it later turned out, that was caused by a short circuit in the
tail [*sic*; tag?] light.

It is undisputed that Trooper Jones spoke with the female operator
of the Pinto, and with her male friend, Willie Hooks, who was the
owner of the vehicle and seated in the front passenger seat, and that at
some point in time the female was seated in the trooper's cruiser. Why
she entered the police cruiser, and what happened while she was there
and shortly thereafter are facts sharply in dispute.

The complainant testified that Jones directed her to enter the
cruiser to discuss his contention that she was operating in violation of
the conditions of her New Jersey learner's permit. She said Jones told
her she could drive only if accompanied by a New Jersey licensed
driver, and because Hooks was licensed only in New York she was
violating the law. She further related that Jones then said he would
have to search her, and after handcuffing her put his hands in her
pockets, unbuckled her belt, unzipped her jeans and pulled them down,
and accomplished digital penetration after placing his hands under her
panties. When she protested, he released her and she returned to the
Pinto. She instructed Hooks, who was now behind the wheel, to obtain
the trooper's tag number. At that point, however, the police cruiser

left at a high rate of speed and without lights. Hooks gave chase, having observed that the complainant's belt buckle was loose and her jeans unzipped, and having learned from her that the officer "messed with her." According to the complainant and Hooks, their Pinto was no match for the police cruiser, and although they achieved speeds up to 70–80 miles per hour as they passed the Maryland House, they were never able to catch up to the cruiser. They then stopped at the first roadside emergency phone and reported the incident to the police. According to the complainant, she did not receive a summons or a warning ticket from Jones.

Jones testified that the complainant approached and entered his cruiser on her own initiative, while he was writing a warning ticket. He said she became upset when he explained that Hooks would have to drive the Pinto. He denied any physical contact with her, except to return her permit and to hand her a warning ticket.[1] Concerning his departure from the scene, Jones said he followed the Pinto into traffic and eventually passed it. He denied operating his vehicle without headlights.

Officer Kenneth Kinesman of the Maryland Toll Facility Police testified that at 11:30 p.m. on the night in question, he was dispatched to an emergency call box on the Harbor Tunnel Thruway, where he met the complainant and Hooks. He described the complainant as agitated, distraught, excited, and upset, and related her complaint that she had been "assaulted by a cop" on Interstate 95, north of the Maryland House. Officer Kinesman confirmed that the emergency call box used by the complainant was the first one available to southbound traffic after passing the Maryland House.

The evidence in controversy is that given by Trooper First Class William Byrd. It involves CB radio transmissions that Trooper Byrd said he heard while in his police cruiser at the Maryland House on the night in question, at some time between 11:00 and 11:30 p.m. To determine admissibility of the proffered evidence, Judge Brodnax Cameron, Jr. conducted a hearing out of the presence of the jury. At the hearing, Trooper Byrd testified he was monitoring channel 19 when he heard consecutive radio transmissions by persons he assumed were truckers. The two transmissions were:

1st Speaker: Look at Smokey Bear southbound with no lights on at a high rate of speed.

2nd Speaker: Look at that little car trying to catch up with him.

Trooper Byrd explained that among truckers and other citizens band radio aficionados "Smokey Bear" means a state trooper. Judge Cameron admitted the testimony, acknowledging that it was hearsay, but holding it was admissible under the present sense impression exception to the hearsay rule.[3] Jones was convicted of a third degree

1. During the course of a subsequent investigation, Jones produced a copy of the warning ticket he said he issued to the complainant. The ticket was not signed by Jones or the complainant, an omission that Jones said represented an oversight on his part.

3. Judge Cameron noted in passing that the "man-bites-dog" character of a small

sexual offense, battery, and misconduct in office. He was given a
sentence of two years imprisonment, of which 90 days was to be served
and the balance suspended. He appealed, and the Court of Special
Appeals reversed, Jones v. State, 65 Md.App. 121, 499 A.2d 511 (1985).
Shortly thereafter, we decided Booth v. State, 306 Md. 313, 508 A.2d
976 (1986), discussing and approving the present sense impression
exception to the hearsay rule. We granted certiorari in this case to
consider the admissibility of the evidence in the light of *Booth.*

The principal reasons assigned by the Court of Special Appeals for
the rejection of the evidence were the absence of an equally percipient
witness to furnish corroboration and the absence of evidence sufficient
to show the relevance of the statements. We address separately these
and the other issues generated by this appeal.

Variance In Testimony

At a bench conference requested by Respondent's counsel as Trooper Byrd was being called to the stand, the trial judge was informed that
the State would attempt to elicit testimony concerning the statements
heard on the CB radio. Respondent's counsel objected to any reference
being made to the statements in the presence of the jury, and Judge
Cameron agreed to excuse the jury when the testimony of Trooper Byrd
reached that point. Consistent with this understanding, Trooper Byrd's
initial testimony concerning the statements was given out of the
presence of the jury. Following that testimony, and following argument by both counsel, Judge Cameron ruled the statements admissible,
and the jury was recalled. As Jones points out, Trooper Byrd's testimony before the jury differed in some respects from that given before the
judge. In first describing the statements he heard, Trooper Byrd cast
them in the language of each declarant: "Look at Smokey Bear
southbound with no lights on at a high rate of speed." "Look at that
little car trying to catch up with him." Before the jury, Trooper Byrd
cast his testimony in the narrative form:

> On the CB radio in the state police car, Channel 19, I
> overheard a trucker on the CB said [sic] that it was Smokey the
> Bear southbound in a police car with no lights on and right
> after that . . . another trucker on Channel 19 advised that
> there was a little car just took off behind Smokey the Bear
> trying to catch him at a high rate of speed.

Because the content of a statement may contain the requisite evidence
of spontaneity, or of the fact that the statement is the product of
personal perception by the declarant, *Booth,* supra, 306 Md. at 330, 508
A.2d 976, the wording of the statement may be important. Here, the
statements in the form first related by Trooper Byrd are self-evidently
spontaneous. However, the statements as related to the jury, at least

civilian car chasing after a police car operating without headlights was the kind of
startling event normally associated with
the excited utterance exception to the
hearsay rule. His holding, however, was
grounded on the present sense impression
exception, there being no evidence that the
declarants spoke under the influence of
excitement.

when standing alone, give rise to questions concerning their spontaneity.[4]

The record discloses that Judge Cameron ruled on the admissibility of the statements based upon the initial testimony of Trooper Byrd. After the jury was recalled, and Trooper Byrd was asked to recount what he had heard, Respondent's counsel interposed a timely objection. However, counsel did not make any additional objection, or move to strike the answer, when Trooper Byrd gave what Respondent now suggests was a different version of the statements. Thus, Judge Cameron was given an opportunity to rule only on the basis of the testimony presented to him. He was never given an opportunity to determine whether the change in language would affect his ruling on admissibility. Nor was the prosecutor given an opportunity to inquire through further questioning whether the change in language reflected simply a different method of presenting the same information, or represented a change in Trooper Byrd's recollection of what had occurred. Although Respondent's counsel has fully preserved for review the question of admissibility based upon the testimony given at the hearing, he has not preserved any question concerning the possible legal effect of the change in words used to recount the statements.

Contemporaneousness

In Booth v. State, supra, 306 Md. at 324, 508 A.2d 976, we discussed the requirement that a statement of present sense impression be essentially contemporaneous with the event it describes:

> [B]ecause the presumed reliability of a statement of present sense impression flows from the fact of spontaneity, the time interval between observation and utterance must be very short. The appropriate inquiry is whether, considering the surrounding circumstances, sufficient time elapsed to have permitted reflective thought. See McCormick on Evidence § 298, at 862 (3d ed. E. Cleary 1984). In the words of Professor Jon Waltz, "absent some special corroborative circumstance, there should be no delay beyond an acceptable hiatus between perception and the cerebellum's construction of an uncalculated verbal description." Waltz, The Present Sense Impression Exception to the Rule Against Hearsay: Origins and Attributes, 66 Iowa L.Rev. 869, 880 (1981)

We also held that in some instances the content of the statement may furnish sufficient evidence of its spontaneity. Id. at 330–31, 508 A.2d 976. As conceded by Respondent's counsel at oral argument, the statements as related by Trooper Byrd to Judge Cameron are "self-evidently contemporaneous."

---

4. The State suggests that the second declarant's reference to the fact that "a little car just took off" furnishes sufficient evidence that the speaker was describing something almost immediately after he observed it, and that because of the content and chronology of the two statements, a finding that the second statement was essentially contemporaneous with the occurrence necessarily implies a similar finding for the first statement. We need not address that contention.

Personal Knowledge—Identity of Declarant

Jones contends, correctly, that the party offering the statement must show that the declarant spoke from personal knowledge. He also contends, incorrectly, that in every instance the identity of the declarant must be established. The contents of the two statements at issue in this case are sufficient to support the conclusion of the trial judge that the declarants spoke from first-hand knowledge. Additionally, we held in *Booth* that identification of the declarant is not an absolute prerequisite to introduction of the statement. What we said in *Booth* is dispositive of these issues:

> Although the declarant need not have been a participant in the perceived event, it is clear that the declarant must speak from personal knowledge, i.e., the declarant's own sensory perceptions. The more difficult question involves the quantity and quality of evidence required to demonstrate the existence of the requisite personal knowledge. We conclude that in some instances the content of the statement may itself be sufficient to demonstrate that it is more likely than not the product of personal perception, and in other instances extrinsic evidence may be required to satisfy this threshold requirement of admissibility. Identification of the declarant, while often helpful in establishing that he or she was a percipient witness, is not a condition of admissibility. When the statement itself, or other circumstantial evidence demonstrates the percipiency of a declarant, whether identified or unidentified, this condition of competency is met. 306 Md. at 324–25, 508 A.2d 976 (footnote omitted).

Corroboration

The question of corroboration, considered in the context of the present sense impression exception, ordinarily relates to proof of first-hand knowledge or spontaneity. We have rejected the contention that corroboration by an equally percipient witness is invariably required as a condition to the admissibility of such a statement, while at the same time noting that in some instances extrinsic evidence in the nature of corroboration may be required. *Booth,* supra, 306 Md. at 327–30, 508 A.2d 976. Respondent puts a different spin on the argument in this case, contending that corroboration should be required to show that the *witness* is being truthful in recounting what he says he heard. In support of his contention, Respondent cites the following language of the Court of Special Appeals in this case:

> To permit evidence such as that of Byrd would throw open the door to imaginative, if not fabricated, present sense declarations between unknowns. Cross-examination of those witnesses is almost guaranteed to test absolutely nothing. *Jones v. State,* supra, 65 Md.App. at 126–27, 499 A.2d 511.

We cannot be certain whether the concern of the intermediate appellate court was directed to the possibility of fabrication by unknown declarants, or the danger that the witness on the stand could falsely testify that such a statement was made without serious fear of detection of his perjury. If it was the former, we are satisfied that the inherent trustworthiness of a statement of perception given contemporaneously with the event being described is sufficient to outweigh that concern. If it is the latter, we are willing to place our trust in the efficacy of the oath and of cross-examination, as we do in the case of any other witness who is present and testifying. There is no absolute safeguard against lying. An officer who would testify that he heard something when he did not could as well testify that he saw something when he did not. Trooper Byrd was sworn and subject to cross-examination. Respondent was at liberty to develop any bias the witness may have had, and to show whether Trooper Byrd knew the details of the alleged assault before he recounted the statements he allegedly heard. He was at liberty to argue the dangers of fabrication and the absence of corroboration. The jury was at liberty to reject, or accept and give appropriate weight to, the testimony that the statements were made.

We reverse and remand to permit consideration of additional issues raised by Respondent but not reached by the Court of Special Appeals.

See Federal Rules of Evidence 803(1) & (2); California Evidence Code § 1240.

Hypotheticals

(1) A, a pedestrian, sues X for damages arising out of being struck by an automobile. X's defense is that he was in the curb lane in his red car and that a blue car passed him in the next lane, struck A, knocking her into the air and onto his red car, and then sped away. A calls B, an ambulance driver, and represents that B will testify that she arrived on the scene ten minutes after the accident, and saw A lying on the ground; that A appeared to be in great pain but not in shock; that B said to A, "Relax now, and take it easy;" and that A then said, "Oh, my God! Help me! That red car hit me while I was in the crosswalk." X makes a hearsay objection.

(2) Assume the same facts as in hypothetical (1). X calls C, a police officer, and represents that C will testify that she arrived at the scene five minutes after the accident occurred; that a number of people were gathered around A; and that she heard someone say, "That lady was hit by a blue car which didn't stop and she was thrown up in the air and landed on the red car," but doesn't know who made the statement. A makes a hearsay objection to C's proposed testimony.

(3) Prosecution of X for the kidnapping of and assault upon Y. Y suffered brain damage, and was hospitalized for seven weeks. W, Y's sister, testified that one week after Y came home from the hospital, W showed her a newspaper article containing a photograph of X. W testified that Y's "immediate reaction was one of great distress," and that Y "pointed to the picture and said very clearly, 'He killed me, he killed me.'" X objects that the statement is hearsay, and that it is not a spontaneous declaration because the startling event was the assault, which occurred eight weeks prior to the statement. What is the proper ruling on X's motion? See United States v. Napier, 518 F.2d 316 (9th Cir. 1975).

(4) Prosecution for the theft of a truck. A state trooper testifies that after receiving a radio report of an abandoned stolen truck, he appealed for information over his citizen's band ("CB") radio. A "CB'er" reported that he saw two men walking away from the point where the truck had been abandoned.

A second "CB'er" informed him that the two men were seen walking five to six miles east of the truck's location. The two men were arrested five miles away from the truck, a few minutes after the first CB statement. Should the first statement have been admitted? See United States v. Cain, 587 F.2d 678 (5th Cir. 1979).

3. ADMISSIONS

REED v. McCORD

Court of Appeals of New York, 1899.
160 N.Y. 330, 54 N.E. 737.

MARTIN, J. This action was to recover damages for personal injuries to the plaintiff's intestate which occasioned his death, and was based upon the alleged negligence of the defendant. * * *

The only remaining question is whether the statements of the defendant of the circumstances and cause of the accident to the plaintiff's intestate, made while a witness before the coroner, were competent and properly received. The defendant was called and sworn as a witness, and gave evidence as to the accident. Upon the trial of this action the official stenographer for the board of coroners was called and permitted, under the defendant's objection and exception, to testify that upon the hearing before the coroner the defendant gave evidence to the effect that all machines of the make of the one in use when the decedent was killed were alike; that at the time of the injury the dog of the machine was not in position, which caused the accident; and that "the man who had charge of it supposed the dog * was in position, and he released his hold on the thing, and it commenced to revolve, and then he got down so as to put his foot on it, and it was going so rapidly that it slipped past." It was admitted that the defendant was not present when the accident occurred, and hence, it is obvious that his statement before the coroner was not based upon his personal knowledge, but upon what he had learned as to the situation and how the accident occurred. The contention of the appellant is that, as his admissions were not based upon his personal knowledge, proof of them should have been excluded, and that his exception to their admission was well taken. The defendant being a party to this action, his admissions against his own interest were evidence in favor of his adversary, if of a fact material to the issue. If he had merely admitted that he heard that the accident occurred in the manner stated, it would have been inadmissible, as then it would only have amounted to an admission that he had heard the statement which he repeated, and not to an admission of the facts included in it. That would have been in no sense an admission of any fact pertinent to the issue, but a mere admission of what he had heard, without adoption or indorsement. Such evidence is clearly inadmissible. Stephens v. Vroman, 16 N.Y.

* A clamp or catch.

381. But the admissions proved in this case were not of that character. They were plain admissions of facts and circumstances which attended the intestate's injury. In a civil action the admissions by a party of any fact material to the issue are always competent evidence against him, wherever, whenever, or to whomsoever made. ＊ ＊ ＊ The theory upon which this class of evidence is held to be competent is that it is highly improbable that a party will admit or state anything against himself or against his own interest unless it is true. As the admissions testified to by the stenographer were of facts and circumstances which were material to the issue in this action, they were clearly competent, although not conclusive, evidence of the facts admitted. We find no error in the admission of this evidence, and, as no other questions are raised that we have jurisdiction to review, our conclusion is that the judgment should be affirmed. The judgment should be affirmed, with costs. All concur, except Parker, C. J., not voting, and O'Brien, J., dissenting. Judgment affirmed.

NOTE

The following quotation is from William Shakespeare's Othello, Act III, Sc. iii. The speaker is Iago.

＊ ＊ ＊ I lay with Cassio lately,

And being troubled with a raging tooth,

I could not sleep.

There are a kind of men so loose of soul,

That in their sleeps will mutter their affairs:

One of this kind is Cassio:

In sleep I heard him say 'Sweet Desdemona,

Let us be wary, let us hide our loves;'

An then, sir, would he gripe and wring my hand,

Cry 'O sweet creature!' and then kiss me hard,

As if he pluk'd up kisses by the roots,

That grew upon my lips: then laid his leg

Over my thigh, and sigh'd and kiss'd, and then

Cried 'Cursed fate that gave thee to the Moor!'

Is this "testimony" of Iago hearsay? Would it on any ground be admissible against Cassio? Or Desdemona? Is it relevant?

UNITED STATES v. HOOSIER

United States Court of Appeals, Sixth Circuit, 1976.
542 F.2d 687.

PER CURIAM.

Appellant seeks to overturn his jury conviction on one count of armed robbery of a federally insured bank. Four witnesses identified him, three of them positively, as the person who robbed the bank in Clarksville, Tennessee.

Another witness, Robert E. Rogers, testified that he had been with
the robbery defendant before and after the bank robbery, that before
the bank robbery defendant told him that he was going to rob a bank,
and that three weeks after the bank robbery, he saw defendant with
money and wearing what he thought were diamond rings, and that in
the presence of defendant, the defendant's girl friend said concerning
defendant's affluence at that point, "That ain't nothing, you should
have seen the money we had in the hotel room," and that she spoke of
"sacks of money." Although both defendant and his girl friend disputed these facts in their testimony, obviously the resolution of that fact
dispute was for the jury, and we must assume the jury resolved it in
favor of the government by its verdict of "guilty."

Appellant's sole appellate argument to this court, however, is that
the testimony elicited from the fifth witness concerning appellant's girl
friend's statement was inadmissible hearsay, and that it was reversible
error for the District Judge to fail to grant the objection to its admission.

Relevant to this issue is Rule 801(d)(2)(B) of the Federal Rules of
Evidence, which reads in applicable part:

> (2) Admission by party-opponent. The statement is of-
> fered against a party and is * * * (B) a statement of which
> he has manifested his adoption or belief in its truth, or * * *

The Advisory Committee's note concerning this rule is as follows:

> (B) Under established principles an admission may be
> made by adopting or acquiescing in the statement of another.
> While knowledge of contents would ordinarily be essential, this
> is not inevitably so: "X is a reliable person and knows what he
> is talking about." See McCormick § 246, p. 527, n. 15. Adop-
> tion or acquiescence may be manifested in any appropriate
> manner. When silence is relied upon, the theory is that the
> person would, under the circumstances, protest the statement
> made in his presence, if untrue. The decision in each case
> calls for an evaluation in terms of probable human behavior.
> In civil cases, the results have generally been satisfactory. In
> criminal cases, however, troublesome questions have been
> raised by decisions holding that failure to deny is an admission:
> the inference is a fairly weak one, to begin with; silence may
> be motivated by advice of counsel or realization that "anything
> you say may be used against you"; unusual opportunity is
> afforded to manufacture evidence; and encroachment upon the
> privilege against self-incrimination seems inescapably to be
> involved. However, recent decisions of the Supreme Court
> relating to custodial interrogation and the right to counsel
> appear to resolve these difficulties. Hence the rule contains no
> special provisions concerning failure to deny in criminal cases.

Fed.R.Evid. (2)(B), Advisory Committee's Notes (1975).

Our analysis of our present problem is made in the context of the
Advisory Committee note which is an appropriately guarded one.
First, we note that the statement was made in appellant's presence,

with only his girl friend and Rogers present. Since appellant had previously trusted Rogers sufficiently to tell him his plan to rob a bank, we see little likelihood that his silence in the face of these statements was due to "advice of counsel" or fear that anything he said might "be used against him." Under the total circumstances, we believe that probable human behavior would have been for appellant promptly to deny his girl friend's statement if it had not been true—particularly when it was said to a person to whom he had previously related a plan to rob a bank. While we agree with appellant's counsel that more is needed to justify admission of this statement than the mere presence and silence of the appellant, we observe that there was more in this record.

Finding no reversible error, the judgment of conviction is affirmed.

LA BUY, JURY INSTRUCTIONS IN FEDERAL CRIMINAL CASES

65 (1963).*

Section 6.15 Accusatory Statements

Evidence has been presented that statements accusing the defendant of the crime charged in the indictment were made in his presence, and that such statements were neither denied, nor objected to by him. If the jury finds that defendant actually heard and understood the accusatory statements, and that they were made under such circumstances that defendant would have denied them if they were not true, then the jury should consider whether defendant's silence was an admission of the truth of the statements. However, where defendant is under arrest, his silence in the face of accusatory statements does not in any way constitute an admission of the truth of the statements, nor create any inference of guilt.

THE GOSPEL ACCORDING TO LUKE **

" 'You are the Son of God, then?' they all said, and he replied, 'It is you who say I am.' They said, 'Need we call further witnesses? We have heard it ourselves from his own lips.'

"With that the whole assembly rose, and they brought him before Pilate. They opened the case against him by saying, 'We found this man subverting our nation, opposing the payment of taxes to Caesar, and claiming to be the Messiah, a king.' Pilate asked him, 'Are you the king of the Jews?' He replied, 'The words are yours.' "

ADMISSION BY SILENCE—ANOTHER VIEW

"In his funeral oration on Roscoe Conkling, Robert G. Ingersoll said: 'He was maligned, misrepresented and misunderstood, but he would not answer. He was as silent then as he is now—and his silence,

* 7th Cir. Judicial Conference, West Pub. Co., 1963.   ** *Luke*, 22:70–23:3; The New English Bible, 106–107 (1970).

better than any form of speech, refuted every charge.' George Bernard Shaw said: 'Silence is the most perfect expression of scorn.' " *

KAPLAN, OF MABRUS AND ZORGS
66 Cal.L.Rev. 987.
1002–03 (1978).

9. Prosecution of D for rape. Witness, W, wishes to testify that while he sat in a bar with D, the prosecutrix's father, F, entered, pointed at D and said: "You are the man who attacked my daughter," but that D made no reply.

Our black letter law is that when a party is accused of something in circumstances where, had he been innocent of the accusation, he would have denied it, his failure to make any denial is admissible as an admission. The jury must decide the preliminary fact questions so long, of course, as reasonable jurors could differ about them. Thus, whether the party heard the accusation, whether the circumstances were such that if it were untrue he would have been likely to deny it, and whether he did, in fact, deny it, are all issues for the jury.

It would seem, however, that the problem is somewhat more complex than this. Remember that in hypothetical 9, the jury passing on the admission by silence will have to hear not only evidence about the fact of silence and the surrounding circumstances, but it also must hear F's accusation as the necessary predicate for understanding what it is that D allegedly has admitted. Certainly, one can imagine situations where the jurors might decide that D had not heard the accusation or that he had denied it, but that the accusation itself, because of F's reliability, was nonetheless highly probative. In such a situation, they would, of course, ignore the judge's instructions that F's statement should not be considered for the truth of the fact it asserts, but only to show what D did or did not admit.[1]

Are we to conclude that our standard rules as to admission by silence are wrong and that the preliminary questions are to be decided by the judge rather than the jury? Not quite. There are indeed some admissions by silence which are—or at least should be—decided by the jury. Take the case where F's accusation is independently admissible as an exception to the hearsay rule. Let us say it is a spontaneous declaration or, should the jurisdiction's evidence rules permit, a contemporaneous statement. In these cases, the jury would be permitted to consider the hearsay accusation anyway, and hence, the admission by silence would carry no freight of inadmissible hearsay. In such a case, the jury could be trusted to apply the judge's instructions in its

---

* Commonwealth v. Dravecz, 424 Pa. 582, 585 n. 1, 227 A.2d 904, 906 n. 1 (1967).

1. It can be argued that if the jurors had nothing further to go on than the mere fact of accusation, it would be extremely unlikely that they would rely on its credibility and, hence, the jurors might, in such cases, be permitted to decide the preliminary fact question. This would be quite diffi- cult to determine in many cases, however, since the jury might make many inferences about the credibility of the accuser which were not strictly rational. As a result, the better rule in all such cases where the accusation would be inadmissible would be to have the judge determine the prelimina- ry facts before the jury could hear the evidence.

consideration of the significance of D's silence. So too, perhaps, where F has already testified about the facts giving rise to the accusation. Here, though the accusation itself is still hearsay, it is likely in most cases that the jury would not give it any independent weight, over and above F's testimony.

A somewhat more difficult question is presented by the cases where the admission by silence involves a failure to reply, not to an accusation, but to a question. Examine the next hypothetical:

> 10. Same as hypothetical 9 except that F asks: "Are you the man who attacked my daughter?"

Although D's failure to reply certainly might be an admission by silence, it is a close case whether the preliminary fact questions should be decided by the judge or the jury. One might argue that since the question is not itself a statement, the jury would not be tempted to rely on the credibility of the questioner. On the other hand, by singling out D to ask, F makes an implied assertion about the existence of some basis for the question. In any event, the question is a difficult one and I am prepared to overlook it here if the reader is as well.

STATE v. CARLSON

Supreme Court of Oregon, In Banc, 1991.
311 Or. 201, 808 P.2d 1002.

UNIS, Justice.

Defendant appeals from his convictions for unlawful possession of a controlled substance, methamphetamine, ORS 475.992(4), and endangering the welfare of a minor, ORS 163.575. * * *

FACTS

On August 3, 1988, Officer Lewis was dispatched to an apartment in response to a report of a domestic dispute between defendant and his wife, Lisa. On his arrival, Lewis was met by Lisa, whom he later described as having a "very white" complexion, looking tired, "fairly depressed," "distraught," and "at her wit's end," being occasionally tearful, and "coming down off of methamphetamine." Also present were the minor daughter of Lisa and defendant, and Lisa's sister and her minor daughter. Defendant was not in the apartment at that time.

Lewis asked Lisa if there were any methamphetamine in the apartment. She responded by saying that "he probably took it all, but go ahead and look around; I don't care anymore." During his search of the apartment, Lewis found traces of methamphetamine on a mirror in the master bedroom that defendant and Lisa shared.

About 15 to 20 minutes later, Lewis, accompanied by a second police officer, met defendant in the parking lot of the apartment complex. Lewis noticed what appeared to be needle marks on defendant's arms. Without first advising defendant of his constitutional rights, Lewis asked defendant about the needle marks. Defendant initially responded, "Yeah, I got a few tracks," and then said that the marks were injuries that he had received from working on a car. Lisa,

who was present during the exchange and close enough to hear what
was being said, broke in by yelling: "You liar, you got them from
shooting up in the bedroom with all your stupid friends." Defendant
"hung his head and shook his head back and forth."

[Over defendant's objection, the trial judge had admitted testimony
about Lisa Carlson's accusation and the defendant's reaction to it.

The court first considered defendant's argument that the evidence
of defendant's statements to the police officer should have been excluded because defendant was not advised of his *Miranda* rights. It
rejected this argument on grounds that the defendant was not in
custody at the time of the incident. The court then turned to the issue
whether Lisa Carlson's statement was inadmissible.]

The state first contends that Lewis' testimony about Lisa's accusatory statement ("[y]ou liar, you got [the marks on your arms] from
shooting up in the bedroom [where the methamphetamine was found]
with all your stupid friends") and defendant's nonverbal reaction thereto ("hung his head and shook his head back and forth") was properly
admitted in evidence as an "adoptive admission" under OEC 801(4)(b)
(B). Defendant responds that Lewis' testimony is inadmissible hearsay.
See OEC 802 (rule against admission of hearsay). He argues, in
essence, that his head shaking manifested his rejection, rather than his
adoption, of his wife's accusation.

A threshold question in this case is whether the intent to adopt,
agree or approve is a preliminary question of fact for the trial judge to
decide under OEC 104(1) or a question of conditional relevancy under
OEC 104(2).[a] * * *

Few courts have addressed the issue whether manifestation of an
adoption or a belief is a preliminary question of fact for the trial judge
under a provision comparable to OEC 104(1) or a question of conditional
relevancy under a provision comparable to OEC 104(2). Louisell &
Mueller, supra, at 294, § 424. Courts, scholars and commentators who
have spoken on the issue disagree on the answer. Some suggest that
the question is one of conditional relevancy. See, e.g., United States v.
Sears, 663 F.2d 896, 905 (9th Cir.1981), cert. den., 455 U.S. 1027, 102
S.Ct. 1731, 72 L.Ed.2d 148 (1982); United States v. Barletta, 652 F.2d
218, 219–20 (1st Cir.1981); Graham, Handbook of Federal Evidence 784,
§ 801.20 (3d ed 1991); McCormick, supra, at 799 n 14, § 269; but see id.
at 135–36, § 53 (author's language suggests adoption is a question for
the trial judge).

Others take the view that the issue is a preliminary question of
fact for the trial judge under the federal counterpart to OEC 104(1).
See, e.g., Wright & Graham, 21 Federal Practice and Procedure 260,
§ 5053 (judge determines issues including the admissibility of hearsay); McCormick, Evidence 527, § 246 (1954) (implicit in principles
stated); Garland & Schmitz, Of Judges and Juries: A Proposed

a. OEC 104(1) and 104(2) are identical
to Fed.R.Evid. 104(a) and 104(b) in all relevant respects.—Eds.

Revision of Federal Rule of Evidence 104, 23 UC Davis L Rev 77, 84 (1989).

For reasons that follow, we hold that whether the party intended to adopt, agree with or approve of the contents of the statement of another, a precondition to the admissibility of evidence offered under OEC 801(4)(b)(B), is a preliminary question of fact for the trial judge under OEC 104(1).

First, the wording of OEC 104(1) and the Legislative Commentary to that rule suggest that result. OEC 104(1) assigns to the trial judge the responsibility for making preliminary determinations regarding, inter alia, the "admissibility of evidence." Intent to adopt, agree or approve is a preliminary fact within the scope of OEC 104(1), because its proof concerns "the admissibility of evidence." * * *

Second, "[b]asically, Rule 104 divides the determination of preliminary facts between judge and jury along the rough line between 'competence' and 'relevance,' though it does not use this terminology." Wright and Graham, supra, at 259, § 5053. " 'Competency,' [in this context,] refers to whether evidence is admissible under one of the policy-based exclusionary rules [such as the rule against hearsay.]" Garland & Schmitz, supra, at 93. The intent to adopt, agree or approve involves a preliminary question of fact on which the competency, and thus the admissibility, of the evidence depends.

There exists an even more persuasive reason for holding that the predicate for admissibility of evidence under OEC 801(4)(b)(B) is an OEC 104(1) preliminary question of fact. The objection to admissibility, based on the rule against hearsay, furthers an important legal policy of preventing the trier of fact from considering the possible truthfulness of out-of-court statements, unless the statements have sufficient guarantees of trustworthiness. The purpose of the hearsay rule is to guard against the risks of misperception, misrecollection, misstatement, and insincerity, which are associated with statements of persons made out of court. Safeguards in the trial procedure, such as the immediate cross-examination of the witness and the opportunity of the trier of fact to observe the demeanor of the witness who swears or affirms under the penalty of perjury to tell the truth, are designed to reduce those risks.

There are several difficulties with leaving the question of intent to adopt, agree or approve to the jury as a question of conditional relevancy under OEC 104(2). If the OEC 104(2) conditional relevancy standard is employed, the legal policy underlying the hearsay rule would be furthered incompletely, if at all. The jury passing on the admission by conduct will have to hear not only evidence about the conduct and the surrounding circumstances, but also the out-of-court statement, as necessary predicates for understanding what the party allegedly adopted. For example, in the present case, the wife's accusatory statement to which defendant's nonverbal conduct is a response, would have to be admitted to give meaning to defendant's conduct, and the accusation is relevant to prove the truth of the accusation even though it may not be admissible for that purpose. A juror could (a) overlook the question of intent to adopt, agree or approve, and consider the truth of the matter asserted in the out-of-court statement, (b) use the out-of-court statement before considering and resolving the preliminary question of intent to adopt, agree or approve, or (c) consider the hearsay statement regardless of what conclusion is reached on the preliminary question of adoption or belief. See Garland & Schmitz, supra (pointing out these potential risks). If the evidence is inadmissible, i.e., the jury does not find the preliminary fact (intent to adopt, agree or approve) to exist, preventing jury contamination may prove impossible. Garland & Schmitz, supra, at 94. Additionally, a general verdict would not indicate the jury's resolution of whether intent to adopt existed. A record for appellate review would require a special set of preliminary jury findings.

In short, we believe that judicial intervention is required to prevent improper use of evidence. The preliminary question of intent to adopt, agree or approve, therefore, should be left to the trial judge under OEC 104(1).

In the present case, the preliminary question of fact for resolution by the trial judge under OEC 104(1) was whether the proponent of the evidence, the state, had established by a preponderance of the evidence (more likely than not) that defendant's nonverbal reaction to his wife's accusatory statement manifested defendant's intention to adopt, agree with or approve of the statement.

In the face of his wife's accusatory statement, defendant "hung his head and shook his head back and forth." Although the record discloses that Lewis twice demonstrated defendant's nonverbal reaction, it does not disclose whether defendant's shaking his head back and forth was positive or negative in character. Defendant essentially testified that he had not intended to adopt, agree with or approve of his wife's remarks and that he did not see any benefit in arguing with an irrational, mentally ill and angry woman.

Various factual hypotheses are suggested by defendant's ambiguous, nonverbal reaction. Head shaking back and forth generally means a negative reply. Village of New Hope v. Duplessie, 304 Minn. 417, 231 N.W.2d 548, 552 (1975) (quoting Bill v. Farm Bureau Ins. Co., 254 Iowa 1215, 119 N.W.2d 768, 773 (1963)). "[T]he lateral motion might * * * mean merely bewilderment or confusion, an 'I don't know' answer," id., a reluctance to engage in, or to continue, a dispute with his wife, a decision to stand mute in a situation that was intimidating by the presence of a police officer, or, as the state asserts in this case on appeal, an expression of dismay or resignation that his wife told the police the truth about how defendant obtained the needle marks on his arms.

We view the record consistent with the trial court's ruling on a preliminary question of fact under OEC 104(1), accepting reasonable inferences and reasonable credibility choices that the trial judge could have made. * * * In the circumstances of this case, defendant's nonverbal reaction is so ambiguous that it cannot reasonably be deemed sufficient to establish that any particular interpretation, consistent with the trial judge's ruling, is more probably correct. We hold, therefore, that there was insufficient evidence to support a finding by a preponderance of the evidence that defendant intended to adopt, agree with or approve the contents of his wife's accusatory statement. Accordingly, we hold that evidence of his wife's hearsay statement and defendant's nonverbal reaction thereto was not admissible under OEC 801(4)(b)(B).   *   *   *

[In the final part of its opinion, the court held Lisa Carlson's statement admissible as an excited utterance.]

Hypotheticals

(1) P sues D for damages for personal injuries arising out of an accident in which D was driving and P was a passenger. D testifies that as she was driving on an offramp of the freeway the throttle of her car stuck and she bent over to jiggle it loose; that as she bent over P reached through the steering wheel and blew the horn; that this so surprised her that she took her eyes off the road to look at P and the car then smashed into a telephone pole. P testifies that he never blew the horn or reached through the steering wheel. In an evidence-admissibility hearing before trial P makes an offer of proof as to an alleged admission made by D; that P and D had a conversation after P saw the police report for the first time; that the report contained D's statement about her leaning over and P's blowing the horn; that P made a telephone call to D and told her this was an untrue statement, and that D responded "Well, I did it because I was fearful over my insurance." D objects to P's offer of proof on grounds of hearsay. Should D's objection be sustained?

(2) A sues B for the price of goods sold to X Enterprises. A claims that B is a partner in X Enterprises. A testifies that, before he sold the goods to X Enterprises, he was at the X Enterprises office and X, the president, introduced him to B with the statement: "Meet my partner in X Enterprises, Ms. B," and that B then shook hands with A and said nothing. B moves to strike A's testimony as hearsay. What result?

McQUEENEY v. WILMINGTON TRUST COMPANY

United States Court of Appeals, Third Circuit, 1985.
779 F.2d 916.

BECKER, Circuit Judge.

This appeal by the owner and operator of a supertanker from a verdict in favor of plaintiff Francis McQueeney, a seaman aboard the vessel, presents * * * interesting questions in the law of evidence. The first, arising under Fed.R.Evid. 401 and 403, is whether evidence from which it might be inferred that McQueeney has suborned perjury of a proffered witness is admissible as substantive evidence that his claim is unfounded even though the witness never testified. * * * The district court excluded the evidence of subornation of perjury * * * but we conclude that it erred.

* * *

I. BACKGROUND

A. *Plaintiff's Accident, His Lawsuit, and the Deposition of Mauro De la Cerda.*

Appellee McQueeney was a second officer on the TT WILLIAMS-BURG, a supertanker owned by appellant Wilmington Trust Company and operated by Anndep Steamship Corporation. McQueeney claims that on March 20, 1981, while the WILLIAMSBURG was docked at Hounds Point, Scotland, he was knocked to the deck while manning a water hose. McQueeney asserts that his fall was caused by both overpressure of the hose and by oil that had been spilled on the deck, making firm footing impossible, and that as a result of his accident, he suffered a herniated cervical disc. He brought this suit in June, 1982 in the district court for the Eastern District of Pennsylvania. The district court conducted a jury trial at the end of which the jury awarded plaintiff a verdict of $305,788.00 against the two defendants. Judgment was entered in the same amount, and the defendants' motions for a new trial and for relief from the judgment were denied. The present appeal followed.

At trial, McQueeney was his only witness on the issue of liability. On the day the trial was scheduled to begin, however, McQueeney's counsel informed the court that he had just located an eyewitness to the accident, a fellow seaman of McQueeney's named Mauro De la Cerda, who was on board a ship in Freeport, Texas, and was therefore not able to appear as a witness. Counsel requested permission to depose De la Cerda.

The district court granted plaintiff's counsel permission to depose De la Cerda. * * * The appropriate arrangements were made, trial was recessed, and the next day De la Cerda was deposed in Houston. His testimony corroborated McQueeney's in all significant respects.

* * *

B. *Evidence of the Falsity of De la Cerda's Deposition, Plaintiff's Decision Not to Offer it, and the District Court's Ruling.*

The trial resumed, and McQueeney took the stand. His testimony lasted several days. During cross-examination, and after court had adjourned for the day, defense counsel received crew lists from his client. The lists reflected that De la Cerda had not joined the crew of the WILLIAMSBURG until three months after the alleged accident. The lists proved, therefore, that De la Cerda's "eyewitness" testimony that he had given at his deposition had been fabricated. The next morning, defense counsel brought this information to the attention of the court in a discussion in chambers. After reviewing the crew lists, plaintiff's counsel immediately stated his intention not to use the deposition.[1] Defense counsel rejoined that he intended to use the deposition to show fraud on the court. Plaintiff's counsel responded

---

1. Plaintiff's counsel also claimed that defendant had withheld the crew lists in- tentionally in order to hinder plaintiff's case.

that, so long as he was not using the deposition himself, and so long as there was no evidence that McQueeney had perjured himself on the stand, there had been no fraud and the deposition was irrelevant. The district court agreed with plaintiff's counsel and stated that it would not receive the deposition and the crew lists into evidence.

The district court did not articulate the basis for its ruling at trial. However, as appears from the colloquy at the time, the district court felt that so long as the deposition was not introduced by plaintiff, any perjury associated with the deposition was irrelevant to the suit at bar.[2] That this was the court's thinking is evident from its opinion denying defendants' post-trial motion for relief from the judgment or, in the alternative, a new trial. In support of the motion, defendants argued that it was reversible error to bar the deposition and crew lists, but the court ruled that the deposition and crew lists were either irrelevant or only minimally relevant.

* * *

[T]he court may fairly be said to have excluded the evidence as either irrelevant under Fed.R.Evid. 401, or as relevant but misleading or unfairly prejudicial, in accordance with Fed.R.Evid. 403.[3]

* * *

2. The colloquy was as follows:

MR. BARISH [plaintiff's counsel]: * * * I will just not use his deposition. It doesn't affect our case. We'll go in on the plaintiff's case.

THE COURT: All right.

MR. DOWNEY [defendant's counsel]: Well, I'm going to have to use the deposition to show a fraud upon the court.

MR. BARISH: By whom?

MR. DOWNEY: By the plaintiff's side of this case.

MR. BARISH: How can you say that?

MR. DOWNEY: Because you've produced a witness—sent me down to Texas last Friday to take a witness who saw an accident, and if my information is correct, the man perjured himself, there's no doubt about it, if he wasn't on that ship to say he saw an accident in March when he didn't join the ship until May. That's serious business, and as defense counsel in this case how can I not bring that to the jury's attention?

MR. BARISH: If I may, your Honor, I think that if what you are saying is accurate that's serious business.

MR. DOWNEY: Yes.

MR. BARISH: But it doesn't affect the plaintiff's case because the plaintiff hasn't perjured himself. And, quite frankly, all it means, as far as I'm concerned, is that I just won't use that deposition. Now there is nothing in that deposition—are you going to introduce into evidence a deposition that supports the plaintiff's case and then say he is not telling the truth?

MR. DOWNEY: Yes, to show a part of fraud.

THE COURT: Well, I'm not going to permit you to do that. I'm going to say to you that if this person perjured himself then we can do one of several things, one of which we can report it to the United States Attorney for perjury, for purposes of perjury, because it was done to influence the outcome of this case. I think that's the appropriate procedure. I don't think we are going to start introducing a document which you think is incorrect and intentionally incorrect in this case.

Now if it's introduced into this case by plaintiff's side then you can bring in the document showing, if you can, that the man wasn't on the ship at the time of the incident and could not have witnessed it, but we're not going to solve all the problems of the world in this case. If it is not brought in then I don't say it's an issue in this case for this jury to consider whether or not the plaintiff is involved. I don't know whether the plaintiff is involved in this matter. That's whose case we're trying. We're trying the plaintiff's case.

MR. DOWNEY: Yes, your Honor.

3. Rule 401 states

" 'Relevant evidence' means evidence having any tendency to make the existence of any fact that is of consequence to the determination of the action more

II. DEFENDANTS' PROFFER THAT MCQUEENEY HAD SUBORNED PERJURY

A. The Rule 401 Ruling

The stated purpose of defense counsel's proffer of De la Cerda's deposition, the crew lists for the date of the alleged accident, and defense counsel's own testimony about what De la Cerda had told him the night before the deposition, was to show that the plaintiff had suborned perjured testimony. Defense counsel intended to argue that plaintiff's subornation was evidence of his knowledge of the weakness of his case, and that such knowledge could be taken into account by the jury.

The district court's decision to exclude the evidence as irrelevant is governed by Fed.R.Evid. 401. We review that decision according to the abuse of discretion standard. See United States v. Steele, 685 F.2d 793, 808 (3d Cir.) (once the threshold of logical relevance is satisfied, "the matter is largely within the discretion of the trial court"), cert. denied, 459 U.S. 908 (1982). We believe that the district court abused its discretion in excluding the proffered evidence. We base our conclusion on common sense, eminent commentators, case law, and the explicit language of Rule 401.

The intuitive appeal of defendants' proffer is immediate. One who believes his own case to be weak is more likely to suborn perjury than one who thinks he has a strong case, and a party knows better than anyone else the truth about his own case. Thus, subornation of perjury by a party is strong evidence that the party's case is weak. Admittedly the conclusion is not inescapable: parties may be mistaken about the merits or force of their own cases. But evidence need not lead inescapably towards a single conclusion to be relevant, it need only make certain facts more probable than not. The evidence of subornation here does cast into doubt the merits of McQueeney's claim, even if it does not extinguish them.[4]

There is ample support among both scholars and courts for this line of argument. * * *

McCormick makes [the] point:

> [W]rongdoing by the party in connection with his case, amounting to an obstruction of justice[,] is also commonly regarded as an admission by conduct. By resorting to wrongful devices he is said to give ground for believing that he thinks his case is weak and not to be won by fair means. Accordingly, a party's false statement about the matter in litigation, whether before

probable or less probable than it would be without the evidence." Rule 403 provides

"Although relevant, evidence may be excluded if its probative value is substantially outweighed by the dangers of unfair prejudice, confusion of the issues, or misleading the jury * * *."

4. Obviously, the fact that McQueeney may demonstrate at trial that the crew lists were simply mistaken and that De la Cerda was in fact on board the ship, or that De la Cerda was mistaken or disoriented, or that he perjured himself without subornation by McQueeney, does not mean that defendants' proffer must be excluded.

suit or on the stand, his fabrication of false documents, his undue pressure, by bribery or intimidation or other means, to influence a witness to testify for him * * * all these are instances of this type of admission by conduct.

McCormick's Handbook on the Law of Evidence § 273 at 660 (2d ed. 1972).

This court has upheld the inference and admitted evidence accordingly. See Newark Stereotypers' Union v. Newark Morning Ledger, 397 F.2d 594, 599 (3d Cir.1968) ("an attempt by a litigant to persuade a witness not to testify is properly admissible against him as an indication of his own belief that his claim is weak or unfounded or false").

McQueeney points out that *Newark Stereotypers' Union* involved a party's subornation of perjured testimony from a witness who testified at trial, whereas in the case at bar De la Cerda's testimony was never introduced into evidence. This is correct, but it is a distinction of no consequence. Evidence of subornation of perjury is substantive evidence, not mere impeachment material; the inference that one may draw from the subornation does not depend upon anyone else's testimony. The fact that a party suborned perjury is what matters, not the ultimate success or failure of that subornation.

* * *

B. *The Rule 403 Balance*

That the evidence was relevant does not necessarily mean that it should have been admitted. As noted above, the district court, after voicing its doubts that the evidence had any relevance, ruled that even assuming it was relevant, the evidence should not have been admitted because its prejudicial impact would likely outweigh its probative value. This is a standard Fed.R.Evid. 403 balance which we review with substantial deference. Despite this deferential standard, we find that the district court erred, for it underestimated the probative value of the evidence, and misevaluated its prejudicial impact.

The district court assigned virtually no probative value to the evidence of subornation. It should be clear from what we said above, however, that evidence of subornation of perjury may be quite valuable to the defendant in this case. Intuition and the unanimity of the commentators and numerous courts that have considered it suggest not only that subornation of perjury is relevant but that it is powerful evidence indeed. Evidence that McQueeney suborned perjury might well have made the jurors re-evaluate McQueeney's case. Of course, it is not certain that McQueeney did suborn perjury; De la Cerda may have had other reasons for making up his story. But the circumstances of the case and the correlation between McQueeney's story and De la Cerda's deposition suggest that subornation of perjury by McQueeney is a possibility that the jury should have been allowed to consider.

By contrast, although the district court referred to potential confusion and "severe prejudice," and although there was danger of prejudice—the mere suggestion that McQueeney suborned perjury might have led the jury to reflect on his character in an improper manner—it is unlikely that the evidence would result in the "unfair prejudice" proscribed by Rule 403. * * * Moreover, it appears to us that the danger of improper influence was not sufficient to "substantially outweigh[ ]" the probative value of the evidence, as required by Fed.R.Evid. 403. The court did not articulate any reasons for its finding of prejudice, and this does not appear to us to be the kind of evidence with obvious or overwhelming potential for unfair prejudice. In the absence of a showing of particularized danger of unfair prejudice, the evidence must be admitted. Were we to rule otherwise, evidence could be excluded on an unfounded fear of prejudice and we would effectively preclude all evidence of subornation of perjury.[5]

In sum, the district court misconstrued both elements of the Rule 403 balance hence its balancing exercise was skewed. The court's Rule 403 ruling was thus an abuse of discretion.

[Reversed].

Question: Isn't the "statement" in *McQueeney* really a kind of non-assertive conduct? Only the fact that historically such conduct by a party was admissible as an admission at a time when non-assertive conduct was still regarded as hearsay makes it appropriate to treat it in this section.

LA BUY, JURY INSTRUCTIONS IN FEDERAL CRIMINAL CASES
63–64 (1963).*

Section 6.14 Exculpatory Statements

Evidence has been introduced that defendant made certain exculpatory statements outside of the courtroom explaining his actions to show that he was innocent of the crime charged in the indictment. Evidence contradicting such statements has also been introduced. If the jury finds that the exculpatory statements were untrue, and that the defendant made them voluntarily with knowledge of their falsity, the jury may consider the statements as circumstantial evidence of defendant's consciousness of guilt.

COKE, THIRD INSTITUTE, 1747

In the county of Warwick there were two brethren, the one having issue a daughter, and being seized of lands in fee devised the government of his daughter and his lands, until she came to her age of sixteen years, to his brother, and died. The uncle brought up his niece very well both at her book and needle, etc., and she was about eight or nine years of age: her uncle for some offence correcting her, she was heard to say, Oh good uncle kill me not. After which time the child after

---

5. The district court was also concerned that the evidence would confuse the jury because it would lead them to wonder about De la Cerda's integrity rather than about the subjects of the suit—whether McQueeney fell, for what reason, and what his damages were. However, the court could easily have instructed the jury on the limited purposes of the evidence, and thus have avoided any possible jury confusion.

* 7th Cir. Judicial Conference, West Pub. Co., 1963.

1 much inquiry, could not be heard of: whereupon the uncle being
2 suspected of the murder of her, the rather for that he was her next
3 heir, was upon examination committed to the gaol for suspicion of
4 murder, and was admonished by the justices of assise to find out the
5 child, and thereupon bailed him until the next assises. Against which
6 time, for that he could not find her, and fearing what would fall out
7 against him, took another child as like unto her both in person and
8 years as he could find, and apparelled her like unto the true child, and
9 brought her to the next assises, but upon view and examination, she
10 was found not to be the true child; and upon these presumptions he
11 was indicted and found guilty, had judgment, and was hanged. But the
12 truth of the case was, that the child being beaten over night, the next
13 morning when she should go to school, ran away into the next county;
14 and being well educated was received and entertained of a stranger:
15 and when she was sixteen years old, at what time she should come to
16 her land, she came to demand it, and was directly proved to be the true
17 child. Which case we have reported for a double caveat: first to judges,
18 that they in case of life judge not too hastily upon bare presumption:
19 and secondly, to the innocent and true man, that he never seek to
20 excuse himself by false or undue means, lest thereby he offending God
21 (the author of truth) overthrow himself, as the uncle did.

Hypotheticals

(1) P sues D, a physician, for damages for malpractice in failing to diagnose a lump in her breast as cancerous and thus allowing its spread into other parts of her body. At the trial, D admits negligence but denies that his negligence was a proximate cause of the spread of the cancer. P offers evidence that D destroyed his original records as to P and produced alleged copies only. D makes an irrelevancy objection, urging that his admission of negligence rendered any adverse inference from suppression of records irrelevant. What result?

(2) D, a physician, is charged with the offense of prescribing narcotics to persons not under treatment for a pathology. Various prescriptions written by D are admitted in evidence as exhibits at D's preliminary hearing. At D's trial, the prosecutor seeks to introduce evidence that during D's preliminary hearing, at D's request, the clerk permitted D to examine the exhibits; that the clerk subsequently discovered that the exhibits comprising the prescriptions were missing; that pieces of the prescriptions were subsequently found floating in a toilet bowl in the men's rest-room in the courthouse. D makes an irrelevancy objection to the prosecutor's proffered evidence, urging that such evidence is too speculative to prove that he took the exhibits. How should the court rule?

(3) D is charged with murder. The prosecutor offers evidence that just prior to his arrest D attempted to flee and conceal his identity. This evidence is offered as corroboration of the testimony of an accomplice, on the theory that such evidence constitutes proof of D's consciousness of guilt. D makes an irrelevancy objection, and offers to prove that the more plausible inference to be drawn from his attempted flight was his belief that a nonsupport warrant for his arrest was outstanding, that he was afraid of being arrested for narcotics hidden in his car, and also that he knew that he had violated his parole. What result?

MAHLANDT v. WILD CANID SURVIVAL & RESEARCH CENTER, INC.

United States Court of Appeals, Eighth Circuit, 1978.
588 F.2d 626.

VAN SICKLE, District Judge.

This is a civil action for damages arising out of an alleged attack by a wolf on a child. The sole issues on appeal are as to the correctness of three rulings which excluded conclusionary statements * * *. Two of them were made by a defendant, who was also an employee of the corporate defendant; and the third was in the form of a statement appearing in the records of a board meeting of the corporate defendant.

On March 23, 1973, Daniel Mahlandt, then 3 years, 10 months, and 8 days old, was sent by his mother to a neighbor's home on an adjoining street to get his older brother, Donald. Daniel's mother watched him cross the street, and then turned into the house to get her car keys. Daniel's path took him along a walkway adjacent to the Poos' residence. Next to the walkway was a five foot chain link fence to which Sophie had been chained with a six foot chain. In other words, Sophie was free to move in a half circle having a six foot radius on the side of the fence opposite from Daniel.

Sophie was a bitch wolf, 11 months and 28 days old, who had been born at the St. Louis Zoo, and kept there until she reached 6 months of age, at which time she was given to the Wild Canid Survival and Research Center, Inc. It was the policy of the Zoo to remove wolves from the Children's Zoo after they reached the age of 5 or 6 months. Sophie was supposed to be kept at the Tyson Research Center, but Kenneth Poos, as Director of Education for the Wild Canid Survival and Research Center, Inc., had been keeping her at his home because he was taking Sophie to schools and institutions where he showed films and gave programs with respect to the nature of wolves. Sophie was known as a very gentle wolf who had proved herself to be good natured and stable during her contacts with thousands of children, while she was in the St. Louis Children's Zoo.

* * *

A neighbor who was ill in bed in the second floor of his home heard a child's screams and went to his window, where he saw a boy lying on his back within the enclosure, with a wolf straddling him. The wolf's face was near Daniel's face, but the distance was so great that he could not see what the wolf was doing, and did not see any biting. Within about 15 seconds the neighbor saw Clarke Poos, about seventeen, run around the house, get the wolf off of the boy, and disappear with the child in his arms to the back of the house. Clarke took the boy in and laid him on the kitchen floor.

* * * An expert in the behavior of wolves stated that when a wolf licks a child's face that it is a sign of care, and not a sign of attack; that a wolf's wail is a sign of compassion, and an effort to get attention, not a sign of attack. * * * The defendant, Mr. Poos, arrived home while Daniel and his mother were in the kitchen. After Daniel was taken in an ambulance, Mr. Poos talked to everyone present, including a neighbor who came in. Within an hour after he arrived home, Mr. Poos went to Washington University to inform Owen Sexton, President of Wild Canid Survival and Research Center, Inc., of the incident. Mr. Sexton was not in his office so Mr. Poos left the following note on his door:

> Owen, would you call me at home, 727–5080? Sophie bit a child that came in our back yard. All has been taken care of.
> I need to convey what happened to you. (Exhibit 11)

Denial of admission of this note is one of the issues on appeal.

Later that day, Mr. Poos found Mr. Sexton at the Tyson Research Center and told him what had happened. Denial of plaintiff's offer to prove that Mr. Poos told Mr. Sexton, that, "Sophie had bit a child that day," is the second issue on appeal.

A meeting of the Directors of the Wild Canid Survival and Research Center, Inc., was held on April 4, 1973. Mr Poos was not present at that meeting. The minutes of that meeting reflect that there was a "great deal of discussion * * * about the legal aspects of the incident of Sophie biting the child." Plaintiff offered an abstract of the minutes containing that reference. Denial of the offer of that abstract is the third issue on appeal.

Daniel had lacerations of the face, left thigh, left calf, and right thigh, and abrasions and bruises of the abdomen and chest. Mr. Mahlandt was permitted to state that Daniel had indicated that he had gone under the fence. Mr. Mahlandt and Mr. Poos, about a month after the incident, examined the fence to determine what caused Daniel's lacerations. Mr. Mahlandt felt that they did not look like animal bites. The parallel scars on Daniel's thigh appeared to match the configuration of the barbs or tines on the fence. The expert as to the behavior of wolves opined that the lacerations were not wolf bites or wounds caused by wolf claws. * * *

The jury brought in a verdict for the defense.

The trial judge's rationale for excluding the note, the statement, and the corporate minutes, was the same in each case. He reasoned that Mr. Poos did not have any personal knowledge of the facts, and accordingly, the first two admissions were based on hearsay; and the third admission contained in the minutes of the board meeting was subject to the same objection of hearsay, and unreliability because of lack of personal knowledge.

The Federal Rules of Evidence became effective in July 1975 (180 days after passage of the Act). Thus, at this time, there is very little case law to rely upon for resolution of the problems of interpretation.

The relevant rule here is: Rule 801(d)(2).

* * * [T]he statement in the note pinned on the door is not hearsay, and is admissible against Mr. Poos. It was his own statement, and as such was clearly different from the reported statement of another. Example, "I was told that * * *." It was also a statement of which he had manifested his adoption or belief in its truth. And the

same observations may be made of the statement made later in the day to Mr. Sexton that, "Sophie had bit a child * * *."

Are these statements admissible against Wild Canid Survival and Research Center, Inc.? They were made by Mr. Poos when he was an agent or servant of the Wild Canid Survival and Research Center, Inc., and they concerned a matter within the scope of his agency, or employment, i.e., his custody of Sophie, and were made during the existence of that relationship.

* * * This is not an 801(d)(2)(C) situation because Mr. Poos was not authorized or directed to make a statement on the matter by anyone. * * * Weinstein's discussion of Rule 801(d)(2)(D) (Weinstein's Evidence § 801(d)(2)(D)(01), p. 801–137), states that:

> Rule 801(d)(2)(D) adopts the approach * * * which, as a general proposition, makes statement made by agents within the scope of their employment admissible * * *. Once agency, and the making of the statement while the relationship continues, are established, the statement is exempt from the hearsay rule so long as it relates to a matter within the scope of the agency.

After reciting a lengthy quotation which justifies the rule as necessary, and suggests that such admissions are trustworthy and reliable, Weinstein, states categorically that although an express requirement of personal knowledge on the part of the declarant of the facts underlying his statement is not written into the rule, it should be. He feels that is mandated by Rules 805 and 403.

Rule 805 recites, in effect, that a statement containing hearsay within hearsay is admissible, if each part of the statement falls within an exception to the hearsay rule. Rule 805, however, deals only with hearsay exceptions. A statement based on the personal knowledge of the declarant of facts underlying his statement is not the repetition of the statement of another, thus not hearsay. It is merely opinion testimony. Rule 805 cannot mandate the implied condition desired by Judge Weinstein.

Rule 403 provides for the exclusion of relevant evidence if its probative value is substantially outweighed by the danger of unfair prejudice, confusion of the issues, or misleading the jury, or by consideration of undue delay, waste of time, or needless presentation of cumulative evidence. Nor does Rule 403 mandate the implied condition desired by Judge Weinstein.

Thus, while both Rule 805 and Rule 403 provide additional bases for excluding otherwise acceptable evidence, neither rule mandates the introduction into Rule 801(d)(2)(D) of an implied requirement that the declarant have personal knowledge of the facts underlying his statement. So we conclude that the two statements made by Mr. Poos were admissible against Wild Canid Survival and Research Center, Inc.

As to the entry in the records of a corporate meeting, the directors as primary officers of the corporation had the authority to include their conclusions in the record of the meeting. So the evidence would fall within 801(d)(2)(C) as to Wild Canid Survival and Research Center, Inc., and be admissible. * * *

But there was no servant, or agency, relationship which justified admitting the evidence of the board minutes as against Mr. Poos.

None of the conditions of 801(d)(2) cover the claim that minutes of a corporate board meeting can be used against a non-attending, nonparticipating employee of that corporation. The evidence was not admissible as against Mr. Poos.

There is left only the question of whether the trial court's rulings which excluded all three items of evidence are justified under Rule 403. He clearly found that the evidence was not reliable, pointing out that none of the statements were based on the personal knowledge of the declarant.

Again, that problem was faced by the Advisory Committee on Proposed Rules. In its discussion of 801(d)(2) exceptions to the hearsay rule, the Committee said:

> The freedom which admissions have enjoyed from technical demands of searching for an assurance of trustworthiness in some against-interest circumstances, and from the restrictive influences of the opinion rule and the rule requiring first hand knowledge, when taken with the apparently prevalent satisfaction with the results, calls for generous treatment of this avenue to admissibility. 28 U.S.C.A., Volume of Federal Rules of Evidence, Rule 801, p. 527, at p. 530.

So, here, remembering that relevant evidence is usually prejudicial to the cause of the side against which it is presented, and that the prejudice which concerns us is unreasonable prejudice; and applying the spirit of Rule 801(d)(2), we hold that Rule 403 does not warrant the exclusion of the evidence of Mr. Poos' statements as against himself or Wild Canid Survival and Research Center, Inc.

* * *

The judgment of the District Court is reversed and the matter remanded to the District Court for a new trial consistent with this opinion.

Hypotheticals

(1) A, a painting subcontractor, sues X, a general contractor, for the balance due on a subcontract with X. A had been paid four progress payments, but X refused to pay the fifth and last progress payment on the ground that A's work was unsatisfactory. B was general superintendent for X and was authorized by X to approve and reject subcontractors' work and to approve progress payments to subcontractors accordingly. When A's painting job for X was 98 percent complete, B wrote a letter of recommendation for A, stating that A had completed the painting job for X to everyone's satisfaction. A offers B's letter in evidence. X objects that the letter is hearsay. What result under federal law? Under California law?

(2) A sues the X market for damages for personal injuries arising out of a slip-and-fall incident. A few minutes after A fell, B, the store manager, arrived and A pointed out a banana peel on the floor. C, a witness to the incident,

proposes to testify for A that B then said to A, "Don't worry about this. We
will pay your bills. It's the store's fault." X objects that C's testimony is
hearsay. What result under federal law? Under California Law?

BIG MACK TRUCKING CO., INC. v. DICKERSON

Supreme Court of Texas, 1973.
497 S.W.2d 283.

SAM D. JOHNSON, Justice.

The wife and children of Willie Lee Dickerson have recovered
damages for his wrongful death in an action against his employer, Big
Mack Trucking Company, Inc. The court of civil appeals affirmed. We
reverse.

Willie Dickerson and Ormand Leday were employees of Big Mack.
Each was driving a truck-tractor pulling a flatbed trailer loaded with
sheet steel across Texas from Eagle Pass to Arp. Both trucks stopped
in Waco. Leday parked his truck fifteen to eighteen feet behind
Dickerson's. Leday left his vehicle unattended. Dickerson got out of
his truck and was standing behind his trailer with his back toward
Leday's vehicle. Leday's unattended truck rolled forward striking
Dickerson's trailer and crushing Dickerson between the two trucks.
Dickerson was killed in the accident.

* * * The jury found that Leday was acting as an employee of
Big Mack at the time of the accident, that Leday was guilty of two acts
of negligence which also amounted to heedless and reckless disregard of
the rights of others, and that those acts were proximate causes of the
occurrence. The jury found actual damages in the aggregate amount of
$220,000.

Big Mack applied for writ of error.

Big Mack asserts that there is "no evidence" to support the
judgment against it because all the evidence of Leday's negligence and
proximate cause was hearsay as to Big Mack. *Leday did not testify.
No attempt was made to explain or justify the failure to call Leday, his
absence, or his failure to give testimony.* The plaintiffs' theory of
liability was predicated upon the fact that Leday's brakes were defective at the time he parked his truck. The only evidence tending to
prove the circumstances of the accident or the elements necessary for
plaintiffs' recovery came from two witnesses who could only testify
what Leday had previously related to them. These two witnesses were
Mr. David Stiles, the vice president of Big Mack, and Officer Henry
Harwell, the investigating officer of the Waco Police Department.

Vice President Stiles testified that following the accident, Leday
told him he had been having "air pressure troubles" and that he had
not been maintaining the proper air pressure in his braking system.
He further told Stiles that he had parked his truck behind Dickerson's
truck, had gone off and left it and that when he returned he found the
deceased crushed between the two trucks. In addition, Stiles, who was
familiar with the proper operation of trucks, testified that if a truck
was being operated under circumstances where the driver was having
trouble with the brakes such as those related that it would be improper

to park the truck on any kind of incline without scotching the wheels or putting it in gear.

The testimony of Officer Harwell was introduced by way of deposition. He testified that when he arrived that Dickerson was no longer there; that he had been removed by an ambulance. The two vehicles were still at the scene of the accident. Officer Harwell then related what Leday had told him: that he had been experiencing brake trouble with his truck in that the air pressure was running law [*sic*], that he was the operator of the back truck, that he parked his truck approximately fifteen to eighteen feet behind the decedent's truck and that when he left his truck Dickerson was standing at the back of Dickerson's truck eating off of the trailer.

Respondents assert that in an action against a servant and master, the master having been joined under respondeat superior, it is not necessary that the evidence proving the servant's negligence and proximate cause be competent evidence against the master in order to support a judgment against the master. The notion is that the master's derivative liability is imposed by law once the liability facts are proven by evidence competent against the servant.

We cannot accept such a view. The suggestion is that with respect to proof of the servant's liability, which we deem an essential element of plaintiffs' *case against the master,* the master loses the protection of the hearsay rule. Any reason which suggests that the master should lose the protection of that rule would also militate against the master's right to offer contrary evidence, to cross-examine plaintiffs' witnesses, to object to evidence on grounds other than hearsay, or, indeed, even to plead the general denial which requires the plaintiffs to prove the servant's liability in the first place. Although we have found no Texas case specifically holding that evidence of the servant's negligence must be admissible against the master in order to sustain a judgment against the master, we believe that the unspoken principle was necessarily followed in Isaacs v. Plains Transport Co., and Waggoner v. Snody.

Since the evidence of Leday's negligence and proximate cause must be admissible against Big Mack in order to support the judgment against it, and since all evidence offered to prove those facts was hearsay, the question becomes whether the hearsay is admissible against Big Mack under any hearsay-rule exception known to Texas law.

The court of civil appeals held that Leday's statements to Stiles qualify against Big Mack as admissions of a party.[1] The theory is that Big Mack authorized Leday to speak to Stiles about the accident in Waco, and when Leday spoke he voiced, in contemplation of law, the position of Big Mack. We cannot agree. An agent's hearsay statements should be received against the principal as vicarious admissions only when the trial judge finds, as a preliminary fact, that the statements were authorized. The Restatement of Agency [§ 287] cautions

1. No doubt such statements are admissions of the party Leday, and so would be admissible over his hearsay objection. The pertinent question under our holding above is whether they are also admissions of Big Mack.

that, in considering the breadth of an agent's authority when reporting details of an event to the principal, the court should notice the very likely limitation that the principal *intends* the agent's report to be made *only* to the principal or other person investigating the accident for the principal. If there be any special facts to show that Big Mack authorized Leday to speak to the world as well as to Stiles, those facts have not been introduced and so we follow the Restatement and hold that the Stiles testimony is not admissible under the admissions exception. In so holding we do not adopt § 287 of the Restatement as a hard and fast rule, but only observe it to the extent that it creates a rebuttable presumption of lack of authority.

The second theory of admissibility is that Leday's statements to Officer Harwell qualify as vicarious admissions. The Restatement rule noted above has no application since Officer Harwell was not investigating for the principal, Big Mack. Nevertheless, we must find that such statements were authorized by Big Mack, and in this inquiry we are mindful of the Wigmore-McCormick caveat against confusing the admissions exception with the res gestae, or spontaneous utterance, exception.

Of course, the authority to make admissions may be implied from express authority to do some other act. The question evolves, then, whether Leday's express authority to operate the truck may be a basis for implied authority to explain how the accident came to pass. Most authorities take the position that a driver's statements after an accident are not authorized by his employer. In terms of strictly consensual authority, we believe the well-advised employer would generally not authorize the driver to speak in these circumstances. There is, moreover, no basis for a claim of apparent authority since all events operating to establish liability for the injury have occurred at the time the statements are made, and there can be no pertinent detrimental reliance upon the driver's statements. There is no reason peculiar to the case at bar why the general rule should not be followed.

Respondent assigns, as contrary authority, the cases of West Texas Produce Co. v. Wilson; Dixie Motor Coach Corporation v. Meredith; Firestone Tire & Rubber Co. v. Rhodes; J. Weingarten, Inc. v. Reagan. We do not think those cases require a different result. In *Wilson,* the president of defendant corporation directed the investigating officers to question the foreman on the day of the accident, and so the foreman's responses were expressly authorized. The statements the driver made the following day were not authorized and so were excluded. In *Meredith,* the bus driver's post rem hearsay declarations were admitted, but the court of civil appeals was of the opinion that there was no real dispute on the issue to which the hearsay was relevant (i.e., defective brakes); the court's holding is only a holding that, if error, it was harmless. The opinion in *Rhodes* indicates that the witness never answered the question which sought to elicit the driver's hearsay declarations; the court there held that "[a]n unanswered question, although improper and duly excepted to, is not sufficient grounds for reversal of the case." In *Reagan,* the hearsay declarations of an employee of the grocery store was admitted to show that the employee had knowledge of the dangerous condition; its admission does not appear to have been challenged upon the basis that it also proved the fact of the dangerous condition. That is a viable distinction, and could properly have controlled the decision of that case.[2]

The final theory of admissibility advanced by respondents is that Leday's statements to Officer Harwell were spontaneous exclamations. In order to so qualify, there must be some evidence of facts from which a trial judge might infer that the declarant (Leday) was in such an emotional state that he was incapable of that deliberation which might permit fabrication. Spontaneity is the essence of the exception. The only evidence which tends to show the time elapsed between the exciting event (Leday's discovery of the accident) and Leday's statements to Officer Harwell is that when Harwell arrived, the ambulance had already taken Dickerson away. That alone is clearly insufficient, and it is unaided by any mention by Officer Harwell that the declarant appeared to be distraught. At all events. It appears that the trial judge did not find the preliminary facts constituting a spontaneous-exclamation predicate, but rather allowed the Harwell deposition into evidence only as an admission. * * * After [the] ruling by the trial judge, the only basis upon which we could hold the Harwell deposition admissible is to hold that Leday's hearsay declarations were "spontaneous" as a matter of law. That we cannot do.

A great measure of trustworthiness stems from the fact that Leday's hearsay declarations were against his pecuniary interests. Our evidence law acknowledges this in the declarations against interest exception to the hearsay rule. However, it has long been the position of Texas jurisprudence that there should be a special *need* to rely on such hearsay, and consequently we require proof that the declarant was not available to testify at the trial. The instant record is wholly without proof of any attempt to establish that the hearsay declarant (Leday) was unavailable to testify. The exception therefore does not apply.

The judgments of the courts below are reversed, and the cause is remanded to the district court for a new trial.

UNITED STATES v. DOERR

United States Court of Appeals, Seventh Circuit, 1989.
886 F.2d 944.

RIPPLE, Circuit Judge.

[Defendants were charged with an unlawful prostitution conspiracy using the facilities of interstate commerce, and with tax crimes related to the enterprise.]

The prostitution activities underlying the offense alleged in Count One of the indictment were concentrated in three businesses that were

---

2. We are aware that issue #2 inquired if Leday knew his brakes were defective, but an essential subsidiary question is whether the brakes were, in fact, defective. Evidence admitted under a special rule-of-necessity, which liberalizes the admissions exception in a proponent's effort to prove knowledge of a fact, cannot be used by indirection to prove existence of the fact itself.

part of an entity known as Worldwide Enterprises, Incorporated: the WW I Club, located in Kenosha County, Wisconsin; the Relaxation Health Systems massage parlor located next to the WW I Club in Kenosha County; and the WW II Club, located in Lake County, Illinois. The clubs were nude dancing establishments that served no food or alcoholic beverages. The testimony at trial revealed that the prostitution activities at the clubs were conducted pursuant to the following general procedure. A customer entering the club would be required to pay a cover charge. He would then be directed to a table and joined by a "dancer." After being seated, a waitress would approach the customer and ask him if he would like to purchase a drink (water or a soft drink) for himself and the dancer. Once the customer had purchased a drink, the waitress would return and ask the customer if he would like to go to a private area with the dancer. If the customer agreed and purchased a bottle of soda or water, at a cost of forty to fifty dollars, he would be taken to a "terrace," consisting of a number of booths, in the rear of the club. The customer would then be asked to buy additional bottles, and, once sufficient bottles had been purchased, the dancer would engage in sexual acts with the customer.

At the massage parlor, the customer would pay a flat fee for thirty minutes in a private room with a masseuse. The masseuse would then negotiate a "tip" with the customer. The amount of the tip would determine the degree of sexual contact that the masseuse had with the customer. At both the clubs and the massage parlor, customers could pay in cash or by credit card.

[Defendant-appellant asserted error in the admission of statements offered as co-conspirators' statements.]

The coconspirator exception to the hearsay rule, Fed.R.Evid. 801(d)(2)(E), provides that a statement is not hearsay if it is "offered against a party and is . . . a statement by a coconspirator of a party [made] during the course and in furtherance of the conspiracy." The appellants maintain that two out-of-court statements admitted at trial failed to satisfy the "in furtherance" requirement of the coconspirator exception. In the first challenged statement, Robert Meyer, a frequent customer at the Kenosha club, testified about a conversation between himself and Mr. Pixley in which the two discussed a red curtain at one of the clubs. Meyer testified that Mr. Pixley "mentioned that when he was hired back there that Josephine had a curtain put up in the terrace or the patio area, how ridiculous it was, it was asking for problems with the police." In the second challenged statement, John Patrick Doerr, Dale Doerr's half brother, testified that, in a conversation with his brother, Dale had laughed at him and said "I can't believe—I don't believe—I can't believe you don't know what's going on, or you didn't know what's going on." While conceding that these two statements may have been admissible against their declarants, Mr. Pixley and Dale Doerr, the appellants maintain that they should not have been admitted against the nondeclarant appellants because the statements were not made "in furtherance" of the conspiracy. Thus, they contend, Rule 801(d)(2)(E) was not satisfied.

We recently emphasized that the "in furtherance" requirement of Rule 801(d)(2)(E) is a limitation on the admissibility of coconspirators' statements that is meant to be taken seriously. See Garlington v. O'Leary, 879 F.2d 277, 283 (7th Cir.1989). As we explained in *Garlington*, a coconspirator's statement satisfies the "in furtherance" requirement "when the statement is 'part of the information flow between conspirators intended to help each perform his role.'" We further explained that statements "in furtherance" of a conspiracy can take many forms, including statements made to recruit potential coconspirators, statements seeking to control damage to an ongoing conspiracy, statements made to keep coconspirators advised as to the progress of the conspiracy, and statements made in an attempt to conceal the criminal objectives of the conspiracy. Narrative declarations, mere "idle chatter," and superfluous casual conversations, however, are not statements "in furtherance" of a conspiracy.

A district court's finding that a particular statement was made "in furtherance" is reviewed under a clearly erroneous standard. In addition, a court may conclude that the challenged statement was "in furtherance" even though "'the statement [was] susceptible of alternative interpretations.'" Id. at 628 (quoting United States v. Mackey, 571 F.2d 376, 383 (7th Cir.1978)). Moreover, the "in furtherance" requirement is satisfied so long "as some reasonable basis exists for concluding that the statement furthered the conspiracy.'" Id., quoted in Garlington, supra, at 283.

The government contends that the district court had a reasonable basis for concluding that Mr. Pixley's statements, described at trial by Meyer, were made "in furtherance" of the conspiracy. The government explains that, in addition to being a frequent customer, Robert Meyer had an interest in investing in the Kenosha club. Given this interest, the government asserts that "the trial court had a 'reasonable basis' for concluding that Pixley's comments were made in furtherance of the conspiracy since Pixley and Meyer had an interest in discussing ways that the club could improve and remain in operation." The government also contends that Dale Doerr's statement was "in furtherance" of the conspiracy, because it was a description of the clubs' illegal activities to John Patrick Doerr, a coconspirator who worked at the clubs as a manager and doorman.

We cannot accept the government's contentions. Therefore, we conclude that the district court erred in admitting the challenged testimony. Neither Mr. Pixley's statement nor Dale Doerr's statement was made "in furtherance" of the conspiracy. After reviewing Robert Meyer's testimony, we conclude that Mr. Pixley's discussion of the red curtain with Meyer cannot reasonably be characterized as part of an attempt to induce Meyer to join or assist the conspiracy. Instead, the statements are more accurately characterized as a narrative discussion of a past event. As such, they do not satisfy the "in furtherance" requirement of Rule 801(d)(2)(E).[7]

7. The district court itself had concluded that discussions between Mr. Pixley and Meyer regarding investment by Meyer in the club were not in furtherance of the conspiracy. The court had, however, concluded that Mr. Pixley's statements about

Similarly, Dale Doerr's statement to John Patrick Doerr fails to satisfy the "in furtherance" requirement. In making the statement recounted by John Patrick Doerr at trial, Dale was mocking his half-brother's ignorance of the clubs' unlawful activities; such a statement cannot be characterized as part of the normal information flow between coconspirators and in no way furthered the ends of the conspiracy. Thus, neither Mr. Pixley's statement nor Dale Doerr's statement should have been admitted under Rule 801(d)(2)(E). [The court went on to conclude, however, that admission of the statements was harmless error.]

BOURJAILY v. UNITED STATES

Supreme Court of the United States, 1987.
483 U.S. 171, 107 S.Ct. 2775, 97 L.Ed.2d 144.

Chief Justice REHNQUIST delivered the opinion of the Court [in which Justices WHITE, POWELL, STEVENS, O'CONNOR, and SCALIA joined. Justice STEVENS also filed a concurring opinion. Justice BLACKMUN filed a dissenting opinion, in which Justices BRENNAN and MARSHALL joined].

Federal Rule of Evidence 801(d)(2)(E) provides, "A statement is not hearsay if * * * [t]he statement is offered against a party and is * * * a statement by a coconspirator of a party during the course and in furtherance of the conspiracy." We granted certiorari to answer three questions regarding the admission of statements under Rule 801(d)(2)(E): (1) whether the court must determine by independent evidence that the conspiracy existed and that the defendant and the declarant were members of this conspiracy; (2) the quantum of proof on which such determinations must be based; and (3) whether a court must in each case examine the circumstances of such a statement to determine its reliability.

In May 1984, Clarence Greathouse, an informant working for the Federal Bureau of Investigation, arranged to sell a kilogram of cocaine to Angelo Lonardo. Lonardo agreed that he would find individuals to distribute the drug. When the sale became imminent, Lonardo stated in a tape-recorded telephone conversation that he had a "gentleman friend" who had some questions to ask about the cocaine. In a subsequent telephone call, Greathouse spoke to the "friend" about the quality of the drug and the price. Greathouse then spoke again with Lonardo, and the two arranged the details of the purchase. They agreed that the sale would take place in a designated hotel parking lot, and Lonardo would transfer the drug from Greathouse's car to the "friend," who would be waiting in the parking lot in his own car. Greathouse proceeded with the transaction as planned, and FBI agents arrested Lonardo and petitioner immediately after Lonardo placed a

the red curtain were "in furtherance," because they illustrate a "desire to increase the efficiency in the remunerative nature of the conspiracy." While the statements may in fact illustrate such a desire on the part of Mr. Pixley, the district court's finding does not explain how making this statement to Meyer in any way furthered the conspiracy.

kilogram of cocaine into petitioner's car in the hotel parking lot. In petitioner's car, the agents found over $20,000 in cash.

Petitioner was charged with conspiring to distribute cocaine, in violation of 21 U.S.C. § 846, and possession of cocaine with intent to distribute, a violation of 21 U.S.C. § 841(a)(1). The Government introduced, over petitioner's objection, Angelo Lonardo's telephone statements regarding the participation of the "friend" in the transaction. The District Court found that, considering the events in the parking lot and Lonardo's statements over the telephone, the Government had established by a preponderance of the evidence that a conspiracy involving Lonardo and petitioner existed, and that Lonardo's statements over the telephone had been made in the course of and in furtherance of the conspiracy. Accordingly, the trial court held that Lonardo's out-of-court statements satisfied Rule 801(d)(2)(E) and were not hearsay. Petitioner was convicted on both counts and sentenced to 15 years. The United States Court of Appeals for the Sixth Circuit affirmed. The Court of Appeals agreed with the District Court's analysis and conclusion that Lonardo's out-of-court statements were admissible under the Federal Rules of Evidence. The court also rejected petitioner's contention that because he could not cross-examine Lonardo, the admission of these statements violated his constitutional right to confront the witnesses against him. We affirm.

Before admitting a co-conspirator's statement over an objection that it does not qualify under Rule 801(d)(2)(E), a court must be satisfied that the statement actually falls within the definition of the Rule. There must be evidence that there was a conspiracy involving the declarant and the nonoffering party, and that the statement was made "in the course and in furtherance of the conspiracy." Federal Rule of Evidence 104(a) provides: "Preliminary questions concerning * * * the admissibility of evidence shall be determined by the court." Petitioner and respondent agree that the existence of a conspiracy and petitioner's involvement in it are preliminary questions of fact that, under Rule 104, must be resolved by the court. The Federal Rules, however, nowhere define the standard of proof the court must observe in resolving these questions.

We are therefore guided by our prior decisions regarding admissibility determinations that hinge on preliminary factual questions. We have traditionally required that these matters be established by a preponderance of proof. Evidence is placed before the jury when it satisfies the technical requirements of the evidentiary Rules, which embody certain legal and policy determinations. The inquiry made by a court concerned with these matters is not whether the proponent of the evidence wins or loses his case on the merits, but whether the evidentiary Rules have been satisfied. Thus, the evidentiary standard is unrelated to the burden of proof on the substantive issues, be it a criminal case, see In re Winship, 397 U.S. 358 (1970), or a civil case. See generally Colorado v. Connelly, 479 U.S. 157, 167–169 (1986). The preponderance standard ensures that before admitting evidence, the court will have found it more likely than not that the technical issues and policy concerns addressed by the Federal Rules of Evidence have been afforded due consideration. As in Lego v. Twomey, 404 U.S. 477, 488 (1972), we find "nothing to suggest that admissibility rulings have been unreliable or otherwise wanting in quality because not based on some higher standard." We think that our previous decisions in this area resolve the matter. See, e.g., Colorado v. Connelly, supra (preliminary fact that custodial confessant waived rights must be proved by preponderance of the evidence); Nix v. Williams, 467 U.S. 431, 444, n. 5 (1984) (inevitable discovery of illegally seized evidence must be shown to have been more likely than not); United States v. Matlock, 415 U.S. 164 (1974) (voluntariness of consent to search must be shown by preponderance of the evidence); Lego v. Twomey, supra (voluntariness of confession must be demonstrated by a preponderance of the evidence). Therefore, we hold that when the preliminary facts relevant to Rule 801(d)(2)(E) are disputed, the offering party must prove them by a preponderance of the evidence.

Even though petitioner agrees that the courts below applied the proper standard of proof with regard to the preliminary facts relevant to Rule 801(d)(2)(E), he nevertheless challenges the admission of Lonardo's statements. Petitioner argues that in determining whether a conspiracy exists and whether the defendant was a member of it, the court must look only to independent evidence—that is, evidence other than the statements sought to be admitted. Petitioner relies on Glasser v. United States, 315 U.S. 60 (1942), in which this Court first mentioned the so-called "bootstrapping rule." The relevant issue in Glasser was whether Glasser's counsel, who also represented another defendant, faced such a conflict of interest that Glasser received ineffective assistance. Glasser contended that conflicting loyalties led his lawyer not to object to statements made by one of Glasser's co-conspirators. The Government argued that any objection would have been fruitless because the statements were admissible. The Court rejected this proposition:

> "[S]uch declarations are admissible over the objection of an alleged co-conspirator, who was not present when they were made, only if there is proof aliunde that he is connected with the conspiracy. . . . Otherwise, hearsay would lift itself by its own bootstraps to the level of competent evidence." Id., at 74–75.

The Court revisited the bootstrapping rule in United States v. Nixon, 418 U.S. 683 (1974), where again, in passing, the Court stated, "Declarations by one defendant may also be admissible against other defendants upon a sufficient showing, *by independent evidence,* of a conspiracy among one or more other defendants and the declarant and if the declarations at issue were in furtherance of that conspiracy." Id., at 701, and n. 14 (emphasis added) (footnote omitted). Read in the light most favorable to petitioner, Glasser could mean that a court should not consider hearsay statements at all in determining preliminary facts under Rule 801(d)(2)(E). Petitioner, of course, adopts this view of the bootstrapping rule. Glasser, however, could also mean that a court must have *some* proof aliunde, but may look at the hearsay statements themselves in light of this independent evidence to determine whether a conspiracy has been shown by a preponderance of the evidence. The Courts of Appeals have widely adopted the former view and held that in determining the preliminary facts relevant to co-conspirators' out-of-court statements, a court may not look at the hearsay statements themselves for their evidentiary value.

Both Glasser and Nixon, however, were decided before Congress enacted the Federal Rules of Evidence in 1975. These Rules now govern the treatment of evidentiary questions in federal courts. Rule 104(a) provides: "Preliminary questions concerning * * * the admissibility of evidence shall be determined by the court. * * * In making its determination it is not bound by the rules of evidence except those with respect to privileges." Similarly, Rule 1101(d)(1) states that the Rules of Evidence (other than with respect to privileges) shall not apply to "[t]he determination of questions of fact preliminary to admissibility of evidence when the issue is to be determined by the court under rule 104." The question thus presented is whether any aspect of Glasser's bootstrapping rule remains viable after the enactment of the Federal Rules of Evidence.

Petitioner concedes that Rule 104, on its face, appears to allow the court to make the preliminary factual determinations relevant to Rule 801(d)(2)(E) by considering any evidence it wishes, unhindered by considerations of admissibility. That would seem to many to be the end of the matter. Congress has decided that courts may consider hearsay in making these factual determinations. Out-of-court statements made by anyone, including putative co-conspirators, are often hearsay. Even if they are, they may be considered, Glasser and the bootstrapping rule notwithstanding. But petitioner nevertheless argues that the bootstrapping rule, as most Courts of Appeals have construed it, survived this apparently unequivocal change in the law unscathed and that Rule 104, as applied to the admission of co-conspirator's statements, does not mean what it says. We disagree.

Petitioner claims that Congress evidenced no intent to disturb the bootstrapping rule, which was embedded in the previous approach, and we should not find that Congress altered the rule without affirmative evidence so indicating. It would be extraordinary to require legislative history to *confirm* the plain meaning of Rule 104. The Rule on its face allows the trial judge to consider any evidence whatsoever, bound only by the rules of privilege. We think that the Rule is sufficiently clear that to the extent that it is inconsistent with petitioner's interpretation of Glasser and Nixon, the Rule prevails.[2]

---

2. The Advisory Committee Notes show that the Rule was not adopted in a fit of absent-mindedness. The Note to Rule 104 specifically addresses the process by which a federal court should make the factual determinations requisite to a finding of admissibility:

"If the question is factual in nature, the judge will of necessity receive evidence pro and con on the issue. The rule provides that the rules of evidence in general do not apply to this process. McCormick § 53, p. 123, n. 8, points out that the authorities are 'scattered and inconclusive,' and observes:

"'Should the exclusionary law of evidence, "the child of the jury system" in Thayer's phrase, be applied to this hearing before the judge? Sound sense backs the view that it should not, and that the judge should be empowered to hear *any relevant evidence*, such as affidavits *or other reliable hearsay*.'" 28 U.S.C.App., p. 681 (emphasis added).

* * *

We think that there is little doubt that a co-conspirator's statements could themselves be probative of the existence of a conspiracy and the participation of both the defendant and the declarant in the conspiracy. Petitioner's case presents a paradigm. The out-of-court statements of Lonardo indicated that Lonardo was involved in a conspiracy with a "friend." The statements indicated that the friend had agreed with Lonardo to buy a kilogram of cocaine and to distribute it. The statements also revealed that the friend would be at the hotel parking lot, in his car, and would accept the cocaine from Greathouse's car after Greathouse gave Lonardo the keys. Each one of Lonardo's statements may itself be unreliable, but taken as a whole, the entire conversation between Lonardo and Greathouse was corroborated by independent evidence. The friend, who turned out to be petitioner, showed up at the prearranged spot at the prearranged time. He picked up the cocaine, and a significant sum of money was found in his car. On these facts, the trial court concluded, in our view correctly, that the Government had established the existence of a conspiracy and petitioner's participation in it.

We need not decide in this case whether the courts below could have relied solely upon Lonardo's hearsay statements to determine that a conspiracy had been established by a preponderance of the evidence. To the extent that Glasser meant that courts could not look to the hearsay statements themselves for any purpose, it has clearly been superseded by Rule 104(a). It is sufficient for today to hold that a court, in making a preliminary factual determination under Rule 801(d)(2)(E), may examine the hearsay statements sought to be admitted. As we have held in other cases concerning admissibility determinations, "the judge should receive the evidence and give it such weight as his judgment and experience counsel." United States v. Matlock, 415 U.S. 164, 175 (1974). The courts below properly considered the statements of Lonardo and the subsequent events in finding that the Government had established by a preponderance of the evidence that Lonardo was involved in a conspiracy with petitioner. We have no reason to believe that the District Court's factfinding of this point was clearly erroneous. We hold that Lonardo's out-of-court statements were properly admitted against petitioner.

[A concurring opinion by Justice STEVENS has been omitted].

Justice BLACKMUN, with whom Justice BRENNAN and Justice MARSHALL join, dissenting.

* * * [T]he independent-evidence requirement directly corresponds to the agency concept that an agent's statement cannot be used alone to prove the existence of the agency relationship.

The Advisory Committee further noted, "An item, offered and objected to, *may itself be considered in ruling on admissibility,* though not yet admitted in evidence." Ibid. (emphasis added). We think this language makes plain the drafters' intent to abolish any kind of bootstrapping rule. Silence is at best ambiguous, and we decline the invitation to rely on speculation to import ambiguity into what is otherwise a clear rule.

"Evidence of a statement by an agent concerning the existence or extent of his authority is not admissible against the principal to prove its existence or extent, unless it appears *by other evidence* that the making of such statement was within the authority of the agent or, as to persons dealing with the agent, within the apparent authority or other power of the agent" (emphasis added). Restatement (Second) of Agency § 285 (1957).

See Levie, 52 Mich.L.Rev., at 1161. The reason behind this concept is that the agent's authority must be traced back to some act or statement by the alleged principal. See 1 F. Mechem, Law of Agency § 285, p. 205 (1914).

   * * * [B]y explicitly retaining the agency rationale for the exemption, the Advisory Committee expressed its intention that the exemption would remain identical to the common-law rule and that it would not be expanded in any way. The Advisory Committee recognized that this agency rationale had been subject to criticism. The drafters of the American Law Institute's Model Code of Evidence had gone so far as to abandon the agency justification and had eliminated the "in furtherance of" requirement, observing that "[t]hese statements are likely to be true, and are usually made with a realization that they are against the declarant's interest." Model Code of Evidence, Rule 508(b) commentary, p. 251 (1942). The Advisory Committee, however, declined to accept without reservation a reliability foundation for Rule 801(d)(2)(E).

   * * * [W]hen Rule 801(d)(2)(E) and Rule 104(a) are considered together—an examination that the Court neglects to undertake—there appears to be a conflict between the fact that no change in the co-conspirator hearsay exemption was intended by Rule 801(d)(2)(E) and the freedom that Rule 104(a) gives a trial court to rely on hearsay in resolving preliminary factual questions. Although one must be somewhat of an interpretative funambulist to walk between the conflicting demands of these Rules in order to arrive at a resolution that will satisfy their respective concerns, this effort is far to be preferred over accepting the easily available safety "net" of Rule 104(a)'s "plain meaning." The purposes of *both* Rules can be achieved by considering the relevant preliminary factual question for Rule 104(a) analysis to be the following: "whether a conspiracy that included the declarant and the defendant against whom a statement is offered has been demonstrated to exist on the basis of evidence *independent of the declarant's hearsay statements* " (emphasis added). Saltzburg & Redden, Federal Rules of Evidence Manual 735 (4th ed. 1986). This resolution sufficiently answers Rule 104(a)'s concern with allowing a trial court to consider hearsay in determining preliminary factual questions, because the only hearsay not available for its consideration is the statement at issue. The exclusion of the statement from the preliminary analysis maintains the common-law exemption unchanged.

KAPLAN, OF MABRUS AND ZORGS

66 Cal.L.Rev. 987, 997–99 (1978).

* * * Let us examine the following hypothetical:

> Prosecution of D for aiding and abetting a bank robbery. W testifies that he (W) was in on the plan and that, to bolster his (W's) courage, A, his coconspirator, told him, "You know D is an excellent driver. Well, D told me he'll be waiting outside the bank with the motor going."

Let us temporarily put aside the problem of what to do when the crime charged is conspiracy so that the preliminary question and ultimate issue are the same. Here the crime charged is not conspiracy but bank robbery, and under the California code, as under the common law, the admissibility of W's testimony for the most part turns on whether A, the declarant, and D, the defendant, were members of the conspiracy and whether A's statement was made "in furtherance" of that conspiracy. (Note that W, himself, need not be a member of the conspiracy: the same rule of admissibility would apply if he merely had overheard A's statement to someone else—provided that A's statement was, in fact, in furtherance of the conspiracy and was not simply bragging. W's participation, however, makes it more likely that A's statement was in furtherance of the plan.)

Surely, in principle, the California Statute,* which makes these preliminary fact questions jury questions, is in error. The jury will likely give short shrift to questions such as whether the declarant, A, was himself a member of the conspiracy or whether the statement was made in furtherance of the conspiracy. Rather, the jurors probably will ignore our hearsay rule and decide whether to give the statement weight depending on whether they think A was knowledgeable and truthful, regardless of whether he was a coconspirator.

Interestingly, in the most common type of case, where the declarant, A, was clearly a conspirator, but the disputed preliminary question is whether the defendant, D, was also a member of the bank robbing conspiracy, the error in the California statute is not so serious. If D's guilt of bank robbery were based on his membership in the conspiracy, and the jury did not believe him to have been a conspirator, it would acquit him. In this case, it would be hard to get upset about whether or not the jury improperly considered A's hearsay statement as to D's guilt.

Of course, it is the other possibility that many find upsetting: that the jurors would believe D to be guilty in part because they considered A's hearsay statement on this issue. This does not mean, however, that the jury would have ignored the policy of the law requiring D's status as a coconspirator as a condition of using A's statement against D. After all, the jury has found that D was a conspirator. The only issue is whether the jury must decide the question as a preliminary fact

---

* Cal.Evid. Code § 1223 (West 1966).
See p. 1144, infra.

question—before it decides the same question on the merits of the case. Looked at another way, the issue is whether the jury may consider the hearsay evidence—or more precisely, A's hearsay statement—on the issue of the preliminary fact of D's conspiratorial status. Certainly it is a departure from orthodoxy to do so, but to allow a jury to consider hearsay evidence in making its preliminary fact determination is very different from misallocating our preliminary fact determination so that the jury will consider inadmissible evidence on the merits of the case.

It is in the related exception to the hearsay rule—for authorized admissions—that the California Evidence Code reaches the indefensible result of allowing the preliminary fact to be ignored completely. Section 1222 [1] makes the question of authorization a jury question. * * * Here, even more clearly than in the case of the coconspirator exception, a rational jury will pay no attention to the artificial preliminary fact requirement of authorization. Consequently, the question should, of course, be decided by the judge. Nor can one defend the California code's transformation of this issue into a jury question on the ground that the hearsay exception itself is much too narrow. It is true that in the usual case the truck driver's statement as to his own negligence probably should be admissible against his employer even if it is not authorized. By treating the question of authorization as a jury question the California code partially rectifies this arguable error by allowing the jury to hear such statements in a much larger number of cases. On the other hand, if indeed it is the scope of the hearsay exception that is at fault, the proper remedy is to change the exception. When the proponent of the truck driver's statement lacks any evidence of authorization, even the treatment of the question as a jury question will not help produce the "correct" result of admitting the statement. In this case at least, two wrongs do not make a right. Moreover, the California Evidence Code allows the jury to hear what may be unauthorized statements, even in cases in which most of us would regard the lack of authorization as important enough to deny them admissibility, at least so long as we are willing to enforce the hearsay rule.

The federal rules reach a better result in handling both coconspirator statements and authorized admissions, although the matter is somewhat complicated by the peculiar definition of hearsay in the federal rules which allows both kinds of out-of-court statements into evidence, not as hearsay exceptions, but rather as nonhearsay. In both cases the preliminary issues are not ones merely of relevance, and hence the judge must decide the preliminary fact questions rather than leaving them to the jury.

* * *

1. Cal.Evid. Code § 1222 (West 1966).

4. FORMER TESTIMONY

TRAVELERS FIRE INSURANCE CO. v. WRIGHT

Supreme Court of Oklahoma, 1958.
322 P.2d 417, 70 A.L.R.2d 1170.

[Action by J.B. Wright and J.C. Wright to recover under the terms of two fire insurance policies. The defendant insurers defended on the ground that the fire that destroyed plaintiffs' property had been deliberately caused by plaintiff J.B. Wright with the intent to defraud the defendants. Defendants alleged and proved that the plaintiffs were, at all pertinent times, business partners. There was a verdict and a judgment for plaintiffs, from which defendants appealed—Ed.]

JACKSON, Justice. * * * Defendants called Wm. Holland Eppler and Albert Brown as witnesses. Each witness claimed his constitutional privilege against self-incrimination and refused to testify. The claim of each was granted by the trial court. Defendant then offered certified transcripts of testimony given by each witness in the trial of a criminal case wherein one of the plaintiffs herein, J.B. Wright, was charged with the crime of arson in connection with the fire involved in the instant case. Such testimony was to the effect that J.B. Wright, with the aid and assistance of the two named witnesses, actively procured the burning of the property. Each offer was rejected by the trial court. The court reporter who took the evidence in the criminal case testified as to the correctness of his transcript, the nature of the case in which the testimony was taken and the parties involved. In addition to offering the transcript, defendants offered to have the reporter read same in evidence.

In 20 Am.Jur. § 686, at page 580, it is said that the real basis for the admission of testimony given by a witness at a former trial is to prevent the miscarriage of justice where the circumstances of the case have made it unreasonable and unfair to exclude the same, and where the court perceives no need for the introduction of testimony taken at a former trial of the same issue, such evidence is properly excluded.

There is a difference of opinion upon the right to use in a civil case the testimony given in a criminal case by a witness whose testimony is no longer available. Indeed this court has had difficulty with this question. In Ray v. Henderson, handed down in 1914, without dissent, it was held in the first paragraph of the syllabus as follows:

"The testimony of a witness, since deceased, given at an examining trial before a justice of the peace on the charge of felonious assault, may be used against the defendant, in a civil suit against him, for damages by the person assaulted."

In Concordia Fire Insurance Co. v. Wise, Adm'r, handed down in 1926, with a divided court, 5 to 3, we overruled Ray v. Henderson, supra, and held in the fifth paragraph of the syllabus as follows:

"In an action to recover on a fire insurance policy, the testimony of a witness who had since died, given in the criminal proceedings against the insured for burning the building covered by insurance, is properly excluded."

Since our decisions are binding upon trial courts and litigants, we appreciate the necessity of establishing a rule and following it. However, if we have established the wrong rule, or if our rule is unsound, we should avail ourselves of the first opportunity to correct it lest we perpetuate the wrong. In 142 A.L.R. 673, there appears an Annotation on the question involved herein. At page 701 of the Annotation the author states that he considers it unfortunate that we overruled Ray v. Henderson in the Concordia case.

It is interesting to note that in the Concordia case we followed the rule laid down by the Supreme Court of Illinois (McInturff v. Insurance Co. of North America), *believing it to be the majority rule.* However, in 46 A.L.R. (published subsequent to the Concordia decision) there appears an Annotation on page 463, under the subject "Use in civil case of testimony given in criminal case by witness no longer accessible", wherein it is said:

> "The weight of authority seems to be to the effect that, on a proper showing of inability to procure the attendance of a witness at the trial of a civil case, his testimony given in a criminal prosecution involving the same transaction is admissible against the person who was defendant therein."

The author lists decisions from five states, Georgia, Iowa, New York, South Dakota, and Wisconsin, as constituting the weight of authority. Three states, Illinois, Pennsylvania, and Oklahoma (citing the Concordia case), are listed as following the minority view.

It is quite often stated that before testimony can be taken from a former trial or proceeding and introduced in a subsequent trial there must be (1) an inability to obtain the testimony of the witness; (2) there must have been an opportunity to cross-examine the witness in the former trial; (3) there must be an identity, or substantial identity of issues, and (4) parties. These requirements are recognized in the Concordia case. The primary difficulty arises when we attempt to determine if there is an identity of issues. In a Pennsylvania decision, Harger v. Thomas, heavy stress was laid upon the conclusion that a criminal prosecution is not an action, and that the issue in a criminal case is between the government and the prisoner on the question of guilt, and not a question of property. In the Illinois case, McInturff v. Insurance Co. of North America, supra, it was pointed out that the issue in a criminal case is "guilt" and in a civil case the issue is "property." The "issue" as defined by those courts appears to us to be more in the nature of the ultimate issue, or result sought to be obtained by the action or proceeding. In our view it would be more accurate to consider the "issue" as that issue sought to be established by the witness when he testified in the criminal case and weigh it against the issue sought to be proved in the witness in the civil case.

In the case before us, it appears that Eppler and Brown testified in the criminal case to establish the issue of whether J.B. Wright procured the burning of the building. Affirmative proof of this issue was necessary to establish his guilt. In the civil case before us the issue is whether J.B. Wright procured the burning of the building. Affirmative proof of this issue is necessary if defendants herein are to prevail. It may be that there were other issues sought to be proved by other witnesses in the instant case, but the issue sought to be established by Eppler and Brown in both the criminal and civil cases was whether J.B. Wright procured the burning of the building.

From a re-examination of our former decisions, and decisions from other jurisdictions, it becomes apparent that it is impossible to write a rule that will fit all situations. As pointed out in 20 Am.Jur., p. 580, supra, the reason for admitting testimony given at a former trial is to prevent a miscarriage of justice. It naturally follows that testimony from a former trial should not be admitted if to do so would result in a miscarriage of justice.

As a general proposition we think testimony from a criminal case can be introduced in a subsequent civil case where it appears that it is impossible to obtain the testimony of the witness who testified in the criminal case; that there was an opportunity to cross-examine the witness by the party against whom the testimony is sought to be used in the civil case, or by one whose motive and interest in cross-examining was the same; and that there is an identity of issues. As will be hereinafter shown, identity of *all* parties is not an independent requirement in all cases.

As a further safeguard the trial court should give the objecting party an opportunity to point out wherein it would be unjust to admit such testimony. We have examined the transcript of the testimony given by the witnesses Eppler and Brown, in the criminal case and find nothing therein indicating that it would have been unjust to admit the testimony against the plaintiffs in this case.

From our examination of the record herein it appears that the trial court erred in refusing to let the court reporter relate the testimony given by Eppler and Brown in the criminal case. It also follows that the rule that is expressed in the fifth paragraph of the syllabus in Concordia Fire Insurance Co. v. Wise must be, and accordingly is, overruled insofar as it conflicts with the views herein expressed.

Is it material that one of the plaintiffs herein, J.C. Wright, was not a party defendant in the criminal case, and apparently did not participate in the alleged burning of the insured property? We think not.

The insurance policies herein, on which recovery is sought, provide that the defendant companies will not be liable for loss by fire caused by neglect of the insured to use all reasonable means to save and preserve the property at and after a loss. In 29 Am.Jur.Insurance § 1028, pp. 777 and 778, it is said:

> "On the other hand, an innocent partner cannot recover on an insurance policy upon partnership property wilfully burned by his copartner, especially where the policy provides that the insured shall use all reasonable means at and after a fire to preserve the property."

This rule of law is supported by cases cited in American Jurisprudence and in an Annotation in 27 A.L.R. beginning at page 948.

Is it important that J.C. Wright did not have an opportunity to cross-examine in the criminal case? J.B. Wright had the same motive and interest in cross-examining the witnesses in the criminal case as would J.C. Wright in the instant case. The issues were the same in both cases. J.B. Wright had, and has, the same property interest as that of J.C. Wright. In 142 A.L.R. at page 696, the author quotes from 5 Wigmore on Evidence, 3rd ed. § 1368, as follows:

> "* * * The principle, then, is that where the interest of the person was calculated to induce equally as thorough a testing by cross-examination, then the present opponent has had adequate protection for the same end. Thus the requirement of identity of parties is after all only an incident or corollary of the requirement as to identity of issue. * * * It ought then, to be sufficient to inquire whether the former testimony was given upon such an issue that the party-opponent in that case had the same interest and motive in his cross-examination that the present opponent has."

The author of the Annotation concludes that the argument and position taken by Wigmore is supported by a considerable number of cases from various jurisdictions and cites the cases in support of that rule. We conclude that J.B. Wright's opportunity to cross-examine the witness in the criminal case on the same issue, and with the same interest and motives that J.C. Wright would have in the instant case, satisfies the rule of substantial identity of issues and parties and opportunity for satisfactory cross-examination.

From the foregoing it is seen that the question of substantial identity of parties is important only with regard to the parties as against whom such testimony is offered; therefore the fact that the state was J.B. Wright's adversary in the first case rather than the insurance companies is immaterial. Such fact has no bearing upon the question of whether there has been an adequate opportunity to thoroughly sift and test such testimony by cross-examination.

In view of our conclusion to remand for new trial, we think it is necessary that we give attention to other questions presented in the briefs which undoubtedly will be presented when the case is retried.

We have herein held that the court reporter should be permitted to relate and testify as to what both witnesses testified to in the criminal trial. This conclusion is upon the assumption that both witnesses, at the subsequent trial of this case, will be subpoenaed and will claim their privilege against self-incrimination, and that their claims will be granted. If so, their testimony is as unavailable as if they were dead.

The judgment is reversed and the cause remanded for a new trial in accordance with the views herein expressed.

Davison, Halley, Johnson, Williams and Carlile, JJ., concur.

Corn V.C.J., and Blackbird, J., dissent.

See Federal Rules of Evidence 804(b)(1); California Rules of Evidence §§ 1290–1292.

NOTE

When an issue that has been examined in a prior action arises in a second action:

1. Under the former testimony exception, testimony given in the first action may be admissible as evidence in the second. See Fed.R.Evid. 804(b)(1).

2. Under the exception for judgments of conviction, the judgment in the first action may be admissible as evidence in the second. See Fed.R.Evid. 803(22).

3. Under the doctrine of issue preclusion (also known as collateral estoppel) the judgment in the first action may preclude relitigation. If so, the issue has already been decided for purposes of the second action, and evidence on the precluded issue is not admissible. In contrast, when the judgment is used merely as evidence, it can be contradicted with other evidence and the second trier can reach a result different from the first trier.

Obviously, if issue preclusion applied in every case in which an issue had been examined in a prior lawsuit, there would be no occasion to create hearsay exceptions for prior testimony or for judgments. Often, however, issue preclusion does not apply despite the existence of overlapping lawsuits. For example, issue preclusion does not apply when the issue sought to be precluded was not actually litigated in the first action. For this reason, a conviction upon a plea of guilty does not have preclusive effect in later litigation, since nothing was litigated in the first action. (This continues to be the prevailing view, despite some distinguished opposition. See Shapiro, Should a Guilty Plea have Preclusive Effect? 70 Iowa L. Rev. 27 (1984).) Preclusive effect may also be denied when determination of the issue was not essential to the judgment in the first action, or when the first action did not come to final judgment. See Restatement, Judgments, Second, § 27 (1982). Even when these conditions are satisfied, there are a variety of exceptions to the rule of preclusion. See Restatement, Judgments, Second, § 28 (1982) (exceptions for cases in which, for example, the procedures in the two courts are substantially different, the burden of proof has shifted, the public interest would be detrimentally affected, the second action was not foreseeable, or in which there was not an adequate opportunity or incentive to litigate in the first action).

Another obstacle to preclusion is the doctrine of mutuality of estoppel. Under traditional mutuality doctrine, a person who was not a party or privy to a prior lawsuit was neither bound by the prior suit nor permitted to take advantage of any determination made in the suit. The doctrine of mutuality was based on the notion that since the prior judgment could not have been used against a stranger to the prior suit had the decision been unfavorable to the stranger, fair play required that the stranger not be allowed to benefit from a favorable judgment. The doctrine treated persons equally when in fact they were in quite different situations. It treated a party who had an opportunity to litigate in the first action in the same way that it treated a non-party who had no opportunity.

The mutuality doctrine has been wholly or partly abandoned in many jurisdictions. A stranger to prior litigation is now often permitted to use issue preclusion against a party who had a full and fair opportunity to litigate in the prior action. Again, however, there are a number of exceptions for situations in which preclusion would have a detrimental effect on the public interest, or in which preclusion would be unfair to the precluded party. For example, if the first action was held in a court that did not allow discovery or follow rules of evidence, then many jurisdictions would not allow the issue to be precluded. See Restatement, Judgments, Second, § 29 (1982).

The once-prevalent refusal to treat criminal convictions as preclusive in subsequent civil cases was a specific application of the mutuality doctrine. (Perhaps other considerations, such as the absence of discovery in criminal actions and the danger that the criminal process would be abused by those with civil claims, have also had an impact.) The modern tendency, by no means universal, is toward expanding the situations in which prior convictions can be used to preclude relitigation of issues in civil cases. Where the convicted person seeks to profit from the crime, as when an arsonist sues the insurance company for the proceeds of fire insurance, courts are generally receptive toward preclusion. Many allow it in other situations, so long as there was a full and fair opportunity to defend the criminal prosecution and the convicted person cannot point to any defect in the proceeding. See Restatement of Judgments, Second, § 85(2)(a), Comment e thereto, and authorities cited in Comment e.

Hypotheticals

(1) X is prosecuted for robbery of A, a bartender. At X's preliminary hearing A testified as to the commission of the crime. In addition A stated the address of B Bar where he was then working, and his residence address, but indicated he planned to change his residence address very soon. At X's trial, the prosecutor offers in evidence the preliminary hearing transcript of A's testimony after calling C, a district attorney's investigator, who testifies that he had been unable to locate A; that A no longer worked at B Bar; and that the local phone book and voters' registration list did not contain A's name. On cross-examination by X, C testifies that he did not make inquiry at the Bartenders' Union nor the residence address A gave at the preliminary hearing, because A had said he was planning to move very soon. X makes a hearsay objection to the preliminary hearing transcript testimony of A. What result?

(2) X is prosecuted for robbery of A. The prosecutor offers in evidence the transcript of A's testimony given at the preliminary hearing after calling B, a district attorney's investigator, who testifies that a subpoena had been sent to A's place of employment but was not served because A was in New York; that an hour before testifying, he, B, had made a telephone call to A in New York and A told him that she planned to remain in New York for six months. Should X's hearsay objection to A's transcript testimony be sustained?

(3) A sues X for $1500 property damage to his automobile arising out of a rear-end collision. X takes A's deposition. A moves to New York after his deposition is taken and is living there at the time of trial. A's counsel offers A's deposition testimony in evidence after testifying that a few days before trial, A telephoned and said it was too expensive for him to come back to California and testify. X makes a hearsay objection to A's deposition testimony. What result?

(4) X, a police officer, pursued a suspect felon into a bar. X became involved in a dispute with A, the bar owner, regarding the whereabouts of the suspected felon. X claims that A struck him with a chair. X arrested A on the charge of battery upon a police officer. In the criminal trial of A, A testifies that he didn't touch X and that X struck him with his billy club. B, a bar patron who was present, testifies for A and corroborates A's version of what

happened. A was acquitted and then sues X and Y City, X's employer, for damages for battery, false arrest, and imprisonment. At the trial of A's action against X and Y City, A establishes that B's whereabouts are unknown and that he used reasonable diligence to find B to serve him with a subpoena, but to no avail. A then offers in evidence a transcript of B's testimony given in A's criminal trial. X and Y City make hearsay objections. How should the court rule?

(5) D is charged with possession of narcotics. D is first arrested at his residence for an unrelated offense. At the time of his arrest, X resided with D. While D is in jail on the unrelated charge, P, a police officer, secures a search warrant for D's residence and discovers a home-constructed bedframe with hollowed out compartments in which P finds the narcotics. D testifies that he had no knowledge of the items in the bedframe compartments, that shortly before his arrest he had observed a pill vial in X's possession similar to the one found in the bedframe compartment, and that he had previously observed X injecting "speed". D offers in evidence in his defense under the former-testimony hearsay exception evidence given by X in another criminal case in a different county. In this prior case X testified for the prosecution as a witness to the murder of her husband, which took place one week after D's arrest. On cross-examination of X at the former trial, testimony was elicited from her that on the evening of the killing she was under the influence of narcotics, having earlier injected "speed"; that she was a narcotics addict and had possession of narcotics and the necessary paraphernalia for their use. At D's trial it is conceded that X is unavailable as a witness. D contends that X's former testimony is relevant on the question of D's lack of knowledge, possession, and control of the items discovered in the bedframe. The prosecutor makes a hearsay objection to the proffered former testimony of X. Should the prosecutor's motion be sustained?

5. DECLARATIONS AGAINST INTEREST

G.M. McKELVEY CO. v. GENERAL CASUALTY CO. OF AMERICA

Supreme Court of Ohio, 1957.
166 Ohio St. 401, 2 O.O.2d 345, 142 N.E.2d 854.

MATTHIAS, Judge. The issue raised by this appeal is whether, in a civil action against an insurer by an insured employer upon a policy of fidelity insurance protecting such employer from defalcations by his employees, written and signed confessions by certain employees admitting misappropriations of their employer's funds and stating the amounts of such misappropriations are admissible in evidence to prove both the fact and the amount of the loss.

* * *

Early in the history of the law of evidence the courts recognized that, although in most instances hearsay evidence should not be admitted, due to the inability to test the trustworthiness of such evidence, there are conditions and circumstances in which hearsay evidence as a matter of necessity must and can be relied upon as being trustworthy.

One of the exceptions to the hearsay rule, which has been found to be based on trustworthiness or a probability of truthfulness and veracity, and which has arisen due to necessity, is a declaration against interest by a third party.

The courts, where confronted with a situation where death, absence from the jurisdiction or insanity makes a witness unavailable, and where such witness is the only source from which his evidence can be obtained, have held that as a matter of necessity a declaration by such witness against his interest should be admitted in evidence. The courts have reasoned that a person does not make statements against his own pecuniary interest unless they are true and have thus considered such statements trustworthy, even though there is no opportunity to confront the witness or to cross-examine him. 5 Wigmore on Evidence, 204, Section 1421.

Thus, the rule has arisen that a declaration against interest by one not a party or in privity with a party to an action is admissible in evidence, where (1) the person making such declaration is either dead or unavailable as a witness due to sickness, insanity or absence from the jurisdiction, (2) the declarant had peculiar means of knowing the facts which he stated, (3) the declaration was against his pecuniary or proprietary interest and (4) he had no probable motive to falsify the facts stated.

*   *   *

We realize that element (1) of the rule above is somewhat broader than the dicta spoken by the court in the Stetson case, i.e., "we are clear in the opinion that it could not properly be received while he was a living and competent witness," but we are compelled by logic and reason to the conclusion that there may be circumstances other than death which render a witness as unavailable to testify as if he were in fact dead, and that under such circumstances a declaration, if it meets the other requirements of the rule, loses none of its trustworthiness or probability of truthfulness and veracity. Thus, anything in the dicta of the court in the Stetson case, hereinbefore set out, which is contrary to this conclusion cannot be said to be the law of Ohio on the subject.

At least as applied to written and signed confessions, we are in accord with the rule as stated above, and we will consider the confessions of the employees in the instant case in relation to this rule. First, it is apparent from the record that the employees making them were unavailable as witnesses, having been summoned and not found in the jurisdiction by the sheriff. Second, certainly a person who commits an embezzlement has a peculiar means of knowing whether he embezzled and how much he took, and, from the record in the instant case, plaintiff's employees are the only persons who can accurately indicate both the fact and the amount of the embezzlements. Third, it was clearly not in their interest to state such facts, since such declarations render them civilly liable for the amounts of their defalcations. Fourth, there would certainly be no probable motive for plaintiff's employees to falsify the facts stated unless it would be to minimize the amount of their defalcations, and that question is not raised herein.

*   *   *

It is our conclusion that, in a civil action by an insured against his fidelity insurer to recover for defalcations by employees of the former, where such employees are unavailable as witnesses, they having been summoned and not found in the jurisdiction by the sheriff, written and signed confessions of such employees are admissible in evidence as declarations against interest as to both the fact and the amount of the loss.

For the reasons herein set out, the judgment of the Court of Appeals is affirmed.

Judgment affirmed.

WEYGANDT, C.J., and ZIMMERMAN, STEWART, BELL, TAFT and HERBERT, JJ., concur.

UNITED STATES v. BARRETT

United States Court of Appeals, First Circuit, 1976.
539 F.2d 244.

Before COFFIN, Chief Judge, McENTEE and CAMPBELL, Circuit Judges.

LEVIN H. CAMPBELL, Circuit Judge.

Arthur Barrett appeals from his conviction after a jury trial for crimes arising from the theft and sale of a collection of postage stamps from the Cardinal Spellman Philatelic Museum in Weston, Massachusetts. [Barrett's nickname was "Bucky." Ben Tilley was allegedly a co-conspirator of Barrett's, but died prior to trial. "Buzzy" Adams testified at Barrett's trial as a government witness, in exchange for immunity from prosecution.]

* * *

Barrett * * * argues that the court below erred by refusing to admit the testimony of three defense witnesses. The first was James Melvin. Melvin testified that in February, 1974, he was at a card game on Bowdoin Street, in Dorchester, Massachusetts, with Ben Tilley. When Melvin was asked to recount a conversation which he had there with Tilley, the Government objected. Barrett made an offer of proof that Melvin would testify that Tilley had told Melvin "that he, Tilley, and Buzzy [Adams] were going to have some trouble from the people from California" with respect to the "stamp theft or matter" and that "[Melvin] asked him did he mean Bucky or Buzzy, and then he said, 'No, Bucky [Barrett] wasn't involved. It was Buzzy.'" Barrett argued at the bench that this testimony was admissible under Fed.R.Evid. 804(b)(3) as a declaration against self-interest, apparently on the theory that Tilley's display of inside knowledge of "the people from California," the stamp theft, and the identity of persons "involved", all tended against Tilley's penal interest at the time by advertising his likely complicity. The court excluded the proffered testimony as hearsay on the ground that the relevant part, that Buzzy, not Bucky, was involved, was not against Tilley's interest. The court said, "You are offering it not to prove anything prejudicial to the alleged maker of the statement but to prove that [Buzzy] rather than [Bucky] did it * * *." Barrett argues on appeal that the entire statement, including the portion exculpating Barrett, should have been admitted.

Rule 804(b)(3) of the new Federal Rules of Evidence provides, with an important qualification, for the admission of a statement by an unavailable declarant that at the time of making tended to subject him to criminal liability. The rule provides in pertinent part,

> "(b) *Hearsay exceptions.* The following are not excluded by the hearsay rule if the declarant is unavailable as a witness:
>
>   *   *   *
>
> (3) *Statement against interest.* A statement which was at the time of its making so far contrary to the declarant's pecuniary or proprietary interest, or so far tended to subject him to civil or criminal liability *   *   * that a reasonable man in his position would not have made the statement unless he believed it to be true. A statement tending to expose the declarant to criminal liability and offered to exculpate the accused is not admissable [sic] unless corroborating circumstances clearly indicate the trustworthiness of the statement."

Rule 804(b)(3) is a departure from the principle laid down in *Donnelly v. United States,* in which the Supreme Court endorsed the exclusion from evidence of a third party's extra-judicial confession to the murder for which the defendant was on trial. In conformity with English precedent, the *Donnelly* court limited the hearsay exception for declarations against interest to declarations against interest of a pecuniary character. Statements subjecting the declarant to criminal liability were held to be outside the exception.

Half a century later, when the present Federal Rules of Evidence were being formulated, *Donnelly* was in disfavor, and provision was made in the various drafts of the new code for the admission of declarations against penal interest. The text underwent several revisions prior to enactment. A provision forbidding prosecutorial use of third party statements or confessions which implicated an accused as well as the declarant was deleted, with the result that subject to sixth amendment and other constraints, a third party's out of court statements against penal interest may now be used against, as well as in favor of, an accused. And, more relevant here, the second sentence of clause (3) was rewritten to require that statements offered to exculpate the accused be corroborated so as to "clearly indicate the trustworthiness of the statement".

As submitted to Congress by the Supreme Court, the Rule required simply that a statement offered to exculpate the accused be corroborated. The Advisory Committee explained this requirement as a way of accommodating the common law's distrust of confessions offered to exculpate an accused:

> "The refusal of the common law to concede the adequacy of a penal interest was no doubt indefensible in logic [citing Holmes' *Donnelly* dissent], but one senses in the decisions a distrust of evidence of confessions by third persons offered to exculpate the accused arising from suspicions of fabrication either of the fact of the making of the confession or in its contents, enhanced in either instance by the required unavailability of the declarant. Nevertheless, an increasing amount of decisional law recognizes exposure to punishment for crime as

a sufficient stake. The requirement of corroboration is included in the rule in order to effect an accommodation between
these competing considerations. When the statement is offered by the accused by way of exculpation, the resulting
situation is not adapted to control by rulings as to the weight
of the evidence, and hence the provision is cast in terms of a
requirement preliminary to admissibility. The requirement of
corroboration should be construed in such a manner as to
effectuate its purpose of circumventing fabrication." [Cita-
tions omitted.]

Notes of Advisory Committee on Proposed Rules, at 28 U.S.C.A. Fed.R.
Evid. 804.

The House Judiciary Committee strengthened this corroboration
requirement by adding the present language. The Committee noted,

"[The Committee] believed * * * as did the [Supreme] Court
[in its earlier version] that statements of this type tending to
exculpate the accused are more suspect and so should have
their admissibility conditioned upon some further provision
insuring trustworthiness. The proposal in the Court Rule to
add a requirement of simple corroboration was, however,
deemed ineffective to accomplish this purpose since the accused's own testimony might suffice while not necessarily
increasing the reliability of the hearsay statement. The Committee settled upon the language 'unless corroborating circumstances clearly indicate the trustworthiness of the statement'
as affording a proper standard and degree of discretion. It was
contemplated that the result in such cases as Donnelly v.
United States where the circumstances plainly indicated reliability, would be changed."

Notes of Committee on the Judiciary, H.R.Rep. No. 93–650, Note to
Subdivision (b)(3), at 28 U.S.C.A. Fed.R.Evid. 804, U.S.Code Cong. &
Admin.News 1974, pp. 7051, 7089.

As finally enacted, Rule 804(b)(3) requires a two-stage analysis:
first, do the offered remarks come within the hearsay exception as a
"statement against interest"? and second, if they do, is there sufficient
corroboration to clearly indicate trustworthiness? Here we believe that
the remarks offered were statements against interest within the Rule,
and that the district court should have gone on to determine whether
there was sufficient corroboration so as to warrant their admission.

Turning to the first stage of analysis, we think that Tilley's alleged
remarks sufficiently tended to subject him to criminal liability "that a
reasonable man in his position would not have made the statement
unless he believed it to be true." * * * A reasonable person would
have realized that remarks of the sort attributed to Tilley strongly
implied his personal participation in the stamp crimes and hence would
tend to subject him to criminal liability. Though by no means conclusive, the statement would be important evidence against Tilley were he
himself on trial for the stamp crimes. We cannot say, therefore, that it

did not pose the sort of threat to Tilley's interest that the hearsay exception contemplates.

We do not overlook the fact that the proffered remarks came in the course of conversation with acquaintances over cards. In such circumstances, Tilley might not so readily have perceived the disserving character of what was said nor have expected his words to be repeated to the police. But we are unable to say that the contextual circumstances so far impugn the reliability presumed from the remarks' disserving character as to take them outside the first part of the Rule. * * * The factors in question seem better considered under the second part of the Rule in determining whether, overall, there is enough corroboration to "clearly indicate * * * trustworthiness."

Nor do we overlook the fact that exculpating Barrett was not in itself against Tilley's interest, since both could have participated in the crime. Tilley's remarks differ in this respect from the third-party confession in * * * Donnelly. In Barrett's trial, the relevance of Tilley's participation is limited to the credence it gives to his views on who else took part. The district court seemed to suggest that in order for exculpatory remarks such as Tilley's to be admissible as against interest, the innocence of the accused must itself be prejudicial to the declarant. On the present facts, we read the first part of Rule 804(b)(3) more broadly, and conclude that so much of Tilley's remarks as exculpated "Bucky" and inculpated "Buzzy" should here be considered as part of the statement against Tilley's interest.

Under the common law exception for declarations against interest, the treatment to be given portions of a declaration collateral to the declarant's interest has been the subject of much debate. A leading commentator, after acknowledging the traditional liberality with which courts have admitted collateral statements, has expressed the opinion that,

> "As long as the courts adhere to the exceptions to the hearsay rule it would be more reasonable to confine the use of statements against interest in all cases to the proof of the fact which is against interest, since the reliability of other parts of the statement is conjectural."

B. Jefferson, Declarations Against Interest: An Exception to the Hearsay Rule, 58 Harv.L.Rev. 1, 62–63 (1944). And more pointedly, in an article criticizing certain conventional exceptions to the hearsay rule, another author has said,

> "Nonetheless, the naming of another as a compatriot will almost never be against the declarant's own interest and thus will contain little assurance of reliability on this ground. * * * The invocation of a name may be gratuitous, may be deliberately false in order to gain advantages for the declarant greater than those that would flow from naming a real participant or no one at all, may be a cover for concealment purposes (another kind of 'advantage'), or may represent an effort to gain some kind of personal revenge." [Footnote omitted.]

D. Davenport, The Confrontation Clause and the Coconspirator Exception in Criminal Prosecutions: A Functional Analysis, 85 Harv.L.Rev. 1378, 1396 (1972).

There are two reasons, however, which make it difficult for us to agree with the district court's view of the statement in issue. First, the Buzzy-Bucky statement, especially in context, is itself arguably disserving to Tilley, since it strengthened the impression that he had an insider's knowledge of the crimes. And second, the case law, while far from settled, has tended to grant at least "[a] certain latitude as to contextual statements, neutral as to invest giving meaning to the declaration against interest * * *", McCormick on Evidence § 279(a), at 676 (2d ed. 1972). While we do not read the federal rule as incorporating the rather broad formulation put forward by Wigmore, who saw the against-interest exception as permitting reception not only of the "specific fact against interest, but also * * * *every fact contained in the same statement*", Wigmore, supra, § 1465, at 339 (emphasis in original), neither does it appear that Congress intended to constrict the scope of a declaration against interest to the point of excluding "collateral" material that, as here, actually tended to fortify the statement's disserving aspects. See Notes of Advisory Committee, supra; Notes of Committee on the Judiciary, supra. We hold that the Buzzy-Bucky remark was sufficiently integral to the entire statement, and the latter sufficiently against interest, as to come within the first part of Rule 804(b)(3).

It follows that the district court was under an obligation to determine, under the second sentence of the Rule, whether "corroborating circumstances clearly indicate[d] the trustworthiness of the statement", including we would add, the trustworthiness of that part exculpating Barrett. We emphasize that admissibility is conditional upon separate compliance with that standard, which, it is clear from both the statutory language and the legislative history, is not an insignificant hurdle. * * * We would * * * make two observations to guide the district court's judgment, should the question arise upon retrial. [Elsewhere in its opinion, the court had decided that the conviction should be reversed because the trial court had erroneously excluded evidence about prior inconsistent statements of a government witness.—Eds.]

First we would not read the standard of trustworthiness as imposing a standard so strict as to be utterly unrealistic. Even in *Donnelly* * * * the evidence, while strongly corroborated, could have been disbelieved by the jury. On the other hand, there is no question but that Congress meant to preclude reception of exculpatory hearsay statements against penal interest unless accompanied by circumstances solidly indicating trustworthiness. This requirement goes beyond minimal corroboration. * * *

Second, in ruling on trustworthiness courts should be mindful of the possible relationship between constitutional cases * * * and the new federal rule. * * * Rule 804(b)(3) reflects Congress' attempt to strike a fair balance between exclusion of trustworthy evidence, as in * * * *Donnelly*, and indiscriminate admission of less trustworthy evidence which, because of the lack of opportunity for cross-examination and the absence of the declarant, is open to easy fabrication. Clearly the federal rule is no more restrictive than the Constitution permits, and may in some situations be more inclusive. * * *

Hypotheticals

(1) X is prosecuted for possession of a marijuana cigarette that was found in a jacket in X's car. X's defense is that the jacket belonged to A. X calls A as a witness and A refuses to answer questions about the jacket on the ground of the self-incrimination privilege. X then calls B, who will testify that A told him on the day before X's arrest that he had been riding with X and left his jacket in X's car. The prosecution makes a hearsay objection to B's proposed testimony. How should the court rule?

(2) X is charged with possession of heroin. The heroin was found in X's house while A was present. X establishes that A is in another state at the time of trial. X calls B, the wife of A, and offers to have her testify that A told her that the heroin found in X's house belonged to A. The prosecution makes a hearsay objection to B's testimony. What result? [Should it matter whether under the laws of the jurisdiction A's statement to his wife was privileged and inadmissible against A?]

(3) A is a guest in a car driven by B, which collides in an intersection with a car driven by X. A, B, and X all receive personal injuries. A sues X for damages, claiming that X ran the red light. X claims that B ran the red light. X offers testimony that B is in Europe. X then calls C and proposes that C will testify that a week after the accident B told him that his accident with X was all B's fault because he "blew the red light". Should A's hearsay objection to C's proposed testimony be sustained?

(4) A sues X in a paternity action, claiming that X is the father of a child born to A. X calls B who testifies that he (B) was a friend of C, a married man who now lives in Europe. X proposes to have B testify that C was formerly A's boss and that C told him (B) he (C) was having an affair with A during the time that A's child was conceived. A makes a hearsay objection to B's proposed testimony. What result?

(5) D is charged with murder of V, who was shot to death. The prosecution introduced testimony that D, along with another, was seen beating V prior to the shooting. There was no eyewitness testimony as to whether D did the shooting. Upon D's request, the trial judge conducts an evidence-admissibility hearing out of the presence of the jury. D calls X to testify about whether X did the shooting. X refuses to answer any questions on the ground of self-incrimination. D then calls A, who testifies that he was in the county jail with X and heard X state (1) that he had shot V in the chest and (2) that D was present trying to break up the fight. On cross-examination, A testifies that he also heard X say that X would "take the beef" because he was going to the Youth Authority and couldn't get hurt; that later, at the Youth Authority, he heard X state to a counselor that D had asked him to testify falsely on his behalf and had threatened to get him if he refused. D then offers to have A testify before the jury as to X's statements (1) that X had shot V and (2) that D was trying to break up the fight. The prosecutor makes a hearsay objection and D urges that X's statements would be admissible under the hearsay exception for a declaration against penal interest. The trial judge sustains the prosecutor's hearsay objection. Is this ruling appropriate?

———

See Federal Rules of Evidence 804(b)(3); California Evidence Code § 1230.

6. STATE OF MIND

ADKINS v. BRETT

Supreme Court of California, 1920.
184 Cal. 252, 193 P. 251.

OLNEY, J. The action involved in the present appeal is one for damages for the alienation by the defendant of the plaintiff's wife. The cause was tried before a jury, a verdict was returned for the plaintiff, and from the judgment entered upon the verdict the defendant appeals.

The first point made on behalf of the defendant is that the verdict is not supported by the evidence. No question is made but that the evidence supports the conclusion that the husband had lost the affection of his wife, as a result of which she insisted upon a separation, or, if the testimony on behalf of the plaintiff be believed, as it must be taken it was by the jury, that acts of criminal conversation had taken place between the plaintiff's wife and the defendant. The particular in which it is claimed the evidence is insufficient is that, according to counsel's contention, it does not show that the defendant lured and enticed the plaintiff's wife from her husband, was her seducer, so to speak. Passing by the question as to whether or not evidence of adultery by a wife not shown to have theretofore lost her affection for her husband is not sufficient of itself to justify an inference of active seduction on the part of the man involved, it is sufficient for the purposes of this case to say that there was evidence of statements by the defendant to a male companion by the name of Tucker made by the day after a call by the two upon the wife as to what had taken place the night before, which, if true, justified the conclusion that the defendant was the active aggressor against the wife's resistance on the occasion when first they had criminal intercourse. It is only fair to say that the making of the statements was denied by the defendant, as was any guilty relation whatever on his part with the wife, and that the witness Tucker appears in anything but a creditable light. But evidence of the statements by the defendant was competent against him as admissions by him, and we cannot say that the jury was not justified in believing the evidence. It should also be said that there was considerable corroboration. The case is not one of a want of evidence in any particular, but of a flat conflict of evidence in nearly every particular, with gross perjury on one side or the other. Where the truth lay it was for the jury to determine.

The serious questions in the case arise in connection with the admission of evidence of conversations between the plaintiff and his wife, wherein the latter admitted or stated that she had gone automobile riding with the defendant, had dined with him, had received flowers from him, that he was able to give her a good time, and the plaintiff was not, that she intended to continue to accept the defendant's attentions and the plaintiff could do what he pleased about it, and that he was distasteful to her.

One objection to the evidence of these conversations, which may as well be disposed of at the outset as involving the most elementary principles of evidence, is that they were had without the presence of the defendant. The answer to this objection is that it is wholly immaterial whether the defendant was present or not. The competency of evidence of declarations or statements by a person other than the party to the action against whom they are introduced is not affected merely by the latter's presence or absence. If the evidence be not competent if the party against whom it is sought to introduce it was not present when the statements or declarations were made, no more is it competent if he were present. There are apparent exceptions to this, but they are only apparent, and not real, exceptions. One instance is that, when the party to the litigation was present and his conduct in response to the declarations or statements of others or his replies to them are of such character as to amount to admissions by him, his conduct, including his silence or want of action where an inference can fairly be drawn from them, or his replies, may be shown in evidence against him, and as a part of such conduct or replies the statements or declarations of others to which they are a response. But the primary thing which is admitted in evidence in such a case is the party's own conduct or statements, and, unless these are of such a character as to be relevant evidence against him, the declarations or statements of others are not admissible simply because made in his presence. Another instance is where it is sought to charge a party with notice or knowledge, and for that purpose evidence is introduced of a statement made to him notifying or informing him.

The real objection to such evidence as that under consideration is that it is hearsay. The evidence was plainly relevant; that is, it tended to prove matters in issue, and was therefore admissible unless there is some rule of exclusion applicable to it. The only rule of exclusion to which it can be subject is the rule against hearsay. The evidence was, in fact, hearsay, both as to the past matters stated in the conversations and as to the wife's statements of her then feelings toward the plaintiff and the defendant. But the rule is thoroughly well settled that, when the intention, feelings, or other mental state of a certain person at a particular time, including his bodily feelings, is material to the issues under trial, evidence of such person's declarations at the time indicative of his then mental state, even though hearsay, is competent as within an exception to the hearsay rule. In the present case the state of the wife's feelings at the time of these conversations, both toward her husband and toward the defendant, was material, and the conversations were indicative of her feelings, and, this being so, evidence of them, was admissible to show her then state of feelings. This much can hardly be questioned, in view of the settled character of the general rule just stated, its plain applicability to just such cases as the present, and the fact that it has very generally been so applied.

The difficulty in regard to such declarations as those involved here lies in the fact that, while they may be competent upon the point of the wife's feelings, they go very much further. They contain statements as to matters, such as automobile rides, dinners, flowers, and attentions generally by the defendant to the wife, as proof of which the statements are not within any exception to the hearsay rule and are wholly incompetent. The situation is intensified by the fact that those matters are themselves material to the issues, and, if true, very detrimental to the defendant, so that the admission of the evidence involves the placing before the jury of evidence tending to prove matters in issue, for proving which such evidence is not competent, and the proof of which is very prejudicial to the party against whom it is introduced.

Nevertheless, it is clear enough that the evidence, competent for the purpose of showing the state of the wife's feelings, is not rendered incompetent by the fact that it also tends to prove other material matters, to prove which it is not competent. The rule upon this point, which is one of well-nigh everyday application in actual trial, is thus stated by Wigmore (volume 1, p. 42):

> "In other words, when an evidentiary fact is offered for one purpose, and becomes admissible by satisfying all the rules applicable to it in that capacity, it is not inadmissible because it does not satisfy the rules applicable to it in some other capacity, and because the jury might improperly consider it in the latter capacity. This doctrine, although involving certain risks, is indispensable as a practical rule."

Cripe v. Cripe, supra, is an illustration of this. A father was sued by the wife of his son for the alienation from her of the son, and at the trial the following question was asked of the father as a witness:

> "After the marriage of your son and daughter, and before Dolly [the son's wife] left the ranch at Huasua in August, 1911, did your son ever tell you that Dolly drank to such an extent that he could not control her, or did he ever tell you during that time that she abused him so bad that he could not live with her?"

It is plain that as to the facts that the wife drank to excess and abused her husband, so that he could not live with her, the evidence was hearsay, was not within any exception to the hearsay rule, and was wholly incompetent, and at the same time those facts were material to the case, and, if true, very detrimental to the cause of the wife, so that the introduction of the evidence would be very prejudicial to her as to facts which the evidence was wholly incompetent to prove. Nevertheless the question was held to be proper, and the refusal of the trial court to permit it to be answered reversible error, on the ground that the testimony which it called for was competent to show the state of the son's feelings.

* * * In this situation there is little question but that Cripe v. Cripe should be followed. It is in accord with the great weight of authority and is but the application in this particular class of cases of a general rule of evidence, thoroughly well settled and applied in every kind of case, civil and criminal. One of the most frequent applications of it in civil cases is the admission of declarations by a testator when

his mental capacity or his feelings are material. A notable instance of
its application in a criminal case is Commonwealth v. Trefethen, where
upon a trial for murder a statement of the decedent, a young unmarried woman, made shortly before her death, that she was five months
pregnant, was held admissible for the purpose of showing that she
believed this to be her condition, and therefore had a motive for
committing suicide. Upon the point that such evidence, admissible to
prove one fact, is not rendered inadmissible because tending to prove
some other fact, to prove which it is not competent, the court said:

> "The most obvious distinction between speech and conduct
> is that speech is often not only an indication of the existing
> state of mind of the speaker, but a statement of a fact external
> to the mind, and as evidence of that it is clearly hearsay.
> There is, of course, danger that a jury may not always observe
> this distinction, but that has not availed to exclude testimony
> which is admissible for one purpose, and not admissible for
> another to which there is danger the jury may apply it."

The rule, then, is that the admissibility of such evidence as that
under discussion, admissible because competent as to one point, is not
destroyed by its incompetency as to other points which it yet logically
tends to prove. The danger, however, of the jury misusing such
evidence and giving it weight in determining the points as to which it is
incompetent is manifest. In such a situation, as Prof. Wigmore puts it
immediately following the quotation already made, "the only question
can be what the proper means are for avoiding the risk of misusing the
evidence." Answering this question, Prof. Wigmore says:

> "It is uniformly conceded that the instruction [to the jury] of
> the court [that the evidence is competent only as proof of one
> point and must not be considered as proof of others] suffices for
> that purpose; and the better opinion is that the opponent of the
> evidence must ask for that instruction; otherwise he may be
> supposed to have waived it as unnecessary for his protection."

The general correctness of this statement cannot be doubted. But we
doubt if the learned author intended to say more than that the opponent
of such evidence is always entitled to such an instruction for his protection, if he asks for it, and that generally it will suffice. But it is not
difficult to imagine cases where it would not suffice, and the opponent
could justly ask for more. The matter is largely one of discretion on the
part of the trial judge. If the point to prove which the evidence is
competent can just as well be proven by other evidence, or if it is of but
slight weight or importance upon that point, the trial judge might well be
justified in excluding it entirely, because of its prejudicial and dangerous
character as to other points. A number of the authorities cited by
defendant's counsel are distinguishable from the present case upon this
ground. This would emphatically be true where there is good reason for
believing that the real object for which the evidence is offered is not to
prove the point for which it is ostensibly offered and is competent, but is
to get before the jury declarations as to other points, to prove which the
evidence is incompetent. The same thing would be true as to the

introduction of repeated declarations, when once the point for which they are competent has been amply shown. It may also be that the portions of the declaration which there is danger may be misused by the jury are not so interwoven with the balance of the declaration but that they can be disassociated from it without impairing the meaning or effect of the declaration for the purpose for which it is admissible. In such a case evidence of such portions of the declaration may be excluded on proper objection, when offered, if there is opportunity for such objection, or, if there is not, may be stricken out on motion subsequently. The point of the matter is that the opponent of such evidence, so likely to be misused against him, is entitled to such protection against its misuse as can reasonably be given him without impairing the ability of the other party to prove his case, or depriving him of the use of competent evidence reasonably necessary for that purpose.

The question, then, in the present case in connection with the evidence of declarations of the wife reduces itself to a question as to whether the defendant was properly protected from the danger of this evidence being misused by the jury, and considered by them as proof of matters other than that for proving which it was admitted. We think that there can be no doubt but that the defendant was not properly protected in this respect. * * *

[The court holds that the instruction of the trial court was inadequate, and the judgment is reversed.]

———

On the question of limited admissibility, see Federal Rules of Evidence 105; California Evidence Code § 355.

MUTUAL LIFE INSURANCE CO. OF NEW YORK v. HILLMON

Supreme Court of the United States, 1892.
145 U.S. 285, 12 S.Ct. 909, 36 L.Ed. 706.

[Actions by Sallie E. Hillmon against two insurance companies to recover on policies on the life of her husband, John W. Hillmon. The chief issue was whether a body found at Crooked Creek was that of the insured Hillmon or, as contended by defendants, that of one Walters. To show that the body was that of Walters, defendants offered in evidence letters from Walters to his sister and fiance which expressed his intention to leave Wichita and go with Hillmon to Colorado, where Crooked Creek is located. The trial court rejected these letters. (For an interesting account of the history of this protracted litigation, involving the ouster during the Populist movement of three insurance companies from Kansas, see Wigmore, Problems of Judicial Proof, pp. 856–896 (1913))—Ed.]

Mr. Justice GRAY, after holding for the court that there had been a procedural error, continued:

There is, however, one question of evidence so important, so fully argued at the bar, and so likely to arise upon another trial, that it is proper to express an opinion upon it.

This question is of the admissibility of the letters written by Walters on the first days of March, 1879, which were offered in evidence by the defendants, and excluded by the court. In order to determine the competency of these letters, it is important to consider the state of the case when they were offered to be read.

The matter chiefly contested at the trial was the death of John W. Hillmon, the insured; and that depended upon the question whether the body found at Crooked Creek on the night of March 18, 1879, was his body, or the body of one Walters.

Much conflicting evidence had been introduced as to the identity of the body. The plaintiff had also introduced evidence that Hillmon and one Brown left Wichita in Kansas on or about March 5, 1879, and travelled together through Southern Kansas in search of a site for a cattle ranch, and that on the night of March 18, while they were in camp at Crooked Creek, Hillmon was accidentally killed, and that his body was taken thence and buried. The defendants had introduced evidence, without objection, that Walters left his home and his be- trothed in Iowa in March, 1878, and was afterwards in Kansas until March, 1879; that during that time he corresponded regularly with his family and his betrothed; that the last letters received from him were one received by his betrothed on March 3 and postmarked at Wichita March 2, and one received by his sister about March 4 or 5, and dated at Wichita a day or two before; and that he had not been heard from since.

The evidence that Walters was at Wichita on or before March 5, and had not been heard from since, together with the evidence to identify as his the body found at Crooked Creek on March 18, tended to show that he went from Wichita to Crooked Creek between those dates. Evidence that just before March 5 he had the intention of leaving Wichita with Hillmon would tend to corroborate the evidence already admitted, and to show that he went from Wichita to Crooked Creek with Hillmon. Letters from him to his family and his betrothed were the natural, if not the only attainable, evidence of his intention.

The position, taken at the bar, that the letters were competent evidence, within the rule stated in Nicholls v. Webb, as memoranda made in the ordinary course of business, cannot be maintained, for they were clearly not such.

But upon another ground suggested they should have been admit- ted. A man's state of mind or feeling can only be manifested to others by countenance, attitude or gesture, or by sounds or words, spoken or written. The nature of the fact to be proved is the same, and evidence of its proper tokens is equally competent to prove it, whether expressed by aspect or conduct, by voice or pen. When the intention to be proved is important only as qualifying an act, its connection with that act must be shown, in order to warrant the admission of declarations of the intention. But whenever the intention is of itself a distinct and material fact in a chain of circumstances, it may be proved by contem- poraneous oral or written declarations of the party.

The existence of a particular intention in a certain person at a certain time being a material fact to be proved, evidence that he expressed that intention at that time is as direct evidence of the fact, as his own testimony that he then had that intention would be. After his death there can hardly be any other way of proving it; and while he is still alive, his own memory of his state of mind at a former time is no more likely to be clear and true than a bystander's recollection of what he then said, and is less trustworthy than letters written by him at the very time and under circumstances precluding a suspicion of misrepresentation.

The letters in question were competent, not as narratives of facts communicated to the writer by others, nor yet as proof that he actually went away from Wichita, but as evidence that, shortly before the time when other evidence tended to show that he went away, he had the intention of going, and of going with Hillmon, which made it more probable both that he did go and that he went with Hillmon, than if there had been no proof of such intention. In view of the mass of conflicting testimony introduced upon the question whether it was the body of Walters that was found in Hillmon's camp, this evidence might properly influence the jury in determining that question.

The rule applicable to this case has been thus stated by this court: "Wherever the bodily or mental feelings of an individual are material to be proved, the usual expressions of such feelings are original and competent evidence. Those expressions are the natural reflexes of what it might be impossible to show by other testimony. If there be such other testimony, this may be necessary to set the facts thus developed in their true light, and to give them their proper effect. As independent explanatory or corroborative evidence, it is often indispensable to the due administration of justice. Such declarations are regarded as verbal acts, and are as competent as any other testimony, when relevant to the issue. Their truth or falsity is an inquiry for the jury."

* * *

Even in the probate of wills, which are required by law to be in writing, executed and attested in prescribed forms, yet where the validity of a will is questioned for want of mental capacity or by reason of fraud and undue influence, or where the will is lost and it becomes necessary to prove its contents, written or oral evidence of declarations of the testator before the date of the will has been admitted, in Massachusetts and in England, to show his real intention as to the disposition of his property, although there has been a difference of opinion as to the admissibility, for such purposes, of his subsequent declarations.

In Shailer v. Bumstead, upon the competency of evidence offered to show that a will propounded for probate "was not the act of one possessed of testamentary capacity, or was obtained by such fraud and undue influence as to subvert the real intentions and will of the maker," Mr. Justice Colt said: "The declarations of the testator accompanying the act must always be resorted to as the most satisfactory evidence to sustain or defend the will, whenever the issue is presented.

So it is uniformly held that the previous declarations of the testator, offered to prove the mental facts involved, are competent. Intention, purpose, mental peculiarity and condition, are mainly ascertainable through the medium afforded by the power of language. Statements and declarations, when the state of the mind is the fact to be shown, are therefore received as mental acts or conduct."

In Sugden v. St. Leonards, which arose upon the probate of the lost will of Lord Chancellor St. Leonards, the English Court of Appeal was unanimous in holding oral as well as written declarations made by the testator before the date of the will to be admissible in evidence. Lord Chief Justice Cockburn said: "I entertain no doubt that prior instructions, or a draft authenticated by the testator, or verbal declarations of what he was about to do, though of course not conclusive evidence, are yet legally admissible as secondary evidence of the contents of a lost will." Sir George Jessel, M.R., said: "It is not strictly evidence of the contents of the instrument, it is simply evidence of the intention of the person who afterwards executes the instrument. It is simply evidence of probability—no doubt of a high degree of probability in some cases, and of a low degree of probability in others. The cogency of the evidence depends very much on the nearness in point of time of the declaration of intention to the period of the execution of the instrument." Lord Justice Mellish said: "The declarations which are made before the will are not, I apprehend, to be taken as evidence of the contents of the will which is subsequently made—they obviously do not prove it; and wherever it is material to prove the state of a person's mind, or what was passing in it, and what were his intentions, there you may prove what he said, because that is the only means by which you can find out what his intentions were."

Upon an indictment of one Hunter for the murder of one Armstrong at Camden, the Court of Errors and Appeals of New Jersey unanimously held that Armstrong's oral declarations to his son at Philadelphia, on the afternoon before the night of the murder, as well as a letter written by him at the same time and place to his wife, each stating that he was going with Hunter to Camden on business, were rightly admitted in evidence. Chief Justice Beasley said: "In the ordinary course of things, it was the usual information that a man about leaving home would communicate, for the convenience of his family, the information of his friends, or the regulation of his business. At the time it was given, such declarations could, in the nature of things, mean harm to no one; he who uttered them was bent on no expedition of mischief or wrong, and the attitude of affairs at the time entirely explodes the idea that such utterances were intended to serve any purpose but that for which they were obviously designed. If it be said that such notice of an intention of leaving home could have been given without introducing in it the name of Mr. Hunter, the obvious answer to the suggestion, I think, is that a reference to the companion who is to accompany the person leaving is as natural a part of the transaction as is any other incident or quality of it. If it is legitimate to show by a man's own declarations that he left his home to be gone a week, or for a certain destination, which seems incontestable, why may

it not be proved in the same way that a designated person was to bear
him company? At the time the words were uttered or written, they
imported no wrongdoing to any one, and the reference to the companion who was to go with him was nothing more, as matters then stood,
than an indication of an additional circumstance of his going. If it was
in the ordinary train of events for this man to leave word or to state
where he was going, it seems to me it was equally so for him to say with
whom he was going."

Upon principle and authority, therefore, we are of opinion that the
two letters were competent evidence of the intention of Walters at the
time of writing them, which was a material fact bearing upon the
question in controversy; and that for the exclusion of these letters, as
well as for the undue restriction of the defendants' challenges, the
verdicts must be set aside, and a new trial had.

As the verdicts and judgments were several, the writ of error sued
out by the defendants jointly was superfluous, and may be dismissed
without costs; and upon each of the writs of error sued out by the
defendants severally the order will be:

Judgment reversed, and case remanded to the Circuit Court, with
directions to set aside the verdict and to order a new trial.

SHEPARD v. UNITED STATES

Supreme Court of the United States, 1933.
290 U.S. 96, 54 S.Ct. 22, 78 L.Ed. 196.

Mr. Justice CARDOZO delivered the opinion of the Court.

The petitioner, Charles A. Shepard, a major in the medical corps of
the United States army, has been convicted of the murder of his wife,
Zenana Shepard, at Fort Riley, Kansas, a United States military
reservation. The jury having qualified their verdict by adding thereto
the words "without capital punishment" (18 U.S.C. § 567), the defendant was sentenced to imprisonment for life. The judgment of the
United States District Court has been affirmed by the Circuit Court of
Appeals for the Tenth Circuit, one of the judges of that court dissenting.
A writ of certiorari brings the case here.

The crime is charged to have been committed by poisoning the
victim with bichloride of mercury. The defendant was in love with
another woman, and wished to make her his wife. There is circumstantial evidence to sustain a finding by the jury that to win himself his
freedom he turned to poison and murder. Even so, guilt was contested
and conflicting inferences are possible. The defendant asks us to hold
that by the acceptance of incompetent evidence the scales were weighted to his prejudice and in the end to his undoing.

The evidence complained of was offered by the Government in
rebuttal when the trial was nearly over. On May 22, 1929, there was a
conversation in the absence of the defendant between Mrs. Shepard,
then ill in bed, and Clara Brown, her nurse. The patient asked the
nurse to go to the closet in the defendant's room and bring a bottle of
whisky that would be found upon a shelf. When the bottle was
produced, she said that this was the liquor she had taken just before
collapsing. She asked whether enough was left to make a test for the

1 presence of poison, insisting that the smell and taste were strange.
2 And then she added the words "Dr. Shepard has poisoned me."

3 The conversation was proved twice. After the first proof of it, the
4 Government asked to strike it out, being doubtful of its competence,
5 and this request was granted. A little later, however, the offer was
6 renewed, the nurse having then testified to statements by Mrs. Shepard
7 as to the prospect of recovery. "She said she was not going to get well;
8 she was going to die." With the aid of this new evidence, the conversa-
9 tion already summarized was proved a second time. There was a
10 timely challenge of the ruling.

11 She said, "Dr. Shepard has poisoned me." The admission of this
12 declaration, if erroneous, was more than unsubstantial error *   *   *
13 [The court held that the statement was not admissible under the dying
14 declaration exception to the hearsay rule, supra.]

15 We pass to the question whether the statements to the nurse,
16 though incompetent as dying declarations, were admissible on other
17 grounds.

18 The Circuit Court of Appeals determined that they were. Witness-
19 es for the defendant had testified to declarations by Mrs. Shepard
20 which suggested a mind bent upon suicide, or at any rate were thought
21 by the defendant to carry that suggestion. More than once before her
22 illness she had stated in the hearing of these witnesses that she had no
23 wish to live; and had nothing to live for, and on one occasion she added
24 that she expected some day to make an end to her life. This testimony
25 opened the door, so it is argued, to declarations in rebuttal that she had
26 been poisoned by her husband. They were admissible, in that view, not
27 as evidence of the truth of what was said, but as betokening a state of
28 mind inconsistent with the presence of suicidal intent.

29 (a) The testimony was neither offered nor received for the strained
30 and narrow purpose now suggested as legitimate. It was offered and
31 received as proof of a dying declaration. What was said by Mrs.
32 Shepard lying ill upon her deathbed was to be weighed as if a like
33 statement had been made upon the stand. The course of the trial
34 makes this an inescapable conclusion. The Government withdrew the
35 testimony when it was unaccompanied by proof that the declarant
36 expected to die. Only when proof of her expectation had been supplied
37 was the offer renewed and the testimony received again. For the
38 reasons already considered, the proof was inadequate to show a con-
39 sciousness of impending death and the abandonment of hope; but
40 inadequate though it was, there can be no doubt of the purpose that it
41 was understood to serve. There is no disguise of that purpose by
42 counsel for the Government. They concede in all candor that Mrs.
43 Shepard's accusation of her husband, when it was finally let in, was
44 received upon the footing of a dying declaration, and not merely as
45 indicative of the persistence of a will to live. Beyond question the jury
46 considered it for the broader purpose, as the court intended that they
47 should. A different situation would be here if we could fairly say in the
48 light of the whole record that the purpose had been left at large,
49 without identifying token. There would then be room for argument,
50 that demand should have been made for an explanatory ruling. Here

the course of the trial put the defendant off his guard. The testimony
was received by the trial judge and offered by the Government with the
plain understanding that it was to be used for an illegitimate purpose,
gravely prejudicial. A trial becomes unfair if testimony thus accepted
may be used in an appellate court as though admitted for a different
purpose, unavowed and unsuspected. Such at all events is the result
when the purpose in reserve is so obscure and artificial that it would be
unlikely to occur to the minds of uninstructed jurors, and even if it did,
would be swallowed up and lost in the one that was disclosed.

(b) Aside, however, from this objection, the accusatory declaration
must have been rejected as evidence of a state of mind, though the
purpose thus to limit it had been brought to light upon the trial. The
defendant had tried to show by Mrs. Shepard's declarations to her
friends that she had exhibited a weariness of life and a readiness to end
it, the testimony giving plausibility to the hypothesis of suicide. By the
proof of these declarations evincing an unhappy state of mind the
defendant opened the door to the offer by the Government of declarations evincing a different state of mind, declarations consistent with the
persistence of a will to live. The defendant would have no grievance if
the testimony in rebuttal had been narrowed to that point. What the
Government put in evidence, however, was something very different.
It did not use the declarations by Mrs. Shepard to prove her present
thoughts and feelings, or even her thoughts and feelings in times past.
It used the declarations as proof of an act committed by some one else,
as evidence that she was dying of poison given by her husband. This
fact, if fact it was, the Government was free to prove, but not by
hearsay declarations. It will not do to say that the jury might accept
the declarations for any light that they cast upon the existence of a
vital urge, and reject them to the extent that they charged the death to
some one else. (Discrimination so subtle is a feat beyond the compass
of ordinary minds.) The reverberating clang of those accusatory words
would drown all weaker sounds. It is for ordinary minds, and not for
psychoanalysts, that our rules of evidence are framed. They have their
source very often in considerations of administrative convenience, of
practical expediency, and not in rules of logic. When the risk of
confusion is so great as to upset the balance of advantage, the evidence
goes out. Thayer, Preliminary Treatise on the Law of Evidence, 266,
516; Wigmore, Evidence, §§ 1421, 1422, 1714.

These precepts of caution are a guide to judgment here. There are
times when a state of mind, if relevant, may be proved by contemporaneous declarations of feeling or intent. Mutual Life Ins. Co. v. Hillmon.
Thus, in proceedings for the probate of a will, where the issue is undue
influence, the declarations of a testator are competent to prove his
feelings for his relatives, but are incompetent as evidence of his conduct
or of theirs. In suits for the alienation of affections, letters passing
between the spouses are admissible in aid of a like purpose. * * *
In damage suits for personal injuries, declarations by the patient to
bystanders or physicians are evidence of sufferings or symptoms (Wigmore, §§ 1718, 1719), but are not received to prove the acts, the
external circumstances, through which the injuries came about.

* * * Even statements of past sufferings or symptoms are generally excluded, (Wigmore, § 1722[b]); though an exception is at times allowed when they are made to a physician. * * * So also in suits upon insurance policies, declarations by an insured that he intends to go upon a journey with another, may be evidence of a state of mind lending probability to the conclusion that the purpose was fulfilled. Mutual Life Ins. Co. v. Hillmon, supra. The ruling in that case marks the high water line beyond which courts have been unwilling to go. It has developed a substantial body of criticism and commentary.* Declarations of intention, casting light upon the future, have been sharply distinguished from declarations of memory, pointing backwards to the past. There would be an end, or nearly that, to the rule against hearsay if the distinction were ignored.

The testimony now questioned faced backward and not forward. This at least it did in its most obvious implications. What is even more important, it spoke to a past act, and more than that, to an act by some one not the speaker. Other tendency, if it had any, was a filament too fine to be disentangled by a jury.

The judgment should be reversed and the case remanded to the District Court for further proceedings in accordance with this opinion.

Reversed.

UNITED STATES v. PHEASTER

United States Court of Appeals, Ninth Circuit, 1976.
544 F.2d 353.

RENFREW, District Judge:

I. FACTS

This case arises from the disappearance of Larry Adell, the 16-year-old son of Palm Springs multi-millionaire Robert Adell. At approximately 9:30 P.M. on June 1, 1974, Larry Adell left a group of his high school friends in a Palm Springs restaurant known as Sambo's North. He walked into the parking lot of the restaurant with the expressed intention of meeting a man named Angelo who was supposed to deliver a pound of free marijuana. Larry never returned to his friends in the restaurant that evening, and his family never saw him thereafter.

The long, agonizing, and ultimately unsuccessful effort to find Larry began shortly after his disappearance. At about 2:30 A.M. on June 2, 1974, Larry's father was telephoned by a male caller who told him that his son was being held and that further instructions would be left in Larry's car in the parking lot of Sambo's North. Those instructions included a demand for a ransom of $400,000 for the release of Larry. Further instructions regarding the delivery of the ransom were promised within a week. Although the caller had warned Mr. Adell that he would never see Larry again if the police or the F.B.I. were notified, Mr. Adell immediately called the F.B.I., and that agency was actively involved in the investigation of the case from the beginning.

---

* Maguire, The Hillmon Case, 38 Harvard L.Rev., 709, 721, 727; Seligman, An Exception to the Hearsay Rule, 26 Harvard L.Rev. 146; Chafee, Review of Wigmore's Treatise, 37 Harvard L.Rev., 513, 519.

Numerous difficulties were encountered in attempting to deliver the ransom, necessitating a number of communications between the kidnappers and Mr. Adell. The communications from the kidnappers included a mixture of instructions and threats, as well as messages from Larry. Before the kidnappers finally broke off communications on June 30, 1974, Mr. Adell had received a total of ten letters from the kidnappers, nine of which were typed in a "script" style and one of which was handwritten. In addition, Mr. Adell had received two telephone calls from the kidnappers, one of which was tape-recorded by the F.B.I. In these communications, the kidnappers gave instructions for a total of four attempts to deliver the ransom, but it was never delivered for a number of reasons, and Larry was never released.

The instructions for the first delivery, set for June 8th, were nullified by the late delivery of the letter containing them on June 9th. The second delivery failed when, on June 12th, Mr. Adell balked at turning over the money without more adequate assurances that his son would be released. The third delivery on June 23rd was aborted, apparently because of the kidnappers' awareness that the pick-up site was being monitored. A duffel bag containing the ransom money was thrown into the designated spot, but it was never retrieved by the kidnappers. The fourth and final attempt never really began. On June 30th, pursuant to instructions, Mr. Adell went to a designated hotel pay telephone to await further instructions but was never contacted. No further communications were received from the kidnappers, despite Mr. Adell's attempt to renew contact by messages published in the Los Angeles Times.

When it appeared that further efforts to communicate with the kidnappers would be futile, the F.B.I. arrested appellants, who had been under surveillance for some time, in a coordinated operation on July 14, 1974.

* * *

Admissibility of Hearsay Testimony Concerning Statements of Larry Adell

Appellant Inciso argues that the district court erred in admitting hearsay testimony by two teenaged friends of Larry Adell concerning statements made by Larry on June 1, 1974, the day that he disappeared. Timely objections were made to the questions which elicited the testimony on the ground that the questions called for hearsay. In response, the Government attorney stated that the testimony was offered for the limited purpose of showing the "state of mind of Larry". After instructing the jury that it could only consider the testimony for that limited purpose and not for "the truth or falsity of what [Larry] said", the district court allowed the witnesses to answer the questions. Francine Gomes, Larry's date on the evening that he disappeared, testified that when Larry picked her up that evening, he told her that he was going to meet Angelo at Sambo's North at 9:30 P.M. to "pick up a pound of marijuana which Angelo had promised him for free". * * * She also testified that she had been with Larry on another occasion when he met a man named Angelo, and she identified the defendant as that man. Miss Gomes stated that it was approximately

9:15 P.M. when Larry went into the parking lot. Doug Sendejas, one of Larry's friends who was with him at Sambo's North just prior to his disappearance, testified that Larry had made similar statements to him in the afternoon and early evening of June 1st regarding a meeting that evening with Angelo. Mr. Sendejas also testified that when Larry left the table at Sambo's North to go into the parking lot, Larry stated that "he was going to meet Angelo and he'd be right back." * * *

Inciso's contention that the district court erred in admitting the hearsay testimony of Larry's friends is premised on the view that the statements could not properly be used by the jury to conclude that Larry did in fact meet Inciso in the parking lot of Sambo's North at approximately 9:30 P.M. on June 1, 1974. The correctness of that assumption is, in our view, the key to the analysis of this contention of error. The Government argues that Larry's statements were relevant to two issues in the case. First the statements are said to be relevant to an issue created by the defense when Inciso's attorney attempted to show that Larry had not been kidnapped but had disappeared voluntarily as part of a simulated kidnapping designed to extort money from his wealthy father from whom he was allegedly estranged. In his brief on appeal, Inciso concedes the relevance and, presumably, the admissibility of the statements to "show that Larry did not voluntarily disappear." However, Inciso argues that for this limited purpose, there was no need to name the person with whom Larry intended to meet, and that the district court's limiting instruction was insufficient to overcome the prejudice to which he was exposed by the testimony. Second, the Government argues that the statements are relevant and admissible to show that, as intended, Larry did meet Inciso in the parking lot at Sambo's North on the evening of June 1, 1974. If the Government's second theory of admissibility is successful, Inciso's arguments regarding the excision of his name from the statements admitted under the first theory is obviously mooted.

In determining the admissibility of the disputed evidence, we apply the standard of Rule 26 of the Federal Rules of Criminal Procedure which governed at the time of the trial below.* Under that standard, the District Court was required to decide issues concerning the "admissibility of evidence" according to the "principles of the common law as they may be interpreted by the courts of the United States in the light of reason and experience."

The Government's position that Larry Adell's statements can be used to prove that the meeting with Inciso did occur raises a difficult and important question concerning the scope of the so-called "*Hillmon* doctrine*", a particular species of the "state of mind" exception to the general rule that hearsay evidence is inadmissible. The doctrine takes its name from the famous Supreme Court decision in Mutual Life Ins. Co. v. Hillmon, 145 U.S. 285 (1892). That the *Hillmon* doctrine should create controversy and confusion is not surprising, for it is an extraordinary doctrine. Under the state of mind exception, hearsay evidence is

* The trial was held before the effective date of the Federal Rules of Evidence (Eds.).

admissible if it bears on the state of mind of the declarant and if that
state of mind is an issue in the case. For example, statements by a
testator which demonstrate that he had the necessary testamentary
intent are admissible to show that intent when it is in issue. The
exception embodied in the *Hillmon* doctrine is fundamentally different,
because it does not require that the state of mind of the declarant be an
actual issue in the case. Instead, under the *Hillmon* doctrine the state
of mind of the declarant is used inferentially to prove other matters
which are in issue. Stated simply, the doctrine provides that when the
performance of a particular act by an individual is an issue in a case,
his intention (state of mind) to perform that act may be shown. From
that intention, the trier of fact may draw the inference that the person
carried out his intention and performed the act. Within this conceptual framework, hearsay evidence of statements by the person which tend
to show his intention is deemed admissible under the state of mind
exception. Inciso's objection to the doctrine concerns its application in
situations in which the declarant has stated his intention to do something *with another person*, and the issue is whether he did so. There
can be no doubt, that the theory of the *Hillmon* doctrine is different
when the declarant's statement of intention necessarily requires the
action of one or more others if it is to be fulfilled.

* * *

The *Hillmon* doctrine has been applied by the California Supreme
Court in People v. Alcalde, 24 Cal.2d 177, 148 P.2d 627 (1944). * * *
In *Alcalde* the defendant was tried and convicted of first degree murder
for the brutal slaying of a woman whom he had been seeing socially.
One of the issues before the California Supreme Court was the asserted
error by the trial court in allowing the introduction of certain hearsay
testimony concerning statements made by the victim on the day of her
murder. As in the instant case, the testimony was highly incriminating, because the victim reportedly said that she was going out with
Frank, the defendant, on the evening she was murdered. On appeal, a
majority of the California Supreme Court affirmed the defendant's
conviction, holding that *Hillmon* was "the leading case on the admissibility of declarations of intent to do an act as proof that the act
thereafter was accomplished."

* * *

* * * The court found no error in the trial court's admission of
the disputed hearsay testimony. "Unquestionably the deceased's statement of her intent and the logical inference to be drawn therefrom,
namely, that she was with the defendant that night, were relevant to
the issue of the guilt of the defendant."

* * *

In addition to the decisions in *Hillmon* and *Alcalde*, support for the
Government's position can be found in the California Evidence Code
and the new Federal Rules of Evidence, although in each instance
resort must be made to the comments to the relevant provisions.

Section 1250 of the California Evidence Code carves out an exception to the general hearsay rule for statements of a declarant's "then
existing mental or physical state". The *Hillmon* doctrine is codified in
Section 1250(2) which allows the use of such hearsay evidence when it

"is offered to prove or explain acts or conduct of the declarant." The comment to Section 1250(2) states that, "Thus, a statement of the declarant's intent to do certain acts is admissible to prove that he did those acts." Although neither the language of the statute nor that of the comment specifically addresses the particular issue now before us, the comment does cite the *Alcalde* decision and, therefore, indirectly rejects the limitation urged by Inciso.

* * * Rule 803(3) provides an exemption from the hearsay rule for the following evidence:

> "*Then existing mental, emotional, or physical condition.* A statement of the declarant's then existing state of mind, emotion, sensation, or physical condition (such as intent, plan, motive, design, mental feeling, pain, and bodily health), but not including a statement of memory or belief to prove the fact remembered or believed unless it relates to the execution, revocation, identification, or terms of declarant's will."

Although Rule 803(3) is silent regarding the *Hillmon* doctrine, both the Advisory Committee on the Proposed Rules and the House Committee on the Judiciary specifically addressed the doctrine. After noting that Rule 803(3) would not allow the admission of statements of memory, the Advisory Committee stated broadly that

> "The rule of Mutual Life Ins. Co. v. Hillmon [citation omitted] allowing evidence of intention as tending to prove the doing of the act intended, is, of course, left undisturbed." Note to Paragraph (3), 28 U.S.C.A. at 585.

Significantly, the Notes of the House Committee on the Judiciary regarding Rule 803(3) are far more specific and revealing:

> "However, the Committee intends that the Rule be construed to limit the doctrine of Mutual Life Insurance Co. v. Hillmon [citation omitted] so as to render statements of intent by a declarant admissible *only to prove his future conduct, not the future conduct of another person.*" House Report No. 93–650, Note to Paragraph (3), 28 U.S.C.A. at 579 (emphasis added).

Although the matter is certainly not free from doubt, we read the note of the Advisory Committee as presuming that the *Hillmon* doctrine would be incorporated in full force, including necessarily the application in *Hillmon* itself. The language suggests that the Advisory Committee presumed that such a broad interpretation was the prevailing common law position. The notes of the House Committee on the Judiciary are significantly different. The language used there suggests a legislative intention to cut back on what that body also perceived to be the prevailing common law view, namely, that the *Hillmon* doctrine could be applied to facts such as those now before us.

Although we recognize the force of the objection to the application of the *Hillmon* doctrine in the instant case,[1] we cannot conclude that

---

1. Criticism of the *Hillmon* doctrine has come from very distinguished quarters, both judicial and academic. However, the position of the judicial critics is definitely the minority position, stated primarily in dicta and dissent.

the district court erred in allowing the testimony concerning Larry Adell's statements to be introduced.

* * *

[Judgment affirmed.]

[Concurring and dissenting opinion omitted.]

Hypotheticals

Let us assume that the issue is, "Was the declarant with Angelo that night?" Examine the following hypothetical statements made by the declarant the previous evening:

a. "I am going to the parking lot at Sambo's North tonight." (Other evidence shows that Angelo went there that night).

In his opinion for the Court in Shepard v. United States, Justice Cardozo indicated in dicta an apparent hostility to the *Hillmon* doctrine. *Shepard* involved hearsay testimony of a dramatically different character from that in the instant case. The Court reviewed the conviction of an army medical officer for the murder of his wife by poison. The asserted error by the trial court was its admission, over defense objection, of certain hearsay testimony by Mrs. Shepard's nurse concerning statements that Mrs. Shepard had made during her final illness. The nurse's testimony was that, after asking whether there was enough whiskey left in the bottle from which she had drunk just prior to her collapse to make a test for poison, Mrs. Shepard stated, "Dr. Shepard has poisoned me." One theory advanced by the Government on appeal was that the testimony was admissible to show that Mrs. Shepard did not have suicidal tendencies and, thus, to refute the defense argument that she took her own life. The Court rejected that theory, holding that the testimony had not been admitted for the limited purpose suggested by the Government and that, even if it had been admitted for that purpose, its relevance was far outweighed by the extreme prejudice it would create for the defendant. In rejecting the Government's theory, the Court refused to "extend the state of mind exception to statements of memory. In his survey of the state of mind exception, Justice Cardozo appeared to suggest the *Hillmon* doctrine is limited to "suits upon insurance policies", although the cases cited by the Court in *Hillmon* refute that suggestion.

The decision in *Shepard* was relied upon by Justice Traynor of the California Supreme Court in his vigorous dissent from the decision reached by the majority in People v. Alcalde. Justice Traynor argued that the victim's declarations regarding her meeting with Frank could not be used to "induce the belief that the defendant went out with the deceased, took her to the scene of the crime and there murdered her * * * without setting aside the rule against hearsay." Any other legitimate use of the declaration, in his opinion, was so insignificant that it was outweighed by the enormous prejudice to the defendant in allowing the jury to hear it.

Finally, the exhaustive analysis of a different, but related, hearsay issue by the Court of Appeals for the District of Columbia in United States v. Brown, provides inferential support for the position urged by Inciso. The issue in that case was the admissibility of hearsay testimony concerning a victim's extrajudicial declarations that he was "[f]rightened that he may be killed" by the defendant. After surveying the relevant cases, the court stated a "synthesis" of the governing principles. One of the cases which was criticized by the court was the decision of the California Supreme Court in People v. Merkouris, a case relied upon by the Government in the instant case. The court in *Merkouris* held that hearsay testimony showing the victim's fear of the defendant could properly be admitted to show the probable identity of the killer. The court in *Brown* expressed the following criticism of that holding, a criticism which might also apply to the application of the *Hillmon* doctrine in the instant case:

"Such an approach violates the fundamental safeguards necessary to the use of such testimony [citation omitted]. Through a circuitous series of inferences, the court reverses the effect of the statement so as to reflect on *defendant's* intent and actions rather than the state of mind of the declarant (victim). This is the very result that it is hoped the limiting instruction will prevent." 490 P.2d at 771 (emphasis in original).

For a frequently cited academic critique of the *Hillmon* doctrine, see Maguire, The Hillmon Case—Thirty-Three Years After, 38 Harv.L.Rev. 709 (1925).

b. "Angelo is going to the parking lot at Sambo's North tonight." (Other evidence shows that the declarant went there that night).

c. "I am going to Angelo's apartment tonight."

d. "I will not go out with anyone other than Angelo tonight." (Other evidence showing that he went out with someone.)

e. "I am going to wait at home for Angelo until he picks me up and we will go out." (Other evidence shows that the declarant left his apartment that night).

f. "I am going out to meet Angelo in the parking lot at Sambo's tonight."

See Federal Rules of Evidence 803(3); California Evidence Code § 1250.

ZIPPO MANUFACTURING CO. v. ROGERS IMPORTS, INC.

United States District Court, Southern District of New York, 1963.
216 F.Supp. 670.

FEINBERG, District Judge. This case involves the attempt of a manufacturer of a popular cigarette lighter to keep others from imitating the lighter's shape and appearance. Plaintiff Zippo Manufacturing Company ("Zippo"), a Pennsylvania corporation, alleges both trademark infringement and unfair competition on the part of defendant Rogers, Inc.[1] ("Rogers"), a New York corporation by reason of Rogers' sale of pocket lighters closely resembling Zippo's. Plaintiff seeks injunctive relief, an accounting, and damages. * * *

Plaintiff Zippo has been primarily engaged in the manufacture of pocket lighters since 1932, and it has grown spectacularly over the years. Its annual national sales of these lighters grew from about 27,000 units in 1934 to over 3,180,00 in 1958, the year just prior to suit, and well over 4,000,000 in 1961. Today, Zippo produces more units than any other domestic lighter manufacturer. Its pocket lighters are made in two models, the "standard" and the "slim-lighter." The latter accounts for slightly less than twenty-five per cent of the number of pocket lighters sold by Zippo. * * *

After Rogers commenced marketing its allegedly offending lighters in 1957, Zippo began receiving Rogers lighters from consumers who wished to have them repaired through Zippo's free repair policy. At the time of trial, a total of 191 Rogers lighters had been received by Zippo in this manner. Zippo's policy was to return the lighter to the person from whom it was received, together with a form letter stating that the lighter was not a Zippo product, and, therefore, the company would not repair it. * * *

Plaintiff's unfair competition action will be considered first, * * *

* * * plaintiff can obtain relief only if it meets its burden of proving that:

(1) Defendant's lighter copies plaintiff's lighter;

(2) A copied feature has acquired a special significance in the market identifying plaintiff as the source of the lighter,

1. Defendant was formerly known as Rogers Imports, Inc.

and that purchasers are moved in any degree to buy the lighter
because of its source ("secondary meaning");

(3) Such copied feature in defendant's lighter is likely to
cause prospective purchasers to regard the lighter as coming
from plaintiff;

(4) Such copied feature is nonfunctional. It should be
noted, however, that even if the copied feature is functional,
plaintiff may still be entitled to relief if defendant has not
taken reasonable steps to set its lighter apart from plaintiff's
in the public mind. * * *

Plaintiff has relied heavily on a consumer study to prove the
elements of its case. This study was prepared and conducted by the
sampling and market research firm of W.R. Simmons & Associates
Research, Inc. Mr. Simmons, the head of this firm, and Donald F.
Bowdren, the project supervisor, appeared as witnesses; both are qualified experts in the field of consumer surveys. Mr. Bowdren testified
that the purpose of the study was to determine whether the physical
attributes of the Zippo standard and slim-lighters serve as indicators of
the source of the lighters to potential customers and whether the
similar physical attributes of the Rogers lighters cause public confusion. The study or project consisted of three separate surveys. In
Survey A, the respondents, or interviewees, were shown a Zippo standard lighter which had all the Zippo identification markings removed
and were asked, among other things, what brand of lighter they
thought it was and why. In Survey B, the same procedure was followed
for the Zippo slim-lighter. In Survey C, respondents were shown a
Rogers standard lighter that was being sold at the time of the survey,
with all of its identifying markings, and they were asked, among other
things, what brand of lighter they thought it was and why.

Mr. Simmons' testimony and the project report made clear the
principles and procedures by which the surveys were conceived and
conducted. Testimony to this effect is important, because it is well
settled that the weight to be given a survey, assuming it is admissible,
depends on the procedures by which the survey was created and
conducted. * * *

There was no overlapping of respondents in the three surveys so
that no one respondent would be influenced in one survey by his
answers to another survey. The developmental phase of the project
involved preparation of questions that could be handled properly by an
interviewer, correctly understood by respondents and easily answered
by them. This required several drafts of questionnaires and some
pretesting. The "universe" to be studied consisted of all smokers aged
eighteen years and older residing in the continental United States,
which the research project indicated was approximately 115,000,000
("the smoking population"). All percentage results in the surveys
represent projected percentages of the smoking population.

The three separate surveys were conducted across a national
probability sample of smokers, with a sample size of approximately 500
for each survey. The samples were chosen on the basis of data obtained
from the Bureau of Census by a procedure which started with the

selection of fifty-three localities (metropolitan areas and non-metropolitan counties), and proceeded to a selection of 100 clusters within each of these localities—each cluster consisting of about 150–250 dwelling units—and then to approximately 500 respondents within the clusters. The manner of arriving at these clusters and respondents within each cluster was described in detail. The entire procedure was designed to obtain a representative sample of all smoking adults in the country. The procedures used to avoid sampling error and errors arising from other sources, the methods of processing, the instructions for the interviewers, and the approximate tolerance limits for a sample base of 500 were also described. Two of the interviewers testified that they were experienced in interviewing, explained the manner in which the interviews were conducted, and stated that they did not know the purpose of the surveys. All of the original responses to the questions as reported by these interviewers were made available in court.

Plaintiff also called Dr. Robert C. Sorensen as an expert in the field of survey research.[2] Dr. Sorensen stated that the project was conducted objectively and scientifically. Defendant does not deny this generally, but points to specific procedures and questions as being improper and buttresses its arguments with the testimony of its own expert, Professor Charles Winick.

Defendant objects to the admission of the surveys into evidence. It first contends that the surveys are hearsay. The weight of case authority, the consensus of legal writers, and reasoned policy considerations all indicate that the hearsay rule should not bar the admission of properly conducted public surveys. Although courts were at first reluctant to accept survey evidence or to give it weight, the more recent trend is clearly contrary. Surveys are now admitted over the hearsay objection on two technically distinct bases. Some cases hold that surveys are not hearsay at all; other cases hold that surveys are hearsay but are admissible because they are within the recognized exception to the hearsay rule for statements of present state of mind, attitude, or belief. Still other cases admit surveys without stating the ground on which they are admitted.

The cases holding that surveys are not hearsay do so on the basis that the surveys are not offered to prove the truth of what respondents said and, therefore, do not fall within the classic definition of hearsay. This approach has been criticized because, it is said, the answers to questions in a survey designed to prove the existence of a specific idea in the public mind are offered to prove the truth of the matter contained in these answers. Under this argument, when a respondent is asked to identify the brand of an unmarked lighter, the answer of each respondent who thinks the lighter is a Zippo is regarded as if he said, "I believe that this unmarked lighter is a Zippo." Since the matter to be proved in a secondary meaning case is respondent's belief that the lighter shown him is a Zippo lighter, a respondent's answer is hearsay in the classic sense. Others have criticized the non-hearsay characterization, regardless of whether surveys are offered to prove the

2. Dr. Sorensen is the co-author, *inter alia*, of R.C. Sorensen & T.C. Sorensen, The Admissibility and Use of Opinion Research Evidence, 28 N.Y.U.L.Rev. 1213 (1953).

truth of what respondents said because the answers in a survey depend
for their probative value on the sincerity of respondents. One of the
purposes of the hearsay rule is to subject to cross-examination statements which depend on the declarant's narrative sincerity. * * *
The answer of a respondent that he thinks an unmarked lighter is a
Zippo is relevant to the issue of secondary meaning only if, in fact, the
respondent really does believe that the unmarked lighter is a Zippo.
Under this view, therefore, answers in a survey should be regarded as
hearsay.

Regardless of whether the surveys in this case could be admitted
under the non-hearsay approach, they are admissible because the
answers of respondents are expressions of presently existing state of
mind, attitude, or belief. There is a recognized exception to the
hearsay rule for such statements, and under it the statements are
admissible to prove the truth of the matter contained therein.

Even if the surveys did not fit within this exception, well reasoned
authority justifies their admission under the following approach: the
determination that a statement is hearsay does not end the inquiry into
admissibility; there must still be a further examination of the need for
the statement at trial and the circumstantial guaranty of trustworthiness surrounding the making of the statement. This approach has
been used to justify the admissibility of a survey. Necessity in this
context requires a comparison of the probative value of the survey with
the evidence, if any, which as a practical matter could be used if the
survey were excluded. If the survey is more valuable, then necessity
exists for the survey, i.e., it is the inability to get "evidence of the same
value" which makes the hearsay statement necessary. When, as here,
the state of mind of the smoking population (115,000,000 people) is the
issue, a scientifically conducted survey is necessary because the practical alternatives do not produce equally probative evidence. With such
a survey, the results are probably approximately the same as would be
obtained if each of the 115,000,000 people were interviewed. The
alternative of having 115,000,000 people testify in court is obviously
impractical. The alternatives of having a much smaller section of the
public testify (such as eighty witnesses) or using expert witnesses to
testify to the state of the public mind are clearly not as valuable
because the inferences which can be drawn from such testimony to the
public state of mind are not as strong or as direct as the justifiable
inferences from a scientific survey.

The second element involved in this approach is the guaranty of
trustworthiness supplied by the circumstances under which the out-of-
court statements were made. A logical step in this inquiry is to see
which of the hearsay dangers are present. With regard to these
surveys: there is no danger of faulty memory; the danger of faulty
perception is negligible because respondents need only examine two or
three cigarette lighters at most; the danger of faulty narration is
equally negligible since the answers called for are simple. The only
appreciable danger is that the respondent is insincere. But this danger
is minimized by the circumstances of this or any public opinion poll in
which scientific sampling is employed, because members of the public

who are asked questions about things in which they have no interest have no reason to falsify their feelings. While the sampling procedure substantially guarantees trustworthiness insofar as the respondent's sincerity is concerned, other survey techniques substantially insure trustworthiness in other respects. If questions are unfairly worded to suggest answers favorable to the party sponsoring the survey, the element of trustworthiness in the poll would be lacking. The same result would follow if the interviewers asked fair questions in a leading manner. Thus, the methodology of the survey bears directly on trustworthiness, as it does on necessity. Since the two elements of necessity and trustworthiness are satisfied, I would admit these surveys under this approach to the hearsay rule, even apart from the state of mind exception.[3]

Defendant's next objection to the surveys is that they should not have been conducted in respondents' homes but in stores, the actual places of purchase. While it may be that in general the store is the best place to measure the state of mind at the time of purchase, it would be virtually impossible to obtain a representative national sample if stores were used. An interview at a respondent's home is probative of his state of mind at the time of purchase, although the deviation from the actual purchase situation should be considered in weighing the force of this evidence. Therefore, the surveys are not inadmissible merely because they were conducted in homes.

Defendant also objects to the surveys on the ground that they measured only the popularity of Zippo, as compared with the popularity of Rogers, and that this is not relevant to secondary meaning. However, I find that, by and large, the surveys did, as Dr. Sorenson testified, test brand identification and not brand popularity. They are, therefore, not incompetent because of the small elements of popularity which may have crept in, although that possibility should be considered in the weight to be given their results.

Defendant's next objection is to Survey C. In that survey, 34.7 per cent of respondents thought a Rogers lighter was a Zippo lighter, and plaintiff argues that this is probative of likelihood of confusion between the two lighters. However, respondents were not shown a Rogers display card when they made their mistaken identification. Therefore, defendant contends that the percentage of people who would mistakenly identify a Rogers lighter as a Zippo lighter would be smaller if the Rogers lighter were shown to them on a Rogers display card. This

3. Irvin v. State raises a possible objection not stressed by defendant—"multiple hearsay." The multiple hearsay argument is as follows: when answers made by respondents to interviewers are admissible under a hearsay exception, the interviewers can testify to these answers; but when the interviewers themselves do not testify but instead "tell" these answers to another person in the market research organization who then testifies as to the answers, this testimony is inadmissible hearsay because the witness is relating what the interviewers told him rather than what respondents in the survey told him. I conclude that this argument should not preclude the admission of a properly conducted survey, possibly because the business entries exception to the hearsay rule covers the transmission of the answers from the interviewers to other people in the organization, at least where the organization involved is in the business of conducting and reporting on surveys, or because considerations of necessity and trustworthiness justify an exception for the "second stage" of hearsay as well as for the original answers.

argument is probably correct. This does not mean, however, that the results of Survey C are inadmissible to prove that the appearance of the Rogers lighter is likely to confuse people into thinking that it is a Zippo lighter.

Defendant's argument is implicitly based on two assumptions: (1) that use of the Rogers display card in the interviews would have caused a great number of the respondents who thought the Rogers lighter was a Zippo lighter to give different answers; and (2) that the number left who, even after a display card was shown to them, would still confuse the Rogers lighter with a Zippo lighter would be statistically insignificant. However, these assumptions at best are too speculative to require exclusion of Survey C. Moreover, they are contradicted by other answers in Survey C, which show that about one-half of respondents who mistakenly thought that the Rogers lighter was a Zippo lighter actually saw something stamped on the bottom of the lighter (where the Rogers name was imprinted) and that over one-third of those who thought the Rogers lighter was a Zippo lighter actually saw the Rogers name stamped on the lighter. These results certainly give rise to the inference that if the Rogers display card had been shown to respondents, a significant number of people would have thought the Rogers lighter was a Zippo lighter anyway: although exposed to the display card, some would not have actually perceived the Rogers name, and others would have seen the Rogers name but would nonetheless think that the lighter was made by Zippo. Therefore, Survey C is not excluded. However, its weight on the issue of likelihood of confusion is less than it would be had a display card been used, and had the same number of respondents nonetheless identified the Rogers lighter as a Zippo lighter.

Defendant has other objections to admissibility of the surveys, e.g., that a survey is not the best way to prove secondary meaning, but none of these merit further discussion. Surveys A, B, and C were scientifically conducted by a competent and professional research firm, substantially in accordance with the recommendations of Recommended Procedures for the Trial of Protracted Cases. I conclude, therefore, that the surveys are admissible to show secondary meaning for the shape and appearance of the Zippo standard and slim-lighters and likelihood of confusion between these lighters and their Rogers counterparts.

[Judgment was rendered in accordance with the opinion]

Hypotheticals

(1) A sues X for damages for wrongful death arising out of an automobile accident in which A's husband, B, was killed. A testifies that they had a warm and affectionate relationship during their five-year marriage, which ended with B's death. X calls C, a business associate of B, to testify that about six months before B's death, B said several times that he hated A and that he was very unhappy in his marriage. A makes a hearsay objection to C's testimony. What result?

(2) Assume the same facts as in Illustration (1). X proposes to have C also testify that on one occasion three months before B's death, B said: "I just can't forget that three months ago I caught A out with another man and that this

has changed my love for her into hate." A makes a hearsay objection. What is the appropriate ruling?

(3) X is prosecuted for murder of A, his brother. X admits that he shot A but his defense is that the shooting was accidental. X calls B, a police officer, to testify that several hours after the shooting he had a conversation with X in which X stated that he was just sick and grief-stricken over A's death. The prosecution makes a hearsay objection. Should the objection be sustained?

(4) X is prosecuted for the murder of A, his girl friend. A was shot to death in X's apartment. X's defense is that A was at his apartment and requested to see his gun collection, that he handed A a pistol, and that while A was examining it she dropped it and it went off, killing her. The prosecution calls B, A's girl friend, to testify that a week before the shooting A told her that she was afraid of X and was deathly afraid of guns. X makes a hearsay objection to B's proposed testimony. How should the court rule?

(5) Assume the same facts as in Illustration (4). X calls C, a friend of A, to testify that two weeks before the shooting, A told her that she was planning to go to Utah the following week and go deerhunting; that upon asking A how were things between her and X, A replied that she was very fond of X and liked to be around him. The prosecution makes a hearsay objection to C's proposed testimony. What result?

(6) Sarah is prosecuted for the murder of Sam. Sarah's defense is self-defense—that Sam was advancing on her with a knife, and that she shot him to protect herself. The prosecution calls W, a friend of Sam, to testify that on the day before the killing, Sam said to W "I am going to tell Sarah that I won't pay her the money I lost to her in that poker game. I might get killed over it but I'm going to do it." Sarah makes a hearsay objection to W's proposed testimony. How should the court rule?

7. PHYSICAL CONDITION

Reasons for the Exception. Out-of-court statements concerning then-existing bodily conditions—symptoms, pain, and the like—are thought to have some built-in guarantees of reliability. Often such declarations are truly spontaneous: "Oh, my aching back!" They appear to be especially reliable when made to a treating physician. If the declarant knows that the physician is going to treat him, he is unlikely to give the physician deliberately incorrect information; the joke could prove to be on the patient. Furthermore, the patient is likely to believe that the physician knows a great deal about physical conditions. It is arguable, therefor, that the patient will not supply false data since the physician will only discover its falsity after possibly painful and costly tests. Finally, the physician's expertise is available to corroborate the accuracy of the out-of-court declarant's statements concerning his physical condition.

The hearsay risks are at a minimum here. There is no perception problem since the declarant is relating what he feels at the time. There is no memory problem where the declaration relates to present symptoms. And there is probably no great veracity problem, for the reasons already suggested.

Statements Made to a Nonphysician. Statements concerning present (then-existing) bodily condition are usually received in evidence no matter to whom they were made. They need not have been made to a treating physician; they may have been made to a spouse, to other relatives, to a friend, to a co-worker on the job, to a nurse, or to a hospital roommate. The declaration can relate to symptomology, including the existence of pain. *Past* symptoms are excluded.

Some jurisdictions require that the declarant be unavailable to take the witness stand before this branch of the bodily condition exception can be used.

Statements Made to a Physician. Statements concerning bodily condition may be made to a treating physician or to one whose assignment is only to examine the patient and render a diagnostic opinion.

1. *Statements to a Treating Physician.* Statements of present bodily condition to a treating physician—one who is going to diagnose the patient's problem and prescribe treatment for it—are admissible in evidence to prove the existence of the condition and are generally considered weightier than such statements made to a nontreating physician. Most courts, but not all of them, will exclude declarations about past bodily condition as proof of the existence of that condition. However, all courts will permit receipt of declarations of past symptoms, made to a treating physician, to show the basis for the physician's opinion (diagnosis, prognosis).

Example:

In Ritter v. Coca Cola Co. (Kenosha-Racine) Inc., 24 Wis.2d 157, 128 N.W.2d 439 (1964) the plaintiff, who had discovered a mouse in her bottle of Coca Cola, consulted a psychiatrist *after* having consulted her lawyer. The psychiatrist treated plaintiff and testified, over objection, that she had sustained psychological injury. The psychiatrist's testimony was ruled admissible.

The Wisconsin Supreme Court said that intrinsic guarantees of trustworthiness apply when treatment was at least part of the reason for consulting a physician. There was enough evidence that the plaintiff had not consulted the psychiatrist solely to secure his expert testimony.

2. *Statements to a Nontreating Physician.* Most courts hold that a nontreating physician's testimony about his patient's narration of present bodily condition is not admissible as proof that the condition actually existed. Such statements can come in only indirectly, where the nontreating physician relied on them in making his diagnosis or prognosis and they help to explain that diagnosis or prognosis.

A minority of courts will permit a nontreating physician—one who has been retained solely to provide an expert opinion and perhaps thereafter to testify in court—to testify only as to objective facts clinically observable to him. The nontreating physician, in other words, cannot testify as to declarations by the patient as to subjective matters, such as pain.

Example a.:

In Gonzales v. Hodsdon, 91 Idaho 330, 420 P.2d 813 (1966), a neuropsychiatrist's report was excluded because the consultation had been exclusively for purposes of getting the neuro-psychiatrist's testimony for trial.

Example b.:

In Davidson v. Cornell, 132 N.Y. 228, 30 N.E. 573 (1892), a personal injury case, the plaintiff, just before trial, was examined by a non-treating physician. Plaintiff, mostly in response to questions by the physician, described his physical sensations and abilities—mainly sexual—during the fifteen months between his injury and the physician's examination. The physician's testimony was ruled inadmissible, the New York court saying that declarations of physical condition are receivable only if made to a *treating* physician about *present* conditions.

The new evidence codes make no distinction between statements made to treating physicians and those made to nontreating physicians. Under these codes the jurors are permitted to decide what weight to accord such statements.

Finally, it should be emphasized that involuntary indications of pain, such as groans or grimaces, are not subject to the hearsay rule at all. Anyone who hears them or sees them and then testifies about them is simply giving direct eyewitness or ear-witness testimony.

EMERGING PROBLEMS UNDER THE FEDERAL RULES OF EVIDENCE *

Rule 803(4). Medical diagnosis or treatment. Statements made for purposes of medical diagnosis or treatment, including statements of past condition and medical history, are exceptions to the hearsay rule "in view of the patient's strong motivation to be truthful." Advisory Committee Note to Rule 803(4).

Given this underlying policy, it appears that the statements need not refer to the declarant's physical condition, although no courts have addressed the issue. For example, a parent's statement concerning her child's physical condition, made for purposes of diagnosis or treatment of the child, are probably admissible under Rule 803(4) because the same guarantees of trustworthiness exist. In the absence of authorities, however, the breadth of the rule is not entirely clear in this regard.

A significant limitation under Rule 803(4) is that statements with respect to the cause of a condition are admissible only "insofar as reasonably pertinent to diagnosis or treatment." The Advisory Committee Note states that this constraint will generally exclude "statements as to fault." In Roberts v. Hollocher, 664 F.2d 200 (8th Cir.1981), the report of the treating physician, which was based on the plaintiff's statements, reported that the plaintiff suffered "[m]ultiple contusions and hematoma, *consistent with excessive force*" (emphasis added). The Eighth Circuit affirmed the trial court's exclusion of the underscored phrase because it related to "fault," not causation, and, unlike the first

* Section of Litigation: American Bar Association © 1983.

portion of the statement, lacked the guarantees of proper motive and trustworthiness. Compare United States v. Iron Shell, 633 F.2d 77, 82–85 (8th Cir.1980), in which the same court upheld the admissibility of the victim's statement to her doctor that the defendant unclothed her. The court held that what happened was reasonably related to treatment; who did it was not. Accord: United States v. Nick, 604 F.2d 1199, 1201–02 (9th Cir.1979) (*per curiam*) (doctor permitted to testify that three year old victim told him about the cause of sexual assault but not to testify as to victim's identification of the defendant). See generally Annot., 55 A.L.R.Fed. 693, 697–98 (1981).

Under Rule 803(4), the statements made need not relate to physical—as opposed to psychiatric or other medical—diagnosis or treatment. In United States v. Lechoco, 542 F.2d 84, 89 n.6 (D.C.Cir.1976), the District of Columbia Circuit, in an appeal of a pre-Rules trial, stated that on remand statements made by the defendant to his psychiatrist should be admitted pursuant to Rule 803(4).

A possible limitation on the admissibility of statements made for purposes of treatment was suggested by the Second Circuit in O'Gee v. Dobbs Houses, Inc., 570 F.2d 1084, 1085 (2d Cir.1978). In obiter, the court stated that Rule 803(4) was not "intended to permit a doctor to testify to his patient's version of other doctor's opinions." Judge Feinberg, concurring and dissenting, "[did] not share the majority's misgivings regarding [the doctor's] testimony, which was clearly admissible for all purposes under Rule 803(4)." Id. at 1091 n. 1. Compare United States v. Cochran, 475 F.2d 1080, 1083–1084 (8th Cir.1973), cert. denied 414 U.S. 833, a pre-Rules decision, in which the court, citing proposed Rule 803(4), held it proper to admit, on cross-examination, testimony by a defense psychiatrist concerning statements made by the defendant with respect to a prior doctor's diagnosis that the defendant suffered from no psychiatric problems.

Florida's version of Rule 803(4) provides that the declarant may be "an individual who has knowledge of the facts and is legally responsible for the person who is unable to communicate the facts." Fla.Stat.Ann. § 90.803(4). Michigan limits the hearsay exception to statements made in connection with treatment, thereby excluding statements made for purposes of diagnosis alone. Mich.R.Evid. 803(4).

8. PRIOR IDENTIFICATION

WEINSTEIN'S EVIDENCE
Weinstein-Berger, 1975 (801–3).*

1975 AMENDMENT

Congress amended [Fed.Rule] 801(d)(1)** by adding subparagraph (C) which excludes from the definition of hearsay a statement "of identification of a person made after perceiving him." This subpara-

---

** 801(d) Statements which are not hearsay. A statement is not hearsay if—

(1) *Prior statement by witness.* The declarant testifies at the trial or hearing and is subject to cross-examination con-

graph had been contained in the rules as promulgated by the Supreme Court and as passed by the House of Representatives, but had been struck by the Senate. See *Congressional Changes,* infra. The House had acquiesced in the Senate version in order to ensure passage of the Rules of Evidence. Statement of Rep. Hungate, Cong.Rec.H. 9653 (daily ed. October 6, 1975). The amendment was signed into law on October 16, 1975 with an effective date of October 31, 1975, P.L. 94–113.

At the Congressional debate on the amendment, it was noted that enactment would return "this section of the hearsay rule to the status it had reached by process of natural judicial evolution," and that this provision had been deleted only because of strenuous objection by Senator Ervin which jeopardized passage of the Rules of Evidence. Cong.Rec. H9654 (daily ed. Oct. 6, 1975).

The Report of the Senate Committee on the Judiciary considering the amendment explained this opposition as stemming from concern "that a conviction could be based upon such unsworn, out-of-court testimony." However, the Report noted that this was a misconception since all constitutional protections were retained and in addition, the requirements of Rule 801(d)(1) that the identifier be available for cross-examination at the trial is continued. The Report reads:

> The purpose of the provision was to make clear, in line with the recent law in the area, that nonsuggestive lineup, photographic and other identifications are not hearsay and therefore are admissible. In the lineup case of Gilbert v. California, the Supreme Court, noting the split of authority in admitting prior out-of-court identifications, stated, "The recent trend, however, is to admit the prior identification under the exception [to the hearsay rule] that admits as substantive evidence a prior communication by a witness who is available for cross-examination at the trial." And the Federal Courts of Appeals have generally admitted these identifications.

* * *

> In the course of processing the Rules of Evidence in the final weeks of the 93d Congress, the provision excluding such statements of identification from the hearsay category was deleted. Although there was no suggestion in the committee report that prior identifications are not probative, concern was there expressed that a conviction could be based upon such unsworn, out-of-court testimony. Upon further reflection, that concern appears misdirected. First, this exception is addressed to the "admissibility" of evidence and not to the "sufficiency" of evidence to prove guilt. Secondly, except for the former testimony exception to the hearsay exclusion, all hearsay exceptions allow into evidence statements which may not have been made under oath. Moreover, under this rule, unlike a significant majority of the hearsay exceptions, the prior identification is admissible only when the person who made it

cerning the statement, and the statement is * * *

testifies at trial and is subject to cross-examination. This
assures that if any discrepancy occurs between the witness' in-
court and out-of-court testimony, the opportunity is available
to probe, with the witness under oath, the reasons for that
discrepancy so that the trier of fact might determine which
statement is to be believed.

Upon reflection, then, it appears the rule is desirable.
Since these identifications take place reasonably soon after an
offense has been committed, the witness' observations are still
fresh in his mind. The identification occurs before his recollection has been dimmed by the passage of time. Equally as
important, it also takes place before the defendant or some
other party has had the opportunity, through bribe or threat,
to influence the witness to change his mind.

* * *

UNITED STATES v. OWENS

Supreme Court of the United States, 1988.
484 U.S. 554, 108 S.Ct. 838, 98 L.Ed.2d 951.

JUSTICE SCALIA delivered the opinion of the Court.

This case requires us to determine whether either the Confrontation Clause of the Sixth Amendment or Rule 802 of the Federal Rules
of Evidence bars testimony concerning a prior, out-of-court identification when the identifying witness is unable, because of memory loss, to
explain the basis for the identification.

I

On April 12, 1982, John Foster, a correctional counselor at the
federal prison in Lompoc, California, was attacked and brutally beaten
with a metal pipe. His skull was fractured, and he remained hospitalized for almost a month. As a result of his injuries, Foster's memory
was severely impaired. When Thomas Mansfield, an FBI agent investigating the assault, first attempted to interview Foster, on April 19, he
found Foster lethargic and unable to remember his attacker's name.
On May 5, Mansfield again spoke to Foster, who was much improved
and able to describe the attack. Foster named respondent as his
attacker and identified respondent from an array of photographs.

Respondent was tried in Federal District Court for assault with
intent to commit murder under 18 U.S.C. § 113(a). At trial, Foster
recounted his activities just before the attack, and described feeling the
blows to his head and seeing blood on the floor. He testified that he
clearly remembered identifying respondent as his assailant during his
May 5th interview with Mansfield. On cross-examination, he admitted
that he could not remember seeing his assailant. He also admitted
that, although there was evidence that he had received numerous
visitors in the hospital, he was unable to remember any of them except
Mansfield, and could not remember whether any of these visitors had
suggested that respondent was the assailant. Defense counsel unsuccessfully sought to refresh his recollection with hospital records, including one indicating that Foster had attributed the assault to someone

1 other than respondent. Respondent was convicted and sentenced to 20
2 years' imprisonment to be served consecutively to a previous sentence.

3   On appeal, the United States Court of Appeals for the Ninth
4 Circuit considered challenges based on the Confrontation Clause and
5 Rule 802 of the Federal Rules of Evidence. By divided vote it upheld
6 both challenges (though finding the Rule 802 violation harmless error),
7 and reversed the judgment of the District Court. We granted certiorari
8 to resolve the conflict with other Circuits on the significance of a
9 hearsay declarant's memory loss both with respect to the Confrontation
10 Clause and with respect to Rule 802.

II

14   The Confrontation Clause of the Sixth Amendment gives the ac-
15 cused the right "to be confronted with the witnesses against him."
16 This has long been read as securing an adequate opportunity to cross-
17 examine adverse witnesses. * * *

18   [The Court went on to hold that the Confrontation Clause was not
19 violated by the admission of Foster's out-of-court statement. In the
20 course of its opinion, it stated that:]

21   * * * "[T]he Confrontation Clause guarantees only 'an opportuni-
22 ty for effective cross-examination, not cross-examination that is effec-
23 tive in whatever way, and to whatever extent, the defense might
24 wish.' " * * * It is sufficient that the defendant has the opportunity
25 to bring out such matters as the witness's bias, his lack of care and
26 attentiveness, his poor eyesight, and even (what is often a prime
27 objective of cross-examination, see 3A J. Wigmore, Evidence § 995, pp.
28 931–932 (J. Chadbourn rev. 1970)) the very fact that he has a bad
29 memory.

III

33   Respondent urges as an alternative basis for affirmance a violation
34 of Federal Rule of Evidence 802, which generally excludes hearsay.
35 Rule 801(d)(1)(C) defines as not hearsay a prior statement "of identifica-
36 tion of a person made after perceiving the person," if the declarant
37 "testifies at the trial or hearing and is subject to cross-examination
38 concerning the statement." The Court of Appeals found that Foster's
39 identification statement did not come within this exclusion because his
40 memory loss prevented his being "subject to cross-examination concern-
41 ing the statement." Although the Court of Appeals concluded that the
42 violation of the Rules of Evidence was harmless (applying for purposes
43 of that determination a "more-probable-than-not" standard, rather
44 than the "beyond-a-reasonable-doubt" standard applicable to the Con-
45 frontation Clause violation), respondent argues to the contrary.

46   It seems to us that the more natural reading of "subject to cross-
47 examination concerning the statement" includes what was available
48 here. Ordinarily a witness is regarded as "subject to cross-examina-
49 tion" when he is placed on the stand, under oath, and responds
50 willingly to questions. Just as with the constitutional prohibition,
51 limitations on the scope of examination by the trial court or assertions

of privilege by the witness may undermine the process to such a degree
that meaningful cross-examination within the intent of the Rule no
longer exists. But that effect is not produced by the witness' assertion
of memory loss—which, as discussed earlier, is often the very result
sought to be produced by cross-examination, and can be effective in
destroying the force of the prior statement. Rule 801(d)(1)(C), which
specifies that the cross-examination need only "concer[n] the statement," does not on its face require more.

This reading seems even more compelling when the Rule is compared with Rule 804(a)(3), which defines "[u]navailability as a witness"
to include situations in which a declarant "testifies to a lack of memory
of the subject matter of the declarant's statement." Congress plainly
was aware of the recurrent evidentiary problem at issue here—witness
forgetfulness of an underlying event—but chose not to make it an
exception to Rule 801(d)(1)(C).

The reasons for that choice are apparent from the Advisory Committee's Notes on Rule 801 and its legislative history. The premise for
Rule 801(d)(1)(C) was that, given adequate safeguards against sugges-
tiveness, out-of-court identifications were generally preferable to courtroom identifications. Advisory Committee's Notes on Rule 801, 28
U.S.C.App., p. 717. Thus, despite the traditional view that such statements were hearsay, the Advisory Committee believed that their use
was to be fostered rather than discouraged. Similarly, the House
Report on the Rule noted that since, "[a]s time goes by, a witness'
memory will fade and his identification will become less reliable,"
minimizing the barriers to admission of more contemporaneous identification is fairer to defendants and prevents "cases falling through
because the witness can no longer recall the identity of the person he
saw commit the crime." H.R.Rep. No. 94–355, p. 3 (1975). See also
S.Rep. No. 94–199, p. 2 (1975). To judge from the House and Senate
Reports, Rule 801(d)(1)(C) was in part directed to the very problem here
at issue: a memory loss that makes it impossible for the witness to
provide an in-court identification or testify about details of the events
underlying an earlier identification.

Respondent argues that this reading is impermissible because it
creates an internal inconsistency in the Rules, since the forgetful
witness who is deemed "subject to cross-examination" under 801(d)(1)(C)
is simultaneously deemed "unavailable" under 804(a)(3). This is the
position espoused by a prominent commentary on the Rules, see 4 J.
Weinstein & M. Berger, Weinstein's Evidence 801–120 to 801–121, 801–
178 (1987). It seems to us, however, that this is not a substantive
inconsistency, but only a semantic oddity resulting from the fact that
Rule 804(a) has for convenience of reference in Rule 804(b) chosen to
describe the circumstances necessary in order to admit certain categories of hearsay testimony under the rubric "Unavailability as a witness." These circumstances include not only absence from the hearing,
but also claims of privilege, refusals to obey a court's order to testify,
and inability to testify based on physical or mental illness or memory
loss. Had the rubric instead been "unavailability as a witness, memory
loss, and other special circumstances" there would be no apparent

inconsistency with Rule 801, which is a definition section excluding certain statements entirely from the category of "hearsay." The semantic inconsistency exists not only with respect to Rule 801(d)(1)(C), but also with respect to the other subparagraphs of Rule 801(d)(1). It would seem strange, for example, to assert that a witness can avoid introduction of testimony from a prior proceeding that is inconsistent with his trial testimony, see Rule 801(d)(1)(A), by simply asserting lack of memory of the facts to which the prior testimony related. But that situation, like this one, presents the verbal curiosity that the witness is "subject to cross-examination" under Rule 801 while at the same time "unavailable" under Rule 804(a)(3). Quite obviously, the two characterizations are made for two entirely different purposes and there is no requirement or expectation that they should coincide.

For the reasons stated, we hold that neither the Confrontation Clause nor Federal Rule of Evidence 802 is violated by admission of an identification statement of a witness who is unable, because of a memory loss, to testify concerning the basis for the identification. The decision of the Court of Appeals is reversed, and the case is remanded for proceedings consistent with this opinion.

So ordered.

JUSTICE KENNEDY took no part in the consideration or decision of this case.

[The dissenting opinion of JUSTICE BRENNAN, with whom JUSTICE MARSHALL joined, has been omitted.]

See Federal Rules of Evidence 801(d)(1); California Evidence Code § 1238.

Hypotheticals

(1) X is prosecuted for robbery of A. A testifies that he was held up at gunpoint, that the next day he went to the police station and identified the man who robbed him, and that he is sure he picked the right man but can't remember now the person he identified. The prosecution then calls B, a police officer, and represents that B will testify that A came to the station the day after the crime and that, while X was being led through the hall, A yelled: "There goes the man who robbed me" and pointed at X. X makes a hearsay objection to B's proposed testimony. What result?

(2) Assume the same facts as in Illustration (1), except that A has no recollection of making a pretrial identification of X or any other person at the police station. The prosecution then offers B's testimony of A's pretrial identification of X at the police station. X makes a hearsay objection to B's testimony. How should the court rule?

9. PAST RECOLLECTION RECORDED

BAKER v. STATE

Court of Special Appeals of Maryland, 1977.
35 Md.App. 593, 371 A.2d 699.

MOYLAN, Judge.

This appeal addresses the intriguing question of what latitude a judge should permit counsel when a witness takes the stand and says, "I don't remember." What are the available keys that may unlock the testimonial treasure vaults of the subconscious? What are the brush strokes that may be employed "to retouch the fading daguerreotype of memory?" The subject is that of Present Recollection Revived.[1]

The appellant, Teretha McNeil Baker, was convicted by a Baltimore City jury of both murder in the first degree and robbery. Although she raises two appellate contentions, the only one which we find it necessary to consider is her claim that the trial judge erroneously refused her the opportunity to refresh the present recollection of a police witness by showing him a report written by a fellow officer.

The ultimate source of most of the evidence implicating the appellant was the robbery and murder victim himself, Gaither Martin, a now-dead declarant who spoke to the jury through the hearsay conduit of Officer Bolton.[2] When Officer Bolton arrived at the crime scene, the victim told him that he had "picked these three ladies up * * * at the New Deal Bar"; that when he took them to their stated destination, a man walked up to the car and pulled him out; that "the other three got out and proceeded to kick him and beat him." It was the assertion made by the victim to the officer that established that his money, wallet and keys had been taken. The critical impasse, for present purposes, occurred when the officer was questioned, on cross-examination, about what happened en route to the hospital. The officer had received a call from Officer Hucke, of the Western District, apparently to the effect that a suspect had been picked up. Before proceeding to the hospital, Officer Bolton took the victim to the place where Officer Hucke was holding the appellant. The appellant, as part of this cross-examination, sought to elicit from the officer the fact that the crime victim confronted the appellant and stated that the appellant was not one of those persons who had attacked and robbed him. To stimulate the present memory of Officer Bolton, appellant's counsel attempted to show him the police report relating to that confrontation and prepared by Officer Hucke.

The record establishes loudly and clearly that appellant's counsel sought to use the report primarily to refresh the recollection of Officer

1. Frequently and alternatively referred to as Present Recollection Refreshed.

2. The exception to the Hearsay Rule urged by the State and utilized by the court to make the out-of-court assertion admissible was the "excited utterance" exception and not the "dying declaration" exception. We are not here considering the admissibility of this hearsay, but are rather assuming it to have been admissible.

Bolton and that he was consistently and effectively thwarted in that attempt:

"BY MR. HARLAN:

Q. Do you have the report filed by Officer Hucke and Officer Saclolo or Sacolo?

A. Right, I have copies.

Q. Okay.

MR. DOORY: I would object to that, Your Honor.

THE COURT: I will sustain the objection. This is not his report.

BY MR. HARLAN:

Q. Can you look at this report and refresh your recollection as to whether or not you ever had the victim in a confrontation with Mrs. Baker?

MR. DOORY: Objection, Your Honor.

MR. HARLAN: He can refresh—

THE COURT: Well, he can refresh his recollection as to his personal knowledge. That's all right.

A. That is what I am saying, I don't know who it was that we confronted really.

BY MR. HARLAN:

Q. All right. Would you consult your report and maybe it will refresh your recollection.

THE COURT: I think the response is he doesn't know who—

MR. HARLAN: He can refresh his recollection if he looks at the report.

THE COURT: He can't refresh his recollection from someone else's report, Mr. Harlan.

MR. HARLAN: I would object, Your Honor. Absolutely he can.

THE COURT: You might object, but—

MR. HARLAN: You are not going to permit the officer to refresh his recollection from the police report?

THE COURT: No. It is not his report.

* * *

MR. HARLAN: Your Honor, I think I am absolutely within my rights to have a police officer read a report which mentions his name in it to see if it refreshes his recollection. If it doesn't refresh his recollection, then fine.

THE COURT: Well, he did that.

MR. HARLAN: You have not afforded him the opportunity to do that yet, Your Honor.

THE COURT: He says he does not know who it was before. So, he can't refresh his recollection if he does not know simply because someone else put some name in there.

MR. HARLAN: He has to read it to see if it refreshes his recollection, Your Honor.

THE COURT: We are reading from a report made by two other officers which is not the personal knowledge of this officer.

MR. HARLAN: I don't want him to read from that report. I want him to read it and see if it refreshes his recollection."

On so critical an issue as possible exculpation from the very lips of the crime victim, appellant was entitled to try to refresh the memory of the key police witness. She was erroneously and prejudicially denied that opportunity. The reason for the error is transparent. Because they both arise from the common seedbed of failed memory and because of their hauntingly parallel verbal rhythms and grammatical structures, there is a beguiling temptation to over analogize Present Recollection Revived and Past Recollection Recorded. It is a temptation, however, that must be resisted. The trial judge in this case erroneously measured the legitimacy of the effort to revive present recollection against the more rigorous standards for the admissibility of a recordation of past memory.

It is, of course, hornbook law that when a party seeks to introduce a record of past recollection, he must establish (1) that the record was made by or adopted by the witness at a time when the witness did have a recollection of the event and (2) that the witness can presently vouch for the fact that when the record was made or adopted by him, he knew that it was accurate. McCormick, Law of Evidence (1st Ed., 1954), describes the criteria, at 15:

> "Appropriate safeguarding rules have been developed for this latter kind of memoranda, requiring that they must have been written by the witness or examined and found correct by him, and that they must have been prepared so promptly after the events recorded that these must have been fresh, in the mind of the witness when the record was made or examined and verified by him. We have treated such memoranda separately, as an exception to the hearsay rule."

Had the appellant herein sought to offer the police report as a record of past recollection on the part of Officer Bolton, it is elementary that she would have had to show, *inter alia*, that the report had either been prepared by Officer Bolton himself or had been read by him and that he can now say that at that time he knew it was correct. Absent such a showing, the trial judge would have been correct in declining to receive it in evidence.

When dealing with an instance of Past Recollection Recorded, the reason for the rigorous standards of admissibility is quite clear. Those standards exist to test the competence of the report or document in question. Since the piece of paper itself, in effect, speaks to the jury, the piece of paper must pass muster in terms of its evidentiary competence.

Not so with Present Recollection Revived! By marked contrast to Past Recollection Recorded, no such testimonial competence is demanded of a mere stimulus to present recollection, for the stimulus itself is never evidence. Notwithstanding the surface similarity between the two phenomena, the difference between them could not be more basic. *It is the difference between evidence and non-evidence.* Of such mere stimuli or memory-prods, McCormick says "[T]he cardinal rule is that they are not evidence, but only aids in the giving of evidence." When we are dealing with an instance of Present Recollection Revived, the only source of evidence is the testimony of the witness himself. The stimulus may have jogged the witness's dormant memory, but the stimulus itself is not received in evidence. Dean McCormick makes it clear that even when the stimulus is a writing, when the witness "speaks from a memory thus revived, his testimony is what he says, not the writing." McCormick describes the psychological phenomenon in the following terms:

> "It is abundantly clear from every-day observation that the latent memory of an experience may be revived by an image seen, or a statement read or heard. It is a part of the group of phenomena which the classical psychologists have called the law of association. The recall of any part of a past experience tends to bring with it the other parts that were in the same field of awareness, and a new experience tends to stimulate the recall of other like experiences."

The psychological community is in full agreement with the legal community in assessing the mental phenomenon. See Cairn, Law and the Social Sciences 200 (1935):

> "In permitting a witness to refresh his recollection by consulting a memorandum, the courts are in accord with present psychological knowledge. A distinction is drawn, in the analysis of the memory process, between *recall,* which is the reproduction of what has been learned, and *recognition,* which is recall with a time-factor added, or an awareness that the recall relates to past experience. It is with recognition that the law is principally concerned in permitting a witness to revive his recollection. The psychological evidence is clear that in thus allowing to be brought to mind what has been forgotten, the law is following sound psychological procedure."

*   *   *

The catalytic agent or memory stimulator is put aside, once it has worked its psychological magic, and the witness then testifies on the basis of the now-refreshed memory. The opposing party, of course, has the right to inspect the memory aid, be it a writing or otherwise, and even to show it to the jury. This examination, however, is not for the purpose of testing the competence of the memory aid (for competence is immaterial where the thing in question is not evidence) but only to test whether the witness's memory has in truth been refreshed. As McCormick warns, "But the witness must swear that he is genuinely refreshed. * * * And he cannot be allowed to read the writing in the guise of refreshment, as a cloak for getting in evidence an inadmissible document." One of the most thorough reviews of this aspect of evidence law is found in the United States v. Riccardi, where the court said at 888:

> "In the case of present recollection revived, the witness, by hypothesis, relates his present recollection, and under oath and subject to cross-examination asserts that it is true; his capacities

for memory and perception may be attacked and tested; his
determination to tell the truth investigated and revealed; protes-
tations of lack of memory, which escape criticism and indeed
constitute a refuge in the situation of past recollection, recorded,
merely undermine the probative worth of his testimony."

*   *   *

When the writing in question is to be utilized simply "to awaken a
slumbering recollection of an event" in the mind of the witness, the
writing may be a memorandum made by the witness himself, 1) even if
it was not made immediately after the event, 2) even if it was not made
of firsthand knowledge and 3) even if the witness cannot now vouch for
the fact that it was accurate when made. It may be a memorandum
made by one other than the witness, even if never before read by the
witness or vouched for by him. It may be an Associated Press account.
It may be a highly selective version of the incident at the hands of a
Hemingway or an Eliot. All that is required is that it ignite the flash
of accurate recall—that it accomplish the revival which is sought.

McCormick wrote to just such effect:

"[I]t is probable that most courts today when faced with the
clear distinction between the two uses of the memoranda, will
adhere to the 'classical' view that any memorandum or other
object may be used as a stimulus to present memory, without
restriction by rule as to authorship, guaranty of correctness, or
time of making."

The Texas dean is in good company, for no less eminent an
authority than Lord Ellenborough said in Henry v. Lee:

"If upon looking at *any* document he can so far refresh his
memory as to recollect a circumstance, it is sufficient; and it
makes no difference that the memorandum is not written by
himself, for it is not the memorandum that is the evidence but
the recollection of the witness."

Not only may the writing to be used as a memory aid fall short of
the rigorous standards of competence required of a record of past
recollection, the memory aid itself need not even be a writing. What
may it be? It may be anything. It may be a line from Kipling or the
dolorous refrain of "The Tennessee Waltz"; a whiff of hickory smoke;
the running of the fingers across a swatch of corduroy; the sweet
carbonation of a chocolate soda; the sight of a faded snapshot in a long-
neglected album. All that is required is that it may trigger the
Proustian moment.[3] It may be anything which produces the desired
testimonial prelude, "It all comes back to me now."

*   *   *

Although the use of a memorandum of some sort will continue
quantitatively to dominate the field of refreshing recollection, we are

---

3. Marcel Proust, in his monumental epic In Remembrance of Things Past, sat, as a middle-aged man, sipping a cup of lime-flavored tea and eating a madeleine, a small French pastry. Through both media, two long-forgotten tastes from childhood were reawakened. By association, long forgotten memories from the same period of childhood came welling and surging back. Once those floodgates of recall were opened, seven volumes followed.

better able to grasp the process conceptually if we appreciate that the use of a memorandum as a memory aid is not a legal phenomenon unto itself but only an instance of a far broader phenomenon. In a more conventional mode, the process might proceed, "Your Honor, I am about to show the witness a written report, ask him to read it and then inquire if he can now testify from his own memory thus refreshed." In a far less conventional mode, the process could just as well proceed, "Your Honor, I am pleased to present to the court Miss Rosa Ponselle who will now sing 'Celeste Aida' for the witness, for that is what was playing on the night the burglar came through the window." Whether by conventional or unconventional means, precisely the same end is sought. One is looking for the effective elixir to revitalize dimming memory and make it live again in the service of the search for truth.

Even in the more conventional mode, it is quite clear that in this case the appropriate effort of the appellant to jog the arguably dormant memory of the key police witness on a vital issue was unduly and prejudicially restricted.

Judgments reversed; case remanded for a new trial; costs to be paid by mayor and city council of Baltimore.

'Perhaps *This* Will Refresh Your Memory' *

ADAMS v. THE NEW YORK CENTRAL RAILROAD CO.

Court of Common Pleas, Cuyahoga County, Cleveland, Ohio, 1961.
Docket No. 724,072.

[This was an action for the recovery of damages for personal injuries. Defendant's theory was that the injury claimed by plaintiff

had in fact never occurred and that plaintiff's quadraplegia stemmed
from an injury antedating the claimed injury. One of the few ways in
which defendant could hope to establish its theory was by introduction,
as past recollection recorded, of a memorandum made by an insurance
company employee of an interview with plaintiff. According to the
memorandum, plaintiff had mentioned the antecedent injury but had
made no reference to any injury of the sort claimed at trial. Following
are key portions of the trial transcript showing the efforts of chief
defense counsel, James C. Davis, Esq., of the Cleveland Bar, to secure
admission of the memorandum—Ed.]

DIRECT EXAMINATION

BY MR. DAVIS:

Q. Will you state your name?

A. Eugene F. Raith.

Q. Where do you live?

A. I live at 20705 Harvard Road, Warrensville Heights,
Ohio.

* * *

Q. What is your business?

A. Home Office Inspector, employed by the John Hancock Mutual Life Insurance Company.

Q. How long have you been employed with John Hancock?

A. 40 years.

Q. In your capacity with John Hancock, did you in 1957
call on a gentleman named Theodore H. Adams at a time when
he was a patient in Highland View Hospital?

A. I did.

Q. What was your purpose in calling on Mr. Adams?

A. To seek any information to be used in evaluation of
his disability claim that he had presented to our insurance
company as an insured.

Q. At that time did you interview him?

A. I did.

Q. During the interview, or immediately thereafter, did
you make a written record of what he told you—of the information you obtained?

A. Yes, sir.

* * *

Q. Do you have with you your file on this particular
matter?

A. Yes.

Q. May I have it? First, the written record which you
made, either during your interview or thereafter, was a record
in longhand, was it not?

A. Yes.

Q. Have you ever testified as a witness before?

A. No.

Q. Well, it really is not as painful as it looks.

A. Thank you. I would change places with you.

* * *

Q. Now, Mr. Raith, do you at this time have any independent recollection of the subject-matter of the conversation between you and Mr. Adams—that is, what he told you and what you asked him—independent of the notes which you made at that time?

A. I do not.

Q. Do you recognize the gentleman at the end of the [counsel] table as the gentleman that you talked to?

A. I believe so.

Q. I hand you what has been marked Defendant's Exhibit OO. Now that piece of paper has writing on both sides, does it not?

A. Yes.

Q. Tell me, if you will, whether or not the notes that you made of your conversation with Mr. Adams appear on only one side or both sides of that page.

A. Only on one side.

* * *

Q. Now, was the information that is contained on the page that is marked Defendant's Exhibit OO * * * obtained entirely from the interview with Mr. Adams?

A. Yes, entirely from Mr. Adams.

Q. At the time you wrote that Exhibit OO * * * did it accurately record what he had told you?

A. Yes.

* * *

Q. Was [the interview] recorded in exactly the words which Mr. Adams gave you, or not?

A. I would be inclined to believe that when I talked to Mr. Adams I made notes rougher than these, and at the conclusion of the interview I made a recap. I say that because of the sequence; it would have been a recap of what I made previously. However, it came from Mr. Adams, no one else.

* * *

Q. Are there certain facts recorded on Exhibit OO?

A. Right.

Q. When did you record the facts on Exhibit OO with reference to the time of your interview with Mr. Adams?

A. At the time or shortly thereafter.

Q. Were the facts obtained from Mr. Adams accurately recorded by you on Exhibit OO?

A. Yes.

Q. At the time you made Defendant's Exhibit OO, did you or did you not know it was accurate so far as facts obtained by you from Mr. Adams were concerned?

A. I did.

Q. Without telling me what it is, Mr. Raith, is it not a fact that Defendant's Exhibit OO records the fact of an injury which Mr. Adams told you he had received?

A. Yes.

Q. Did you record whatever he told you about injuries?

A. I did.

MR. DAVIS: At this time defendant offers in evidence Defendant's Exhibit OO as evidence of past recollection recorded.

MR. DUDNIK: It is entirely improper.

THE COURT: We will recess until 1:30.

(Thereupon the jury left the Courtroom and the following further proceedings were had in the absence of the jury:)

THE COURT: Proceed, Mr. Davis.

MR. DAVIS: If the Court please, in these circumstances there are two ways in which a witness may properly proceed. First, he may look at a memorandum made at the time and, on the basis of his refreshed recollection, testify. Then he is testifying from his present recollection refreshed. On the other hand, the law is perfectly clear that a witness having no such present refreshed recollection may testify that he made a record of the event at a time in the past and that he knew at the time the record was made that the record was accurate. That record is admissible as past recollection recorded as distinguished from present recollection refreshed. Dean Wigmore says, in Volume 3, Section 734 of the third edition of his work on evidence. ∗ ∗ ∗ [Quotation omitted.]

THE COURT: I will hear from Mr. Dudnik.

MR. DUDNIK: My associate, Mr. Nurenberg, will argue the point, your Honor.

MR. NURENBERG: These notes do not fill the bill. Office records might be permitted into evidence, providing certain qualifications are met. The witness stated that even by looking at the exhibit he can't refresh his recollection. ∗ ∗ ∗ The witness said he saw Mr. Adams at Highland View Hospital and, apparently, he has some recollection. ∗ ∗ ∗ The most important thing is that the document [Defendant's Exhibit OO], on its face is not a document at all. It is merely a piece of paper with some pencil jotting; this is not a document. ∗ ∗ ∗ If I talk to you and I go home and jot down with pencil on a piece of paper what you told me, even though they are an accurate recollection ∗ ∗ ∗ I can't come into Court and say they are what you told me, Judge White. I can't come into Court and introduce a pencil note. That is what they are trying to do. That is not past recollection recorded. Past recollection recorded is when a man, in the routine order of business, makes a certain document at or contemporaneous with the subject-matter, not a pencil jotting. ∗ ∗ ∗ That is hearsay in its purest form. Every record is not *ipso facto* a business record.

* * *

MR. DAVIS: Your Honor, Mr. Dudnik has given you a case in 156 Northwestern at page 867. That is a case cited by Wigmore. If you will notice, Wigmore does not restrict past recollection recorded to papers that, in the technical sense, constitute business records. The very case cited to you by Mr. Dudnik involved a memorandum taken down by an insurance agent in connection with a policy.

* * *

THE COURT: The Court has examined, necessarily with some haste, the cases cited to it. * * * The fact that the witness has testified that his own recollection is not refreshed [by Defendant's Exhibit OO] persuades the Court that the exhibit is not admissible at this time.

* * *

Thereupon the defendant, further to maintain the issues on its part to be maintained, recalled as a witness, EUGENE F. RAITH, who, having been previously duly sworn, was examined and testified further as follows:

BY MR. DAVIS:

Q. Now, Mr. Raith, I hand you once more Defendant's Exhibit OO, and ask you if you will read it through again. To yourself, not out loud.

Q. Have you finished?

A. Yes, sir.

Q. Having read Exhibit OO, will you tell me whether or not your memory has been refreshed so that you now have a present recollection of your interview with Mr. Adams at Highland View Hospital, and of what he told you on that occasion?

A. No, it has not.

Q. It has not what?

A. It has not been refreshed by reading these notes.

Q. Then do you or do you not at this time have any present recollection of what Mr. Adams told you at the time you interviewed him at Highland View Hospital?

A. Other than these notes, I do not.

Q. Do the notes refresh your recollection so that you now have a recollection, or do they not?

A. No, they do not refresh my recollection.

* * *

Q. Now, at the time you made the writings on Exhibit OO, did you have a clear recollection of what Mr. Adams had told you?

A. Very clear.

MR. DAVIS: I reoffer Defendant's Exhibit OO, your Honor.

MR. DUDNIK: The same objection.

THE COURT: The objection is sustained.

MR. DAVIS: That is all, Mr. Raith.

NOTE

Do you agree with the rulings of the trial court? Did attorney Davis fail in some significant respect to lay the proper foundation for admission into evidence of the memorandum?

The trial of Adams v. The New York Central R.R. Co. resulted in a verdict for plaintiff in the sum of $300,000. In its motion for a new trial defendant argued that rejection of the proffered memorandum was prejudicial error. Before further proceedings were had, the case was settled for a sum substantially less than the verdict.

———

See Federal Rules of Evidence 803(5); California Evidence Code § 1237.

———

See Federal Rules of Evidence 612; California Evidence Code § 771.

Hypothetical

(1) X is prosecuted for robbery. The prosecution calls A, who testifies that she saw the getaway car and noticed the license number, and that ten minutes later a police officer came to the scene and she told him exactly what license number she observed, but that she has no recollection now of that number. The prosecution then calls B, a police officer, who testifies that at the robbery scene A told him the license number of the getaway car she had seen and that he wrote correctly on a sheet in his book the number stated by A, and produces the sheet. The prosecutor asks B to read the license number written on the sheet. X makes a hearsay objection to the prosecutor's question. What result under California law? Under federal law?

10.   BUSINESS AND PUBLIC RECORDS

MARYLAND—DISTRICT OF COLUMBIA—VIRGINIA CRIMINAL PRACTICE INSTITUTE TRIAL MANUAL
2–5, 2–9 (1964).*

2.02 Introducing Business Records**

1.   Your Honor, I would like to have this instrument marked as defense exhibit # 1 for identification.

2.   State your name.

3.   Where do you reside, Mr. [witness]?

4.   And what is your occupation?

5.   Where are you employed?

6.   What is the nature of your employer's business?

7.   And what is the nature of your work there?

---

* Copyright, 1964, by Lerner Law Book Company.

** On the authentication of writings, see Chapter I, Making the Record, supra.

8. Were you so employed thereon [date in question]?

9. Now, as the [position title], do you have responsibility of keeping the records concerning [subject matter]?

10. What is the method utilized for keeping these records?

11. Is this followed with respect to every [entry] [patient, etc.]?

12. I show you defendant's exhibit # 1 for identification, purporting to be [document title], and ask you whether these are the original records which you have kept in your position?

13. Were these records in your custody on [date]?

14. And were they in your custody prior to your bringing them to court this morning?

15. Where were they kept?

16. Were the entries made herein made shortly after the transaction they record?

17. Who provided the information contained therein?

18. Was it his duty to collect this data and pass it on to you?

19. And were these entries made in the usual and ordinary course of business?

20. To the best of your knowledge, are they true and correct?

[Then move the admission of defense exhibit # 1 for identification into evidence.]

JOHNSON v. LUTZ
Court of Appeals of New York, 1930.
253 N.Y. 124, 170 N.E. 517.

HUBBS, J. This action is to recover damages for the wrongful death of the plaintiff's intestate, who was killed when his motorcycle came into collision with the defendants' truck at a street intersection. There was a sharp conflict in the testimony in regard to the circumstances under which the collision took place. A policeman's report of the accident filed by him in the station house was offered in evidence by the defendants under section 374–a of the Civil Practice Act, and was excluded. The sole ground for reversal urged by the appellants is that said report was erroneously excluded That section reads: "Any writing or record, whether in form of an entry in a book or otherwise, made as a memorandum or record of any act, transaction, occurrence or event, shall be admissible in evidence in proof of said act, transaction, occurrence or event, if the trial judge shall find that it was made in the regular course of any business, and that it was the regular course of such business to make such memorandum or record at the time of such act, transaction, occurrence or event, or within a reasonable time thereafter. All other circumstances of the making of such writing or record, including lack of personal knowledge by the entrant or maker, may be shown to affect its weight, but they shall not affect its admissibility. The term business shall include business, profession, occupation and calling of every kind."

Prior to the decision in the well-known case of Vosburgh v. Thayer, shopbooks could not be introduced in evidence to prove an account. The decision in that case established that they were admissible where

preliminary proof could be made that there were regular dealings
between the parties; that the plaintiff kept honest and fair books; that
some of the articles charged had been delivered; and that the plaintiff
kept no clerk. At that time it might not have been a hardship to
require a shopkeeper who sued to recover an account to furnish the
preliminary proof required by that decision. Business was transacted
in a comparatively small way, with few, if any, clerks. Since the
decision in that case, it has remained the substantial basis of all
decisions upon the question in this jurisdiction prior to the enactment
in 1928 of section 374–a, Civil Practice Act.

Under modern conditions, the limitations upon the right to use
books of account, memoranda, or records, made in the regular course of
business, often resulted in a denial of justice, and usually in annoyance,
expense, and waste of time and energy. A rule of evidence that was
practical a century ago had become obsolete. The situation was appre-
ciated, and attention was called to it by the courts and textwriters.

The report of the Legal Research Committee of the Commonwealth
Fund, published in 1927, by the Yale University Press, under the title,
"The Law of Evidence—Some Proposals for Its Reform," dealt with the
question in chapter 5, under the heading, "Proof of Business Transactions to Harmonize with Current Business Practice." That report,
based upon extensive research, pointed out the confusion existing in
decisions in different jurisdictions. It explained and illustrated the
great need of a more practical, workable, and uniform rule, adapted to
modern business conditions and practices. The chapter is devoted to a
discussion of the pressing need of a rule of evidence which would "give
evidential credit to the books upon which the mercantile and industrial
world relies in the conduct of business." At the close of the chapter,
the committee proposed a statute to be enacted in all jurisdictions. In
compliance with such proposal the Legislature enacted section 374–a of
the Civil Practice Act in the very words used by the committee.

It is apparent that the Legislature enacted section 374–a to carry
out the purpose announced in the report of the committee. That
purpose was to secure the enactment of a statute which would afford a
more workable rule of evidence in the proof of business transactions
under existing business conditions.

In view of the history of section 374–a and the purpose for which it
was enacted, it is apparent that it was never intended to apply to a
situation like that in the case at bar. The memorandum in question
was not made in the regular course of any business, profession, occupation, or calling. The policeman who made it was not present at the
time of the accident. The memorandum was made from hearsay
statements of third persons who happened to be present at the scene of
the accident when he arrived. It does not appear whether they saw the
accident and stated to him what they knew, or stated what some other
persons had told them.

The purpose of the Legislature in enacting section 374–a was to
permit a writing or record, made in the regular course of business, to be
received in evidence, without the necessity of calling as witnesses all of
the persons who had any part in making it, provided the record was

made as a part of the duty of the person making it, or on information imparted by persons who were under a duty to impart such information. The amendment permits the introduction of shopbooks without the necessity of calling all clerks who may have sold different items of account. It was not intended to permit the receipt in evidence of entries based upon voluntary hearsay statements made by third parties not engaged in the business or under any duty in relation thereto. It was said, in Mayor, etc., of New York City v. Second Ave. R. Co.: "It is a proper qualification of the rule admitting such evidence that the account must have been made in the ordinary course of business, and that it should not be extended so as to admit a mere private memorandum, not made in pursuance of any duty owing by the person making it, or when made upon information derived from another who made the communication casually and voluntarily, and not under the sanction of duty or other obligation."

An important consideration leading to the amendment was the fact that in the business world credit is given to records made in the course of business by persons who are engaged in the business upon information given by others engaged in the same business as part of their duty.

"Such entries are dealt with in that way in the most important undertakings of mercantile and industrial life. They are the ultimate basis of calculation, investment, and general confidence in every business enterprise. Nor does the practical impossibility of obtaining constantly and permanently the verification of every employee affect the trust that is given to such books. It would seem that expedients which the entire commercial world recognizes as safe could be sanctioned, and not discredited, by courts of justice. When it is a mere question of whether provisional confidence can be placed in a certain class of statements, there cannot profitably and sensibly be one rule for the business world and another for the court-room. The merchant and the manufacturer must not be turned away remediless because the methods in which the entire community places a just confidence are a little difficult to reconcile with technical judicial scruples on the part of the same persons who as attorneys have already employed and relied upon the same methods. In short, courts must here cease to be pedantic and endeavor to be practical." 3 Wigmore on Evidence (1923) § 1530, p. 278.

The Legislature has sought by the amendment to make the courts practical. It would be unfortunate not to give the amendment a construction which will enable it to cure the evil complained of and accomplish the purpose for which it was enacted. In construing it, we should not, however, permit it to be applied in a case for which it was never intended.

The judgment should be affirmed, with costs.

CARDOZO, C.J., and POUND, CRANE, LEHMAN, KELLOGG, and O'BRIEN, JJ., concur.

Judgment affirmed.

Hypotheticals

Examine the following hypotheticals involving a suit by A against B arising out of an automobile accident. What should be the result in each case?

The police report contains the following statement which the plaintiff seeks to introduce:

a. "I was standing at my beat and saw the red Chevrolet [which we now know to be the defendant's car] go through the red light and strike the green Ford [which other testimony shows to be the plaintiff's car]."

b. "I arrived at one thirty [which other evidence indicates was twenty minutes after the accident] and noticed a skid mark, which I measured at 93 feet leading directly to the rear wheels of the Chevrolet."

c. "I arrived within five seconds of the impact and heard a bystander scream, 'Did you see that crazy red car go through the red light?' "

d. "I arrived a few minutes after the accident and asked the driver in the red Chevrolet what happened. He stated that he had fallen asleep at the wheel and did not rightly know."

e. "I arrived a few minutes after the accident and Officer Jones approached me and said that he had seen the accident and that the red Chevrolet had gone through the red light and hit the green Ford."

f. "I arrived a few minutes after the accident and Officer Jones told me that she had gotten there just before I did and asked the Chevrolet driver what had happened and that he had said, 'I fell asleep at the wheel and I don't rightly know.' "

g. "I arrived twenty-five minutes after the accident and I asked a bystander what had happened. He said that he had seen it all and the red Chevrolet was going too fast and couldn't stop for the red light and went right through the red light and hit the green Ford."

DEAN JEROME PRINCE, "THE HEARSAY RULE" IN TRIAL EVIDENCE
18–1, 18–8 (Schreiber ed. 1967). *

Johnson v. Lutz has been very severely criticized by commentators on the grounds that the court read into the statute a requirement not expressly to be found in it, a requirement that the informant, or one imparting the information must be under a business duty or obligation to impart the information.

I think that that requirement has much merit.

Business records are trustworthy because they are based upon reports made by persons who are under a routine duty to record it.

The business cannot function if there are reports that are inaccurate and the informant will not long last in the business if his observations or reports are inaccurate.

No such high probability of trustworthiness attaches to reports based upon information supplied by a person uncon-

* Foundation Press, Brooklyn, N.Y.

nected with the business who gives the information voluntarily and casually.

And the Court of Appeals in Cox v. State, 3 N.Y.2d 693, 148 N.E.2d 879, 171 N.Y.S.2d 818 (1958), reaffirmed the rule announced in Johnson v. Lutz.

The Rule in Kelly v. Wasserman

The requirement that the informant be under a duty to give information has apparently been disregarded in a recent case. In Kelly v. Wasserman, the plaintiff conveyed her house to the defendant in exchange for the defendant's oral promise to pay her debts and to allow her to live rent-free in the house.

Later, a dispute arose concerning the terms of the occupancy. The plaintiff said that the oral agreement was that she was to live rent-free in the house for life. The defendant said, "No," the agreement was that she was to live rent-free in that house only so long as the Housing Department did not object to the number of tenants in the house.

The plaintiff was a welfare beneficiary. On the trial the plaintiff offered in evidence an entry in the records of the Welfare Department pertaining to her welfare case. These were entries made by Welfare Department employees in the regular course of their business and were made by persons supervising the plaintiff's welfare case.

The entries offered in evidence were entries to this effect: that in several conversations had between the Welfare Department employees and the defendant, the defendant said that he had agreed to allow the plaintiff to live rent-free for life in that house.

The Court of Appeals held that this entry, or these entries, were admissible under the Statutory Business Records Rule, saying that the entries pertaining to the plaintiff's shelter were germane to the welfare business and the entries were made in the regular course of the business of the Welfare Department.

Now, it is quite plain that the entries were made by the employees of the Welfare Department in the regular course of their business. But, was the defendant a person under a business duty or obligation to impart that information within the contemplation of the rule laid down by Johnson v. Lutz?

The Court of Appeals in Kelly v. Wasserman did not discuss at all, or even mention, the requirement that the informant must be under a business duty or obligation to impart the information.

Regarding Multiple Hearsay, see Federal Rules of Evidence 805; California Evidence Code § 1201.

UNITED STATES v. DUNCAN

United States Court of Appeals, Fifth Circuit, 1990.
919 F.2d 981.

DUHÉ, Circuit Judge.

The defendants raise a litany of issues to challenge their convictions for mail fraud and conspiracy. They contend that the district

court improperly denied their motion for change of venue and erred in
fourteen different evidentiary rulings. They also argue that the court
erred by denying their motion for mistrial based on a comment by the
judge and by refusing their proposed jury instructions. Finally, they
assert that the evidence adduced at trial was insufficient to sustain
their convictions and that the court imposed excessive sentences. We
find no error and affirm the judgment of the district court.

FACTS

The defendants participated in a scheme to defraud insurance
companies. Over a period of several years, each defendant purchased
numerous hospitalization policies. Each policy provided that the insured would receive a predetermined sum of money for each day spent
in the hospital, regardless of other coverage.

The indictment charged that on many occasions, the defendants
sought admission to hospitals after reporting accidents that never
occurred or after staging accidents. According to several witnesses, the
defendants participated in planned collisions in which a driver, carrying a carload of conspirators, intentionally swerved out of his lane and
careened into another car.

The evidence indicated that Samuel Duncan and Grace Duncan,
husband and wife, were the ringleaders of the conspiracy. Each was
hospitalized over twenty times and collected over $300,000 in insurance
proceeds. Mr. Duncan's sister Gay Nell, another defendant, entered
the hospital three times within a seven-month period and collected over
$50,000. The insurance companies mailed the Duncans checks for
these amounts.

The other four defendants were close friends and relatives of the
Duncans. Each of the four was hospitalized between ten and nineteen
times during a five-year period and each collected over $75,000. These
defendants also received payments by mail.

The government indicted the seven defendants for mail fraud and
conspiracy. After a two-week trial, the jury found all seven defendants
guilty.

DISCUSSION

* * *

1. Admission of Records

The defendants first claim that the court erred in admitting into
evidence the records of insurance companies. They challenge the
admissibility of these records on a variety of grounds, arguing that (1)
they were not sufficiently authenticated under rule 901; (2) they are
not proper business records under rule 803(6); and (3) they were made
by a person without personal knowledge in violation of rule 602.

Representatives of insurance companies came to court and authenticated the records. The prosecutor clearly established the prerequisites for admitting the records under the business records exception.[4]

4. For example, the following exchange   Q.   Your full name, Sir?
occurred between the prosecutor and a wit-   A.   George Beverly Walker, Jr.
ness: Q.   And by whom are you employed?

But the defendants argue that the insurance company records contained other unauthenticated medical records and statements by doctors. They contend that these medical records and statements are hearsay not falling within the business records exception of rule 803(6).

We reject this argument. The insurance companies compiled their records from the business records of hospitals. Because the medical records from which the insurance company records were made were themselves business records, there was no accumulation of inadmissible hearsay.

There is no requirement that the witness who lays the foundation be the author of the record or be able to personally attest to its accuracy. Furthermore, there is no requirement that the records be created by the business having custody of them.

Instead, the "primary emphasis of rule 803(6) is on the reliability or trustworthiness of the records sought to be introduced." The district court has great latitude on the issue of trustworthiness. Hospitals and insurance companies rely on these records in conducting business. We hold, therefore, that the district court did not err in admitting them under Federal Rule of Evidence 803(6) upon proper authentication by their custodian.

Even if the insurance company records contained some medical information not taken from actual hospital records, that information was admissible as nonhearsay evidence. The Federal Rules of Evidence exclude from the category of hearsay any "statement by a person authorized by the party to make a statement concerning the subject" and any "statement by the party's agent . . . concerning a matter within the scope of the agency." Fed.R.Evid. 801(d)(2)(C)–(D).

A patient routinely authorizes the release of medical records for use by insurance companies. A medical provider without express authority to release information would be acting as the patient's agent in obtaining payment of medical expenses from insurance companies. We therefore conclude that all information in the insurance company records was admissible either under the business records exception or as nonhearsay evidence. * * *

A.   J.C. Penney Life Insurance Company.

Q.   And in what position?

A.   Senior Vice President, Insurance Operations.

Q.   Have you produced records of your corporation?

A.   Yes I have.

Q.   Pursuant to a subpoena?

A.   Yes, Sir.

Q.   Are these records kept in the regular course of your company's business?

A.   Yes, they are.

Q.   Are these records accurate?

A.   Yes.

Q.   Is it the regular practice of your company to keep such records?

A.   Yes, it is.

. . . .

Q.   [Let me] show you what's been marked for identification purposes as G–36–SDA, and ask you what is that?

A.   This is a copy of the application by Samuel Duncan. . . . We have two applications as Mr. Duncan had two policies with our company. . . .

Q.   Are you familiar with how your company generates and maintains and stores records?

A.   Yes.

Q.   How are these applications generated?

A.   Through direct mail.

Hypotheticals

Should a newspaper reporter's notes be admissible as a business record? A newspaper itself? A clipping from the newspaper's back-issue library?

WILLIAMS v. ALEXANDER

Court of Appeals of New York, 1955.
309 N.Y. 283, 129 N.E.2d 417.
[Footnotes omitted.]

FULD, Judge. Dessi Williams was struck by defendant's automobile as he was crossing a street in Brooklyn, with the traffic light in his favor. His right leg fractured, he was taken to Kings County Hospital for treatment. At the trial, the testimony of the parties as to the manner in which the accident occurred was sharply discrepant. According to plaintiff, defendant's automobile approached the intersection, at which he was crossing, without diminishing speed and ran into him. Defendant, on the other hand, insisting that he had brought his car to a complete stop at the light, maintained that another vehicle had struck it from the rear and propelled it forward and upon plaintiff.

In the early stages of the trial, plaintiff introduced so much of the Kings County Hospital record as bore upon his injuries and their treatment. Counsel for defendant thereupon offered the balance of the record and it was received in evidence over plaintiff's objection. Specifically challenged by plaintiff as inadmissible hearsay was an entry to the effect that he had stated to a physician at the hospital that "he was crossing the street and an automobile ran into another automobile that was at a standstill, causing this car (standstill) to run into him". Plaintiff denied making any such statement, and the doctor who recorded it was not called as a witness.

Upon this appeal—following a verdict in defendant's favor and an affirmance by a divided Appellate Division—we are called upon to decide whether the statement attributed to plaintiff, relating the manner in which the accident occurred, was properly admitted in evidence as a memorandum or record made "in the regular course of * * * business". Civil Practice Act, § 374–a.

Section 374–a of the Civil Practice Act permits the introduction in evidence of "Any writing or record * * * made as a memorandum or record of any act, transaction, occurrence or event," despite its hearsay character, "if the trial judge shall find that it was made in the regular course of any business, and that it was the regular course of such business to make such memorandum or record at the time of such act, transaction, occurrence or event, or within a reasonable time thereafter." The term "business" is broadly defined as including "business, profession, occupation and calling of every kind", and among the records within the section's ambit are those that a hospital keeps in diagnosing and treating the ills of its patients.

The statute, similar to those in effect in most jurisdictions, is designed to harmonize the rules of evidence with modern business practice and give "evidential credit" to the memoranda or other writings upon which reliance is placed in the systematic conduct of business undertakings. It rests upon the probability of trustworthiness which inheres in such records, by virtue of the fact, first, that they are the "routine reflections of the day to day operations of a business", and, second, that it is the entrant's own obligation, and to his interest, to have them truthful and accurate, made and kept as they are with the knowledge, indeed, for the purpose, that they will be relied upon in the conduct of the enterprise. * * * [I]t is this element of trustworthiness, serving in place of the safeguards ordinarily afforded by confrontation and cross-examination, which justifies admission of the writing or record without the necessity of calling all the persons who may have had a hand in preparing it. And it was to assure such accuracy and reliability that the legislature made explicit the condition that the memorandum may be received in evidence—and this is the heart of the provision—only if it was "made in the regular course of [the] business, and * * * it was the regular course of such business to make such memorandum".

As the statute makes plain, and we do not more than paraphrase it, entries in a hospital record may not qualify for admission in evidence unless made in the regular course of the "business" of the hospital, and for the purpose of assisting it in carrying on that "business." The business of a hospital, it is self-evident, is to diagnose and treat its patients' ailments. Consequently, the only memoranda that may be regarded as within the section's compass are those reflecting acts, occurrences or events that relate to diagnosis, prognosis or treatment or are otherwise "helpful to an understanding of the medical or surgical aspects of * * * [the particular patient's] hospitalization."

It follows from this that a memorandum made in a hospital record of acts or occurrences leading to the patient's hospitalization—such as a narration of the accident causing the injury—not germane to diagnosis or treatment, is not admissible under section 374–a, and so it has been almost universally held under the identical or similar statutes of other jurisdictions.

In the words of the Ohio court in Green v. City of Cleveland, typical of those found in the other cases, "it was the business of the hospital to diagnose plaintiff's condition and to treat her for her ailments, not to record a statement describing the cause of the accident in which plaintiff's injuries were sustained."

In some instances, perhaps, the patient's explanation as to how he was hurt may be helpful to an understanding of the medical aspects of his case; it might, for instance, assist the doctors if they were to know that the injured man had been struck by *an* automobile. However, whether the patient was hit by car A or car B, by car A under its own power or propelled forward by car B, or whether the injuries were caused by the negligence of the defendant or of another, cannot possibly bear on diagnosis or aid in determining treatment. That being so, entries of this sort, purporting to give particulars of the accident, which serve no medical purpose, may not be regarded as having been made in the regular course of the hospital's business. Indeed, in discussing the matter, Wigmore observed that the essential "Guarantee of Trustworthiness" rests upon the fact that "the physicians and nurses * * * themselves rely upon the record" and that the record is designed to be "relied upon in affairs of life and death." Such reasoning, however, will not support the use, or justify the receipt, of a statement detailing the circumstances of the accident where they are immaterial to, and were never intended to be relied upon in, the treatment of the patient. There is no need in that case for the physician to exercise care in obtaining and recording the information or to question the version, whatever it might be, that is given to him. The particulars may be a natural subject of the doctor's curiosity, but neither the inquiry nor the response properly belong in a record designed to reflect the regular course of the hospital's business.

In conclusion, then, that portion of the hospital record containing the statement assertedly made by plaintiff as to the manner in which the accident happened was erroneously admitted, and, since we cannot say that it did not influence the jury in arriving at its verdict for defendant, there must be a new trial.

The judgment of the Appellate Division and that of Trial Term should be reversed and a new trial granted, with costs to abide the event.

DESMOND, Judge (dissenting).

I see no error here, and no reason for retrying this simple question of fact.

Plaintiff, for his own convenience, chose to prove his injuries and the hospital treatment he received therefor, by putting a hospital record in evidence and without calling as a witness the physician who made the entries. In so doing, he of course vouched for the accuracy and regularity of that record. Defendant made no objection but in his turn offered in evidence so much of the same hospital record as showed a statement to the hospital physician by plaintiff that the accident had occurred in a manner quite different from that testified to at the trial by plaintiff. Plaintiff objected to any such "history" going into evidence. His alleged ground of objection was stated in the one word: "hearsay". That of course was meaningless in this context. An undoubted exception to the "hearsay" rule makes admissible extra-judicial declarations against interest. Plaintiff's declaration to the hospital physician as to the way the accident happened was directly probative evidence of a main fact in issue. It is, of course, conceivable (but unlikely) that by plaintiff's use of the word "hearsay" he referred to the failure of defendant to call as a witness the physician who had written up the notes. But plaintiff himself had put into evidence the (helpful to him) parts of that identical paper without calling the physician. Surely, plaintiff could not then demand that the other party prove the authenticity of the very record plaintiff had himself presented to the court. Since plaintiff had been allowed to prove by the record alone the diagnosis and treatment of his injuries, it would be absurd to forbid defendant using the same record, written in the same handwriting by the same physician at the same time, to prove an equally relevant, competent and material fact, that is, that plaintiff had stated to the physician that his injuries were caused in the manner asserted by defendant.

It follows from the above that section 374–a of the Civil Practice Act, our statutory rule as to admissibility of records made in the regular course of a business, has little or nothing to do with this case. What we have here is an admission against interest, proved not by the oral testimony of the person to whom it was made but by an authentic document already vouched for to the court by the opposing party himself.

But let us suppose that this is a section 374–a case. "Hospital records concededly are included within the records to which section 374–a of the Civil Practice Act is applicable." The physician who made the entries need not be called as a witness. True, as Judge Fuld points out, this court has not yet directly decided whether the section 374–a makes admissible that part of a hospital record which gives the history of the injury. But why should this court not adopt a practical and useful construction, rather than a narrow and unnecessarily restrictive one? And the statute itself seems to furnish the answer: "Any writing or record, whether in the form of an entry in a book or otherwise, made as a memorandum or record of any act, transaction, occurrence or event, shall be admissible in evidence in proof of said act, transaction, occurrence or event, if the trial judge shall find that it was made in the regular course of any business, and that it was the regular course of such business to make such memorandum or record at the time of such act, transaction, occurrence or event, or within a reasonable time thereafter." There is no reason why the "history" part of a hospital record, obtained not from unidentified persons but from the patient himself, should not be used in evidence against the patient. Of course, the writing must have been made in the regular course of the hospital's business and it must have been the regular course of the business of the hospital to make such entries. But in this case plaintiff did not object because of any failure to prove those requirements. Indeed, he could not, after himself bringing the record to court, reasonably urge that it was not the regularly made record of this hospital. And he knew, as we all do, that an examining physician, especially in a hospital receiving department, always inquires as to the cause of a trauma. Certainly, in the absence of any suspicious circumstance, it is not up to the courts to decide just how thoroughly a qualified physician may delve into the cause or occasion of the injuries he is diagnosing and treating. Anyhow, all this is by the statute's own words committed to the trial judge's discretion. It is he who is charged with passing on the question of whether the entry was regularly made. Here, no one suggested that it was not so made or called for proof that it was. The trial justice, therefore, had no reason for excluding it, particularly since there was no suggestion that the physician or the hospital had any interest in the case or any possible reason for falsifying these records.

This was a routine trial of a simple issue of fact. Plaintiff said the accident happened one way, defendant said that it happened another way. A hospital book brought to court by plaintiff showed that he himself had described the occurrence in the way that defendant described it. Plaintiff denied that he had made such a statement at the hospital. The jury settled that dispute. It is most unfortunate, especially in these days of congested calendars, that such a case must now be retried.

The judgment should be affirmed, with costs.

CONWAY, C.J., and FROESSEL and VAN VOORHIS, JJ., concur with FULD, J.

DESMOND, J., dissents in an opinion in which DYE and BURKE, JJ., concur.

Judgments reversed, etc.

PERITZ, COMPUTER DATA AND RELIABILITY: A CALL FOR AUTHENTICATION OF BUSINESS RECORDS UNDER THE FEDERAL RULES OF EVIDENCE

80 Nw.U.L.Rev. 956 (1986).
[Footnotes omitted.]

The traditional business records exception to the hearsay rule is based upon the recognition of two practicalities: Necessity and reliance. Shop books as evidence are thought necessary for adjudication on the merits: unless business records can be used in court without the testimony of every employee involved in the transaction, no one need ever satisfy obligations to large or complex firms. Moreover, records are seen as reliable evidence because of the business community's day-to-day reliance on them. This inference of trustworthiness or reliability makes sense with traditional leatherbound shop books, in part because the opposing party is thought to have a reasonable opportunity to uncover errors and deletions.

But does the same inference make sense with computerized record-keeping and accounting systems? This question deserves attention not only because most business records are now computerized, but also because our reliance on computers belies the lingering mystification of electronic data processing and the questionable reliability of its output—whether the output be an erroneous monthly credit statement or the false reports generated in the Equity Funding fraud. Should courts continue to infer trustworthiness simply from the traditional elements of the shop-book rule, or should proof of computer system reliability constitute part of a more comprehensive foundation for qualifying computerized business records?

Certainly the practicalities that engendered the business record exception remain with us. Given their size, complexity, and geographic dispersion, many businesses would face not only great expense but perhaps the impossibility of proof without recourse to their computerized information. Moreover, because of the business community's reliance on computerized shop books, these books meet the traditional conditions for circumstantial trustworthiness.

Although some commentators have expressed concern over the reliability of computerized business records, federal judges substantially agree that computer output should be qualified like any other business record, despite the fact that computer systems store, retrieve, and manipulate information in ways significantly different from earlier manual or mechanical systems. This judicial consensus has evolved since the passage of the Federal Rules of Evidence in 1975. Before the passage of the Rules, some courts required a more comprehensive foundation for qualifying business records stored and maintained by computer. More recently, all courts have required proponents to meet only the business records standard, and thereby have required the objector to assume the burden of persuading the trier of fact that such records lack probative value.

Under the Rules, a trial court rarely excludes an offer of computerized business records or reports not specially prepared for trial. Moreover, courts of appeals almost always uphold a lower court's finding of proper foundation for computerized business records, even when the lower court's finding is questionable. Appellate court opinions offer two rationales for their rubberstamps of approval. First, they grant trial judges broad discretion in admitting evidence. Thus, the party opposing admission must carry the formidable burden of persuading an appellate court that the trial court judge abused her discretion. Second, federal judges define objections to admissibility as arguments about probative value. In practical terms, this means that the opponent is left with a Sisyphean task—arguing that the judge erred in granting any probative value to the business records and thus that she should not have permitted the jury to consider them at all. Given the context of trial court discretion, the probability of carrying that burden approaches zero. * * *

The presumption of trustworthiness simply carries too much weight in our recently computerized society. Judges, juries, attorneys, and parties cannot make sound judgments regarding the credibility of computerized records by comparing fairly brief and understandable testimony with recognizable documents, as they could with traditional shop books. Unlike ledgers and books of payables and receivables with individual items, intermediate accounts, and scrivened entries or changes, computer printouts are not records at all, but rather neatly packaged concatenations of information excerpted from numerous records in multiple files. Because program changes or data manipulations can be accomplished without leaving any trace and without affecting the day-to-day operation of a computer system, both unintentional error and intentional fraud are difficult to discover behind a perfect-looking printout. Even if document discovery and deposition of data processing personnel are forthcoming, system examination may be too expensive and time consuming, especially given the frequent confrontation between the individual objector and large firm or government agency proponent. Computerization clearly magnifies the significance of the evidential tenet that the proponent is in the best position to offer proof about his own system's reliability because his personnel are already familiar with the machinery, programs, operation, and documentation.

Given the judiciary's perception that computerized records have an aura of reliability as well as the broad discretion granted to trial court judges regarding evidentiary questions, the current practice simply does not accord the objecting party a fair chance to argue the reliability question. Because more and better evidence is central to our fundamental commitment to trials on the merits, relying on business reliance is no longer good enough.

It may be argued that an expanded foundation for admitting computerized business records into evidence, like the one proposed here,[a] would have the undesirable effect of significantly raising litigation costs. This concern is misplaced, because higher litigation costs would turn out to be the exception, rather than the rule, for two reasons. First of all, uncontested offers of computerized business records could be accomplished in much the same way as they are currently—by stipulation of the parties. Second, although contested offers might sometimes involve slightly higher costs on account of a modest increase in the amount of evidence and testimony, the typical case would reflect, for the most part, not an increase, but rather a shift of burden and some expense from the objecting to the offering party.

———

See Federal Rules of Evidence 803(6)–(7); California Evidence Code §§ 1270–1272.

PALMER v. HOFFMAN

Supreme Court of the United States, 1943.
318 U.S. 109, 63 S.Ct. 477, 87 L.Ed. 645.
[Most of the Court's footnotes are omitted.]

Mr. Justice DOUGLAS delivered the opinion of the Court.

This case arose out of a grade crossing accident which occurred in Massachusetts. Diversity of citizenship brought it to the federal District Court in New York. There were several causes of action. The first two were on behalf of respondent individually, one being brought under a Massachusetts statute (Mass.Gen.L. (1932) c. 160, §§ 138, 232), the other at common law. The third and fourth were brought by

a. Editors' note: Elsewhere in his article, Professor Peritz supports the recommendations of the Federal Judicial Center's Manual for Complex Litigation (5th Ed.1982) that

Computer-maintained records kept in the regular course of business and printouts prepared especially for litigation should be admitted if the court finds that reliable computer equipment and techniques have been used and that the material is of probative value. The court should therefore require, well in advance of trial, that (a) the offering party demonstrate that the input procedures conform to the standard practice of persons engaged in the business or profession of the party or person from whom the printout is obtained; (b) in the case of a printout prepared especially for trial, the offering party demonstrate that the person from whom the printout is obtained relied on the data base in making a business or professional judgment within a reasonably short period of time before producing the printout sought to be introduced; (c) the offering party provide expert testimony that the processing program reliably and accurately processes the data in the data base; and (d) the opposing party be given the opportunity to depose the offeror's witness and to engage a witness of its own to evaluate the processing procedure.

See 80 Nw.U.L.Rev. 956, 974, n. 88 (1986).

respondent as administrator of the estate of his wife and alleged the same common law and statutory negligence as the first two counts. On the question of negligence the trial court submitted three issues to the jury—failure to ring a bell, to blow a whistle, to have a light burning in the front of the train. The jury returned a verdict in favor of respondent individually for some $25,000 and in favor of respondent as administrator for $9,000. The District Court entered judgment on the verdict. The Circuit Court of Appeals affirmed, one judge dissenting. 129 F.2d 976. The case is here on a petition for a writ of certiorari which presents three points.

I. The accident occurred on the night of December 25, 1940. On December 27, 1940, the engineer of the train, who died before the trial, made a statement at a freight office of petitioners where he was interviewed by an assistant superintendent of the road and by a representative of the Massachusetts Public Utilities Commission. This statement was offered in evidence by petitioners under the Act of June 20, 1936, 49 Stat. 1561, 28 U.S.C. § 695.[1] They offered to prove (in the language of the Act) that the statement was signed in the regular course of business, it being the regular course of such business to make such a statement. Respondent's objection to its introduction was sustained.

We agree with the majority view below that it was properly excluded.

We may assume that if the statement was made "in the regular course" of business, it would satisfy the other provisions of the Act. But we do not think that it was made "in the regular course" of business within the meaning of the Act. The business of the petitioners is the railroad business. That business like other enterprises entails the keeping of numerous books and records essential to its conduct or useful in its efficient operation. Though such books and records were considered reliable and trustworthy for major decisions in the industrial and business world, their use in litigation was greatly circumscribed or hedged about by the hearsay rule—restrictions which greatly increased the time and cost of making the proof where those who made the records were numerous. It was that problem which started the movement towards adoption of legislation embodying the principles of the present Act. And the legislative history of the Act indicates the same purpose.

The engineer's statement which was held inadmissible in this case falls into quite a different category. It is not a record made for the systematic conduct of the business as a business. An accident report

---

1. "In any court of the United States and in any court established by Act of Congress, any writing or record, whether in the form of an entry in a book or otherwise, made as a memorandum or record of any act, transaction, occurrence, or event, shall be admissible as evidence of said act, transaction, occurrence, or event, if it shall appear that it was made in the regular course of any business, and that it was the regular course of such business to make such memorandum or record at the time of such act, transaction, occurrence, or event or within a reasonable time thereafter. All other circumstances of the making of such writing or record, including lack of personal knowledge by the entrant or maker, may be shown to affect its weight, but they shall not affect its admissibility. The term 'business' shall include business, profession, occupation, and calling of every kind."

may affect that business in the sense that it affords information on
which the management may act. It is not, however, typical of entries
made systematically or as a matter of routine to record events or
occurrences, to reflect transactions with others, or to provide internal
controls. The conduct of a business commonly entails the payment of
tort claims incurred by the negligence of its employees. But the fact
that a company makes a business out of recording its employees'
versions of their accidents does not put those statements in the class of
records made "in the regular course" of the business within the
meaning of the Act. If it did, then any law office in the land could
follow the same course, since business as defined in the Act includes the
professions. We would then have a real perversion of a rule designed
to facilitate admission of records which experience has shown to be
quite trustworthy. Any business by installing a regular system for
recording and preserving its version of accidents for which it was
potentially liable could qualify those reports under the Act. The result
would be that the Act would cover any system of recording events or
occurrences provided it was "regular" and though it had little or
nothing to do with the management or operation of the business as
such. Preparation of cases for trial by virtue of being a "business" or
incidental thereto would obtain the benefits of this liberalized version
of the early shop book rule. The probability of trustworthiness of
records because they were routine reflections of the day to day operations of a business would be forgotten as the basis of the rule. Regularity of preparation would become the test rather than the character of
the records and their earmarks of reliability acquired from their source
and origin and the nature of their compilation. We cannot so completely empty the words of the Act of their historic meaning. If the Act is to
be extended to apply not only to a "regular course" of a business but
also to any "regular course" of conduct which may have some relationship to business, Congress not this Court must extend it. Such a major
change which opens wide the door to avoidance of cross-examination
should not be left to implication. Nor is it any answer to say that
Congress has provided in the Act that the various circumstances of the
making of the record should affect its weight, not its admissibility.
That provision comes into play only in case the other requirements of
the Act are met.

   In short, it is manifest that in this case those reports are not for
the systematic conduct of the enterprise as a railroad business. Unlike
payrolls, accounts receivable, accounts payable, bills of lading and the
like, these reports are calculated for use essentially in the court, not in
the business. Their primary utility is in litigating, not in railroading.

   It is, of course, not for us to take these reports out of the Act if
Congress has put them in. But there is nothing in the background of
the law on which this Act was built or in its legislative history which
suggests for a moment that the business of preparing cases for trial
should be included. In this connection it should be noted that the Act
of May 6, 1910, 36 Stat. 350, 45 U.S.C. § 38, requires officers of common
carriers by rail to make under oath monthly reports of railroad accidents to the Interstate Commerce Commission, setting forth the nature

and causes of the accidents and the circumstances connected therewith. And the same Act (45 U.S.C. § 40) gives the Commission authority to investigate and to make reports upon such accidents. It is provided, however, that "Neither the report required by section 38 of this title nor any report of the investigation provided for in section 40 of this title nor any part thereof shall be admitted as evidence or used for any purpose in any suit or action for damages growing out of any matter mentioned in said report or investigation." 45 U.S.C. § 41. A similar provision (36 Stat. 916, 54 Stat. 148, 45 U.S.C. § 33) bars the use in litigation of reports concerning accidents resulting from the failure of a locomotive boiler or its appurtenances. 45 U.S.C. §§ 32, 33. That legislation reveals an explicit Congressional policy to rule out reports of accidents which certainly have as great a claim to objectivity as the statement sought to be admitted in the present case. We can hardly suppose that Congress modified or qualified by implication these long standing statutes when it permitted records made "in the regular course" of business to be introduced. Nor can we assume that Congress having expressly prohibited the use of the company's reports on its accidents impliedly altered that policy when it came to reports by its employees to their superiors. The inference is wholly the other way.

The several hundred years of history behind the Act indicate the nature of the reforms which it was designed to effect. It should of course be liberally interpreted so as to do away with the anachronistic rules which gave rise to its need and at which it was aimed. But "regular course" of business must find its meaning in the inherent nature of the business in question and in the methods systematically employed for the conduct of the business as a business.

LEWIS v. BAKER
United States Court of Appeals, Second Circuit, 1975.
526 F.2d 470.

WATERMAN, Circuit Judge:

Plaintiff, Clifford J. Lewis Jr., brought this action in the United States District Court for the Southern District of New York alleging he suffered a disabling injury while employed by the Penn Central Railroad. Judgment was entered in favor of defendants after a jury trial. Plaintiff appeals and seeks a new trial on the * * * ground [that the] accident reports were improperly admitted into evidence. * * * Finding no merit to the above contention, we affirm.

On the date of his injury, October 26, 1969, plaintiff was employed as a freight brakeman or car dropper in the Penn Central railroad freight yard in Morrisville, Pennsylvania. His work called for him to move freight cars in a railroad yard by riding them down a slope while applying the brake manually. Plaintiff testified that immediately before the incident in question, he climbed onto the lead car of two box-cars, stationed himself on the rear brake platform of that car, applied the brake to test it, and found that the brake held. Upon his signal, another employee of the railroad released the two box-cars from the rest of the train at the top of a hill, at which time they started to roll down the slope. Plaintiff then started to turn the vertical brake wheel so that the car would slow down as it descended the slope and would ease into the train with which it was to couple on a track beyond the bottom of the slope. He claims that the brake did not hold, that the car continued to gather momentum, and that he then decided to leap off the car to avoid injury. As a result of the fall, he claims to have sustained substantial knee injury and the aggravation of a preexisting psychiatric condition which has precluded his returning to his job. There were no witnesses to the accident other than the plaintiff.

At the trial, defendants sought to rebut plaintiff's allegations of a faulty brake with evidence that the brake had functioned properly immediately prior to the accident when the plaintiff tested it, and immediately after the accident when it was checked in connection with the preparation of an accident report. It was the defendants' contention that plaintiff improperly set, or forgot to set, a necessary brake handle, panicked, and then leapt from the car.

In support of their interpretation of the events, defendants offered into evidence a "personal injury report" and an "inspection report." Frank Talbott, a trainmaster, testified that the personal injury report was signed by him and prepared under his supervision. The information had been provided to him by William F. Campbell, the night trainmaster. Talbott confirmed the authenticity of the record and testified that he was required to make out such reports of injuries as part of the regular course of business. At the trial David W. Halderman, an assistant general foreman for the defendants, identified the inspection report which had been prepared by Campbell and by Alfred Zuchero, a gang foreman. This report was based upon an inspection of the car Campbell and Zuchero had conducted less than four hours after the accident. Halderman testified that Zuchero was dead and that Campbell was employed by a railroad in Virginia. The latter was thus beyond the reach of subpoena. Halderman also confirmed that following every accident involving injury to an employee his office was required to complete inspection reports, and that such reports were regularly kept in the course of business. Over objection, the court admitted both reports into evidence.

*   *   *

As a preliminary matter, there is little doubt that these reports are each a "writing or record, whether in the form of an entry in a book or otherwise, made as a memorandum or record of any act, transaction, occurrence, or event *   *   * " 28 U.S.C. § 1732 (1966). Furthermore, it is beyond dispute that these reports were made pursuant to a regular procedure at the railroad yard, and that Talbott, Campbell and Zuchero made the reports within a reasonable time after the accident. Appellant argues, however, that notwithstanding the presence of those factors which would indicate a full compliance with 28 U.S.C. § 1732, the Supreme Court's decision in Palmer v. Hoffman, 318 U.S. 109, 63 S.Ct. 477, 87 L.Ed. 645 (1943), precludes their admission into evidence. There the Court upheld the inadmissibility of an accident report offered by the defendant railroad that had been prepared by one of its locomotive engineers. The Court stated that since the report was not prepared "for the systematic conduct of the business as a business," it was not "made 'in the regular course' of the business" of the railroad. We find significant differences between the report and the circumstances of its making in that case and the facts here, and we uphold the district court's admission of the records below.

In *Palmer v. Hoffman,* the engineer preparing the report had been personally involved in the accident, and, as Circuit Judge Frank stated in his opinion for the Court of Appeals, the engineer knew "at the time of making it that he [was] very likely, in a probable law suit relating to that accident, to be charged with wrongdoing as a participant in the accident, so that he [was] almost certain, when making the memorandum or report, to be sharply affected by a desire to exculpate himself and to relieve himself or his employer of liability." Here there could have been no similar motivation on the part of Talbott, Campbell or Zuchero, for not one of them was involved in the accident, or could have possibly been the target of a lawsuit by Lewis. In United States v. New York Foreign Trade Zone Operators, 304 F.2d 792 (2d Cir.1962), we sustained the admissibility of a similar report by the co-employee of the injured party which had been prepared as part of the regular business of the defendant pier-owner and operator. As we explained there, the mere fact that a record might ultimately be of some value in the event of litigation does not *per se* mandate its exclusion. In *Palmer v. Hoffman,* "[o]bviously the Supreme Court was concerned about a likely untrustworthiness of materials prepared specifically by a prospective litigant for courtroom use." The fact that a report embodies an employee's version of the accident, or happens to work in favor of the entrant's employer, does not, without more, indicate untrustworthiness. In the absence of a motive to fabricate, a motive so clearly spelled out in *Palmer v. Hoffman,* the holding in that case is not controlling to emasculate the Business Records Act. Therefore the trial court must look to those earmarks of reliability which otherwise establish the trustworthiness of the record.

Here the ICC requires the employer to prepare and file monthly reports of all accidents involving railroad employees. Assistant general foreman Halderman testified that following every injury he was required to inspect the equipment involved and to report the results of the inspection on a regular printed form.[2] As we stated in Taylor v.

2. 45 U.S.C. § 38 provides in relevant part:

It shall be the duty of the general manager, superintendent, or other proper officer of every common carrier engaged in interstate or foreign commerce by railroad to make to the Secretary of Transportation a monthly report, under oath, of all . . . accidents resulting in death or injury to any person. . . .

Although 45 U.S.C. § 41 provides that neither the report required by section 38 nor any part thereof "shall be admitted as evidence . . . in any suit or action for damages growing out of any matter mentioned in said report or investigation," we think it clear that the reports prepared by Talbott and by Campbell and Zuchero were not themselves monthly reports under section 41, and there is no indication that any part of the information contained in those reports will ever become part of the monthly report. Rather, it would appear that the forms completed by those employees were supplied by the employer, and that wholly different forms are utilized in complying with the federal reporting regulations, as prescribed by 49 C.F.R. § 225.1 et seq. Only the latter are barred by section 41 from admission in accident-related litigation.

Baltimore & Ohio R.R. Co., 344 F.2d 281 (2d Cir.1965), "[i]t would ill become a court to say that the regular making of reports required by law is not in the regular course of business." In addition to their use by the railroad in making reports to the ICC, the reports here were undoubtedly of utility to the employer in ascertaining whether the equipment involved was defective so that future accidents might be prevented. These factors, we think, are sufficient indicia of trustworthiness to establish the admissibility of the reports into evidence under the Federal Business Records Act.

Affirmed.

YATES v. BAIR TRANSPORT, INC.

United States District Court, Southern District of New York, 1965.
249 F.Supp. 681.
[Footnotes omitted.]

Judge TENNEY.

* * * We next proceed to the second class of proffered documents—the reports of various doctors who examined plaintiff.

As appears in the pre-trial order filed herein on March 18, 1964, the plaintiff, who was injured in the course of his employment, made a claim in workmen's compensation for the same injuries arising from the same occurrence as is the subject of this suit. The Liberty Mutual Insurance Company (hereinafter at times referred to as "the Insurance Company"), was the insurance carrier for Charles Noeding Trucking Co. Inc., in connection with that claim and was and is the insurance carrier for defendant Knickerbocker Despatch, Inc.

In accordance with the regular procedure under the Workmen's Compensation Law, and in compliance with Rule 2(b) of the Rules of the Workmen's Compensation Board of the State of New York, reports were submitted by certain physicians to the Insurance Company as well as to the Workmen's Compensation Board. Plaintiff wishes to introduce the reports of Doctors Youmans, Guthrie, Lewis, Fleck and Richman into evidence in lieu of calling them as witnesses, and has requested a pre-trial ruling as to their admissibility.

It appears from ¶ 4C of the Pre-Trial Order herein that all the parties agreed as to the authenticity of the medical reports which are now being proffered. It further appears from the reports themselves, and it can very easily be verified, that Doctors Guthrie and Youmans examined plaintiff on behalf of Liberty Mutual Insurance Company, that Doctor Richman examined plaintiff on behalf of Interboro Mutual Indemnity Insurance Company, and that Doctors Fleck and Lewis were plaintiff's treating physicians. Accordingly, the reports have been sufficiently authenticated.

In ruling on the admissibility of the documents, the reports will be grouped, based on the identity of the party on whose behalf the report was prepared.

In reaching a determination herein, I am assuming, based on the concessions made by defendant Knickerbocker in its memorandum of law (at pg. 3), that Knickerbocker does not seriously contest the fact that the proffered reports of Doctors Youmans and Guthrie were in fact made by them and were made on behalf of Liberty Mutual in the Workmen's Compensation proceeding.

That the report was prepared in the ordinary course of the business of both doctors is indicated by the Court of Appeals decision in White v. Zutell, which involved a medical report made by a specialist who had examined the plaintiff on behalf of the defendant's insurance carrier.

In sustaining the admissibility of the report, the Court stated: "The making of this report was clearly a part of this specialist's 'business'; indeed that is what he was commissioned to do. And it bears its own inherent guaranty of being what it purports to be—a detailed report of what he found medically upon examining the subject. That it might come up in the course of litigation does not affect this guaranty, unless to enhance it; what would be the use of such a report except to aid in fixing legal damage?"

As stated in McCormick, Evidence § 287 at 604 (1954): "[W]ell reasoned modern decisions have admitted in accident cases the written reports of doctors of their findings from an examination of the injured party when it appears that is the doctor's professional routine or duty to make such report." But, it is argued, all the doctors' reports were prepared specifically for litigation (whether before the Workmen's Compensation Board, or in this suit) and at a time when the motive to misrepresent was present and the reports thus lack the trustworthiness necessary to permit their introduction. Palmer v. Hoffman is cited in support of this argument.

In Palmer v. Hoffman, supra, the Court was concerned with the likely untrustworthiness of materials prepared specifically by a prospective litigant for courtroom use and thus held that the mere fact of regularity of preparation would not in itself be enough to justify the use of the evidence. The Business Records Act was interpreted in Palmer as facilitating the "admission of records which experience has shown to be quite trustworthy."

Accordingly, what must be found in the case at bar is an added element of trustworthiness which will counterbalance the fact that these reports were prepared in clear anticipation of litigation. With respect to the reports of Doctors Guthrie and Youmans, this added element is present.

> "In Pekelis v. Transcontinental & W. Air Inc., we held that the district court was erroneous in refusing to admit the plaintiff's offer of certain accident reports prepared by boards set up by the defendant airline to investigate the crash of one of defendant's airplanes. We interpreted the decision in Palmer v. Hoffman to exclude accident reports only when they were prepared for use in litigation or when there was other indicia of their untrustworthiness. The Pekelis reports, the court pointed out, ' * * * were against the interest of the entrant when made, * * * were clearly not part of a story cooked up in advance of litigation in the disguise of business records' and

were offered as evidence by the party opposing the one which had had the reports prepared.

In Korte v. New York, N.H. & H.R.R., another accident case, the district court had admitted certain doctors' reports, offered by the plaintiff, which had been prepared at the request of the defendant railroad. We affirmed the district court. Again, we pointed out that the decision in Palmer v. Hoffman was directed against the admission of hearsay evidence prepared for a litigious or other self-serving purpose. The court in Korte doubted whether the Palmer v. Hoffman rationale extended to reports made by independent doctors. Regardless of this, the Korte court stated that its holding could rest on Pekelis, where it had been held that reports offered by the party adverse to the party for whom the reports were prepared were admissible."

Thus the thrust of both opinions supports the admissibility of a doctor's report made in the regular course of business (when litigation was on the horizon) "when offered by one other than the entrant or one for whom the entrant is then working, i.e., the carrier * * *."

That other courts have refused to follow Korte and instead have followed Masterson v. Pennsylvania R. Co., is not binding on this Court since *Masterson* was sufficiently distinguished, if not disapproved, in *Korte.*

Thus in the case at bar the fact that litigation involving Liberty Mutual was pending when these three reports were made, if anything, enhances the trustworthiness of the documents, since it is the plaintiff, not the defendant, who seeks their introduction (i.e., the party whose interest is adverse to that of the party on whose behalf the reports were made).

Reference must once again be made to White v. Zutell, since it is a case on all fours with the case at bar.

In *White,* the plaintiff was asked whether he had ever been examined by a Doctor Gilshannon, and the defendants conceded that Doctor Gilshannon "a doctor of * * * [their] choosing" had examined the plaintiff and made a report to the defendants. The report was turned over to plaintiff, and based on the foregoing foundation, was offered into evidence "as an admission against interest" as well as "a document kept by them [the insurance carrier] in the regular course of business * * *." On the basis of the *Korte* case (which decision was also cited by the Court of Appeals), the report was admitted into evidence. In the case at bar, the foundation is, of course, a more solid one. * * *

Accordingly, I am inclined to overrule the objection to the report of Doctors Youmans and Guthrie.

No case, however, has been found or cited wherein a plaintiff was permitted to introduce self-serving reports made by doctors of his own choosing, in anticipation of litigation to shore up his own case. In fact, as noted above, analysis of both *Pekelis* and *Korte* supports the argument that, but for the characteristic of admission against the interest of the maker's principle, they would not have been admitted even though they were technically records kept in the ordinary course of business.

The fact that the record is self-serving is, of course, not determinative if made in the ordinary course of business without a view toward litigation.

As stated in the recent case of Taylor v. Baltimore & Ohio R.R.:

> "The report here was made when, so far as the record shows no one thought Taylor had suffered any serious injury, and it can hardly be assumed that a freight agent would appreciate the witty diversity whereby the difference of a few feet in the place of an employee's injury would result in the imposition of a distinct legal regime."

Thus the situation with respect to the reports of the doctors employed by plaintiff is different than that of defendant's doctors (Doctors Guthrie and Youmans) and warrants a different result, since statements by them would (if statements by defendant's doctors can be deemed admissions) be self-serving with no added degree of trustworthiness. They are thus statements made on behalf of a party by persons more inclined to favor that party's position, and the fact that they were made for the purposes of litigation causes me sufficient concern to refuse to admit them at this time.

The Court, with respect to documents falling under the Business Records Act, has a limited discretion. "The district court's discretion with respect to § 1732 is a discretion in judging whether the document offered 'has an inherent probability of trustworthiness.' It is therefore a necessary premise for its exercise that the document's trustworthiness be in doubt. * * *

Accordingly, where, as here, there is no counterbalancing force to the desire to promote the self-interest of the party on whose behalf the report was made, discretion dictates that the objection at this time be sustained and plaintiff be required to call Doctors Lewis and Fleck. Insofar as Doctor Richman is concerned, his status is not clear with respect to the parties involved in the litigation, and with respect to his report there may not be present this added element of trustworthiness. Therefore, I will place him in the latter group of doctors employed by plaintiff and hold his report at this time inadmissible as well.

The rulings of the Court are as noted above.

So ordered.

BEECH AIRCRAFT CORP. v. RAINEY

Supreme Court of the United States, 1988.
488 U.S. 153, 109 S.Ct. 439, 102 L.Ed.2d 445.

Justice BRENNAN delivered the opinion of the Court [which was unanimous on the issue presented in this excerpt.]

I

This litigation stems from the crash of a Navy training aircraft at Middleton Field, Alabama, on July 13, 1982, which took the lives of both pilots on board, Lieutenant Commander Barbara Ann Rainey and Ensign Donald Bruce Knowlton. The accident took place while Rainey, a Navy flight instructor, and Knowlton, her student, were flying "touch-and-go" exercises in a T–34C Turbo–Mentor aircraft, number 3E955. Their aircraft and several others flew in an oval pattern, each plane making successive landing/takeoff maneuvers on the runway. Following its fourth pass at the runway, 3E955 appeared to make a left turn prematurely, cutting out the aircraft ahead of it in the pattern and threatening a collision. After radio warnings from two other pilots, the plane banked sharply to the right in order to avoid the other aircraft. At that point it lost altitude rapidly, crashed, and burned.

Because of the damage to the plane and the lack of any survivors, the cause of the accident could not be determined with certainty. The two pilots' surviving spouses brought a product liability suit against petitioners Beech Aircraft Corporation, the plane's manufacturer, and Beech Aerospace Services, which serviced the plane under contract with the Navy. The plaintiffs alleged that the crash had been caused by a loss of engine power, known as "rollback," due to some defect in the aircraft's fuel control system. The defendants, on the other hand, advanced the theory of pilot error, suggesting that the plane had stalled during the abrupt avoidance maneuver.

At trial, the only seriously disputed question was whether pilot error or equipment malfunction had caused the crash. Both sides relied primarily on expert testimony. One piece of evidence presented by the defense was an investigative report prepared by Lieutenant Commander William Morgan on order of the training squadron's commanding officer and pursuant to authority granted in the Manual of the Judge Advocate General. This "JAG Report," completed during the six weeks following the accident, was organized into sections labeled "finding of fact," "opinions," and "recommendations," and was supported by some 60 attachments. The "finding of fact" included statements like the following:

> "13. At approximately 1020, while turning crosswind without proper interval, 3E955 crashed, immediately caught fire and burned.

> * * *

> "27. At the time of impact, the engine of 3E955 was operating but was operating at reduced power." App. 10–12.

[The "opinions" section of Morgan's report included a statement, which the trial judge admitted, that "The most probable cause of the accident was the pilots [sic] failure to maintain proper interval."]

II

Federal Rule of Evidence 803 provides that certain types of hearsay statements are not made excludable by the hearsay rule, whether or not the declarant is available to testify. Rule 803(8) defines the "public records and reports" which are not excludable, as follows:

> "Records, reports, statements, or data compilations, in any form, of public offices or agencies, setting forth (A) the activities of the office or agency, or (B) matters observed pursuant to duty imposed by law as to which matters there was a duty to report, * * * or (C) in civil actions and proceedings and against the Government in criminal cases, factual findings resulting from an investigation made pursuant to authority granted by law, unless the sources of information or other circumstances indicate lack of trustworthiness."

Controversy over what "public records and reports" are made not excludable by Rule 803(8)(C) has divided the federal courts from the beginning. In the present case, the Court of Appeals followed the "narrow" interpretation of Smith v. Ithaca Corp., 612 F.2d 215, 220–223 (CA5 1980), which held that the term "factual findings" did not encompass "opinions" or "conclusions." Courts of appeal other than those of the Fifth and Eleventh Circuits, however, have generally adopted a broader interpretation. For example, the Court of Appeals for the Sixth Circuit, in Baker v. Elcona Homes Corp., 588 F.2d 551, 557–558 (1978), cert. denied, 441 U.S. 933 (1979), held that "factual findings admissible under Rule 803(8)(C) may be those which are made by the preparer of the report from disputed evidence * * *." The other courts of appeal that have squarely confronted the issue have also adopted the broader interpretation. We agree and hold that factually based conclusions or opinions are not on that account excluded from the scope of Rule 803(8)(C).

Because the Federal Rules of Evidence are a legislative enactment, we turn to the "traditional tools of statutory construction," INS v. Cardoza–Fonseca, 480 U.S. 421, 446 (1987), in order to construe their provisions. We begin with the language of the Rule itself. Proponents of the narrow view have generally relied heavily on a perceived dichotomy between "fact" and "opinion" in arguing for the limited scope of the phrase "factual findings." Smith v. Ithaca Corp., supra, contrasted the term "factual findings" in Rule 803(8)(C) with the language of Rule 803(6) (records of regularly conducted activity), which expressly refers to "opinions" and "diagnoses." "Factual findings," the court opined, must be something other than opinions. Smith, supra, at 221–222.

For several reasons, we do not agree. In the first place, it is not apparent that the term "factual findings" should be read to mean simply "facts" (as opposed to "opinions" or "conclusions"). A common definition of "finding of fact" is, for example, "[a] conclusion by way of reasonable inference from the evidence." Black's Law Dictionary 569 (5th ed. 1979). To say the least, the language of the Rule does not compel us to reject the interpretation that "factual findings" includes conclusions or opinions that flow from a factual investigation. Second, we note that, contrary to what is often assumed, the language of the Rule does not state that "factual findings" are admissible, but that "reports * * * setting forth * * * factual findings" (emphasis added) are admissible. On this reading, the language of the Rule does not create a distinction between "fact" and "opinion" contained in such reports.

Turning next to the legislative history of Rule 803(8)(C), we find no clear answer to the question of how the Rule's language should be interpreted. Indeed, in this case the legislative history may well be at the origin of the dispute. Rather than the more usual situation where a court must attempt to glean meaning from ambiguous comments of legislators who did not focus directly on the problem at hand, here the Committees in both Houses of Congress clearly recognized and expressed their opinions on the precise question at issue. Unfortunately, however, they took diametrically opposite positions. Moreover, the two Houses made no effort to reconcile their views, either through changes in the Rule's language or through a statement in the Report of the Conference Committee.

The House Judiciary Committee, which dealt first with the proposed rules after they had been transmitted to Congress by this Court, included in its Report but one brief paragraph on Rule 803(8):

> "The Committee approved Rule 803(8) without substantive change from the form in which it was submitted by the Court. The Committee intends that the phrase 'factual findings' be strictly construed and that evaluations or opinions contained in public reports shall not be admissible under this Rule." H.R.Rep. No. 93–650, p. 14 (1973).

The Senate Committee responded at somewhat greater length, but equally emphatically:

> "The House Judiciary Committee report contained a statement of intent that 'the phrase "factual findings" in subdivision (c) be strictly construed and that evaluations or opinions contained in public reports shall not be admissible under this rule.' The committee takes strong exception to this limiting understanding of the application of the rule. We do not think it reflects an understanding of the intended operation of the rule as explained in the Advisory Committee notes to this subsection * * *. We think the restrictive interpretation of the House overlooks the fact that while the Advisory Committee assumes admissibility in the first instance of evaluative reports, they are not admissible if, as the rule states, 'the sources of information or other circumstances indicate lack of trustworthiness.'
>
> * * *
>
> "The committee concludes that the language of the rule together with the explanation provided by the Advisory Committee furnish sufficient guidance on the admissibility of evaluative reports." S.Rep. No. 93–1277, p. 18 (1974).

Clearly this legislative history reveals a difference of view between the Senate and the House that affords no definitive guide to the congressional understanding. It seems clear however that the Senate understanding is more in accord with the wording of the Rule and with the comments of the Advisory Committee.

The Advisory Committee's comments are notable, first, in that they contain no mention of any dichotomy between statements of "fact" and "opinions" or "conclusions." What was on the Committee's mind was simply whether what it called "evaluative reports" should be admissible. Illustrating the previous division among the courts on this subject, the Committee cited numerous cases in which the admissibility of such reports had been both sustained and denied. It also took note of various federal statutes that made certain kinds of evaluative reports admissible in evidence. What is striking about all of these examples is that these were *reports that stated conclusions.* E.g., Moran v. Pittsburgh–Des Moines Steel Co., 183 F.2d 467, 472–473 (CA3 1950) (report of Bureau of Mines concerning the cause of a gas tank explosion admissible); Franklin v. Skelly Oil Co., 141 F.2d 568, 571–572 (CA10 1944) (report of state fire marshal on the cause of a gas explosion inadmissible); 42 U.S.C. § 269(b) (bill of health by appropriate official admissible as prima facie evidence of vessel's sanitary history and condition). The Committee's concern was clearly whether reports of this kind should be admissible. Nowhere in its comments is there the slightest indication that it even considered the solution of admitting only "factual" statements from such reports. Rather, the Committee referred throughout to "reports," without any such differentiation regarding the statements they contained. What the Committee referred to in the Rule's language as "reports ＊ ＊ ＊ setting forth ＊ ＊ ＊ factual findings" is surely nothing more or less than what in its commentary it called "evaluative reports." Its solution as to their admissibility is clearly stated in the final paragraph of its report on this Rule. That solution consists of two principles: First, "the rule ＊ ＊ ＊ assumes admissibility in the first instance ＊ ＊ ＊." Second, it provides "ample provision for escape if sufficient negative factors are present."

That "provision for escape" is contained in the final clause of the Rule: evaluative reports are admissible "unless the sources of information or other circumstances indicate lack of trustworthiness." This trustworthiness inquiry—and not an arbitrary distinction between "fact" and "opinion"—was the Committee's primary safeguard against the admission of unreliable evidence, and it is important to note that it applies to all elements of the report. Thus, a trial judge has the discretion, and indeed the obligation, to exclude an entire report or portions thereof—whether narrow "factual" statements or broader "conclusions"—that she determines to be untrustworthy. Moreover, safeguards built in to other portions of the Federal Rules, such as those dealing with relevance and prejudice, provide the court with additional means of scrutinizing and, where appropriate, excluding evaluative reports or portions of them. And of course it goes without saying that the admission of a report containing "conclusions" is subject to the ultimate safeguard—the opponent's right to present evidence tending to contradict or diminish the weight of those conclusions.

Our conclusion that neither the language of the Rule nor the intent of its framers calls for a distinction between "fact" and "opinion" is strengthened by the analytical difficulty of drawing such a line. It has frequently been remarked that the distinction between statements of fact and opinion is, at best, one of degree:

> "All statements in language are statements of opinion, i.e., statements of mental processes or perceptions. So-called 'statements of fact' are only more specific statements of opinion. What the judge means to say, when he asks the witness to state the facts, is: 'The nature of this case requires that you be more specific, if you can, in your description of what you saw.'" W. King & D. Pillinger, Opinion Evidence in Illinois 4 (1942) (footnote omitted), quoted in 3 J. Weinstein & M. Berger, Weinstein's Evidence ¶ 701[01], p. 701–6 (1988).

See also E. Cleary, McCormick on Evidence 27 (3d ed. 1984) ("There is no conceivable statement however specific, detailed and 'factual,' that is not in some measure the product of inference and reflection as well as observation and memory"); R. Lempert & S. Saltzburg, A Modern Approach to Evidence 449 (2d ed. 1982) ("A factual finding, unless it is a simple report of something observed, is an opinion as to what more basic facts imply"). Thus, the traditional requirement that lay witnesses give statements of fact rather than opinion may be considered, "[l]ike the hearsay and original documents rules * * * a 'best evidence' rule." McCormick, Opinion Evidence in Iowa, 19 Drake L.Rev. 245, 246 (1970).

In the present case, the trial court had no difficulty in admitting as a factual finding the statement in the JAG Report that "[a]t the time of impact, the engine of 3E955 was operating but was operating at reduced power." Surely this "factual finding" could also be characterized as an opinion, which the investigator presumably arrived at on the basis of clues contained in the airplane wreckage. Rather than requiring that we draw some inevitably arbitrary line between the various shades of fact/opinion that invariably will be present in investigatory reports, we believe the Rule instructs us—as its plain language states— to admit "reports * * * setting forth * * * factual findings." The Rule's limitations and safeguards lie elsewhere: First, the requirement that reports contain factual findings bars the admission of statements not based on factual investigation. Second, the trustworthiness provision requires the court to make a determination as to whether the report, or any portion thereof, is sufficiently trustworthy to be admitted.

A broad approach to admissibility under Rule 803(8)(C), as we have outlined it, is also consistent with the Federal Rules' general approach of relaxing the traditional barriers to "opinion" testimony. Rules 702– 705 permit experts to testify in the form of an opinion, and without any exclusion of opinions on "ultimate issues." And Rule 701 permits even a lay witness to testify in the form of opinions or inferences drawn from her observations when testimony in that form will be helpful to the trier of fact. We see no reason to strain to reach an interpretation of Rule 803(8)(C) that is contrary to the liberal thrust of the Federal Rules.

We hold, therefore, that portions of investigatory reports otherwise admissible under Rule 803(8)(C) are not inadmissible merely because they state a conclusion or opinion. As long as the conclusion is based on a factual investigation and satisfies the Rule's trustworthiness requirement, it should be admissible along with other portions of the report. As the trial judge in this case determined that certain of the JAG Report's conclusions were trustworthy, he rightly allowed them to be admitted into evidence. * * *

[In a final portion of its opinion, the Court decided that the District Court erred in restricting the cross-examination of a witness concerning a document about which the witness had testified on direct.]

UNITED STATES v. OATES

United States Court of Appeals, Second Circuit, 1977.
560 F.2d 45.

WATERMAN, Circuit Judge:

This is an appeal from a judgment of the United States District Court for the Eastern District of New York convicting appellant, following a six-day jury trial, of possession of heroin with intent to distribute, and of conspiracy to commit that substantive offense.

* * *

Appellant * * * claims that the trial court committed error by admitting into evidence at trial two documentary exhibits purporting to be the official report and accompanying worksheet of the United States Customs Service chemist who analyzed the white powdery substance seized * * *. The documents, the crucial nature of which is beyond cavil, concluded that the powder examined was heroin. Appellant contends * * * that under the new Federal Rules of Evidence (herein-after "FRE") the documents should have been excluded as hearsay * * *.

At trial the government had planned upon calling as one of its final witnesses a Mr. Milton Weinberg, a retired United States Customs Service chemist who allegedly had analyzed the white powder seized from Isaac Daniels. It seems that Mr. Weinberg had been present on the day the trial had been scheduled to commence but he was not able to testify then because of a delay occasioned by the unexpected length of the pretrial suppression hearing. The government claims that by the time Weinberg was rescheduled to testify he had become "unavaila-ble." The Assistant United States Attorney explained the circum-stances of this unavailability as follows: "I am told by his wife [he is] very sick. Apparently he has some type of bronchial infection." After a short adjournment the prosecutor added the following comment: "Mr. Weinberg called my office this morning and I was made known about it about 10:30 this morning prior to coming up stairs." Considering these two explanations to be consistent with each other, it appears that Weinberg called the United States Attorney's office to inform them of his unavailability and that subsequently the Assistant United States

Attorney attempted to speak to Weinberg personally but was able, for
some reason, to speak only to Weinberg's wife who advised that Weinberg had "some type of bronchial infection."   There is no indication in
the record as to why the Assistant United States Attorney was at that
time unable to speak to Weinberg himself, although earlier that day
Weinberg had been able to carry on a telephone conversation.   Nor is
there any other indication in the record that the prosecutor made any
further attempts to confirm the fact that Weinberg was ill, and, if so,
how ill he might be.   No request was made of the district court for a
brief continuance for the purpose of determining the nature and expected duration of Weinberg's illness.

　　 * * * [T]he prosecutor had planned to call Weinberg for the
purpose of eliciting from him testimony that Weinberg had analyzed
the powder seized * * * and found it to be heroin.   When Weinberg
became "unavailable," the government decided to call another Customs
chemist, Shirley Harrington, who, although she did not know Weinberg
personally, was able to testify concerning the regular practices and
procedures used by Customs Service chemists in analyzing unknown
substances.   Through Mrs. Harrington the government was successful
in introducing Exhibits 13 and 12 which purported to be, respectively,
the handwritten worksheet used by the chemist analyzing the substance seized from Daniels and the official typewritten report of the
chemical analysis.   The report summarizes salient features of the
worksheet.   Mrs. Harrington claimed to be able to ascertain from the
face of the worksheet the various steps taken by Weinberg to determine
whether the unknown substance was, as suspected, heroin.   When the
defense voiced vigorous objection to the attempt to introduce the
documents through Mrs. Harrington, the government relied * * * on
the modified "business records" exception found in FRE 803(6).   [T]he
evidence was also claimed to be admissible under FRE 803(8) as a
"public record" * * *.

　　 Mrs. Harrington was obviously an experienced chemist, having
conducted thousands of tests while working for the Customs Service,
including hundreds designed to identify heroin.   She was also an
experienced witness, having testified "probably a hundred or so" times
in the course of her duties with the Customs Service.   She had never
worked with Weinberg personally and had never observed him perform
any chemical tests.   She had never received any notes or letters from
him, but she identified Weinberg's writing on Exhibit 13 and his
signature on Exhibit 12, presumably because she had, in accordance
with Customs Service practices, re-analyzed, prior to destruction, substances Weinberg had previously analyzed shortly after the substances
were seized.

　　 The defense, in addition to having no opportunity to cross-examine
Weinberg, the chemist who had performed the analysis, was also
disturbed about two other circumstances surrounding the introduction
of Exhibits 12 and 13.   In particular, the defense was surprised that
Exhibit 12, the official typewritten report, contained Weinberg's signature, for no such signature had appeared on the copy of this exhibit
given to the defense beforehand.   Moreover, the defense was particular-

1 ly, and understandably distressed about the absence of Weinberg in
2 view of the fact that the two exhibits differed in one important
3 particular, a particular in which they certainly should have been
4 identical. A notation pertaining to the chain of custody of the powder
5 within the agency appeared on both exhibits, in typewritten form on
6 the official report and in handwriting, presumably Weinberg's on the
7 worksheet. The notation read "Received from and returned to CSO
8 Fromkin." On the typewritten official report, however, this statement
9 had been crossed out, although it still was legible beneath the scrib-
10 bling. Mrs. Harrington knew nothing about this deletion. There is
11 nothing in the exhibits themselves or in the testimony of any witnesses
12 that would explain why, when and by whom this deletion was made.
13   * * *

14   It is eminently clear that the report and worksheet were "written
15 assertions" constituting "statements," FRE 801(a)(1), which were "of-
16 fered [by the prosecution] in evidence [at trial] to prove the truth of the
17 matters asserted [in them]." FRE 801(c). As such, they were hearsay,
18 and, for our present purposes, under FRE 802 were inadmissible "ex-
19 cept as [otherwise] provided by" other provisions of the Federal Rules of
20 Evidence. * * *

21   * * * On this appeal the government and the appellant are in
22 complete disagreement over the materiality of FRE 803(8) to the issue
23 of whether the chemist's report and worksheet were excludable as
24 hearsay. Although at trial the government placed some reliance on
25 FRE 803(8), the so-called "public records and reports" exception to
26 exclusion, in its brief in this court it completely ignores the provision,
27 apparently abandoning any reliance on it for reasons we shall discuss
28 below. Instead, it urges us to find that the challenged evidence falls
29 easily within the scope of what has traditionally been labeled the
30 "business records exception" to the hearsay exclusionary rule, the
31 codification of which in the Federal Rules of Evidence is found in FRE
32 803(6). Appellant, on the other hand, vigorously asserts that the issue
33 of whether the chemist's report and worksheet were fatal hearsay can
34 be correctly evaluated only by a careful study of the precise wording of
35 FRE 803(8) and the legislative intent underlying the enactment of that
36 rule.
37

38   While the problem presented is not susceptible of any facile solu-
39 tion, we believe that, on balance, appellant's emphasis on the impor-
40 tance of FRE 803(8) is well-founded. It would certainly seem to be the
41 exception which would logically come to mind if a question arose as to
42 the admissibility of reports of the kind we are considering in this case.
43 Moreover, although as a general rule there is no question that hearsay
44 evidence failing to meet the requirements of one exception may none-
45 theless satisfy the standards of another exception, and there thus might
46 be no need to examine FRE 803(8) at all, we agree with appellant that
47 both the language of Rule 803(8) and the congressional intent, as
48 gleaned from the explicit language of the rule and from independent
49 sources, which impelled that language have impact that extends beyond
50 the immediate confines of exception (8) itself. We therefore regard
51 FRE 803(8) as the proper starting point for our evidentiary analysis.

That the chemist's report and worksheet could not satisfy the
requirements of the "public records and reports" exception seems
evident merely from examining, on its face, the language of FRE 803(8).
That rule insulates from the exclusionary effect of the hearsay rule
certain:

> (8) *Public records and reports.*—Records, reports, state-
> ments, or data compilations, in any form, of public offices or
> agencies, setting forth (A) the activities of the office or agency,
> or (B) matters observed pursuant to duty imposed by law as to
> which matters there was a duty to report, excluding, however,
> in criminal cases matters observed by police officers and other
> law enforcement personnel, or (C) in civil cases and proceed-
> ings and against the Government in criminal cases, factual
> findings resulting from an investigation made pursuant to
> authority granted by law, unless the sources of information or
> other circumstances indicate lack of trustworthiness.

While there may be no sharp demarcation between the records covered
by exception 8(B) and those referenced in exception 8(C), and indeed
there may in some cases be actual overlap, we conclude without
hesitation that surely the language of item (C) is applicable to render
the chemist's documents inadmissible as evidence in this case, and they
might also be within the ambit of the terminology of item (B), a claim
appellant argues to us persuasively.

It is manifest from the face of item (C) that "factual findings
resulting from an investigation made pursuant to authority granted by
law" are not shielded from the exclusionary effect of the hearsay rule
by "the public records exception" if the government seeks to have those
"factual findings" admitted *against* the accused in a criminal case. It
seems indisputable to us that the chemist's official report and worksheet in the case at bar can be characterized as reports of "factual
findings resulting from an investigation made pursuant to authority
granted by law." The "factual finding" in each instance, the conclusion of the chemist that the substance analyzed was heroin, obviously is
the product of an "investigation," * * * supposedly involving on the
part of the chemist employment of various techniques of scientific
analysis. Furthermore, in view of its reliance on the chemist's report
at trial and its representation to the district court that "chemical
analys[e]s of unidentified substances are indeed a regularly conducted
activity of the Customs laboratory of Customs chemists," the government here is surely in no position to dispute the fact that the analyses
regularly performed by United States Customs Service chemists on
substances lawfully seized by Customs officers are performed pursuant
to authority granted by law.

Though with less confidence, we believe that the chemist's documents might also fail to achieve status as public records under FRE
803(8)(B) because they are records of "matters observed by police
officers and other law enforcement personnel." Although in character-
izing the chemist's report and worksheet here it is quite accurate to
designate those reports as the reports of factual findings made pursuant

to an investigation, the reports in this case conceivably could also be susceptible of the characterization that they are "reports * * * setting forth * * * (B) matters observed pursuant to duty imposed by law as to which matters there was a duty to report." If this characterization is justified, the difficult question would be whether the chemists making the observations could be regarded as "other law enforcement personnel." We think this phraseology must be read broadly enough to make its prohibitions against the use of government-generated reports in criminal cases coterminous with the analogous prohibitions contained in FRE 803(8)(C). We would thus construe "other law enforcement personnel" to include, at the least, any officer or employee of a governmental agency which has law enforcement responsibilities. Applying such a standard to the case at bar, we easily conclude that full-time chemists of the United States Customs Service are "law enforcement personnel." The chemist in this case was employed by the Customs Service, a governmental agency which had clearly defined law enforcement authority in the field of illegal narcotics trafficking; the officers who actually seized the suspected contraband were employed by the Customs Service, and the unidentified substance was delivered by them to a laboratory operated by the Customs Service. The unidentified substance was then subjected to analysis by a chemist, one of whose regular functions is to test substances seized from suspected narcotics violators. Chemists at the laboratory are, without question, important participants in the prosecutorial effort. * * * Moreover, the role of the chemist typically does not terminate upon completion of the chemical analysis and submission of the resulting report but participation continues until the chemist has testified as an important prosecution witness at trial. * * * In short, these reports are not "made by persons and for purposes unconnected with a criminal case [but rather they are a direct] result of a test made for the specific purpose of convicting the defendant and conducted by agents of the executive branch, the very department of government which seeks defendant's conviction." It would therefore seem that if the chemist's report and worksheet here can be deemed to set forth "matters observed," the documents would fail to satisfy the requirements of exception FRE 803(8) for the chemist must be included within the category of "other law enforcement personnel."

Our conclusion that the chemist's report and worksheet do not satisfy the standards of FRE 803(8) comports perfectly with what we discern to be clear legislative intent not only to exclude such documents from the scope of FRE 803(8) but from the scope of FRE 803(6) as well.

* * *

* * * We * * * think it manifest that it was the clear intention of Congress to make evaluative and law enforcement reports absolutely inadmissible against defendants in criminal cases. Just as importantly, it must have been the unquestionable belief of Congress that the language of FRE 803(8)(B) and (C) accomplished that very result.

Despite what we perceive to be clear congressional intent that reports not qualifying under FRE 803(8)(B) or (C) should, and would, be inadmissible against defendants in criminal cases, the government completely ignores those provisions * * * and argues instead that the chemist's report and worksheet in the case at bar fall clearly within the literal terms of the modified business records exception to the hearsay rule contained in FRE 803(6), entitled *"Records of regularly conducted activity."*

* * *

* * * [T]he government's argument that the documents in this case satisfy the requirements of the modified "business records" exception is not altogether unappealing if it is assessed strictly on the basis of the literal language of FRE 803(6) and without reference to either the legislative history or the language of FRE 803(8)(B) and (C). For instance, it is true that, traditionally, a proponent's inability to satisfy the requirements of one hearsay exception does not deny him the opportunity to attempt to meet the standards of another. Secondly, it is clear from the explicit inclusion of the words "opinions" and "diagnoses" in FRE 803(6) that, in one sense anyway, Congress intended to expand, or at least ratify, the view of prior court cases that had expanded the concept of what constitutes a "business record." The Advisory Committee's Notes confirm this. Advisory Committee's Notes, Note to Paragraph (6) of Rule 803, 56 F.R.D. at 309. It is reasonable to assume that a laboratory analysis may well be an "opinion." Thirdly, the testimony of Mrs. Harrington, a "qualified witness," established that it was a regular practice of the Customs laboratory to make written reports of their analyses and that these particular written reports were made in the regular course of the laboratory's activities.

However, not nearly as clear is whether under the facts here the "method or circumstances of preparation" might not "indicate lack of trustworthiness." The language contained within the subordinate "unless" clause creates an exception to the general language of FRE 803(6) and, as such, "is * * * subject to the rule of strict construction; that is, any doubt will be resolved in favor of the general provision and against the exception, and anyone claiming to be relieved from the statute's operation must establish that he comes within the exception." * * * Here there are some "circumstances of preparation [which tend to] indicate lack of trustworthiness." As already noted, Exhibits 12 and 13 differ from each other in one significant respect in which they should be identical. On both, in handwriting on the worksheet and in typewritten form on the official report, the notation "Received from and returned to CSO Fromkin" appears. Yet, on the report this notation has been crossed out.

Nothing indicates who deleted the notation, when it was deleted, or why it was deleted and, as it relates to the issue of chain of custody, it is a matter of some importance. Moreover, before trial defense counsel was given what was purported to be a copy of the official chemist's report. Yet, this document did not contain the signature of the certifying chemist Weinberg. At trial the official report the government offered was signed. Assuming that Weinberg did sign the document the government offered, there is obviously a question as to when

1   this document was signed, it not being unreasonable to assume that it
2   was signed after the government had already given the defense a copy
3   of an originally unsigned report.   However, while we are troubled by
4   these concededly unusual circumstances, and it may well be that they
5   raise ample doubts to require exclusion on the face of FRE 803(6) alone,
6   we prefer not to predicate our decision on a finding that the "circum-
7   stances of preparation indicate lack of trustworthiness."   Instead, we
8   assume for purposes of argument here, that, as sedulously asserted by
9   the government, the chemist's report and worksheet might fall within
10   the literal language of FRE 803(6).

11   For purposes of our present analysis, we thus consider the situation
12   to be that the chemist's documents might appear to be within the
13   literal language of FRE 803(6) although there is clear congressional
14   intent that such documents be deemed inadmissible against a defendant
15   in a criminal case.   This would not be the first time that a court has
16   encountered a situation pitting some literal language of a statute
17   against a legislative intent that flies in the face of that literal language.
18   Our function as an interpretive body is, of course, to construe legisla-
19   tive enactments in such a way that the intent of the legislature is
20   carried out.   In recognition of this responsibility numerous courts have
21   either applied, or at least recognized the principle that, despite the
22   existence of literal language that might dictate a contrary result, a
23   court should interpret a statute in such a way as to effectuate clear
24   legislative intent.

25   *   *   *

26   *   *   * Representative William Hungate, in presenting the report
27   of the Committee of Conference to the House of Representatives, left no
28   doubt that it was the belief of the Committee of Conference that under
29   the new Federal Rules of Evidence the *effect* of FRE 803(8)(B) and (C)
30   was to render law enforcement reports and evaluative reports inadmis-
31   sible against defendants in criminal cases.   It is thus clear that the only
32   way to construe FRE 803(6) so that it is reconcilable with this intended
33   effect is to interpret FRE 803(6) and the other hearsay exceptions in
34   such a way that police and evaluative reports not satisfying the stan-
35   dards of FRE 803(8)(B) and (C) may not qualify for admission under
36   FRE 803(6) or any of the other exceptions to the hearsay rule.   *   *   *
37
38   Even if the remarks of Representative Hungate *   *   * were not as
39   clear as they are, we could still reach the same conclusion that, in view
40   of the articulated purpose behind the narrow drafting of FRE 803 in
41   general and FRE 803(8) in particular, FRE 803(6) must be read in
42   conjunction with FRE 803(8)(B) and (C).   Specifically, the pervasive fear
43   of the draftsmen and of Congress that interference with an accused's
44   right to confrontation would occur was the reason why in criminal
45   cases evaluative reports of government agencies and law enforcement
46   reports were expressly denied the benefit to which they might other-
47   wise be entitled under FRE 803(8).   It follows that this explanation of
48   the reason for the special treatment of evaluative and law enforcement
49   reports under FRE 803(8) applies with equal force to the treatment of
50   such reports under *any* of the other exceptions to the hearsay rule.
51   The prosecution's utilization of any hearsay exception to achieve admis-

sion of evaluative and law enforcement reports would serve to deprive the accused of the opportunity to confront his accusers as effectively as would reliance on a "public records" exception. Thus, there being no apparent reason why Congress would tolerate the admission of evaluative and law enforcement reports by use of some other exception to the hearsay rule * * * it simply makes no sense to surmise that Congress ever intended that these records could be admissible against a defendant in a criminal case under *any* of the Federal Rules of Evidence's exceptions to the hearsay rule. * * *

We are not the first court to indulge in a less than literal construction of a hearsay exception so as to effectuate congressional intent. An issue addressed by the D.C. Circuit in the United States v. Smith, was whether the police reports of FRE 803(8)(B) are admissible *against* the government. While conceding that "[o]n its face, 803(8)(B) appears to [say that they are not, the court was] convinced, however, that 803(8)(B) should be read, in accordance with the obvious intent of Congress and in harmony with 803(8)(C) to authorize the admission of the reports of police officers and other law enforcement personnel at the request of the defendant in a criminal case." 521 F.2d at 968 n. 24. The "obvious intent of Congress" in enacting FRE 803(8)(B) was found to be that "use of reports against defendants would be unfair." 521 F.2d at 969 n. 24. "Since there [was] no apparent reason to allow defendants to use the reports admitted by 803(8)(C) but not those governed by 803(8)(B) [the court concluded] that a police report * * * is an exception to the new hearsay rules when introduced at the request of the defense."

* * *

* * * Inasmuch as the chemist's documents here can be characterized as governmental reports which set forth matters observed by law enforcement personnel or which set forth factual findings resulting from an authorized investigation, they were incapable of qualifying under any of the exceptions to the hearsay rule specified in FRE 803 and 804. The documents were crucial to the government's case, they were of course, hearsay, and, inasmuch as they were ineligible to qualify for any exception to the hearsay rule, their admission at trial against appellant was prejudicial error.

* * * [W]e reverse the judgment of conviction and remand for a new trial.

UNITED STATES v. GRADY

United States Court of Appeals, Second Circuit, 1976.
544 F.2d 598.

OAKES, Circuit Judge:

The waves of tragedy from the internecine conflict in Northern Ireland have their ripple effects in this country. Appellants here are Frank Grady, a sympathizer with the Catholic minority in Ulster, and John Jankowski, a licensed firearms dealer in Yonkers, New York. Each was convicted of conspiracy to violate the federal firearms law, particularly 18 U.S.C. §§ 922(m) and 923, which together require a licensed firearms dealer to make true entries in a federal firearms

1 record, and of ten substantive counts of making or causing to be made
2 false entries as to ten .30-caliber semiautomatic rifles in Jankowski's
3 record or "logbook"; Grady was also convicted of one count of unlawful
4 exportation without a permit of these same rifles. * * *

5   * * *

6 *IV. Admission of Irish Police Records.*

7

8   Much is made in the briefs of the admission into evidence of
9 records of the formidable-sounding Department of Industrial and Foren-
10 sic Science of the Ministry of Commerce and of the Royal Ulster
11 Constabulary. These were entitled "Material Forwarded for Examina-
12 tion" and "Order for Disposal of Firearms/Ammunition." The ground
13 of objection was that the documents constituted inadmissible hearsay.
14 * * *

15   For the limited purpose of showing that the specified weapons were
16 found in Northern Ireland on dates subsequent to the May, 1970,
17 purchases, however, we think the records were admissible under the
18 public records exception to the hearsay rule, codified in Fed.R.Evid.
19 803(8)(B). Rule 803(8)(B) allows admission of records and reports of
20 public offices or agencies setting forth "matters observed pursuant to
21 duty imposed by law as to which matters there was a duty to report,"
22 but is subject to an exception for "matters observed by police officers
23 and other law enforcement personnel." In adopting this exception,
24 Congress was concerned about prosecutors attempting to prove their
25 cases in chief simply by putting into evidence police officers' reports of
26 their contemporaneous observations of crime. The reports admitted
27 here were not of this nature; they did not concern observations by the
28 Ulster Constabulary of the appellants' commission of crimes. Rather,
29 they simply related to the routine function of recording serial numbers
30 and receipt of certain weapons found in Northern Ireland. They did
31 not begin to prove the Government's entire case; they were strictly
32 routine records.

33   * * *

34   Judgments affirmed.

35

36   Hypotheticals

37

38   (1) A sues X Department Store for damages for injuries received in slipping
39 on X's floor. A claims she slipped and fell because the floor was highly waxed
40 and polished and unduly slippery as a result. X offers in evidence a report
41 prepared for X by B, the store manager. B is no longer in X's employ and could
42 not be found to testify. X's evidence establishes that B's report was prepared
43 the day after the accident, and that X's store manager customarily makes a
44 report after an accident. B's report states that B arrived at the scene a few
45 minutes after A fell and while A was still on the floor, and that B examined the
46 floor and it was not highly waxed or polished but had a dull finish and was not
47 slippery. A objects to the report as hearsay. Should the objection be sus-
     tained?

48   (2) X is prosecuted for robbery of A. X's defense is an alibi. X testifies
49 that he was in a distant city, having just registered at the B Motel at the time
50 of the robbery. X calls C, a clerk at the B Motel, who identifies a registration
51 card that shows that one X, with defendant's address, registered at the motel at

the time of the robbery of A. The registration card does not bear any signature of the guest X on it. C further testifies that motel clerks frequently fill out the registration card from information supplied by the guest and do not require a guest's signature. X offers the registration card in evidence. The prosecution makes a hearsay objection. What result?

(3) A sues X for fire damage to A's house. A had employed X, a general contractor, to remodel A's kitchen. Just before the work was completed, a fire started in the kitchen and caused the damage. A claims the fire resulted from X's negligence in leaving an open can of highly inflammable cabinet stain too close to the pilot of the water heater. X's defense is that the fire was the result of arson. After laying a proper foundation, X offers in evidence a report by B, a captain in the city fire department. B's report stated that his investigation of the fire included an inspection of the premises and conversations with A's neighbors, and that based upon this investigation, his conclusion was that the fire was of incendiary origin. A objects to the report as hearsay. Is A's objection proper?

(4) P sues D for damages for injuries suffered in an automobile accident. P does not call a doctor to testify but offers into evidence the doctor's report. Foundation is established that the doctor's report is the only record kept by him in the ordinary course of business. The report recites that the doctor examined P on a certain date, had X-rays taken, and diagnosed a fracture of the femur. In a separate paragraph of the doctor's report, a prognosis is stated that, in the doctor's opinion, P will suffer permanent residuals of a limitation of motion. D makes a hearsay objection. How should the court rule?

(5) A sues X to recover the contract price of goods sold. A and X entered into a written contract for A to sell X 1,000 metric tons of lead fume. The contract price depended on the exact weight and metallic content of the lead fume delivered by A. To prove the weight and metallic content, A testifies that she employed B, a highly respected assayer, to assay a sample of the lead fume; that she later went by B's office and received from a secretary a report on the letterhead of B, purporting to bear B's signature; that he is not, however, familiar with B's signature. A offers in evidence this report, which sets forth the weight and metallic content of a sample of the lead fume allegedly assayed by B. X makes a hearsay objection. What result?

(6) A sues X for damages for personal injuries and car property damage arising out of an automobile accident. A testifies that he went to Dr. B and C Hospital for treatment, and had his car repaired at D Garage. A offers in evidence bills or invoices, which he testifies as having been received from Dr. B, C Hospital, and D Garage. Each bill is stamped with the words "Payment Received." X makes a hearsay objection to the admissibility of the bills. How should the court rule?

(7) D is charged with robbery of V, a liquor store owner, at his store. V testifies that after the robbery he ran out of the store and obtained D's license number as D drove off. V testifies that the license number of the car was 468 ABC. D's car bore this license number. D calls PO, a police officer, who identifies a police report of the event and establishes the foundation that it was made in the usual course of business and at or near the time of the robbery. A sentence in the report states that 30 minutes after the robbery, the police received a telephone call from A, a neighbor of V, who reported the license number of the robber's car as 416 ABC. D offers the police report in evidence. In response to the prosecutor's hearsay objection, D states that the report is being offered as nonhearsay to establish that a different license number had been reported, but that, if hearsay, the report is admissible under the official-record hearsay exception. Should the prosecutor's objection be sustained?

(8) Sam D is charged with perjury because he allegedly gave false testimony in the trial of a civil action. The prosecution's contention of the false testimony is that, in the civil action, Sam D identified himself by the name of John D, while his real name was Sam D, and that in qualifying to testify as an expert he said he was a standing consultant in engineering at the U.S. Bureau of Mines. The prosecution offers in evidence a writing stating that C, the signer, was the official custodian of records for the U.S. Bureau of Mines and that C had made a diligent search of the records of the U.S. Bureau of Mines and failed to find any record that any person by the name of Sam D or John D had been an engineering consultant. The writing bears a signature, C, as custodian of records of the U.S. Bureau of Mines, and has stamped thereon a seal purporting to be the seal of the U.S. Bureau of Mines. D makes a hearsay objection to the writing. What result?

11. MISCELLANEOUS EXCEPTIONS

JUDGMENT OF PREVIOUS CONVICTION

See Federal Rules of Evidence 803(22); California Evidence Code §§ 1300–1302.

COMMENT TO CALIF.EVID.CODE § 1300

Analytically, a judgment that is offered to prove the matters determined by the judgment is hearsay evidence. It is in substance a statement of the court that determined the previous action ("a statement that was made other than by a witness while testifying at the hearing") that is offered "to prove the truth of the matter stated." Evidence Code § 1200. Therefore, unless an exception to the hearsay rule is provided, a judgment would be inadmissible if offered in a subsequent action to prove the matters determined.

Of course, a judgment may, as a matter of substantive law, conclusively establish certain facts insofar as a party is concerned. The sections of this article do not purport to deal with the doctrines of res judicata and estoppel by judgment. These sections deal only with the evidentiary use of judgments in those cases where the substantive law does not require that the judgments be given conclusive effect.

Section 1300 provides an exception to the hearsay rule for a final judgment adjudging a person guilty of a crime punishable as a felony. Hence, if a plaintiff sues to recover a reward offered by the defendant for the arrest and conviction of a person who committed a particular crime, Section 1300 permits the plaintiff to use a judgment of conviction as evidence that the person convicted committed the crime. The exception does not, however, apply in criminal actions. Thus, Section 1300 does not permit the judgment to be used in a criminal action as evidence of the identity of the person who committed the crime or as evidence that the crime was committed.

Section 1300 will change the California law. Under existing law, a conviction of a crime is inadmissible as evidence in a subsequent action. The change, however, is desirable, for the evidence involved is peculiarly reliable. The seriousness of the charge assures that the facts will be thoroughly litigated, and the fact that the judgment must be based upon a determination that there was no reasonable doubt concerning the defendant's guilt assures that the question of guilt will be thoroughly considered.

Section 1300 applies to any crime punishable as a felony. The fact that a misdemeanor sentence is imposed does not affect the admissibility of the judgment of a conviction under this section. Cf. Penal Code § 17. The exclusion of judgments based on a plea of nolo contendere from the exception in Section 1300 is a reflection of the policy expressed in Penal Code Section 1016.

COMMENT TO CALIF.EVID.CODE § 1301

If a person entitled to indemnity, or if the obligee under a warranty contract, complies with certain conditions relating to notice and defense, the indemnitor or warrantor is conclusively bound by any judgment recovered.

Where a judgment against an indemnitee or person protected by a warranty is not made conclusive on the indemnitor or warrantor, Section 1301 permits the judgment to be used as hearsay evidence in an action to recover on the indemnity or warranty. Section 1301 reflects the existing law relating to indemnity agreements. Civil Code § 2778(6). Section 1301 probably restates the law relating to warranties, too, but the law in that regard is not altogether clear.

TREATISES AND OTHER PROFESSIONAL LITERATURE

WELLMAN, THE ART OF CROSS–EXAMINATION
67–70 (1923).*

During the lifetime of Dr. J.W. Ranney there were few physicians in this country who were so frequently seen on the witness stand as he, especially in damage suits. So expert a witness had he become that Chief Justice Van Brunt many years ago told me that "Any lawyer who attempts to cross-examine Dr. Ranney is a fool." A case occurred in my practice a few years before Dr. Ranney died, however, where a failure to cross-examine would have been tantamount to a confession of judgment, and, though fully aware of the dangers, I was left no alternative, and as so often happens where "fools rush in," I made one of those lucky "bull's-eyes" that is perhaps worth recording. * * *

My first questions emphasized to the jury the fact that the witness had been the medical expert for the New York, New Haven, and Hartford R.R. thirty-five years, for the New York Central R.R. forty years, for the New York and Harlem River R.R. twenty years, for the Erie R.R. fifteen years and so on until the doctor was forced to admit that he was so much in court as a witness in defence of these various railroads, and was so occupied with their affairs that he had but comparatively little time to devote to his reading and private practice.

1   *Counsel* (perfectly quietly). "Are you able to give us, doctor, the
2   name of any medical authority that agrees with you when you say that
3   the particular group of symptoms existing in this case points to one
4   disease and one only?"

5   *Doctor.* "Oh, yes, Dr. Ericson agrees with me."

6
7   *Counsel.* "Who is Dr. Ericson, if you please?"

8   *Doctor* (with a patronizing smile). "Well, Mr. Wellman, Ericson
9   was probably one of the most famous surgeons that England has ever
10 produced." (There was a titter in the audience at the expense of
11 counsel.)

12 *Counsel.* "What book has he written?"

13 *Doctor* (still smiling). "He has written a book called 'Ericson on
14 the Spine,' which is altogether the best known work on the subject."
15 (The titter among the audience grew louder.)

16
17 *Counsel.* "When was this book published?"

18 *Doctor.* "About ten years ago."

19 *Counsel.* "Well, how is it that a man, whose time is so much
20 occupied as you have told us yours is, has leisure enough to look up
21 medical authorities to see if they agree with him?"

22 *Doctor* (fairly beaming on counsel). "Well, Mr. Wellman, to tell
23 you the truth, I have often heard of you, and I half suspected you would
24 ask me some such foolish question; so this morning after my breakfast,
25 and before starting for court, I took down from my library my copy of
26 Ericson's book, and found that he agreed entirely with my diagnosis in
27 this case." (Loud laughter at expense of counsel, in which the jury
28 joined.)
29

30 *Counsel* (reaching under the counsel table and taking up his own
31 copy of "Ericson on the Spine," and walking deliberately up to the
32 witness). "Won't you be good enough to point out to me where Ericson
33 adopts your view of this case?"

34 *Doctor* (embarrassed). "Oh, I can't do it now; it is a very thick
35 book."

36 *Counsel* (still holding out the book to the witness). "But you forget,
37 doctor, that thinking I might ask you some such foolish question, you
38 examined your volume of Ericson this very morning after breakfast and
39 before coming to court."

40 *Doctor* (becoming more embarrassed and still refusing to take the
41 book). "I have not time to do it now."
42

43 *Counsel.* *"Time!* —why, there is all the time in the world."

44 *Doctor.* (no answer).

45 Counsel and witness eye each other closely.

46
47 *Counsel* (sitting down, still eying witness). "I am sure the court
48 will allow me to suspend my examination until you shall have had time
49 to turn to the place you read this morning in that book, and can reread
50 it now aloud to the jury."

51 *Doctor.* (no answer).

The court room was in deathly silence for fully three minutes. The witness *wouldn't* say anything, counsel for plaintiff *didn't dare* to say anything, and counsel for the city *didn't want* to say anything; he saw that he had caught the witness in a manifest falsehood, and that the doctor's whole testimony was discredited with the jury unless he could open to the paragraph referred to which counsel well knew did not exist in the whole work of Ericson.

At the expiration of a few minutes, Mr. Justice Barrett, who was presiding at the trial, turned quietly to the witness and asked him if he desired to answer the question, and upon his replying that he did not intend to answer it any further than he had already done, he was excused from the witness stand amid almost breathless silence in the court room.

See Federal Rules of Evidence 803(17) & (18); California Evidence Code §§ 1340, 1341.

McCORMICK'S HANDBOOK OF THE LAW OF EVIDENCE
745–747 (2d ed. 1972).

Statements and Reputation as to Pedigree and Family History.

One of the oldest exceptions to the hearsay rule encompasses, under certain conditions, statements concerning family history, such as the date and place of births and deaths of members of the family and facts about marriage, descent, and relationship. Under the traditional rule, declarations of the person whose family situation is at issue are admissible, as are declarations by other members of the family and even, under a liberal view adopted by some courts, declarations by nonfamily members with a close relationship to the family. These statements are admissible, however, only upon a showing that the declarant is unavailable, that the statement was made before the origin of the controversy giving rise to the litigation in which the statement is offered (i.e., *ante litem motam*) and that there was no apparent motive for the declarant to misrepresent the facts. The firsthand knowledge requirement is not enforced; it is unnecessary to show that the declarant had personal knowledge of the facts of birth, death, kinship or the like. Special need for this type of evidence is found in the general difficulty of obtaining other evidence of family matters reflected in the unavailability requirement. Special assurances of reliability are found in the probability that in the absence of any motive for lying, the discussions of relatives (and others intimately related to them) as to family members will be accurate.

The traditional exception goes beyond oral declarations and permits the use of contemporary records of family history, such as entries in a family Bible or on a tombstone, even though the author may not be identifiable. Further, evidence of the traditional reputation in the family as to such facts is admissible, and some courts have extended this to the reputation in the community of matters of family history.

Both the Uniform Rules of Evidence and the Proposed Federal Rules of Evidence adopt liberal positions, abandoning the requirement

that declarations have been made *ante litem motam* and providing for
the admission of statements of a nonfamily member if the declarant
was so intimately associated with the family as to be likely to have
accurate information concerning the subject of the statement.

———

See Federal Rules of Evidence 803(11) & (12), California Evidence
Code §§ 1310–1316.

McCORMICK'S HANDBOOK OF THE LAW OF EVIDENCE
747–748 (2d ed. 1972).

Recitals in Ancient Writings and Documents Affecting an Interest in Property.

As discussed in a preceding section, a writing is usually regarded as
sufficiently authenticated if the offering party proves that it is at least
30 years old, the trial judge finds that it is unsuspicious in appearance,
and the party proves that it was produced from a place of custody
natural for such a writing. This "ancient documents" rule, however,
traditionally relates only to authentication. American courts have
nevertheless sometimes held that if a writing meets these requirements
it is admissible to prove the truth of statements made in it. Thus what
originated as an exception to general requirements of authentication
has become in some jurisdictions also an exception to the hearsay rule.

Is the exception justified? The age requirement probably assures
that there will be a special need for dispensing with the hearsay rule,
for the same reasons which give rise to the special authentication rule.
After passage of such a period of time, witnesses are unlikely to be
available or, if available, to recall reliably the events at issue. But it is
more doubtful whether there are sufficient assurances of special trustworthiness to justify admissibility. The mere age of the writing it may
be contended, offers little assurance of truth; it is unlikely that lying
was less common 30 years ago. Advocates of the exception argue,
however, that given the special need for the evidence sufficient assurances of reliability exist. First the dangers of mistransmission are
minimized since the rule applies only to written statements. Second,
the age requirement virtually assures that the assertion will have been
made long before the beginning of the present controversy. Consequently, it is unlikely that the declarant had a motive to falsify, and, in
any case, the statements are almost certainly uninfluenced by partisanship. Finally, some additional assurance of reliability is provided by
insistence, insofar as practicable, that the usual qualifications for
witnesses and out-of-court declarants be met. Thus the writing would
be inadmissible if the declarant lacked the opportunity to know firsthand the facts asserted.

Nearly all courts will apply an exception to the hearsay rule when
the matter involves ancient deed recitals. Thus deed recitals of the
contents and execution of an earlier instrument, of heirship, and of
consideration are nearly everywhere received to prove those facts. It is
arguable that, especially where possession has been taken under the

deed, these cases involve unusual assurances of reliability and the rule should be limited to them. A number of courts, however, have applied the exception to other types of documents. Both Wigmore and the Uniform Rules do not recognize any exception to the hearsay rule for ancient documents as such, but do recognize an exception for recitals in deeds without regard to the age of the deed.[1] The Uniform Rules would extend this to recitals in wills and other documents purporting to transfer land or personal property, but would require that the judge find that the matter stated would be relevant upon an issue as to an interest in the property and that dealings with the property since the statement was made have not been inconsistent with the truth of the statement. The Proposed Federal Rules of Evidence provide a similar exception for statements affecting an interest in property,[2] and also would recognize a specific exception for ancient documents with the common law age requirement reduced from 30 to 20 years.[3]

See Federal Rules of Evidence 803(15) and (16); California Evidence Code § 1331.

McNAUGHTON, EVIDENCE EXAM, HARVARD LAW SCHOOL, FIRST SEMESTER, 1960–1961

B. 50 HEARSAY QUESTIONS

Each of the following questions has two parts. (a) Is the item hearsay? Answer "Yes" or "No." And (b), if hearsay, under what exception or exceptions might the item reasonably fall? In the blank following the question, write one of the following three things: (i) "Not applicable" (or "N/A") if the item is not hearsay; (ii) "None" if the hearsay link falls under no exception; (iii) the appropriate hearsay exception(s) under which the hearsay link might reasonably fall.

SPECIAL INFORMATION: (1) Even if the facts given are insufficient to supply all of the prerequisites of an exception, you should mention the exception if the facts given reasonably suggest and are not inconsistent with it. (2) Treat past recollection recorded, the business entry statute and present sense impression—pg—as separate exceptions to the hearsay rule.

If the item is multiple, or "totem pole," hearsay, indicate in some appropriate way which exceptions (if any) apply to which hearsay link.

Hearsay?

(Yes or No) ——

___   76. Prosecution of D for killing V. On the issue of D's fear of V, W1 testifies that he heard W2 say to D, "V has knifed three people in the last year." (Exception(s)_____
_____)

---

1. 5 Wigmore, Evidence §§ 1573–1574; **3.** F.R.Ev. (R.D.1971) 803(16).
Uniform Rule 63(29).

2. F.R.Ev. (R.D.1971) 803(15).

77. Same as 76 except the issue is whether V or D was the aggressor. (Exception(s)_____)

78. On the issue whether P and D are bound by a contract, W testifies to D's statement to P, "I accept your offer." (Exception(s)_____)

79. Action P v. D for injuries sustained when P fell through termite-eaten boards on D's porch. (a) to prove that P was involved in such an accident, P offers the testimony of W: "D said that when he got home from work he heard that P had gone through the porch and that he thought it was too bad." (Exception(s) *Hearsay + admission*)

80. ―― (b) to prove that P was involved in such an accident, P offers the testimony of W that N, a neighbor who had been on the porch with P, came rushing across the lawn shouting to D, "P has fallen through your porch." (Exception(s) *Hearsay + excited utterance*)

81. ―― (c) to rebut evidence by D that he had no knowledge of P's alleged accident until 18 months after it was supposed to have occurred, P offers the testimony in 80. (Exception(s) *Not HEARSAY*)

82. ―― (d) to prove that P was involved in such an accident, P offers the transcript of D's testimony in prior litigation between him and his insurance company: "The boards on the porch were so weak that P went right through them." (Exception(s) *Hearsay + Admission Former Testimony (has to be unavailable)*)

83. Same as 79 except that W is dead and P is offering a transcript of W's testimony, to the indicated effect, given in a prior trial of the same cause. (Exception(s) *Hearsay*)

84. As tending to show that D had a revolver in his possession, the state offers the testimony of W that, as D passed W's house, W called her husband's attention to a revolver sticking out of D's pocket. (Exception(s) *Hearsay + Present Sense*)

85. On the issue whether plaintiff's decedent (V) was still alive after his car was struck by the first of two cars, W (who was in V's car with V) testifies that, before the second car struck, V said, "My head hurts." (Exception(s) *Not Hearsay*)

86. On the issue of the existence of injuries to V's head caused by the first car, the testimony in 85. (Exception(s) *Hearsay, Present physc. cond.*)

87. On the issue of the sanity of D, a woman, W testifies that D on numerous occasions said publicly, "I am the Pope."

(Exception(s)_____ 1

_____) 2

____ 88. On the issue of D's guilt of the crime of killing V, W testifies 3
that D told him that he (D) fled the scene immediately after 4
V's murder. (Exception(s) *Necessary / Admission* 5
_____) 6
7

____ 89. On the issue of X's sanity, W testifies that X was confined to 8
an insane asylum. (Exception(s) *Necessary,* 9
_____) 10

____ 90. On the issue whether a transfer of a fountain pen from 11
defendant (D) to plaintiff (P) was a sale or gift, P testifies 12
that D made a statement accompanying the transfer, "I am 13
giving you this pen as a birthday present." (Exception(s) 14
Operative facts (delivery) + words of meaning 15
16

____ 91. In 90, P testifies instead that D, the day following the 17
transfer, said, "I gave you the pen as a birthday present." 18
(Exception(s) *Necessary / admission* 19
_____) 20

____ 92. In 90, P testifies instead that D, the day before the transfer, 21
said, "I plan to give you the pen as a birthday present." 22
(Exception(s) *Necessary, Present State* 23
of Mind) 24
25

* * * 26

____ 94. On the issue of plaintiff's (P's) having cancer, N (a nurse) 27
testifies for D that E, a doctor, gave P X-Ray treatments. 28
(Exception(s)_____ 29
_____) 30

____ 95. In 94, N testifies instead that she heard E tell P that P had 31
cancer. (Exception(s)_____ 32
_____) 33
34

____ 96. In 94, instead of using N's testimony, D offers in evidence 35
the hospital record containing a notation made by E to the 36
effect that he had found a malignant tumor in P. 37
(Exception(s) *Necessary, Business record* 38
excep.) 39

____ 97. Same as 96 except that the hospital record contains a 40
notation by the hospital receptionist to the effect that P, on 41
entering the hospital, said that he had "a cancerous tumor." 42
(Exception(s) *Necessary, Admission — un CA* 43
FRE Admission isn't necessary) 44
45

____ 98. On the issue of X's good eyesight, W testifies that Y, X's 46
commanding officer, assigned X to the position of lookout on 47
the ship. (Exception(s) *Necessary* 48
_____) 49

____ 99. Action P v. D. On the issue of P's knowledge that D was in 50
the city, D offers X's testimony that Z said to P, "D is in the 51

city." (Exception(s) *Circumstantial knowledge of state of mind — not hearsay*)

___ 100. The testimony in 99 offered to prove that D was in the city. (Exception(s) *Hearsay*)

___ 101. Action P v. D. To prove that D was present in the city, D offers W's testimony that P said, "I know that D is in the city." (Exception(s) *Hearsay, Prior Inconsis. Statement / Admission*)

___ 102. On the issue of witness W1's hostility toward defendant (D), W2 testifies for D that W1 said to D in an angry tone, while D remained silent, "Well, at least I've never stolen money from my employer like you have!" (Exception(s) *Not Hearsay*)

___ 103. On the issue of D's stealing money from his employer plaintiff (P) offers the evidence in 102. (Exception(s) *Hearsay / Adoptive Admission (if no response)*)

___ 104. To prove the license number of the car involved in a hit-run accident, P offers a crumpled slip of paper on which appears the number EE2468 and the testimony of a woman that, though she cannot now recall the number of the car, she did, while the number was fresh in her mind, write the number down on the piece of paper offered in evidence. (Exception(s) *Hearsay, Prior Recorded Recollection*) *this is a sketchy element*

___ 105. To prove the license number of the car involved in a hit-run accident, P offers a photograph of a retreating automobile bearing the license plate EE2468 and the testimony of a woman that, though she cannot now remember the number of the car, she did know it at the time and that she took the photograph offered in evidence of the accident car as it left the scene. (Exception(s) *Hearsay / Prior Recorded Recollection (subject to accuracy of camera)*)

___ 108. On the issue of the speed of a locomotive, P introduces the tape printed by an automatic speed-recording device in the train. (Exception(s) *Not Hearsay*)

___ 109. On the issue of D's guilt of a crime, P offers a moving picture of D re-enacting the crime. (Exception(s) *Hearsay / Admission (Confession)*)

___ 110. On the issue of the voluntariness of D's confession, P offers the moving picture in 109. (Exception(s) *Not Hearsay*) *Not offered for voluntariness*

___ 111. On the issue of D's good faith in discharging X, an employee (W) testifies that the police chief told D that X had been caught burglarizing a store. (Exception(s) *Only for (D)'s Knowledge*)

___ 112. On the issue of D's good faith in discharging X, an employee, D testifies that W told him (D) that the police chief told W that X had been caught burglarizing a store. (Exception(s) *Goes to state of mind*)

___ 113. On the issue of D's good faith in discharging X, an employee, W testifies that the police chief told W that he (the police chief) had told D that X had been caught burglarizing a store. (Exception(s) *Hearsay*)

* * *

___ 115. Action P v. D. W1 testifies for P that D's car was going "over 50 miles an hour." To impeach W1, D offers the testimony of W2 that W1 said a day after the accident that D was going "slow." (Exception(s) *Not Hearsay*)

___ 116. The evidence in 115 offered by D to prove that he (D) was going slowly. (Exception(s) *Hearsay* *(A) if offered to impeach also for truth*)

___ 117. In 115, W2 is a police officer with no present recollection of W1's statement, so D offers the officer's (W2's) accident report, made up the day after the accident, containing the alleged W1 statement. (Exception(s) *Hearsay of Prior Inconsis Stale, Prior Rec Recorded*)

___ 118. To prove that X was ill, W testifies that X, at the time, complained of a pain in his chest. (Exception(s) *Hearsay, Present Physc. Cond.*)

___ 119. Action P v. D for $800, the price of a used automobile. Plea, payment. On the issue of payment, W testifies that he saw D hand P $800 in cash and say, "This is the payment for that car." (Exception(s) *Not Legally operative words*)

___ 120. Action P v. D for conversion of a new automobile. To prove value, P offers a receipt for the purchase price, $3000, signed by X, the dealer from whom P bought it. (Exception(s))

___ 121. Same as 120 except X is D. (Exception(s))

___ 122. Action for personal injuries by a guest in an automobile against the owner. On the issue of contributory negligence and assumption of risk, W testifies than an hour before the accident, a mechanic said to the owner in the presence of the guest, "The spindle on that front wheel may break at any moment." (Exception(s))

123. The evidence in 122 offered to show that the spindle was defective. (Exception(s)_____

_____)

124. As tending to prove title to Blackacre in defendant (D) by adverse possession under claim of title, D offers the testimony of W that plaintiff (P) said to his sister, "I've been down to the town meeting, and D is telling everyone that he owns Blackacre." (Exception(s)_____

_____)

125. Action P v. D. To prove that A was an agent of D's, P offers the testimony of W that A said, "I am an agent of D's." (Exception(s)_____

_____)

PART C.   THE FUTURE OF HEARSAY

Saturday Review

June 4, 1966, p. 341 *

"Sure, it's hearsay—but it's great hearsay!"

[C1914]

McCORMICK, LAW AND THE FUTURE: EVIDENCE
51 Nw.U.L.Rev. 218 (1956).*

* * * The group of rules about hearsay evidence may be liberalized and simplified. A distinctive and cherished ideal of our trial tradition is that evidence in the main should be limited to the statements in court of witnesses who have observed the facts and are produced for cross-examination. But the rational investigation of facts cannot always be so limited. In ordinary life we must base many of our important decisions upon letters, technical books and articles, word of mouth, account books—in short, upon hearsay. So ten to twenty (depending upon minuteness of classification) sharply defined exceptions have been hammered out. But a half-century ago the exceptions had become more or less crystallized and had ceased to grow. Already they were too numerous and too complex to be remembered reliably at the counsel table. They badly need to be consolidated and enlarged. One move in that direction is the Massachusetts hearsay statute which admits the declaration of a deceased person if the judge finds it was made in good faith upon personal knowledge. The English Evidence Act of 1938 admits a written hearsay statement, on personal knowledge, if the writer is unavailable for any reason. The Model Code would admit any hearsay statement, written or oral, based on personal knowledge, if the declarant is unavailable for any cause. Even bolder in conception are those decisions which seem to sanction the practice that when a statement does not fall within an existing exception it still may be admitted if the judge finds that there is a necessity for its use and that it was made under circumstances showing exceptional trustworthiness. These courageous judges have marked the way, and we may eventually see our hearsay canon restated in this fashion: a hearsay statement will be received if the judge finds that the need for and the probative value of the statement render it a fair means of proof under the circumstances. * * *

TURBYFILL v. INTERNATIONAL HARVESTER CO.
United States District Court, Eastern District of Michigan, 1980.
486 F.Supp. 232.

MEMORANDUM OPINION AND ORDER

JOINER, District Judge.

The facts underlying plaintiff's claim for damages are as follows. Plaintiff visited defendant's used car lot with the purpose of purchasing a truck. [He] became interested in one particular truck, but because the truck wouldn't start, defendant's mechanic Oakley Anderson attempted, with the help of plaintiff, to get the truck started. Plaintiff was pouring gasoline from a small can into the carburetor when [a] companion attempted to start the engine. The engine backfired and ignited the can held by plaintiff, and plaintiff suffered severe burns on the upper part of his body.

* * * [P]laintiff * * * asserts that it was error for the court to admit into evidence the handwritten, unsworn account of the accident made by defendant's mechanic, Oakley Anderson. As noted above, Anderson was asked to get the truck started for plaintiff and was present when plaintiff was injured. Prior to trial, but after this suit was instituted, Anderson died. Defendant sought to have admitted Anderson's handwritten account of the accident. During the trial, Gordon Brown, Anderson's supervisor, testified that, upon learning of the accident on the afternoon that it happened, he instructed Anderson to "go into a room, fill out a statement and not talk to anyone else; write down anything that he knew about it, and everything." Anderson made a handwritten report of the incident as he was instructed to do. Brown testified that the document proffered by defendant was the account written by Anderson, stating that he was familiar with Anderson's handwriting and identifying the document as written by Anderson. Brown further stated that Anderson signed the account in his presence, although Anderson wrote it while he was alone in a room. The written statement was read to the jury, but the court did not allow the jury to see copies of the statement, declining to give Anderson's account of the accident any more weight than it would have had if Anderson had been alive to testify.

Anderson's written account of the accident was admitted into evidence to prove the truth of the matter asserted therein. It thus constituted hearsay evidence under Rule 801(c) of the Federal Rules of Evidence. Plaintiff objects to the admission of the Anderson statement on the ground that it does not fall within any of the hearsay exceptions embodied in F.R.E. 803 or 804, and is thus barred by F.R.E. 802, the general evidentiary rule barring the admission of hearsay.

The circumstances under which Anderson wrote his account of the accident were such as to persuade the court that the statement should be admitted under Rule 804(b)(5):

> A statement not specifically covered by any of the foregoing exceptions but having equivalent circumstantial guarantees of trustworthiness [is not excluded by the hearsay rule] if the court determines that (A) the statement is offered as evidence of a material fact; (B) the statement is more probative on the point for which it is offered than any other evidence which the proponent can procure through reasonable efforts; and (C) the general purposes of these rules and the interests of justice will best be served by admission of the statement into evidence.

Anderson's statement was written on the afternoon of the accident while the events were still fresh in his mind. Moreover, he wrote the account while he was alone in a room, without prompting or pressure by his superiors. These factors amply demonstrate that Anderson's statement had circumstantial guarantees of trustworthiness equivalent to those underlying the hearsay exceptions of both Rule 804 and Rule 803. Moreover, the statement was offered as proof of a material fact, and was more probative on the points for which it was offered than any other evidence which defendant could reasonably have obtained. Under these circumstances, it clearly served the interests of justice to admit the statement into evidence.

Moreover, it is worthy of note that admission of the Anderson statement was consistent with the policy underlying Rule 803(5) which provides:

> A memorandum or record concerning a matter about which a witness once had knowledge but now has insufficient recollection to enable him to testify fully and accurately, shown to have been made or adopted by the witness when the matter was fresh in his memory and to reflect that knowledge correctly [is not excluded by the hearsay rule].

If Anderson had been alive and present to testify at the trial, and if he had suffered a loss of memory concerning the circumstances of the accident, his written account would have been admissible and could have been read to the jury. He wrote the statement on the afternoon of the accident, while the circumstances were still fresh in his mind. Moreover, the fact that he made his written account while alone in a room indicates that the account accurately reflects his knowledge of the events transcribed.

The above discussion demonstrates that Anderson's statement was properly admitted into evidence. Accordingly, plaintiff's motion for a new trial is denied.

UNITED STATES v. GUINAN

United States Court of Appeals, Seventh Circuit, 1988.
836 F.2d 350.

COFFEY, Circuit Judge.

Defendant–Appellant, Michael J. Guinan, appeals his conviction of six counts of filing false income tax returns, in violation of 26 U.S.C. § 7206(1), and two counts of fraudulent use of social security numbers, in violation of 42 U.S.C. § 408(g)(2). We affirm.

I. Background

On April 26, 1984, a four-count indictment was filed charging the defendant with filing false income tax returns for the tax years 1977, 1979, 1980, and 1981, in violation of 26 U.S.C. § 7206(1). On August 16, 1984, Guinan's longtime paramour and wife of seven months, Loretta Clarke Guinan ("Lori Guinan"), telephoned IRS Special Agent Patrick McDermott, told him that she and her husband had become estranged and she had filed for a divorce, and indicated that she wanted to provide evidence about Guinan's finances. During the remainder of August and early September, Lori Guinan met or spoke with Agent McDermott at least ten times. Although some of the information provided by Lori Guinan was self-incriminating, she was not promised immunity; she was told, however, that her cooperation would be considered in deciding whether she would be prosecuted. Based on his notes of his interviews and telephone conversations with Lori Guinan, McDermott prepared a written statement. Lori Guinan reviewed the statement three times. She went over the statement with Agent McDermott on September 19, 1984 for one-half hour, and again on September 20, this time for an hour. Finally, later that day, Lori reviewed the statement for about two hours with an Assistant U.S. Attorney. She was allowed to make changes in the statement and did make some minor revisions. Lori Guinan then signed the statement and read it under oath before a grand jury on September 20, 1984. In her grand jury testimony, Lori Guinan identified herself as the wife of Michael J. Guinan and stated that she was separated from and planning to divorce him. She stated that she had known Guinan since June 1976 and testified to various aspects of Guinan's expenditures and financial arrangements between that time and 1984. The next day, September 21, 1984, a superseding indictment was filed against Michael Guinan adding two counts of filing false tax returns for the tax years 1978 and 1982.

After her grand jury appearance, Lori Guinan met with Agent McDermott approximately five more times; she never recanted her testimony. During this time she retained an attorney and was promised immunity. McDermott last saw Lori Guinan on November 2, 1984. On November 6, Lori Guinan disappeared. After attempting unsuccessfully to locate her, on November 30, 1984, the U.S. Attorney's office gave notice to defendant's counsel that it intended to offer Lori Guinan's testimony at trial pursuant to Fed.R.Evid. 804(b)(5), an exception to the hearsay rule.

On December 27, 1984, the defendant failed to appear for trial, and a warrant for his arrest was issued. Guinan was apprehended in California in April 1985. In May of 1985 a second superceding indictment was filed adding two counts of perjury, in violation of 18 U.S.C. § 1623, one count of failure to appear, in violation of 18 U.S.C. § 3146(a)(1), and four counts of fraudulent use of social security numbers, in violation of 42 U.S.C. § 408(g)(2).

On June 18, 1985, the government filed a motion to admit the grand jury testimony of Lori Guinan. The defendant responded with a memorandum of law in opposition to the government's motion, and a hearing was held on June 26, 27, and 28, 1985 regarding the admissibility of Lori Guinan's testimony under Rule 804(b)(5).

The trial court, ruling orally at the conclusion of the hearing, found Lori Guinan's grand jury testimony admissible. In reaching that conclusion, the court found that:

1) notice to the defendant was adequate; 2) the government had made a satisfactory showing that the witness was unavailable; 3) the statement contained evidence of facts material to the government's proof that the defendant's income was falsely reported on his tax returns; 4) due to Lori Guinan's relationship with the defendant, her statement was more probative than any other available evidence; 5) the interests of justice warranted admission of the statement into evidence; and 6) the corroboration offered in support of the statement was "substantial", and the statement was made voluntarily and under oath. The court also found that the defendant's counsel had ample

opportunity to cross examine Agent McDermott at the hearing regarding the grand jury statement and the circumstances under which it was prepared. Although the court expressed some concern about the form of the grand jury testimony—a statement previously prepared by Agent McDermott and read verbatim—it found that that format was used in order to organize material developed over a period of time. In sum, the court concluded that the requirements of Rule 804(b)(5) were met, and the grand jury testimony was admissible under that Rule. The court did, however, excise portions of the statement that it found conclusory, irrelevant, or unduly prejudicial.

At the defendant's trial, the redacted version of Lori Guinan's grand jury testimony was read to the jury by a female Special Agent of the IRS. The jury convicted Guinan of six counts of filing false income tax returns, two counts of fraudulent use of social security numbers, and one count of failure to appear. Guinan received an aggregate sentence of sixteen years in prison.

On appeal Guinan does not challenge his conviction on the charge of failure to appear, but argues that his conviction on all of the other counts should be reversed because the admission of Lori Guinan's grand jury statement violated both the Federal Rules of Evidence and his Sixth Amendment right to confront the witnesses against him.

II. Rule 804

Guinan contends that the trial court's admission of Lori Guinan's testimony violated the Federal Rules of Evidence. In support of that contention, he argues, first, that the admissibility of grand jury testimony must be determined under Rule 804(b)(1), rather than 804(b)(5).

Rule 804(b), under the heading, "Hearsay exceptions," lists types of statements not excluded by the hearsay rule if, as in this case, the declarant is unavailable as a witness. The first four subsections of Rule 804(b) list specific categories of statements excepted from the hearsay rule, namely: 1) former testimony; 2) statements under belief of impending death; 3) statements against interest; and 4) statements of personal or family history. Rule 804(b)(5) then sets out a catch-all exception for "statement[s] not specifically covered by any of the foregoing exceptions but having equivalent circumstantial guarantees of trustworthiness," provided the other requirements of subsection (b)(5) are met. The defendant argues, essentially, that since the statements at issue here consist of grand jury testimony, they fall into the general category of "former testimony," and are "specifically covered by" exception (b)(1); therefore, he argues, their admissibility must be tested only under that subsection, rather than under the catch-all provision, (b)(5). The government responds that the defendant waived this argument by failing to raise it before the trial court. In his reply brief, defendant points out that he did raise the issue in his memorandum in support of his motion in limine to exclude Lori Guinan's testimony. There, Guinan asserted, inter alia, "It is illogical to argue that the Federal Rules (804(b)(1) [sic] provide specifically that grand jury testimony is not admissible [sic] due to lack of confrontation, and then turn to 804(b)

(5) and argue it is admissable [sic] under a general catch-all 'exception' rule." Defendant did not press the argument at the hearing six months later. Assuming that this sufficed, nonetheless, to bring the issue to the trial court's attention, this court has already decided it adversely to the defendant. In United States v. Boulahanis, 677 F.2d 586, 588 (7th Cir.) cert. denied, 459 U.S. 1016, 103 S.Ct. 375, 74 L.Ed.2d 509 (1982), we explicitly stated, "Since grand jury transcripts do not come within one of the specific hearsay exceptions in Rule 804, they are admissible if at all only under the stringent criteria of 804(b)(5), the catch-all provision." The trial court therefore properly considered the admissibility of the grand jury testimony under Rule 804(b)(5).

The defendant also contends, however, that even if Rule 804(b)(5) provides the proper test, the court erroneously concluded that Lori Guinan's grand jury testimony met its requirements. In particular, he argues that the statement does not have "circumstantial guarantees of trustworthiness" equivalent to those of statements within the specified exceptions of subsections (b)(1)–(b)(4). We disagree.

"A trial judge has considerable discretion, within the parameters of the rules of evidence, in determining whether . . . hearsay statements contain the necessary circumstantial guarantees of trustworthiness. We find no error in the trial judge's exercise of that discretion.

In *Boulahanis*, this court affirmed the trial court's admission of the grand jury testimony of an unavailable declarant under Rule 804(b)(5). We found the requirement of "equivalent circumstantial guarantees of trustworthiness" satisfied because the declarant: 1) had testified before the grand jury under oath and subject to prosecution for perjury; 2) had not been pressured to testify; 3) was disinterested—"a mere bystander, with no axe to grind"; and 4) had given testimony that was corroborated by a tape of the conversation, and by testimony of eyewitnesses. *Boulahanis*, 677 F.2d at 588. On appeal, the defendant argues that the guarantees of trustworthiness present in this case are not equivalent to those noted by the court in *Boulahanis*. He focuses on the last two factors listed: the witness' lack of a personal interest and the degree of corroboration of the testimony.

We note first that, although we rely on our previous decision in *Boulahanis*, we do not suggest that the factors listed there are all either exhaustive or necessary prerequisites to admissibility under Rule 804(b)(5). Every case must be analyzed on its own facts. See, e.g., *Howard*, 774 F.2d at 845–46 (relying on factors other than those listed in *Boulahanis*). Thus, for example, we have found hearsay statements admissible despite the fact that the unavailable declarant was not a disinterested bystander. See *Vretta*, 790 F.2d at 656–59 (declarant was the murder victim and had himself been under investigation by the District Attorney's office).

The crucial question in considering the effect of Lori Guinan's personal interests on the admissibility of her testimony under Rule 804(b)(5) is not whether she was a "mere bystander" but whether she had a motive to lie that calls the trustworthiness of her statements into question. The defendant speculates that Lori Guinan had two such motives—vindictiveness due to the failure of her marriage and a financial interest in overstating her husband's assets. We admit that this argument gives us pause. Lori Guinan volunteered to give evidence against her husband, when, after only months of marriage, the two became estranged and she filed for divorce. Certainly, it seems plausible that her motive for volunteering to testify may have been personal vindictiveness. But it does not follow that any motive for volunteering to testify other than a pristine sense of civic duty is also an incentive to manufacture *false* testimony. Moreover, the grand jury statement read to the jury at trial included Lori Guinan's statement that she had filed for divorce so that the jury could take that fact into account in weighing the credibility of her testimony, and the defendant himself testified at trial and therefore had an opportunity to testify to any discord between himself and Lori Guinan that might have discredited her testimony. Considering these facts and the absence of any additional indication that the declarant had an interest in testifying *falsely,* we do not believe that the mere fact that the declarant volunteered to testify after her marriage to the defendant deteriorated so seriously calls into question the credibility of her testimony that admission under Rule 804(b)(5) was erroneous.

Defendant does suggest, in conclusory fashion, that in this case there was an additional motive for Lori Guinan to testify falsely, claiming, "Her own pecuniary interests militate toward the exaggeration of Defendant's financial resources." It is not apparent to us, however, and the defendant does not explain, how Lori Guinan would have benefited by testifying as she did. As the government points out, her grand jury testimony was substantially limited to a period some years prior to her marriage and largely concerned the defendant's expenditures rather than his assets. Moreover, it is unclear what the value of a federal conviction for filing false tax returns for tax years prior to the parties' marriage would be in proceedings in a state divorce court. We are, therefore, unpersuaded by defendant's argument that Lori Guinan's "pecuniary interest" so seriously undermines the trustworthiness of her testimony that it is inadmissible under Rule 804(b)(5).

This brings us to defendant's main contention, namely, that Lori Guinan's testimony was insufficiently corroborated. * * *

In this case there is substantial other evidence linking the defendant to the expenditures that Lori Guinan testified he had made. Independent evidence was introduced at the June 26–28 hearing that corroborated Lori Guinan's testimony that the defendant supported her and gave her an allowance and grocery money, that they traveled extensively, and that the defendant, through various financial arrangements, purchased two condominiums during the relevant period. Moreover, independent evidence was introduced regarding the defendant's intent in filing false tax returns.

Lori Guinan's testimony that the defendant supported her and gave her an allowance and grocery money was corroborated by the fact that she never filed an individual income tax return, that there was no substantial activity in her personal bank account, that she stated to her parents and in a loan application that the defendant was her sole source of support, that checks payable to Lori were drawn on bank accounts associated with Guinan, that checks payable to Treasure Island Stores, (where Lori testified she did most of her grocery shopping) were drawn on the defendant's account, by the statements of a secretary-receptionist in the defendant's office to the effect that Lori came to the office to get cash from Guinan, and by the statement of the defendant's law clerk that Lori had complained to him that she was not receiving a sufficient allowance.   Lori Guinan's testimony regarding the couple's extensive travels was corroborated by the logbook for one of the defendant's boats, by the defendant's own sworn statement in a divorce proceeding, by entries on a calendar kept by the defendant's ex-wife, by telephone records of the defendant's office showing collect calls from the Caribbean, by credit card records, and by the statements of the defendant's receptionists, secretaries, law clerk, and friends.

* * *

[The court noted that Lori Guinan had also testified that defendant purchased two condominiums. It described in detail corroborating evidence that the defendant, using fictitious names and straw owners, had in fact purchased the condominiums.]

Finally, Lori Guinan's testimony regarding the defendant's intent was corroborated by the statement of one of the defendant's former secretaries to the effect that Guinan had remarked to her that he would "beat the IRS," and by the statement of another former secretary that she had helped Guinan destroy various records that might disclose receipts to the IRS.

Despite all of this, Guinan argues that the crucial aspect of Lori Guinan's testimony—the *amount* of money she testified he had expended on the various items—is not corroborated. At least in this case, where there is nothing facially suspicious about the amounts the witness testified to, and indeed many of them seem fairly conservative, we do not believe that Rule 804(b)(5) requires that degree of corroboration.   At oral argument, defendant's counsel admitted that a court cannot require that every detail of an item of hearsay testimony be corroborated before admitting it under Rule 804(b)(5); the proponent of the evidence will always be relying on "a little more" than is independently corroborated. The question, according to counsel, is "how much more?" We need not, and indeed cannot, provide a general answer to that question. We can and do, however, hold that the additional information contained in Lori Guinan's testimony that was not independently corroborated—i.e., the exact dollar amounts—in the context of this case, did not go so far beyond that which was corroborated that the trial court's decision that the testimony was sufficiently trustworthy to meet the requirements of Rule 804(b)(5) was erroneous.

III. *Confrontation Clause*

The defendant finally contends that the admission of Lori Guinan's grand jury testimony into evidence violated the Confrontation Clause of the Sixth Amendment to the United States Constitution, which pro-

vides that in criminal prosecutions "the accused shall enjoy the right
. . . to be confronted with the witnesses against him. . . ." Our
determination that the grand jury testimony was admissible under
Rule 804(b)(5) does not immediately dispose of the constitutional issue.
For, while "the hearsay rules and the Confrontation Clause . . . 'stem
from the same root,' . . . the two are not equivalent." *Vretta,* 790
F.2d at 660 (quoting Dutton v. Evans, 400 U.S. 74, 86, 91 S.Ct. 210, 218,
27 L.Ed.2d 213 (1970)); see also, United States v. Keplinger, 776 F.2d
678, 695 (7th Cir.1985), cert. denied, 476 U.S. 1183, 106 S.Ct. 2919, 91
L.Ed.2d 548 (1986). Thus, evidence that is admissible under a hearsay
exception may still be violative of the Sixth Amendment. On the other
hand, although any use of hearsay testimony literally denies the
defendant an opportunity to confront a witness against him if the
hearsay declarant is unavailable to be cross-examined, this court "has
been unwilling to hold that the admission of hearsay evidence is a per
se violation of the confrontation clause." *Boulahanis,* 677 F.2d at 589.
Instead, in a case such as this, where the witness is unavailable, the
court enquires whether the hearsay bears "sufficient 'indicia of reliability.'" *Keplinger,* 776 F.2d at 695 (quoting Ohio v. Roberts, 448 U.S. 56,
65–66, 100 S.Ct. 2531, 2538–39, 65 L.Ed.2d 597 (1986)).

On appeal, the defendant stresses the importance of cross-examination in testing the reliability of testimony. While we hardly disagree, it
is also clear that the constitutional "test [is] 'not whether there was an
opportunity for . . . cross-examination, but whether there are adequate indicia of reliability to justify the placement of the hearsay
statement before the jury.'" Thus, even absent an opportunity for
cross-examination, where the government has "made a strong 'showing
of particularized guarantees of trustworthiness' concerning the statements," their admission is not barred by the Confrontation Clause.
Howard, 774 F.2d at 846 (quoting Ohio v. Roberts, 448 U.S. at 66, 100
S.Ct. at 2539), quoted in *Vretta,* 790 F.2d at 660. "Under this Court's
test derived from *Roberts,* statements are [constitutionally] admissible
even where there was no cross-examination if it is clear (1) that the
declarant actually made the statement in question; and (2) there is
circumstantial evidence supporting its veracity." *Feldman,* 761 F.2d at
387. Here, the challenged evidence consists of transcripts of grand jury
testimony read at trial; the accuracy of the transcripts is not challenged. The first requirement is therefore met. The second requirement is satisfied as well. Given our previous discussion of the guarantees of trustworthiness present in this case—in particular, the fact that
the testimony was given voluntarily under oath and was substantially
corroborated by other independent evidence, see *Boulahanis,* 677 F.2d
at 589—we conclude that the admission of Lori Guinan's grand jury
testimony did not violate the Sixth Amendment.

IV. Conclusion

We are satisfied that there are present in this case sufficient
indicia of trustworthiness to meet the requirements of both Rule 804(b)

(5) and the Sixth Amendment. The defendant's convictions are therefore

AFFIRMED.

EMERGING PROBLEMS UNDER THE FEDERAL RULES OF EVIDENCE *

Rules 803(24) and 804(b)(5). Other exceptions. One of the most controversial aspects of Rules 803 and 804 as proposed by the Advisory Committee was the inclusion of the residual exceptions providing simply for the receipt of statements "not specifically covered by any of the foregoing exceptions but having equivalent circumstantial guarantees of trustworthiness."

The House deleted the proposed exceptions entirely but the Senate, while rejecting the Advisory Committee versions as overly broad, added several prerequisites to admissibility and passed both 803(24) and 804(b)(5). The Joint Conferees added a pre-trial notice requirement, otherwise adopting the Senate version of both rules.

Congress clearly intended that the residual exceptions be used cautiously.[216] In fact, however, they have been the focal point of considerable judicial activism, a trend which has been met with varying degrees of enthusiasm. While the trend is not universal, the cases reflect a widespread willingness to admit hearsay deemed reliable and necessary, but the standards applied in determining reliability and need vary. Clarification of the parameters of admissibility, as discussed below, would be desirable.

A major concern of some members of Congress was that certain types of hearsay deliberately excluded from the specific class exceptions might nevertheless be admitted under Rules 803(24) or 804(b)(5), thus frustrating Congress's intention to prevent the admission of such material. In Zenith Radio Corp. v. Matsushita Electric Industrial Co., 505 F.Supp. 1190 (E.D.Pa.1980), the court discussed this issue, which it described as the "near miss" question—that is, the question whether evidence which is generically of a type covered by a specific exception but which fails to meet the precise requirements of that exception is nonetheless admissible under the residual exception. Analyzing the legislative history, the court found that Congress had intended the residual exceptions to be used in "exceptional and unanticipated" situations, not where a specific exception sets forth conditions governing the admissibility of a clearly defined category of hearsay.

---

* Section of Litigation: American Bar Association © 1983.

216. It is intended that the residual hearsay exceptions will be used very rarely, and only in exceptional circumstances. The committee does not intend to establish a broad license for trial judges to admit hearsay statements that do not fall within one of the other exceptions contained in Rules 803 and 804(b). The residual exceptions are not meant to authorize major judicial revisions of the hearsay rule, including its present exceptions. Such major revisions are best accomplished by legislative action. It is intended that in any case in which evidence is sought to be admitted under these subsections, the trial judge will exercise no less care, reflection and caution than the courts did under the common law in establishing the now-recognized exceptions to the hearsay rule.

However, the *Zenith* Court distinguished those exceptions dealing with well-defined categories, such as Rules 803(18) (learned treatises), 803(22) (judgment of previous convictions) and 804(b)(1) (former testimony, declarant unavailable), and those exceptions dealing with "amorphous" categories, such as Rules 803(1) (present sense impression), 803(5) (recorded recollection) and 803(6) (business records). The *Zenith* Court reasoned that to apply the "near miss" doctrine to these latter categories would, in effect, negate the residual exceptions altogether.[219]

The introductory clause of Rule 803 appears to dispense with the availability of the declarant as a factor in the admissibility of out-of-court statements. However, application of the residual exception of Rule 803(24) seems to require some consideration of availability because Rule 803(24) requires that the proffered statement be "more probative" on the point for which it's offered than any other evidence reasonably obtainable. Thus, in deMars v. Equitable Life Assurance Society, 610 F.2d 55 (1st Cir.1979), the First Circuit reversed the district court's ruling admitting the written report of an unavailable medical expert on the grounds that the proponent could have procured the opinion of another expert witness. Similarly in United States v. Fredericks, 599 F.2d 262 (8th Cir.1979), a defendant's offer of hearsay statements of an unavailable witness was rejected not only because the declarant had a possible motive to make a statement exculpating the defendant, but because there was better evidence available—i.e., the testimony of other eyewitnesses.

In *Zenith,* supra, the court observed:

> In view of the rigor with which the requirements of the residual exceptions should be construed, we agree with these courts that the proponent of hearsay evidence under the residual exception must attempt to procure the testimony by deposition not only of the declarant, but also of any other witness with knowledge of the subject matter of the statement, unless such testimony plainly cannot be procured by reasonable means.

505 F.Supp. at 1190.

Similarly, in United States v. Mathis, 559 F.2d 294 (5th Cir.1977), the Fifth Circuit reversed a trial court determination that Rule 803(24) permitted the admission of out-of-court statements where there were strong reasons for not compelling the declarant, who was technically "available," to testify against the defendant.[220] The *Mathis* Court ruled

---

219. See also United States v. Oates, 560 F.2d 45 (2d Cir.1977), discussed in conjunction with Rule 803(8), supra, in which the Second Circuit ruled that police and evaluative reports not admissible under Rule 803(8)(B) or (C) could not, in light of Congress' intent, be admitted under any other hearsay exception.

220. The declarant in *Mathis* had been married to the defendant at the time that certain crimes had been committed and made incriminating statements regarding her husband to Government investigators after she had obtained a divorce. The declarant repeated her incriminating statements before a grand jury.

However, before the trial, the declarant was coerced into a remarriage with her former husband. At the trial, the declarant indicated that she did not wish to testify against him, claiming the marital (spousal immunity) privilege. The government argued that the marital privilege was unavailable on the grounds that the second

that, while the statements were trustworthy and highly material, they were not admissible under either Rule 804(b)(5)—because the declarant was not "unavailable"—or under Rule 803(24)—because the statements were not "more probative" than the live testimony of the declarant, which was reasonably obtainable given her presence in the courtroom throughout the trial and her willingness to testify if compelled to do so.

In contrast, other courts, in interpreting Rule 803(24) have determined that the availability of the declarant is a factor to be weighed in favor of admissibility because it affords the adverse party the opportunity to cross-examine. Generally, in these cases hearsay statements were offered either to rebut or corroborate in-court testimony rather than to substitute for it. However, even assuming the reliability of such material, the use of prior statements as corroborative or rebuttal evidence raises certain questions with respect to probativeness and necessity.

For example, in United States v. Boulahanis, 677 F.2d 586 (7th Cir. 1982), cert. denied 459 U.S. 1016, 103 S.Ct. 375, 74 L.Ed.2d 509, the court, in discussing the reliability of prior statements offered under Rule 804(b)(5), noted that the statements were corroborated on virtually every point by tapes and by other eyewitnesses. However, while affirming the admission of the statements, the Seventh Circuit noted that the extent of corroboration "undermined" the argument that they were the most probative evidence possible.

Prior consistent statements are usually admissible only to rebut charges of recent fabrication. Rule 801(d)(1)(B). However, the Second Circuit has allowed the admission of a witness' two prior consistent statements for substantive purposes under Rule 803(24). In United States v. Iaconetti, 540 F.2d 574 (2d Cir.1976), cert. denied 429 U.S. 1041, 97 S.Ct. 739, 50 L.Ed.2d 752 (1977), a witness testified that the defendant had solicited a bribe and repeated the defendant's words— demands to the witness' business partners. The defendant took the stand, denied the witness' accusation and claimed that the witness had offered the bribe. In rebuttal, the prosecution offered the testimony of the witness' partners, who repeated the witness' conversations with them concerning the defendant's demands. The Second Circuit affirmed the admission of the two prior statements under Rule 803(24), upholding the trial court's determination that the statements were the most reliable method of corroborating the witness' testimony with respect to the conversation with the defendant. The Court reasoned that the prior statements were reliable because they were made closer in time to the actual event and were subject to cross-examination. However, that is true of virtually all prior consistent statements. Although Congress decided against admitting prior consistent statements for substantive purposes even when the declarant is available at

marriage was a fraud. While declarant stated that she "would tell the truth" if forced to testify and reaffirmed the veracity of her prior statements the trial judge, fearing her safety, declined to compel her testimony and instead allowed admission of her prior statements to the government investigators as substantive evidence, despite a simultaneous finding that the remarriage had been a fraud, thus rendering the marital privilege inapplicable.

trial for cross-examination, *Iaconetti* contemplates opening the door to most such statements whenever the in-court testimony of the declarant is challenged or disputed, regardless of whether recent fabrication is alleged.

Similarly, in United States v. Muscato, 534 F.Supp. 969 (E.D.N.Y. 1982), a prior consistent statement by a co-conspirator was admitted as substantive evidence linking another defendant to the conspiracy. The declarant, whose history of mental instability cast doubt on his credibility as a witness, had described receiving a unique pen gun from the co-defendant. His out-of-court description of the gun to a government agent, made before he was shown a gun taken from the co-defendant, was offered to corroborate his in-court testimony identifying the co-defendant as a conspirator.

Chief Judge Weinstein offered several theories of admissibility, including admissibility under Rule 803(24). He noted both the reliability and the probativeness of the statements, although he admitted that their effect was "cumulative" with respect to other evidence. Nevertheless, he declined to interpret the "more probative" requirement narrowly.

The trend to admit prior consistent statements was rejected in United States v. Gomez, 529 F.2d 412 (5th Cir.1976). Informants' out-of-court statements describing the time and place of a marijuana pick-up, as well as the pick-up car, were held admissible to explain why government agents had been at the scene. However, out-of-court statements by the same informants that the owner of the pick-up car owned the marijuana were ruled inadmissible when proffered as substantive evidence against the car owner. The Fifth Circuit observed that the information, while probative, was possibly prejudicial, and "not necessary" to the prosecution's case.

A non-party witness's prior inconsistent statements, made out of court, are admissible only for impeachment purposes unless given under oath at a formal hearing or proceeding. Rule 801(d)(1)(A). Nevertheless, courts have admitted such statements for substantive purposes where they have found them to be particularly trustworthy. Moreover, such statements have also been admitted for substantive purposes even where there has been reason to question the motivation for the prior statements.

For example, in United States v. Leslie, 542 F.2d 285 (5th Cir.1976), the appellant challenged the admission of prior incriminating statements made by his alleged accomplices at the time of their arrest. The statements were offered to impeach the accomplices after they gave testimony at trial exculpating the appellant. The Fifth Circuit decided that the prior statements were substantively admissible against the appellant. Despite the declarants' explanation that their prior statements had been uttered under the influence of drugs and that they had been attempting to curry favor with the government, the court nevertheless found sufficient indicia of trustworthiness—including transcripts of the statements, contemporaneously signed waivers, proximity in time to the events, and the opportunity for cross-examination—to justify admission of the statements. In discounting the declarants' claims, the *Leslie* Court assumed that (a) the existence of an attempt to secure favorable treatment from the police is dependent on the likelihood of the declarants' success and (b) statements made closer in time to the events described are less likely to be tainted by an ulterior motive.

The *Leslie* Court's downplaying of the possibility of an ill-motivated incrimination stands in marked contrast to the concern of other courts about admitting incriminating statements offered under the "statement against penal interest" exception of Rule 804(b)(3). In a number of these cases, courts have found inculpatory statements against penal interest to be untrustworthy, especially if made while the declarant was in police custody, unless accompanied by other "indicia of reliability." [221] However, it should be noted that in these cases, unlike *Leslie*, no opportunity for cross-examination existed.

Grand jury testimony, unlike testimony at a prior trial or hearing, is not subject to cross-examination. Although made under oath, grand jury testimony under Rule 804(b)(5) lacks many of the indicia of reliability generally required under Rule 804. [222] In addition, the use of hearsay without the opportunity for cross-examination may raise Confrontation Clause problems.

In United States v. Gonzalez, 559 F.2d 1271 (5th Cir.1977), a drug conviction was overturned on the ground that grand jury testimony had been improperly admitted under Rule 804(b)(5). Among the factors noted by the Fifth Circuit indicating a lack of reliability were the pressure put on the declarant (who refused to testify at trial) by the prosecutor, the fact that leading questions had been asked, the prosecutor's threats to call the witness repeatedly before grand juries and to seek contempt citations for failure to testify, threats of physical harm, and the absence of cross-examination.

Grand jury testimony was admitted, however, in United States v. Carlson, 547 F.2d 1346 (8th Cir.1976), cert. denied 431 U.S. 914, 97 S.Ct. 2174, 53 L.Ed.2d 224 (1977), where the declarant, who had refused to testify at trial because of threats made against him, had not been subjected to the same sort of prosecutorial pressure. Moreover, in *Carlson*, unlike *Gonzalez*, the only threats against the declarant could be traced directly to the defendant. The court ruled that under the circumstances, the defendant had waived his right to object on Confrontation Clause grounds to the absence of cross-examination. [223]

---

221. See the discussion of Rule 804(b)(3), pp. 67–74, infra.

222. In United States v. West, 574 F.2d 1131 (4th Cir.1978), the grand jury testimony of the declarant, who was murdered prior to trial, was deemed highly reliable because of careful government surveillance of his activities (including photographs of contracts with the defendants, and taped conversations).

223. Similarly, in United States v. Thevis, 665 F.2d 616 (5th Cir.1982), the court found that where there was clear and convincing evidence that the defendant was responsible for the death of a witness, both Confrontation Clause objections and hearsay objections were waived. Accord: United States v. Mastrangelo, 533 F.Supp. 389 (E.D.N.Y.1982) See also United States v. West, supra note 28, p. 55 (waiver theory not employed).

United States v. Garner, 574 F.2d 1141 (4th Cir.1978), cert. denied 439 U.S. 936, 99 S.Ct. 333, 58 L.Ed.2d 333, presents somewhat unusual facts. The declarant, who had agreed to testify for the government pursuant to a plea bargaining agreement, voluntarily appeared before the grand jury but reneged at the time of trial. Ultimately, he agreed to answer questions from defense counsel before the jury, disavowing his grand jury statements, evading certain questions, and disclaiming knowledge of the defendants' criminal activities. Despite his appearance before the jury, the declarant was ruled unavailable within the meaning of Rule 804, and his prior statements before the grand jury were admitted as substantive evidence by the trial court.[224] On appeal, the Fourth Circuit found the proffered hearsay reliable, on the basis of several species of corroboration.[225]

These diverse decisions strongly suggest the need for greater uniformity in the application of the residual exceptions. It is by no means clear, however, that uniformity would be promoted by changes in the rule itself. The rule places several burdens on party wishing to utilize it, and the legislative history indicates that Congress was not opening the door to all hearsay that a federal judge might consider suitable for a jury. There is some reason to believe that certain appellate decisions have too quickly stretched the rules to protect trial court rulings that would have been difficult to justify under specific hearsay exceptions.

The danger inherent in such stretching is that the limits set forth in the residual rules may tend to lose significance. It seems that greater attention to the details of the residual exceptions and to articulation of reasons why the exceptions are satisfied in particular cases would promote decision-making by trial courts. At some point the Supreme Court may find it desirable to indicate the scope of the residual exception in cases raising issues that appear to arise with some frequency—e.g., the admissibility of grand jury testimony of a witness not present and subject to cross-examination at trial.

The residual exceptions contain a notice requirement which was added by Congress to ensure fairness by allowing parties sufficient time before trial to prepare objections to the use of such hearsay statements.[226] A number of courts have read the notice requirement strictly, requiring formal pre-trial notice. In United States v. Oates, 560 F.2d 45 (2d Cir.1977), and United States v. Ruffin, 575 F.2d 346 (2d Cir. 1978), detailed examinations of the legislative history led the Second Circuit to conclude that there was "absolutely no doubt that the

224. But see United States v. Mathis, 559 F.2d 294 (5th Cir.1977), supra (declarant's presence in courtroom held to preclude application of Rule 804(b)(5)).

225. The Fourth Circuit found that the trial testimony supplied "substantial assistance" to the jury in assessing the reliability of the grand jury testimony, a curious reversal of the usual role of prior statements offered under Rule 803(24) to corroborate or rebut trial testimony. Interestingly, the *Garner* Court noted that, absent strong indicia of reliability of the grand

jury testimony (which were present in that case), the defense questioning of the declarant at trial would not have constituted adequate cross-examination to overcome the Confrontation Clause hurdle.

226. House Rep. No. 1597, 93rd Cong., 2d Sess. 11–12, 13 (1974). A proposal that notice *during* trial should suffice with respect to material submitted under the residual exceptions was rejected by the Joint Conference as inadequate to protect the rights of adverse parties. 120 Cong. Rec.H. 12256 (Dec. 18, 1974).

requirement of advance notice [should] be rigidly enforced." However, both that court and others have read the notice requirement less strictly. In United States v. Muscato, 534 F.Supp. 969 (E.D.N.Y.1982), supra, Chief Judge Weinstein ruled that, where the objecting party had himself called the witness from whom the hearsay was adduced, had not taken the stand himself, and had not objected to the admission of the hearsay at trial on notice grounds, the objector had effectively waived any right to claim lack of notice. In United States v. Iaconetti, supra, the Second Circuit, while noting the legislative history and the general need to comply with the notice requirement, upheld Judge Weinstein's trial court ruling that hearsay material be admitted under the residual exception, despite the lack of notice, where the need for offering the material had not arisen until trial had commenced, the adverse party had received five days notice and the adverse party had not requested a continuance or otherwise indicated an inability to prepare for the testimony.

Similarly, in United States v. Leslie, 542 F.2d 285 (5th Cir.1976), supra, the Fifth Circuit deemed failure to comply with the notice requirements of Rule 803(24) harmless error, finding that the defendant had had "ample opportunity" to attack the trustworthiness of the material since he could not have failed to anticipate that the witnesses in question (his alleged accomplices) would be called. Although such anticipation may not necessarily include anticipation that specific hearsay may be offered under the residual exception, nevertheless several courts have interpreted the notice requirement flexibly where they found that the adverse party had not, or should not have been, surprised by the offer.[227]

It may be that all of the decisions rendered no injustice. Yet, there is a danger that these decisions will effectively write the notice requirement out of the rule. In future cases, it may be wise for trial judges to ascertain first why the rule-required notice was not given. If the party who failed to give notice sought the advantage of surprise, any claim of unfairness ought not be rejected out of hand. If, however, notice was not given because a party reasonably was unaware of the need to rely on a hearsay statement, the most timely notice under the circumstances is all that reasonably should be demanded. In close cases, however, the extent to which notice could not realistically have been given in advance may weigh heavily with a judge trying to decide whether tardy notice is sufficient to satisfy the rule and, in some criminal cases, the Confrontation Clause.

In adopting their versions of the Rules, seven states—Colorado, Florida, Maine, Michigan, Nevada, Ohio and Washington—decided against including either of the residual exceptions, Rule 803(24) or Rule 804(b)(5). Delaware adopted Rule 803(24) but not Rule 804(b)(5) on the theory that the latter provision merely duplicated the former.

227. See, e.g., Furtado v. Bishop, 604 F.2d 80 (1st Cir.1979), cert. denied 444 U.S. 1035, 100 S.Ct. 710, 62 L.Ed.2d 672 (1980); Piva v. Xerox Corp., 654 F.2d 591 (9th Cir. 1981).

CIVIL EVIDENCE ACT, ENGLAND, 1968.

2.—(1) In any civil proceedings a statement made, whether orally or in a document or otherwise, by any person whether called as a witness in those proceedings or not, shall, subject to this section and to rules of court, be admissible as evidence of any fact stated therein of which direct oral evidence by him would be admissible.

(2) Where in any civil proceedings a party desiring to give a statement in evidence by virtue of this section has called or intends to call as a witness in the proceedings the person by whom the statement was made, the statement—

    (a) shall not be given in evidence by virtue of this section on behalf of that party without the leave of the court; and

    (b) without prejudice to paragraph (a) above, shall not be given in evidence by virtue of this section on behalf of that party before the conclusion of the examination-in-chief of the person by whom it was made, except—

        (i) where before that person is called the court allows evidence of the making of the statement to be given on behalf of that party by some other person; or

        (ii) in so far as the court allows the person by whom the statement was made to narrate it in the course of his examination-in-chief on the ground that to prevent him from doing so would adversely affect the intelligibility of his evidence.

(3) Where in any civil proceedings a statement which was made otherwise than in a document is admissible by virtue of this section, no evidence other than direct oral evidence by the person who made the statement or any person who heard or otherwise perceived it being made shall be admissible for the purpose of proving it:

Provided that if the statement in question was made by a person while giving oral evidence in some other legal proceedings (whether civil or criminal), it may be proved in any manner authorized by the court.

OHIO v. ROBERTS

Supreme Court of the United States, 1980.
448 U.S. 56, 100 S.Ct. 2531, 65 L.Ed.2d 597.

Mr. Justice BLACKMUN delivered the opinion of the Court.

This case presents issues concerning the constitutional propriety of the introduction in evidence of the preliminary hearing testimony of a witness not produced at the defendant's subsequent state criminal trial.

I

Herschel Roberts * * * was charged with forgery of a check in the name of Bernard Isaacs, and with possession of stolen credit cards belonging to Isaacs and his wife Amy.

A preliminary hearing was held. Respondent's appointed counsel had seen the Isaacs' daughter, Anita, in the courthouse hallway, and called her as the defense's only witness. Defense counsel questioned Anita at some length and attempted to elicit from her an admission that she had given respondent checks and the credit cards without informing him that she did not have permission to use them. Anita, however, denied this. The prosecutor did not question Anita.

A county grand jury subsequently indicted respondent for forgery [and] for receiving stolen property.

Between November 1975 and March 1976, five subpoenas for four different trial dates were issued to Anita at her parents' Ohio residence. [S]he did not appear at trial.

[At trial] respondent took the stand and testified that Anita Isaacs had given him her parents' checkbook and credit cards with the understanding that he could use them. Relying on Ohio Rev. Code Ann. § 2945.49 (1975) which permits the use of preliminary examination testimony of a witness who "cannot for any reason be produced at the trial," the State, on rebuttal, offered the transcript of Anita's testimony.

Asserting a violation of the Confrontation Clause * * * the defense objected to the use of the transcript. The trial court conducted a *voir dire* hearing as to its admissibility. Amy Isaacs, the sole witness at *voir dire,* was questioned by both the prosecutor and defense counsel concerning her daughter's whereabouts. Anita, according to her mother, left home for Tucson, Ariz., soon after the preliminary hearing. When Anita called, some seven or eight months before trial, she told her parents that she "was traveling" outside Ohio, but did not reveal the place from which she called. Mrs. Isaacs stated that she knew of no way to reach Anita in case of an emergency. Nor did she "know of anybody who knows where she is." The trial court admitted the transcript into evidence. Respondent was convicted on all counts.

* * *

[The Supreme Court of Ohio] held that the transcript was inadmissible. Reasoning that normally there is little incentive to cross-examine a witness at a preliminary hearing, where the "ultimate issue" is only probable cause, and citing the dissenting opinion in California v. Green, 399 U.S. 149 (1970), the court held that the mere opportunity to cross-examine at a preliminary hearing did not afford constitutional confrontation for purposes of trial. The court distinguished *Green*, where this Court had ruled admissible the preliminary hearing testimony of a declarant who was present at trial, but claimed forgetfulness. The Ohio court perceived a "dictum" in *Green* that suggested that the mere opportunity to cross-examine renders preliminary hearing testimony admissible. But the court concluded that *Green* "goes no further than to suggest that cross-examination actually conducted at preliminary hearing *may* afford adequate confrontation for purposes of a later trial." Since Anita had not been cross-examined at the preliminary hearing and was absent at trial, the introduction of the transcript of her testimony was held to have violated respondent's confrontation right.

II

The Court here is called upon to consider once again the relationship between the Confrontation Clause and the hearsay rule with its many exceptions. The basic rule against hearsay, of course, is riddled with exceptions developed over three centuries. These exceptions vary among jurisdictions as to number, nature, and detail. But every set of exceptions seems to fit an apt description offered more than 40 years ago: "an old-fashioned crazy quilt made of patches cut from a group of paintings by cubists, futurists and surrealists."

The Sixth Amendment's Confrontation Clause, made applicable to the States through the Fourteenth Amendment, provides: "In all criminal prosecutions, the accused shall enjoy the right * * * to be confronted with the witnesses against him." If one were to read this language literally, it would require, on objection, the exclusion of any statement made by a declarant not present at trial. But, if thus applied, the Clause would abrogate virtually every hearsay exception, a result long rejected as unintended and too extreme.

The historical evidence leaves little doubt, however, that the Clause was intended to exclude some hearsay.

* * *

The Confrontation Clause operates in two separate ways to restrict the range of admissible hearsay. First, in conformance with the Framers' preference for face-to-face accusation, the Sixth Amendment establishes a rule of necessity. In the usual case (including cases where prior cross-examination has occurred), the prosecution must either produce, or demonstrate the unavailability of, the declarant whose statement it wishes to use against the defendant.

The second aspect operates once a witness is shown to be unavailable. Reflecting its underlying purpose to augment accuracy in the factfinding process by ensuring the defendant an effective means to test adverse evidence, the Clause countenances only hearsay marked with such trustworthiness that "there is no material departure from the reason of the general rule." The principle recently was formulated in Mancusi v. Stubbs:

> "The focus of the court's concern has been to insure that there 'are indicia of reliability which have been widely viewed as determinative of whether a statement may be placed before the jury though there is no confrontation of the declarant,' and to 'afford the trier of fact a satisfactory basis for evaluating the truth of the prior statement,'. It is clear from these statements, and from numerous prior decisions of this Court, that even though the witness be unavailable his prior testimony must bear some of these 'indicia of reliability.' "

The Court has applied this "indicia of reliability" requirement principally by concluding that certain hearsay exceptions rest upon such solid foundations that admission of virtually any evidence within them comports with the "substance of the constitutional protection." This reflects the truism that "hearsay rules and the Confrontation

Clause are generally designed to protect similar values," California v. Green, and "stem from the same roots." It also responds to the need for certainty in the workaday world of conducting criminal trials.

In sum, when a hearsay declarant is not present for cross-examination at trial, the Confrontation Clause normally requires a showing that he is unavailable. Even then, his statement is admissible only if it bears adequate "indicia of reliability." Reliability can be inferred without more in a case where the evidence falls within a firmly rooted hearsay exception. In other cases, the evidence must be excluded, at least absent a showing of particularized guarantees of trustworthiness.

III

We turn first to that aspect of confrontation analysis deemed dispositive by the Supreme Court of Ohio, and answered by it in the negative—whether Anita Isaacs' prior testimony at the preliminary hearing bore sufficient "indicia of reliability." Resolution of this issue requires a careful comparison of this case to California v. Green.

A

In *Green*, at the preliminary hearing, a youth named Porter identified Green as a drug supplier. When called to the stand at Green's trial, however, Porter professed a lapse of memory. Frustrated in its attempt to adduce live testimony, the prosecution offered Porter's prior statements. The trial judge ruled the evidence admissible, and substantial portions of the preliminary hearing transcript were read to the jury. This Court found no error. Citing the established rule that prior trial testimony is admissible upon retrial if the declarant becomes unavailable, the Court rejected Green's Confrontation Clause attack. It reasoned:

> "Porter's statement at the preliminary hearing had already been given under circumstances closely approximating those that surround the typical trial. Porter was under oath; respondent was represented by counsel—the same counsel in fact who later represented him at the trial; respondent had every opportunity to cross-examine Porter as to his statement; and the proceedings were conducted before a judicial tribunal, equipped to provide a judicial record of the hearings."

These factors, the Court concluded, provided all that the Sixth Amendment demands: "substantial compliance with the purposes behind the confrontation requirement."

This passage and others in the *Green* opinion suggest that the *opportunity* to cross-examine at the preliminary hearing—even absent actual cross-examination—satisfies the Confrontation Clause. Yet the record showed, and the Court recognized, that defense counsel in fact had cross-examined Porter at the earlier proceeding.

We need not decide whether the Supreme Court of Ohio correctly dismissed statements in *Green* suggesting that the mere opportunity to cross-examine rendered the prior testimony admissible. Nor need we decide whether *de minimis* questioning is sufficient, for defense counsel in this case tested Anita's testimony with the equivalent of significant cross-examination.

B

Counsel's questioning clearly partook of cross-examination as a matter of *form*. His presentation was replete with leading questions, the principal tool and hallmark of cross-examination. In addition, counsel's questioning comported with the principal *purpose* of cross-examination: to challenge "whether the declarant was sincerely telling what he believed to be the truth, whether the declarant accurately perceived and remembered the matter he related, and whether the declarant's intended meaning is adequately conveyed by the language he employed." Anita's unwillingness to shift the blame away from respondent became discernible early in her testimony. Yet counsel continued to explore the underlying events in detail. [H]e directly challenged Anita's veracity by seeking to have her admit that she had given the credit cards to respondent to obtain a television. When Anita denied this, defense counsel elicited the fact that the only television she owned was a "Twenty Dollar * * * old model."

Respondent argues that, because defense counsel never asked the court to declare Anita hostile, his questioning necessarily occurred on direct examination. But however state law might formally characterize the questioning of Anita, it afforded "substantial compliance with the purposes behind the confrontation requirement," no less so than classic cross-examination. Although Ohio law may have authorized objection by the prosecutor or intervention by the court, this did not happen. As in *Green,* respondent's counsel was not "significantly limited in any way in the scope or nature of his cross-examination."

We are also unpersuaded that *Green* is distinguishable on the ground that Anita Isaacs—unlike the declarant Porter in *Green*—was not personally available for questioning *at trial.* This argument ignores the language and logic of *Green:*

> "Porter's statement would, we think, have been admissible at trial even in Porter's absence if Porter had been actually unavailable. * * * That being the case, we do not think a different result should follow where the witness is actually produced."

Nor does it matter that, unlike Green, respondent had a different lawyer at trial from the one at the preliminary hearing. Although one might strain one's reading of *Green* to assign this factor some significance, respondent advances no reason of substance supporting the distinction. Indeed, if we were to accept this suggestion, *Green* would carry the seeds of its own demise; under a "same attorney" rule, a defendant could nullify the effect of *Green* by obtaining new counsel after the preliminary hearing was concluded.

Finally, we reject respondent's attempt to fall back on general principles of confrontation, and his argument that this case falls among those in which the Court must undertake a particularized search for "indicia of reliability." Under this theory, the factors previously cited—absence of face-to-face contact at trial, presence of a new attorney, and the lack of classic cross-examination—combine with considerations uniquely tied to Anita to mandate exclusion of her statements. Anita, respondent says, had every reason to lie to avoid prosecution or parental reprobation. Her unknown whereabouts is explicable as an effort to avoid punishment, perjury, or self-incrimination. Given these facts, her prior testimony falls on the unreliable side, and should have been excluded.

In making this argument, respondent in effect asks us to disassociate preliminary hearing testimony previously subjected to cross-examination from previously cross-examined prior-trial testimony, which the Court has deemed generally immune from subsequent confrontation attack. Precedent requires us to decline this invitation. In *Green* the Court found guarantees of trustworthiness in the accouterments of the preliminary hearing itself; there was no mention of the inherent reliability or unreliability of Porter and his story.

In sum, we perceive no reason to resolve the reliability issue differently here than the Court did in *Green*. "Since there was an adequate opportunity to cross-examine [the witness], and counsel * * * availed himself of that opportunity, the transcript * * * bore sufficient 'indicia of reliability' and afforded '"the trier of fact a satisfactory basis for evaluating the truth of the prior statement."'" [1]

We conclude that the prosecution carried its burden of demonstrating that Anita was constitutionally unavailable for purposes of respondent's trial.

The judgment of the Supreme Court of Ohio is reversed, and the case is remanded for further proceedings not inconsistent with this opinion.

It is so ordered.

[Justice BRENNAN'S dissent, joined by Justices MARSHALL and STEVENS, is omitted].

LILLY, AN INTRODUCTION TO THE LAW OF EVIDENCE
273–278 (1978).

Any assessment of the future role of hearsay evidence, at least in criminal trials, must take account of the Constitution's Sixth Amend-

---

1. We need not consider whether defense counsel's questioning at the preliminary hearing surmounts some inevitably nebulous threshold of "effectiveness." In *Mancusi*, to be sure, the Court explored to some extent the adequacy of counsel's cross-examination at the earlier proceeding. That discussion, however, must be read in light of the fact that the defendant's representation at the earlier proceeding, provided by counsel who had been appointed only four days prior thereto, already had been held to be ineffective. Under those unusual circumstances, it was necessary to explore the character of the actual cross-examination to ensure that an adequate opportunity for full cross-examination had been afforded to the defendant. We hold that in all but such extraordinary cases, no inquiry into "effectiveness" is required. A holding that every case involving prior testimony requires such an inquiry would frustrate the principal objective of generally validating the prior-testimony exception in the first place—increasing certainty and consistency in the application of the Confrontation Clause.

ment guarantee to an accused of the right "to be confronted with the witnesses against him."[1] Although "the confrontation cases are in disarray and the policies to be served by the constitutional protection are far from clear," certain conclusions may be drawn from the cases.

The confrontation clause never has been read so literally as to preclude generally the use of hearsay evidence in criminal trials. Indeed, the cases are replete with instances of hearsay statements admitted under the recognized exceptions. It is fairly certain that there is no constitutional prohibition against either the substantive use of a prior extrajudicial declaration of a witness present at trial (at least where it clearly is shown that the prior statements were made) or, in cases of unavailability, against the use of prior testimony in circumstances in which the accused had an earlier opportunity to conduct a fair and full cross-examination.[2] Even admission against the accused of dying declarations apparently is permissible, and most courts have turned aside confrontation clause challenges to such hearsay exceptions as declarations against interest, business entries,[3] and party admissions by coconspirators.[4]

Nonetheless, the confrontation clause places limits, however uncertain, upon the freedom with which the prosecution may deny the accused adequate opportunity to cross-examine witnesses (including, in some circumstances, hearsay declarants) and the right to have adverse statements secured under oath and in the presence of the trier of fact. The Supreme Court apparently has rejected both of the most extreme readings of the confrontation clause. Under one of these constructions, every hearsay declarant would be viewed as a witness against the accused and his presence at trial would be compelled constitutionally, thus blocking substantially all hearsay evidence. Under the opposite reading, the constitutional command would require merely a guarantee that evidence used to convict the accused be presented through trial witnesses. The source of the witness's information, while perhaps raising issues under an exclusionary rule of evidence such as the hearsay rule, would not present a constitutional problem.

In several cases, the Supreme Court has struck down under the confrontation clause evidence of inculpatory statements that the ac-

1. This provision applies not only to the federal government but to the states as well. The clause also can be read as guaranteeing the accused's right to be present at his own trial.

2. California v. Green. See Barber v. Page, which contrary to the language in *Green* indicates that prior testimony at the preliminary hearing may not afford a defendant adequate opportunity to cross-examine because the issue at the preliminary hearing is limited to whether there is probable cause for a trial.

3. United States v. Lipscomb. See also Reed v. Beto (public records); State v. Finkley (hospital's medical records). Contra, State v. Tims (confrontation clause violated by use of business-hospital record).

4. Dutton v. Evans. Further, the confrontation clause does not extend to statements by persons whose declarations are not used to establish guilt at trial, such as witnesses before a grand jury, informers who provide information sufficient for probable cause to search, or probation officers who supply information relevant to sentencing. As one commentator notes, participants in the criminal process whose statements are not considered by a jury in connection with a determination of guilt or innocence are not "witnesses" against the accused as that term is used in the constitution.

cused could not subject to meaningful cross-examination. Use of a transcript of prior testimony elicited from a witness during the accused's preliminary hearing at which the accused was not repre-sented by counsel [6] was found constitutionally objectionable. Similar-ly rejected was improper "evidence" (although not formally admitted) of a prosecutor's use of the confession of the accused's codefendant: after the codefendant-witness invoked the fifth amendment and re-fused to testify, the prosecutor used the guise of refreshing the witness's recollection to read aloud the codefendant's earlier confes-sion which implicated the accused. In a third case, in which the accused did not take the stand, the use of a codefendant's confession which inculpated the accused was held to violate the latter's right of confrontation; [8] an instruction to the jury that it consider the confes-sion only with regard to the codefendant's guilt was deemed ineffec-tive. The Supreme Court also has indicated that the confrontation clause limits when a witness can be considered "unavailable" for purposes of a hearsay exception. In one case, state authorities who knew that a prosecution witness was in a federal penitentiary in another state made no attempt to secure his presence at trial. The Court held that the state denied the accused's right of confrontation when it used the witness's out-of-state custody as a ground for invok-ing the exception for prior recorded testimony.[9]

The Court has yet to clarify the reach of the confrontation clause, but reason suggests an analytical framework for future decisions. Like other constitutional provisions, the right of an accused "to be confronted with witnesses against him" should not be inflexible. Confrontation is a relative term to be given a functional meaning. Although the values to be protected by the confrontation clause are not altogether clear, the notion of confronting a witness implies a right to interrogate him effectively under oath and to bring him within the observation of the trier of fact. At a minimum, it guarantees that the accused may effectively confront and cross-examine those who testify against him at trial. Cross-examination may not be limited so as to significantly emasculate its effectiveness.[11] In all probability, the right of confronta-tion also ensures that an accused will not be convicted on the basis of statements by absent declarants that fall within no recognized exception to the hearsay rule. Thus, prosecutorial use at trial of the ex parte affidavit of an absent declarant to supply significant proof against the

6. Pointer v. Texas. This case also holds that the confrontation clause is fully applicable to the states through the Four-teenth Amendment.

8. Bruton v. United States. But see Nelson v. O'Neil (*Bruton* not controlling where codefendant takes stand, denies in-culpatory admission, and testifies favora-bly to accused); Harrington v. California (*Bruton* violation can be harmless error; also *Bruton* may not apply when codefend-ant takes the stand and admits state-ments).

9. Barber v. Page. But see Mancusi v. Stubbs (witness who had left country genu-inely unavailable therefore defendant could not invoke Barber v. Page). See also California v. Green (admission at trial of statement taken from witness at prelimi-nary hearing did not violate confrontation clause where accused had counsel and ade-quate opportunity to cross-examine at ear-lier proceeding).

11. Davis v. Alaska (accused must be permitted to show probationary status of juvenile witness against him); Smith v. Illinois (accused must be allowed to ask a principal prosecution witness the latter's true name and address).

accused probably would violate his sixth amendment right to confrontation.

Beyond these situations, application of the confrontation clause should depend upon whether considerations of trustworthiness and adversarial fairness are satisfied. In ascertaining whether the confrontation of a witness at trial who merely presents documents or who gives testimony which embodies the assertions of absent declarants satisfies the sixth amendment, at least three factors should be determinative: trustworthiness, the ease with which a declarant can be produced, and the importance of the evidence in question. If there is strong reason to distrust the reliability of the evidence, the preference for live testimony should be compelling. If the declarant reasonably can be produced, his courtroom presence should be demanded. In instances where the declarant is deceased or otherwise not available, the question whether the right of confrontation has been violated should depend on the degree of risk that the evidence will produce an erroneous finding. If the statements in question fall within a hearsay exception and thus have the imprimatur of judicial and legislative experience, this fact should weigh heavily in favor of a determination that the right to confrontation has been satisfied.[13] Finally, the significance of an accused's right to confront a witness should bear a direct relation to the significance of the evidence supplied by the witness. When this evidence is comparatively inconsequential, cross-examination of the in-court witness should be sufficient confrontation even though the source of the witness's testimony may be traced to an absent declarant.[14]

The foregoing analysis may fit as comfortably within a due process analysis as it does within the framework of the confrontation clause. Nonetheless, the Supreme Court already has embarked upon a course that accords the confrontation clause content beyond that found in a restrictive interpretation described earlier. A middle ground permitting ample flexibility to accommodate the growth of the hearsay rule seems consonant with the existing cases and highly desirable.

UNITED STATES v. INADI

Supreme Court of the United States, 1986.
475 U.S. 387, 106 S.Ct. 1121, 89 L.Ed.2d 390.

Justice POWELL delivered the opinion of the Court.

This case presents the question whether the Confrontation Clause requires the Government to show that a nontestifying co-conspirator is unavailable to testify, as a condition for admission of that co-conspirator's out-of-court statements.

13. See Hoover v. Beto (confession of principal admissible at accomplice's trial). But see Park v. Huff (confrontation clause violated by admission of co-conspirator's statements).

14. In Dutton v. Evans, the Supreme Court noted that the hearsay evidence admitted against the accused was not "critical" or "devastating," especially in light of the other inculpatory evidence in the rec-

ord. Although the significance of evidence which arguably violates the confrontation clause may be an important factor in determining if a constitutional violation has occurred, it would appear that a trial judge, faced with a timely constitutional objection, should reject even insignificant evidence if he thinks that it violates the accused's sixth amendment right.

I

Following a jury trial in the Eastern District of Pennsylvania, respondent Joseph Inadi was convicted of conspiring to manufacture and distribute methamphetamine, and related offenses. He was sentenced to three years' imprisonment to be followed by a 7–year parole term. The evidence at trial showed that in September 1979, respondent was approached by unindicted co-conspirator Michael McKeon, who was seeking a distribution outlet for methamphetamine. Respondent's role was to supply cash and chemicals for the manufacture of methamphetamine and to be responsible for its distribution. McKeon and another unindicted co-conspirator, William Levan, were to manufacture the substance.

In the course of manufacturing and selling methamphetamine, McKeon, Levan, and respondent met with another unindicted co-conspirator, John Lazaro, at an empty house in Cape May, New Jersey. There they extracted additional methamphetamine from the liquid residue of previous batches. In the early morning hours of May 23, 1980, two Cape May police officers, pursuant to a warrant, secretly entered the house and removed a tray covered with drying methamphetamine. With the permission of the issuing Magistrate, the officers delayed returning an inventory, leaving the participants to speculate over what had happened to the missing tray.

* * *

From May 23 to May 27, 1980, the Cape May County Prosecutor's Office lawfully intercepted and recorded five telephone conversations between various participants in the conspiracy. These taped conversations were played for the jury at trial. The conversations dealt with various aspects of the conspiracy, including planned meetings and speculation about who had taken the missing tray from the house. Respondent sought to exclude the recorded statements of Lazaro and the other unindicted co-conspirators on the ground that the statements did not satisfy the requirements of Federal Rule of Evidence 801(d)(2) (E), governing admission of co-conspirator declarations.[1] After listening to the tapes the trial court admitted the statements, finding that they were made by conspirators during the course of and in furtherance of the conspiracy, and thereby satisfied Rule 801(d)(2)(E).

Respondent also objected to admission of the statements on Confrontation Clause grounds, contending that the statements were inadmissible absent a showing that the declarants were unavailable. The court suggested that the prosecutor bring Lazaro to court in order to demonstrate unavailability. The court also asked defense counsel whether she wanted the prosecution to call Lazaro as a witness, and defense counsel stated that she would discuss the matter with her client. The co-conspirators' statements were admitted, conditioned on the prosecution's commitment to produce Lazaro. The Government subpoenaed Lazaro, but he failed to appear, claiming car trouble. The

---

1. Federal Rule of Evidence 801(d)(2)(E) provides that a statement is not hearsay if it is offered against a party and is "a statement by a co-conspirator of a party during the course and in furtherance of the conspiracy."

record does not indicate that the defense made any effort on its own part to secure Lazaro's presence in court.

Respondent renewed his Confrontation Clause objections, arguing that the Government had not met its burden of showing that Lazaro was unavailable to testify. The trial court overruled the objection, ruling that Lazaro's statements were admissible because they satisfied the co-conspirator rule.[2]

The Court of Appeals for the Third Circuit reversed. The court agreed that the Government had satisfied Rule 801(d)(2)(E), but decided that the Confrontation Clause established an independent requirement that the Government, as a condition to admission of any out-of-court statements, must show the unavailability of the declarant. The court derived this "unavailability rule" from Ohio v. Roberts, 448 U.S. 56 (1980). The Court of Appeals rejected the Government's contention that *Roberts* did not require a showing of unavailability as to a nontestifying co-conspirator, finding that *Roberts* created a "clear constitutional rule" applicable to out-of-court statements generally. The court found no reason to create a special exception for co-conspirator statements, and therefore ruled Lazaro's statements inadmissible.

We granted certiorari, 471 U.S. 1142, 105 S.Ct. 2653, 86 L.Ed.2d 271 (1985), to resolve the question whether the Confrontation Clause requires a showing of unavailability as a condition to admission of the out-of-court statements of a nontestifying co-conspirator, when those statements otherwise satisfy the requirements of Federal Rule of Evidence 801(d)(2)(E).[3] We now reverse.

II

A

The Court of Appeals derived its rule that the Government must demonstrate unavailability from our decision in *Roberts*. It quoted *Roberts* as holding that "in conformance with the Framers' preference for face-to-face accusation, the Sixth Amendment establishes a rule of necessity. In the usual case * * * the prosecution must either produce, or demonstrate the unavailability of, the declarant whose statement it wishes to use against the defendant." The Court of Appeals viewed this language as setting forth a "clear constitutional rule" applicable before any hearsay can be admitted. 748 F.2d, at 818. Under this interpretation of *Roberts,* no out-of-court statement would be admissible without a showing of unavailability.

Roberts, however, does not stand for such a wholesale revision of the law of evidence, nor does it support such a broad interpretation of

---

2. The trial court also noted that two of the four co-conspirator declarants (Mrs. Lazaro and McKeon) had testified and that a third (Levan) was unavailable because he had asserted his Fifth Amendment privilege outside the presence of the jury.

3. The reliability of the out-of-court statements is not at issue in this case. The Court of Appeals determined that whether or not the statements are reliable, their admission violated the Sixth Amendment because the government did not show that the declarant was unavailable to testify. 748 F.2d, at 818–819. The sole issue before the Court is whether that decision is correct.

the Confrontation Clause. *Roberts* itself disclaimed any intention of proposing a general answer to the many difficult questions arising out of the relationship between the Confrontation Clause and hearsay. "The Court has not sought to 'map out a theory of the Confrontation Clause that would determine the validity of all * * * hearsay "exceptions." ' " The Court in *Roberts* remained "[c]onvinced that 'no rule will perfectly resolve all possible problems' " and rejected the "invitation to overrule a near-century of jurisprudence" in order to create such a rule. In addition, the Court specifically noted that a "demonstration of unavailability * * * is not always required." In light of these limiting statements, *Roberts* should not be read as an abstract answer to questions not presented in that case, but rather as a resolution of the issue the Court said it was examining: "the constitutional propriety of the introduction in evidence of the preliminary hearing testimony of a witness not produced at the defendant's subsequent state criminal trial."

The Confrontation Clause analysis in *Roberts* focuses on those factors that come into play when the prosecution seeks to admit testimony from a prior judicial proceeding in place of live testimony at trial. See Fed.Rule Evid. 804(b)(1). In particular, the *Roberts* Court examined the requirement, found in a long line of Confrontation Clause cases involving prior testimony, that before such statements can be admitted the government must demonstrate that the declarant is unavailable.[4] All of the cases cited in *Roberts* for this "unavailability rule" concern prior testimony. In particular, the Court focused on two cases, *Barber* and *Mancusi*, that directly "explored the issue of constitutional unavailability." Both cases specifically limited the unavailability exception to prior testimony.

Roberts must be read consistently with the question it answered, the authority it cited, and its own facts. *Roberts* cannot fairly be read to stand for the radical proposition that no out-of-court statement can be introduced by the government without a showing that the declarant is unavailable.

B

There are good reasons why the unavailability rule, developed in cases involving former testimony, is not applicable to co-conspirators' out-of-court statements. Unlike some other exceptions to the hearsay rules, or the exemption from the hearsay definition involved in this case, former testimony often is only a weaker substitute for live testimony. It seldom has independent evidentiary significance of its own, but is intended to replace live testimony. If the declarant is available and the same information can be presented to the trier of fact in the form of live testimony, with full cross-examination and the

4. Federal Rule of Evidence 804 also imposes an unavailability requirement before allowing the admission of prior testimony. The Rule 804 requirement is part of the law of evidence regarding hearsay. While it "may readily be conceded that hearsay rules and the Confrontation Clause are generally designed to protect similar values," California v. Green, 399 U.S., at 155, 90 S.Ct., at 1933, the overlap is not complete.

opportunity to view the demeanor of the declarant, there is little
justification for relying on the weaker version. When two versions of
the same evidence are available, longstanding principles of the law of
hearsay, applicable as well to Confrontation Clause analysis, favor the
better evidence. See Graham, The Right of Confrontation and the
Hearsay Rule: Sir Walter Raleigh Loses Another One, 8 Crim.L.Bull.
99, 143 (1972). But if the declarant is unavailable, no "better" version
of the evidence exists, and the former testimony may be admitted as a
substitute for live testimony on the same point.

Those same principles do not apply to co-conspirator statements.
Because they are made while the conspiracy is in progress, such
statements provide evidence of the conspiracy's context that cannot be
replicated, even if the declarant testifies to the same matters in court.
When the Government—as here—offers the statement of one drug
dealer to another in furtherance of an illegal conspiracy, the statement
often will derive its significance from the circumstances in which it was
made. Conspirators are likely to speak differently when talking to
each other in furtherance of their illegal aims than when testifying on
the witness stand. Even when the declarant takes the stand, his in-
court testimony seldom will reproduce a significant portion of the
evidentiary value of his statements during the course of the conspiracy.

In addition, the relative positions of the parties will have changed
substantially between the time of the statements and the trial. The
declarant and the defendant will have changed from partners in an
illegal conspiracy to suspects or defendants in a criminal trial, each
with information potentially damaging to the other. The declarant
himself may be facing indictment or trial, in which case he has little
incentive to aid the prosecution, and yet will be equally wary of coming
to the aid of his former partners in crime. In that situation, it is
extremely unlikely that in-court testimony will recapture the evidentiary significance of statements made when the conspiracy was operating
in full force.

These points distinguish co-conspirators' statements from the statements involved in *Roberts* and our other prior testimony cases. Those
cases rested in part on the strong similarities between the prior judicial
proceedings and the trial. No such strong similarities exist between co-
conspirator statements and live testimony at trial. To the contrary, co-
conspirator statements derive much of their value from the fact that
they are made in a context very different from trial, and therefore are
usually irreplaceable as substantive evidence. Under these circumstances, "only clear folly would dictate an across the board policy of
doing without" such statements. The admission of co-conspirators'
declarations into evidence thus actually furthers the "Confrontation
Clause's very mission" which is to "advance 'the accuracy of the truth-
determining process in criminal trials.'"

C

There appears to be little, if any, benefit to be accomplished by the
Court of Appeals' unavailability rule. First, if the declarant either is

unavailable, or is available and produced by the prosecution, the statements can be introduced anyway. Thus, the unavailability rule cannot be defended as a constitutional "better evidence" rule, because it does not actually serve to exclude anything, unless the prosecution makes the mistake of not producing an otherwise available witness.

Second, an unavailability rule is not likely to produce much testimony that adds anything to the "truth-determining process" over and above what would be produced without such a rule. Some of the available declarants already will have been subpoenaed by the prosecution or the defense, regardless of any Confrontation Clause requirements. Presumably only those declarants that neither side believes will be particularly helpful will not have been subpoenaed as witnesses. There is much to indicate that Lazaro was in that position in this case. Neither the Government nor the defense originally subpoenaed Lazaro as a witness.[5] When he subsequently failed to show, alleging car trouble, respondent did nothing to secure his testimony.   *   *   *

While the benefits seem slight, the burden imposed by the Court of Appeals' unavailability rule is significant. A constitutional rule requiring a determination of availability every time the prosecution seeks to introduce a co-conspirator's declaration automatically adds another avenue of appellate review in these complex cases. The co-conspirator rule apparently is the most frequently used exception to the hearsay rule. A rule that required each invocation of Rule 801(d)(2)(E) to be accompanied by a decision on the declarant's availability would impose a substantial burden on the entire criminal justice system.

Moreover, an unavailability rule places a significant practical burden on the prosecution. In every case involving co-conspirator statements, the prosecution would be required to identify with specificity each declarant, locate those declarants, and then endeavor to ensure their continuing availability for trial. Where declarants are incarcerated there is the burden on prison officials and marshals of transporting them to and from the courthouse, as well as the increased risk of escape. For unincarcerated declarants the unavailability rule would require that during the sometimes lengthy period before trial the Government must endeavor to be aware of the whereabouts of the declarant or run the risk of a court determination that its efforts to produce the declarant did not satisfy the test of "good faith."

An unavailability rule would impose all of these burdens even if neither the prosecution nor the defense wished to examine the declarant at trial. Any marginal protection to the defendant by forcing the government to call as witnesses those co-conspirator declarants who are available, willing to testify, hostile to the defense and yet not already subpoenaed by the prosecution, when the defendant himself can call and cross-examine such declarants, cannot support an unavailability

---

5. In fact, the actions of the parties in this case demonstrate what is no doubt a frequent occurrence in conspiracy cases— neither side wants a co-conspirator as a witness.   *   *   *   [T]he interests of the prosecution and the co-conspirator seldom will run together. Nor do the co-conspirator's interests coincide with his former partners, since each is in a position that is potentially harmful to the others.

rule. We hold today that the Confrontation Clause does not embody such a rule.

* * *

We accordingly reverse the judgment of the Court of Appeals for the Third Circuit.

It is so ordered.

Justice MARSHALL, with whom Justice BRENNAN joins, dissenting.

With respect to the case before us, the majority takes but a small step. In Ohio v. Roberts, 448 U.S. 56, 100 S.Ct. 2531, 65 L.Ed.2d 597 (1980), the Court held: "[W]hen a hearsay declarant is not present for cross-examination at trial, the Confrontation Clause normally requires a showing that he is unavailable. Even then, his statement is admissible only if it bears adequate 'indicia of reliability.'" The majority now assures us that "[t]he reliability of the out-of-court statements is not at issue in this case." Respondent is thus free to return to the Court of Appeals and argue that the co-conspirator declarations admitted against him lack the "indicia of reliability" demanded by the Confrontation Clause.[1]

BOURJAILY v. UNITED STATES

Supreme Court of the United States, 1987.
483 U.S. 171, 107 S.Ct. 2775, 97 L.Ed.2d 144.

[Editors' Note: The portion of this opinion that deals with non-constitutional issues has been excerpted on p. 188. Please refer to that excerpt for the facts of the case.]

Chief Justice REHNQUIST delivered the opinion of the Court.

* * *

While a literal interpretation of the Confrontation Clause could bar the use of any out-of-court statements when the declarant is unavailable, this Court has rejected that view as "unintended and too extreme." Ohio v. Roberts, 448 U.S. 56, 63 (1980). Rather, we have attempted to harmonize the goal of the Clause—placing limits on the kind of evidence that may be received against a defendant—with a societal interest in accurate factfinding, which may require consideration of out-of-court statements. To accommodate these competing interests, the Court has, as a general matter only, required the prosecution to demonstrate both the unavailability of the declarant and the "indicia of

---

1. Today's decision does nothing to resolve the conflict among the lower courts as to whether declarations of co-conspirators who are not present in court for cross-examination must be shown to have particularized "indicia of reliability" before they can be admitted for substantive purposes against a criminal defendant. Compare United States v. DeLuna, 763 F.2d 897 (CA8 1985) (particularized inquiry into reliability of co-conspirator statements demanded in addition to unavailability requirement); United States v. Ordonez, 722 F.2d 530, 535 (CA9 1983) (particularized assessment of reliability needed for every statement admitted under co-conspirator hearsay exemption); United States v. Perez, 702 F.2d 33 (CA2) (same), cert. denied, 462 U.S. 1108, 103 S.Ct. 2457, 77 L.Ed.2d 1336 (1983), with Boone v. Marshall, 760 F.2d 117, 119 (CA6 1985) (declaration admitted under co-conspirator exemption "automatically satisfies the Sixth Amendment requirements"); United States v. Molt, 758 F.2d 1198 (CA7 1985) (same).

reliability" surrounding the out-of-court declaration. Id., at 65–66. Last Term in United States v. Inadi, 475 U.S. 387 (1986), we held that the first of these two generalized inquiries, unavailability, was not required when the hearsay statement is the out-of-court declaration of a co-conspirator. Today, we conclude that the second inquiry, independent indicia of reliability, is also not mandated by the Constitution.

The Court's decision in Ohio v. Roberts laid down only "a general approach to the problem" of reconciling hearsay exceptions with the Confrontation Clause. See 448 U.S., at 65. In fact, Roberts itself limits the requirement that a court make a separate inquiry into the reliability of an out-of-court statement. Because "hearsay rules and the Confrontation Clause are generally designed to protect similar values,' California v. Green, 399 U.S. [149, 155 (1970),] and 'stem from the same roots,' Dutton v. Evans, 400 U.S. 74, 86 (1970)," id., at 66, we concluded in Roberts that no independent inquiry into reliability is required when the evidence "falls within a firmly rooted hearsay exception." Ibid. We think that the co-conspirator exception to the hearsay rule is firmly enough rooted in our jurisprudence that, under this Court's holding in Roberts, a court need not independently inquire into the reliability of such statements. Cf. Dutton v. Evans, 400 U.S. 74 (1970) (reliability inquiry required where evidentiary rule deviates from common-law approach, admitting co-conspirators' hearsay statements made after termination of conspiracy). The admissibility of co-conspirators' statements was first established in this Court over a century and a half ago in United States v. Gooding, 12 Wheat. 460 (1827) (interpreting statements of co-conspirator as res gestae and thus admissible against defendant), and the Court has repeatedly reaffirmed the exception as accepted practice. In fact, two of the most prominent approvals of the rule came in cases that petitioner maintains are still vital today, Glasser v. United States, 315 U.S. 60 (1942), and United States v. Nixon, 418 U.S. 683 (1974). To the extent that these cases have not been superseded by the Federal Rules of Evidence, they demonstrate that the co-conspirator exception to the hearsay rule is steeped in our jurisprudence. * * *

[Justice BLACKMUN, with whom Justice MARSHALL and Justice BRENNAN joined, dissented.]

IDAHO v. WRIGHT

Supreme Court of the United States, 1990.
___ U.S. ___, 110 S.Ct. 3139, 111 L.Ed.2d 638.

Justice O'Connor delivered the opinion of the Court.

This case requires us to decide whether the admission at trial of certain hearsay statements made by a child declarant to an examining pediatrician violates a defendant's rights under the Confrontation Clause of the Sixth Amendment.

I

Respondent Laura Lee Wright was jointly charged with Robert L. Giles of two counts of lewd conduct with a minor under 16, in violation

of Idaho Code § 18–1508 (1987).   The alleged victims were respondent's
two daughters, one of whom was 5½ and the other 2½ years old at the
time the crimes were charged.

[The allegations surfaced after one of the children told an adult
that Giles had sexually abused the children and that Wright had
helped.   Medical examinations revealed physical evidence of abuse.
The issue in this case turned on the admissibility of statements by the
younger daughter to Dr. John Jambura, a pediatrician.   In response to
Dr. Jambura's questions, the younger daughter indicated that Giles had
had sexual contact with her, and then volunteered that Giles "does do
this with me, but he does it a lot more with my sister than with me."
The trial judge found, and the parties agreed, that the younger daughter was "not capable of communicating to the jury."   The trial judge
then admitted Dr. Jambura's testimony about the child's statements
under Idaho Rule Evid. 803(24), which is identical in relevant respects
to Fed.R.Evid. 803(24).   On Wright's appeal from the conviction involving her younger daughter, the Idaho Supreme Court held that the
admission of this testimony violated the federal Confrontation Clause.
The United States Supreme Court granted certiorari.]

In Ohio v. Roberts, we set forth "a general approach" for determining when incriminating statements admissible under an exception to
the hearsay rule also meet the requirements of the Confrontation
Clause.   We noted that the Confrontation Clause "operates in two
separate ways to restrict the range of admissible hearsay."   Ibid. "First,
in conformance with the Framers' preference for face-to-face accusation, the Sixth Amendment establishes a rule of necessity.   In the usual
case . . ., the prosecution must either produce or demonstrate the
unavailability of, the declarant whose statement it wishes to use
against the defendant."   Ibid. (citations omitted).   Second, once a witness is shown to be unavailable, "his statement is admissible only if it
bears adequate 'indicia of reliability.'   Reliability can be inferred without more in a case where the evidence falls within a firmly rooted
hearsay exception.   In other cases, the evidence must be excluded, at
least absent a showing of particularized guarantees of trustworthiness."
*   *   *

Applying the Roberts approach to this case, we first note that this
case does not raise the question whether, before a child's out-of-court
statements are admitted, the Confrontation Clause requires the prosecution to show that a child witness is unavailable at trial—and, if so,
what that showing requires.   The trial court in this case found that
respondent's younger daughter was incapable of communicating with
the jury, and defense counsel agreed.   The court below neither questioned this finding nor discussed the general requirement of unavailability.   For purposes of deciding this case, we assume without deciding
that, to the extent the unavailability requirement applies in this case,
the younger daughter was an unavailable witness within the meaning
of the Confrontation Clause.

The crux of the question presented is therefore whether the State,
as the proponent of evidence presumptively barred by the hearsay rule

and the Confrontation Clause, has carried its burden of proving that the younger daughter's incriminating statements to Dr. Jambura bore sufficient indicia of reliability to withstand scrutiny under the Clause. The court below held that, although the trial court had properly admitted the statements under the State's residual hearsay exception, the statements were "fraught with the dangers of unreliability which the Confrontation Clause is designed to highlight and obviate." The State asserts that the court below erected too stringent a standard for admitting the statements and that the statements were, under the totality of the circumstances, sufficiently reliable for Confrontation Clause purposes.

In Roberts, we suggested that the "indicia of reliability" requirement could be met in either of two circumstances: where the hearsay statement "falls within a firmly rooted hearsay exception," or where it is supported by "a showing of particularized guarantees of trustworthiness."

We note at the outset that Idaho's residual hearsay exception, Idaho Rule Evid 803(24), under which the challenged statements were admitted, is not a firmly rooted hearsay exception for Confrontation Clause purposes. Admission under a firmly rooted hearsay exception satisfies the constitutional requirement of reliability because of the weight accorded longstanding judicial and legislative experience in assessing the trustworthiness of certain types of out-of-court statements. The residual hearsay exception, by contrast, accommodates ad hoc instances in which statements not otherwise falling within a recognized hearsay exception might nevertheless be sufficiently reliable to be admissible at trial. Hearsay statements admitted under the residual exception, almost by definition, therefore do not share the same tradition of reliability that supports the admissibility of statements under a firmly rooted hearsay exception. Moreover, were we to agree that the admission of hearsay statements under the residual exception automatically passed Confrontation Clause scrutiny, virtually every codified hearsay exception would assume constitutional stature, a step this Court has repeatedly declined to take.

The State in any event does not press the matter strongly and recognizes that, because the younger daughter's hearsay statements do not fall within a firmly rooted hearsay exception, they are "presumptively unreliable and inadmissible for Confrontation Clause purposes," and "must be excluded, at least absent a showing of particularized guarantees of trustworthiness," Roberts, 448 U.S., at 66. The court below concluded that the State had not made such a showing, in large measure because the statements resulted from an interview lacking certain procedural safeguards. The court below specifically noted that Dr. Jambura failed to record the interview on videotape, asked leading questions, and questioned the child with a preconceived idea of what she should be disclosing.

Although we agree with the court below that the Confrontation Clause bars the admission of the younger daughter's hearsay statements, we reject the apparently dispositive weight placed by that court on the lack of procedural safeguards at the interview. Out-of-court statements made by children regarding sexual abuse arise in a wide variety of circumstances, and we do not believe the Constitution imposes a fixed set of procedural prerequisites to the admission of such statements at trial. The procedural requirements identified by the court below, to the extent regarded as conditions precedent to the admission of child hearsay statements in child sexual abuse cases, may in many instances be inappropriate or unnecessary to a determination whether a given statement is sufficiently trustworthy for Confrontation Clause purposes. See, e.g., Nelson v. Farrey, 874 F.2d 1222, 1229 (7th Cir.1989) (videotape requirement not feasible, especially where defendant had not yet been criminally charged), cert denied, 493 US ___ (1990); J. Myers, Child Witness Law and Practice § 4.6, 129–134 (1987) (use of leading questions with children, when appropriate, does not necessarily render responses untrustworthy). Although the procedural guidelines propounded by the court below may well enhance the reliability of out-of-court statements of children regarding sexual abuse, we decline to read into the Confrontation Clause a preconceived and artificial litmus test for the procedural propriety of professional interviews in which children make hearsay statements against a defendant.

The State responds that a finding of "particularized guarantees of trustworthiness" should instead be based on a consideration of the totality of the circumstances, including not only the circumstances surrounding the making of the statement, but also other evidence at trial that corroborates the truth of the statement. We agree that "particularized guarantees of trustworthiness" must be shown from the totality of the circumstances, but we think the relevant circumstances include only those that surround the making of the statement and that render the declarant particularly worthy of belief. This conclusion derives from the rationale for permitting exceptions to the general rule against hearsay:

> "The theory of the hearsay rule . . . is that the many possible sources of inaccuracy and untrustworthiness which may lie underneath the bare untested assertion of a witness can best be brought to light and exposed, if they exist, by the test of cross-examination. But this test or security may in a given instance be superfluous; it may be sufficiently clear, in that instance, that the statement offered is free enough from the risk of inaccuracy and untrustworthiness, so that the test of cross-examination would be a work of supererogation." 5 J. Wigmore, Evidence § 1420, p 251 (J. Chadbourne rev 1974).

In other words, if the declarant's truthfulness is so clear from the surrounding circumstances that the test of cross-examination would be of marginal utility, then the hearsay rule does not bar admission of the statement at trial. The basis for the "excited utterance" exception, for example, is that such statements are given under circumstances that eliminate the possibility of fabrication, coaching, or confabulation, and that therefore the circumstances surrounding the making of the statement provide sufficient assurance that the statement is trustworthy and that cross-examination would be superfluous. Likewise, the "dying declaration" and "medical treatment" exceptions to the hearsay rule are based on the belief that persons making such statements are highly unlikely to lie. * * * "The circumstantial guarantees of trustworthiness on which the various specific exceptions to the hearsay rule are based are those that existed at the time the statement was made and do not include those that may be added by using hindsight."   Huff v. White Motor Corp., 609 F.2d 286, 292 (7th Cir.1979).

We think the "particularized guarantees of trustworthiness" required for admission under the Confrontation Clause must likewise be drawn from the totality of circumstances that surround the making of the statement and that render the declarant particularly worthy of belief.   Our precedents have recognized that statements admitted under a "firmly rooted" hearsay exception are so trustworthy that adversarial testing would add little to their reliability.   Because evidence possessing "particularized guarantees of trustworthiness" must be at least as reliable as evidence admitted under a firmly rooted hearsay exception, we think that evidence admitted under the former requirement must similarly be so trustworthy that adversarial testing would add little to its reliability. * * *

As our discussion above suggests, we are unpersuaded by the State's contention that evidence corroborating the truth of a hearsay statement may properly support a finding that the statement bears "particularized guarantees of trustworthiness."   To be admissible under the Confrontation Clause, hearsay evidence used to convict a defendant must possess indicia of reliability by virtue of its inherent trustworthiness, not by reference to other evidence at trial.   A statement made under duress, for example, may happen to be a true statement, but the circumstances under which it is made may provide no basis for supposing that the declarant is particularly likely to be telling the truth—indeed, the circumstances may even be such that the declarant is particularly unlikely to be telling the truth.   In such a case, cross-examination at trial would be highly useful to probe the declarant's state-of-mind when he made the statements; the presence of evidence tending to corroborate the truth of the statement would be no substitute for cross-examination of the declarant at trial.

In short, the use of corroborating evidence to support a hearsay statement's "particularized guarantees of trustworthiness" would permit admission of a presumptively unreliable statement by bootstrapping on the trustworthiness of other evidence at trial, a result we think at odds with the requirement that hearsay evidence admitted under the Confrontation Clause be so trustworthy that cross-examination of the declarant would be of marginal utility. * * * [W]e think the presence of corroborating evidence more appropriately indicates that any error in admitting the statement might be harmless, rather than that any basis exists for presuming the declarant to be trustworthy. * * *

Corroboration of a child's allegations of sexual abuse by medical evidence of abuse, for example, sheds no light on the reliability of the child's allegations regarding the identity of the abuser.   There is a very real danger that a jury will rely on partial corroboration to mistakenly infer the trustworthiness of the entire statement. * * *

Finally, we reject respondent's contention that the younger daughter's out-of-court statements in this case are per se unreliable, or at least presumptively unreliable, on the ground that the trial court found the younger daughter incompetent to testify at trial. First, respondent's contention rests upon a questionable reading of the record in this case. The trial court found only that the younger daughter was "not capable of communicating to the jury." App 39. Although Idaho law provides that a child witness may not testify if he "appear[s] incapable of receiving just impressions of the facts respecting which they are examined, or of relating them truly," Idaho Code § 9–202 (Supp 1989); Idaho Rule Evid 601(a), the trial court in this case made no such findings. Indeed, the more reasonable inference is that, by ruling that the statements were admissible under Idaho's residual hearsay exception, the trial court implicitly found that the younger daughter, at the time she made the statements, was capable of receiving just impressions of the facts and of relating them truly. In addition, we have in any event held that the Confrontation Clause does not erect a per se rule barring the admission of prior statements of a declarant who is unable to communicate to the jury at the time of trial. * * *

III

The trial court in this case, in ruling that the Confrontation Clause did not prohibit admission of the younger daughter's hearsay statements, relied on the following factors:

> "In this case, of course, there is physical evidence to corroborate that sexual abuse occurred. It would also seem to be the case that there is no motive to make up a story of this nature in a child of these years. We're not talking about a pubescent youth who may fantasize. The nature of the statements themselves as to sexual abuse are such that they fall outside the general believability that a child could make them up or would make them up. This is simply not the type of statement, I believe, that one would expect a child to fabricate.
>
> We come then to the identification itself. Are there any indicia of reliability as to identification? From the doctor's testimony it appears that the injuries testified to occurred at the time that the victim was in the custody of the Defendants. The [older daughter] has testified as to identification of [the] perpetrators. Those—the identification of the perpetrators in this case are persons well known to the [younger daughter]. This is not a case in which a child is called upon to identify a stranger or a person with whom they would have no knowledge of their identity or ability to recollect and recall. Those factors are sufficient indicia of reliability to permit the admission of the statements."

Of the factors the trial court found relevant, only two relate to circumstances surrounding the making of the statements: whether the child had a motive to "make up a story of this nature," and whether, given the child's age, the statements are of the type "that one would expect a child to fabricate." Ibid. The other factors on which the trial court relied, however, such as the presence of physical evidence of abuse, the opportunity of respondent to commit the offense, and the older daughter's corroborating identification, relate instead to whether other evidence existed to corroborate the truth of the statement. These factors, as we have discussed, are irrelevant to a showing of the "particularized guarantees of trustworthiness" necessary for admission of hearsay statements under the Confrontation Clause.

We think the Supreme Court of Idaho properly focused on the presumptive unreliability of the out-of-court statements and on the suggestive manner in which Dr. Jambura conducted the interview. Viewing the totality of the circumstances surrounding the younger daughter's responses to Dr. Jambura's questions, we find no special reason for supposing that the incriminating statements were particularly trustworthy. The younger daughter's last statement regarding the abuse of the older daughter, however, presents a closer question. According to Dr. Jambura, the younger daughter "volunteered" that statement "after she sort of clammed-up." Although the spontaneity of the statement and the change in demeanor suggest that the younger daughter was telling the truth when she made the statement, we note that it is possible that "[i]f there is evidence of prior interrogation, prompting, or manipulation by adults, spontaneity may be an inaccurate indicator of trustworthiness." Robinson, 153 Ariz, at 201, 735 P.2d, at 811. Moreover, the statement was not made under circumstances of reliability comparable to those required, for example, for the admission of excited utterances or statements made for purposes of medical diagnosis or treatment. Given the presumption of inadmissibility accorded accusatory hearsay statements not admitted pursuant to a firmly rooted hearsay exception, we agree with the court below that the State has failed to show that the younger daughter's incriminating statements to the pediatrician possessed sufficient "particularized guarantees of trustworthiness" under the Confrontation Clause to overcome that presumption.

The State does not challenge the Idaho Supreme Court's conclusion that the Confrontation Clause error in this case was not harmless beyond a reasonable doubt, and we see no reason to revisit the issue. We therefore agree with that court that respondent's conviction involving the younger daughter must be reversed and the case remanded for further proceedings. Accordingly, the judgment of the Supreme Court of Idaho is affirmed.

It is so ordered.

[The dissenting opinion of Justice KENNEDY, with whom THE CHIEF JUSTICE, Justice WHITE, and Justice BLACKMUN joined, has been omitted.]

CHAMBERS v. MISSISSIPPI

Supreme Court of the United States, 1973.
410 U.S. 284, 93 S.Ct. 1038, 35 L.Ed.2d 297.

Mr. Justice POWELL delivered the opinion of the Court.

Petitioner, Leon Chambers, was tried by a jury in a Mississippi trial court and convicted of murdering a policeman. The jury assessed punishment at life imprisonment, and the Mississippi Supreme Court affirmed, one justice dissenting. * * * Subsequently, the petition for certiorari was granted * * * to consider whether petitioner's trial was conducted in accord with principles of due process under the Fourteenth Amendment. We conclude that it was not.

I

The events that led to petitioner's prosecution for murder occurred in the small town of Woodville in Southern Mississippi. On Saturday evening, June 14, 1969, two Woodville policemen, James Forman and Aaron "Sonny" Liberty, entered a local bar and pool hall to execute a warrant for the arrest of a youth named C.C. Jackson. Jackson resisted and a hostile crowd of some 50 or 60 persons gathered. The officers' first attempt to handcuff Jackson was frustrated when 20 or 25 men in the crowd intervened and wrestled him free. Forman then radioed for assistance and Liberty removed his riot gun, a 12-gauge sawed-off shotgun, from the car. Three deputy sheriffs arrived shortly thereafter and the officers again attempted to make their arrest. Once more, the officers were attacked by the onlookers and during the commotion five or six pistol shots were fired. Foreman was looking in a different direction when the shooting began, but immediately saw that Liberty had been shot several times in the back. Before Liberty died, he turned around and fired both barrels of his riot gun into an alley in the area from which the shots appeared to have come. The first shot was wild and high and scattered the crowd standing at the face of the alley. Liberty appeared, however, to take more deliberate aim before the second shot and hit one of the men in the crowd in the back of the head and neck as he ran down the alley. That man was Leon Chambers.

Officer Forman could not see from his vantage point who shot Liberty or whether Liberty's shots hit anyone. One of the deputy sheriffs testified at trial that he was standing several feet from Liberty and that he saw Chambers shoot him. Another deputy sheriff stated that, although he could not see whether Chambers had a gun in his hand, he did see Chambers "break his arm down" shortly before the shots were fired. The officers who saw Chambers fall testified that they thought he was dead but they made no effort at that time either to examine him or to search for the murder weapon. Instead, they attended to Liberty, who was placed in the police car and taken to a hospital where he was declared dead on arrival. A subsequent autopsy showed that he had been hit with four bullets from a .22-caliber revolver.

Shortly after the shooting, three of Chambers' friends discovered that he was not yet dead. James Williams,[1] Berkley Turner, and Gable McDonald loaded him into a car and transported him to the same hospital. Later that night, when the county sheriff discovered that Chambers was still alive, a guard was placed outside his room. Chambers was subsequently charged with Liberty's murder. He pleaded not guilty and has asserted his innocence throughout.

The story of Leon Chambers in intertwined with the story of another man, Gable McDonald. McDonald, a lifelong resident of Woodville, was in the crowd on the evening of Liberty's death. Sometime shortly after that day, he left his wife in Woodville and moved to Louisiana and found a job at a sugar mill. In November of that same year, he returned to Woodville when his wife informed him that an acquaintance of his, known as Reverend Stokes, wanted to see him. Stokes owned a gas station in Natchez, Mississippi, several miles north of Woodville, and upon his return McDonald went to see him. After talking to Stokes, McDonald agreed to make a statement to Chambers' attorneys, who maintained offices in Natchez. Two days later, he appeared at the attorneys' offices and gave a sworn confession that he shot Officer Liberty. He also stated that he had already told a friend of his, James Williams, that he shot Liberty. He said that he used his own pistol, a nine-shot .22-caliber revolver, which he had discarded shortly after the shooting. In response to questions from Chambers' attorneys, McDonald affirmed that his confession was voluntary and that no one had compelled him to come to them. Once the confession had been transcribed, signed, and witnessed, McDonald was turned over to the local police authorities and was placed in jail.

One month later, at a preliminary hearing, McDonald repudiated his prior sworn confession. He testified that Stokes had persuaded him to confess that he shot Liberty. He claimed that Stokes had promised that he would not go to jail and that he would share in the proceeds of a lawsuit that Chambers would bring against the town of Woodville. On examination by his own attorney and on cross-examination by the State, McDonald swore that he had not been at the scene when Liberty was shot but had been down the street drinking beer in a cafe with a friend, Berkley Turner. When he and Turner heard the shooting, he testified, they walked up the street and found Chambers lying in the alley. He, Turner, and Williams took Chambers to the hospital. McDonald further testified at the preliminary hearing that he did not know what had happened, that there was no discussion about the shooting either going to or coming back from the hospital, and that it was not until the next day that he learned that Chambers had been felled by a blast from Liberty's riot gun. In addition, McDonald stated that while he once owned a .22-caliber pistol he had lost it many months before the shooting and did not own or possess a weapon at that time. The local justice of the peace accepted McDonald's repudiation

---

1. James Williams was indicted along with Chambers. The State, however, failed to introduce any evidence at trial implicating Williams in the shooting. At the conclusion of the State's case-in-chief, the trial court granted a directed verdict in his favor.

and released him from custody. The local authorities undertook no
further investigation of his possible involvement.

Chambers' case came on for trial in October of the next year.[2] At
trial, he endeavored to develop two grounds of defense. He first
attempted to show that he did not shoot Liberty. Only one officer
testified that he actually saw Chambers fire the shots. Although three
officers saw Liberty shoot Chambers and testified that they assumed he
was shooting his attacker, none of them examined Chambers to see
whether he was still alive or whether he possessed a gun. Indeed, no
weapon was ever recovered from the scene and there was no proof that
Chambers had ever owned a .22-caliber pistol. One witness testified
that he was standing in the street near where Liberty was shot, that he
was looking at Chambers when the shooting began, and that he was
sure that Chambers did not fire the shots.

Petitioner's second defense was that Gable McDonald had shot
Officer Liberty. He was only partially successful, however, in his
efforts to bring before the jury the testimony supporting this defense.
Sam Hardin, a life-long friend of McDonald's testified that he saw
McDonald shoot Liberty. A second witness, one of Liberty's cousins,
testified that he saw McDonald immediately after the shooting with a
pistol in his hand. In addition to the testimony of these two witnesses,
Chambers endeavored to show the jury that McDonald had repeatedly
confessed to the crime. Chambers attempted to prove that McDonald
had admitted responsibility for the murder on four separate occasions,
once when he gave the sworn statement to Chambers' counsel and
three other times prior to that occasion in private conversations with
friends.

In large measure, he was thwarted in his attempt to present this
portion of his defense by the strict application of certain Mississippi
rules of evidence. Chambers asserts in this Court, as he did unsuccessfully in his motion for new trial and on appeal to the State Supreme
Court, that the application of these evidentiary rules rendered his trial
fundamentally unfair and deprived him of due process of law. It is
necessary, therefore, to examine carefully the rulings made during the
trial.

II

Chambers filed a pretrial motion requesting the court to order
McDonald to appear. Chambers also sought a ruling at that time that,
if the State itself chose not to call McDonald, he be allowed to call him
as an adverse witness. Attached to the motion were copies of McDonald's sworn confession and of the transcript of his preliminary hearing
at which he repudiated that confession. The trial court granted the
motion requiring McDonald to appear but reserved ruling on the
adverse-witness motion. At trial, after the State failed to put McDon-

---

2. Upon Chambers, motion, a change of
venue was granted and the trial was held
in Amite County, to the east of Woodville.
The change of trial setting was in response
to petitioner's claim that, because of adverse publicity and the hostile attitude of
the police and sheriff's staffs in Woodville,
he could not obtain a fair and impartial
trial there.

ald on the stand, Chambers called McDonald, laid a predicate for the introduction of his sworn out-of-court confession, had it admitted into evidence, and read it to the jury. The State, upon cross-examination, elicited from McDonald the fact that he had repudiated his prior confession. McDonald further testified, as he had at the preliminary hearing, that he did not shoot Liberty, and that he confessed to the crime only on the promise of Reverend Stokes that he would not go to jail and would share in a sizable tort recovery from the town. He also retold his own story of his actions on the evening of the shooting, including his visit to the cafe down the street, his absence from the scene during the critical period, and his subsequent trip to the hospital with Chambers.

At the conclusion of the State's cross-examination, Chambers renewed his motion to examine McDonald as an adverse witness. The trial court denied the motion, stating: "He may be hostile, but he is not adverse in the sense of the word, so your request will be overruled." On appeal, the State Supreme Court upheld the trial court's ruling, finding that "McDonald's testimony was not adverse to appellant" because "[n]owhere did he point the finger at Chambers."

Defeated in his attempt to challenge directly McDonald's renunciation of his prior confession, Chambers sought to introduce the testimony of the three witnesses to whom McDonald had admitted that he shot the officer. The first of these, Sam Hardin, would have testified that, on the night of the shooting, he spent the late evening hours with McDonald at a friend's house after their return from the hospital and that, while driving McDonald home later that night, McDonald stated that he shot Liberty. The State objected to the admission of this testimony on the ground that it was hearsay. The trial court sustained the objection.[3]

Berkley Turner, the friend with whom McDonald said he was drinking beer when the shooting occurred, was then called to testify. In the jury's presence, and without objection, he testified that he had not been in the cafe that Saturday and had not had any beers with McDonald. The jury was then excused. In the absence of the jury, Turner recounted his conversations with McDonald while they were riding with James Williams to take Chambers to the hospital. When asked whether McDonald said anything regarding the shooting of Liberty, Turner testified that McDonald told him that he "shot him." Turner further stated that one week later, when he met McDonald at a friend's house, McDonald reminded him of their prior conversation and urged Turner not to "mess him up." Petitioner argued to the court that, especially where there was other proof in the case that was corroborative of these out-of-court statements, Turner's testimony as to McDonald's self-incriminating remarks should have been admitted as an exception to the hearsay rule. Again, the trial court sustained the State's objection.

3. Hardin's testimony, unlike the testimony of the other two men who stated that McDonald had confessed to them, was actually given in the jury's presence. After the State's objection to Hardin's account of McDonald's statement was sustained, the trial court ordered the jury to disregard it.

The third witness, Albert Carter, was McDonald's neighbor. They had been friends for about 25 years. Although Carter had not been in Woodville on the evening of the shooting, he stated that he learned about it the next morning from McDonald. That same day, he and McDonald walked out to a well near McDonald's house and there McDonald told him that he was the one who shot Officer Liberty. Carter testified that McDonald also told him that he had disposed of the .22-caliber revolver later that night. He further testified that several weeks after the shooting, he accompanied McDonald to Natchez where McDonald purchased another .22 pistol to replace the one he had discarded.[4] The jury was not allowed to hear Carter's testimony. Chambers urged that these statements were admissible, the State objected and the court sustained the objection.[5] On appeal, the State Supreme Court approved the lower court's exclusion of these witnesses' testimony on hearsay grounds.

In sum, then, this was Chambers' predicament. As a consequence of the combination of Mississippi's "party witness" or "voucher" rule and its hearsay rule, he was unable either to cross-examine McDonald or to present witnesses in his own behalf who would have discredited McDonald's repudiation and demonstrated his complicity. Chambers had, however, chipped away at the fringes of McDonald's story by introducing admissible testimony from other sources indicating that he had not been seen in the cafe where he said he was when the shooting started, that he had not been having beer with Turner, and that he possessed a .22 pistol at the time of the crime. But all that remained from McDonald's own testimony was a single written confession countered by an arguably acceptable renunciation. Chambers' defense was far less persuasive than it might have been had he been given an opportunity to subject McDonald's statements to cross-examination or had the other confessions been admitted.

III

The right of an accused in a criminal trial to due process is, in essence, the right to a fair opportunity to defend against the State's accusations. The rights to confront and cross-examine witnesses and to call witnesses in one's own behalf have long been recognized as essential to due process. Mr. Justice Black, writing for the Court in In re Oliver, identified these rights as among the minimum essentials of fair trial:

> "A person's right to reasonable notice of a charge against him, and an opportunity to be heard in his defense—a right to his day in court—are basic in our system of jurisprudence; and

4. A gun dealer from Natchez testified that McDonald had made two purchases. The witness' business records indicated that McDonald purchased a nine-shot .22-caliber revolver about a year prior to the murder. He purchased a different style .22 three weeks after Liberty's death.

5. It is not entirely clear whether the trial court's ruling was premised on the same hearsay rationale underlying the exclusion of the other testimony. In this instance, the State argued that Carter's testimony was an impermissible attempt by petitioner to impeach a witness (McDonald) who was not adverse to him. The trial court did not state why it was excluding the evidence but the State Supreme Court indicated that it was excluded as hearsay.

these rights include, as a minimum, a right to examine the witnesses against him, to offer testimony, and to be represented by counsel."

* * * Both of these elements of a fair trial are implicated in the present case.

A

Chambers was denied an opportunity to subject McDonald's damning repudiation and alibi to cross-examination. He was not allowed to test the witness' recollection, to probe into the details of his alibi, or to "sift" his conscience so that the jury might judge for itself whether McDonald's testimony was worthy of belief. The right of cross-examination is more than a desirable rule of trial procedure. It is implicit in the constitutional right of confrontation, and helps assure the "accuracy of the truth-determining process." It is indeed, "an essential and fundamental requirement for the kind of fair trial which is this country's constitutional goal." Of course, the right to confront and to cross-examine is not absolute and may, in appropriate cases, bow to accommodate other legitimate interests in the criminal trial process. But its denial or significant diminution calls into question the ultimate " 'integrity of the fact-finding process' " and requires that the competing interest be closely examined.

In this case, petitioner's request to cross-examine McDonald was denied on the basis of a Mississippi common-law rule that a party may not impeach his own witness. The rule rests on the presumption— without regard to the circumstances of the particular case—that a party who calls a witness "vouches for his credibility." Although the historical origins of the "voucher" rule are uncertain, it appears to be a remnant of primitive English trial practice in which "oath-takers" or "compurgators" were called to stand behind a particular party's position in any controversy. Their assertions were strictly partisan and, quite unlike witnesses in criminal trials today, their role bore little relation to the impartial ascertainment of the facts.

Whatever validity the "voucher" rule may have once enjoyed, and apart from whatever usefulness it retains today in the civil trial process, it bears little present relationship to the realities of the criminal process.[6] It might have been logical for the early common law to require a party to vouch for the credibility of witnesses he brought before the jury to affirm his veracity. Having selected them especially for that purpose, the party might reasonably be expected to stand firmly behind their testimony. But in modern criminal trials, defendants are rarely able to select their witnesses: they must take them where they find them. Moreover, as applied in this case, the "voucher" rule's[7] impact was doubly harmful to Chambers' efforts to develop his

6. The "voucher" rule has been condemned as archaic, irrational, and potentially destructive of the truth-gathering process.

7. The "voucher" rule has been rejected altogether by the newly proposed Federal Rules of Evidence, Rule 607, Rules of Evidence for United States Courts and Magistrates (approved Nov. 20, 1972, and transmitted to Congress to become effective July 1, 1973, unless the Congress otherwise determines).

defense. Not only was he precluded from cross-examining McDonald, but, as the State conceded at oral argument, he was also restricted in the scope of his direct examination by the rule's corollary requirement that the party calling the witness is bound by anything he might say. He was, therefore, effectively prevented from exploring the circumstances of McDonald's three prior oral confessions and from challenging the renunciation of the written confession.

In this Court, Mississippi has not sought to defend the rule or explain its underlying rationale. Nor has it contended that its rule should override the accused's right of confrontation. Instead, it argues that there is no incompatibility between the rule and Chambers' rights because no right of confrontation exists unless the testifying witness is "adverse" to the accused. The State's brief asserts that the "right of confrontation applies to witnesses *'against'* an accused." Relying on the trial court's determination that McDonald was not "adverse," and on the State Supreme Court's holding that McDonald did not "point the finger at Chambers," the State contends that Chambers' constitutional right was not involved.

The argument that McDonald's testimony was not "adverse" to, or "against," Chambers is not convincing. The State's proof at trial excluded the theory that more than one person participated in the shooting of Liberty. To the extent that McDonald's sworn confession tended to incriminate him, it tended also to exculpate Chambers. And, in the circumstances of this case, McDonald's retraction inculpated Chambers to the same extent that it exculpated McDonald. It can hardly be disputed that McDonald's testimony was in fact seriously adverse to Chambers. The availability of the right to confront and to cross-examine those who give damaging testimony against the accused has never been held to depend on whether the witness was initially put on the stand by the accused or by the State. We reject the notion that a right of such substance in the criminal process may be governed by that technicality or by any narrow and unrealistic definition of the word "against." The "voucher" rule, as applied in this case, plainly interfered with Chambers' right to defend against the State's charges.

B

We need not decide, however, whether this error alone would occasion reversal since Chambers' claimed denial of due process rests on the ultimate impact of that error when viewed in conjunction with the trial court's refusal to permit him to call other witnesses. The trial court refused to allow him to introduce the testimony of Hardin, Turner, and Carter. Each would have testified to the statements purportedly made by McDonald, on three separate occasions shortly after the crime, naming himself as the murderer. The State Supreme Court approved the exclusion of this evidence on the ground that it was hearsay.

The hearsay rule, which has long been recognized and respected by virtually every State, is based on experience and grounded in the notion that untrustworthy evidence should not be presented to the triers of fact. Out-of-court statements are traditionally excluded because they lack the conventional indicia of reliability: they are usually not made under oath or other circumstances that impress the speaker with the solemnity of his statements; the declarant's word is not subject to cross-examination; and he is not available in order that his demeanor and credibility may be assessed by the jury. California v. Green. A number of exceptions have developed over the years to allow admission of hearsay statements made under circumstances that tend to assure reliability and thereby compensate for the absence of the oath and opportunity for cross-examination. Among the most prevalent of these exceptions is the one applicable to declarations against interest—an exception founded on the assumption that a person is unlikely to fabricate a statement against his own interest at the time it is made. Mississippi recognizes this exception but applies it only to declarations against pecuniary interest. It recognizes no such exception for declarations, like McDonald's in this case, that are against the penal interest of the declarant.

This materialistic limitation on the declaration-against-interest hearsay exception appears to be accepted by most States in their criminal trial processes, although a number of States have discarded it. Declarations against penal interest have also been excluded in federal courts under the authority of Donnelly v. United States, although exclusion would not be required under the newly proposed Federal Rules of Evidence.[8] Exclusion, where the limitation prevails, is usually premised on the view that admission would lead to the frequent presentation of perjured testimony to the jury. It is believed that confessions of criminal activity are often motivated by extraneous considerations and, therefore, are not as inherently reliable as statements against pecuniary or proprietary interest. While that rationale has been the subject of considerable scholarly criticism, we need not decide in this case whether, under other circumstances, it might serve some valid state purpose by excluding untrustworthy testimony.

The hearsay statements involved in this case were originally made and subsequently offered at trial under circumstances that provided considerable assurance of their reliability. First, each of McDonald's confessions was made spontaneously to a close acquaintance shortly after the murder had occurred. Second, each one was corroborated by some other evidence in the case—McDonald's sworn confession, the testimony of an eyewitness to the shooting, the testimony that McDonald was seen with a gun immediately after the shooting, and proof of his prior ownership of a .22-caliber revolver and subsequent purchase of a new weapon. The sheer number of independent confessions provided additional corroboration for each. Third, whatever may be the parameters of the penal-interest rationale,[9] each confession here was in a very

---

8. Rule 804, supra, n. 9.

9. The Mississippi case which refused to adopt a hearsay exception for declarations against penal interest concerned an out-of-court declarant who purportedly stated that he had committed the murder with which his brother had been charged. The Mississippi Supreme Court believed that the declarant might have been motivated by a desire to free his brother rather than by any compulsion of guilt. The Court also noted that the declarant had fled, was unavailable for cross-examination, and might well have known at the time he made the

real sense self-incriminatory and unquestionably against interest. Mc-
Donald stood to benefit nothing by disclosing his role in the shooting to
any of his three friends and he must have been aware of the possibility
that disclosure would lead to criminal prosecution. Indeed, after telling Turner of his involvement, he subsequently urged Turner not to
"mess him up." Finally, if there was any question about the truthfulness of the extrajudicial statements, McDonald was present in the
courtroom and was under oath. He could have been cross-examined by
the State, and his demeanor and responses weighed by the jury. The
availability of McDonald significantly distinguishes this case from the
prior Mississippi precedent, Brown v. State, supra, and from the *Donnelly*-type situation, since in both cases the declarant was unavailable
at the time of trial.[10]

Few rights are more fundamental than that of an accused to
present witnesses in his own defense. In the exercise of this right, the
accused, as is required of the State, must comply with established rules
of procedure and evidence designed to assure both fairness and reliability in the ascertainment of guilt and innocence. Although perhaps no
rule of evidence has been more respected or more frequently applied in
jury trials than that applicable to the exclusion of hearsay, exceptions
tailored to allow the introduction of evidence which in fact is likely to
be trustworthy have long existed. The testimony rejected by the trial
court here bore persuasive assurances of trustworthiness and thus was
well within the basic rationale of the exception for declarations against
interest. That testimony also was critical to Chambers' defense. In
these circumstances, where constitutional rights directly affecting the
ascertainment of guilt are implicated, the hearsay rule may not be
applied mechanistically to defeat the ends of justice.

We conclude that the exclusion of this critical evidence, coupled
with the State's refusal to permit Chambers to cross-examine McDonald, denied him a trial in accord with traditional and fundamental
standards of due process. In reaching this judgment, we establish no
new principles of constitutional law. Nor does our holding signal any
diminution in the respect traditionally accorded to the States in the
establishment and implementation of their own criminal trial rules and
procedures. Rather, we hold quite simply that under the facts and

statement that he would not suffer for it.
There is, in the present case, no such basis
for doubting McDonald's statement.

10. McDonald's presence also deprives
the State's argument for retention of the
penal-interest rule of much of its force. In
claiming that "[t]o change the rule would
work a travesty on justice," the State posited the following hypothetical:

"If the rule were changed, A could be
charged with the crime; B could tell C
and D that he committed the crime; *B
could go into hiding* and at A's trial C
and D would testify as to B's admission
of guilt; A could be acquitted and B
would return to stand trial; B could then

provide several witnesses to testify as to
his whereabouts at the time of the crime.
The testimony of those witnesses along
with A's statement that he really committed the crime could result in B's acquittal. A would be barred from further
prosecution because of the protection
against double jeopardy. No one could
be convicted of perjury as A did not
testify at his first trial, B did not lie
under oath, and C and D were truthful
in their testimony."

Obviously, B's absence at trial is critical
to the success of the justice-subverting
ploy.

circumstances of this case the rulings of the trial court deprived Chambers of a fair trial.

The judgment is reversed and the case is remanded to the Supreme Court of Mississippi for further proceedings not inconsistent with this opinion.

It is so ordered.

[The concurring opinion of Justice White and the dissenting opinion of Justice Rehnquist are omitted.]

NOTE

See the excerpt from Williams, The Proof of Guilt, below. Does Chambers v. Mississippi enact the British prosecutor's ethical rule?

WILLIAMS, THE PROOF OF GUILT
209–10 (1955).*

Hearsay as Evidence for the Defense

The books on evidence do not distinguish between the rules of hearsay as applied to the evidence for the Crown and as applied to the evidence for the defense. In fact it has sometimes been ruled with great distinctness that defendants in criminal trials are subject to the same rules of evidence (including the hearsay rule) as the prosecution. Most people would say, however, that there should be a great difference between the position of the defense and that of the prosecution. A miscarriage of justice should not be risked by shutting out any evidence for the defense, even though it may be hearsay. Accordingly, Crown counsel frequently take no objection to defense evidence even when they might technically be able to do so. As Sir Herbert Stephen wrote:

> "The counsel for the prosecution ought to make it obvious, and in England he almost always does so, that his object is not to get a conviction, without qualification, but to get a conviction only if justice requires it. He therefore seldom if ever raises any objection to questions proposed to be asked in the course of the defense upon any ground except that they are a waste of time, or likely to distract the attention of the jury from the substantial issues of the case."

GREEN v. GEORGIA
Supreme Court of the United States, 1979.
442 U.S. 95, 99 S.Ct. 2150, 60 L.Ed.2d 738.

PER CURIAM.

Petitioner and Carzell Moore were indicted together for the rape and murder of Teresa Carol Allen. Moore was tried separately, was convicted of both crimes, and has been sentenced to death. Petitioner subsequently was convicted of murder, and also received a capital sentence. The Supreme Court of Georgia upheld the conviction and

* London, Stevens, 1955.

sentence, and petitioner has sought review of so much of the judgment as affirmed the capital sentence. * * *

The evidence at trial tended to show that petitioner and Moore abducted Allen from the store where she was working alone and, acting either in concert or separately, raped and murdered her. After the jury determined that petitioner was guilty of murder, a second trial was held to decide whether capital punishment would be imposed. At this second proceeding, petitioner sought to prove he was not present when Allen was killed and had not participated in her death. He attempted to introduce the testimony of Thomas Pasby, who had testified for the State at Moore's trial. According to Pasby, Moore had confided to him that he had killed Allen, shooting her twice after ordering petitioner to run an errand. The trial court refused to allow introduction of this evidence, ruling that Pasby's testimony constituted hearsay that was inadmissible under Ga.Code § 38–301 (1978).[1] The State then argued to the jury that in the absence of direct evidence as to the circumstances of the crime, it could infer that petitioner participated directly in Allen's murder from the fact that more than one bullet was fired into her body.[2]

Regardless of whether the proffered testimony comes within Georgia's hearsay rule, under the facts of this case its exclusion constituted a violation of the Due Process Clause of the Fourteenth Amendment. The excluded testimony was highly relevant to a critical issue in the punishment phase of the trial, and substantial reasons existed to assume its reliability. Moore made his statement spontaneously to a close friend. The evidence corroborating the confession was ample, and indeed sufficient to procure a conviction of Moore and a capital sentence. The statement was against interest, and there was no reason to believe that Moore had any ulterior motive in making it. Perhaps most important, the State considered the testimony sufficiently reliable to use it against Moore, and to base a sentence of death upon it.[3] In these unique circumstances, "the hearsay rule may not be applied mechanistically to defeat the ends of justice." Chambers v. Mississippi. Because the exclusion of Pasby's testimony denied petitioner a fair trial on the

---

1. Georgia recognizes an exception to the hearsay rule for declarations against pecuniary interest, but not for declarations against penal interest.

2. The District Attorney stated to the jury:

"We couldn't possibly bring any evidence other than the circumstantial evidence and the direct evidence that we had pointing to who did it, and I think it's especially significant for you to remember what Dr. Dawson said in this case. When the first shot, in his medical opinion, he stated that Miss Allen had positive blood pressure when both shots were fired but I don't know whether Carzell Moore fired the first shot and handed the gun to Roosevelt Green and he fired the second shot or whether it was vice versa or whether Roosevelt Green had the gun and fired the shot or Carzell Moore had the gun and fired the first shot or the second, but I think it can be reasonably stated that you Ladies and Gentlemen can believe that each one of them fired the shots so that they would be as equally involved and one did not exceed the other's part in the commission of this crime." Pet. for Cert. 10.

3. A confession to a crime is not considered hearsay under Georgia law when admitted against a declarant. Ga.Code § 38–414 (1978); Green v. State, 115 S.E.2d 655 (1967).

1 issue of punishment, the sentence is vacated and the case is remanded
2 for further proceedings not inconsistent with this opinion.

3   Reversed and remanded.

5   Mr. Justice REHNQUIST, dissenting.

6   The Court today takes another step toward embalming the law of
7 evidence in the Due Process Clause of the Fourteenth Amendment to
8 the United States Constitution. I think it impossible to find any
9 justification in the Constitution for today's ruling, and take comfort
10 only from the fact that since this is a capital case, it is perhaps an
11 example of the maxim that "hard cases make bad law."

12   * * *

13   * * * No practicing lawyer can have failed to note that Georgia's
14 evidentiary rules, like those of every other State and of the United
15 States, are such that certain items of evidence may be introduced by
16 one party, but not by another.

Chapter IV

A RETURN TO RELEVANCE

PART A. PROBABILISTIC EVIDENCE

PEOPLE v. COLLINS

Supreme Court of California, 1968.
68 Cal.2d 319, 66 Cal.Rptr. 497, 438 P.2d 33.
[Most footnotes omitted.]

SULLIVAN, Justice. We deal here with the novel question whether evidence of mathematical probability has been properly introduced and used by the prosecution in a criminal case. While we discern no inherent incompatibility between the disciplines of law and mathematics and intend no general disapproval or disparagement of the latter as an auxiliary in the fact-finding processes of the former, we cannot uphold the technique employed in the instant case. As we explain in detail infra, the testimony as to mathematical probability infected the case with fatal error and distorted the jury's traditional role of determining guilt or innocence according to long-settled rules. Mathematics, a veritable sorcerer in our computerized society, while assisting the trier of fact in the search for truth, must not cast a spell over him. We conclude that on the record before us defendant should not have had his guilt determined by the odds and that he is entitled to a new trial. We reverse the judgment.

A jury found defendant Malcolm Ricardo Collins and his wife defendant Janet Louise Collins guilty of second degree robbery (Pen. Code, §§ 211, 211a, 1157). Malcolm appeals from the judgment of conviction. Janet has not appealed.[1] * * *

At the seven-day trial the prosecution experienced some difficulty in establishing the identities of the perpetrators of the crime. The victim could not identify Janet and had never seen defendant. The identification by the witness Bass, who observed the girl run out of the alley and get into the automobile, was incomplete as to Janet and may have been weakened as to defendant. There was also evidence, introduced by the defense, that Janet had worn light-colored clothing on the day in question, but both the victim and Bass testified that the girl they observed had worn dark clothing.

In an apparent attempt to bolster the identifications, the prosecutor called an instructor of mathematics at a state college. Through this witness he sought to establish that, assuming the robbery was committed by a Caucasian woman with a blond ponytail who left the scene

1. Hereafter, the term "defendant" is intended to apply only to Malcolm, but the term "defendants" to Malcolm and Janet.

accompanied by a Negro with a beard and mustache, there was an overwhelming probability that the crime was committed by any couple answering such distinctive characteristics. The witness testified, in substance, to the "product rule," which states that the probability of the joint occurrence of a number of *mutually independent* events is equal to the product of the individual probabilities that each of the events will occur. *Without presenting any statistical evidence whatsoever in support of the probabilities for the factors selected,* the prosecutor then proceeded to have the witness *assume* probability factors for the various characteristics which he deemed to be shared by the guilty couple and all other couples answering to such distinctive characteristics.[2]

Applying the product rule to his own factors the prosecutor arrived at a probability that there was but one chance in 12 million that any couple possessed the distinctive characteristics of the defendants. Accordingly, under this theory, it was to be inferred that there could be but one chance in 12 million that defendants were innocent and that another equally distinctive couple actually committed the robbery. Expanding on what he had thus purported to suggest as a hypothesis, the prosecutor offered the completely unfounded and improper testimonial assertion that, in his opinion, the factors he had assigned were "conservative estimates" and that, in reality "the chances of anyone else besides these defendants being there, * * * having every similarity, * * * is somewhat like one in a billion."

Objections were timely made to the mathematician's testimony on the grounds that it was immaterial, that it invaded the province of the jury, and that it was based on unfounded assumptions. The objections were "temporarily overruled" and the evidence admitted subject to a motion to strike. When that motion was made at the conclusion of the direct examination, the court denied it, stating that the testimony had been received only for the "purpose of illustrating the mathematical probabilities of various matters, the possibilities for them occurring or re-occurring." * * *

---

2. Although the prosecutor insisted that the factors he used were only for illustrative purposes—to demonstrate how the probability of the occurrence of mutually independent factors affected the probability that they would occur together—he nevertheless attempted to use factors which he personally related to the distinctive characteristics of defendants. In his argument to the jury he invited the jurors to apply their own factors, and asked defense counsel to suggest what the latter would deem as reasonable. The prosecutor himself proposed the individual probabilities set out in the table below. Although the transcript of the examination of the mathematics instructor and the information volunteered by the prosecutor at that time create some uncertainty as to precisely which of the characteristics the prosecutor assigned to the individual probabilities, he restated in his argument to the jury that they should be as follows:

Characteristics	Individual Probability
A. Partly yellow automobile	1/10
B. Man with mustache	1/4
C. Girl with ponytail	1/10
D. Girl with blond hair	1/3
E. Negro man with beard	1/10
F. Interracial couple in car	1/1000

In his brief on appeal defendant agrees that the foregoing appeared on a table presented in the trial court.

As we shall explain, the prosecution's introduction and use of mathematical probability statistics injected two fundamental prejudicial errors into the case: (1) The testimony itself lacked an adequate foundation both in evidence and in statistical theory; and (2) the testimony and the manner in which the prosecution used it distracted the jury from its proper and requisite function of weighing the evidence on the issue of guilt, encouraged the jurors to rely upon an engaging but logically irrelevant expert demonstration, foreclosed the possibility of an effective defense by an attorney apparently unschooled in mathematical refinements, and placed the jurors and defense counsel at a disadvantage in sifting relevant fact from inapplicable theory.

We initially consider the defects in the testimony itself. As we have indicated, the specific technique presented through the mathematician's testimony and advanced by the prosecutor to measure the probabilities in question suffered from two basic and pervasive defects—an inadequate evidentiary foundation and an inadequate proof of statistical independence. First, as to the foundation requirement, we find the record devoid of any evidence relating to any of the six individual probability factors used by the prosecutor and ascribed by him to the six characteristics as we have set them out in footnote 10, ante. To put it another way, the prosecution produced no evidence whatsoever showing, or from which it could be in any way inferred, that only one out of every ten cars which might have been at the scene of the robbery was partly yellow, that only one out of every four men who might have been there wore a mustache, that only one out of every ten girls who might have been there wore a ponytail, or that any of the other individual probability factors listed were even roughly accurate.[3]

The bare, inescapable fact is that the prosecution made no attempt to offer any such evidence. Instead, through leading questions having perfunctorily elicited from the witness the response that the latter could not assign a probability factor for the characteristics involved,[4] the prosecutor himself suggested what the various probabilities should be and these became the basis of the witness' testimony (see fn. 10, ante). It is a curious circumstance of this adventure in proof that the prosecutor not only made his own assertions of these factors in the hope that they were "conservative" but also in later argument to the jury invited the jurors to substitute their "estimates" should they wish to do so. We can hardly conceive of a more fatal gap in the prosecution's scheme of proof. A foundation for the admissibility of the witness'

3. We seriously doubt that such evidence could ever be compiled since no statistician could possibly determine after the fact which cars, or which individuals "might" have been present at the scene of the robbery; certainly there is no reason to suppose that the human and automotive populations of San Pedro, California, include all potential culprits—or, conversely, that all members of these populations are proper candidates for inclusion. Thus the sample from which the relevant probabilities would have to be derived is itself undeterminable.

4. The prosecutor asked the mathematics instructor: "Now, let me see if you can be of some help to us with some independent factors, and you have some paper you may use. Your specialty does not equip you, I suppose, to give us some probability of such things as a yellow car as contrasted with any other kind of car, does it? * * * I appreciate the fact that you can't assign a probability for a car being yellow as contrasted to some other car, can you? A. No, I couldn't."

testimony was never even attempted to be laid, let alone established. His testimony was neither made to rest on his own testimonial knowledge nor presented by proper hypothetical questions based upon valid data in the record. In State v. Sneed, the court reversed a conviction based on probabilistic evidence, stating: "We hold that mathematical odds are not admissible as evidence to identify a defendant in a criminal proceeding *so long as the odds are based on estimates, the validity of which have [sic] not been demonstrated.*"

But, as we have indicated, there was another glaring defect in the prosecution's technique, namely an inadequate proof of the statistical independence of the six factors. No proof was presented that the characteristics selected were mutually independent, even though the witness himself acknowledged that such condition was essential to the proper application of the "product rule" or "multiplication rule."[5] To the extent that the traits or characteristics were not mutually independent (e.g. Negroes with beards and men with mustaches obviously represent overlapping categories[6]), the "product rule" would inevitably yield a wholly erroneous and exaggerated result even if all of the individual components had been determined with precision.

In the instant case, therefore, because of the aforementioned two defects—the inadequate evidentiary foundation and the inadequate proof of statistical independence—the technique employed by the prosecutor could only lead to wild conjecture without demonstrated relevancy to the issues presented. It acquired no redeeming quality from the prosecutor's statement that it was being used "for illustrative purposes" since, as we shall point out, the prosecutor's subsequent utilization of the mathematical testimony was not confined within such limits.

We now turn to the second fundamental error caused by the probability testimony. Quite apart from our foregoing objections to the specific technique employed by the prosecution to estimate the probability in question, we think that the entire enterprise upon which the prosecution embarked, and which was directed to the objective of measuring the likelihood of a random couple possessing the characteristics allegedly distinguishing the robbers, was gravely misguided. At best, it might yield an estimate as to how infrequently bearded Negroes drive yellow cars in the company of blond females with ponytails.

The prosecution's approach, however, could furnish the jury with absolutely no guidance on the crucial issue: *Of the admittedly few such*

5. It is stated that: "A trait is said to be independent of a second trait when the occurrence or non-occurrence of one does not affect the probability of the occurrence of the other trait. The multiplication rule cannot be used without some degree of error where the traits are not independent."

6. Assuming *arguendo* that factors B and E (see fn. 10, ante), were correctly estimated, nevertheless it is still arguable that most Negro men with beards *also* have mustaches (exhibit 3 herein, for instance, shows defendant with both a mustache and a beard, indeed in a hirsute continuum); if so, there is no basis for multiplying ¼ by ¹⁄₁₀ to estimate the proportion of Negroes who wear beards *and* mustaches. Again, the prosecution's technique could *never* be meaningfully applied, since its accurate use would call for information as to the degree of interdependence among the six individual factors. (See Yamane, op. cit. supra.) Such information cannot be compiled, however, since the relevant sample necessarily remains unknown. (See fn. 10, ante.)

couples, which one, if any, was guilty of committing this robbery? 1
Probability theory necessarily remains silent on that question, since no 2
mathematical equation can prove beyond a reasonable doubt (1) that 3
the guilty couple *in fact* possessed the characteristics described by the 4
People's witnesses, or even (2) that only *one* couple possessing those 5
distinctive characteristics could be found in the entire Los Angeles 6
area. 7

As to the first inherent failing we observe that the prosecution's 8
theory of probability rested on the assumption that the witnesses called 9
by the People had conclusively established that the guilty couple 10
possessed the precise characteristics relied upon by the prosecution. 11
But no mathematical formula could ever establish beyond a reasonable 12
doubt that the prosecution's witnesses correctly observed and accurate- 13
ly described the distinctive features which were employed to link 14
defendants to the crime. Conceivably, for example, the guilty couple 15
might have included a light-skinned Negress with bleached hair rather 16
than a Caucasian blond; or the driver of the car might have been 17
wearing a false beard as a disguise; or the prosecution's witnesses 18
might simply have been unreliable.[7] 19
20

The foregoing risks of error permeate the prosecution's circumstan- 21
tial case. Traditionally, the jury weighs such risks in evaluating the 22
credibility and probative value of trial testimony, but the likelihood of 23
human error or of falsification obviously cannot be quantified; that 24
likelihood must therefore be excluded from any effort to assign a 25
number to the probability of guilt or innocence. Confronted with an 26
equation which purports to yield a numerical index of probable guilt, 27
few juries could resist the temptation to accord disproportionate weight 28
to that index; only an exceptional juror, and indeed only a defense 29
attorney schooled in mathematics, could successfully keep in mind the 30
fact that the probability computed by the prosecution can represent, *at* 31
best, the likelihood that a random couple would share the characteris- 32
tics testified to by the People's witnesses—*not necessarily the character-* 33
istics of the actually guilty couple. 34
35

As to the second inherent failing in the prosecution's approach, 36
even assuming that the first failing could be discounted, the most a 37
mathematical computation could *ever* yield would be a measure of the 38
probability that a random couple would possess the distinctive features 39
in question. In the present case, for example, the prosecution at- 40
tempted to compute the probability that a random couple would include 41
a bearded Negro, a blond girl with a ponytail, and a partly yellow car; 42
the prosecution urged that this probability was no more than one in 12 43
million. Even accepting this conclusion as arithmetically accurate, 44
however, one still could not conclude that the Collinses were probably 45
the guilty couple. On the contrary, as we explain in the Appendix, the 46

7. In the instant case, for instance, the 47
victim could not state whether the girl had 48
a ponytail, although the victim observed 49
the girl as she ran away. The witness 50
Bass, on the other hand, was sure that the 51
girl whom he saw had a ponytail. The demonstration engaged in by the prosecutor also leaves no room for the possibility,
although perhaps a small one, that the girl
whom the victim and the witness observed
was, in fact, the same girl.

prosecution's figures actually implied a likelihood of over 40 percent that the Collinses could be "duplicated" by at least *one other couple who might equally have committed the San Pedro robbery*. Urging that the Collinses be convicted on the basis of evidence which logically establishes no more than this seems as indefensible as arguing for the conviction of X on the ground that a witness saw either X or X's twin commit the crime.

Again, few defense attorneys, and certainly few jurors, could be expected to comprehend this basic flaw in the prosecution's analysis. Conceivably even the prosecutor erroneously believed that his equation established a high probability that *no* other bearded Negro in the Los Angeles area drove a yellow car accompanied by a ponytailed blond. In any event, although his technique could demonstrate no such thing, he solemnly told the jury that he had supplied mathematical proof of guilt.

Sensing the novelty of that notion, the prosecutor told the jurors that the traditional idea of proof beyond a reasonable doubt represented "the most hackneyed, stereotyped, trite, misunderstood concept in criminal law." He sought to reconcile the jury to the risk that, under his "new math" approach to criminal jurisprudence, "on some rare occasion * * * an innocent person may be convicted." "Without taking that risk," the prosecution continued, "life would be intolerable * * * because * * * there would be immunity for the Collinses, for people who chose not to be employed to go down and push old ladies down and take their money and be immune because how could we ever be sure they are the ones who did it?"

In essence this argument of the prosecutor was calculated to persuade the jury to convict defendants whether or not they were convinced of their guilt to a moral certainty and beyond a reasonable doubt. (Pen.Code, § 1096.) Undoubtedly the jurors were unduly impressed by the mystique of the mathematical demonstration but were unable to assess its relevancy or value. Although we make no appraisal of the proper applications of mathematical techniques in the proof of facts, we have strong feelings that such applications, particularly in a criminal case, must be critically examined in view of the substantial unfairness to the defendant which may result from ill conceived techniques with which the trier of fact is not technically equipped to cope. We feel that the technique employed in the case before us falls into the latter category.

We conclude that the court erred in admitting over defendant's objection the evidence pertaining to the mathematical theory of probability and in denying defendant's motion to strike such evidence. * * *

The judgment is reversed.

TRAYNOR, C.J., and PETERS, TOBRINER, MOSK and BURKE, JJ., concur.

McCOMB, Justice. I dissent. I would affirm the judgment in its entirety.

APPENDIX

If "Pr" represents the probability that a certain distinctive combination of characteristics, hereinafter designated "C," will occur jointly in a random couple, then the probability that C will *not* occur in a random couple is (1–Pr). Applying the product rule (see fn. 8, ante), the probability that C will occur in *none* of N couples chosen at random is $(1-Pr)^N$, so that the probability of C occurring in *at least one* of N random couples is $[1-(1-Pr)^N]$.

Given a particular couple selected from a random set of N, the probability of C occurring in that couple (i.e., Pr), multiplied by the probability of C occurring in none of the remaining N–1 couples (i.e., $(1-Pr)^{N-1}$), yields the probability that C will occur in the selected couple and in no other. Thus the probability of C occurring in any particular couple, and in that couple alone, is $[(Pr) \times (1-Pr)^{N-1}]$. Since this is true for each of the N couples, the probability that C will occur in precisely *one* of the N couples, without regard to which one, is $[(Pr) \times (1-Pr)^{N-1}]$ added N times, because the probability of the occurrence of one of several *mutually exclusive* events is equal to the *sum* of the individual probabilities. Thus the probability of C occurring in *exactly one* of N random couples (*any* one, but *only* one) is $[(N) \times (Pr) \times (1-Pr)^{N-1}]$.

By subtracting the probability that C will occur in *exactly one* couple from the probability that C will occur in *at least one* couple, one obtains the probability that C will occur in *more than one* couple: $[1-(1-Pr)^N-(N) \times (Pr) \times (1-Pr)^{N-1}]$. Dividing this difference by the probability that C will occur in at least one couple (i.e., dividing the difference by $[1-(1-Pr)^N]$) then yields *the probability that C will occur more than once in a group of N couples in which C occurs at least once.*

Turning to the case in which C represents the characteristics which distinguish a bearded Negro accompanied by a ponytailed blond in a yellow car, the prosecution sought to establish that the probability of C occurring in a random couple was 1/12,000,000—i.e., that Pr = 1/12,000,000. Treating this conclusion as accurate, it follows that, in a population of N random couples, the probability of C occurring *exactly once* is $[(N) \times (1/12,000,000) \times (1-1/12,000,000)^{N-1}]$. Subtracting this product from $[1-(1-1/12,000,000)^N]$, the probability of C occurring in *at least one* couple, and dividing the resulting difference by $[1-(1-1/12,000,000)^N]$, the probability that C will occur in at least one couple, yields the probability that C will occur more than once in a group of N random couples of which at least one couple (namely, the one seen by the witnesses) possesses characteristics C. In other words, the probability of *another* such couple in a population of N is the quotient A/B, where A designates the numerator $[1-(1-1/12,000,000)^N]-[(N) \times 1/12,000,000 \times (1-1/12,000,000)^{N-1}]$, and B designates the denominator $[1-(1-1/12,000,000)^N]$.

N which represents the total number of all couples who might conceivably have been at the scene of the San Pedro robbery, is not determinable, a fact which suggests yet another basic difficulty with the use of probability theory in establishing identity.   One of the imponderables in determining N may well be the number of N-type couples in which a single person may participate.   Such considerations make it evident that N, in the area adjoining the robbery, is in excess of several million; as N assumes values of such magnitude, the quotient A/B computed as above, representing the probability of a second couple as distinctive as the one described by the prosecution's witnesses, soon exceeds 4/10.   Indeed, as N approaches 12 million, this probability quotient rises to approximately 41 percent.   We note parenthetically that if $1/N = Pr$, then as N increases indefinitely, the quotient in question approaches a limit of $(e-2)/(e-1)$, where "e" represents the transcendental number (approximately 2.71828) familiar in mathematics and physics.

Hence, even if we should accept the prosecution's figures without question, we would derive a probability of over 40 percent that the couple observed by the witnesses could be "duplicated" by at least one other equally distinctive interracial couple in the area, including a Negro with a beard and mustache, driving a partly yellow car in the company of a blond with a ponytail.   Thus the prosecution's computations, far from establishing beyond a reasonable doubt that the Collinses were the couple described by the prosecution's witnesses, imply a very substantial likelihood that the area contained *more than one* such couple, and that a couple *other* than the Collinses was the one observed at the scene of the robbery.

NOTE

Even before People v. Collins, evidence scholars had taken an interest in the application of probability theory to courtroom situations. See, e.g., Kaplan, Decision Theory and the Factfinding Process, 20 Stan.L.Rev. 1065 (1968). The Collins case augmented this interest. It inspired an article, Finkelstein & Fairley, A Bayesian Approach to Identification Evidence, 83 Harv.L.Rev. 489 (1970), that argued that while Collins was correct on its facts, experts might in other cases properly use probability theory, in particular Bayes' theorem, to aid the jury in making identification decisions. The authors suggested a hypothetical case in which the defendant is accused of murdering his girlfriend. A partial palmprint was found on the knife that was used in the murder. It matches the defendant's palm. But it would also match the palm of one in a thousand people chosen at random, which means that in a metropolitan area hundreds of people would have the same palmprint characteristics. How is the jury to use that one in a thousand figure? Bayes' theorem, which provides a way of determining how an evaluation of probability based upon initial evidence should be modified in light of additional evidence, could be used to guide the jury. If the trier of fact believed that the prior probability of defendant's guilt was 25% (before taking the palmprint into account) then Bayes' theorem tells us that trier should believe that the posterior probability of guilt (after taking the palmprint into account) is 99.9%. The method often yields higher probabilities than intuition would yield. For example, if the prior probability is 25% and the palmprint is one in a hundred, then the posterior probability of guilt is 97%.

The proposition that the jury should be instructed about Bayes' theorem attracted the attention of a talented and resourceful debater, Laurence Tribe,

then an assistant professor at the Harvard Law School. See Tribe, Trial by
Mathematics: Precision and Ritual in the Legal Process, 84 Harv.L.Rev. 1329
(1971). Tribe pointed out a host of problems. It would be difficult to get jurors
who are unused to formal probabilities to arrive at a consistent understanding
of what they are supposed to do in formulating a prior probability. There is
also a danger of "dwarfing soft variables"; that is, issues that cannot be
quantified might be overlooked as the jury became mesmerized with those that
could. Moreover, uncertainty about predicate facts can require the jury to
make so many quantification decisions about so many issues that use of the
theorem would be more confusing than helpful.

Although Tribe's view seems to have carried the day with regard to the use
of Bayes' theorem in instructing the jury, the debate did stimulate interest in
Bayes' theorem and probability theory. It has spawned a considerable body of
"new evidence scholarship" that explores how probability theory might be used
as a means of proof or as a way to help scholars model and evaluate trial
processes—or even, as the following material indicates, to prove identity.

LEMPERT, THE NEW EVIDENCE SCHOLARSHIP: ANALYZING THE PROCESS OF PROOF *

The article which triggered widespread interest in the applicability
of Bayesian reasoning to trial processes—and arguably still accounts for
residual passion—was the comment of Finklestein and Fairley on
People v. Collins, in which they argued that the real problem in that
case lay not in the prosecutor's attempt to use statistical reasoning but
in his failure to offer the jury statistical information in the form best
suited to its decision-making task—i.e., Bayes's Theorem. Professor
Laurence Tribe, in his justly celebrated article *Trial by Mathematics,*
took issue with Finklestein and Fairley on both counts.

Among legal academics it is generally agreed that Tribe won this
particular debate. As Professor Allen writes in his contribution to this
volume, "It is becoming increasingly obvious, for example, that Bayesian approaches can best be used heuristically as guides to rational
thought and not as specific blueprints for forensic decisionmaking."
This conclusion, is however, premature. Statistical evidence has fig-
ured in litigation for more than a century, and in recent years has
become increasingly common and complex. For example, a recent
LEXIS search of statistical terms done for the National Research
Council reports:

> A search of published opinions in federal courts with a comput-
> er-based legal information retrieval system reveals the dramat-
> ic growth since 1960 in cases involving some form of statistical
> evidence. Between January 1960 and September 1979 the
> terms 'statistic(s)' or 'statistical' appeared in about 3,000 or 4%
> of 83,769 reported District Court opinions. In the Courts of
> Appeals, the same terms appeared in 1,671 reported opinions.

These uses include not only statistical descriptions of samples and
populations, but also uses of the kind Finklestein and Fairley pro-

* From P. Tillers & E. Green (eds.),
Probability and Inference in the Law of
Evidence, The Uses and Limits of Baye-
sianism 61, 62–63 (1988). Copyright 1988,
Kluwer Academic Publishers.

posed—as identification evidence.[9] With both sorts of uses problems arise because juries are presented with frequentist statistics in situations where Bayesian approaches may be more appropriate to the task at hand.

I shall not dwell on this issue except to make one point. Many participants in [this] symposium paint with a broad brush in rejecting any place for Bayesian models in trial processes. Often their arguments, or portions of their arguments, read as if statistical evidence has no place at all in trials. Those who criticize Bayesian models of the legal process and the suggested application of Bayesian approaches at trial must confront the reality that statistical evidence is offered in trials every day.

I do not mean to argue that this reality cannot be accommodated by critics of Bayesian models or proposed applications. It is not difficult to imagine a place for statistical evidence in a theory that focuses, as do most non-Bayesian theories of rational proof, on the relative weight of conflicting evidence, the plausible generalizations that trial evidence allows, or the coherence of evidence with some larger plausible story. More difficult challenges for those who reject the Bayesian perspective are to explain why, if statistical evidence is presented at trials, frequentist approaches should be preferred to Bayesian ones, and to reevaluate arguments used to reject Bayesian approaches to proof where they do not accommodate the reality of the regular use of statistical evidence. Thus, arguments from the intuition that the law will not allow verdicts to rest on naked statistical evidence must accommodate or condemn a world in which the only admissible evidence of discrimination is embodied in a statistical model, or where the only admissible evidence linking the defendant to a crime is a hair match. If the answer is, as it appears implicitly to be in the case of fingerprint evidence, that the statistical probabilities are sufficiently high as to be unproblematic, an explanation is required of why one level of irreducible and undeniable uncertainty is tolerable and another is not.

KAMMER v. YOUNG

Court of Special Appeals of Maryland, 1988.
73 Md.App. 565, 535 A.2d 936.

BISHOP, Judge.

A Baltimore City jury found appellant, Thomas Robert Kammer, to be the father of the child of Christine J. Young, appellee. From the decree of the circuit court based on this verdict, Kammer appeals.

* * *

FACTS

Appellee gave birth to a child on May 24, 1982. She alleged that appellant was the only man with whom she had had sexual intercourse

9. Examples include efforts to identify the accused as the criminal through blood traces or hair samples. * * * Other kinds of identification evidence like finger-prints also depend on statistical inferences but the reliability of these tests is thought to be so high that their statistical base may be neglected.

in the year immediately preceding the child's birth. Appellant responded that his sexual relations with appellee had ended more than 15 months before the birth.

The court admitted into evidence, over objection, the results of the blood tests of appellant, appellee and the child, obtained in accordance with MD.FAM.LAW CODE ANN. Section 5–1029. Additional facts will be given in the course of the discussion of the issues.

I.

Admissibility of Blood Test Evidence

(a)

Admission of Opinion Evidence Concerning the Interpretation of the Blood Tests

In his attack on the admissibility of the interpretation of the blood tests, appellant claims that:

(1) the expert witnesses appellee called at trial were not qualified to perform statistical analysis, to interpret the results or to express an opinion on the ultimate issue of the "statistical probability" of the appellant's paternity; and

(2) the number presented to the jury was predicated upon a scientifically invalid formula and was not a competent "statistical probability of paternity" thereby rendering the laboratory report inadmissible at trial.

Appellant also asks that we reconsider our decision in Haines v. Shanholtz, 57 Md.App. 92, 468 A.2d 1365, cert. denied 300 Md. 90, 475 A.2d 1201 (1984), in which we held that by virtue of legislative enactment, blood test results which meet certain threshold requirements are admissible. We decline to do so.

This controversy is governed by § 5–1029 of the MD.FAM.LAW CODE ANN. (1984) which provides in pertinent part:

5–1029. **Blood tests.**

(a) *In general.*—On the motion of a party to the proceeding or on its own motion, the court shall order the mother, child, and alleged father to submit to blood tests to determine whether the alleged father can be excluded as being the father of the child.

(b) *Approved laboratory required.*—The blood tests shall be made in a laboratory selected by the court from a list of laboratories provided by the Administration.

(c) *Form of results.*—The laboratory shall report the results of each blood test in writing and in the form the court requires.

(d) *Copies of results.* A copy of the results of each blood test shall be provided to the parties or their counsel in the manner that the court directs.

(handwritten margin note: Blood Tests use as evidence when—)

(e) *Results as evidence.*—(1) The results of each blood test shall be received in evidence if:

(i) definite exclusion is established; or

(ii) the testing is sufficiently extensive to exclude 97.3% of alleged fathers who are not biological fathers, and the statistical probability of the alleged father's paternity is at least 97.3%.

(2) A laboratory report is prima facie evidence of the results of a blood test.

(3) If a laboratory report is admitted in evidence, the laboratory technician who made the test is subject to cross-examination by any party to the proceeding.

We begin our analysis of the applicability of this section to the appellant's claims by setting out the following facts which are undisputed by the parties:

(handwritten margin note: Facts of specific case)

(1) Appellee's witnesses are employed by an approved blood testing laboratory and are qualified in the field of paternity testing, but are not trained statisticians. Appellant's witness is a trained statistician and although he is not employed by a blood testing laboratory he does consult, as part of his employment, with the paternity testing laboratory at Johns Hopkins Hospital.

(2) The blood tests were performed by an approved laboratory and the testing was done for blood group markers in seven different systems, six in the red cell laboratory and for HLA [2] in the white cell laboratory.

(3) The combination of the HLA and red cell tests is sufficiently extensive to exclude more than "97.3% of alleged fathers who are not biological fathers".

(4) The "paternity index" [3] in this case is 460 to 1, i.e. it is 460 times more likely that appellant could produce the single sperm carrying the necessary genetic information than a random man in the population.

(5) The prior probability [4] used by the laboratory in converting the paternity index to a percentage was .5, and that number is the standard used for such tests.

(6) Using a prior probability of .5, the percentage which results from application of Bayes' Theorem [5] to the paternity index of 460 to 1 is 99.78%.

---

2. HLA is the abbreviation for human leucocyte antigen.

3. A paternity index is a ratio which expresses the odds that the accused is the father of the child based on his chance of producing a sperm that carries all the necessary genetic information in conjunction with the mother's genetic information as compared to finding such a sperm in the random population.

4. Prior probability is expressed as a number, in the form of a percentage, which represents the accumulated non-genetic evidence that tends to indicate the accused man's paternity.

5. Bayes' Theorem is a mathematical technique accepted in the blood testing field for calculating conditional probabilities. See Ellman and Kaye, Probabilities and Proof: Can HLA and Blood Group Testing Prove Paternity? 54 N.Y.U.L.Rev. 1131, 1149 (1979).

[The court's discussion of the qualification of witnesses and the adequacy of the laboratory procedure has been omitted.]

(b)

Admission of the Blood Test as a Violation of Due Process

Appellant contends that even if appellee properly complied with the blood test statute, the admission of any opinion evidence concerning the father's alleged "statistical probability" of paternity violates the due process provisions of the United States and Maryland Constitutions. He also claims that apart from the due process violation, the introduction of statistical and mathematical evidence on the ultimate issue before the jury effectively deprived him of a fair and impartial trial by jury as guaranteed by Article 23 of the Maryland Declaration of Rights.

Appellant's due process challenge is actually a two-pronged attack. He asks whether: (1) due process of law permits a paternity index to be converted to a statistical probability of paternity through the use of Bayes' Theorem with an assigned prior probability; and (2) the limited reference population used in this case[12] can be used to compute the "paternity index" used in the equation.

Once appellant's paternity index has been calculated, it must then be converted to a statistical probability in order to determine whether it meets the 97.3% benchmark for admissibility set forth in § 5–1029(e)(1)(ii). The mathematical equation used in making this transformation is Bayes' Theorem, a basic formula of probability theory. It is expressed as follows:

$$P(F/M) = \frac{1}{(1-f) + (f/P(F))}$$

where

$$f = \frac{P(M/not-F)}{P(M/F)}$$

In this formula, P(F) represents the prior probability and it is factored into the equation in order to account for the non-genetic evidence of the accused man's paternity.

Ideally, the prior probability should reflect an assessment of all the relevant non-genetic evidence in each individual case and should take into consideration such factors as the accused man's opportunity for access to the child's mother during the period of conception, the evidence linking the child's mother to other men during that time period and the credibility of the witnesses. In the case *sub judice*, however, an assumed prior probability of fifty percent (.5) was used in converting appellant's paternity index to a statistical probability. He contends that this was a violation of his due process rights. We disagree.

Appellant claims that the methodology employed by all of appellee's experts assumes a fact not in evidence (the prior probability) and it is therefore scientifically inaccurate and invalid. We disagree. The

---

12. Appellant's blood markers were compared against a gene frequency chart which shows how often his specific gene pattern arose in the United States in tests of 12,000 persons of his same race.

evidence presented at trial makes plain that within the relevant community of blood testers, the paternity probability calculations in the
present case were based upon scientific methods, accepted world-wide,
which incorporate both Bayes' Theorem and the .5 prior probability.[14]
All of the experts who testified at trial agreed that the paternity index,
representing only the purely genetic evidence (the HLA and the red cell
tests), was 460 to 1. Furthermore, using Bayes' Theorem and a prior
probability of .5, all of the experts (including appellant's expert Dr.
Chase) calculated the same probability percentage of 99.78%. The
mathematical basis for the .5 figure was explained by Dr. Chase in the
following manner:

> If you know nothing about a set of possibilities then the
> principle of insufficient reason says you are entitled to assign
> equal prior probability to those alternatives. [T]hat's what's
> used to get this .5. This .5 comes from a principle that says we
> don't know whether he was the father or somebody else was
> the father. So we are going to split the probability fifty-fifty
> between the two possibilities. We are going to load him with
> 50 percent of it and give the other percent to all the other men.

When calculating a statistical probability of paternity, the blood
testing laboratory does not have before it any of the individualized non-
genetic evidence, and it therefore uses a standard figure (.5) whenever
it makes its calculations. This fact neither renders the methodology
"scientifically invalid" nor does it deny appellant an opportunity to
present the non-genetic evidence. If the laboratory's calculations meet
the prerequisites for admissibility set forth in § 5–1029(e)(1)(ii) the
blood test evidence is admitted, but it is neither conclusive nor does it
create a presumption, it is merely one piece of evidence that is put
before the jury. Appellant was free to, and in fact did, put on non-
genetic evidence which not only disputed generally his paternity but, in
effect, was an attack upon the use of the .5 prior probability figure.
This allowed him an opportunity to counterbalance appellee's introduction of the blood test results and the prior probability on which they
were based and served to protect his due process rights.

[The court also rejected appellant's arguments that the reference
population was insufficient.]

Judgment affirmed; costs to be paid by the appellant.

1,000,000,000,000,000,000,000,000,000,000 TO 1

ODDS TRIP UP PAIR IN NEW YORK RACE BET CASE *

MINEOLA, L.I. A Queens woman and a Baldwin, L.I., man have
been convicted in an unusual case over disputed claims to a winning
parimutuel ticket worth $5,050.

14. Because the use of the .5 as a basis
for prior probability meets the requirement of general acceptance in the relevant
community, it satisfies the test for admission of scientific evidence set out in Frye v.
United States, 293 F. 1013 (D.C.Cir.1923)
and adopted by the Court of Appeals in
Reed v. State, 283 Md. 374, 391 A.2d 364
(1978).

Key elements in the Nassau County Court trial were a Belmont Park racetrack computer printout of more than 350 bets made at a particular betting window on the day in question, and a Hofstra University mathematics professor's testimony that the odds against two different people independently choosing the same combination of nine $2 bets in nine races on the same day were a decillion to one.

The jury trial stemmed from a complaint to racetrack security personnel and later to the Nassau County Police and district attorney's office by a Brooklyn nurse, Rose Grant. She said she had been cheated out of her winning ticket on the track's ninth-race triple bet for May 21, 1974.

The triple is a high-return betting arrangement in which the bettor must pick the first, second and third-place finishers in exact order. At other tracks it is known as the trifecta.

According to Grant's complaint, she went to the track that day but had to leave early. She said she wrote down her picks in each of the nine races on a piece of lavatory paper before leaving. She said she gave the paper and an old, wrinkled $20 bill to a track lavatory matron, Evelyn Jones, with a request that Jones place the $2 bets as listed for her. She said Jones consented.

The next day or so she learned that her triple bet had paid off and was worth $5,050, Grant said. So she went to the track to get her winning ticket from the matron. But she said that Jones told her she had not been able to place the bets after all and that Jones handed her back her paper with the choices and a $20 bill. The bill, Grant said, was a new one and not the one she had had originally. Grant filed a complaint with the track.

Within about a week, Howard R. Graham, a retired restauranteur, tried to cash a winning ticket on that triple. Graham said he had placed his own bet. That ticket was the only winning triple ticket sold at Window 18.

Jones and Graham were indicted in January on charges of second-degree grand larceny and first-degree criminal possession of stolen property.

A computer printout of bets placed at Window 18 on May 21, 1974, showed that the precise series of 27 betting choices noted on Grant's paper had indeed been made that day. Track personnel also testified that the ticket produced by Graham came from Window 18. Assistant Dist. Atty. James Boland produced an expert witness, Hofstra mathematics Professor Sylvia Pines, who said the chances of two strangers deciding on their own to bet the same 27 choices in sequence at the same window the same day were 1,000,000,000,000,000,000,000,000,000,000 to 1.

The jury found Jones guilty of grand larceny and Graham guilty of criminal possession.

PART B. CHARACTER, HABIT, AND CUSTOM

---

1. CHARACTER IN ISSUE

CLEGHORN v. NEW YORK CENTRAL & H. RIVER RY. CO.

Court of Appeals of New York, 1874.
56 N.Y. 44.

CHURCH, Ch. J. The accident was caused by the carelessness of the switchman, in neglecting to close the switch after the stock train had passed on to the side track, and in giving a false signal to the approaching passenger train, that the track was all right. It was a clear case of negligence; and for the injury to the plaintiff produced thereby the defendant is liable in this action. It is insisted that the court erred in admitting evidence of the intemperate habits of the switchman, and that the case of Warner v. N.Y.C.R.R. Co. is a direct authority against it. That was a case of injury at a road crossing. It was proved that the flagman neglected to give the customary signal, and was intoxicated at the time. The Commission of Appeals held it error to show previous habits of intemperance known to the officers of the company, upon the ground that such evidence had no bearing upon the question of negligence at the time. In that view the decision was right. Previous intoxication would not tend to establish an omission to give the signal on the occasion of the accident. In this case it was sought to be proved, not only that Hartman was intoxicated at the time of the accident, but that he was a man of intemperate habits, which were known by the agent of the company, having the power to employ and discharge him and other subordinates, with a view of claiming exemplary damages. For this purpose the evidence was competent. * * * Judgment reversed. [On other grounds.]

WELLMAN, THE ART OF CROSS-EXAMINATION
199–200 (1962).*

[Suit for libel. The defendant newspaper had published a front page attack upon the plaintiff opera manager which included the sentence:]

"My opinion of you is that you are the sort of man who would steal his mother's bones from the grave and sell them to buy flowers for a harlot."

The plaintiff testified in his own behalf. On cross-examination by Mr. Nicoll it developed that the plaintiff had written the editor who had composed the article an offensive note almost as violent as the one sued upon; that while manager of a trade journal he, himself, had been sued for libel, where the verdict was four thousand five hundred dollars against him; and that he was put upon the jail limits for failure to pay

* Copyright, 1962 by Collier.

the judgment. It also appeared that he had been convicted of assault 1
upon the opposing lawyer, a most respectable member of the bar; that 2
he had been twice bankrupt; that his sister had recovered a judgment 3
against him for money borrowed; and that his wife had been persuaded 4
to help him in his business affairs and had been driven into bankruptcy 5
on his account. During seven of the twenty years of his married life he 6
kept a mistress, and even occupied, with her, on many occasions, a box 7
in his own opera house directly over his wife's box. He also wrote her 8
impassioned letters, and allowed her to use his wife's horses and 9
carriages. The object of the cross-examiner was, of course, to show that 10
the reputation of such a man could not be injured by anything a 11
newspaper might say about him. The jury agreed with counsel that 12
one thousand dollars out of the two hundred and fifty sued for was 13
balm enough for his injured feelings. 14

Newspaper didn't print anything that wasn't already known

In actions for defamation such as the one just described, it is 15
always legitimate to attack the character of the plaintiff, whether or 16
not he becomes a witness in his own behalf. The question in such cases 17
is one of sound tactics rather than of professional ethics. The plain- 18
tiff's character is directly material on the issue as to how much he has 19
been damaged by what the defendant has said or written of him. 20

In libel cases (P's) character is an issue to determine how much he's been damaged.

Hypothetical

P, the widow of H, sues D in a wrongful death action arising out of H's 24
death in 1970. P testifies on the issue of damages that she and H had a happy 25
and affectionate marital relationship. D then proffers evidence that in 1961– 26
63, H left P and lived with another woman in a meretricious relationship, and 27
that H was convicted in 1967 of the offense of issuing checks without sufficient 28
funds and received a year's jail sentence. P makes an inadmissible-character- 29
evidence objection to D's proffered evidence. D contends that the proffered 30
evidence establishes H's character traits for immorality and dishonesty and 31
that these character traits are relevant to the issue of the pecuniary value of 32
H's companionship to P, his widow. The trial judge overrules P's objection. Is 33
this ruling correct? 34

— Most cts. exclude this

2. CHARACTER AS CIRCUMSTANTIAL EVIDENCE 35 36 37

MICHELSON v. UNITED STATES 38

Supreme Court of the United States, 1948. 39
335 U.S. 469, 69 S.Ct. 213, 93 L.Ed. 168. 40
[Some of the Court's footnotes have been omitted.] 41

Mr. Justice JACKSON delivered the opinion of the Court. 42 43

In 1947 petitioner Michelson was convicted of bribing a federal 44
revenue agent. The Government proved a large payment by accused to 45
the agent for the purpose of influencing his official action. The 46
defendant, as a witness on his own behalf, admitted passing the money 47
but claimed it was done in response to the agent's demands, threats, 48
solicitations, and inducements that amounted to entrapment. It is 49
enough for our purposes to say that determination of the issue turned 50
on whether the jury should believe the agent or the accused. 51

On direct examination of defendant, his own counsel brought out that, in 1927, he had been convicted of a misdemeanor having to do with trading in counterfeit watch dials. On cross-examination it appeared that in 1930, in executing an application for a license to deal in second-hand jewelry, he answered "No" to the question whether he had theretofore been arrested or summoned for any offense.

Defendant called five witnesses to prove that he enjoyed a good reputation. Two of them testified that their acquaintance with him extended over a period of about thirty years and the others said they had known him at least half that long. A typical examination in chief was as follows:

"Q. Do you know the defendant Michelson? A. Yes.

"Q. How long do you know Mr. Michelson? A. About 30 years.

"Q. Do you know other people who know him? A. Yes.

"Q. Have you had occasion to discuss his reputation for honesty and truthfulness and for being a law-abiding citizen? A. It is very good.

"Q. You have talked to others? A. Yes.

"Q. And what is his reputation? A. Very good."

These are representative of answers by three witnesses; two others replied, in substance, that they never had heard anything against Michelson.

On cross-examination, four of the witnesses were asked, in substance, this question: "Did you ever hear that Mr. Michelson on March 4, 1927, was convicted of a violation of the trademark law in New York City in regard to watches?" This referred to the twenty-year-old conviction about which defendant himself had testified on direct examination. Two of them had heard of it and two had not.

To four of these witnesses the prosecution also addressed the question the allowance of which, over defendant's objection, is claimed to be reversible error:

"Did you ever hear that on October 11th, 1920, the defendant, Solomon Michelson, was arrested for receiving stolen goods?"

None of the witnesses appears to have heard of this.

The trial court asked counsel for the prosecution, out of presence of the jury, "Is it a fact according to the best information in your possession that Michelson was arrested for receiving stolen goods?" Counsel replied that it was, and to support his good faith exhibited a paper record which defendant's counsel did not challenge.

The judge also on three occasions warned the jury, in terms that are not criticized, of the limited purpose for which this evidence was received.[3]

3. In ruling on the objection when the question was first asked, the Court said: "* * * I instruct the jury that what is happening now is this: the defendant has called character witnesses, and the basis for the evidence given by those character

Defendant-petitioner challenges the right of the prosecution so to
cross-examine his character witnesses. The Court of Appeals held that
it was permissible. The opinion, however, points out that the practice
has been severely criticized and invites us, in one respect, to change the
rule.[4] Serious and responsible criticism has been aimed, however, not
alone at the detail now questioned by the Court of Appeals but at
common-law doctrine on the whole subject of proof of reputation or
character.[5] It would not be possible to appraise the usefulness and

witnesses is the reputation of the defendant in the community, and since the defendant tenders the issue of his reputation the prosecution may ask the witness if she has heard of various incidents in his career. I say to you that regardless of her answer you are not to assume that the incidents asked about actually took place. All that is happening is that this witness' standard of opinion of the reputation of the defendant is being tested. Is that clear?"

In overruling the second objection to the question the Court said: "Again I say to the jury there is no proof that Mr. Michelson was arrested for receiving stolen goods in 1920, there isn't any such proof. All this witness has been asked is whether he had heard of that. There is nothing before you on that issue. Now would you base your decision on the case fairly in spite of the fact that that question has been asked? You would? All right."

The charge included the following: "In connection with the character evidence in the case I permitted a question whether or not the witness knew that in 1920 this defendant had been arrested for receiving stolen goods. I tried to give you the instruction then that that question was permitted only to test the standards of character evidence that these character witnesses seemed to have. There isn't any proof in the case that could be produced before you legally within the rules of evidence that this defendant was arrested in 1920 for receiving stolen goods, and that fact you are not to hold against him; nor are you to assume what the consequences of that arrest were. You just drive it from your mind so far as he is concerned, and take it into consideration only in weighing the evidence of the character witnesses."

4. Footnote 8 to that court's opinion reads as follows:

"Wigmore, Evidence (3d ed. 1940) § 988, after noting that 'such inquiries are almost universally admitted,' not as 'impeachment by extrinsic testimony of particular acts of misconduct,' but as means of testing the character 'witness' grounds of knowledge,' continues with these comments: 'But the serious objection to them is that practically the above distinction—between rumors of such con-

duct, as affecting reputation, and the fact of it as violating the rule against particular facts—cannot be maintained in the mind of the jury. The rumor of the misconduct, when admitted, goes far, in spite of all theory and of the judge's charge, towards fixing the misconduct as a fact upon the other person, and thus does three improper things,—(1) it violates the fundamental rule of fairness that prohibits the use of such facts, (2) it gets at them by hearsay only, and not by trustworthy testimony, and (3) it leaves the other person no means of defending himself by denial or explanation, such as he would otherwise have had if the rule had allowed that conduct to be made the subject of an issue. Moreover, these are not occurrences of possibility, but of daily practice. This method of inquiry or cross-examination is frequently resorted to by counsel for the very purpose of injuring by indirection a character which they are forbidden directly to attack in that way; they rely upon the mere putting of the question (not caring that it is answered negatively) to convey their covert insinuation. The value of the inquiry for testing purposes is often so small and the opportunities of its abuse by underhand ways are so great that the practice may amount to little more than a mere subterfuge, and should be strictly supervised by forbidding it to counsel who do not use it in good faith.'

"Because, as Wigmore says, the jury almost surely cannot comprehend the judge's limiting instruction, the writer of this opinion wishes that the United States Supreme Court would tell us to follow what appears to be the Illinois rule, i.e., that such questions are improper unless they relate to offenses similar to those for which the defendant is on trial."

5. A judge of long trial and appellate experience has uttered a warning which, in the opinion of the writer, we might well have heeded in determining whether to grant certiorari here: " * * * evidence of good character is to be used like any other, once it gets before the jury, and the less they are told about the grounds for its admission, or what they shall do with it,

propriety of this cross-examination without consideration of the unique practice concerning character testimony, of which such cross-examination is a minor part.

Courts that follow the common-law tradition almost unanimously have come to disallow resort by the prosecution to any kind of evidence of a defendant's evil character to establish a probability of his guilt. Not that the law invests the defendant with a presumption of good character, but it simply closes the whole matter of character, disposition and reputation on the prosecution's case-in-chief. The State may not show defendant's prior trouble with the law, specific criminal acts, or ill name among his neighbors, even though such facts might logically be persuasive that he is by propensity a probable perpetrator of the crime.[8] The inquiry is not rejected because character is irrelevant;[9] on the contrary, it is said to weigh too much with the jury and to so overpersuade them as to prejudge one with a bad general record and deny him a fair opportunity to defend against a particular charge. The overriding policy of excluding such evidence, despite its admitted probative value, is the practical experience that its disallowance tends to prevent confusion of issues, unfair surprise and undue prejudice.

But this line of inquiry firmly denied to the State is opened to the defendant because character is relevant in resolving probabilities of guilt. He may introduce affirmative testimony that the general estimate of his character is so favorable that the jury may infer that he would not be likely to commit the offense charged. This privilege is sometimes valuable to a defendant for this Court has held that such testimony alone, in some circumstances, may be enough to raise a reasonable doubt of guilt and that in the federal courts a jury in a proper case should be so instructed.

When the defendant elects to initiate a character inquiry, another anomalous rule comes into play. Not only is he permitted to call witnesses to testify from hearsay, but indeed such a witness is not allowed to base his testimony on anything but hearsay. What commonly is called "character evidence" is only such when "character" is employed as a synonym for "reputation." The witness may not testify about defendant's specific acts or courses of conduct or his possession of a particular disposition or of benign mental and moral traits; nor can

the more likely they are to use it sensibly. The subject seems to gather mist which discussion serves only to thicken, and which we can scarcely hope to dissipate by anything further we can add."

In opening its cyclopedic review of authorities from many jurisdictions, CORPUS JURIS SECUNDUM summarizes that the rules regulating proof of character "have been criticized as illogical, unscientific, and anomalous, explainable only as archaic survivals of compurgation or of states of legal development when the jury personally knew the facts on which their verdict was based." 32 C.J.S., Evidence, § 433.

8. This would be subject to some qualification, as when a prior crime is an element

of the later offense; for example, at a trial for being an habitual criminal. There are also well-established exceptions where evidence as to other transactions or a course of fraudulent conduct is admitted to establish fraudulent intent as an element of the crime charged. [Citations omitted.]

9. As long ago as 1865, Chief Justice Cockburn said, "The truth is, this part of our law is an anomaly. Although, logically speaking, it is quite clear that an antecedent bad character would form quite as reasonable a ground for the presumption and probability of guilt as previous good character lays the foundation of innocence, yet you cannot, on the part of the prosecution, go into evidence as to character."

he testify that his own acquaintance, observation, and knowledge of defendant leads to his own independent opinion that defendant possesses a good general or specific character, inconsistent with commission of acts charged. The witness is, however, allowed to summarize what he has heard in the community, although much of it may have been said by persons less qualified to judge than himself. The evidence which the law permits is not as to the personality of defendant but only as to the shadow his daily life has cast in his neighborhood. This has been well described in a different connection as "the slow growth of months and years, the resultant picture of forgotten incidents, passing events, habitual and daily conduct, presumably honest because disinterested, and safer to be trusted because prone to suspect. * * * It is for that reason that such general repute is permitted to be proven. It sums up a multitude of trivial details. It compacts into the brief phrase of a verdict the teaching of many incidents and the conduct of years. It is the average intelligence drawing its conclusion."

While courts have recognized logical grounds for criticism of this type of opinion-based-on-hearsay testimony, it is said to be justified by "overwhelming considerations of practical convenience" in avoiding innumerable collateral issues which, if it were attempted to prove character by direct testimony, would complicate and confuse the trial, distract the minds of jurymen and befog the chief issues in the litigation.

Another paradox in this branch of the law of evidence is that the delicate and responsible task of compacting reputation hearsay into the "brief phrase of a verdict" is one of the few instances in which conclusions are accepted from a witness on a subject in which he is not an expert. However, the witness must qualify to give an opinion by showing such acquaintance with the defendant, the community in which he has lived and the circles in which he has moved, as to speak with authority of the terms in which generally he is regarded. To require affirmative knowledge of the reputation may seem inconsistent with the latitude given to the witness to testify when all he can say of the reputation is that he has "heard nothing against defendant." This is permitted upon assumption that, if no ill is reported of one, his reputation must be good.[13] But this answer is accepted only from a witness whose knowledge of defendant's habitat and surroundings is intimate enough so that his failure to hear of any relevant ill repute is an assurance that no ugly rumors were about.

Thus the law extends helpful but illogical options to a defendant. Experience taught a necessity that they be counterweighted with equally illogical conditions to keep the advantage from becoming an unfair and unreasonable one. The price a defendant must pay for attempting to prove his good name is to throw open the entire subject which the law has kept closed for his benefit and to make himself vulnerable where the law otherwise shields him. The prosecution may pursue the

---

13. The law apparently ignores the existence of such human ciphers as Kipling's Tomlinson, of whom no ill is reported but no good can be recalled. They win seats with the righteous for character evidence purposes, however hard their lot in literature.

inquiry with contradictory witnesses to show that damaging rumors, whether or not well-grounded, were afloat—for it is not the man that he is, but the name that he has which is put in issue. Another hazard is that his own witness is subject to cross-examination as to the contents and extent of the hearsay on which he bases his conclusions, and he may be required to disclose rumors and reports that are current even if they do not affect his own conclusion.[16] It may test the sufficiency of his knowledge by asking what stories were circulating concerning events, such as one's arrest, about which people normally comment and speculate. Thus, while the law gives defendant the option to show as a fact that his reputation reflects a life and habit incompatible with commission of the offense charged, it subjects his proof to tests of credibility designed to prevent him from profiting by a mere parade of partisans.

To thus digress from evidence as to the offense to hear a contest as to the standing of the accused, at its best opens a tricky line of inquiry as to a shapeless and elusive subject matter. At its worst it opens a veritable Pandora's box of irresponsible gossip, innuendo and smear. In the frontier phase of our law's development, calling friends to vouch for defendant's good character, and its counterpart—calling the rivals and enemies of a witness to impeach him by testifying that his reputation for veracity was so bad that he was unworthy of belief on his oath—were favorite and frequent ways of converting an individual litigation into a community contest and a trial into a spectacle. Growth of urban conditions, where one may never know or hear the name of his next-door neighbor, have tended to limit the use of these techniques and to deprive them of weight with juries. The popularity of both procedures has subsided, but courts of last resort have sought to overcome danger that the true issues will be obscured and confused by investing the trial court with discretion to limit the number of such witnesses and to control cross-examination. Both propriety and abuse of hearsay reputation testimony, on both sides, depend on numerous and subtle considerations, difficult to detect or appraise from a cold record, and therefore rarely and only on clear showing of prejudicial abuse of discretion will Courts of Appeals disturb rulings of trial courts on this subject.[17]

Wide discretion is accompanied by heavy responsibility on trial courts to protect the practice from any misuse. The trial judge was

---

16. A classic example in the books is a character witness in a trial for murder. She testified she grew up with defendant, knew his reputation for peace and quiet, and that it was good. On cross-examination she was asked if she had heard that the defendant had shot anybody, and, if so, how many. She answered, "Three or four," and gave the names of two but could not recall the names of the others. She still insisted, however, that he was of "good character." The jury seems to have valued her information more highly than her judgment, and on appeal from conviction the cross-examination was held proper.

17. It has been held that the question may not be hypothetical nor assume unproven facts and ask if they would affect the conclusion. And that it may not be so asked as to detail evidence or circumstances of a crime of which defendant was accused. It has been held error to use the question to get before the jury a particular derogatory newspaper article. The proof has been confined to general reputation and that among a limited group such as fellow employees in a particular building held inadmissible.

scrupulous to so guard it in the case before us. He took pains to ascertain, out of presence of the jury, that the target of the question was an actual event, which would probably result in some comment among acquaintances if not injury to defendant's reputation. He satisfied himself that counsel was not merely taking a random shot at a reputation imprudently exposed or asking a groundless question to waft an unwarranted innuendo into the jury box.[18]

The question permitted by the trial court, however, involves several features that may be worthy of comment. Its form invited hearsay; it asked about an arrest, not a conviction, and for an offense not closely similar to the one on trial; and it concerned an occurrence many years past.

Since the whole inquiry, as we have pointed out, is calculated to ascertain the general talk of people about defendant, rather that the witness' own knowledge of him, the form of inquiry, "Have you heard?" has general approval, and "Do you know?" is not allowed.

A character witness may be cross-examined as to an arrest whether or not it culminated in a conviction, according to the overwhelming weight of authority. This rule is sometimes confused with that which prohibits cross-examination to credibility by asking a witness whether he himself has been arrested.

Arrest without more does not, in law any more than in reason, impeach the integrity or impair the credibility of a witness. It happens to the innocent as well as the guilty. Only a conviction, therefore, may be inquired about to undermine the trustworthiness of a witness.

Arrest without more may nevertheless impair or cloud one's reputation. False arrest may do that. Even to be acquitted may damage one's good name if the community receives the verdict with a wink and chooses to remember defendant as one who ought to have been convicted. A conviction, on the other hand, may be accepted as a misfortune or an injustice, and even enhance the standing of one who mends his ways and lives it down. Reputation is the net balance of so many debits and credits that the law does not attach the finality to a conviction when the issue is reputation, that is given to it when the issue is the credibility of the convict.

---

18. This procedure was recommended by Wigmore. But analysis of his innovation emphasizes the way in which law on this subject has evolved from pragmatic considerations rather than from theoretical consistency. The relevant information that it is permissible to lay before the jury is talk or conversation about the defendant's being arrested. That is admissible whether or not an actual arrest had taken place; it might even be more significant of repute if his neighbors were ready to arrest him in rumor when the authorities were not in fact. But before this relevant and proper inquiry can be made, counsel must demonstrate privately to the court an irrelevant and possibly unprovable fact—the reality of arrest. From this permissible inquiry about reports of arrest, the jury is pretty certain to infer that defendant had in fact been arrested and to draw its own conclusions as to character from that fact. The Wigmore suggestion thus limits legally relevant inquiries to those based on legally irrelevant facts in order that the legally irrelevant conclusion which the jury probably will draw from the relevant questions will not be based on unsupported or untrue innuendo. It illustrates Judge Hand's suggestion that the system may work best when explained least. Yet, despite its theoretical paradoxes and deficiencies, we approve the procedure as calculated in practice to hold the inquiry within decent bounds.

The inquiry as to an arrest is permissible also because the prosecution has a right to test the qualifications of the witness to bespeak the community opinion. If one never heard the speculations and rumors in which even one's friends indulge upon his arrest, the jury may doubt whether he is capable of giving any very reliable conclusions as to his reputation.

In this case the crime inquired about was receiving stolen goods; the trial was for bribery. The Court of Appeals thought this dissimilarity of offenses too great to sustain the inquiry in logic, though conceding that it is authorized by preponderance of authority. It asks us to substitute the Illinois rule which allows inquiry about arrest, but only for very closely similar if not identical charges, in place of the rule more generally adhered to in this country and in England.[21] We think the facts of this case show the proposal to be inexpedient.

The good character which the defendant had sought to establish was broader than the crime charged and included the traits of "honesty and truthfulness" and "being a law-abiding citizen." Possession of these characteristics would seem as incompatible with offering a bribe to a revenue agent as with receiving stolen goods. The crimes may be unlike, but both alike proceed from the same defects of character which the witnesses said this defendant was reputed not to exhibit. It is not only by comparison with the crime on trial but by comparison with the reputation asserted that a court may judge whether the prior arrest should be made subject of inquiry. By this test the inquiry was permissible. It was proper cross-examination because reports of his arrest for receiving stolen goods, if admitted, would tend to weaken the assertion that he was known as an honest and law-abiding citizen. The cross-examination may take in as much ground as the testimony it is designed to verify. To hold otherwise would give defendant the benefit of testimony that he was honest and law-abiding in reputation when such might not be the fact; the refutation was founded on convictions equally persuasive though not for crimes exactly repeated in the present charge.

The inquiry here concerned an arrest twenty-seven years before the trial. Events a generation old are likely to be lived down and dropped from the present thought and talk of the community and to be absent from the knowledge of younger or more recent acquaintances. The court in its discretion may well exclude inquiry about rumors of an event so remote, unless recent misconduct revived them. But two of these witnesses dated their acquaintance with defendant as commencing thirty years before the trial. Defendant, on direct examination, voluntarily called attention to his conviction twenty years before. While the jury might conclude that a matter so old and indecisive as a 1920 arrest would shed little light on the present reputation and hence propensities of the defendant, we cannot say that, in the context of this evidence and in the absence of objection on this specific ground, its admission was an abuse of discretion.

21. The Supreme Court of Illinois, in considering its own rule which we are urged to adopt, recognized that "the rule adhered to in this State is not consistent with the great weight of authority in this country and in England."

We do not overlook or minimize the consideration that "the jury almost surely cannot comprehend the Judge's limiting instructions," which disturbed the Court of Appeals. The refinements of the evidentiary rules on this subject are such that even lawyers and judges, after study and reflection, often are confused, and surely jurors in the hurried and unfamiliar movement of a trial must find them almost unintelligible. However, limiting instructions on this subject are no more difficult to comprehend or apply than those upon various other subjects; for example, instructions that admissions of a co-defendant are to be limited to the question of his guilt and are not to be considered as evidence against other defendants, and instructions as to other problems in the trial of conspiracy charges. A defendant in such a case is powerless to prevent his cause from being irretrievably obscured and confused; but, in cases such as the one before us, the law foreclosed this whole confounding line of inquiry, unless defendant thought the net advantage from opening it up would be with him. Given this option, we think defendants in general and this defendant in particular have no valid complaint at the latitude which existing law allows to the prosecution to meet by cross-examination an issue voluntarily tendered by the defense.

We end, as we began, with the observation that the law regulating the offering and testing of character testimony may merit many criticisms. England, and some states have overhauled the practice by statute.[22] But the task of modernizing the longstanding rules on the subject is one of magnitude and difficulty which even those dedicated to law reform do not lightly undertake.[23]

The law of evidence relating to proof of reputation in criminal cases has developed almost entirely at the hands of state courts of last resort, which have such questions frequently before them. This Court, on the other hand, has contributed little to this or to any phase of the law of evidence, for the reason, among others, that it has had extremely rare occasion to decide such issues, as the paucity of citations in this opinion to our own writings attests. It is obvious that a court which can make only infrequent sallies into the field cannot recast the body of case law on this subject in many, many years, even if it were clear what the rules should be.

22. Criminal Evidence Act, 61 & 62, Vict. c. 36. See also 51 L.Q.Rev. 443, for discussion of right to cross-examine about prior arrests. For review of English and State legislation, see 1 Wigmore, Evidence (3d ed., 1940) § 194, et seq. The Pennsylvania statute, Act of March 15, 1911, P.L. 20, § 1, discussed by Wigmore has been amended. Act of July 3, 1947, P.L. 1239, § 1, 19 P.S. § 711. The current statute and Pennsylvania practice were considered recently by the Superior Court of that state.

23. The American Law Institute, in promulgating its "Model Code of Evidence," includes the comment, "Character, whenever used in these Rules, means disposition not reputation. It denotes what a person is, not what he is reputed to be. No rules are laid down as to proof of reputation, when reputation is a fact to be proved. When reputation is a material matter, it is proved in the same manner as is any other disputed fact." Rule 304. The latter sentence may seem an oversimplification in view of the decisions we have reviewed.

We concur in the general opinion of courts, textwriters and the profession that much of this law is archaic, paradoxical and full of compromises and compensations by which an irrational advantage to one side is offset by a poorly reasoned, counterprivilege to the other. But somehow it has proved a workable even if clumsy system when moderated by discretionary controls in the hands of a wise and strong trial court. To pull one misshapen stone out of the grotesque structure is more likely simply to upset its present balance between adverse interests than to establish a rational edifice.

The present suggestion is that we adopt for all federal courts a new rule as to cross-examination about prior arrest, adhered to by the courts of only one state and rejected elsewhere.[24] The confusion and error it would engender would seem too heavy a price to pay for an almost imperceptible logical improvement, if any, in a system which is justified, if at all, by accumulated judicial experience rather than abstract logic.[25]

The judgment is

Affirmed.

Mr. Justice Frankfurter, concurring.

Despite the fact that my feelings run in the general direction of the views expressed by MR. JUSTICE RUTLEDGE in his dissent, I join the Court's opinion. I do so because I believe it to be unprofitable, on balance, for appellate courts to formulate rigid rules for the exclusion of evidence in courts of law that outside them would not be regarded as clearly irrelevant in the determination of issues. For well-understood reasons this Court's occasional ventures in formulating such rules hardly encourage confidence in denying to the federal trial courts a power of control over the allowable scope of cross-examination possessed by trial judges in practically all State courts. After all, such uniformity of rule in the conduct of trials is the crystallization of experience even when due allowance is made for the force of imitation. To reject such an impressive body of experience would imply a more dependable wisdom in a matter of this sort than I can claim.

To leave the District Courts of the United States the discretion given to them by this decision presupposes a high standard of professional competence, good sense, fairness and courage on the part of the federal district judges. If the United States District Courts are not manned by judges of such qualities, appellate review, no matter how stringent, can do very little to make up for the lack of them.

[The dissenting opinion of Mr. Justice Rutledge who was joined by Mr. Justice Murphy, though worthy of examination, is not reproduced here.]

---

24. See note 21.

25. It must not be overlooked that abuse of cross-examination to test credibility carries its own corrective. Authorities on practice caution the bar of the imprudence as well as the unprofessional nature of attacks on witnesses or defendants which are likely to be resented by the jury. Wellman, Art of Cross Examination (1927) p. 167 et seq.

CAMUS, THE STRANGER
79–81.*

[The protagonist is awaiting trial before an Algerian Court on a charge of murdering an Arab in a brawl. The defense is self-defense. His lawyer visits him in jail] * * * [H]e said that they'd been making investigations into my private life. They had learned that my mother died recently in a home. Inquiries had been conducted at Marengo and the police informed that I'd shown "great callousness" at my mother's funeral.

"You must understand," the lawyer said, "that I don't relish having to question you about such a matter. But it has much importance, and, unless I find some way of answering the charge of 'callousness,' I shall be handicapped in conducting your defense. And that is where you, and only you, can help me."

He went on to ask if I had felt grief on that "sad occasion." The question struck me as an odd one; I'd have been much embarrassed if I'd had to ask anyone a thing like that.

I answered that, of recent years, I'd rather lost the habit of noting my feelings, and hardly knew what to answer. I could truthfully say I'd been quite fond of Mother—but really that didn't mean much. All normal people, I added as on afterthought, had more or less desired the death of those they loved, at some time or another.

Here the lawyer interrupted me, looking greatly perturbed.

"You must promise me not to say anything of that sort at the trial, or to the examining magistrate."

I promised, to satisfy him, but I explained that my physical condition at any given moment often influenced my feelings. For instance, on the day I attended Mother's funeral, I was fagged out and only half awake. So, really, I hardly took stock of what was happening. Anyhow, I could assure him of one thing: that I'd rather Mother hadn't died.

The lawyer, however, looked displeased. "That's not enough," he said curtly.

After considering for a bit he asked me if he could say that on that day I had kept my feelings under control.

"No," I said. "That wouldn't be true."

He gave me a queer look, as if I slightly revolted him; then informed me, in an almost hostile tone, that in any case the head of the Home and some of the staff would be cited as witnesses.

"And that might do you a very nasty turn," he concluded.

When I suggested that Mother's death had no connection with the charge against me, he merely replied that this remark showed I'd never had any dealings with the law.

A.L.I., MODEL PENAL CODE
Tentative Draft No. 9, art. 207.12.*

(7) Evidence. On the issue whether a place is a house of prostitution the following shall be admissible evidence: its general repute; the repute of the persons who reside in or frequent the place; the frequency, timing, and duration of visits by nonresidents * * *.

MARYLAND—DISTRICT OF COLUMBIA—VIRGINIA CRIMINAL PRACTICE INSTITUTE TRIAL MANUAL
2–7 (1964).**

2.03 *Eliciting Testimony Regarding the Character Trait of Truth and Veracity.*

1. What is your name, please?

2. Where do you reside, Mr. [name]?

3. Where are you employed?

4. How long have you worked there?

5. In what capacity?

6. Do you know the defendant, [name]?

7. How long have you know him?

8. During that period, how often did you see him?

9. What was the nature of your association with him?

10. Did you know other people who knew him?

11. Did you discuss with these people, or hear discussed, the defendant's reputation for truth and veracity?

12. What generally is his reputation for truth and veracity among those people?

THEODORE ROOSEVELT AS CHARACTER WITNESS
10 Journal of the Cleveland Bar Assoc. 36 (Dec. 1938).

[Note—In this installment of the address which was delivered by President Frank J. Hogan, of the American Bar Association, before our members at the October meeting, we start with the entrance of the late President Theodore Roosevelt into the courtroom at Washington to testify as a character witness for Charles G. Glover, president of the largest national bank in the capital city.]

As Teddy Roosevelt stepped up into the room it appeared as though he had stepped on a button that would set off the applause, and first the applause started with hand clapping, and then everybody in the courtroom stood up. * * *

* The American Law Institute, Philadelphia, 1959. See Calif.Penal Code § 315.

** Copyright, 1964, by Lerner Law Book Co.

When quiet was restored and a few minutes passed and Roosevelt   1
had waved to everybody whether he knew them or not, the Judge   2
ascended the bench and we put Teddy on as the first witness.   3

Now, all of you, I don't know whether your rule is as strict with   4
respect to reputation witnesses here, but in most states, of course, the   5
witness is allowed to identify himself and then say he knows the   6
defendant, and then he is asked whether the defendant's character or   7
reputation for the trait involved is good or bad, and in some states they   8
tie it down to good, bad or excellent, or very good, or something of that   9
kind. In our jurisdiction we are allowed a little greater latitude, our   10
Court of Appeals having held that one might have a good reputation or   11
a superlatively good reputation, and that also we have a right to show   12
who the character witness is so that the jury can give greater or less   13
weight to the man who thus testifies.   14

But whether we had those rules of "good" or "bad" or monosyllabic   15
responses would have made no difference to Roosevelt. Rules of evi-   16
dence might be worshipped by a Wigmore, but if Roosevelt ever heard   17
of them he heard of them only to laugh at them. (Laughter).   18
19

He was asked his name, and then many in the audience noticed   20
what the older of this audience must know, that Theodore Roosevelt   21
had a perpetually boy's changing voice—got a great reputation for over-   22
emphasis which he could not help. He had a slight St. Vitus's dance   23
which made him go as though he were going to spit something out, and   24
he could not help it any more than I can help winking one eye every   25
now and then—one of those tics that the psychoanalyst says shows   26
something's wrong up here. When one's voice was changing as a boy,   27
when he was going through that period that makes mother angry when   28
she calls up and says, "Johnny, it's dinner time," and he says, "All   29
right (bass voice). I will be down in a minute (high-pitched voice)," and   30
she says, "Dont's both answer at once," and scolds the daughter for   31
joining in—he had almost that kind of a voice, and, as I say, it gave a   32
sort of an added, not practiced, unintentional emphasis to what he had   33
to say.   34

And when we asked him his name, he said, "Theodore Roosevelt."   35
(Voice breaking from bass to high-pitched). We asked what his profes-   36
sion was, and he said, "Write." (High-pitched voice). We asked where   37
he lived; he said, "Used to be New York." (High-pitched voice). And   38
then without imitating him any more I will tell you he went on that   39
way, getting that up and down. It was fascinating when you realized   40
that the man was intensely interested in what he was saying.   41

He was asked whether or not he had ever lived in Washington, and   42
he twisted around to the jury, and he said, "May I state what happened   43
without any further question?"   44
45

And I said, "Yes, go ahead."   46

He said, "I came to Washington as Civil Service Commissioner   47
when conditions were very bad. Politics, politics, alone, governed   48
whether—are any of you in the government service? Oh, no. I forgot   49
jurymen can't be in the government service. Well, those of your   50
neighbors would be shoved in and out of office all the time, and we were   51

1 trying to make something permanent in the tenure of government
2 officials, and we did it. But it was very routine: it wasn't exciting at
3 all; and I was called back to New York—Judge, you will remember
4 this; you are old enough to remember it—called back to New York, and
5 when I got there I became Police Commissioner. Oh, gentlemen of the
6 jury, I know I can't tell you stories about it today, but it was bully fun—
7 it was bully fun. And I was interested in that. It's fine work where
8 the policemen are generally honest policemen, and we made them
9 honest in New York. We did, gentlemen of the jury, and the citizens of
10 New York would be proud of our work. Oh, but I am getting off. I am
11 coming back, Judge. I am coming back.

12   "Then I came to Washington as Assistant Secretary of the Navy.
13 That got my interest. When this country gets a great big strong navy
14 it won't have any reason to fear anybody, and people won't be going
15 around saying, 'I didn't raise my son to be a soldier.' You won't hear
16 that any more because the navy will take care of it. We need a strong
17 navy.

18
19   "I know, Judge, you are just about to tell me, but I am coming now
20 to it. That's when I was in Washington, though." (Laughter). "And
21 at that time I opened—I know you want me, Mr. Hogan, to say this—I
22 opened an account at the Riggs National Bank. You know, I had a
23 deposit at the Riggs National Bank ever since, and I had it because my
24 faith in Mr. Glover was so great, I wouldn't take it out no matter where
25 I lived."

Glover's Character is mentioned

26   There was still no stopping him. The district attorney had sense
27 enough to know that if you stopped him you would be bowled over in
28 some way.

29   He said, "Then came the Spanish-American War. That was terri-
30 ble, but it was interesting, it was fine, and I had a real life for a while.
31 Then I became governor of New York, so I was back there again for
32 quite a while. Then, gentlemen of the jury, they made me Vice-
33 President. It was the most terrible experience, a perfectly terrible
34 experience. I don't think I would have lived through it if I had to take
35 four years, but I had my account here at the Riggs National Bank as
36 Vice-President just as I had it when I was President; and as you know,
37 I was President for about seven and a half years, living here all the
38 time, keeping my account at the Riggs National Bank.

39
40   "And by the way, Judge, I knew I had met you somewhere. I
41 appointed you because of your civic righteousness, because of your
42 interest in the poor of this city, on my committee to clean out the
43 slums. That's what I did, and you were one of the best men on the
44 committee I ever had. I know, gentlemen of the jury, you are glad to
45 hear that about your Judge. I knew I recognized him. And you did
46 splendid work." And the Judge, who was just on the soft and kindly
47 side, was agreeing with my man, particularly when he said, "You did
48 that splendid work." He went on for some time. Then he said, "Now,
49 have I covered it?"

50   And I said, "Well, you have covered the fact that you had an
51 account at the Riggs National Bank."

Glover's Character mentioned

"And didn't I tell you why I put it there? Because of my confidence in Mr. Glover, because of his integrity, because of the splendid man he was and the fine bank he ran and what a fine credit it had all over the United States."

I said, "Yes, Colonel, you have told us that." Well; we were getting away with it. Now, we weren't doing anything wrong; we were simply presenting a man as nature had made him, and we could no more control him, parenthesis, if we wanted to, end parenthesis, (laughter) than could the judge or the jury, or the district attorney, had he attempted it.

Well, we went a little further—I won't go into all the details—and finally he was asked, "Do you know the reputation of Mr. Glover for honesty, probity, and integrity and veracity?" Getting them all in, you know.

He said, "Do I know it? Why, everybody in the city of Washington knows it. Of course. Nobody could live here, nobody could at any time have had any dealings that amounted to anything, and not know what his reputation is. It was"—

I said, "Just a moment, Colonel. You know that reputation, do you not? I am speaking now of his reputation in the community among people who knew him as you knew him."

"Well," he said "even everybody knew him, so everybody must have known the reputation as I knew it."

"All right. Now, Colonel, will you tell us what that reputation was?"

Glover's character

He pulled his chair forward almost to the edge of the jury platform, leaned over to the jury—he had very heavy hands, put them down on his knees, and he said "I knew Mr. Glover as a civic minded citizen who did more to make the national capitol the perfectly beautiful, outstanding capitol of the world that it is today than any other man that ever lived in America. I knew Mr. Glover as one who in all philanthropic and charitable enterprises—like the Judge; like you, Judge—would always come forward and respond, whether a neighbor or the President of the United States called him.

"I knew Mr. Glover in his home. We visited. My daughter was out there staying with his daughter. We visited out there. We visited as good old chums, because we have been very friendly, and I knew him as a family man loved by all of his own relatives and reverenced by all of his neighbors, and I knew Mr. Glover as a banker whose credit was so high, whose reputation was so fine, whose word was so good, that nobody ever questioned for a moment the safety of his deposit, whether it be large or small. That is the way I knew Mr. Glover."

And then the district attorney couldn't stand it any longer. He arose with a solemnity that I recall vividly to this day. He said, "If your Honor please, I move to strike out the entire answer of the witness. Colonel Roosevelt has said that he knew Mr. Glover in these various capacities, these various ways. He has not said a word about what his reputation was, and I move"—

The Court said, "I am with you, Mr. District Attorney; I will grant your motion," turned apologetically to Colonel Roosevelt and said, "Colonel, you have testified to your own knowledge of Mr. Glover. The rule is that you can testify only to general reputation, general repute. That's what you can do, and nothing more. So I'll have to strike out your answer. Now, please keep that in mind."

[handwritten margin note: One can only testify to general reputation]

I said, "go ahead, Colonel. Please give us your answer again, keeping the Judge's admonition in mind."

Again he turned to the Judge, again the thick finger went out. He said, "You are right. I should have known that. Thanks ever so much.

"Gentlemen of the jury, I knew Mr. Glover by general reputation and general repute—I'm right now, Judge, am I not? I am right now." (Laughter). And he went all over the whole thing again, with elaborations.

The district attorney whispered to me, "Oh, hell."

And I said, "I should have known better."

But there was no cross-examination. And then, as though that were not enough, Colonel Roosevelt, whom we had promised to let get the 11:00 o'clock train back to New York if he got through with his testimony as we thought he would, came over, and he was wearing his great big sombrero that all of you who ever saw him or pictures of him would recognize, that he always wore in campaign years, and he grabbed it and swished it in to the ladies. One of my associates was to take him to the train, and he had to pass right in front of the jury on his way out. Getting right in the middle in front of the jury, clenching his hand, using that terrific thick finger, he squatted himself as though for a football rush, and he said, "Judge or no Judge,"— * * * "Goodbye, gentlemen of the jury. I always like to appear before a jury of my fellow citizens, for you are rendering a public service. You are rendering a really great public service, just as much as the Judge there. You are here to do justice. That's why you are here—and I know you are going to do it, I know you are going to do it." (Laughter and applause).

With that he went out leaving the courtroom in a perfect storm of disorder. * * * Of course, may I add, again in parenthesis, that justice was done. (Laughter). * * *

————

On methods of proving character, see Federal Rules of Evidence 405, and Advisory Committee's Note to Rule 405.

McCORMICK'S HANDBOOK OF THE LAW OF EVIDENCE *
557–565 (3rd ed. 1984).

§ 190. Bad Character as Evidence of Criminal Conduct: Other Crimes

This broad prohibition [against the prosecution's initially using character evidence] includes the specific and frequently invoked rule

* West Publishing Co. Reprinted with permission.

Prosecution can introduce other crim. acts of accused only for specific purposes

that the prosecution may not introduce evidence of other criminal acts of the accused unless the evidence is introduced for some purpose other [1] than to suggest that because the defendant is a person of criminal character, it is more probable that he committed the crime for which he is on trial.

As the rule indicates, there are numerous other uses to which evidence of criminal acts may be put, and those enumerated are neither mutually exclusive nor collectively exhaustive. The permissible purposes include:

(1) To complete the story of the crime on trial by placing it in the context of nearby and nearly contemporaneous happenings.[2] The phrases "same transaction" or, less happily, "res gestae" often are used to denote evidence introduced for this purpose.

(2) To prove the existence of a larger plan,[3] scheme, or conspiracy, of which the crime on trial is a part. This will be relevant as showing motive, and hence the doing of the criminal act, the identity of the actor, or his intention.

(3) To prove other crimes by the accused so nearly identical in method as to earmark them as the handiwork of the accused.[4] Much more is demanded than the mere repeated commission of crimes of the same class, such as repeated murders,[5] robberies [6] or

1. Evidence of other crimes brought forth as circumstantial proof of guilt for the offense charged is sometimes called "extrinsic offense evidence." • • •

2. United States v. Masters, 622 F.2d 83 (4th Cir.1980) (upholding admission of taped conversations of the defendant with undercover agents despite reference to other sales and acts on grounds that the evidence was necessary to complete the story of the crime on trial as well as to prove that the defendant was "dealing"; State v. Villavicencio, 95 Ariz. 199, 388 P.2d 245 (1964) (upholding introduction of evidence of sale of narcotics to one person in prosecution for sale to another, where evidence showed that both sales took place at same time and place) • • •.

3. Compare United States v. Lewis, 693 F.2d 189 (D.C.Cir.1982) (testimony concerning stolen money orders not charged in indictment admissible to show that defendant was "the mastermind of a common scheme"); United States v. Parnell, 581 F.2d 1374 (10th Cir. 1978) (previous fraudulent scheme admissible as "direct precursor" of conspiracy to purchase grain with forged cashiers checks); State v. Toshishige Yoshino, 45 Hawaii 206, 364 P.2d 638 (1961) (evidence of first robbery admissible in prosecution for second where defendant and others robbed first victim and obtained from him the name and address of their next victim); [and] State v. Manrique, 271 Or. 201, 531 P.2d 239, 242–243 (1975) (previous heroin sales not part of common scheme or plan); Note, 53 Ind.L.J. 805 (1978).

4. Whiteman v. State, 119 Ohio St. 285, 164 N.E. 51 (1928) (evidence of other robberies by defendants wearing uniforms, impersonating officers and stopping cars, thus "earmarking" them as the perpetrators of the offense charged); Rex v. Smith, 11 Cr.App.R. 229, 84 L.J.K.B. 2153 (1915), described in Marjoribanks, For the Defence: The Life of Edward Marshall Hall 321 (1937) (in this "brides of the bath" case it was shown that the man accused of drowning in the bathtub a woman whom he had bigamously "married" had later "married" several wives who left him their property and whom he then purportedly discovered drowned in the bath).

The phrase of which authors of detective fiction are fond, *modus operandi*, may be employed in this context. • • •

5. United States v. Woods, 484 F.2d 127, 134 (4th Cir. 1973), cert. denied 415 U.S. 979 (evidence that defendant accused of suffocating her eight-month-old pre-adoptive foster son had custody of or access to nine children who suffered at least 20 cyanotic episodes resulting in the death of seven of them "admissible generally under the accident and signature exceptions") • • •.

6. United States v. Myers, 550 F.2d 1036, 1046 (5th Cir. 1977), appeal after remand 572 F.2d 506, ("An early afternoon robbery of an outlying bank situated on a

rapes.[7] The pattern and characteristics of the crimes must be so unusual and distinctive as to be like a signature.

(4) To show a passion or propensity for unusual and abnormal sexual relations.[8] Initially, proof of other sex crimes always was confined to offenses involving the same parties, but a number of jurisdictions now admit other sex offenses with other persons, at least as to offenses involving sexual aberrations.[9]

(5) To show, by similar acts or incidents, that the act in question was not performed inadvertently, accidentally,[10] involuntarily,[11] or without guilty knowledge. The similarities between the act charged and the extrinsic acts need not be as extensive and striking as is required under purpose (3), and the various acts need not be manifestations of a unifying plan, as required for purpose (2).

highway, by revolver-armed robbers wearing gloves and stocking masks, and carrying a bag for the loot, is not such an unusual crime that it tends to prove that one of the two individuals involved must have been the single bandit in a similar prior robbery") * * *.

7. State v. Sauter, 125 Mont. 109, 232 P.2d 731, 732 (1951) (in charge of forcible rape in automobile after picking up victim in barroom, other rapes following similar pickups were "too common * * * to have much evidentiary value in showing a systematic scheme or plan") * * *.

8. Woods v. State, 250 Ind. 132, 235 N.E.2d 479 (1968) (other acts of rape and incest with same victim admissible to show "depraved sexual instinct"); State v. Schut, 71 Wn.2d 400, 429 P.2d 126 (1967) (prior acts of incest with victim admissible to show lustful inclination toward victim), * * *. For criticism of this exception to the propensity rule, see Lempert & Saltzburg, A Modern Approach to Evidence 289–90 (2d ed. 1983). Admissibility under Fed. and Rev.Unif.R.Evid. (1974) 404 is highly doubtful.

9. State v. McFarlin, 110 Ariz. 225, 517 P.2d 87 (1973) (overruling cases establishing an unqualified propensity rule). Defining aberrant sexual activity presents a considerable problem. At least one state has retreated further, entirely withdrawing its more lenient treatment of evidence of other sex crimes. Commonwealth v. Shively, 492 Pa. 411, 424 A.2d 1257, 1259–1260 (1981), overruling Commonwealth v. Kline, 361 Pa. 434, 65 A.2d 348 (1949).

10. United States v. Johnson, 634 F.2d 735 (4th Cir. 1980), (evidence that physician accused of tax evasion submitted fraudulent medicaid billing properly admitted to rebut her claim that she was too devoted to patients to worry about finances); * * * People v. Williams, 6 Cal.2d 500, 58 P.2d 917 (1936) (where defendant accused of larceny by posing as a customer standing near owner of bag and taking purse from bag while owner was shopping, testimony of detectives that defendant took another purse from another woman's bag in the same manner admissible to refute defendant's claim that he picked the purse off the floor, thinking it lost); State v. Lapage, 57 N.H. 245, 294 (1876) (where there were repeated deaths of children in defendant's care, the court referred to a "class of cases * * * in which it becomes necessary to show that the act for which the prisoner was indicted was not accidental, e.g., where the prisoner had shot the same person twice within a short time, or where the same person had fired a rick of grain twice, or where several deaths by poison had taken place in the same family, or where the children of the same mother had mysteriously died"); Makin v. Attorney General of New South Wales [1894] App. C. 57 (P.C. 1893) (in prosecution for murder of infant left with professional foster parent, evidence that twelve other babies entrusted to him without adequate payment for their support were found buried in the gardens of three houses he had formerly occupied was properly received on question of whether adoption was bona fide and death accidental) * * *.

11. United States v. Holman, 680 F.2d 1340, 1349 (11th Cir. 1982), (other smuggling incidents to rebut defense of coercion); * * * United States v. Hearst, 563 F.2d 1331 (9th Cir. 1977), rehearing denied 573 F.2d 579, cert. denied 435 U.S. 1000 (evidence of other crimes to negate anticipated defense of duress by publisher's daughter held for ransom by terrorist group and charged in bank robbery committed by group).

(6) To establish motive.[12] The evidence of motive may be probative of the identity of the criminal [13] or of malice or specific intent.[14] An application of this principle permits proof of criminal acts of the accused that constitute admissions by conduct designed to obstruct justice [15] or avoid punishment for a crime * * *.[16]

(7) To establish opportunity, in the sense of access to or presence at the scene of the crime [17] or in the sense of possessing distinctive or unusual skills or abilities employed in the commission of the crime charged.[18]

(8) To show, without considering motive, that defendant acted with malice, deliberation, or the requisite specific intent.[19]

(9) To prove identity. Although this is indisputably one of the ultimate purposes for which evidence of other criminal conduct will be received, the need to prove identity should not be, in itself, a ticket to admission. Almost always, identity is the inference that flows from one or more of the theories just listed. The second (larger plan), third (distinctive device), and sixth (motive) seem to be most often relied upon to show identity. In addition, the courts tend to apply stricter standards when the desired inference pertains to identity as opposed to state of mind. * * *

A number of procedural and other substantive considerations also affect the admissibility of other crimes evidence pursuant to these * * * exceptions. * * * [T]he other crimes evidence should be

[handwritten margin note: even if (D) acquitted may be admissible]

12. United States v. Haldeman, 559 F.2d 31, 88 (D.C.Cir.1976), cert. denied 431 U.S. 933 (evidence of conspiracy of government officials to break into psychiatrist's office to obtain records of an opponent of government's war policy admissible to show motive for Watergate cover-up conspiracy); * * * State v. Long, 195 Or. 81, 244 P.2d 1033 (1952) (testimony that defendant accused of murder used victim's truck to commit a robbery shortly afterward admissible) * * *.

13. State v. Green, 232 Kan. 116, 652 P.2d 697, 701 (1982) (where the "defendant claimed in essence that someone had broken into his wife's house to rob her and inflicted the fatal wounds prior to his arrival * * * evidence of the defendant's prior assaults on his wife was of great probative value on the issue of identity").

14. United States v. Benton, 637 F.2d 1052, 1056 (5th Cir. 1981), ("While motive is not an element of any offense charged * * * appellant's knowledge that Zambito might implicate him in the Florida homicides constituted a motive for appellant wanting to kill Zambito * * *. This evidence of motivation was relevant as tending to show the participation of appellant in the crime and to show malice or intent which are elements of the crimes charged"). * * *.

15. People v. Spaulding, 309 Ill. 292, 141 N.E. 196 (1923) (killing sole eyewitness to crime) * * *.

16. People v. Gambino, 12 Ill.2d 29, 145 N.E.2d 42 (1957), (escape and attempted escape while awaiting trial); State v. Brown, 231 Or. 297, 372 P.2d 779 (1962) (stealing cars to escape) * * *.

17. United States v. DeJohn, 638 F.2d 1048, 1053 (7th Cir. 1981) (testimony of YMCA security guard and city police officer revealing that on other occasions defendant had obtained checks from a mailbox at YMCA was "highly probative of defendant's opportunity to gain access to the mailboxes and obtain the checks that he cashed" with forged endorsements).

18. United States v. Barrett, 539 F.2d 244 (1st Cir. 1976) (evidence admissible to show familiarity with sophisticated means of neutralizing burglar alarms).

19. United States v. Beechum, 582 F.2d 898 (5th Cir. 1978) (en banc), (evidence that defendant had possessed two stolen credit cards for 10 months admissible to prove that he intended to keep a planted silver dollar taken from the mails rather than to return it to postal authorities, as he claimed, on the theory that "because the defendant had unlawful intent in the extrinsic offense, it is less likely that he had lawful intent in the present offense") (1979) * * *.

potentially admissible even if the defendant was acquitted of the other charge.[20]

Second, the connection between the evidence and the permissible purpose should be clear, and the issue on which the other crimes evidence is said to bear should be the subject of a genuine controversy. For example, if the prosecution maintains that the other crime reveals defendant's guilty state of mind, then his intent must be disputed. Likewise, if the accused does not deny performing the acts charged, the exceptions pertaining to identification are unavailing.

Finally, even if one or more of the valid purposes for admitting other crimes evidence is appropriately invoked, there is still the need to balance its probative value against the usual counterweights. When the sole purpose of the other crimes evidence is to show some propensity to commit the crime at trial, there is no room for ad hoc balancing. The evidence is then unequivocally inadmissible—this is meaning of the rule against other crimes evidence. But the fact that there is an accepted logical basis for the evidence other than the forbidden one of showing a proclivity for criminality may not preclude the jury from relying on a defendant's apparent propensity toward criminal behavior. Accordingly, most recent authority recognizes that the problem is not merely one of pigeonholing, but of classifying and then balancing. In deciding whether the danger of unfair prejudice and the like substantially outweighs the incremental probative value, a variety of matters must be considered, including the strength of the evidence as to the commission of the other crime, the similarities between the crimes, the interval of time that has elapsed between the crimes, the need for the evidence, the efficacy of alternative proof, and the degree to which the evidence probably will rouse the jury to overmastering hostility.

* * *

PEOPLE v. MASSEY
District Court of Appeal of California, 1961.
196 Cal.App.2d 230, 16 Cal.Rptr. 402.

KAUFMAN, P.J. By an information dated August 9, 1960, the appellant, Richard L. Massey, was charged with the burglary (Pen.Code, § 459) of an apartment at 620 Jones Street, San Francisco, on May 2, 1960; and with two prior felony convictions in Iowa. He admitted the prior convictions and entered a plea of not guilty. A jury found him guilty of burglary in the first degree and the court sentenced him for the term prescribed by law, and decreeing that the sentence was to run concurrently with any prior incompleted sentence. On this appeal from the judgment of conviction entered on the verdict and the order denying his motion for a new trial, appellant argues that: * * * the evidence relating to another burglary of which he was acquitted was erroneously admitted. * * *

The record reveals the following facts: About 4:30 a.m. on the morning of May 2, 1960, Mrs. Sarah Finley, who lived alone in a one-room apartment, was awakened when she felt "a terrific jerk." She

20. The cases are divided. * * *

saw a Negro man hovering over her face and screamed. The intruder
hurried to the open window, leaped out and ran off. Mrs. Finley took a
pill for her heart condition and telephoned for help. The police arrived
and discovered that $13 was missing from her purse, as well as a few
other small items from the apartment. A large rectangular piece had
been cut out of the sheet on Mrs. Finley's bed, probably with the
scissors on the nearby table. Later the same day, Mrs. Finley's apartment was dusted for latent fingerprints by an officer from the crime
laboratory. A fingerprint was found on the inside of the window in
Mrs. Finley's room and a knife outside the window.

Mrs. Finley had lived for several years in the apartment on the
first floor of the Gaylord Hotel at 620 Jones Street in San Francisco.
Her apartment had only two windows which overlooked the porch and
the hotel next door. On the prior evening, May 1, 1960, she retired
about 10 p.m.; as the night was very warm, she opened both windows,
locked them with the chain, and covered herself only with a sheet.

The above occurrence remained unsolved for several weeks. About
3 a.m. on the morning of May 26, 1960, Elsie Cox, who lived alone in a
two-room apartment at 757 Sutter Street, awoke and in the large
mirror facing her bed, saw the reflection of a man entering the living
room where she slept. She could see him very clearly as the living-
room window extended almost the entire wall and overlooked the
brightly lit Trader Vic's parking area next door. The venetian blinds
on the window were down but open. She watched the prowler creep
around her bed, and noticed that he kept a white cloth over his hand as
he flashed a light into the closet and took a leisurely survey. He then
turned and lifted up the pillow next to hers and pushed his hand under
it. Then he straightened up, proceeded to the end of the bed, and the
other side of the room. After he climbed out the kitchen window, she
called the police. Later, she discovered that only a dish towel was
missing, although several things were awry. Miss Cox's apartment was
on the second floor; there were a fire escape and some pipes near the
kitchen window. Shortly thereafter, a police officer saw the appellant
walking down Post Street near Mason Street, and returned with him to
Miss Cox's apartment. Miss Cox positively identified the appellant as
the prowler at that time and at the later trial.

On June 9, 1960, while in custody on the Cox matter, the appellant
was questioned about the Finley burglary. He denied being at Mrs.
Finley's apartment on the morning in question and indicated he did not
wish to make any further statements. On July 26, 1960, the preliminary hearing was held in Mrs. Finley's room because of her heart
condition. At this time, Mrs. Finley testified that the prowler who was
in her room on the morning of May 2 did not look like the appellant but
was huskier, fatter and older. At the trial, she testified that the
prowler looked very much like the appellant but admitted that she had
observed the prowler for only about half a second and that it was so
dark that she couldn't tell. She explained that the inconsistency in her
identification was due to her nervousness at the preliminary.

The prosecution's expert witness testified that in his opinion, the latent fingerprint found on the window of Mrs. Finley's apartment was appellant's. The appellant took the stand, admitted the two prior felony convictions and being on parole from the Iowa Men's Reformatory for one of them. He testified that on May 1, he had gone to bed around 10 o'clock at the home of his sister and brother-in-law at 184 Hoff Street. The appellant's sister and her husband also testified that the appellant was in his bed on the night of May 1 at their home in the Ingleside district. It was also brought out at the trial that one week earlier, the appellant had been tried and acquitted of the Cox burglary. * * *

Appellant next argues that the evidence relating to the subsequent burglary of Miss Cox's apartment was not admissible because of his acquittal and because of its prejudicial effect. It is well established, however, that an acquittal does not prevent the admissibility of evidence concerning another wrongful act, as conviction of the offense is not a prerequisite to the introduction of such evidence.

As stated in People v. Brown, supra at pages 552–553: "The ultimate fact to be proved is the defendant's guilt of the crime with which he is charged and not the other offense. The evidence of the other offense is admissible even though the defendant was not convicted of it, provided such evidence is relevant. Therefore, the rule concerning the admissibility of other offenses expressed in the *Raleigh* case must be limited to those circumstances where the proof is relevant and material to the crime for which the defendant is being tried."

Appellant here argues that the Cox burglary is not relevant to the Finley burglary; the attorney general argues that the evidence was relevant and admissible as the Cox burglary was committed in the same neighborhood (about 2 blocks from the Gaylord Hotel where Mrs. Finley lived), was committed within the same month in the early hours of the morning, and both involved the use of a white cloth, Miss Cox's dish cloth, and by inference, the piece cut from Mrs. Finley's sheet.

The general rule of the admissibility of other criminal acts is stated in People v. Sanders:

> "If the evidence of another crime is necessary or pertinent to the proof of the one charged, the law will not thwart justice by excluding that evidence, simply because it involves the commission of another crime. The general tests of the admissibility of evidence in a criminal case are: 1. Is it a part of the *res gestae?* 2. If not, does it tend logically, naturally, and by reasonable inference, to establish any fact material for the people, or to overcome any material matter sought to be proved by the defense? If it does, then it is admissible, whether it embraces the commission of another crime or does not, whether the other crime be similar in kind or not, whether it be part of a single design or not * * *."

We think the evidence of the Cox burglary was pertinent to the issue of intent. * * *

[Affirmed.]

CALIFORNIA CONSTITUTION ART. 1, § 28

(d) **Right to Truth-in-Evidence.** Except as provided by statute hereafter enacted by a two-thirds vote of the membership in each house of the Legislature, relevant evidence shall not be excluded in any criminal proceeding, including pretrial and post conviction motions and hearings, or in any trial or hearing of a juvenile for a criminal offense, whether heard in juvenile or adult court. Nothing in this section shall affect any existing statutory rule of evidence relating to privilege or hearsay, or Evidence Code, Sections 352, 782 or 1103. Nothing in this section shall affect any existing statutory or constitutional right of the press.

(Added by Initiative Measure, approved by the people, June 8, 1982, known as "The Victims' Bill of Rights").

UNITED STATES v. BEASLEY

United States Court of Appeals, Seventh Circuit, 1987.
809 F.2d 1273.

EASTERBROOK, Circuit Judge. Meese, Inc., of Madison, Indiana, hired as a consultant Marvin Leo Beasley, whose Ph.D. is in chemistry. Beasley had some 75 scientific publications to his credit, including one—M.L. Beasley & R.L. Collins, *Water-Degradable Polymers for Controlled Release of Herbicides and Other Agents,* 169 Science 769 (Aug. 21, 1970)—that claimed a substantial scientific advance in the application of herbicides. Other publications, such as W.O. Milligan, M.L. Beasley, M.H. Lloyd & R.G. Haire, *Crystalline Americium Trihydroxide,* 24 Acta Cristallographica 979 (1968), and K. Maer, M.L. Beasley, R.L. Collins & W.O. Milligan, *The Structure of the Titanium-Iron Cyanide Complexes,* 90 J.Am. Chemical Soc. 3201 (1968), demonstrated Beasley's accomplishments in his field. His new employer wanted to take precautions against the day it might lose access to Beasley's skills and paid for a $1 million life insurance policy, with itself as beneficiary.

To obtain the policy Beasley had to submit the results of a physical examination. Warren Rucker, a physician who was also the Mayor of Madison, administered the examination. Beasley took the occasion to explain to Rucker one of his theories: that administering large doses of tranquilizers and analgesics to vegetables would help them deal with stress better and absorb nutrients more quickly, increasing their rate of growth. Beasley needed only the drugs to test this thesis. Dr. Rucker decided to help Beasley conduct his experiments and wrote out many prescriptions. Most were in Beasley's name, with one each in the names F.E. Brooks and Marilyn Pierce, who Beasley said were his assistants and would need access to drugs while Beasley was out of town. The amounts of drugs prescribed, and the amounts Beasley obtained from three pharmacies between August 1980 and January 1981, are:

Drug	Prescribed	Dispensed
Dilaudid 4 mg	13,970.	7,470.
Dilaudid 1/24 gr	37.	37.
Codeine 1 gr	800.	800.
Morphine ½ gr	1,300.	300.
Morphine Sulfate 15mg/cc	240. cc	240. cc
Percodan	1,100.	600.
Demerol 100 mg	1,300.	300.
Preludin 75 mg	1,900.	1,000.
Desoxyn 15 mg	1,850.	850.
Desoxyn 5 mg	34.	34.
Desoxyn 2.5 mg	104.	104.
Quaalude 300 mg	800.	200.
Parest 400 mg	1,600.	800.
Tuinal 3 gr	100.	100.
Valium 10 mg	3,700.	3,000.
Librium 25 mg	700.	1,000.
Tenuate 75 mg	100.	100.
Ionamin 30 mg	600.	530.
Meprobamate 400 mg	800.	300.
Seconal 1.5 gr	600.	100.

All of the drugs are controlled substances—either narcotics or treated in the same way as narcotics.

Beasley says the vegetables took their medicine. The U.S. Attorney believes that the drugs were sold on the black market and turned at least one person into a vegetable. An indictment charged Beasley with seven counts of obtaining Dilaudid (hydromorphone HCL), a Schedule II controlled substance, with intent to distribute, in violation of 21 U.S.C. § 841(a)(1), and two counts of attempting to obtain Dilaudid by misrepresenting the name of the person to appear on the prescription, in violation of 21 U.S.C. §§ 843(a)(3) and 846. Beasley was convicted on all nine counts by a jury; the judge sentenced him to nine concurrent seven-year terms and fined him $1,000. Dr. Rucker and the three pharmacists who made all this possible were not charged; the U.S. Attorney believes they were simply credulous. But see 21 C.F.R. § 1306.02(f) (defining a prescription as an order to dispense drugs "to or for an ultimate user"), and § 1306.04(a) (no prescription is lawful unless issued "for a legitimate medical purpose by an individual practitioner acting in the usual course of his medical practice")—both of which suggest that even if Dr. Rucker believed every word Beasley told him (and the pharmacists believed Rucker, who relayed the tale), all knew or should have known that they lacked authority to distribute these drugs to Beasley. But there may be other matters of which we are unaware, and our function is to examine the claims of those who were convicted rather than to inquire into the position of those not charged.

* * *

There is a substantial challenge to the government's trial strategy, however. The prosecutor was worried about the jury's reaction to Beasley's academic credentials and success as a biochemist, which lent

verisimilitude to what would otherwise be a preposterous excuse for
acquiring mountains of drugs. The other problem was that the principal evidence that Beasley distributed the Dilaudid he acquired in
Indiana would come from F.E. Brooks, a convicted drug dealer. The
word of a felon versus the word of a biochemist is not the strongest
case. So the prosecutor decided to introduce extensive evidence that
Beasley acquired and distributed drugs between 1981 and 1984. This
presents questions under Fed.R.Evid. 404(b), which provides:

> Evidence of other crimes, wrongs, or acts is not admissible to
> prove the character of a person in order to show that he acted
> in conformity therewith. It may, however, be admissible for
> other purposes, such as proof of motive, opportunity, intent,
> preparation, plan, knowledge, identity, or absence of mistake
> or accident.

It also presents questions under Fed.R.Evid. 403, which provides that
relevant evidence may be excluded "if its probative value is substantially outweighed by the danger of unfair prejudice".

The case that Beasley acquired Dilaudid with intent to distribute
comes from the size and irregular manner of his purchases coupled
with the testimony of F.E. Brooks that over a ten-month period starting
in the summer of 1980, Beasley sold Brooks large quantities of the drug.
Brooks testified that he bought between 50 and 600 tablets at a time, at
a price of approximately $33 per tablet. According to Brooks, some
tablets were given to his girlfriend, his son, and his daughter Marilyn
Pierce; the rest were sold to strangers for between $40 and $50 per
tablet. Other evidence came from Rocky Terrell, one of Beasley's
assistants, who said that although he helped Beasley plant test plots of
many kinds of vegetables, he never added any solution to the plants or
observed Beasley do so.

Some evidence showing that Beasley may have committed crimes
other than those charged came in without objection. The prosecutor
introduced the list of drugs given above, showing that Beasley acquired
many drugs other than Dilaudid. The remaining evidence in the case
was met by objections and portrays Beasley as acquiring and distributing drugs between March 1981 (two months after the last acquisition
charged in the indictment) and some time in 1984. Christy Terrell
testified that in March or April 1981 Beasley gave her codeine at his
farm in Oklahoma and showed her how to ingest codeine or dilute it for
injection. Rocky Terrell testified that in December 1982 Beasley
showed him how to fake pain so that a physician would prescribe
Dilaudid. Between December 1982 and March 1983, Rocky Terrell,
Carol Parks, and on occasion Beasley went "shopping for doctors" in
Texas, Kansas, Oklahoma, and Arkansas. Rocky Terrell and Parks
would visit physicians' offices in the hope of obtaining prescriptions for
Dilaudid. When they did, they would either sell the tablets or split
them with Beasley. Rocky Terrell also related a conversation with
Beasley in 1982, attributing to Beasley the statement that he had
"some kind of deal going" with a physician to hold Dilaudid tablets off
the black market until the price rose past $55.

Parks supported Rocky Terrell's testimony, although she said that the "shopping for doctors" may have lasted until 1984. She testified that she used some of the Dilaudid and gave some to Beasley. Between February 1981 and June 1981, she maintained, she received Valium and codeine directly from Beasley (although she had asked him for Dilaudid).

Finally, Margaret Walraven gave an explanation for the absence from trial of Marilyn Pierce, Brooks's daughter, in whose apartment the Beasley-Brooks sales of Dilaudid took place. According to Walraven, Pierce was a Dilaudid addict who could not testify because, shortly before the trial began, she had been committed to Central State Hospital, a mental hospital in Oklahoma, apparently suffering from the effects of the drug.

Although counsel for Beasley objected to this evidence at trial, the principal consideration came beforehand. Counsel asked the judge to prohibit the prosecutor from using the evidence about "shopping for doctors" and from offering evidence that would tend to show that Beasley used Parks, Pierce, and Walraven as prostitutes. The judge stated that he would exclude any evidence that Walraven saw Pierce "shooting up Dilaudid outside the presence of Dr. Beasley." The prosecutor promised to keep from the jury any evidence tending to show prostitution but argued that evidence tending to show that Beasley dealt in any of the kinds of drugs for which Dr. Rucker had written prescriptions should be admitted to show a "pattern". The prosecutor stated: "with regard to the testimony of Rocky Terrell and Carol Parks, the government believes it is pattern evidence and it is admissible because it shows a pattern that started in our time [i.e., October 1980 to January 1981, the period covered by the indictment] and continued through the next—picked up again in the fall of 1982 through the spring of 1983". The judge responded: "Well, that seems to me to be admissible pattern evidence." After counsel and the court dealt with questions concerning the potential testimony of a physician who may have helped Beasley acquire drugs in Oklahoma,[1] the colloquy continued:

Mr. Molloy [Beasley's lawyer]: We have still got the question about these * * * bad acts.

* * *

The Court: * * * I think they are especially close in time to be admissible under Rule 404(b) which does not make any distinction as to whether the other acts are prior or subsequent to the time or times set out in the indictment.

The decision to admit the evidence rested on a belief that the bad acts showed a "pattern" of crimes "especially close in time". Come the

1. Beasley had been convicted in an Oklahoma court of obtaining Dilaudid, codeine, and Quaalude in October 1980 by misrepresenting to a physician that they would be used in research and misrepresenting to a pharmacist that he had the necessary permission by the state to use the drugs in research. The conviction was reversed solely [on technical grounds]. Beasley v. State, 665 P.2d 852. The district judge apparently believed that the reversal of the conviction precluded use of the episode as a similar act showing intent. He did not give a reason, and we do not know of one.

trial, however, the judge repeatedly told the jury that the sole purpose
of admitting the evidence was to show Beasley's "intent". The judge
tried to limit the jury's consideration in cautionary instructions as the
evidence was admitted, and one of the instructions in the charge
repeated this limitation.

The prosecutor tries to defend the decision on appeal by resur-
recting the argument about "pattern". "Pattern" is missing not only
in the instructions to the jury but also in Rule 404(b)'s list of permissible uses of bad act evidence. "Pattern" usually is a shorthand for a
series of acts that collectively identify the offender—the ten bank
robberies by a gang disguised by red polka dot bandannas, the series of
counterfeit bills made by an engraver who never gets the Great Seal
quite right, and so on. The pattern serves as the signature that enables
the jury to determine that this offense, too, was committed by the
defendant. This use of pattern to show identity, or sometimes the
extent and membership of a conspiracy, is the usual one in this circuit,
as in others.

When the similarity of the acts is used to identify the culprit, the
proximity of the acts in time is important. Given enough time, similar
crimes will be committed by other people, and the value of the other
acts as an earmark is diminished. Thus many cases use language
emphasizing proximity. But the many bad acts of which Beasley was
accused during trial were not similar in the sense of demonstrating a
modus operandi. None of the other bad acts involved duping a physician into making drugs available for "experiments." The episodes of
"shopping for doctors" were similar to each other, but not to the crimes
of which Beasley stood accused; Beasley's provision of Valium and
codeine to his associates is not like the fraudulent acquisition of
Dilaudid. * * * We therefore bypass the dispute that has occupied
the parties about whether two or three years is "too remote" for the
latter acts to be proximate in time. Questions about "how long is too
long" do not have uniform answers; the answers depend on the theory
that makes the evidence admissible. Here the acts are so dissimilar
that their timing becomes unimportant.

Some language in the government's brief suggests that any commission of similar crimes is the sort of "pattern" that permits the
evidence to come in. On this reasoning, one drug offense may be used
to prove another, although a bank robbery could not be admitted in a
drug prosecution. The prosecutor admits as limits the factors enumerated in cases such as United States v. Draiman, 784 F.2d 248, 254 (7th
Cir.1986): the bad act evidence must be clear and convincing, must
show a similar act close enough in time, must have value that outweighs the risk of unfair prejudice (the Rule 403 standard), and must be
used to show something other than the defendant's propensity to
commit similar crimes (the Rule 404(b) requirement). Yet in the
prosecutor's view, to show similarity is to negate prejudice and the
tendency of the evidence to condemn by besmirching character. Not so.
The requirements are distinct. A rule that a judge may admit all
evidence that the defendant committed crimes of similar varieties
produces the gravest risk of offending the central prohibition of Rule

404(b): "Evidence of other crimes, wrongs, or acts is not admissible to prove the character of a person in order to show that he acted in conformity therewith." The inference from "pattern" by itself is *exactly* the forbidden inference that one who violated the drug laws on one occasion must have violated them on the occasion charged in the indictment. Unless something more than a pattern and temporal proximity is required, the fundamental rule is gone. This is why "pattern" is not listed in Rule 404(b) as an exception. Patterns of acts may *show* identity, intent, plan, absence of mistake, or one of the other listed grounds, but a pattern is not itself a reason to admit the evidence.

This brings into focus the instructions limiting the use of the evidence to proof of "intent". Patterns of similar acts may show intent, just as they may show identity. That the other bad acts came after the crimes charged in the indictment does not preclude their use to show intent.

Intent was an issue here. Beasley testified that he bought the drugs to conduct experiments, fed the drugs to his plants, and never distributed drugs to anyone. If this is true, he did not purchase with intent to distribute. The prosecutor claims that Beasley sold the Dilaudid to Brooks and perhaps others and did not conduct or intend to conduct experiments on the effects of narcotics on rutabagas or cauliflowers. A demonstration that in 1982 and 1983 Beasley, Rocky Terrell, and Carol Parks bilked other physicians into prescribing Dilaudid, which they resold, tends to show that Beasley acquired the Dilaudid in Indiana with the same intent. At the same time, the evidence inescapably creates a risk of the forbidden inference, that a person who violates the law at one time has a bad character and therefore violated the law at a different time. So although the episodes of "shopping for doctors" were relevant to show intent, they also had a potential for "unfair prejudice"—which the advisory committee's note to Rule 403 describes as "an undue tendency to suggest decision on an improper basis, commonly, though not necessarily, an emotional one." The sale of drugs brings emotions into play, especially when the evidence reveals that the drugs may have ruined Marilyn Pierce's life.

When the same evidence has legitimate and forbidden uses, when the introduction is valuable yet dangerous, the district judge has great discretion. There are no bright line rules; it is easy to identify polar cases but impossible to draw a line of demarcation. Appellate courts can contribute only modestly to the making of the best decision case by case. The decision must be made on the scene, and once the imponderables have been weighed there is little to be gained from weighing them again on appellate scales. The balance would not be systematically better the second time around, and the costs of second-guessing include new trials that may be less accurate as events become more remote. Trial judges have a comparative advantage because they alone see all the evidence in context, and the judicial system as a whole takes advantage of the division of labor.

Yet although appellate courts cannot often tell whether it was best, all things considered, to let in a given piece of evidence, it may be

possible to tell whether the district court and the parties took the right
things into account. A flaw in the process is easier to detect than is a
flaw in the result—and over the run of cases the consistent operation of
process is more important, too. The principled and just functioning of
the judicial system depends on careful observation of the rules that
focus attention on the proper grounds of decision. The rules deal in
probabilities. We cannot know whether admission of the bad act
evidence against Beasley changed the outcome or produced an improper
conviction; we can be confident that repeated, careless use of bad act
evidence will increase the probability of such unhappy outcomes.

The objective is not to enforce "rules"; Rules 403 and 404(b)
establish standards rather than rules. It is to ensure that standards
not be applied as if they were rules, as if they established mechanical
indicia (such as "One drug offense may be used as evidence to prove any
other"). The list of exceptions in Rule 404(b), if mechanically applied,
would overwhelm the central principle. Almost *any* bad act evidence
simultaneously condemns by besmirching character and by showing one
or more of "motive, opportunity, intent, preparation, plan, knowledge,
identity, or absence of mistake or accident", not to mention the "other
purposes" of which this list is meant to be illustrative. We therefore
repeat the theme that there must be a principled exercise of discretion.
The district judge must both identify the exception that applies to the
evidence in question and evaluate whether the evidence, although
relevant and within the exception, is sufficiently probative to make
tolerable the risk that jurors will act on the basis of emotion or an
inference via the blackening of the defendant's character. Discretion,
when exercised, will rarely be disturbed.

The record in this case does not show that the district judge took
into account the power of this bad act evidence to impugn Beasley's
character. The pretrial hearing was perfunctory. The district judge
did not ask the prosecutor to explain what she expected to show. The
only two comments by the court are "that seems to be admissible
pattern evidence" and "[the acts] are especially close in time to be
admissible". We have already explained why "pattern" evidence as
such is excludable unless it shows one of the listed exceptions; the
district court appeared to act on the opposite view. We have also
explained why temporal proximity—if two or three years could be
called "especially close in time"—does not support use of the evidence.
And the court did not demonstrate an effort to determine the likely
effect of the evidence in poisoning Beasley's character. The effect on
Beasley's character may well have been the dominant one, indeed the
principal reason why the prosecutor wanted to use the evidence. If
Beasley's Ph.D. and scientific achievements might suggest to the jury
that Beasley had a good character, the prosecutor wanted something
that cut the other way.

If the power of the bad act evidence to show intent were obvious,
and the danger of improper inferences low, we would not be concerned
by the lack of balancing on the record. Judges need not explain the
obvious, even briefly. We are not dealing, however, with transparently
admissible evidence. Some seems almost transparently inadmissible.

Evidence that Beasley gave Valium and codeine to two people in 1981 is not proof of the intent with which Beasley acquired Dilaudid—not unless any drug offense proves any other. Proof that Marilyn Pierce was addicted to Dilaudid and had to be committed to a mental hospital was gratuitous, much more likely to provoke an emotional reaction from the jurors than to help them understand Beasley's intent. Doubtless it was important to tell the jurors that Pierce, named on one prescription and whose apartment was a locus of sales, could not be present. It would have sufficed, however, for the judge to tell the jury that "for reasons beyond the prosecutor's control Marilyn Pierce cannot attend the trial" and to warn the jurors not to draw inferences for or against either party because of her absence. Or the court might have told the jury that Pierce was in a hospital and for medical reasons could not attend. The full reason for her absence—and the proof of the reason through Margaret Walraven, another Dilaudid addict—invited all the wrong kinds of inferences. Only the evidence that Beasley, Parks, and Rocky Terrell went "shopping for doctors" to acquire Dilaudid between 1982 and 1983 (or 1984) substantially implies intent to distribute in 1980, and even here the potential for an improper inference is strong enough to make its admission as part of the prosecutor's affirmative case not a foregone conclusion. The thoughtful exercise of discretion would have mattered. (Beasley took the stand and denied selling drugs to anyone * * *.)

It was certainly a mistake to admit the evidence about Pierce's mental condition; it was probably a mistake to admit the evidence about Valium and codeine; the use of the "shopping for doctors" incidents was sufficiently problematic that a more discriminating treatment by the district court was called for.

With respect to the two convictions for fraudulently obtaining Dilaudid, the error was harmless. Intent to distribute was not in issue on these counts. The government proved beyond any doubt that Brooks and Pierce were not Beasley's research assistants, as he had represented, and that the prescriptions were not designed to obtain drugs for their lawful use. Convictions on these counts were inevitable.

The error is not harmless with respect to the remaining counts, however. An error (other than a constitutional error) is not harmless if it "results in actual prejudice because it 'had substantial and injurious effect or influence in determining the jury's verdict.'" The extensive use of other-crime evidence to show intent weighed heavily against Beasley. It was an important component of the prosecutor's case. Tellingly, the prosecutor does not argue that any error was harmless.

Although two of the nine counts were not affected by the admission of the bad act evidence, we vacate the sentences on these counts as well. This will permit the district judge to resentence Beasley on the two fraud counts with knowledge that these counts supply the sole justification for imprisonment rather than being tag-along concurrent sentences. If there should be a second trial, and Beasley again be convicted on charges of possession with intent to distribute, the district court will be able to reconstruct a package of sentences. Beasley

[handwritten margin note: Conclusion]

should not be resentenced on the fraud convictions until the final disposition of all counts.

Reversed in part and remanded.

TUCKER v. STATE

Supreme Court of Nevada, 1966.
82 Nev. 127, 412 P.2d 970.

THOMPSON, Justice.

On May 7, 1957, Horace Tucker telephoned the police station and asked a detective to come to the Tucker home in North Las Vegas. Upon arrival the detective observed that Tucker had been drinking, was unshaven, and looked tired. Tucker led the detective to the dining room where one, Earl Kaylor, was dead on the floor. Kaylor had been shot several times. When asked what had happened, Tucker said that he (Tucker) had been sleeping in the bedroom, awakened, and walked to the dining room where he noticed Kaylor lying on the floor. Upon ascertaining that Kaylor was dead, Tucker telephoned the police station. He denied having killed Kaylor. A grand jury conducted an extensive investigation. However, an indictment was not returned as the grand jury deemed the evidence inconclusive. No one, including Tucker, has ever been charged with that killing.

On October 8, 1963, Horace Tucker telephoned the police and asked a sergeant to come to the Tucker home in North Las Vegas; that there was an old man dead there. Upon arrival the sergeant noticed that Tucker had been drinking. The body of Omar Evans was dead on the couch in the living room. Evans had been shot. Tucker stated that he (Tucker) had been asleep, awakened, and found Evans dead on the couch. Subsequently Tucker was charged with the murder of Evans. A jury convicted him of second degree murder.

At trial, over vehement objection, the court allowed the state to introduce evidence of the Kaylor homicide. The court reasoned that the circumstances of the deaths of Kaylor and Evans were sufficiently parallel to render admissible evidence of the Kaylor homicide to prove that Tucker intended to kill Evans, that the killing of Evans was part of a common scheme or plan in Tucker's mind, and also to negate any defense of accidental death. These limited purposes, for which the evidence was received and could be considered by the jury, were specified by court instruction as required by case law. We rule that evidence of the Kaylor homicide was not admissible for any purpose and that prejudicial error occurred when the court permitted the jury to hear and consider it.

Nevada exclude[s] any evidence which shows that the defendant committed other offenses unless relevant to prove the commission of the crime charged. The "unless" portion of the rule is stated in the form of exceptions. Thus we have held that evidence of an offense, other than that for which the accused is on trial, may be allowed as an exception if relevant to prove motive, identity, the absence of mistake or accident, or a common scheme or plan.

Whenever the problem of evidence of other offenses confronts a trial court, grave considerations attend. The danger of prejudice to the defendant is ever present, for the jury may convict now because he has escaped punishment in the past. Nor has the defendant been advised that he must be prepared to meet extraneous charges. Indeed, as our system of justice is accusatorial rather than inquisitorial, there is much to be said for the notion that the prosecution must prove the defendant guilty of the specific crime charged without resort to past conduct. Thus when the other offense sought to be introduced falls within an exception to the rule of exclusion, the trial court should be convinced that the probative value of such evidence outweighs its prejudicial effect. The reception of such evidence is justified by necessity and, if other evidence has substantially established the element of the crime involved (motive, intent, identity, absence of mistake, etc.), the probative value of showing another offense is diminished, and the trial court should rule it inadmissible even though relevant and within an exception to the rule of exclusion.

In the case at hand we need not consider whether evidence of the Kaylor homicide comes within one of the exceptions to the rule of exclusion, because the first requisite for admissibility is wholly absent—namely, that the defendant on trial committed the independent offense sought to be introduced. There is nothing in this record to establish that Tucker killed Kaylor. Anonymous crimes can have no relevance in deciding whether the defendant committed the crime with which he is charged. Kaylor's assailant remains unknown. A fortiori, evidence of that crime cannot be received in the trial for the murder of Evans.

We have not before had occasion to discuss the quantum of proof needed to establish that the defendant on trial committed the separate offense sought to be introduced. Here there was only conjecture and suspicion, aroused by the fact that Kaylor was found dead in Tucker's home. We now adopt the rule that, before evidence of a collateral offense is admissible for any purpose, the prosecution must first establish by plain, clear and convincing evidence, that the defendant committed that offense. Fundamental fairness demands this standard in order to preclude verdicts which might otherwise rest on false assumptions.

Reversed and remanded for new trial.

HUDDLESTON v. UNITED STATES

Supreme Court of the United States, 1988.

485 U.S. 681, 108 S.Ct. 1496, 99 L.Ed.2d 771.

[REHNQUIST, C.J., delivered the opinion for a unanimous Court.]

Federal Rule of Evidence 404(b) provides:

"Other crimes, wrongs, or acts.—Evidence of other crimes, wrongs, or acts is not admissible to prove the character of a person in order to show that he acted in conformity therewith. It may, however, be admissible for other purposes, such as

FRE
404

proof of motive, opportunity, intent, preparation, plan, knowledge, identity, or absence of mistake or accident."

This case presents the question whether the district court must itself make a preliminary finding that the Government has proved the "other act" by a preponderance of the evidence before it submits the evidence to the jury. We hold that it need not do so.

Petitioner, Guy Rufus Huddleston, was charged with one count of selling stolen goods in interstate commerce, 18 U.S.C. § 2315, and one count of possessing stolen property in interstate commerce, 18 U.S.C. § 659. The two counts related to two portions of a shipment of stolen Memorex video cassette tapes that petitioner was alleged to have possessed and sold, knowing that they were stolen.

The evidence at trial showed that a trailer containing over 32,000 blank Memorex video cassette tapes with a manufacturing cost of $4.53 per tape was stolen from the Overnight Express yard in South Holland, Illinois, sometime between April 11 and 15, 1985. On April 17, 1985, petitioner contacted Karen Curry, the manager of the Magic Rent-to-Own in Ypsilanti, Michigan, seeking her assistance in selling a large number of blank Memorex video cassette tapes. After assuring Curry that the tapes were not stolen, he told her he wished to sell them in lots of at least 500 at $2.75 to $3.00 per tape. Curry subsequently arranged for the sale of a total of 5,000 tapes, which petitioner delivered to the various purchasers—who apparently believed the sales were legitimate.

There was no dispute that the tapes which petitioner sold were stolen; the only material issue at trial was whether petitioner knew they were stolen. The district court allowed the Government to introduce evidence of "similar acts" under Rule 404(b), concluding that such evidence had "clear relevance as to [petitioner's knowledge],". The first piece of similar act evidence offered by the Government was the testimony of Paul Toney, a record store owner. He testified that in February 1985, petitioner offered to sell new 12″ black and white televisions for $28 a piece. According to Toney, petitioner indicated that he could obtain several thousand of these televisions. Petitioner and Toney eventually traveled to the Magic Rent-to-Own, where Toney purchased 20 of the televisions. Several days later, Toney purchased 18 more televisions.

The second piece of similar act evidence was the testimony of Robert Nelson, an undercover FBI agent posing as a buyer for an appliance store. Nelson testified that in May 1985, petitioner offered to sell him a large quantity of Amana appliances—28 refrigerators, 2 ranges, and 40 icemakers. Nelson agreed to pay $8,000 for the appliances. Petitioner was arrested shortly after he arrived at the parking lot where he and Nelson had agreed to transfer the appliances. A truck containing the appliances was stopped a short distance from the parking lot, and Leroy Wesby, who was driving the truck, was also arrested. It was determined that the appliances had a value of approximately $20,000 and were part of a shipment that had been stolen.

Petitioner testified that the Memorex tapes, the televisions, and the appliances had all been provided by Leroy Wesby, who had represented that all of the merchandise was obtained legitimately. Petitioner stated that he had sold 6,500 Memorex tapes for Wesby on a commission basis. Petitioner maintained that all of the sales for Wesby had been on a commission basis and that he had no knowledge that any of the goods were stolen.

In closing, the prosecution explained that petitioner was not on trial for his dealings with the appliances or the televisions. The district court instructed the jury that the similar acts evidence was to be used only to establish petitioner's knowledge, and not to prove his character. The jury convicted petitioner on the possession count only.

We granted certiorari, to resolve a conflict among the Courts of Appeals as to whether the trial court must make a preliminary finding before "similar acts" and other Rule 404(b) evidence is submitted to the jury. We conclude that such evidence should be admitted if there is sufficient evidence to support a finding by the jury that the defendant committed the similar act.

Federal Rule of Evidence 404(b)—which applies in both civil and criminal cases—generally prohibits the introduction of evidence of extrinsic acts that might adversely reflect on the actor's character, unless that evidence bears upon a relevant issue in the case such as motive, opportunity, or knowledge. Extrinsic acts evidence may be critical to the establishment of the truth as to a disputed issue, especially when that issue involves the actor's state of mind and the only means of ascertaining that mental state is by drawing inferences from conduct. The actor in the instant case was a criminal defendant, and the act in question was "similar" to the one with which he was charged. Our use of these terms is not meant to suggest that our analysis is limited to such circumstances.

Before this Court, petitioner argues that the district court erred in admitting Toney's testimony as to petitioner's sale of the televisions. The threshold inquiry a court must make before admitting similar acts evidence under Rule 404(b) is whether that evidence is probative of a material issue other than character. The Government's theory of relevance was that the televisions were stolen, and proof that petitioner had engaged in a series of sales of stolen merchandise from the same suspicious source would be strong evidence that he was aware that each of these items, including the Memorex tapes, was stolen. As such, the sale of the televisions was a "similar act" only if the televisions were stolen. Petitioner acknowledges that this evidence was admitted for the proper purpose of showing his knowledge that the Memorex tapes were stolen. He asserts, however, that the evidence should not have been admitted because the Government failed to prove to the district court that the televisions were in fact stolen.

Petitioner argues from the premise that evidence of similar acts has a grave potential for causing improper prejudice. For instance, the jury may choose to punish the defendant for the similar rather than the charged act, or the jury may infer that the defendant is an evil person inclined to violate the law. Because of this danger, petitioner maintains, the jury ought not to be exposed to similar act evidence until the

be so harmful trial crt must make prelim find of guilt before prepond.

trial court has heard the evidence and made a determination under Federal Rule of Evidence 104(a) that the defendant committed the similar act. Rule 104(a) provides that "[p]reliminary questions concerning the qualification of a person to be a witness, the existence of a privilege, or the admissibility of evidence shall be determined by the court, subject to the provisions of subdivision (b)." According to petitioner, the trial court must make this preliminary finding by at least a preponderance of the evidence.

Crt. says— No prelim finding necess.

We reject petitioner's position, for it is inconsistent with the structure of the Rules of Evidence and with the plain language of Rule 404(b). Article IV of the Rules of Evidence deals with the relevancy of evidence. Rules 401 and 402 establish the broad principle that relevant evidence—evidence that makes the existence of any fact at issue more or less probable—is admissible unless the Rules provide otherwise. Rule 403 allows the trial judge to exclude relevant evidence if, among other things, "its probative value is substantially outweighed by the danger of unfair prejudice." Rules 404 through 412 address specific types of evidence that have generated problems. Generally, these latter Rules do not flatly prohibit the introduction of such evidence but instead limit the purpose for which it may be introduced. Rule 404(b), for example, protects against the introduction of extrinsic act evidence when that evidence is offered solely to prove character. The text contains no intimation, however, that any preliminary showing is necessary before such evidence may be introduced for a proper purpose. If offered for such a proper purpose, the evidence is subject only to general strictures limiting admissibility such as Rules 402 and 403.

Petitioners claim inconsistent w/ legis. history

Petitioner's reading of Rule 404(b) as mandating a preliminary finding by the trial court that the act in question occurred not only superimposes a level of judicial oversight that is nowhere apparent from the language of that provision, but it is simply inconsistent with the legislative history behind Rule 404(b). The Advisory Committee specifically declined to offer any "mechanical solution" to the admission of evidence under 404(b). Advisory Committee's Notes on Fed.Rule Evid. 404(b), 18 U.S.C.App., p. 691. Rather, the Committee indicated

The only determination necessary

that the trial court should assess such evidence under the usual rules for admissibility: "The determination must be made whether the danger of undue prejudice outweighs the probative value of the evidence in view of the availability of other means of proof and other factors appropriate for making decisions of this kind under Rule 403." Ibid; see also S.Rep. No. 93–1277, p. 25 (1974) ("[I]t is anticipated that with respect to permissible uses for such evidence, the trial judge may exclude it only on the basis of those considerations set forth in Rule 403, i.e., prejudice, confusion or waste of time").

Congress much more concer restrictions wouldn't be put on FRE 404 evidence

Petitioner's suggestion that a preliminary finding is necessary to protect the defendant from the potential for unfair prejudice is also belied by the Reports of the House of Representatives and the Senate. The House made clear that the version of Rule 404(b) which became law was intended to "plac[e] greater emphasis on admissibility than did the final Court version." H.R.Rep. No. 93–650, p. 7 (1973). The Senate echoed this theme: "[T]he use of the discretionary word 'may' with respect to the admissibility of evidence of crimes, wrongs, or other acts is not intended to confer any arbitrary discretion on the trial judge." S.Rep. No. 93–1277, at 24. Thus, Congress was not nearly so concerned with the potential prejudicial effect of Rule 404(b) evidence as it was with ensuring that restrictions would not be placed on the admission of such evidence.

We conclude that a preliminary finding by the court that the Government has proved the act by a preponderance of the evidence is not called for under Rule 104(a).[6] This is not to say, however, that the Government may parade past the jury a litany of potentially prejudicial similar acts that have been established or connected to the defendant only by unsubstantiated innuendo. Evidence is admissible under Rule 404(b) only if it is relevant. "Relevancy is not an inherent characteristic of any item of evidence but exists only as a relation between an item of evidence and a matter properly provable in the case." Advisory Committee's Notes on Fed.Rule Evid. 401, 28 U.S.C.App., p. 688. In the Rule 404(b) context, similar act evidence is relevant only if the jury can reasonably conclude that the act occurred and that the defendant was the actor. See United States v. Beechum, 582 F.2d 898, 912–913 (CA5 1978) (en banc). In the instant case, the evidence that petitioner was selling the televisions was relevant under the Government's theory only if the jury could reasonably find that the televisions were stolen.

Such questions of relevance conditioned on a fact are dealt with under Federal Rule of Evidence 104(b). Beechum, supra, at 912–913; see also E. Imwinkelried, Uncharged Misconduct Evidence § 2.06 (1984). Rule 104(b) provides:

> "When the relevancy of evidence depends upon the fulfill-
> ment of a condition of fact, the court shall admit it upon, or
> subject to, the introduction of evidence sufficient to support a
> finding of the fulfillment of the condition."

In determining whether the Government has introduced sufficient evidence to meet Rule 104(b), the trial court neither weighs credibility nor makes a finding that the Government has proved the conditional fact by a preponderance of the evidence. The court simply examines all the evidence in the case and decides whether the jury could reasonably find the conditional fact—here, that the televisions were stolen—by a preponderance of the evidence. The trial court has traditionally exercised the broadest sort of discretion in controlling the order of proof at trial, and we see nothing in the Rules of Evidence that would change this practice. Often the trial court may decide to allow the proponent to introduce evidence concerning a similar act, and at a

---

6. Petitioner also suggests that in performing the balancing prescribed by Federal Rule of Evidence 403, the trial court must find that the prejudicial potential of similar acts evidence substantially outweighs its probative value unless the court concludes by a preponderance of the evidence that the defendant committed the similar act. We reject this suggestion because Rule 403 admits of no such gloss and because such a holding would be erroneous for the same reason that a preliminary finding under Rule 104(a) is inappropriate. We do, however, agree with the Government's concession at oral argument that the strength of the evidence establishing the similar act is one of the factors the court may consider when conducting the Rule 403 balancing.

later point in the trial assess whether sufficient evidence has been
offered to permit the jury to make the requisite finding. If the
proponent has failed to meet this minimal standard of proof, the trial
court must instruct the jury to disregard the evidence.

We emphasize that in assessing the sufficiency of the evidence
under Rule 104(b), the trial court must consider all evidence presented
to the jury. "[I]ndividual pieces of evidence, insufficient in themselves
to prove a point, may in cumulation prove it. The sum of an evidentiary presentation may well be greater than its constituent parts."
Bourjaily v. United States, 483 U.S. 171 (1987). In assessing whether
the evidence was sufficient to support a finding that the televisions
were stolen, the court here was required to consider not only the direct
evidence on that point—the low price of the televisions, the large
quantity offered for sale, and petitioner's inability to produce a bill of
sale—but also the evidence concerning petitioner's involvement in the
sales of other stolen merchandise obtained from Wesby, such as the
Memorex tapes and the Amana appliances. Given this evidence, the
jury reasonably could have concluded that the televisions were stolen,
and the trial court therefore properly allowed the evidence to go to the
jury.

We share petitioner's concern that unduly prejudicial evidence
might be introduced under Rule 404(b). See Michelson v. United
States, 335 U.S. 469, 475–476 (1948). We think, however, that the
protection against such unfair prejudice emanates not from a requirement of a preliminary finding by the trial court, but rather from four
other sources: first, from the requirement of Rule 404(b) that the
evidence be offered for a proper purpose; second, from the relevancy
requirement of Rule 402—as enforced through Rule 104(b); third, from
the assessment the trial court must make under Rule 403 to determine
whether the probative value of the similar acts evidence is substantially
outweighed by its potential for unfair prejudice, and fourth, from
Federal Rule of Evidence 105, which provides that the trial court shall,
upon request, instruct the jury that the similar acts evidence is to be
considered only for the proper purpose for which it was admitted.

Affirmed.

JAMES AND DICKINSON, ACCIDENT PRONENESS AND ACCIDENT LAW

63 Harv.L.Rev. 769, 791–94 (1950).*
[Footnotes omitted.]

* * * There is also a question whether evidence of a person's
accident proneness is to be admitted to show what he probably did on
this occasion. The difficulties spring chiefly from the rule limiting the
use of character to show conduct on a specific occasion and the inhibi-
tions against the use of prior specific instances to throw light on what
was done in the case at bar.

In civil cases the general rule is that evidence of a party's character is not admissible to show what his conduct was on a particular
occasion, but that evidence of his habit or custom of doing or omitting a
particular thing may be received for this purpose. The general propensity to be negligent or careful has usually been assimilated to character,
and evidence of it excluded, though on no very satisfactory ground. It
could scarcely be urged that propensity is totally without probative
value, though perhaps its rational probative effect is too slight to
warrant the risks of an unduly long excursion into collateral matters
and a too facile overpersuasion of uncritical minds. Such reasoning
would obviously exclude evidence offered to show that a party was
accident-prone for the purpose of proving that he was negligent at the
time of the accident. And this would be true however the accident
proneness was sought to be evidenced—whether by the opinion of
experts, by tests, by a showing of past accidents, or otherwise.

It may be urged with considerable force that the recent studies
invite reconsideration of the rule stated in the last paragraph, since
they afford a scientific basis for attributing more probative value to
accident proneness, when properly shown, than loose conclusions about
propensity toward negligence deserve. Moreover, the general rule has
not commanded universal acceptance. Some courts, for example, admit
evidence of a person's general disposition to be careful in order to show
care at the time of the accident, where there are no eyewitnesses to his
conduct at that time; and very occasionally courts have admitted this
kind of evidence for such a purpose in cases beyond the scope of this
exception. Under such rulings, proper evidence of accident proneness
should be admitted to show carelessness.

Where it is proper to show accident proneness for this or any other
purpose, there is a question of how it may be proven. The results of
specific tests of the individual in question should be admissible if
introduced through the testimony of a qualified expert who can show
that the tests are scientifically approved ones, that they were properly
administered in this case, and what the significance of the result is.
The last might well be in the form of an expert opinion whether the
individual was accident-prone.

As we have seen, a conclusion as to accident proneness may also be
based on, or contributed to by, a clinical interview and observation or a
past accident record. The former should be admissible in evidence as
an admission against a party to the action if a qualified expert will
testify as to its meaning. Where, however, the conduct of a nonparty is
in issue (as where an employer is sued for his employee's negligence),
the subject's narrative as to his case history will run afoul of the
hearsay rule if offered through the observer. This difficulty could be
obviated by eliciting the narrative, on the stand, from the subject
himself and calling the expert simply to interpret it.

The admissibility of past accident records presents more difficulty
in view of the traditional reluctance of the law of evidence to receive
individual instances for the purpose of showing propensity, character,
or the like. Exclusion has been based in part on a supposed lack of

Past accid. records often excluded because lack probative value & too many collateral issues —

strong probative value and on fear of encountering too many collateral
issues. The recent studies should reduce the force of both objections.
They tend to indicate that accident records have substantial bearing on
the actor's conduct at the time of accident. And they show that
collateral inquiry into the particular circumstances surrounding the
other accidents is largely unnecessary since the crucial fact is the mere
repetition itself of involvement in accident. * * *

PERRIN v. ANDERSON

United States Court of Appeals, Tenth Circuit, 1986.
784 F.2d 1040.

LOGAN, Circuit Judge.

* * *

This is a 42 U.S.C. § 1983 civil rights action for compensatory and
punitive damages arising from the death of Terry Kim Perrin. Plaintiff, administratrix of Perrin's estate and guardian of his son, alleged
that defendants, Donnie Anderson and Roland Von Schriltz, members
of the Oklahoma Highway Patrol, deprived Perrin of his civil rights
when they shot and killed him while attempting to obtain information
concerning a traffic accident in which he had been involved. The jury
found in favor of defendants.

In this appeal plaintiff contends that the district court erred in
admitting testimony by four police officers recounting previous violent
encounters they had had with Perrin. * * *

A simple highway accident set off the bizzarre chain of events that
culminated in Perrin's death. The incident began when Perrin drove
his car into the back of another car on an Oklahoma highway. After
determining that the occupants of the car he had hit were uninjured,
Perrin walked to his home, which was close to the highway.

Trooper Von Schriltz went to Perrin's home to obtain information
concerning the accident. He was joined there by Trooper Anderson.
They knocked on and off for ten to twenty minutes before persuading
Perrin to open the door. Once Perrin opened the door, the defendant
officers noticed Perrin's erratic behavior. The troopers testified that
his moods would change quickly and that he was yelling that the
accident was not his fault. Von Schriltz testified that he sensed a
possibly dangerous situation and slowly moved his hand to his gun in
order to secure its hammer with a leather thong. This action apparently provoked Perrin who then slammed the door. The door bounced
open and Perrin then attacked Anderson. A fierce battle ensued
between Perrin and the two officers, who unsuccessfully applied several
chokeholds to Perrin in an attempt to subdue him. Eventually Anderson, who testified that he feared he was about to lose consciousness as a
result of having been kicked repeatedly in the face and chest by Perrin,
took out his gun, and, without issuing a warning, shot and killed
Perrin. Anderson stated that he was convinced Perrin would have
killed both officers had he not fired.

At trial the court permitted four police officers to testify that they had been involved previously in violent encounters with Perrin. These officers testified to Perrin's apparent hatred or fear of uniformed officers and his consistently violent response to any contact with them. For example, defendants presented evidence that on earlier occasions Perrin was completely uncontrollable and violent in the presence of uniformed officers. On one occasion he rammed his head into the bars and walls of his cell, requiring administration of a tranquilizer. Another time while barefoot, Perrin kicked loose a porcelain toilet bowl that was bolted to the floor. One officer testified that he encountered Perrin while responding to a public drunk call. Perrin attacked him, and during the following struggle Perrin tried to reach for the officer's weapon. The officer and his back-up had to carry Perrin handcuffed, kicking and screaming, to the squad car, where Perrin then kicked the windshield out of the car. Another officer testified that Perrin attacked him after Perrin was stopped at a vehicle checkpoint. During the ensuing struggle three policemen were needed to subdue Perrin, including one 6'2" officer weighing 250 pounds and one 6'6" officer weighing 350 pounds.

Defendants introduced this evidence to prove that Perrin was the first aggressor in the fight—a key element in defendants' self-defense claim. The court admitted the evidence over objection, under Federal Rules of Evidence provisions treating both character and habit evidence. Plaintiff contends this was error.

A

Section 404(a) of the Federal Rules of Evidence carefully limits the circumstances under which character evidence may be admitted to prove that an individual, at the time in question, acted in conformity with his character. This rule is necessary because of the high degree of prejudice that inheres in character evidence. *See* Fed.R.Evid. 404 advisory committee note.* In most instances we are unwilling to permit a jury to infer that an individual performed the alleged acts based on a particular character trait. The exceptions to Rule 404(a)'s general ban on the use of character evidence permit criminal defendants to offer evidence of their own character or of their victim's character. Fed.R.Evid. 404(a)(1)–(2). Not until such a defendant takes this initial step may the prosecution rebut by offering contrary character evidence. Although the Advisory Committee on the Rules of Evidence has observed that this rule "lies more in history and experience than in logic," it does seem desirable to afford a criminal defendant every opportunity to exonerate himself.[1] In offering such potentially prejudicial testimony, the defendant of course proceeds at his own

---

* See p. B–19.

1. We agree with Professor Uviller's explanation of why a criminal defendant is entitled to use character evidence to a greater extent than a civil defendant:

"About the best one can do with this puzzle is to guess that somewhere, somehow the rule was relaxed to allow the criminal defendant with so much at stake and so little available in the way of

risk. Once he offers evidence of his or his victim's character, the
prosecution may offer contrary evidence. Fed.R.Evid. 404(a)(1)–(2).

Although the literal language of the exceptions to Rule 404(a)
applies only to criminal cases, we agree with the district court here
that, when the central issue involved in a civil case is in nature
criminal, the defendant may invoke the exceptions to Rule 404(a).

In a case of this kind, the civil defendant, like the criminal
defendant, stands in a position of great peril. A verdict against the
defendants in this case would be tantamount to finding that they killed
Perrin without cause. The resulting stigma warrants giving them the
same opportunity to present a defense that a criminal defendant could
present. Accordingly we hold that defendants were entitled to present
evidence of Perrin's character from which the jury could infer that
Perrin was the aggressor. The self-defense claim raised in this case is
not functionally different from a self-defense claim raised in a criminal
case.[2]

Although we agree with the district court that character evidence
was admissible in this case, we hold that the district court should not
have permitted testimony about prior specific incidents.

Federal Rule of Evidence 405 establishes the permissible methods
of proving character:

> "(a) **Reputation or opinion.** In all cases in which evidence of
> character or a trait of character of a person is admissible, proof
> may be made by testimony as to reputation or by testimony in
> the form of an opinion. On cross-examination, inquiry is
> allowable into relevant specific instances of conduct.

> (b) **Specific instances of conduct.** In cases in which charac-
> ter or a trait of character of a person is an essential element of
> a charge, claim, or defense, proof may also be made of specific
> instances of his conduct."

Testimony concerning specific instances of conduct is the most convincing, of course, but it also "possesses the greatest capacity to arouse
prejudice, to confuse, to surprise and to consume time." Rule 405
therefore concludes that such evidence may be used only when character is in issue "in the strict sense."

Character is directly in issue in the strict sense when it is "a
material fact that under the substantive law determines rights and
liabilities of the parties." In such a case the evidence is not being
offered to prove that the defendant acted in conformity with the
character trait; instead, the existence or nonexistence of the character

---

conventional proof to have special dispensation to tell the factfinder just what
sort of person he really is."

Uviller, Evidence of Character to Prove
Conduct: Illusion, Illogic, and Injustice in
the Courtroom, 130 U.Pa.L.Rev. 845, 855
(1982).

2. Plaintiff also argues that, because
defendants had no personal knowledge of

Perrin's character, evidence of his character was irrelevant. Although plaintiff is
correct that this evidence has no bearing
on whether defendants had a reasonable
fear of Perrin, it is directly relevant to the
issue of who was the aggressor in the fight.

trait itself "determines the rights and liabilities of the parties." In a defamation action, for example, the plaintiff's reputation for honesty is directly at issue when the defendant has called the plaintiff dishonest.

Defendants here offered character evidence for the purpose of proving that Perrin was the aggressor. "[E]vidence of a violent disposition to prove that the person was the aggressor in an affray" is given as an example of the circumstantial use of character evidence in the advisory committee notes for Fed.R.Evid. 404(a). When character is used circumstantially, only reputation and opinion are acceptable forms of proof. We therefore find that the district court erroneously relied upon the character evidence rules in permitting testimony about specific violent incidents involving Perrin.

B

Character and habit are closely akin. The district court found, alternatively, that the testimony recounting Perrin's previous violent encounters with police officers was admissible as evidence of a habit under Fed.R.Evid. 406. Here, we concur.

Rule 406 provides:

> "Evidence of the habit of a person * * *, whether corroborated or not and regardless of the presence of eyewitnesses, is relevant to prove that the conduct of the person * * * on a particular occasion was in conformity with the habit * * *."

The limitations on the methods of proving character set out in Rule 405 do not apply to proof of habit. Testimony concerning prior specific incidents is allowed.

This court has defined "habit" as "a regular practice of meeting a particular kind of situation with a certain type of conduct, or a reflex behavior in a specific set of circumstances." The advisory committee notes to Rule 406 state that, "[w]hile adequacy of sampling and uniformity of response are key factors, precise standards for measuring their sufficiency for evidence purposes cannot be formulated." That Perrin might be proved to have a "habit" of reacting violently to uniformed police officers seems rather extraordinary. We believe, however, that defendants did in fact demonstrate that Perrin repeatedly reacted with extreme aggression when dealing with uniformed police officers.

Four police officers testified to at least five separate violent incidents, and plaintiff offered no evidence of any peaceful encounter between Perrin and the police. Five incidents ordinarily would be insufficient to establish the existence of a habit. See Reyes v. Missouri Pacific Railway Co., 589 F.2d 791, 794–95 (5th Cir.1979) (four convictions for public intoxication in three and one-half years insufficient to prove habit). But defendants here had made an offer of proof of testimony from eight police officers concerning numerous different incidents. To prevent undue prejudice to plaintiff, the district court permitted only four of these witnesses to testify, and it explicitly stated that it thought the testimony of the four officers had been sufficient to

establish a habit. We hold that the district court properly admitted   1
this evidence pursuant to Rule 406. There was adequate testimony to   2
establish that Perrin invariably reacted with extreme violence to any   3
contact with a uniformed police officer.   4

　　Affirmed.   5
                                                                          6
                                                                          7
　　　　　　　　　　　　　　　　NOTE   8

　　See Federal Rules of Evidence 404, 405, and 803(21); California Evidence   9
Code §§ 1100–1104 and § 1324.   10

　　Until fairly recently, the character of the victim was admissible on behalf   11
of the defendant in one type of case other than that of self-defense—forcible   12
rape. The cases were virtually unanimous that where the defendant had   13
alleged consent as a defense, the "consenting character of the victim" could be   14
shown to make consent more likely. After 1970, statutes in virtually every   15
jurisdiction prohibited this, and did a good deal more as well. See Note, p. 439   16
and *State v. Cassidy*, p. 440. See Fed. Rules of Evidence 412, Cal. Evidence   17
Code Sec. 1103.   18
                                                                          19
                                                                          20
LILLY, AN INTRODUCTION TO THE LAW   21
OF EVIDENCE   22
(121–124).*

Evidence of Habit   23

　　The line between character and habit is not always easy to discern,   24
but the division can mark the difference between exclusion and admis-   25
sibility. * * * [E]vidence of habit, used circumstantially to prove   26
particular conduct, generally is admissible. The jurisdictions differ,   27
however, in their degree of receptivity. In some courts, evidence of   28
habit is admissible only if there is no eyewitness to the conduct in   29
question.[64]   30
                                                                          31
　　Character may be thought of as a trait or disposition which can   32
manifest itself in a variety of activities. Thus viewed, character is   33
more general than habit; the latter is a particular activity, routine, or   34
response that is frequently repeated over a protracted period of time.   35
A person with a character trait for punctuality and orderliness may   36
have a habit of picking up and sorting his mail each day at noon.   37

　　The probative value of habit is considered greater than that of   38
character. When evidence of habit is introduced, the desired inference   39
from habit to the conduct in question is grounded upon a series of   40
specific, repetitious actions. The trier is asked to infer that on the   41
occasion in question the actor conformed to habitual practice or proce-   42
dure. When evidence of character is considered, the desired inference   43
                                                                          44

64. McCormick, § 195, at 463. This   proof were considered reliable, should evi-
view is difficult to defend because its pre-   dence of habit be rejected? It seems that
mise is the superior reliability of eyewit-   this added evidence still should be present-
ness testimony—a proposition which is   ed for the trier's evaluation. The case for
highly dubious. A very good summary of   habit evidence especially is strong when
the weaknesses of testimonial proof, which   the eyewitness is one of the parties (or
collects many authorities, appears in   identified with one of the parties) and evi-
Maguire et al. at 52. Even if testimonial   dence of habit is offered by the adversary.

is grounded upon a trait, tendency, or disposition which may be displayed in somewhat varied circumstances. A general tendency to drive carefully could be displayed in a variety of driving activities. Thus, evidence that a person generally exercises care in driving is usually classified as evidence of character and rejected. Conversely, evidence that each workday a person traversed a particular railroad track and always stopped before crossing is generally classified as habit. The character-habit line becomes blurred when the evidence offered is that the actor always stopped at railroad crossings, but surely this is an area where the judge's discretion should be sustained.

The business environment, which is characterized by standardized procedures and routines, offers many opportunities to develop evidence of habit. Frequently, courts refer to habit within a business organization as "custom," but this difference in label does not alter the requirement of a repeated response to a particular circumstance. Some courts have required that the admissibility of evidence of custom be dependent upon corroborating evidence that the custom was followed on the particular occasion in question. This is an inadvisable limitation which loses sight of the rationale of evidence showing a habit or custom: the theory is that a pattern of continuous activity increases the likelihood that the custom was followed on the particular occasion.

The modern approach to the admissibility of habit and custom is expressed in the following provision of the Federal Rules of Evidence:

> Evidence of the habit of a person or of the routine practice of an organization, whether corroborated or not and regardless of the presence of eyewitnesses, is relevant to prove that the conduct of the person or organization on a particular occasion was in conformity with the habit or routine practice.[69]

Note that the Federal Rule expressly rejects the eyewitness requirement [70] and leaves open the question of what kind of evidence is admissible to prove habit or custom.[71] The usual method of proof is by the testimony of a witness who has observed the habit or custom over a sufficient period to state that it is a routine, repeated practice. Sometimes, however, the proponent must resort to proof of a number of specific instances which, taken together, demonstrate the required regularity. This manner of proof is generally accepted, although dissimilarities between the instances or the apparent lack of a sufficient number to establish a routine may result in the judge's discretionary rejection. The Federal Rule also rejects the requirement, imposed by some courts, that business custom be corroborated as a condition

---

69. In a recent criminal case the trial judge was reversed for excluding evidence of business custom.

70. See supra n. 64 and accompanying text.

71. The House Committee on the Judiciary deleted a provision that would have authorized the proof of habit by opinion evidence and evidence of specific instances of conduct. This deletion was made to allow the courts to deal with this issue on a case-by-case basis. The Committee noted that it did not intend to sanction a general authorization for the use of opinion evidence to show habit. H.Rep. 93–650, 93d Cong., 2d Sess. reprinted in 1974 U.S. Code Cong. & Admin. News 7075, 7079. In any event, it would appear that an opinion whether a habit was followed on the occasion in question would not be appropriate unless there was evidence of repetitious conduct.

precedent to its admission. Corroboration is viewed correctly as relating to the sufficiency of evidence rather than to its admissibility.[73]

————

See Federal Rules of Evidence 406; California Evidence Code § 1105.

Hypotheticals

(1) X, a prison inmate is charged with aggravated assault upon A, a fellow prisoner. The prosecution's case is that X and B, another inmate, assaulted A and stabbed him numerous times. X's defense is that his only part in the fray was to break up a fight between A and B. X calls Y, an inmate who did not witness the fight, to testify that he has known X for one month and that, in his opinion, X is a nonviolent man. The prosecutor makes an inadmissible-character-evidence objection to Y's proposed testimony. What result?

(2) X is charged with first degree murder of A, a police officer. B, a police officer, testifies that he was with A in a police car and that they stopped X, who was driving an automobile in an erratic fashion; that A asked X to step out and X complied; that A then asked X to raise his hands so he could be checked for weapons; that instead, X sprang back, drew a gun from a concealed holster under his shirt and began firing; that A was hit and died the next day; and that B succeeded in disarming X and placed him under arrest. The prosecution offers evidence that (a) X was on parole from a felony sentence in Illinois and his presence in California was in violation of his parole; (b) seven days before the charged offense X committed armed robbery of a market in Denver, Colorado; and (c) the automobile in which X was riding had been stolen from a San Francisco car dealer three days before the charged offense. The prosecutor announces that he is offering the above items of evidence on the issues of motive, intent, and premeditation. X makes an irrelevancy and inadmissible character evidence objection. How should the court rule?

(3) X is charged with grand theft from the person of A. X's defense is an alibi. A testifies that he is 85 years of age; that X approached him on the street, said he was celebrating the birth of a boy, put his arm around A, offered him a cigar and then left; and that immediately thereafter A noticed his wallet from his hip pocket was missing with its contents of $75. The prosecutor calls B and makes an offer of proof that he will testify that he is 84 years of age; that two months after the A incident, he was approached on the street by X who told him he was celebrating the birth of his first boy, offered him a cigar, put his arm around his waist, and asked for some street directions; that X pushed him slightly and then left; that B immediately felt for his wallet in his hip pocket and it was missing; and that he ran after X, saw him get into a car but could not catch him. The prosecutor states that B's testimony is offered on the issue of identity to prove modus operandi and common scheme or plan. X makes an irrelevancy and an inadmissible character-evidence objection. What result?

(4) X is charged with murder of A. X's version of events is that A, who lived in the same apartment building, was visiting X; that an argument developed and A took a karate stance and sprang at X; and that X wrestled A to the floor and stomped his foot in A's stomach. A died from injuries to the abdomen about two weeks later. In rebuttal, the prosecutor offers the following testimony: (1) the testimony of B that about two months before X's fight

73. Adv.Comm. Note to Fed.R.Evid. 406.

with A, he and X had a drunken quarrel; that X kicked him in the ribs, causing him to be hospitalized; and that X pleaded guilty to assault and battery; and (2) the testimony of C that he was a longtime acquaintance of X; that a year before X's fight with A, X and several others knocked him, C, down without reason; and that X then kicked him in the stomach. The prosecutor states that he is offering the testimony of B and C to establish X's modus operandi to use his feet in a fight. X makes an irrelevancy and an inadmissible character-evidence objection to the proposed testimony of B and C. What result?

(5) A sues X and the Y Bus Company for damages for personal injuries suffered in a collision between a bus driven by X, an employee of the Y Bus Company, and a car driven by A. A claims that X failed to stop at a stop sign. A calls B, who testifies that he has been a regular and daily rider on the bus driven by X during the six-month period preceding the accident, but that he was not on the bus the day of A's accident. A asks B whether, in this six-month period, X habitually failed to come to a stop at the intersection where the accident took place. X and the Y Bus Company make an inadmissible-character and a habit-evidence objection to A's question. Should the objections be sustained?

PART C. SIMILAR HAPPENINGS

SIMON v. KENNEBUNKPORT

Supreme Judicial Court of Maine, 1980.
417 A.2d 982.

GLASSMAN, Justice.

On the morning of July 22, 1977, the appellant, Irene Simon, sustained a broken hip when she stumbled and fell while walking on a sidewalk along Ocean Avenue in Kennebunkport. The elderly woman filed a complaint against the appellee, Town of Kennebunkport (Town), alleging that her injury was proximately caused by a defect in the design or construction of the sidewalk. Following a trial in the Superior Court, York County, the jury determined by special verdict that no defect in the sidewalk had proximately caused the appellant to fall, and judgment was entered for the appellee. The appellant contends that the presiding Justice erred in excluding evidence, offered to establish the defective condition of the sidewalk, that during the two years prior to the accident many other persons stumbled or fell at the location. We vacate the judgment.

Greg Quevillon and Anthony Cooper both operated businesses in the building in front of which the appellant fell. At trial Quevillon testified that the condition of the uneven, inclined sidewalk had not changed from the time it was constructed in 1974 or 1975 until the time of the accident in 1977. The appellant then attempted to elicit from this witness whether he had observed other persons fall at the location. The presiding Justice sustained the Town's objection, ruling that although the appellant could establish that the condition of the sidewalk had remained unchanged since its construction she could not offer evidence that other persons had fallen during this period. The appellant then represented that "if permitted to testify both Mr. Quevillon and Mr. Cooper would state that they saw nearly one person a day fall

on that particular sidewalk, and * * * evidence of prior fall[s] is
admissible where it goes to show a defect." Later, referring to the
proposed testimony of Cooper, the appellant stated:

> My offer of proof is that if permitted to testify this witness would
> indicate that on similar conditions of weather, and under condi-
> tions where the road was identical to that, the condition of July
> 22, 1979 [sic], he saw approximately 100 people stumble or fall on
> that particular portion of the roadway.

* * *

In a negligence action, evidence of other similar accidents or
occurrences may be relevant circumstantially to show a defective or
dangerous condition, notice thereof or causation on the occasion in
question. The absence of other accidents or occurrences may also be
probative on these issues. Nevertheless, Maine courts, with only rare
exceptions, traditionally excluded such evidence on the ground that it
"tends to draw away the minds of the jury from the point in issue
(negligence of the defendant at the time and place of the accident), and
to excite prejudice, and mislead them; and, moreover, the adverse
party, having no notice of such a course of evidence, is not prepared to
rebut it."

The genesis of an inflexible rule excluding other-accident evidence
is commonly believed to be the early Massachusetts case of Collins v.
Inhabitants of Dorchester, 60 Mass. (6 Cush.) 396 (1850), which reasoned
that such evidence was largely irrelevant, involved proof of collateral
facts and engendered unfair surprise. The overwhelming majority of
jurisdictions, including Massachusetts, have since either rejected or
abandoned a positive rule of exclusion in favor of a standard of
discretion. These courts hold that where the proponent can show that
other accidents occurred under circumstances substantially similar to
those prevailing at the time of the injury in question such evidence is
admissible subject to exclusion by the trial court when the probative
value of the evidence on the issues of defect, notice or causation is
substantially outweighed by the danger of unfair prejudice or confusion
of the issues or by consideration of undue delay.

A blanket rule of irrelevance is manifestly incompatible with
modern principles of evidence. Although the introduction of other-
accident evidence may carry with it the problems associated with
inquiry into collateral matters, such evidence may also be highly
probative on material issues of a negligence action, as illustrated by the
instant case. Early cases failed to discern that admitting this evidence
for its circumstantial force is not inconsistent with the fundamental
principle that negligence liability is to be predicated on absence of due
care under the circumstances at the time and place of injury. Although not rejecting prior case law, several later decisions of this Court
appeared to eschew a *per se* rule as unnecessarily broad and to recognize that the similarity requirement, together with the trial court's
discretion, adequately safeguards the proper use of this evidence.

Whatever the continued vitality following these cases of an absolute prohibition against other-accident evidence, it is clear that such a

rule did not survive the adoption of our new Rules of Evidence in 1976. Because the comprehensive reformulation does not specifically bar the use of this evidence, its admissibility must be determined by reference to the general provisions governing the admission of relevant evidence. M.R.Evid. 401 defines relevancy in terms of probative value and materiality. With exceptions not here pertinent, M.R.Evid. 402 provides that all relevant evidence is admissible. Although relevant, evidence may nevertheless be excluded under M.R.Evid. 403 when the danger of unfair prejudice, confusion or undue delay is disproportionate to the value of the evidence. Under this formulation, therefore, when a party seeks to introduce evidence of other accidents over objection on the ground of irrelevance, M.R.Evid. 401 requires the presiding Justice to determine the relevancy of the evidence on the basis of whether there is a substantial similarity in the operative circumstances between the proffer and the case at bar and whether the evidence is probative on a material issue in the case.[1] He must then consider whether the probative value of such evidence is substantially outweighed by the countervailing considerations of M.R.Evid. 403. As with other determinations of admissibility involving the balancing of probative value against prejudicial effect, the admission of other-accident evidence is committed to the sound discretion of the presiding Justice.[2]

In the case at bar, it is readily apparent that the ruling of the presiding Justice constituted an abuse of discretion which rose to the level of prejudicial error. Evidence that in the two years prior to the accident as many as one hundred persons stumbled or fell under similar circumstances at the same location, unchanged in condition, clearly satisfies the substantial-similarity foundational requirement and is highly probative on the material issue whether the sidewalk was in a defective condition at the time of the appellant's fall. As demonstrated by its prepared objection to the introduction of this evidence, the Town was well aware of the evidence before trial and therefore would not have been unfairly surprised by its admission. Because the evidence was to be offered through the personal observations of two witnesses, its introduction would not have consumed an inordinate amount of time or tended to confuse or excite the jury. The excluded evidence was crucial to the case of the appellant. The judgment of the Superior Court cannot stand.

* * *

All concurring.

1. As part of this determination, the presiding Justice must examine the temporal relationship between the proffered evidence and the injury in the case at bar. For example, evidence that other accidents occurred after the injury in question may be relevant to show causation but is without probative force on the issue of notice.

2. At a later stage of the trial, the Town offered evidence that the appellant's husband, who was walking directly in front of the appellant at the time of the accident, did not fall as tending to show the absence of a defect in the sidewalk. Over the appellant's objection, the presiding Justice admitted this evidence, ruling that, unlike the excluded evidence of prior falls, the "non-fall" evidence related to the immediate time frame of the accident. In view of our disposition of this appeal, we need not decide whether this ruling, assigned as an additional ground of error by the appellant, constituted an abuse of discretion and, if so, whether the error was harmless. See M.R.Evid. 103(a).

HALLORAN v. VIRGINIA CHEMICALS INC.

Court of Appeals of New York, 1977.
41 N.Y.2d 386, 393 N.Y.S.2d 341, 361 N.E.2d 991.

BREITEL, Chief Judge.

Defendant Virginia Chemicals appeals in a personal injury products liability action. Plaintiff Frank Halloran, an automobile mechanic, obtained a verdict in his favor, after a jury trial on the issue of liability only, for injuries he sustained while using a can of refrigerant packaged and sold by the chemical company. A divided Appellate Division affirmed, and certified a question of law for review in this court.

* * *

There is one * * * issue meriting extended discussion: whether evidence that the injured mechanic had previously used an immersion heating coil to heat the can of the refrigerant should be admissible to show that on the particular occasion he was negligent and ignored the labeled warnings on the can [which cautioned against using an immersion coil]. Evidently relying on the rubric excluding prior instances of carelessness to create an inference of carelessness on a particular occasion, both the Trial Judge and the Appellate Division, save for two dissenting Justices, agreed that such evidence was not admissible.

There should be a reversal and a new trial. If plaintiff, when necessary to stimulate the flow of the refrigerant, a highly compressed liquefied gas, habitually or regularly used an immersion coil to heat the water in which the container was placed, evidence of that habit or regular usage should be admissible to prove he followed such a procedure on the day of the explosion. Evidence of habit or regular usage, if properly defined and therefore circumscribed, involves more than unpatterned occasional conduct, that is, conduct however frequent yet likely to vary from time to time depending upon the surrounding circumstances; it involves a repetitive pattern of conduct and therefore predictable and predictive conduct. On this view, the excluded evidence was offered to show a particular method of executing a task followed by the mechanic, who, on his own testimony, had serviced "hundreds" of air-conditioning units and used "thousands" of cans of the refrigerant. If on remittal the evidence tends to show that the mechanic used an immersion coil a sufficient number of times to warrant a finding of habit, or regular usage, it would be admissible to aid the jury on its inquiry whether he did so on the occasion in question.

On June 1, 1970, the day of the accident, Frank Halloran, a mechanic for 15 years, had been employed by the Hillcrest Service station for over three years. Among his duties was the servicing and charging of automobile air-conditioning units, a job for which he had been specially trained, and for which he used "all [his] own tools." The particular task involved that day was the changing of the air-conditioning compressor on a 1967 Chrysler automobile. Plaintiff testified that he had emptied the system, removed the old compressor, and installed a new one. He then began to charge the unit.

The first two cans of the refrigerant, Freon, flowed into the system without difficulty. By the time he was emptying the third can, however, plaintiff found it necessary to accelerate the flow of the refrigerant. The mechanic described how he filled an empty two-pound coffee tin with warm tap water, used a thermometer to determine that the water temperature was about 90 to 100 degrees, and inserted into the coffee tin the third can of Freon. Having a similar problem with the flow of the fourth can, Halloran again dropped the Freon into the warm water. Noticing that his low pressure gauge showed a rapid increase in the pressure, and aware that "something was wrong", Halloran reached down to remove the can from the water, but was too late. The can exploded before he could touch it.

Neither the thermometer Halloran claimed to have used nor the bottom of the exploded can of Freon was produced at trial. Halloran knew that excessive heating of the can would cause damage, and that the warnings on the can specified 130 degrees as the maximum permissible safe temperature. As discussed earlier, he proved no particular defect in the can, its contents, or in so much of the exploded can which was produced at the trial. Having worked alone that day, Halloran was the only eyewitness to the explosion.

Defendant Virginia Chemicals * * * sought to establish that it was Halloran's "usage and practice" to use an immersion coil to heat the water in which the Freon was placed. * * *

Of course, had an immersion heating coil been used at the time of the accident the unexplained and thus far unexplainable explosion would have been fully explained.

* * *

To be sure, Halloran's practice prior to June 1, 1970 is not conclusive proof of the method he employed in working on the 1967 Chrysler. * * * While courts of this State have in negligence cases traditionally excluded evidence of carefulness or carelessness as not probative of how one acted on a particular occasion, in other cases evidence of a consistent practice or method followed by a person has routinely been allowed * * *. That a kind of habit, practice, or method was proffered in this case to establish negligence should not, without more, affect its admissibility.

Because one who has demonstrated a consistent response under given circumstances is more likely to repeat that response when the circumstances arise again, evidence of habit has, since the days of the common-law reports, generally been admissible to prove conformity on specified occasions * * *. Hence, a lawyer, to prove due execution of a will, may testify that he always has wills executed according to statutory requirements. So, too, to prove that notice is mailed on a specified day of the month, one is allowed to testify that he is in the habit of being home on that day of the month to transact such business.

When negligence is at issue, however, New York courts have long resisted allowing evidence of specific acts of carelessness or carefulness

to create an inference that such conduct was repeated when like
circumstances were again presented. Hence, evidence of a plaintiff's
habit of jumping on streetcars may not be offered to prove he was
negligent on the day of the accident. Nor could testimony that the
deceased had usually looked both ways before crossing railroad tracks
be introduced to establish his care on the particular occasion. Whether
a carryover from the prohibition against using so-called "character"
evidence in civil cases, or grounded on the assumption that even
repeated instances of negligence or care do not sufficiently increase the
probability of like conduct on a particular occasion, the statement that
evidence of habit or regular usage is never admissible to establish
negligence is too broad (see 1 Wigmore, Evidence [3d ed.], § 97, esp. p.
532).

At least, as in this kind of case, where the issue involves proof of a
deliberate and repetitive practice, a party should be able, by introducing evidence of such habit or regular usage, to allow the inference of its
persistence, and hence negligence on a particular occasion (see McCormick, Evidence [2d ed.], § 195, advocating an even more expansive
approach; see, also, 1 Wigmore, Evidence [3d ed.], § 97). Far less likely
to vary with the attendant circumstances, such repetitive conduct is
more predictive than the frequency (or rarity) of jumping on streetcars
or exercising stop-look-and-listen caution in crossing railroad tracks.
On no view, under traditional analysis, can conduct involving not only
oneself but particularly other persons or independently controlled instrumentalities produce a regular usage because of the likely variation
of the circumstances in which such conduct will be indulged. Proof of a
deliberate repetitive practice by one in complete control of the circumstances is quite another matter and it should therefore be admissible
because it is so highly probative.

As previously noted, Halloran, in the course of his work as a
mechanic, had serviced "hundreds" of automobile air conditioners and
had used "thousands" of cans of Freon. From his testimony at trial it
seems clear that in servicing these units he followed, as of course he
would, a routine. If, indeed, the use of an immersion coil tended to be
part of this routine whenever it was necessary to accelerate the flow of
the refrigerant, as he indicated was often the case, the jury should not
be precluded from considering such evidence as an aid to its determination.

Of course, to justify introduction of habit or regular usage, a party
must be able to show on *voir dire,* to the satisfaction of the Trial Judge,
that he expects to prove a sufficient number of instances of the conduct
in question * * *. If defendant's witness was prepared to testify to
seeing Halloran using an immersion coil on only one occasion, exclusion
was proper. If, on the other hand, plaintiff was seen a sufficient
number of times, and it is preferable that defendant be able to fix, at
least generally, the times and places of such occurrences, a finding of
habit or regular usage would be warranted and the evidence admissible
for the jury's consideration.

* * *

* * * [T]he action remitted for a new trial on the issue of liability.

JASEN, GABRIELLI, JONES, WACHTLER, FUCHSBERG and COOKE, JJ., concur.

MORRIS, STUDIES IN THE LAW OF TORTS
87–89 (1952).*
[Some footnotes omitted.]

* * * In the simple cases, safety-history evidence favorable to the defendant may be of greater weight than safety-history evidence favorable to the plaintiff. In Field v. Davis, the plaintiff was hurt when his mules backed his wagon out of the defendant's grain elevator and over the side of a railing-protected inclined roadway. The defendant was allowed to prove that thousands of wagons had been driven into his elevator and no other accident had ever happened on the incline. The jury might have been able to visualize the incline and appreciate its safety without such evidence; nevertheless, the fact that the plaintiff was injured is itself some slight evidence of danger, and the defendant deserves the protection of safety-history evidence—which tends to check the jury from formulating unsound general theories as to the danger of inclined roadways.

The difference between evidence of safety history offered by a plaintiff and that offered by a defendant is illustrated perhaps more sharply in Charlton v. St. L. & S.F.R.R. The plaintiff's deceased, a brakeman, was knocked off a ladder on the side of a moving boxcar by a standpipe maintained near the tracks. Another brakeman was allowed to testify that he brushed his arm on the same standpipe under similar circumstances. The problem of danger seems so simple that, after proof of the distance between cars and the standpipe, jurors could probably decide this case without the second brakeman's testimony as well as they could with it. While this testimony probably did no harm, a trial judge who excluded it would not have abused his discretion. But if the railroad had offered to prove that no brakeman other than the deceased had ever been brushed by the standpipe, in spite of constant exposure, the evidence should be received. The deceased's injury was proof that such an accident could happen. Unless the distance was so large that a trainman could be hit only by assuming an unlikely posture, jurors with the actual dimensions of the clearance before them are not likely to judge the clearance safe. But the situation may be safer than it seems to those without actual experience in railroading. Therefore, a defendant's proof of favorable safety history has greater probative value in this kind of case than a plaintiff's proof of unfavorable safety history. * * *

Hypothetical

A sues the X Golf Course for damages for personal injuries arising out of a slip-and-fall accident. A, a business invitee of X, was proceeding from the parking lot to the starting area and was walking across a new, level, cement veranda that has a smooth surface. A was wearing golf shoes with half-worn spikes and her feet slipped from under her, causing her serious injury. X calls B, the manager of the golf course, to testify that, during the year the cement veranda has been in existence, she had never been informed of any accidents on this area other than A's, and that between 3500 and 4000 persons per month had traversed the area wearing golf shoes. A objects to B's proposed testimony on the grounds of irrelevancy and that such negative evidence is precluded by law. What result?

PART D. SUBSEQUENT PRECAUTIONS

FLAMINIO v. HONDA MOTOR COMPANY

United States Court of Appeals, Seventh Circuit, 1984.
733 F.2d 463.

POSNER, Circuit Judge.

* * * In 1978 a middle-aged man named Forrest Flaminio bought a "Gold Wing" motorcycle, a large and powerful touring motorcycle manufactured by the Honda Motor Company of Japan (Japanese Honda) and distributed in the United States by its wholly owned subsidiary, American Honda Motor Company (American Honda). The motorcycles are shipped from Japan partially assembled, but assembly is completed by the dealers to whom American Honda distributes the motorcycles rather than by American Honda itself. Three days after taking delivery, and shortly after a dinner at which he had one or two drinks, Flaminio was driving the motorcycle down a two-lane road at night when he came up behind a car traveling at about 40 miles per hour. He passed it at a speed of somewhere between 50 and 70 m.p.h. (the speed limit was 50), and as he did so felt a vibration in the front end of the motorcycle. He tried to look at the front wheel to see what was wrong. This was an awkward maneuver because his feet were up on the motorcycle's "highway pegs" (supplied and installed by the motorcycle dealer rather than by either of the defendants), so that he was leaning backward. By his own admission the effort in this position to see the front wheel probably brought him up off the seat. In any event the motorcycle began to wobble uncontrollably and then it shot off the road and crashed, inflicting injuries that have left Flaminio a paraplegic.

* * * Flaminio sued Japanese Honda and American Honda, alleging that either the wobble was due to the defective design of the motorcycle, which should have been corrected, or the defendants should have warned users about the motorcycle's propensity to wobble.

* * *

The issue with respect to the allegation of defective design is whether the district court erred in excluding evidence (consisting of two blueprints) that, the plaintiffs say, shows that after the accident Honda, in an effort to reduce wobble, made the struts ("front forks") that connect the Gold Wing's handlebars to its front wheel two millimeters thicker. Rule 407 of the Federal Rules of Evidence makes evidence of subsequent remedial measures "not admissible to prove negligence or culpable conduct in connection with the event," but adds: "This rule does not require the exclusion of evidence of subsequent measures when offered for another purpose, such as proving ownership, control, or feasibility of precautionary measures, if controverted, or impeachment." Flaminio argues that the blueprints were admissible under the exceptions for "proving * * * feasibility of precautionary measures, if controverted," and for impeaching the defendants' evidence. But the first of these exceptions is inapplicable because the defendants did not deny the feasibility of precautionary measures against wobble. Their argument was that there is a tradeoff between wobble and "weave," and that in designing the model on which Flaminio was injured Japanese Honda had decided that weave was the greater danger because it occurs at high speeds and because the Gold Wing model—what motorcycle buffs call a "hog"—was designed for high speeds. The feasibility, as distinct from the net advantages, of reducing the danger of wobble was not in issue. As for the second exception, if the defendants had testified that they would never have thickened the struts on the Gold Wing, the blueprints would have been impeaching. But the defendants offered no such testimony. Although any evidence of subsequent remedial measures might be thought to contradict and so in a sense impeach a defendant's testimony that he was using due care at the time of the accident, if this counted as "impeachment" the exception would swallow the rule.

Flaminio also argues that Rule 407 does not apply to strict liability cases. There is a conflict among circuits on the question. Most hold that it does. But the Tenth Circuit holds that it does not apply, see Herndon v. Seven Bar Flying Service, Inc., 716 F.2d 1322, 1331 (10th Cir.1983), at least where state law would, in a strict liability case, allow evidence of subsequent remedial measures. * * *

In any event, we agree with the majority view that the rule does apply to strict liability cases. We are not persuaded by the purely semantic argument to the contrary that since "culpable conduct" is not the issue in such a case—the defendant is liable, at least prima facie, even if he is not blameworthy in the sense of being willful or negligent, provided that he caused the plaintiff's injury—the rule is inapplicable by its own terms. Wisconsin law rejects this argument in holding that a defendant's blameworthiness must, under the state's comparative-negligence statute, be compared with the plaintiff's blameworthiness in strict liability cases, even though the defendant was not blameworthy in a negligence sense. A major purpose of Rule 407 is to promote safety by removing the disincentive to make repairs (or take other safety measures) after an accident that would exist if the accident victim could use those measures as evidence of the defendant's liability. One might think it not only immoral but reckless for an injurer, having been alerted by the accident to the existence of danger, not to take steps to correct the danger. But accidents are low-probability events.

The probability of another accident may be much smaller than the
probability that the victim of the accident that has already occurred
will sue the injurer and, if permitted, will make devastating use at trial
of any measures that the injurer may have taken since the accident to
reduce the danger.

The analysis is not fundamentally affected by whether the basis of
liability is the defendant's negligence or his product's defectiveness or
inherent dangerousness. In either case, if evidence of subsequent
remedial measures is admissible to prove liability, the incentive to take
such measures will be reduced.

Affirmed.

MAINE RULES OF EVIDENCE
June 1975.

RULE 407

SUBSEQUENT REMEDIAL MEASURES;
NOTIFICATION OF DEFECT

(a) **Subsequent remedial measures.** When, after an event, measures are taken which, if taken previously, would have made the event
less likely to occur, evidence of the subsequent measures is admissible.

(b) **Notification of defect.** A written notification by a manufacturer of any defect in a product produced by such manufacturer to
purchasers thereof is admissible against the manufacturer on the issue
of existence of the defect to the extent that it is relevant.

———

Compare with Federal Rules of Evidence 407; California Evidence
Code § 1151.

DAGGETT v. ATCHISON, TOPEKA AND SANTA FE
RAILWAY CO.
Supreme Court of California, 1957.
48 Cal.2d 655, 313 P.2d 557.

CARTER, Justice. Defendants, The Atchison, Topeka and Santa
Fe Railway Company, G.H. Benton (motorman), and Irwin M. Pike
(conductor) appeal from a judgment in favor of John S. Daggett for the
loss of his two minor children in an action arising out of a collision
between one of defendant's passenger trains and an automobile driven
by Paula Smith Daggett, who died in the same accident, at a railway
crossing in Solana Beach. Olga Smith and Paul R. Smith, the parents
of Paula Smith Daggett (wife of John S. Daggett) were also plaintiffs in
the action but as to them the jury found in favor of defendant railway
company.

Neither the negligence of defendants, nor the contributory negligence of Paula Smith Daggett, are issues on this appeal. The only two
assignments of error with respect to the evidence relate to the examination of defendant railway's employees called under section 2055 of the

Code of Civil Procedure. The facts therefore will be set forth as briefly as possible but with particular emphasis on the disputed evidence.

The accident occurred at approximately 11:18 a.m. on June 25, 1954. It was a clear day. Mrs. Daggett, who was 24 years of age and eight months pregnant, was driving in a westerly direction on Plaza Street, Solana Beach, accompanied by her two minor children, aged 3 years and 10 months, respectively. Defendant's train, which was traveling in a southerly direction at a speed of between 86 and 90 miles an hour crossed the intersection of Plaza Street on its railroad tracks at the same time as Mrs. Daggett's automobile which was estimated to be traveling at a speed of from 10 to 15 miles per hour. Mrs. Daggett and the two minor children were killed in the accident. On the north side of Plaza Street was a lumber company building about 75 feet from the crossing; on the same side of Plaza Street was a railroad siding on which stood a freight car about 100 feet from the crossing. Both the building and the freight car were on Mrs. Daggett's right (the direction from which the train approached the crossing) as she drove westerly on Plaza Street toward the railroad crossing. On the northeast corner (on Mrs. Daggett's right) of the intersection of the tracks and Plaza Street was an automatic wigwag signal located 12 feet 9 inches above the ground; on the southwest corner of the crossing was a standard crossarm. Running parallel to, and a very short distance from, defendant's railroad tracks is the Pacific Coast Highway which intersects Plaza Street after it crosses the tracks. At this intersection there is a traffic light for vehicular traffic.[1] Ringing circuits for the operation of the wigwag signal were set off by a southbound train at a point 3,023 feet north of Plaza Street where it intersects with the tracks. In view of the speed at which defendant's train was approaching the intersection, this would result in the operation of the automatic wigwag signal for approximately 22 seconds.

Glenn H. Benton, a defendant, and the motorman who was operating the train at the time of the accident, was the first witness called by plaintiffs under section 2055 of the Code of Civil Procedure.[2] Mr. Benton testified that the train which he was operating at the time of the accident was a four-unit Diesel with ten passenger cars; that it was capable of a speed of 100 miles an hour; that at the time of the accident he had the train in throttle "position 8" (the highest speed position) and that the train was going from 85 to 90 miles an hour; that the railroad speed limit for that crossing was 90 miles an hour and that this was considered a safe speed.[3] The witness also testified that on the day in question the train was 15 minutes late and that he was trying to make

1. There was evidence in the record that this light, rather than the automatic wigwag signal predominated the view of vehicular traffic proceeding in a westerly direction on Plaza Street.

2. A party to the record of any civil action or proceeding * * * may be examined by the adverse party as if under cross-examination, subject to the rules applicable to the examination of other witnesses. The party calling such adverse witness shall not be bound by his testimony, and the testimony given by such witness may be rebutted by the party calling him for such examination by other evidence * * *.

3. The record shows that an average of 2,500 automobiles crossed the tracks daily at this intersection.

up time. Mr. Benton testified that the area involved was part of the   1
fourth district and that the speed limit for that district was 90 miles an   2
hour. The witness testified that the speed "*is* 90 now on the first,   3
second, and fourth districts." (Emphasis added.) Over objection by   4
defense counsel the following occurred: "Q. [By plaintiffs' counsel]:   5
Well, Mr. Benton, the restriction now is 50 miles an hour, isn't it?"   6
Plaintiffs' counsel, in answer to the court's question concerning the   7
district to which he was referring, replied: "He is referring to the   8
fourth. He says the restriction in the fourth district now is 90 miles an   9
hour. We are prepared to show that the restriction in this district at   10
this crossing now, rather than being 90 miles an hour, is 50 miles an   11
hour." In response to defense counsel's request to take "this matter"   12
up out of the presence of the jury, the court ruled that "He has a right   13
to say what he expects to prove or what he expects to get this witness to   14
testify to. It is cross-examination, a legitimate statement." Over   15
objection by defense counsel, the following took place: "Q. [Plaintiff's   16
counsel]: Mr. Benton, you say that the speeds in these areas then and   17
now are 90 miles an hour?" After objection and a holding that the   18
question was a compound one, the witness answered a simplified   19
question that the speed "now" at the "Plaza area" was 50 miles an   20
hour.   21

The second witness called by plaintiffs was William Price, signal   22
engineer for the defendant railway company. Mr. Price, who qualified   23
as an expert witness, and who testified under section 2055 of the Code   24
of Civil Procedure said that he was "absolutely sure" that the type of   25
signal in use at the Plaza crossing at the time of the accident was "the   26
safest type of signal." Counsel for plaintiffs, over objection, questioned   27
the witness and brought out that since the accident the California   28
Public Utilities Commission had requested defendant railway company   29
to change the single wigwag signal to two "flashing light signals"   30
located 8 feet above the ground level. Over objection, the court   31
permitted the jury to view the scene of the accident at a time when a   32
train crossed the intersection. At this time, of course, the speed limit   33
had been reduced and the new signals installed. However, photographs   34
of the crossing with the new signals installed had been theretofore   35
admitted in evidence without objection by defense counsel.[4]   36

Defendants contend that the court committed prejudicial error in   37
admitting evidence of changes made subsequent to the time of the   38
accident. Plaintiffs argue that the evidence was not admitted for the   39
purpose of showing changed conditions but to impeach the witnesses   40
called by them under section 2055. It is also argued by defendants that   41
evidence of changed conditions may not be used to impeach a witness   42
called under section 2055, and that the error was magnified by plain-   43
tiffs' counsel during argument to the jury.   44
   45
It is the general rule in this state that evidence of precautions   46
taken and repairs made after the happening of the accident is not   47
admissible to show a negligent condition at the time of the accident.   48

4. In Church v. Headrick & Brown, it   out objection the admission of similar evi-   49
was held that where evidence of changed   dence from another witness, over objection,   50
conditions was admitted by the court with-   was not ground for a reversal.   51

The reason for the rule was well stated in Sappenfield v. Main St. & A.P.R. Co.: "It would be unjust to hold that, because the employer seeks by all the aid he gets from the light of experience to make the implement free from danger, he is therefore to be charged with negligence in the use of all prior appliances, even though they were adopted with the best light then under his control. * * * He may have exercised all the care which the law requires, and yet in the light of a new experience, after an unexpected accident has occurred, he may adopt additional safeguards. To hold that the adoption of such new appliances which experience has demonstrated are more efficient than those previously in use, or which invention has developed from observing the defects in those originally adopted, shall be an admission that he was negligent prior thereto would prevent the very conduct in employers which they should be urged to follow."

This court has held, however, that "Although evidence of the character here in question may not be admissible to prove negligence at the time of the accident, it is proper to impeach the testimony of a witness. Inyo Chemical Co. v. City of Los Angeles, supra. * * * [W]here evidence is admissible for a limited purpose only, it is not the duty of a judge to instruct the jury as to such purpose unless requested to do so [citations omitted]. Having failed to request an instruction that the impeaching evidence was admitted only for that purpose and was not otherwise competent, defendants may not complain.

* * *

The judgment is affirmed.

GIBSON, C.J., and SHENK and TRAYNOR, JJ., concur.

SCHAUER, Justice (dissenting).

It is my view that it was prejudicial error to bring before the jury the fact that after the accident defendant railroad company reduced its speed limitation from 90 to 50 miles an hour at the intersection in Solana Beach where the railroad tracks crossed Plaza Street and where the accident occurred. The attempt to defend such an error as being merely the presentation of impeaching evidence appears to me to be without support in the record. To the contrary, the record affirmatively shows that at no time did the witness, Benton, testify that the limitation for the crossing remained at 90 miles an hour at the time of trial. His testimony was clearly to the effect that the general limitation for the entire fourth district—i.e., the area from Fullerton to San Diego—was 90 miles both at the time of the accident and at the time of trial, and he had further made clear that there were other limitations calling for lesser speeds at various smaller areas within the district. Moreover, any confusion as to speeds, times, and districts or areas appears from the record to have been invited and brought about by counsel for plaintiffs, who then seized upon such alleged confusion as an excuse to get before the jury otherwise inadmissible evidence of a change in the speed limitation after the accident. The following excerpts from the examination of Benton by counsel for plaintiffs, who had called him as a witness under section 2055 of the Code of Civil Procedure, will so demonstrate (all italics have been added):

"Q. [By counsel for plaintiff] What *was* [at the time of the accident] that crossing posted for as far as the railroad was concerned? A. 90 miles an hour. * * *

"Q. Now, with reference to whether you were early or late, were you late on that run, on that day? A. We were. We were late. * * *

"Q. And where was the place to the Los Angeles side of Solana Beach where you had last attempted to pick up some time? A. The speed restriction down *at the district* is 90 miles per hour, *with the exception of where there is curve restrictions or restrictions otherwise.* * * *

"Q. Well, how fast *did* you usually go across that intersection in Solana Beach? A. Between 80—between 80 and 90 miles per hour. * * *

"Q. But across this intersection your speed varies [note present tense used by counsel for plaintiff] between 80 and 90 miles an hour; right? A. Yes, sir. * * *

"Q. Could you go as fast as 90 miles an hour around this curve that comes into Solana Beach or *is* [note the present tense] that restricted to less? A. That is 90 miles an hour.

"Q. And do I understand that you could go 90 miles an hour all the way from Los Angeles to San Diego? A. *No*, sir, because *there is restrictions, curve restrictions and other forms of restrictions.*

"Q. How about that curve from Cardiff into the place of the accident; *isn't* [note present tense] that curve restricted to 85? A. That's a 90 mile an hour curve. * * *

"Q. * * * Now, you have driven these diesels similar to the one you were driving on that day for some time, haven't you? A. Yes, sir.

"Q. And in driving those diesels, have you gone over 90 miles an hour with them? * * * A. I have. Those diesels are a hundred-mile-an-hour diesel, but *that* particular *district is 90 mile restriction* down there. *That's known as the fourth district.* * * *

"Q. What does fourth district mean; can you tell us? A. Well, that's the district from one station to the other.

"Q. That has nothing to do with the type of speed, does it? A. No.

"Q. Merely nomenclature of the area, merely geographically a description or appellation of the area, what it is called; is that right? A. What the company, what particular restriction they put on that particular district, why [the reason why] I don't know.

"Q. *Is* [note present tense employed by counsel for plaintiff] that put on the whole district from Los Angeles all the way to San Diego? A. That just runs from Fullerton to San

Diego, but from Los Angeles to Fullerton is a portion of the third district.

"Q. And then you *have* [note present tense] to go slower in that area? A. That's right.

"Q. What speed *do you go* [note present tense] in the area between Fullerton and Los Angeles? * * * A. The speed *restriction on* all *districts* in the Santa Fe Los Angeles Division *is 90 miles* an hour.

"Q. How about between Fullerton and Los Angeles? A. That *is* 90 miles an hour, too.

"Q. So there *is* no more restriction there than there *is* down here? A. Not at this time. I don't recall whether—it was a hundred on all districts but the third and fourth districts it was less, but it *is* the same all over now, with the exception of the third district. That *is* 80.

"Q. Your are not speaking of what it *is* now, are you? A. No. It *is 90 now on the* first, second, and *fourth districts.*

"Q. Well, Mr. Benton, the *restriction now is 50 miles an hour, isn't it?* * * * "

From the above-quoted portion of the record it is apparent that counsel for plaintiffs, by swinging back and forth between past tense and present tense, and by discussing speed restrictions without specific indication of whether he referred to restrictions within entire railroad districts or to restrictions at a smaller area within a district (such as at the Plaza Street crossing here involved), succeeded in confusing not only Benton, the witness, but also the court itself. Counsel then seized upon the confusion which he himself had engendered, to not only bring before the jury the fact that the restriction at the Plaza Street crossing had been changed to 50 miles, but to emphasize that the change had taken place subsequent to the accident. The admission of such improper evidence could not, and did not, tend to impeach the witness, who at no time had testified that the *Plaza Street* intersection speed had remained at 90 miles an hour up to the time of trial; on the contrary, the witness had clearly stated that the overall restriction in the fourth district (i.e., from Fullerton to San Diego) remained at 90 miles, but he had also several times referred to "curve restrictions and other forms of restrictions" within districts—references which were plainly understood by plaintiff's counsel, who himself likewise referred to such lesser restrictions. Inasmuch as the issue of negligence on the part of defendants was close, it appears that the error of admitting such evidence of changed conditions was prejudicial.

SPENCE and McCOMB, JJ., concur.

ANDERSON v. MALLOY

United States Court of Appeals, Eighth Circuit, 1983.
700 F.2d 1208.

LAY, Chief Judge.

Linda and Derriel Anderson appeal from a judgment on a jury verdict rendered against them in the United States District Court for the Eastern District of Missouri. The Andersons claim the trial court abused its discretion in excluding portions of the plaintiffs' evidence. We agree, and accordingly vacate the district court's judgment and remand the case for a new trial.

In January and February of 1979, the Andersons were guests in a motel in the St. Louis area owned and operated by the defendants, Malloy, Zes, and Gibson. On the evening of February 7, 1979, while Linda Anderson was alone in the motel room, an unknown assailant forcibly entered the room and assaulted and raped her.

The Andersons thereupon filed suit alleging diversity jurisdiction in federal district court in St. Louis, alleging that the defendants negligently failed to provide them with reasonably safe lodging, that the defendants breached an express warranty to provide reasonably safe lodging, and that the defendants fraudulently misrepresented the level of security provided to the motel's guests. * * *

The motel owners argued in defense that they had done everything reasonably necessary to make their motel secure. The defendants also affirmatively claimed that Linda Anderson's injuries were proximately caused by her own negligence in opening her door in a strange city to a person she did not know.[2] * * *

Evidence of Subsequent Remedial Measures.

The plaintiffs attempted to introduce evidence to show that, after Linda Anderson was assaulted and raped, the defendants installed safety chains and "peep holes" on the doors of all units in the motel. The trial court refused to admit the evidence on the ground that Federal Rule of Evidence 407 "generally prohibits" the admission of such evidence.

Rule 407 prohibits the admission of evidence of subsequent remedial measures when the evidence is offered to prove negligence or culpable conduct. However, the rule expressly does not require the exclusion of such evidence when offered for another purpose. Of course, to be admissible any evidence not excluded by rule 407 must still be relevant (Fed.R.Evid. 402) and its probative value must outweigh any dangers associated with its admission (Fed.R.Evid. 403).

The plaintiffs assert on appeal that the defendants controverted the feasibility of the use of peep holes and safety chains. Thus, the

---

2. Linda Anderson testified at trial that she heard a knock on the door. When she asked who was there, she heard a muffled voice that she thought was that of her husband. When she opened the door slightly, the assailant asked her a few questions and then forced his way into the room.

plaintiffs argue that the evidence comes within the exception of rule 407. Although the trial court held to the contrary, we find that the defendants did affirmatively controvert the feasibility of the chain locks and peep holes. We conclude that the trial court committed a prejudicial abuse of discretion when it excluded the evidence.

The first witness called by the plaintiffs was the defendant, Malloy, one of the owners of the motel. Malloy was asked by the plaintiffs' counsel about the security measures taken by the defendants since they purchased the motel in 1974, but he was not asked about the absence of peep holes or chain locks on the doors. On cross-examination defense counsel opened up the issue in the following exchange:

> Q. We've already talked about the additional lighting that was installed. Did [the village police chief] indicate to you anything about putting these peepholes, as they are called, in the solid core doors?
>
> A. He felt like we had six-foot picture windows right next to the door. If we'd put peepholes in, it would be false security.
>
> Q. Did you follow the officer's recommendation in that regard?
>
> A. Yes. We did not put the peepholes in at that time.
>
> Q. Did he indicate to you anything about these chains you see on doors on occasion?
>
> A. He felt like they were unnecessary, also. False security.

On redirect, in rebuttal, the plaintiffs' counsel then asked:

> Do I understand, [the police chief] indicated to you that it wouldn't be feasible to put in peepholes and chain guards on the front doors?

Mr. Malloy replied:

> A. At that time he felt like the picture windows were adequate for—that the peephole would be sort of a false security, because they could look out these picture windows and see the door, the step there.

Whether something is feasible relates not only to actual possibility of operation, and its cost and convenience, but also to its ultimate utility and success in its intended performance. That is to say, "feasible" means not only "possible," but also means "capable of being . . . utilized, or dealt with successfully." Webster's Third New International Dictionary 831 (unabridged ed. 1967); see Black's Law Dictionary 549 (5th ed. 1979) ("reasonable assurance of success.").

For the defendant to suggest that installation of peep holes and chain locks would provide only a false sense of security not only infers that the devices would not successfully provide security, it also infers that the devices would in fact create a lesser level of security if they were installed. With this testimony the defendants controverted the feasibility of the installation of these devices, because the defendant

Malloy in effect testified that these devices were not "capable of being utilized or dealt with successfully."

The defendants' counsel took advantage of the situation and in closing argument to the jury said that the evidence showed that the defendants in providing security "did everything anybody recommended that they do. What more can they do? . . . Is there any evidence from any reliable source that [the defendants] could or should have done anything more?" With such a suggestion implanted in the minds of the jurors by Malloy's testimony, the plaintiffs' counsel had every right to rebut that suggestion by showing that the defendants had in fact installed these devices after Linda Anderson was raped.

The plaintiffs were entitled to show affirmatively that these devices were feasible, and furthermore to impeach the credibility of the defendants by showing that, although the defendants testified that they had done everything necessary for a secure motel, and that chain locks and peep holes would not be successful, they in fact took further security measures after Linda Anderson was raped, and in fact installed the same devices that they testified could not be used successfully. Under rule 407 the evidence could not be used by the plaintiffs to prove the defendants' negligence, and a limiting instruction would warn the jury of this restriction in its admission. But we think it was an abuse of discretion for the trial court to refuse to admit the only evidence that would effectively rebut the inferences created by the defendants.

* * *

We find the trial court committed prejudicial error in the ruling discussed above; accordingly, we vacate the judgment of the district court, and remand the case for a new trial.

[Dissenting Opinion by Gibson, J., omitted]

Hypotheticals

(1) A sues X for damages for personal injuries arising out of A's slipping and falling on steps in a store owned and operated by X. A testifies that a strip of abrasive tape on the step on which she slipped was worn, and that the step was slippery. X calls B, the store manager, who testifies that the tape strips on the steps were not worn and that the steps were not slippery. In rebuttal, A offers to prove that a week after A's accident, X replaced the old strips of tape with new ones, and A offers in evidence photographs of the steps with the new strips of tape. X objects to A's offer of proof on the ground of the policy exclusion of evidence of subsequent remedial conduct. What result?

(2) Assume the same facts as in Illustration (1), except that A adds to her offer of proof the fact that B, the store manager who testified for X, was the person who authorized installation of the new abrasive tape strips after A's accident. X makes the same objection that he makes in Illustration (1). How should the court rule?

(3) P, a savings company, sues D, a bank, for damages arising out of a long-period embezzlement of $500,000 by M, a manager of P's branch office. From time to time, M placed the embezzled funds in a personal account with D and subsequently made withdrawals by checks to herself until all funds were withdrawn. P claims D was negligent in permitting M to make deposits and withdrawals from this account. D's defense is that P was negligent in its

accounting and auditing procedures which allowed M to embezzle such a large amount without detection. After the embezzlement, P retained X, an accounting firm, to audit P and recommend accounting and auditing changes. P placed such recommended changes into effect after getting X's report. D makes a discovery motion to inspect and copy X's report. What result?

PART E. OFFERS IN COMPROMISE

HATFIELD v. CONTINENTAL IMPORTS, INC.

Superior Court of Pennsylvania, 1990.
396 Pa.Super. 309, 578 A.2d 530.

DEL SOLE, Judge:

Following this court's grant of permission to take an interlocutory appeal, these appeals were filed challenging a trial court order which determined that it was appropriate for a settlement agreement to be brought into evidence at trial. We reverse.

This action was initiated by Agnes and Herbert Hatfield seeking to recover damages which were alleged to be a result of injuries Mrs. Hatfield sustained to her back following a fall from a chair which suddenly collapsed. The Hatfields set forth causes of action in negligence and products liability against Continental Imports Inc., and Marvin Gross and Leonard Gross individually and trading as Warehouse Imports (hereinafter called original defendants.). Original defendants subsequently joined as an additional defendant, Talin Industria Arredamenti, an Italian manufacturer, (hereinafter Talin).

The day before trial was scheduled to begin Talin presented a motion in limine to the court, seeking permission to introduce a settlement agreement and release into evidence. This agreement entered into between the Hatfields and the original defendants provided in part:

> In addition to the foregoing, the plaintiffs also agree to pursue an action against Talin Industria Arredamenti. If the action against Talin Industria Arredamenti is successful the plaintiffs will return fifty-thousand ($50,000.00) dollars to releasees, free and clear of all fees and expenses except that releasors agree to pay 50% of the expenses of the litigation against Talin Industria Arredamenti, incurred after the signing of this release. If releasees are able to settle their claim against Talin prior to trial, they will return to the releasees twenty-five thousand ($25,000.00) dollars free and clear of all fees and expenses.

The trial court granted Talin's motion, ruling that the release would be admissible at trial. Subsequently, the Hatfields and the original defendants sought, and were granted, permission to appeal this interlocutory order.

Our sole concern in this appeal is the admissibility of the agreement and release. The trial court ruled that it was admissible, accepting Talin's argument that the release constituted a "Mary Carter Agreement". The term "Mary Carter Agreement" was made popular after a Florida decision in *Booth v. Mary Carter Paint Co.*, 202 So.2d 8

(Fla.App.1967). Such an agreement has certain classic features. They include a secret agreement which dictates that the defendant must remain in the action and will pay to the plaintiff a certain monetary recovery regardless of the outcome of the action and will have his or her own maximum liability diminished proportionately by increasing the liability of the other co-defendants. The trial court adopted the position taken in the later Florida case of *Ward v. Ochoa*, 284 So.2d 385 (Fla.1973), and found that such an agreement should be admitted into evidence by citing the following passage:

> Secrecy is the essence of such an agreement because the court or jury as trier of the fact, if apprised of this, would likely weigh differently the testimony and conduct of the signing defendant as related to the non-signing defendant. *Ward v. Ochoa*, supra, at 387.

We decline to accept the position adopted by the trial court in this case. While the Appellants opine that the instant agreement is not a classic "Mary Carter Agreement" since the agreement was fully disclosed to the court, this jurisdiction has not considered or defined what is a "Mary Carter Agreement". We will not undertake such consideration here or determine the effect such an agreement would have on this action because we find this case to be controlled by 42 Pa.C.S.A. § 6141(c). This statute provides:

> **Admissibility in evidence.**—Except in an action in which final settlement and release has been pleaded as a complete defense, any settlement or payment referred to in subsections (a) [relating to personal injuries] and (b) [relating to damages to property] shall not be admissible in evidence on the trial of any matter.

This statute plainly states that settlements and releases shall not be disclosed to a jury. The only exception concerns a situation which is inapplicable here, where the settlement and release are pleaded as a complete defense. Although the settlement and release was not sought to be admitted as a complete defense to this action, the trial court believed a further exception should exist with respect to this settlement agreement which it found to be unduly prejudicial and biased against Talin. The trial court concluded that "in the interests of fairness and justice, to ensure that the jury fairly weighs the credibility of the witnesses, and properly determines liability, the jury must be apprised of the settlement agreement." This ruling was contrary to the express mandate of § 6141(c) which prohibits admission of such an agreement.

* * *

We conclude the outcome of this decision is mandated by the language of 42 Pa.C.S.A. § 6141(c) and the cases which interpret it to be without further exceptions. Accordingly, we reverse the trial court's order which granted Talin's motion in limine to introduce into evidence the settlement agreement and release.

KEETON, TRIAL TACTICS AND METHODS
52–54 (1954).*
[Most footnotes omitted.]

CASE 13. *P* is suing for injuries sustained in a collision between his car and *D's* truck. *P's* car, after the impact with *D's* truck, veered into *W's* car. When *P's* lawyer interviews *W,* he learns that *D* paid *W* $75 for a release and that *W* tells a version of the facts favorable to *D.* *P's* lawyer anticipates that *D* will call *W* as a witness in the trial, and he wants to be prepared to get in evidence the payment of $75 by *D* to *W,* though the possibility of an objection on the ground that it was paid in compromise of a disputed claim is apparent.

In some exceptional instances, the asking of questions which are clearly improper and prejudicial is regarded as such misconduct of counsel as to warrant the granting of a mistrial or new trial. There is a widespread attitude that it is fair practice to offer objectionable evidence so long as there is no violation of these comparatively innocuous rules against misconduct of counsel. Some lawyers frankly state, and still more practice, the ethically indefensible proposition that such an improper question should be asked unless the question is of such prejudicial character that the refusal of the trial court to declare a mistrial would be reversible error. This practice is sometimes used for the very purpose of confronting adverse counsel with the difficult choice of waiving objection by failing to make it, or else making an objection which may lead the jury to conclude that he is attempting to withhold information from them. An advocate of this practice may seek to justify it on the basis that the exclusionary rule of evidence applying to his case is archaic, that the jury should have the benefit of the evidence, and that his adversary ought to have to pay the price if he wants to take advantage of some technical rule of evidence. Another argument often advanced is that since the right to exclude evidence may be waived by failure to object, it is not improper to make the offer and hope that objection will be waived. Both of these arguments, and the practice of deliberate use of improper questions, probably should be regarded as inconsistent with the provision of Canon 22 [1] that "A lawyer should not offer evidence which he knows the Court should reject, in order to get the same before the jury by argument for its admissibility, * * *" and that kindred practices are condemned.

Protection against the deliberate use of clearly improper questions is inadequate under existing rules of law, unless the trial judge uses his discretionary powers to deal with the practice sternly. Even if ethical considerations are disregarded, however, some limitations exist as to advisability of asking objectionable questions, because of tactical considerations. The jury may recognize the unfairness of such tactics, after

---

* Copyright, 1954 by Prentice-Hall, Inc.

1. Canons of Professional Ethics of the American Bar Association. The second of the arguments stated above is the more troublesome. It might be urged that if the offering lawyer thinks his opponent may waive his ground of objection by failing to object either through design or by oversight, then the evidence offered is not "evidence which he knows the Court should reject," since the court should not reject it in the absence of an objection.

the court has sustained objection to the question, and may be influenced against the lawyer using such tactics and against his case. The jury's recognition of such unfairness might even occur without objection to the evidence, as in the case of a practice of continually leading the witness.

If admissibility is subject to reasonable doubt, on strictly ethical considerations the asking of the question is proper if the lawyer actually desires to insist on admission of the evidence, since it is the lawyer's right and duty to present the best case for his client that the facts and rules of law will support. Although it might be argued that he should first present such evidence to the court in the absence of the jury, for its admissibility to be determined, this attitude is rarely taken except in cases where the other attorney has presented an objection to the court in advance of the offer. On tactical considerations, offering evidence of doubtful admissibility should usually be avoided by the party (normally the plaintiff) who desires speedy termination of the case and has jury sympathy on his side, unless the evidence is actually important to persuasion of the jury, in the judgment of the lawyer. This is true for the reason that the admission of such evidence over objection may result in the granting of a new trial, if either the trial or appellate court later concludes that such admission was harmful error. The question might be asked with the purpose of not insisting upon admission of the evidence over objection, but it may be difficult to withdraw the question after it is asked. If the judge promptly overrules the objection when made, the lawyer who then tries to get the judge to withdraw the evidence by an instruction to the jury to disregard it will find it difficult to maintain even the appearance of good faith in making the offer.

If you conclude that the evidence of doubtful admissibility is likely to have a strong influence on the conclusion reached by the jury in the case, you may conclude that the chance of reversal is worth taking; the decision is based upon weighing the probable value of the evidence to you in its influence on the jury against the disadvantage of possible reversal of a favorable verdict and judgment. The evidence of payment of $75 to *W* by *D*, in Case 13, presents an illustration of this problem. If admissibility of this evidence is doubtful in the jurisdiction of trial, even on the alternative theory, the evidence probably should be offered unless plaintiff has a very strong case without it and a client whose circumstances make important prompt termination of the litigation (and avoidance of the possibility of new trial because of a decision that receipt of the evidence was harmful error).

ANDO v. WOODBERRY

Court of Appeals of New York, 1960.
8 N.Y.2d 165, 203 N.Y.S.2d 74, 168 N.E.2d 520.

FULD, Judge. This appeal calls upon us to decide a question of first impression in this court: May a defendant's prior plea of guilt to a traffic offense be introduced as evidence of his carelessness in a civil action for damages?

The relevant facts are simple and undisputed. Robert Ando, a police officer, driving a motorcycle, and Edward Nichols, driving an automobile owned by Essie Woodberry, were both proceeding north on Fifth Avenue, New York City, on the afternoon on December 28, 1955. Car and motorcycle collided when Mr. Nichols attempted to make a left turn at 110th Street, and Officer Ando was injured as a result of the collision. Mr. Nichols was given a summons which charged him with failing to make a proper turn and failing to signal before turning, and he subsequently appeared in the Manhattan Traffic Division of Magistrates' Court and pleaded guilty to both charges.

Upon the negligence trial, held in the Supreme Court, the only witnesses to the occurrence of the accident were the plaintiff and the defendant Nichols who drove the car. According to the plaintiff, Mr. Nichols, after first pulling over to the right, made a left turn without prior warning or signal and struck his motorcycle. Mr. Nichols not only denied that he had moved to the right, but asserted that he had given a signal upon making the turn. In order to strengthen his case, the plaintiff attempted to prove Mr. Nichols' plea of guilt in Traffic Court on the theory that it constituted an admission, but, upon the defendants' objection, the trial court excluded the proffered evidence. The jury returned a verdict in favor of the defendants and the Appellate Division, two Justices dissenting, affirmed the judgment subsequently rendered.

In deciding whether proof of a plea of guilty to a traffic violation should be received as evidence in chief in a subsequent civil action, it is well to recall the principle, basic to our law of evidence, that "All facts having rational probative value are admissible" unless there is sound reason to exclude them unless, that is "some specific rule forbids" (1 Wigmore, Evidence [3d ed., 1940], p. 293). It is this general principle which gives rationality, coherence and justification to our system of evidence and we may neglect it only at the risk of turning that system into a trackless morass of arbitrary and artificial Rules.

In view of the fact that Mr. Nichols' plea of guilty to the charges leveled against him—failing to signal and making an improper turn—is relevant to the issue of his negligence in turning off Fifth Avenue, we must simply decide whether there is any justification for excluding it. Two possible grounds of exclusion suggest themselves; the first, that such testimony is hearsay and, the second, that its introduction violates public policy.

Since a prior plea of guilt represents an admission, it is not obnoxious to the hearsay rule. Accordingly, the courts of this State, as well as of other jurisdictions, have generally sanctioned the receipt in evidence in a negligence action of a prior plea of guilty to a traffic violation. [Citations omitted.] Thus, when Mr. Nichols pleaded guilty to the traffic infractions charged against him, his plea of guilty amounted to a statement or admission by him that he did the act charged. As such, it should be treated like any other admission or confession, and subject to the same rules relating to its weight and effect.

The defendants insist, however, that there is a public policy which requires us to treat the admission implicit in pleading guilty to a traffic offense differently from others. It is the policy of this State, they urge, that a traffic infraction be distinguished from a crime and that it be recognized that a plea of guilt is entered in traffic court for numerous reasons unrelated to actual guilt. To support their contention, they point to subdivision 29 of section 2 of the Vehicle and Traffic Law, Consol. Laws, c. 40, Hart v. Mealey, and Walther v. News Syndicate Co.

The portion of the Vehicle and Traffic Law relied upon provides that "a traffic infraction is not a crime and the penalty or punishment imposed therefor * * * shall not affect or impair the credibility as a witness, or otherwise, of any person convicted thereof." (Vehicle and Traffic Law, § 2, subd. 29; see, also Civil Practice Act, § 355). Whatever else this provision may mean, it is clear that it is directed solely against the use of a conviction of a traffic infraction to "affect or impair * * * credibility as a witness" of the person convicted and not against the use of a plea as evidence in chief. The statute does no more than restate the rule of the common law that a prior conviction may be shown to attack the credibility of a witness only if it was a conviction of a *crime.*

Since a traffic infraction was declared not to be a crime, it was but natural for the Legislature to, in effect, codify the settled rule prohibiting the use of a conviction of such an offense to impeach the offender when called to testify as a witness. Had more than this been intended, had it been the legislative design to render evidence of a traffic infraction unavailable for *any* purpose in a subsequent civil action, it could easily have so provided. See, e.g., Minn.Stats.Ann. § 169.94, subd. 1; Colo.Rev.Stat., 13–4–140.[1] The Legislature of this State having written a clearly limited rule of exclusion, we may not apply it beyond its terms to exclude the use of a guilty plea as evidence in chief.

Nor may legislative policy be taken to justify its exclusion. Certain violations of the Vehicle and Traffic Law were denominated traffic infractions and distinguished from crimes in order to establish a new type of offense, one "with the stigma of criminality removed." The legislation simply represented a recognition of the fact that most traffic violations do not involve the degree of moral turpitude associated with crime.

In addition to their reliance on policy and precedent, the defendants also offer an argument based on what they label "experience". They contend that one charged with a traffic violation pleads guilty even though he believes himself innocent, in order to avoid the expenditure of time and money which would be involved if guilt were denied and the charge contested. Based on this assumption, they suggest that the plea of guilt must be looked upon as one *nolo contendere.* The contention has no merit. In the first place, the plea of *nolo contendere* has long been abolished in this State and may not be resurrected

1. The Minnesota statute declares that "No record of the conviction of any person for any violation of [the Highway Traffic Regulation Act] shall be admissible as evidence in any court in any civil action" (Minn.Stats.Ann. § 169.94, subd. 1).

without legislative sanction. In the second place, while we are willing to assume that pleas to traffic charges are not infrequently prompted by considerations of expediency, we have no reliable means of judging how significant a portion of all guilty pleas to traffic charges are of this character. But, quite apart from this, there is no basis for the defendants' unverified generalization or "hunch" in cases where, as here, the alleged violation was attended with injury to the person or property of a third party and the plea carries with it serious consequences to the offender's future status as a motor vehicle operator (Vehicle and Traffic Law, § 71).[2]

What the defendant Nichols is actually arguing is that, when he pleaded guilty, he "really didn't mean what he said". This claim, however, goes to the weight of evidence and entitles the defendant not to exclusion of the plea, but to an "opportunity to explain" it. After the defendant has given his explanation, his reasons for pleading guilty, it is for the jurors to evaluate his testimony and decide whether the plea is entitled to any weight. As this court wrote some years ago with respect to extra-judicial admissions, it is for the jury, noting "the conditions and circumstances under which [such admissions] were made", to determine their "effect * * * and their probative weight and value, which may range from the lowest, or none at all, to conclusiveness." The traditional treatment accorded to admissions by our courts takes account of the very claim here made, namely, that the defendant's guilty plea was not an admission that he committed the acts charged against him.

To the claim that the jury will be unduly prejudiced by the introduction of a plea of guilt despite the opportunity to explain it away, we content ourselves with the statement that this underestimates the intelligence of jurors and overlooks their awareness of those very circumstances said to destroy the meaning and significance of the plea. If voluntarily and deliberately made, the plea was a statement of guilt, an admission by the defendant that he committed the acts charged, and it should be accorded no less force or effect than if made outside of court to a stranger.

The judgment of the Appellate Division should be reversed and a new trial granted, with costs to abide the event.

VAN VOORHIS, Judge (dissenting).

The law of evidence has its roots in experience, and in common experience men and women charged with minor traffic violations plead guilty to avoid inconvenience whether they are innocent or guilty. In the Federal courts it is possible for a defendant in a criminal action to plead *nolo contendere,* the accepted meaning of which is that the defendant chooses not to contest and takes the consequences of conviction but without admitting the truth of the charge against him. Such a

2. Under the so-called "point system", in effect in New York, a plea of guilt, for instance, to the charge of failing to signal or of making an improper turn, is taken into account in determining whether the offender's license should be suspended or revoked. (See pamphlet issued by the Commissioner of Motor Vehicles, entitled, "What You Need to Know About New York State's Point System for Persistent Traffic Law Violators".)

plea could not be received in evidence as a voluntary admission against
interest under the reasoning of the opinion by Judge Fuld in this case.
The State procedure does not give opportunity to plead *nolo contendere*
but that is exactly what persons accused of minor traffic violations
generally mean to do and are understood to have done when they enter
guilty pleas in such instances. They are subject to the punishment
provided by law for the offenses to which they have pleaded guilty, but
the criminal statutes do not impose the additional burden of having the
conviction used in a civil action as a factual admission by the person
charged that he or she did or omitted the act on which the traffic
infraction depends. It is irrelevant that *nolo contendere* is not a form
of plea that is used in the State courts, inasmuch as we are not
confronted in this case with any of the consequences of conviction
under the criminal law. We have before us merely the collateral effect
of such a plea as bearing upon the civil rights of the party in an action
for damages. It is contrary to ordinary experience to give that effect to
this plea of guilty in the Magistrates' Court, as the Appellate Division
has correctly held. When Mr. Nichols pleaded guilty in the Manhattan
Traffic Division of Magistrates' Court, to failure to make a proper turn
or to signal, he rendered himself liable to whatever penalties were
involved but in my view it cannot be said with justice or a sense of
reality that he conceded whatever facts he was accused of by the
arresting officer. I think that it was not intended that the first steps in
the enforcement or defense of damage claims in automobile negligence
accident cases should be taken in traffic courts or police courts, nor
does it aid their most effective functioning if that is so.

DESMOND, C.J., and DYE, FROESSEL, BURKE and FOSTER, JJ.,
concur with FULD, J.

VAN VOORHIS, J., dissents in an opinion.

Judgment reversed, etc.

NOTE

See Federal Rules of Evidence 410; California Evidence Code § 1153.

In connection with Ando v. Woodberry, supra, and its problem of the
admissibility in civil cases of prior pleas of guilty in criminal cases, two related
problems should be considered: (1) the admissibility of judgments of conviction;
and (2) the possible res judicata effect of judgments of conviction.

Judgments of conviction. See Hearsay Exceptions, supra, pp. 291–92.
Historically, judgments of conviction (other than for impeachment purposes)
have been inadmissible as constituting hearsay and opinion. However, a
growing number of courts are admitting in civil cases a judgment of conviction
offered against the person convicted. California Evidence Code § 1300 provides
that a final judgment of conviction for a felony is not made inadmissible by the
hearsay rule when offered in a civil action to prove any fact essential to the
judgment.

Res judicata. Beyond the problem of admissibility is the doctrine in those
jurisdictions where mutuality as a condition of res judicata has been abandoned, that the criminal judgment of conviction may be conclusive in the civil
case. See Note, supra, pp. 200–01. But in California an exception has been

legislated for violations of the Vehicle Code; judgments of conviction for such offenses are not res judicata in civil cases. West's Ann.Cal.Vehicle C. § 40834.

Hypotheticals

(1) A sues X and the Y Bus Company for damages for personal injuries suffered in a collision between an automobile driven by A and a bus owned by the Y Bus Company and driven by X, its employee. A makes an offer of proof that at the scene of the accident X made the statement, "I know I blew the stop sign, but will you take $100 in settlement? I know the company will pay that much." Both X and the Y Bus Company make objections that X's statement is hearsay and also barred by the rule against admissions made during settlement negotiations. Should the objection be sustained?

(2) A sues the X Insurance Company for damages for intentional infliction of mental distress. A carried a disability-insurance policy with X, which provided for monthly payments of $150 to A as long as a disability continued. A is hurt and has a permanent disability. X pays A $150 per month until she has been paid $2,500. X then stops the payments, and seeks cancellation of the policy on the ground that A had made misrepresentations at the time of the policy application. A offers evidence that X was acting in bad faith in asserting that A had made any misrepresentations to secure the policy. A offers in evidence a letter from X to A, in which X offered to compromise A's claim that the policy was valid by permitting A to retain the $2,500 in payments, in return for X's cancellation of the policy and A's execution of a release of X. X makes an objection that its letter is inadmissible as an offer to compromise a claim. What result?

PART F. PRIOR SEXUAL CONDUCT

NOTE *

Some common-law courts allowed rape defendants to introduce evidence about the victim's character for chastity. The evidence might take the form of testimony about the victim's reputation, or it might include testimony about specific sexual activity. The practice of receiving this evidence deterred victims from pursuing well-founded complaints because of fear of abuse and degradation in the courtroom. Its premise that consent with one partner is worthy evidence of consent with another is untenable in an age in which "one can presume that a woman will freely choose her partners, picking some and rejecting others, in line with highly personal standards not susceptible of generalization."[1] As part of a reform effort supported by the women's movement and by law enforcement officials, almost all state legislatures and Congress adopted "rape shield" legislation in the 1970's that limited the use of evidence of prior sexual conduct in sexual assault cases.[2]

Rape shield legislation differs from state to state, but all statutes have at least one common feature: Evidence of reputation and sexual behavior is not admissible purely for purposes of showing unchaste character, as the basis for a further inference that the complainant consented to sex on the occasion in

---

* Based on R. Park, Trial Objections Handbook 37–38 (Shephard's McGraw–Hill, 1991).

1. Berger, Man's Trial, Woman's Tribulation: Rape Cases in the Courtroom, 77 Colum.L.Rev. 1, 56 (1977).

2. See Galvin, Shielding Rape Victims in the State and Federal Courts: A Proposal for the Second Decade, 70 Minn.L.Rev. 763, 765 (1986). Professor Galvin reports that 48 states have adopted reform legislation. Id. at 808.

question. The statutes generally do allow prior sexual behavior to be admitted
for certain limited purposes. Two widely recognized examples of admissible
behavior are (a) the complainant's prior sexual behavior with the defendant, as
opposed to behavior with other persons, and (b) evidence of the complainant's
sexual behavior with other persons, when offered for purposes of explaining the
physical consequences of the alleged rape—e.g., injury, the presence of semen,
pregnancy, or venereal disease. Other examples of admissible behavior, though
not universally recognized, involve evidence that is offered to show a possible
motive for fabrication of the complaint, or to show other behavior closely
similar to the behavior on the occasion in question. The statutes generally also
have a procedural element, providing for hearings in limine on the issue of
admissibility, and in some cases providing for in camera hearings to protect the
victim's privacy. Indeed, some statutes do little more than set up a procedural
mechanism for pretrial decision and call attention to the problem, providing
only some general standard of admissibility, such as weighing prejudice against
probative value.

STATE v. CASSIDY

Appellate Court of Connecticut, 1985.
3 Conn.App. 374, 489 A.2d 386, cert. denied
196 Conn. 803, 492 A.2d 1239 (1985).

BORDEN, Judge.

* * *

The information arose out of an incident occurring on February 20,
1983. The jury could reasonably have found the following facts: The
victim had previously been acquainted with the defendant, with whom
she had engaged in sexual relations one or two times prior to the
evening in question. Early in the morning hours of February 20, 1983,
the victim went to a bar with a friend, where she saw the defendant.
She accompanied him and some of his friends to an after-hours bar.
They stayed there briefly and then went to the defendant's house. The
victim went upstairs to the defendant's bedroom, undressed and got
into the bed. She was, at that point, willing to have sexual relations
with him.

At this stage in the events, the victim's and the defendant's
recollections diverge. The victim recounted as follows: After she was
in the bed, the defendant [started yelling threats and abuse. He then
physically forced her to have oral, anal and vaginal intercourse with
him.] Throughout the incident, the defendant called her obscene
names and, in her estimation, acted "[l]ike a crazy person." The
defendant then told her that she had two seconds to put her clothes on
and leave or he would kill her. She quickly put on some of her clothes;
the defendant got her coat and, pushing her out the door, said he never
wanted to see her again and threatened to kill her if she called the
police. She left the house and, after unsuccessfully attempting to get
neighbors' help, flagged down a car which happened to be driven by a
police officer. He took her to the police station. She was later taken to
a hospital and treated for injuries.

The defendant's account was as follows: After the victim got into
the bed, the defendant, * * * got into the bed with her [and engaged
in intercourse]. She then asked if she could tie him up. He said no but

asked if she would like to be tied up. She consented, and he tied her hands loosely in front of her with her stockings. * * * Then, * * * the complainant's "whole attitude changed * * * like she didn't consent to what we were doing." She started getting hysterical, screaming about her husband who was killed in Vietnam. She said she "shouldn't be doing this," and that she wanted to die and wanted to be with her husband. She untied her hands and started swinging at the defendant. He tried to get her off of him and slapped her. She fell onto the bed. The defendant got up, told the victim to put her clothes on and get out of his house, and went into the bathroom. When he returned to the bedroom, she was gone.

The defendant's principal claim on appeal arises from the exclusion of certain evidence by the trial court. Prior to trial, the defendant moved, pursuant to General Statutes § 54–86f,[1] to offer evidence of the complainant's prior sexual conduct. The court permitted evidence of the prior sexual conduct between the defendant and the complainant but refused to admit evidence of a sexual encounter between the victim and another man, who testified in the absence of the jury as part of the defendant's offer of proof. This testimony was to the effect that she and he had gone to her home together about a year before the night in question. They had sexual relations, during which she began "going crazy" and screaming about her husband who was killed in Vietnam. The witness told her to forget about it and went to sleep. Nothing eventful happened for the rest of the night. The next morning she showed him pictures of her husband.

The trial court excluded this testimony in the absence of an offer of proof by the defendant that the victim made a prior false complaint of sexual assault. The defendant argues that the evidence should have been admitted to show a pattern of conduct by the victim, and because it was highly relevant, probative and essential to the defense. He claims that applying the statute in this case violated his constitutional

1. General Statutes § 54–86f, as amended by Public Acts 1983, No. 83–113, provides as follows: "ADMISSIBILITY OF EVIDENCE OF PRIOR SEXUAL CONDUCT. In any prosecution for sexual assault under sections 53a–70, 53a–70a, and 53a–71 to 53a–73a, inclusive, no evidence of the prior sexual conduct of the victim may be admissible unless such evidence is (1) offered by the defendant on the issue of whether the defendant was, with respect to the victim, the source of semen, disease, pregnancy or injury, or (2) offered by the defendant on the issue of credibility of the victim, provided the victim has testified on direct examination as to his or her prior sexual conduct, or (3) evidence of prior sexual conduct with the defendant offered by the defendant on the issue of consent by the victim, when consent is raised as a defense by the defendant, or (4) otherwise so relevant and material to a critical issue in the case that excluding it would violate the defendant's constitutional rights. Such evidence shall be admissible only after a hearing on a motion to offer such evidence containing an offer of proof. On motion of either party the court may order such hearing held in camera, subject to the provisions of section 51–164x. If the proceeding is a trial with a jury, such hearing shall be held in the absence of the jury. If, after hearing, the court finds that the evidence meets the requirements of this section and that the probative value of the evidence outweighs its prejudicial effect on the victim, the court may grant the motion. The testimony of the defendant during a hearing on a motion to offer evidence under this section may not be used against the defendant during the trial if such motion is denied, except that such testimony may be admissible to impeach the credibility of the defendant if the defendant elects to testify as part of the defense."

rights of confrontation and to present witnesses in his own behalf. We
disagree.

Statutes such as General Statutes § 54–86f, commonly known as
rape shield statutes, have been enacted specifically to bar or limit the
use of prior sexual conduct of an alleged victim of a sexual assault
because it is such highly prejudicial material. Our legislature has
determined that, except in specific instances, and taking the defendant's constitutional rights into account, evidence of prior sexual conduct is to be excluded for policy purposes. Some of these policies
include protecting the victim's sexual privacy and shielding her from
undue harassment, encouraging reports of sexual assault, and enabling
the victim to testify in court with less fear of embarrassment. Other
policies promoted by the law include avoiding prejudice to the victim,
jury confusion and waste of time on collateral matters. The state's
interests are substantial, but cannot by themselves outweigh the defendant's competing constitutional interests. The United States Supreme
Court has looked to the facts and circumstances of the particular cases
before it when determining if the state's interests in excluding evidence
must yield to those interests of the defendant. See, e.g., Chambers v.
Mississippi, 410 U.S. 284, 93 S.Ct. 1038, 35 L.Ed.2d 297 (1973). Likewise, we must analyze the defendant's constitutional claims in light of
the facts of this particular case.

Under General Statutes § 54–86f, which has not been previously
interpreted, evidence of the victim's prior sexual conduct is inadmissible unless the trial court determines from an offer of proof at a hearing
that it fits into one of the statute's exceptions. The defendant's
argument focuses on exception (4) of § 54–86f, which permits evidence
of prior sexual conduct if it is "so relevant and material to a critical
issue in the case that excluding it would violate the defendant's
constitutional rights."

This statute directs the court to examine the defendant's constitutional rights, implicating both his sixth amendment right to confront
witnesses and his fourteenth amendment due process right to call
witnesses on his own behalf. See Chambers v. Mississippi, supra, 410
U.S. 294, 93 S.Ct. 1045. ∗   ∗   ∗

The court, in this case, was correct in noting that, unless the
proffered testimony was to show that the victim previously made a false
claim of sexual assault following the claimed similar, consensual sexual
conduct, the evidence should be excluded. The relevant conduct was
that between the defendant and the victim. Unless she had raised a
false claim before, her conduct with another man had no bearing on her
conduct with this defendant or on the credibility of her testimony in
this case. ∗   ∗   ∗

∗   ∗   ∗ The defendant claims he had a right to present this
evidence because it established a pattern of conduct by the victim, and
it supported his defense of consent by showing another instance where
the victim became irascible during a consensual sexual encounter.

∗   ∗   ∗

"As a general principle, evidence is relevant if it has a tendency to establish the existence of a material fact. 'One fact is relevant to another fact whenever, according to the common course of events, the existence of the one, taken alone or in connection with other facts, renders the existence of the other either certain or more probable.'" State v. Lombardo, 163 Conn. 241, 243, 304 A.2d 36 (1972)." The fact that about one year before the alleged assault occurred, the victim began a sexual episode with another man, became upset and changed her mind because of her feelings about her dead husband, does not tend to establish that, on this night, the victim became hysterical about her husband, screamed that she wanted to die and be with her dead husband, and struck the defendant. Particularly since there was also evidence of more recent nights which the defendant and the victim had spent together with no similar behavior by her, the defendant's version would not have been made more probable by this evidence.

One cannot logically infer that the victim acted in the manner described by the defendant simply because of a somewhat similar incident one year beforehand. The evidence, therefore, was legally irrelevant and was properly excluded without denying the defendant his constitutional rights.

Moreover, one similar instance is not sufficient to prove a pattern of conduct. Even in states which expressly permit evidence of prior sexual conduct to establish a pattern of conduct, evidence of one sexual encounter is not enough to do so. * * * No other instances of similar conduct were offered; the instances of prior sexual conduct between the defendant and the victim showed no pattern of the same type of behavior. The evidence was properly excluded, therefore, as insufficient to provide a basis for the inference that the victim acted as claimed by the defendant.

In holding that this single past instance of the victim's sexual conduct was properly excluded, we do not suggest that such evidence is never relevant or admissible. To be admissible, however, such evidence must fulfill the requirements of the statute within the context of the facts and circumstances of the case in which it arises. The evidence sought to be introduced in this case did not meet those requirements.[2]

There is no error.

OLDEN v. KENTUCKY

Supreme Court of the United States, 1988.
488 U.S. 227, 109 S.Ct. 480, 102 L.Ed.2d 513.

PER CURIAM. Petitioner James Olden and his friend Charlie Ray Harris, both of whom are black, were indicted for kidnapping, rape and forcible sodomy. The victim of the alleged crimes, Starla Matthews, a

---

2. Before admitting evidence of prior sexual conduct, which otherwise meets the requirements of one of the statutory exceptions, General Statutes § 54–86f also requires balancing the probative value of the evidence with its prejudicial potential. We find this balancing test inapplicable to evidence fulfilling the requirements of subsection (4) because, if the defendant's constitutional rights would be violated by the exclusion of the evidence, no amount of prejudice to the victim could require its exclusion.

young white woman, gave the following account at trial: She and a
friend, Regina Patton, had driven to Princeton, Kentucky, to exchange
Christmas gifts with Bill Russell, petitioner's half-brother. After meeting Russell at a local car wash and exchanging presents with him,
Matthews and Patton stopped in J.R.'s, a "bootlegging joint" serving a
predominantly black clientele, to use the restroom. Matthews consumed several glasses of beer. As the bar became more crowded, she
became increasingly nervous because she and Patton were the only
white people there. When Patton refused to leave, Matthews sat at a
separate table, hoping to demonstrate to her friend that she was upset.
As time passed, however, Matthews lost track of Patton and became
somewhat intoxicated. When petitioner told her that Patton had
departed and had been in a car accident, she left the bar with petitioner
and Harris to find out what had happened. She was driven in Harris's
car to another location, where, threatening her with a knife, petitioner
raped and sodomized her. Harris assisted by holding her arms. Later
she was driven to a dump, where two other men joined the group.
There, petitioner raped her once again. At her request, the men then
dropped her off in the vicinity of Bill Russell's house.

On cross-examination, petitioner's counsel focused on a number of
inconsistencies in Matthews' various accounts of the alleged crime.
Matthews originally told the police that she had been raped by four
men. Later, she claimed that she had been raped by only petitioner
and Harris. At trial, she contended that petitioner was the sole rapist.
Further, while Matthews testified at trial that petitioner had threatened her with a knife, she had not previously alleged that petitioner had
been armed.

Russell, who also appeared as a State's witness, testified that on
the evening in question he heard a noise outside his home and, when he
went out to investigate, saw Matthews get out of Harris's car. Matthews immediately told Russell that she had just been raped by petitioner and Harris.

Petitioner and Harris asserted a defense of consent. According to
their testimony, Matthews propositioned petitioner as he was about to
leave the bar, and the two engaged in sexual acts behind the tavern.
Afterwards, on Matthews' suggestion, Matthews, petitioner, and Harris
left in Harris's car in search of cocaine. When they discovered that the
seller was not at home, Matthews asked Harris to drive to a local dump
so that she and petitioner could have sex once again. Harris complied.
Later that evening, they picked up two other men, Richard Hickey and
Chris Taylor, and drove to an establishment called "The Alley." Harris, Taylor, and Hickey went in, leaving petitioner and Matthews in the
car. When Hickey and Harris returned, the men gave Hickey a ride to
a store and then dropped Matthews off, at her request, in the vicinity of
Bill Russell's home.

Taylor and Hickey testified for the defense and corroborated the
defendants' account of the evening. While both acknowledged that
they joined the group later than the time when the alleged rape
occurred, both testified that Matthews did not appear upset. Hickey

further testified that Matthews had approached him earlier in the evening at J.R.'s and told him that she was looking for a black man with whom to have sex. An independent witness also appeared for the defense and testified that he had seen Matthews, Harris and petitioner at a store called Big O's on the evening in question, that a policeman was in the store at the time, and that Matthews, who appeared alert, made no attempt to signal for assistance.

Although Matthews and Russell were both married to and living with other people at the time of the incident, they were apparently involved in an extramarital relationship. By the time of trial the two were living together, having separated from their respective spouses. Petitioner's theory of the case was that Matthews concocted the rape story to protect her relationship with Russell, who would have grown suspicious upon seeing her disembark from Harris's car. In order to demonstrate Matthews' motive to lie, it was crucial, petitioner contended, that he be allowed to introduce evidence of Matthews' and Russell's current cohabitation. Over petitioner's vehement objections, the trial court nonetheless granted the prosecutor's motion in limine to keep all evidence of Matthews' and Russell's living arrangement from the jury. Moreover, when the defense attempted to cross-examine Matthews about her living arrangements, after she had claimed during direct examination that she was living with her mother, the trial court sustained the prosecutor's objection.

Based on the evidence admitted at trial, the jury acquitted Harris of being either a principal or an accomplice to any of the charged offenses. Petitioner was likewise acquitted of kidnapping and rape. However, in a somewhat puzzling turn of events, the jury convicted petitioner alone of forcible sodomy. He was sentenced to ten years' imprisonment.

Petitioner appealed, asserting, inter alia, that the trial court's refusal to allow him to impeach Matthews' testimony by introducing evidence supporting a motive to lie deprived him of his Sixth Amendment right to confront witnesses against him. The Kentucky Court of Appeals upheld the conviction. The court specifically held that evidence that Matthews and Russell were living together at the time of trial was not barred by the State's rape shield law. Moreover, it acknowledged that the evidence in question was relevant to petitioner's theory of the case. But it held, nonetheless, that the evidence was properly excluded as "its probative value [was] outweighed by its possibility for prejudice." By way of explanation, the court stated: "[T]here were the undisputed facts of race; Matthews was white and Russell was black. For the trial court to have admitted into evidence testimony that Matthews and Russell were living together at the time of the trial may have created extreme prejudice against Matthews." Judge Clayton, who dissented but did not address the evidentiary issue, would have reversed petitioner's conviction both because he believed the jury's verdicts were "manifestly inconsistent," and because he found Matthews' testimony too incredible to provide evidence sufficient to uphold the verdict.

Petitioner's 6th Amendment not weighed properly

The Kentucky Court of Appeals failed to accord proper weight to petitioner's Sixth Amendment right "to be confronted with the witnesses against him." That right, incorporated in the Fourteenth Amendment and therefore available in state proceedings, Pointer v. Texas, 380 U.S. 400 (1965), includes the right to conduct reasonable cross-examination. Davis v. Alaska, 415 U.S. 308, 315–316 (1974).

In Davis v. Alaska, we observed that, subject to "the broad discretion of a trial judge to preclude repetitive and unduly harassing interrogation * * *, the cross-examiner has traditionally been allowed to impeach, i.e., discredit, the witness." Id., at 316. We emphasized that "the exposure of a witness' motivation in testifying is a proper and important function of the constitutionally protected right of cross-examination." Recently, in Delaware v. Van Arsdall, 475 U.S. 673 (1986), we reaffirmed Davis, and held that "a criminal defendant states a violation of the Confrontation Clause by showing that he was prohibited from engaging in otherwise appropriate cross-examination designed to show a prototypical form of bias on the part of the witness, and thereby 'to expose to the jury the facts from which jurors * * * could appropriately draw inferences relating to the reliability of the witness.' "

Credibility of Matthews would be perceived as different

In the instant case, petitioner has consistently asserted that he and Matthews engaged in consensual sexual acts and that Matthews—out of her fear of jeopardizing her relationship with Russell—lied when she told Russell she had been raped and has continued to lie since. It is plain to us that "[a] reasonable jury might have received a significantly different impression of [the witness'] credibility had [defense counsel] been permitted to pursue his proposed line of cross-examination." Delaware v. Van Arsdall, supra, at 680.

Court felt that even too prejudicial against Matthews

The Kentucky Court of Appeals did not dispute, and indeed acknowledged, the relevance of the impeachment evidence. Nonetheless, without acknowledging the significance of, or even adverting to, petitioner's constitutional right to confrontation, the court held that petitioner's rights to effective cross-examination was outweighed by the danger that revealing Matthews' interracial relationship would prejudice the jury against her. While a trial court may, of course, impose reasonable limits on defense counsel's inquiry into the potential bias of a prosecution witness, to take account of such factors as harassment, prejudice, confusion of the issues, the witness' safety, or interrogation that [would be] repetitive or only marginally relevant," Delaware v. Van Arsdall, supra, at 679, the limitation here was beyond reason. Speculation as to the effect of jurors' racial biases cannot justify exclusion of cross-examination with such strong potential to demonstrate the falsity of Matthews' testimony.

In Delaware v. Van Arsdall, supra, we held that "the constitutionally improper denial of a defendant's opportunity to impeach a witness for bias, like other Confrontation Clause errors, is subject to Chapman [v. California, 386 U.S. 18 (1967)] harmless-error analysis." Id., at 684. Thus we stated:

> "The correct inquiry is whether, assuming that the damaging potential of the cross-examination were fully realized, a reviewing court might nonetheless say that the error was harmless beyond a reasonable doubt. Whether such an error is harmless in a particular case depends upon a host of factors, all readily accessible to reviewing courts. These factors include the importance of the witness' testimony in the prosecution's case, whether the testimony was cumulative, the presence or absence of evidence corroborating or contradicting the testimony of the witness on material points, the extent of cross-examination otherwise permitted, and, of course, the overall strength of the prosecution's case." Ibid.

Here, Matthews' testimony was central, indeed crucial, to the prosecution's case. Her story, which was directly contradicted by that of petitioner and Harris, was corroborated only by the largely derivative testimony of Russell, whose impartiality would also have been somewhat impugned by revelation of his relationship with Matthews. Finally, as demonstrated graphically by the jury's verdicts, which cannot be squared with the State's theory of the alleged crime, and by Judge Clayton's dissenting opinion below, the State's case against petitioner was far from overwhelming. In sum, considering the relevant Van Arsdall factors within the context of this case, we find it impossible to conclude "beyond a reasonable doubt" that the restriction on petitioner's right to confrontation was harmless.

The motion for leave to proceed in forma pauperis and the petition for certiorari are granted, the judgment of the Kentucky Court of Appeals is reversed, and the case is remanded for further proceedings not inconsistent with this opinion.

It is so ordered.

[Justice BRENNAN took no part in the consideration or decision of this case.]

Justice MARSHALL, dissenting. I continue to believe that summary dispositions deprive litigants of a fair opportunity to be heard on the merits and create a significant risk that the Court is rendering an erroneous or ill-advised decision that may confuse the lower courts. I therefore dissent from the Court's decision today to reverse summarily the decision below.

NOTE

See Fed.Rules of Evidence 412, Cal.Evidence Code Sec. 1103. See also Berger, "Man's Trial, Woman's Tribulation: Rape Cases in the Courtroom," 77 Colum.L.Rev. 1 (1977); S. Brownmiller, Against Our Will: Men, Women and Rape, (1975); and S. Estrich, Real Rape (1987).

Chapter V

IMPEACHMENT AND CROSS EXAMINATION

PART A. THE RULE AGAINST IMPEACHING ONE'S OWN WITNESS AND OTHER FORENSIC PROBLEMS

KAPLAN AND WALTZ, THE TRIAL OF JACK RUBY
120–121 (1965).*

* * * Unlike the practice in most European countries, where the witness merely stands up and delivers a long narrative concerning what he knows about the case, in Anglo-American law the witnesses relate their stories through the question-and-answer method. Although some lawyers argue that by focusing the witnesses' attention on specific details, our method actually is simpler and faster, most lawyers would agree that it is in fact slower and more cumbersome. The reason it is used is that the rules of evidence in our jurisprudence are vastly more detailed, complicated and strict than those of most other countries. Relying on a jury untrained in the law, we make every possible effort to keep from the jurors the sort of information which they might rely on but which experience teaches is either unfair to the defendant or for some reason dangerously misleading. We therefore require the witness to give his answers in response to relatively pointed questions so that the opposing attorney, forewarned by the question that the jury may be about to hear inadmissible material, can object in time to prevent receipt of the damaging answer.

In Anglo-American law not only must the parties proceed by question and answer, but they must adhere to certain forms of questions. And the restrictions are far more severe on the side calling the witness to the stand. The examination of one's own witness—direct examination as distinguished from cross-examination—must be made without the use of leading questions, that is, questions which suggest their own answer. A typical leading question is, "Was the defendant's black automobile going about fifty miles an hour when you first saw it on the right, bearing down on you?" The witness may answer "Yes," but it is the attorney's version of the story that the jury hears. Leading questions, although technically prohibited, are generally used to save time on unimportant and background matters. "Is your name Joe Smith?" However, as soon as important matters are reached, most trial lawyers automatically switch from leading questions to avoid a barrage of objections which are properly sustained by the court.

---

* Copyright, 1965 by the Macmillan Co.

A second major restriction encountered in direct examination is that the side calling the witness is, as lawyers say, "bound by his testimony." This means not that the lawyer must assume the truth of every fact testified to by his own witnesses but rather that he cannot argue with them or seek by further questioning to modify their testimony unless he can convince the judge that the witness is hostile or has taken him by surprise.

In cross-examination these restrictive rules do not apply. The cross-examiner can ask as many leading questions as he wishes and, if the answers prove unsatisfactory, he can go at the matter again and again in as many different ways as he can devise to press the witness into delivering the desired answers.   * * *

MAGUIRE, EVIDENCE: COMMON SENSE AND COMMON LAW
41–43 (1947).*

Examination of Witnesses

In judicial and legislative provisions for the handling of witnesses the notion appears again and again that a litigant producing a witness vouches for, or in a sense commits his cause to, the probity of that witness and must consequently grin and bear it if the witness proves unfavorable. This may be a hazy heritage from the time when witnesses were not questioned as now, but rather, in the process termed compurgation, by the very weight of their oaths carried the day for the party in whose behalf they appeared. Or it may be a consequence of the fact that the presentation of evidence, particularly in jury trials began as a special privilege instead of as a right, with the result that a litigant would be denied leave to attack the credibility of a witness whom he had been granted the privilege of presenting. The notion does not stand up well under analytical criticism, because an honest man engaged in litigation cannot count upon having his choice of witnesses. Experts, to be sure, he may select within the limits of scientific controversy and scientific ethics, and in most commercial cases he may rest part of his reliance upon the testimony of associates likely to see matters his way. But in catch-as-catch-can litigation such as accident cases and criminal prosecutions the litigant who takes real witnesses as they come instead of trying to make artificial ones is often forced to put forward highly dubious human material.

One result of the vouching notion has been a doctrine that the party who places a witness on the stand and examines him directly or in chief may not impeach him if his testimony is disappointing or harmful. "Impeach" is a lawyers' word of art which may not be quite clear on first encounter. It really means something like "derogate from credibility". One impeaches a witness, for example, by seeking to show that he has a poor reputation for truth and veracity, or has been convicted of crime which reflects on veracity, or has out of court made statements inconsistent with his testimony, or is affected by some sort

of bias with respect to the present litigation. Impeachment must be
distinguished from contradicting one of your witnesses by counter-
testimony of the others as to matters at issue on the merits. The latter
process is always allowed. The anti-impeachment rules does not forbid
contradiction.

The best argument concocted to sustain this "no impeachment of
your own witness" doctrine is that if a witness finds himself exposed to
battering by both sides, he may, to obtain the protective championship
of one side, warp his testimony away from the truth to make it entirely
favorable for that one side. The argument is not moving. To begin
with, it stinks of the lamp, being manifestly some laborious scholar's
rationalization of existing practice. Besides, if witnesses are such
shrinking violets as this, the really thorough-going protective step
would be to forbid impeachment by *anybody*. That is not usually done,
although it may be brought about when *both* sides have called and
examined the *same* witness to make out their respective cases. Finally
and very practically, this argument is at loggerheads with the exception
to the rule against impeaching one's own witnesses manifested in the
case of the "necessary" witness. An example will suggest the scope of
this exception. Very commonly in a will contest the proponent is
required by law to call all the attesting witnesses of the alleged
testamentary instrument, although he distrusts them and would like to
pass them by. They thus become necessary or legally compelled
witnesses, and because of the compulsion the proponent is allowed to
impeach them if their testimony turns out adverse to the validity of the
instrument they attested. But that opens such witnesses to hammering
by both sides, and thus disregards the argument stated at the opening
of this paragraph. And so, it is fair to remark, does the practice of
having the trial judge call dubious witnesses to the stand, with permission for impeachment by all parties.

According to the best professional thought, sweeping prohibition of
impeachment by a party of his own witnesses is nonsense—most regret-
tably not simple nonsense, but very complex nonsense; the underlying
connotations extend far, as we shall see. It has been somewhat broken
down here and there by decision and statute. Yet it has perverse
vitality and will be with us in some jurisdictions for a long time to
come. * * *

UNITED STATES v. GOMEZ–GALLARDO

United States Court of Appeals, Ninth Circuit, 1990.
915 F.2d 553.

NELSON, Circuit Judge:

OVERVIEW

Defendant/appellant Emilano Gomez–Gallardo (Gallardo) was indicted and convicted for conspiracy with Jose Delacruz–Gutierrez (Gutierrez) to distribute cocaine. Gallardo appeals three alleged errors in
his jury trial. He argues that Gutierrez was called as a witness in
order to introduce otherwise inadmissible evidence, that the govern-

ment introduced evidence of Gutierrez's guilty plea for illegitimate and
highly prejudicial purposes and that the government elicited prejudicial
and irrelevant evidence of Gallardo's drug use. We reverse the conviction and remand for new trial.

FACTUAL AND PROCEDURAL HISTORY

On the basis of an investigation by Agent James Baker with the
assistance of an informant, "Lucky" Vrell, the government alleged that
Gallardo, the appellant, and Gutierrez conspired to distribute cocaine
between September 23 and 27, 1988. Gutierrez pled guilty to this
charge.

The government's case against Gallardo was based on the testimony of Vrell, Baker and Gutierrez. Vrell testified that he had participated in drug deals with Gallardo and Gutierrez and that they were
supposed to complete a deal on the night of September 27, 1988. Vrell
also testified that he had used cocaine with Gallardo. On direct
examination Vrell stated that he had not talked to Gallardo at all
about the September 27 deal, although he recanted that statement on
redirect.

Agent Baker testified at the trial that he had overheard a conversation between Vrell and a man who identified himself as Emilio arrang-
ing a drug deal.[1] Baker also stated that he had surveyed Vrell's house
on September 27 and that he had seen Gallardo arrive and spend about
three hours. When Gallardo left the house Baker arrested him. Gallardo had no drugs in his possession and no cocaine connected to the
alleged conspiracy was ever found.

Prior to Gallardo's trial, the government told the court that it did
not expect Gutierrez to agree to testify. On the final day of trial, the
government asked to call Gutierrez out of the presence of the jury.
Under oath Gutierrez testified that he knew Gallardo. He admitted
participating in one cocaine deal with Vrell but claimed that he had
never participated in any cocaine transaction with Gallardo. Gutierrez
stated that on September 27 his car was overheating and he had called
Gallardo to meet him at Vrell's house to give him a ride.[2] On the basis
of this testimony the government decided to call Gutierrez.

On the stand in the presence of the jury, Gutierrez first testified
that he had pled guilty to a conspiracy with the defendant to distribute
cocaine. Gutierrez then repeated his testimony from earlier in the day,
including his assertions of Gallardo's innocence and that Gallardo was
at Vrell's house only because of the overheating car.

The government had three witnesses impeach Gutierrez's testimony and character. Agent Perry Skipton testified as to statements made
by Gutierrez involving a different proposed sale of cocaine. Agent
Bruce Stubbs testified about Gutierrez's involvement in a scheme to

1. The conversation took place in English. The evidence indicates that Gallardo
spoke only Spanish.

2. Gutierrez claimed he began having
car trouble in Ellensberg, Washington and
that he had called Gallardo in Yakima,
Washington to request that Gallardo drive
to Seattle and wait at Vrell's house. Apparently the distances between these cities
makes this story obviously implausible.

trade machine guns for cocaine. The government never claimed that
Gallardo was involved in either of the schemes described by Agent
Skipton and Agent Stubbs. Finally Agent Samuel Soto testified that he
had driven the car Gutierrez claimed was overheating and that there
was no indication of any mechanical difficulties.

The defense presented no evidence, arguing only that the government had not proven its case. The defense did not object to the
government calling Gutierrez as a witness, to the admission of his
guilty plea into evidence or to the introduction into evidence of appellant's use of cocaine.

In closing arguments, the government stated that no question
existed as to Gutierrez's guilt. It reviewed all the evidence in the case,
closely examining Gutierrez's testimony and urging the jury to reject it
as false. The jury convicted Gallardo. He was sentenced to 97 months
imprisonment to be followed by three years of supervised release. He
timely appeals.

DISCUSSION

I. Standard of Review

Because none of the issues on appeal was raised before the district
court, we employ a plain error standard of review. * * *

II. Government's Impeachment of Gutierrez

Gallardo claims that the government called Gutierrez as a witness
for the sole purpose of impeaching him with otherwise inadmissible
evidence. The defendant also argues that this was a highly prejudicial
error requiring reversal even under the plain error standard. The
government claims it called Gutierrez to "facilitate its proof of the
elements of the crime charged."

Federal Rule of Evidence 607 permits the government to impeach
its own witness. However, "the government must not knowingly elicit
testimony from a witness in order to impeach him with otherwise
inadmissible testimony." United States v. Whitson, 587 F.2d 948, 952–
53 (9th Cir. 1978). "[T]he maximum legitimate effect of the impeaching
testimony can never be more than the cancellation of the adverse
answer by which the party is surprised." United States v. Crouch, 731
F.2d 621, 623 (9th Cir. 1984), cert. denied, 469 U.S. 1105, 105 S.Ct. 778,
83 L.Ed.2d 773 (1985) (internal quotations omitted). That is, impeachment is not permitted where it is "employed as a guise for submitting
to the jury substantive evidence that is otherwise unavailable." United
States v. Peterman, 841 F.2d 1474, 1479 (10th Cir. 1988), cert. denied,
488 U.S. 1004, 109 S.Ct. 783, 102 L.Ed.2d 774 (1989) (internal quotations
omitted).

In evaluating the reason a witness is called, we determine whether
the government examined the witness for the primary purpose of
placing before the jury substantive evidence which is not otherwise
admissible.

After carefully reviewing the trial transcript, we are convinced
that the government did call Gutierrez for the primary purpose of

impeaching him. In determining the government's purpose, we examine its use of the evidence during the trial rather than any post-trial explanation.

The government argues that Gutierrez's testimony was intended to corroborate Vrell's testimony. Although part of Gutierrez's testimony did so corroborate, a review of the transcript indicates that the government did not use the testimony for corroborative purposes at trial.

In closing argument the government did not rely on Gutierrez's testimony in support of its case, but instead urged the jury to consider him a liar. At one point, the prosecutor specifically argued, "if you don't believe the testimony of Jose Delacruz–Gutierrez . . . then you're entitled to conclude that the defendant was here to do a deal." Later in closing argument, the government reiterated:

> Has the government proved beyond a reasonable doubt that the defendant conspired to distribute cocaine? Jose Delacruz–Gutierrez says no, that there was no conspiracy. Do you accept his testimony? Does it hang together? Does it correspond to common sense or does it sound like he's just trying to get a buddy out of trouble? Moreover, the government cannot claim that it intended to use Gutierrez's testimony to prove its case but was surprised by his testimony; it knew in advance that Gutierrez would testify falsely.[5]

In sum, Gutierrez's testimony that the prosecution now claims was material in its proof of the case was never so argued to the jury. Instead, the government thoroughly discredited his testimony. On this basis, and in light of the testimony itself, we are compelled to conclude that the government called Gutierrez for the primary purpose of impeaching Gutierrez's credibility to prove the substance of the charges against Gallardo. This is an illegitimate purpose.

We also find that the government's actions reached the level of plain error. The government's case was weak: Gallardo had not been caught with any cocaine; there was evidence he spoke no English and could not have discussed the transaction with Special Agent Baker or understood the conversations with Gutierrez and Vrell; and Vrell had contradicted himself on the stand. The government's ability to bring in Gutierrez's testimony, to question him about unrelated crimes and to show that his defense of Gallardo was false was crucial to the conviction.

Moreover, the government's actions directly undermined the judicial process. The government is obligated to prove its case beyond a reasonable doubt; the defendant has no concomitant obligation to prove a defense. In the instant case, Gallardo chose to provide no defense

---

5. Before testifying at the trial, Gutierrez was brought to the stand and testified under oath outside the presence of the jury. In that testimony he repeatedly stated that he had not agreed with the defendant to distribute cocaine. He also told the same story about his overheating car that he told during the trial. It is undisputed that the government was not surprised by Gutierrez's testimony. Thus, contrary to the principle stated in Crouch, the impeaching testimony went well beyond a "cancellation of the adverse answer by which the party is surprised." Crouch, 731 F.2d at 623.

theory or witnesses but to argue only that the government had failed to
prove its case. The government, however, created a defense theory and
alibi for him in order to prove his guilt by refuting it. The adversarial
system breaks down when the defendant is prevented from defining and
presenting his own case and the prosecution proves guilt by creating
and then destroying its own creation. This type of error "seriously
affect[s] the fairness, integrity [and] public reputation of judicial proceedings," Smith, 790 F.2d at 193, and thus must be reversed even
under a plain error standard of review.[7] * * *

Reversed and remanded.

MATHEW, FORENSIC FABLES BY O
267–68 (1961).

THE BEGINNER WHO THOUGHT HE WOULD
DO IT HIMSELF

A Beginner, in the Temporary Absence of his Leader, Found
himself Opposed to a Big Pot in the Commercial Court. Though
Greatly Alarmed, the Beginner Bore himself Bravely. To his Surprise
and Delight the Beginner Managed to Cross-Examine the Big Pot's
Principal Witness with Such Effect that he Needed a Good Deal of
Rehabilitation. Rising to Re-Examine, the Big Pot Airily Observed to
the Principal Witness: "I Suppose What You Meant by Your Last
Answer was This," and Proceeded to Tell the Principal Witness Quite
Clearly what he Meant. When the Beginner made a Dignified Protest
the Judge Smilingly Suggested that the Big Pot might Shape his
Question rather Differently. The Next Day the Beginner was in a
County Court. The Plaintiff (for whom the Beginner Appeared) having
Made an Awkward Admission to his Learned Friend on the Other Side,
the Beginner Thought he would Employ the Excellent Formula of the
Big Pot. He Did so. The Scene that Followed Beggars Description.
The County Court Judge in a Voice of Thunder Ordered the Beginner to
Sit Down. He then Rebuked the Beginner for his Gross Misconduct
and Discussed the Question whether he would Commit him for Con-
tempt, or Merely Report him to the General Council of the Bar.
Finally he Expressed the Hope that the Incident would be a Lesson to
the Beginner and Directed that the Case should be re-Heard on a Later
Date before a Fresh Jury.

Moral.—*Wait till You're a Big Pot.*

———

See Federal Rules of Evidence 607, 611; California Evidence Code
§§ 764, 767, 776, 785.

7. Because we find that the government improperly called Gutierrez as a witness, we need not determine whether it was error to introduce the guilty plea.

PART B. CROSS EXAMINATION

SUSANNA AND THE ELDERS *

* * *

Then the two elders stood up in the midst of the people, and laid their hands upon her head. And she weeping looked up toward heaven: for her heart trusted in the Lord. And the elders said, "As we walked in the garden alone, this woman came in with two maids, and shut the garden doors, and sent the maids away. Then a young man, who there was hid, came unto her, and lay with her. Then we that stood in a corner of the garden, seeing this wickedness, ran unto them. And when we saw them together, the man we could not hold: for he was stronger than we, and opened the door, and leaped out. But having taken this woman, we asked who the young man was, but she would not tell us: these things do we testify."

Then the assembly believed them, as those that were the elders and judges of the people: so they condemned her to death.

Then Susanna cried out with a loud voice, and said, "O everlasting God, that knowest the secrets, and knowest all things before they be: thou knowest that they have borne false witness against me, and behold, I must die; whereas I never did such things as these men have maliciously invented against me."

The Lord heard her voice.

Therefore when she was led to be put to death, the Lord raised up the holy spirit of a young youth, whose name was Daniel: who cried with a loud voice, "I am clear from the blood of this woman."

Then all the people turned them toward him, and said, "What mean these words that thou hast spoken?"

So he standing in the midst of them said, "Are ye such fools, ye sons of Israel, that without examination or knowledge of the truth ye have condemned a daughter of Israel? Return again to the place of judgment: for they have borne false witness against her."

Wherefore all the people turned again in haste, and the elders said unto him, "Come, sit down among us, and show it us, seeing God hath given thee the honour of an elder."

Then said Daniel unto them, "Put these two aside one far from another, and I will examine them."

So when they were put asunder one from another, he called one of them, and said unto him, "O thou that art waxed old in wickedness, now thy sins which thou hast committed aforetime are come to light: for thou hast pronounced false judgment, and hast condemned the innocent, and hast let the guilty go free; albeit the Lord saith, 'The

* THE BIBLE: DESIGNED TO BE READ AS LIVING LITERATURE 860–61. (Simon and Schuster. N.Y. 1936)

The story of Susanna and the Elders appears in what some regard as the Apoc-

ryphal writings of the Bible. Depending on your beliefs the story appears as *Daniel* 13:34–63 or 1:34–63 or as the Apocryphal Book of Susanna.

innocent and righteous shalt thou not slay.' Now then, if thou hast
seen her, tell me under what tree sawest thou them companying
together?

Who answered, "Under the mastic tree."

And Daniel said, "Very well; thou hast lied against thine own
head; for even now the angel of God hath received the sentence of God
to cut thee in two."

So he put him aside, and commanded to bring the other, and said
unto him, "O thou seed of Chanaan, and not of Juda, beauty hath
deceived thee, and lust hath perverted thine heart. Thus have ye dealt
with the daughters of Israel, and they for fear companied with you: but
the daughter of Juda would not abide your wickedness. Now therefore,
tell me under what tree didst thou take them companying together?"

Who answered, "Under a holm tree."

Then said Daniel unto him, "Well; thou hast also lied against thine
own head: for the angel of God waiteth with the sword to cut thee in
two, that he may destroy you."

With that all the assembly cried out with a loud voice, and praised
God, who saveth them that trust in him. And they arose against the
two elders, for Daniel had convicted them of false witness by their own
mouth: and according to the law of Moses they did unto them in such
sort as they maliciously intended to do their neighbour: and they put
them to death. Thus the innocent blood was saved the same day.

Therefore Chelcias and his wife praised God for their daughter
Susanna, with Joacim her husband, and all the kindred, because there
was no dishonesty found in her.

GILBERT WITHOUT SULLIVAN *

First briefs are always alarming, but few draw so much public
attention as the following, which was delivered in 1863.

Mrs. Briggs had instructed her counsel that she was in the omnibus, a hymn book in her pocket, on her way to tea and prayers, when
she was seized and monstrously accused of having just picked someone's
pocket. The purse found on her must have been planted by some evil
worldling. Counsel was holding his first brief and, determined to draw
attention to the hymn-book, cross-examined the policeman with all the
assurance he could muster.

GILBERT: You say you found the purse in her pocket, my
man?

CONSTABLE: Yes, sir.

GILBERT: Did you find anything else?

CONSTABLE: Yes, sir.

GILBERT: What?

* Stephen Tumim, *Great Legal Disasters,*
Arthur Barker Limited, London.

CONSTABLE: Two other purses, a watch with the bow broken, three handkerchiefs, two silver pencil-cases, and a hymn-book.

Before Mrs. Briggs went below to start her eighteen-month sentence, she paused briefly to remove her boot and hurl it at her counsel, W.S. Gilbert (for it was he). 'The language in which her ovation was couched was perfectly shocking,' he noted soon afterwards. 'The boot missed me, but hit a reporter on the head, and to this fact I am disposed to attribute the unfavourable light in which my search for the defence was placed in two or three leading daily papers next morning.'

Gilbert practised at the bar for four years, with an average of five clients a year, and earned £75. Happily it was not long before he found more lucrative employment through meeting Arthur Sullivan in 1871.

MATHEW, FORENSIC FABLES BY O
87–88 (1961).

MR. WHITEWIG AND THE RASH QUESTION

MR. WHITEWIG was Greatly Gratified when the Judge of Assize Invited him to Defend a Prisoner who was Charged with Having Stolen a Pair of Boots, a Mouse-Trap, and Fifteen Packets of Gold Flakes. It was his First Case and he Meant to Make a Good Show. Mr. Whitewig Studied the Depositions Carefully and Came to the Conclusion that a Skillful Cross-Examination of the Witnesses and a Tactful Speech would Secure the Acquittal of the Accused. When the Prisoner (an Ill-Looking Person) was Placed in the Dock, Mr. Whitewig Approached that Receptacle and Informed the Prisoner that he Might, if he Wished, Give Evidence on Oath. From the Prisoner's Reply (in which he Alluded to Grandmothers and Eggs) Mr. Whitewig Gathered that he did not Propose to Avail Himself of this Privilege. The Case Began. At First All Went Well. The Prosecutor Admitted to Mr. Whitewig that he Could not be Sure that the Man he had Seen Lurking in the Neighbourhood of his Emporium was the Prisoner; and the Prosecutor's Assistant Completely Failed to Identify the Boots, the Mouse-Trap, or the Gold Flakes by Pointing to any Distinctive Peculiarities which they Exhibited. By the Time the Police Inspector Entered the Witness-Box Mr. Whitewig Felt that the Case was Won. Mr. Whitewig Cunningly Extracted from the Inspector the Fact that the Prisoner had Joined Up in 1914, and that the Prisoner's Wife was Expecting an Addition to her Family. He was about to Sit Down when a Final Question Occurred to him. "Having Regard to this Man's Record," he Sternly Asked, "How Came You to Arrest him?" The Inspector Drew a Bundle of Blue Documents from the Recesses of his Uniform, and, Moistening his Thumb, Read therefrom. Mr. Whitewig Learned in Silent Horror that the Prisoner's Record Included Nine Previous Convictions. When the Prisoner was Asked whether he had Anything to

say why Sentence should not be Passed Upon him, he Said some Very
Disagreeable Things about the Mug who had Defended him.

Moral.—Leave Well Alone.

KEETON, TRIAL TACTICS AND METHODS
87–90 (1954).*

Cross-examination is that phase of the trial which has potentiali-
ties of being the most spectacular. It affords the opportunity for the
most successful employment of an aptitude for quick thinking, sharp
repartee, and dramatics. To excel in these, one must have native
ability. Nearly everyone interested in trial work does have a degree of
such ability, however, and it can be developed by practice and experience, just as a talent for music or acting may be so developed. But the
talent for cross-examination, in this sense, is the lesser part of the
secret of effective cross-examination. Nearly all effective cross-examination is planned, to one degree or another. For one interested in
entering trial practice without experience, adequate planning can often
produce effective cross-examination from the first. For one who is
experienced, greater success in cross-examination is possible as he
prepares more diligently and thoroughly for it. This chapter is devoted
to consideration of methods customarily used in effective cross-examination, and ways of planning for their use. In this broader sense of
"talent," one can enter the courtroom with considerable talent for
cross-examination even in his earliest cases.

The potential aims of cross-examination may be classified into four
groups: (1) discrediting the testimony of the witness being examined;
(2) using testimony of this witness to discredit the unfavorable testimony of other witnesses; (3) using the testimony of this witness to
corroborate the favorable testimony of other witnesses; and (4) using
the testimony of this witness to contribute independently to the
favorable development of your own case.

Accomplishing one of these aims may require an entirely different
method of dealing with the witness from that appropriate for another
aim. A method of cross-examination designed to serve one aim may
defeat another. In such instances, adequate planning requires an
appraisal of the relative advantages associated with each of these aims,
as a factor in the choice of methods.

Your selection of methods of cross-examination of the witness will
be influenced also by the type of witness before you—for example,
whether the witness is an argumentative one, an expert, a woman, or
one of a series of witnesses who appear to have a memorized story. The
age, education, and mentality of the witness are other important
factors. The most ignorant witness is often the hardest to cross-
examine because you cannot get him set up to knock over. Also, you
must exercise great care to avoid creating jury sympathy for him
because you are exposing his ignorance or illiteracy. Your aim is to
condemn his testimony as unreliable without condemning the witness

for being ignorant. The infliction of personal ridicule upon an ignorant witness, or sarcastic treatment of the witness, may be regarded by jurors as your taking an unfair advantage of the differences in intelligence and education between yourself and the witness.

Some consideration should be given to your general attitude and demeanor toward the witness. Should you let your contempt for the reprobate be obvious for the jury to see, if you feel that way about him? Or should you be the paragon of courtesy? Usually an attitude of courtesy toward the witness should be adopted, for although the jurors expect a lawyer to be an advocate, they very quickly take up sympathy for the witness if they get the idea that the lawyer is badgering the witness unfairly. It is quite possible to be very polite and yet convey to the jury your distrust of the witness' testimony.

Most trial yarns concerning cross-examination are tales of the brilliant cross-examination which won the lawsuit. Others tell of the inept cross-examination which lost the lawsuit. While both types of yarns are usually influenced by a recognized license, like that of the poet and fisherman, they are founded on truths.

These are some of the risks which you incur in cross-examination:

(1) Confronting a witness with a prior written statement inconsistent with his present testimony may result in proof of other facts recorded in the statement and not previously proven, or it may result in incidental disclosure of the existence of liability insurance, where its existence would have been unknown to the jury otherwise.

(2) Confronting the witness with inconsistency between his testimony and that of your own witness may result in impeachment of the testimony of your own witness.

(3) The cross-examination intended to show want of good opportunity for observation of the facts related may serve only to demonstrate that the opportunity was good.

(4) An attempt to prove or even actual proof of bad character of the witness may provoke the sympathy of the jury for the witness and the case he supports.

(5) The cross-examination intended to reveal indirectly the bias of the witness by committing him to an untenable extreme may result in strengthening the direct examination.

(6) The cross-examination intended to bring out matters about which your adversary failed to inquire, in the belief that the answers will be favorable to your client, may result only in more evidence favorable to the adverse party who called the witness.

(7) Calling on the witness to repeat and elaborate his testimony, as a foundation for proof of prior contradictions or inconsistencies, may emphasize and strengthen the witness' testimony if he has a plausible explanation for the apparent inconsistencies.

(8) Cross-examination intended to show bias from animosity associated with termination of employment may provoke sympathy for the discharged employee.

(9) Asking a "why" question in the belief that the witness can have no reasonable explanation may result in expression of prejudicial arguments which would have been clearly inadmissible in the absence of the invitation by the open question.

(10) Insistence upon a clear answer from an evasive witness may lead to an unexpected and unfavorable disclosure.

(11) Defendant's cross-examination of plaintiff's medical expert regarding fees may emphasize plaintiff's expenses and cause a higher damages finding.

(12) Cross-examination of an expert concerning his qualifications may serve only to bolster less adequate proof of those qualifications during direct examination.

(13) Methods of cross-examination intended to exact disclosures from an unwilling witness may be harmful because of a jury reaction that they are unfair methods.

PART C. CROSS EXAMINATION AND IMPEACHMENT

---

1. IMPEACHMENT BY CONTRADICTION

STATE v. OSWALT

Supreme Court of Washington, 1963.
62 Wn.2d 118, 381 P.2d 617.

HAMILTON, Judge. Defendant appeals, upon a short record, from a conviction of robbery and first degree burglary. During trial, a defense of alibi was introduced. Error is assigned to the admission of certain rebuttal testimony, defendant contending such evidence constituted impeachment on a collateral matter.

The short record before us (testimony of two witnesses) indicates that on July 14, 1961, two armed men entered the King County residence of Frank L. Goodell. One man stood guard over a number of people at the home. The other man took Mr. Goodell to a Tradewell store and forced him to open the safe and turn over the money therein. Defendant was identified as one of the two men.

In presenting his defense of alibi, defendant called a Mr. August Ardiss of Portland, Oregon. On direct examination, Mr. Ardiss testified in substance that: his wife and he operated a restaurant in Portland; he was acquainted with the defendant, as a fairly regular patron of the restaurant; defendant was in the restaurant at such times on July 14, 1961, as to render it impossible, as a practical matter, for defendant to be in Seattle at the time of the offense charged; and he remembered this occasion because defendant had accompanied a restaurant employee to work, assisted in a part of her work, and escorted her home.

On cross-examination by the state, the following exchange took place:

"Q. To the best of your knowledge would you say Oswalt had been in every day for the last couple of months or did he miss occasional periods of three or four days, or what was it? A. No, I think he was in there every day. I really think he was in there every day. Q. For the last couple months? A. Yes."

In rebuttal, a police detective was permitted to testify, over defense objections, as follows:

"Q. Did you see and talk to the defendant Mr. Oswalt on June 12, 1961? A. I did. Q. And in what city did you talk to him? A. In the City of Seattle. Q. And did you during that conversation ask him how long he had been in this city of Seattle at that time? * * * A. I did. Q. And how long did he state he had been in the City of Seattle? A. He stated he had arrived in Seattle a couple days before I talked to him. Q. Did he state where he had come from? A. Portland, Oregon."

During colloquy between the trial court and counsel relative to the admissibility of the detective's testimony, the trial court commented: "There is no claim by Oswalt he wasn't in Seattle, Gilman [a codefendant] claims that, but Oswalt doesn't."

It is to the rebuttal testimony of the police detective that defendant assigns error. The state, in response, contends such testimony to be admissible not only because it challenges the credibility of witness Ardiss, but also establishes defendant's presence in Seattle preparatory to the offense.

It is a well recognized and firmly established rule in this jurisdiction, and elsewhere, that a witness cannot be impeached upon matters collateral to the principal issues being tried. [Citations omitted.]

The purpose of the rule is basically two-fold: (1) avoidance of undue confusion of issues, and (2) prevention of unfair advantage over a witness unprepared to answer concerning matters unrelated or remote to the issues at hand.

We, in common with other jurisdictions, have stated the test of collateralness to be: Could the fact, as to which error is predicated, have been shown in evidence for any purpose independently of the contradiction?

We are handicapped by the limited record before us in evaluating the relationship of the contradictory evidence in question to the general issues presented in the trial.

So far as appears by this record, the sole issue raised by defendant's defense of alibi, through the direct testimony of witness Ardiss, was whether or not the defendant was or could have been in Seattle at the time of the offense on July 14, 1961. The defendant did not contend or seek to prove by this witness that he had not been in Seattle prior to such date. Thus, for purposes of impeaching this witness, whether the defendant was in Seattle on a given occasion one month prior to July 14th, was irrelevant and collateral. While a cross-examiner is, within the sound discretion of the trial court, permitted to inquire into collateral matters testing the credibility of a witness, he does so at the risk of being concluded by the answers given.

The state, however, contends that the quoted testimony of Ardiss, as elicited by its cross-examination, carries with it an inference that defendant could not have been in Seattle sufficiently in advance of July 14, 1961, to have participated in necessary planning of and preparation for the offense. Upon the inference so erected, the state asserts the questioned testimony becomes material and admissible independently of its contradictory nature. The state further supports this argument by testimony elicited from the police detective to the effect that defendant admitted, in the interview of June 12, 1961, that he had purchased some adhesive tape.

Admittedly, relevant and probative evidence of preparations by an accused for the commission of a crime is admissible. Based upon the limited record before us, however, the state's argument requires us to speculate that the defendant could not readily commute between Portland and Seattle, and that his presence in Seattle and acquisition of adhesive tape, upon an isolated occasion approximately a month before the offense in question, constituted significant evidence of planning and preparation for the offense in question, the particular mechanics of which are unrevealed by the record. This we decline to do, absent effort upon the part of the state to obtain a more complete record.

Upon the record before us, we must conclude it was error to admit the questioned testimony.

Having so concluded, we must next determine whether the error was prejudicial.

In State v. Britton, we said:

> "A harmless error is an error which is trivial, or formal, or merely academic, and was not prejudicial to the substantial rights of the party assigning it, and in no way affected the final outcome of the case.
>
> * * *
>
> "A prejudicial error is an error which affected the final result of the case and was prejudicial to a substantial right of the party assigning it. * * *"

In the instant case, the state's charge apparently rested upon an identification of the defendant by witnesses at the scene of the crime. The defense apparently rested upon alibi. The state seemingly considered the testimony of witness Ardiss sufficiently credible to require this attack. The defendant was convicted. It is difficult, therefore, to classify admission of the testimony in question trivial, formal, academic, or harmless, and to conclude that such did not affect the outcome of the case. The alternative is that it was prejudicial. We so hold.

The judgment is reversed and the cause remanded for new trial.

OTT, C.J., and DONWORTH, HUNTER, and FINLEY, JJ., concur.

---

2. CHARACTER OF THE WITNESS

---

a. PRIOR BAD ACTS

UNITED STATES v. OWENS

United States Court of Military Appeals, 1985.
21 M.J. 117.

COX, Judge:

* * *

The circumstances surrounding appellant's conviction for unpremeditated murder were summarized by the court below as follows:

> On 4 September 1981, Gari Owens was apprehended for the murder of his wife, Mary Owens. She died in the early morning hours of 4 September as a result of a single gunshot which entered her back causing a large laceration of the liver and perforation of the breathing muscle. Death was due to excessive bleeding. At the time Mary Owens had been driving the couple's Volkswagen Rabbit down the street from their quarters at Fort Campbell, Kentucky. Gari Owens held the 30.06 rifle mounted with a "Bushnell 4" telescopic sight which fired the fatal bullet.

> At the trial the government introduced evidence to show that Gari Owens fired the weapon in anger following a domestic quarrel and that Owens intended his wife's death or grievous bodily harm. In defense Owens took the stand. An experienced hunter and marksman, Owens claimed that he had been standing in front of his house examining his rifle and that he had chambered a round and cleared the weapon by pulling the trigger. He maintained that his wife's death was a tragic accident.

* * *

* * * [A]fter appellant testified on direct examination, * * *

* * *

* * * [A]ppellant was cross-examined as follows:

Questions by assistant trial counsel:

Q. Mr. Owens, isn't it a fact that as to your application for appointment as a Warrant Officer in the United States Army and the statement of personal history attached to it, that you knowingly omitted the fact from questions 19 and 18, that you had been convicted in Daleville, Alabama, for the possession of marihuana and marihuana paraphernalia in 1976?

A. No, sir.

Q. Is it not a fact that you intentionally omitted from both of these documents the fact that you had been arrested in 1976 in Daleville, Alabama, for assault and battery on your second wife, Mrs. Jennifer Conant Braun?

A. No, sir.

Q. Is it not a fact that you omitted from both of these documents, the fact that you had been convicted in Enterprise, Alabama, for carrying a .22 caliber pistol in your automobile without a permit in 1976?

A. It was admitted—it was omitted, rather. I did not knowingly omit it.

Q. You did not knowingly omit it?

A. I did not omit it.

Q. Mr. Owens, isn't it a fact that you knowingly omitted all three of these matters from those two documents because you realized that if you put them in there, you likely would not become the Warrant Officer that you wanted so badly to become?

A. No, Sir. That's not true.

After this cross-examination, defense counsel questioned appellant in detail about these omissions. He admitted to two prior convictions and provided explanations for the underlying conduct. He further explained the omission of this information from these forms. He testified that he informed the personnel specialists processing his application that he had a local marihuana offense and pistol offense. He asserted that he relied on these personnel specialists to properly process his application and signed the final papers without reading them. He made no admission concerning his prior arrest for assault or any claim that he disclosed this matter to them.

Finally, prior to deliberation on findings, the military judge gave the following instruction:

Now, there was certain evidence in this case which I admitted for certain limited purposes. Specifically on cross-examination of the accused, the trial counsel presented the accused with a document which was not offered in evidence but this line of questioning was engaged in for the limited purpose of determining the credibility of the accused as a witness. And specifically as to this issue, the accused replied that when he submitted his application for a warrant officer and the accompanying statement of personal history, when answering the question whether or not he had ever been arrested or convicted for offenses, he answered "yes," but did not give complete answers. And specifically, the prosecution inquired as to the accused omitting his having been convicted in a civilian court in Daleville, Alabama, and another conviction in a civilian court in Enterprise, Alabama, both in 1976 for offenses of possession of marihuana and carrying an unregistered firearm, as well as omitting having been arrested in 1976 in Daleville,

Alabama, for assault and battery on an individual. And by the same token, the accused then explained his omission of this, alluding to administrative processes in which these applications were prepared and stated that although it was an oversight, it was not an intentional oversight on his part. Now, as I mentioned, that line of questioning and answers were admitted only for the purpose of your assessing the credibility of the accused as a witness, whether he did or did not intentionally lie in those documents.

This Court granted review on the following question of law:

WHETHER THE APPELLANT WAS IMPROPERLY IMPEACHED TO HIS SUBSTANTIAL PREJUDICE BY QUESTIONS CONCERNING OMISSIONS FROM HIS APPLICATION FOR WARRANT OFFICER CANDIDATE.

We hold that it was proper for trial counsel to attempt to impeach appellant by eliciting on cross-examination his admission to a prior act of intentional falsehood. Mil.R.Evid. 607 and 608(b). However, in asking these questions for this purpose, he was prohibited from suggesting evidence to the members which was inadmissible. Mil.R.Evid. 103(c). We find that the evidence of appellant's prior convictions and arrest, and the underlying conduct, was not admissible to show appellant's prior criminal disposition or his untruthful character. Nevertheless, we find that such evidence could be admitted at this court-martial and was suggested for a purpose other than showing appellant's character. Moreover, we find with a single exception that the military judge did not abuse his discretion under Mil.R.Evid. 403 by permitting these matters to be evidenced or suggested for this purpose. On the basis of the entire record of trial, we conclude that such limited error was harmless.

* * *

* * * [O]n cross-examination, appellant generally denied that he had ever lied under oath and particularly denied that he knowingly provided incomplete answers on his warrant-officer application.[1]

* * *

We note that there were several purposes for which the suggested evidence was clearly inadmissible. First, evidence of these prior bad acts was not admissible under Mil.R.Evid. 404(a) to show appellant's criminal disposition. Not only were the requirements of this evidentiary rule not satisfied in this case, but also trial counsel did not attempt to offer the suggested evidence for the purposes stated in this rule. Second, evidence of the prior facts of convictions and arrest was not

1. The Government was not required to accept appellant's earlier denials of the impeaching act of deceit. Mil.R.Evid. 608(b) only precluded it from introducing "extrinsic evidence" to prove this discrediting fact. See generally IIIA Wigmore, Evidence § 981 (Chadbourn rev. 1970). Such a prohibition does not mean that further cross-examination of appellant is impermissible. See United States v. Cottle, 14 M.J. 260, 264 (C.M.A.1982); People v. Sorge, 301 N.Y. 198, 93 N.E.2d 637, 639 (1950). Within reason, it could rephrase its questions in terms of the specific matters omitted so as to gradually but dramatically induce appellant to abandon his previous more general denials. See Mil.R. Evid. 611(b) and McCormick's Handbook of the Law of Evidence § 28 at 55–56 (E. Cleary 2d ed. 1972).

admissible under Mil.R.Evid. 609 to show appellant's poor character for veracity. Not only were the requirements of this rule not satisfied in this case, but also trial counsel conceded the suggested evidence was inadmissible under this rule. Finally, evidence of the prior misconduct was not offered under Mil.R.Evid. 608(b) to *directly* show appellant's poor character for truthfulness. Trial counsel did not contend that the suggested acts of misconduct, i.e., drug possession, unlicensed firearm possession, and assault and battery, were themselves the type of conduct which could be considered probative of a person's character for truthfulness.

* * *

In the present case, trial counsel * * * was clearly authorized under Mil.R.Evid. 608(b) to impeach appellant by extracting on cross-examination his admission to a prior act of intentional falsehood under oath. In particular, he had a good-faith belief that appellant had previously failed to provide complete and truthful answers on his warrant-officer application. Since the prior convictions and arrests were the matters omitted in his answers, they were necessary and inseparable parts of this act of deceit. As such, they were clearly matters which were relevant within the meaning of Mil.R.Evid. 401 to establish appellant's prior act of falsehood. More importantly, the adverse nature of these omissions coupled with appellant's admitted interest in being selected reasonably tended to show these omissions were intentional.[2] The relevance of the suggested evidence was not obviated simply because the omissions pertained to additional acts of prior misconduct which might unfavorably reflect on appellant's character.

The relevance of the suggested evidence to show a prior act of deceit by appellant does not *per se* dictate its admissibility under the Military Rules of Evidence. Under Mil.R.Evid. 403, evidence relevant for a permissible purpose may still be found inadmissible "if its probative value is substantially outweighed by the danger of unfair prejudice." This additional requirement for admissibility precludes admission of relevant evidence which would tend to "*unduly*" prejudice an accused under the circumstances of a particular case.

* * *

The record of trial in this case provides a firm basis for the conclusion that the suggested evidence had substantial probative value. First, the issue of appellant's prior falsehood was clearly a matter contested by the parties. Although after some evasion appellant admitted there were some omissions on his application, he steadfastly denied

---

2. The suggested evidence of prior misconduct tended to show the omissions were substantial and material to the success of appellant's warrant-officer application. The Government argued that the more substantial and material the omission, the more likely that the omission was intentional on appellant's part. We note further that the more substantial and material the omissions, the less likely that personnel specialists would negligently omit responses given by appellant on the final form. In this light, the particular matters omitted were external circumstances which reflected on appellant's intent in submitting his application in an incomplete form. See generally II Wigmore, supra, §§ 242 and 242(2), and IIIA Wigmore, supra, § 1023; cf. n. 5, supra.

that he consciously and intentionally omitted the complete answers.[3] Second, other evidence to show appellant engaged in this act of deceit was not available to the Government. Under Mil.R.Evid. 608(b), the prosecution could not introduce extrinsic evidence of appellant's prior falsehood, by, for example, calling the personnel specialists who processed appellant's application. Finally, the strength of the suggested evidence to show appellant's prior falsehood was considerable. The number of omissions, their serious nature in terms of involvement with law enforcement authorities, and the potentially disqualifying character of the underlying offenses in terms of military promotion were substantial circumstances indicating deliberate deceit by appellant.

The military judge was also required to consider the tendency of the suggested evidence to unfairly prejudice appellant. He had to assess the suggested evidence in terms of its tendency to incite the members to irrational decision by its force on human emotion. The prior convictions and the prior arrest could naturally have led the members to find the appellant guilty because he was a "bad man." * * * In these circumstances and in view of the considerable probative value of the suggested evidence for a proper purpose, we hold that the military judge did not abuse his discretion under Mil.R.Evid. 403.

This holding does not extend to all the suggested evidence to which trial counsel was permitted to refer. The victim of appellant's purported assault and battery was identified as his second wife, Mrs. Jennifer Conant Braun. It is highly doubtful that the questions on the warrant-officer application intended to elicit this information as an essential part of a truthful and complete answer. In any event, its probative value, if any, on the issue of deceit was marginal if in fact the arrest and the basic underlying offense, assault and battery, had been omitted. Of course, the potential for prejudice was great in view of the fact that appellant was on trial for the murder of his third wife. This conclusion is buttressed by the fact that the military judge in his closing instructions referred to the suggested evidence of assault and battery as occurring "on an individual." Therefore, acknowledging the broad discretion of the military judge under Mil.R.Evid. 403, we nonetheless hold that the suggested evidence in this limited regard was inadmissible.

* * *

We have concluded that it was error for the military judge to allow trial counsel to suggest to the members in his cross-examination questions that appellant had previously been arrested for assault and battery on his second wife. However, appellant was entitled to a fair trial, not "an error-free, perfect trial." After considering the trial record as a whole, we are convinced beyond a reasonable doubt that

3. Appellant admitted that complete and truthful answers to several questions on his warrant-officer application had been omitted. He asserted, however, that he did provide complete answers orally to the personnel specialists who processed his application; that they omitted the complete answers; and that he failed to read the completed forms before he signed them. In other words, he denied the impeaching fact sought to be proven by the Government, namely, that he knowingly and intentionally lied under oath or affirmation. See Mil.R.Evid. 608(b).

this error did not prejudice appellant. Accordingly, he is not entitled to relief.

The decision of the United States Army Court of Military Review is affirmed.

* * *

WELLMAN, THE ART OF CROSS–EXAMINATION
56–60 (1903, 1962).*

Henry E. Lazarus, a prominent merchant in this city, was indicted a few years ago by the Federal Grand Jury, charged with the offense of bribing a United States officer and violation of the Sabotage Act, but was honorably acquitted by a jury after a thirty minute deliberation. It was during the height of the war and Mr. Lazarus was a very large manufacturer of rubber coats and had manufactured hundreds of thousands for the Government under contract. The Government for its protection employed large numbers of inspectors, and in the heat and excitement of war times these inspectors occasionally tried to "make good." One of these efforts resulted in the indictment of Lazarus.

The chief witness against Lazarus was Charles L. Fuller, Supervising Inspector attached to the Depot Quartermaster's Office in New York City. Fuller testified that Lazarus gave money to him to influence him in regard to his general duties as an inspector, and to overlook the fact that Lazarus was manufacturing defective coats and thereby violating the Sabotage Act.

Martin W. Littleton acted as chief counsel for the defense and was fully appreciative of Mr. Lazarus's high character and of his conscientious discharge of his duties in the manufacture of material for the Government. He was also well informed as to the general character and history of Fuller. After Fuller testified in chief, he was first questioned closely as to the time when he became an employee of the Government, counsel knowing that he was *required to make and sign and swear to an application as to his prior experience.*

A messenger had been sent to the Government files to get the original of this application, signed by the witness, and came into court with the document in his hand just as counsel was putting the following question:

> Q. "Did you sign such an application?"
>
> A. "I did, sir."
>
> Q. "Did you swear to it?"
>
> A. "No, I did not swear to it."
>
> Q. "I show you your name signed on the bottom of this blank, and ask you if you signed that?"
>
> A. "Yes, sir."
>
> Q. "Do you see it is sworn to?"
>
> A. "I had forgotten it."

* Copyright, 1962 by Collier.

Q. "You see there is a seal on it?"

A. "I had forgotten that also."

Q. "This application appears to be subscribed on the 24th of May, 1918, by Charles Lawrence Fuller."

A. "It must be right if I have sworn to it on that date."

Q. "Do you remember in May, 1918, that you signed and swore to this application?"

A. "That is so, I must have sworn to it, sir."

Q. "Do you remember?"

A. "Let me look at it and I can probably refresh my memory." (Paper handed to witness)

Q. "Look at the signature. Does that help you?"

A. "That is my signature."

Q. "You said that. Do you remember in May, 1918, you signed and swore to this?"

A. "Well, the date is there."

Q. "Do you know that?"

A. "Yes, sir, I must have sworn to it. I don't remember the date."

Q. "Don't you remember you signed your name, Charles Lawrence Fuller, there?"

A. "I did, sir."

Q. "And you swore to this paper and signed it?"

A. "That date is correct there, yes, sir."

Q. "Don't you remember you swore to it the date you signed it?"

A. "I swore to it."

Q. "Was your name Fuller?"

A. "Yes, sir."

Q. "Has your name always been Fuller?"

A. "No, sir."

Q. "What was your name?"

The witness protested against any further inquiry along that line, but counsel was permitted to show that his name at one time was Finkler and that he changed his name, back and forth, from Finkler to Fuller.

Counsel then proceeded to bring the witness down to the actual oath he had taken in his application.

Q. "Now, Mr. Fuller, in your application you made to the Government, on which I showed you your signature and affidavit, you attached your picture, did you not?"

A. "Yes, sir."

Q. "And you stated in your application you were born in
Atlanta, Georgia, did you not?"

A. "Yes, sir."

Q. "You were asked, when you sought this position, these
questions: 'When employed, the years and the months,' and
you wrote in, 'February, 1897 to August, 1917, number of years
20; Where employed—Brooklyn; Name of employer—Vulcan
Proofing Company; Amount of salary,—$37.50 a week; also
superintendent in the rubber and compound room.'"

Q. "You wrote that, didn't you?"

A. "Yes, sir."

Q. "And swore to that, didn't you?"

A. "Yes, sir."

Q. "Now, were you employed from February, 1897, to
August, 1917, twenty years, with the Vulcan Proofing Company?"

A. "No sir."

Q. "That was not true, was it?"

A. "No, sir."

Q. "And had you been assistant superintendent of the
rubber and compound room?"

A. "No, sir."

Q. "That was false, wasn't it?"

A. "Yes, sir."

Q. "'And through my experience as chief inspector of the
rubber and slicker division,' that was false, wasn't it?"

A. "Yes, sir."

Q. "You knew it was false didn't you?"

A. "Yes, sir."

Q. "And you knew you were swearing to a falsehood
when you swore to it?"

A. "Yes, sir."

Q. "And you swore to it intentionally?"

A. "Yes, sir."

Q. "And you knew you were committing perjury when
you swore to it?"

A. "I did not look at it in that light."

Q. "Didn't you know you were committing perjury by
swearing and pretending you had been twenty years in this
business?"

A. "Yes, sir."

Q. "And you are swearing now, aren't you?"

A. "Yes, sir."

Q. "In a matter in which a man's liberty is involved?"

A. "Yes, sir."

Q. "And you know that the jury is to be called upon to consider whether you are worthy of belief or not, don't you?"

A. "Yes, sir."

Q. "When you swore to this falsehood deliberately, and wrote it in your handwriting, you knew it was false, you swore to it intentionally, and you knew that you were committing perjury, didn't you?"

A. "I did not look at it in that light."

Q. "Well, now, when you know you are possibly swearing away the liberty of a citizen of this community, do you look at it in the same light?"

A. "Yes, sir, I do."

Mr. Littleton then uncovered the fact that the witness, instead of having been twenty years superintendent of a rubber room with the Vulcan Proofing Company, as he had sworn in his own handwriting, was a stag entertainer in questionable houses, was a barker at a Coney Island show, was an advance agent of a cheap road show and had been published in the paper as having drawn checks that were worthless, the witness fully admitting all of the details of his twenty years of questionable transactions. The result was his utter collapse so far as his credibility was concerned, and the Government's case collapsed with him.

The point of the cross-examination and the design of the cross-examiner was to get the witness at the outset of his cross-examination in a position from which he could not possibly extricate himself, by confronting him with this document, written in his own handwriting in which he would be obliged to admit that he had sworn falsely. The witness having been thoroughly subjugated by this process would then, as he actually did, confess to twenty years of gadding about in questionable employment, under different names, and thus completely destroy himself as a reliable witness in the eyes of the jury.

HOUSE, GREAT TRIALS OF FAMOUS LAWYERS

180–81 (1962).

Max Steuer had the task of cross-examining Representative Foelker, a very popular member of Congress, who was the crucial witness against Steuer's client in a prosecution for bribery. When Steuer began his preparation for trial his * * * mental picture of Foelker's career was on the usual pattern of the crusader in politics. The first essential is that he be beholden to none. This most frequently results in a young man, from a secure background of position and affluence, both generally inherited. Mr. Thain * gave an outline of Foelker's history. He was a German immigrant reaching this country in his early teens. After a short period in Troy, he settled in Brooklyn

* [The Prosecutor].

and attended public school. He left school early to go to work. He got
a job in a law office, where he progressed from the minor tasks to a
clerkship, eventually studying for the bar and being admitted. At the
same time he interested himself in politics with the results already
seen. So, in addition to being a knight errant he was also an Horatio
Alger hero.

Now whatever Steuer may or may not have known about a
Galahad career he was perfectly familiar with the life of the "Rags-to-
Riches" type. He had lived it and when he got back to his office he
compared his meager information with his intimate knowledge of the
background. Two points loomed up. The first was that a man of that
background gets rapid political preferment by being an asset first to a
ward-heeler, then to a district leader. The most obvious service is the
production of votes and the first vote to be produced is one's own. He
decided to look into Foelker's voting record. It proved interesting.
Foelker had followed the adage about voting early—by a year at least.

Secondly, in order to take the bar examination a candidate who is
not a law-school graduate must pass a certain number of examinations
set by the Board of Regents. The Regents examinations of those days
were about the present equivalent of the graduation examinations for a
junior high school. But they were all factual. An unprepared candidate could not pass them. There is obviously no way of knowing who
won the battle of Lookout Mountain, the conjugations of the French
irregular verbs or how to obtain the square root of $X^2–Y^2$ unless you
have learned the answers. In the thumbnail sketch of Foelker, the
necessary schooling was missing. He decided to find out how Foelker
passed his Regents examinations.

Inquiry at the Board of Regents showed that the examination
papers had been destroyed but the notation of the results, the correspondence and the like had been preserved. Foelker did remarkably
well but the subject in which he must have been most proficient,
German, did not appear in the list of his subjects. What writings there
were from Foelker were not in a German script. And although Foelker
had a residence and a business address at the time, the Regents Board
were directed to correspond with him, care of Solinsky, at 54 Rutgers
Street. Max Solinsky was traced and found. He proved to be a
professional examination taker and was currently in Sing Sing prison
for taking a civil-service examination under a false name.

That was all the ammunition there was, and it needed careful
handling. In the first place there are the rules of evidence. When a
witness takes the stand he puts his character in issue, and he can be
cross-examined about anything in his life that will show he is not fit to
be believed. But as to anything that he was not asked about on his
direct examination, his answer is final and cannot be contradicted. For
instance, if a lady takes the stand and testifies that the defendant stole
her purse, you can call witnesses to show that she never had a purse, or
that she was in Chicago at the time, or anything else to show that the
purse was not stolen. But if you want to prove that she is no lady you
must prove it out of her own mouth. You may have a dozen witnesses

to show that she ran a gambling house, or tortured stray cats, or engaged in any number of activities that are not looked upon with approbation, but if she denies them (and you must ask her) that is the end of it.

Mr. Steuer had no illusions about Foelker's knowledge of this rule. If he was not already acquainted with it, he would be when he took the stand. Therefore he had to be so enmeshed by the time he was confronted with something important that a denial would be unavailing. But to get him in the toils would involve a series of questions about his schooling to which entirely credible answers would be that he did not remember. Who does remember at the age of 35 what he learned in school? Foelker had to have no excuse for not remembering. Mr. Steuer wrote Thain a letter telling him that he was going to question Foelker on these subjects, and asked him to refresh his recollection. If he ignored the request the jury would see that he had a good reason for doing it. On the other hand it would certainly warn Foelker that this incident was known and his care would make the questioning more difficult. It could not be helped. * * *

See Federal Rules of Evidence 608(b); California Evidence Code § 787.

Hypotheticals

(1) D is prosecuted for forcible rape of V, a 21-year-old female. D's defense is an alibi. At the preliminary hearing and at trial, V testifies on direct examination that D was the perpetrator and that she suffered great emotional distress and great physical pain because she had never had sexual intercourse with any man before. After V's direct examination, D files a motion to present an offer of proof with an affidavit by B that he, B, was V's former boyfriend and that he and V had engaged in several acts of sexual intercourse, setting forth specific dates and circumstances prior to the date of the charged offense. The trial judge conducts an in camera hearing at which V testifies that B was a former boyfriend but denies any intimacy with B. B testifies as set forth in his affidavit. The prosecutor makes impermissible-attempted-impeachment objection. How should the court rule?

(2) D is charged with rape of an unmarried female, V. V testifies and identifies D, by his voice, as the perpetrator. After the prosecution completes its case in chief, D calls V and elicits testimony that she had engaged in sexual relations within two days prior to the date of the alleged rape. D then asks V if she had taken a pregnancy test within two weeks prior to the date of the alleged rape. The prosecutor makes an improper impeachment objection. D then makes an oral offer of proof to the effect that his cross-examination question was relevant on the theory that V, on the date of the alleged rape, may have known that she was pregnant and had thus concocted the story of being raped to cover up for the fact of her pregnancy. What result?

(3) X is prosecuted for the murder of A. B is called by the prosecution and testifies that he saw the fight between A and X and that X struck the first blow. X calls C, who testifies that he was with B in a bar an hour before the fight. X proposes to have C testify that he saw B drink five shots of straight whiskey during that hour. The prosecutor objects that this is improper impeachment evidence. What result?

b. PSYCHIATRIC CONDITION

MOSLEY v. COMMONWEALTH

Court of Appeals of Kentucky, 1967.
420 S.W.2d 679.

WADDILL, Commissioner.

Appellant was convicted of the crime of rape and sentenced to ten years' servitude in the state penitentiary. The sole ground for reversal of the conviction is that the trial court erred in excluding the testimony of James Gay, a psychologist, concerning the mental condition of the prosecuting witness at the time of the alleged rape.

The record reflects that for several months prior to May 11, 1966, the date of the alleged offense, Geraldine Eden, the prosecuting witness, had been staying in the home of Elihu Asher where she was employed as a full-time baby-sitter. Geraldine, who is 27 years of age, testified that during the evening of May 11, 1966, the Ashers had left their residence to go bowling. Appellant, an acquaintance of Geraldine and a relative of Asher entered the Asher home for the purpose of staying overnight. Geraldine stated that after the Asher children went to bed, appellant tried to make love to her and when she resisted his amorous advances he forcibly tied her hands behind her back, pushed her down on a couch, removed her underclothing and raped her.

Appellant, age 54, testified that upon his arrival at the Asher residence Geraldine informed him that she wanted to talk with him before he retired. He had waited only a short time when Geraldine came over and sat beside him on a couch where they immediately began making love and Geraldine voluntarily submitted to sexual intercourse with him as she had on several previous occasions. He stated that following the intercourse they went to the kitchen and Geraldine prepared a snack for them. When they were later questioned that night as to their conduct, appellant stated that much to his surprise Geraldine claimed he had raped her.

Appellant urges that the court erred in refusing to permit the jury to consider, for the purpose of impeaching Geraldine's credibility, the testimony of Doctor Gay concerning Geraldine's mental condition. Doctor Gay has obtained a Ph.D. degree in psychology and has been licensed by the state of Kentucky as clinical psychologist. * * *

Doctor Gay, who is in charge of the treatment of Geraldine's mental disorder, testified, by way of avowal out of the presence of the jury, that Geraldine had entered a state hospital for mental treatment during October 1961. At that time she was complaining that her father and brothers had molested her sexually during her adolescence. She was discharged from the hospital in January 1962 and readmitted for treatment on a voluntary basis during 1964. She has been treated by Doctor Gay since September 1965.

While Doctor Gay believed that Geraldine was in a state of remission at the time of the alleged rape, it was his opinion that she is schizophrenic and is an immature individual. She could not tolerate frustration, was easily disturbed and had a guilt complex. Doctor Gay stated that schizophrenia is a complex phenomenon, that it is a disturbance of behavioral effect and thinking which has not been found to be caused or related to any physical or organic condition, but it has a psychiatric origin, i.e. an emotional basis. He further stated that one of the manifestations of schizophrenic reaction is fantasies and when asked whether Geraldine's fantasies extend to the area of sex, he answered, "In this particular case I think it does."

Since the Commonwealth relied upon the uncorroborated testimony of Geraldine to establish its case against appellant, the principal question at issue had reference to the credit to be given to the testimony of Geraldine. Therefore, Doctor Gay's testimony [, if admitted, might] have had an important impact on the jury as it tended to impeach Geraldine's credibility.

It is our opinion that the proffered testimony of Doctor Gay was relevant and competent and should have been received, not in extenuation of rape, but for its bearing upon the question of the weight to be accorded Geraldine's testimony. For this reason the court should admonish the jury that the expert testimony should be considered by it only for the purpose of affecting the credibility of this witness, if it does so.

Generally a witness may be impeached only as specified in our Rules of Civil Procedure (CR 43.07). However, the modern trend is to permit the jury to consider expert testimony in the field of mental disorders and relax the rule in sex offense cases. McCormick in his treatise on Evidence, Section 45 at page 99, observes:

> " * * * Naturally, the use of psychiatric testimony as to mental disorders and defects suggests itself as a potential aid in determining the credibility of crucial witnesses in any kind of litigation. In one type of case, namely that of sex offenses, the indispensible value of this kind of testimony has been urged by Wigmore, and other commentators, and such testimony has been widely received by the courts. * * *."

* * *

In State v. Armstrong, the importance of permitting an accused to impeach a witness for the state was pointed out as follows:

> " * * * It is always open to a defendant to challenge the credibility of the witnesses offered by the prosecution who testify against him. * * *.
>
> "What could be more effective for the purpose than to impeach the mentality or the intellectual grasp of the witness? If his interest, bias, indelicate way of life, insobriety and general bad reputation in the community may be shown as bearing upon his unworthiness of belief, why not his imbecility, want of understanding, or moronic comprehension, which go more directly to the point? * * *."

A similar conclusion was reached by the United States District Court in United States v. Hiss, wherein it was observed:

> "The existence of insanity or mental derangement is admissible for the purpose of discrediting a witness. Evidence of insanity is not merely for the judge on the preliminary question of competency, but goes to the jury to affect credibility. * * *."

Also see Giles v. State of Maryland, which concerns itself with the prosecution's suppression of evidence relating to the credibility of the prosecution's witnesses.

We conclude that the jury was entitled to hear and consider the testimony of Doctor Gay and that its exclusion constituted prejudicial error in the case.

The judgment is reversed with directions to grant appellant a new trial.

WILLIAMS, C.J., and EDWARD P. HILL, MILLIKEN, STEINFELD, PALMORE and OBSORNE, JJ., concur.

1950 ANNUAL SURVEY OF AMERICAN LAW
EVIDENCE, BY JUDSON FALKNOR
804–808 (1950).*

Witnesses: Impeachment by Psychiatric Testimony.—Although similar testimony had been rejected at the first trial of Alger Hiss, Judge Goddard at the second trial held admissible psychiatric testimony designed to impeach the credibility of the Government witness Whittaker Chambers, and in pursuance of this ruling a psychiatrist, Dr. Carl Binger, testified that Chambers was a "psychopath with a tendency toward making false accusations."[3] Dr. Binger testified that his opin-

---

3. N.Y. Times, Jan. 6, 1950, p. 1, col. 2. Amplifying this, the psychiatrist testified that Chambers suffered from a condition known as "a psychopathic personality, a disorder of character, the outstanding features of which are amoral and asocial behavior." This condition, said the witness, has "nothing to do with the conventional judgment of sanity"; it is rather a "personality deviation" that would not prevent Chambers from earning the $30,000 a year he got as senior editor of Time magazine up to Dec. 12, 1948. The symptoms of "a psychopathic personality" are variegated, including chronic, persistent and repetitious lying, stealing and deception, abnormal sexuality, alcoholism, panhandling, vagabondage, inability to form regular habits and a tendency to make false accusations. Such a person, the doctor continued, is quite aware of what he is doing but does not always know why he is doing it. He is frequently impulsive and bizarre. The psychopathic holds some kind of middle ground between the psychotic and neurotic. He plays a role: he may be a hero one moment and a gangster the next, but he acts as though the fancied situation were true. He will claim friendships that do not exist and will make false accusations because he is under constant compulsion to make his fancies come true. He is "amazingly isolated and egocentric." Ibid.

The cross-examination of the psychiatrist (N.Y. Times, Jan. 11, 1950, p. 12, col. 4 and Jan. 12, 1950, p. 9, col. 1) appears to have been rather effective. For example, the witness on his direct examination had emphasized and apparently attached importance to Chambers' "untidiness." He agreed on cross-examination that that trait was manifested by such persons as Albert Einstein, Heywood Broun, Will Rogers, Owen D. Young, Bing Crosby and Thomas A. Edison. The expert had testified that Mr. Chambers habitually gazed at the ceiling while testifying and seemed to have no direct relation with his examiner. "We have made a count of the number of times you looked at the ceiling," the prosecutor

ion was based on "personal observation of Mr. Chambers at the first trial for five days and on one day at this trial" and that "he had read plays, poems, articles and book reviews written by Mr. Chambers and books he had translated from German." While it has been said that Dr. Binger's diagnosis was "based entirely on courtroom observation" it appears from a trustworthy contemporary newspaper account that Dr. Binger gave his opinion after listening to a 70-minute hypothetical question "that accentuated unpalatable aspects of Mr. Chamber's life." These accounts leave obscure the tenor of the assumptions in the hypothetical question as well as the character and source of evidence in support thereof.

"Since the use of psychiatric testimony to impeach the credibility of a witness is a comparatively modern innovation," said Judge Goddard in his opinion, "there appear to be no Federal cases dealing with this precise question. However, the importance of insanity on the question of credibility of witnesses is often stressed.[6] There are some state cases in which such testimony has been held to be admissible or which indicate that if this question had been presented it would have been admissible."[7] Judge Goddard noted the contrary conclusion of the

told Dr. Binger. "During the first ten minutes you looked at the ceiling nineteen times. In the next fifteen minutes you looked up twenty times. For the next fifteen minutes ten times and for the last fifteen minutes ten times more. We counted a total of fifty-nine times that you looked at the ceiling in fifty minutes. Now I was wondering whether that was any symptom of a psychopathic personality?" Shifting in the witness chair, Dr. Binger smiled frostily and said: "Not alone." When the expert insisted that stealing was a psychopathic symptom the prosecutor asked: "Did you ever take a hotel towel or a Pullman towel?" "I can't swear whether I did or not," Dr. Binger replied, "I don't think so." "And if any member of this jury had stolen a towel, would that be evidence of psychopathic personality?" Mr. Murphy asked. "That would have no bearing on it," the psychiatrist said. It should be noted also that Dr. Binger conceded on cross-examination that he "could not form an opinion of a person merely by watching him from the witness stand."

6. Wigmore, Evidence §§ 931, 932 (3d ed. 1940).

7. The cases cited by the Court scarcely support this statement. The cases cited follow: People v. Cowles: In this rape case two physicians who had observed the prosecuting witness expressed the opinion that she was a "pathological falsifier, a nymphomaniac and a sexual pervert." But this testimony was received without objection. It is to be noted, however, that in holding improper the prosecutor's argument deprecating the medical testimony the Court said that "the term 'nymphomaniac' is a standard one in medical parlance * * * the opinion evidence that she was such is entitled to consideration"; State v. Wesler: This was also a rape case and the question on appeal was whether the verdict of guilty was against the weight of the evidence. In determining that it was not, the Court made reference to the testimony of two psychiatrists to the effect that the prosecuting witnesses were "psychopaths and immoral and that psychopaths are prone to be untruthful," but the admissibility of the evidence is not discussed. As far as the opinion discloses it was received without objection. In any case, the admissibility of the psychiatric testimony was not involved on the appeal; Ellarson v. Ellarson: This case appears to go no further than to hold that extrinsic evidence of "insanity," in the traditional sense, is admissible for impeachment purposes. The holding is orthodox; Jeffers v. State: In this rape case a physician testified apparently as a State's witness, as to the result of a physical examination of the prosecutrix, a girl of thirteen, and also "relative to her mental condition he testified she was below the average and that he considered her a child." On appeal the convicted defendant questioned the admissibility of this evidence but it was held proper. The case does not seem apposite; Bouldin v. State: In a robbery prosecution defendant proposed to show that a state's witness was, if not insane, an idiot or feeble-minded and also that the mother of the witness was an idiot. On appeal the exclusion of this evidence was held erroneous. This is like the *Ellarson* case, supra.

West Virginia court in State v. Driver,[8] but said, "This was in 1921— before the value of psychiatry had been recognized."[9]

Judge Goddard's instructions relative to the weight to be given the psychiatric testimony are set forth in the margin.[10] * * *

8. In this prosecution for rape the trial court excluded the opinions of a neurologist and a psychologist that the prosecuting witness was a moron and as such "untrustworthy of belief." This ruling was affirmed on appeal. The Court said that "we are not convinced that the time-honored and well-settled and defined rule of impeachment of the veracity of a witness [by evidence of bad reputation for truth and veracity] should be thus innovated upon. It is yet to be demonstrated that psychological and medical tests are practical, and will detect the lie on the witness stand."

9. Psychiatric Evaluation of the Mentally Abnormal Witness, 59 Yale L.J. 1324 (1950) contains a helpful summary of psychological and psychiatric theory touching the reliability of this sort of impeaching evidence. It is the conclusion of the writer that while the psychiatrist's opinion would be most helpful where he has had the benefit of a clinical examination, nevertheless his "diagnosis should be admitted whenever it is offered, whether based on clinical examination or courtroom observation alone. * * * Enough data may be presented in court to provide the basis for a psychological diagnosis which will be helpful to the jury. For example, by correlating all the factors of a witness' personality a psychiatrist may sometimes be able to detect a pathological liar in the courtroom as easily as in the clinic. These factors may include the witness' ability to adjust quickly to exposure of his lies, a case history denoting bizarre, insensitive or paranoidal tendencies and any convictions or indications of a bad reputation for veracity extrinsically revealed. Thus, whenever a qualified psychiatrist believes that he can make a competent courtroom diagnosis the Court should allow him to do so. Despite any shortcomings in a diagnosis of this sort, the psychiatrist is better qualified than a lay jury to assess personality disorders."

In a letter published in 123 N.Y.L.J., p. 414, col. 3, Feb. 2, 1950, A.S. Cutler criticizes the ruling as giving to the well-to-do litigant an unfair advantage. The poor litigant, because of the cost, will be unable to utilize this "new weapon in the armory of trial procedure." And in a letter published in 123 N.Y.L.J., p. 702, col. 2, Feb. 27, 1950, David L. Delman, besides agreeing with Cutler's point, calls attention to the frequent disagreement among experts "on scientific facts or pseudo-scientific facts" and says "especially is this true when we come to the nebulous field of psychology, psychiatry and psychoanalysis. * * * It is not generally known that this whole field of psychology is not a science at all because it is so inexact. * * * To have a psychologist or psychiatrist testify to the fact that a man is lying because the experts saw him look at the ceiling comes about as close to burlesquing justice as possible. * * * The jurors, by hearing testimony of the various witnesses and by using their own common sense are much more able to determine truth or falsehood than psychological experts." For a contrary view, see letter of Harry Silberschutz, 123 N.Y.L.J., p. 812, col. 2, March 7, 1950. He says: "The novelty of the offer of the testimony argued by counsel for the prosecution [in the Hiss case] is no insuperable obstacle. Progress in science has compelled changes in legal concepts and growth in medical knowledge is not legally of lesser significance. The psychopathic personality was not known in the days of Blackstone, so it is futile to dig deep into the past for cases on 'all fours'. * * * The constitutional infirmity of the psychopathic personality is not less a factor in destruction of credibility than interest or bias or what is loosely denominated 'insanity'. * * * Psychiatrists are already well accepted as experts virtually everywhere in our courts, and deservedly so. That they sometimes differ among themselves in their findings is no more damaging than it is in the case of other experts."

10. "The defense has called Dr. Binger a psychiatrist, and Dr. Murray, a psychologist, for the purpose of attacking Mr. Chambers' credibility. Dr. Binger, basing his opinion upon certain testimony which for the purpose of a hypothetical question he assumed to be true and on his observations of Mr. Chambers while Mr. Chambers was on the witness stand; and Dr. Murray, basing his opinion upon the same hypothetical situation which he assumed to be true, testified that in their opinion Mr. Chambers was a psychopathic personality and that this tended to reduce his credibility. As is the case with all expert testimony, these opinions are purely advisory. You may reject their opinions entirely if you find the hypothetical situation presented to them in the question to be incomplete or incorrect or if you believe their reasons to be unsound or not convincing. An expert does not pass on the truth of the testimony included in a hypothetical ques-

WITNESS' CLAIM THAT HE ONCE WAS HARLOW
CAST A REASONABLE DOUBT *

United Press International

MIAMI—A federal prosecutor labored to establish the credibility of his star witness, only to hear him proclaim in court that he is the reincarnation of the actress Jean Harlow.

The prosecutor, Peter Kostopulos, an assistant US attorney, cringed and jurors stifled guffaws, but the witness, Perry Bond, was deadly serious.

During two hours of testimony in a Miami fraud scam trial, Bond told how the scam worked.

Then it was defense lawyer James Jay Hogan's turn.

Hogan brought out a large square of cardboard covered with a sheet of paper. With a flourish, he uncovered his life-size exhibit—a picture of Jean Harlow in a bathing suit.

Hogan asked Bond if he recognized the picture of the platinum blond bombshell, a Hollywood sex symbol who died in 1937 at age 26.

Bond solemnly said he did.

Hogan asked if Bond had once occupied the body displayed in the picture.

Bond, born five years after Harlow's death, said he had.

Hogan continued his cross-examination.

"There was nothing I could do," Kostopulos said yesterday. "I asked him if there was anything else at all about his life I should know, but he never mentioned this. He really believes it."

A mistrial was declared after US District Judge Jose Gonzalez suffered an apparent heart attack * * *.

Hypothetical

X is prosecuted for battery upon A, his girl friend. A testifies that she was trying to break off her relationship with X and that he got mad and beat her. On cross-examination, X asks A if it isn't true that she has been under the care of a psychiatrist for the last three years. The prosecutor makes an improper impeachment objection. X represents that he intends to prove that it was he

tion. Similarly, he does not, and as a matter of law, he cannot pass on the truth of any part or parts of the testimony of the witness about whose mental condition he expresses his opinion. Assuming the facts in the hypothetical question to be true, the expert testifies that in his opinion the witness is suffering from a mental disorder which would tend to reduce his credibility in general. You yourselves have seen and heard Mr. Chambers for several days while he was on the witness stand and you have heard all the evidence. It is for you to say how much weight, if any, you will give to the testimony of the experts—and of Mr. Chambers. * * * Was Mr. Chambers telling the truth when he testified that he did see Mr. Hiss and that he did receive from him documents as charged? Those are the questions you must answer. Even though you may accept the experts' opinion as to Mr. Chambers' mental condition, you may still find that Mr. Chambers was telling the truth when he testified regarding those particular matters." N.Y. Times, Jan. 21, 1950, p. 2, col. 2.

* Boston Globe—Oct 18, 1984 P 7.

who was trying to break off the relationship, because he found out that A had
been under the care of a psychiatrist; that he never struck A at all; and that
A's claim is a figment of her imagination.

c. PRIOR CONVICTIONS

PEOPLE v. BARRICK

Supreme Court of California, In Bank, 1982.
33 Cal.3d 115, 187 Cal.Rptr. 716, 654 P.2d 1243.

BROUSSARD, J. Defendant appeals from a judgment of conviction after a jury found him guilty of theft and unlawful driving or
taking of a vehicle. Defendant was acquitted of the charge of receiving
stolen property. The prosecutor also charged two prior felony convictions for the purpose of sentence enhancement and to preclude probation. These were admitted by the defendant.

The primary issue in this appeal is whether the trial court erred in
ruling that if the defendant testified, he could be impeached by the
prosecutor asking whether defendant had ever been convicted of a
"felony involving theft." This is but the latest twist involving the
propriety of admitting prior felony convictions for the purpose of
impeachment. We conclude that where similar offenses are involved,
the technique of "sanitizing" the prior felony is ineffective to dispel the
prejudice in admitting evidence of the prior conviction. Therefore, the
procedure is unacceptable, and the trial court erred in permitting it.

* * *

Before trial, defense counsel made a motion to prohibit the prosecutor from impeaching defendant with a prior felony conviction of automobile theft. The trial court recognized the potential prejudice in
telling the jury that defendant had been previously convicted of automobile theft. In an attempt to avoid that prejudice, the court ruled
that should the defendant testify, the prosecutor could ask him if he
had ever been convicted of "a felony involving theft." At that point,
defense counsel indicted that he would advise his client not to testify.

We granted a hearing to consider the propriety of impeaching a
defendant by a "sanitized" reference to a prior conviction as a "felony
involving theft."

We begin by examining the statutory authorization for allowing
impeachment by prior felony convictions, and the statutory and judicial
limitations on that authority. Evidence Code section 788 provides in
pertinent part that "[f]or the purpose of attacking the credibility of a
witness, it *may* be shown by the examination of the witness or by the
record of the judgment that he has been convicted of a felony * * *."
(Italics added.) This authorization of judicial discretion is tempered,
however, by Evidence Code section 352, which permits the trial judge to
exclude otherwise admissible evidence "if its probative value is substantially outweighed by the probability that its admission will * * *
create substantial danger of undue prejudice * * *." We first examined the relationship between these sections in People v. Beagle,
where we held that read together, sections 788 and 352 "clearly provide

discretion to the trial judge to exclude evidence of prior felony convictions when their probative value on credibility is outweighed by the risk of undue prejudice." (Id., at p. 453.) This court adopted the discussion by Judge (now Chief Justice) Burger in Gordon v. United States, identifying some of the more important factors for the trial court to consider in exercising its discretion whether to allow evidence of the prior felony conviction for the purpose of impeachment: " 'In common human experience acts of deceit, fraud, cheating, or stealing, for example, are universally regarded as conduct which reflects adversely on a man's honesty and integrity. Acts of violence * * * generally have little or no direct bearing on honesty and veracity. A "rule of thumb" thus should be that convictions which rest on dishonest conduct relate to credibility whereas those of violent or assaultive crimes generally do not. * * * The nearness or remoteness of the prior conviction is also a factor of no small importance. Even one involving fraud or stealing, for example, if it occurred long before and has been followed by a legally blameless life, should generally be excluded on the ground of remoteness. A special and even more difficult problem arises when the prior conviction is for the same or substantially similar conduct for which the accused is on trial. Where multiple convictions of various kinds can be shown, strong reasons arise for excluding those which are for the same crime because of the inevitable pressure on lay jurors to believe "if he did it before he probably did so this time." As a general guide, those convictions which are for the same crime should be admitted sparingly. * * * One important consideration is what the effect will be if the defendant does not testify out of fear of being prejudiced because of impeachment by prior convictions. Even though a judge might find that the prior convictions are relevant to credibility and the risk of prejudice to the defendant does not warrant their exclusion, he may nevertheless conclude that it is more important that the jury have the benefit of the defendant's version of the case than to have the defendant remain silent out of fear of impeachment.' " Before admitting evidence of the prior felony conviction, courts have the duty to determine whether the proffered evidence has "any tendency in reason to prove or disprove" the defendant's credibility.

[Evidence Code section 786 provides that] the sole trait relevant to the witness' credibility is truthfulness: "Evidence of traits of his character other than honesty or veracity, or their opposites, is inadmissible to attack or support the credibility of a witness." Thus, if a prior felony conviction does not reflect on the trait of truthfulness, it must be excluded as irrelevant under Evidence Code section 350, which provides that "[n]o evidence is admissible except relevant evidence." However, not all felony convictions reflecting on the truthfulness of the defendant are equally probative of that issue. "[D]ifferent felonies have different degrees of probative value on the issue of credibility. Some, such as perjury, are intimately connected with that issue; others, such as robbery and burglary, are somewhat less relevant; * * *" Thus, even when a prior conviction is conceded to adversely reflect on the defendant's honesty, the court must make an initial determination as to the "degree or probative value" that the prior conviction has on the question of the defendant's honesty or veracity.

The initial determination regarding the probative value of the prior felony conviction is made by examining the elements of the offense itself. Unless the conviction contains an element reflecting on defendant's honesty, it may not be admitted. "Only a conviction which has as a necessary element an intent to deceive, defraud, lie, steal, etc., impacts on the credibility of a witness." It is not sufficient that the prior offense shows a "disrespect for law" or a "character trait of willingness to do anything." Some theft offenses, such as robbery, contain elements that are both larcenous and assaultive, and thus bear only in part on the individual's veracity. Hence, such offenses are entitled to somewhat less weight in the balancing process. However, the mere removal of the noncredibility aspects of certain theft offenses does not increase the probative value of the credibility-bearing elements of the offense. "Even those elements of a robbery conviction which do reflect on a witness' credibility are less probative of that issue than the elements of other convictions, such as perjury. Thus, while a robbery or other theft conviction may be relevant to credibility, it is entitled to less weight in the *Beagle* balancing process than such other offenses."

[I]t is the obligation of the trial judge to make an initial determination whether the prior felony conviction is sufficiently probative of the question of credibility for the jury to consider it in assessing the truthfulness of the defendant. This is but the threshold question in the balancing test required by *Beagle* and its progeny. Of course, once this determination is made, and assuming that the remaining conditions to admissibility are satisfied, it is for the jury to make the final determination to what extent the prior conviction affects credibility in a particular case.

[T]he technique of not identifying the prior crime "frustrates a prime function of the jury." That function is to make a final determination as to the credibility of the witness. One of the factors that the jury considers in assessing that credibility is the persuasiveness of the prior conviction. Although the trial judge must make an initial determination as to the probative value of the prior conviction, the jury cannot weigh the probative value of the particular prior conviction if it is deprived of knowledge of the identity of that crime.

Another problem caused by not revealing the prior conviction is that stating only that the defendant has been convicted of "a felony" will arouse the jury's curiosity about the identity of the prior offense: "Normal human curiosity will inevitably lead to brisk speculation on the nature of that conviction, and the range of such speculation will be limited solely by the imaginations of the individual jurors."

The second factor for the trial court to consider is the nearness or remoteness in time of the prior felony conviction. In this case, the prior conviction occurred two years prior to the trial. [T]his factor would point toward admissibility of the prior felony conviction.

The third factor to be assessed in applying the balancing formula, crucial to the determination in this case, is the " 'special and even more difficult problem [that] arises when the prior conviction is for the same or substantially similar conduct for which the accused is on trial.' " This problem arises when the witness whose testimony is sought to be impeached is also the defendant. In such a case, the trial court must exercise extreme caution in assessing the potential prejudice because "[s]uch circumstances present a unique risk of undue prejudice and confusion of issues. Despite limiting instructions, the jury is likely to consider this evidence for the improper purpose of determining whether the accused is the type of person who could engage in criminal activity. This is particularly likely where the prior conviction is for the same crime as that which forms the basis of the charges against defendant. The probability of such misuse also increases where the prosecution's case is weak. In these circumstances, only the most disciplined minds would be able to restrict their use of the prior felony evidence to assessing the defendant's credibility as a witness and disregard its obvious implications with respect to his tendencies in the area of unlawful conduct."

Moreover, "[t]here is also the 'obvious danger' that the jury will decide that based on his prior convictions, the accused 'ought to be put away without too much concern with present guilt.' Further, the admission of prior convictions often confuses the issues at trial and 'draw[s] [the jurors'] minds away from the real issue' of guilt or innocence.

A strict limitation on the admission of similar prior convictions is thus necessary because "[w]hile the risk of undue prejudice is substantial when any prior conviction is used to impeach the credibility of a defendant-witness, it is far greater when the prior conviction is similar or identical to the crime charged." "A jury which is made aware of a similar prior conviction will inevitably feel pressure to conclude that if an accused committed the prior crime he likely committed the crime charged."

In [People v.] Rist we found the admission of a similar prior conviction to be an abuse of discretion when there were dissimilar prior convictions available for the purpose of impeachment. This court did not, however, imply that a similar or identical conviction should be admitted merely because no dissimilar prior conviction is available to impeach credibility.

In People v. Fries, defendant was charged with robbery. The trial court denied defendant's motion to exclude evidence of his prior robbery conviction. We reversed the conviction, holding that the trial court erred in permitting the defendant to be impeached by use of a prior identical felony conviction. Thus, the rule emerges that identical prior offenses may not be used; similar prior convictions should only be used sparingly.

In People v. Betts, the trial court attempted to "sanitize" the prior conviction by allowing the prosecutor to ask the defendant if he had ever been convicted of a felony involving the trait of honesty. In concluding that the trial court erred in allowing the question, the Court of Appeal not[ed] that although some speculation is removed, "it is yet the case the trier of fact could well imagine 'that the [appellant's] prior conviction[s] [were] similar to or identical with the charge for which he [was] on trial' * * *."

* * *

In our view, the method used in this case, does not avoid the prejudice warned against and despite the facile evenhandedness, "the scales remain sharply weighted against the defendant."

The effort to "sanitize" the prior auto theft conviction as a "felony involving theft" was an attempt to tread between the pitfalls of identifying the prior conviction as an offense similar or identical to the charged offense and not identifying the felony at all. We conclude that the technique, while having a superficial appeal as an acceptable accommodation of the competing interests of the prosecution and the defense, does not avoid creating a "substantial danger of undue prejudice." Although the partial identification in this case would forestall the possibility that the jury would assume that the undisclosed prior offense was heinous, the technique only increased the possibility that the jury would assume that the undisclosed prior offense was indeed identical to the crime charged. Why else, when defendant is charged with a theft-type offense, reveal that he had previously been convicted of a felony involving theft? The flaw in the procedure is that it not only does not remove the speculation warned against in *Rollo*, supra, but it in fact tends to focus the speculation toward the conclusion that the prior crime was identical, which inevitably leads to the improper presumption that "if he did it once, he will do it again."

Indeed, the procedure whereby the jury is suggestively led to speculate that the prior offense was similar to the one charged may be as detrimental to the fact-finding process as explicitly identifying the prior crime as identical to the current charge offense.

Even were we to conclude that the technique used by the trial court is a generally acceptable method of revealing the credibility-bearing aspect of the prior conviction without creating the substantial danger of undue prejudice, we cannot sanction the approach in this case. Although "sanitized," the prior conviction closely resembled the offense for which the defendant was on trial. There is no doubt that defendant's conviction of auto theft is similar to the charged offense of violating Vehicle Code section 10851 (theft and unlawful driving or taking of a vehicle). Indeed, "Vehicle Code section 10851 is a lesser included offense of Penal Code section 487, subdivision 3, grand theft, auto."

* * * The jury would, in all likelihood, consider the charged offense to be a "theft." Thus, there can be no lessening of the prejudicial effect in describing a prior conviction as a "felony involving theft" when defendant is charged with the similar offense of "theft and unlawful driving or taking of a vehicle."

Finally, * * * the trial court must also consider in the balancing equation the effect if the defendant does not testify out of fear of being prejudiced because of impeachment by prior convictions. We have previously noted that even if the first three factors suggest admissibility of the prior conviction, the trial judge may nevertheless decide that it is "more important that the jury have the benefit of defendant's version of the case than to have the defendant remain silent out of fear of impeachment."

Several reasons compel this heightened significance of the fourth factor. Like the third factor, this one becomes particularly important when the witness whose testimony is sought to be impeached is also the defendant. In such a case, the loss of the defendant's testimony will undoubtedly have a greater impact on the fact-finding process than would the failure to testify of a nondefendant witness. The threat of impeachment by a prior felony conviction has significant coercive force when the witness' liberty is at stake.

In addition, the defendant's constrained silence has a detrimental impact on our criminal justice system. When "the accused elects not to testify in order to keep the evidence of prior convictions from the jury, the jury is deprived of competent, probative evidence—the testimony of the accused.

Third, despite limiting instructions, the defendant's silence caused by the threat of impeachment by prior convictions may itself tend to prejudice the defendant. The jury "will expect the defendant to present all the evidence he can to escape conviction, and it will naturally infer that his failure to explain or deny evidence against him when the facts are peculiarly within his knowledge arises from his inability to do so."

Finally, if the trial court errs in admitting the prior felony conviction and the defendant does not testify, it is extremely difficult for an appellate court to measure the impact that defendant's testimony might have had.

Our holding that the prejudicial effect of the "sanitized" prior conviction outweighs its probative value does not mean that we are encouraging "a form of blackmail by defendants" or permitting the defendant to be clothed with "a false aura of veracity." "The exclusion of a prior conviction to impeach credibility does not prevent a prosecutor from subjecting a defendant-witness to piercing cross-examination. Through cross-examination, the prosecutor can raise doubts as to the general truthfulness of the witness and question the credibility of his version of the facts. Also, the defendant's memory and capacity for observation can be challenged. Prior inconsistent statements may be used to impeach credibility."

The judgment is reversed.

CALIFORNIA CONSTITUTION ART. 1, § 28

(f) **Use of Prior Convictions.** Any prior felony conviction of any person in any criminal proceeding, whether adult or juvenile, shall subsequently be used without limitation for purposes of impeachment or enhancement of sentence in any criminal proceeding. When a prior felony conviction is an element of any felony offense, it shall be proven to the trier of fact in open court.

(Added by Initiative Measure, approved by the people, June 8, 1982, known as "The Victims' Bill of Rights").

UNITED STATES v. WONG

United States Court of Appeals, Third Circuit, 1983.
703 F.2d 65.

PER CURIAM:

This case presents the issue whether a district court has any discretion to exclude, as unduly prejudicial, evidence that a witness had previously been convicted of a crime involving dishonesty or false statement. The district court held that it had no discretion to weigh the probative value of the prior conviction against its prejudicial effect. Agreeing with every other circuit to consider the matter, we affirm.

I.

John Barry Wong was charged with seventeen counts of violation of the mail fraud statute, 18 U.S.C. § 1341 (1976), and two counts of violation of the Racketeer Influenced and Corrupt Organizations statute, 18 U.S.C. §§ 1961–68 (1976 & Supp. V 1981). A jury found him guilty on all counts, and he was sentenced to seven years imprisonment followed by five years probation and ordered to make restitution of $100,000.

Wong had previously been convicted at least twice—a 1978 mail fraud conviction in a federal court in Pennsylvania and a 1981 Medicare fraud conviction in a federal court in Hawaii. At trial in this case, prior to putting his client on the stand, counsel for Wong moved to preclude use of these convictions for impeachment. The trial court stated that the probative value of the convictions did not outweigh their prejudicial effect. The trial court held, however, that since the two convictions were crimes involving dishonesty or false statement [so-called *crimen falsi*], under Fed.R.Evid. 609(a)(2) no balancing of prejudice against probative value was appropriate. Wong then took the stand; during his cross-examination the two convictions were introduced against him.

Wong now attacks as erroneous the legal conclusion of the trial judge that *crimen falsi* under Fed.R.Evid. 609(a)(2) are admissible as impeachment without reference to their prejudicial effect.

II.

Fed.R.Evid. 609(a) provides as follows:

Rule 609. Impeachment by Evidence of Conviction of Crime

(a) General Rule. For the purpose of attacking the credibility of a witness, evidence that he has been convicted of a crime shall be admitted if elicited from him or established by public record during cross-examination but only if the crime (1) was punishable by death or imprisonment in excess of one year under the law under which he was convicted, and the court determines that the probative value of admitting this evidence outweighs its prejudicial effect to the defendant, or (2) involved dishonesty or false statement, regardless of the punishment.

Defendant does not dispute that his previous mail fraud and Medicare fraud convictions are crimes involving dishonesty or false statement and are therefore within 609(a)(2).

Rule 609(a) differentiates on its face between convictions for crimes punishable by imprisonment of more than one year, which are admissible under 609(a)(1), and convictions for *crimen falsi*, which are admissible under 609(a)(2). The former may be admitted only if the trial court determines that their probative value outweighs their prejudicial effect. The latter simply "shall be admitted."

Wong suggests that the apparently mandatory admission of *crimen falsi* under Fed.R.Evid. 609(a)(2) is qualified by the general balancing test of Fed.R.Evid. 403. Rule 403 provides as follows:

Rule 403. Exclusion of Relevant Evidence on Grounds of Prejudice, Confusion, or Waste of Time

Although relevant, evidence may be excluded if its probative value is substantially outweighed by the danger of unfair prejudice, confusion of the issues, or misleading the jury, or by considerations of undue delay, waste of time, or needless presentation of cumulative evidence.

Wong asserts that the trial court therefore has the power to exclude *crimen falsi* convictions if it determines that their probative force is substantially outweighed by their prejudicial effect.

We disagree. As the First Circuit has recently noted, Rule 403 was not designed to override more specific rules; rather it was "designed as a guide for the handling of situations for which no specific rules have been formulated."

Rule 609(a) is such a specific rule. It was the product of extensive Congressional attention and considerable legislative compromise, clearly reflecting a decision that judges were to have no discretion to exclude *crimen falsi*.

In an earlier draft, Rule 609 included a subsection, 609(a)(3), which would have allowed the court to exclude either convictions carrying an imprisonment of more than one year or *crimen falsi* convictions if it determined that their probative value was substantially outweighed by their prejudicial effect.

Proposed section 609(a)(3) was severely criticized by Senator McClellan of Arkansas on the floor of the Senate. Thereafter, when the Supreme Court officially promulgated the Federal Rules of Evidence and transmitted them to the Congress, section 609(a)(3) had disappeared; at that point there was no reference in the section to any weighing by the trial judge of probative value against prejudicial effect.

Rule 609(a) then came under considerable scrutiny in Congress. Various ways of treating impeachment by conviction were proposed. The compromise that resulted in the final version of Rule 609(a) came in the Conference Committee and was described in the following terms by the Chairman of the Subcommittee on Criminal Justice of the House Judiciary Committee:

> The House version of the rule permitted the use of convictions for crimes of dishonesty or false statement. The Senate version permitted the use of convictions for any felony or for any crime of dishonesty or false statement. * * *

The conference rule strikes a middle ground between the two versions, but a ground as close or closer to the House version than to the Senate's. *The conference rule provides that evidence of a conviction of a crime involving dishonesty or false statement may always be used to impeach.* * * * This constitutes no change from either the House or Senate version. The conference rule further provides that evidence of a prior felony conviction may be used for impeachment but only if the court determines that the probative value of the conviction outweighs its prejudicial effect to the defendant.

The Conference Report is likewise clear:

> The admission of prior convictions involving dishonesty and false statement is not within the discretion of the Court. Such convictions are peculiarly probative of credibility and, under this rule, are always to be admitted.

Thus the legislative history of Rule 609(a)(2) unambiguously demonstrates that a judge has no authority to prohibit the government's effort to impeach the credibility of a witness by questions concerning a prior *crimen falsi* conviction. In light of this clear Congressional judgment we hold that the general balancing test of Fed.R.Evid. 403 is not applicable to impeachment by *crimen falsi* convictions under Fed.R. Evid. 609(a)(2).

The judgment of the district court will be affirmed.

ABBY'S VIEW

DEAR ABBY: My husband and I went on a two-week trip last year and hired a woman to stay in our home and look after our children.

After we came home, I couldn't find my favorite pair of earrings. They were only costume jewelry, but I liked them and wore them with many outfits.

Last evening my husband and I went to a movie, and as we came out, there was this friend who stayed at our home last year, wearing my earrings! Up until that time I wanted to believe that I had just misplaced them. Needless to say, I was shocked. Shall I ask her to return my earrings? Or should I just wait and hope she reads your column and brings them back?

MRS. A

DEAR MRS. A: Ask, but don't expect her to return them. Any one who would steal would probably lie.

Hypothetical

X is prosecuted for the offense of having sexual intercourse with A, his 13-year-old stepdaughter. A testifies, with minimal impeachment of her testimony. X testifies in denial of the charge. To impeach X, the prosecution proposes to establish, through cross-examination of X, that he has suffered prior felony convictions of rape, sale of heroin, and grand theft, all occurring within the 10-year-period prior to the offense charged. X requests the court to preclude such cross-examination. How should the court rule?

GREEN v. BOCK LAUNDRY MACHINE CO., 490 U.S. 504, 109 S.Ct. 1981, 104 L.Ed.2d 557 (1989). Plaintiff, a prisoner, obtained a work-release job at a car wash. While working there, he reached inside a large dryer. A rotating drum tore off his arm. He brought a civil action to recover damages for the injury. At trial, he testified about the cause of the accident. The defendant impeached plaintiff with plaintiff's prior felony convictions for burglary and conspiracy to commit burglary. Plaintiff claimed that the prior convictions should have been excluded as prejudicial. In arguing that the convictions were properly received, defendant relied upon the language of original Rule 609(a)(1), which provided that prior convictions "shall be admitted" unless probative value is outweighed by "prejudicial effect *to the defendant* " (emphasis added). In a 5–1–3 decision, the Supreme Court held that the convictions were admissible. The majority decided that Congress intended the balancing test to apply only to criminal defendants, and that the rule mandated the reception of 609(a)(1) convictions in *civil* cases even when prejudice outweighed probative value. The Court subsequently promulgated an amendment to Rule 609(a), effective December 1, 1990. The rule as amended provides a Rule 403 balancing test for witnesses other than the accused.

LUCE v. UNITED STATES

Supreme Court of the United States, 1984.
469 U.S. 38, 105 S.Ct. 460, 83 L.Ed.2d 443.

Chief Justice BURGER delivered the opinion of the Court.

We granted certiorari to resolve a conflict among the Circuits as to whether the defendant, who did not testify at trial, is entitled to review of the District Court's ruling denying his motion to forbid the use of a prior conviction to impeach his credibility.

I

Petitioner was indicted on charges of conspiracy, and possession of cocaine with intent to distribute, in violation of 21 U.S.C. §§ 846 and 841(a)(1). During his trial in the United States District Court for the Western District of Tennessee, petitioner moved for a ruling to preclude the Government from using a 1974 state conviction to impeach him if he testified. There was no commitment by petitioner that he would testify if the motion were granted, nor did he make a proffer to the court as to what his testimony would be. In opposing the motion, the Government represented that the conviction was for a serious crime— possession of a controlled substance.

The District Court ruled that the prior conviction fell within the category of permissible impeachment evidence under Federal Rule of Evidence 609(a).[1] The District Court noted, however, that the nature

1. Rule 609(a) provides:

and scope of petitioner's trial testimony could affect the court's specific evidentiary rulings; for example, the court was prepared to hold that the prior conviction would be excluded if petitioner limited his testimony to explaining his attempt to flee from the arresting officers. However, if petitioner took the stand and denied any prior involvement with drugs, he could then be impeached by the 1974 conviction. Petitioner did not testify, and the jury returned guilty verdicts.

II

The United States Court of Appeals for the Sixth Circuit affirmed. 713 F.2d 1236 (1983). The Court of Appeals refused to consider petitioner's contention that the District Court abused its discretion in denying the motion *in limine* [2] without making an explicit finding that the probative value of the prior conviction outweighed its prejudicial effect. The Court of Appeals held that when the defendant does not testify, the court will not review the District Court's *in limine* ruling.

Some other Circuits have permitted review in similar situations; we granted certiorari to resolve the conflict. We affirm.

III

It is clear, of course, that had petitioner testified and been impeached by evidence of a prior conviction, the District Court's decision to admit the impeachment evidence would have been reviewable on appeal along with any other claims of error. The Court of Appeals would then have had a complete record detailing the nature of petitioner's testimony, the scope of the cross-examination, and the possible impact of the impeachment on the jury's verdict.

A reviewing court is handicapped in any effort to rule on subtle evidentiary questions outside a factual context.[3] This is particularly true under Rule 609(a)(1), which directs the court to weigh the probative value of a prior conviction against the prejudicial effect to the defendant. To perform this balancing, the court must know the precise nature of the defendant's testimony, which is unknowable when, as here, the defendant does not testify.[4]

"General Rule.—For the purpose of attacking the credibility of a witness, evidence that he has been convicted of a crime shall be admitted if elicited from him or established by public record during cross-examination but only if the crime (1) was punishable by death or imprisonment in excess of one year under the law under which he was convicted, and the court determines that the probative value of admitting this evidence outweighs its prejudicial effect to the defendant, or (2) involved dishonesty or false statement, regardless of the punishment."

2. "*In limine*" has been defined as "[o]n or at the threshold; at the very beginning; preliminarily." Black's Law Dictionary 708 (5th ed. 1979). We use the term in a broad sense to refer to any motion, whether made before or during trial, to exclude anticipated prejudicial evidence before the evidence is actually offered.

3. Although the Federal Rules of Evidence do not explicitly authorize *in limine* rulings, the practice has developed pursuant to the district court's inherent authority to manage the course of trials. See generally Fed.Rule Evid. 103(c); cf. Fed. Rule Crim.Proc. 12(e).

4. Requiring a defendant to make a proffer of testimony is no answer; his trial testimony could, for any number of reasons, differ from the proffer.

Any possible harm flowing from a district court's *in limine* ruling permitting impeachment by a prior conviction is wholly speculative. The ruling is subject to change when the case unfolds, particularly if the actual testimony differs from what was contained in the defendant's proffer. Indeed even if nothing unexpected happens at trial, the district judge is free, in the exercise of sound judicial discretion, to alter a previous *in limine* ruling. On a record such as here, it would be a matter of conjecture whether the District Court would have allowed the Government to attack petitioner's credibility at trial by means of the prior conviction.

When the defendant does not testify, the reviewing court also has no way of knowing whether the Government would have sought to impeach with the prior conviction. If, for example, the Government's case is strong, and the defendant is subject to impeachment by other means, a prosecutor might elect not to use an arguably inadmissible prior conviction.

Because an accused's decision whether to testify "seldom turns on the resolution of one factor," New Jersey v. Portash, 440 U.S. 450, 467, 99 S.Ct. 1292, 1301, 59 L.Ed.2d 501 (1979) (BLACKMUN, J., dissenting), a reviewing court cannot assume that the adverse ruling motivated a defendant's decision not to testify. In support of his motion a defendant might make a commitment to testify if his motion is granted; but such a commitment is virtually risk free because of the difficulty of enforcing it.

Even if these difficulties could be surmounted, the reviewing court would still face the question of harmless error. Were *in limine* rulings under Rule 609(a) reviewable on appeal, almost any error would result in the windfall of automatic reversal; the appellate court could not logically term "harmless" an error that presumptively kept the defendant from testifying. Requiring that a defendant testify in order to preserve Rule 609(a) claims, will enable the reviewing court to determine the impact any erroneous impeachment may have had in light of the record as a whole; it will also tend to discourage making such motions solely to "plant" reversible error in the event of conviction.

* * *

We hold that to raise and preserve for review the claim of improper impeachment with a prior conviction, a defendant must testify. Accordingly, the judgment of the Court of Appeals is

Affirmed.

* * *

Justice BRENNAN, with whom Justice MARSHALL joins, concurring.

I join the opinion of the Court because I understand it to hold only that a defendant who does not testify at trial may not challenge on appeal an *in limine* ruling respecting admission of a prior conviction for purposes of impeachment under Rule 609(a) of the Federal Rules of Evidence. The Court correctly identifies two reasons for precluding appellate review unless the defendant testifies at trial. The careful weighing of probative value and prejudicial effect that Rule 609(a)

requires of a district court can only be evaluated adequately on appeal
in the specific factual context of a trial as it has unfolded. And if the
defendant declines to testify, the reviewing court is handicapped in
making the required harmless error determination should the district
court's *in limine* ruling prove to have been incorrect.

I do not understand the Court to be deciding broader questions of
appealability *vel non* of *in limine* rulings that do not involve Rule
609(a). * * *

d. BAD REPUTATION FOR TRUTH AND VERACITY

MATHES AND DEVITT, FEDERAL JURY PRACTICE
§ 9.10 (1965).*

§ 9.10 Impeachment—Evidence of Witness' Reputation for Truth and Veracity

When an attempt is made to impeach a witness by showing a bad
general reputation for truth and veracity in the community where the
witness now resides, or has recently resided, the jury should consider
such evidence along with all evidence of good reputation as to those
traits of character. Evidence that the witness' reputation for truth and
veracity has not been discussed or, if discussed, those traits of the
witness' character have not been questioned, may be sufficient to
warrant an inference of good reputation as to those traits of character.

————

See Federal Rules of Evidence 608; California Evidence Code
§ 786.

Hypothetical

X is prosecuted for the sale of heroin to A, an informer for the police. A
testifies that he made a purchase of heroin from X in a dimly lit bar, and that
this was part of a "buy" program that covered a three-month period, with A's
purchase from X coming in the second month. X's defense is an alibi. X calls
B to testify that he has been a next-door neighbor to A for 10 years and has
attended many social affairs which A also attended, and that A has a reputation in the community for having a bad memory. The prosecutor objects to the
proposed testimony of B as improper impeachment evidence. What result?

3. PRIOR INCONSISTENT STATEMENTS

COLES v. HARSCH
Supreme Court of Oregon, 1929.
129 Or. 11, 276 P. 248.

In this action the plaintiff sought to recover a judgment for $50,000
upon charges that the defendant had maliciously alienated the affections of plaintiff's wife by improper attentions shown to her in the
years 1923, 1924, and 1925. * * * The verdict and judgment were
in favor of the plaintiff in the sum of $17,500. The defendant appealed.

* Copyright, 1965 by West Publishing Co.

ROSSMAN, J. (after stating the facts as above). The defendant presents for our disposal several assignments of error. We shall first consider the one which is based upon the endeavor of the plaintiff to impeach the testimony of one James A. Thompson, who was one of the defendant's principal witnesses. In order to better understand the situation presented by this assignment of error, it seems desirable to state the following undisputed facts: While the parties were married to their former wives, the two couples belonged to the same social group; they frequently met at card parties, dances, and other social diversions, and frequently visited back and forth. The plaintiff contended that at some time in 1923 he noticed that the defendant was developing a propensity for wrestling with the plaintiff's wife, and engaging in other similar play with her. It was his contention that this propensity of the defendant did not abate with the passing of time, but that it grew more pronounced, and the plaintiff contended that it constituted one of the means which the defendant employed for winning the affections of the plaintiff's wife. This seems to be a rather unusual method of love making, yet if current reports are reliable, it is not the first instance where a cicisbeo has delved into the distant stone age and brought forth a somewhat rough and uncouth method of endearment, which well served his purpose, and brought about the desired result. Be this as it may, it will suffice to say that much time was consumed in the trial court in taking testimony concerning these wrestling and similar encounters and the extent to which other members of the parties participated in them; there was also testimony, not all in harmony, however, concerning the plaintiff's protests against the activities along these lines of his wife and the defendant and the latter's replies and rejoinders thereto.

As we have said, one of the defendant's principal witnesses was a Mr. James A. Thompson. The latter and his wife were members of this social group. His testimony, apparently important to the defendant, covered these wrestling encounters, the social diversions of the group, and the relationship between the defendant and Mrs. Coles, plaintiff's former wife. If his testimony was accepted as truthful by the jury, the defendant's conduct towards Mrs. Coles was the same as his conduct towards other women friends, and was proper and harmless. Apparently nothing developed upon cross-examination which obviously discredited this witness; but, upon rebuttal, the plaintiff was permitted over objection to testify that, "at the time I was in the garage where he works," Thompson told him that at a picnic held on the banks of the Pudding river the conduct of the defendant and Mrs. Coles towards each other was disgraceful. Before defendant's objection was ruled upon, plaintiff's counsel stated that the purpose of the contemplated answer was to "go to the credibility of Thompson." The objections of the defendant to the questions, which elicited the above answer, were specific and were reiterated; they were to the effect that, if the plaintiff sought this information to substantiate the charges of his complaint, the inquiry was in violation of the hearsay evidence rule: That if the plaintiff sought the answer for the purpose of impeaching Thompson, he had not laid the proper foundation by making a similar inquiry of

Thompson accompanied with the details of time, place, and persons present. The merits of the first alternative of the objection are so self-evident, that we deem it necessary to set forth our consideration only of the second phase of the objection.

Section 864, Or.L., provides: "A witness may also be impeached by evidence that he has made, at other times, statements inconsistent with his present testimony; but before this can be done, the statements must be related to him, with the circumstances of times, places, and persons present; and he shall be asked whether he has made such statements, and if so, allowed to explain them. If the statements be in writing, they shall be shown to the witness before any question is put to him concerning them."

It is necessary, therefore, to examine the inquiries propounded to Thompson and determine whether a similar question was put to him which complied with this statutory rule. Pausing for a moment, it is worthwhile to observe that this requirement does not invoke an idle ceremony, but is intended to serve a useful purpose. Every witness, whose testimony is shown in conflict with a previous statement made by him, is not necessarily revealed thereby as a dishonest person; the impeachment, in many instances, may uncover only a faulty memory in the discredited witness. The requirement that the identifying circumstances of time, place, those present, and the statement that the witness then made shall be related to him, is founded upon the experience, which frequently presents itself in the courtroom, that a witness, who has stoutly denied having made an alleged statement, may finally blushingly and apologetically admit it, when the questioner throws into association with it identifying circumstances. It is a common observation that associated ideas, as they are related, one after another, not infrequently succeed in upturning a fact which previously had defied all efforts of recollection. And so this rule of evidence is intended to reveal not only the dishonest witness, but is also intended to afford all witnesses ample opportunity to recall a fact before they may be assailed as dishonest. The requirement also tends to reduce to the minimum a confusion of issues by eliminating unnecessary impeachments.

Approaching the statutory requirement thus broadly as one intended to serve a practical, useful end, let us see what the record presents. On direct examination Thompson was asked concerning a conversation he had had with the plaintiff at the Bybee Avenue Garage. The witness stated that the conversation occurred so long ago that his recollection had become somewhat vague, but he recalled that at that time the plaintiff said that his wife was going to get a divorce. No further questions were asked him on direct examination concerning that conversation. The time of this conversation was not fixed, nor were those present mentioned, and he was asked nothing concerning the Pudding river incident. On cross-examination he was asked whether he recalled "talking to Mr. Coles about that trip to the Pudding river." He replied in the negative. This was the only foundation laid for the impeaching question; we believe it was insufficient. It may be that Thompson was untruthful, but before the plaintiff could avail himself of such an argument he should have prepared the necessary premise by submitting to Thompson the alleged statement accompanied by the identifying circumstances. Since this was not done, error was committed when the impeaching witness was permitted to answer. * * *

[Reversed.]

GOLDSTEIN, TRIAL TECHNIQUE
§ 601 (1935).*

§ 601. Former contradictory oral statements

In those instances where the lawyer is in possession of information as to verbal statements made by the witness which are directly contrary to his present testimony, the following procedure is suggested: First—get the witness to repeat upon cross-examination the statements that he has made on direct examination, then put a casual and general question as to whether or not he has ever made a statement to the contrary, at any time or place, then identify the person to whom the contradictory statement is purported to have been made, then direct his attention to the time, the place, and the exact language used or in substance, and again ask him whether or not he had made such contradictory statement. Upon his denial he might again be interrogated on the same question for psychological effect and upon a similar denial the witness should be excused.

After opponent's case is in and he rests, the lawyer should then produce the impeaching witness and prove the contradictory statement by him.

See Federal Rules of Evidence 613; California Evidence Code §§ 769, 770.

BARMORE v. SAFETY CASUALTY CO.
Court of Civil Appeals of Texas, 1962.
363 S.W.2d 355.

McNEILL, Justice. Appellant sought benefits under the Workmen's Compensation law for total and permanent incapacity resulting from an alleged injury of March 9, 1960. Since judgment was against him, the parties here will be referred to as they were in the trial court.

In answer to the first special issue submitted to it, the jury found that plaintiff had not sustained an injury on or about March 9, 1960. Seeking to set aside the judgment of the lower court and for remand, plaintiff urges a single point of error. This point asserts that, since the charge of "recent fabrication" had been leveled by defendant at plaintiff, the trial court erred in excluding the testimony of plaintiff's wife in rebuttal that he told her the morning after his claimed injury that he had been hurt on the job.

The question whether plaintiff had had an accident and sustained any injury on the occasion in question was vigorously contested. To

* Copyright 1935 by Callaghan & Co.

put the question in proper perspective, we set forth a summary of
pertinent events as they developed at the trial. Plaintiff was the first
witness taking the stand and on direct examination, after having told
about being employed by Socony-Mobil Oil Company as a tank-truck
driver, stated that the night of March 9th, while driving along the
highway some electric wires in the motor of the truck shorted and
caught on fire. Upon discovering this he immediately pulled his truck
off the highway and, just before he stopped its roll, he jumped out of the
cab and claimed to have injured himself doing so. After waiting about
an hour beside the road, another employee of the company, Sterling
Hoke, coming from the opposite direction stopped his truck and plaintiff told him about the motor catching on fire. Plaintiff was then asked
whether he told Sterling Hoke at that time that he had gotten hurt, in
answer to which he said he did. He testified that Hoke flagged a car
for him and the driver of that car brought plaintiff to the inspection
station in Logansport, Louisiana. After he reached this inspection
station plaintiff telephoned his boss, Zee P. Brooks, and reported the
break down of the truck. After staying at the inspection station about
four hours he caught a ride with his co-employee Hoke, who was then
returning from a trip and going back to Center, where plaintiff lived.

On the following cross-examination, plaintiff stated, while he did
not remember, he might have mentioned to Brooks that he had gotten
hurt. He was then asked whether he had seen a doctor L.S. Oates after
his claimed injury and whether he told him of his injury. Plaintiff said
he did not remember doing so. He was then asked whether he had any
explanation for this, and he stated, "No, sir, I don't." In reference to
the way the accident happened, he was asked on this examination, "Of
course, you had no skinned places on you? No, sir, * * *" Then he
was asked, "You had no bruises to show anybody. You had no signs on
you anywhere? A. No, sir." When asked whether he fell on his
hands when he jumped from the truck, he said he could not answer
that. Then: "Uh-huh. But you did not skin your hand and you had no
skins any place on you? A. No sir." A short time later in this cross-
examination, defendant's counsel stated "As a matter of fact, don't you
know you didn't have any accident there. You just had your truck
short out and you stopped and first man come along, you didn't tell him
you had any injury did you? A. I told him the truck was on fire." He
was then asked if after he went to the inspection station "You didn't
tell that man about being injured did you? A. I did." Then he was
asked whether he told Brooks on the 'phone that he had gotten hurt, to
which he stated he did not remember. Plaintiff was pressed for not
having told Brooks about any injury, and in answer to this he said he
had no reasonable opportunity to do so and that he knew that there
was going to be some men laid off and he wanted to hold his job. As a
matter of fact he was let out about two weeks after March 9th. Then
defendant's counsel stated:

> "Q. Yeah. And he finally let you out and then you
> decided to file this claim and then you left him—you ever seen
> Dr. Dickerson up till then? A. No, sir.

"Q. Till you decided to make a case and when you decided to make a case, you started hunting those kind of doctors didn't you? One that would swear there was something wrong with you? A. I didn't hunt Dr. Dickerson at all.

"Q. Well, did you hunt the lawyers and the lawyers hunted the doctor for you? Who gave you this doctor's name? A. Well, I had heard of Dr. Dickerson.

"Q. Well, did you see your lawyer here first? A. Yes, sir.

"Q. And from him did you get Dr. Dickerson's name? A. Yes, sir.

"Q. Uh-huh. And so at the time you got Dr. Dickerson you really wasn't trying to get treated, you was trying to file a lawsuit wasn't you? Trying to make out a case? A. We had talked about it."

After the above took place, plaintiff was then questioned as to who the man was who took him into the weighing station at Logansport. While he could not recall the man's name, he described him well and where he was located and the man, C.R. Baker, later testified for the defendant to the effect that he did not remember plaintiff mentioning anything about an injury to him. In this connection plaintiff himself had previously testified that he did not remember telling Baker about his injury. Defendant also produced the weighing station witness who stated that while he recalled the incident when plaintiff stayed at the station March 9, 1960, to his knowledge plaintiff did not mention that he had gotten hurt. He heard his conversation with Mr. Brooks on the 'phone but did not remember that plaintiff mentioned his injury to Mr. Brooks. Defendant also placed Brooks on the stand, who testified that while plaintiff had several opportunities to tell him of the injury, he never mentioned it to him either on the telephone or in person. Defendant produced Dr. L.A. Oates, who also testified that insofar as he could recall plaintiff never mentioned an injury to him; that his record listed no such injury and if he had been told thereof, he would have made a note of it.

After defendant rested, plaintiff placed his wife on the stand in rebuttal. The following transpired, while plaintiff's counsel was examining her:

"Q. Now then, after he had been in Louisiana, the time when his truck got on fire, when he came back, did he tell you anything about getting hurt? A. Yes he did.

"Q. What did he tell you? A. Well, he—

"MR. LANE: Just a minute, I was listening here. We would object to what he told her some several hours or 6 or 8 hours after he came in. Wouldn't be res gestae.

"COURT: Sustain the objection as to what he told her.

"Q. But did he tell you he got hurt? A. He did.

"MR. LANE: Well we—that's the same thing.

"MR. SEALE: Now your Honor, the whole case, every witness he's brought up here, he said 'Did he tell you he got hurt' 'Did he tell you he got hurt.' That's the big issue in the case. Now if he can ask his witnesses whether he told them, I think I ought to be able to.

"MR. LANE: That's different. He's the plaintiff. We're the defendants. We've got a right to ask that but he can't ask a self-serving declaration of that type. We've got them as admissions from him but he can't put this witness on unless it's res gestae.

"MR. SEALE: Silence of a witness can't be admission—

"MR. LANE: Certainly can be.

"MR. FITZPATRICK: If your Honor please Mr. Barmore testified he told these people things. We brought witnesses on to show that he had not. That's admissible under the hearsay rule.

"COURT: I'm going to exclude what he told her.

"MR. SEALE: Note our exception. And so that we won't disturb the proceedings, may it be understood I may complete by bill later in the absence of the jury.

"COURT: Very well."

The following stipulation was made at the close of the evidence:

"MR. SEALE: Can we stipulate her testimony would have been that he told her he got hurt?

"MR. FITZPATRICK: I guess so John.

"MR. SEALE: I assume—it seems obvious that's what she was going to do.

"MR. FITZPATRICK: Yes."

Plaintiff insists that as the issue of injury was hotly contested with the charge of "recent fabrication" having been thrown at him, plaintiff's wife should have been permitted to so testify in rebuttal, and that her testimony may thus have been sufficient to cause the jury to find that he had received an injury on the occasion in question. Defendant counters this upon several grounds: first, it denies that the charge of "recent fabrication" was made. In view of defendant's vigorous cross-examination of plaintiff, we hold that the charge was made. In fact, the charge was expressly made in this cross-examination twice. This is so in the above quoted statement: "As a matter of fact, don't you know you didn't have any accident there" and in the latter quotation, "Till you decided to make a case and when you decided to make a case, you started hunting those kind of doctors didn't you? One that would swear there was something wrong with you."

Undoubtedly the defendant has the right to produce testimony to meet evidence presented by plaintiff that he had sustained an accident, but the cross-examination went much further than this. In addition, although plaintiff did not say that he told Baker, who brought him into the inspection station, that he had gotten hurt, defendant produced him and he testified he had no memory that plaintiff mentioned that he had gotten hurt. Plaintiff stated he did not remember whether he told his boss that he had gotten hurt when he talked to him on the 'phone. Brooks, when placed on stand by defendant, testified plaintiff never mentioned receiving any injury. And though plaintiff had testified that he did not remember telling Dr. Oates he had gotten hurt, defendant produced Dr. Oates, who stated that plaintiff had not told him about his injury. Thus, the defendant, and not plaintiff, undoubtedly initiated the charge of "recent fabrication."

When a witness is charged at the trial with recent fabrication, his former consistent declarations are admissible to corroborate his testimony, provided such declarations were made at a time when he had no motive to misrepresent the fact stated by him. It was held in Aetna Ins. Co. v. Eastman and in Skillern & Sons, Inc. v. Rosen that prior consistent statements of the plaintiff were inadmissible for the reason that in each case plaintiff had the motive (whether influenced thereby or not) to falsify the fact. Or as alternatively stated in the Skillern case, after the time when its ultimate effect and operation could be foreseen. The prior consistent declarations in both Eastman and Rosen took place shortly after the event the plaintiffs claimed took place. Although the fire loss had not occurred in the former case and the consistent declaration was made the day after notice of taking out the second policy was given to the insurance company's agent, the court said: "It is nevertheless true that at the time of the alleged statement it was to his interest to make it."

There is, however, a modification of the proposition above that prior consistent declarations to be admissible must be made before motive to misrepresent exists. This modification comes into play if defendant raises the charge of recent fabrication and produces witnesses who testify plaintiff was silent about his accident at a time when he could have been reasonably expected to speak of it and did not do so. It is then permissible for plaintiff to show by other witnesses that he did speak of the accident and injury at or near those particular times. This we think are the holdings in Houston & T. C. Ry. Co. v. Fox and Texas Employers' Ins. Ass'n. v. Thames, as interpreted in Skillern v. Rosen, supra. In the latter circumstances the consistent declarations appear to be admissible even after plaintiff's claim is filed, provided there was not then, (at the time of making such declaration or claim), a motive to rebut the issue of recent fabrication. At the time, 6 or 8 hours after he had returned home, when plaintiff told his wife he had gotten hurt, there existed no charge of recent fabrication. In fact, defendant produced Dr. Oates to show that several days later, when plaintiff went to the doctor plaintiff did not mention getting hurt. This evidence was tendered upon the ground that it would have been the usual and customary thing for plaintiff to have then told his doctor, if he had gotten hurt. What Judge Hamilton said in the Skillern opinion, of the holding in the Texas Employers' Ins. Ass'n. v. Thames, supra, is presently pertinent:

" * * * The notice of injury and claim in the Thames case was prepared before any motive could have existed to rebut the issue of recent fabrication raised by the failure of the plaintiff to tell the doctors of his general injury." * * *

[The court, however, holds the error "harmless", and the judgment is affirmed.]

————

See Federal Rules of Evidence 801(d)(1); California Evidence Code § 791, §§ 1235–36.

Hypotheticals

(1) X is indicted for child molestation. The victim is A, his 12-year-old stepdaughter. At X's trial the prosecution calls A, who testifies that she has no recollection of any molestation by X, or of having testified before the grand jury. The prosecution seeks to read into the record a transcript of A's testimony before the grand jury, describing X's acts of molestation. X objects. Is X correct?

(2) X is charged with the murder of A by use of a beer bottle in a barroom fight. X claims that he struck in self-defense when A came at him with a knife. There were no witnesses to the killing. B testifies for X that shortly before the final encounter he saw A and X fighting in the bar with their fists, and that A was getting the best of it; that X was retreating as if he were trying to stop fighting; and that he, B, stepped in between A and X, stopped the fighting and then left the bar. On cross-examination, B has no recollection of making any prior statement to C. The prosecution calls C to testify that a week after the killing B told him that X started the earlier fight with A and he (B) heard X say during that fight that he was going to get a gun and shoot A. X objects. What result?

(3) X is prosecuted for robbery of a gas station. Y, a codefendant, is tried first and convicted. At X's trial, the prosecutor calls Y who proves to be a recalcitrant witness and testifies that he and a friend had gone to the gas station together and that he, Y, had committed the robbery. Y gives an "I-don't-remember" answer to the prosecutor's question as to whether X was the friend with him at the gas station. In answer to the prosecutor's questions seeking a description of the friend, Y gives evasive and "I-don't-remember" answers. Y gives an "I-don't-remember" answer to the prosecutor's question as to whether Y had given a statement to B, a police officer, as to who was with him at the robbery. The prosecutor calls B and represents that B will testify that Y told him that X was his accomplice and told him the part each played in committing the robbery. X objects to B's proposed testimony, on the ground that Y's prior statements are not inconsistent with any of Y's testimony. How should the court rule?

(4) X is prosecuted for assault with a deadly weapon upon A. X calls B, who testifies that A was approaching X with a gun in his hand when struck by X with a billiard cue. On cross-examination, the prosecutor asks B, "Didn't you state after X's encounter with A that A had no weapon in his hand when he was struck by X with the billiard cue?" X makes a lack-of-foundation objection, in that no time, place, or persons present are given. Is X correct?

4. BIAS

UNITED STATES v. ABEL

Supreme Court of the United States, 1984.
469 U.S. 45, 105 S.Ct. 465, 83 L.Ed.2d 450.

Justice REHNQUIST delivered the opinion of the Court.

A divided panel of the Court of Appeals for the Ninth Circuit reversed respondent's conviction for bank robbery. The Court of Appeals held that the District Court improperly admitted testimony which impeached one of respondent's witnesses. We hold that the District Court did not err, and we reverse.

Respondent John Abel and two cohorts were indicted for robbing a savings and loan in Bellflower, Ca., in violation of 18 U.S.C. §§ 2113(a) and (d). The cohorts elected to plead guilty, but respondent went to trial. One of the cohorts, Kurt Ehle, agreed to testify against respondent and identify him as a participant in the robbery.

Respondent informed the District Court at a pretrial conference that he would seek to counter Ehle's testimony with that of Robert Mills. Mills was not a participant in the robbery but was friendly with respondent and with Ehle, and had spent time with both in prison. Mills planned to testify that after the robbery Ehle had admitted to Mills that Ehle intended to implicate respondent falsely, in order to receive favorable treatment from the government. The prosecutor in turn disclosed that he intended to discredit Mills' testimony by calling Ehle back to the stand and eliciting from Ehle the fact that respondent, Mills, and Ehle were all members of the "Aryan Brotherhood," a secret prison gang that required its members always to deny the existence of the organization and to commit perjury, theft, and murder on each member's behalf.

Defense counsel objected to Ehle's proffered rebuttal testimony as too prejudicial to respondent. After a lengthy discussion in chambers the District Court decided to permit the prosecutor to cross-examine Mills about the gang, and if Mills denied knowledge of the gang, to introduce Ehle's rebuttal testimony concerning the tenets of the gang and Mills' and respondent's membership in it. The District Court held that the probative value of Ehle's rebuttal testimony outweighed its prejudicial effect, but that respondent might be entitled to a limiting instruction if his counsel would submit one to the court.

At trial Ehle implicated respondent as a participant in the robbery. Mills, called by respondent, testified that Ehle told him in prison that Ehle planned to implicate respondent falsely. When the prosecutor sought to cross-examine Mills concerning membership in the prison gang, the District Court conferred again with counsel outside of the jury's presence, and ordered the prosecutor not to use the term "Aryan Brotherhood" because it was unduly prejudicial. Accordingly, the prosecutor asked Mills if he and respondent were members of a "secret type of prison organization" which had a creed requiring members to deny its existence and lie for each other. When Mills denied knowledge of such an organization the prosecutor recalled Ehle.

Ehle testified that respondent, Mills, and he were indeed members of a secret prison organization whose tenets required its members to deny its existence and "lie, cheat, steal [and] kill" to protect each other. The District Court sustained a defense objection to a question concerning the punishment for violating the organization's rules. Ehle then further described the organization and testified that "in view of the fact of how close Abel and Mills were" it would have been "suicide" for Ehle to have told Mills what Mills attributed to him. Respondent's counsel did not request a limiting instruction and none was given.

The jury convicted respondent. On his appeal a divided panel of the Court of Appeals reversed. The Court of Appeals held that Ehle's rebuttal testimony was admitted not just to show that respondent's and Mills' membership in the same group might cause Mills to color his testimony; the court held that the contested evidence was also admitted to show that because Mills belonged to a perjurious organization, he must be lying on the stand. This suggestion of perjury, based upon a group tenet, was impermissible. The court reasoned:

"It is settled law that the government may not convict an individual merely for belonging to an organization that advocates illegal activity. * * * Rather, the government must show that the individual knows of and personally accepts the tenets of the organization. Neither should the government be allowed to impeach on the grounds of mere membership, since membership, without more, has no probative value. It establishes nothing about the individual's own actions, beliefs, or veracity."

The court concluded that Ehle's testimony implicated respondent as a member of the gang; but since respondent did not take the stand, the testimony could not have been offered to impeach him and it prejudiced him "by mere association."

We hold that the evidence showing Mills' and respondent's membership in the prison gang was sufficiently probative of Mills' possible bias towards respondent to warrant its admission into evidence. Thus it was within the District Court's discretion to admit Ehle's testimony, and the Court of Appeals was wrong in concluding otherwise.

Both parties correctly assume, as did the District Court and the Court of Appeals, that the question is governed by the Federal Rules of Evidence. But the Rules do not by their terms deal with impeachment for "bias," although they do expressly treat impeachment by character evidence and conduct, Rule 608, by evidence of conviction of a crime, Rule 609, and by showing of religious beliefs or opinion, Rule 610. Neither party has suggested what significance we should attribute to this fact. Although we are nominally the promulgators of the Rules, and should in theory need only to consult our collective memories to analyze the situation properly, we are in truth merely a conduit when we deal with an undertaking as substantial as the preparation of the Fed.Rules of Evid. In the case of these Rules, too, it must be remembered that Congress extensively reviewed our submission, and considerably revised it.

Before the present Rules were promulgated, the admissibility of evidence in the federal courts was governed in part by statutes or rules, and in part by case law. This Court had held in Alford v. United States, 282 U.S. 687 (1931) that a trial court must allow some cross-examination of a witness to show bias. This holding was in accord with the overwhelming weight of authority in the state courts as reflected in Wigmore's classic treatise on the law of evidence. Our decision in Davis v. Alaska, 415 U.S. 308 (1974) holds that the Confrontation Clause of the Sixth Amendment requires a defendant to have some opportunity to show bias on the part of a prosecution witness.

With this state of unanimity confronting the drafters of the Fed. Rules of Evid., we think it unlikely that they intended to scuttle entirely the evidentiary availability of cross-examination for bias. One commentator, recognizing the omission of any express treatment of impeachment for bias, prejudice, or corruption, observes that the Rules "clearly contemplate the use of the above-mentioned grounds of impeachment." E. Cleary, McCormick on Evidence, § 40 p. 85 (3d ed. 1984).

We think this conclusion is obviously correct. Rule 401 defines as "relevant evidence" evidence having any tendency to make the existence of any fact that is of consequence to the determination of the action more probable or less probable than it would be without the evidence. Rule 402 provides that all relevant evidence is admissible, except as otherwise provided by the United States Constitution, Act of Congress, or by applicable rule. A successful showing of bias on the part of a witness would have a tendency to make the facts to which he testified less probable in the eyes of the jury than it would be without such testimony.

* * *

Ehle's testimony about the prison gang certainly made the existence of Mills' bias towards respondent more probable. Thus it was relevant to support that inference. Bias is a term used in the "common law of evidence" to describe the relationship between a party and a witness which might lead the witness to slant, unconsciously or otherwise, his testimony in favor or against a party. Bias may be induced by a witness' like, dislike, or fear of a party, or by the witness' self-interest. Proof of bias is almost always relevant because the jury, as finder of fact and weigher of credibility, has historically been entitled to assess all evidence which might bear on the accuracy and truth of a witness' testimony. The "common law of evidence" allowed the showing of bias by extrinsic evidence, while requiring the cross-examiner to "take the answer of the witness" with respect to less favored forms of impeachment.

Mills' and respondent's membership in the Aryan Brotherhood supported the inference that Mills' testimony was slanted or perhaps fabricated in respondent's favor. A witness' and a party's common membership in an organization, even without proof that the witness or party has personally adopted its tenets, is certainly probative of bias. We do not read our holdings in Scales v. United States, 367 U.S. 203 (1961), and Brandenburg v. Ohio, 395 U.S. 444 (1969), to require a different conclusion. Those cases dealt with the constitutional requirements for convicting persons under the Smith Act and state syndicalism laws for belonging to organizations which espoused illegal aims and engaged in illegal conduct. Mills' and respondent's membership in the Aryan Brotherhood was not offered to convict either of a crime, but to impeach Mills' testimony. Mills was subject to no sanction other than that he might be disbelieved. Under these circumstances there is no requirement that the witness must be shown to have subscribed to all the tenets of the organization, either casually or in a manner sufficient to permit him to be convicted under laws such as those involved in *Scales* and *Brandenburg.* For purposes of the law of evidence the jury may be permitted to draw an inference of subscription to the tenets of the organization from membership alone, even though such an inference would not be sufficient to convict beyond a reasonable doubt in a criminal prosecution under the Smith Act.

Respondent argues that even if the evidence of membership in the prison gang were relevant to show bias, the District Court erred in permitting a full description of the gang and its odious tenets. Respondent contends that the District Court abused its discretion under Federal Rules of Evidence 403, because the prejudicial effect of the contested evidence outweighed its probative value. In other words, testimony about the gang inflamed the jury against respondent, and the chance that he would be convicted by his mere association with the organization outweighed any probative value the testimony may have had on Mills' bias.

Respondent specifically contends that the District Court should not have permitted Ehle's precise description of the gang as a lying and murderous group. Respondent suggests that the District Court should have cut off the testimony after the prosecutor had elicited that Mills knew respondent and both may have belonged to an organization together. This argument ignores the fact that the *type* of organization in which a witness and a party share membership may be relevant to show bias. If the organization is a loosely knit group having nothing to do with the subject matter of the litigation, the inference of bias arising from common membership may be small or nonexistent. If the prosecutor had elicited that both respondent and Mills belonged to the Book of the Month Club, the jury probably would not have inferred bias even if the District Court had admitted the testimony. The attributes of the Aryan Brotherhood—a secret prison sect sworn to perjury and self-protection—bore directly not only on the *fact* of bias but also on the *source* and *strength* of Mills' bias. The tenets of this group showed that Mills had a powerful motive to slant his testimony towards respondent, or even commit perjury outright.

A district court is accorded a wide discretion in determining the admissibility of evidence under the Federal Rules. Assessing the probative value of common membership in any particular group, and weighing any factors counseling against admissibility is a matter first for the district court's sound judgment under Rules 401 and 403 and ultimately, if the evidence is admitted, for the trier of fact.

Before admitting Ehle's rebuttal testimony, the District Court gave heed to the extensive arguments of counsel, both in chambers and at the bench. In an attempt to avoid undue prejudice to respondent the court ordered that the name "Aryan Brotherhood" not be used. The court also offered to give a limiting instruction concerning the testimony, and it sustained defense objections to the prosecutor's questions concerning the punishment meted out to unfaithful members. These precautions did not prevent *all* prejudice to respondent from Ehle's testimony, but they did in our opinion ensure that the admission of this highly probative evidence did not *unduly* prejudice respondent. We hold there was no abuse of discretion under Rule 403 in admitting Ehle's testimony as to membership and tenets.

* * *

The judgment of the Court of Appeals is

Reversed.

WALTZ, INTRODUCTION TO CRIMINAL EVIDENCE *

136–37 (3d ed.).

* * *

Proof of bias and the like is always relevant to credibility and can be inquired into thoroughly. This can run the gamut from showing that the accused's solitary alibi witness is his devoted wife to demonstrating that the witness on the stand has been bribed by the side whose cause his testimony favors.

Thus it can be brought out that an accomplice who has turned "State's evidence" was granted immunity from prosecution or promised a reduced sentence as a *quid pro quo* for testimony advantageous to the prosecution. Less dramatic circumstances can be revealed. Perhaps the defendant's witnesses can all be shown to be his relatives or close friends. Or perhaps—and this will be more difficult for the criminal investigator to develop—the defendant's witnesses, such as alibi witnesses, are persons over whom the defendant has some sort of hold. He has threatened them, or gotten others to threaten them, with bodily harm unless they testify in his favor. Threats to the witness's loved ones can be shown, as can threats to destroy the witness's business or reputation. Promises of a monetary or other type of reward for favorable testimony can be brought out.

Sometimes defense counsel, lacking anything more solid, will bear down on the fact that the prosecution's key witness has been housed in a good hotel, wined and dined, and supported financially pending and during the trial.

Example:

> BY THE PROSECUTING ATTORNEY: Let's get this straight, Ms. Adams. You state, as I understand it, that the accused was with you during all of the night in question?

* Copyright 1991 by Jon R. Waltz.

A. That's correct.

Q. It is a fact, is it not, that you have been living with the accused, although not married to him, for the past five years?

A. That's true. But we're going to get married sometime. He's promised me.

Q. That is your hope, is it?

A. Yes.

Q. You won't be able to get married if he goes to jail on this charge, will you?

A. No. Maybe I could wait for him.

Q. And the fact also is that the accused has been and is now your sole source of financial support, isn't that so?

A. Yes.

Q. And he could not continue to support you if he goes to prison, could he?

A. I guess not. They don't earn much in there.

Q. You have everything to gain if Charlie is acquitted and everything to lose if he is convicted, is that not correct?

A. Yes, but I'm not lying.

Q. Can you give the court and jury the name of any person who saw you and Charlie together on the night in question?

A. No.

It is proper to ask expert witnesses, such as a psychiatrist who has supported an insanity defense, whether he is being paid a fee for his testimony, although a carefully coached expert will usually sidestep this sort of cross-examination fairly artfully.

––––––––

See Federal Rules of Evidence 806; California Evidence Code § 1202.

Hypotheticals

(1) A sues X, a police officer, and Y City, X's employer, for damages for false imprisonment growing out of X's arrest of A in a barroom brawl. B, a witness for A, testifies that A was a mere bystander and not a party to the brawl. On cross-examination, X asks B if he had not, on two occasions, slashed tires on marked police cars and been convicted of malicious mischief for so doing. A objects that this is improper cross-examination and improper attempted impeachment of B. What result?

(2) A sues X, a police officer, and Y City, X's employer, for damages for false arrest and imprisonment growing out of X's arrest of A in a barroom brawl. B, a witness for A, testifies that A was a mere bystander and not a party to the brawl. On cross-examination, X seeks to question B to elicit that he had had three felony arrests by Y City police resulting in no convictions, and six arrests by Y City police resulting in misdemeanor convictions. A objects to this cross-examination as being irrelevant and improper impeachment by

specific instances of conduct. X asserts he is offering the evidence to prove bias by B against Y City police and against X as a police officer. Should A's objections be sustained?

Chapter VI

CONFIDENTIALITY AND CONFIDENTIAL COMMUNICATION

PART A. THE ATTORNEY–CLIENT PRIVILEGE

JEREMY BENTHAM, 5 RATIONALE OF JUDICIAL EVIDENCE

pp. 302–304 (1827) (quoted in part in 8 Wigmore, Evidence, § 2291 pp. 549–550, McNaughton rev. 1961).

Lawyer and Client

English judges have taken care to exempt the professional members of the partnership from so unpleasant an obligation as that of rendering service to justice * * * When in consulting with a law advisor, attorney or advocate, a man has confessed his delinquency, or disclosed some fact which, if stated in court, might tend to operate in proof of it, such law adviser is not to be suffered to be examined as to any such point. The law adviser is neither to be compelled, nor so much as suffered, to betray the trust thus reposed in him. Not Suffered? Why not? Oh, because to betray a trust is treachery; and an act of treachery is an immoral act * * * But if such confidence, when reposed, is permitted to be violated, and if this be known, (which, if such be the law, it will be), the consequence will be, that no such confidence will be reposed. Not reposed?—Well: and if it be not, wherein will consist the mischief? The man by the supposition is guilty; if not, by the supposition there is nothing to betray: let the law adviser say every thing he has heard, every thing he can have heard from his client, the client cannot have any thing to fear from it * * * What then, will be the consequence? That a guilty person will not in general be able to derive quite so much assistance from his law adviser, in the way of concerting a false defence, as he may do at present.

* * *

508

LOUISELL, CONFIDENTIALITY, CONFORMITY AND CONFUSION: PRIVILEGES IN FEDERAL COURT TODAY.

31 Tul.L.Rev. 101, 109–115 (1956).*

THE NATURE OF THE PRIVILEGES

Although European legal thought seems to regard at least certain privileges as consistent with the goal of accurate fact-finding because they help avoid perjury, Anglo-American analysis commonly proceeds from the premise that recognition of the privileges constitutes a perpetual threat to the ascertainment of truth in litigation. Assuming for present purposes the validity of this premise (which should be further tested by comparative law inquiry), it is nevertheless submitted that there are things even more important to human liberty than accurate adjudication. One of them is the right to be left by the state unmolested in certain human relations. At least, there is no violence to history, logic or common sense in a legislative judgment to that effect. It is the historic judgment of the common law, as it apparently is of European law and is generally in western society, that whatever handicapping of the adjudicatory process is caused by recognition of the privileges, it is not too great a price to pay for secrecy in certain communicative relations—husband-wife, client-attorney, and penitent-clergyman.

Therefore, to conceive of the privileges merely as exclusionary rules, is to start out on the wrong road and, except by happy accident, to reach the wrong destination. They are, or rather by the chance of litigation may become, exclusionary rules; but this is incidental and secondary. Primarily they are a right to be let alone, a right to unfettered freedom, in certain narrowly prescribed relationships, from the state's coercive or supervisory powers and from the nuisance of its eavesdropping. Even when thrown into the lap of litigation, they are not the property of the adversaries as such; even in litigation, they may be exclusively the property of perfectly neutral persons who wish to preserve despite litigation, just as they preserved prior to litigation, their right to be left alone in their confidences.

> "* * * The privilege is that the confidential matter be not revealed, not that it be not used against the holder of the privilege or any other. * * *"

It may be that Wigmore, despite his monumental contribution to the law of privileges, has conducted to the current confusion by his emphasis on strictly utilitarian bases for the privileges—bases which are sometimes highly conjectural and defy scientific validation. It will be remembered that he predicates four fundamental conditions necessary to establish a privilege as an exception to the general liability of all persons to testify fully on all facts in a judicial proceeding:

* Copyright, 1957 by the Tulane Law Review Association.

(1) The communications must originate in a *confidence* that they will not be disclosed;

(2) This element of *confidentiality must be essential* to the full and satisfactory maintenance of the relation between the parties;

(3) The *relation* must be one which in the opinion of the community ought to be sedulously *fostered*; and

(4) The *injury* that would inure to the relation by the disclosure of the communications must be *greater than the benefit* thereby gained for the correct disposal of litigation.

As is well known, he concludes that all of the requisites exist for the husband-wife, client-attorney, and penitent-priest communications, but that only the third requisite exists in the patient-physician relationship which he considers should not be privileged. The thesis of his main justification of the client-attorney privilege, for example, is that "In order to promote freedom of consultation of legal advisers by clients, the apprehension of compelled disclosure by the legal advisers must be removed; and hence the law must prohibit such disclosure except on the client's consent." A telling attack on this thesis is made by one of the most precise analysts in the history of common law evidence.* The theory that this privilege is necessary to ensure that the attorney gets all essential information, inevitably rests ultimately on sheer speculation. Wigmore comes much closer to the heart of the matter when, in responding to Bentham's onslaught on this privilege, Wigmore states:

> "The consideration of 'treachery,' so inviting an argument for Bentham's sarcasms, is after all not to be dismissed with a sneer. The *sense of treachery* in disclosing such confidences is impalpable and somewhat speculative; but it is there nevertheless. * * * If the counsellors were compellable to disclose, 'no man * * * of a noble or elevated mind would stoop to such an employment.' Certainly the position of the legal adviser would be a difficult and disagreeable one; for it must be repugnant to any honorable man to feel that the confidences which his relation naturally invites are liable at the opponent's behest to be laid open through his own testimony. He cannot but feel the disagreeable inconsistency of being at the same time solicitor and the revealer of the secrets of the cause. This double-minded attitude would create an unhealthy moral state in the practitioner. Its concrete impropriety could not be overbalanced by the recollection of its abstract desirability. If only for the sake of the peace of mind of the counsellor, it is better that the privilege should exist."

Why would compellability to reveal his clients' secrets "create an unhealthy moral state in the practitioner?" Because, it is submitted, he would know that he was perverting the function of counselling.

* * *

* Morgan, Suggested Remedy for Obstructions to Expert Testimony by Rules of Evidence, 10 U.Chi.L.Rev. 285, 288–290 (1943).

If it will help clarify thinking about the nature of the privileges, let us by all means use terminology appropriate to describe protection for significant human freedoms. The privileges are guarantees for the benefit of their holders; they exist from the moment of their inception in the confidential communication; they normally survive all the vicissitudes of life save only waiver by the owner; they survive even his death. The law will protect them at all stages of their existence. If they are in the form of written documents, the law will protect them against theft, trespass, subpoena, or other infringement; if oral, from all types of seizure to which such are susceptible: coercion, physical or psychological, trickery or fraud. If the holder becomes involved in litigation, a new type of attack on his privilege may or may not be made, in the discretion of his adversary. But if the attack is made, if the infringing question is propounded, the law through the judge will continue its protection by now affirmatively enveloping the holder in a cloak of silence. Realization that all this protection is for the holder of the privilege as such, regardless of whether or not in litigation he becomes an adversary or neutral witness, perhaps most keenly focuses up that the exclusionary feature of the privileges, far from defining them, is only an incident of their vitality. It is also noteworthy that, whether or not evidence rules primarily exclusionary in nature, such as the hearsay rule, are attributable to the jury trial, the composition of the tribunal has nothing to do with the privileges. It is equally important to prevent disclosure in a judge or jury trial, an administrative hearing, deposition or other discovery proceeding, or any other procedure whatsoever. Of course the privileges can be waived by the holder; but so can an automobile be sold, given away, abandoned or destroyed; so can realty be deliberately conveyed or let go for taxes.

I write primarily of the genuine privileges whose validity is proved at least to the extent that general acceptance by the common and apparently European law proves it. The courts should, it is true, accept in a democratic society the legislative judgment in providing privileged status for additional communications, although concededly the new privileges may be spurious, unwarranted and abusive of the social interest in accurate adjudication. But it is submitted that in the long run insistence upon precise analysis of the reason for privileged communications, and close inquiry into the true nature and psychological, social, historical and moral importance to human freedom of claims to privilege, will best separate the genuine from the spurious. Conversely, it is the hodge-podge treatment of all the privileges, throwing them into a single pot labelled "exclusionary rules," that conduces toward making all privilege a mere matter of professional jealousy and contention, with the resultant spawning of spurious privileges. It is in the area indicated in this paragraph that further careful inquiry into non-common law sources, particularly in respect of the ultimate historical roots of each privilege, should I believe prove exceptionally fruitful.

* * *

UNITED STATES v. WOODRUFF

United States District Court, Eastern District of Pennsylvania, 1974.
383 F.Supp. 696.

MEMORANDUM AND ORDER

CLIFFORD SCOTT GREEN, District Judge.

In this case, defendant Woodruff, who was free on bail pending trial of this matter, did not appear for trial. The government, which intends to seek an indictment against this defendant on charges of bail jumping, has requested this Court to order the public defender who represented this defendant to respond to the questions put to him by the government relating to whether or not he advised his client as to the time and place of the trial in this matter and further as to whether or not his client responded and acknowledged that he understood the time and place of the trial.

[T]he sole question before us is whether counsel is obligated to furnish this type of information when properly requested by the government. The essence of the question is whether the compelled disclosure which is sought will violate the attorney-client privilege. We grant the government's motion.

There is no doubt that the purpose of this rule is to promote the freedom of consultation of legal advisers by clients. We set out Judge Wyzanski's statement of the privilege.

> "The privilege applies only if (1) the asserted holder of the privilege is or sought to become a client; (2) the person to whom the communication was made (a) is a member of the bar of a court, or his subordinate and (b) in connection with this communication is acting as a lawyer; (3) the communication relates to a fact of which his attorney was informed (a) by his client (b) without the presence of strangers (c) for the purpose of securing primarily either (i) an opinion on law or (ii) legal services or (iii) assistance in some legal proceeding, and not (d) for the purpose of committing a crime or tort; and (4) the privilege has been (a) claimed and (b) not waived by the client. United States v. United Shoe Machinery Corporation, (D.Mass. 1950).

Two Circuit Courts have held that there is no breach of the attorney-client privilege in permitting a defendant's former counsel to testify that he had informed the defendant of the necessity of his appearance at a court proceeding and the time thereof. Both these cases involved prosecutions for violations of the statute under which the government intends to proceed against the present defendant. Both courts noted: that it is the duty of counsel to relay such instructions as an officer of the court; that, in this regard, defense counsel merely served as a conduit for the transmission of a message; and that, the transmission of such an instruction is not in the nature of a confidential communication.

Wigmore has helpfully analyzed the problem presented by this motion.

"The courts have not always used consistent language in answering the question whether the privilege is limited in some way to communications *necessary* or *material* or *relevant* to some purpose of the consultation.

It should be clear, on the one hand, that the actual necessity of making a particular statement, or the materiality to the cause of a particular fact, cannot determine the answer, for the client cannot know what is necessary or material, and the object of the privilege is that he should be unhampered in his quest for advice. On the other hand, when he knowingly departs from that purpose and interjects other matters not relevant to it, he is in that respect not seeking legal advice, and the privilege does not design to protect him. The test is, therefore, not whether the fact or the statement is actually necessary or material or relevant to the subject of the consultation, but whether the statement is made as *a part of the purpose of the client* to obtain advice on that subject. Some such rule would seem to have been in the minds of all the judges in spite of the occasional apparent inconsistency of their utterances." 8 Wigmore, Evidence § 2310.

"A lawyer is sometimes employed without reference to his knowledge and discretion in the law—as where he is charged with finding a profitable investment for trust funds. * * * It is not easy to frame a definite test for distinguishing *legal from nonlegal advice*. Where the general purpose concerns legal rights and obligations, a particular incidental transaction would receive protection, though in itself it were merely commercial in nature—as where the financial condition of a shareholder is discussed in the course of a proceeding to enforce a claim against a corporation. But apart from such cases, the most that can be said by way of generalization is that a matter committed to a professional legal adviser *is prima facie so committed for the sake of the legal advice* which may be more or less desirable for some aspect of the matter, and is therefore within the privilege unless it clearly appears to be lacking in aspects requiring legal advice.

Obviously, much depends upon the circumstances of the individual transactions." 8 Wigmore, Evidence § 2296.

There is no doubt that one could argue that holding these communications to be within the privilege would further the purpose of the privilege in that the disclosure by counsel will inhibit the development of trust on the part of clients and, as a consequence, inhibit full communication. However, the law has always recognized competing considerations, such as the necessity of the testimony of men [*sic*] in the enforcement of the criminal laws. Consequently, the scope and structure of the privilege is narrowed because of competing considerations.

Communications between counsel and defendant as to the trial date do not involve the subject matter of defendant's legal problem. Moreover, this is so clear that we need not be concerned in this regard with the factor of a client's uncertainty as to the relevancy of information which he imparts to his attorney. Such communications are non-legal in nature. Counsel is simply performing a notice function. In fact, we take judicial notice that the courts generally rely upon counsel to perform such a function.

For this reason, and the fact that any communication from the attorney to the client in this regard was based on facts obtained by the attorney from a source other than his client, we hold that the transmission to defendant from the attorney of the fact of the time of trial is not privileged.

Defense counsel requests that we limit this disclosure to the situation when the attorney, himself, communicated this fact to the defendant. However, the rationale of our holding requires that the transmission of this information to defendant by defense counsel's office personnel is also outside the privilege. Also, defense counsel would have us exempt from disclosure other transmissions of this information to defendant by defense counsel which transmissions took place during strategy sessions concerning defendant's defense to this indictment. Both the rationale set out above and the fact that the questions proposed are specific and discrete, lead us to conclude that the transmission of the information in that context is also outside the privilege.

The communications involved here are not of the type that the client might arguably consider relevant to his legal problem. The information is not the type of non-legal information which is related to the client's legal problem and the advice he needs thereon and, for that reason, is not a protected incidental communication.

Finally, we also hold based on the reasoning above, that the communications of the defendant to defense counsel with respect to the trial date are outside the privilege.

Defense counsel has also indicated the peculiarly sensitive problem that a situation such as this presents for defense counsel of the Defender Association. We understand the singular problems that such counsel has in establishing a relationship of trust with their clients. Defense counsel suggests that this factor should be considered in shaping the attorney-client privilege in this context and/or that we should hold that disclosure under these circumstances would violate public policy. We decline to so hold. The impact of such a holding is difficult to foresee and, at least with respect to notice for court appearances, less drastic solutions to the problem should be created.

UPJOHN CO. v. UNITED STATES

Supreme Court of the United States, 1981.
449 U.S. 383, 101 S.Ct. 677, 66 L.Ed.2d 584.

Justice REHNQUIST delivered the opinion of the Court.

We granted certiorari in this case to address important questions concerning the scope of the attorney-client privilege in the corporate context. We decline to lay down a broad rule or series of rules to govern all conceivable future questions in [the privilege] area. We can and do, however, conclude that the attorney-client privilege protects the communications involved in this case from compelled disclosure.

I

In January 1976 independent accountants conducting an audit of one of petitioner's foreign subsidiaries discovered that the subsidiary made payments to or for the benefit of foreign government officials in order to secure government business. The accountants so informed Mr. Gerard Thomas, petitioner's Vice President, Secretary, and General Counsel. He consulted with outside counsel and R.T. Parfet, Jr., petitioner's Chairman of the Board. It was decided that the company would conduct an internal investigation of what were termed "questionable payments." As part of this investigation the attorneys prepared a letter containing a questionnaire which was sent to "All Foreign General and Area Managers" over the Chairman's signature. The letter began by noting recent disclosures that several American companies made "possibly illegal" payments to foreign government officials and emphasized that the management needed full information concerning any such payments made by Upjohn. The letter indicated that the Chairman had asked Thomas, identified as "the company's General Counsel," "to conduct an investigation." The questionnaire sought detailed information concerning such payments. Managers were instructed to treat the investigation as "highly confidential" and not to discuss it with anyone other than Upjohn employees who might be helpful in providing the requested information. Responses were to be sent directly to Thomas. Thomas and outside counsel also interviewed the recipients of the questionnaire and some 33 other Upjohn officers or employees as part of the investigation.

On March 26, 1976, the company voluntarily submitted a preliminary report to the Securities and Exchange Commission on Form 8–K disclosing certain questionable payments. A copy of the report was simultaneously submitted to the Internal Revenue Service, which immediately began an investigation to determine the tax consequences of the payments. Special agents conducting the investigation were given lists by Upjohn of all those interviewed and all who had responded to the questionnaire. On November 23, 1976, the Service issued a summons demanding production of:

> "All files relative to the investigation conducted under the supervision of Gerard Thomas to identify payments to employees of foreign governments and any political contributions made by the Upjohn Company or any of its affiliates since January 1, 1971 and to determine whether any funds of the Upjohn Company had been improperly accounted for on the corporate books during the same period.

> "The records should include but not be limited to written questionnaires sent to managers of the Upjohn Company's foreign affiliates. * * *

The company declined to produce the documents specified in the second paragraph on the grounds that they were protected from disclosure by the attorney-client privilege. [T]he United States filed a petition seeking enforcement of the summons. [The District C]ourt adopted the recommendation of a Magistrate who concluded that the summons should be enforced. Petitioner appealed to the Court of Appeals for the Sixth Circuit which rejected the Magistrate's finding of a waiver of the attorney-client privilege, but agreed that the privilege did not apply "[t]o the extent that the communications were made by officers and agents not responsible for directing Upjohn's actions in response to legal advice * * * for the simple reason that the communications were not the 'client's.'" The court reasoned that accepting petitioner's claim for a broader application of the privilege would encourage upper-echelon management to ignore unpleasant facts and create too broad a "zone of silence." Noting that petitioner's counsel had interviewed officials such as the Chairman and President, the Court of Appeals remanded to the District Court so that a determination of who was within the "control group" could be made.

II

Federal Rule of Evidence 501 provides that "the privilege of a witness * * * shall be governed by the principles of the common law as they may be interpreted by the courts of the United States in light of reason and experience." The attorney-client privilege is the oldest of the privileges for confidential communications known to the common law. * * *

* * *

The Court of Appeals, however, considered the application of the privilege in the corporate context to present a "different problem," since the client was an inanimate entity and "only the senior management, guiding and integrating the several operations, * * * can be said to possess an identity analogous to the corporation as a whole." The first case to articulate the so-called "control group test" adopted by the court below, Philadelphia v. Westinghouse Electric Corp., reflected a similar conceptual approach:

> "Keeping in mind that the question is, Is it the corporation which is seeking the lawyer's advice when the asserted privileged communication is made?, the most satisfactory solution, I think, is that if the employee making the communication, of whatever rank he may be, is in a position to control or even to take a substantial part in a decision about any action which the corporation may take upon the advice of the attorney, * * * then, in effect, *he is (or personifies) the corporation* when he makes his disclosure to the lawyer and the privilege would apply." (Emphasis supplied.)

Such a view, we think, overlooks the fact that the privilege exists to protect not only the giving of professional advice to those who can act on it but also the giving of information to the lawyer to enable him to give sound and informed advice. The first step in the resolution of any legal problem is ascertaining the factual background and sifting through the facts.

In the case of the individual client the provider of information and the person who acts on the lawyer's advice are one and the same. In the corporate context, however, it will frequently be employees beyond the control group as defined by the court below—"officers and agents * * * responsible for directing [the company's] actions in response to legal advice"—who will possess the information needed by the corporation's lawyers. Middle-level—and indeed lower-level—employees can, by actions within the scope of their employment, embroil the corporation in serious legal difficulties, and it is only natural that these employees would have the relevant information needed by corporate counsel if he is adequately to advise the client with respect to such actual or potential difficulties. * * *

The control group test—adopted by the court below—frustrates the very purpose of the privilege by discouraging the communication of relevant information by employees of the client to attorneys seeking to render legal advice to the client corporation. The attorney's advice will also frequently be more significant to noncontrol group members than to those who officially sanction the advice, and the control group test makes it more difficult to convey full and frank legal advice to the employees who will put into effect the client corporation's policy.

The narrow scope given the attorney-client privilege by the court below not only makes it difficult for corporate attorneys to formulate sound advice when their client is faced with a specific legal problem but also threatens to limit the valuable efforts of corporate counsel to ensure their client's compliance with the law. In light of the vast and complicated array of regulatory legislation confronting the modern corporation, corporations, unlike most individuals, "constantly go to lawyers to find out how to obey the law," particularly since compliance with the law in this area is hardly an instinctive matter. The test adopted by the court below is difficult to apply in practice, though no abstractly formulated and unvarying "test" will necessarily enable courts to decide questions such as this with mathematical precision. But if the purpose of the attorney-client privilege is to be served, the attorney and client must be able to predict with some degree of certainty whether particular discussions will be protected. An uncertain privilege, or one which purports to be certain but results in widely varying applications by the courts, is little better than no privilege at all. The very terms of the test adopted by the court below suggest the unpredictability of its application. The test restricts the availability of the privilege to those officers who play a "substantial role" in deciding and directing a corporation's legal response. Disparate decisions in cases applying this test illustrate its unpredictability.

The communications at issue were made by Upjohn employees[1] to counsel for Upjohn acting as such, at the direction of corporate superiors in order to secure legal advice from counsel. As the Magistrate found, "Mr. Thomas consulted with the Chairman of the Board and outside counsel and thereafter conducted a factual investigation to determine the nature and extent of the questionable payments *and to be in a position to give legal advice to the company with respect to the payments.*" (Emphasis supplied.) Information, not available from upper-echelon management, was needed to supply a basis for legal advice concerning compliance with securities and tax laws, foreign laws, currency regulations, duties to shareholders, and potential litigation in each of these areas. The communications concerned matters within the scope of the employees' corporate duties, and the employees them-

1. Seven of the eighty-six employees interviewed by counsel had terminated their employment with Upjohn at the time of the interview. Petitioner argues that the privilege should nonetheless apply to communications by these former employees concerning activities during their period of employment. Neither the District Court nor the Court of Appeals had occasion to address this issue, and we decline to decide it without the benefit of treatment below.

selves were sufficiently aware that they were being questioned in order that the corporation could obtain legal advice. The questionnaire identified Thomas as "the company's General Counsel" and referred in its opening sentence to the possible illegality of payments such as the ones on which information was sought. A statement of policy accompanying the questionnaire clearly indicated the legal implications of the investigation. The policy statement was issued "in order that there be no uncertainty in the future as to the policy with respect to the practices which are the subject of this investigation." It began "Upjohn will comply with all laws and regulations," and stated that commissions or payments "will not be used as a subterfuge for bribes or illegal payments" and that all payments must be "proper and legal." Any future agreements with foreign distributors or agents were to be approved "by a company attorney" and any questions concerning the policy were to be referred "to the company's General Counsel." This statement was issued to Upjohn employees worldwide, so that even those interviewees not receiving a questionnaire were aware of the legal implications of the interviews. Pursuant to explicit instructions from the Chairman of the Board, the communications were considered "highly confidential" when made, and have been kept confidential by the company. Consistent with the underlying purposes of the attorney-client privilege, these communications must be protected against compelled disclosure.

The Court of Appeals declined to extend the attorney-client privilege beyond the limits of the control group test for fear that doing so would entail severe burdens on discovery and create a broad "zone of silence" over corporate affairs. Application of the attorney-client privilege to communications such as those involved here, however, puts the adversary in no worse position than if the communications had never taken place. The privilege only protects disclosure of communications; it does not protect disclosure of the underlying facts by those who communicated with the attorney:

> "[T]he protection of the privilege extends only to *communications* and not to facts. A fact is one thing and a communication concerning that fact is an entirely different thing. The client cannot be compelled to answer the question, 'What did you say or write to the attorney?' but may not refuse to disclose any relevant fact within his knowledge merely because he incorporated a statement of such fact into his communication to his attorney." Philadelphia v. Westinghouse Electric Corp.

Here the Government was free to question the employees who communicated with Thomas and outside counsel. While it would probably be more convenient for the Government to secure the results of petitioner's internal investigation by simply subpoenaing the questionnaires and notes taken by petitioner's attorneys, such considerations of convenience do not overcome the policies served by the attorney-client privilege. As Justice Jackson noted in his concurring opinion in Hickman v. Taylor: "Discovery was hardly intended to enable a learned profession to perform its functions * * * on wits borrowed from the adversary."

* * * [W]e conclude that the narrow "control group test" sanctioned by the Court of Appeals in this case cannot, consistent with "the principles of the common law as * * * interpreted * * * in the light of reason and experience," govern the development of the law in this area. * * *

* * *

Accordingly, the judgment of the Court of Appeals is reversed, and the case remanded for further proceedings.

It is so ordered.

Chief Justice BURGER, concurring in part and concurring in the judgment.

I join in [P]art I of the opinion of the Court and in the judgment. I agree fully with the Court's rejection of the so-called "control group" test, its reasons for doing so, and its ultimate holding that the communications at issue are privileged. As the Court states, however, "if the purpose of the attorney-client privilege is to be served, the attorney and client must be able to predict with some degree of certainty whether particular discussions will be protected." For this very reason, I believe that we should articulate a standard that will govern similar cases and afford guidance to corporations, counsel advising them, and federal courts.

The Court properly relies on a variety of factors in concluding that the communications now before us are privileged. Because of the great importance of the issue, in my view the Court should make clear now that, as a general rule, a communication is privileged at least when, as here, an employee or former employee speaks at the direction of the management with an attorney regarding conduct or proposed conduct within the scope of employment. The attorney must be one authorized by the management to inquire into the subject and must be seeking information to assist counsel in performing any of the following functions: (a) evaluating whether the employee's conduct has bound or would bind the corporation; (b) assessing the legal consequences, if any, of that conduct; or (c) formulating appropriate legal responses to actions that have been or may be taken by others with regard to that conduct. Other communications between employees and corporate counsel may indeed be privileged—as the petitioners and several *amici* have suggested in their proposed formulations—but the need for certainty does not compel us now to prescribe all the details of the privilege in this case. * * * Simply asserting that this failure "may to some slight extent undermine desirable certainty," neither minimizes the consequences of continuing uncertainty and confusion nor harmonizes the inherent dissonance of acknowledging that uncertainty while declining to clarify it within the frame of issues presented.

———

NOTE ON FEDERAL WORK PRODUCT DOCTRINE

During discovery, a claim of attorney-client privilege is likely to be accompanied by a claim that the material is protected under the Federal Rules of Civil Procedure as "work product" of the attorney or party. A limited "work product" protection is also recognized in criminal cases.

The civil "work product" protection has been codified in Fed.R.Civ.P. 26(b) (3). Under that rule, a party may obtain discovery of documents and tangible things prepared "in anticipation of litigation" by an attorney or agent of the opposing party only upon a showing of "substantial need" and a showing that the party seeking discovery cannot, without undue hardship, obtain the substantial equivalent from other sources.[1] Moreover, even if the requisite showing of need is made, the court must protect against disclosure of "the mental impressions, conclusions, opinions, or legal theories of an attorney or other representative of a party concerning the litigation."

There are several differences between the "work product" protection and the attorney-client privilege:

(1) Material that is covered by the attorney-client privilege cannot be discovered even if the opponent demonstrates that she has a special need for the material to prepare her case. Material that is covered only by work product protection can be discovered upon such a showing, at least if it does not reveal the mental impressions of the party's attorney or other representative.

(2) The attorney-client privilege applies only to confidential communications between the attorney (or attorney's representative) and the client (or client's representative). A much larger category of material is covered by the work product protection. For example, statements to an attorney by a witness who is not a client are covered. For that matter, an attorney need not be involved at all for the work product protection to take effect. For example, information gathered by the party or the party's agent (such as a claim adjuster) are covered by the work product doctrine so long as the information is gathered in anticipation of litigation, even if no attorney had been retained at the time of the information-gathering.

(3) The work product protection applies only to information gathered in "anticipation of litigation." The attorney-client privilege covers confidential communications to the lawyer seeking legal advice or services, whether or not litigation is expected.

See Federal Rules of Evidence 501; California Evidence Code §§ 911–913, 915–919.

1. A person is, however, entitled to discover his or her own statement as a matter of course. For example, if the plaintiff gave a statement to the defendant's investigator, the plaintiff is entitled to have a copy of that statement without any showing of need.

CITY AND COUNTY OF SAN FRANCISCO v. SUPERIOR COURT

Supreme Court of California, 1951.
37 Cal.2d 227, 231 P.2d 26, 25 A.L.R.2d 1418.

TRAYNOR, Justice. James Hession brought an action for personal injuries against the City and County of San Francisco and the Western Pacific Railroad Company. He alleged that he suffered brain concussion, nerve root damage, and nervous shock. At the request of Hession's attorneys, Dr. Joseph Catton, a physician specializing in nervous and mental diseases, twice gave Hession a neurological and psychiatric examination. In his deposition Dr. Catton testified that there was no physician-patient relationship between him and Hession; that he did not advise or treat Hession; that the sole purpose of the examination was to aid Hession's attorneys in the preparation of a lawsuit for Hession; and that he was the agent of the attorneys. He refused to answer questions regarding Hession's condition on the grounds that the information sought was privileged under subdivisions 2 and 4 of Section 1881 of the Code of Civil Procedure and that the questions called for "the use of faculties of a physician, neurologist, and psychiatrist and for an opinion based thereon, which opinion is a portion of my property which I do not wish to be deprived of without due compensation and arrangement having been made in relation thereto." Hession's counsel also claimed that the information was privileged.

Petitioner, the City and County of San Francisco, seeks a writ of mandamus to compel respondent court to order Dr. Catton to answer the questions.

The Physician-Patient Privilege

[The court finds that the physician-patient privilege is inapplicable]

The Attorney-Client Privilege

Although Dr. Catton can invoke no privilege of his own and there was no physician-patient privilege in this case, we have concluded that Dr. Catton was an intermediate agent for communication between Hession and his attorneys and that Hession may therefore invoke the attorney-client privilege under section 1881, subdivision (2) of the Code of Civil Procedure. That subdivision reads: "An attorney cannot, without the consent of his client, be examined as to any communication made by the client to him, or his advice given thereon in the course of professional employment; nor can an attorney's secretary, stenographer, or clerk be examined, without the consent of his employer, concerning any fact the knowledge of which has been acquired in such capacity." See also, Bus. & Prof.Code, § 6068(e). This privilege is strictly construed, since it suppresses relevant facts that may be necessary for a just decision. It cannot be invoked unless the client intended the communication to be confidential, and only communications made to an attorney in the course of professional employment are privileged.

The privilege is given on grounds of public policy in the belief that the benefits derived therefrom justify the risk that unjust decisions may sometimes result from the suppression of relevant evidence. Adequate legal representation in the ascertainment and enforcement of rights or the prosecution or defense of litigation compels a full disclosure of the facts by the client to his attorney. "Unless he makes known to the lawyer all the facts, the advice which follows will be useless, if not misleading; the lawsuit will be conducted along improper lines, the trial will be full of surprises, much useless litigation may result. Thirdly, unless the client knows that his lawyer cannot be compelled to reveal what is told him, the client will suppress what he thinks to be unfavorable facts." Morgan, Foreword, Am.Law.Inst.Code of Evidence, pp. 25–26. Given the privilege, a client may make such a disclosure without fear that his attorney may be forced to reveal the information confided to him. "[T]he absence of the privilege would convert the attorney habitually and inevitably into a mere informer for the benefit of the opponent." 8 Wigmore, supra, § 2380a, p. 813.

The privilege embraces not only oral or written statements but actions, signs, or other means of communicating information by a client to his attorney. "(A)lmost any act, done by the client in the sight of the attorney and during the consultation, may conceivably be done by the client as the subject of a communication, and the only question will be whether, in the circumstances of the case, it was intended to be done as such. The client, supposedly, may make a specimen of his handwriting for the attorney's information, or may exhibit an identifying scar, or may show a secret token. If any of these acts are done as part of a communication to the attorney, and if further the communication is intended to be confidential * * *, the privilege comes into play." 8 Wigmore, supra, § 2306, p. 590.

Petitioner contends that under the express terms of section 1881(2) it is only the attorney and the attorney's secretary, stenographer, or clerk who cannot be examined, and that since Dr. Catton was not engaged in any of these capacities he cannot withhold the information requested.

The statute specifically extends the client's privilege to preclude examination of the attorney's secretary, stenographer, or clerk regarding information of communications between attorney and client acquired in such capacities, to rule out the possibility of their coming within the general rule that the privilege does not preclude the examination of a third person who overhears or otherwise has knowledge of communications between a client and his attorney. It does not follow, however, that intermediate agents of communication between attorney and client fall within that general rule. Had Hession himself described his condition to his attorneys there could be no doubt that the communication would be privileged and that neither the attorney nor Hession could be compelled to reveal it, even though a client is not listed in section 1881(2) among those who cannot be examined. It is no less the client's communication to the attorney when it is given by the client to an agent for transmission to the attorney, and it is immaterial whether the agent is the agent of the attorney, the client, or both. "(T)he client's freedom of communication requires a liberty of employing other means than his own personal action. The privilege of confidence would be a vain one unless its exercise could be thus delegated. A communication, then by *any form of agency* employed or set in motion by the client is within the privilege.

"This of course includes communications through an *interpreter,* and also communications *through a messenger* or any other *agent of transmission,* as well as communications *originating with the client's agent* and made to the attorney. It follows, too, that the communications of the *attorney's agent* to the attorney are within the privilege, because the attorney's agent is also the client's sub-agent and is acting as such for the client." 8 Wigmore, supra, § 2317, pp. 616–617; * * * Thus, when communication by a client to his attorney regarding his physical or mental condition requires the assistance of a physician to interpret the client's condition to the attorney, the client may submit to an examination by the physician without fear that the latter will be compelled to reveal the information disclosed. In Arnold v. City of Maryville, and McMillen v. Industrial Comm. of Ohio, on which petitioner relies, it was held, as we hold in the present case, that there was no physician-patient privilege. In neither case, however, was the attorney-client privilege invoked or considered.

It is contended that the purpose of the patient-litigant exception in subdivision 4 of section 1881 would be defeated if the attorney-client privilege in subdivision 2 can be invoked to prevent a physician from divulging the results of his examination of a person for the purpose of aiding his attorneys in the preparation of an action for personal injuries. The two subdivisions relate to two separate and distinct privileges. Since there was no physician-patient relationship, there was no physician-patient privilege to waive; the whole of subdivision 4 including the exception was therefore inapplicable. It does not follow that if there is no physician-patient privilege there can be no attorney-client privilege. The patient-litigant exception applies only to the physician-patient privilege in subdivision 4 and there is no corresponding client-litigant exception in subdivision 2. Had Dr. Catton treated Hession before being asked to serve as an intermediate agent between Hession and his attorneys, the patient-litigant exception would apply and Dr. Catton would then have been like any other witness with knowledge of facts pertinent to an issue to be tried. The exception could not be defeated by asking the physician to reveal his knowledge of the facts to the attorneys, for a litigant cannot silence a witness by having him reveal his knowledge to the litigant's attorney. Similarly, if Dr. Catton should now treat Hession, any information acquired in the course of that treatment would not be privileged, although the results of his previous examinations and his reports to Hession's attorneys would be.

The alternative writ of mandamus is discharged, and the petition for the peremptory writ is denied.

GIBSON, C.J., and SHENK, EDMONDS, CARTER, SCHAUER and SPENCE, JJ., concur.

CLARK v. STATE

Court of Criminal Appeals, Texas, 1953.
159 Tex.Cr.R. 187, 261 S.W.2d 339.
Cert. denied 346 U.S. 855, 905, 74 S.Ct. 69(3), 217(2), 98 L.Ed. 360, 404.

MORRISON, Judge.   The offense is murder; the punishment, death.

The deceased secured a divorce from appellant on March 25, 1952. That night she was killed, as she lay at home in her bed, as the result of a gunshot wound.   From the mattress on her bed, as well as from the bed of her daughter, were recovered bullets which were shown by a firearms expert to have been fired by a .38 special revolver having Colt characteristics.   Appellant was shown to have purchased a Colt .38 Detective Special some ten months prior to the homicide.

* * *

Marjorie Bartz, a telephone operator in the City of San Angelo, testified that at 2:49 in the morning of March 26, 1952, while on duty, she received a call from the Golden Spur Hotel; that at first she thought the person placing the call was a Mr. Cox and so made out the slip; but that she then recognized appellant's voice, scratched out the word "Cox" and wrote "Clark."   She stated that appellant told her he wanted to speak to his lawyer, Jimmy Martin in Dallas, and that she placed the call to him at telephone number Victor 1942 in that city and made a record thereof, which record was admitted in evidence.   Miss Bartz testified that, contrary to company rules, she listened to the entire conversation that ensued, and that it went as follows:

> The appellant: "Hello, Jimmy, I went to the extremes."
>
> The voice in Dallas: "What did you do?"
>
> The appellant: I just went to the extremes."
>
> The voice in Dallas: "You got to tell me what you did before I can help."
>
> The appellant: "Well, I killed her."
>
> The voice in Dallas: "Who did you kill; the driver?"
>
> The appellant: "No, I killed her."
>
> The voice in Dallas: "Did you get rid of the weapon?"
>
> The appellant: "No, I still got the weapon."
>
> The voice in Dallas: "Get rid of the weapon and sit tight and don't talk to anyone, and I will fly down in the morning."

It was stipulated that the Dallas telephone number of appellant's attorney was Victor 1942.

* * *

We now discuss the contentions raised by appellant's able counsel in their carefully prepared brief.

* * *

Proposition (1b) is predicated upon the contention that the court erred in admitting the testimony of the telephone operator, because the conversation related was a privileged communication between appellant and his attorney.

As a predicate to a discussion of this question, we note that the telephone operator heard this conversation through an act of eavesdropping.

In 20 Am.Jur., p. 361, we find the following:

> "Evidence procured by eavesdropping, if otherwise relevant to the issue, is not to be excluded because of the manner in which it was obtained or procured * * *."

This Court has recently, in Schwartz v. State, supra, affirmed by the Supreme Court of the United States on December 15, 1952, authorized the introduction of evidence secured by means of a mechanical interception of a telephone conversation.

We now discuss the question of the privileged nature of the conversation. Wigmore on Evidence (Third Edition), Section 2326, reads as follows:

> "The law provides subjective freedom for the client by assuring him of exemption from its processes of disclosure against himself or the attorney or their agents of communication. This much, but not a whit more, is necessary for the maintenance of the privilege. Since the means of preserving secrecy of communication are entirely in the client's hands, and since the privilege is a derogation from the general testimonial duty and should be strictly construed, it would be improper to extend its prohibition to third persons who obtain knowledge of the communications."

The precise question here presented does not appear to have been passed upon in this or other jurisdictions.

In Hoy v. Morris, a conversation between a client and his attorney was overheard by Aldrich, who was in the adjoining room. The Court therein said:

> "Aldrich was not an attorney, not in any way connected with Mr. Todd; and certainly in no situation where he was either necessary or useful to the parties to enable them to understand each other. On the contrary, he was a mere bystander, and casually overheard conversation not addressed to him nor intended for his ear, but which the client and attorney meant to have respected as private and confidential. Mr. Todd could not lawfully have revealed it. But, in consequence of a want of proper precaution, the communications between him and his client were overheard by a mere stranger. As the latter stood in no relation of confidence to either of the parties, he was clearly not within the rule of exemption from giving testimony; and he might therefore, when summoned as a witness, be compelled to testify as to what he overheard, so far as it was pertinent to the subject matter of inquiry upon the trial * * *."

In Walker v. State, we find the following:

> "Mrs. Bridges was not incompetent or disqualified because she was present and heard the confessions made by defendant, even assuming that the relation of attorney and client subsisted in fact between him and Culberson."

The above holding is in conformity with our statute, Article 713, Code Cr.Proc.

> "All other persons, except those enumerated in articles 708 and 714, whatever may be the relationship between the defendant and witness, are competent to testify, except that an attorney at law shall not disclose a communication made to him by his client during the existence of that relationship, nor disclose any other fact which came to the knowledge of such attorney by reason of such relationship."

Attention is also called to Russell v. State.

Appellant relies upon Gross v. State, wherein we held that a letter written by the accused to his wife remained privileged even though it had fallen into the hands of a third party. We think that such opinion is not authority herein, because therein we said:

> "There is a broad distinction between the introduction of conversations overheard by third parties occurring between husband and wife and the introduction of letters written by one to the other, as shown by practically, if not all, the authorities. It is unnecessary to take up or discuss the question as to conversations going on between husband and wife which are overheard by other parties. That question is not in the case, and it is unnecessary to discuss it. We hold that the introduction of the contents of the letter through the witness Mrs. Maud Coleman was inadmissible. It was a privileged communication under the statute, and therefore interdicted. Article 774, Code of Criminal Procedure."

And, further on the opinion, we find the following:

> "Not minimizing the same relation of client and attorney, but we do say that the relation between husband and wife is far more sacred, and to be the more strongly guarded, than that of relation between attorney and client."

We hold that the trial court properly admitted the evidence of the telephone operator.

* * *

Finding no reversible error, the judgment of the trial court is affirmed.

On Appellant's Motion for Rehearing

WOODLEY, Judge. We are favored with masterful briefs and arguments in support of appellant's motion for rehearing including amicus curiae brief by an eminent and able Texas lawyer addressed to the question of privileged communications between attorney and client.

* * *

As to the testimony of the telephone operator regarding the conversation between appellant and Mr. Martin, the conversation is set forth in full in our original opinion. Our holding as to the admissibility of the testimony of the operator is not to be considered as authority except in comparable fact situations.

For the purpose of this opinion we assume that the Dallas voice was that of Mr. Martin, appellant's attorney. If it was not appellant's attorney the conversation was not privileged.

It is in the interest of public justice that the client be able to make a full disclosure to his attorney of all facts that are material to his defense or that go to substantiate his claim. The purpose of the privilege is to encourage such disclosure of the facts. But the interests of public justice further require that no shield such as the protection afforded to communications between attorney and client shall be interposed to protect a person who takes counsel on how he can safely commit a crime.

We think this latter rule must extend to one who, having committed a crime, seeks or takes counsel as to how he shall escape arrest and punishment, such as advice regarding the destruction or disposition of the murder weapon or of the body following a murder.

One who knowing that an offense has been committed conceals the offender or aids him to evade arrest or trial becomes an accessory. The fact that the aider may be a member of the bar and the attorney for the offender will not prevent his becoming an accessory.

Art. 77, P.C. defining an accessory contains the exception "One who aids an offender in making or preparing his defense at law" is not an accessory.

The conversation as testified to by the telephone operator is not within the exception found in Art. 77, P.C. When the Dallas voice advised appellant to "get rid of the weapon" (which advice the evidence shows was followed) such aid cannot be said to constitute aid "in making or preparing his defense at law". It was aid to the perpetrator of the crime "in order that he may evade arrest or trial."

Is such a conversation privileged as a communication between attorney and client?

If the adviser had been called to testify as to the conversation, would it not have been more appropriate for him to claim his privilege against self-incrimination rather than that the communication was privileged because it was between attorney and client?

Appellant, when he conversed with Mr. Martin, was not under arrest nor was he charged with a crime. He had just inflicted mortal wounds on his former wife and apparently had shot her daughter. Mr. Martin had acted as his attorney in the divorce suit which had been tried that day and had secured a satisfactory property settlement. Appellant called him and told him that he had gone to extremes and had killed "her", not "the driver". Mr. Martin appeared to understand these references and told appellant to get rid of "the weapon".

We are unwilling to subscribe to the theory that such counsel and advice should be privileged because of the attorney-client relationship which existed between the parties in the divorce suit. We think, on the other hand, that the conversation was admissible as not within the realm of legitimate professional counsel and employment.

The rule of public policy which calls for the privileged character of the communication between attorney and client, we think, demands that the rule be confined to the legitimate course of professional employment. It cannot consistent with the high purpose and policy supporting the rule be here applied.

The murder weapon was not found. The evidence indicates that appellant disposed of it as advised in the telephone conversation. Such advice or counsel was not such as merits protection because given by an attorney. It was not in the legitimate course of professional employment in making or preparing a defense at law.

Nothing is found in the record to indicate that appellant sought any advice from Mr. Martin other than that given in the conversation testified to by the telephone operator. We are not therefore dealing with a situation where the accused sought legitimate advice from his attorney in preparing his legal defense.

Some of the citations and quotations have been deleted from our original opinion.

We remain convinced that the appeal was properly disposed of on original submission.

Appellant's motion for rehearing is overruled.

UNITED STATES v. ZOLIN

Supreme Court of the United States, 1989.
491 U.S. 554, 109 S.Ct. 2619, 105 L.Ed.2d 469.

[The Church of Scientology sought to prevent the IRS from obtaining access to tape recordings of meetings between Church representatives and legal counsel. The IRS argued that the tapes fell within the crime-fraud exception to the attorney-client privilege. It urged the District Court to listen to the tapes in camera to determine whether the exception applied. In support of its position, it submitted affidavits from an undercover agent who gave his reasons for believing that the tapes were relevant, and who provided a partial transcript of the contents of the tapes. The transcript had been obtained from a confidential source. For purposes of its decision, the Supreme Court assumed that the partial transcript had been obtained legally.]

Justice BLACKMUN delivered the opinion of the Court [in which all the other Justices joined, except Justice BRENNAN, who took no part in the consideration or decision of the case].

[The Court first decided that neither Rule 104(a) nor the federal common law flatly prohibited in camera review of material claimed to be privileged. It continued:]

We turn to the question whether in camera review at the behest of the party asserting the crime-fraud exception is always permissible, or, in contrast, whether the party seeking in camera review must make some threshold showing that such review is appropriate. In addressing this question, we attend to the detrimental effect, if any, of in camera review on the policies underlying the privilege and on the orderly administration of justice in our courts. We conclude that some such showing must be made.

Our endorsement of the practice of testing proponents' privilege claims through in camera review of the allegedly privileged documents has not been without reservation. This Court noted in United States v. Reynolds, 345 U.S. 1 (1953), a case which presented a delicate question concerning the disclosure of military secrets, that "examination of the evidence, even by the judge alone, in chambers" might in some cases "jeopardize the security which the privilege is meant to protect." Analogizing to claims of Fifth Amendment privilege, it observed more generally: "Too much judicial inquiry into the claim of privilege would force disclosure of the thing the privilege was meant to protect, while a complete abandonment of judicial control would lead to intolerable abuses."

The Court in Reynolds recognized that some compromise must be reached. In Reynolds, it declined to "go so far as to say that the court *may automatically require* a complete disclosure to the judge before the claim of privilege will be accepted *in any case*" (emphasis added). 345 U.S., at 10. We think that much the same result is in order here.

A blanket rule allowing in camera review as a tool for determining the applicability of the crime-fraud exception, as Reynolds suggests, would place the policy of protecting open and legitimate disclosure between attorneys and clients at undue risk. There is also reason to be concerned about the possible due process implications of routine use of in camera proceedings. Finally, we cannot ignore the burdens in camera review places upon the district courts, which may well be required to evaluate large evidentiary records without open adversarial guidance by the parties.

There is no reason to permit opponents of the privilege to engage in groundless fishing expeditions, with the district courts as their unwitting (and perhaps unwilling) agents. Courts of Appeals have suggested that in camera review is available to evaluate claims of crime or fraud only "when justified," In re John Doe Corp., 675 F.2d, at 490, or "[i]n appropriate cases." In re Sealed Case, 219 U.S.App.D.C. 195, 217, 676 F.2d 793, 815 (1982) (opinion of WRIGHT, J.). Indeed, the Solicitor General conceded at oral argument (albeit reluctantly) that a district court would be mistaken if it reviewed documents in camera solely because "the government beg[ged it]" to do so, "with no reason to suspect crime or fraud." We agree.

In fashioning a standard for determining when in camera review is appropriate, we begin with the observation that "in camera inspection ∗ ∗ ∗ is a smaller intrusion upon the confidentiality of the attorney–client relationship than is public disclosure." Fried, Too High a Price for Truth: The Exception to the Attorney–Client Privilege for Contemplated Crimes and Frauds, 64 N.C.L.Rev. 443, 467 (1986). We therefore conclude that a lesser evidentiary showing is needed to trigger in camera review than is required ultimately to overcome the privilege. Ibid. The threshold we set, in other words, need not be a stringent one.

We think that the following standard strikes the correct balance. Before engaging in in camera review to determine the applicability of the crime-fraud exception, "the judge should require a showing of a factual basis adequate to support a good faith belief by a reasonable person," Caldwell v. District Court, 644 P.2d 26, 33 (Colo.1982), that in camera review of the materials may reveal evidence to establish the claim that the crime-fraud exception applies.

Once that showing is made, the decision whether to engage in in camera review rests in the sound discretion of the district court. The court should make that decision in light of the facts and circumstances of the particular case, including, among other things, the volume of materials the district court has been asked to review, the relevant importance to the case of the alleged privileged information, and the likelihood that the evidence produced through in camera review, together with other available evidence then before the court, will establish that the crime-fraud exception does apply. The district court is also free to defer its in camera review if it concludes that additional evidence in support of the crime-fraud exception may be available that is not allegedly privileged, and that production of the additional evidence will not unduly disrupt or delay the proceedings.

C

The question remains as to what kind of evidence a district court may consider in determining whether it has the discretion to undertake an in camera review of an allegedly privileged communication at the behest of the party opposing the privilege. Here, the issue is whether the partial transcripts may be used by the IRS in support of its request for in camera review of the tapes.

The answer to that question, in the first instance, must be found in Rule 104(a), which establishes that materials that have been determined to be privileged may not be considered in making the preliminary determination of the existence of a privilege. Neither the District Court nor the Court of Appeals made factual findings as to the privileged nature of the partial transcripts, so we cannot determine on this record whether Rule 104(a) would bar their consideration.

Assuming for the moment, however, that no rule of privilege bars the IRS' use of the partial transcripts, we fail to see what purpose would be served by excluding the transcripts from the District Court's consideration. There can be little doubt that partial transcripts, or other evidence directly but incompletely reflecting the content of the contested communications, generally will be strong evidence of the subject matter of the communications themselves. Permitting district courts to consider this type of evidence would aid them substantially in rapidly and reliably determining whether in camera review is appropriate.

Respondents suggest only one serious countervailing consideration. In their view, a rule that would allow an opponent of the privilege to rely on such material would encourage litigants to elicit confidential information from disaffected employees or others who have access to the information. We think that deterring the aggressive pursuit of relevant information from third-party sources is not sufficiently central to the policies of the attorney-client privilege to require us to adopt the exclusionary rule urged by respondents. We conclude that the party opposing the privilege may use any nonprivileged evidence in support of its request for in camera review, even if its evidence is not "independent" of the contested communications as the Court of Appeals uses that term.

D

In sum, we conclude that a rigid independent evidence requirement does not comport with "reason and experience," Fed.Rule Evid. 501, and we decline to adopt it as part of the developing federal common law of evidentiary privileges. We hold that in camera review may be used to determine whether allegedly privileged attorney-client communications fall within the crime-fraud exception. We further hold, however, that before a district court may engage in in camera review at the request of the party opposing the privilege, that party must present evidence sufficient to support a reasonable belief that in camera review may yield evidence that establishes the exception's applicability. Finally, we hold that the threshold showing to obtain in camera review may be met by using any relevant evidence, lawfully obtained, that has not been adjudicated to be privileged.

Because the Court of Appeals employed a rigid independent-evidence requirement which categorically excluded the partial transcripts and the tapes themselves from consideration, we vacate its judgment on this issue and remand the case for further proceedings consistent with this opinion. On remand, the Court of Appeals should consider whether the District Court's refusal to listen to the tapes in toto was justified by the manner in which the IRS presented and preserved its request for in camera review. In the event the Court of Appeals hold that the IRS' demand for review was properly preserved, the Court of Appeals should then determine, or remand the case to the District Court to determine in the first instance, whether the IRS has presented a sufficient evidentiary basis for in camera review, and whether, if so, it is appropriate for the District Court, in its discretion, to grant such review.

It is so ordered.

Hypotheticals

(1) D is charged with furnishing a restricted dangerous drug to V, a minor. V testifies and identifies D as the person who gave her pills. After the first day of trial, D disappears. A, D's attorney, testifies that D had expressed to him apprehension about whether V would show up to testify against him, and that upon seeing V enter the courtroom on the second day of trial, D departed. D is convicted by the jury. On appeal, D contends that it was error for the trial

court to permit A to testify about D's communication to him as it violated D's lawyer-client privilege rights. Is D's contention correct?

(2) D is charged with exploding a destruction device, causing great bodily injury to V. V testifies about a bomb in a package exploding as he opened the package. While testifying, V draws on the blackboard a diagram of the bomb. The prosecutor calls B, the court bailiff, who testifies, without objection, that while V was drawing the diagram, B was seated near the far end of the jury box and heard D tell his lawyer: "It was not quite like that." D is convicted and makes a motion for a new trial on the ground that B's testimony was admitted in evidence in violation of D's lawyer-client privilege. How should the court rule?

(3) X is prosecuted for perjury. X previously had been convicted of assault with a deadly weapon and sentenced to prison. X filed a habeas corpus petition, alleging that he had entered a plea of guilty to the assault charge because A, his lawyer, had assured him that the judge, with the prosecutor's concurrence, had agreed to a county jail sentence. In the habeas corpus proceeding, A denied giving X any such assurance. The perjury prosecution is based on X's allegations in the habeas corpus petition. At the perjury trial, the prosecutor calls A to testify to the communications between him and X when he represented X on the assault charge. X claims the lawyer-client privilege to prevent A's testimony. What result?

(4) A was injured from a gas explosion occurring in a building under construction. A sues X, the contractor, and the Y Gas Co., which was installing gas equipment and machinery. Y Gas Co. files a cross-complaint against X. X takes the deposition of Z, an employee of Y Gas Co., who conducted an investigation of the explosion for Y. In answer to questions from X, Z testifies that he investigated the explosion upon the direction of his employer, Y Gas Co.; that he made a written report of the investigation; that one copy was sent to the accident-prevention department of the Y Gas Co. and the original was sent to the lawyer for Y Gas Co.; and that his job was to investigate all explosion-type accidents involving Y Gas Co.'s employees and equipment. Upon being asked what he discovered about the explosion and its cause, he answered that he had no present recollection and that he would have to look at his report. Y Gas Co.'s lawyer objects to Z's use of the report on the ground of the lawyer-client privilege. X seeks a court order to compel Z to answer the deposition questions through use of his report. How should the court rule?

(5) A sues the X Gas Service Station for damages for personal injuries arising out of a freeway accident. A's car was stopped on the freeway, with part of it in a travel lane. A was standing in back of his car when he was struck by an oncoming car driven by Y. A settled with Y. A testifies that before getting on the freeway he got oil and gas from X and that X's employee failed to fasten the hood, which suddenly flew open on the freeway, causing him to stop. X calls P, a police officer, to testify that several weeks after the accident he (P) telephoned Z, A's attorney, and advised him that if P couldn't get a statement from A about how the accident happened, he would be forced to issue a traffic citation against A; that Z replied that A had been too ill to give a statement, but that Z knew the facts about the accident; that Z then said that A's engine had suddenly stopped and this was why A stopped; and that A first looked under the hood and then went to the back of his car to get some pliers when he was struck by Y's car. A objects to P's proposed testimony, on the ground that the lawyer-client privilege protects Z's disclosure to P of A's communication to Z. Is A's objection proper?

(6) A sues the X Hospital, a corporation, for damages for injuries suffered in falling out of a hospital bed while she was a patient. A makes a pretrial

discovery motion for inspection and copying of a report of the incident prepared by B, an employee of the X Hospital, in possession of X's lawyer. X opposes the motion by asserting the lawyer-client privilege. X files a declaration by C, the X Hospital administrator, that states that a few days after the accident to A, he directed B, who is head of nursing services, to prepare a report of the accident on a form provided by the Y Insurance Co., the hospital's liability-insurance carrier. The form read at the top, "Confidential—to be prepared for use of hospital attorneys in case of litigation." The declaration also states that B prepared the report and that it was sent to Y Insurance Co. without any copy being held by the hospital. Other declarations filed by X indicate that B was not a witness to A's fall, and that Y Insurance Co. sent B's report to the X Hospital's lawyer. Should A's motion be granted?

(7) P sues D, a corporation, for damages arising out of a slip-and-fall accident at one of D's stores. At request of D's insurance carrier, D has M, the store manager, make a report of the accident. The report is transmitted to the carrier and then to defense counsel. P makes a discovery motion for inspection and copying of the report. D objects on the ground of the lawyer-client privilege. What result?

PART B.　PATIENT–PHYSICIAN AND PSYCHOTHERAPIST–PATIENT PRIVILEGES

PRINK v. ROCKEFELLER CENTER INC.

Court of Appeals of New York, 1979.
48 N.Y.2d 309, 422 N.Y.S.2d 911, 398 N.E.2d 517.

MEYER, J.

The question presented by this appeal is whether evidentiary privileges prevent disclosure in a wrongful death action concerning the mental condition of the decedent whose unwitnessed death occurred under circumstances consistent with either negligence of the defendant or suicide. * * *

Plaintiff is the administratrix of the estate of her husband, Robert Prink, who was an associate of a law firm whose offices were at 30 Rockefeller Plaza in New York City. On March 1, 1976, he was found dead on the sixth floor setback of the building. The window of the 36th floor office Mr. Prink had occupied was open. There were no eyewitnesses, but the deputy chief medical examiner noted on Mr. Prink's death certificate that Dr. Thomas Doyle, Mr. Prink's psychiatrist, had reported to him that Mr. Prink had been acutely tense and depressed.

Thereafter plaintiff commenced the present action against defendants, the owners and architects respectively of 30 Rockefeller Center, claiming that negligence in the design and installation of the window alcove desk at which decedent worked and in the maintenance of the window required that he kneel on the desk in order to open the window which was jammed, and that he lost his balance and fell when he attempted to do so. During the examination of plaintiff before trial she admitted that her husband had told her sometime before his death that he was seeing Dr. Doyle, a psychiatrist. * * * She also admitted that after her husband's death she had spoken with Dr. Doyle, but

refused to disclose the content of the conversation, claiming privilege.[1]
On defendants' motion for an order compelling plaintiff to testify
concerning the content of her conversations with * * * Dr. Doyle,
Special Term ordered the questions answered. The Appellate Division
affirmed, but certified to us the question "Was the order of the
Supreme Court, as affirmed by this Court, properly made?" We answer
the certified question in the affirmative and, therefore, affirm the
Appellate Division's order.

The initial inquiry is whether privilege ever attached. * * *
Mrs. Prink did not consult Dr. Doyle as a patient. Mr. Prink did,
however, and Dr. Doyle's information concerning him was therefore,
"acquired in attending a patient in a professional capacity" within the
meaning of * * * [the New York Statute] and for purposes of the
present inquiry at least may be presumed to have been "necessary to
enable him to act in that capacity" as required by that provision.

* * * [T]he physician-patient privilege is [not] terminated by
death alone. * * * [The privilege applies] unless waived in some
manner. To be borne in mind in deciding whether there has been a
waiver is that * * * the physician-patient privilege belongs to the
patient. * * * [I]t follows that Dr. Doyle's voluntary disclosures to
the chief medical examiner and to Mrs. Prink after her husband's
death, proper though they undoubtedly were as a matter of professional
ethics cannot constitute a waiver making an otherwise privileged
statement admissible. To hold that a recipient of confidential information by his sole fiat may destroy the privilege would be directly
contrary to the salutary purpose for which the privilege was adopted.[2]

There is, however, another basis upon which we hold * * * the
doctor-patient * * * privilege waived. The instant action is brought
pursuant to EPTL 5–4.1, which authorizes an action for wrongful death
only "for a wrongful act, neglect or default which *caused the decedent's
death* against a person *who would have been liable to the decedent by
reason of such wrongful conduct* if death had not ensued" (emphasis
supplied). Thus to succeed in this action, which is wholly statutory in
nature, plaintiff must establish that it could have been maintained by
decedent had he survived * * * and that defendants' wrongful act
caused his death. In final analysis, therefore, the issue is whether had
Mr. Prink survived and brought the action he could successfully have

1. While plaintiff's testimony concerning what Dr. Doyle told her is clearly hearsay, that would not protect her from the
disclosure required by CPLR 3101 which
requires revelation of inadmissible testimony that may lead to discovery of admissible
evidence.

2. To be distinguished, of course, is the
common-law rule permitting an eavesdropper to testify concerning an otherwise privileged communication * * *. Thus, had
Mrs. Prink overheard Dr. Doyle's conversation with her husband as an eavesdropper
rather than having learned its content
from the doctor she could be required to
disclose its content. The distinction, perhaps filagree in nature, is between the
unauthorized act of the recipient of the
confidence and the act of the eavesdropper
who unauthorizedly intrudes himself upon
the confidential conference. It results, apparently, from the confidant's negligence
in the eavesdropper situation in not assuring absolute secrecy at the time of disclosure, and the contradiction in terms that
would be involved in taxing the confidant
with negligence in relying upon the trust
which is the very root of his relationship to
the person in whom he has confided.

resisted defendants' demand, in their effort to establish that his injuries resulted from attempted suicide rather than defendant's negligence, for disclosure of his conversations with Dr. Doyle * * *.

* * * [Because of] the unfairness of mulcting a defendant in damages without affording him an opportunity to prove his lack of culpability [cf. Chambers v. Mississippi], Mr. Prink as plaintiff could (not) assert * * * the physician-patient privilege (Koump v. Smith) to foreclose inquiry concerning whether his injury was the result of an attempt at suicide.

In *Koump* plaintiff demanded authorization * * * to obtain defendant's hospital record in an effort to show that defendant was intoxicated at the time his car crossed a center divider striking plaintiff's car and injuring plaintiff. We upheld defendant's claim of privilege in that case because defendant had done no more than deny plaintiff's allegation that defendant was intoxicated and plaintiff's only evidence of intoxication was an attorney's affidavit reciting that the police report of the accident contained a hearsay statement that defendant appeared intoxicated. Nevertheless, we recognized: "that by bringing or defending personal injury action in which mental or physical condition is affirmatively put in issue, a party *waives* the privilege" (emphasis in original).

Whatever the ultimate determination of the triers of fact may be in the present case and notwithstanding the presumption against suicide which they will have to consider in reaching their determination, we conclude that it is a matter of common knowledge which we can judicially notice * * * that many apparently accidental deaths are in fact suicides and that a wrongful death complaint predicated upon an alleged accidental fall from a 36th story window is sufficiently equivocal in that respect to put in issue, by plaintiff's affirmative act in bringing the action, decedent's mental condition * * *. To hold otherwise is to ignore the realities of the factual situation and to come perilously close to a taking of defendants' property without due process of law (cf. Chambers v. Mississippi). An additional reason, not however essential to our conclusion, for holding the (privilege) waived by the bringing of the action is that determination of the pecuniary injury sustained by Mr. Prink's death necessarily involved his mental condition.

Bearing in mind the purpose for which the (privilege) in question (was) created, the affirmative stance of plaintiff who claims on behalf of decedent's distributees to have sustained pecuniary injury as a result of defendants' negligence, and the unfairness of permitting plaintiff to succeed by hiding behind the (privilege) asserted, we are satisfied on balance that the better policy is to hold the (privilege) waived. The basis for that conclusion * * * is set forth in Koump v. Smith, supra; see, also, Wigmore, *op. cit.*, § 2380a). * * *

Accordingly the certified question should be answered in the affirmative and the order of the Appellate Division should be affirmed.

* * *

IN RE LIFSCHUTZ

Supreme Court of California, 1970.
2 Cal.3d 415, 85 Cal.Rptr. 829, 467 P.2d 557.

TOBRINER, Justice.

Dr. Joseph E. Lifschutz, a psychiatrist practicing in California, seeks a writ of habeas corpus to secure his release from the custody of the Sheriff of the County of San Mateo. Dr. Lifschutz was imprisoned after he was adjudged in contempt of court for refusing to obey an order of the San Mateo County Superior Court instructing him to answer questions and produce records relating to communications with a former patient.   *   *   *

The instant proceeding arose out of a suit instituted by Joseph F. Housek against John Arabian on June 3, 1968, for damages resulting from an alleged assault. Housek's complaint alleged that the assault caused him "physical injuries, pain, suffering and severe mental and emotional distress." Defendant Arabian deposed the plaintiff and during the course of that deposition Housek stated that he had received psychiatric treatment from Dr. Lifschutz over a six-month period approximately 10 years earlier. Nothing in the record indicates that the plaintiff revealed the nature or contents of any conversation with or treatment by Dr. Lifschutz.

Arabian then subpoenaed for deposition Dr. Lifschutz and all of his medical records relating to the treatment of Housek. (Code Civ.Proc. §§ 2016, 2019, subd. (a).) Although Dr. Lifschutz appeared for the deposition, he refused to produce any of his medical records and refused to answer any questions relating to his treatment of patients; the psychiatrist declined even to disclose whether or not Housek had consulted him or had been his patient. Although notified, neither plaintiff Housek nor his attorney were present at this deposition and neither has appeared in any of the subsequent hearings related to this proceeding. Housek has neither expressly claimed a psychotherapist-patient privilege, statutory or constitutional, nor expressly waived such a privilege.

*   *   *

Dr. Lifschutz presents a novel challenge, attempting to raise far-reaching questions of constitutional law. From the affidavits and correspondence included in the record we note that a large segment of the psychiatric profession concurs in Dr. Lifschutz's strongly held belief that an absolute privilege of confidentiality is essential to the effective practice of psychotherapy.

We recognize the growing importance of the psychiatric profession in our modern, ultracomplex society. The swiftness of change—economic, cultural, and moral—produces accelerated tensions in our society, and the potential for relief of such emotional disturbances offered by psychotherapy undoubtedly establishes it as a profession essential to the preservation of societal health and well-being. Furthermore, a growing consensus throughout the country, reflected in a trend of legislative enactments,[3] acknowledges that an environment of confidentiality of treatment is vitally important to the successful operation of psychotherapy. California has embraced this view through the enactment of a broad, protective psychotherapist-patient privilege.

* * *

Properly viewed, the broadest issue before our court is whether the Legislature, in attempting to accommodate the conceded need of confidentiality in the psychotherapeutic process with general societal needs of access to information for the ascertainment of truth in litigation, has unconstitutionally weighted its resolution in favor of disclosure by providing that a psychotherapist may be compelled to reveal relevant confidences of treatment when the patient tenders his mental or emotional condition in issue in litigation. For the reasons discussed below, we conclude that, under a properly limited interpretation, the litigant-patient exception to the psychotherapist-patient privilege, at issue in this case, does not unconstitutionally infringe the constitutional rights of privacy of either psychotherapists or psychotherapeutic patients. As we point out, however, because of the potential of invasion of patients' constitutional interests, trial courts should properly and carefully control compelled disclosures in this area in the light of accepted principles.

I.   *The order requiring Dr. Lifschutz to answer appropriate questions concerning communications with a patient does not infringe the psychotherapist's constitutional rights.*

The primary contention of Dr. Lifschutz's attack on the judgment of contempt consists of the assertion of a constitutional right of a psychotherapist to absolute confidentiality in his communications with, and treatment of, patients. Although, as we understand it, the alleged right draws its substance primarily from the psychological needs and expectations of patients, Dr. Lifschutz claims that the Constitution grants him an absolute right to refuse to disclose such confidential

3. Until 20 years ago, no statutes dealt specifically with the question of the privilege for psychotherapeutic communications; protection was available only under the terms of existing physician-patient privileges. Such privilege only applied to medical practitioners who fell within the terms of various state statutes; often psychiatrists were covered, but clinical psychologists, though using many of the same techniques of psychotherapy, were not. In the nineteen-fifties and sixties several states, responding to the demands of organized spokesmen of psychology, enacted new privilege statutes, often granting psychologist-patient communications much broader protection than was provided by existing physician-patient privileges. (See Ferster, "Statutory Summary of Physician-Patient Privileged Communication Laws" in Allen, Ferster & Ruben, Readings in Law & Psychiatry (1968) pp. 161–165). In 1960 California enacted such a statute, providing: "[T]he confidential relations and communications between psychologist and client shall be placed upon the same basis as those provided by law between attorney and client * * *." (Bus & Prof.Code, § 2904 (since repealed).)

Although commentators who analyzed the need for a privilege in this specific area unanimously supported the position that greater protection be extended to communications of psychotherapeutic treatment (see, e.g., Louisell, The Psychologist in Today's Legal World: Part II (1957) 41 Minn. L.Rev. 731; Slovenko, Psychiatry and a Second Look at the Medical Privilege (1960) 6 Wayne L.Rev. 175), they pointed out the anomaly of affording more protection to patients of psychologists than to patients of psychiatrists, as most of the existing statutory schemes did. To eliminate this irrational distinction, California enacted the current psychotherapist-patient privilege (Evid.Code, § 1014) in 1965.

communications, regardless of the wishes of a patient in a particular case. In separating the interest of the psychotherapist from that of the patient for the purposes of analyzing this contention, we conclude that the compelled disclosure of relevant information obtained in a confidential communication does not violate any constitutional privacy rights of the psychotherapist.

*   *   *

[The court in Griswold v. Connecticut, on which Dr. Lifschutz relies] * * * explained, however, that the constitutional privacy interests and rights underlying its decision were those of the "patients" of the birth control clinic, rather than of physicians. * * * It is the depth and intimacy of the *patients'* revelations that give rise to the concern over compelled disclosure; the psychotherapist, though undoubtedly deeply involved in the communicative treatment, does not exert a significant privacy interest separate from his patient.[6] We cannot accept petitioner's reliance on the *Griswold* decision as establishing broad constitutional privacy rights of psychotherapists.

In addition to his claim as to a "right of privacy," petitioner urges that the provisions of the Evidence Code requiring a psychotherapist to reveal confidential matters under some circumstances unconstitutionally impair the practice of his profession. This position rests on two distinct legal contentions: first, that the impairment is so severe as to constitute an unconstitutional "taking" of a valuable property right, the doctor's right to practice psychotherapy; and second, that compelled disclosure of any psychotherapeutic communication renders the continued practice of psychotherapy impossible and thus unconstitutionally constricts the realm of available medical treatment. Although psychotherapists should, of course, be entitled to the constitutional protections requisite to the right to practice their profession we doubt that the disclosure involved here goes so far as to constitute the claimed unconstitutional deprivation of that right.

Insofar as petitioner's argument rests on the economic loss that psychotherapists may suffer as a result of the disclosure requirement, his position runs contra to the current trend of constitutional adjudication involving the regulation of economic interests. Legal requirements prescribing mandatory disclosure of confidential business records are of course regular occurrences and although all compelled disclosures may interfere to some extent with an individual's performance of his work, such requirements have been universally upheld so long as the compelled disclosure is reasonable in the light of a related and important governmental purpose. * * *

The second basis of petitioner's contention raises a more serious problem. Petitioner claims that if the state is authorized to compel disclosure of some psychotherapeutic communications, psychotherapy can no longer be practiced successfully.[7] He asserts that the unique

6. Indeed, in many instances a patient may desire to have a psychotherapist testify as to confidential communications. The granting of petitioner's broad contention could foreclose access to psychotherapeutic sessions even when the patient has no desire to preserve his "privacy."

7. Petitioner's contention that the recognition of a privilege is necessary to the

nature of psychotherapeutic treatment, involving a probing of the patient's subconscious thoughts and emotions, requires an environment of total confidentiality and absolute trust. Petitioner claims that unless a psychotherapist can truthfully assure his patient that all revelations will be held in strictest confidence and never disclosed, patients will be inhibited from participating fully in the psychotherapeutic process and proper treatment will be impossible. Petitioner concludes that the patient-litigant exception involved here conflicts with the preservation of an environment of absolute confidentiality and unconstitutionally constricts the field of medical practice.

Petitioner's argument, resting as it does on assertions of medical necessity, exemplifies the type of question to which the judiciary brings little expertise. Although petitioner has submitted affidavits of psychotherapists who concur in his assertion that total confidentiality is essential to the practice of their profession, we cannot blind ourselves to the fact that the practice of psychotherapy has grown, indeed flourished, in an environment of a non-absolute privilege. No state in the country recognizes as broad a privilege as petitioner claims is constitutionally compelled.[8]   *   *   *

                         *   *   *

The statutory provisions challenged here do not attempt to narrow the scope of psychotherapeutic treatment, by proscribing, for example, the discussion of certain subjects (cf. Poe v. Ullman (1961) (Douglas, J., dissenting) (state statute barring advice on the use of contraceptives)). Instead, the provisions are intended to serve the important state interest of facilitating the ascertainment of truth in legal proceedings. Although petitioner argues that, as a matter of social as well as medical policy, the benefits to be derived from a broadening of the existing privilege would outweigh the detriments resulting from a narrowing of evidence available in litigation, the balancing of those alternatives remains with the Legislature.

II. *The presence of a legislatively created absolute clergyman-penitent privilege does not render the absence of such an absolute psychotherapist-patient privilege a denial of equal protection.*

Section 1034 of the Evidence Code provides that: "a clergyman * * * has a privilege to refuse to disclose a penitential communication if he claims the privilege"; the code provides no exceptions to the clergyman-penitent privilege comparable to the numerous exceptions to the psychotherapist-patient privilege. (See Evid.Code, §§ 1016–1026.)

preservation of a given occupation or profession is by no means unique to psychotherapy. In the past, organized occupational groups of journalists, accountants, and social workers, among others, have sought the establishment of a legal privilege and have proclaimed, on principle, that required revelation of information received in confidence would mean the destruction of their calling. (See generally, 8 Wigmore, Evidence (McNaughton rev. 1961) § 2286, pp. 532–537.) In many instances such organized groups have been able to convince state legislatures of the wisdom of their position and as a result statutory privileges have been created; the broad psychotherapist-patient privilege enacted in California is such an example.

8. Indeed, only six states have any laws specifically granting to the psychiatric relationship any special protection, over and above that given to medical communications generally. (See Slawson, Patient-Litigant Exception: Hazard to Psychotherapy (1969), 21 Arch.Gen.Psychiat. 347, 348.)

Petitioner contends that the Legislature, in so distinguishing between clergymen and psychotherapists, has denied psychotherapists the equal protection of the laws in violation of the Fourteenth Amendment.

* * *

Petitioner maintains, however, that, given the purpose of the clergyman-penitent privilege, the distinction between clergymen and psychotherapists cannot stand. Dr. Lifschutz characterizes the "modern" purpose of the clergyman-penitent privilege as fostering a "sanctuary for the disclosure of emotional distress": as so characterized, relevant distinctions between clergymen and psychotherapists do diminish. Petitioner's portrayal of the clergyman-penitent privilege, however, while perhaps identifying one of the supporting threads of the statutory provision, does not reflect a complete analysis of the foundation of the privilege.

Realistically, the statutory privilege must be recognized as basically an explicit accommodation by the secular state to strongly held religious tenets of a large segment of its citizenry. As the Law Revision Commission Comment accompanying the adoption of California's current privilege explains: "At least one underlying reason seems to be that the law will not compel a clergyman to violate—nor punish him for refusing to violate—the tenets of his church which require him to maintain secrecy as to confidential statements made to him in the course of his religious duties." Wigmore, in his treatise, similarly relates the purpose of the privilege in a question and answer format: "Does the penitential relation deserve recognition and countenance? In a state where toleration of religion exists by law, and where a substantial part of the community professes a religion practising a confessional system, this question must be answered in the affirmative." (8 Wigmore, Evidence, supra, § 2396 at p. 878; * * *.

Recognizing that the toleration of religious beliefs and practices forms the basis for this privilege, we cannot say that the Legislature acted irrationally in granting the privilege to clergymen and not to psychotherapists. Although in some circumstances clergymen and psychotherapists perform similar functions and serve similar needs, fundamental and significant differences remain. While many psychotherapists are no doubt strongly committed to the "tenets" of their profession,[9] as indeed Dr. Lifschutz has exhibited by his determined action in the instant proceeding, the source of this commitment can be reasonably distinguished from the distinctive religious conviction out of which the penitential privilege flows.

* * *

9. We note that this court has not been apprised of any present, established "tenet" of the medical profession that would be violated by petitioner's compliance with the order of the trial court. Section 9 of the "Principles of Medical Ethics" adopted by the American Medical Association, which petitioner submitted to the trial court, proclaims: "A physician may not reveal the confidences entrusted to him in the course of medical attendance, or the deficiencies he may observe in the character of patients, *unless he is required to do so by law* or unless it becomes necessary in order to protect the welfare of the individual or of the community." (Italics added.) Although there has been some criticism of this present principle (see, e.g., Sidel, Confidential Information and the Physician, supra, 264 New England J. of Med. 1133), we are not aware of any modification of the "official" principle of confidentiality.

III.   *Under the facts of this case petitioner could assert no statutory authority to refuse to comply with requested disclosures.*

Although, as we have discussed above, Dr. Lifschutz on his own behalf can claim no constitutional privilege to avoid disclosure, he may in some circumstances assert the statutory privilege of his patient.[11] Evidence Code, section 1012 recognizes communications between patient and psychotherapist, diagnosis by the psychotherapist, and advice given during the therapy relationship as privileged communications. Section 1015 provides that: "[t]he psychotherapist who received or made a communication subject to the privilege under this article shall claim the privilege whenever he is present when the communication is sought to be disclosed and is authorized to claim the privilege under subdivision (c) of Section 1014." Section 1014, subdivision (c), indicates that the psychotherapist cannot claim the privilege of the patient "if there is no holder of the privilege in existence or if he is otherwise instructed by a person authorized to permit disclosure." The record in the present case shows no express instructions from plaintiff Housek directing Dr. Lifschutz to decline the privilege against disclosure. Thus, under Evidence Code, section 1015 Dr. Lifschutz could generally assert the privilege of his patient to prevent disclosure of privileged communications.

The psychotherapist, however, cannot assert his patient's privilege if that privilege has been waived or if the communication in question falls within the statutory exceptions to the privilege. Evidence Code, section 912, subdivision (a), provides that: " * * * the right of any person to claim a privilege provided by Section * * * 1014 (psychotherapist-patient privilege) * * * is waived with respect to a communication protected by such privilege if any holder of the privilege, without coercion has disclosed a significant part of the communication or has consented to such disclosure made by anyone. Consent to disclosure is manifested by any statement or other conduct of the holder of the privilege indicating his consent to the disclosure, including his failure to claim the privilege in any proceeding in which he has the legal standing and opportunity to claim the privilege."

Since Housek, the holder of the privilege (see Evid.Code, § 1013), disclosed at a prior deposition that he had consulted Dr. Lifschutz for psychiatric treatment, he has waived whatever privilege he might have had to keep such information confidential.

The questions posed to Dr. Lifschutz, however, have inquired only into whether he treated Mr. Housek and whether he possessed records regarding this patient. Defendant has not yet asked Dr. Lifschutz about the nature of his treatment of the plaintiff, his diagnosis, or the content of any communication. Certainly, in admitting the existence of a psychotherapist-patient relationship, plaintiff has not disclosed "a significant part of the communication" (Evid.Code, § 912) between himself and Dr. Lifschutz so as to waive his right subsequently to claim the privilege as to other elements of the communication.

---

11. The statutory privilege established in section 1014 of the Evidence Code is a privilege of the patient, not of the psychotherapist. (Evid.Code, § 1013.)

Defendant contended in the superior court, however, that *any* communication between the plaintiff and Dr. Lifschutz has lost its privileged status because the plaintiff has filed a personal injury action in which he claims recovery for "mental and emotional distress." Defendant relies on section 1016 of the Evidence Code, the patient-litigant exception to the psychotherapist-patient privilege, which provides that: "[t]here is no privilege under this article as to a communication relevant to an issue concerning the mental or emotional condition of the patient if such issue has been tendered by: (a) the patient * * *." To avoid the necessity for further contempt proceedings or delaying appellate review in the instant case, we have considered whether defendant has accurately identified the proper reach of the patient-litigant exception.

* * * [T]he patient-litigant exception allows only a limited inquiry into the confidences of the psychotherapist-patient relationship, compelling disclosure of only those matters directly relevant to the nature of the specific "emotional or mental" condition which the patient has voluntarily disclosed and tendered in his pleadings or in answer to discovery inquiries. Furthermore, even when confidential information falls within this exception, trial courts, because of the intimate and potentially embarrassing nature of such communications, may utilize the protective measures at their disposal to avoid unwarranted intrusions into the confidences of the relationship.

In interpreting this exception we are necessarily mindful of the justifiable expectations of confidentiality that most individuals seeking psychotherapeutic treatment harbor. * * *

We believe that a patient's interest in keeping such confidential revelations from public purview, in retaining this substantial privacy, has deeper roots than the California statute and draws sustenance from our constitutional heritage. In Griswold v. Connecticut, supra, the United States Supreme Court declared that "Various guarantees [of the Bill of Rights] create zones of privacy," and we believe that the confidentiality of the psychotherapeutic session falls within one such zone. Although *Griswold* itself involved only the marital relationship, the open-ended quality of that decision's rationale evidences its far-reaching dimension.[12] * * *

Even though a patient's interest in the confidentiality of the psychotherapist-patient relationship rests, in part, on constitutional underpinnings, all state "interference" with such confidentiality is not prohibited. In section 1016 we do not deal with a provision which seeks to proscribe the association of a psychotherapist and patient entirely, but instead we encounter a provision carefully tailored to serve the historically important state interest of facilitating the ascertainment of truth in connection with legal proceedings.[14] In the past this state interest has been viewed as substantial enough to compel the disclosure

---

12. The breadth of the principles of privacy and individual freedom recognized in *Griswold* is illustrated by the variety of the cases which have subsequently embraced that decision's conclusions.

14. The justification for compelling disclosure of relevant psychotherapeutic communications when the patient himself has raised an issue of his mental condition has been recognized even by commentators

of a great variety of confidential material.   Moreover, since the exception compels disclosure only in cases in which the patient's own action initiates the exposure, "intrusion" into a patient's privacy remains essentially under the patient's control.   As such, we find no constitutional infirmity in it.

Although no previous cases have arisen under the patient-litigant exception to the psychotherapist-patient privilege, decisions applying an analogous exception to the physician-patient privilege [15] have identified two distinct grounds for the exception.   First, the courts have noted that the patient, in raising the issue of a specific ailment or condition in litigation, in effect dispenses with the confidentiality of that ailment and may no longer justifiably seek protection from the humiliation of its exposure.   Second, the exception represents a judgment that, in all fairness, a patient should not be permitted to establish a claim while simultaneously foreclosing inquiry into relevant matters. As we explained in City and County of San Francisco v. Superior Court, supra, (the *Catton* case), "The whole purpose of the [physician-patient] privilege is to preclude the humiliation of the patient that might follow disclosure of his ailments.   When the patient himself discloses those ailments by bringing an action in which they are in issue, there is no longer any reason for the privilege.   The patient-litigant exception precludes one who has placed in issue his physical condition from invoking the privilege on the ground that disclosure of his condition would cause him humiliation.   He cannot have his cake and eat it too."

Although defendant reads the above quoted language of the *Catton* case as implying that the patient-litigant exception contemplates an automatic, complete waiver of privilege whenever a patient institutes a claim for any physical or mental injury, we find nothing in either the rationale of the exception as explained in the *Catton* case, or in the cases applying the exception, to justify the breadth of this description. In previous physician-patient privilege cases the exception has been generally applied only to compel disclosure of medical treatment and communication concerning the very injury or impairment that was the subject matter of the litigation.[19]   There is certainly nothing to suggest

who are strongly in favor of broadening the current psychotherapist-patient privilege.   Two "model" psychotherapist-patient privilege acts, drafted by such proponents, have included a provision recognizing a patient-litigant exception.

15. The present patient-litigant exception to the physician-patient privilege (Evid.Code, § 996) which parallels the exception to the psychotherapist-patient privilege precisely, superseded section 1881, subdivision 4, of the Code of Civil Procedure, the initial patient-litigant exception enacted in 1917 and the section under which most of the relevant case law arose. Section 1881, subdivision 4, limited the physician-patient privilege by providing: "[W]here any person brings an action to

recover damages for personal injuries, such action shall be deemed to constitute a consent by the person bringing said action that any physician who has prescribed for or treated said person and *whose testimony is material in said action* shall testify." (Italics added.)

19. For example, in Ballard v. Pacific Greyhound Lines, the plaintiff, injured in a bus accident, had consulted a physician concerning the injuries she sustained therein.   When the patient later sued the bus company for damages, the court permitted the defendant to examine the physician concerning the injuries of which plaintiff complained, finding the patient-litigant exception directly applicable.

that in the context of the more liberal psychotherapist-patient privilege this exception should be given a broader reading.[20]

If the provision had as broad an effect as is suggested by petitioner, it might effectively deter many psychotherapeutic patients from instituting any general claim for mental suffering and damage out of fear of opening up all past communications to discovery. This result would clearly be an intolerable and overbroad intrusion into the patient's privacy, not sufficiently limited to the legitimate state interest embodied in the provision and would create opportunities for harassment and blackmail.

In light of these considerations, the "automatic" waiver of privilege contemplated by section 1016 must be construed not as a complete waiver of the privilege but only as a limited waiver concomitant with the purposes of the exception. Under section 1016 disclosure can be compelled only with respect to *those mental conditions* the patient-litigant has "disclose[d] * * * by bringing an action in which *they* are in issue" (City and County of San Francisco v. Superior Court, supra; communications which are not directly relevant to those specific conditions do not fall within the terms of section 1016's exception and therefore remain privileged. Disclosure cannot be compelled with respect to other aspects of the patient-litigant's personality even though they may, in some sense, be "relevant" to the substantive issues of litigation.[21] The patient thus is not obligated to sacrifice all privacy to seek redress for a specific mental or emotional injury; the scope of the inquiry permitted depends upon the nature of the injuries which the patient-litigant himself has brought before the court.

* * *

Because only the patient, and not the party seeking disclosure, knows both the nature of the ailments for which recovery is sought and

---

20. Our reliance on precedents rendered in the context of the physician-patient privilege is not intended to suggest that authorities involving the physician-patient privilege will always be helpful in resolving issues concerning the psychotherapist-patient privilege. In the past the physician-patient privilege has been the subject of rather severe criticism (see, e.g., Chafee, Privileged Communications: Is Justice Served or Obstructed by Closing the Doctor's Mouth on the Witness Stand? (1943) 52 Yale L.J. 607; 8 Wigmore, Evidence, supra, § 2380a, at pp. 828–832), and in response the application of the privilege has been limited in a variety of circumstances (see, e.g., Evid.Code, §§ 998, 999, 1007). The psychotherapist-patient privilege, on the other hand, won legislative recognition in the face of legal antipathy toward privileges generally (see Louisell, The Psychologist in Today's Legal World: Part II, supra, 41 Minn.L.Rev. 731, 731–732); the Legislature acknowledged that the unique nature of psychotherapeutic treatment required and justified a greater degree of confidentiality than was legally afforded other medical treatment (see Legislative Committee Com. to Evid.Code, § 1014). Even commentators who concurred in the criticism of the general physician-patient privilege noted that the psychotherapeutic privilege rested on a much sounder basis and supported its adoption. (See, e.g., Louisell, supra, at pp. 740–746.) The differences that exist between these two medically oriented privileges caution against blind application of the precedents of the physician-patient privilege in future psychotherapist-patient privilege cases.

21. Thus in the instant case, for example, defendant would not be authorized to undertake an examination of psychotherapeutic communications to determine if the plaintiff has ever exhibited aggressive tendencies or had other personal attributes that might be related to the assault. The plaintiff has not disclosed such elements of his mental condition merely by instituting an action for damages resulting from an assault and thus the exception of section 1016 is not applicable.

the general content of the psychotherapeutic communications, the burden rests upon the patient initially to submit some showing that a given confidential communication is not directly related to the issue he has tendered to the court. (Cf. Evid.Code, § 404 (person claiming privilege against incrimination bears burden of showing proffered evidence might tend to incriminate him).) A patient may have to delimit his claimed "mental or emotional distress" or explain, in general terms, the object of the psychotherapy [23] in order to illustrate that it is not reasonably probable that the psychotherapeutic communications sought are directly relevant to the mental condition that he has placed in issue. In determining whether communications sufficiently relate to the mental condition at issue to require disclosure, the court should heed the basic privacy interests involved in the privilege in general, the statutory psychotherapist-patient privilege "[is to] be liberally construed in favor of the patient."

* * *

* * * Moreover, as with any evidence, the court retains discretion to "exclude evidence if its probative value is substantially outweighed by the probability that its admission will * * * (b) create substantial danger of undue prejudice, * * *." (Evid.Code, § 352.) [25] In this area, the careful exercise of this discretion is necessary to provide substantial protection for the patient's legitimate interests; [26] without this element of court supervision intensive examinations of psychotherapists and patients may often ultimately result in substantially more harm than benefit.

In sum, we conclude that no constitutional right enables the psychotherapist to assert an absolute privilege concerning all psychotherapeutic communications. We do not believe the patient-psychotherapist's privilege should be frozen into the rigidity of absolutism. So extreme a conclusion neither harmonizes with the expressed legislative intent nor finds a clear source in constitutional law. Such an application would lock the patient into a vice which would prevent him from waiving the privilege without the psychotherapist's consent. The ques-

23. Although ordinarily a patient cannot be required to disclose privileged information in order to claim the privilege (Evid.Code, § 915, subd. (a)), because the privileged status of psychotherapeutic communications under the patient-litigant exception depends upon the *content* of the communication, a patient may have to reveal some information about a communication to enable the trial judge to pass on his claim of irrelevancy. Upon such revelation, the trial judge should take necessary precautions to protect the confidentiality of these communications; for example, he might routinely permit such disclosure to be made *ex parte* in his chambers. (Compare the procedure suggested in Evid.Code, § 915, subd. (b).) (See also Developments in the Law—Discovery (1964), 74 Harv.L. Rev. 940, 1017–1018.)

25. Necessary information will often be accessible without delving deeply into specific intimate factual circumstances and such searching probes ought to be avoided whenever possible. The psychotherapist's general conclusions about specific emotional symptoms will often suffice to convey the needed information while preserving the patient's dignity and interest in privacy.

26. The draftsmen of two separate versions of "model" legislation in this field each suggested that only a "conditional" patient-litigant exception be adopted; under this suggestion, disclosure would be compelled only upon a finding of the court that it would be in "the best interests of justice." Similar protection can be afforded under the California statutory scheme through a sensitive exercise of the trial court's discretionary authority.

tion whether such a ruling would have the medical merit claimed by petitioner must be addressed to the Legislature; we can find no basis for such a ruling in legal precedent or principle.

Furthermore, the existence of a broad statutory privilege in clergy-men does not deny psychotherapists the equal protection of the laws. Finally, although we recognize the legitimacy and importance of the concern over governmentally sanctioned intrusions into a patient's psychotherapeutic history, the patient-litigant exception, as properly limited, does not necessarily entail an overbroad intrusion into the patient's privacy.

Inasmuch as plaintiff had already disclosed that he had consulted Dr. Lifschutz for psychotherapeutic treatment, petitioner could not properly have refused to answer at least that question concerning the communications; since neither plaintiff nor the psychotherapist has as yet made any claim that the subpoenaed records are not directly relevant to the specific "mental and emotional" injuries for which plaintiff is claiming relief, Dr. Lifschutz had no right to refuse to produce the records. Thus the trial court's order requiring the production of records and the answering of questions was valid; the trial court properly adjudged Dr. Lifschutz in contempt of court for intentionally violating that valid court order.

The order to show cause is discharged and the petition for writ of habeas corpus is denied.

MOSK, Acting C.J., McCOMB, PETERS, BURKE, and SULLIVAN, JJ., and * MOLINARI, J. pro tem., concur.

———

See California Evidence Code §§ 1010–1017, 1024, 1027, 1028.

Hypothetical

A sues Dr. X for damages for injuries in a medical malpractice action. A's injuries were received when Dr. X performed angiogram tests on A. During the deposition of Dr. X, taken by A, Dr. X, claiming the physician-patient privilege, refuses to answer questions as to the names and addresses of other patients upon whom he performed angiogram tests, both before and after those performed on A, including two patients who developed complications from such tests. A moves for an order to compel Dr. X to answer these questions. Should A's motion be granted?

PART C. THE MARITAL PRIVILEGES

TRAMMEL v. UNITED STATES

Supreme Court of the United States, 1980.
445 U.S. 40, 100 S.Ct. 906, 63 L.Ed.2d 186.

Mr. Chief Justice BURGER delivered the opinion of the Court.

We granted certiorari to consider whether an accused may invoke the privilege against adverse spousal testimony so as to exclude the

* Assigned by the Chairman of the Judicial Council.

voluntary testimony of his wife. This calls for a re-examination of Hawkins v. United States.

I

On March 10, 1976, petitioner Otis Trammel was indicted with two others, Edwin Lee Roberts and Joseph Freeman, for importing heroin into the United States from Thailand and the Philippine Islands and for conspiracy to import heroin in violation of 21 U.S.C. §§ 952(a), 962(a), and 963. The indictment also named six unindicted co-conspirators, including petitioner's wife Elizabeth Ann Trammel.

According to the indictment, petitioner and his wife, flew from the Philippines to California in August 1975, carrying with them a quantity of heroin. Freeman and Roberts assisted them in its distribution. Elizabeth Trammel then travelled to Thailand where she purchased another supply of the drug. On November 3, 1975, with four ounces of heroin on her person, she boarded a plane for the United States. During a routine customs search in Hawaii, she was searched, the heroin was discovered, and she was arrested. After discussions with Drug Enforcement Administration agents, she agreed to cooperate with the Government.

Prior to trial on this indictment, petitioner moved to sever his case from that of Roberts and Freeman. He advised the court that the Government intended to call his wife as an adverse witness and asserted his claim to a privilege to prevent her from testifying against him. At a hearing on the motion, Mrs. Trammel was called as a Government witness * * *. She testified that she and petitioner were married in May 1975 and that they remained married.[1] She explained that her cooperation with the Government was based on assurances that she would be given lenient treatment.[2] She then described, in considerable detail, her role and that of her husband in the heroin distribution conspiracy.

After hearing this testimony, the District Court ruled that Mrs. Trammel could testify in support of the Government's case to any act she observed during the marriage and to any communication "made in the presence of a third person"; however, confidential communications between petitioner and his wife were held to be privileged and inadmissible. The motion to sever was denied.

At trial, Elizabeth Trammel testified within the limits of the court's pretrial ruling; her testimony, as the Government concedes, constituted virtually its entire case against petitioner. He was found guilty on both the substantive and conspiracy charges * * *.

In the Court of Appeals petitioner's only claim of error was that the admission of the adverse testimony of his wife, over his objection, contravened this Court's teaching in Hawkins v. United States, and

1. In response to the question whether divorce was contemplated, Mrs. Trammel testified that her husband had said that "I would go my way and he would go his." (App., at 27).

2. The Government represents to the Court that Elizabeth Trammel has not been prosecuted for her role in the conspiracy.

therefore constituted reversible error. The Court of Appeals rejected this contention. It concluded that *Hawkins* did not prohibit "the voluntary testimony of a spouse who appears as an unindicted co-conspirator under grant of immunity from the Government in return for her testimony."

II

The privilege claimed by petitioner has ancient roots. Writing in 1628, Lord Coke observed that "it hath been resolved by the Justices that a wife cannot be produced either against or for her husband." 1 Coke, A Commentarie upon Littleton 6b (1628). This spousal disqualification sprang from two canons of medieval jurisprudence; first, the rule that an accused was not permitted to testify in his own behalf because of his interest in the proceeding; second, the concept that husband and wife were one, and that since the woman had no recognized separate legal existence, the husband was that one. From those two now long-abandoned doctrines, it followed that what was inadmissible from the lips of the defendant-husband was also inadmissible from his wife.

Despite its medieval origins, this rule of spousal disqualification remained intact in most common-law jurisdictions well into the 19th century. It was applied by this Court in Stein v. Bowman, in Graves v. United States, and again in Jin Fuey Moy v. United States, where it was deemed so well established a proposition as to "hardly requir[e] mention." Indeed, it was not until 1933, in Funk v. United States, that this Court abolished the testimonial disqualification in the federal courts, so as to permit the spouse of a defendant to testify in the defendant's behalf. *Funk,* however, left undisturbed the rule that either spouse could prevent the other from giving adverse testimony. The rule thus evolved into one of privilege rather than one of absolute disqualification. * * *

The modern justification for this privilege against adverse spousal testimony is its perceived role in fostering the harmony and sanctity of the marriage relationship. Notwithstanding this benign purpose, the rule was sharply criticized. Professor Wigmore termed it "the merest anachronism in legal theory and an indefensible obstruction to truth in practice." 8 Wigmore, § 2228 at 221. The Committee on the Improvement of the Law of Evidence of the American Bar Association called for its abolition. 63 American Bar Association Reports, at 594–595 (1938). In its place, Wigmore and others suggested a privilege protecting only private marital communications, modeled on the privilege between priest and penitent, attorney and client and physician and patient.[5]

These criticisms influenced the American Law Institute, which, in its 1942 Model Code of Evidence, advocated a privilege for marital

---

5. This Court recognized just such a confidential marital communications privilege in Wolfle v. United States and in Blau v. United States. In neither case, however, did the Court adopt the Wigmore view that the communications privilege be substituted *in place of* the privilege against adverse spousal testimony. The privilege as to confidential marital communications is not at issue in the instant case; accordingly, our holding today does not disturb *Wolfle* and *Blau.*

confidences, but expressly rejected a rule vesting in the defendant the right to exclude all adverse testimony of his spouse. See American Law Institute, Model Code of Evidence, Rule 215 (1942). In 1953 the Uniform Rules of Evidence, drafted by the National Conference of Commissioners on Uniform State Laws, followed a similar course; it limited the privilege to confidential communications and "abolishe[d] the rule, still existing in some states, and largely a sentimental relic, of not requiring one spouse to testify against the other in a criminal action." See Rule 23(2) and comments. Several state legislatures enacted similarly patterned provisions into law.

In Hawkins v. United States, this Court considered the continued vitality of the privilege against adverse spousal testimony in the federal courts. There the District Court had permitted petitioner's wife, over his objection, to testify against him. With one questioning concurring opinion, the Court held the wife's testimony inadmissible; it took note of the critical comments that the common-law rule had engendered but chose not to abandon it. Also rejected was the Government's suggestion that the Court modify the privilege by vesting it in the witness spouse, with freedom to testify or not independent of the defendant's control. The Court viewed this proposed modification as antithetical to the widespread belief, evidenced in the rules then in effect in a majority of the States and in England, "that the law should not force or encourage testimony which might alienate husband and wife, or further inflame existing domestic differences."

Hawkins, then, left the federal privilege for adverse spousal testimony where it found it, continuing "a rule which bars the testimony of one spouse against the other unless both consent." Accord, Wyatt v. United States.[7] However, in so doing, the Court made clear that its decision was not meant to "foreclose whatever changes in the rule may eventually be dictated by 'reason and experience.'"

III

A

The Federal Rules of Evidence acknowledge the authority of the federal courts to continue the evolutionary development of testimonial privileges in federal criminal trials "governed by the principles of the common law as they may be interpreted * * * in the light of reason and experience." Fed.Rule Evid. 501. The general mandate of Rule 501 was substituted by the Congress for a set of privilege rules drafted by the Judicial Conference Advisory Committee on Rules of Evidence and approved by the Judicial Conference of the United States and by this Court. That proposal defined nine specific privileges, including a

---

7. The decision in *Wyatt* recognized an exception to *Hawkins* for cases in which one spouse commits a crime against the other. This exception placed on the ground of necessity, was a longstanding one at common law. See Lord Audley's Case, 8 Wigmore § 2239. It has been expanded since then to include crimes against the spouse's property, see Herman v. United States, and in recent years crimes against children of either spouse, United States v. Allery. Similar exceptions have been found to the confidential marital communications privilege. See 8 Wigmore, § 2338.

husband-wife privilege which would have codified the *Hawkins* rule and eliminated the privilege for confidential marital communications. See Fed.Rule of Evid., Proposed Rule 505. In rejecting the proposed rules and enacting Rule 501, Congress manifested an affirmative intention not to freeze the law of privilege. Its purpose rather was to "provide the courts with the flexibility to develop rules of privilege on a case-by-case basis," 120 Cong.Rec. 40891 (1974) (statement of Rep. Hungate), and to leave the door open to change. * * *

Although Rule 501 confirms the authority of the federal courts to reconsider the continued validity of the *Hawkins* rule, the long history of the privilege suggests that it ought not to be casually cast aside. That the privilege is one affecting marriage, home, and family relationships—already subject to much erosion in our day—also counsels caution. At the same time we cannot escape the reality that the law on occasion adheres to doctrinal concepts long after the reasons which gave them birth have disappeared and after experience suggests the need for change. This was recognized in *Funk* where the Court "decline[d] to enforce * * * ancient rule[s] of the common law under conditions as they now exist." For, as Mr. Justice Black admonished in another setting, "[w]hen precedent and precedent alone is all the argument that can be made to support a court-fashioned rule, it is time for the rule's creator to destroy it." Francis v. Southern Pacific Co. (Black, J., dissenting).

B

Since 1958, when *Hawkins* was decided, support for the privilege against adverse spousal testimony has been eroded further. Thirty-one jurisdictions, including Alaska and Hawaii, then allowed an accused a privilege to prevent adverse spousal testimony. The number has now declined to 24.[9] In 1974, the National Conference on Uniform States Laws revised its Uniform Rules of Evidence, but again rejected the *Hawkins* rule in favor of a limited privilege for confidential communications. See Uniform Rules of Evidence, Rule 504. That proposed rule has been enacted in Arkansas, North Dakota, and Oklahoma—each of which in 1958 permitted an accused to exclude adverse spousal testimony.[10] The trend in state law toward divesting the accused of the privilege to bar adverse spousal testimony has special relevance be-

9. Eight states provide that one spouse is incompetent to testify against the other in a criminal proceeding: * * *.

Sixteen states provide a privilege against adverse spousal testimony and vest the privilege in both spouses or in the defendant-spouse alone; * * *.

Nine states entitle the witness-spouse alone to assert a privilege against adverse spousal testimony: * * *.

The remaining 17 states have abolished the privilege in criminal cases: * * *.

In 1901, Congress enacted a rule of evidence for the District of Columbia that made husband and wife "competent but not compellable to testify for or against each other," except as to confidential communications. This provision, which vests the privilege against adverse spousal testimony in the witness spouse, remains in effect. See 31 Stat. 1358, §§ 1068, 1069, recodified as D.C.Code § 14–306 (1973).

10. In 1965, California took the privilege from the defendant-spouse and vested it in the witness-spouse, accepting a study commission recommendation that the "latter [was] more likely than the former to determine whether or not to claim the privilege on the basis of the probable effect on the marital relationship." See Cal. Evid.Code §§ 970–973 * * *.

cause of the law of marriage and domestic relations are concerns traditionally reserved to the states. Scholarly criticism of the *Hawkins* rule has also continued unabated.

C

Testimonial exclusionary rules and privileges contravene the fundamental principle that "the public * * * has a right to every man's evidence." United States v. Bryan. As such, they must be strictly construed and accepted "only to the very limited extent that permitting a refusal to testify or excluding relevant evidence has a public good transcending the normally predominant principle of utilizing all rational means for ascertaining truth." Elkins v. United States. Accord, United States v. Nixon. Here we must decide whether the privilege against adverse spousal testimony promotes sufficiently important interests to outweigh the need for probative evidence in the administration of criminal justice.

It is essential to remember that the *Hawkins* privilege is not needed to protect information privately disclosed between husband and wife in the confidence of the marital relationship—once described by this Court as "the best solace of human existence." Those confidences are privileged under the independent rule protecting confidential marital communications. The *Hawkins* privilege is invoked, not to exclude private marital communications, but rather to exclude evidence of criminal acts and of communications made in the presence of third persons.

No other testimonial privilege sweeps so broadly. The privileges between priest and penitent, attorney and client, and physician and patient limit protection to private communications. These privileges are rooted in the imperative need for confidence and trust. The priest-penitent privilege recognizes the human need to disclose to a spiritual counselor, in total and absolute confidence, what are believed to be flawed acts or thoughts and to receive priestly consolation and guidance in return. The lawyer-client privilege rests on the need for the advocate and counselor to know all that relates to the client's reasons for seeking representation if the professional mission is to be carried out. Similarly, the physician must know all that a patient can articulate in order to identify and to treat disease; barriers to full disclosure would impair diagnosis and treatment.

The *Hawkins* rule stands in marked contrast to these three privileges. Its protection is not limited to confidential communications; rather it permits an accused to exclude all adverse spousal testimony. As Jeremy Bentham observed more than a century and a half ago, such a privilege goes far beyond making "every man's house his castle," and permits a person to convert his house into "a den of thieves." 5

Support for the common-law rule has also diminished in England. In 1972 a study group there proposed giving the privilege to the witness-spouse, on the ground that "if [the wife] is willing to give evidence * * * the law would be showing excessive concern for the preservation of marital harmony if it were to say she must not do so." Criminal Law Revision Committee, Eleventh Report Evidence (General), at 93.

Rationale of Judicial Evidence 340 (1827). It "secures, to every man, one safe and unquestionable and ever ready accomplice for every imaginable crime." Id., at 338.

The ancient foundations for so sweeping a privilege have long since disappeared. Nowhere in the common-law world—indeed in any modern society—is a woman regarded as chattel or demeaned by denial of a separate legal identity and the dignity associated with recognition as a whole human being. Chip by chip, over the years those archaic notions have been cast aside so that "[n]o longer is the female destined solely for the home and the rearing of the family, and only the male for the marketplace and the world of ideas."

The contemporary justification for affording an accused such a privilege is also unpersuasive. When one spouse is willing to testify against the other in a criminal proceeding—whatever the motivation— their relationship is almost certainly in disrepair; there is probably little in the way of marital harmony for the privilege to preserve. In these circumstances, a rule of evidence that permits an accused to prevent adverse spousal testimony seems far more likely to frustrate justice than to foster family peace.[12] Indeed, there is reason to believe that vesting the privilege in the accused could actually undermine the marital relationship. For example, in a case such as this, the Government is unlikely to offer a wife immunity and lenient treatment if it knows that her husband can prevent her from giving adverse testimony. If the Government is dissuaded from making such an offer, the privilege can have the untoward effect of permitting one spouse to escape justice at the expense of the other. It hardly seems conducive to the preservation of the marital relation to place a wife in jeopardy solely by virtue of her husband's control over her testimony.

IV

Our consideration of the foundations for the privilege and its history satisfy us that "reason and experience" no longer justify so sweeping a rule as that found acceptable by the Court in *Hawkins*. Accordingly, we conclude that the existing rule should be modified so that the witness spouse alone has a privilege to refuse to testify adversely; the witness may be neither compelled to testify nor foreclosed from testifying. This modification—vesting the privilege in the witness spouse—furthers the important public interest in marital harmony without unduly burdening legitimate law enforcement needs.

Here, petitioner's spouse chose to testify against him. That she did so after a grant of immunity and assurances of lenient treatment does not render her testimony involuntary. Accordingly, the District Court

---

12. It is argued that abolishing the privilege will permit the Government to come between husband and wife, pitting one against the other. That, too, misses the mark. Neither *Hawkins,* nor any other privilege, prevents the Government from enlisting one spouse to give information concerning the other or to aid in the other's apprehension. It is only the spouse's testimony in the courtroom that is prohibited.

and the Court of Appeals were correct in rejecting petitioner's claim of privilege, and the judgment of the Court of Appeals is affirmed.

Affirmed.

The concurring opinion of Mr. Justice STEWART is omitted.

———

See California Evidence Code §§ 970–973, 980–982, 984–987.

Hypothetical

X is prosecuted for murder of A, a liquor-store clerk, during a holdup. The murder remained unsolved for several years. X's participation became known after B, X's wife at the time, secured an annulment. The prosecutor calls B to testify that she had her marriage to X annulled about six months ago because she married X before her divorce from Y became final, and that on the night of A's murder, X came home and told her he had pulled a robbery at the liquor store and killed the clerk. X objects to B's proposed testimony on the ground of the privilege for marital communications. What result?

PART D.   MISCELLANEOUS PRIVILEGES

STOKES, CHURCH & STATE IN THE UNITED STATES
555–6 (1964).*

The Seal of the Confessional

The question of the sacredness of confessions made to a priest has frequently been a matter of judicial consideration. In general, what is called the "seal of the confessional" has been recognized by the civil courts, though by the old common law confessions were not considered privileged. New York is said to have been the first of all English-speaking states from the time of the Reformation to protect by its courts and laws the secrecy and sanctity of auricular confession. The decision was made in June, 1813, by De Witt Clinton, then presiding in the mayor's court in New York City. It was judicially determined that auricular confession, being a recognized part of Church discipline, protects a priest from being compelled in a court of law to testify as to statements made to him in the confessional. Many states, following this decision, specifically protect a priest against the necessity of disclosing confessions made to him in confidence and in his professional capacity. In some states a characteristic provision is that found in an Arkansas statute:

No minister of the gospel or priest of any denomination shall be compelled to testify in relation to any confession made to him in his professional character, in the course of discipline by the rules or practice of such denomination.

In other states, such as Michigan and New York, the provision goes even farther and substitutes the word "allowed" for "compelled," which means that even if the clergyman were willing to testify concerning the confession made to him and none of the attorneys objected to the testimony, the court would still have to forbid him to do so.

There are states with no specific legislation, but attempts are extremely rare where any responsible court tries to compel a priest to disclose knowledge gained through the confessional. Perhaps the most interesting case that has come before the courts was in Richmond, Virginia, in 1855, when the vicar general, the Very Reverend John Teeling, D.D., was summoned to testify against a man who had fatally wounded his wife. The vicar general had taken her confession as she was dying and was ordered to reveal it. He replied, "Any statement made in her sacramental confession whether inculpatory or exculpatory of the prisoner, I am not at liberty to reveal." The presiding judge of the circuit court then gave a decision in which he said,

"I regard any infringement upon the tenets of any denomination as a violation of the fundamental law, which guarantees perfect freedom to all classes in the exercise of their religion. To encroach upon the confessional, which is well understood to be a fundamental tenet in the Catholic church, would be to ignore the Bill of Rights, so far as it is applicable to that Church. In view of these circumstances, as well as of other considerations connected with the subject, I feel no hesitation in ruling that a priest enjoys a privilege of exemption from revealing what is communicated to him in the confessional."

The records of the court were lost in the Civil War, and little information is available about either the defendant or the priest. Hence, it cannot be said what the ultimate outcome of the trial was or whether the defendant was convicted and executed. It should be noted that the priest refused to testify even if the testimony would have been "exculpatory of the prisoner." In these circumstances it can hardly be said that the moral issue was clearly in favor of upholding the execution of a man for a crime he never committed. Nevertheless, there is no exception made in the law in respect to exculpatory confessions, and in general the courts hold that the confidence which was recognized by the English common law as existing between lawyer and client should also exist between physician and patient and between priest as confessor and his parishioner or other penitent. This applies not only to the Roman Catholic Church with its regular confessional but to similar confidence between non-Catholic clergymen, when acting as such, and their parishioners.

———

See California Evidence Code §§ 1030–1034.

NOTE, FUNCTIONAL OVERLAP BETWEEN THE LAW- YER AND OTHER PROFESSIONALS: ITS IMPLICATIONS FOR THE PRIVILEGED COMMUNICATIONS DOCTRINES

71 Yale L.J. 1226, 1247–49 (1962).*

THE ACCOUNTANT

At common law there was no testimonial privilege for communications between a man and his accountant, and courts continue to reject this claim of privilege unanimously. By enacting privileged communications statutes protecting confidences between accountants and their clients, fifteen American jurisdictions have changed the common law rule. Almost no case law exists which interprets these statutes. However, they may be narrowly construed if cases arise which invite their construction, since lawyers and jurists responding to our survey, leading commentators, legal organizations, and a number of federal courts disfavor this privilege. Almost certainly all the exceptions and limitations of the attorney-client privilege will be grafted onto these statutes. In a number of cases raising the question in States with such a privilege, federal courts have refused to apply the state accountant privilege statute, but have adhered to the common law rule. These cases involved either tax investigations or criminal prosecutions.

At first glance, it seems unfair that a conversation with a lawyer is protected while the same conversation if held with an accountant would not be. The possibility of an accountant-client privilege, however, is one which has not been enthusiastically embraced by all accountants. The American Institute of Certified Public Accountants officially opposes the privilege. The Executive Director of the National Society of Public Accountants explains this policy:

> Perhaps the reason for not pushing for privileged communication for our members practicing public accounting is the fact that much of their income is from tax work, and they maintain a good relationship with the Internal Revenue Service. There might be some question about cooperation and working relationships should there be privileged communication. Usually a client will tell the agent, "Go see my accountant." The agent would not be so amendable to this suggestion if the accountant were privileged.

Arguably, since the privilege is for the client's protection, not the professional's, the accountant's preference should defer to his client's. But no tension seems to exist between the views of the accountant and the client; a majority of the laymen surveyed who expressed an opinion disfavored the accountant privilege. Lawyers and judges, too, were heavily opposed, and accountants ambivalent at best. Thus, the practical political obstacles either to passage or successful administration of such a law are great.

* Copyright, 1962 by The Yale Law Journal Company, Inc.

Even discounting the public opinion against it, the accountant-client privilege is of dubious inherent desirability. It is likely that federal courts at least believe that an accountant-client privilege would greatly increase the government's difficulties in proving tax evasions. Tacit recognition of this privilege's obstructive effect is also found in the statutes of six of the fifteen States with this privilege. Those six suspend the privilege in criminal and bankruptcy cases. While personal counseling and advice about lawsuits may require guarantees of absolute confidentiality in order to be effectual, this is probably untrue of the tasks performed by the accountant—evidenced by the attitudes of their professional associations to the privilege. Although there is a functional overlap between accountants and attorneys, this is insufficient to justify a privilege for the former. The attorney-client privilege must cover all legitimate attorney tasks in order to shield those functions for which protection is essential. If the area of overlap could be separated, neither profession would be entitled to a privilege. In fact, courts have withdrawn the privilege from attorneys who were acting more like accountants than attorneys. Further, courts have curtailed accountant activity which resembled too closely the lawyer's work by declaring such tasks to have been unauthorized practice of law. In sum, therefore, the privilege should not be extended to the accountant.

See also California Evidence Code §§ 1050 (privilege to protect secrecy of vote), 1060 (privilege to protect trade secret), 1070 (newsman's refusal to disclose news source.)

PARENT–CHILD PRIVILEGE FOUND

The National Law Journal, November 19, 1979.*

A NEW YORK state court, in an apparently unprecedented ruling, has held that a parent cannot be forced to testify against his child, even if the child is an adult.

Judge Gerard Delaney of the Westchester County Court, said that "the confidences extended between a parent and child are just as sacrosanct as between a doctor and a patient or a priest and a penitent. The privilege does not terminate simply because the child reaches majority." People v. Fitzgerald, 76–43.

Judge Jack B. Weinstein of the U.S. District Court in Brooklyn reportedly characterized the Nov. 1 ruling as "very unusual."

"It would never occur to most lawyers" to claim the privilege, he was quoted as saying. "It's not recognized in the federal courts at all or by any of the states."

Judge Delaney dismissed the case against Michael Fitzgerald of Briarcliff Manor, N.Y., who had been charged with criminally negligent homicide in a 1975 automobile accident in which an 18-year-old woman died. Mr. Fitzgerald was then 23 years old.

* Copyright 1979, National Law Journal.

The dismissal came after Mr. Fitzgerald's father refused to testify against him. The elder Fitzgerald had previously testified before a grand jury about conversations he had with his son after the accident but before his son was arrested.

The younger Fitzgerald's attorney, John Keegan of White Plains, N.Y., said he relied on a state appellate division ruling, Matter of A&M. The appellate court supported the confidentiality between parent and child in principle, though it did not rule on the matter or address the issue of the child's majority, he said.

THE NEWS–PERSON'S PRIVILEGE

MATTER OF FARBER

Supreme Court of New Jersey, 1978.
78 N.J. 259, 394 A.2d 330.

MOUNTAIN, J.

In these consolidated appeals The New York Times Company and Myron Farber, a reporter employed by the newspaper, challenge judgments entered against them in two related matters—one a proceeding in aid of a litigant (civil contempt), the other for criminal contempt of court. The proceedings were instituted in an ongoing murder trial now in its seventh month, as a result of the appellants' failure to comply with two *subpoena duces tecum,* directing them to produce certain documents and materials compiled by one or both of these appellants in the course of Farber's investigative reporting of certain allegedly criminal activities. Farber's investigations and reporting are said to have contributed largely to the indictment and prosecution of Dr. Mario E. Jascalevich for murder. Appellants moved unsuccessfully before Judge William J. Arnold, the trial judge in State v. Jascalevich, to quash the two subpoenas; an order was entered directing that the subpoenaed material be produced for *in camera* inspection by the court. The appellant's applications for a stay of Judge Arnold's order were denied successively by the Appellate Division of the Superior Court, by this Court, and by two separate Justices of the Supreme Court of the United States.

Impelled by appellants' persistent refusal to produce the subpoenaed materials for *in camera* inspection, Judge Arnold issued an order returnable before Judge Theodore W. Trautwein, directing appellants to show cause why they should not be deemed in contempt of court. During the subsequent hearing, Judge Trautwein ordered counsel for Jascalevich to apply to Judge Arnold, pursuant to *R* 1:10–5, for an additional order to show cause, this to be in aid of litigants' rights. The order was issued, served and the hearing on the matter consolidated with the hearing on the criminal contempt charge.

Judge Trautwein determined that both appellants had wilfully contemned Judge Arnold's order directing that materials be produced for *in camera* inspection and found them guilty as charged. A fine of $100,000 was imposed on The New York Times and Farber was ordered to serve six months in the Bergen County jail and to pay a fine of

$1,000. Additionally, in order to compel production of the materials subpoenaed on behalf of Jascalevich, a fine of $5,000 per day for every day that elapsed until compliance with Judge Arnold's order was imposed upon The Times; Farber was fined $1,000 and sentenced to confinement in the county jail until he complied with the order.

* * *

I

The First Amendment

Appellants claim a privilege to refrain from revealing information sought by the *subpoenas duces tecum* essentially for the reason that were they to divulge this material, confidential sources of such information would be made public. Were this to occur, they argue, newsgathering and the dissemination of news would be seriously impaired, because much information would never be forthcoming to the news media unless the persons who were the sources of such information could be entirely certain that their identities would remain secret. The final result, appellants claim, would be a substantial lessening in the supply of available news on a variety of important and sensitive issues, all to the detriment of the public interest. They contend further that this privilege to remain silent with respect to confidential information and the sources of such information emanates from the "free speech" and "free press" clauses of the First Amendment.[1]

In our view the Supreme Court of the United States has clearly rejected this claim and has squarely held that no such First Amendment right exists. In Branzburg v. Hayes, 408 U.S. 665 (1972), three news media representatives argued that, for the same reason here advanced, they should not be required to appear and testify before grand juries, and that this privilege to refrain from divulging information, asserted to have been received from confidential sources, derived from the First Amendment. Justice White, noting that there was no common law privilege, stated the issue and gave the Court's answer in the first paragraph of his opinion:

> The issue in these cases is whether requiring newsmen to appear and testify before state or federal grand juries abridges the freedom of speech and press guaranteed by the First Amendment. We hold that it does not. [Branzburg v. Hayes, supra]

In that case one reporter, from Frankfort, Kentucky, had witnessed individuals making hashish from marijuana and had made a rather comprehensive survey of the drug scene in Frankfort. He had written an article in the Louisville Courier-Journal describing this illegal activity. Another, a newsman-photographer employed by a New Bedford, Massachusetts television station, had met with members of the

---

1. The First Amendment of the United States Constitution reads as follows:

Congress shall make no law respecting an establishment of religion, or prohibiting the free exercise thereof, or abridging the freedom of speech, or of the press; or the right of the people peaceably to assemble, and to petition the Government for a redress of grievances.

Black Panther movement at the time that certain riots and disorders occurred in New Bedford. The material he assembled formed the basis for a television program that followed. The third investigative reporter had met with members of the Black Panthers in northern California and had written an article about the nature and activities of the movement. In each instance there had been a commitment on the part of the media representative that he would not divulge the source of his article or story.

By a vote of 5 to 4 the Supreme Court held that newspaper reporters or other media representatives have no privilege deriving from the First Amendment to refrain from divulging confidential information and the sources of such information when properly subpoenaed to appear before a grand jury. The three media representatives were directed to appear and testify. The holding was later underscored and applied directly to this case by Justice White in a brief opinion filed in this cause upon the occasion of his denial of a stay sought by these appellants. He said:

> There is no present authority in this Court either that newsmen are constitutionally privileged to withhold duly subpoenaed documents material to the prosecution or defense of a criminal case or that a defendant seeking the subpoena must show extraordinary circumstances before enforcement against newsmen will be had. [New York Times and Farber v. Jascalevich].

We pause to point out that despite the holding in *Branzburg,* those who gather and disseminate news are by no means without First Amendment protections. Some of these are referred to by Justice White in the *Branzburg* opinion. They include, among others, the right to publish what the press chooses to publish, to refrain from publishing what it chooses to withhold, to seek out news in any legal manner and to refrain from revealing its sources except upon legitimate demand. Demand is not legitimate when the desired information is patently irrelevant to the needs of the inquirer or his needs are not manifestly compelling. Nor will the First Amendment sanction harassment of the press. These do not exhaust the list of such First Amendment protective rights.

The point to be made, however, is that among the many First Amendment protections that may be invoked by the press, there is not to be found the privilege of refusing to reveal relevant confidential information and its sources to a grand jury which is engaged in the fundamental governmental function of "[f]air and effective law enforcement aimed at providing security for the person and property of the individual * * *" The reason this is so is that a majority of the members of the United States Supreme Court have so determined.

Faced with this conclusion, appellants appear to argue that Justice Powell's concurring opinion in *Branzburg* somehow fails to support this result. The argument is without merit. We do not read Justice Powell's opinion as in any way disagreeing with what is said by Justice White. But even if it did, it would not matter for present purposes.

The important and conclusive point is that five members of the Court have all reached the conclusion that the First Amendment affords no privilege to a newsman to refuse to appear before a grand jury and testify as to relevant information he possesses, even though in so doing he may divulge confidential sources. The particular path that any Justice may have followed becomes unimportant when once it is seen that a majority have reached the same destination.

Thus we do no weighing or balancing of societal interests in reaching our determination that the First Amendment does not afford appellants the privilege they claim. The weighing and balancing has been done by a higher court. * * *

II

The Shield Law [2]

In Branzburg v. Hayes, supra, the Court dealt with a newsman's claim of privilege based solely upon the First Amendment. As we have seen, this claim of privilege failed. In *Branzburg* no shield law was involved. Here we have a shield law, said to be as strongly worded as any in the country.

We read the legislative intent in adopting this statute in its present form as seeking to protect the confidential sources of the press as well as information so obtained by reporters and other news media representatives to the greatest extent permitted by the Constitution of the United States and that of the State of New Jersey. It is abundantly clear that appellants come fully within the literal language of the enactment. Extended discussion is quite unnecessary. Viewed solely as a matter of statutory construction, appellants are clearly entitled to the protections afforded by the act unless statutory exceptions including waiver are shown to apply. In view of the fundamental basis of our decision today, the question of waiver of privilege under the Shield Law need not be addressed by us.

2. The term "shield law" is commonly and widely applied to statutes granting newsmen and other media representatives the privilege of declining to reveal confidential sources of information. The New Jersey shield law reads as follows:

Subject to Rule 37, a person engaged on, engaged in, connected with, or employed by news media for the purpose of gathering, procuring, transmitting, compiling, editing or disseminating news for the general public or on whose behalf news is so gathered, procured, transmitted, compiled, edited or disseminated has a privilege to refuse to disclose, in any legal or quasi-legal proceeding or before any investigative body, including, but not limited to, any court, grand jury, petit jury, administrative agency, the Legislature or legislative committee, or elsewhere:

a. The source, author, means, agency or person from or through whom any information was procured, obtained, supplied, furnished, gathered, transmitted, compiled, edited, disseminated, or delivered; and

b. Any news or information obtained in the course of pursuing his professional activities whether or not it is disseminated.

The provisions of this rule insofar as it relates to radio or television stations shall not apply unless the radio or television station maintains and keeps open for inspection, for a period of at least 1 year from the date of an actual broadcast or telecast, an exact recording, transcription, kinescopic film or certified written transcript of the actual broadcast or telecast.

III

The Sixth Amendment [3] and its New Jersey Counterpart [4]

Viewed on its face, considered solely as a reflection of legislative intent to bestow upon the press as broad a shield as possible to protect against forced revelation of confidential source materials, this legislation is entirely constitutional. Indeed, no one appears to have attacked its facial constitutionality.

It is, however, argued, and argued very strenuously, that if enforced under the facts of this case, the Shield Law violates the Sixth Amendment of the Federal Constitution as well as Article 1, ¶ 10 of the New Jersey Constitution. These provisions are set forth above. Essentially the argument is this: The Federal and State Constitutions each provide that in all criminal prosecutions the accused shall have the right "to have compulsory process for obtaining witnesses in his favor." Dr. Jascalevich seeks to obtain evidence to use in preparing and presenting his defense in the ongoing criminal trial in which he has been accused of multiple murders. He claims to come within the favor of these constitutional provisions—which he surely does. Finally, when faced with the Shield Law, he invokes the rather elementary but entirely sound proposition that where Constitution and statute collide, the latter must yield. Subject to what is said below, we find this argument unassailable.

The compulsory process clause of the Sixth Amendment has never been elaborately explicated by the Supreme Court. Not until 1967, when it decided Washington v. Texas, had the clause been directly construed. Westen, Confrontation and Compulsory Process: A Unified Theory of Evidence for Criminal Cases, 91 Harv.L.Rev. 567, 586 (1978). In *Washington* the petitioner sought the reversal of his conviction for murder. A Texas statute at the time provided that persons charged or convicted as co-participants in the same crime could not testify for one another. One Fuller, who had already been convicted of the murder, was prevented from testifying by virtue of the statute. The record indicated that had he testified his testimony would have been favorable to petitioner. The Court reversed the conviction on the ground that petitioner's Sixth Amendment right to compulsory process had been denied. At the same time it determined that the compulsory process clause in the Sixth Amendment was binding on state courts by virtue of

---

3. The Sixth Amendment of the United States Constitution reads as follows:

In all criminal prosecutions, the accused shall enjoy the right to a speedy and public trial, by an impartial jury of the State and district wherein the crime shall have been committed, which district shall have been previously ascertained by law, and to be informed of the nature and cause of the accusation; to be confronted with the witnesses against him; to have compulsory process for obtaining witnesses in his favor; and to have the Assistance of Counsel for his defense.

4. Article 1, § 10 of the Constitution of the State of New Jersey reads as follows:

In all criminal prosecutions the accused shall have the right to a speedy and public trial by an impartial jury; to be informed of the nature and cause of the accusation; to be confronted with the witnesses against him; to have compulsory process for obtaining witnesses in his favor; and to have the assistance of counsel in his defense.

the due process clause of the Fourteenth Amendment. It will be seen that *Washington* is like the present case in a significant respect. The Texas statute and the Sixth Amendment could not both stand. The latter of course prevailed. So must it be here.

Quite recently, in United States v. Nixon, the Court dealt with another compulsory process issue. There the Special Prosecutor, Leon Jaworski, subpoenaed various tape recordings and documents in the possession of President Nixon. The latter claimed an executive privilege and refused to deliver the tapes. The Supreme Court conceded that indeed there was an executive privilege and that although "[n]owhere in the Constitution * * * is there any explicit reference to a privilege of confidentiality, yet to the extent this interest relates to the effective discharge of a President's powers, it is constitutionally based." Despite this conclusion that at least to some extent a president's executive privilege derives from the Constitution, the Court nonetheless concluded that the demands of our criminal justice system required that the privilege must yield.

> We have elected to employ an adversary system of criminal justice in which the parties contest all issues before a court of law. The need to develop all relevant facts in the adversary system is both fundamental and comprehensive. The ends of criminal justice would be defeated if judgments were to be founded on a partial or speculative presentation of the facts. The very integrity of the judicial system and public confidence in the system depend on full disclosure of all the facts, within the framework of the rules of evidence. To ensure that justice is done, it is imperative to the function of courts that compulsory process be available for the production of evidence needed either by the prosecution or by the defense. [United States v. Nixon, supra.]

It is important to note that the Supreme Court in this case compelled the production of privileged material—the privilege acknowledged to rest in part upon the Constitution—even though there was no Sixth Amendment compulsion to do so. The Sixth Amendment affords rights to an accused but not to a prosecutor. The compulsion to require the production of the privileged material derived from the necessities of our system of administering criminal justice.

Article 1, ¶ 10 of the Constitution of the State of New Jersey contains, as we have seen, exactly the same language with respect to compulsory process as that found in the Sixth Amendment. There exists no authoritative explication of this constitutional provision. Indeed it has rarely been mentioned in our reported decisions. We interpret it as affording a defendant in a criminal prosecution the right to compel the attendance of witnesses and the production of documents and other material for which he may have, or may believe he has, a legitimate need in preparing or undertaking his defense. It also means that witnesses properly summoned will be required to testify and that material demanded by a properly phrased *subpoena duces tecum* will be forthcoming and available for appropriate examination and use.

Testimonial privileges, whether they derive from common law or from statute, which allow witnesses to withhold evidence seem to conflict with this provision. This conflict may arise in a variety of factual contexts with respect to different privileges. We confine our consideration here to the single privilege before us—that set forth in the Shield Law. We hold that Article 1, ¶ 10 of our Constitution prevails over this statute, but in recognition of the strongly expressed legislative viewpoint favoring confidentiality, we prescribe the imposition of the safeguards set forth in Point IV below.

IV

Procedural Mechanism

Appellants insist that they are entitled to a full hearing on the issues of relevance, materiality and overbreadth of the subpoena. We agree. The trial court recognized its obligation to conduct such a hearing, but the appellants have aborted that hearing by refusing to submit the material subpoenaed for an *in camera* inspection by the court to assist it in determining the motion to quash. That inspection is no more than a procedural tool, a device to be used to ascertain the relevancy and materiality of that material. Such an *in camera* inspection is not in itself an invasion of the statutory privilege. Rather it is a preliminary step to determine whether, and if so to what extent, the statutory privilege must yield to the defendant's constitutional rights.

Appellants' position is that there must be a full showing and definitive judicial determination of relevance, materiality, absence of less intrusive access, and need, prior to any *in camera* inspection. The obvious objection to such a rule, however, is that it would, in many cases, effectively stultify the judicial criminal process. It might well do so here. The defendant properly recognizes Myron Farber as a unique repository of pertinent information. But he does not know the extent of this information nor is it possible for him to specify all of it with particularity, nor to tailor his subpoena to precise materials of which he is ignorant. Well aware of this, Judge Arnold refused to give ultimate rulings with respect to relevance and other preliminary matters until he had examined the material. We think he had no other course. It is not rational to ask a judge to ponder the relevance of the unknown.

The same objection applies with equal force to the contention that the subpoena is overbroad. Appellants do not assert that the subpoena is vague and uncertain, but that the data requested may not be relevant and material. To deal effectively with this assertion it is not only appropriate but absolutely necessary for the trial court to inspect *in camera* the subpoenaed items so that it can make its determinations on the basis of concrete materials rather than in a vacuum.

While we agree, then, that appellants should be afforded the hearing they are seeking, one procedural aspect of which calls for their compliance with the order for *in camera* inspection, we are also of the view that they, and those who in the future may be similarly situated, are entitled to a preliminary determination before being compelled to submit the subpoenaed materials to a trial judge for such inspection. Our decision in this regard is not, contrary to the suggestion in some of the briefs filed with us, mandated by the First Amendment; for in addition to ruling generally against the representatives of the press in *Branzburg,* the Court particularly and rather vigorously, rejected the claims there asserted that before going before the grand jury, each of the reporters, at the very least, was entitled to a preliminary hearing to establish a number of threshold issues. Branzburg v. Hayes, supra. Rather, our insistence upon such a threshold determination springs from our obligation to give as much effect as possible, within ever-present constitutional limitations, to the very positively expressed legislative intent to protect the confidentiality and secrecy of sources from which the media derive information. To this end such a determination would seem a necessity.

The threshold determination would normally follow the service of a subpoena by a defendant upon a newspaper, a reporter or other representative of the media. The latter foreseeably would respond with a motion to quash. If the status of the movant—newspaper or media representative—were not conceded, then there would follow the taking of proofs leading to a determination that the movant did or did not qualify for the statutory privilege. Assuming qualification, it would then become the obligation of the defense to satisfy the trial judge, by a fair preponderance of the evidence including all reasonable inferences, that there was a reasonable probability or likelihood that the information sought by the subpoena was material and relevant to his defense, that it could not be secured from any less intrusive source, and that the defendant had a legitimate need to see and otherwise use it.

* * *

Although in this case the trial judge did not articulate the findings prescribed above, it is perfectly clear that on the record before him a conclusion of materiality, relevancy, unavailability of another source, as well as need was quite inescapable. * * *

* * * Two and a half months before his June 30th decision, Judge Arnold observed:

> The facts show that Farber has written articles for the *New York Times* about this matter, commencing in January 1976. According to an article printed in the *New York Times* (hereinafter the *Times*) on January 8, 1976, Farber showed Joseph Woodcock, the Bergen County Prosecutor at that time, a deposition not in the State's file and *provided additional information that convinced the prosecutor to reopen an investigation into some deaths that occurred at Riverdell Hospital.* [State v. Jascalevich; In the Matter of the Application of Myron Farber and the New York Times Company re: Sequestration (emphasis added).]

And

> The court has examined the news stories in evidence and they demonstrate exceptional quality, a grasp of intricate scientific knowledge, and a style of a fine journalist. *They, also,*

*demonstrate considerable knowledge of the case before the court
and deep involvement by Farber,* showing his attributes as a
first-rate investigative reporter. However, if a newspaper reporter assumes the duties of an investigator, he must also
assume the responsibilities of an investigator and be treated
equally under the law, unless he comes under some exception.

In the same vein is a letter before the trial court dated January 14,
1977 from Assistant Prosecutor Moses to Judge Robert A. Matthews,
sitting as a Presiding Judge in the Appellate Division, undertaking to
explain "how the investigation, from which the [Jascalevich] indictment
resulted, came to be reopened." In the course of that explanation it is
revealed that sometime in the latter part of 1975 "a reporter for the
New York Times began an investigation into the 1965–66 deaths and
circumstances surrounding them. The results of the *New York Times*
inquiry were made available to the Prosecutor. *It was thus determined
that there were certain items which were not in the file of the Prosecutor.*" [Emphasis added.]

Further support for the determination that there is a reasonable
probability that the subpoenaed materials meet the test formulated
above appears in the following factual circumstances pointed to by this
defendant and supported by documents and transcripts of testimony
found in the appendix filed by the defendant:

1. A principal witness for the State is Dr. Michael Baden,
a New York City Medical Examiner, who testified that Farber
communicated with him prior to any official communication
from the Prosecutor's office. The defendant would have one
infer from this that Farber stimulated Baden's research into
the causal connection among curare, the deaths, and Dr. Jascalevich, then turned the results of this joint effort over to the
Prosecutor. (Trial testimony elicited from Dr. Baden after
June 30th, the date of Judge Arnold's order, is said to furnish
further support for this inference.) While no sinister implications need flow from this, it arguably serves to buttress the
defense assertion that the driving power behind this prosecution is Farber, and hence such materials, if any, that he may
be secreting are reasonably likely to bear on the guilt or
innocence of Dr. Jascalevich.

2. Dr. Stanley Harris was a surgeon at the hospital where
the criminal activities are said to have occurred. His suspicions are said to have been aroused by the unexplained deaths
of some of his patients. Dr. Harris admits having spoken to
Farber five times before the New York Times articles appeared
and before his reinterview by the Prosecutor's office in 1976.
He is characterized by the criminal defendant as his "principal
accuser," and therefore whatever otherwise unavailable information Farber extracted from him would, with reasonable
probability, bear upon Dr. Jascalevich's guilt or innocence.

3. Lee Henderson was an attendant at Seton Hall Medical School at a time when, according to one statement allegedly

made by Dr. Jascalevich, the latter was performing certain tests on dogs in the School laboratory. The tests supposedly involved the effects of curare (a drug said to have been administered by the criminal defendant in producing the deaths of the victims). Henderson may very well have information touching upon Dr. Jascalevich's activities, if any, in the laboratory. After considerable effort Farber succeeded in tracking down Henderson in South Carolina. When a Prosecutor's investigator was later able to communicate with Henderson (having presumably been led to him by information furnished by Farber), the witness initially refused to give a statement (later supplied) for fear that it would conflict with a written statement previously furnished to Farber. The criminal defendant wishes to examine this earlier statement.

4. Herman Fuhr was an operating room attendant who opened Dr. Jascalevich's locker at Riverdell Hospital, where curare was allegedly stored. Farber interviewed him. He will not speak to defense representatives.

5. Dr. Charles Umberger was a toxicologist who worked on slides of one of the alleged victims. He gave notes to Farber who did not return them. Some of these notes are missing. Dr. Umberger died in 1977 before the defense could interview him.

6. Barbara Kenderes was a lab technician at the hospital. She gave a statement to a Prosecutor's detective in 1966, which the State either has not furnished or cannot furnish to the defense. She testified before the grand jury in March, 1976. Several days later Mrs. Kenderes received a telephone call on her private, unlisted number from Myron Farber. During the course of the conversation he accused her of hiding something from him. She replied that, indeed, she was. Shortly thereafter, she received a call from Assistant Prosecutor Sybil Moses, who is handling the case. Mrs. Moses told Mrs. Kenderes that Myron Farber called her and said Mrs. Kenderes was hiding something. Mrs. Moses wanted to know what that was. Mrs. Kenderes replied that it was only the fact that she had appeared before the grand jury, which Mrs. Moses had cautioned her not to speak about. The only person to whom Mrs. Kenderes had given her private phone number in connection with this matter was Mrs. Moses. Again the inference defendant Jascalevich would have us draw is that early on there was complete cooperation and exchange of information between the Prosecutor's office and Farber, with the resultant likelihood that Farber is now, and for some time has been, in possession of material and relevant information not otherwise obtainable bearing on the guilt or innocence of Dr. Jascalevich.

We hasten to add that we need not, and do not, address (much less determine) the truth or falsity of these assertions. The point to be made is that these are the assertions of the criminal defendant supported by testimonial or documentary proof; and based thereon it is perfectly clear that there was more than enough before Judge Arnold to satisfy the tests formulated above. Of course all of this information detailed above has long been known to appellants. Accordingly we find that preliminary requirements for *in camera* inspection have been met.

* * *

The judgment of conviction of criminal contempt and that in aid of litigants' rights are affirmed. Stays heretofore entered are vacated effective as of 4:00 p.m., Tuesday, September 26, 1978.

For affirmance: Chief Justice Hughes and Justices Mountain, Sullivan, Clifford and Schreiber—5.

For reversal: Justices Pashman and Handler—2.

[Concurring and dissenting opinions omitted.]

Chapter VII

THE PRIVILEGE AGAINST COMPULSORY SELF–INCRIMINATION

PART A. INTRODUCTION

CONSTITUTION OF THE UNITED STATES, AMENDMENT V

No person ∗ ∗ ∗ shall be compelled in any criminal case to be a witness against himself ∗ ∗ ∗.

HISTORICAL BACKGROUND

The privilege against self-incrimination can only be understood against the background of English history which produced it. In very brief and simplified form, this is what happened:

Early in the reign of Henry VIII, about 450 years ago, England was a Roman Catholic state. Protestants were vigorously persecuted. Then, when Henry broke with the Roman Catholic Church and Parliament established the Church of England, the Protestants reversed the situation and began to persecute the Catholics, until Queen Mary once again persecuted the Protestants. This situation was reversed after the death of Mary, when Elizabeth took the throne. From the 1560's Elizabeth's Church began persecuting (in addition to the Catholics) dissident Protestants called Puritans. This continued under James I and Charles I and helped provoke the Revolution in which Puritans and their allies were victorious.

After the Puritan victory, the authorities continued to persecute Catholics, while also persecuting both the Anglican clergy, less reform-minded than themselves, and the "left wing" dissenters who broke away from the main body of Puritans. Then, after the accession to power of Oliver Cromwell, the center of the Puritan establishment moved left and began its own campaigns against the "ungodly," persecuting the Catholics, the High Anglicans and the right wing Puritans. By the time of the Restoration of the monarchy under Charles II, all England was sick of religious persecution and for the most part it ceased.

This history is quite remarkable. In the course of about 150 years, members of every major religious group in England had been both the initiators and the victims of persecution—and the roles had changed with bewildering rapidity.

Of course, these persecutions were only partly religious. They were also political. The divorce of religion from politics is, in historical terms, a relatively recent phenomenon. It is obvious that the break of

568

Henry VIII with Rome (not to mention the later excommunication of Elizabeth) had political as well as religious significance.

In any event, a major method of these persecutions was the oath. During the persecution of the Puritans by the Church of England under Elizabeth and James, for example, Puritan ministers were called before the High Commission and asked questions under oath about their beliefs. Being men of God, they could not lie—and, if they admitted to their deviant and nonconformist views, they could be very seriously punished. As a result, increasingly, they claimed the right not to answer and the existence or non-existence of such a right gradually became a major issue in 17th century England. One of the most celebrated cases involving the right was that of John Lilburne: *

"In 1637, Lilburne, A Puritan dissenter, was brought before the Star Chamber. Having just returned from Holland, he was charged with sending "factitious and scandalous books" from there to England. Lilburne repeatedly contended that he was entitled to notice, indictment, and court trial under the known laws of England; that he had a right to have witnesses summoned in his behalf and be confronted by witnesses against him; and that he could not be compelled to testify against himself.

"For refusing to respond to the questions, Lilburne was fined, was tied to a cart and, his body bared, was whipped through the streets of London. At Westminster he was placed in a pillory—his body bent down, his neck in the hole, and his lacerated back bared to the midday sun; there he stood for two hours and exhorted all who would listen to resist the tyranny of the bishops. Refusing to be quiet, he was gagged so cruelly that his mouth bled. After all this, he was kept in solitary confinement in the Fleet Prison with irons on his hands and legs and without anything to eat for ten days. After Lilburne's release, his cruel treatment and bold resistance had two consequences. The first was the vote of the Long Parliament that his sentence was illegal and that he be paid reparations. The second was the abolition of both the Star Chamber and the Court of the High Commission by the same Parliament. * * *"

The development of the privilege was by no means complete at this point. As has been pointed out,

"[The] objections to compulsory self-incrimination were not, however, aimed at the practice in the regular criminal courts but, rather, at the practice as it was carried out by the Star Chamber and the High Commission. After the abolition of the Courts of the Star Chamber and of the High Commission, [q]uestioning of the accused at his trial continued unaltered for nearly two decades; the examination of the prisoner

* *The Bill of Rights, A Source Book for Teachers,* California State Department of Education (1967, pp. 79–83).

by the committing magistrate continued for as long as two
centuries. Nevertheless, a gradual repugnance to compulsory
self-incrimination developed. By the end of the reign of
Charles II, the privilege was recognized in all courts when
claimed by defendant or witness."

———

See California Evidence Code §§ 404, 930, and 940.

MALLOY v. HOGAN

Supreme Court of the United States, 1964.
378 U.S. 1, 84 S.Ct. 1489, 12 L.Ed.2d 653.
[Most of the Court's footnotes are omitted.]

Mr. Justice BRENNAN delivered the opinion of the Court.

In this case we are asked to reconsider prior decisions holding that
the privilege against self-incrimination is not safe-guarded against state
action by the Fourteenth Amendment. Twining v. New Jersey; Adam-
son v. California.

The petitioner was arrested during a gambling raid in 1959 by
Hartford, Connecticut, police. He pleaded guilty to the crime of pool
selling, a misdemeanor, and was sentenced to one year in jail and fined
$500. The sentence was ordered to be suspended after 90 days, at
which time he was to be placed on probation for two years. About 16
months after his guilty plea, petitioner was ordered to testify before a
referee appointed by the Superior Court of Hartford County to conduct
an inquiry into alleged gambling and other criminal activities in the
county. The petitioner was asked a number of questions related to
events surrounding his arrest and conviction. He refused to answer
any question "on the grounds it may tend to incriminate me." The
Superior Court adjudged him in contempt, and committed him to prison
until he was willing to answer the questions. Petitioner's application
for a writ of habeas corpus was denied by the Superior Court, and the
Connecticut Supreme Court of Errors affirmed. The latter court held
that the Fifth Amendment's privilege against self-incrimination was
not available to a witness in a state proceeding, that the Fourteenth
Amendment extended no privilege to him, and that the petitioner had
not properly invoked the privilege available under the Connecticut
Constitution. We reverse. We hold that the Fourteenth Amendment
guaranteed the petitioner the protection of the Fifth Amendment's
privilege against self-incrimination, and that under the applicable federal standard, the Connecticut Supreme Court of Errors erred in
holding that the privilege was not properly invoked.

* * *

The marked shift to the federal standard in state cases began with
Lisenba v. California, where the Court spoke of the accused's "free
choice to admit, to deny, or to refuse to answer." The shift reflects
recognition that the American system of criminal prosecution is accusatorial, not inquisitorial, and that the Fifth Amendment privilege is its
essential mainstay. Governments, state and federal, are thus constitutionally compelled to establish guilt by evidence independently and

freely secured, and may not by coercion prove a charge against an accused out of his own mouth. Since the Fourteenth Amendment prohibits the States from inducing a person to confess through "sympathy falsely aroused" Spano v. New York, or other like inducement far short of "compulsion by torture," Haynes v. Washington, it follows *a fortiori* that it also forbids the States to resort to imprisonment, as here, to compel him to answer questions that might incriminate him. The Fourteenth Amendment secures against state invasion the same privilege that the Fifth Amendment guarantees against federal infringement—the right of a person to remain silent unless he chooses to speak in the unfettered exercise of his own will, and to suffer no penalty, as held in Twining, for such silence. * * * In thus returning to the Boyd view that the privilege is one of the "principles of a free government," [1] Mapp necessarily repudiated the Twining concept of the privilege as a mere rule of evidence "best defended not as an unchangeable principle of universal justice, but as a law proved by experience to be expedient." * * *

We turn to the petitioner's claim that the State of Connecticut denied him the protection of his federal privilege. It must be considered irrelevant that the petitioner was a witness in a statutory inquiry and not a defendant in a criminal prosecution, for it has long been settled that the privilege protects witnesses in similar federal inquiries. We recently elaborated the content of the federal standard in Hoffman v. United States:

> "The privilege afforded not only extends to answers that would in themselves support a conviction * * * but likewise embraces those which would furnish a link in the chain of evidence needed to prosecute. * * * [I]f the witness, upon interposing his claim, were required to prove the hazard * * * he would be compelled to surrender the very protection which the privilege is designed to guarantee. To sustain the privilege, it need only be evidence from the implications of the question, in the setting in which it is asked, that a responsive answer to the question or an explanation of why it cannot be answered might be dangerous because injurious disclosure could result."

We also said that, in applying that test, the judge must be

> " '*perfectly clear,* from a careful consideration of all the circumstances in the case, that the witness is mistaken, and that the answer[s] *cannot possibly* have such tendency' to incriminate."

---

1. Boyd had said of the privilege, " * * * any compulsory discovery by extorting the party's oath * * * to convict him of crime * * * is contrary to the principles of a free government. It is abhorrent to the instincts of an Englishman; it is abhorrent to the instincts of an American. It may suit the purposes of despotic power, but it cannot abide the pure atmosphere of political liberty and personal freedom."

Dean Griswold has said: "I believe the Fifth Amendment is, and has been through this period of crisis, an expression of the moral striving of the community. It has been a reflection of our common conscience, a symbol of the America which stirs our hearts." The Fifth Amendment Today 73 (1955).

The State of Connecticut argues that the Connecticut courts properly applied the federal standards to the facts of this case. We disagree.

The investigation in the course of which petitioner was questioned began when the Superior Court in Hartford County appointed the Honorable Ernest A. Inglis, formerly Chief Justice of Connecticut, to conduct an inquiry into whether there was reasonable cause to believe that crimes, including gambling, were being committed in Hartford County. Petitioner appeared on January 16 and 25, 1961, and in both instances he was asked substantially the same questions about the circumstances surrounding his arrest and conviction for pool selling in late 1959. The questions which petitioner refused to answer may be summarized as follows: (1) for whom did he work on September 11, 1959; (2) who selected and paid his counsel in connection with his arrest on that date and subsequent conviction; (3) who selected and paid his bondsman; (4) who paid his fine; (5) what was the name of the tenant of the apartment in which he was arrested; and (6) did he know John Bergoti. The Connecticut Supreme Court of Errors ruled that the answers to these questions could not tend to incriminate him because the defenses of double jeopardy and the running of the one-year statute of limitations on misdemeanors would defeat any prosecution growing out of his answers to the first five questions. As for the sixth question, the court held that petitioner's failure to explain how a revelation of his relationship with Bergoti would incriminate him vitiated his claim to the protection of the privilege afforded by state law.

The conclusions of the Court of Errors, tested by the federal standard, fail to take sufficient account of the setting in which the questions were asked. The interrogation was part of a wide-ranging inquiry into crime, including gambling, in Hartford. It was admitted on behalf of the State at oral argument—and indeed it is obvious from the questions themselves—that the State desired to elicit from the petitioner the identity of the person who ran the pool-selling operation in connection with which he had been arrested in 1959. It was apparent that petitioner might apprehend that if this person were still engaged in unlawful activity, disclosure of his name might furnish a link in a chain of evidence sufficient to connect the petitioner with a more recent crime for which he might still be prosecuted.

Analysis of the sixth question, concerning whether petitioner knew John Bergoti, yields a similar conclusion. In the context of the inquiry, it should have been apparent to the referee that Bergoti was suspected by the State to be involved in some way in the subject matter of the investigation. An affirmative answer to the question might well have either connected petitioner with a more recent crime, or at least have operated as a waiver of his privilege with reference to his relationship with a possible criminal. We conclude, therefore, that as to each of the questions, it was "evident from the implications of the question, in the setting in which it [was] asked, that a responsive answer to the question or an explanation of why it [could not] be answered might be dangerous because injurious disclosure could result."

Reversed.

(The dissenting opinions of Mr. Justice Harlan joined by Mr. Justice Clark and of Mr. Justice White, joined by Mr. Justice Stewart, are omitted.)

MIRANDA v. ARIZONA

Supreme Court of the United States, 1966.
384 U.S. 436, 438–457, 527–535, 86 S.Ct. 1602, 1609–1618, 1655–1659,
16 L.Ed.2d 694.

Mr. Chief Justice WARREN delivered the opinion of the Court.

The cases before us raise questions which go to the roots of our concepts of American criminal jurisprudence: the restraints society must observe consistent with the Federal Constitution in prosecuting individuals for crime. More specifically, we deal with the admissibility of statements obtained from an individual who is subjected to custodial police interrogation and the necessity for procedures which assure that the individual is accorded his privilege under the Fifth Amendment to the Constitution not to be compelled to incriminate himself.

* * *

Our holding will be spelled out with some specificity in the pages which follow but briefly stated it is this: the prosecution may not use statements, whether exculpatory or inculpatory, stemming from custodial interrogation of the defendant unless it demonstrates the use of procedural safeguards effective to secure the privilege against self-incrimination. By custodial interrogation, we mean questioning initiated by law enforcement officers after a person has been taken into custody or otherwise deprived of his freedom of action in any significant way.[1] As for the procedural safeguards to be employed, unless other fully effective means are devised to inform accused persons of their right of silence and to assure a continuous opportunity to exercise it, the following measures are required. Prior to any questioning, the person must be warned that he has a right to remain silent, that any statement he does make may be used as evidence against him, and that he has a right to the presence of an attorney, either retained or appointed. The defendant may waive effectuation of these rights, provided the waiver is made voluntarily, knowingly and intelligently. If, however, he indicates in any manner and at any stage of the process that he wishes to consult with an attorney before speaking there can be no questioning. Likewise, if the individual is alone, and indicates in any manner that he does not wish to be interrogated, the police may not question him. The mere fact that he may have answered some questions or volunteered some statements on his own does not deprive him of the right to refrain from answering any further inquiries until he has consulted with an attorney and thereafter consents to be questioned.

1. This is what we meant in *Escobedo* when we spoke of an investigation which had focused on an accused.

I.

The constitutional issue we decide in each of these cases is the admissibility of statements obtained from a defendant questioned while in custody or otherwise deprived of his freedom of action in any significant way. In each, the defendant was questioned by police officers, detectives, or a prosecuting attorney in a room in which he was cut off from the outside world. In none of these cases was the defendant given a full and effective warning of his rights at the outset of the interrogation process. In all the cases, the questioning elicited oral admissions, and in three of them, signed statements as well which were admitted at their trials. They all thus share salient features— incommunicado interrogation of individuals in a police-dominated atmosphere, resulting in self-incriminating statements without full warnings of constitutional rights.

An understanding of the nature and setting of this in-custody interrogation is essential to our decisions today. The difficulty in depicting what transpires at such interrogations stems from the fact that in this country they have largely taken place incommunicado. From extensive factual studies undertaken in the early 1930's, including the famous Wickersham Report to Congress by a Presidential Commission, it is clear that police violence and the "third degree" flourished at that time. In a series of cases decided by this Court long after these studies, the police resorted to physical brutality—beatings, hanging, whipping—and to sustained and protracted questioning incommunicado in order to extort confessions. The Commission on Civil Rights in 1961 found much evidence to indicate that "some policemen still resort to physical force to obtain confessions." The use of physical brutality and violence is not, unfortunately, relegated to the past or to any part of the country. Only recently in Kings County, New York, the police brutally beat, kicked and placed lighted cigarette butts on the back of a potential witness under interrogation for the purpose of securing a statement incriminating a third party. People v. Portelli, 15 N.Y.2d 235 (1965).[2]

The examples given above are undoubtedly the exception now, but they are sufficiently widespread to be the object of concern. Unless a proper limitation upon custodial interrogation is achieved—such as

---

2. In addition, see People v. Wakat, 415 Ill. 610, 114 N.E.2d 706 (1953); Wakat v. Harlib, 253 F.2d 59 (C.A. 7th Cir. 1958) (defendant suffering from broken bones, multiple bruises and injuries sufficiently serious to require eight months' medical treatment after being manhandled by five policemen); Kier v. State, 213 Md. 556, 132 A.2d 494 (1957) (police doctor told accused, who was strapped to a chair completely nude, that he proposed to take hair and skin scrapings from anything that looked like blood or sperm from various parts of his body); Bruner v. People, 113 Colo. 194, 156 P.2d 111 (1945) (defendant held in custody over two months, deprived of food for 15 hours, forced to submit to a lie detector test when he wanted to go to the toilet); People v. Matlock, 51 Cal.2d 682, 336 P.2d 505, 71 A.L.R.2d 605 (1959) (defendant questioned incessantly over an evening's time, made to lie on cold board and to answer questions whenever it appeared he was getting sleepy). Other cases are documented in American Civil Liberties Union, Illinois Division, Secret Detention by the Chicago Police (1959); Potts, The Preliminary Examination and "The Third Degree," 2 Baylor L.Rev. 131 (1950); Sterling, Police Interrogation and the Psychology of Confession, 14 J.Pub.L. 25 (1965).

these decisions will advance—there can be no assurance that practices of this nature will be eradicated in the foreseeable future. The conclusion of the Wickersham Commission Report, made over 30 years ago, is still pertinent:

"To the contention that the third degree is necessary to get to the facts, the reporters aptly reply in the language of the present Lord Chancellor of England (Lord Sankey): 'It is not admissible to do a great right by doing a little wrong. * * * It is not sufficient to do justice by obtaining a proper result by irregular or improper means.' Not only does the use of the third degree involve a flagrant violation of law by the officers of the law, but it involves also the dangers of false confessions, and it tends to make police and prosecutors less zealous in the search for objective evidence. As the New York prosecutor quoted in the report said, 'It is a short cut and makes the police lazy and unenterprising.' Or, as another official quoted remarked: 'If you use your fists, you are not so likely to use your wits.' We agree with the conclusion expressed in the report, that 'The third degree brutalizes the police, hardens the prisoner against society, and lowers the esteem in which the administration of justice is held by the public.' " IV National Commission on Law Observance and Enforcement, Report on Lawlessness in Law Enforcement 5 (1931).

Again we stress that the modern practice of in-custody interrogation is psychologically rather than physically oriented. As we have stated before, "Since Chambers v. State of Florida, 309 U.S. 227, this Court has recognized that coercion can be mental as well as physical, and that the blood of the accused is not the only hallmark of an unconstitutional inquisition." Blackburn v. State of Alabama, 361 U.S. 199 (1960). Interrogation still takes place in privacy. Privacy results in secrecy and this in turn results in a gap in our knowledge as to what in fact goes on in the interrogation rooms. A valuable source of information about present police practices, however, may be found in various police manuals and texts which document procedures employed with success in the past, and which recommend various other effective tactics. These texts are used by law enforcement agencies themselves as guides. It should be noted that these texts professedly present the most enlightened and effective means presently used to obtain statements through custodial interrogation. By considering these texts and other data, it is possible to describe procedures observed and noted around the country.

The officers are told by the manuals that the "principal psychological factor contributing to a successful interrogation is privacy—being alone with the person under interrogation." The efficacy of this tactic has been explained as follows:

"If at all practicable, the interrogation should take place in the investigator's office or at least in a room of his own choice. The subject should be deprived of every psychological advantage. In his own home he may be confident, indignant,

or recalcitrant. He is more keenly aware of his rights and
more reluctant to tell of his indiscretions or criminal behavior
within the walls of his home. Moreover his family and other
friends are nearby, their presence lending moral support. In
his office, the investigator possesses all the advantages. The
atmosphere suggests the invincibility of the forces of the law."

To highlight the isolation and unfamiliar surroundings, the manuals instruct the police to display an air of confidence in the suspect's
guilt and from outward appearance to maintain only an interest in
confirming certain details. The guilt of the subject is to be posited as a
fact. The interrogator should direct his comments toward the reasons
why the subject committed the act, rather than court failure by asking
the subject whether he did it. Like other men, perhaps the subject has
had a bad family life, had an unhappy childhood, had too much to
drink, had an unrequited desire for women. The officers are instructed
to minimize the moral seriousness of the offense, to cast blame on the
victim or on society. These tactics are designed to put the subject in a
psychological state where his story is but an elaboration of what the
police purport to know already—that he is guilty. Explanations to the
contrary are dismissed and discouraged.

The texts thus stress that the major qualities an interrogator
should possess are patience and perseverance. One writer describes the
efficacy of these characteristics in this manner:

> "In the preceding paragraphs emphasis has been placed on
> kindness and stratagems. The investigator will, however, en-
> counter many situations where the sheer weight of his person-
> ality will be the deciding factor. Where emotional appeals and
> tricks are employed to no avail, he must rely on an oppressive
> atmosphere of dogged persistence. He must interrogate steadi-
> ly and without relent, leaving the subject no prospect of
> surcease. He must dominate his subject and overwhelm him
> with his inexorable will to obtain the truth. He should inter-
> rogate for a spell of several hours pausing only for the subject's
> necessities in acknowledgment of the need to avoid a charge of
> duress that can be technically substantiated. In a serious case,
> the interrogation may continue for days, with the required
> intervals for food and sleep, but with no respite from the
> atmosphere of domination. It is possible in this way to induce
> the subject to talk without resorting to duress or coercion. The
> method should be used only when the guilt of the subject
> appears highly probable."

The manuals suggest that the suspect be offered legal excuses for
his actions in order to obtain an initial admission of guilt. Where there
is a suspected revenge-killing, for example, the interrogator may say:

> "Joe, you probably didn't go out looking for this fellow with the
> purpose of shooting him. My guess is, however, that you
> expected something from him and that's why you carried a
> gun—for your own protection. You knew him for what he was,
> no good. Then when you met him he probably started using

foul, abusive language and he gave some indication that he was about to pull a gun on you, and that's when you had to act to save your own life. That's about it, isn't it, Joe?"

Having then obtained the admission of shooting, the interrogator is advised to refer to circumstantial evidence which negates the self-defense explanation. This should enable him to secure the entire story. One text notes that "Even if he fails to do so, the inconsistency between the subject's original denial of the shooting and his present admission of at least doing the shooting will serve to deprive him of a self-defense 'out' at the time of trial."

When the techniques described above prove unavailing, the texts recommend they be alternated with a show of some hostility. One ploy often used has been termed the "friendly-unfriendly" or the "Mutt and Jeff" act:

"* * * In this technique, two agents are employed. Mutt, the relentless investigator, who knows the subject is guilty and is not going to waste any time. He's sent a dozen men away for this crime and he's going to send the subject away for the full term. Jeff, on the other hand, is obviously a kindhearted man. He has a family himself. He has a brother who was involved in a little scrape like this. He disapproves of Mutt and his tactics and will arrange to get him off the case if the subject will cooperate. He can't hold Mutt off for very long. The subject would be wise to make a quick decision. The technique is applied by having both investigators present while Mutt acts out his role. Jeff may stand by quietly and demur at some of Mutt's tactics. When Jeff makes his plea for cooperation, Mutt is not present in the room." [3]

The interrogators sometimes are instructed to induce a confession out of trickery. The technique here is quite effective in crimes which require identification or which run in series. In the identification situation, the interrogator may take a break in his questioning to place the subject among a group of men in a line-up. "The witness or complainant (previously coached, if necessary) studies the line-up and confidently points out the subject as the guilty party." Then the questioning resumes "as though there were now no doubt about the guilt of the subject." A variation on this technique is called the "reverse line-up":

"The accused is placed in a line-up, but this time he is identified by several fictitious witnesses or victims who associated him with different offenses. It is expected that the subject will

---

3. O'Hara, supra, at 104, Inbau & Reid, supra, at 58–59. See Spano v. People of State of New York, 360 U.S. 315, 79 S.Ct. 1202, 3 L.Ed.2d 1265 (1959). A variant on the technique of creating hostility is one of engendering fear. This is perhaps best described by the prosecuting attorney in Malinski v. People of State of New York, 324 U.S. 401, 407, 65 S.Ct. 781, 784, 89 L.Ed. 1029 (1945): "Why this talk about being undressed? Of course, they had a right to undress him to look for bullet scars, and keep the clothes off him. That was quite proper police procedure. That is some more psychology—let him sit around with a blanket on him, humiliate him there for a while; let him sit in the corner, let him think he is going to get a shellacking."

become desperate and confess to the offense under investigation in order to escape from the false accusations."

The manuals also contain instructions for police on how to handle the individual who refuses to discuss the matter entirely, or who asks for an attorney or relatives. The examiner is to concede him the right to remain silent. "This usually has a very undermining effect. First of all, he is disappointed in his expectation of an unfavorable reaction on the part of the interrogator. Secondly, a concession of this right to remain silent impresses the subject with the apparent fairness of his interrogator." After this psychological conditioning, however, the officer is told to point out the incriminating significance of the suspect's refusal to talk:

> "Joe, you have a right to remain silent. That's your privilege and I'm the last person in the world who'll try to take it away from you. If that's the way you want to leave this, O.K. But let me ask you this. Suppose you were in my shoes and I were in yours and you called me in to ask me about this and I told you, 'I don't want to answer any of your questions.' You'd think I had something to hide, and you'd probably be right in thinking that. That's exactly what I'll have to think about you, and so will everybody else. So let's sit here and talk this whole thing over."

Few will persist in their initial refusal to talk, it is said, if this monologue is employed correctly.

In the event that the subject wishes to speak to a relative or an attorney, the following advice is tendered:

> "[T]he interrogator should respond by suggesting that the subject first tell the truth to the interrogator himself rather than get anyone else involved in the matter. If the request is for an attorney, the interrogator may suggest that the subject save himself or his family the expense of any such professional service, particularly if he is innocent of the offense under investigation. The interrogator may also add, 'Joe, I'm only looking for the truth, and if you're telling the truth, that's it. You can handle this by yourself.'" * * *

[The dissenting opinions of Justices Harlan, Clark, Stewart, and White are omitted.]

WILLIAMS, THE PROOF OF GUILT

THE RIGHT NOT TO BE QUESTIONED *
[Most footnotes omitted.]

According to the rule, neither the judge nor the prosecution is entitled at any stage to question the accused unless he chooses to give evidence. "At the common law," says Blackstone, "*nemo tenebatur prodere seipsum:* and his fault was not to be wrung out of himself, but rather to be discovered by other means and other men." This rule may be called the accused's right not to be questioned; in America it is

* London, Stevens, 1955.

termed the privilege against self-incrimination. The latter expression is more apt as the name for another rule, the privilege of any witness to refuse to answer an incriminating question; this is different from the rule under discussion, which, applying only to persons accused of crime, prevents the question from being asked. The person charged with crime has not merely the liberty to refuse to answer a question incriminating himself; he is freed even from the embarrassment of being asked the question. The privilege against self-incrimination, as applied to witnesses generally, must be expressly claimed by the witness when the question is put to him in the box [1]; whereas the accused's freedom from being questioned prevents the prosecution from asking (much less compelling) him to enter the box, and from addressing questions to him in the dock.

* * * The first great opponent of the rule was Bentham, and his criticism of it is still the fullest and best in our literature. Bentham did not hesitate to adopt a strong attitude, calling the rule "one of the most pernicious and most irrational notions that ever found its way into the human mind." This attack took considerable courage, for then, as indeed to a lesser degree now, the rule was firmly entrenched in public favour as one of the most important safeguards of the English legal system.

Bentham recognized that the rule derived part of its attraction from the fact that it stood at the opposite pole from the tyranny practised on the Continent, and in England under the Star Chamber, which "presented the hateful spectacle of torture, and of judges eager to seize, and turn against the accused, every word which might escape him in the agony of pain." This reaction has lost none of its psychological force at the present day. It is a natural, if irrational, response to barbarity of this kind to refuse to permit any questioning of a defendant. However, as Bentham pointed out, the rule cannot, if dispassionately regarded, be supported by an argument referring to torture. No one supposes that in present-day England a permission to question an accused person, if accompanied, as it would be, by safeguards, would result in any ill treatment of him. The risk, if there is one, is just the opposite: that if dangerous criminals cannot be questioned before a magistrate or judge, the frustrated police may resort to illegal questioning and brutal "third degree" methods in order to obtain convictions. This has happened in the United States of America; and even if we have sufficient confidence in our own police to discount the possibility of rubber-hose beatings here, we must recognise that the restraint on their part exists in spite of the defendant's freedom from examination in court and not because of it.

Bentham had no difficulty in disposing of the other argument for the rule, that it prevented the enforcement of bad laws, and above all restricted the operation of the too numerous laws carrying capital punishment. The simple answer was that the rule tended to prevent the enforcement of good law equally with bad, and thus acted as a

---

1. The judge will not generally take the objection for the witness: Att.-Gen. v. Radloff (1854) 10 Ex. at 107, 156 E.R. 375, *per* Parke B.; but he ought to inform the witness of his rights. Cf. [1954] Crim.L.R. 916. Whereas the witness' privilege causes little difficulty in England, it has caused innumerable problems in the United States, partly because of the multiplicity of jurisdictions which makes it impossible to be certain as a practical matter that the witness will not be charged.

debilitative upon the whole body of the penal law. As Stephen afterwards remarked, "people always protest with passionate eagerness
against being deprived of technical defences against what they regard
as bad laws, and such complaints often give a spurious value to
technicalities when the cruelty of the laws against which they have
offered protection has come to be commonly admitted."

The old laws of capital punishment were examples of such bad
laws: and one of their evil effects was that they reduced the administration of justice to a gamble. Although almost all felonies were
punishable with death, it was not in fact practicable to carry out
executions on the scale that legal theory required, and public justice
was regarded as satisfied if a comparatively small number of felons was
executed each year. The rest might be allowed benefit of clergy,
pardoned, or acquitted on technicalities or by the "pious perjury" of the
jury. Historically regarded, the rule against questioning the defendant
is one example of the indifference of society to the need for securing the
conviction of the guilty. Bentham set his face against this system of
haphazard punishment, arguing that "the more certain punishment is,
the less severe it need be." Consequently he was against all rules
making for the acquittal of offenders.

The third argument in favour of the law was again mere sentiment:
that to try to get an accused person to give evidence against himself
was not playing the game; it was hitting below the belt, or hitting a
man when he was down. Bentham was scornful of the analogy between a criminal trial and a private combat. He pointed to the evil
results of the rule: in so far as it hindered the conviction of the guilty it
might operate to prevent the conviction of the apprentice in crime
while he was yet open to redemption, besides neglecting the immediate
interest of society that dangerous criminals should not be left free.
"When the guilty is acquitted, society is punished." Moreover, the
supposed rule of fair play was not logically applied, because no objection was seen to giving evidence against the accused of documents
written by him, or even of conversations ascribed to him by other
witnesses. "Thus," said Bentham, "what the technical procedure rejects is his own evidence in the purest and most authentic form; what it
admits is the same testimony, provided that it be indirect, that it have
passed through channels which may have altered it, and that it be
reduced to the inferior and degraded state of hearsay." In fact, of
course, the conventional notion of fairness could not be consistently
applied in these other respects without destroying the law altogether.
But, said Bentham, "if it is wished to protect the accused against
punishment, it can be done at once, and with perfect efficacy, by not
allowing any investigation."

With his clarity of mind Bentham perceived that the common use
of the maxim *Nemo tenetur seipsum accusare* (or, *prodere*) was tenden-
tious. Read as a proposition that no one was bound to start a prosecution against himself, the thing was so obvious that its mere statement
was puerile. Read as an assertion that no one should be punished for
refusing to make a confession of guilt, the maxim was again not in
question. In this sense the maxim applies to all witnesses in all legal

proceedings, not merely to the defendant to a criminal charge: no witness is punishable for refusing to answer a question which he claims may incriminate him. This rule has not been doubted for four centuries, because it is regarded as inhumane to place a person in a legal dilemma which must result in punishment one way or the other.[2] Those who seek to alter the accused's freedom from interrogation ask only that the prosecution should be permitted in court, to put questions to the accused person, whether (since 1898) he elects to give evidence or not. There would be no direct compulsion on the accused to answer the questions if he preferred to maintain a stolid silence; though of course this silence would almost certainly have a most serious effect upon his defence.

The crux of the matter is that immunity from being questioned is a rule which from its nature can protect the guilty only. It is not a rule that may operate to acquit some guilty for fear of convicting some innocent. To quote Bentham's words, "If all criminals of every class had assembled, and framed a system after their own wishes, is not this rule the very first which they would have established for their security? Innocence never takes advantage of it; innocence claims the right of speaking, as guilt invokes the privilege of silence."

NOONAN, INFERENCES FROM THE INVOCATION OF THE PRIVILEGE AGAINST SELF–INCRIMINATION

(41) Va.L.Rev. 311 (1955).*

* * *

The most commonly accepted rationale today is Wigmore's—that unrestricted interrogation has a demoralizing effect on the prosecution. Wigmore illustrates this proposition by these specifications: such interrogation encourages incomplete investigations; and it induces a resort to bullying and even physical force. Neither of these specific examples of demoralization, however, has much persuasiveness. If investigation results in the conviction of a guilty person through his own admission, how can it be termed incomplete? Torture is already barred by the due process clause, and many observers have commented that the barrier to judicial interrogation interposed by the privilege achieves the contrary effect of encouraging the police to use the third degree to get the information they need. The famous red pepper story of Judge Stephen,[1] used to illustrate so many defenses of the privilege, is relevant only if it be supposed that abandonment of the privilege would entail abandonment of due process.

2. But Canada has resolved this problem in a different way, by providing that the witness who takes objection is compellable to answer but is protected from having his statement given in evidence against him in any subsequent criminal prosecution (Canada Evidence Act, 1952, s. 5, replacing earlier legislation).

1. An Indian officer observed to Judge Stephen, "It is far pleasanter to sit comfortably in the shade rubbing red pepper into a poor devil's eyes than to go about in the sun hunting up evidence." Stephen quotes the statement to illustrate the value of the privilege. 1 Stephen, History of the Criminal Law of England 442 n. 1 (1883).

Similarly, the argument cited by Wigmore that the privilege protects against the undignified and prejudicial examination of the accused by the court, a practice alleged to characterize the French courts, seems to be founded on a misconception; if the privilege did not exist, questioning would still be by counsel and no more a battle of wits between accused and court than any other examination of a witness. Another suggestion by Wigmore is that in an inquisitorial system blackmail is practiced on the timid by the unscrupulous. But he offers no empirical evidence of his own in support of this statement, and as far as can be seen, not study of French civic life, for example, would support him. His assertion can scarcely be given more weight than any speculation on general habits which seems to rest on no very common experience.

But Wigmore in the same section does go on to give more substantial support to his main proposition. "Under any system which permits John Doe to be forced to answer on the mere suspicion of an officer of the law, or on public rumor, or on secret betrayal," he writes, " * * * the petty judicial officer becomes a local tyrant and misuses his discretion for political or mercenary or malicious ends. * * *" The proposition has support in experience. Yet it must be examined in the light of a careful distinction between adversary and nonadversary proceedings.

Take his statement first in regard to criminal trials. Here there is some danger that an unjust prosecutor, by the use of circumstantial evidence obtained from the defendant or by collateral impeachment evidence of a prejudicial nature, could secure the conviction of an innocent man. In fact, the American Bar Association's Committee on the Improvement of the Law of Evidence in 1937 recommended against the abolition of the privilege on this ground, that overzealous prosecutors might convict the innocent if it were abolished. Yet the most intensive study of the conviction of the innocent, Borchard's, actually recommends the abolition of the privilege.[2] In a criminal trial where both a grand jury and a petit jury stand in the way of the success of arbitrary prosecution, the Wigmore reason does not seem very substantial.

Wigmore's illustration carries more weight, however, in regard to inquisitorial proceedings. A Committee of the New York Constitutional Convention, in a thoughtful analysis of the advantages of the privilege noted the danger, if the privilege did not exist, of " * * * investigations that can be instituted for no other purpose than to appease groups, satisfy curiosity, or harass the unpopular." The history of the privilege is particularly pertinent here. It was originally asserted only against the inquisitorial proceedings of the High Commission and the Star Chamber, and the enthusiasm of the common lawyers for it apparently developed from dislike of these institutions. Hence, a

---

2. Borchard, Convicting the Innocent xvi–xvii (1932). Of course there might have been more convictions of the innocent without the privilege, a possibility Borchard's study cannot disprove. But what is significant is that one who has studied the conditions contributing to injustice to the innocent finds the privilege not a safeguard, but a nuisance.

rationale for the privilege which has little weight for a jury trial reacquires its historic validity when applied to an inquisition.

Historically, the privilege was a shield for religious dissent. The privilege peculiarly protects the contents of a man's mind, his beliefs, at which the High Commission directed its questioning; and early respect for use of the privilege in heresy cases may have arisen partly from the secular community's unspoken reluctance to punish mere belief, partly from a sympathy for the witness' fear of entrapment by subtle theological questions. Yet protection of beliefs extended to acts of belief. The celebrated cases establishing the privilege, concerned overt acts of heresy, such as publishing heretical libels, or hearing Mass, or even treason. Given the closer relation of religious and political dissent in the seventeenth century, this protection was equally a defense for political heresy.

Later, in America, the colonial experience with the privilege was mainly in opposition to political inquiries by the prerogative courts of the governor and council of a colony. And two of the principal cases seem to have been free-speech cases, in which the right to silence was asserted against the inquisition of the governor.

Considering this historical background, we may conclude that one purpose of the constitutional provisions for the privilege was not merely to impede inquisitions, but to impede them especially in relation to crimes in which religious or political belief was a large element. It is here that the official tyranny of which Wigmore speaks is likely to be especially acute. Acceptance of the privilege on this ground would explain why the courts have found no invasion of the privilege in requiring corporations to incriminate themselves, in forcing business to keep incriminating records; or in holding motorists to have waived the privilege to the extent that anti-hit-and-run laws require. At the same time, this explanation of the privilege is largely valid only in relation to grand jury and legislative investigations, and for only a special type of these.

A second appealing basis for the privilege has been scouted by Bentham as the "old woman's reason," but still has much support. It is that a man should not be forced to do the unnatural act of bringing about his own conviction of crime. The most basic human urge is that of self-preservation; should the law command a man to stifle it? The argument has particular force when it is observed that even when the privilege as such did not exist before the ecclesiastical inquisitions, a moral privilege to deny a public accusation was recognized by some scholastic moralists, because it would be too harsh to make a man condemn himself. And as Dean Griswold has very recently expressed it,

> *　*　* We do not make even the most hardened criminal sign his own death warrant, or dig his own grave, or pull the lever that springs the trap on which he stands. We have through the course of history developed a considerable feeling of the dignity and intrinsic importance of the individual man.

The State in many ways may demand a curbing of the urge to self-preservation, as when it conscripts for war. But nowhere else is a man's voluntary act made so certain and deliberate a means of his own ruin. True, a man is evidence against himself when his body is used as evidence, as when he is compelled to submit to identification or finger-printing, or even to blood tests. Yet there is a difference, at least in degree, between this and the use of the man's intelligence and memory. Finally, the exceptions to the privilege are consistent with this explanation. Corporations have no biological tendency to self-preservation; in the business records and automobile cases, a man is at least warned in advance that by running a business or a car he forfeits the right to protect his criminal secrets.

The strength of this natural tendency argument may vary with the temperament or philosophy of the reader. It is more a product of intuition than a fact capable of empirical demonstration. One can always answer to it, with Bentham, that the man who by his own acts has placed himself in an incriminating position has done so by voluntary choice, and the law does no more than attach consequences to his first choice. But as long as a number of authorities on the privilege find its justification here, this reason must be treated seriously as a major purpose of the privilege. It is applicable equally to adversary and nonadversary proceedings.

So far the purposes of the privilege have been but half-expressed. It is to protect against tyrannous inquisition and self-betrayal, but only if the inquisition and betrayal lead to punishment. The protection of the privilege is not, as it were, a privilege in the air; it is a protection against penal sanctions. Two types of cases seem to make this clear: (1) The cases denying that the privilege protects against disgrace; and, (2) The cases sustaining immunity statutes if they grant immunity to criminal prosecution and nothing more.

The first class of cases, ordering the witness to testify although his reputation will be destroyed, shows that the privilege is not intended to protect against the social consequences of compulsory testimony. Thus, disclosure of disgraceful conduct is not protected by the privilege, nor is disclosure of criminal behavior if the statute of limitations has run or the defendant has already been tried for the offense. The second class of cases shows that the legislature may investigate unrestrainedly if it counts the investigation serious enough to pay the price of immunity. Once immunity is granted, the testimony obtained may be used against the witness economically, as in the regulation of his business, and even professionally in disbarment proceedings.

These cases may be objected to on the ground that the main purposes of preventing self-destruction and restraining persecutive prosecutions are then defeated. The self-destruction of reputation can be forced, and a persecutive investigating group can achieve many of its ends, if testimony may ever be forced. The difference lies in degree. There is an attempt to balance a public interest in the truth against the interests served by protection; as happens wherever interests are balanced, no interest gets its full measure. Here the law protects the witness only from the most formidable types of State coercion; it is silent as to other sanctions.

PART B. WAIVER

ROGERS v. UNITED STATES

Supreme Court of the United States, 1951.
340 U.S. 367, 71 S.Ct. 438, 95 L.Ed. 344.

Mr. Chief Justice VINSON delivered the opinion of the Court.

This case arises out of an investigation by the regularly convened grand jury of the United States District Court for the District of Colorado. The books and records of the Communist Party of Denver were sought as necessary to that inquiry and were the subject of questioning by the grand jury. In September, 1948, petitioner, in response to a subpoena, appeared before the grand jury. She testified that she held the position of Treasurer of the Communist Party of Denver until January, 1948, and that, by virtue of her office, she had been in possession of membership lists and dues records of the Party. Petitioner denied having possession of the records and testified that she had turned them over to another. But she refused to identify the person to whom she had given the Party's books, stating to the court as her only reason: "I don't feel that I should subject a person or persons to the same thing that I'm going through." [1] The court thereupon committed petitioner to the custody of the marshal until ten o'clock the next morning, expressly advising petitioner of her right to consult with counsel.[2]

The next day, counsel for petitioner informed the court that he had read the transcript of the prior day's proceedings and that, upon his advice, petitioner would answer the questions to purge herself of contempt.[3] However, upon reappearing before the grand jury, petition-

1. Transcript, p. 39 (September 21, 1948):

"The Court: Now, what is the question?

"Mr. Goldschein: Who has the books and records of the Communist Party of Denver now? Who did Mrs. Rogers give those books up to as she says she gave them up in January of this year?

"The Court: Do you care to answer that question, madam?

"Mrs. Rogers: I do not.

"The Court: What?

"Mrs. Rogers: I do not, and that's what I told them.

"The Court: Why won't you answer?

"Mrs. Rogers: I don't feel that I should subject a person or persons to the same thing that I'm going through.

"The Court: It is the order or finding of the Court that you should answer those questions. Now, will you do that?

"Mrs. Rogers: No."

2. Transcript, p. 40 (September 21, 1948):

"The Court: You will be detained until tomorrow morning until ten o'clock. In the meantime, you may consult counsel and have a hearing tomorrow morning at ten o'clock on your reasons for refusal to answer questions.

"Mrs. Rogers: I can consult counsel between now and then? The Court: Yes, but you will be in the custody of the marshal all the time. Get your counsel and bring him over here if you want to, but you will have to be in the custody of the marshal and spend the night in jail, I'm afraid."

3. Transcript, pp. 43, 49 (September 22, 1948):

"Mr. Menin (After entering his appearance on behalf of petitioner): In regard to the witness Rogers, I've read the transcript of what has transpired in

er again refused to answer the question. The following day she was again brought into court. Called before the district judge immediately after he had heard oral argument concerning the privilege against self-incrimination in another case, petitioner repeated her refusal to answer the question, asserting this time the privilege against self-incrimination.[4] After ruling that her refusal was not privileged, the district judge imposed a sentence of four months for contempt. The Court of Appeals for the Tenth Circuit affirmed, and we granted certiorari.

If petitioner desired the protection of the privilege against self-incrimination, she was required to claim it. The privilege "is deemed waived unless invoked." United States v. Murdock. Furthermore, the decisions of this Court are explicit in holding that the privilege against self-incrimination "is solely for the benefit of the witness," [6] and "is purely a personal privilege of the witness." Petitioner expressly placed her original declination to answer on an untenable ground, since a refusal to answer cannot be justified by a desire to protect others from punishment, much less to protect another from interrogation by a grand jury. Petitioner's claim of the privilege against self-incrimination was pure afterthought. Although the claim was made at the time of her second refusal to answer in the presence of the court, it came only after she had voluntarily testified to her status as an officer of the Communist Party of Denver. To uphold a claim of privilege in this case would open the way to distortion of facts by permitting a witness to select any stopping place in the testimony.

The privilege against self-incrimination, even if claimed at the time the question as to the name of the person to whom petitioner turned over the Party records was asked, would not justify her refusal to

court here yesterday; and I believe that upon my advice she will answer questions which were propounded to her."

＊ ＊ ＊

"Mr. Menin: As to the witness Jane Rogers, I think she will purge herself of her contempt by answering the questions.

"The Court: In the case of the witness Rogers, then, the order of the Court is that she return to the Grand Jury room and if she purges herself of contempt, then upon bringing the matter back to the Court, she will be discharged. In the meantime, she will remain in custody."

4. "No person ＊ ＊ ＊ shall be compelled in any criminal case to be a witness against himself ＊ ＊ ＊." U.S. Const. Amend. V. The proceedings leading to the claim of privilege by petitioner appear at Transcript, pp. 77–78 (September 23, 1948):

"The Court: Madam, do you still persist in not answering these questions? Mrs. Rogers: Well, on the basis of Mr. Menin's statements this morning—

"The Court: Will you please answer the question yes or no? Mrs. Rogers:

Well, I think that's rather undemocratic. I'm a very honest person. Would you mind letting me consider—

"The Court: Make any statement you wish.

"Mrs. Rogers: Well, as I said before, I'm a very honest person and I'm not acquainted with the tricks of legal procedure, but I understand from the reading of these cases this morning that I am— and I do have a right to refuse to answer these questions, on the basis that they would tend to incriminate me, and you read it yourself, that I have a right to decide that.

"The Court: You have not the right to say.

"Mrs. Rogers: According to what you read, I do. I stand on that.

"The Court: All right. If you will make no changes, it is the judgment and sentence of the court you be confined to the custody of the Attorney General for four months. Call the next case."

6. United States v. Murdock, 1931, 284 U.S. 141, 148, 52 S.Ct. 63, 64, 76 L.Ed. 210.

answer. As a preliminary matter, we note that petitioner had no privilege with respect to the books of the Party, whether it be a corporation or an unincorporated association. Books and records kept "in a representative rather than in a personal capacity cannot be the subject of the personal privilege against self-incrimination, even though production of the papers might tend to incriminate (their keeper) personally." United States v. White.[11] Since petitioner's claim of privilege cannot be asserted in relation to the books and records sought by the grand jury, the only claim for reversal of her conviction rests on the ground that mere disclosure of the name of the recipient of the books tends to incriminate.

In Blau v. United States, we held that questions as to connections with the Communist Party are subject to the privilege against self-incrimination as calling for disclosure of facts tending to criminate under the Smith Act.[12] But petitioner's conviction stands on an entirely different footing, for she had freely described her membership, activities and office in the Party. Since the privilege against self-incrimination presupposes a real danger of legal detriment arising from the disclosure, petitioner cannot invoke the privilege where response to the specific question in issue here would not further incriminate her. Disclosure of a fact waives the privilege as to details. As this Court stated in Brown v. Walker: "Thus, if the witness himself elects to waive his privilege, as he may doubtless do, since the privilege is for his protection and not for that of other parties, and discloses his criminal connections, he is not permitted to stop, but must go on and make a full disclosure."

Following this rule, federal courts have uniformly held that, where incriminating facts have been voluntarily revealed, the privilege cannot be invoked to avoid disclosure of the details. The decisions of this Court in Arndstein v. McCarthy, and McCarthy v. Arndstein further support the conviction in this case for, in sustaining the privilege on each appeal, the Court stressed the absence of any previous "admission of guilt *or incriminating facts*," [15] and relied particularly upon Brown v. Walker, supra, and Foster v. People. The holding of the Michigan court is entirely apposite here: "(W)here a witness has voluntarily answered as to materially criminating facts, it is held with uniformity that he cannot then stop short and refuse further explanation, but must disclose fully what he has attempted to relate." [16]

11. * * * The privilege does not attach to the books of an organization, whether or not the books in question are "required records" of the type considered in Shapiro v. United States.

12. Membership in the Communist Party was not, of itself, a crime at the time questions in this case case were asked. And Congress has since expressly provided, in the Internal Security Act of 1950, Act of Sept. 23, 1950, 64 Stat. 987, 992, § 4(f), 50 U.S.C.A. § 783(f), that "Neither the holding of office nor membership in any Communist organization by any person shall constitute per se a violation (of this Act) or of any other criminal statute." We, of course, express no opinion as to the implications of this legislation upon the issues presented by these cases.

15. The Arndstein appeals, like the present case, arose out of an involuntary examination. The Court reserved, as we do here, the problems arising out of a possible abuse of the privilege against self-incrimination in adversary proceedings.

16. VIII Wigmore, Evidence (1940) § 2276, quotes from Foster v. People as authoritative and summarizes the law as follows: "The case of the *ordinary witness*

Requiring full disclosure of details after a witness freely testifies as
to a criminating fact does not rest upon a further "waiver" of the
privilege against self-incrimination. Admittedly, petitioner had already "waived" her privilege of silence when she freely answered
criminating questions relating to her connection with the Communist
Party. But when petitioner was asked to furnish the name of the
person to whom she turned over Party records, the court was required
to determine, as it must whenever the privilege is claimed, whether the
question presented a reasonable danger of further crimination in light
of all the circumstances, including any previous disclosures. As to each
question to which a claim of privilege is directed, the court must
determine whether the answer to that particular question would subject the witness to a "real danger" of further crimination. After
petitioner's admission that she held the office of Treasurer of the
Communist Party of Denver, disclosure of acquaintance with her successor presents no more than a "mere imaginary possibility" of increasing the danger of prosecution.

Petitioner's contention in the Court of Appeals and in this Court
has been that, conceding her prior voluntary crimination as to one
element of proof of a Smith Act violation, disclosure of the name of the
recipient of the Party records would tend to incriminate as to the
different crime of conspiracy to violate the Smith Act. Our opinion in
Blau v. United States, supra, explicitly rejects petitioner's argument for
reversal here in its holding that questions relating to activities in the
Communist Party are criminating both as to "violation of (or conspiracy
to violate) the Smith Act." Of course, at least two persons are required
to constitute a conspiracy, but the identity of the other members of the
conspiracy is not needed, inasmuch as one person can be convicted of
conspiring with persons whose names are unknown.

Affirmed.

Mr. Justice CLARK took no part in the consideration or decision of
this case.

Mr. Justice BLACK, with whom Mr. Justice FRANKFURTER and
Mr. Justice DOUGLAS concur, dissenting.

* * *

Apparently, the Court's holding is that at some uncertain point in
petitioner's testimony, regardless of her intention, admission of associations with the Communist Party automatically effected a "waiver" of
her constitutional protection as to all related questions. To adopt such
a rule for the privilege against self-incrimination, when other constitutional safeguards must be knowingly waived, relegates the Fifth
Amendment's privilege to a second-rate position. Moreover, today's
holding creates this dilemma for witnesses: On the one hand, they risk
imprisonment for contempt by asserting the privilege prematurely; on

can hardly present any doubt. He may
waive his privilege; this is conceded. He
waives it by exercising his option of answering; this is conceded. Thus the only
inquiry can be whether, by *answering as to
fact X, he waived it for fact Y.* If the two
are related facts, parts of a whole fact
forming a single relevant topic, then his
waiver as to a part is a waiver as to the
remaining parts; because the privilege exists for the sake of the criminating fact as
a whole." [Emphasis in original.]

the other, they might lose the privilege if they answer a single question. The Court's view makes the protection depend on timing so refined that lawyers, let alone laymen, will have difficulty in knowing when to claim it.   In this very case, it never occurred to the trial judge that petitioner waived anything.   And even if voluntary testimony can under some circumstances work a waiver, it did not do so here because what petitioner stated to the grand jury "standing alone did not amount to an admission of guilt or furnish clear proof of crime * * *."

Furthermore, unlike the Court, I believe that the question which petitioner refused to answer did call for additional incriminating information.   She was asked the names of the persons to whom she had turned over the Communist Party books and records.   Her answer would not only have been relevant in any future prosecution of petitioner for violation of the Smith Act but also her conviction might depend on testimony of the witnesses she was thus asked to identify.   For these reasons the question sought a disclosure which would have been incriminating to the highest degree.   Certainly no one can say that the answer "[could not] possibly be used as a basis for, or in aid of, a criminal prosecution against the witness * * *."

I would reverse the judgment of conviction.

[An appendix to the opinion of Mr. Justice Black giving the full transcript of the proceedings under review is omitted.]

KENNEDY, THE ENEMY WITHIN
314–16 (1960).*

* * *

Some attorneys advise their clients to plead the Fifth Amendment on every question and not to be selective.   There is some legal precedent indicating that such advice is well founded.   Although I could never be sure until a particular question was asked whether the witness would claim the Fifth Amendment, I could often tell early in the questioning whether I was going to get many answers out of him. When a witness resorted to the Fifth Amendment on every request, I felt he should be interrogated only on matters I would have asked about if he were answering questions.   In other words, I questioned him on a point only when the facts had already been established in the record or when I had some definite information to support the question.   For instance, if we had a gangster or underworld figure from Chicago or New York who was taking the Fifth Amendment, I would not ask him whether he had been involved in a murder or armed robbery, or had been the gunman for Albert Anastasia, unless I had some specific information that he had been.

I am not claiming that when I questioned a witness I always had positive proof on the subject matter of interrogation.   In many instances, where a gangster was concerned, the information came from police files and could not be positively verified.   These people not only

* Harper & Brothers, New York; 1960.

wouldn't talk to us, they wouldn't and haven't talked to anyone. However, if I had some information to support the question, I believed that I was justified in asking it.

But this is where abuses creep in.

For instance, a witness from the Midwest was pleading the Fifth Amendment on every question when suddenly Senator Curtis asked him what his relationship was with the Governor of Iowa. I knew this was an unfair question at the time, for we had no information that the man even knew the Governor of Iowa or had had any dealings with him. The witness, of course, did not have to plead the Fifth Amendment on that question, but since he was pleading it regularly, once more made no difference to him. In any case, he exercised his privilege and refused to answer on grounds of self-incrimination. And in Iowa, as I had expected, the story was "Gangster Takes Fifth Amendment on Ties with Governor." I immediately put out a statement that we had absolutely no information about any relationship between the Governor and the witness. But the damage had been done. It was low politics and a perversion of the use of the Congressional investigating committee.

Very early in the hearings in 1957, my brother pointed out the unfairness of this kind of procedure, but as late as one of our last hearings in 1959 it was still being practiced. For example, in September of that year a former UAW official who had taken some pay-offs from an employer invoked the Fifth Amendment in answer to all questions. In the course of his interrogation, he was asked by Senator Mundt if he had made kickbacks to Richard Gosser, vice president of the UAW. He took the Fifth Amendment. Robert Manual, an assistant counsel appointed by the Republicans, then asked if Reuther had not instructed him to take the Fifth Amendment, with the implication that it was a cover-up for the UAW. My brother asked if there was any evidence whatever that the witness, Zvara, had kicked back to Richard Gosser. Senator Curtis and Robert Manual had to admit that there was not. My brother showed the unfairness of the questioning by asking Zvara if he had ever kicked back to Robert Manual. Again, on this, Zvara pleaded the Fifth Amendment. Manual also admitted that there was no evidence whatever that Walter Reuther had had any conversations with Zvara in connection with his appearance before the Committee, let alone instructing him to plead the Fifth Amendment.

If my brother had not pointed these things out at the time, the record would have carried a completely unfair implication. As it was, one news story did report that Zvara pleaded the Fifth Amendment on kickbacks to Gosser.   *   *   *

UNITED STATES v. HEARST

United States Court of Appeals, Ninth Circuit, 1977.
563 F.2d 1331.

PER CURIAM:

*   *   *

Privilege against Self-Incrimination

During the trial appellant elected to testify in her own behalf. She described in exhaustive detail the events immediately following her kidnapping of February 4, 1974. These included physical and sexual abuses by members of the Symbionese Liberation Army (SLA), extensive interrogations, forced tape recordings and written communications designed to convince her family that she had become a revolutionary, and training in guerrilla warfare. She next described how the SLA compelled her under threat of death to participate in the robbery of the Hibernia Bank on April 15, 1974, and to identify herself by reading a revolutionary speech. She explained that by the time the group moved to Los Angeles, the SLA had convinced her that they would kill her if she tried to escape and that the Federal Bureau of Investigation also desired to murder her. Appellant added that the SLA required her to make various post-robbery admissions about her voluntary role in the crime.

Appellant's story continued by describing her participation one month after the robbery in the disturbance at Mel's Sporting Goods Store. She claimed that her reaction in firing at the store resulted from fear of the SLA, as did her admission to Thomas Matthews of complicity in the bank robbery. She then told how she, the Harrises, and Jack Scott traveled from Los Angeles to Berkeley, then to New York, to Pennsylvania, and finally to Las Vegas in September of 1974. Again, she emphasized that she was an unwilling companion of the group. After mentioning her arrival in Las Vegas, her testimony jumped a year to the time of her arrest in San Francisco on September 18, 1975.

On cross-examination, appellant refused to answer most questions concerning the period between her arrival in Las Vegas and her arrest in San Francisco. In response to questions about her activities, residences, and association with other suspected members of the SLA during this year, she invoked the Fifth Amendment privilege against self-incrimination 42 times.

Prior to government questioning, appellant had moved for an order limiting the scope of the cross-examination so as to avoid the necessity of invoking the Fifth Amendment in response to questions implicating her in other crimes for which she was not on trial. Finding that appellant had waived her privilege against self-incrimination as to all relevant matters by testifying in her own behalf, the court denied this motion and allowed the government to ask her questions which resulted in her assertion of the Fifth Amendment. Appellant now offers grounds for finding that the court committed reversible error in making this ruling.

The Fifth Amendment provides that "[n]o person * * * shall be compelled in any criminal case to be a witness against himself." But it is also true, as the trial court stressed, that a defendant who testifies in his own behalf waives his privilege against self-incrimination with respect to the relevant matters covered by his direct testimony and subjects himself to cross-examination by the government. Appellant contends that she "did not voluntarily waive her Fifth Amendment privilege by testifying because her testimony was compelled by the introduction of certain evidence, i.e., post-crime conduct, which was challenged as inadmissible and highly prejudicial." She pleads that she was caught between the "rock and the whirlpool" when forced to decide whether to testify or allow the evidence to stand unrebutted.

The validity of this argument depends largely on appellant's assumption that evidence of her post-robbery behavior was admitted erroneously, and that she had no choice but to respond to this inadmissible evidence.

* * *

Appellant's assumption about the nature of her testimony is completely erroneous. The central theme of her lengthy testimony was that from the moment of her kidnapping to the time of her arrest she was an unwilling victim of the SLA who acted under continual threats of death. She tried to show, not merely that she made her admissions involuntarily, but that she acted under duress in robbing the Hibernia Bank, firing at the sporting goods store, and traveling with the Harrises * for over one year. She disputed the main element of the government's case: that she had the necessary criminal intent when she participated in the bank robbery. Thus, her reliance on Calloway v. Wainwright is misplaced, for that case dealt with the much narrower situation in which a defendant takes the witness stand solely to deny the voluntariness of his confession.

Appellant next claims that even if she did waive her privilege against self-incrimination by testifying in her own behalf, the waiver did not extend to the period between her arrival in Las Vegas and her arrest in San Francisco. She argues that since she did not testify concerning her activities during this "lost year," the government had no right or reason to ask any questions about it. She would confine the proper scope of cross-examination to the events which she specifically discussed during her direct testimony.

We find that appellant misinterprets the controlling case law on waiver and the permissible limits of the cross-examination of a testifying defendant. The Supreme Court has stated that when a defendant takes the witness stand, "his credibility may be impeached and his testimony assailed like that of any other witness, and the breadth of his waiver is determined by the scope of relevant cross-examination." "[A] defendant who takes the stand in his own behalf cannot then claim the privilege against cross-examination on matters reasonably related to the subject matter of his direct examination." This rule is premised on basic goals of fairness and ascertainment of the truth. * * * Nowhere in this rule is there even a suggestion that the waiver and the permissible cross-examination are to be determined by what the defendant actually discussed during his direct testimony. Rather, the focus is on whether the government's questions are "reasonably related" to the subjects covered by the defendant's testimony.

* "Soldiers" in the SLA.

Applying this principle to the present case, we conclude that the trial court did not abuse its broad discretion in allowing the government to ask questions about the year which appellant failed to cover in her direct testimony. [A]ppellant's testimony was not limited to disputing the voluntariness of her post-robbery admissions. Instead, she attempted to show that from her kidnapping until her arrest she acted exactly as her captors directed. She tried to persuade the jury that her post-robbery conduct and feelings of fear, dependence, and obedience proved that she had also acted involuntarily and without criminal intent in robbing the Hibernia Bank.

We agree with the trial court's conclusion that appellant's testimony placed in issue her behavior during the entire period from abduction to arrest, and gave the government a right to question her about the "lost year." * * *

Appellant argues that even if she had no right to refuse to answer the government's questions, the court erred in allowing the prosecution to continue to ask questions which it knew would elicit repeated assertions of the privilege against self-incrimination. We find that appellant's authorities do not support her proposition. Her cases involve situations in which the government or the defendant questioned a witness or a co-defendant, knowing that a valid, unwaived Fifth Amendment privilege would be asserted.

* * *

[W]hen a defendant has voluntarily waived his Fifth Amendment privilege by testifying in his own behalf, the rationale for prohibiting privilege-invoking queries on cross-examination does not apply. The defendant has chosen to make an issue of his credibility; he has elected to take his case to the jury in the most direct fashion. The government, accordingly, has a right to challenge the defendant's story on cross-examination. The government may impeach the defendant by developing inconsistencies in his testimony; the government may also successfully impeach him by asking questions which he refuses to answer. If the refusals could not be put before the jury, the defendant would have the unusual and grossly unfair ability to insulate himself from challenges merely by declining to answer embarrassing questions. He alone could control the presentation of evidence to the jury.

* * *

Affirmed.

PEOPLE v. BAGBY

Court of Appeals of New York, 1985.
65 N.Y.2d 410, 492 N.Y.S.2d 562, 482 N.E.2d 41.

ALEXANDER, Justice.

The issue on this appeal is whether a nonparty witness who testifies for the prosecution and is fully cross-examined without invoking her 5th Amendment privilege thereby waives the right to invoke that privilege, in the face of a threat of a perjury prosecution, when recalled as a defense witness and asked the same questions she had

previously answered. We hold that under these circumstances, the 5th
Amendment privilege against self-incrimination is not waived.

On December 26, 1978, members of the Mount Vernon Police
Department went to an upstairs apartment leased by Sandra Mann in a
two-family house in order to execute a warrant to search both the
premises and defendant Vernon Bagby. The officers entered the unoccupied apartment and found quantities of several controlled substances
and assorted drug paraphernalia. Defendant was thereafter arrested
and charged with criminal possession of a controlled substance in the
first, third, fifth and eighth degrees and two counts of criminally using
drug paraphernalia. Defendant and Mann had been married, divorced
and remarried at the time of defendant's arrest, but by the time of his
trial they were again divorced. A critical issue at defendant's nonjury
trial was whether he had been residing at Mann's apartment in
December 1978 or had exercised sufficient dominion and control over
the premises during that period to infer that he had constructive
control over the drugs found therein.

The prosecution subpoenaed Mann to testify during its case-in-
chief. She testified that defendant had lived with her for a three-week
period during December 1978, that she had given him a set of keys to
the premises and that they were the only two persons who had keys.
She denied possessing any of the drugs found in the apartment and
claimed that defendant had been at her apartment and had threatened
to harm her "if anything went wrong with the case." She was thoroughly cross-examined by the defense but maintained the essential
thrust of her direct testimony. She confirmed that she had been
interviewed at her place of employment about a week before the trial
by a police officer who told her she would have to testify, but denied
that they had threatened her with prosecution for drug possession if
she refused.

On the day following her testimony, Mann contacted defense counsel and requested to go back on the stand and "tell the truth". Defense
counsel informed the Trial Judge of Mann's request and his intention to
recall her as a defense witness. The court appointed an attorney to
protect Mann's interests. The prosecutor informed the attorney on the
record that prior to testifying, Mann had given him a sworn statement
that was consistent with the favorable testimony she had given for the
People and that "if the testimony [on recall] is materially different
there is a good likelihood of a perjury prosecution." The court then
recessed so that Mann's attorney could speak with her and further
advise her.

When trial resumed, the defense called Mann to the stand and
began to question her as follows:

"Q. Miss Mann, you recall you testified previously in this case, I
think last Wednesday, do you remember that? A. Yes.

"Q. At that time, I believe, that you testified that during the
month of December, 1978, up until December 26th, that your husband,
the defendant had been living with you at 127 South 12th Avenue in

Mt. Vernon, was that a correct statement? A. I take the Fifth Amendment.

"Q. Was the defendant living with you during December of 1978? A. I take the Fifth Amendment.

"Q. Did the defendant have keys to the outer door of the premises at 127 South 12th. A. No, he did not."

At this point the prosecutor objected, asserting that the witness should not be allowed to selectively invoke her 5th Amendment privilege. Traynor (Mann's attorney) then advised the court that she did in fact wish to invoke her privilege against self-incrimination and had not expected to be questioned further following the assertion of the privilege. The court sustained the objection to the last question, and following an in camera discussion with the witness and her counsel and their statements made on the record that she intended to assert her privilege in response to all questions, the court discharged the witness.

The Appellate Division reversed the judgment of conviction and ordered a new trial based on its view that "[b]y testifying for the prosecution on its direct case, Mann waived her right to subsequently invoke the privilege * * * By allowing withdrawal of the waiver, the trial court effectively deprived defendant of the opportunity to impeach Mann, even though she had earlier been subjected to cross-examination".

As the Appellate Division correctly noted, "a witness is the judge of her own right to invoke the [5th Amendment] privilege * * * [and] the witness may claim the privilege based upon the fact that the proposed testimony would be so inconsistent with prior statements under oath as to expose him to conviction for perjury. We do not agree, however, that in the circumstances here presented it would have been proper for the trial court to have directed Mann to testify under threat of contempt, if necessary, or to strike her earlier testimony if she continued to claim her privilege.

Although in some instances a witness, by giving testimony, will be found to have waived the right subsequently to invoke the privilege in the same proceeding, the cases establishing this principle and their underlying rationale are inapposite to the circumstances of this case. In its classic application, the waiver principle prevents a witness from testifying in his or her own defense and thereafter refusing to answer questions on cross-examination regarding matters made relevant by the direct examination because the answers might tend to be incriminating. Thus, a witness who foregoes the protection of the constitutional privilege against self-incrimination by giving testimony to his advantage or to the advantage of his friends cannot in the same proceeding assert the privilege and refuse to answer questions that are to his disadvantage or the disadvantage of his friends.

However, a witness may assert the privilege anew in a separate proceeding, where circumstances and surroundings can often differ dramatically. Thus, in Matter of Neff, 3rd Cir., 206 F.2d 149, a witness was allowed to assert the privilege against self-incrimination at a criminal trial although no claim of the privilege had been asserted

earlier when testifying regarding the same subject matter during a
Grand Jury hearing. The *Neff* court noted that at trial, "the setting in
which the questions were asked of her had greatly changed and she
could well have had apprehensions as to the incriminating effect of her
requested testimony which she did not have on the earlier occasion".

A further distinction has been drawn between defendants in criminal cases and "ordinary witnesses"—nonparties in criminal cases and
witnesses in civil cases. Because the criminal defendant can never be
compelled to take the stand, when he does so voluntarily he waives his
5th Amendment privilege and cannot refuse to answer questions regarding any matters relevant to the case. A nonparty witness in a
criminal case, however, can be compelled to testify against his will and
thus does not waive his 5th Amendment privilege merely by acceding to
the command of a subpoena. Thus, "where the previous disclosure by
an ordinary witness is not an actual admission of guilt or incriminating
facts, he is not deprived of the privilege of stopping short in his
testimony whenever it may fairly tend to incriminate him".

A waiver should be found only when a witness' statements are
" 'incriminating', meaning that they did not merely deal with matters
'collateral' to the events surrounding commission of the crime * * *
but directly inculpated the witness on the charges at issue * * * and
* * * [thus] contain[ed] information that the witness was privileged
not to reveal". Thus in Matter of Bohland v. Markewich (26 A.D.2d
545), a Grand Jury witness was found to have waived the privilege
when he gave answers to general inquiries concerning his participation
in acts of bribery, which were the subject of the investigation, but
thereafter declined to answer questions about a specific incident.

Applying these general principles to the present case, it is clear
that in testifying initially Mann did not waive her right to later assert
her 5th Amendment privilege to avoid exposing herself to possible
perjury—criminality wholly unrelated to the subject matter of her
original nonincriminating testimony. As a nonparty witness, Mann
had no option but to testify when subpoenaed by the prosecution. At
that time she could not rightfully have asserted a 5th Amendment
privilege unless her answers would have exposed her to a real danger of
criminal liability or implicated her with respect to the events of which
she was testifying, neither of which they did. It was not until she was
recalled by the defense and faced with the danger of exposing herself to
possible perjury by answering the questions then put to her in a
manner materially different from her previous answers that her privilege against self-incrimination became relevant, and thus waivable.

We conclude that by testifying and being fully cross-examined as a
nonparty witness concerning facts that were not self-incriminating, in
that they did not directly inculpate her on the charges at issue, Mann
did not waive her right, upon being recalled by the defendant, to invoke
her 5th Amendment privilege so as to avoid giving testimony that
might have involved her in criminality (perjury) that was not the
subject of her initial testimony.

Accordingly, the order of the Appellate Division, rendered on the law alone, should be reversed, the judgment of conviction reinstated.

* * *

PART C. IMMUNITY

McCORMICK'S HANDBOOK ON THE LAW OF EVIDENCE
354–60 (3d ed.).*

Removing the Danger of Incrimination: Immunity and
Immunity Statutes

Since criminal liability for an act is a matter of legal mandate rather than an inherent characteristic of the act itself, it follows that the liability may also be removed by legal action. Removing liability removes the danger against which the privilege protects and makes the privilege unavailable. Thus if no conviction is possible because of a prior conviction or acquittal, passage of the period of limitations, or executive pardon, the privilege cannot be invoked. The same holds true if the one from whom testimony is sought is effectively granted legal immunity from any danger arising from his testimony which is within the protection of the privilege.

Although in some jurisdictions prosecuting attorneys have been found to have inherent power to confer immunity, in most jurisdictions their ability to do so depends upon specific legislative authorization. Legislative activity in this area, however, has been piecemeal and the statutory provisions for conferring immunity are consequently varied and often confusing. Most jurisdictions have a number of different provisions each relating to a single crime or a limited category of crimes difficult to prove unless a participant "turns State's evidence;" these provisions often differ in phraseology and substance within a jurisdiction. Some states and the United States, however, have enacted general immunity statutes and Rule 732 of the Uniform Rules of Criminal Procedure (1974) is also available as a guide. It will be observed that the Uniform Rule provides for transactional immunity, a choice which was made with great care.

The major question in regard to immunity has been the scope of immunity that is necessary or desirable in order to render the privilege inapplicable. In 1892, the Supreme Court held that an immunity statute which conferred limited "use immunity"—that is, protection from the subsequent use of the witness' immunized testimony against the witness in a criminal prosecution—was inadequate where it did not protect the witness from the use of evidence obtained by using immunized testimony—that is, derivative evidence—as well as the testimony itself. Dictum in the Court's opinion was widely regarded as committing the Court to the position that "transactional immunity"—that is, immunity from prosecution for those transactions about which the witness testified under immunity—is necessary to render the privilege effectively unavailable to a witness.

* Copyright West Publishing Co. 1984.

The major concern regarding immunity from the use of testimony and other evidence derived from that testimony is that it may be ineffective in practice. The prosecution may in fact be able to exploit a person's immunized testimony to his disadvantage in later prosecutions because of the person's inability to convince the courts that evidence offered by the prosecution was in fact obtained by exploiting the person's earlier immunized testimony. The matter was finally addressed in Kastigar v. United States,[14] in which the Court held that the Fifth Amendment does not require a grant of transactional immunity before a witness may be compelled to testify. The sole concern of the privilege, reasoned the majority, is the prevention of compulsion to give testimony that leads to the infliction of penalties affixed to criminal acts. "Immunity from the use of compelled testimony, as well as evidence derived directly and indirectly therefrom, affords this protection." Turning to the long-standing concerns regarding the implementation of such grants of use immunity, the Court indicated that once a defendant establishes that he has previously testified under a grant of immunity concerning matters relating to the prosecution, the prosecution—upon defense objection—must affirmatively prove that the evidence it offers against the defendant is derived from a legitimate source wholly independent of the previously compelled testimony.

Kastigar has rendered a substantial amount of immunity legislation unnecessarily (although perhaps not undesirably) broad. Courts have quite properly regarded the Fifth Amendment as requiring no more than use immunity, although a statute which fails clearly to protect the witness from the use of derivative evidence is insufficient foundation for a grant of immunity that removes the privilege. As a matter of state constitutional law or legislative policy, however, it may still be appropriate to rely upon the concern expressed in Justice Marshall's *Kastigar* dissent: the "inevitable uncertainties of the fact-finding process" mean that even compelling the prosecution to establish an independent source for its evidence cannot adequately assure that one prosecuted for a matter concerning which he has previously been compelled to testify under immunity is actually in the exact same position as if he had not so testified. Under this view, of course, transactional immunity may still be required as a matter of policy or of state constitutional construction.

Although procedures for bringing immunity into effect depend upon the specific statute involved, the better drafted statutes have in common several important requirements that must be complied with in order to divest the witness of his privilege:

> (1) The witness must be faced with an attempt by the state to use its power of testimonial inquiry. Thus the witness's position must be such that if he wrongfully refused to answer he would be subject to legal sanctions.

> (2) The witness must invoke the privilege. If the witness is willing to testify without the grant of immunity, there would

---

14. 406 U.S. 441 (1972), rehearing denied 408 U.S. 931.

be little reason for the state to grant immunity and much reason not to do so. It is often required, therefore, that before immunity can be conferred the questions must be put to the witness and he must decline to answer them, relying on his privilege.

(3) The application for immunity must be made by the prosecution authorities. The decision to seek immunity in return for testimony involves a determination that the value of the testimony would ultimately be greater than the value of the right to prosecute the witness or to use any testimony that he might be persuaded to give without the immunity. This is essentially a matter within the province of prosecution authorities, and many statutes make explicit their option to decide whether to attempt to forfeit possible actions against the witness.

(4) The grant must be approved by the court, which under the Uniform Rule and some statutes may decline to approve it if to do so would be clearly to the contrary of the public interest. This requirement serves the purpose of formalizing the "agreement" and making it a matter of formal court record. It also provides the witness with notice that immunity has been granted and that he may no longer rely on the privilege. In addition, however, many statutes appear to be based on the policy that there should be some check on the prosecutor's power to forfeit the state's right to proceed against individuals who may well be guilty of criminal offenses.

No such carefully defined procedure is defined in many of the statutes, especially the so-called "automatic" immunity statutes which by their terms provide only that in a given situation a witness shall not be excused from testifying and then direct that the witness is to be protected from prosecution or the use of his testimony. Nevertheless, a witness may not be held in contempt for failure to testify under even these automatic statutes unless "it has been demonstrated to him that an immunity, as broad in scope as the privilege it replaces, is available and applicable to him." It is reasonable that this demonstration must include a representation by the court that in fact the statutory requirements have been complied with and the immunity has been validly conferred.

It is generally held that immunity does not protect the witness from prosecution for perjury committed in the giving of the immunized testimony. Thus a witness granted either transactional or use immunity may be prosecuted for perjury committed during the testimony and the testimony may be admitted as evidence during that prosecution. Further, in United States v. Apfelbaum,[25] the Supreme Court held that neither the Fifth Amendment nor the federal immunity statute limited the government to using, in a perjury prosecution, the immunized testimony alleged to be the "corpus delicti" or "core" of the offense. Other immunized testimony could be used against the witness if it was

25. 445 U.S. 115 (1980), on remand 621 F.2d 62 (3d Cir.).

relevant to the charge of perjury. Special problems remain, however, when immunized testimony tends to prove that the witness committed perjury during other testimony, either before or after the immunized testimony. The majority's language in *Apfelbaum* suggests that the Fifth Amendment imposes no barrier to the use of immunized testimony in either situation: "[N]either the [federal] immunity statute nor the Fifth Amendment precludes the use of [a witness'] immunized testimony at a subsequent prosecution for making false statements, so long as that testimony conforms to otherwise applicable rules of evidence." Three members of the Court expressed reservations concerning this broad dictum. There is lower court authority for the proposition that a grant of immunity must protect the witness against the use of immunized testimony in a prosecution for perjury committed at a previous time. It may follow that full protection also requires that a prosecution for prior perjury be barred if the entire matter was disclosed and stipulated only by the witness' immunized testimony. Further, it has been urged that a witness must also be protected against the use of prior testimony to prove perjury during immunized testimony, apparently on the rationale that the incriminating significance of the prior testimony was discovered by exploiting the witness' immunized testimony. It seems quite unlikely that the Fifth Amendment will be held to bar the use of admitted accurate immunized testimony to prove subsequent perjury. Just as there is no doctrine of "anticipatory contempt" in this area, there is probably no "anticipatory perjury" doctrine that permits a person to gain immunity from later perjury by submitting to a demand for immunized testimony. Nor does the need for immunity to correspond to the protection it replaces demand any such doctrine.

If after giving immunized testimony, a witness is later prosecuted and testifies in his own defense, the immunized testimony may not be used for impeachment purposes. Even if the immunized testimony tends reliably to suggest that the witness-defendant is committing perjury and thus should not be believed, the Supreme Court has made clear, this use of the testimony is not permissible. Immunized testimony is "the essence of coerced testimony" and thus inadmissible in light of the Fifth and Fourteenth Amendments' bar upon the use of compelled self-incrimination.

A special problem arises if a witness is granted transactional immunity on the assumption that the testimony will be incriminating but the testimony given turns out not to incriminate the witness. It has been suggested, on the basis of scant authority, that legislatures do not intend to confer immunity in such situations without obtaining a benefit in return and therefore the transactional immunity becomes ineffective if the testimony is not incriminating.

Immunity is generally granted at the instance of the prosecution and for the purpose of obtaining information or testimony for the government's purposes. Often, the government's purpose is to make testimony available that incriminates someone other than the witness. Criminal defendants are urging with increasing frequency, however, that in at least some situations defendants are or should be entitled to have immunity granted to witnesses whose testimony would be favorable to the defense. Failing to grant such immunity sometimes, it is argued, violates defendants' Sixth Amendment right to compel testimony for defensive purposes. Certain procedural difficulties are created by such claims, as immunity statutes often provide for grants of immunity only upon motion of the prosecution; thus the defense may lack statutory authority for a motion to have witnesses granted immunity. In Gov't of Virgin Islands v. Smith,[34] however, the court held that at least where the government's refusal to grant immunity to a defense witness is made with the deliberate intent of distorting judicial factfinding procedures, the trial court should dismiss the prosecution unless the government pursues its statutory right to request immunity for the defense witness. Further, the court held that the trial court should exercise inherent authority to grant judicial immunity to defense witnesses where it is shown that their testimony would be both exculpatory and "essential" to the defense and that there is no strong governmental interest militating against the grant of immunity. Other courts have refused to follow *Smith,* however, and the overwhelming tendency has been to find that the Sixth Amendment creates no general right in defendants to have their witnesses granted immunity to secure testimony.

UNITED STATES v. TURKISH

United States Court of Appeals, Second Circuit, 1980.
623 F.2d 769.

NEWMAN, Circuit Judge:

This criminal appeal concerns primarily the issue of whether a defendant is entitled to have immunity conferred upon defense witnesses who invoke their privilege against self-incrimination. The appeal is brought by Norman Turkish, who was convicted by a jury in the Southern District of New York (Vincent L. Broderick, Judge) of evading income taxes and filing false income tax returns, and conspiring to defraud the United States. Turkish [was] found guilty [and] appeals.

The Government's evidence established that Turkish was a principal participant in a scheme that used fraudulent means to enable an oil company, to create artificial tax losses in one year, offset by equally artificial taxable gains in a subsequent year, thereby postponing for a year the taxes on millions of dollars of corporate income. * * * Turkish not only orchestrated the fraudulent aspects of the scheme but also evaded taxes on the money he received as compensation for his role.

Defense Witness Immunity

The claim for defense witness immunity arose in the following circumstances. The Government presented its case by calling a number of witnesses involved in the fraudulent transactions, several of whom were co-conspirators. Of these, three had pleaded guilty to participation in the conspiracy and had received letter agreements that they would not be prosecuted for any other commodity market crimes

34. 615 F.2d 964 (3d Cir.1980).

or related tax offenses if they testified truthfully. Two other prosecution witnesses who had not been indicted received similar letters, one of which was sufficient to persuade its recipient to return from Switzerland for the trial. In addition, one prosecution witness was formally granted "use" immunity under 18 U.S.C. § 6002.

During the trial, and after the Government had concluded its case, Turkish and [three] co-defendants moved that seventeen of the prospective defense witnesses be granted "use" immunity and required to testify under 6002. They argued that these witnesses could provide exculpatory testimony, but would invoke their Fifth Amendment privilege and decline to testify unless compelled to do so. Judge Broderick invited the Government to consider granting "use" immunity to these witnesses pursuant to 6002. The Government did consider the matter, but decided not to grant immunity. Judge Broderick then reserved decision on defendants' motion until after the trial, at which time the defendants moved for a new trial or acquittal. Judge Broderick denied the defendants' motion.

In a subsequent opinion, United States v. Turkish (S.D.N.Y.1979), Judge Broderick set forth his analysis of the issue and his reasons for denying the motion. Judge Broderick concluded that the Compulsory Process Clause of the Sixth Amendment does not give a defendant the right to require immunization of a witness, but that such a right is "probably" contained in the Due Process Clause of the Fifth Amendment. However, he declined to accord the defendants the benefit of this "probable" Fifth Amendment right to defense witness immunity for two reasons. First, he ruled that the defendants' motion was untimely, since it should properly have been made at the beginning of the trial. Second, he concluded that defense witness immunity would be available only to secure testimony that was material and exculpatory and that the defendants had not shown that any of the witnesses for whom they sought immunity would give material, exculpatory testimony.

To assess Turkish's challenges to these rulings we deem it appropriate to explore the concept of defense witness immunity, a matter arising with increasing frequency before this and other courts.

Granting immunity to a defense witness at the defendant's request seems to have been considered for the first time, in a reported decision, by Chief Justice Burger, then a Circuit Judge, as dictum in Earl v. United States. Since then it has been much discussed by courts and commentators. Interest in defense witness immunity was considerably heightened after Congress enacted the "use" immunity statute in 1970, and the Supreme Court subsequently upheld its constitutionality, Kastigar v. United States. No longer did an immunity grant forbid prosecution of the witness for crimes referred to in his testimony ("transactional" immunity). Now the Government could still prosecute the witness; it was barred only from making any use of his immunized testimony, either directly by putting the testimony in evidence at the witness's trial, or indirectly by obtaining other evidence from leads that the testimony supplied.

Claims for defense witness use immunity have been uniformly rejected by this Court, and by almost all circuits to consider the matter.

The only federal appellate decisions ruling in favor of defense witness immunity appear to be the Third Circuit decisions in [United States v.] Morrison and [Government of the Virgin Islands v.] Smith. In *Morrison* a divided panel of the Third Circuit reversed a conviction on the ground that prosecutorial misconduct had caused a defense witness to withhold testimony out of fear of self-incrimination. As a remedy for the misconduct, the Court ordered that upon a retrial, the Government face the choice of either granting the witness use immunity or having the defendant acquitted.

Smith involved a totally bizarre situation. A juvenile defendant sought use immunity for a juvenile defense witness. The office of the Virgin Islands Attorney General, who had exclusive jurisdiction to prosecute both the defendant and the witness, was agreeable to use immunity for the witness. However, this local prosecuting office, as a matter of "prosecutorial courtesy," conditioned its approval upon the consent of the United States Attorney, who inexplicably declined to consent. In a thoughtful opinion Judge Garth reversed the conviction and remanded for determination of whether use immunity should have been conferred under standards explicated in the Court's decision.

* * *

The established content of the Sixth Amendment does not support a claim for defense witness immunity. Traditionally, the Sixth Amendment's Compulsory Process Clause gives the defendant the right to bring his witness to court and have the witness's non-privileged testimony heard, but does not carry with it the additional right to displace a proper claim of privilege, including the privilege against self-incrimination. While the prosecutor may not prevent or discourage a defense witness from testifying, it is difficult to see how the Sixth Amendment of its own force places upon either the prosecutor or the court any affirmative obligation to secure testimony from a defense witness by replacing the protection of the self-incrimination privilege with a grant of use immunity.

Arguably there is a more plausible basis for defense witness immunity in the more general and perhaps developing requirement of basic fairness protected by the Fifth Amendment's Due Process Clause. The appeal to constitutionally protected fairness proceeds from two basic arguments. First, as this Circuit hinted in *Gleason* and *Lang,* unfairness may inhere in some situations because the Government's grant of use immunity to its witnesses affords it an advantage over the defendant's ability to present a defense. Secondly, to the extent that a trial is viewed as a search for the truth, denial of defense witness immunity may in some circumstances unfairly thwart that objective.

The first contention, based on equalizing the powers of the prosecution and the defense, is entirely unpersuasive. A criminal prosecution, unlike a civil trial, is in no sense a symmetrical proceeding. * * *

The system of criminal law administration involves [a] procedural imbalance in favor of the defendant. * * * Viewed in isolation, there is a surface appeal to the equal availability of use immunity for prosecution and defense witnesses. But in the context of criminal investigation and criminal trials, where accuser and accused have inherently different roles, with entirely different powers and rights, equalization is not a sound principle on which to extend any particular procedural device. At a minimum, such a principle will not support a constitutional interpretation of Fifth Amendment fairness.

The second argument, based on the need to pursue the truth, has somewhat greater force. As a general rule the Government is properly obliged to divulge exculpatory evidence. Brady v. Maryland. That principle, however, has heretofore been limited to evidence in the Government's possession and has not been extended to create a Government obligation to assist the defense in extracting from others evidence the Government does not have. Moreover the concept of a trial as a search for the truth has always failed of full realization whenever important facts are shielded from disclosure because of a lawful privilege. The key fact needed to prove a defendant's innocence may be contained in a client's privileged admission to his attorney, or a husband's privileged admission to his wife, as well as in the testimony of a witness protected by the privilege against self-incrimination. Nevertheless, it must be acknowledged that since the advent of immunity statutes, the self-incrimination privilege, unlike any other, can be displaced without any impairment of the legally protected rights of the holder of the privilege. And unlike transactional immunity, use immunity does not improve the legal position of the holder of the privilege; it leaves his legal rights precisely as they were before he testified. However, the grant of use immunity does implicate public interests, and any assessment of a claim for defense witness use immunity must reckon with those public concerns.

In the first place, while the prosecution remains theoretically free under *Kastigar* to prosecute a witness granted use immunity, the obstacles to a successful prosecution can be substantial. The Government has a "heavy burden" to prove that its evidence against the immunized witness has not been obtained as a result of his immunized testimony. While this burden can be met by cataloguing or "freezing" the evidence known to the Government prior to the immunized testimony, that technique is not available when continuing investigations disclose vital evidence after, though not resulting from, the immunized testimony. Moreover, to meet its burden of proving that prosecution of the immunized witness was not benefitted in any way by his immunized testimony the prosecutors most knowledgeable about an investigation may in some circumstances be obliged to forgo any further contact with the witness and arrange for a new team of investigators and prosecutors to pursue the case against him.

Secondly, awareness of the obstacles to successful prosecution of an immunized witness may force the prosecution to curtail its cross-examination of the witness in the case on trial to narrow the scope of the testimony that the witness will later claim tainted his subsequent prosecution. While the witness cannot prevent prosecution and secure an immunity "bath" by broadening the scope of his answers, as he could if testifying under a grant of transactional immunity, his fulsome answers may substantially lessen the likelihood of any successful prosecution.

Finally, there is considerable force to the Government's apprehension that defense witness immunity could create opportunities for undermining the administration of justice by inviting cooperative perjury among law violators. Co-defendants could secure use immunity for each other, and each immunized witness could exonerate his co-defendant at a separate trial by falsely accepting sole responsibility for the crime, secure in the knowledge that his admission could not be used at his own trial for the substantive offense. The threat of a perjury conviction, with penalties frequently far below substantive offenses, could not be relied upon to prevent such tactics. Moreover, this maneuver would substantially undermine the opportunity for joint trials, with consequent expense, delay, and burden upon disinterested witnesses and the judicial system.

How these substantial concerns are to be weighed against the defendant's interest in securing truthful exculpatory testimony through defense witness immunity turns in large part upon whether the balancing of these interests is appropriately a judicial function. The Government suggests it is not, contending that the granting of immunity is pre-eminently a function of the Executive Branch. On the other hand, the judiciary has constitutional responsibilities for the fairness of a trial. Moreover, as Judge Garth has argued in *Smith,* the court can accord use immunity without directly acting in the domain of either the Legislative or Executive Branch. A court can rule that testimony may not be used against a witness without adding any gloss to the use immunity statute or directing the prosecutor to use his statutory authority. Judicially created use immunity, albeit premised on constitutional considerations, was fashioned by the Supreme Court in Murphy v. Waterfront Commission of New York Harbor, and in Simmons v. United States.

However, a court cannot determine whether any constitutional provision requires a judicial grant of use immunity without assessing the implications upon the Executive Branch, both those that flow from a grant of use immunity and those that flow from an adjudication of whether such immunity might be appropriate in a particular case. The concerns previously expressed about the risk to other successful prosecutions are matters normally better assessed by prosecutors than by judges. Surely a court is in no position to weigh the public interest in the comparative worth of prosecuting a defendant or his witness, although if a court decides that immunity is required, it can always leave that ultimate assessment with the prosecutor by advising that trial of the defendant will continue only if the witness's testimony is immunized. But confronting the prosecutor with a choice between terminating prosecution of the defendant or jeopardizing prosecution of the witness is not a task congenial to the judicial function.

Still it may be contended, as Judge Garth did in *Smith,* that a court ought to determine in each case whether the risks to the public interest in conferring defense witness immunity outweigh the needs of the defendant. *Smith* suggests two types of inquiry: whether the prosecutor's opposition to defense witness immunity stems from "the deliberate intention of distorting the fact finding process," or whether the prosecutor can present "strong countervailing interest," to the defendant's need for clearly exculpatory evidence. Either inquiry will propel a trial court into uncharted waters. Focusing upon the prosecutor's intent will often lead to exploration and premature disclosure of the pending status of an investigation against the witness. Moreover, a prosecutor without enough evidence to seek indictment of a witness may legitimately prefer to maintain his option to prosecute on the basis of later information. It cannot fairly be argued, where the prosecutor declines to consent to use immunity, that the absence of present intention to prosecute is evidence of intention to distort the fact-finding process. Alternatively, weighing the "countervailing interest" in not granting defense witness immunity will in all likelihood prove to be as elusive a task as formulating any meaningful standards for the assessment. In the extraordinary fact situation presented by the *Smith* case, where the prosecutor opposing use immunity does not even have jurisdiction to prosecute the witness, the public interest in not granting defense witness immunity appears to be non-existent. But in most situations where defense witness immunity is likely to be sought, some legitimate opposing prosecution interest will exist, and constitutional fairness is not a satisfactory standard against which to assess such interests.

When any novel legal proposition is urged upon a court, there is a natural judicial reluctance to say "never." Indeed, the extraordinary fact situation presented by the *Smith* case illustrates a situation where denial of defense witness immunity can be said to deny the defendant the fair trial guaranteed by the Due Process Clause. Yet it is important to recognize that *Smith* really does not involve a use of the Due Process Clause to balance the public interest in withholding immunity against the defense need for it. In *Smith* the prosecutor with jurisdiction over the witness was willing to grant use immunity. Opposition came from a prosecutor without jurisdiction. This was simply an instance of a prosecutor interfering, for no apparent reason, to suppress evidence that was about to become available to the accused. We have no dispute with the holding in *Smith*. However, in light of all the considerations previously discussed, we find ourselves in fundamental disagreement with the standards outlined in that decision. Without precluding the possibility of some circumstances not now anticipated, we simply do not find in the Due Process Clause a general requirement that defense witness immunity must be ordered whenever it seems fair to grant it. The essential fairness required by the Fifth Amendment guards the defendant against overreaching by the prosecutor, and insulates him against prejudice. It does not create general obligations for prosecutors or courts to obtain evidence protected by lawful privileges.

* * *

We have expressed our thoughts on the issue at some length because we do not agree with Judge Broderick's views on the general availability of defense witness immunity, nor do we wish to see criminal trials regularly interrupted by wide-ranging inquiries concerning the specific pros and cons of defense witness immunity in a particular case. In fact, we think trial judges should summarily reject claims for defense witness immunity whenever the witness for whom immunity is sought is an actual or potential target of prosecution. No hearing should be held to establish such status. The prosecutor need only show that the witness has been indicted or present to the court *in camera* an *ex parte* affidavit setting forth the circumstances that support the prosecutor's suspicion of the witness's criminal activity. No duty is imposed upon the prosecutor; he simply has an option to rely upon the witness's status as an actual or potential target of prosecution to foreclose any inquiry concerning immunity for that witness. If a case should arise where the witness is not an indicted defendant and the prosecutor cannot or prefers not to present any claim that the witness is a potential defendant, and if the defendant on trial demonstrates that the witness's testimony will clearly be material, exculpatory, and not cumulative, it will be time enough to decide whether in those circumstances a court has any proper role with respect to defense witness immunity.

Affirmed.*

* Question: Despite citation to nearly fifty cases, *Turkish* fails to cite or to mention Chambers v. Mississippi. See p. 340. Why?

Chapter VIII

GOVERNMENTAL PRIVILEGES

UNITED STATES v. REYNOLDS

Supreme Court of the United States, 1953.
345 U.S. 1, 73 S.Ct. 528, 97 L.Ed. 727.
[Some of the Court's footnotes are omitted.]

Mr. Chief Justice VINSON delivered the opinion of the Court.

These suits under the Tort Claims Act[1] arise from the death of three civilians in the crash of a B–29 aircraft at Waycross, Georgia, on October 6, 1948. Because an important question of the Government's privilege to resist discovery[2] is involved, we granted certiorari.

The aircraft had taken flight for the purpose of testing secret electronic equipment, with four civilian observers aboard. While aloft, fire broke out in one of the bomber's engines. Six of the nine crew members, and three of the four civilian observers were killed in the crash.

The widows of the three deceased civilian observers brought consolidated suits against the United States. In the pretrial stages the plaintiffs moved, under Rule 34 of the Federal Rules of Civil Procedure,[3] for production of the Air Force's official accident investigation report and the statements of the three surviving crew members, taken in connection with the official investigation. The Government moved to quash the motion, claiming that these matters were privileged against disclosure pursuant to Air Force regulations promulgated under R.S. § 161.[4] The District Judge sustained plaintiffs' motion, holding

1. 28 U.S.C. §§ 1346, 2674, 28 U.S.C.A. §§ 1346, 2674.

2. Federal Rules of Civil Procedure, Rule 34, 28 U.S.C.A.

3. "Rule 34. *Discovery and Production of Documents and Things for Inspection, Copying, or Photographing.* Upon motion of any party showing good cause therefor and upon notice to all other parties, and subject to the provisions of Rule 30(b), the court in which an action is pending may (1) order any party to produce and permit the inspection and copying or photographing, by or on behalf of the moving party, of any designated documents, papers, books, accounts, letters, photographs, objects, or tangible things, not privileged, which constitute or contain evidence relating to any of the matters within the scope of the examination permitted by Rule 26(b) and which are in his possession, custody, or control; or (2) order any party to permit entry upon designated land or other property in his possession or control for the purpose of inspecting, measuring, survey-

ing, or photographing the property or any designated object or operation thereon within the scope of the examination permitted by Rule 26(b). The order shall specify the time, place, and manner of making the inspection and taking the copies and photographs and may prescribe such terms and conditions as are just."

4. 5 U.S.C. § 22, 5 U.S.C.A. § 22:

"The head of each department is authorized to prescribe regulations, not inconsistent with law, for the government of his department, the conduct of its officers and clerks, the distribution and performance of its business, and the custody, use, and preservation of the records, papers, and property appertaining to it."

Air Force Regulation No. 62–7(5)(b) provides:

"Reports of boards of officers, special accident reports, or extracts therefrom will not be furnished or made available to persons outside the authorized chain

that good cause for production had been shown.[5] The claim of privilege under R.S. § 161 was rejected on the premise that the Tort Claims Act, in making the Government liable "in the same manner" as a private individual [6] had waived any privilege based upon executive control over governmental documents.

Shortly after this decision, the District Court received a letter from the Secretary of the Air Force, stating that "it has been determined that it would not be in the public interest to furnish this report. * * *" The court allowed a rehearing on its earlier order, and at the rehearing the Secretary of the Air Force filed a formal "Claim of Privilege." This document repeated the prior claim based generally on R.S. § 161, and then stated that the Government further objected to production of the documents "for the reason that the aircraft in question, together with the personnel on board, were engaged in a highly secret mission of the Air Force." An affidavit of the Judge Advocate General, United States Air Force, was also filed with the court, which asserted that the demanded material could not be furnished "without seriously hampering national security, flying safety and the development of highly technical and secret military equipment." The same affidavit offered to produce the three surviving crew members, without cost, for examination by the plaintiffs. The witnesses would be allowed to refresh their memories from any statement made by them to the Air Force, and authorized to testify as to all matters except those of a "classified nature."

The District Court ordered the Government to produce the documents in order that the court might determine whether they contained privileged matter. The Government declined, so the court entered an order, under Rule 37(b)(2)(i),[7] that the facts on the issue of negligence would be taken as established in plaintiffs' favor. After a hearing to determine damages, final judgment was entered for the plaintiffs. The Court of Appeals affirmed, both as to the showing of good cause for production of the documents, and as to the ultimate disposition of the case as a consequence of the Government's refusal to produce the documents.

We have had broad propositions pressed upon us for decision. On behalf of the Government it has been urged that the executive depart-

---

of command without the specific approval of the Secretary of the Air Force."

5. 10 F.R.D. 468.

6. 28 U.S.C. § 2674, 28 U.S.C.A. § 2674:

"The United States shall be liable, respecting the provisions of this title relating to tort claims, in the same manner and to the same extent as a private individual under like circumstances, but shall not be liable for interest prior to judgment or for punitive damages."

7. "Rule 37. *Refusal to Make Discovery: Consequences*

* * *

"(b) Failure to Comply With Order.

* * *

"(2) *Other Consequences.* If any party or an officer or managing agent of a party refuses to obey * * * an order made under Rule 34 to produce any document * * *, the court may make such orders in regard to the refusal as are just, and among others the following:

"(i) An order that the matters regarding which the questions were asked, or the character or description of the thing or land, or the contents of the paper, or the physical or mental condition of the party, or any other designated facts shall be taken to be established for the purposes of the action in accordance with the claim of the party obtaining the order; * * *"

ment heads have power to withhold any documents in their custody from judicial view if they deem it to be in the public interest.[9] Respondents have asserted that the executive's power to withhold documents was waived by the Tort Claims Act. Both positions have constitutional overtones which we find it unnecessary to pass upon, there being a narrower ground for decision.

The Tort Claims Act expressly makes the Federal Rules of Civil Procedure applicable to suits against the United States. The judgment in this case imposed liability upon the Government by operation of Rule 37, for refusal to produce documents under Rule 34. Since Rule 34 compels production only of matters "not privileged," the essential question is whether there was a valid claim of privilege under the Rule. We hold that there was, and that, therefore, the judgment below subjected the United States to liability on terms to which Congress did not consent by the Tort Claims Act.

We think it should be clear that the term "not privileged" as used in Rule 34, refers to "privileges" as that term is understood in the law of evidence. When the Secretary of the Air Force lodged his formal "Claim of Privilege," he attempted therein to invoke the privilege against revealing military secrets, a privilege which is well established in the law of evidence. The existence of the privilege is conceded by the court below, and, indeed, by the most outspoken critics of governmental claims to privilege.

Judicial experience with the privilege which protects military and state secrets has been limited in this country. English experience has been more extensive, but still relatively slight compared with other evidentiary privileges. Nevertheless, the principles which control the application of the privilege emerge quite clearly from the available precedents. The privilege belongs to the Government and must be asserted by it; it can neither be claimed nor waived by a private party. It is not to be lightly invoked. There must be a formal claim of privilege, lodged by the head of the department which has control over the matter, after actual personal consideration by that officer. The court itself must determine whether the circumstances are appropriate for the claim of privilege, and yet do so without forcing a disclosure of the very thing the privilege is designed to protect. The latter requirement is the only one which presents real difficulty. As to it, we find it helpful to draw upon judicial experience in dealing with an analogous privilege, the privilege against self-incrimination.

The privilege against self-incrimination presented the courts with a similar sort of problem. Too much judicial inquiry into the claim of privilege would force disclosure of the thing the privilege was meant to protect, while a complete abandonment of judicial control would lead to intolerable abuses. Indeed, in the earlier stages of judicial experience with the problem, both extremes were advocated, some saying that the bare assertion by the witness must be taken as conclusive, and others

---

9. While claim of executive power to suppress documents is based more immediately upon R.S. § 161 (see supra, note 4), the roots go much deeper. It is said that R.S. § 161 is only a legislative recognition of an inherent executive power which is protected in the constitutional system of separation of power.

saying that the witness should be required to reveal the matter behind his claim of privilege to the judge for verification. Neither extreme prevailed, and a sound formula of compromise was developed. This formula received authoritative expression in this country as early as the Burr trial. There are differences in phraseology, but in substance it is agreed that the court must be satisfied from all the evidence and circumstances, and "from the implications of the question, in the setting in which it is asked, that a responsive answer to the question or an explanation of why it cannot be answered might be dangerous because injurious exposure could result." Hoffman v. United States. If the court is so satisfied, the claim of the privilege will be accepted without requiring further disclosure.

Regardless of how it is articulated, some like formula of compromise must be applied here. Judicial control over the evidence in a case cannot be abdicated to the caprice of executive officers. Yet we will not go so far as to say that the court may automatically require a complete disclosure to the judge before the claim of privilege will be accepted in any case. It may be possible to satisfy the court, from all the circumstances of the case, that there is a reasonable danger that compulsion of the evidence will expose military matters which, in the interest of national security, should not be divulged. When this is the case, the occasion for the privilege is appropriate, and the court should not jeopardize the security which the privilege is meant to protect by insisting upon an examination of the evidence, even by the judge alone, in chambers.

In the instant case we cannot escape judicial notice that this is a time of vigorous preparation for national defense. Experience in the past war has made it common knowledge that air power is one of the most potent weapons in our scheme of defense, and that newly developing electronic devices have greatly enhanced the effective use of air power. It is equally apparent that these electronic devices must be kept secret if their full military advantage is to be exploited in the national interest. On the record before the trial court it appeared that this accident occurred to a military plane which had gone aloft to test secret electronic equipment. Certainly there was a reasonable danger that the accident investigation report would contain references to the secret electronic equipment which was the primary concern of the mission.

Of course, even with this information before him, the trial judge was in no position to decide that the report was privileged until there had been a formal claim of privilege. Thus it was entirely proper to rule initially that petitioner had shown probable cause for discovery of the documents. Thereafter, when the formal claim of privilege was filed by the Secretary of the Air Force, under circumstances indicating a reasonable possibility that military secrets were involved, there was certainly a sufficient showing of privilege to cut off further demand for the document on the showing of necessity for its compulsion that had then been made.

In each case, the showing of necessity which is made will determine how far the court should probe in satisfying itself that the occasion for invoking the privilege is appropriate. Where there is a strong showing of necessity, the claim of privilege should not be lightly accepted, but even the most compelling necessity cannot overcome the claim of privilege if the court is ultimately satisfied that military secrets are at stake.[26] *A fortiori*, where necessity is dubious, a formal claim of privilege, made under the circumstances of this case, will have to prevail. Here, necessity was greatly minimized by an available alternative, which might have given respondents the evidence to make out their case without forcing a showdown on the claim of privilege. By their failure to pursue that alternative, respondents have posed the privilege question for decision with the formal claim of privilege set against a dubious showing of necessity.

There is nothing to suggest that the electronic equipment, in this case, had any causal connection with the accident. Therefore, it should be possible for respondents to adduce the essential facts as to causation without resort to material touching upon military secrets. Respondents were given a reasonable opportunity to do just that, when petitioner formally offered to make the surviving crew members available for examination. We think that offer should have been accepted.

Respondents have cited us to those cases in the criminal field, where it has been held that the Government can invoke its evidentiary privileges only at the price of letting the defendant go free. The rationale of the criminal cases is that, since the Government which prosecutes an accused also has the duty to see that justice is done, it is unconscionable to allow it to undertake prosecution and then invoke its governmental privileges to deprive the accused of anything which might be material to his defense. Such rationale has no application in a civil forum where the Government is not the moving party, but is a defendant only on terms to which it has consented.

The decision of the Court of Appeals is reversed and the case will be remanded to the District Court for further proceedings consistent with the views expressed in this opinion.

Reversed and remanded.

Mr. Justice BLACK, Mr. Justice FRANKFURTER, and Mr. Justice JACKSON dissented.

EVIDENTIARY PRIVILEGE OF "STATE SECRETS" IN CONTRACT ACTION

55 Colum.L.Rev. 570–573 (1955).*

Defendant contracted to manufacture arming mechanisms for the United States Army. Plaintiff with whom he had subcontracted

---

26. See Totten v. United States, where the very subject matter of the action, a contract to perform espionage, was a matter of state secret. The action was dismissed on the pleadings without ever reaching the question of evidence, since it was so obvious that the action should never prevail over the privilege.

* Copyright, 1955 by the Trustees of the Columbia Law Review.

brought an action for breach of contract. Defendant moved to dismiss or, in the alternative, to stay all proceedings on the ground that prosecution and defense of the action would require disclosure of classified information in violation of the Espionage Act. *Held,* motions denied. Proceedings may continue along their ordinary course and the court if necessary will, at the appropriate time, take measures to ensure that national security is not endangered.

The courts have long recognized a privilege against disclosure of information affecting national security in essentially private litigation as well as when the government is a party. The basic policy underlying the decisions granting protection to state secrets is the paramount interest of the nation in safeguarding its military and diplomatic position, even to the subordination of individual interests.

Although the government has not raised the state secrets privilege while acting as plaintiff or prosecutor, it has asserted other privileges of nondisclosure resting upon different grounds. Ordinarily in these situations, however, the courts have not sustained the privilege where the defendant requested material documents in the government's possession. Apparently, the rationale of these decisions is that it is unconscionable to allow the government to initiate an action and then invoke a privilege that might deprive an accused of anything material to his defense. Although one case suggested that the government introduce secondary evidence in order to prevent disclosure, generally the courts have accommodated the conflicting interests of individuals and the government in favor of individuals. Thus, if the court finds that the information requested is material, the government is in the dilemma of either having to risk unsuccessful prosecution or being forced to disclose privileged information.

The government as defendant has not been estopped from raising the states secrets privilege by virtue of its consent to be sued. In United States v. Reynolds, the Supreme Court distinguished the role of government as prosecutor and reversed the trial court's finding of certain facts in favor of plaintiffs after the government had refused to produce documents in conformity with an order of the court. The Court noted the existence of international tension and emphasized that plaintiff had not demonstrated sufficient necessity to justify an order requiring initial disclosure to the judge of information involving ostensibly secret electronic data.

In private litigation the question of whether information comes within the states secrets privilege has been raised by motion or objection of a private party or by the court itself. The government's position in the matter, which may be stated by affidavit of the cognizant executive head—whether the government intervenes as a party or not—is apparently the crucial factor in determining whether the privilege is to be sustained. Thus, if the court has evidence that the government does not object to the introduction of documents, a refusal to disclose may subject the objector to contempt proceedings.

Once a claim of privilege is properly made by the appropriate executive department head, the English view appears to be that wheth-

er there is a state secret involved is not justiciable. This view, granting
the executive almost unlimited discretion, has been defended on the
grounds that showing the information to the court may defeat the very
secrecy required and that the court lacks the expertise that the executive possesses for a sound determination of the necessity for secrecy.
Reynolds, while asserting the justiciable nature of the question, formu-
lates a rule which considerably limits the court's discretion. If the
government makes a showing that there is a reasonable danger that the
evidence sought would expose military secrets, the privilege will be
sustained without disclosure to the court. Although, theoretically, the
showing required would be balanced against the opposing party's need,
practically it appears that the government's burden of persuasion is
relatively slight since the executive claim of secrecy is likely to be
accepted on its face. Consequently, almost any assertion of privilege by
the government will foreclose a private party's ability to litigate successfully.

The instant case in some measure reasserts judicial control over
the privilege when a private party makes the claim, and the government apparently has not reviewed the question of secrecy in the light of
the impending litigation. The decision does not require a disclosure of
state secrets since production of classified documents or information
was not requested by the opposing party or by the court. The court
recognized that unauthorized disclosure by defendant would violate the
espionage laws, but it apparently hoped to avoid the issue by taking a
course of action which would stimulate the government to declassify
the evidence, intervene in the action or arrange for a settlement
between the parties. The court also reasoned that a dismissal might
unjustly deprive plaintiff of his rights by precluding relief if declassifi-
cation did not occur until after expiration of the statute of limitations
and would encourage other litigants in the defendant's position to
breach contracts and seek refuge under a privilege designed for the
benefit of the state.

Although the prematureness of defendant's motions enabled the
court to adjust the competing interests of nation and litigants, it is
clear that the problem may be merely postponed. If plaintiff had
utilized discovery mechanisms the court would have been faced with
the issue of compulsion of the requested information. Assuming the
court determines that state secrets are not involved and orders production, a refusal risks possible contempt of court or loss of the suit
whereas compliance may entail violation of the espionage laws and
exposure of the nation's secrets. A dismissal by the court after a
decision that state secrets are involved may cause an injustice to a
deserving plaintiff. Present procedures seem inadequate to equitably
adjust the interests of nation and individual both in ascertaining the
presence of state secrets and in disposing of the controversy once it is
decided they are involved.

Perhaps, in the sub-contract situation, a solution might be reached
along the following lines: A federal statute, based upon the power of
the nation to protect itself, could require that sub-contracts let under a
government prime contract and classified as affecting the national

security contain a clause requiring the parties to arbitrate all disputes arising under the contract, the dispute would, however, only proceed to arbitration if the appropriate executive department head certified that there was a continued need for secrecy. If the executive declassified the contract or took no action within a reasonable time, the information would be deemed unprivileged and the clause inapplicable; the disputants would be free to litigate in the courts. Otherwise, an arbitrator would be chosen by the parties from a list provided by the executive department concerned, or if no choice could be agreed upon one would be designated by the department. The parties would be represented by counsel of their choice, or if necessary, because of security considerations, by appointed counsel. The arbitrator would be empowered to enter a default award after prescribed notice to a recalcitrant party. An award would be confirmable in any federal district court. Although the arbitrator's determination of the scope of the arbitration clause and the merits of the controversy would be final, an award would not be enforced if (1) the subject of the dispute had been declassified prior to arbitration proceedings, (2) reasonable notice was not given to a party against whom a default award was taken or, (3) the award was procured by means of fraud or corruption of the arbitrator.

At the minimum the proposal would ensure that individual interests receive a disposition on the merits while preserving the nation's interest in secrecy. Although parties would have to accept an arbitrator's disposition of the controversy with few of the safeguards of an independent judiciary, it is submitted that while the adjustment of individual and governmental interests requires something more than complete denial of relief to deserving litigants an effective security system precludes full judicial inquiry.

UNITED STATES v. NIXON

Supreme Court of the United States, 1974.
418 U.S. 683, 94 S.Ct. 3090, 41 L.Ed.2d 1039.

Mr. Chief Justice BURGER delivered the opinion of the Court.

* * *

On March 1, 1974, a grand jury of the United States District Court for the District of Columbia returned an indictment charging seven named individuals [3] with various offenses, including conspiracy to defraud the United States and to obstruct justice. Although he was not designated as such in the indictment, the grand jury named the President, among others, as an unindicted coconspirator. On April 18, 1974, upon motion of the Special Prosecutor, see n. 8, infra, a subpoena *duces tecum* was issued pursuant to Rule 17(c) to the President by the United States District Court and made returnable on May 2, 1974. This subpoena required the production, in advance of the September 9

---

3. The seven defendants were John N. Mitchell, H.R. Haldeman, John D. Ehrlichman, Charles W. Colson, Robert C. Mardian, Kenneth W. Parkinson, and Gordon Strachan. Each had occupied either a position of responsibility on the White House staff or the Committee for the Re-election of the President. Colson entered a guilty plea on another charge and is no longer a defendant.

trial date, of certain tapes, memoranda, papers, transcripts or other writings relating to certain precisely identified meetings between the President and others. The Special Prosecutor was able to fix the time, place, and persons present at these discussions because the White House daily logs and appointment records had been delivered to him. On April 30, the President publicly released edited transcripts of 43 conversations; portions of 20 conversations subject to subpoena in the present case were included. On May 1, 1974, the President's counsel, filed a "special appearance" and a motion to quash the subpoena under Rule 17(c). This motion was accompanied by a formal claim of privilege. At a subsequent hearing, further motions to expunge the grand jury's action naming the President as an unindicted coconspirator and for protective orders against the disclosure of that information were filed or raised orally by counsel for the President.

On May 20, 1974, the District Court denied the motion to quash and the motions to expunge and for protective orders. It further ordered "the President or any subordinate officer, official, or employee with custody or control of the documents or objects subpoenaed," to deliver to the District Court, on or before May 31, 1974, the originals of all subpoenaed items, as well as an index and analysis of those items, together with tape copies of those portions of the subpoenaed recordings for which transcripts had been released to the public by the President on April 30. * * *

* * *

[The Court held that the order of the district judge was a final appealable order, despite the fact that no contempt adjudication had been made; that the matter was within the Supreme Court's jurisdiction, despite the fact that the two contending parties, the President and the Special Prosecutor, were both within the executive branch; and that the subpoena in question met the requirements of specificity of Rule 17 of the Federal Rules of Criminal Procedure. Then, it moved on to the privilege issue.]

IV

THE CLAIM OF PRIVILEGE

A

* * * [W]e turn to the claim that the subpoena should be quashed because it demands "confidential conversations between a President and his close advisors that it would be inconsistent with the public interest to produce." The first contention is a broad claim that the separation of powers doctrine precludes judicial review of a President's claim of privilege. The second contention is that if he does not prevail on the claim of absolute privilege, the court should hold as a matter of constitutional law that the privilege prevails over the subpoena *duces tecum.*

In the performance of assigned constitutional duties each branch of the Government must initially interpret the Constitution, and the interpretation of its powers by any branch is due great respect from the others. The President's counsel, as we have noted, reads the Constitution as providing an absolute privilege of confidentiality for all Presidential communications. Many decisions of this Court, however, have unequivocally reaffirmed the holding of Marbury v. Madison, that "[i]t is emphatically the province and duty of the judicial department to say what the law is."

* * *

* * * Notwithstanding the deference each branch must accord the others, the "judicial Power of the United States" vested in the federal courts by Art. III, § 1, of the Constitution can no more be shared with the Executive Branch than the Chief Executive, for example, can share with the Judiciary the veto power, or the Congress share with the Judiciary the power to override a Presidential veto. Any other conclusion would be contrary to the basic concept of separation of powers and the checks and balances that flow from the scheme of a tripartite government. * * *

B

In support of his claim of absolute privilege, the President's counsel urges two grounds, one of which is common to all governments and one of which is peculiar to our system of separation of powers. The first ground is the valid need for protection of communications between high Government officials and those who advise and assist them in the performance of their manifold duties; the importance of this confidentiality is too plain to require further discussion. Human experience teaches that those who expect public dissemination of their remarks may well temper candor with a concern for appearances and for their own interests to the detriment of the decisionmaking process.[15] Whatever the nature of the privilege of confidentiality of Presidential communications in the exercise of Art. II powers, the privilege can be said to derive from the supremacy of each branch within its own assigned area of constitutional duties. Certain powers and privileges flow from the nature of enumerated powers;[16] the protection of the confidentiality of Presidential communications has similar constitutional underpinnings.

The second ground asserted by the President's counsel in support of the claim of absolute privilege rests on the doctrine of separation of

---

15. There is nothing novel about governmental confidentiality. The meetings of the Constitutional Convention in 1787 were conducted in complete privacy. 1 M. Farrand, The Records of the Federal Convention of 1787, pp. xi–xxv (1911). Moreover, all records of those meetings were sealed for more than 30 years after the Convention. See 3 Stat. 475, 15th Cong., 1st Sess., Res. 8 (1818). Most of the Framers acknowledge that without secrecy no constitution of the kind that was developed could have been written. C. Warren, The Making of the Constitution 134–139 (1937).

16. The Special Prosecutor argues that there is no provision in the Constitution for a Presidential privilege as to the President's communications corresponding to the privilege of Members of Congress under the Speech or Debate Clause. But the silence of the Constitution on this score is not dispositive. "The rule of constitutional interpretation announced in McCulloch v. Maryland, that that which was reasonably appropriate and relevant to the exercise of a granted power was to be considered as accompanying the grant, has been so universally applied that it suffices merely to state it." Marshall v. Gordon.

powers. Here it is argued that the independence of the Executive
Branch within its own sphere, insulates a President from a judicial
subpoena in an ongoing criminal prosecution, and thereby protects
confidential Presidential communications.

However, neither the doctrine of separation of powers, nor the need
for confidentiality of high-level communications, without more, can
sustain an absolute, unqualified Presidential privilege of immunity
from judicial process under all circumstances. The President's need for
complete candor and objectivity from advisers calls for great deference
from the courts. However, when the privilege depends solely on the
broad, undifferentiated claim of public interest in the confidentiality of
such conversations, a confrontation with other values arises. Absent a
claim of need to protect military, diplomatic, or sensitive national
security secrets, we find it difficult to accept the argument that even
the very important interest in confidentiality of Presidential communications is significantly diminished by production of such material for *in
camera* inspection with all the protection that a district court will be
obliged to provide.

The impediment that an absolute, unqualified privilege would place
in the way of the primary constitutional duty of the Judicial Branch to
do justice in criminal prosecutions would plainly conflict with the
function of the courts under Art. III. In designing the structure of our
Government and dividing and allocating the sovereign power among
three co-equal branches, the Framers of the Constitution sought to
provide a comprehensive system, but the separate powers were not
intended to operate with absolute independence.

> "While the Constitution diffuses power the better to secure
> liberty, it also contemplates that practice will integrate the
> dispersed powers into a workable government. It enjoins upon
> its branches separateness but interdependence, autonomy but
> reciprocity." Youngstown Sheet & Tube Co. v. Sawyer (Jack-
> son, J., concurring).

To read the Art. II powers of the President as providing an absolute
privilege as against a subpoena essential to enforcement of criminal
statutes on no more than a generalized claim of the public interest in
confidentiality of nonmilitary and nondiplomatic discussions would
upset the constitutional balance of "a workable government" and
gravely impair the role of the courts under Art. III.

C

Since we conclude that the legitimate needs of the judicial process
may outweigh Presidential privilege, it is necessary to resolve those
competing interests in a manner that preserves the essential functions
of each branch. The right and indeed the duty to resolve that question
does not free the Judiciary from according high respect to the representations made on behalf of the President.

The expectation of a President to the confidentiality of his conversations and correspondence, like the claim of confidentiality of judicial
deliberations, for example, has all the values to which we accord

deference for the privacy of all citizens and, added to those values, is the necessity for protection of the public interest in candid, objective, and even blunt or harsh opinions in Presidential decision-making. A President and those who assist him must be free to explore alternatives in the process of shaping policies and making decisions and to do so in a way many would be unwilling to express except privately. These are the considerations justifying a presumptive privilege for Presidential communications. The privilege is fundamental to the operation of Government and inextricably rooted in the separation of powers under the Constitution.[17] In Nixon v. Sirica, the Court of Appeals held that such Presidential communications are "presumptively privileged" and this position is accepted by both parties in the present litigation. We agree with Mr. Chief Justice Marshall's observation, therefore, that "[i]n no case of this kind would a court be required to proceed against the president as against an ordinary individual."

But this presumptive privilege must be considered in light of our historic commitment to the rule of law. This is nowhere more profoundly manifest than in our view that "the twofold aim [of criminal justice] is that guilt shall not escape or innocence suffer." We have elected to employ an adversary system of criminal justice in which the parties contest all issues before a court of law. The need to develop all relevant facts in the adversary system is both fundamental and comprehensive. The ends of criminal justice would be defeated if judgments were to be founded on a partial or speculative presentation of the facts. The very integrity of the judicial system and public confidence in the system depend on full disclosure of all the facts, within the framework of the rules of evidence. To ensure that justice is done, it is imperative to the function of courts that compulsory process be available for the production of evidence needed either by the prosecution or by the defense.

Only recently the Court restated the ancient proposition of law, albeit in the context of a grand jury inquiry rather than a trial,

> "that 'the public * * * has a right to every man's evidence,' except for those persons protected by a constitutional, common-law, or statutory privilege, United States v. Bryan, 339 U.S. [323, 331, 70 S.Ct. 724, 730 (1949)]; Blackmer v. United States, 284 U.S. 421, 438 [52 S.Ct. 252, 76 L.Ed. 375] (1932) * * *" Branzburg v. Hayes. United States, 408 U.S. 665, 688 [92 S.Ct. 2646, 33 L.Ed.2d 626] (1972).

The privileges referred to by the Court are designed to protect weighty and legitimate competing interests. Thus, the Fifth Amendment to the Constitution provides that no man "shall be compelled in any criminal case to be a witness against himself." And, generally, an attorney or a priest may not be required to disclose what has been revealed in professional confidence. These and other interests are recognized in

17. "Freedom of communication vital to fulfillment of the arms of wholesome relationships is obtained only by removing the specter of compelled disclosure. * * * [G]overnment * * * needs open but protected channels for the kind of plain talk that is essential to the quality of its functioning." Carl Zeiss Stiftung v. V.E.B. Carl Zeiss, Jena.

law by privileges against forced disclosure, established in the Constitution, by statute, or at common law. Whatever their origins, these exceptions to the demand for every man's evidence are not lightly created nor expansively construed, for they are in derogation of the search for truth.[18]

In this case the President challenges a subpoena served on him as a third party requiring the production of materials for use in a criminal prosecution; he does so on the claim that he has a privilege against disclosure of confidential communications. He does not place his claim of privilege on the ground they are military or diplomatic secrets. As to these areas of Art. II duties the courts have traditionally shown the utmost deference to Presidential responsibilities. In C. & S. Air Lines v. Waterman S.S. Corp., dealing with Presidential authority involving foreign policy considerations, the Court said:

> "The President, both as Commander-in-Chief and as the Nation's organ for foreign affairs, has available intelligence services whose reports are not and ought not to be published to the world. It would be intolerable that courts, without the relevant information, should review and perhaps nullify actions of the Executive taken on information properly held secret."

In United States v. Reynolds, dealing with a claimant's demand for evidence in a Tort Claims Act case against the Government, the Court said:

> "It may be possible to satisfy the court, from all the circumstances of the case, that there is a reasonable danger that compulsion of the evidence will expose military matters which, in the interest of national security, should not be divulged. When this is the case, the occasion for the privilege is appropriate, and the court should not jeopardize the security which the privilege is meant to protect by insisting upon an examination of the evidence, even by the judge alone, in chambers."

No case of the Court, however, has extended this high degree of deference to a President's generalized interest in confidentiality. Nowhere in the Constitution, as we have noted earlier, is there any explicit reference to a privilege of confidentiality, yet to the extent this interest relates to the effective discharge of a President's powers, it is constitutionally based.

The right to the production of all evidence at a criminal trial similarly has constitutional dimensions. The Sixth Amendment explicitly confers upon every defendant in a criminal trial the right "to be confronted with the witnesses against him" and "to have compulsory process for obtaining witnesses in his favor. Moreover, the Fifth

---

18. Because of the key role of the testimony of witnesses in the judicial process, courts have historically been cautious about privileges. Mr. Justice Frankfurter, dissenting in Elkins v. United States, said of this: "Limitations are properly placed upon the operation of this general principle only to the very limited extent that permitting a refusal to testify or excluding relevant evidence has a public good transcending the normally predominant principle of utilizing all rational means for ascertaining truth."

Amendment also guarantees that no person shall be deprived of liberty without due process of law. It is the manifest duty of the courts to vindicate those guarantees, and to accomplish that it is essential that all relevant and admissible evidence be produced.

In this case we must weigh the importance of the general privilege of confidentiality of Presidential communications in performance of the President's responsibilities against the inroads of such a privilege on the fair administration of criminal justice.[19] The interest in preserving confidentiality is weighty indeed and entitled to great respect. However, we cannot conclude that advisers will be moved to temper the candor of their remarks by the infrequent occasions of disclosure because of the possibility that such conversations will be called for in the context of a criminal prosecution.[20]

On the other hand, the allowance of the privilege to withhold evidence that is demonstrably relevant in a criminal trial would cut deeply into the guarantee of due process of law and gravely impair the basic function of the courts. A President's acknowledged need for confidentiality in the communications of his office is general in nature, whereas the constitutional need for production of relevant evidence in a criminal proceeding is specific and central to the fair adjudication of a particular criminal case in the administration of justice. Without access to specific facts a criminal prosecution may be totally frustrated. The President's broad interest in confidentiality of communications will not be vitiated by disclosure of a limited number of conversations preliminarily shown to have some bearing on the pending criminal cases.

We conclude that when the ground for asserting privilege as to subpoenaed materials sought for use in a criminal trial is based only on the generalized interest in confidentiality, it cannot prevail over the fundamental demands of due process of law in the fair administration of criminal justice. The generalized assertion of privilege must yield to the demonstrated, specific, need for evidence in a pending criminal trial.

19. We are not here concerned with the balance between the President's generalized interest in confidentiality and the need for relevant evidence in civil litigation, nor with that between the confidentiality interest and congressional demands for information, nor with the President's interest in preserving state secrets. We address only the conflict between the President's assertion of a generalized privilege of confidentiality and the constitutional need for relevant evidence in criminal trials.

20. Mr. Justice Cardozo made this point in an analogous context, speaking for a unanimous Court in Clark v. United States, he emphasized the importance of maintaining the secrecy of the deliberations of a petit jury in a criminal case. "Freedom of debate might be stifled and independence of thought checked if jurors were made to feel that their arguments and ballots were to be freely published to the world." Nonetheless, the Court also recognized that isolated inroads on confidentiality designed to serve the paramount need of the criminal law would not vitiate the interests served by secrecy:

A juror of integrity and reasonable firmness will not fear to speak his mind if the confidences of debate are barred to the ears of mere impertinence or malice. He will not expect to be shielded against the disclosure of his conduct in the event that there is evidence reflecting upon his honor. The chance that now and then there may be found some timid soul who will take counsel of his fears and give way to their repressive power is too remote and shadowy to shape the course of justice."

D

We have earlier determined that the District Court did not err in authorizing the issuance of the subpoena. If a President concludes that compliance with a subpoena would be injurious to the public interest he may properly, as was done here, invoke a claim of privilege on the return of the subpoena. Upon receiving a claim of privilege from the Chief Executive, it became the further duty of the District Court to treat the subpoenaed material as presumptively privileged and to require the Special Prosecutor to demonstrate that the Presidential material was "essential to the justice of the [pending criminal] case." United States v. Burr. Here the District Court treated the material as presumptively privileged, proceeded to find that the Special Prosecutor had made a sufficient showing to rebut the presumption, and ordered an *in camera* examination of the subpoenaed material. On the basis of our examination of the record we are unable to conclude that the District Court erred in ordering the inspection. Accordingly we affirm the order of the District Court that subpoenaed materials be transmitted to that court. We now turn to the important question of the District Court's responsibilities in conducting the *in camera* examination of Presidential materials or communications delivered under the compulsion of the subpoena *duces tecum*.

E

Enforcement of the subpoena *duces tecum* was stayed pending this Court's resolution of the issues raised by the petitions for certiorari. Those issues now having been disposed of, the matter of implementation will rest with the District Court. "[T]he guard, furnished to [the President] to protect him from being harassed by vexatious and unnecessary subpoenas, is to be looked for in the conduct of a [district] court after those subpoenas have issued; not in any circumstance, which is to precede their being issued." United States v. Burr, supra. Statements that meet the test of admissibility and relevance must be isolated; all other material must be excised. At this stage the District Court is not limited to representations of the Special Prosecutor as to the evidence sought by the subpoena; the material will be available to the District Court. It is elementary that *in camera* inspection of evidence is always a procedure calling for scrupulous protection against any release or publication of material not found by the court, at that stage, probably admissible in evidence and relevant to the issues of the trial for which it is sought. That being true of an ordinary situation, it is obvious that the District Court has a very heavy responsibility to see to it that Presidential conversations, which are either not relevant or not admissible, are accorded that high degree of respect due the President of the United States. Mr. Chief Justice Marshall, sitting as a trial judge in the *Burr* case, supra, was extraordinarily careful to point out that

> "[i]n no case of this kind would a court be required to proceed against the president as against an ordinary individual."

Marshall's statement cannot be read to mean in any sense that a President is above the law, but relates to the singularly unique role under Art. II of a President's communications and activities, related to the performance of duties under that Article. Moreover, a President's communications and activities encompass a vastly wider range of sensitive material than would be true of any "ordinary individual." It is therefore necessary [21] in the public interest to afford Presidential confidentiality the greatest protection consistent with the fair administration of justice. The need for confidentiality even as to idle conversations with associates in which casual reference might be made concerning political leaders within the country or foreign statesmen is too obvious to call for further treatment. We have no doubt that the District Judge will at all times accord to Presidential records that high degree of deference suggested in United States v. Burr, supra and will discharge his responsibility to see to it that until released to the Special Prosecutor no *in camera* material is revealed to anyone. This burden applies with even greater force to excised material; once the decision is made to excise, the material is restored to its privileged status and should be returned under seal to its lawful custodian.

* * *

Affirmed.

Mr. Justice REHNQUIST took no part in the consideration or decision of these cases.

———

See California Evidence Code § 1040.

ROVIARO v. UNITED STATES

Supreme Court of the United States, 1957.
353 U.S. 53, 77 S.Ct. 623, 1 L.Ed.2d 639.

Mr. Justice BURTON delivered the opinion of the Court.

This case concerns a conviction for violation of the Narcotic Drugs Import and Export Act, as amended. The principal issue is whether the United States District Court committed reversible error when it allowed the Government to refuse to disclose the identity of an undercover employee who had taken a material part in bringing about the possession of certain drugs by the accused, had been present with the accused at the occurrence of the alleged crime, and might be a material witness as to whether the accused knowingly, transported the drugs as charged. For the reasons hereafter stated, we hold that, under the circumstances here present, this was reversible error.

In 1955, in the Northern District of Illinois, petitioner, Albert Roviaro, was indicted on two counts by a federal grand jury. The first count charged that on August 12, 1954, at Chicago, Illinois, he sold

---

21. When the subpoenaed material is delivered to the District Judge *in camera*, questions may arise as to the excising of parts, and it lies within the discretion of that court to seek the aid of the Special Prosecutor and the President's counsel for *in camera* consideration of the validity of particular excisions, whether the basis of excision is relevancy or admissibility or under such cases as United States v. Reynolds, or C. & S. Air Lines v. Waterman S.S. Corp.

heroin to one "John Doe" in violation of 26 U.S.C. § 2554(a), 26 U.S. C.A. § 2554(a). The second charged that on the same date and in the same city he "did then and there fraudulently and knowingly receive, conceal, buy and facilitate the transportation and concealment after importation of * * * heroin, knowing, the same to be imported into the United States contrary to law; in violation of Section 174, Title 21, United States Code."

Before trial, petitioner moved for a bill of particulars requesting, among other things, the name, address and occupation of "John Doe." The Government objected on the ground that John Doe was an informer and that his identity was privileged. The motion was denied.

Petitioner, who was represented by counsel, waived a jury and was tried by the District Court. During the trial John Doe's part in the charged transaction was described by government witnesses, and counsel for petitioner, in cross-examining them, sought repeatedly to learn John Doe's identity. The court declined to permit this cross-examination and John Doe was not produced, identified, or otherwise made available. Petitioner was found guilty on both counts and was sentenced to two years' imprisonment and a fine of $5 on each count, the sentences to run concurrently. The Court of Appeals sustained the conviction, holding that the concurrent sentence was supported by the conviction on Count 2 and that the trial court had not abused its discretion in denying petitioner's requests for disclosure of Doe's identity. * * *

At the trial, the Government relied on the testimony of two federal narcotics agents, Durham and Fields, and two Chicago police officers, Bryson and Sims, each of whom knew petitioner by sight. On the night of August 12, 1954, these four officers met at 75th Street and Prairie Avenue in Chicago with an informer described only as John Doe. Doe and his Cadillac car were searched and no narcotics were found. Bryson secreted himself in the trunk of Doe's Cadillac, taking with him a device with which to raise the trunk lid from the inside. Doe then drove the Cadillac to 70th Place and St. Lawrence Avenue, followed by Durham in one government car and Field and Sims in another. After an hour's wait at about 11 o'clock, petitioner arrived in a Pontiac, accompanied by an unidentified man. Petitioner immediately entered Doe's Cadillac, taking a front seat beside Doe. They then proceeded by a circuitous route to 74th Street near Champlain Avenue. Both government cars trailed the Cadillac but only the one driven by Durham managed to follow it to 74th Street. When the Cadillac came to a stop on 74th Street, Durham stepped out of his car onto the sidewalk and saw petitioner alight from the Cadillac about 100 feet away. Durham saw petitioner walk a few feet to a nearby tree, pick up a small package, return to the open right front door of the Cadillac, make a motion as if depositing the package in the car, and then waive to Doe and walk away. Durham went immediately to the Cadillac and recovered a package from the floor. He signaled to Bryson to come out of the trunk and then walked down the street in time to see petitioner reenter the Pontiac, parked nearby, and ride away.

Meanwhile, Bryson, concealed in the trunk of the Cadillac, had heard a conversation between John Doe and petitioner after the latter had entered the car. He heard petitioner greet John Doe and direct him where to drive. At one point, petitioner admonished him to pull over to the curb, cut the motor, and turn out the lights so as to lose a "tail." He then told him to continue "further down." Petitioner asked about money Doe owed him. He advised Doe that he had brought him "three pieces this time." When Bryson heard Doe being ordered to stop the car, he raised the lid of the trunk slightly. After the car stopped, he saw petitioner walk to a tree, pick up a package, and return toward the car. He heard petitioner say, "Here it is," and "I'll call you in a couple of days." Shortly thereafter he heard Durham's signal to come out and emerged from the trunk to find Durham holding a small package found to contain three glassine envelopes containing a white powder.

A field test of the powder having indicated that it contained an opium derivative, the officers, at about 12:30 a.m., arrested petitioner at his home and took him, along with Doe, to Chicago police headquarters. There petitioner was confronted with Doe, who denied that he knew or had ever seen petitioner. Subsequent chemical analysis revealed that the powder contained heroin.

I.

Petitioner contends that the trial court erred in upholding the right of the Government to withhold the identity of John Doe. He argues that Doe was an active participant in the illegal activity charged and that, therefore, the Government could not withhold his identity, his whereabouts, and whether he was alive or dead at the time of trial.[1] The Government does not defend the nondisclosure of Doe's identity with respect to Count 1, which charged a sale of heroin to John Doe, but it attempts to sustain the judgment on the basis of the conviction on Count 2, charging illegal transportation of narcotics. It argues that the conviction on Count 2 may properly be upheld since the identity of the informer, in the circumstances of this case, has no real bearing on that charge and is therefore privileged.

1. The following colloquy occurred between Chester E. Emanuelson, the government counsel, and Maurice J. Walsh, petitioner's counsel:

"Mr. Emanuelson: ⁎ ⁎ ⁎

⁎ ⁎ ⁎

"The reason we do not want to reveal his [Doe's] name is that there are other matters that are pending. I have been told—I know of one myself—and the cases hold that we do not have to reveal the informer's name. Now, if there is some reason—

"Mr. Walsh: Well, is there any activity of the informer which will be curtailed by reason of the disclosure of his name?

Would you answer that?

"Mr. Emanuelson: Any activities?

"Mr. Walsh: Yes.

"Mr. Emanuelson: From this point forward, no.

"Mr. Walsh: Is there any occasion upon which he will be called to testify?

"Mr. Emanuelson: No."

In a later colloquy Mr. Emanuelson stated: "[A]s I understand it, the reason his [Doe's] name has not been disclosed is because he is acting as a Government employee in other cases and it would help other persons in other matters that are pending."

What is usually referred to as the informer's privilege is in reality the Government's privilege to withhold from disclosure the identity of persons who furnish information of violations of law to officers charged with enforcement of that law. The purpose of the privilege is the furtherance and protection of the public interest in effective law enforcement. The privilege recognizes the obligation of citizens to communicate their knowledge of the commission of crimes to law enforcement officials and, by preserving their anonymity, encourages them to perform that obligation.

The scope of the privilege is limited by its underlying purpose. Thus, where the disclosure of the contents of a communication will not tend to reveal the identity of an informer, the contents are not privileged. Likewise, once the identity of the informer has been disclosed to those who would have cause to resent the communication, the privilege is no longer applicable.[2]

A further limitation on the applicability of the privilege arises from the fundamental requirements of fairness. Where the disclosure of an informer's identity, or of the contents of his communication, is relevant and helpful to the defense of an accused, or is essential to a fair determination of a cause, the privilege must give way. In these situations the trial court may require disclosure and, if the Government withholds the information, dismiss the action. Most of the federal cases involving this limitation on the scope of the informer's privilege have arisen where the legality of a search without a warrant is in issue and the communications of an informer are claimed to establish probable cause. In these cases the Government has been required to disclose the identity of the informant unless there was sufficient evidence apart from his confidential communication.

Three recent cases in the Courts of Appeals have involved the identical problem raised here—the Government's right to withhold the identity of an informer who helped to set up the commission of the crime and who was present at its occurrence. In each case it was stated that the identity of such an informer must be disclosed whenever the informer's testimony may be relevant and helpful to the accused's defense.

We believe that no fixed rule with respect to disclosure is justifiable. The problem is one that calls for balancing the public interest in protecting the flow of information against the individual's right to

---

2. The record contains several intimations that the identity of John Doe was known to petitioner and that John Doe died prior to the trial. In either situation, whatever privilege the Government might have had would have ceased to exist, since the purpose of the privilege is to maintain the Government's channels of communication by shielding the identity of an informer from those who would have cause to resent his conduct. The Government suggests that if petitioner knew John Doe's identity, the court's failure to require disclosure would not be prejudicial even if erroneous. See Sorrentino v. United States, 9 Cir., 163 F.2d 627. However, any indications that petitioner, at the time of the trial, was aware of John Doe's identity are contradicted by the testimony of Officer Bryson that John Doe at police headquarters denied knowing, or ever having seen, petitioner. The trial court made no factual finding that petitioner knew Doe's identity. On this record we cannot assume that John Doe was known to petitioner, and, if alive, available to him as a witness. Nor can we conclude that John Doe died before the trial.

prepare his defense. Whether a proper balance renders nondisclosure erroneous must depend on the particular circumstances of each case, taking into consideration the crime charged, the possible defenses, the possible significance of the informer's testimony, and other relevant factors.

II.

The materiality of John Doe's possible testimony must be determined by reference to the offense charged in Count 2 and the evidence relating to that count. The charge is in the language of the statute. It does not charge mere possession; it charges that petitioner did "fraudulently and knowingly receive, conceal, buy and facilitate the transportation and concealment after importation of * * * heroin, knowing the same to be imported into the United States contrary to law. * * *" While John Doe is not expressly mentioned, this charge, when viewed in connection with the evidence introduced at the trial, is so closely related to John Doe as to make his identity and testimony highly material.

It is true that the last sentence of subdivision (c) of § 2 authorizes a conviction when the Government has proved that the accused possessed narcotics, unless the accused explains or justifies such possession. But this statutory presumption does not reduce the offense to one of mere possession or shift the burden of proof; it merely places on the accused, at a certain point, the burden of going forward with his defense. The fact that petitioner here was faced with the burden of explaining or justifying his alleged possession of the heroin emphasizes his vital need for access to any material witness. Otherwise, the burden of going forward might become unduly heavy.

The circumstances of this case demonstrate that John Doe's possible testimony was highly relevant and might have been helpful to the defense. So far as petitioner knew, he and John Doe were alone and unobserved during the crucial occurrence for which he was indicted. Unless petitioner waived his constitutional right not to take the stand in his own defense, John Doe was his one material witness. Petitioner's opportunity to cross-examine Police Officer Bryson and Federal Narcotics Agent Durham was hardly a substitute for an opportunity to examine the man who had been nearest to him and took part in the transaction. Doe had helped to set up the criminal occurrence and had played a prominent part in it. His testimony might have disclosed an entrapment. He might have thrown doubt upon petitioner's identity or on the identity of the package. He was the only witness who might have testified to petitioner's possible lack of knowledge of the contents of the package that he "transported" from the tree to John Doe's car. The desirability of calling John Doe as a witness, or at least interviewing him in preparation for trial, was a matter for the accused rather than the Government to decide.

Finally, the Government's use against petitioner of his conversation with John Doe while riding in Doe's car particularly emphasizes the unfairness of the nondisclosure in this case. The only person, other than petitioner himself, who could controvert, explain or amplify Bryson's report of this important conversation was John Doe. Contradiction or amplification might have borne upon petitioner's knowledge of the contents of the package or might have tended to show an entrapment.

This is a case where the Government's informer was the sole participant, other than the accused, in the transaction charged. The informer was the only witness in a position to amplify or contradict the testimony of government witnesses. Moreover, a government witness testified that Doe denied knowing petitioner or ever having seen him before. We conclude that, under these circumstances, the trial court committed prejudicial error in permitting the Government to withhold the identity of its undercover employee in the face of repeated demands by the accused for his disclosure.[3] * * *

Reversed and remanded.

Mr. Justice BLACK and Mr. Justice WHITTAKER took no part in the consideration or decision of this case.

Mr. Justice CLARK, dissenting.

It is with regret that I dissent from the opinion of the Court, not because I am alone, but for the reason that I have been unable to convince the majority of the unsoundness of its conclusion on the facts here and the destructive effect which that conclusion will have on the enforcement of the narcotic laws. The short of it is that the conviction of a self-confessed dope peddler is reversed because the Government refused to furnish the name of its informant whose identity the undisputed evidence indicated was well known to the peddler. Yet the Court reverses on the ground of "unfairness" because of the Government's failure to perform this fruitless gesture. In my view this does violence to the common understanding of what is fair and just. * * *

McCRAY v. ILLINOIS

Supreme Court of the United States, 1967.
386 U.S. 300, 87 S.Ct. 1056, 18 L.Ed.2d 62.
[Some of the Court's footnotes are omitted.]

Mr. Justice STEWART delivered the opinion of the Court.

The petitioner was arrested in Chicago, Illinois, on the morning of January 16, 1964, for possession of narcotics. The Chicago police officers who made the arrest found a package containing heroin on his person and he was indicted for its unlawful possession. Prior to trial

---

3. Thus far we have dealt largely with the trial court's refusal, at the trial, to require disclosure of the informer's identity. In view of the Government's exclusive reliance here upon Count 2, we have considered this question only with respect to that count. However, we think that the court erred also in denying, prior to the trial, petitioner's motion for a bill of particulars, insofar as it requested John Doe's identity and address. Since Count 1 was then before the court and expressly charged petitioner with a sale of heroin to John Doe, it was evident from the face of the indictment that Doe was a participant in and a material witness to that sale. Accordingly, when his name and address were thus requested, the Government should have been required to supply that information or suffer dismissal of that count.

he filed a motion to suppress the heroin as evidence against him, claiming that the police had acquired it in an unlawful search and seizure in violation of the Fourth and Fourteenth Amendments. See Mapp v. Ohio. After a hearing, the court denied the motion, and the petitioner was subsequently convicted upon the evidence of the heroin the arresting officers had found in his possession. The judgment of conviction was affirmed by the Supreme Court of Illinois, and we granted certiorari to consider the petitioner's claim that the hearing on his motion to suppress was constitutionally defective.

The petitioner's arrest occurred near the intersection of 49th Street and Calumet Avenue at about seven in the morning. At the hearing on the motion to suppress, he testified that up until a half hour before he was arrested he had been at "a friend's house" about a block away, that after leaving the friend's house he had "walked with a lady from 48th to 48th and South Park," and that, as he approached 49th Street and Calumet Avenue, "[t]he Officers stopped me going through the alley." "The officers," he said, "did not show me a search warrant for my person or an arrest warrant for my arrest." He said the officers then searched him and found the narcotics in question.[1] The petitioner did not identify the "friend" nor the "lady," and neither of them appeared as a witness.

The arresting officers then testified. Officer Jackson stated that he and two fellow officers had had a conversation with an informant on the morning of January 16 in their unmarked police car. The officer said that the informant had told them that the petitioner, with whom Jackson was acquainted, "was selling narcotics and had narcotics on his person and that he could be found in the vicinity of 47th and Calumet at this particular time." Jackson said that he and his fellow officers drove to that vicinity in the police car and that when they spotted the petitioner, the informant pointed him out and then departed on foot. Jackson stated that the officers observed the petitioner walking with a woman, then separating from her and meeting briefly with a man, then proceeding alone, and finally, after seeing the police car, "hurriedly walk[ing] between two buildings." "At this point," Jackson testified, "my partner and myself got out of the car and informed him we had information he had narcotics on his person, placed him in the police vehicle at this point." Jackson stated that the officers then searched the petitioner and found the heroin in a cigarette package.

Jackson testified that he had been acquainted with the informant for approximately a year, that during this period the informant had supplied him with information about narcotics activities "fifteen, sixteen times at least," that the information had proved to be accurate and had resulted in numerous arrests and convictions. On cross-examination, Jackson was even more specific as to the informant's previous reliability, giving the names of people who had been convicted of narcotics violations as the result of information the informant had

---

1. The weather was "real cold," and the petitioner testified he "had on three coats." In order to conduct the search, the arresting officers, required the petitioner to remove some of his clothing, but even the petitioner's version of the circumstances of the search did not disclose any conduct remotely akin to that condemned by this Court in Rochin v. California.

supplied.   When Jackson was asked for the informant's name and
address, counsel for the State objected, and the objection was sustained
by the court.[2]

Officer Arnold gave substantially the same account of the circumstances of the petitioner's arrest and search, stating that the informant
had told the officers that the petitioner "was selling narcotics and had
narcotics on his person now in the vicinity of 47th and Calumet."   The
informant, Arnold testified, "said he had observed [the petitioner]
selling narcotics to various people, meaning various addicts, in the area
of 47th and Calumet."   Arnold testified that he had known the informant "roughly two years," that the informant had given him information
concerning narcotics "20 or 25 times," and that the information had
resulted in convictions.   Arnold too was asked on cross-examination for
the informant's name and address, and objections to these questions
were sustained by the court.   *   *   *   It is the petitioner's claim,
however, that even though the officers' sworn testimony fully supported
a finding of probable cause for the arrest and search, the state court
nonetheless violated the Constitution when it sustained objections to
the petitioner's questions as to the identity of the informant.   We
cannot agree.

In permitting the officers to withhold the informant's identity, the
court was following well-settled Illinois law.   When the issue is not
guilt or innocence, but, as here, the question of probable cause for an
arrest or search, the Illinois Supreme Court has held that police officers
need not invariably be required to disclose an informant's identity if
the trial judge is convinced, by evidence submitted in open court and
subject to cross-examination, that the officers did rely in good faith
upon credible information supplied by a reliable informant.   This
Illinois evidentiary rule is consistent with the law of many other States.
*   *   *

The reasoning of the Supreme Court of New Jersey in judicially
adopting the same basic evidentiary rule was instructively expressed by
Chief Justice Weintraub in State v. Burnett:

> "If a defendant may insist upon disclosure of the inform-
> ant in order to test the truth of the officer's statement that
> there is an informant or as to what the informant related or as
> to the informant's reliability, we can be sure that every defen-
> dant will demand disclosure.   He has nothing to lose and the

---

2. "Q. What is the name of this informant that gave you this information?

"Mr. Engerman: Objection, Your Hon-
or.

"The Court: State for the record the
reasons for your objection.

"Mr. Engerman: Judge, based upon
the testimony of the officer so far that
they had used this informant for approximately a year, he has, worked with this
individual, in the interest of the public, I
see no reason why the officer should be
forced to disclose the name of the informant, to cause harm or jeopardy to an
individual who has cooperated with the
police. The City of Chicago has a tremendous problem with narcotics. If the
police are not able to withhold the name
of the informant they will not be able to
get informants. They are not willing to
risk their lives if their names become
known.

"In the interest of the City and the law
enforcement of this community, I feel
the officer should not be forced to reveal
the name of the informant. And I also
cite People vs. Durr.

"The Court: I will sustain that.

"Mr. Adam: Q. Where does this informant live?

"Mr. Engerman: Objection, your Hon-
or, same basis.

"The Court: Sustained."

prize may be the suppression of damaging evidence if the State cannot afford to reveal its source, as is so often the case. And since there is no way to test the good faith of a defendant who presses the demand, we must assume the routine demand would have to be routinely granted. The result would be that the State could use the informant's information only as a lead and could search only if it could gather adequate evidence of probable cause apart from the informant's data. Perhaps that approach would sharpen investigatorial techniques, but we doubt that there would be enough talent and time to cope with crime upon that basis. Rather we accept the premise that the informer is a vital part of society's defensive arsenal. The basic rule protecting his identity rests upon that belief.

* * *

"We must remember also that we are not dealing with the trial of the criminal charge itself. There the need for a truthful verdict outweighs society's need for the informer privilege. Here, however, the accused seeks to avoid the truth. The very purpose of a motion to suppress is to escape the inculpatory thrust of evidence in hand, not because its probative force is diluted in the least by the mode of seizure, but rather as a sanction to compel enforcement officers to respect the constitutional security of all of us under the Fourth Amendment. If the motion to suppress is denied, defendant will still be judged upon the untarnished truth.

* * *

"The Fourth Amendment is served if a judicial mind passes upon the existence of probable cause. Where the issue is submitted upon an application for a warrant, the magistrate is trusted to evaluate the credibility of the affiant in an *ex parte* proceeding. As we have said the magistrate is concerned, not with whether the informant lied, but with whether the affiant is truthful in his recitation of what he was told. If the magistrate doubts the credibility of the affiant, he may require that the informant be identified or even produced. It seems to us that the same approach is equally sufficient where the search was without a warrant, that is to say, that it should rest entirely with the judge who hears the motion to suppress to decide whether he needs such disclosure as to the informant in order to decide whether the officer is a believable witness."

What Illinois and her sister States have done is no more than recognize a well-established testimonial privilege, long familiar to the law of evidence. Professor Wigmore, not known as an enthusiastic advocate of testimonial privileges generally,[3] has described that privilege in these words:

"A genuine privilege, on * * * fundamental principle * * *, must be recognized for the *identity of persons supply-*

3. See 8 Wigmore, Evidence § 2192 (McNaughton rev.1961).

*ing the government with information concerning the commis-
sion of crimes.* Communications of this kind ought to receive
encouragement. They are discouraged if the informer's identity is disclosed. Whether an informer is motivated by good
citizenship, promise of leniency or prospect of pecuniary reward, he will usually condition his cooperation on an assurance
of anonymity—to protect himself and his family from harm, to
preclude adverse social reactions and to avoid the risk of
defamation or malicious prosecution actions against him. The
government also has an interest in nondisclosure of the identity of its informers. Law enforcement officers often depend
upon professional informers to furnish them with a flow of
information about criminal activities. Revelation of the dual
role played by such persons ends their usefulness to the government and discourages others from entering into a like
relationship.

   "That the government has this privilege is well established
and its soundness cannot be questioned." (Footnotes omitted.)
8 Wigmore, Evidence § 2374 (McNaughton rev.1961).

   In the federal courts the rules of evidence in criminal trials are
governed "by the principles of the common law as they may be
interpreted by the courts of the United States in the light of reason and
experience." This Court, therefore, has the ultimate task of defining
the scope to be accorded to the various common law evidentiary
privileges in the trial of federal criminal cases. This is a task which is
quite different, of course, from the responsibility of constitutional
adjudication. In the exercise of this supervisory jurisdiction the Court
had occasion 10 years ago, in Roviaro v. United States, to give thorough
consideration to one aspect of the informer's privilege, the privilege
itself having long been recognized in the federal judicial system.

   The *Roviaro* case involved the informer's privilege, not at a preliminary hearing to determine probable cause for an arrest or search, but
at the trial itself where the issue was the fundamental one of innocence
or guilt. * * *

   What *Roviaro* thus makes clear is that this Court was unwilling to
impose any absolute rule requiring disclosure of an informer's identity
even in formulating evidentiary rules for federal criminal trials.

   * * * Yet we are now asked to hold that the Constitution
somehow compels Illinois to abolish the informer's privilege from its
law of evidence, and to require disclosure of the informer's identity in
every such preliminary hearing where it appears that the officers made
the arrest or search in reliance upon facts supplied by an informer they
had reason to trust. The argument is based upon the Due Process
Clause of the Fourteenth Amendment, and upon the Sixth Amendment
right of confrontation, applicable to the State through the Fourteenth
Amendment. We find no support for the petitioner's position in either
of those constitutional provisions.

   The arresting officers in this case testified, in open court, fully and
in precise detail as to what the informer told them and as to why they

had reason to believe his information was trustworthy. Each officer was under oath. Each was subjected to searching cross-examination. The judge was obviously satisfied that each was telling the truth, and for that reason he exercised the discretion conferred upon him by the established law of Illinois to respect the informer's privilege.

Nothing in the Due Process Clause of the Fourteenth Amendment requires a state court judge in every such hearing to assume the arresting officers are committing perjury. "To take such a step would be quite beyond the pale of this Court's proper function in our federal system. It would be a wholly unjustifiable encroachment by this Court upon the constitutional power of States to promulgate their own rules of evidence * * * in their own state courts. * * * "

The petitioner does not explain precisely how he thinks his Sixth Amendment right to confrontation and cross-examination was violated by Illinois' recognition of the informer's privilege in this case. If the claim is that the State violated the Sixth Amendment by not producing the informer to testify against the petitioner, then we need no more than repeat the Court's answer to that claim a few weeks ago in Cooper v. California:

"Petitioner also presents the contention here that he was unconstitutionally deprived of the right to confront a witness against him, because the State did not produce the informant to testify against him. This contention we consider absolutely devoid of merit."

On the other hand, the claim may be that the petitioner was deprived of his Sixth Amendment right to cross-examine the arresting officers themselves, because their refusal to reveal the informer's identity was upheld. But it would follow from this argument that no witness on cross-examination could ever constitutionally assert a testimonial privilege, including the privilege against compulsory self-incrimination guaranteed by the Constitution itself. We have never given the Sixth Amendment such a construction, and we decline to do so now.

Affirmed.

[The opinion of Mr. Justice Douglas, with whom The Chief Justice, Mr. Justice Brennan and Mr. Justice Fortas concur, dissenting, is omitted.]

NON–DISCLOSURE OF COMPLAINANTS' NAMES IN SCHOOL DESEGREGATION CASES: TITLE IV OF THE CIVIL RIGHTS ACT OF 1964

Comment, 1967 Washington Univ. Law Quarterly 459.

United States v. School Dist. No. 1, 40 F.R.D. 391 (D.S.C.1966).

Title IV of the 1964 Civil Rights Act[1] permits the Attorney General to bring desegregation suits against local school boards "in the

---

1. 42 U.S.C. § 2000c–6 (1964).

name of the United States" provided, among other requirements,[2] he believes the aggrieved persons cannot "initiate and maintain appropriate legal proceedings." Satisfied that the various requirements were met, the Attorney General commenced this action against the Lexington County School Board. The Board, stating it could not prepare its defense, posed numerous interrogatories, some of which the government refused to answer. The contested questions sought the name or names of the complainants and the nature of the complaint.[3] the government based its refusal to answer on subsection (b) of Title IV, which declares that a person is unable to initiate and maintain appropriate proceedings " * * * whenever he [the Attorney General] is satisfied that the institution of such litigation would jeopardize the personal safety, employment, or economic standing of such person or persons, their families, or their property." This provision, the government argued, was intended to protect the complainant by concealment, allowing suit to be brought in the name of the United States.

The court ordered the government to answer. Finding no reference to reprisals in desegregation cases to date, the court reasoned that there was no basis for the concealment provision of the statute. Earlier cases involving non-disclosure were not directly in point. Moreover, the purpose and scope of pre-trial discovery demanded that this information be made available to the defendant school board.

The court's decision raises three problems: congressional intent, troublesome language in earlier cases, and the scope of discovery. In his address to the Senate introducing the 1964 Civil Rights bill, the then Senator Hubert H. Humphrey stated:

> The bill requires the Attorney General to state in his complaint that in his judgment the persons who complained are unable to initiate or maintain appropriate legal proceedings. These statements by the Attorney General will not be subject to challenge either by the defendants or by the court. *Under no circumstances will the Attorney General be required to reveal the names of the particular complainants.*

This unequivocal language is the sole statement about the non-disclosure provision. Congress accepted it without further debate. One federal court, after considering this provision, said:

> Section 407 of the Civil Rights Act of 1964 clearly expresses the legislative intent that the Attorney General be vested with exclusive and final determination of the sufficiency of the

---

2. The Act also requires that the Attorney General: 1) receive a written complaint signed by parents stating that their children are being denied the equal protection of the laws, 2) believe the complaint is meritorious, 3) believe the action will "materially further the orderly achievement of desegregation of public education," 4) notify the school board of the complaint, 5) certify that he believes the school board has had a "reasonable time to adjust the conditions." 42 U.S.C. § 2000c–6(a) (1964).

3. A third question challenged the basis upon which the Attorney General determined the complainants' inability to initiate and maintain a suit. In sustaining the government's refusal to answer, the court followed precedent. * * * It would have been difficult to draw a contrary conclusion because the House Judiciary Committee's Report states: "It is not intended that the determination on which the certification was based should be reviewable." 1964 (U.S.) Code Cong. & Ad.News 2355.

complaint. Thus, the Attorney General need not detail the
facts behind the certificate nor disclose the names or identity
of the person or persons complaining to him. The legislative
history of the Act leaves no doubt that such was the contemplation of Congress.

But in *School Dist. No. 1,* the court questioned the need for
concealment. Although it found no reprisals in desegregation cases,
the court went on to say that even if there were reprisals, the "United
States court is now available for the protection of the complainants."
What this precisely means remains obscure. * * *

Arguably, the "informer" in desegregation cases is substantially like
the informer in an action brought under the Fair Labor Standards Act of
1938. In these cases, after an employee complains to the Department of
Labor about a violation of the Act, the Secretary is authorized to bring
suit in his own name. After suits have commenced, employers, as part
of the discovery process, have sought the names of the employees who
complained. The Secretary has successfully raised the privilege to
protect the informers' names. In Wirtz v. Continental Finance & Loan
Co., the court reasoned that employees are "particularly susceptible to
the fear of retaliation," so that to obtain the information needed to
insure compliance with the Act, the government must assure informers
that their names would not be divulged. Summarizing the facts to be
considered concerning informer's privilege, the court stated:

> This privilege may be invoked where a balancing of conflicting
> policy considerations shows that the public interest in protect-
> ing the flow of information outweighs the individual's rights to
> prepare his defense. If this type of weighing of conveniences is
> warranted in an action where the defendant may be subject to
> criminal penalties, it goes without saying that it is appropriate
> where only civil remedies are sought.

* * *

The government has decided to answer the interrogatories as
ordered by the Court rather than suffer dismissal and appeal. There
may be several reasons for this course of action: the government may
not have feared reprisals in this locality, it may have decided that it
must use the complainants at the trial, it may not have wished to delay
this suit unless absolutely necessary. These are all matters of strategy
whose importance is restricted to this particular case. They do not
necessarily indicate any policy to be followed by the government in
future cases.

———

See California Evidence Code §§ 1041–1042.

Hypotheticals

(1) D is charged with committing battery against PO, a police officer. D
makes a pretrial discovery motion to have the prosecution obtain from the Police
Department its personnel or disciplinary record file on PO for inspection and
copying by D. D asserts in his motion that his defense will be self-defense in
response to the use of excessive force by PO. D's motion is supported by

affidavits setting forth (a) that two named persons who had filed complaints against PO for use of excessive force are unavailable for interview by D and that these persons' prior statements to police investigators are necessary for D's effective cross-examination of PO at trial; (b) that two other named persons had previously reported misconduct on the part of PO and are available as witnesses but are unable to recall the details of the events and that the Police Department's files are necessary to refresh their recollection. The prosecutor claims the official information privilege as the person authorized by the Police Department to assert the privilege in opposition to D's motion. The trial judge makes an in camera inspection of the file in question and finds that the file does contain allegations by the four persons as set forth in D's affidavits. The trial judge then overrules the prosecutor's claim of privilege on the ground that the public-interest necessity for preserving the confidentiality of the information sought by D does not outweigh D's need for disclosure of the information to aid his defense in the interest of justice. Is this ruling of the trial judge correct?

(2) P sues D for damages for injuries received in an automobile accident on December 31, 1972. P alleges in her complaint that she lost a year's income of $20,000 for the year 1973, the year she was unable to work as a result of the accident. By a pretrial discovery motion, D seeks to inspect and copy P's copies of her federal and state income tax returns for the years 1971 and 1972, before the accident, and for 1973, the year after the accident. P resists D's motion on the ground of the official-information privilege. What result?

(3) A sues X for damages for injuries received in a collision between A's car and X's car. Shortly after the accident, A filed a claim for state disability-insurance benefits. The State Office for Disability Insurance Claims requests Dr. B to examine A for his ability or inability to work, and to make a confidential report to the state office. Dr. B examines A and sends his report to the state office. X takes Dr. B's deposition and has the state office served with a subpoena *duces tecum* to produce Dr. B's report at the deposition examination. A gives a written consent for the state office to disclose Dr. B's report to X. At the deposition examination, the state office claims an absolute privilege for nondisclosure. X seeks a court order to compel the state office to disclose Dr. B's report. How should the court rule?

(4) X is prosecuted for possession of heroin. At a pretrial hearing on X's motion to suppress, A, a police officer, testifies that he received a telephone call from a reliable informer who told him that X was selling heroin from her apartment and that she kept it in a telephone jack on the south wall of the bedroom; and that A then proceeded to X's apartment, without a warrant, found the heroin in the telephone jack and arrested X in the apartment. On cross-examination, A testifies that he did not learn from the informer whether he had ever been in X's apartment or in what way he obtained his information about the heroin location. X demands disclosure of the informer's identity, on the ground that there is the possibility that the informer could testify that another person put the heroin in the telephone jack, which would exonerate X of the heroin-possession charge. The prosecutor asserts the privilege for nondisclosure. Should the prosecutor's claim of privilege be sustained?

(5) "X" is prosecuted for the sale of heroin. At the preliminary hearing, A, a police officer, testifies that he gave an informer a ten-dollar bill dusted with fluorescent powder, that he watched the informer go into an apartment and later come out with a bindle of heroin, that A then knocked on the apartment door, that X opened the door and was placed under arrest, and that X had traces of fluorescent powder on his hands. In cross-examination of A, X asks the name of the informer. A claims the identity-of-informer privilege. What result?

Chapter IX

WRITINGS

PART A. THE BEST EVIDENCE RULE

McCORMICK, EVIDENCE

409, 411–12 (1954).*
[All footnotes omitted.]

The specific tenor of [the best evidence rule] needs to be definitely stated and its limits clearly understood. The rule is this: in proving the terms of a writing, where such terms are material, the original writing must be produced, unless it is shown to be unavailable for some reason other than the serious fault of the proponent.

* * *

A rule which permitted the judge to insist that all evidence must pass his scrutiny as the "best" or most reliable means of proving the fact would be a sore incumbrance upon the parties, who in our system have the responsibility of proof. In fact, * * * no such general scrutiny is sanctioned, but only as to "writings" is a demand for the "best," the original, made. Accordingly, as to objects bearing no writing, the judge (unless in some exceptional cases when the exact features of the object have become as essential to the issue, as the precise words of a writing usually are) may not exclude oral testimony describing the object and demand that the object itself be produced. * * * If, however, the object, such as a policeman's badge, a revolver, an engagement ring, or a tombstone, bears a number or inscription the terms of which are relevant, we face the question, shall we treat it as a chattel or as a "writing"? Probably most modern cases would support the view advocated by Wigmore, that the judge shall have discretion, to follow the one analogy or the other in the light of such factors as the need for precise information as to the exact inscription, the ease or difficulty of production, and the simplicity or complexity of the inscription.

SIRICO v. COTTO

Civil Court of the City of New York, 1971.
67 Misc.2d 636, 324 N.Y.S.2d 483.
[Some citations omitted.]

Irving YOUNGER, Judge.

In the course of trying this personal injury action, there arose a problem in evidence the solution of which seemed to elude plaintiff's attorney. For whatever assistance it will be to him, and because others may find it useful, I am filing this memorandum.

637

To support her case on damages, plaintiff called as a witness Dr. Stanley Wolfson, a specialist in radiology. Dr. Wolfson testified that plaintiff had been sent to him by the treating physician and that, in due course, Dr. Wolfson had taken a number of X-ray photographs of plaintiff's spine. After studying them, he wrote a report setting forth his conclusions and sent it, together with the X-ray plates, directly to the treating physician. All that Dr. Wolfson had with him as he sat on the witness stand was a copy of his report. Having refreshed his recollection from it, he was asked to describe what he had found in the X-rays and to state his opinion with respect to plaintiff's physical condition. At this point, defense counsel objected. In order to afford plaintiff an opportunity to make her record, the jury was excused, and Dr. Wolfson completed his testimony in its absence. He said that the X-rays showed a flattening of plaintiff's lumbar lordosis and a scoliosis of her midlumbar spine with convexity towards the left, from which he would conclude that plaintiff was suffering from the consequences of a lumbar-sacral sprain. As to the whereabouts of the X-ray plates, Dr. Wolfson knew only that he had sent them to the treating physician. That gentleman did not testify. Plaintiff's counsel did not have the plates in his possession, nor did he explain his failure to produce them. I sustained defendants' objection and, upon the jury's return to the courtroom, excused Dr. Wolfson.

The problem, then, is whether Dr. Wolfson, without the X-ray plates, might describe what he had seen in them and state the significance he ascribed to his observations. Two lines of analysis are available, each of which leads to the same conclusion—that Dr. Wolfson's testimony is inadmissible.

First, the best evidence rule. This oft-mentioned and much misunderstood rule merely requires a party who seeks to prove the contents of a document to offer in evidence the original copy of that document. If he does not, but rather offers secondary evidence (such as a photostat, a carbon, or a witness' *viva voce* description of the document), the adversary's objection must be sustained. But if the proponent explains his failure to offer the original copy of the document, he may then proceed to prove its contents by whatever secondary evidence is available to him. IV Wigmore, Evidence, Secs. 1192 et seq. (3d ed. 1940). A "document," within the meaning of the best evidence rule, is any physical embodiment of information or ideas—a letter, a contract, a receipt, a book of account, a blueprint, or an X-ray plate.

So much for basics. Here, plaintiff asked Dr. Wolfson to describe what he saw when he looked at the X-ray plates. This was secondary evidence of their contents. The best evidence rule, we see, requires plaintiff to offer the originals, which, in the instance of X-rays, would be the familiar negative plates one "reads" by affixing to a shadow box. Plaintiff's failure to offer these original plates would have been excused had counsel explained his failure (by proof competent for that purpose, needless to say.) This he did not do, and hence I sustained defendants' objection.

* * *

* * * [T]he consequence of my sustaining defendants' objection to Dr. Wolfson's testimony was a rather complicated excision from the jury's ken of part of another physician's opinion based upon Dr. Wolfson's. That, however, is a matter of interest only to counsel in this case and so I leave it in the obscurity of the stenographer's minutes.

CASE NOTE

64 Harv.L.Rev. 1369 (1951).*

EVIDENCE—DOCUMENTS—"BEST EVIDENCE" RULE AP-PLIED TO PREVENT INTRODUCTION OF A RECORDING OF A DESTROYED RECORDING.—*A* and *B* were arrested and indicted for murder and robbery. A tape recording of damaging admissions was obtained by means of a microphone concealed in their cell. As was customary, the contents of the tape were recorded onto a disc, and the conversation was erased from the tape, which was then placed back in stock for reuse. The disc recording was admitted in evidence by the trial court over objection by defendant *A*. On appeal, *held,* conviction affirmed. Admission of the recording violated the "best evidence" rule, but there was enough other evidence to sustain the conviction.

It is generally agreed that if the speakers are properly identified and adequate safeguards are taken to ensure authenticity, a recording may be introduced into evidence. Hence, it would seem that the original tape recording could properly have been admitted. However, in the instant case the disc recording raises the additional problem of the "best evidence" rule, which requires that to prove the contents of a writing, the writing itself must be offered in evidence unless adequate excuse is given for not presenting it. Although a recording is not colloquially considered to be a writing, it is defined as such in the Model Code of Evidence, Rule 1(17) (1942), and should be similarly treated in relation to the best evidence rule since the policy of the rule—to obtain the most truly probative evidence of a preserved communication—is equally applicable to recordings. It may be argued that the disc recording in the instant case is no more than a mechanical reproduction of the conversation on the tape and thus is a "duplicate original," which, under the best evidence rule, may be introduced to prove the contents of a writing without requiring an excuse for not producing the original. However, the only reproductions that have been categorized as duplicate originals are carbon and printed copies. The courts have ordinarily labeled all other mechanically produced copies as secondary evidence lacking the necessary reliability to be treated as originals. But since most mechanical processes of reproduction are highly accurate and all are susceptible in some degree to tampering, it would appear that the judicial distinction, based upon relative reliability, is of doubtful validity. It would seem that uniform treatment should be accorded all such devises either treating them as originals, or as secondary evidence, in which case the duplicate original doctrine would be restricted to copies possessing identical legal significance, such as a duplicate will with the requisite testamentary formalities.

The court indicates that it will not accept secondary evidence when the original has been intentionally destroyed by the proponent even if such destruction was done in good faith. This is contrary to the generally accepted view that the proponent may introduce secondary evidence upon a showing that the destruction was not fraudulent. Furthermore, where the destruction occurs pursuant to a usual course of business operations and without thought of evidentiary significance, as was alleged in the instant case the burden on the proponent to justify his action should be materially lessened. It has been suggested that the entire problem of admissibility of copies should be left to the discretion of the trial court. Such discretion would allow courts to alleviate the rigidity of the best evidence rule and eliminate the necessity to classify so-called "super-reliable" copies as duplicate originals. Utilizing such an approach, mechanical reproductions would be treated as secondary evidence, and the proponent would have to account to the satisfaction of the trial court for failure to produce the original. If, however, trial courts are to remain bound by stringent rules governing the admissibility of secondary evidence, it would seem that mechanically reproduced copies should be admitted as duplicate originals, with the question of tampering left to the triers of fact.

HERZIG v. SWIFT & CO.

United States Court of Appeals, Second Circuit, 1945.
146 F.2d 444.
[All footnotes omitted.]

[Wrongful death action. Deceased had been a partner in a building construction firm. At trial, on the issue of damages, plaintiff offered testimony by one of the partners as to the amount of the partnership earnings and the deceased's share. This testimony was rejected on the ground that it was not the best evidence and that the firm's books should have been produced. Plaintiff appealed from a dismissal of her action.—Ed.]

FRANK, Circuit Judge. 1. Perhaps the most to be said for the "best evidence rule" is that it may serve on occasion as a good mnemonic device. It did not so serve the trial judge here, for it awoke in him an incorrect recollection when, in rejecting the oral testimony as to partnership earnings and in refusing to allow the plaintiff's counsel to argue for its admissibility, he said, "I am not going to hear an elementary argument on law school evidence."

"In its modern application, the best evidence rule amounts to little more than the requirement that the contents of a writing must be proved by the introduction of the writing itself, unless its absence can be satisfactorily accounted for." Here there was no attempt to prove the contents of a writing; the issue was the earnings of the partnership, which for convenience were recorded in books of account after the relevant facts occurred. Generally, this differentiation has been adopted by the courts. On the precise question of admitting oral testimony to prove matters that are contained in books of account, the courts have divided, some holding the oral testimony admissible, others excluding it. The federal courts have generally adopted the rationale limiting the "best evidence rule" to cases where the contents of the writing are to be proved. We hold, therefore, that the district judge erred in excluding the oral testimony as to the earnings of the partnership. A closer question arises as to whether proof of the decedent's share in the partnership must be proved by the partnership agreement; but we are not called upon to decide this question since the trial never reached the point where this question would be raised.   *   *   *

Reversed and remanded.

MEYERS v. UNITED STATES

United States Court of Appeals, District of Columbia, 1948.
84 U.S.App.D.C. 101, 171 F.2d 800, cert. denied 336 U.S. 912, 69 S.Ct. 602, 93 L.Ed. 1076.
[All footnotes omitted.]

[This was a prosecution for subornation of perjury. At trial the prosecution sought to establish the content of one Lamarre's testimony for a committee of the United States Senate. Although a transcript of the stenographic record of Lamarre's testimony was available, the committee's counsel was permitted to recount orally the substance of Lamarre's testimony—Ed.]

Wilbur K. MILLER, Circuit Judge.   *   *   * At the opening of the dissent it is said, "The testimony given by Lamarre before the Senate Committee was presented to the jury upon the trial in so unfair and prejudicial a fashion as to constitute reversible error."

The reference is to the fact that William P. Rogers, chief counsel to the senatorial committee, who had examined Lamarre before the subcommittee and consequently had heard all the testimony given by him before that body, was permitted to testify as to what Lamarre had sworn to the subcommittee. Later in the trial the government introduced in evidence a stenographic transcript of Lamarre's testimony at the senatorial hearing.

In his brief here the appellant characterizes this as a "bizarre procedure" but does not assign as error the reception of Rogers' testimony. The dissenting opinion, however, asserts it was reversible error to allow Rogers to testify at all as to what Lamarre had said to the subcommittee, on the theory that the transcript itself was the best evidence of Lamarre's testimony before the subcommittee.

That theory is, in our view, based upon a misconception of the best evidence rule. As applied generally in federal courts, the rule is limited to cases where the contents of a writing are to be proved. Here there was no attempt to prove the contents of a writing; the issue was what Lamarre had said, not what the transcript contained. The transcript made from shorthand notes of his testimony was, to be sure, evidence of what he had said, but it was not the only admissible evidence concerning it. Rogers' testimony was equally competent, and was admissible whether given before or after the transcript was received in evidence. Statements alleged to be perjurious may be proved by any person who heard them, as well as by a reporter who recorded them in shorthand. ✳ ✳ ✳

As we have pointed out, there was no issue as to the contents of the transcript, and the government was not attempting to prove what it contained; the issue was what Lamarre actually had said. Rogers was not asked what the transcript contained but what Lamarre's testimony had been.

After remarking, " ✳ ✳ ✳ there is a line of cases which holds that a stenographic transcript is not the best evidence of what was said. There is also a legal cliche that the best evidence rule applies only to documentary evidence", the dissenting opinion asserts that the rule is outmoded and that "the courts ought to establish a new and correct rule." We regard the principle set forth in the cases which we have cited as being, not a legal cliche, but an established and sound doctrine which we are not prepared to renounce. ✳ ✳ ✳

Affirmed.

PRETTYMAN, Circuit Judge (dissenting).

✳ ✳ ✳ From the theoretical viewpoint, I realize that there is a line of authority that (absent or incompetent the original witness) a bystander who hears testimony or other conversation may testify as to what was said, even though there be a stenographic report. And there is a line of cases which holds that a stenographic transcript is not the best evidence of what was said. There is also a legal cliche that the best evidence rule applies only to documentary evidence. The trial judge in this case was confronted with that authority, and a trial court is probably not the place to inaugurate a new line of authority. But I do not know why an appellate court should perpetuate a rule clearly outmoded by scientific development. I know that courts are reluctant to do so. I recognize the view that such matters should be left to Congress. But rules of evidence were originally judge-made and are an essential part of the judicial function. I know of no reason why the judicial branch of Government should abdicate to the legislative branch so important a part of its responsibility.

I am of opinion, and quite ready to hold, that the rules of evidence reflected by the cases to which I have just referred are outmoded and at variance with known fact, and that the courts ought to establish a new and correct rule. The rationale of the so-called "best evidence rule" requires that a party having available evidence which is relatively certain may not submit evidence which is far less certain. The law is concerned with the true fact, and with that alone; its procedures are directed to that objective, and to that alone. It should permit no procedure the sole use of which is to obscure and confuse that which is otherwise plain and certain.

We need not venture into full discussion of all the principles involved. As between two observers of an event, the law will not accept the evidence of one and exclude that of the other, because the law cannot say which is more accurate. But as between a document itself and a description of it, the law accepts the former and excludes the

latter, because the former is certain and the latter is subject to many
frailties. So as between the recollection of the parties to a contract
evidenced by a writing and the writing itself, the law rejects the former
and accepts the latter. To be sure, the writing may be attacked for
forgery, alteration or some such circumstance. But absent such impeachment, the writing is immutable evidence from the date of the
event, whereas human recollection is subject to many infirmities and
human recitation is subject to the vices of prejudice and interest.
Presented with that choice, the law accepts the certain and rejects the
uncertain. The repeated statement in cases and elsewhere that the
best evidence rule applies only to documents is a description of practice
and not a pronouncement of principle. The principle is that as between
human recollections the law makes no conclusive choice; it makes a
conclusive choice only as between evidence which is certain and that
which is uncertain.

It may be remarked at this point that the transcript in the case at
bar is a document, not challenged for inaccuracy or alteration. It
possesses every characteristic which the most literal devotee of established rules of evidence could ascribe to written evidence of a contract
as justification for preference of such writing over the recollection of
the parties.

In my view, the court iterates an error when it says that the best
evidence rule is limited to cases where the contents of a writing are to
be proved. The purpose of offering in evidence a "written contract" is
not to prove the contents of the writing. The writing is not the
contract; it is merely evidence of the contract. The contract itself is
the agreement between the parties. Statutes such as the statute of
frauds do not provide that a contract be in writing; they provide that
the contract be evidenced by a writing, or that a written memorandum
of it be made. The writing is offered as evidence of an agreement, not
for the purpose of proving its own contents.

* * * From the theoretical point of view, the case poses this
question: Given both (1) an accurate stenographic transcription of a
witness' testimony during a two-day hearing and (2) the recollection of
one of the complainants as to the substance of that testimony, is the
latter admissible as evidence in a trial of the witness for perjury? I
think not. To say that it is, is to apply a meaningless formula and
ignore crystal-clear actualities. The transcript is, as a matter of
simple, indisputable fact, the best evidence. The principle and not the
rote of the law ought to be applied. * * *

PEOPLE v. ENSKAT

Appellate Department, Superior Court, Los Angeles County, California, 1971.
20 Cal.App.3d Supp. 1, 98 Cal.Rptr. 646.

ZACK, Judge. The complaint charges appellant with two counts of
[exhibiting obscene motion pictures].

* * *

The motion picture involved was not seized under a warrant, or
otherwise offered or placed in evidence by the prosecution. The officers

entered the theater and then took pictures of portions of the film. Such pictures, including pictures of the theater exterior, are People's 1 through 9, 11, and 12. The balance of the film, audio and visual, was the subject of testimony. A best evidence objection was overruled on the ground that the rule does not apply. Such ruling was error.

Evidence Code section 1500 states that " * * * no evidence other than the writing itself is admissible to prove the content of a writing." There is no question but that the contents of the material must be considered in an obscenity case. * * * Motion pictures are accorded the same constitutional protection as books and other forms of expression. * * * As the content of a film is always an issue in an obscenity case, the best evidence rule will apply if a film is a writing under the Evidence Code.

Evidence Code section 250 defines a "writing" as including " * * * photographing, and every other means of recording upon any tangible thing, any form of communication or representation, including letters, words, pictures, sounds, or symbols." A photographic transparency, e.g., a "slide," is a writing under this definition, because it is a picture recorded upon a tangible thing, the celluloid.[1] A motion picture film is a series of such pictures recorded upon a celluloid film strip. * * * Each picture in each frame is slightly different from the preceding one, so that when the film is moved through a projector, these individual pictures appear to merge into a continuous "moving" picture. This movement is only an optical illusion, for in actuality each separate picture is projected onto the screen for a split second, rapidly followed by the next one. That there *appears* to be a "motion picture" does not alter the fact that a series of single pictures on the filmstrip, each one a "writing," is casting an image on a screen.

Respondent argues, however, that it is not the film, but these light images on the screen, that constitute the offense of exhibiting an obscene motion picture. Respondent argues that as this moving image is unrecorded, it cannot be a writing, and therefore is not subject to the best evidence rule. This argument ignores the essential fact that the moving image is merely the consequence of passing a writing (the film) through a machine. Without the projector and the filmstrip, no moving image is cast at all. The content of the moving image, "evanescent" or not, is totally dependent upon the content of the filmstrip. Just as it is better for the trier of fact to read a document than have it described, it is better for the trier of fact to see a movie than have it described. The policy considerations upholding the rule for written documents apply with full force to movies as well. It is to be noted that the instant prosecution under Penal Code section 311.2 is for exhibiting *obscene matter.* The latter is defined in section 311, subdivisions (a)(2), (b) to include a "motion picture." It is the character of the contents of the motion picture exhibited which, strictly speaking is in issue, not the character of the images on the screen resulting from its exhibition.

---

1. A photograph printed from a negative is still considered secondary evidence.

Our ruling herein does not mean that obscenity cases may not, under any circumstances, be prosecuted by means of secondary evidence of the obscene material. It means that in this case, the prosecution, in presenting such secondary evidence, did not comply with the Evidence Code. An example of how the prosecution may proceed is contained in Evidence Code section 1503, subdivision (a): If (1) a defendant is in possession or control of the material at the time he is expressly or impliedly notified of the existence of a criminal action against him involving such alleged obscene material, and (2) if a request that he produce it is made at the trial (out of the presence of the jury), secondary evidence can be used.

But the prosecution has, as does the proponent of secondary evidence in any civil or criminal case, the burden of making a prima facie showing as to both (1) and (2). * * * Here, the proponent of the secondary evidence made no factual showing as to (1) nor did it do [so as to] (2). Nor did the proponent attempt to make any other showing which might be construed as a foundation for use of secondary evidence other than the example we have mentioned. * * *

The judgment is reversed, and the cause remanded for a new trial.

WHYTE, P.J., and KATZ, J., concur.

See Federal Rules of Evidence 1001–08. California Evidence Code §§ 1500–10, 1530 and 1550; Chapter 1, pp. 33–37.

Hypothetical

A, as administrator of B's estate, sues X to cancel a deed that B had delivered to X. A claims that the deed was given to X by reason of X's fraudulent representation that she would care for B during his declining years. X testifies that the deed was given in consideration of prior services performed by her. In rebuttal, A produces a cancelled check for $5000 from B to X. X then testifies that the $5000 check was a loan from B so that she could add a room to her house, that she had executed a promissory note for $5000 to B for this loan, and that the loan had been repaid and the note marked paid and returned to her. A moves to strike X's testimony on the ground that the paid note is the best evidence. What result?

PART B. AUTHENTICATION

McCORMICK, EVIDENCE
395–96 (1954).*
[Footnotes omitted.]

One who seeks to introduce evidence of a particular fact, or item of proof, must generally give evidence (or offer assurance that he will do so) of those circumstances which make this fact or item relevant to some issue in the case. In respect to writings one of the commonest and most obvious of these circumstances on which relevancy may depend is the *authorship* of the writing. By whom was it written,

signed or adopted? Certainly any intelligible system of procedure must
require that if the legal significance of the writing depends upon its
authorship by a particular person, some showing must be made that he
was the author, if the writing is to be accepted for consideration. The
question is, what showing? In the everyday affairs of business and
social life, the practice is to look first to the writing itself and if it bears
the purported signature of X, or recites that it was made by him, we
assume if no question of authenticity is raised that the writing is what
it purports to be, that is, the writing of X.

It is just here that the common law trial procedure departs sharply
from men's customs in ordinary affairs, and adopts the opposite attitude, namely, that the purported signature or the recitation of authorship on the face of the writing will not be accepted as sufficient
preliminary proof of authenticity to secure the admission of the writing
in evidence. * * *

The term authentication is here used in the limited sense of proof
of authorship. It is sometimes employed in a wider meaning, embracing all proof which may be required as a preliminary to the admission
of a writing, chattel, photograph or the like. Thus in the case of
business records not only is proof of authorship required for admission,
but at common law various other facts such as that they were made in
the course of the business must also be proved as part of the "foundation." Similarly the identity of a bullet offered in a murder case as the
fatal bullet, or the correctness of a photograph would be part of the
necessary foundation-proof for admission. * * *

MANCARI v. FRANK P. SMITH, INC.

United States Court of Appeals, District of Columbia Circuit, 1940.
114 F.2d 834.

STEPHENS, Associate Justice. This is an appeal from a judgment
of the District Court of the United States for the District of Columbia
entered upon a verdict directed for the appellee at the close of the
appellant's case. Hereafter we refer to the appellant as plaintiff and to
the appellee as defendant.

The plaintiff sued upon an alleged violation of his right of privacy.
His complaint charged that the defendant Frank P. Smith, Inc., was
engaged in business in the District of Columbia, and that for commercial and advertising purposes, and wrongfully and maliciously and
without the plaintiff's knowledge or consent, it caused to be published
in the District of Columbia a so-called advertising "tear sheet" in the
form of the following purported newspaper article:

"Salvatore Mancari is Missing—Wide Search being Made

"Frank P. Smith, Inc., Offers Reward for Producing Valued
Prospect

"One of the most intensive manhunts in years was instituted today by Frank P. Smith, Inc., in an effort to solve a

mysterious disappearance that has baffled the organization for months.

"Today's bold step climaxes a long series of attempts to locate this missing man and discover some reason for his continued absence. The announcement of a worth-while reward in the nature of substantial savings on the kind of shoes he wears will do much, we believe, to bring about his return and solve the mystery.

"Representatives of Frank P. Smith, Inc., were confident they could find their man, they honestly believe that once a man enjoys the style, fit, comfort and longer wear of 'Foot-Joy,' the shoe that's different, he will wear them again—in fact there is no fairer test of 'Foot-Joy's' economy than to compare the low cost of wear per day with that of many shoes in America.

"Men who have worn 'Foot-Joy' know what a value they are at their regular price; they will be quick to take advantage of the present price before the increase. They know the quality is unchanged, they realize they are getting superior materials and workmanship that have built 'the shoe that's different,' they realize that 'Foot-Joy's' give them absolute comfort—that different feeling. When a man has once been fitted properly with 'Foot-Joy's' he will wear them on all occasions.

"Wanted!

"Reward Offered for Producing Salvatore Mancari

"We want this man; he's too valuable to lose! When last seen he was wearing a pair of shoes and apparently well pleased. When found he probably will still be wearing them! If he will make his first visit to the Frank P. Smith, Inc., a substantial reward in foot comfort waits him. See details below.

* * *"

The plaintiff charged that as a result of the publication of this material, he suffered mortification and humiliation—and for this he prayed damages.[1]

The defendant demurred to the plaintiff's complaint, but the demurrer was overruled. The defendant abided this ruling and entered three pleas. In the first of these it admitted that it was engaged in business in the District of Columbia, as alleged in the complaint; it denied each and every other allegation made in the complaint. In the second plea the defendant averred that: The defendant was a retailer of shoes, including "Foot-Joy" shoes manufactured by Field and Flint

---

1. According to the record and briefs there was a second count in the plaintiff's complaint charging libel through publication of the "tear sheet." To this count a demurrer was sustained. The count, however, does not appear in the record and no point is made concerning it on this appeal.

Company of Brockton, Massachusetts, and purchased outright by the defendant and held for sale on its own account and risk. Field and Flint Company, the manufacturer, had entered into an advertising contract with the Reuben H. Donnelley Corporation of New York, whereby the latter agreed to issue in behalf of the former advertising matter of the kind described in the plaintiff's complaint, with the names of prospective customers inserted by rubber stamp, this matter to be mailed by the Donnelley Corporation to prospective customers in Washington and elsewhere, these to be selected by the Donnelley Corporation itself. The defendant was not a party to this agreement, and had no knowledge until after the fact that such advertising matter had been sent to the plaintiff or to any other person. The defendant never authorized either Field and Flint Company or the Donnelley Corporation to act in the defendant's behalf in respect of this advertising. The third plea set up matter not material to the question involved in this appeal.

On the issues thus joined, the case went to trial before a jury. By Frances Mancari (the plaintiff's wife), and corroborating witnesses, the plaintiff proved that Mrs. Mancari had received through the mail, addressed to the plaintiff, the purported newspaper item, and that she had had it read to her—not herself readily reading English. Evidence was introduced on the subject of damages also. To prove that the defendant was responsible for the publication of the "tear sheet," the plaintiff introduced in evidence the "tear sheet" itself, pointing to the presence therein of the defendant's name. No other evidence was offered.

At the close of the plaintiff's case, the defendant moved for a directed verdict upon the ground that the evidence introduced failed to prove that the defendant was responsible for the publication of the article. The plaintiff urged that the presence of the defendant's name in the body of the advertisement was sufficient to raise a presumption of authorship and to take the case to the jury. The court granted the defendant's motion and directed a verdict. This appeal was then taken.

The ruling of the trial court that the evidence was insufficient to warrant submitting the case to the jury was correct. The mere presence in printed material of the name of a particular person constitutes no substantial evidence that that person caused such material to be written or published. Saenger Amusement Co. v. Murray; 4 Wigmore, Evidence (2d ed. 1923) § 2150. In the case cited, Murray sued the Amusement Company for personal injuries charged to have been caused by the negligence of the Amusement Company as his employer. It was shown that at the time of his injury, in September 1919, Murray was employed as a janitor in the Lomo Theater, a moving picture house in Hattiesburg, Tennessee. To prove that this theater was operated by the Amusement Company and that he was accordingly its employee, Murray offered in evidence September issues of a newspaper, the Hattiesburg American, containing advertisements of moving picture attractions to appear in the Lomo Theater. That portion of the advertisements relied upon to show that the Amusement Company operated the Lomo Theater was in the following terms:

"Saenger Amusement Company presents today at Lomo Theater," etc. "Saenger's Lomo Theater." "Saenger's Lomo Theater, Progressive Amusements, Progressive People. Saenger Amusement Company presents Evelyn Nesbitt."

As in the instant case, no other evidence was offered that the defendant company had any connection with the publishing of the advertisements. Over the objection of the Amusement Company they were received in evidence. On an appeal by the company from a judgment rendered against it, the admission of the evidence was held erroneous as constituting no proof. The Supreme Court of Mississippi said:

"We are of the opinion that these advertisements proved nothing except the fact that they appeared in the newspaper in question. For aught that appears to the contrary, they may have been wholly unauthorized by appellant, or appellant may have furnished to the management of the Lomo Theater, by rental or otherwise, the picture reels which were being used therein, without having any control or interest whatever in the business, or appellant may have rented such reels to the management of said picture show, and as a part of the consideration for such rental authorized and paid for said advertisements. The advertisements utterly fail to establish the vital fact that appellee at the time of his injury was an employee of appellant by virtue of the alleged ownership or control by appellant of the said Lomo Theater. Therefore these newspaper advertisements, standing alone, should have been excluded by the trial court." Wigmore, cit. supra, states:

"Printed matter in general bears upon itself no marks of authorship other than contents. But there is ordinarily no necessity for resting upon such evidence, since the responsibility for printed matter, under the substantive law, usually arises from the act of causing publication, not merely of writing, and hence there is usually available as much evidence of the act of printing or of handing to a printer as there would be of any other act, such as chopping a tree or building a fence. There is therefore no judicial sanction for considering the contents alone as sufficient evidence." * * *

Affirmed.

RUTLEDGE, Associate Justice (dissenting).

Assuming that a cause of action was stated, as to which I express no opinion, I think the evidence was sufficient to put the defendant to proof of its denial of publication.

The rule that the contents of a document, purporting to be a particular person's, are not of themselves sufficient evidence of genuineness, is based on two principles: (1) that other, and better, evidence generally is available to prove authorship; (2) the danger that "too many would be found to take fraudulent advantage of this rule." 4 Wigmore, Evidence (2d ed. 1923) § 2148. But, as to the latter, there is also "danger of abuse in the opposite direction" (Id., § 2149) and, as to the former, there are situations in which other evidence is not availa-

ble. In such a case, the first reason for the rule fails, and the contents
become the best, in fact the only available, evidence of authorship.
When this is true, evidence that the defendant did not publish the
document generally would be within his peculiar knowledge and the
situation, therefore, such as to require him to come forward with it.
The rule is not invariable and in special circumstances the contents
may be used as evidence of authorship or publication, particularly
when they relate to other facts which, when admitted or proved, serve
to identify the person named in the document as author. Cf. 4
Wigmore, Evidence (2d ed. 1923) §§ 2148–2150.

In the case of printed matter, the document itself generally contains no evidence of authorship other than its contents. Nothing in the
record shows that the "tear sheet" contained a printer's label or any
other means of identifying the printer, and through him the author.
The article contained not only defendant's name, repeated in four
places, but advertising solicitation for "Foot-Joy" shoes, together with
specific mention of the plaintiff as prospective customer. It therefore
identified defendant by name, by the general description of his business, by reference to the particular product in which he dealt, and it
solicited business for the defendant and for that product. There was no
indication of the manufacturer's identity or that the advertisement was
issued by the manufacturer. The clear inference from the contents was
that the defendant mailed the sheet. Nine out of ten persons, and
possibly the tenth, on receiving such a document through the mails
would assume that defendant had sent it. Furthermore, these facts
were verified by statements in defendant's plea, which we may consider
insofar as they are admissions, though we may not consider his denials.
Defendant admits that it was engaged in retailing shoes in Washington
and that "Foot-Joy" shoes were sold by it. To this extent its plea bears
out the identification of defendant by the contents of the tear sheet, and
made unnecessary production of proof by plaintiff to establish these
facts. When the verdict was directed, therefore, the evidence, together
with admissions in the pleadings, had established that defendant was a
retail shoe dealer in Washington, selling "Foot-Joy" shoes, and that the
tear sheet advertising this product and soliciting trade in it at defendant's store was sent through the mails and received at the intended
address. Furthermore, there was nothing in the contents or in the
advertising matter to indicate that another person was interested in the
business, the product, the advertising, or having it distributed.

Under these circumstances, the natural and normal inference is
that the sheet was mailed by the defendant. It is not customary or
usual for strangers to advertise gratuitously another's business or
product in a manner which involves, as this did, very considerable
expense. According to common experience, that is done, generally by
the owner or by another at his procurement. "National advertising" is
an apparent exception, but the usual manner in which that is done is
by indicating—and by emphasizing—the name of the manufacturer,
with or without the local dealer's name. Unless the mere mention of
"Foot-Joy" shoes in the sheet, which did not mention or purport to be
made on behalf of the manufacturer or anyone other than the defen-

dant, can be taken as rebutting the clear inference created by the entire remaining contents and admitted facts, that inference would appear to be, if not the only, certainly a reasonable, one to make from them. If it was reasonable, the jury should have been allowed to make or refuse to make it, providing defendant did not succeed in rebutting it by his proof.

In Saenger Amusement Co. v. Murray, relied upon by the majority, several inferences were possible, equally consistent with that which the plaintiff insisted the jury should be permitted to draw. The decision held that the advertisement could not be admitted to prove that plaintiff was an employee of defendant, not that its contents did not prove authorship.

In my opinion, the judgment should be reversed and the cause remanded for further proceedings.

NOTE

In Keegan v. Green Giant Co., 150 Me. 283, 110 A.2d 599 (1954), plaintiff complained of injury produced by a piece of metal which had allegedly been included in a can of peas. To establish that the named defendant was the packer and distributor of the offending peas, plaintiff offered the metal can and the label surrounding it. The label read in part, "Green Giant Brand Great Big Tender Sweet Peas. Distributed by Green Giant Company." The Court held that exclusion of the exhibit was not error since the label had not been authenticated.

FIRST STATE BANK OF DENTON v. MARYLAND CASUALTY CO.

United States Court of Appeals, Fifth Circuit, 1990.
918 F.2d 38.

JERRY E. SMITH, Circuit Judge:

The plaintiff, First State Bank of Denton, acting as executor of the will of J.T. Mills, appeals from a jury verdict finding that a fire at the Millses' home was set intentionally. The plaintiff contends that the district court erred by allowing defendant Maryland Casualty Company (the "insurance company") to introduce a telephone conversation that occurred between a police dispatcher and an unknown male at the Mills' home. * * * Finding no reversible error, we affirm.

I.

The parties agree on the basic facts. The Millses' residence, which was insured by the Maryland Casualty Company, was completely destroyed by fire. Pursuant to Texas law, the policy provided that in case of total loss, Mills would receive $133,000, the entire face amount of the policy. After inspecting the site, however, the insurance company concluded that the fire was set intentionally and thus refused to make any payment on the policy.

The Millses brought suit to recover on their policy, but both of them died before the trial. The First State Bank of Denton continued the claim as executor. At trial, the insurance company introduced evidence showing that the Millses' house was unoccupied for several weeks prior to the fire but that a neighbor had seen a light in the home a few hours before the flames struck. The company also introduced the testimony of a witness who, right before the fire started, saw a pickup truck leaving the road which accesses the residence. Only Mills and his wife had a key to the house, and Mills owned a pickup truck.

The insurance company also showed that Mills was in financial trouble, as he had bought a second home before he had sold his first. For two years, Mills had attempted to sell his first home, but it had enkindled little interest; because of poor market conditions, the value of the home now was significantly less than the face value of the Millses' policy.

The company concluded by introducing evidence showing that Mills was not at his new home at the time of the fire. About fifteen minutes after the fire began, a police dispatcher attempted to contact Mills at his new residence to notify him of the fire. The dispatcher testified that when she called Mills there, at 1:00 a.m., an unidentified person replied that Mr. Mills was not home. Denton objected, believing this testimony to be unauthenticated and hearsay. The trial court allowed the insurance company to introduce the evidence.   * * *

Fed.R.Evid. 901 provides that all evidence must be authenticated before being admitted and that this requirement is satisfied by evidence reliable enough to show that it is what its proponent claims it to be. The rule provides a laundry list of examples of proper authentication. Rule 901(b)(6) provides that authentication can occur for a

> [t]elephone conversation[ ], by evidence that a call was made to the number assigned at the time by the telephone company to a particular person or business, if (A) in the case of a person, circumstances, including self-identification, show the person answering to be the one called, or (B) in the case of a business, the call was made to a place of business and the conversation related to business reasonably transacted over the telephone.

The illustrations contained in rule 901(b) also provide that they only are examples and do not exhaust all possibilities.

Under the plain language of rule 901(b)(6), when a person places a call to a listed number, and the answering party identifies himself as the expected party, the call is properly authenticated. What is different about the present case is that the person who answered the phone did not identify himself as Mr. Mills; rather, he simply identified the residence as "the Millses' residence." The plaintiff contends that this does not fit within the illustration and that the phone call thus was unauthenticated.

What plaintiff ignores is that the illustrations are not exclusive, but are intended only to provide clear examples of properly authenticated evidence. All that is necessary in authenticating a phone call is that the proponent offer "sufficient authentication to make a *prima facie* case that would allow the issue of identity to be decided by the jury." *United States v. Register*, 496 F.2d 1072, 1077 (5th Cir.1974), *cert. denied*, 419 U.S. 1120, 95 S.Ct. 802, 42 L.Ed.2d 819 (1975).

The plaintiff's position, in demanding that the person answering the phone himself be the defendant, implicitly treats the authentication requirement as requiring an admission by a party opponent. This ignores the true reason for requiring the self-identification: The primary authentication occurs because the phone company usually is accurate. "The calling of a number assigned by the telephone company reasonably supports the assumption that the listing is correct and that the number is the one reached." Rule 901, advisory committee note example (6).

The self-identification supports this maxim by showing that the correct number was dialed. "In such a situation the accuracy of the telephone system, the probable absence of motive to falsify and the lack of opportunity for premeditated fraud all tend to support the conclusion that the self-identification of the speaker is reliable." E. Cleary, McCormick on Evidence § 226 at 698 (3d ed. 1984); accord Register, 496 F.2d at 1076–77.

The evidence in this case meets the *prima facie* standard established in *Register*. The dispatcher who called the Millses' residence on the night of the fire testified that she correctly dialed the Millses' number and that when she asked whether she had reached the Millses' residence, the person replied that "[t]his is the Millses' residence." Furthermore, when she asked whether Mr. Mills was home, the person answered, "J.T. Mills is not at home." *   *   *

There is little doubt that the dispatcher actually reached Mills's home. The trial court thus did not abuse its discretion by overruling the authentication objection. *   *   *

NOTE

See Federal Rules of Evidence 901–903; California Evidence Code §§ 1400–1402 and 1410–1421. For additional discussion of procedures for authentication of writings, see Chapter I, Making the Record, supra.

Hypothetical

A sues X for damages for personal injuries suffered in a two-car collision. A testifies that X ran a red light. A produces a letter addressed to him and bearing a signature, "X," which states that X ran the red light. A testifies that he received this letter through the mail about a week after the accident. A offers the letter in evidence. X makes a lack-of-authentication objection. What result?

Chapter X

COMPETENCY OF WITNESSES

HILL v. SKINNER

Court of Appeals of Ohio, 1947.
81 Ohio App. 375, 79 N.E.2d 787.

DOYLE, Presiding Judge. This is an action under the Ohio statute, Section 5838, General Code, seeking to hold the owners and harborers of a dog called "Chang" with liability for damages arising out of an episode in which the dog, Chang, is alleged to have seized with his teeth and injured a youngster aged approximately four, the petitioner herein.

A jury, upon trial, awarded damages in the amount of $500. The judgment rendered thereon, in the Court of Common Pleas of Summit county, is part of the final order from which this appeal is taken, and consideration will be first given to the legality of this money judgment.

1. The appellants say "There was no evidence of a 'bite' anywhere in the record from any of the witnesses save the plaintiff himself. Without this * * * minor's testimony there was evidence of injury only with barbed wire, glass, a gashed steel barrel and other dogs being present as explanation."

It is a fact that there is no *direct* testimony of this dog's attack except that given by the child. If this evidence has probative worth, and is competent, it, coupled with the circumstances and other facts shown to exist, is sufficient to furnish the degree of proof necessary to sustain the judgment.

Section 11493, General Code, reads:

"All persons are competent witnesses except those of unsound mind, and children under ten years of age who appear incapable of receiving just impressions of the facts and transactions respecting which they are examined, or of relating them truly."

The Supreme Court of this state has recently ruled on that part of this statute pertaining to witnesses claimed to be of "unsound mind."

"2. The competency of an insane person to testify as a witness lies in the discretion of the trial judge and a reviewing court will not disturb the ruling thereon where there is no abuse of discretion. State v. Wildman.

And in 2 Wigmore on Evidence (3 Ed.), Section 505, it is said:

"With reference to the general capacity to observe, recollect, and narrate, the same principles apply to Mental Immaturity that are applied to Mental Derangement."

The essential test of the competency of an infant witness is his comprehension of the obligation to tell the truth and his intellectual

654

capacity of observation, recollection and communication. The nature of his conception of the obligation to tell the truth is of little importance if he shows that he will fulfill the obligation to speak truthfully as a duty which he owes a Diety or something held in reverence or regard, and if he has the intellectual capacity to communicate his observations and experiences.

The trial court, in chambers, examined the child at length, touching upon his qualifications to testify. Among other questions he was asked: "Do you know about telling the truth, what happens if you don't tell the truth?" and he answered, "They won't love me." Question: "Who won't love you?" Answer: "God won't love me." And in further answer to dozens of questions propounded by both the judge and counsel, the child demonstrated a capacity for memory of events, observation, recollection and communication.

Following this necessary and proper examination by the trial judge of the prospective witness, the court permitted him to testify. The child thereupon, direct examination, testified in part as follows:

"Q. Cary do you remember when you went over to Skinner's? A. Sure.

"Q. Tell the judge and jury what happened. A. The doggy bit me.

"Q. What doggy bit you? A. Skinner's doggy.

"Q. What were you doing with Skinner's dog? A. I was loving him.

"Q. How? A. Like that (indicating.)

"Q. You mean around his neck? A. Yes."

On cross-examination appears the following:

"Q. Where did Chang bite you, can you tell the ladies, take your fingers and show me where he bit you? A. He bit me when I was loving him.

"Q. Where did he bite you, did he bite you on the leg? A. No, he bite me on the head and on my mouth here (indicating.)"

As we view the testimony, the youthful narrator, except for a few nonresponsive answers, clearly described and explained the circumstances giving rise to this action. The evidence considered as a whole describes the wandering of the child out onto his neighbor's yard and the subsequent attack of the dog, under circumstances clearly related by the child. There is nothing in the record to show, except through pure guess and speculation, that the head injuries resulted from any other cause.

Paraphrasing a syllabus in State v. Wildman, supra, to fit this case, the rule may be pronounced to be that the competency of a child of mental immaturity to testify as a witness lies in the discretion of the trial judge, and a reviewing court will not disturb the ruling thereon when there is no abuse of discretion. In the instant case we find no

such abuse. We further find that the evidence in the record is such as
to warrant the jury in finding in favor of the petitioner.

Judgment modified to provide for the destruction of the dog, as
required by the Ohio statute, and as modified, affirmed.

TRACY, HANDBOOK OF THE LAW OF EVIDENCE

120–133 (1952).*
[Footnotes omitted.]

COMPETENCY

In general. As we said in the Introduction, in the early days, the
facts in a case were brought out only by the knowledge of the members
of the jury; the calling of outside witnesses was a later development.
It is not surprising that at first these outsiders were greeted with
suspicion. Apparently the early courts looked on nearly every proffered witness as a possible prospective perjurer, and if there were any
reason to suspect that certain characteristics or circumstances of a
witness might incline him to lie, that person was considered incompetent to testify. Nearly all the old incompetencies have now been
removed, but they will be discussed here briefly for their historical
interest.

Religious belief. At common law, the religious belief of a prospective witness was most important, for unless he was found to believe
in a Supreme Being who was a rewarder of truth and an avenger of
falsehood, he was incapable of taking an oath and therefore of testifying. Ancient reports are full of cases dealing with this disability, but
the common law rules on the subject have been made obsolete by the
universal enactment of constitutional and statutory provisions. Such
legislation has been along two lines: (1) abolishing any religious test as
a prerequisite to taking an oath; (2) giving to those who have scruples
against taking an oath the privilege to affirm.

In no American jurisdiction is religious belief now a test of the
competency of a witness.

Infamy. At early common law a part of the punishment for crime
was that the person found guilty was thereby rendered infamous. He
lost the rights of an ordinary citizen: the right to vote, the right to hold
office, the right to serve on a jury, the right to testify in a court of law.
The rule that he was incompetent to serve as a witness was based on
the theory that such a person could not be expected to regard the
obligation of an oath.

The reports and digests are full of cases construing this rule, but it
has now been generally abolished. The reasons for its abolishment are
obvious: (1) There is no logical connection between committing a crime
(except probably the crime of perjury) and mendacity; there is no
reason for believing that a person who has murdered will also lie. (2)
Prosecutors in criminal cases discovered that by the enforcement of this
rule they were being deprived of indispensable evidence in criminal
cases, for the testimony of an accomplice who had himself pleaded

guilty or who had stood trial and had been convicted could never be used. The rule is still applied by statute in a number of states to convictions for the crime of perjury, including subornation of perjury and, in a few southern states, to a specified list of infamous crimes. Most of these last-named jurisdictions, however, apply the rule in criminal trials only.

The attorney should examine the statutes of his state on this point. If there is no statute, there is no disability, for the common law rule on this subject no longer exists anywhere.

Interest. In the administration of justice at common law, it was considered essential to prevent a witness from testifying if he were interested in the outcome of the cause, as a party or otherwise. The reasons asserted to support this rule of disability were interestingly set out in a leading treatise on evidence published as late as 1824:

The law will not receive the evidence of any person, even under the sanction of an oath, who has an interest in giving the proposed evidence, and consequently whose interest conflicts with his duty. This rule of exclusion, considered in its principle, requires little explanation. It is founded on the known infirmities of human nature, which is too weak to be generally restrained by religious or moral obligations, when tempted and solicited in a contrary direction by temporal interests. There are, no doubt, many whom no interests could seduce from a sense of duty, and their exclusion by the operation of this rule may in particular cases shut out the truth. But the law must prescribe general rules; and experience proves that more mischief would result from the general reception of interested witnesses than is occasioned by their general exclusion.

Generations of experience in applying this rule of exclusion demonstrated to the satisfaction of jurists not only that the courts were wrong in assuming that pecuniary interest necessarily assures falsehood in testimony but that many apparently meritorious cases were rendered impossible of proof because the only persons who knew the facts could not testify, and that, consequently, more mischief resulted from the exclusion of the testimony of such witnesses than would have resulted from its reception. Therefore, by statutory enactment in practically every jurisdiction, such disability has been abolished, and interested persons may now testify fully, except in one class of cases—namely, where the survivor of a transaction with a deceased person undertakes to testify against the latter's estate. This exception exists by statute in all but a very few states, being popularly known as the "Dead Man's Act."

Testimony of interested survivor. * * *

Mental capacity. A witness will ordinarily be presumed to have the mental capacity to testify. That capacity to testify may be challenged, however, in which event the mental capacity of the witness is to be determined by the trial judge as a preliminary question of fact. The three situations in which such challenge may be made are where the proffered witness is an infant, where he is alleged to be insane, or where he is alleged to be intoxicated.

Infancy. An infant of very tender years is, of course, incompetent to understand the nature of an oath or to narrate with understanding the facts of what he has seen. At what age does he become competent so to understand or narrate? Courts have struggled with that question, and certain judges have endeavored to lay down a rule determining the age at which a child should be admitted as a witness. There is so great a difference, however, in the mental growth of children that it is impossible to fix a proper age limit. Before a witness is permitted to testify, the court should be convinced on two points: that he understands the nature of an oath and the possible consequences of lying, and that he possesses the capacities of observation, recollection, and communication. In other words, he must be sufficiently mature to make an intelligent statement of what he saw take place. The proper person to decide these two questions is the trial judge, after talking with the child and observing him. Sometimes, on the question of whether the child understands the nature of an oath, the judge may consult the child's minister or priest.

A word of caution on the use of child witnesses: The ordinary child is a great weaver of romances. He may often relate something he has read in a story as a personal experience. His story should be searched for its truth before he is called to the stand. If he is a witness for the opponent, he should be skillfully cross-examined.

Caution should also be used in preparing the child witness for his examination. An experienced attorney will not ordinarily call a witness to the stand unless he has first thoroughly gone over with him the story he is to tell to the court and jury and has prepared him for the cross-examination to which he may be subjected. But it is not safe to do this too thoroughly with a child witness, for if he is asked on cross-examination "Why did you say so-and-so?", he is likely to reply "Because Mr. Blank told me to."

A child witness is usually frightened at finding himself the center of attention in the court room, and it may be difficult to get him to talk at all or to talk loud enough to be heard. In such a case it is a common practice for the attorney to start out with some friendly, irrelevant questions to put the witness at his ease before bringing the examination around to the facts in the case. In this practice he will usually be indulged by the trial judge.

Mental derangement. In the early days, one whose mind was affected was regarded as not capable of giving testimony in a court of law. But as the knowledge of mental disease developed, it was seen how wrong such a rule may be. A person may be insane only on certain subjects or at certain times. For example, in a leading English case an attendant in an asylum for the insane was being prosecuted for manslaughter inflicted on an inmate. The prosecution called as one of its witnesses another inmate. There was no question but that this inmate was properly in the asylum. He stated on examination that he had 20,000 spirits speaking to him, who ascended from his stomach and head. Yet he appeared to understand the obligations of an oath and the consequences of perjury, and he gave a perfectly collected and rational account of the affair, which he reported himself to have witnessed. This testimony was admitted.

The rule is therefore now thoroughly established that an insane man can be a competent witness if he can pass these two tests: knowledge and appreciation of the obligation of an oath and the consequences of testifying falsely, and ability to tell an intelligent story of what he saw take place.

One question on which the courts have had some difficulty is whether, assuming that the witness can meet these two tests when called to the stand, he may still be held to be a competent witness if he was incapable of observing intelligently at the time of the event concerning which he is to testify. Ordinarily the courts will admit evidence of a derangement occurring before the time of testifying as affecting only the credibility of the witness, not his competency to testify.

Intoxication. The same rules that apply to mental derangement would seem to apply to a witness who is intoxicated when he appears on the stand or who was intoxicated at the time of the occurrence to which he testifies. The test to be applied to a witness who is intoxicated on the stand is whether he is capable of intelligent and truthful narration. That is a preliminary question of fact for the trial judge. If the witness is sober on the stand but was intoxicated at the time of the transaction to which he testifies, the fact of his intoxication at that time would be admissible as bearing on the credibility of his testimony, but not to bar him as a witness.

Marital relationship. Two questions are involved here: the competency of the husband or wife as a witness, and the privilege of husband or wife not to have the other spouse testify. Here only the question of competency will be discussed. The matter of privilege will be discussed later.

At common law a wife was not permitted to testify for or against her husband, or a husband for or against his wife, without the other's consent, except in such cases of necessity as assaults by one upon the other, actions for divorce, and the like. The disability was directed to the social end of preventing marital discord arising from one party's testifying against the other or being coerced to testify for him. It was most often applicable to the wife. As her social status improved and her independence of her husband increased, it was seen that often a greater harm was done to the cause of justice by depriving the courts of needed testimony than was warranted by the need of preserving family concord. So gradually legislation began to be enacted limiting the applicability of the rule. Practically every state now has some statute on the subject. Some of these statutes merely increase the number of common law exceptions; others abolish the common law rule altogether except as to confidential communications made by one spouse to the other during coverture. Inasmuch as Congress has never enacted any statute on the subject, the federal courts continued to apply the common law until 1933. In that year the Supreme Court handed down a decision that reviewed the history of the rule, recognized its abolishment or limitation by statute in nearly every common law jurisdiction and the fact that the reason for its original adoption no longer existed, and approved the admission of the testimony of the wife in the case before it.

The enactment of legislation on this subject has been so general that it can be said that, except in one or two jurisdictions, the incompetency of husband or wife as a witness in a case when a spouse is a party no longer exists. The marital relations problems that continue to confront the courts are those of privilege rather than of competency. [See supra pp. 579–585.—Ed.]

It should be noted, however, that it is the rule of many courts that on one subject married persons are still considered incompetent to testify: Neither husband nor wife will be permitted, as a witness, to bastardize the issue of the wife after marriage by testifying to the nonaccess of the husband. The rule is said to be one of public policy, in the interests of morality and decency.

Official connection with tribunal. Is a judge, a court clerk or bailiff, an attorney, or a juror a competent witness?

Judge

A judge is not incompetent to testify merely because he holds a judicial office, and this is so whether he is called upon to testify to actual facts or as a witness to character. The question may be asked whether he can take the stand as a witness in a case being tried before him. Fortunately this question rarely arises, since the judge will generally know in advance that he is to be called and will arrange to have another judge hear the case. If the possibility of his being called as a witness arises during the trial, the judge may either call in another judge to take over or order a retrial before another judge. On the strict question whether the judge is actually incompetent to testify if he is to continue to sit in the case, the modern rule is that a judge is not a competent witness in a case in which he is presiding unless there is a statute permitting it, but that if he does testify with the consent of all parties no reversible error occurs and he does not lose jurisdiction. A federal statute requires a judge to disqualify himself under such circumstances.

Court Officers

A court attaché, clerk, bailiff, or stenographer may testify generally in the case being tried, and there is no question but that he is a competent witness.

Attorney

Whether an attorney may take the stand in a trial in which he is engaged as counsel has caused some controversy and a certain amount of loose thinking by the courts. There are two questions involved, one of evidence law, the other of professional ethics. It is a rule of legal ethics that, except on merely formal matters, he should not testify in a case in which he is engaged as counsel. It will not be unusual for him to testify to formal matters, such as the identification of a document or the calculation of interest on a mortgage, on which there will be no controversy. If, however, he is called upon to testify to matters of a controversial nature, he should immediately withdraw from the trial and have his case conducted by counsel already engaged in the trial or obtain a new trial counsel in his place. But there is nothing in the law of evidence that makes him incompetent to testify as a witness. If the attorney violates the canons of ethics by continuing in the trial after testifying, he is subject to bar discipline. Only a few courts have held that such action constitutes reversible error, and even these courts regard the conduct of the attorney as the error, not the admission of his testimony.

Jurors

A juror may be called as a witness in a trial in which he is engaged, returning to the box after he has finished his testimony. Although there are strong arguments against permitting this practice, the consequences of a refusal to let him testify—namely, that he would tell his story to his fellow jurors in their deliberations without being subject to cross-examination or impeachment—are such that the courts have chosen the lesser of two evils. If the testimony of the juror is on a vital point in the case, the court may consider it wise to declare a mistrial.

The situation of a juror's giving testimony on an ordinary issue in the case rarely arises, for usually his knowledge of the facts of the case will have been brought out on his voir dire examination, and he will have been challenged and excused for cause. The problem of the competency of a juror to testify will most often arise when, on the trial or after the verdict, he is called as a witness on a claim of misconduct on the part of the jury. * * *

NEW YORK CIV. PRAC. ACT & RULES, § 4519
(Formerly N.Y.Civ.Prac.Act § 347).

§ 4519. Personal transaction or communication between witness and decedent or lunatic.

Upon the trial of an action or the hearing upon the merits of a special proceeding, a party or a person interested in the event, or a person from, through or under whom such a party or interested person derives his interest or title by assignment or otherwise, shall not be examined as a witness in his own behalf or interest, or in behalf of the party succeeding to his title or interest against the executor, administrator or survivor of a deceased person or the committee of a lunatic, or a person deriving his title or interest from, through or under a deceased person or lunatic, by assignment, or otherwise, concerning a personal transaction or communication between the witness and the deceased person or lunatic, except where the executor, administrator, survivor, committee or person so deriving title or interest is examined in his own behalf, or the testimony of the lunatic or deceased person is given in evidence, concerning the same transaction or communication. A person shall not be deemed interested for the purposes of this section by

reason of being a stockholder or officer of any banking corporation
which is a party to the action or proceeding, or interested in the event
thereof. No party or person interested in the event, who is otherwise
competent to testify, shall be disqualified from testifying by the possible
imposition of costs against him or the award of costs to him. A party
or person interested in the event or a person from, through or under
whom such a party or interested person derives his interest or title by
assignment or otherwise, shall not be qualified for the purposes of this
section, to testify in his own behalf or interest, or in behalf of the party
succeeding to his title or interest, to personal transactions or communications with the donee of a power of appointment in an action or
proceeding for the probate of a will, which exercises or attempts to
exercise a power of appointment granted by the will of a donor of such
power, or in an action or proceeding involving the construction of the
will of the donee after its admission to probate.

Nothing contained in this section, however, shall render a person
incompetent to testify as to the facts of an accident or the results
therefrom where the proceeding, hearing, defense or cause of action
involves a claim of negligence or contributory negligence in an action
wherein one or more parties is the representative of a deceased or
incompetent person based upon, or by reason of, the operation or
ownership of a motor vehicle being operated upon the highways of the
state, or the operation or ownership of aircraft being operated in the air
space over the state, or the operation or ownership of a vessel on any of
the lakes, rivers, streams, canals or other waters of this state, but this
provision shall not be construed as permitting testimony as to conversations with the deceased. As amended L.1963, c. 532, § 22.

See California Evidence Code § 1261.

Comment to Section 1261—Law Revision Commission

The dead man statute (subdivision 3 of Section 1880 of the Code of
Civil Procedure) prohibits a party who sues on a claim against a
decedent's estate from testifying to any fact occurring prior to the
decedent's death. The theory apparently underlying the statute is that
it would be unfair to permit the surviving claimant to testify to such
facts when the decedent is precluded by his death from doing so. To
balance the positions of the parties, the living may not speak because
the dead cannot.

The dead man statute operates unsatisfactorily. It prohibits testimony concerning matters of which the decedent had no knowledge and,
hence, to which he could not have testified even if he had survived. It
operates unevenly since it does not prohibit testimony relating to
claims under, as distinguished from claims against, the decedent's
estate even though the effect of such a claim may be to frustrate the
decedent's plan for the disposition of his property. See the Law
Revision Commission's Comment to Code of Civil Procedure Section
1880 and 1 Cal.Law Revision Comm'n, Rep., Rec. & Studies, Recommendation and Study Relating to the Dead Man Statute at D–1 (1957). The

dead man statute excludes otherwise relevant and competent evidence—even if it is the only available evidence—and frequently this
forces the courts to decide cases with a minimum of information
concerning the actual facts. See the Supreme Court's complaint in
Light v. Stevens, 159 Cal. 288, 292, 113 P. 659, 660 (1911) ("Owing to the
fact that the lips of one of the parties to the transaction are closed by
death and those of the other party by the law, the evidence on this
question is somewhat unsatisfactory."). Hence, the dead man statute is
not continued in the Evidence Code.

Under the Evidence Code, the positions of the parties are balanced
by throwing more light, not less, on the actual facts. Repeal of the
dead man statute permits the claimant to testify without restriction.
To balance this advantage, Section 1261 permits hearsay evidence of
the decedent's statements to be admitted. Certain safeguards—i.e.,
personal knowledge, recent perception, and circumstantial evidence of
trustworthiness—are included in the section to provide some protection
for the party against whom the statements are offered, for he has no
opportunity to test the hearsay by cross-examination.

STATE EX REL. COLLINS v. SUPERIOR COURT

Supreme Court of Arizona, 1982.
132 Ariz. 180, 644 P.2d 1266.

SUPPLEMENTAL OPINION

FELDMAN, Justice.

In our original opinion in this case, we held that a witness who had
undergone hypnosis should not be permitted to testify. The State
moved for a rehearing. This opinion follows the order granting the
motion for rehearing.

The hypnosis question first arose in State v. La Mountain, where
we held that in a rape prosecution, the court erred in admitting
hypnotically induced recall pertaining to identification. This decision
was followed by State v. Mena, in which we reversed the conviction,
holding that "until hypnosis gains general acceptance in the fields of
medicine and psychiatry as a method by which memories are accurately
improved without undue danger of distortion, delusion or fantasy, we
feel that testimony of witnesses which has been tainted by hypnosis
should be excluded in criminal cases."

Hypnosis was not so easily to be put beyond us. The issue returned
in the case *sub judice,* and in our original opinion, we repeated that
because of its unreliability and the phenomena which interfere with the
right of effective cross-examination, post-hypnotic recall testimony
would be inadmissible in criminal trials. We extended the rule to the
issue of competency, and held that any person who had been hypnotized
would not be permitted to testify to hypnotically induced recall, and
would also be incompetent to testify to *any* fact, even those which
demonstrably had been recalled prior to hypnosis.

One week later, in Lemieux v. Superior Court, we held that these
rules would be applicable to civil cases, at least to the extent that

persons hypnotized subsequent to the mandate could not testify to
matters discussed under hypnosis. Two other cases involving hypnotically induced testimony have been submitted for decision and are under
advisement.

Thus, the motion for rehearing in this case has called into question
both the holdings in the previous decisions and the hypnosis issues of
the pending cases.

* * *

[FACTS]

Over a three year period, from August, 1977 to May, 1980, eighteen
reported rape incidents occurred in unpopulated areas in west Phoenix.
There is some variance among the assaults but essentially they followed
a similar pattern. Couples in vehicles were approached by a masked,
heavy-set male armed with a pistol and carrying what the state characterizes as a "rape kit," consisting of ropes, blindfolds, ground cloth, and
toilet paper. In each instance the assailant informed the couple he was
going to steal their car or take their money and proceeded to tie and
blindfold the couple. After using the ground cloth for the rape, the
assailant would use the toilet paper to clean the woman, and then untie
the victims, return the paraphernalia to his tote bag, and leave the area
on foot.

The Phoenix Police Department and the Maricopa County Sheriff's
Office investigated the case for several years, taking statements, analyzing fingerprints, sending hair samples to the F.B.I. lab, and increasing patrols in the area. To obtain additional information on the
identification of the assailant seven victims were hypnotized.

On July 1, 1980 defendant Silva was arrested as he approached an
undercover decoy vehicle containing a male and female officer in
plainclothes. Silva was wearing a mask, armed with a pistol, and
carrying the "rape kit."

Silva was charged with forty felony counts involving kidnapping,
sexual assault, * * *

* * *

At this point, we need make only the following observations by way
of summary:

1. The nature of hypnosis

Although experts disagree about the many aspects of hypnosis, all concur that hypnosis is a sleeplike state whereby
response to stimuli is more easily achieved than in a waking
state. * * * Categorized as a state of heightened concentra-
tion, hypnosis is achieved by creating a passiveness in the
subject * * *. The subject, with increased receptivity to
instruction, is guided into a trance-like state through a series
of suggestions from [1] the hypnotist. The hypnotized subject

---

1. Use of hypnosis to revive or refresh
memory necessarily involves age regression. The subject is asked to put himself
back to some earlier time, to visualize the
events which transpired at that time and
relate them to the hypnotist. It is then
suggested to the subject that upon awaken-
ing he will recall that which he has been

can be regressed to past times and places and recount the emotions and events experienced then. For this purpose, hypnosis has been utilized by prosecution and defense alike to stimulate recall * * *.

2. There are serious problems inherent in the use of the procedure. For example,

> Two salient conditions that usually characterize the person who is in a hypnotic state or trance are *hypersuggestibility* and *hypercompliance.* * * * Thus, the hypnotized individual is not only more easily influenced but is also more highly motivated to please others, most especially the hypnotist and those who are seen as associated with the hypnotist. Levitt, *The Use of Hypnosis to "Freshen" the Memory of Witnesses or Victims,* Trial, April 1981, at 56.

Thus, the hypnotized subject may not only have heightened recall of events he did experience, but may have pseudomemories of facts he did not experience but which were consciously or unconsciously suggested to him by the hypnotist or which he has actually fantasized or confused and transferred from other events and memories. These become part of his "recall" in an effort to satisfy his desire to fulfill the implied "demand" of the hypnotist to answer the questions asked during the hypnotic trance. This latter phenomenon is known as "confabulation." Thus, the more closely the hypnotized subject is questioned, the greater the danger that information produced will be inaccurate.

3. Once a person has been hypnotized, he becomes absolutely confident in the events as "recalled" during the hypnotic trance.

4. The most dangerous aspect of all is that:

> During the hypnotic session, neither the subject nor the hypnotist can distinguish between true memories and pseudo memories of various kinds in the reported recall; and when the subject repeats that recall in the waking state (e.g., in a trial) neither an expert witness nor a lay observer (e.g., the judge or jury) can make a similar distinction. In each instance, if the claimed memory is not or cannot be verified by wholly independent means, no one can reliably tell whether it is an accurate recollection or mere confabulation. Because of the foregoing pressures on the subject to present the hypnotist with a logically complete and satisfying memory of the prior event, neither the detail, coherence, nor plausibility of the resulting recall is any guarantee of its veracity.

able to see, remember and relate to the hypnotist during the regressed state. An interesting aspect of the problem presented by hypnosis is that while the subject of age regression is often able to give a convincing description of that which allegedly occurred during the past event, experiments have shown that the technique of age *progression* can also be used during hypnosis. This technique involves telling the hypnotized subject that he is being transported to some specific time in the future. He is then asked to relate what he sees. Many subjects are able to give a very convincing description of what they "see" during such age progression. *See* Orne, *The Use and Misuse of Hypnosis in Court,* in 3 Crime & Justice 61, 77 (M. Tonry & N. Morris eds. 1981).

People v. Shirley, 31 Cal.3d 18 (1982).

These problems and the resulting ramifications were more completely discussed with complete citation to the medical literature in our opinion in *Mena* and in the original opinion in this case. Reexamination of the literature originally cited and examination of the most recent publications lead us to reaffirm our original conclusion that the threshold question of reliability must be resolved by precluding courtroom use of hypnotically recalled testimony.

This conclusion is reinforced by the trend in the most recent cases to refuse to follow *Harding* and its progeny. The cases, after exhaustive analysis, hold that hypnotically refreshed testimony is not *per se* admissible, rejecting the *Harding* proposition that the problems inherent to hypnosis go only to the weight rather than the admissibility of the evidence.

Thus, we reaffirm our previous determination that hypnosis has not received sufficient general acceptance in the scientific community to give reasonable assurance that the benefit of the results produced under even the best of circumstances will be sufficiently reliable to outweigh the risks of abuse or prejudice. We reject the *Harding* rule that hypnotically induced recall is admissible as a general matter and that the problems inherent in the use of the technique go to weight rather than admissibility.

Our previous decisions, however, went further and held that hypnotically induced testimony was inadmissible in any circumstance and for any reason. At this point, recent developments in the use of this evidence with appropriate "safeguards" deserve mention.

THE USE OF HYPNOSIS WITH "SAFEGUARDS"

Several of the recent cases have found insufficient acceptance in the relevant scientific community to permit application of a *per se* rule of admissibility, but have nevertheless adopted a rule involving limited admissibility under "safeguards."

* * *

As a result of [Dr. Martin T. Orne's] [2] original article and his testimony or affidavits in various cases, several courts concluded that

---

2. Dr. Orne is a Doctor of Medicine, Professor of Psychiatry at the University of Pennsylvania, Director of the Unit for Experimental Psychiatry at the University of Pennsylvania Hospital and Senior Attending Psychiatrist at that hospital. He also holds a Ph.D. in Psychology. He is Past-President of the Society for Clinical and Experimental Hypnosis, Past-President of the International Society for Hypnosis, and has been Editor of the International Journal of Clinical and Experimental Hypnosis. He has served as a reviewer of research proposals on hypnosis for the National Science Foundation, the National Institute of Mental Health, the Office of Scientific Research of the United States Air Force and the Office of Naval Research. He has been a consultant for a number of law enforcement agencies. He has been principal investigator of a major research group working on the nature of hypnosis and related phenomena since 1960. He has been a member of the editorial boards of various journals of psychiatry and psychology and has, himself, published over one hundred scientific articles. In addition, he has used hypnosis in clinical practice, has taught the subject and has carried out research on the nature of hypnosis. He wrote the article on hypnosis for the Encyclopedia Brittanica and has served as a witness on the nature of hypnosis, its acceptance in the scientific community and its reliability in many of

the use of hypnosis as a procedure to increase recall had achieved such a degree of acceptance in the scientific community that, despite its inherent dangers, the testimony could be admitted. In each of these cases, the court imposed certain safeguards on the hypnotic procedure as a condition precedent to admissibility. In each of the cases, the safeguards are quite similar, primarily because directly or indirectly the safeguards were derived from Dr. Orne's outline of the conditions under which hypnosis should be performed and without which its results should be deemed unreliable. These safeguards are well outlined by the New Jersey Supreme Court:

> Whenever a party in a criminal trial seeks to introduce a witness who has undergone hypnosis to refresh his memory, the party must inform his opponent of his intention and provide him with the recording of the session and other pertinent material. The trial court will then rule on the admissibility of the testimony either at a pretrial hearing or at a hearing out of the jury's presence. In reviewing the admissibility of hypnotically refreshed testimony, the trial court should evaluate both the kind of memory loss that hypnosis was used to restore and the specific technique employed, based on expert testimony presented by the parties. The object of this review is not to determine whether the proffered testimony is accurate, but instead whether the use of hypnosis and the procedure followed in the particular case was a reasonably reliable means of restoring the witness' memory.

> The first question a court must consider is the appropriateness of using hypnosis for the kind of memory loss encountered. The reason for a subject's lack of memory is an important factor in evaluating the reliability of hypnosis in restoring recall. According to defendant's expert, Dr. Orne, hypnosis often is reasonably reliable in reviving normal recall where there is a pathological reason, such as a traumatic neurosis, for the witness' inability to remember. On the other hand, the likelihood of obtaining reasonably accurate recall diminishes if hypnosis is used simply to refresh a witness' memory or concerning details where there may be no recollection at all or to "verify" one of several conflicting accounts given by a witness.

> A related factor to be considered is whether the witness has any discernible motivation for not remembering or for "recalling" a particular version of the events. In either case, the possibility of creating self-serving fantasy is significant
> *   *   *.

> Once it is determined that a case is of a kind likely to yield normal recall if hypnosis is properly administered, then it is necessary to determine whether the procedures followed were reasonably reliable. Of particular importance are the manner of questioning and the presence of cues or suggestions during

the cases cited in this opinion (footnote relocated).

the trance and the post-hypnotic period. * * * [citing Orne and others] An additional factor affecting the reliability of the procedure is the amenability of the subject to hypnosis * * *.

To provide an adequate record for evaluating the reliability of the hypnotic procedure, and to ensure a minimum level of reliability, we also adopt several procedural requirements based on those suggested by Dr. Orne and prescribed by the trial court * * *. *Before it may introduce hypnotically re-freshed testimony, a party must demonstrate compliance with these requirements.*

First, a psychiatrist or psychologist experienced in the use of hypnosis must conduct the session. * * *

Second, the professional conducting the hypnotic session should be independent of and not regularly employed by the prosecutor, investigator or defense.

Third, any information given to the hypnotist by law enforce-ment personnel or the defense prior to the hypnotic session must be recorded, either in writing or in other suitable form. * * *

Fourth, *before* inducing hypnosis the hypnotist should obtain from the subject a detailed description of the facts as the subject remembers them. * * *

Fifth, all contacts between the hypnotist and the subject must be recorded. This will establish a record of the preinduction interview, the hypnotic session, and the post-hypnotic period, enabling a court to determine what information or suggestions the witness may have received * * *.

Sixth, only the hypnotist and the subject should be present during any phase of the hypnotic session, including the prehypnotic testing and the post-hypnotic interview. * * *

Once compliance with these safeguards is shown, the trial court can determine the reliability and therefore the admissi-bility of hypnotically refreshed testimony, according to the standards set forth above.

State v. Hurd, 86 N.J. 525, 543–46, 432 A.2d 86, 95–97 (1981). Similar tests, some as complicated, some considerably shorter, but all based on Dr. Orne's suggestions, have been adopted in other cases. See, e.g., Polk v. State, [in which the Maryland Court of Appeals] determined that the trial court should make a determination of factors (most of which are similar to Orne's safeguards) which would determine the issue of admissibility, not merely weight; State v. Mack (Minnesota Supreme Court reversed admission of hypnosis testimony but did not foreclose the "use of hypnosis as an extremely useful investigative tool" in providing new leads for solving crimes. The court further noted but did not adopt Orne's safeguards.).

Thus, we are faced with three lines of authority. The first one is exemplified by *Harding* and its progeny, holding that recall aided by hypnosis is admissible, and all problems inherent in its use go to the

weight of the evidence. As noted above, we reject this approach to
resolve the question before us. The second line of cases adopts a rule of
total exclusion and is exemplified by the following decisions from
California, Michigan, Minnesota, Nebraska, and Pennsylvania. This is
the rule we adopted in *Mena* and in the original opinion in this case.
The third line of cases adopts a middle road, finding that there is
general acceptance in the relevant scientific community provided certain safeguards are followed. By and large, these courts have enumerated safeguards based on the Orne formulation and have held that if
such safeguards are followed, the testimony may be admitted, leaving
the jury free to hear and weigh all evidence the opponent of the
testimony may offer regarding possibilities of pseudomemory resulting
from suggestion, confabulation, or deliberate untruthfulness.

We must, then, determine which of these two remaining paths we
should take. Before making this decision, we must turn to the literature and examine the current state of acceptance by the relevant
scientific community. We note a recent article by Warner, *The Use of
Hypnosis in the Defense of Criminal Cases,* 27 Int'l J. Clinical &
Experimental Hypnosis, 417 (1979), advocating the admission of such
testimony providing the "safeguards" are followed. In contrast, Dr.
Diamond argues that the process is so unreliable that it has no
scientific acceptance by knowledgeable psychiatrists and psychologists,
so that recall testimony should not be admitted no matter what safeguards are applied and any witness who has been hypnotized should be
declared incompetent for all purposes. Dr. Orne's position is of some
interest:

> Hypnosis may be helpful in the context of criminal investiga-
> tion and under circumstances involving functional memory
> loss. Hypnosis is not useful in assuring truthfulness since,
> particularly in a forensic context, subjects may simulate hyp-
> nosis and are able to lie wilfully even in deep hypnosis;
> [additionally and] most troublesome, actual memories cannot
> be distinguished from confabulations—pseudomemories where
> plausible fantasy has replaced gaps in recall—either by the
> subject or by the hypnotist without full and independent cor-
> roboration. While potentially useful to refresh witnesses' and
> victims' memories to facilitate eyewitness identification, the
> procedure is relatively safe and appropriate only when neither
> the subject nor the authorities nor the hypnotist has any
> preconceptions about the events under investigation. If such
> preconceptions do exist, hypnosis may readily cause the subject
> to confabulate the person who is suspected into his "hypnoti-
> cally enhanced memories." These pseudo memories, originally
> developed in hypnosis, may come to be accepted by the subject
> as his actual recall of the original events; they are then
> remembered with great subjective certainty and reported with
> conviction. Such circumstances can *create* convincing, appar-
> ently objective "eyewitnesses" rather than facilitating actual
> recall. Minimal safeguards are proposed to reduce the likeli-

hood of such an eventuality and other serious potential abuses of hypnosis.

Dr. Orne specifically points out that:

> As a consequence of [its] limitations, hypnosis may be useful in some instances to help bring back forgotten memories following an accident or a crime while in others a witness might, with the same conviction, produce information that is totally inaccurate. * * * As long as this material is subject to independent verification, its utility is considerable and the risk attached to the procedure minimal. There is no way, however, by which anyone—even a psychologist or psychiatrist with extensive training * * * can for any particular piece of information determine whether it is an actual memory or a confabulation unless there is independent verification.

Dr. Orne also notes that the type of induced recall most likely to lead to accurate revival of memory is that which is least useful in the forensic process: "[f]ree narrative recall [under hypnosis] will produce the highest percentage of accurate information but also the lowest amount of detail. Conversely, the more an eyewitness is questioned about details [while under hypnosis] the more details will be obtained—but with a marked decrease in accuracy."

One conclusion reached by Orne bears further mention: "We will show that as emphasis shifts away from the search for clues that will lead to reliable independent evidence and focuses more on helping to prepare witnesses to give eyewitness testimony, the difficulties that hypnosis creates for the administration of justice become increasingly greater [*sic*]."

Orne concludes his article by warning that if there is even the "vaguest possibility" of using hypnotically enhanced recall at trial, certain safeguards must be followed. Since the use of hypnosis "can profoundly affect the individual's subsequent testimony" in a manner which is "not reversible," Orne concludes that "[i]f individuals are to be allowed to testify after having undergone hypnosis to aid their memory, a minimum number of safeguards are absolutely essential." He then proposes the "Orne safeguards" which in one form or another have been adopted in those cases following the middle road.

* * *

Viewed from the perspective afforded us by the foregoing analysis of the case law and review of the literature describing the present state of the art, the questions remaining are easily identified. The first question is whether, having rejected the *Harding* rule of *per se* admissibility, we should retreat from our previous position and follow the "middle road," adopting the New Jersey rule (State v. Hurd) that hypnotically induced recall testimony may be admitted providing there has been strict compliance with court-formulated standards which will, hopefully, minimize the danger of pseudomemory. The second question is whether we should modify the rule announced in our original opinion in this case, that when a witness' memory of any part of an event has been "tainted" by the hypnotic procedure, that witness is rendered incompetent to testify for any purpose and with respect to any fact, even those remembered and related prior to hypnosis. We answer the first question in the negative and the second in the affirmative.

HYPNOTICALLY INDUCED RECALL TESTIMONY IS *PER SE* INADMISSIBLE

In deciding whether to depart from our rule of *per se* inadmissibility, we are faced with some of the same considerations of benefit vs. risk that we faced in connection with our rejection of the *Harding* doctrine of *per se* admissibility. We feel that the value of adopting a set of safeguards is minimal. The State's position here is that standards such as those adopted in *Hurd* should not be adopted in Arizona, but that the trial courts should be permitted to apply those or other proper standards to determine reliability of the proffered testimony on a case-by-case basis. This approximates the *Hurd* rule, but we are not persuaded that it is a wise practice.

> To require the admissibility of hypnotically induced testimony to be determined on a case-by-case basis based on the testimony of expert witnesses produced by the parties, as required by *Hurd,* is neither sound nor practical. To compare the "recollections" of a witness whose testimony has been hypnotically induced to the "recollections" of an "ordinary" witness, and to determine whether the use of hypnosis was a feasibly reliable means of restoring memory comparable to normal recall in its accuracy, is virtually impossible. * * * [T]he consensus of expert testimony indicates that no expert can determine whether memory retrieved by hypnosis or any part of that memory is truth, falsehood, or fantasy.
>
> * * *
>
> [In People v. Shirley,] the California court reasoned that not even the *Hurd* standards would forestall the dangers at which they were directed, that other dangers exist—such as causing the witness to lose his "critical judgment" and therefore to become certain of "memories" that before hypnosis he, himself, viewed as unreliable. * * *
>
> * * * We feel that the case-by-case determination under a set of safeguards will consume too much in the way of judicial resources, will produce conflicting results in different trial courts, and will produce few situations in which hypnotic recall testimony is ever admitted; even when admitted, there will still be substantial dangers of injustice because of the unavoidable risks attendant to the procedure and the present inability of even the most qualified expert to separate truth from fiction in such testimony. The problems inherent in separating truth from fiction and fact from fantasy in "ordinary recall" are already great enough that we see very little to be gained and much to be lost by adding to them. We see no way of avoiding, in some cases, infringement upon the constitutional right to cross-examination. We reaffirm our previous holdings that hypnotically induced recall testimony is inadmissible. This is a rule of *per se* inadmissibility based on what we conceive to be sound public policy in the administration of the

judicial system and in the oversight of the constitutional rights of litigants. To this extent, we reaffirm *Mena* and the original opinion in this case. However, the reexamination which we have undertaken has led us to reconsider the rule of outright incompetency adopted in our prior decisions.

HYPNOSIS DOES NOT RENDER THE WITNESS INCOMPETENT TO TESTIFY TO THOSE FACTS DEMONSTRABLY RECALLED PRIOR TO HYPNOSIS

In its motion for rehearing, the State argues persuasively that hypnosis has received general acceptance in the scientific community as an investigative tool, that the effect of the incompetency rule is to render hypnosis useless for even investigatory purposes and to foster injustice by disqualifying witnesses from testifying for the purpose of establishing the very elements of the crime, even though there is no danger that such testimony was produced or influenced by the subsequent hypnotic session. For example, the State points out that there is no valid public policy for not allowing a rape victim to testify to the fact of rape even though she was subsequently hypnotized for the purpose of providing identifying "facts" which, after verification, might lead the police to apprehension of the criminal. Upon reexamination, we agree with this position.

We recognize that there are conflicting views on this problem. Dr. Diamond argues in his article (cited previously) for the rule of outright incompetency because of the "contamination" of the witness by the hypnotic process. However, our review of the literature and the position of law enforcement experts, lead us to conclude that hypnosis is generally accepted as a reliable investigative tool by the relevant scientific community. When used for prompting recall in order to provide valuable leads for investigation, hypnosis has less serious risks than the problems the technique presents when courtroom testimony is involved. Unlike a jury, an investigator need not make subjective evaluations of the truth or falsity of the hypnotic recall. He need only obtain leads for the purpose of subsequent investigation and verification.[3]

As a practical matter, if we are to maintain the rule of incompetency, the police will seldom dare to use hypnosis as an investigatory tool because they will thereby risk making the witness incompetent if it is

---

3. Another authority cited to us by the State is Elizabeth Loftus. In her recent book, E. Loftus, Memory 37 (1980), Loftus points out that memory is not akin to the operation of a computer where input is stored in some electronic circuit and can be reproduced intact. Memory does not remain in the brain in the same manner it was recorded. It is affected by the passage of time, by motivation, by confusion with memories of other events, and by self-delusion. False information becomes part of recollection. Memory is no more than a person's "current picture of the past." Thus, Loftus acknowledges that the "memory" produced by hypnosis produces a mixture of new, important facts and, all too often, "totally false information." Nevertheless, Loftus indicates that occasionally the hypnotically produced recall can provide a valuable lead for investigation. Many examples of the use of hypnosis to uncover missing pieces of evidence for subsequent use in court are provided. Id. at 7, 55–59.

later determined that the testimony of that witness is essential. [W]eighing the benefit against the risk, we modify our previous decision and hold that a witness will not be rendered incompetent merely because he or she was hypnotized during the investigatory phase of the case. That witness will be permitted to testify with regard to those matters which he or she was able to recall *and* relate prior to hypnosis. Thus, for example, the rape victim would be free to testify to the occurrence of the crime, the lack of consent, the injury inflicted and the like, assuming that such matters were remembered and related to the authorities prior to use of hypnosis.

This position is supported by authority from those states which, like Arizona, have adopted the rule of *per se* inadmissibility of hypnotically induced recall testimony.

We recognize, however, that there is danger even in allowing testimony of facts recalled prior to hypnosis, because the subsequent hypnosis does have an effect upon the witness' confidence in those facts. It is for this reason that we originally adopted Dr. Diamond's suggestion that any witness who had been hypnotized would be incompetent to testify for any purpose. We are persuaded, however, that with respect to investigatory use of hypnosis, the benefit does outweigh the danger. We also recognize that none of the other states which have adopted the rule of *per se* admissibility have gone as far as *Mena*. They allow a witness to testify to those facts which were demonstrably recalled prior to hypnosis. Some of the attendant risks may be minimized by allowing cross-examination of the previously hypnotized witness in order to permit the opposing party to establish the fact of hypnosis and to introduce expert evidence showing the inherent possibility that the witness might have become subjectively certain of events only tentatively recalled before hypnosis.

We further minimize the risk by requiring that before hypnotizing a potential witness for investigatory purposes, the party intending to offer the prehypnotic recall appropriately record in written, tape recorded, or preferably, videotaped form the substance of the witness' knowledge and recollection about the evidence in question so that the prehypnotic recall may be established. Such recordation must be preserved so that at trial the testimony of that witness can be limited to the prehypnotic recall. If such steps are not taken, admission of the prehypnotic recall will be error, which, if prejudicial, will require reversal.

Further, parties intending to use hypnosis for investigatory purposes should make sure that the hypnosis procedure is performed in a manner designed to minimize the danger of contamination of both prehypnotic and posthypnotic recall. A record of that procedure should be made and retained. While we do not impose any particular set of standards for that purpose, we suggest that litigants adopt some, if not all of the Orne standards referred to above. Any litigant intending to offer testimony of a witness who has been hypnotized must make timely disclosure of such information to the court and to opposing counsel.

To those who may feel that we are overly apprehensive and cautious on the subject of hypnosis, we can only state that the law has long recognized that there are few dangers so great in the search for truth as man's propensity to tamper with the memory of others. The prevention of such an evil is necessary for the benefit of all, since hypnosis and other techniques are perhaps as widely used by criminal defendants as by prosecutors. It is in the interest of the judicial system and of society as a whole that such risks be minimized. We are not unaware of Orwell's warning that control of the future depends above all on the training of memory to induce men to "remember" a doctored view of the past. G. Orwell, *1984* (1971). As Dr. Loftus points out, there is more harm than good to come from the "memory doctor."

The prayer for relief is granted and the case is remanded to the trial court to proceed in accordance with the original opinion as modified by this opinion on rehearing.

ROCK v. ARKANSAS

Supreme Court of the United States, 1987.
483 U.S. 44, 107 S.Ct. 2704, 97 L.Ed.2d 37.

Justice BLACKMUN delivered the opinion of the Court [in which Justices BRENNAN, MARSHALL, POWELL, and STEVENS joined. Chief Justice REHNQUIST filed a dissenting opinion, in which Justices WHITE, O'CONNOR, and SCALIA joined.]

The issue presented in this case is whether Arkansas' evidentiary rule prohibiting the admission of hypnotically refreshed testimony violated petitioner's constitutional right to testify on her own behalf as a defendant in a criminal case.

I

Petitioner Vickie Lorene Rock was charged with manslaughter in the death of her husband, Frank Rock, on July 2, 1983. A dispute had been simmering about Frank's wish to move from the couple's small apartment adjacent to Vickie's beauty parlor to a trailer she owned outside town. That night a fight erupted when Frank refused to let petitioner eat some pizza and prevented her from leaving the apartment to get something else to eat. When police arrived on the scene they found Frank on the floor with a bullet wound in his chest. Petitioner urged the officers to help her husband, and cried to a sergeant who took her in charge, "please save him" and "don't let him die." The police removed her from the building because she was upset and because she interfered with their investigation by her repeated attempts to use the telephone to call her husband's parents. According to the testimony of one of the investigating officers, petitioner told him that "she stood up to leave the room and [her husband] grabbed her by the throat and choked her and threw her against the wall and * * * at that time she walked over and picked up the weapon and pointed it toward the floor and he hit her again and she shot him."

Because petitioner could not remember the precise details of the shooting, her attorney suggested that she submit to hypnosis in order to refresh her memory. Petitioner was hypnotized twice by Doctor Betty Back, a licensed neuropsychologist with training in the field of hypnosis. Doctor Back interviewed petitioner for an hour prior to the first hypnosis session, taking notes on petitioner's general history and her recollections of the shooting. Both hypnosis sessions were recorded on tape. Petitioner did not relate any new information during either of the sessions, but, after the hypnosis, she was able to remember that at the time of the incident she had her thumb on the hammer of the gun, but had not held her finger on the trigger. She also recalled that the gun had discharged when her husband grabbed her arm during the scuffle. As a result of the details that petitioner was able to remember about the shooting, her counsel arranged for a gun expert to examine the handgun, a single action Hawes .22 Deputy Marshal. That inspection revealed that the gun was defective and prone to fire, when hit or dropped, without the trigger's being pulled.

When the prosecutor learned of the hypnosis sessions, he filed a motion to exclude petitioner's testimony. The trial judge held a pretrial hearing on the motion and concluded that no hypnotically refreshed testimony would be admitted. The court issued an order limiting petitioner's testimony to "matters remembered and stated to the examiner prior to being placed under hypnosis." At trial, petitioner introduced testimony by the gun expert, but the court limited petitioner's own description of the events on the day of the shooting to a reiteration of the sketchy information in Doctor Back's notes. The jury convicted petitioner on the manslaughter charge and she was sentenced to 10 years imprisonment and a $10,000 fine.

On appeal, the Supreme Court of Arkansas rejected petitioner's claim that the limitations on her testimony violated her right to present her defense. The court concluded that "the dangers of admitting this kind of testimony outweigh whatever probative value it may have," and decided to follow the approach of States that have held hypnotically refreshed testimony of witnesses inadmissible per se. Although the court acknowledged that "a defendant's right to testify is fundamental," it ruled that the exclusion of petitioner's testimony did not violate her constitutional rights. Any "prejudice or deprivation" she suffered "was minimal and resulted from her own actions and not by any erroneous ruling of the court." We granted certiorari, to consider the constitutionality of Arkansas' per se rule excluding a criminal defendant's hypnotically refreshed testimony.

II

Petitioner's claim that her testimony was impermissibly excluded is bottomed on her constitutional right to testify in her own defense. At this point in the development of our adversary system, it cannot be doubted that a defendant in a criminal case has the right to take the witness stand and to testify in his or her own defense. This, of course, is a change from the historic common-law view, which was that all parties to litigation, including criminal defendants, were disqualified from testifying because of their interest in the outcome of the trial.

See generally 2 J. Wigmore, Evidence §§ 576, 579 (J. Chadbourn rev. 1979). The principal rationale for this rule was the possible untrustworthiness of a party's testimony. Under the common law, the practice did develop of permitting criminal defendants to tell their side of the story, but they were limited to making an unsworn statement that could not be elicited through direct examination by counsel and was not subject to cross-examination. Id., at § 579, p. 827.

This Court in Ferguson v. Georgia, 365 U.S. 570, 573–582 (1961), detailed the history of the transition from a rule of a defendant's incompetency to a rule of competency. As the Court there recounted, it came to be recognized that permitting a defendant to testify advances both the " 'detection of guilt' " and " 'the protection of innocence,' " and by the end of the second half of the 19th century, all States except Georgia had enacted statutes that declared criminal defendants competent to testify. * * *

The right to testify on one's own behalf at a criminal trial has sources in several provisions of the Constitution. It is one of the rights that "are essential to due process of law in a fair adversary process." Faretta v. California, 422 U.S. 806, 819, n. 15 (1975). The necessary ingredients of the Fourteenth Amendment's guarantee that no one shall be deprived of liberty without due process of law include a right to be heard and to offer testimony:

> "A person's right to reasonable notice of a charge against him, and *an opportunity to be heard in his defense* —a right to his day in court—are basic in our system of jurisprudence; and these rights include, as a minimum, a right to examine the witnesses against him, to offer testimony, and to be represented by counsel." (Emphasis added.) In re Oliver, 333 U.S. 257, 273 (1948).

* * *

The right to testify is also found in the Compulsory Process Clause of the Sixth Amendment, which grants a defendant the right to call "witnesses in his favor," a right that is guaranteed in the criminal courts of the States by the Fourteenth Amendment. Logically included in the accused's right to call witnesses whose testimony is "material and favorable to his defense," United States v. Valenzuela–Bernal, 458 U.S. 858, 867, is a right to testify himself, should he decide it is in his favor to do so. In fact, the most important witness for the defense in many criminal cases is the defendant himself. There is no justification today for a rule that denies an accused the opportunity to offer his own testimony. Like the truthfulness of other witnesses, the defendant's veracity, which was the concern behind the original common-law rule, can be tested adequately by cross-examination. * * *

The opportunity to testify is also a necessary corollary to the Fifth Amendment's guarantee against compelled testimony. In Harris v. New York, 401 U.S. 222, 230 (1971), the Court stated: "Every criminal defendant is privileged to testify in his own defense, or to refuse to do so." Id., at 225. Three of the dissenting Justices in that case agreed that the Fifth Amendment encompasses this right: "[The Fifth Amendment's privilege against self-incrimination] is fulfilled only when an accused is guaranteed the right 'to remain silent unless he chooses to speak in the unfettered exercise of his own will.' * * * The choice of whether to testify in one's own defense * * * is an exercise of the constitutional privilege." Id., at 230, quoting Malloy v. Hogan, 378 U.S. 1, 8 (1964). (Emphasis removed.)

III

The question now before the Court is whether a criminal defendant's right to testify may be restricted by a state rule that excludes her post-hypnosis testimony. This is not the first time this Court has faced a constitutional challenge to a state rule, designed to ensure trustworthy evidence, that interfered with the ability of a defendant to offer testimony. In Washington v. Texas, 388 U.S. 14 (1967), the Court was confronted with a state statute that prevented persons charged as principals, accomplices, or accessories in the same crime from being introduced as witnesses for one another. The statute, like the original common-law prohibition on testimony by the accused, was grounded in a concern for the reliability of evidence presented by an interested party:

> "It was thought that if two persons charged with the same crime were allowed to testify on behalf of each other, 'each would try to swear the other out of the charge.' This rule, as well as the other disqualifications for interest, rested on the unstated premises that the right to present witnesses was subordinate to the court's interest in preventing perjury, and that erroneous decisions were best avoided by preventing the jury from hearing any testimony that might be perjured, even if it were the only testimony available on a crucial issue."

As the Court recognized, the incompetency of a codefendant to testify had been rejected on nonconstitutional grounds in 1918, when the Court, refusing to be bound by "the dead hand of the common-law rule of 1789," stated:

> " '[T]he conviction of our time [is] that the truth is more likely to be arrived at by hearing the testimony of all persons of competent understanding who may seem to have knowledge of the facts involved in a case, leaving the credit and weight of such testimony to be determined by the jury or by the court. . . .' " 388 U.S., at 22, quoting Rosen v. United States, 245 U.S. 467, 471 (1918).

The Court concluded that this reasoning was compelled by the Sixth Amendment's protections for the accused. In particular, the Court reasoned that the Sixth Amendment was designed in part "to make the testimony of a defendant's witnesses admissible on his behalf in court."

With the rationale for the common-law incompetency rule thus rejected on constitutional grounds, the Court found that the mere presence of the witness in the courtroom was not enough to satisfy the Constitution's Compulsory Process Clause. By preventing the defendant from having the benefit of his accomplice's testimony, "the State *arbitrarily* denied him the right to put on the stand a witness who was physically and mentally capable of testifying to events that he had personally observed, and whose testimony would have been relevant and material to the defense."

Just as a State may not apply an arbitrary rule of competence to exclude a material defense witness from taking the stand, it also may not apply a rule of evidence that permits a witness to take the stand, but arbitrarily excludes material portions of his testimony. In Chambers v. Mississippi, 410 U.S. 284 (1973), the Court invalidated a State's hearsay rule on the ground that it abridged the defendant's right to "present witnesses in his own defense." Chambers was tried for a murder to which another person repeatedly had confessed in the presence of acquaintances. The State's hearsay rule, coupled with a "voucher" rule that did not allow the defendant to cross-examine the confessed murderer directly, prevented Chambers from introducing testimony concerning these confessions, which were critical to his defense. This Court reversed the judgment of conviction, holding that when a state rule of evidence conflicts with the right to present witnesses, the rule may "not be applied mechanistically to defeat the ends of justice," but must meet the fundamental standards of due process. In the Court's view, the State in Chambers did not demonstrate that the hearsay testimony in that case, which bore "assurances of trustworthiness" including corroboration by other evidence, would be unreliable, and thus the defendant should have been able to introduce the exculpatory testimony.

Of course, the right to present relevant testimony is not without limitation. The right "may, in appropriate cases, bow to accommodate other legitimate interests in the criminal trial process." But restrictions of a defendant's right to testify may not be arbitrary or disproportionate to the purposes they are designed to serve. In applying its evidentiary rules a State must evaluate whether the interests served by a rule justify the limitation imposed on the defendant's constitutional right to testify.

IV

The Arkansas rule enunciated by the state courts does not allow a trial court to consider whether posthypnosis testimony may be admissible in a particular case; it is a per se rule prohibiting the admission at trial of any defendant's hypnotically refreshed testimony on the ground that such testimony is always unreliable. Thus, in Arkansas, an accused's testimony is limited to matters that he or she can prove were remembered before hypnosis. This rule operates to the detriment of any defendant who undergoes hypnosis, without regard to the reasons for it, the circumstances under which it took place, or any independent verification of the information it produced.

In this case, the application of that rule had a significant adverse effect on petitioner's ability to testify. It virtually prevented her from describing any of the events that occurred on the day of the shooting, despite corroboration of many of those events by other witnesses. Even more importantly, under the court's rule petitioner was not permitted to describe the actual shooting except in the words contained in Doctor Back's notes. The expert's description of the gun's tendency to misfire would have taken on greater significance if the jury had heard petitioner testify that she did not have her finger on the trigger and that the gun went off when her husband hit her arm.

In establishing its per se rule, the Arkansas Supreme Court simply followed the approach taken by a number of States that have decided that hypnotically enhanced testimony should be excluded at trial on the ground that it tends to be unreliable. Other States that have adopted an exclusionary rule, however, have done so for the testimony of *witnesses,* not for the testimony of a *defendant.* The Arkansas Supreme Court failed to perform the constitutional analysis that is necessary when a defendant's right to testify is at stake.

Although the Arkansas court concluded that any testimony that cannot be proved to be the product of prehypnosis memory is unreliable, many courts have eschewed a per se rule and permit the admission of hypnotically refreshed testimony. Hypnosis by trained physicians or psychologists has been recognized as a valid therapeutic technique since 1958, although there is no generally accepted theory to explain the phenomenon, or even a consensus on a single definition of hypnosis. See Council on Scientific Affairs, Scientific Status of Refreshing Recollection by the Use of Hypnosis, 253 J.A.M.A. 1918, 1918–1919 (1985) (Council Report). The use of hypnosis in criminal investigations, however, is controversial, and the current medical and legal view of its appropriate role is unsettled.

Responses of individuals to hypnosis vary greatly. The popular belief that hypnosis guarantees the accuracy of recall is as yet without established foundation and, in fact, hypnosis often has no effect at all on memory. The most common response to hypnosis, however, appears to be an increase in both correct and incorrect recollections. Three general characteristics of hypnosis may lead to the introduction of inaccurate memories: the subject becomes "suggestible" and may try to please the hypnotist with answers the subject thinks will be met with approval; the subject is likely to "confabulate," that is, to fill in details from the imagination in order to make an answer more coherent and complete; and, the subject experiences "memory hardening," which gives him great confidence in both true and false memories, making effective cross-examination more difficult. See generally M. Orne, et al., Hypnotically Induced Testimony, in Eyewitness Testimony: Psychological Perspectives 171 (G. Wells and E. Loftus, eds., 1985); Diamond, Inherent Problems in the Use of Pretrial Hypnosis on a Prospective Witness, 68 Calif.L.Rev. 313, 333–342 (1980). Despite the unreliability that hypnosis concededly may introduce, however, the procedure has been credited as instrumental in obtaining investigative leads or identifications that were later confirmed by independent evidence. See, e.g., People v. Hughes, 59 N.Y.2d 523, 533, 453 N.E.2d 484, 488 (1983); see generally R. Udolf, Forensic Hypnosis 11–16 (1983).

The inaccuracies the process introduces can be reduced, although perhaps not eliminated, by the use of procedural safeguards. One set of suggested guidelines calls for hypnosis to be performed only by a psychologist or psychiatrist with special training in its use and who is independent of the investigation. See Orne, The Use and Misuse of Hypnosis in Court, 27 Int'l J. Clinical & Experimental Hypnosis 311, 335–336 (1979). These procedures reduce the possibility that biases will be communicated to the hypersuggestive subject by the hypnotist. Suggestion will be less likely also if the hypnosis is conducted in a neutral setting with no one present but the hypnotist and the subject. Tape or video recording of all interrogations, before, during, and after hypnosis, can help reveal if leading questions were asked. Id., at 336. Such guidelines do not guarantee the accuracy of the testimony, because they cannot control the subject's own motivations or any tendency to confabulate, but they do provide a means of controlling overt suggestions.

The more traditional means of assessing accuracy of testimony also remain applicable in the case of a previously hypnotized defendant. Certain information recalled as a result of hypnosis may be verified as highly accurate by corroborating evidence. Cross-examination, even in the face of a confident defendant, is an effective tool for revealing inconsistencies. Moreover, a jury can be educated to the risks of hypnosis through expert testimony and cautionary instructions. Indeed, it is probably to a defendant's advantage to establish carefully the extent of his memory prior to hypnosis, in order to minimize the decrease in credibility the procedure might introduce.

We are not now prepared to endorse without qualifications the use of hypnosis as an investigative tool; scientific understanding of the phenomenon and of the means to control the effects of hypnosis is still in its infancy. Arkansas, however, has not justified the exclusion of all of a defendant's testimony that the defendant is unable to prove to be the product of prehypnosis memory. A State's legitimate interest in barring unreliable evidence does not extend to per se exclusions that may be reliable in an individual case. Wholesale inadmissibility of a defendant's testimony is an arbitrary restriction on the right to testify in the absence of clear evidence by the State repudiating the validity of all posthypnosis recollections. The State would be well within its powers if it established guidelines to aid trial courts in the evaluation of posthypnosis testimony and it may be able to show that testimony in a particular case is so unreliable that exclusion is justified. But it has not shown that hypnotically enhanced testimony is always so untrustworthy and so immune to the traditional means of evaluating credibility that it should disable a defendant from presenting her version of the events for which she is on trial.

In this case, the defective condition of the gun corroborated the details petitioner remembered about the shooting. The tape recordings provided some means to evaluate the hypnosis and the trial judge concluded that Doctor Back did not suggest responses with leading questions. Those circumstances present an argument for admissibility of petitioner's testimony in this particular case, an argument that must be considered by the trial court. Arkansas' per se rule excluding all posthypnosis testimony infringes impermissibly on the right of a defendant to testify on his or her own behalf.

The judgment of the Supreme Court of Arkansas is vacated and the case is remanded to that court for further proceedings not inconsistent with this opinion.

It is so ordered.

Chief Justice REHNQUIST, with whom Justice WHITE, Justice O'CONNOR, and Justice SCALIA join, dissenting.

In deciding that petitioner Rock's testimony was properly limited at her trial, the Arkansas Supreme Court cited several factors that undermine the reliability of hypnotically induced testimony. Like the Court today, the Arkansas Supreme Court observed that a hypnotized individual becomes subject to suggestion, is likely to confabulate, and experiences artifically increased confidence in both true and false memories following hypnosis. No known set of procedures, both courts agree, can insure against the inherently unreliable nature of such testimony. Having acceded to the factual premises of the Arkansas Supreme Court, the Court nevertheless concludes that a state trial court must attempt to make its own scientific assessment of reliability in each case it is confronted with a request for the admission of hypnotically induced testimony. I find no justification in the Constitution for such a ruling.

In the Court's words, the decision today is "bottomed" on recognition of Rock's "constitutional right to testify in her own defense." Ante, at 49. While it is true that this Court, in dictum, has recognized the existence of such a right, see, e.g., Faretta v. California, 422 U.S. 806, 819, n. 15 (1975), the principles identified by the Court as underlying this right provide little support for invalidating the evidentiary rule applied by the Arkansas Supreme Court.

As a general matter, the Court first recites, a defendant's right to testify facilitates the truth-seeking function of a criminal trial by advancing both the " 'detection of guilt' " and " 'the protection of innocence.' " Ante, at 50, quoting Ferguson v. Georgia, 365 U.S. 570, 581 (1961). Such reasoning is hardly controlling here, where advancement of the truthseeking function of Rock's trial was the sole motivation behind limiting her testimony. The Court also posits, however, that "a rule that denies an accused the opportunity to offer his own testimony" cannot be upheld because, "[l]ike the truthfulness of other witnesses, the defendant's veracity * * * can be tested adequately by cross-examination." Ante, at 52. But the Court candidly admits that the increased confidence inspired by hypnotism makes "cross-examination more difficult," ante, at 60, thereby diminishing an adverse party's ability to test the truthfulness of defendants such as Rock. Nevertheless, we are told, the exclusion of a defendant's testimony cannot be sanctioned because the defendant " 'above all others may be in a position to meet the prosecution's case.' " Ante, at 50, quoting Ferguson v. Georgia, supra, at 582. In relying on such reasoning, the Court apparently forgets that the issue before us arises only by virtue of

Rock's memory loss, which rendered her less able "to meet the prosecution's case."

In conjunction with its reliance on broad principles that have little relevance here, the Court barely concerns itself with the recognition, present throughout our decisions, that an individual's right to present evidence is subject always to reasonable restrictions. Indeed, the due process decisions relied on by the Court all envision that an individual's right to present evidence on his behalf is not absolute and must often times give way to countervailing considerations. Similarly, our Compulsory Process Clause decisions make clear that the right to present relevant testimony "may, in appropriate cases, bow to accommodate other legitimate interests in the criminal trial process." Chambers v. Mississippi, 410 U.S. 284, 295 (1973); see Washington v. Texas, 388 U.S. 14, 22 (1967). The Constitution does not in any way relieve a defendant from compliance with "rules of procedure and evidence designed to assure both fairness and reliability in the ascertainment of guilt and innocence." Chambers v. Mississippi, supra, at 302. Surely a rule designed to exclude testimony whose trustworthiness is inherently suspect cannot be said to fall outside this description.

This Court has traditionally accorded the States "respect * * * in the establishment and implementation of their own criminal trial rules and procedures." One would think that this deference would be at its highest in an area such as this, where, as the Court concedes, "scientific understanding * * * is still in its infancy." Ante, at 61. Turning a blind eye to this concession, the Court chooses instead to restrict the ability of both state and federal courts to respond to changes in the understanding of hypnosis.

The Supreme Court of Arkansas' decision was an entirely permissible response to a novel and difficult question. See National Institute of Justice, Issues and Practices, M. Orne et al., Hypnotically Refreshed Testimony: Enhanced Memory or Tampering with Evidence? 51 (1985). As an original proposition, the solution this Court imposes upon Arkansas may be equally sensible, though requiring the matter to be considered res nova by every single trial judge in every single case might seem to some to pose serious administrative difficulties. But until there is a much more general consensus on the use of hypnosis than there is now, the Constitution does not warrant this Court's mandating its own view of how to deal with the issue.

TANNER v. UNITED STATES

Supreme Court of the United States, 1987.
483 U.S. 107, 107 S.Ct. 2739, 97 L.Ed.2d 90.

JUSTICE O'CONNOR delivered the opinion of the Court.

Petitioners William Conover and Anthony Tanner were convicted of conspiring to defraud the United States in violation of 18 U.S.C. § 371, and of committing mail fraud in violation of 18 U.S.C. § 1341. * * *

The day before petitioners were scheduled to be sentenced, Tanner filed a motion, in which Conover subsequently joined, seeking continuance of the sentencing date, permission to interview jurors, an evidentiary hearing, and a new trial. According to an affidavit accompanying the motion, Tanner's attorney had received an unsolicited telephone call from one of the trial jurors, Vera Asbul. Juror Asbul informed Tanner's attorney that several of the jurors consumed alcohol during the lunch breaks at various times throughout the trial, causing them to sleep through the afternoons. The District Court continued the sentencing date, ordered the parties to file memoranda, and heard argument on the motion to interview jurors. The District Court concluded that juror testimony on intoxication was inadmissible under Federal Rule of Evidence 606(b) to impeach the jury's verdict. The District Court invited petitioners to call any nonjuror witnesses, such as courtroom personnel, in support of the motion for new trial. Tanner's counsel took the stand and testified that he had observed one of the jurors "in a sort of giggly mood" at one point during the trial but did not bring this to anyone's attention at the time. * * *

Following the hearing the District Court filed an order stating that "[o]n the basis of the admissible evidence offered I specifically find that the motions for leave to interview jurors or for an evidentiary hearing at which jurors would be witnesses is not required or appropriate." The District Court also denied the motion for new trial.

While the appeal of this case was pending before the Eleventh Circuit, petitioners filed another new trial motion based on additional evidence of jury misconduct. In another affidavit, Tanner's attorney stated that he received an unsolicited visit at his residence from a second juror, Daniel Hardy. Despite the fact that the District Court had denied petitioners' motion for leave to interview jurors, two days after Hardy's visit Tanner's attorney arranged for Hardy to be interviewed by two private investigators. The interview was transcribed, sworn to by the juror, and attached to the new trial motion. In the interview Hardy stated that he "felt like . . . the jury was on one big party." Hardy indicated that seven of the jurors drank alcohol during the noon recess. Four jurors, including Hardy, consumed between them "a pitcher to three pitchers" of beer during various recesses. Of the three other jurors who were alleged to have consumed alcohol, Hardy stated that on several occasions he observed two jurors having one or two mixed drinks during the lunch recess, and one other juror, who was also the foreperson, having a liter of wine on each of three occasions. Juror Hardy also stated that he and three other jurors smoked marijuana quite regularly during the trial. Moreover, Hardy stated that during the trial he observed one juror ingest cocaine five times and another juror ingest cocaine two or three times. One juror sold a quarter pound of marijuana to another juror during the trial, and took marijuana, cocaine, and drug paraphernalia into the courthouse. Hardy noted that some of the jurors were falling asleep during the trial, and that one of the jurors described himself to Hardy as "flying." Hardy stated that before he visited Tanner's attorney at his residence, no one had contacted him concerning the jury's conduct, and Hardy had not been offered anything in return for his statement. Hardy said that he came forward "to clear my conscience" and "[b]ecause I felt . . . that the people on the jury didn't have no business being on the jury. I felt . . . that Mr. Tanner should have a better opportunity to get somebody that would review the facts right."

The District Court, stating that the motions "contain supplemental allegations which differ quantitatively but not qualitatively from those in the April motions," denied petitioners' motion for a new trial.

The Court of Appeals for the Eleventh Circuit affirmed. We granted certiorari, to consider whether the District Court was required to hold an evidentiary hearing, including juror testimony, on juror alcohol and drug use during the trial, and to consider whether petitioners' actions constituted a conspiracy to defraud the United States within the meaning of 18 U.S.C. § 371.

Petitioners argue that the District Court erred in not ordering an additional evidentiary hearing at which jurors would testify concerning drug and alcohol use during the trial. Petitioners assert that, contrary to the holdings of the District Court and the Court of Appeals, juror testimony on ingestion of drugs or alcohol during the trial is not barred by Federal Rule of Evidence 606(b). Moreover, petitioners argue that whether or not authorized by Rule 606(b), an evidentiary hearing including juror testimony on drug and alcohol use is compelled by their Sixth Amendment right to trial by a competent jury.

By the beginning of this century, if not earlier, the near-universal and firmly established common-law rule in the United States flatly prohibited the admission of juror testimony to impeach a jury verdict. See 8 J. Wigmore, Evidence § 2352, pp. 696–697 (J. McNaughton rev. ed. 1961) (common-law rule, originating from 1785 opinion of Lord Mansfield, "came to receive in the United States an adherence almost unquestioned").

Exceptions to the common-law rule were recognized only in situations in which an "extraneous influence," Mattox v. United States, 146 U.S. 140, 149 (1892), was alleged to have affected the jury. In *Mattox,* this Court held admissible the testimony of jurors describing how they heard and read prejudicial information not admitted into evidence. The Court allowed juror testimony on influence by outsiders in Parker v. Gladden, 385 U.S. 363, 365 (1966) (bailiff's comments on defendant), and Remmer v. United States, 347 U.S. 227, 228–230 (1954) (bribe offered to juror). See also Smith v. Phillips, 455 U.S. 209 (1982) (juror in criminal trial had submitted an application for employment at the District Attorney's office). In situations that did not fall into this exception for external influence, however, the Court adhered to the common-law rule against admitting juror testimony to impeach a verdict.

Lower courts used this external/internal distinction to identify those instances in which juror testimony impeaching a verdict would be admissible. The distinction was not based on whether the juror was literally inside or outside the jury room when the alleged irregularity took place; rather, the distinction was based on the nature of the allegation. Clearly a rigid distinction based only on whether the event took place inside or outside the jury room would have been quite unhelpful. For example, under a distinction based on location a juror could not testify concerning a newspaper read inside the jury room. Instead, of course, this has been considered an external influence about which juror testimony is admissible. Similarly, under a rigid locational distinction jurors could be regularly required to testify after the verdict as to whether they heard and comprehended the judge's instructions, since the charge to the jury takes place outside the jury room. Courts wisely have treated allegations of a juror's inability to hear or comprehend at trial as an internal matter.

Most significant for the present case, however, is the fact that lower federal courts treated allegations of the physical or mental incompetence of a juror as "internal" rather than "external" matters. In United States v. Dioguardi, 492 F.2d 70 (CA2 1974), the defendant Dioguardi received a letter from one of the jurors soon after the trial in which the juror explained that she had "eyes and ears that . . . see things before [they] happen," but that her eyes "are only partly open" because "a curse was put upon them some years ago." Armed with this letter and the opinions of seven psychiatrists that the letter suggested that the juror was suffering from a psychological disorder, Dioguardi sought a new trial or in the alternative an evidentiary hearing on the juror's competence. The District Court denied the motion and the Court of Appeals affirmed. The Court of Appeals noted "[t]he strong policy against any post-verdict inquiry into a juror's state of mind," and observed:

> "The quickness with which jury findings will be set aside when there is proof of tampering or *external* influence, . . . parallel the reluctance of courts to inquire into jury deliberations when a verdict is valid on its face. . . . Such exceptions support rather than undermine the rationale of the rule that possible *internal* abnormalities in a jury will not be inquired into except 'in the gravest and most important cases.' "

The Court of Appeals concluded that when faced with allegations that a juror was mentally incompetent, "courts have refused to set aside a verdict, or even to make further inquiry, unless there be proof of an adjudication of insanity or mental incompetence closely in advance . . . of jury service," or proof of "a closely contemporaneous and independent post-trial adjudication of incompetency." * * *

Substantial policy considerations support the common-law rule against the admission of jury testimony to impeach a verdict. As early as 1915 this Court explained the necessity of shielding jury deliberations from public scrutiny:

> "[L]et it once be established that verdicts solemnly made and publicly returned into court can be attacked and set aside on the testimony of those who took part in their publication and all verdicts could be, and many would be, followed by an inquiry in the hope of discovering something which might invalidate the finding. Jurors would be harassed and beset by the defeated party in an effort to secure from them evidence of facts which might establish misconduct sufficient to set aside a

verdict. If evidence thus secured could be thus used, the result would be to make what was intended to be a private deliberation, the constant subject of public investigation—to the destruction of all frankness and freedom of discussion and conference." McDonald v. Pless, 238 U.S., at 267–268. ∗ ∗ ∗

There is little doubt that postverdict investigation into juror misconduct would in some instances lead to the invalidation of verdicts reached after irresponsible or improper juror behavior. It is not at all clear, however, that the jury system could survive such efforts to perfect it. Allegations of juror misconduct, incompetency, or inattentiveness, raised for the first time days, weeks, or months after the verdict, seriously disrupt the finality of the process. Moreover, full and frank discussion in the jury room, jurors' willingness to return an unpopular verdict, and the community's trust in a system that relies on the decisions of laypeople would all be undermined by a barrage of postverdict scrutiny of juror conduct.

Federal Rule of Evidence 606(b) is grounded in the common-law rule against admission of jury testimony to impeach a verdict and the exception for juror testimony relating to extraneous influences. ∗ ∗ ∗

[P]etitioners argue that substance abuse constitutes an improper "outside influence" about which jurors may testify under Rule 606(b). In our view the language of the Rule cannot easily be stretched to cover this circumstance. However severe their effect and improper their use, drugs or alcohol voluntarily ingested by a juror seems no more an "outside influence" than a virus, poorly prepared food, or a lack of sleep.

In any case, whatever ambiguity might linger in the language of Rule 606(b) as applied to juror intoxication is resolved by the legislative history of the Rule. ∗ ∗ ∗

[T]he legislative history demonstrates with uncommon clarity that Congress specifically understood, considered, and rejected a version of Rule 606(b) that would have allowed jurors to testify on juror conduct during deliberations, including juror intoxication. This legislative history provides strong support for the most reasonable reading of the language of Rule 606(b)—that juror intoxication is not an "outside influence" about which jurors may testify to impeach their verdict.

Finally, even if Rule 606(b) is interpreted to retain the common-law exception allowing postverdict inquiry of juror incompetence in cases of "substantial if not wholly conclusive evidence of incompetency," *Dioguardi*, 492 F.2d, at 80, the showing made by petitioners falls far short of this standard. The affidavits and testimony presented in support of the first new trial motion suggested, at worst, that several of the jurors fell asleep at times during the afternoons. The District Court Judge appropriately considered the fact that he had "an unobstructed view" of the jury, and did not see any juror sleeping. The juror affidavit submitted in support of the second new trial motion was obtained in clear violation of the District Court's order and the court's local rule against juror interviews, MD Fla. Rule 2.04(c); on this basis alone the

District Court would have been acting within its discretion in disregarding the affidavit. In any case, although the affidavit of juror Hardy describes more dramatic instances of misconduct, Hardy's allegations of *incompetence* are meager. Hardy stated that the alcohol consumption he engaged in with three other jurors did not leave any of them intoxicated. App. to Pet. for Cert. 47 ("I told [the prosecutor] that we would just go out and get us a pitcher of beer and drink it, but as far as us being drunk, no we wasn't"). The only allegations concerning the jurors' ability to properly consider the evidence were Hardy's observations that some jurors were "falling asleep all the time during the trial," and that his own reasoning ability was affected on one day of the trial. These allegations would not suffice to bring this case under the common-law exception allowing postverdict inquiry when an extremely strong showing of incompetency has been made.

Petitioners also argue that the refusal to hold an additional evidentiary hearing at which jurors would testify as to their conduct "violates the sixth amendment's guarantee to a fair trial before an impartial and *competent* jury."

This Court has recognized that a defendant has a right to "a tribunal both impartial and mentally competent to afford a hearing." Jordan v. Massachusetts, 225 U.S. 167, 176 (1912). In this case the District Court held an evidentiary hearing in response to petitioners' first new trial motion at which the judge invited petitioners to introduce any admissible evidence in support of their allegations. At issue in this case is whether the Constitution compelled the District Court to hold an additional evidentiary hearing including one particular kind of evidence inadmissible under the Federal Rules.

As described above, long-recognized and very substantial concerns support the protection of jury deliberations from intrusive inquiry. Petitioners' Sixth Amendment interests in an unimpaired jury, on the other hand, are protected by several aspects of the trial process. The suitability of an individual for the responsibility of jury service, of course, is examined during *voir dire*. Moreover, during the trial the jury is observable by the court, by counsel, and by court personnel. Moreover, jurors are observable by each other, and may report inappropriate juror behavior to the court *before* they render a verdict. Finally, after the trial a party may seek to impeach the verdict by nonjuror evidence of misconduct. See United States v. Taliaferro, 558 F.2d 724, 725–726 (CA4 1977) (court considered records of club where jurors dined, and testimony of marshal who accompanied jurors, to determine whether jurors were intoxicated during deliberations). Indeed, in this case the District Court held an evidentiary hearing giving petitioners ample opportunity to produce nonjuror evidence supporting their allegations.

In light of these other sources of protection of petitioners' right to a competent jury, we conclude that the District Court did not err in deciding, based on the inadmissibility of juror testimony and the clear insufficiency of the nonjuror evidence offered by petitioners, that an additional postverdict evidentiary hearing was unnecessary. * * *

[The dissenting opinion of Justice MARSHALL, in which Justices BRENNAN, BLACKMUN and STEVENS joined, has been omitted.]

————

See Federal Rules of Evidence 601–606; California Evidence Code §§ 700–704.

Hypotheticals

(1) D is charged with the sale of heroin to X. The prosecution's evidence is that X, a known heroin addict, was given $300 by the police to purchase heroin from D at D's barbershop. The prosecution calls X, and D objects to any testimony from X on the ground that X is incompetent to be a witness by virtue of drug use. The trial court conducts an in-chambers hearing on the question. D calls P, a psychiatrist, who testifies that the use of LSD may confuse one's perception, thereby impairing the capacity to perceive or remember one's observations. In this case, however, P states that he did not personally interview X, and that his opinion testimony is based upon his experience with LSD users who had a history of suffering blackouts. The prosecutor calls X, who testifies to excessive use of drugs, including LSD, but denies ever passing out, freaking out, or having loss of memory from use of LSD. The trial judge then overrules D's incompetency objection. Is this ruling correct?

(2) A sues X for damages for personal injuries arising out of a two-car collision. A took X's deposition one month before trial. During her deposition, X testified that he had retrograde amnesia and could not remember the facts of the accident. At the trial, X takes the witness stand and her attorney asks her to relate how the accident happened. A objects that X is incompetent to testify in view of her deposition testimony. How should the court rule?

(3) Assume the same facts as in Hypothetical (2). A calls as a witness, C, who observed the accident after having escaped from a mental institution to which he had been committed as a manic-depressive psychotic. At the time of trial, C has been captured and is back in the institution. X objects to C as a witness, on the ground that C's commitment to a mental institution renders him incompetent to be a witness. How should the court rule?

(4) A sues X for damages for personal injuries arising out of a two-car, intersectional collision. A claims that X didn't stop at a stop sign. At a jury trial, A calls B to testify. X makes a lack-of-personal-knowledge objection. A represents that she will establish B's personal knowledge as B testifies. The trial judge permits B to testify conditionally, subject to X making a motion to strike. B then testifies that X "blew" the stop sign. On cross-examination, B finally admits that she reached the intersection just as the cars collided, and that she concluded that X blew the stop sign from observing the point of impact and from hearing other witnesses talk about what happened. X moves to strike B's testimony. What result? *— w/out sufficient observation & personal knowledge =*

Chapter XI

JUDICIAL NOTICE

PART A. ADJUDICATIVE FACTS

VARCOE v. LEE

Supreme Court of California, 1919.
180 Cal. 338, 181 P. 223.

OLNEY, J. This is an action by a father to recover damages suffered through the death of his child, resulting from her being run over by an automobile of the defendant Lee, driven at the time by the other defendant, Nichols, the chauffeur of Lee. The automobile was going south on Mission street in San Francisco, and was approaching the crossing of Twenty-First street, when the child, in an endeavor to cross the street, was run over and killed. The cause was tried before a jury, which returned a verdict of $5,000 for the plaintiff. From the judgment upon this verdict, the defendants appeal.

The alleged negligence, upon which plaintiff's right to recover is predicated, consisted in the speed at which it is claimed the automobile was proceeding. * * *

* * *

* * * On this point the testimony was sharply conflicting. * * * [T]he trial judge instructed [the jury] that, if they found that the defendant Nichols was running the automobile along Mission street at the time of the accident at a greater speed than 15 miles an hour, he was violating the city ordinance, and also the state Motor Vehicle Act, and that such speed was negligence in itself. The trial judge then read to the jury the portion of subdivision "b" of section 22 of the Motor Vehicle Act (St.1913, p. 639), which provides that it shall be unlawful to operate a motor vehicle "in the business district" of any incorporated city or town at a greater speed than 15 miles an hour, and defines (see section 1) a business district as "territory * * * contiguous to a public highway, which is at that point mainly built up with structures devoted to business." Having read this definition, the court proceeded with its charge as follows:

"That is the situation on Mission street between Twentieth and Twenty-Second streets, where this accident happened, so that is a business district and the maximum legal rate of speed on that street at the time of the happening of this accident was 15 miles an hour."

* * *

* * * We are brought, therefore, to the * * * point, that the trial judge erred in charging the jury that the location of the accident was in "a business district" as those words are defined in the state act,

689

with the consequent result that 15 miles an hour was the maximum legal speed.

So far as the record itself goes, there is little to show what the character of Mission street between Twentieth and Twenty-Second streets is. The defendant Nichols himself refers to it in his testimony as part of the "downtown district," undoubtedly meaning thereby part of the business district of the city. The evidence shows incidentally that at the scene of the accident there was a drug store, a barber shop, a haberdashery, and a saloon. If there had been any issue or question as to the character of the district, the record in this meager condition would not justify the taking of the question from the jury, as was undoubtedly done by the instruction complained of.

The actual fact of the matter is, however, that Mission street, between Twentieth and Twenty-Second streets, is a business district, within the definition of the Motor Vehicle Act, beyond any possibility of question. It has been such for years. Not only this, but its character is known as a matter of common knowledge by anyone at all familiar with San Francisco. Mission street, from its downtown beginning at the water front to and beyond the district of the city known as the Mission, is second in importance and prominence as a business street only to Market street. The probabilities are that every person in the court-room at the trial, including judge, jury, counsel, witnesses, parties, and officers of the court, knew perfectly well what the character of the location was. It was not a matter about which there could be any dispute or question. If the court had left the matter to the determination of the jury, and they for some inconceivable reason had found that it was not a business district, it would have been the duty of the court to set aside the verdict. We are asked now to reverse the judgment, because the court assumed, without submitting to the jury, what could not be disputed, and what he and practically every resident in the county for which the court was sitting knew to be a fact. If error there was, it is clear that, upon the actual fact, there was no prejudice to the defendants.

It would have been much better if counsel for the plaintiff or the trial judge himself had inquired of defendants' counsel, before the case went to the jury, whether there was any dispute as to the locality being a business district within the meaning of the state law. There could have been but one reasonable answer, and, if any other were given, the matter could have been easily settled beyond any possibility of question. But this was not done, and we are now confronted by the question whether either this court or the trial court can take judicial notice of the real fact.

An appellate court can properly take judicial notice of any matter of which the court of original jurisdiction may properly take notice.

In fact, a particularly salutary use of the principle of judicial notice is to sustain on appeal, a judgment clearly in favor of the right party, but as to which there is in the evidence an omission of some necessary fact which is yet indisputable and a matter of common knowledge, and was probably assumed without strict proof for that very reason.

The question, therefore, is: Was the superior court for the city and county of San Francisco, whose judge and talesmen were necessarily residents of the city, entitled to take judicial notice of the character of one of the most important and best-known streets in the city? If it were, the court was authorized to charge the jury as it did.

It should perhaps be noted that the fact that the trial judge knew what the actual fact was, and that it was indisputable, would not of itself justify him in recognizing it. Nor would the fact that the character of the street was a matter of common knowledge and notoriety justify him in taking the question from the jury, if there were any possibility of dispute as to whether or not that character was such as to constitute it a business district within the definition of the statute applicable. If such question could exist, the fact involved—whether the well-known character of the street was sufficient to make it a business district—was one for determination by the jury. But we have in this case a combination of the two circumstances. In the first place, the fact is indisputable and beyond question. In the second place, it is a matter of common knowledge throughout the jurisdiction in and for which the court is sitting.

A consideration of the reasons underlying the matter of judicial notice and its fundamental principles leaves, we believe, but little doubt as to its applicability here. Judicial notice is a judicial short cut, a doing away, in the case of evidence, with the formal necessity for evidence, because there is no real necessity for it. So far as matters of common knowledge are concerned, it is saying there is no need of formally offering evidence of those things, because practically everyone knows them in advance, and there can be no question about them. The rule in this respect is well stated in 15 R.C.L. 1057, as follows:

"It may be stated generally with regard to the question as to what matters are properly of judicial cognizance that, while the power of judicial notice is to be exercised with caution, courts should take notice of whatever is or ought to be generally known, within the limits of their jurisdiction, for justice does not require that courts profess to be more ignorant than the rest of mankind. This rule enumerates three material requisites: (1) The matter of which a court will take judicial notice must be a matter of common and general knowledge. The fact that the belief is not universal, however, is not controlling, for there is scarcely any belief that is accepted by everyone. Courts take judicial notice of those things which are common knowledge to the majority of mankind, or to those persons familiar with the particular matter in question. But matters of which courts have judicial knowledge are uniform and fixed, and do not depend upon uncertain testimony; as soon as a circumstance becomes disputable, it ceases to fall under the head of common knowledge, and so will not be judicially recognized. (2) A matter properly a subject of judicial notice must be 'known'; that is, well established and authoritatively settled, not doubtful or uncertain. In every instance the test is whether sufficient notoriety attaches to the fact involved as to make it safe and proper to assume its existence without proof. In harmony with that view it has been said that courts must 'judicially recognize whatever has the requisite certainty and

notoriety in every field of knowledge, in every walk of practical life.'
(3) A matter, to be within judicial cognizance, must be known 'within
the limits of the jurisdiction of the court.' "

The three requirements so mentioned—that the matter be one of
common and general knowledge, that it be well established and authoritatively settled, be practically indisputable, and that this common,
general, and certain knowledge exist in the particular jurisdiction—all
are requirements dictated by the reason and purpose of the rule, which
is to obviate the formal necessity for proof when the matter does not
require proof.

It is truly said that the power of judicial notice is, as to matters
claimed to be matters of general knowledge, one to be used with
caution. If there is any doubt whatever, either as to the fact itself or as
to its being a matter of common knowledge, evidence should be required; but, if the court is of the certain opinion that these requirements exist, there can properly be no hesitation. In such a case there
is, on the one hand, no danger of a wrong conclusion as to the fact—and
such danger is the reason for the caution in dispensing with the
evidence—and, on the other hand, purely formal and useless proceedings will be avoided.

Little assistance can be had by a search of the authorities for
exactly similar cases. What may be a proper subject of judicial notice
at one time or place may not be at another. It would be wholly
unreasonable to require proof, if the fact became material, as to the
general location in the city of San Francisco of its city hall before a
judge and jury made up of residents of that city and actually sitting in
the building. But before a judge and jury in another county proof
should be made. The difference lies in the fact being one of common
knowledge in one jurisdiction and not in the other. Similarly it has
been held repeatedly that courts will judicially notice the general
doctrines of any religious denomination prevalent within its jurisdiction, and yet it was held by an Ohio court, and properly held, in the
early days of Christian Science, that notice would not be taken of the
doctrines of that sect. Now that the sect has grown to large numbers,
and its general doctrines are a matter of common knowledge, it is as
proper to notice them as to notice those of older denominations. As is
well said by Wigmore (4 Wigmore on Ev. § 2580):

"Applying the general principle (ante, section 2565), especially in
regard to the element of notoriousness, courts are found noticing, from
time to time, a varied array of unquestionable facts, ranging throughout the data of commerce, industry, history, and natural science. It is
unprofitable, as well as impracticable, to seek to connect them by
generalities and distinctions; for the notoriousness of a truth varies
much with differences of period and of place. It is even erroneous, in
many, if not in most instances, to regard them as precedents. It is the
spirit and example of the rulings, rather than their precise tenor, that
is to be useful in guidance."

The test, therefore, in any particular case where it is sought to
avoid or excuse the production of evidence because the fact to be proven

is one of general knowledge and notoriety, is: (1) Is the fact one of common, everyday knowledge in that jurisdiction, which everyone of average intelligence and knowledge of things about him can be presumed to know? and (2) is it certain and indisputable? If it is, it is a proper case for dispensing with evidence, for its production cannot add or aid. On the other hand, we may well repeat, if there is any reasonable question whatever as to either point, proof should be required. Only so can the danger involved in dispensing with proof be avoided. Even if the matter be one of judicial cognizance, there is still no error or impropriety in requiring evidence.

Applying this test to the facts of the case, the matter is not in doubt. The character of Mission street is as well known to San Franciscans as the character of Spring street to residents of Los Angeles, or of State street to residents of Chicago, or of Forty-Second street to residents of New York, or of F street to residents of Washington. It is a matter of their everyday common information and experience, and one about which there can be no dispute.

The conclusion follows that the charge of the trial court that Mission street, between Twentieth and Twenty-Second streets, was a business district, was not error. The judgment is therefore affirmed.

* * *

STATE v. LAWRENCE

Supreme Court of Utah, 1951.
120 Utah 323, 234 P.2d 600.

CROCKETT, Justice. This case comes to us on an appeal from a conviction of grand larceny, arising out of the theft of an automobile. Two questions are presented: First, where there is no evidence of value except a description of the property involved, is it prejudicial error for the court to instruct the jury that the value of the property is greater than $50 and that if defendant is guilty at all he is guilty of grand larceny. The necessity of answering the first question in the affirmative gives rise to the second: Where such error has been committed, can the cause be remanded for retrial without violating the constitutional guarantee of the accused not to be placed twice in jeopardy for the same offense. After a consideration of the problems involved touching upon those questions we answer both in the affirmative.

At the conclusion of the evidence, the defendant's counsel moved the court for a directed verdict on the ground that there had been no evidence of value of the stolen car. The State's attorney might properly and with little difficulty have moved to reopen and supply the missing evidence. He did not do so but instead argued that judicial notice could be taken of the value of the car. The court denied defendant's motion and included in its instructions to the jury the following:

> "Grand Larceny so far as it might be material in this case
> is committed when the property taken is of a value exceeding
> $50.00.

"In this case you will take the value of this property as being in excess of $50.00 and therefore the defendant, if he is guilty at all, is guilty of grand larceny."

It is conceded by the State that there was no direct evidence of value and that the only testimony in the record upon which a finding of value could be based was that of the owner of the automobile describing it saying it was in excellent condition.

This is not a case where the defendant either expressly or impliedly admitted the value, nor by conduct or statements of himself or counsel, allowed it to be assumed that the matter was not disputed. His plea of not guilty cast upon the State the burden of proving every essential element of the offense by evidence sufficient to convince the jury beyond a reasonable doubt. In a charge of grand larceny, one of those essentials is that the value be greater than $50. A conviction for that offense cannot stand unless there is satisfactory evidence of the value of the property. Ordinarily, judicial notice will not be taken of the value of personal property, 31 C.J.S., Evidence, § 101, page 701, and as will later appear herein, this is unquestionably so in connection with the instruction given in this case.

We direct our attention to the argument of the prosecution that the court could take judicial notice of the value of the car and so instruct the jury: Judicial notice is the taking cognizance by the court of certain facts without the necessity of proof, 31 C.J.S., Evidence, § 6, page 509. One class of factual material which is the subject of judicial notice is that dealt with by statute. Section 104–46–1, U.C.A.1943, provides: "Courts take judicial notice of the following facts:" and proceeds to list in eight separate categories, such things as English words, whatever is established by law, acts of departments of government, seals of courts, states and the United States, etc. It would be of no value to list them all here because the value of the car in question could not be thought to come under any subdivision of that statute by any stretch of the imagination.

Section 104–54–4, U.C.A.1943, under the Code of Civil Procedure provides in part: "* * * Whenever the knowledge of the court is by law made evidence of a fact, the court is to declare such knowledge to the jury, who are bound to accept it."

The word "knowledge" in the foregoing section is apparently used advisedly, there being a distinction between "judicial knowledge" of public records, laws, etc. which the court is deemed to know by virtue of his office and "judicial notice" of things which are commonly known. The further discussion in this opinion will show that this statute has no application to the instant case. We are not here concerned with what the result might be if the evidence in question were such that the statute required that the jury be bound to accept it.

Beyond the scope of the statute providing that certain matters will be taken judicial notice of, there is another class of facts which are so well known and accepted that they are judicially noticed without taking the time, trouble and expense necessary to prove them. Under this doctrine the court will consider, without proof of such generally known facts, its knowledge of what is known to all persons of ordinary intelligence. This court has recognized that class of judicial notice in a great variety of matters, a few examples of which are: Rugg v. Tolman, 39 Utah 295, 117 P. 54 (that assignment or garnishment of wages ordinarily imputes no wrong or misconduct to the debtor); Union Savings & Inv. Co. v. District Court of Salt Lake County, 44 Utah 397, 140 P. 221 (the general purpose and methods of doing business of building and loan associations); Salt Lake City v. Board of Education of Salt Lake City, 52 Utah 540, 175 P. 654 (location of school buildings); Utah State Fair Ass'n v. Green, 68 Utah 251, 249 P. 1016 (that betting follows horse racing); State Tax Commission v. City of Logan, 88 Utah 406, 54 P.2d 1197 (that most consumers of electrical energy are constant users). For numerous cases on judicial notice of many different subjects of common knowledge outside the classes covered by our statute see Pacific Digest, Evidence ⊙1 to 52, inc. The taking of judicial notice of this latter class of commonly known evidentiary facts does not establish them so conclusively as to prevent the presentation of contrary evidence or the making of a finding to the contrary. The subject is treated in Wigmore on Evidence, 3d Ed., Sections 2555 et sequi, and he states in Section 2567: "(a) That a matter is judicially noticed means merely that it is taken as true without the offering of proof by the party who should ordinarily have done so. This is because the court assumes that the matter is so notorious that it will not be disputed. But the opponent is not prevented from disputing the matter by evidence, if he believes it disputable."

In discussing this further, Wigmore refers to statutes which expressly provide that the judicial notice is the final determination and binding on the jury; and in Subsection b of the above section, continues: "* * * Does it signify that the settlement of the matter rests with the judge and not with the jury, that the jury are to accept the fact from the judge, and that so far as any further investigation is concerned, it is for the judge alone? Such is the view sometimes found, in decisions as well as statutes [citing statutes including Utah]. *Yet it seems rather that the jury are not concluded;* that the process of notice is intended chiefly for expedition of proof; *and remains possible for the jury to negative it.*" (Emphasis added.)

Accordingly, if we assume that the value of the car is of that class of facts which is so well known that judicial notice should be taken thereof, that would not necessarily be conclusive upon the jury. It would merely take the place of evidence. Upon that basis the court could have instructed the jury to this effect: If you believe from the evidence beyond a reasonable doubt that the defendant stole the automobile in question and that it was a 1947 Ford Sedan in good condition, then you make take into consideration your knowledge acquired in the every day affairs of life in determining what value you will place upon said automobile.

Suppose any number of thoroughly competent and credible witnesses had testified that the car was worth more than $50, and there had been no evidence to the contrary, no matter how clear and convincing the evidence might have been, in a criminal case it was not the prerogative of the court to tell the jury that they have to believe it and so find. See State v. Estrada, Utah, wherein this court reiterated the time-honored rule that it is the sole and exclusive province of the jury to determine the facts in criminal cases, whether the evidence offered by the State is strong or weak; and expressly stated:

"If the trial judge may not find a verdict of guilty, so, likewise he may not find any of the facts which are necessary elements of the crime for which the accused is being tried. * * * The provision of our State Constitution which grants accused persons the right to a trial by jury extends to each and all of the facts which must be found to be present to constitute the crime charged, and *such right may not be invaded by the presiding judge indicating to the jury that any of such facts are established by the evidence.*"

(Emphasis added.)

* * * It is to be admitted that upon the surface there doesn't appear to be much logic to the thought that a jury would not be bound to find that the car involved here (1947 Ford 2-Door Sedan) is worth more than $50. However, under our jury system it is traditional that in criminal cases juries can, and sometimes do, make findings which are not based on logic, nor even common sense. No matter how positive the evidence of a man's guilt may be, the jury may find him not guilty and no court has any power to do anything about it. Notwithstanding the occasional incongruous result, this system of submitting all of the facts in criminal cases to the jury and letting them be the exclusive judges thereof has lasted for some little time now and with a fair degree of success. If the result in individual cases at times seems illogical, we can be consoled by the words of Mr. Justice Holmes, that in some areas of the law, "a page of history is worth a volume of logic." We, who live with it, have a fervent devotion to the jury system, in spite of its faults. We would not like to see it destroyed nor whittled away. If a court can take one important element of an offense from the jury and determine the facts for them because such fact seems plain enough to him, then which element cannot be similarly taken away, and where would the process stop?

For the court to instruct the jury as it did in its Instruction No. 4 "* * * you will take the value of this property as being in excess of $50.00" was an invasion of their province as the exclusive triers of the fact and was prejudicial error * * *. No case has been cited which supports the action of the trial court. One case has been found, certain language of which seems to indicate that the court could take judicial notice of the value of the car, State v. Phillips, in which the court said: "We must not assume to be more ignorant than everybody else, and everybody else knows that such a car is worth more than $20."

But that case did not involve an instruction as to the value the jury must place on the car as in the instant case. In the Phillips case, the judgment was attacked for failure to prove value but the court recited that the defendant himself testified that he and his accomplice had sold the car for $200 (ten times the amount necessary to make grand larceny in that State) and taken $100 each. The evidence of value was sufficient and the conviction was affirmed. * * *

Judgment of the lower court is reversed and the cause remanded for a new trial.

WADE, McDONOUGH, and HENRIOD, JJ., concur.

WOLFE, Chief Justice (dissenting).

I dissent. It is a well known fact of common and general knowledge that a 1947 2-door Ford sedan in excellent condition was worth more than $50 when it was stolen in March, 1950. There is sufficient notoriety of the value of this model car for the trial court to properly take judicial notice thereof.

* * * Defendant argued that the jury should be directed to find a verdict of not guilty upon the ground that there was no evidence as to the value of this automobile. The court took judicial notice of the obvious fact that the car was worth more than $50 and so instructed the jury. The doctrine of judicial notice of generally well known facts has been invoked in many criminal cases. Wharton's Criminal Evidence, 10th Ed. Vol. 1, Chapter VI. The rule should be the same in civil cases as in criminal cases, American Law Institute, Model Code of Evidence, Rules 1, 2 and 801. The majority opinion incorrectly assumes that in this state our Constitution forbids the trial court in a criminal case to take judicial notice of any of the facts necessary to proof of the offense. * * *

The fact that this car was a 1947 model in excellent condition is itself very good evidence of the fact that it was worth substantially more than $50. This is a chattel with which we are all familiar and no reasonable mind could believe that it was worth less than $50. Thus, the testimony of the owner of the automobile as to its make, model and condition made out a prima facie case as to its value. Instead of presenting evidence to rebut what the value of the car was, defendant seeks a reversal of the conviction contending that the State failed in its burden of proof. But the proof is plainly there. * * *

In order to scrupulously refrain from permitting the trial court to invade the province of the jury, the majority opinion suggests that the court could have instructed the jury that "you may take into consideration your knowledge acquired in the every day affairs of life in determining what value you will place upon said automobile." The question thus arises: If the court takes judicial notice of a fact, or at least believes a fact is so obvious that proof thereof is unnecessary, in what manner must he see that a just verdict does not fail for want of that fact? How should his decision to take judicial notice of a fact be transmitted to the jury? Mr. Justice Crockett believes it to be prejudicial error if the trial court tells the jury forthright, what is obviously so—that the car is worth more than $50. He would rather have the jury instructed that they are to draw from their own everyday experience in determining what the car is worth.

There is no constitutional provision which prohibits the trial judge from taking judicial notice in a criminal case of a fact, sufficiently

notorious. If the fact is so well known that judicial notice should be
taken thereof, it then becomes the duty of the court to inform the jury
that the matter should be taken to be established. Counsel not contending that the fact is controverted, the jury should be instructed as to
what the fact is. The trial court in this case stated in effect that the
evidence as to value of the property stolen warranted conviction of
grand larceny, if defendant was guilty at all. The jury was fully
instructed that before the defendant could be found guilty of grand
larceny they must believe beyond a reasonable doubt that the defendant drove away the Ford automobile, with a felonious intent of
stealing said property and of permanently depriving the owner thereof.
The jury was left free to determine the ultimate fact of guilt or
innocence. * * *

* * *

COMMENT, JUDICIAL NOTICE BY APPELLATE COURTS
OF FACTS AND FOREIGN LAWS NOT
BROUGHT TO THE ATTENTION
OF THE TRIAL COURT

42 Mich.L.Rev. 509 (1943).*
[Footnotes omitted.]

The doctrine of judicial notice represents one of the oldest and most
valuable constituents of our jurisprudence. From the days of the
Yearbooks, courts have noticed matters of many diverse kinds which
they have considered (a) sufficiently notorious and (b) commonly recognized. Thus courts have recognized that games such as ping-pong are
not "toys," that short delays often occur in mail deliveries, * * * that
tobacco is a farm product, that the front fender of an automobile is
about the height of a man's knee * * * that a mule is a dangerous
instrumentality. * * * Today, as in earlier times, the doctrine remains a kind of common-sense "taking-for-granted" of certain facts
which experience has shown need not be proved. To put the matter
another way, it declares that there are certain propositions in a party's
case as to which he will not be required to offer evidence. * * *

SCHWARTZ, A SUGGESTION FOR THE DEMISE OF
JUDICIAL NOTICE OF "JUDICIAL FACTS"

45 Tex.L.Rev. 1212 (1967).**

Judicial notice as presently conceived is a doctrine that allows a
court to decide certain issues without reference to data submitted at an
adversary hearing governed by the conventional rules of evidence. A
court takes judicial notice of an issue for one of two reasons: (1) It is
general in nature, relevant to a legal question such as statutory
construction or constitutionality, and can better be explored by the
judge free of the limitations imposed by the rules of evidence. (2) It is
so indisputably settled that although normally in the province of the
fact finder (usually a jury) it can be resolved by the judge without

hearing evidence. This is commonly referred to as judicial notice of "judicial facts."

The latter aspect of judicial notice is formulated in rule 9(2) of the Uniform Rules of Evidence. The test for permitting judicial notice is whether the facts "are so generally known or of such common notoriety within the territorial jurisdiction * * * that they cannot reasonably be the subject of dispute * * * [or] are capable of immediate and accurate determination by resort to easily accessible sources of indisputable accuracy." [1] This aspect of judicial notice performs essentially two functions. It serves to identify in advance issues that need not be formally tried, and it provides a means for achieving a just result despite the failure of the parties to produce adequate proof.

The doctrine is, however, seriously deficient in accomplishing both of these objectives. It fails as a means of identifying issues that need be tried because of the extraneous limitation to facts that are of "common notoriety" or "capable of immediate and accurate determination." The only significant question should be whether the particular factual issue is genuinely in dispute. As a means of reaching a just result in the face of an inadequate record, judicial notice, of course, suffers from this same deficiency. More fundamental, however, is the failure to face squarely the questions of what should be the judge's responsibility in determining whether a factual record is inadequate and whether to take steps to cure it. Surely that responsibility should not be limited to supplying facts that are of "common notoriety" or "capable of immediate and accurate determination."

The following statute, together with presently available motions for summary judgment and directed verdict, would provide more inclusive and rational means for dealing with these problems:

> (1) If the trial court in a case in which both sides have rested and the case has not been decided shall determine that the evidence with respect to a material issue of fact is significantly less than may be available and that there is a substantial risk that decision based on the evidence of record measured by the applicable burdens of proof and persuasion may not comport with actual fact it may

> (a) in all cases where there is no jury and in jury cases where the additional evidence can be obtained without substantial delay stay all proceedings until the parties have an opportunity to obtain the additional evidence and then permit the evidence to be introduced and considered in the decision of the case, or

> (b) in jury cases where the additional evidence cannot be obtained without substantial delay discharge the jury

---

1. Rule 9 also provides for judicial notice of various matters of local and foreign law. This portion of the rule, however, will not be considered here. This observation is also limited to civil cases.

and direct retrial of the case when the additional evidence is obtained.[2]

(2) If the trial court after the case has been decided or an appellate court shall determine that the evidence with respect to a material issue of fact is significantly less than may be available and that there is a substantial risk that decision based on the evidence of record measured by the applicable burdens of proof and persuasion may not comport with actual fact it may

(a) afford the parties the opportunity to demonstrate to the Court before whom the matter is pending their respective rights to summary judgment[3] with respect to the issue, or

(b) remand the case for the taking of further evidence and reconsideration by the judge before whom the case was originally heard (who may be the judge issuing the order) or a retrial of the issue before a jury as may be appropriate.[4]

(3) The party or parties against whom the issue would be resolved on the state of the record prior to the proceedings authorized by this Rule shall be responsible for all costs, including reasonable attorney's fees, incurred by the other parties in connection with proceedings authorized by this Rule.

There are two main conclusions underlying the proposed solution. First, a party who is aware that there is strong proof of his contention and would be entitled to have judicial notice taken should be able to demonstrate his right to summary judgment or a directed verdict. In addition to covering all cases within the scope of judicial notice as presently conceived, the summary judgment and directed verdict procedures serve to foreclose spurious issues that are beyond reach of judicial notice. The overlap between summary judgment or directed verdict on the one hand and judicial notice on the other creates the risk that a party may invoke judicial notice, overlook the other devices, and thus be denied relief to which he is entitled. Secondly, in those cases where all the evidence is in and the matter is pending before a trial or appellate court, judicial notice provides a poor way to cure a defective record—the real reason for its use. The question whether the record affords an inadequate basis for decision should be squarely faced and

---

2. There are procedural devices that provide alternatives to directing complete retrial. Thus if the issue with respect to which the evidence is to be offered is severable the court can sever it and hear the remainder of the case. The jury verdict may then make the severed issue moot. A second possibility is that the party who will have to bear the expense of the extra proceedings (as provided in paragraph 3) may be agreeable to waiving jury trial. If the other party concurs, the case can simply be continued until the additional evidence is available. It is also possible that after the additional evidence is obtained summary judgment can be awarded and retrial thus avoided.

3. A motion for summary judgment before the appellate court would be an unprecedented innovation. Since no oral testimony is required and the appellate court has gained familiarity with the case by hearing the appeal, there is no reason for a remand to the trial court.

4. Of course, waiver of jury trial will avoid the necessity of repeating the evidence previously admitted on the issue.

the court should have available the full range of practical alternatives for obtaining further factual guidance.

The principal reason for rejecting judicial notice in favor of summary judgment or directed verdict is that the judicial notice concept introduces the essentially extraneous concepts that the facts must be "so generally known or of such common notoriety that they cannot reasonably be the subject of dispute" or "capable of immediate and accurate determination by resort to easily accessible sources of indisputable accuracy." Whether the matter is commonly known or subject to immediate and accurate determination should be irrelevant if the truth of the particular fact in issue can be plainly demonstrated. This is precisely the approach of summary judgment and directed verdict, which foreclose the matter if the particular issue is not "genuine." These devices, moreover, should cover all cases where judicial notice can now be taken. If the matter is of "common notoriety," the affidavit or testimony of a knowledgeable person will be sufficient because presumably no denial will be possible. If the matter can be determined by reference to sources of "indisputable accuracy" the moving party will offer them; if indeed they are indisputable, they will not be disputed.

The use of judicial notice as a pretrial device is probably explicable in historical terms by the unavailability of summary judgment (and perhaps discovery devices such as requests for admissions that can also be used to eliminate spurious issues) as a means of limiting trials to matters genuinely in dispute. One other contemporary justification might be offered. Since the exclusionary rules of evidence generally do not govern what a judge may consider in determining whether to take judicial notice, judicial notice may be viewed as a means of relaxing the hearsay limitations on the use of documentary evidence. This approach to the problem is unfortunate. If reliable documentation is being excluded by the hearsay rule, the rule ought to be changed. It is anomalous indeed for a scholarly work to be characterized as a "source of indisputable accuracy" for the purpose of allowing judicial notice and yet to be excluded as hearsay at trial.

In any event, with the advent of liberal discovery and summary judgment, the judicial notice doctrine is not significant where counsel realizes that his position may be so strong that he can avoid litigating the matter at trial. Its more significant use, however, is when it is discovered after all the evidence is in that a party has failed to offer adequate proof with respect to a contention that the court nevertheless feels is true. In this situation the limitations of the judicial notice doctrine can create more serious problems. The court can supply the missing proof only if the stated requirements are met. If they cannot be met, however, the case must be decided on the existing record no matter how strong the indications are that vital evidence has been omitted.

This is obviously a bad result. If there is still time to produce reliable proof before the case is submitted for decision, the court should advise counsel to obtain it. Or if the inadequacy is detected after an initial determination, the party should be permitted to demonstrate the fact by affidavit or other irrefutable proof. More fundamentally, the court should never decide a case on a record it regards as inadequate. Rather, it should invoke the alternative provided by the proposed Rule, which assures an informed resolution of the issue with the least possible expense and burden.

The proposal is completed by providing that the party who has failed to discharge his responsibility to prove the matter should bear the expense of the extra proceedings to cure the defective record. Indeed, if the party in turn succeeds in recovering these expenses from his own counsel, when his negligence has created the necessity for the additional proceedings, the consequences may be even more salutary.

In conclusion, judicial notice adds nothing as a means of selecting in advance issues that need not be the subject of proof at trial—with the exception of the doubtful contribution of indirect relaxation of the hearsay rule. As a means of achieving a just resolution when the trial record is inadequate it suffers most fundamentally from a failure squarely to face the problem. Moreover, it is far too limited and inflexible to afford appropriate relief in all cases where it is needed. The use of summary judgment and directed verdict to eliminate spurious issues, the relaxation of hearsay limitations on the consideration of reliable scholarly works, and the invocation of the proposed statute dealing directly with the problem of the inadequate trial record, together afford far better means for resolving the problems now handled under the judicial notice doctrine.

————

See Federal Rules of Evidence 201. California Evidence Code §§ 450–460. On judicial notice of foreign law see F.R.Civ.P. 44.1 and F.R.Cr.P. 26.1.

LILLY, AN INTRODUCTION TO THE LAW OF EVIDENCE
18 (2d ed. 1987).[*]

The term "judicial notice" also applies to the process by which a judge, usually with the assistance of counsel, determines or discovers the procedural or substantive law in his or some other jurisdiction. Usually the judge can consult and apply statutes, regulations, and prior case law (precedents) whether or not such materials have been introduced into evidence. If counsel wishes the judge to consult a particular source, he simply calls the judge's attention to it and supplies a citation. However, in instances where there is no widely available source (as there is with most American codes and case reports), it may be necessary for counsel formally to provide evidence of the pertinent rule of law. For example, foreign law, the content of which may pose difficulties of discovery and interpretation, is not routinely judicially noticed. Unless a statute provides for judicial notice, the content of the foreign law must be proved by official documents and, when necessary, expert witnesses. The treatment of municipal ordinances varies. Typically, these will not be noticed absent a statutory authorization; thus one relying upon such an ordinance may have to prove its content by an official or "true" copy.

PART B. JURY NOTICE

IX WIGMORE, EVIDENCE § 2570 (1940) *

[Some footnotes omitted.]

Judicial Notice by the Jury's Own Knowledge. In general, the jury may in modern times act only upon evidence properly laid before them in the course of the trial. But so far as the matter in question is one upon which men in general have a common fund of experience and knowledge, through data notoriously accepted by all, the analogy of judicial notice by the judge obtains here also, to some extent, and the jury are allowed to resort to this information in making up their minds.

This doctrine, of course, has several aspects. From the point of view of the jury's duty, it appears as an exception to the rule that they must act only upon what is presented to them at the trial. From the point of view of the Hearsay rule, it may also be thought of as a partial exception to that.[1] But additionally it must be considered from the present point of view. It authorizes the party to ask the *jury to refer to their general knowledge* upon matters *notorious and unquestioned,* and thus in effect and to that extent makes it unnecessary for the party to have offered evidence on the matter:

> 1878, Hunter's Trial, N.J., 13 Amer.St.Tr. 57, 151; murder of Armstrong by Graham, at Hunter's instigation; a witness as to their doings placed Hunter on the Philadelphia ferry-boat on the evening of the murder. Mr. *George R. Robeson,* for the accused, arguing against this witness' credibility: "As to the testimony of Mrs. Auvache, think of the brilliancy of memory of a witness who could come into court five months after the 23d of January and positively identify Hunter as a man at whom she had taken a passing glance on the evening of that day. And her entry in the diary of her trip to Philadelphia on that day, only two other entries being made in the whole book! She insisted that the ladies' cabin on the boat she came over on was on the left-hand side of the boat, although the ladies' cabin is on the right side of the boat."
>
> Mr. *Jenkins* [for the State]: *"Is there any proof in this case* as to what side the ladies cabin is located?"
>
> Mr. *Robeson:* "Does the prosecutor dispute that fact?"
>
> Mr. *Jenkins:* "I dispute that it is in testimony."
>
> Mr. *Robeson:* "I don't care whether it is or not. I think Moore testified to the fact, but it does not matter; *the Court*

* Copyright, 1940 by John H. Wigmore.

1. Ante, § 1900 (jurors having personal knowledge must take the stand and state it publicly as witnesses subject to cross-examination). Distinguish, however, the propriety of *knowledge acquired at a view* (ante, § 1168).

knows, the jury knows, the people know, and the prosecutor knows, that the ladies' cabin on the boats of the Camden ferry is on the *right*-hand side. I gave Mrs. Auvache every opportunity to rectify her statement by asking her every form of question about it, but she stuck to her falsehood."

1908, Mr. Arthur Train, in the "Sunday Magazine," Nov. 7, 1908: "Most cases turn on an unconsidered point. A prosecutor once lost what seemed to him the clearest sort of a case. When it was all over, and the defendant had passed out of the courtroom rejoicing, he turned to the foreman and asked the reason for the verdict. 'Did you hear your chief witness say he was a carpenter?' inquired the foreman. 'Why, certainly,' answered the district attorney. 'Did you hear me ask him what he paid for that ready-made pine door he claimed to be working on when he saw the assault?' The prosecutor recalled the incident and nodded. 'Well, he said ten dollars—and I knew he was a liar. A door like that don't cost but four-fifty!' It is, perhaps, too much to require a knowledge of carpentry on the part of a lawyer trying an assault case. Yet the juror was undoubtedly right in his deduction."

1884, Lyon, J., in Washburn v. R. Co., 59 Wis. 364, 370: "A jury is not bound to give and cannot give any weight to testimony which, although undisputed by witnesses, is contrary to what every person of ordinary intelligence knows to be true. To illustrate, should a witness testify that at Boston on a certain day the sun arose at midnight, or that the Mississippi river empties into Lake Michigan, or that white is black, the testimony would be rejected at once. * * * Beyond this the jury cannot properly go. To allow jurors to make up their verdict on their individual knowledge of disputed facts material to the case, not testified to by them in court, or upon their private opinions, would be most dangerous and unjust. It would deprive the losing party of the right of cross-examination and the benefit of all the tests of credibility which the law affords. Besides, the evidence of such knowledge or of the grounds of such opinions could not be preserved in a bill of exceptions or questioned on appeal."

1895, Hackney, J., Jenney Electric Co. v. Branham, 145 Ind. 314, 41 N.E. 448 (permitting the use of "your experience and relations among men" in judging of the credibility of witnesses): "It is argued that such a rule would permit the disposition of a cause upon the whims of jurors, rather than upon the law and the evidence as they were learned in the trial. Jurors should be, and, as a rule, are, selected because of their extensive experiences among men. The school of experience which men attend in their varied relations among men imparts a keenness of mental vision which enables them the more readily to see the motives and to judge of the selfish or unselfish interest of men. This education, be it much or little, is a part of the juror, and should not, if possible, be laid aside

in passing upon the inducements which may surround a witness to speak falsely. It is this education which to a great
extent enables a juror to discover in the faltering manner or
the downcast eye whether the statement of the witness is made
in modesty or in the guilt of falsehood. The value of experience is not to be given up when the man becomes a juror, and
is required to apply the tests of credit to the heart and mind of
the witness, but whatever qualification that experience gives
should be employed to the end that the whole truth may be
known and acted upon."

1921, Burnett, C.J., in Rostad v. Portland R.L. & P. Co.,
101 Or. 569, 201 P. 184: "The *personal* knowledge of any juror
concerning any probative fact involved in the case under
consideration is not to be used in deciding the case. Such a
juror should communicate his information to the Court, and if
he is not excused from service and it is deemed proper to use
his cognizance of such a fact in the trial, he must be sworn as a
witness and examined, subject to cross-examination by the
adverse party, the same as any other witness. But any juror
must consider the testimony in the light of that *knowledge and
experience which is common to all men.* For instance, it is a
matter of common knowledge that a bullet piercing the brain
of a human being will in all likelihood prove fatal. It is
common knowledge, also, that a forest tree cut nearly in two at
the butt will fall, if a high wind blows against it. If a witness
should testify to the contrary to these ordinary phenomena,
the common knowledge of the juror derived from his experience in such matters would naturally compel him to discredit
that witness. Many illustrations might be given where men
are normally and legitimately influenced in considering testimony by their general knowledge and experience. * * * It is
utterly impracticable in the administration of courts of justice
to secure a juror whose mind is totally blank as to questions
involved in the ordinary transactions of life. Triers of fact
cannot, in the nature of things, be divested of general knowledge of practical affairs. The Court cannot do otherwise than
to direct them to use such experiences as are common to all
men in the decision of questions of fact. It is part of the jury
system which cannot be dispensed with."

But the scope of this doctrine is narrow; it is strictly limited to a
few matters of elemental experience in human nature, commercial
affairs, and everyday life. Thus, the natural instincts of human conduct, with reference to care or negligence at the time of danger, may be
considered, the dangerousness of smoking a pipe in a barn near the
straw, the conditions affecting the various kinds of values, the intoxi-
cating nature of a certain liquor, and even (though this illustrates how
local conditions may affect the application) that a game played with
bone-counters was played for money. But such a matter of private and
variable belief as the character of a particular witness cannot be so
taken into consideration by the jury.

The range of such general knowledge is not precisely definable. But in these days when too much emphasis is placed, in the selection of jurors, on the blankness of their mental tablets, there can be no harm in the liberal application of the present principle.

As a natural part of its doctrine, of course, these matters may be referred to by counsel in their arguments.

HIGGINS v. LOS ANGELES GAS & ELECTRIC CO.

Supreme Court of California, 1911.
159 Cal. 651, 115 P. 313.

HENSHAW, J. This action was brought to recover damages from defendant for injuries caused to a building, the property of plaintiff. The damage was caused by an explosion of gas. This explosion occurred in a restaurant of a tenant of the plaintiff, Cressaty by name. The facts attending the explosion have recently been set forth by this court in its consideration of the case of Merrill v. Los Angeles Gas & Electric Company, 111 Pac. 534. It is sufficient to refer to that case; but it is to be borne in mind that that action was for personal injuries occasioned to a patron of Cressaty's restaurant, while the present action is to recover damages occasioned to plaintiff's building while in the possession of a tenant.

Trial was had before a jury. The defendant, as part of its evidence, showed that, the gas leak being in a dark and obscure place, its employés approached the leak with an electric flash light, and while the man holding the flash light was in close proximity to the leak the explosion occurred. The flash light used to inspect the leak was never recovered. It was probably destroyed by the explosion. But a similar flash light was introduced in evidence by the defendant, and the contention was made that it was impossible for this flash light as used to give out any spark which would cause the ignition and explosion of the gas. It was also in evidence than an oil stove in the restaurant was burning at the time of the explosion, and that this oil stove was some 44 feet from the place where the gas was escaping. It was contended by plaintiff that the explosion was probably occasioned by a spark from the electric flash light, and he introduced evidence to establish the fact that a flash light such as that before the jury could produce a spark. It was contended by defendant that the explosion was occasioned by the flame of the oil stove, and that Cressaty, plaintiff's tenant, was negligent in not having extinguished the light of the stove after demand by defendant's employés that he do so. To demonstrate that the flash light could give out, and might have given out, a spark sufficient to cause the explosion, plaintiff, in rebuttal of the evidence of defendant's experts to the contrary, put an expert witness on the stand who so testified. Asked to demonstrate before the jury how the spark could be produced and to produce it, he proceeded to unscrew the cap of the flash light and undertook to make a spark by the use of a pair of plyers. Under objection the court stopped this experiment, manifestly for the reason that, to be of value to the jury, a spark should be produced from the flash light under conditions of use like those attending the explosion. Argument was indulged in before the jury pro and con over the possibility of so producing a spark, and the flash light was passed from hand to hand and inspected by the jury. While deliberating over their verdict, the jury requested to have with them in the jury room the flash light. The court permitted them to do so. Special interrogatories were submitted to the jury, amongst them one in answer to which it declared that the explosion was caused by a spark from the flash light and not from the flame of the oil stove. The general verdict was for plaintiff. Defendant moved for a new trial.

The court denied the motion as to all grounds save one, and granted the new trial "on the sole ground that the court erred in sending into the jury in their consultation room the flash light." The terms of this order eliminate from consideration the question of the sufficiency or insufficiency of the evidence to support the verdict. There are left for consideration two matters: First, was it error calling for a new trial for the court to have permitted the jury to take with them to their room and to have with them during their deliberations the flash light introduced in evidence by respondent? Second, alleged errors of the court arising in the trial of the case.

The only express provision of the law bearing upon the right of juries to use exhibits or upon the right of the court to permit juries to use exhibits in their deliberations is found in section 612 of the Code of Civil Procedure, and this has to do solely with "papers" which have been introduced in evidence. One curious in such matters can learn from the common law why this section of the Code was adopted and why also it is confined to papers. The common-law rule was that jurors were allowed to take with them in their deliberations only such instruments as were under seal, and that they were not permitted to take with them any unsealed papers excepting by consent of the parties. The reason for this, according to Lord Hale and Lord Gilbert, was that jurors were supposed to be, and for the most part were, unlettered men. They could not read. A writing conveyed to them nothing. But in the case of sealed instruments, as these jurors were drawn from the vicinage, they were quite apt to be familiar with the armorial bearings of their neighborhood great from which the seals were derived. An instrument under seal, therefore, spoke for itself, and the jurors were permitted to take such instruments with them, not for the purpose of reading the instrument itself, but rather for the purpose of verifying their recollection of the seal and testing its genuineness. The curious inquirer will also find that it was not uncommon for one who had not risen to the dignity of possessing an armorial bearing to set the stamp of his teeth as his seal upon the instrument, and hence the old time phrase of "proving it to (by) his teeth." But, in the case of other exhibits not involving a knowledge of reading or writing, it seems to have been a matter of discretion with the court to allow the jury to take them into the jury room in aid of their deliberations. This rule, as to papers, however, was in force at a time when learning in letters was so rare and the premium upon such learning so high that a felon could save his neck by proving his ability to read a verse of scripture. It was to save the possibility of the

question arising in this state as in 1812 it arose in the state of
Pennsylvania (Alexander et al. v. Jameson et al., 5 Bin. 238) that the
section of the Code was adopted. All distinction between sealed and
unsealed instruments had been abolished, and, as the restrictive rule of
the common law upon the power of the court had gone only to papers
containing printing or writing, it was necessary only to modify that
rule as was done by section 612. Therefore section 612 is not to be
construed as a limitation of the power of the court in the matter of
other exhibits, but as a modification and extension of the common-law
rule touching exhibits containing writings.

It will be noted that depositions are excluded by the section. This
is for the very obvious reason that depositions may, and usually do,
contain matters not admissible in evidence which matters have been
eliminated from the consideration of the jury. To permit the jury to
take depositions with them would be to put them in possession of this
excluded evidence.

In this lies the suggestion of the true rule guiding the court and
governing the jury in the use of exhibits. The court may permit the
jury to take with them and use in their deliberations any exhibit where
the circumstances call for it, observing the proper precaution of instructing the jury in the nature of the use which they shall make of the
exhibit. It is a fundamental rule that all evidence shall be taken in
open court, and that each party to a controversy shall have knowledge
of, and thus be enabled to meet and answer, any evidence brought
against him. It is this fundamental rule which is to govern the use of
such exhibits by the jury. They may use the exhibit according to its
nature to aid them in weighing the evidence which has been given and
in reaching a conclusion upon a controverted matter.

They may carry out experiments within the lines of offered evidence; but if their experiments shall invade new fields, and they shall
be influenced in their verdict by discoveries from such experiments
which will not fall fairly within the scope and purview of the evidence,
then, manifestly, the jury has been itself taking evidence without the
knowledge of either party, evidence which it is not possible for the
party injured to meet, answer, or explain.

Typical instances of the improper and proper experimental use of
exhibits by a jury are found, respectively, in Wilson v. United States,
and Taylor v. Commonwealth. In the first of these cases the indictment charged the defendant with smuggling opium "prepared for
smoking purposes." A sealed can had been introduced in evidence by
the prosecution and asserted to contain a sample of the smuggled
opium. No testimony was given tending to show that the can contained
opium prepared for smoking purposes, and yet it was conceded that it
was essential to a conviction (since the offense was so laid) to show not
only that the can contained opium, and that it was smuggled opium,
but also that it was opium "prepared for smoking purposes." In this
condition of the evidence the court instructed the jury that it might
take the can to the jury room, open it, and extract some of the contents;
that they would not be permitted to make a chemical examination of

1 the contents; but that they could in the jury room test the extracted
2 samples and learn to their satisfaction whether or not it would burn,
3 and use the information so obtained in determining whether the can
4 contained "opium prepared for smoking purposes." The Circuit Court
5 of Appeals, in holding this instruction to be erroneous, said: "Surely, if
6 the attorney for the government, as was his duty, had offered evidence
7 going to show that the can in question contained opium for smoking
8 purposes, the defendants would have been legally and justly entitled to
9 have proved, if they could, that it contained no such thing; in which
10 latter event there must have been a verdict of not guilty, for there was
11 nothing else offered tending to show that there was any opium pre-
12 pared for smoking purposes in the case. Yet the jury was left to
13 determine that essential fact for themselves, by experiment, and in the
14 absence of the defendants, who were thus wholly deprived of the
15 opportunity to contest the correctness of the jury's experiments, and of
16 the possibility of giving any evidence upon one of the essential facts
17 involved in the prosecution." Taylor v. Commonwealth was a case of
18 murder. It was the assassination from ambush at midday of six or
19 seven innocent and unsuspecting people. By the Supreme Court of
20 Virginia it is described as "an inhuman and wholesale massacre of
21 innocent and unsuspecting men, women and children traveling peacea-
22 bly upon the public highway." In the ambuscade of the assassins were
23 found certain cartridge shells which had been discharged from a 45–75
24 Winchester rifle. Defendant was charged with this murder. It was
25 shown by the prosecution that he carried a rifle of this description and
26 caliber. The defendant introduced his rifle in evidence and with it four
27 empty shells which he proved were fired from his rifle. It was contend-
28 ed that the marks of the firing pin upon the cartridge shells found in
29 the ambuscade were so different from the marks of the firing pin upon
30 the shells introduced by the defendant in evidence as to establish to a
31 certainty that the shells found in the ambuscade were not fired from
32 defendant's rifle. During the trial the rifle admitted in evidence was
33 inspected by the jury but was not taken to pieces. After retiring to
34 deliberate the jury asked if the gun could be sent to them. This was
35 done without objection from either side. After a verdict of guilty
36 defendant moved in arrest of judgment, contending that the jury had
37 improperly taken the gun to pieces and examined the plunger or firing
38 pin. It was shown in support of the motion that the jury had actually
39 done this thing, and that from their examination had concluded that
40 the plunger or firing pin had been tampered with. The Supreme Court
41 of Virginia very properly upheld the verdict, the conduct, and the
42 experiment of the jury. The purpose of the introduction of the gun in
43 evidence was to show that its firing pin did not strike the cartridge in a
44 particular way. The gun was offered by the defendant to establish his
45 contention in this regard. A more acute prosecuting attorney might
46 have caused the examination to have been made in open court, and
47 thus have demonstrated the trick and fraud; but his failure to do so
48 afforded no ground for overthrowing the verdict of an intelligent and
49 scrutinizing jury, which, making its own examination of the evidence
50 admitted to prove or disprove the very fact, discovered that the plunger

"had been recently tampered with and fixed for the occasion of the trial." These cases, we have said, are typical. In the one the jury was permitted to make an experiment without knowledge of the parties of the method or process which was employed. It was an experiment addressed to evidence necessary to the prosecution's case which should have been offered in court. To permit the jury to gather this evidence without the presence of the defendant and without the possibility of knowledge upon his part as to the method by which their conclusion was reached and without the possibility of contesting the correctness of their experiment was, as the court justly held, the equivalent of the taking by the jury of evidence out of court, and a deprivation of the constitutional right of the defendant to be present at the taking of all evidence in his case. Upon the other hand, in the Virginia case the jury was not experimenting along lines without the evidence. It merely subjected an exhibit to a more critical examination than had been made of it in court, and by such examination reached a conclusion upon a contested fact by a more careful scrutiny of an exhibit introduced for the very purpose of affording evidence of the fact.

In this state it was held, in People v. Conkling, that it was error demanding a new trial, when certain of the jurors, to satisfy themselves at what distance a rifle discharged would powder-mark cloth, procured a rifle out of the courtroom and experimented with it. Here was a clear case of the jury's obtaining evidence by unauthorized experiments made without the presence and knowledge of the defendant. But, on the other hand, in People v. Mahoney, clothing worn by the deceased at the time of the homicide was, upon the jury's request, sent to the jury room, and in the matter of the Thomas Estate, it was held that a memorandum book admitted in evidence was properly allowed in the jury room in aid of the jury's deliberations.

In most of the cases, because of the very nature of the exhibit and of all the possible uses to which it may be put in the jury room, there is no occasion for the court to admonish the jury or to caution and limit it as to the nature of the use or experiment which shall be made. But where, from its nature, it may be susceptible to improper use, as in the case of the can of opium, it is the duty of the court, by instruction to the jury, to limit and restrict that use.

Coming to the case at bar, it is certain that the trial judge conceived that he had fallen into error in allowing the jury to take with them and to experiment with an exhibit which they might subject to an improper use, without limiting the scope of their experiments by proper instruction. It will be remembered that the court checked one experiment in the courtroom during its progress, and it is probable that the judge thought that by delivering the exhibit to the jury he had prepared the way for them to perform the very experiment which he had forbidden.

Since a jury is not allowed to impeach its verdict by showing what improper methods it employed to reach it, the need of such cautionary instructions in a proper case becomes imperative, and we would by no means disturb the ruling of a trial court granting a new trial if it appeared that injury resulted from its failure to give such instructions.

But if, on the other hand, it could not have resulted in injury to the defendant even if the jury did perform an improper experiment and from it reached its conclusion that the explosion of gas was caused by a spark from the flash light, then clearly no new trial should be granted for an error which could not have resulted in injury. To this consideration we now come.

The special verdict that the explosion was caused by a spark from the flash light was not material to the case, and defendant's position would not have been bettered if the jury had found that the cause of the explosion was not the spark from the flash light, but the fire from Cressaty's stove. It is to be remembered that this is not Cressaty's action to recover, which might be defeated by proof of his own contributory negligence. It is the action of his landlord, and, unless it can be said that the landlord was responsible for the negligent act of the tenant so as to defeat the landlord's recovery, the statement just made is unanswerable.

[The order granting a new trial was reversed.]

PART C.　LEGISLATIVE FACTS

McCORMICK'S HANDBOOK OF THE LAW OF EVIDENCE
766–69 (2d ed. 1972).*

Social and Economic Data Used in Judicial Law-Making: "Legislative" Facts.

It is conventional wisdom today to observe that judges not only are charged to find what the law is, but must regularly make new law when deciding upon the constitutional validity of a statute, interpreting a statute, or extending or restricting a common law rule. The very nature of the judicial process necessitates that judges be guided, as legislators are, by considerations of expediency and public policy. They must, in the nature of things, act either upon knowledge already possessed or upon assumptions,[83] or upon investigation of the pertinent general facts, social,[84] economic,[85] political,[86] or scientific.[87] An older

---

* Copyright West Publishing Co. 1972.

83. See, e.g., Village of Euclid v. Ambler Realty Co., 272 U.S. 365, 47 S.Ct. 114, 71 L.Ed. 303 (1926) (proper exercise of police power to exclude apartment houses from residential districts because they tend to be mere parasites and come near to being nuisances); Potts v. Coe, 78 U.S.App. D.C. 297, 140 F.2d 470 (1944) (incentive to invent supplied by patent law will not work in organized research because it destroys teamwork).

84. Brown v. Board of Education, 347 U.S. 483 [74 S.Ct. 686, 98 L.Ed. 873] (1954), supplemented 349 U.S. 294 [75 S.Ct. 753, 99 L.Ed. 1083, (racially segregated schools can never be equal notwithstanding their equality of teachers or equipment because the very act of segregation brands the segregated minority with a feeling of inferiority).

85. SEC v. Capital Gains Research Bureau, Inc., 300 F.2d 745 (2d Cir. 1961), rev'd 375 U.S. 180 [84 S.Ct. 275, 11 L.Ed.2d 237], (judicial notice taken that advice tendered by small advisory service could not influence stock market generally); same case, 375 U.S. 180 [84 S.Ct. 275, 11 L.Ed.2d 237] (1963) (judicial notice taken that the advice tendered could influence the market price).

86. Baker v. Carr, 369 U.S. 186 [82 S.Ct. 691, 7 L.Ed.2d 663] (1962) (contemporary notions of justice require that equal apportionment of voting districts be made a legal

---

87. See note 87 on page 712.

tradition once prescribed that judges should rationalize their result
solely in terms of analogy to old doctrines leaving the considerations of
expediency unstated.   Contemporary practice indicates that judges in
their opinions should render explicit their policy-judgments and the
factual grounds therefor.   These latter have been helpfully classed as
"legislative facts," as contrasted with the "adjudicative facts" which are
historical facts pertaining to the incident which give rise to lawsuits.

Constitutional cases argued in terms of due process typically involve reliance upon legislative facts for their proper resolution.
Whether a statute enacted pursuant to the police power is valid, after
all, involves a twofold analysis.   First, it must be determined that the
enactment is designed to achieve an appropriate objective of the police
power; that is, it must be designed to protect the public health, morals,
safety, or general welfare.   The second question is whether, in light of
the data on hand, a legislature still beholden to reason could have
adopted the means they did to achieve the aim of their exercise of the
police power.   In Burns Baking Co., v. Bryan, for example, the question
was whether, concerned about consumers being misled by confusing
sizes of bread, the Nebraska legislature could decree not only that the
bakers bake bread according to distinctively different weights but that
they wrap their product in wax paper lest any post-oven expansion of
some loaves undo these distinctions.   A majority of the court held the
enactment unconstitutional because, in their opinion, the wrapping
requirement was unreasonable.   Mr. Justice Brandeis, correctly antici-
pating the decline of substantive due process, dissented, pointing out
that the only question was whether the measure was a reasonable
legislative response in light of the facts available to the legislators
themselves.   Then, in a marvellous illustration of the Brandeis-brief
technique, he recited page after page of data illustrating how widespread was the problem of shortweight and how, in light of nationwide
experience, the statute appeared to be a reasonable response to the
environmental situation.[93]

Given the bent to test due process according to the information
available to the legislature, the truth-content of this data is not directly
relevant.   The question is whether sufficient data exists which could
influence a reasonable legislature to act, not whether ultimately this
data is true.[94]   This is not the same case as when a court proceeds to

and perforce largely mathematical question rather than a purely political one).

87. Durham v. United States, 94 U.S.
App.D.C. 228, 214 F.2d 862 (1954) (psychiatric learning pertinent to the scientific
soundness of the right-and-wrong test of
criminal insanity).

93. The opponents of a statute can resort to extra-record legislative facts to support their argument that it is invalid.   In
Burns Baking Co. v. Bryan, 264 U.S. 504
[44 S.Ct. 412, 68 L.Ed. 813] (1924), the
statute regulating bread sizes was struck
down because it was "contrary to common
experience and unreasonable to assume
there could be any danger of * * * de-

ception." See also Defiance Milk Products
Co. v. DeMond, 309 N.Y. 537, 132 N.E.2d
829 (1956) (statute requiring inordinately
large size cans for retail sale of evaporated
skimmed milk held invalid because judicial
notice was taken that it would be incredible to believe consumers needed protection
against deception practiced with regard to
the nature of this product).

94. In theory, at least, the Uniform
Rules of Evidence would not allow the
judges to take judicial notice of any of the
data with which the cases in this section
are concerned since none of it is "indisputably" true. See the text of these rules
reproduced in § 328, note 3, supra. Given

interpret a constitutional norm and, while they still rely upon data, the judges *qua* legislators themselves proceed to act as if the data were true. In Brown v. Board of Education, for example, the Court faced the issue whether segregated schools, equal facility and teacher-wise, could any longer be tolerated under the equal protection clause. The question was not any longer whether a reasonable legislator could believe these schools could never be equal, but whether the *judges* believed that the very act of segregating branded certain children with a feeling of inferiority so deleterious that it would be impossible for them to obtain an equal education no matter how equal the facilities and teachers. Thus the intellectual legitimacy of this kind of decision turns upon the actual truth-content of the legislative facts taken into account by the judges who propound the decision. While not necessarily indisputably true, it would appear that these legislative facts must at least appear to be more likely than not true if the opinion is going to have the requisite intellectual legitimacy upon which the authority of judge-made rules is ultimately founded.[96]

When making new common law, judges must, like legislators, do the best they can assaying the data available to them and make the best decision they can of which course wisdom dictates they follow. Should they, for example, continue to invoke the common law rule of *caveat emptor* in the field of real property, or should they invoke a notion of implied warranty in the instance of the sale of new houses? [97] Should they require landlords of residential units to warrant their habitability and fitness for the use intended? [98] While sociological, economic, political and moral doctrine may abound about questions like this, none of this data is likely indisputable.[99]

the practice of courts to notice less than indisputably true facts within a legislative context, the Uniform Rules might be interpreted to apply only to adjudicative facts.
* * *

96. See, e.g., the reaction to Durham v. United States, 94 U.S.App.D.C. 228, 214 F.2d 862 (1954), wherein on the basis of psychiatric data the court formulated a new test for criminal insanity. Some psychiatrists accepted the result: Roche, Criminality and Mental Illness—Two Faces of the Same Coin, 22 U.Chi.L.Rev. 320 (1955). The American Law Institute rejected it. Model Penal Code, Tentative Draft No. 4, 159–60 (1955). See also Brown v. Board of Education, 347 U.S. 483 [74 S.Ct. 686, 98 L.Ed. 873 (1954), supplemented 349 U.S. 294 [75 S.Ct. 753, 99 L.Ed. 1083] wherein for the psychological impact of segregation the court relied upon, inter alia, the work of Dr. Kenneth B. Clark. Dr. Clark felt compelled thereafter publicly to respond to critics of his work. Clark, The Desegregation Cases: Criticism of the Social Scientists Role, 5 Vill.L.Rev. 224, 236–40 (1960). But see Van den Haag, Social Science Testimony in the Desegregation Cases—A Reply to Professor Kenneth Clark, 6 Vill.L.Rev. 69 (1960).

97. Schipper v. Levitt & Sons, Inc., 44 N.J. 70, 207 A.2d 314 (1965) (mass developer of homes who assembled final product out of component parts treated as a manufacturer and implied warranty imposed).

98. Lemle v. Breeden, 51 Hawaii 426, 462 P.2d 470 (1969) (application of implied warranty recognizes changes in history of leasing transactions and takes into account contemporary housing realities).

99. See particularly Davis, A System of Judicial Notice Based on Fairness and Convenience, in Perspectives of Law, 69, 82 (Pound ed. 1964) ("judge-made law would stop growing if judges, in thinking about questions of law and policy, were forbidden to take into account the facts they believe, as distinguished from facts which are 'clearly * * * within the domain of the indisputable.'") If the data available on appeal are conflicting, however, a court can remand the case to trial so these data can be more effectively explored by introducing them there in the form of evidence subject to cross-examination. See, e.g., Borden's Farm Products Co. v. Baldwin, 293 U.S. 194 [55 S.Ct. 187, 79 L.Ed. 281] (1934).

Thus it is that, in practice, the legislative facts upon which judges rely when performing their lawmaking function are not indisputable. At the same time, cognizant of the fact that his decision as lawmaker can affect the public at large, in contradistinction to most rulings at trials which affect only the parties themselves, a judge is not likely to rely for his data only upon what opposing counsel tender him. Obviously enough, therefore, legislative facts tend to be the most elusive facts when it comes to propounding a codified system of judicial notice.[1]

Hypotheticals

(1) A sues X to recover on a promissory note in which X is the maker and B is the payee. A is B's assignee. X's defense is that the note was given in payment of B's services as a real estate broker and that B did not possess a broker's license. On direct examination, A is asked whether B, his assignor, was a licensed real estate broker. X makes an objection that A lacks personal knowledge. The judge announces that he knows B personally, and is taking judicial notice of the fact that B is a licensed real estate broker. Is the judge correct?

(2) In an action brought in state court in California, A sues X Construction Co. for damages for breach of a contract to build a brick chicken coop in Provo, Utah. X's defense is that it is illegal and impossible to build. At the trial, set for a two-day trial, X produces a volume labeled "Municipal Ordinances of Provo," and requests the court to take judicial notice of the fact that the building of brick chicken coops is prohibited by ordinance within the city of Provo. A objects on the ground that he has not been given advance notice of this judicial-notice request. What result?

---

1. Note that F.R.Ev. (R.D.1971) 201, re-produced at § 328, n. 3, supra, does not purport to regulate the notice of legislative facts.

Chapter XII

THE BURDEN OF PROOF
AND PRESUMPTIONS

PART A. CIVIL CASES

JAMES, CIVIL PROCEDURE

248–266 (1965).*

[Most footnotes are omitted.]

§ 7.5. Burden of proof: The two meanings of the term. The term "burden of proof" is used in our law to refer to two separate and quite different concepts. The distinction was not clearly perceived until it was pointed out by James Bradley Thayer in 1898. The decisions before that time and many later ones are hopelessly confused in reasoning about the problem. The two distinct concepts may be referred to as (1) the risk of nonpersuasion, or the burden of persuasion or simply persuasion burden; (2) the duty of producing evidence, the burden of going forward with the evidence, or simply the production burden or the burden of evidence.

§ 7.9. Burden of proof: Presumptions. The word "presumption" is used to mean many different things, but this they all have in common: they involve a relationship between a proven or admitted fact or group of facts, A, and another fact or conclusion of fact, B, which is sought to be proven.

At one end of the scale is the presumption of law, or conclusive or irrebuttable presumption. If A is shown, then B is to be presumed without question and the court will not even receive evidence or entertain argument to show the nonexistence of B. And the court will direct a jury that if they find A to be proven they *must* also find B. The conclusive presumption is not really a procedural device at all. Rather it is a process of concealing by fiction a change in the substantive law. When the law conclusively presumes the presence of B from A, this means that the substantive law no longer requires the existence of B in cases where A is present, although it hesitates as yet to say so forthrightly. We shall not here deal further with conclusive presumptions. Our concern is with those often called "rebuttal presumptions of fact."

The word "presumption" is occasionally used to refer to the logical inference of one fact from the existence of another. The process of judicial proof is constantly calling on circumstantial evidence and the inferences which may be drawn from it. If Smith mails at a postbox a letter to Jones, with proper address and postage on the envelope, the

* Copyright, 1965 by Fleming James, Jr.

trier may infer that Jones received the letter. From long skid marks
on a pavement great speed on the part of the vehicle that made them
may be inferred. From the blowing of a horn in certain circumstances
it may be inferred that a driver then saw a pedestrian. From handwriting similarities identity of authorship of two documents may be
inferred. And so on, ad infinitum. As we shall see, courts set limits to
the drawing of inferences and will permit juries to draw only those
which the courts consider rational. But if a court determines that B is
a rational inference from A, then the trier of fact is free to draw that
inference as a matter of general lay reasoning and persuasion without
the aid of any special procedural rules pertaining to litigation. Since
there are such special rules, since the word "presumption" is often used
to refer to them, and since "inference" is the word generally used to
refer to the process of drawing conclusions of fact on the basis of
general lay reasoning and experience, it serves clarity and avoids
confusion to observe this distinction between these two words.

Many careful courts and writers use the word "presumption" to
refer only to a device for allocating the production burden. It operates
thus: If B is presumed from A, then on a showing of A, B *must* be
assumed by the trier in the absence of evidence of non-B. To put it
another way, if A is shown, then the party who asserts non-B has the
production burden on the issue of B vel non—that is, B's existence or
nonexistence. The word "presumption" will be used here only in this
way.

In some situations, to be sure, B may be the only rational inference
from A (absent further evidence), and we have seen that in all such
cases the production burden shifts under rules of general application.
But courts and legislatures have created presumptions in cases where
either (1) B would be a permissible inference from A, but not the *only*
permissible one, or (2) B would not even be a permissible inference from
A. In such situations a presumption has an artificial procedural force
and effect (at the point where proponent rests his case) over and above
the logical probative effect of the evidence. In the first situation just
described a presumption would call for a directed verdict on the issue of
B vel non, if the opponent also rests, while, as we have seen, without
the presumption the proponent on that issue would be entitled only to
have it go to the jury. In the second situation the presumption has a
double effect. It protects the proponent from an adverse directed
verdict on the issue (or nonsuit or dismissal), which he would otherwise
suffer for want of sufficient evidence. It also entitles the proponent to
a directed verdict in his own favor on the issue, absent any countervailing evidence. Later in this section we shall inquire whether a
presumption may have any further, continuing effect after evidence to
rebut it has been introduced.

From the above it appears that a presumption may have important
consequences. What, then, are the bases upon which courts or legislatures will create presumptions? For the most part they are the same
kinds of reasons that influence the allocation of the production burden
generally, and these may be summed up a reasons of convenience,
fairness, and policy. What is *likely*, for instance, is often presumed.

Most men are sane, as the law reckons sanity, and most properly sent letters reach their destination. In the absence of any evidence pointing to an opposite conclusion in the case at hand, it is both convenient and fair to assume that *this* testator, or *this* man accused of crime was sane when he made the will or did the act charged as criminal; or that *this* properly mailed letter reached the addressee. If nothing else, these assumptions will save a lot of time and trouble in making ponderous proof in every case of matters which will be controverted in only a small minority of cases.

Access to evidence is often the basis for creating a presumption. When goods are damaged in a bailee's possession, for instance, the bailee can more easily find out what happened to them than the bailor, so it is fair to presume the bailee's negligence as an initial matter and put him to the production of exculpatory evidence if he has any. The owner of an automobile has better means of knowing whether the driver was in his service when it struck the plaintiff than has the plaintiff. In such a case also there is an increasingly strong policy to make an automobile owner pay for the damage it causes even where there is no agency in the legal sense. Fairness and policy therefore combine to justify a presumption of agency from the mere fact of ownership. Here, it may be noted, is a presumption (usually created by statute) in a situation where most courts would not permit an inference.

If there is a presumption operating in proponent's favor when he rests his case, two questions then arise: (1) what must the opponent do to lift the production burden then resting upon him, and (2) if the opponent does lift this burden, what (if any) further effect does the presumption have?

Let us take up the first of these questions. It can be rephrased in terms of the simple symbols we have been using. If from A there is a presumption of B, and A is shown,[1] what must the opponent do to escape a compulsory finding of B? The answer is that the opponent must introduce evidence which will justify a finding of non-B. This requirement has, to use Maguire's terms, both an extensive and an intensive aspect. To satisfy the extensive aspect, the evidence must cover the whole of B. Thus a presumption of negligence on the part of the charterers of a vessel turned over to them in good condition and sinking while in their control is not met by a showing of care during *part* of the time it was in their control. Such evidence is not enough to lift the production burden. To satisfy the intensive aspect of the requirement, the evidence must satisfy the qualitative tests of sufficiency of the evidence to show non-B.

If, now, the opponent has lifted the production burden by rebutting evidence which satisfies the above standards, what happens to the presumption? The orthodox view, sired by Thayer, has it that the presumption is utterly destroyed and disappears, and this even though the trier disbelieves the countervailing evidence. If, for example, the

---

1. Of course the evidence tending to show A may itself fall short of compelling such a finding. If so it will be a question for the trier to decide whether A exists.

addressee of a properly mailed letter testifies that he never received it, that testimony would, if believed, justify a finding of nonreceipt. It therefore satisfies the test of *sufficiency*—which is not concerned with *credibility*—whether it is believed or not. Under the orthodox view this testimony would, then, *end the presumption* even if everybody in the courtroom was convinced that the testimony was a lie. In the case put, the destruction of the presumption would not, however, compel a finding of nonreceipt because a properly addressed letter is so likely to reach its destination that a *rational inference* may be drawn that it did so. And while countervailing evidence banishes the artificial procedural effect given by a presumption to the facts proven, A (in this case the mailing of the letter, and so on), yet it does not destroy the rational probative effect of A. In our illustration, if the trier rejects the testimony of nonreceipt as false and believes the testimony as to proper mailing, it could and probably would find receipt as an inference from the mailing. On the suppositions here made, this result seems just and proper and the orthodox theory would not prevent it. But there are other situations wherein that view does present serious problems.

Suppose, first, that the mind of the trier in the case just described is in equipoise on all the evidence. If the proponent has the burden of persuading the trier of *B*'s existence, he must lose. Does a presumption of *B*'s existence from proof of *A* have any effect on the persuasion burden? The orthodox doctrine says emphatically not—it declares that the effect of a presumption is entirely spent in shifting the production burden, and it denies that the persuasion burden ever shifts. But why should this necessarily be so? We have seen that the considerations which determine the allocation of the persuasion burden are of the same kind as those which lead to the creation of presumptions. If the developments of a trial bring forth a situation which justifies a presumption in the proponent's favor, might not the same considerations (though not necessarily) be sufficient to call for placing the persuasion burden also on the opponent? Why should a presumption always have the minimum effect prescribed for it by orthodoxy? The reasons that bring it forth will vary from mere administrative convenience, the necessity for getting the ball rolling, so to speak, to very strong policy. Should not the force of a presumption "be tough or tender according to the nature and force of those reasons"? Some courts say frankly that it should, and that a presumption may sometimes shift the persuasion burden; but on this particular point the weight of authority is probably that it may not. This problem is of importance, but only in cases where the trier's mind is in equipoise at the end of its deliberations, a situation which probably does not occur very often.

There is another situation where the orthodox theory gives more trouble. As we have seen, the fact(s), A, which give rise to a presumption of B in many instances are not sufficient to warrant an *inference* of B. A familiar example is the fairly common presumption of agency from the fact of ownership of an automobile. Suppose the Plaintiff, injured by Owner's automobile driven by Driver, has no available evidence on the issue of agency except the adverse testimony of Owner and Driver, and therefore rests on a presumption of agency, ownership being proven or admitted. Suppose further that Owner, sole defendant, puts on his own testimony and that of Driver, both of whom deny agency. If this testimony banishes the presumption, you may have the anomaly that the trier must find nonagency, even though it thoroughly disbelieves the denial as self-serving perjury. Such a result does indeed offend common sense and justice, and most courts reject it, although it is hard to reconcile its rejection with the orthodox view. Once a presumption comes into play the tendency is to send the matter to the jury unless the evidence to rebut the presumption leaves no reasonable room for the jury's function.

If the issue is sent to the jury, the question arises in this situation, as in the illustration involving the mailing of the letter, whether the persuasion burden is to be placed on plaintiff or defendant. And here again most courts will probably put it on plaintiff.[2]

Another different problem has arisen in connection with presumptions. If a case goes to the jury, what if anything should be said to the jury about any presumptions which may have come into the case? The orthodox answer is unequivocal: nothing. If a presumption has been met with sufficient evidence, the presumption has vanished and the issue should go to the jury without mention of it. Of course, if the facts giving rise to the presumption also afford an inference, the jury may be told about the inference and if the word "presumption" is used so as to be clearly understood to mean only this permissible inference, choice of the wrong word may be harmless error.

Even where a court gives a presumption continuing effect after evidence has been introduced to rebut it, there is no need to mention the presumption to the jury and it is probably only confusing to do so. If the persuasion burden is shifted, that is the only burden the instructions need mention. If it is not, but the jury may find B if they disbelieve opponent's evidence of non-B, then a simple direction to that effect is all that is needed. The only justification for telling the jury about the presumption would be a desire to implement the policy behind the presumption by inviting the jury to weigh it, in some vague manner not easy to understand or articulate, as they would a part of the evidence. But if policy demands additional force to the presumption, better ways than this can be devised for giving it.

2. * * *

The two alternative views set forth in the text are not the only possible ones, nor the only ones to attain some judicial support. Morgan, for example, lists the following: (1) The so-called orthodox view. (2) A presumption puts on the opponent the burden of persuading the jury "to believe so much of the evidence against the presumed fact as would justify a reasonable jury in finding against that fact." (3) It disappears when opponent puts in evidence upon which the trier's mind is in equipoise, if that evidence "is of the requisite quantity and quality to justify a reasonable jury in finding the non-existence of the presumed fact." (4) It puts on opponent "the burden of persuading the jury that the existence of the presumed fact is so doubtful that the jury cannot determine whether it exists." (5) It puts on opponent "the burden of persuading the jury that the presumed fact does not exist." (6) In addition to having one of the foregoing effects, the presumption is to be weighed by the jury together with the evidence in the case. (7) It may simply allow an inference of B from A when the ordinary rules of proof would not allow it. (8) It may compel the finding of B unconditionally, if A is found (the conclusive presumption).

SMITH v. RAPID TRANSIT, INC.

Supreme Judicial Court of Massachusetts, 1945.
317 Mass. 469, 58 N.E.2d 754.

SPALDING, Justice. The decisive question in this case is whether there was evidence for the jury that the plaintiff was injured by a bus of the defendant that was operated by one of its employees in the course of his employment. If there was, the defendant concedes that the evidence warranted the submission to the jury of the question of the operator's negligence in the management of the bus. The case is here on the plaintiff's exception to the direction of a verdict for the defendant.

These facts could have been found: While the plaintiff at about 1:00 A.M. on February 6, 1941, was driving an automobile on Main Street, Winthrop, in an easterly direction toward Winthrop Highlands, she observed a bus coming toward her which she described as a "great big, long, wide affair." The bus, which was proceeding at about forty miles an hour, "forced her to turn to the right," and her automobile collided with a "parked car." The plaintiff was coming from Dorchester. The department of public utilities had issued a certificate of public convenience or necessity to the defendant for three routes in Winthrop, one of which includes Main Street, and this was in effect in February, 1941. "There was another bus line in operation in Winthrop at that time but not on Main Street." According to the defendant's time-table, buses were scheduled to leave Winthrop Highlands for Maverick Square via Main Street at 12:10 A.M., 12:45 A.M., 1:15 A.M., and 2:15 A.M. The running time for this trip at that time of night was thirty minutes.

The direction of a verdict for the defendant was right. The ownership of the bus was a matter of conjecture. While the defendant had the sole franchise for operating a bus line on Main Street, Winthrop, this did not preclude private or chartered buses from using this street; the bus in question could very well have been one operated by someone other than the defendant. It was said in Sargent v. Massachusetts Accident Co. that it is "not enough that mathematically the chances somewhat favor a proposition to be proved; for example, the fact that colored automobiles made in the current year outnumber black ones would not warrant a finding that an undescribed automobile of the current year is colored and not black, nor would the fact that only a minority of men die of cancer warrant a finding that a particular man did not die of cancer." The most that can be said of the evidence in the instant case is that perhaps the mathematical chances somewhat favor the proposition that a bus of the defendant caused the accident. This was not enough. A "proposition is proved by a preponderance of the evidence if it is made to appear more likely or probable in the sense that actual belief in its truth, derived from the evidence, exists in the mind or minds of the tribunal notwithstanding any doubts that may still linger there."

Exceptions overruled.

HART & McNAUGHTON, EVIDENCE AND INFERENCE IN THE LAW
54–55 (1958).*

It may be suggested parenthetically at this point that, while it is clear that the law satisfies itself with less than certainty, it is not clear that the formulas mentioned above always describe correctly the degree of certainty which the law actually requires. Consider the formula that in a civil case the facts must be determined on a more-likely-than-not basis. In the first place, the probabilities are determined in a most subjective and unscientific way: the trier of fact simply asks itself which of the contesting contradictory propositions according to the trier's limited experience more nearly squares with the evidence. In the second place, the law refuses to honor its own formula when the evidence is coldly "statistical." A court would not, for example hold the government liable to a farmer for injuries inflicted on him by his mule frightened by a "buzzing" jet plane if the only evidence that the pilot was a member of the Air Force (rather than a civilian) was that most of the pilots flying jets that day were Air Force personnel. This would be true even though the farmer could show that as [many] as 70 or 80 per cent of the jet pilots in the vicinity that day were of the Air Force.

The court, on the other hand, would certainly allow recovery if the evidence was that 100 per cent of the pilots were Air Force personnel, and would probably allow it if all of them were except a negligible few. Similarly, the court might allow recovery if the farmer, instead of introducing the statistical evidence, testified that he got a fleeting glimpse of the pilot's cap and that it was distinctively Air Force headgear. The court somehow feels more comfortable permitting a finding to be based on such eye-witness testimony even though the probative value of such testimony is itself determined ultimately by home-spun "statistics" in the mind of the trier of fact and even though the eye-witness testimony is probably no more indicative of the truth than is the evidence as to the proportion of Air Force pilots in the air.

Even in the case as originally stated—with the farmer producing solely the statistical evidence—the court might allow recovery if the reason for the farmer's dearth of evidence is the irrelevant fact that the government refused without justification to cooperate in the farmer's search for the offending pilot. And, though according to the more-likely-than-not formula it is irrelevant, the court might be swayed in its demand for evidence by the size of the stakes—a more elaborate presentation would naturally be expected if the farmer was claiming $100,000 in damages than if he was claiming $100.

* The Hayden Colloquium on Scientific Concept and Method edited by Daniel Lerner, Copyright, 1958, by American Academy of Arts & Sciences, Copyright, 1959 by The Free Press: Excerpts from Material by Henry M. Hart, Jr., and John McNaughton.

DYER v. MacDOUGALL

United States Court of Appeals, Second Circuit, 1952.
201 F.2d 265.

L. HAND, Circuit Judge.   This case comes up on appeal by the plaintiff from a judgment summarily dismissing the third and fourth counts of a complaint for libel and slander.   Two questions arise: (1) whether we have jurisdiction over the appeal; (2) whether the defendants showed that there was no "genuine issue" to try within the meaning of Rule 56(c) Fed.Rules Civ.Proc. 28 U.S.C.   We may start with the amended complaint, which was filed on November 24, 1950.   It was in four counts, of which the first alleged that the defendant, Albert E. MacDougall, had said of the plaintiff at a directors' meeting of the "Queensboro Corporation": "You are stabbing me in the back."   The second count alleged that MacDougall had written a letter to one, Dorothy Russell Hope, the plaintiff's wife's sister, containing the words: "He"—the plaintiff—"has made false statements to my clients in Philadelphia," and "He has presented bills for work he has not done."   The third count alleged that MacDougall had said to a lawyer, named Almirall, that a letter sent out by the plaintiff to the shareholders of the "Queensboro Corporation" was a "a blackmailing letter."   The fourth count alleged that MacDougall's wife, as MacDougall's agent, had said to Mrs. Hope that the plaintiff had "written and sent out a blackmailing letter."   On December 26, 1950, the defendants, before answer, moved for judgment summarily dismissing the second, third and fourth counts, supporting their motion by affidavits of MacDougall, MacDougall's wife, and Almirall, and by a deposition of Mrs. Hope, which the plaintiff himself had already taken.   Each of the defendants unequivocally denied the utterance of the slanders attributed to him or her; and Almirall and Mrs. Hope denied that he or she had heard the slanders uttered.   On his part the plaintiff replied with several affidavits of his own, the contents of all of which would, however, be inadmissible as evidence at a trial upon the issue of utterance.   On January 24, 1951, the defendants filed an unverified answer denying the defamatory utterances, and on the same day they brought on their motion for hearing before Judge Kennedy.   He offered the plaintiff an opportunity to take depositions of Mr. and Mrs. MacDougall and of Almirall, and a second deposition of Mrs. Hope; and by consent the case was then adjourned to allow the plaintiff to take the depositions.   However, towards the end of October 1951, he told the court that he did not wish to do so, and on December 28, 1951 (the defendants having meanwhile withdrawn their motion as to the second count), the judge decided the defendants' motion by summarily dismissing the third and fourth counts on the ground that upon the trial the plaintiff would have no evidence to offer in support of the slanders except the testimony of witnesses, all of whom would deny their utterance.   On this opinion he entered the judgment in suit on January 7, 1952, from which the plaintiff took no appeal within thirty days.   However, on February 20, 1952, he wrote a letter to the judge, asking an extension under Rule 73(a) of thirty days within which to appeal; and this he followed on the

25th by a motion for a reargument, repeating his request for the extension. On March 4, 1952, the judge filed a second opinion, granting the reargument, but again deciding that counts three and four should be dismissed. However, he granted an extension of thirty days for the time to appeal, and, apparently, *sua sponte,* "certified" "that I did give an express direction for the entry of judgment, and that there is no reason for delay." On March 4, 1952, the plaintiff filed a notice of appeal from the judgment.

* * * The question is whether, in view of the defendants' affidavits and Mrs. Hope's deposition, there was any "genuine issue" under Rule 56(c) as to the utterance of the slanders. The defendants had the burden of proving that there was no such issue; on the other hand, at a trial the plaintiff would have the burden of proving the utterances; and therefore, if the defendants on the motion succeeded in proving that the plaintiff would not have enough evidence to go to the jury on the issue, the judgment was right. As the plaintiff has refused to avail himself of the privilege under Rule 56(f) of examining by deposition the witnesses whom the defendants proposed to call at the trial, we must assume that what they said in their affidavits they would have repeated in their depositions; and that what they would have said in their depositions, they would say at a trial, with one possible exception, the consideration of which we will postpone for the time being. With that reserve we will therefore first discuss the judgment on the assumption that the record before us contains all the testimony that would appear at a trial in support of the slanders. We have not forgotten that the plaintiff swears that his wife told him on March 8, 1950, that Mrs. Hope had said to her on March 7, 1950, that she, Mrs. Hope, could forgive the plaintiff "everything except that letter," meaning a letter, written by the plaintiff and addressed to the shareholders of the "Queensboro Corporation," which Mrs. MacDougall according to the complaint described as a "blackmailing letter." The plaintiff did not submit his wife's affidavit that Mrs. Hope had told her what he says his wife said to him she did; but we shall assume that such an affidavit is in the record. Mrs. Hope's putative declaration to Mrs. Dyer would of course be hearsay, but the plaintiff says that it would nevertheless be competent under the exception as to "spontaneous exclamations." We cannot agree. The time of Mrs. MacDougall's statement to Mrs. Hope is not fixed except that it is said to have been between December 13th and March 7th; and, strictly, we might dispose of the point because there is no reason to say that the interval was not two months. But let us suppose that Mrs. MacDougall had called up Mrs. Hope only the day before Mrs. Hope narrated the talk to her sister. The argument must be that the emotional stress set up in Mrs. Hope's mind by Mr. MacDougall's information endured for twenty-four hours and so far suspended her ordinary powers of deliberation as to make her declaration like the ejaculation of a person injured in an accident, or suddenly faced with a vital crisis. "The utterance must have been *before there has been time to contrive and fabricate,* i.e. while the nervous excitement may be supposed still to dominate and the reflective powers to be yet in abeyance." Wigmore § 1750(b). So we are to suppose that,

when Mrs. Hope learned that her brother-in-law, whom incidentally she
had recently "castigated," had sent out a letter that could be described
as blackmailing MacDougall, it so far obsessed her deliberative faculties
that, although she did not call up her sister that day, she remained
unable to "contrive or fabricate" for twenty-four hours. Unless we are
altogether to abandon the hearsay rule, it is difficult to imagine a
situation more appropriate for its application. Finally, any declaration
of Mrs. Hope would be incompetent as contradictory of her testimony, if
the plaintiff should call her as his witness. It is true that Rule 43(b)
makes competent inconsistent statements of a witness called by a party,
if the witness is the adverse party himself, but Mrs. Hope is not a party.
If the plaintiff called her and she repeated her deposition, he could not
use his wife's contradictory version of the interview between her and
Mrs. MacDougall.

Hence, if the cause went to trial, the plaintiff would have no
witnesses by whom he could prove the slanders alleged in the third and
fourth counts, except the two defendants, Almirall and Mrs. Hope; and
they would all deny that the slanders had been uttered. On such a
showing how could he escape a directed verdict? It is true that the
carriage, behavior, bearing, manner and appearance of a witness—in
short, his "demeanor"—is a part of the evidence. The words used are
by no means all that we rely on in making up our minds about the
truth of a question that arises in our ordinary affairs, and it is
abundantly settled that a jury is as little confined to them as we are.
They may, and indeed they should, take into consideration the whole
nexus of sense impressions which they get from a witness. This we
have again and again declared, and have rested our affirmance of
findings of fact of a judge, or of a jury, on the hypothesis that this part
of the evidence may have turned the scale. Moreover, such evidence
may satisfy the tribunal, not only that the witness' testimony is not
true, but that the truth is the opposite of his story; for the denial of
one, who has a motive to deny, may be uttered with such hesitation,
discomfort, arrogance or defiance, as to give assurance that he is
fabricating, and that, if he is, there is no alternative but to assume the
truth of what he denies.

Nevertheless, although it is therefore true that in strict theory a
party having the affirmative might succeed in convincing a jury of the
truth of his allegations in spite of the fact that all the witnesses denied
them, we think it plain that a verdict would nevertheless have to be
directed against him. This is owing to the fact that otherwise in such
cases there could not be an effective appeal from the judge's disposition
of a motion for a directed verdict. He, who has seen and heard the
"demeanor" evidence, may have been right or wrong in thinking that it
gave rational support to a verdict; yet, since that evidence has disappeared, it will be impossible for an appellate court to say which he was.
Thus, he would become the final arbiter in all cases where the evidence
of witnesses present in court might be determinative. We need not say
that in setting aside a verdict the judge has not a broader discretion
than in directing one, for we have before us only the equivalent of a
direction. It may be argued that such a ruling may deprive a party of a

possibly rational verdict, and indeed that is theoretically true, although the occasions must be to the last degree rare in which the chance so denied is more than fanciful. Nevertheless we do not hesitate to set against the chance so lost, the protection of a review of the judge's decision.

There remains the second point which we reserved for separate discussion: i.e. whether by an examination in open court the plaintiff might extract from the four witnesses admissions which he would not have got on the depositions that he refused. Although this is also at best a tenuous possibility, we need not say that there could never be situations in which it might justify denying summary judgment. It might appear for example that upon a deposition a witness had been recalcitrant, or crafty, or defiant, or evasive, so that the immediate presence of a judge in a court-room was likely to make him tell more. That would be another matter; and it might be enough. But the plaintiff is in no position to invoke such a possibility for he has refused to try out these witnesses upon deposition, where he might discover whether there was any basis for supposing that awe of a judge was necessary to make them more amenable. A *priori* we will not assume that that is true. The course of procedural reform has all indeed been towards bringing witnesses before the tribunal when it is possible; but that is not so much because more testimony can be got out of them as because only so can the "demeanor" evidence be brought before the tribunal.

Judgment affirmed.

FRANK, Circuit Judge (concurring).

1. The facts here are most peculiar, unlikely to recur often: The plaintiff in his complaint asserts that defendant slandered plaintiff in the plaintiff's absence but in the presence of only two other persons. If there were a trial, plaintiff could not himself testify, for he knows of his own knowledge none of the facts necessary to support his case. To prove his case, he would have to call the defendant who, in his oral testimony, would deny that he had uttered the alleged slanderous statement. For plaintiff is aware that the only two other possible witnesses he could summon would corroborate defendant; and, if he called them, he could not impeach them.

Judge Hand's opinion states that, if defendant and the other witnesses testified, the trial court, evaluating their credibility in the light of their demeanor as witnesses, could rationally find not only that defendant's denial was false but that the opposite was true, i.e., that defendant had made the slanderous statement. Yet Judge Hand holds that a trial judge in a jury trial of such a case would be obliged not to let the jury reach a verdict for plaintiff on that rational basis. As I understand Judge Hand, he says that the result of holding otherwise would be that the trial judge's disposition of a motion for a directed verdict (or a verdict n.o.v.) could not be effectively reviewed on appeal. On that ground alone—i.e., the supposed obstacle, in a jury trial of such a case, to review of a directed verdict—Judge Hand's opinion affirms the summary judgment for defendant here.

Since, then, the sole reason given in Judge Hand's opinion for affirmance is something peculiar to a jury trial, I take it that, were there a jury waiver here, so that if there were a trial, it would be a judge trial, Judge Hand would hold erroneous the summary judgment here. This is a curious distinction. It would make the propriety of a summary judgment in such a case turn exclusively on whether or not the parties, if entitled to any trial, are entitled to one by jury.[1] In such a case as this, it would prevent a jury from relying on demeanor but permit a judge in a judge trial to do so (although, if he did, his decision, in so far as he relied on demeanor, would not ordinarily be reviewable).

I agree with Judge Hand that (at least in some cases)[2] a trial judge should be allowed to find that a plaintiff has discharged his burden of proof when the judge disbelieves oral testimony all of which is adverse to plaintiff, solely because of the trial court's reaction to the witnesses' demeanor and there is no evidence for plaintiff except that "demeanor evidence."[3] But I think it most unfortunate to hold that this rule applies in judge trials and not in jury trials. Such a distinction should be avoided if possible.

But I read Judge Hand's opinion as saying it is unavoidable for the following reason: If, in a jury trial, the jury, solely on the basis of its evaluation of credibility as affected by the jury's reaction to a witness' demeanor, were allowed to bring in a plaintiff's verdict, then necessarily (says Judge Hand) the judge in that same trial could also properly take into account demeanor in passing on the defendant's motion for a directed verdict; but, were that true, the judge's action on the motion could never be reviewed, as demeanor cannot appear in the printed record on appeal.[4]

---

1. That is, whether or not they both have failed to demand a jury, or whether or not plaintiff seeks relief (e.g., specific performance) precluding a jury trial.

2. This parenthetical qualification I shall explain later.

3. We have already held that, solely on the basis of a trial judge's disbelief in the oral testimony of a plaintiff's witness—a disbelief resulting entirely from the witness' demeanor—the judge may decide for the defendant. [H]owever, the disbelief in this testimony—uncontradicted by anything other than the witnesses' demeanor—meant that plaintiff had not discharged his burden of proof. In the instant case, the question is whether plaintiff can discharge his burden of proof where the judge disbelieves the testimony of witnesses all of whom testified against him.

4. This reasoning, spelled out more in detail, is as follows:

(a) If a jury, solely on the basis of its evaluation of credibility as affected by its reaction to a witness' demeanor in a case like this, could properly bring in a verdict for the plaintiff, then (says Judge Hand) necessarily a trial judge could also properly take into account credibility in the light of demeanor, and solely because of resulting evaluation of the witnesses' reliability, could grant or deny the defendant's motion for a directed verdict.

(b) But (says Judge Hand) if the trial judge could thus consider demeanor, then in no case where there was oral testimony could the grant or denial of a directed verdict motion ever be reviewed and reversed, because the printed record before the upper court necessarily omits demeanor.

(c) Since, however, such directed-verdict orders can and should be reviewable this follows according to Judge Hand:

(1) The jury in a case like this may not properly return a plaintiff's verdict on the sole basis of "demeanor evidence."

(2) Therefore in such a case, on defendant's motion for a directed verdict, the trial judge must disregard the possibility that, were the case allowed to go to the jury, it might decide for plaintiff on the sole basis of "demeanor evidence."

I cannot accept that distinction for the following reasons: Judge Hand argues from the alleged unreviewability of a directed verdict in a case like this, if demeanor were a factor. But this argument cuts too far. For, if Judge Hand is correct, the same difficulty will attend the review of any directed verdict in any case where any important evidence consists of oral testimony. In any such case, one could say, as Judge Hand says here: If the jury (should the case go to the jury) could rely on "demeanor evidence," then necessarily the trial judge could do likewise, on a motion for a directed verdict; and, if he could, no directed verdict would be reviewable when important testimony is oral. But this is exactly not the rule in the federal courts: The well-settled rule is that, in passing on a motion for a directed verdict, the trial judge always must utterly disregard his own views of witnesses' credibility, and therefore of their demeanor; that he believes or disbelieves some of the testimony is irrelevant. When asked to direct a verdict for the defendant, the judge must assume that if he lets the case go to the jury, the jurymen will believe all evidence—including "demeanor evidence"—favorable to the plaintiff. In other words, the judge must not deprive plaintiff of any advantage that plaintiff might derive from having the jury pass upon the oral testimony. Indeed, the important difference between a trial judge's power on a motion for a new trial and on a motion for a directed verdict is precisely that on a new-trial motion he may base his action on his belief or disbelief in some of the witnesses, while on a directed-verdict motion he may not.

Lurton, J., in a much quoted opinion,[5] expressed the difference thus: "We do not think * * * that it is a proper test of whether the court should direct a verdict, that the court, on weighing the evidence, would, upon motion, grant a new trial. * * * In passing upon such motions [for new trial] he is necessarily required to weigh the evidence * * *. But, in passing upon a motion to direct a verdict, his functions are altogether different. In the latter case we think he cannot properly undertake to weigh the evidence. His duty is to take that view of the evidence most favorable to the party against whom it is moved to direct a verdict, and from that evidence, and the inferences reasonably and justifiably to be drawn therefrom, determine whether or not, under the law, a verdict might be found for the party having the onus."

Taft, J., held similarly in Felton v. Spiro. The cases in accord are legion. They are excellently discussed by Judge Parker in Aetna Cas. & Sur. Co. v. Yeatts and by Judge Sibley in Marsh v. Illinois Central R. Co.

In Brady v. Southern Ry. Co., the Court said: "When the evidence is such that *without weighing the credibility of the witnesses* there can be but one reasonable conclusion as to the verdict, the court should determine the proceeding by non-suit, directed verdict or otherwise in accordance with the applicable practice without submission to the jury, or by judgment notwithstanding the verdict." (Emphasis added.) As

5. Mt. Adams & E.P. Inclined Ry. Co. v. Lowery.

Moore puts it, a motion for new trial may invoke "the exercise of the trial court's discretion, such as that the verdict is inadequate or excessive, or that the verdict is against the weight of the evidence. In reference to this latter matter this function of the motion for a new trial must be sharply distinguished from the motion for a directed verdict."[6] A "verdict may be set aside as contrary to the preponderance of the evidence, although a directed verdict is not justified."[7]

On a motion for new trial, the judge acts "as the thirteenth juror", i.e., he evaluates the credibility of the orally-testifying witnesses and therefore their demeanor. But on a motion for a directed verdict he does not. The rule that a trial judge may legitimately consider demeanor in ordering new trials means that his new-trial orders are seldom reviewable; on the other hand, the rule that he may not legitimately consider demeanor in considering directed verdict motions means that his orders on such motions are readily reviewable.

Frequently this sort of case arises: The defendant urges his motion for a directed verdict on the ground that, although there is oral testimony, the record contains no testimony (or other evidence) from which any rational inference can be drawn for the existence of a fact indispensable to plaintiff's case. If the trial judge, then, directs a defendant's verdict,[8] the upper court, on appeal, in testing the propriety of his direction, adopts the postulate that the trial judge assumed that the jury, were it allowed to render a verdict, would regard the oral testimony—and therefore the witnesses' demeanor—in a manner most favorable to plaintiff. The upper court makes the same assumption; as a consequence, the trial judge's attitude towards that demeanor is not a factor on such an appeal, and so constitutes no obstacle to review.

If I am correct, there is no foundation for Judge Hand's distinction; and, as I gather that he would have held it error to enter summary judgment for defendant here, if there had been no jury demand, he should, I think, hold that the judgment here must be reversed, despite the request for trial by jury.

2. One can imagine a case in which a man would suffer a grave injustice, if it were the invariable rule that a plaintiff can never win a case when (1) he can offer only the oral testimony of the defendant, the one available witness, which is flatly and unswervingly against the plaintiff but (2) the jury (in a jury trial) or the judge (in a judge trial) is thoroughly convinced by that witness' demeanor that he is an unmitigated liar. On that account, I would oppose such a rule.

But this is not such a case. As already noted, the facts here are most unusual: The plaintiff asserts that in his absence he was slandered by defendant in the presence of but two other persons. As this fact is denied by all three, only plaintiff's own suit serves to publicize the alleged slander. In these peculiar circumstances, the plaintiff

---

6. Moore, Federal Practice (2d ed. 1951) § 50.02(1), p. 2317.

7. Moore, loc. cit., § 50.03, p. 2318. See also § 50.11, pp. 2338–2339, and Wigmore, Evidence (3d ed.) § 2494, pp. 298–299.

8. Or if he denies defendant's motion for such a verdict.

should not have the chance at a trial to discharge his burden of proof by nothing except the trial court's disbelief in the oral testimony of witnesses all of whom will deny that the alleged slanderous statement was made. Wherefore I concur.

MAGUIRE, EVIDENCE: COMMON SENSE AND COMMON LAW
177–79, 182–84 (1947).*

* * * Now let us illustrate with a fascinating little case from which can be spun our whole discussion of these topics. Plaintiff sued defendant to quiet plaintiff's title to Blackacre. It seems to be assumed throughout that he had the burden of persuasion that he was the owner at the time he brought suit. Plaintiff alleged that he had acquired title on a specified date, and had ever since retained possession and title, but that defendant without right made some claim to Blackacre. Defendant admitted that plaintiff became owner of Blackacre on the date specified but denied that plaintiff was the present owner and also denied that defendant's claim was without right.

If on the issues shaped by these pleadings defendant had offered at trial evidence of acquisition of title to Blackacre by a sale for taxes, and plaintiff had given evidence tending to prove the sale invalid, apparently plaintiff would have had the burden of persuasion on the consequent issue. But that was not the way the parties tried the case. Plaintiff stood on the admission of the answer as to his acquisition of title and rested, urging that the status of ownership thus established was presumed to continue. Defendant, offering no evidence, moved for a nonsuit. The motion was granted, and plaintiff appealed. Held error; reversed and remanded with a plain intimation that if defendant persisted in giving no evidence, judgment should be entered for plaintiff. Gatrell v. Salt Lake County; the court had trouble with the case; there are a brief main opinion, a slightly longer concurring opinion, and a still longer dissent.

The holding here is that although plaintiff had the ultimate burden of persuasion on the issue of continued ownership, the case had been left in a posture which cast upon defendant the burden of producing evidence on that issue. Evidently the cardinal point of the whole business is defendant's partial admission of plaintiff's allegations. The majority argue that this admission is in the nature of evidence conclusively establishing plaintiff's acquisition of title to Blackacre. Once getting title, plaintiff is presumed to retain title. Defendant has done nothing to displace or rebut this presumption. Therefore defendant could not win.

By reasoning thus the majority allow plaintiff to pick and choose among defendant's allegations, accepting the favorable and rejecting the unfavorable. The dissenter argues that plaintiff might not do this; he must take the bitter with the sweet; the whole matter is to be decided on the pleading level and, for purposes of pleading, defendant's

denial of continued ownership nullifies the effect of his admission of
plaintiff's acquisition of title.   The majority seems to deny that the
problem is one of pleading, treating it rather as a problem of evidence.
They assume in that aspect the propriety of plaintiff's taking what he
likes, and only what he likes, from defendant's various utterances about
the issue of ownership.

This controversy within the court is aside from our immediate
interest.   Let us grant the soundness of the majority's method of attack
on the case and examine its elements.   First, burden of persuasion—
why was it upon plaintiff and what does the term signify when
translated into mental operations of the trier of fact?   As to placement
of burden of persuasion, all sorts of explanatory formulae can be found
in the books.   It is with the party seeking to sustain an affirmative; it
is determined by the form of the pleadings; it is to be borne by the
party having peculiar knowledge of the facts; it is imposed on the party
whose contentions depart further from normal likelihood.   This plurali-
ty of so-called decisive factors proves forthwith that no single simple
formula for allocating burden of persuasion will be found.   All four
factors mentioned might be found in the same case, some pointing to
one litigant, some to the other.   Here, as in many large legal problems,
we must work out our answers issue by issue, taking into consideration
all elements of fairness and expediency.   Of course this does not mean
that the answers have to be worked out case by case.   As already
remarked, precedents will build up for recurrent issues and these
precedents will be serviceable analogies.   It merely means that there is
no wondrous touchstone to solve all problems without pain of thought.

Think back now to our *Gatrell* case about title to Blackacre.   The
decision rendered necessarily connoted that the finding *must* be for
plaintiff unless defendant came forward with evidence to prove that
plaintiff had somehow lost title between the date when he acquired it
and the date when he began his suit.   But, as a purely original
proposition, there might be difference of opinion as to whether proof of
getting title say in 1931 without more made it impossible reasonably to
find that the grantee had lost title by say 1940.   A lot could happen to
shift ownership of Blackacre in nine years.   Here, though, the courts
step in with a judicial control.   They say there is a presumption of
continuance of the status of ownership, and that this presumption has
an effect comparable to overwhelming proof in taking the issue out of
debatability.

Here we had better slow down, make some comparisons, and take
stock of difficulties.   There is trouble with terminology.   This word
presumption has suffered badly from rough and careless handling.   It
has been used as a synonym for inference and sometimes as the
operative part of weasel-worded formulae for saying that from the
judicial or legislative point of view certain things are taken as so and
attempts to contradict them will be futile.   In the former usage the
word has often been expanded into the term "presumption of fact" and
in the latter into "presumption of law" or "conclusive presumption".
As our text has shown, we are rejecting both these usages and employing presumption to denote the concept, illustrated specifically dozens of

times in common and statute law, that when a designated basic fact or aggregate of facts exists, existence of another fact or aggregate of facts, called the presumed fact or facts, must be assumed in absence of adequate rebuttal. In the *Gatrell* case the basic fact was plaintiff's acquisition of title to Blackacre and the presumed fact the continuance of his ownership down to and through the date when he began his suit. This careful, particularized use of the word presumption, by the way, is getting more and more consistent acceptance in the courts; nobody has ever succeeded in making consistent the legislative use of this or any other important word.

Our text has steadily conceded that the state of decisive one-sidedness may not always be permanent. Temporarily overwhelming proof on an issue of fact may be met and controlled by counter-proof. Likewise the text has indicated that presumptions may be rebutted— that is, the presumed facts thrown open for deliberative findings instead of being coercively assumed. But a mighty battle has raged, and is still raging, over this matter of rebutting presumptions. Without being foolhardy enough to offer an infallible solution to terminate the battle for good and all, we should at least see what all the shooting is about.

It may be said that a presumption has both extensity and intensity. Rebuttal, we should expect, ought to be correspondingly wide and forceful. Suppose our presumption is that if a ship, hired under charter party, is turned over to the hirer in seaworthy condition and thereafter sinks, the sinking is due to the fault of the hirer. In case the rebuttal evidence offered by the hirer, when sued for damages because of the loss of the ship, tends to show due care on his part for *only a portion of the time* he controlled the ship, the evidence is not extensive enough to rebut the presumption. * * *

LEGILLE v. DANN

United States Court of Appeals, District of Columbia Circuit, 1976.
544 F.2d 1.
[Footnote omitted.]

SPOTTSWOOD W. ROBINSON, III, Circuit Judge:

* * *

I

* * * On March 1, 1973, appellees' attorney mailed from East Hartford, Connecticut, to the Patent Office in Washington, D.C., a package containing four patent applications. Each of the applications had previously been filed in the Grand Duchy of Luxembourg, three on March 6, 1972, and the fourth on the following August 11. The package was marked "Airmail," bore sufficient airmail postage and was properly addressed. Delivery of air mail from East Hartford to Washington at that time was normally two days.

The applications were date-stamped "March 8, 1973," by the Patent Office. Each of the four applications was assigned that filing date on the ground that the stamped date was the date of receipt by the Patent Office. If the action of the Patent Office is to stand, three of appellees' applications, on which Luxembourg patents had been granted, fail in this country.

Appellees petitioned the Commissioner of Patents to reassign the filing date. The petition was denied. Appellees then sued in the District Court for a judgment directing the Commissioner to accord the applications a filing date not later than March 6, 1973. Both sides moved for summary judgment on the basis of the pleadings and affidavits respectively submitted. Not surprisingly, none of the affidavits reflected any direct evidence of the date on which the applications were actually delivered to the Patent Office.

The District Court correctly identified the central issue: "whether there exists a genuine issue of fact as to when these applications were received by the Patent Office." By the court's appraisal, appellees' suit was "predicated upon the legal presumption that postal employees discharge their duties in a proper manner and that properly addressed, stamped and deposited mail is presumed to reach the addressee in due course and without unusual delay, unless evidence to the contrary is proven." The court believed, however, that the Commissioner's position rested "primarily upon a presumption of procedural regularity based upon the normal manner, custom, practice and habit established for the handling of incoming mail at the Patent Office and upon the absence of evidence showing that the subject applications were not handled routinely in accordance with those established procedures." On this analysis, the court "concluded that the presumption relied upon by the [Commissioner] is insufficient to overcome the strong presumption that mails, properly addressed, having fully prepaid postage, and deposited in the proper receptacles, will be received by the addressee in the ordinary course of the mails." "This latter presumption," the court held, "can only be rebutted by proof of specific facts and not by invoking another presumption"; "the negative evidence in this case detailing the manner, custom, practice and habit of handling incoming mail by the Patent Office fails to overcome or rebut the strong presumption that the applications were timely delivered in the regular course of the mails to the Patent Office." In sum,

> [appellees] rely upon the strong presumption of the regularity of the mails to show that, in the normal course of postal business, these applications would be delivered within two days from March 1, 1973. [The Commissioner] does not show nor offer to show by way of any positive evidence that the presumption is inapplicable in this case. On the contrary, he relies on negative evidence as to custom, habit and usual procedure to create a conflicting presumption that the agency's business and procedure were followed in this case. Under the circumstances of this case, this Court holds, as a matter of law, that this presumption is insufficient to rebut or overcome the presumption of the regularity of the mails.

II

Proof that mail matter is properly addressed, stamped and deposited in an appropriate receptacle has long been accepted as evidence of delivery to the addressee. On proof of the foundation facts, innumerable cases recognize a presumption to that effect. Some presume more specifically that the delivery occurred in due course of the mails. The cases concede, however, that the presumption is rebuttable. We think the District Court erred in adhering to the presumption in the face of the evidentiary showing which the Commissioner was prepared to make.

Rebuttable presumptions [1] are rules of law attaching to proven evidentiary facts certain procedural consequences as to the opponent's duty to come forward with other evidence. In the instant case, the presumption would normally mean no more than that proof of proper airmailing of appellees' applications required a finding, in the absence of countervailing evidence, that they arrived at the Patent Office within the usual delivery time. There is abundant authority undergirding the proposition that, as a presumption, it did not remain viable in the face of antithetical evidence. As Dean Wigmore has explained, "the peculiar effect of a presumption 'of law' (that is, the real presumption) is merely to invoke a rule of law compelling the [trier of fact] to reach a conclusion in the absence of evidence to the contrary from the opponent. If the opponent does offer evidence to the contrary (sufficient to satisfy the judge's requirement of some evidence), the presumption disappears as a rule of law, and the case is in the [factfinder's] hands free from any rule." As more poetically the explanation has been put, "[p]resumptions * * * may be looked on as the bats of the law, flitting in the twilight, but disappearing in the sunshine of actual facts."

We are aware of the fact that this view of presumptions—the so-called "bursting bubble" theory—has not won universal acclaim. Nonetheless, it is the prevailing view, to which jurists preponderantly have subscribed; it is the view of the Supreme Court, and of this court as well. It is also the approach taken by the Model Code of Evidence and, very importantly, by the newly-adopted Federal Rules of Evidence.[2] These considerations hardly leave us free to assume a contrary

---

1. We distinguish the presumption "of law"—the procedural rule dictating a factual conclusion in the absence of contrary evidence—from the presumption "of fact," which in reality is not a presumption at all, see 9 J. Wigmore, Evidence § 2491 at 288–289 (3d ed. 1940), and from the "conclusive" presumption, which is actually a substantive rule of law. See 9 J. Wigmore, Evidence § 2492 (3d ed. 1940); C. McCormick, Evidence § 342 at 804 (2d ed. 1972). We also differentiate presumptions from inferences, a dissimilarity which "is subtle, but not unreal. A presumption, sometimes called a presumption of law, is an inference which the law directs the [trier of

fact] to draw if it finds a given set of facts; an inference is a conclusion which the [trier of fact] is *permitted*, but not compelled, to draw from the facts."

2. "In all civil actions and proceedings not otherwise provided for by Act of Congress or by these rules, a presumption imposes on the party against whom it is directed the burden of going forward with evidence to rebut or meet the presumption, but does not shift to such party the burden of proof in the sense of the risk of nonpersuasion, which remains throughout the trial upon the party on whom it was originally cast." Fed.R.Evid. 301. The history

position. Beyond that, we perceive no legal or practical justification for preferring either of the two involved presumptions over the other. In light of the Commissioner's showing on the motions for summary judgment, then, we conclude that the District Court should have declined a summary disposition in favor of a trial.

III

Conservatively estimated, the Patent Office receives through the mails an average of at least 100,000 items per month. The procedures utilized for the handling of that volume of mail were meticulously described in an affidavit by an official of the Patent Office, whose principal duties included superintendence of incoming mail. Ordinary mail—other than special delivery, registered and certified—arrives at the Patent Office in bags, which are date-marked if the items contained were placed by the postal service in the Patent Office pouch earlier than the date of delivery of the bags. A number of readers open the wrappers, compare the contents against any included listing—such as a letter of transmittal or a return postcard—and note any discrepancy, and apply to at least the principal included paper a stamp recording thereon the receipt date and the reader's identification number. Another employee then applies to the separate papers the official mail-room stamp, which likewise records the date; the two stamps are used in order to minimize the chance of error. The date recorded in each instance is the date on which the Patent Office actually receives the particular bag of mail, or a previous date when the bag is so marked. From every indication, the affidavit avers, appellees' applications were not delivered to the Patent Office until March 8, 1973.

We cannot agree with the District Court that an evidentiary presentation of this caliber would do no more than raise "a presumption of procedural regularity" in the Patent Office. Certainly it would accomplish that much; it would cast upon appellees the burden of producing contradictory evidence, but its effect would not be exhausted

of this provision portrays a fluctuating evolution. As originally proposed by the Supreme Court, the presumptions governed were given the effect of placing on the opposing party the burden of establishing the nonexistence of the presumed fact, and "[t]he so-called 'bursting bubble' theory, under which a presumption vanishes upon the introduction of evidence which would support a finding of the nonexistence of the presumed fact, even though not believed, [was] rejected as according presumptions too 'slight and evanescent' an effect." Advisory Committee's Note to original Rule 301. The House Committee on the Judiciary agreed, but substituted a shift in the burden of going forward in place of a shift of the burden of proof, and conferred evidentiary value on the presumption. H.R.Rep. No. 93–650, 93d Cong., 1st Sess. 7 (1973), U.S. Code Cong. & Admin. News 1974, p. 7075. The Senate Committee on the Judiciary felt, however, that "the House amendment is ill-advised. * * * 'Presumptions are not evidence, but ways of dealing with evidence.' [footnote omitted]. This treatment requires juries to perform the task of considering 'as evidence' facts upon which they have no direct evidence and which may confuse them in performance of their duties." S.Rep. No. 93–1277, 93d Cong., 2d Sess. 9–10 (1974), first quoting Hearings on H.R. 2463 Before the Senate Committee on Judiciary, 93d Cong., 2d Sess. 96 (1974) U.S. Code Cong. & Admin. News 1974, pp. 7051, 7056. The Senate Committee accordingly modified Rule 301 to its present form, and the Conference Committee adopted the Senate version. H.R.Rep. No. 93–1597, 93d Cong., 2d Sess. 5–6 (1974) U.S. Code Cong. & Admin. News 1974, p. 7098.

* * *

at that point. The facts giving rise to the presumption would also have evidentiary force, and as evidence would command the respect normally accorded proof of any fact. In other words, the evidence reflected by the affidavit, beyond creation of a presumption of regularity in date-stamping incoming mail, would have probative value on the issue of date of receipt of appellees' applications; and even if the presumption were dispelled, that evidence would be entitled to consideration, along with appellees' own evidence, when a resolution of the issue is undertaken. And, clearly, a fact-finder convinced of the integrity of the Patent Office's mail-handling procedures would inexorably be led to the conclusion that appellees' applications simply did not arrive until the date which was stamped on them.

In the final analysis, the District Court's misstep was the treatment of the parties' opposing affidavits as a contest postulating a question of law as to the relative strength of the two presumptions rather than as a prelude to conflicting evidence necessitating a trial. Viewed as the mere procedural devices we hold that they are, presumptions are incapable of waging war among themselves. Even more importantly, the court's disposition of the case on a legal ruling disregarded the divergent inferences which the evidentiary tenders warranted, and consequently the inappropriateness of a resolution of the opposing claims by summary judgment. As only recently we said, "[t]he court's function is not to resolve any factual issue, but to ascertain whether any exists, and all doubts in that regard must be resolved against summary judgment." Here the District Court was presented with an issue of material fact as to the date on which appellees' applications were received by the Patent Office, and summary judgment was not in order.

The judgment appealed from is accordingly reversed, and the case is remanded to the District Court for further proceedings. The cross-motions for summary judgment will be denied, and the case will be set down for trial on the merits in regular course.

So ordered.

* * *

NOTE

See Federal Rules of Evidence 301–302, California Evidence Code §§ 110, 115, 500–502, 520–522, 550, 600–607, 620–624, 630–645, 660, 662–668.

DEGNAN, SYLLABUS ON CALIFORNIA EVIDENCE CODE

(11th Annual Summer Program for California Lawyers, U. of Calif. at Berkeley, 1965) pp. 18–25.

B. Presumptions

The Code of Civil Procedure § 1957 divides all "indirect" (i.e., circumstantial) evidence into two forms or kinds, inferences and presumptions. In §§ 1958 and 1959 these two forms are defined. Without repeating the unnecessary division of § 1957, Evidence Code § 600 restates in more modern expression the substance of the existing

definitions. An inference is a deduction which reasonable men could
draw from another fact or facts which have been proved or established;
a presumption is an assumption of fact that the law *requires* to be made
when another fact or facts have been proved or established.

Evidence Code § 601 divides presumptions further into conclusive
and rebuttable presumptions; so does C.C.P. § 1961. Retention of the
term "conclusive presumption" is unfortunate because the kinds of
things described in §§ 621–624 are not presumptions at all but rules of
law. None of the things which will subsequently be said about management of presumptions generally have any reference to conclusive presumptions.

There have been two perennially difficult problems about presumptions in civil cases in California. First to be treated is the difficult
concept of the presumption as evidence. The second is what impact the
presumption has on the burdens of producing evidence and of persuasion. These two will be discussed separately.

1. Presumptions as Evidence

All theories about presumption agree on one thing. If the basic
facts which support the presumption are established, and there is no
contradiction, the jury *must* find the presumed fact to be true. This is
the result of C.C.P. § 1961, and it is much more explicitly stated in
Evidence Code §§ 604 and 606. The difficulty under the C.C.P. was the
meaning of the word "controverted" in § 1961. Did contradictory
evidence so "controvert" the presumption that it disappeared entirely,
never to be mentioned by judge or jury? Or was a controverted
presumption merely no longer binding, but still retaining some probative force? In part because of some language (§§ 1957, 1963) which
refers to presumptions as "evidence," the Supreme Court in Smellie v.
Southern Pac. Co., 212 Cal. 540, 299 P. 529 (1931), held that presumptions are evidence, and that they continue in the case even after
controverting evidence has been introduced. The jury should be so
instructed. Although abundantly criticized, this holding has endured
and is the prime basis for the instructions framed under BAJI series
135. The case also held that while a presumption could be totally
dispelled by testimony, that could be accomplished only by the testimony the holder of the presumption offered on his own behalf, and not by
that extracted from him under C.C.P. § 2055.

To meet this uniquely California view, Evidence Code § 600(a),
after defining presumptions, expressly declares: "A presumption is not
evidence." No longer should juries be instructed that it is evidence,
and that it is to be weighed by them along with all other evidence on
the particular issue. And there should no longer be a problem about
whether the presumption is "dispelled" (i.e., totally eliminated) from
the case in the sense of the *Smellie* opinion, for it was only as to the
existence of the presumption as evidence that this question had any
content.

2. The Two Kinds of Presumptions

Evidence Code § 601, after dividing presumptions into conclusive and rebuttable, further classifies the latter as those affecting only the burden of producing evidence and those also affecting the burden of proof. Each of these classes, and the consequences of the classification, is elaborated in §§ 603–606.

The basic theoretical dispute in other states and in the scholarly literature (somewhat concealed in California because of the doctrine that a presumption is evidence) has been about the effect of contrary or controverting evidence. One view, identified with Professors Thayer and Wigmore, has been that presumptions are created to resolve issues when no evidence has been produced on the point; when evidence is produced, the presumption is exhausted and plays no further role in the case. The burden of persuading the jury about the existence of the fact in question remains where it was at the outset. To the extent that the underlying facts of the presumption have some probative, circumstantial force (e.g., that a properly addressed and mailed letter was received) the jury may consider those facts, balancing them against the testimony of the other party that he did not receive it. But those basic facts, once contradicted, are not reinforced by the presumption.

The other major view, identified largely with Professors Morgan and McCormick and essentially adopted by the Uniform Rules of Evidence, is that a presumption that has a logical basis (again the letter doctrine) should not be robbed of its force merely by a denial or by the production of some evidence that, if believed, would support a finding. This view would continue the presumption in force, in the form of an instruction to the jury that if they believe that the basic facts exist they should find that the letter was received, unless the contrary evidence persuaded them (usually by a preponderance) that it was not achieved. Thus it may be that a party who started with the burden of proof on a given issue will have shifted that burden to the opponent by establishing the basic fact of a presumption.

No state has consistently followed either of these two theories. A court that solemnly declares that the burden of proof never shifts will, when encountering certain kinds of presumptions, declare that the presumption may be overcome only by persuasive evidence, and that the jury should find the presumed fact unless persuaded by the contrary evidence. Thus in California a child born of a married woman, or within ten months of the end of the marriage, is presumed to be the child of the husband, and that presumption can be overcome only by clear and convincing evidence.

The Law Revision Commission resolved the seeming contradiction between theories by determining that some presumptions are created merely to expedite the proof of law suits, or to shift to a person who has superior access to proof the obligation to come forward with an explanation of an event. § 603. These it classified as presumptions affecting only the burden of producing evidence. Under this section, the stages are:

(a) Evidence supporting the basic facts is produced by the party initially bearing the burden of proof. If no contrary evidence is produced the judge must direct the jury to find (or find himself) that the presumed fact exists if it or he believes the basic facts.

(b) If evidence sufficient to support a contrary finding is produced, the case goes to the jury without mention of the presumption; they resolve it as they would any case of conflicting inferences and testimony.

Some other presumptions founded more in policy considerations than in mere expedition are given greater force under §§ 605–606. The presumption of legitimacy found in § 661 is illustrative. The stages here are:

(a) Evidence supporting the basic facts is produced by the party initially bearing the burden of proof. If no contrary evidence is produced, the consequences are the same as above—a peremptory finding.

(b) If contrary evidence sufficient to support a finding is produced, the jury will be instructed that the husband bears the burden of persuading them that he is not the father.

Admittedly the classification of presumptions as one form or the other will not be a simple task. The code helps by classifying some of the standard and commonly encountered presumptions. As to others (either those found in other codes or in the case law), the judges must do as they have done before.

C. Prima Facie Evidence

Code of Civil Procedure § 1833 defines prima facie evidence as "that which suffices for the proof of a particular fact, until contradicted and overcome by other evidence." The phrase is troublesome because it has been and is used with several different meanings. To the original code commissioners, it meant evidence that "in the absence of all controlling evidence or discrediting circumstances, becomes conclusive of the fact; that is, it should operate upon the minds of the jury as decisive to found their verdict as to the fact." As such, it is hard to distinguish from a presumption. The term is often used also as the equivalent of a reasonable inference—evidence which, if believed, is sufficient to support but not to compel, a finding. And the code commissioners themselves often used it when the only probable purpose was to create a hearsay exception. E.g., C.C.P. §§ 1936, 1946. To avoid the confusion, the commission has eliminated from the Evidence Code both the definition and the usage of "prima facie." But the problem remains, for other codes contain many sections making one thing, usually a writing or recording prima facie evidence of some fact or facts. E.g., Health & S.C. § 10577 (death certificate). Sometimes the courts have treated these as presumptions affecting the burden of proof. At other times they appear to be regarded as merely shifting the burden of producing evidence.

Although the Commission eliminated the term from the Evidence Code, it could not eliminate the many instances in which the term is used in other codes. Section 602 therefore provides:

"A statute providing that a fact or group of facts is prima facie evidence of another fact establishes a rebuttable presumption."

Whether it is a presumption shifting the burden of producing evidence only, or one shifting the burden of proof as well, the courts must in each instance decide by ascertaining the legislative purpose. And in most instances, of course, the special statute will serve the additional purpose of creating a hearsay exception. Evidence Code § 1205 expressly disclaims any intention to repeal hearsay exceptions found in other codes.

ATKINSON v. HALL

Supreme Court of Maine, 1989.
556 A.2d 651.

HORNBY, Justice.

This case concerns the applicability of conflicting presumptions about the paternity of a child born during a marriage. Under the Maine Rules of Evidence, the legitimacy of a child born or conceived during marriage can be challenged only by proof beyond a reasonable doubt. Here, however, the results of blood tests produced a conflicting statutory presumption that the defendant—not the mother's husband—was the father, a presumption that can in turn be rebutted only by clear and convincing evidence. We conclude that no reversible error occurred when the Superior Court (Aroostook County; Pierson, J.) put these competing presumptions aside in informing the jury that the mother must prove her paternity case against the defendant by the ordinary standard, a preponderance of the evidence.

The defendant Robert Hall testified that he dated the plaintiff Julie Atkinson off and on from December of 1970 until early October of 1971. In September 1971 they went to Connecticut together. The couple lived in a friend's house while they were in Connecticut and engaged in sexual intercourse at that time. Hall soon returned to Houlton, Maine, because he had a court appearance. Hall testified that he did not see Atkinson after the first of October except on one occasion when she visited him in jail in Maine sometime between the end of October and early December, 1971. He testified that during that visit Atkinson told him that she was going to marry Gerald Marshall and that she was pregnant with Marshall's child. Atkinson, on the other hand, testified that she was pregnant with Hall's child and that she told Hall so when she visited him in jail. Atkinson married Gerald Marshall in January of 1972. The child, Jay, was born July 20, 1972. Jay's name on his birth certificate was Jay Alan Marshall, with his father listed as Gerald Alan Marshall. A certificate of baptism listed Jay's father as Gerald A. Marshall.

Marshall and Atkinson were divorced some five to eight months after Jay's birth. According to Atkinson, the divorce decree required Marshall to pay child support for Jay, but he has made only one

payment of $75.00. Atkinson filed a complaint for nonsupport against
Marshall in early 1974. Atkinson has received AFDC benefits and has
repeatedly used Jay's birth certificate (showing Marshall as his father)
in support of her entitlement. Indeed, she agrees that all legal documentation pertaining to Jay's paternity shows Marshall as his father.

At the time of trial, Hall was 5'8½" tall, weighed 150 lbs. and wore
a size 8½ shoe. Atkinson was 5'4" tall. Jay, age 15 at trial, testified
that he was 6'1" tall, weighed 170 lbs., and wore a size 14 shoe. There
was evidence that Gerald Marshall was heavy and conflicting testimony
that he was either 5'11" or 5'9". Atkinson testified that other members
of her family are 6' tall.

The results of blood tests submitted to the jury showed the
probability of Hall's paternity to be 98.27 percent. No blood test was
conducted on Marshall. Atkinson produced birthday cards and photographs from Hall to Jay in which Hall referred to himself as Jay's
father or "Dad." Hall testified that he signed the cards and photographs in this fashion because Jay had no father figure in his life and
that he did the same thing for his stepchildren by a later marriage.

Atkinson brought her lawsuit in 1986 seeking child support from
Hall under Maine's version of the Uniform Paternity Act, 19 M.R.S.A.
§§ 271–287 (1981 & Supp.1988). At trial Atkinson requested a jury
instruction that Hall's blood test raised a presumption of paternity in
Hall that could be rebutted only by "clear and convincing evidence."
19 M.R.S.A. §§ 280, 280–A. Hall, on the other hand, sought an instruction under M.R.Evid. 302 that because Jay was born to Atkinson while
she was lawfully married to Marshall, Atkinson had the burden of
"producing evidence" and of "persuading the trier of fact beyond a
reasonable doubt" that Jay was not Marshall's son. The Superior
Court Justice disregarded both presumptions under M.R.Evid. 301(c)
and instructed the jury that Atkinson had the burden of proving her
case by a preponderance of the evidence. The jury returned a unanimous verdict for Hall, thus finding that he was not the father of the
child. Atkinson has appealed.

We have some concern whether Maine's paternity statute contemplates an action to establish that the father of a child born during
marriage is someone other than its mother's husband. It is true that
bastardy proceedings predating the adoption of the statute suggest the
possibility of such an action. See *Ventresco v. Bushey,* 159 Me. 241,
191 A.2d 104 (1963) (recognizing such an action where the child was
conceived during the marriage but born after a divorce). But in
adopting the paternity statute in 1967, the Maine Legislature dealt
only with the obligations of "the father of a child which is or may be
born out of wedlock" and declared that such a father is liable "to the
same extent as the father of a child born in wedlock." 19 M.R.S.A.
§ 271. The Uniform Act on Paternity, which the Maine statute otherwise closely follows, specifies that "[a] child born out of wedlock
includes a child born to a married woman by a man other than her
husband." § 1, 9–B U.L.A. 350 (1960). Significantly, the Maine Legislature dropped this sentence entirely in enacting the Maine version.

Thus, it is possible that the Maine Legislature intended to limit paternity actions to instances where children were born to an unmarried woman. Because the parties have not addressed this issue and we have been unable to find any legislative history on the subject, we do not decide the question.

Assuming without deciding that a mother whose child was born during marriage may question the legitimacy of that child and bring a paternity action against a man other than her husband, we examine the conflicting presumptions. Because the blood tests showed that the probability of Hall's paternity was 97 percent or higher, the paternity statute provides first that "the alleged father is presumed to be the father, and this evidence must be admitted," 19 M.R.S.A. s 280(1)(D), and second that the presumption may be rebutted only "by clear and convincing evidence." Id. s 280–A. Because Atkinson was married to Marshall at the time of Jay's birth, however, M.R.Evid. 302 establishes a different presumption. Specifically, [w]henever it is established in an action that a child was born to or conceived by a woman while she was lawfully married, the party asserting the illegitimacy of the child has the burden of producing evidence and the burden of persuading the trier of fact beyond a reasonable doubt of such illegitimacy. Under the presumption of legitimacy established by this rule, Atkinson has the burden of showing that Jay is not Marshall's child by proof beyond a reasonable doubt. These two presumptions directly conflict.

M.R.Evid. 301(c) provides instructions on how to resolve the conflict: If two presumptions arise which are conflicting with each other, the court shall apply the presumption which is founded on the weightier considerations of policy and logic. If there is no such preponderance, both presumptions shall be disregarded. In terms of logic, presuming paternity from a 98.27 percent blood test seems weightier than presuming legitimacy from the mere fact of marriage. In terms of policy, however, there is no particular weight to the blood test presumption (except perhaps to reduce the number of trials), since a jury is able to hear and evaluate the testimony concerning the blood test without the presumption and thus make a rational decision as to who is the biological father in any event. The presumption of legitimacy, on the other hand, is clearly designed to minimize official intrusion into marital and family relations. This Court has consistently stated that the presumption of legitimacy is one of the strongest known to the law, In Re Estate of Parker, 137 Me. 80, 82, 15 A.2d 183, 184 (1940), and that it is "no ordinary presumption." Ventresco v. Bushey, 159 Me. at 250, 191 A.2d at 109. The fact that the legitimacy presumption requires proof beyond a reasonable doubt to overcome it, whereas the paternity presumption requires only clear and convincing evidence, may also bear upon their respective weights.

With logic on one side and policy on the other, we are satisfied that at the very least the paternity presumption is not founded on weightier considerations than the legitimacy presumption. Therefore, Atkinson was not prejudiced when the Superior Court instructed the jury to decide this case under the ordinary civil standard of a preponderance of the evidence; if anything, Hall may have been entitled to an instruction on the presumption of legitimacy. Since no party here is arguing that the legitimacy presumption prevails, however, and given our uncertainty whether Atkinson even had a cause of action under Maine's paternity statute, we leave that issue for another day.

The jury heard all the evidence concerning Atkinson's relationship with both Marshall and Hall, and concerning Hall's relationship with Jay; observed Atkinson, Hall and Jay as well as pictures and descriptions of Marshall; and made its decision accordingly. We see no reason to disturb it.

The entry is:

Judgment affirmed.

All concurring.

PART B. CRIMINAL CASES

PEOPLE v. RODER

Supreme Court of California, In Bank, 1983.
33 Cal.3d 491, 189 Cal.Rptr. 501, 658 P.2d 1302.

OPINION

KAUS, J. After a jury trial, defendant Robert Earl Roder was convicted of receiving stolen property. On appeal he raises a single issue, contending that in light of the United States Supreme Court decisions in Ulster County Court v. Allen (1979) and Sandstrom v. Montana (1979), the trial court committed constitutional error in instructing the jury on the statutory presumption of guilty knowledge embodied in Penal Code section 496. We conclude that defendant's claim is well-founded and accordingly we reverse the receiving count.

I

In January 1980, Roder and his codefendant Betty Rayfield shared a residence and were coproprietors of Betty Boop's Junque Shop, a secondhand store located in what was described at trial as the "skidrow" section of Santa Cruz. On January 29, a woman informed police that she had seen many items that had been stolen from her home earlier that month at Betty Boop's. The police obtained a warrant and, the following day, entered and searched the store and defendants' residence, seizing 60 items that were later identified by their owners as stolen property. Thereafter, Roder and Rayfield were charged with receiving stolen property.

At trial, the prosecution introduced evidence as to a number of the seized items but the jury informed the court on returning its verdict on the receiving charges that it had been able to agree only with respect to one item—a used Selmar clarinet. Accordingly, we summarize the evidence only with respect to this item of property.

The clarinet, easily identifiable because it had a severe crack and was enclosed in a unique case, had been stolen from Bart Goldsteen in November 1979. Goldsteen testified that shortly after it was stolen, he made the rounds of the nearby secondhand stores, including Betty Boop's, describing the clarinet to the proprietors. He identified Roder as the person to whom he had spoken at Betty Boop's, and stated that he had never heard from Roder after that.

Kurt Heisig, a musical instrument dealer in San Jose, testified that sometime before Christmas he spoke with Roder about possibly purchasing the clarinet. Heisig stated that he called the San Jose and Santa Clara police to inquire about the clarinet, but did not call the Santa Cruz police because Roder told him that he had already done so.

Testifying on his own behalf, Roder conceded that he might have had a conversation with Goldsteen about a clarinet but stated that he could not specifically remember it, explaining that he had similar brief conversations about lost items with many people every day. Roder stated that he hardly ever personally bought items to sell in the store and that he had not purchased the clarinet; he testified that the first time he saw the clarinet it was already part of the store inventory. He acknowledged that he had spoken with Heisig about the clarinet and that he had not contacted the Santa Cruz police about the instrument. He maintained, however, that he did not know that the clarinet was stolen property.

The defense also put on evidence indicating that much of the store's inventory was purchased at flea markets in the early hours of the morning, and that Betty Rayfield and others who purchased the goods very often did not comply with the store's "official" policy of obtaining full and accurate identification of the seller of the goods. The defense also produced a receipt book which included an entry for an "old clarinet, $20.00," purchased from a "Merle A. Turner, alien identification number A 13084A13"; the entry was signed by Rayfield. The listing did not describe the manufacturer of the clarinet, nor include an address or phone number of the seller and there was no additional information to establish whether or not the entry referred to Goldsteen's clarinet.

At the conclusion of the trial, the court instructed the jury on the presumption of innocence, the definition of reasonable doubt, and the elements of receiving stolen property: "One, that a person receives property which had been stolen; two, that such person actually knew said property was stolen at the time he or she received such property." The court then gave an instruction based on—but not identical to—section 496, subdivision 2, which informed the jury that if it found (1) that defendant was a dealer in secondhand merchandise, (2) that he had bought or received stolen property, (3) that he bought or received such property under circumstances which should have caused him to make reasonable inquiry that the person from whom the property was bought had the legal right to sell it, and (4) that he did not make such reasonable inquiry, "then you shall presume that defendant[ ] bought or received such property knowing it to have been stolen unless from all the evidence you have reasonable doubt that defendant[ ] knew the property was stolen."

During deliberations, the jury requested clarification of the latter instruction. The court reviewed the court elements noted above, and then explained:

> "If you find those four things, then the presumption does come into play. The presumption is that the defendants bought such property knowing it to have been stolen. However it's a presumption—There are two kinds of presumptions. One is a conclusive presumption that if you have the presumption, that's it, you don't go any further. This isn't that kind of presumption. It's what's called a rebuttable presumption, because you have the presumption, presume to know that the property was stolen, but they can go forward and raise a reasonable doubt that they actually knew that. So you still do have that question. Basically, it boils down to are you satisfied that they acquired or retained the property knowing it was stolen, or do you have a reasonable doubt. * * * *"

The jury resumed its deliberations and thereafter returned a verdict finding Roder guilty of receiving stolen property. As noted, the jury indicated in response to the court's inquiry that the clarinet was the only item of stolen property on which it had reached unanimous agreement.

* * *

Roder's sole contention on appeal is that the trial court erred in instructing the jury on the presumption of guilty knowledge applicable to secondhand dealers embodied in section 496. He asserts that the United States Supreme Court's decisions in Ulster County Court v. Allen, 442 U.S. 140 (1979) and Sandstrom v. Montana, 442 U.S. 510 (1979) establish that such a presumption is unconstitutional because it relieves the prosecution of its burden of proving all elements of the criminal offense beyond a reasonable doubt.

In the past two decades the Supreme Court has repeatedly grappled with the problems raised by the use of presumptions in criminal cases. In *Ulster County* the court explained: "Inferences and presumptions are a staple of our adversary system of factfinding. It is often necessary for the trier of fact to determine the existence of an element of the crime—that is, an 'ultimate' or 'elemental' fact—from the existence of one or more 'evidentiary' or 'basic' facts. The value of these evidentiary devices, and their validity under the Due Process Clause, vary from case to case, however, depending on the strength of the connection between the particular basic and elemental facts involved and on the degree to which the device curtails the factfinder's freedom to assess the evidence independently. Nonetheless, in criminal cases, the ultimate test of any device's constitutional validity remains constant: the device must not undermine the factfinder's responsibility at trial, based on evidence adduced by the State, to find the ultimate facts beyond a reasonable doubt.

In determining whether a particular evidentiary device meets this baseline standard, however, the *Ulster County* court emphasized that a sharp distinction must be drawn between two different types of devices:

(1) "[an] entirely permissive inference or presumption, which allows—but does not require—the trier of fact to infer the elemental fact from proof by the prosecutor of the basic one and which places no burden of any kind on the defendant" and (2) "[a] mandatory presumption * * * [which] tells the trier that he or they *must* find the elemental fact upon proof of the basic fact, at least unless the defendant has come forward with some evidence to rebut the presumed connection between the two facts." (Original italics.)

With respect to a permissive inference, the court reasoned that "[b]ecause this [type of device] leaves the trier of fact free to credit or reject the inference and does not shift the burden of proof, it affects the application of the 'beyond a reasonable doubt' standard only if, under the facts of the case, there is no rational way the trier could make the connection permitted by the inference." "[O]nly in that situation," the court concluded, "is there any risk that an explanation of the permissible inference to a jury, or its use by a jury, has caused the presumptively rational factfinder to make an erroneous factual determination."

On the other hand, the court recognized that "[a] mandatory presumption is a far more troublesome evidentiary device" insofar as the reasonable doubt standard is concerned. Because such a presumption tells the trier of fact that it *must* assume the existence of the ultimate, elemental fact from proof of specific, designated basic facts, it limits the jury's freedom independently to assess all of the prosecution's evidence in order to determine whether the facts of the particular case establish guilt beyond a reasonable doubt. For that reason, the court concluded that a mandatory presumption must be judged "on its face," not "as applied" and that "since the prosecution bears the burden of establishing guilt, it may not rest its case on [such] a presumption unless the fact proved is sufficient to support the inference of guilt beyond a reasonable doubt." [1]

In *Ulster County* itself, the court found that under the jury instructions given in that case the evidentiary device at issue—a statute which provided that the presence of a firearm in an automobile is "presumptive evidence" of the firearm's illegal possession by all persons in the vehicle—gave rise only to a permissive inference, not a mandatory presumption. Relying on its determination that the constitutionality of an instruction embodying such an inference must be judged "as applied" rather than "on its face", the court reviewed the evidence in the case in some detail and upheld the conviction, finding that on the evidence presented "there is a 'rational connection' between the basic facts that the prosecution proved and the ultimate fact presumed, and the latter is 'more likely than not to flow' from the former."

---

1. Although the last-quoted passage from *Ulster County* suggests that a mandatory presumption may be upheld if the basic fact proved "is sufficient *to support* the inference of guilt beyond a reasonable doubt", the reasoning of both *Ulster County* and *Sandstrom* would appear to mandate a more stringent test. Because a mandatory presumption *requires* the trier of fact to find that the elemental fact has been established when the presumption's terms have been met, such a device appears reconcilable with the prosecution's burden of proof under *Winship* only if the basic fact proved *compels* the inference of guilt beyond a reasonable doubt.

Two weeks later, in Sandstrom v. Montana, the court struck down an instruction—given in a murder case in which "intent" was an element of the charged offense—which informed the jury that "the law presumes that a person intends the ordinary consequences of his voluntary acts." Rejecting the prosecution's contention that the instruction merely described a permissive inference, the court found that "a reasonable juror could easily have viewed such an instruction as mandatory" and could have interpreted it either as embodying a "conclusive presumption" of intent or as shifting the burden of persuasion on the issue of intent to the defendant. The court reasoned that under either interpretation the instruction was incompatible with the principles of In re Winship, since it improperly relieved the prosecution of its burden of proving all elements of the offense beyond a reasonable doubt.

In light of *Ulster County* and *Sandstrom*, it is apparent that in evaluating the constitutionality of any presumption in a criminal case, the threshold inquiry which a court must now undertake is to determine the nature of the device—permissive inference or mandatory presumption—involved in the proceeding.

In the present case, if we approach this threshold issue purely as a matter of statutory interpretation, there is little question but that the presumption established by section 496 is a "mandatory presumption" within the meaning of *Ulster County* and *Sandstrom*. As we have seen, under California law one of the elements of the offense of receiving stolen property is that the defendant must know that the property which he receives is stolen. In re Winship, establishes, of course, that the People are constitutionally required to prove this element beyond a reasonable doubt.

Under subdivisions 2 and 3 of section 496,[2] however, the People's burden is lightened in two distinct respects. First, subdivision 3, whose operation logically precedes subdivision 2, provides that once the People prove the first three of the statute's four "basic facts"—(1) that the defendant is a secondhand dealer, (2) that he bought or received stolen

---

2. At the time of the alleged offense, section 496 read in [part]: "[2. Every person whose principal business is dealing in or collecting used or secondhand merchandise or personal property, and every agent, employee or representative of such person, who buys or receives any property which has been stolen or obtained in any manner constituting theft or extortion, under such circumstances as should cause such person, agent, employee or representative to make reasonable inquiry to ascertain that the person from whom such property was bought or received had the legal right to sell or deliver it, without making such reasonable inquiry, shall be presumed to have bought or received such property knowing it to have been so stolen or obtained. This presumption may, however, be rebutted by proof. [¶] 3. When in a prosecution under this section it shall appear from the evidence that the defendant's principal business was as set forth in the preceding paragraph, that the defendant bought, received, or otherwise obtained, or concealed, withheld or aided in concealing or withholding from the owner, any property which had been stolen or obtained in any manner constituting theft or extortion, and that the defendant bought, received, obtained, concealed or withheld such property under such circumstances as should have caused him to make reasonable inquiry to ascertain that the person from whom he bought, received, or obtained such property had the legal right to sell or deliver it to him, then the burden shall be upon the defendant to show that before so buying, receiving, or otherwise obtaining such property, he made such reasonable inquiry to ascertain that the person so selling or delivering the same to him had the legal right to so sell or deliver it.] * * *"

property, and (3) that he did so under circumstances that "should have caused him to make reasonable inquiry that the person from whom he bought ∗ ∗ ∗ such property had the legal right to sell ∗ ∗ ∗ it"— *"then the burden shall be on the defendant* to show that before so buying ∗ ∗ ∗ such property, he made such reasonable inquiry" thus, subdivision 3 appears to place the burden of persuasion with respect to the fourth basic fact on the defendant. Second, if the defendant is unable to meet his burden on the question of reasonable inquiry and the four basic facts are thus "established," subdivision 2 provides that he *"shall be presumed* to have bought or received such property knowing it to have been ∗ ∗ ∗ stolen ∗ ∗ ∗." Although subdivision 2 also provides that this presumption "may ∗ ∗ ∗ be rebutted by proof," the rebuttable nature of the presumption does not alter the fact that if the defendant decides to put the People to their proof, the statute *compels* the jury to presume that he had the requisite guilty knowledge simply from the prosecution's proof that he was a second-hand dealer who received stolen property under circumstances which called for a reasonable inquiry—facts which might permit, but certainly would not require, the jury to find beyond a reasonable doubt that defendant knew the property was stolen. Thus, on its face, section 496 is a classic example of a "mandatory presumption" described in *Ulster County*, for it "tells the trier [of fact] that he or they *must* find the elemental fact upon proof of the basic fact, at least unless the defendant has come forward with some evidence to rebut the presumed connection between the two facts."

Furthermore, in addition to the language of section 496 itself, the general provisions of the Evidence Code which define and prescribe the effect of "presumptions" in this state make it clear that the presumption of section 496 is a mandatory presumption under *Ulster County*. In this regard, Evidence Code section 600 explicitly distinguishes a "presumption" from an "inference," providing that "[a] presumption is an assumption of fact that the law *requires to be made* from another fact or group of facts found or otherwise established in the action" (italics added) (Evid. Code, § 600, subd. (a)), while "[a]n inference is a deduction of fact that *may* logically and reasonably *be drawn* from another fact or group of facts found or otherwise established in the action." (Italics added.) (*Id.*, subd. (b).) Since section 496 explicitly establishes a "presumption" rather than an "inference," the Evidence Code provisions confirm that the Legislature intended *to require* the jury to draw the assumption of guilty knowledge from proof of the basic facts, unless the defendant came forth with sufficient evidence to rebut the presumed fact.[3] This, of course, precisely meets *Ulster County*'s definition of a mandatory presumption. (See also *Sandstrom*, supra.)

3. Under Evidence Code section 607, the defendant's burden would be to raise a reasonable doubt as to the existence of the presumed fact. Section 607 provides: "When a presumption affecting the burden of proof operates in a criminal action to establish presumptively any fact that is essential to the defendant's guilt, the presumption operates only if the facts that give rise to the presumption have been found or otherwise established beyond a reasonable doubt, and, in such case, the defendant need only raise a reasonable doubt as to the existence of the presumed fact."

Thus, if the nature of the presumption involved in this case were solely a matter of statutory interpretation, it would be clear that we are dealing with a "mandatory presumption." Moreover, since the Attorney General apparently concedes that the basic facts which the prosecution is required to prove to bring the presumption into play—defendant was a secondhand dealer and bought stolen property under circumstances calling for reasonable inquiry—do not on their face establish beyond a reasonable doubt that the defendant actually knew the property was stolen, it would follow under *Ulster County* and *Sandstrom* that defendant's conviction is constitutionally infirm.

The constitutional issue before us is a bit more complicated, however, because the Supreme Court in *Sandstrom* explained that a determination of the nature of the presumption at issue in any case "requires careful attention to the words actually spoken to the jury, for whether a defendant has been accorded his constitutional rights depends upon the way a reasonable juror could have interpreted the instruction", and in this case the instructions given to the jury differed from the relevant statutes in a number of respects favorable to Roder. To begin with, the jury was not informed of the statutory definition of "presumption" in Evidence Code section 600, and thus was not explicitly told that it is an assumption "that the law requires to be made" from another fact. Second, in instructing the jury under section 496, the trial court omitted any reference to the provisions of subdivision 3 altogether, and thus did not tell the jurors that if the prosecution proved that defendant was a secondhand dealer and had obtained stolen property under circumstances calling for reasonable inquiry, the burden shifted to the defendant to show that he made such inquiry; instead, the court's instruction informed the jury that the prosecution bore the burden of proving that there had been no reasonable inquiry as well as the other basic facts. Finally, whereas section 496, subdivision 2 provides simply that if the basic facts are established the defendant "shall be presumed" to have the requisite guilty knowledge, the instruction given by the court told the jurors that if they found the basic facts "then you shall presume that defendant bought or received such property knowing it to have been stolen *unless from all the evidence you have reasonable doubt that defendants knew the property was stolen.*" This concluding clause—not contained in the statute—could have been interpreted by the jurors to mean that even if they found the basic facts to exist, they were *not* required to find in accordance with the presumption and could refuse to do so if "from all the evidence"—that is, the evidence presented by either the prosecution or the defense—they had a reasonable doubt that defendant knew the property was stolen. Thus, this language—taken by itself—could be read to suggest that the "presumption" of guilty knowledge was simply a permissive inference, which the jurors could, but were not required to, draw.

For a number of reasons, however, we cannot find that the jury was properly informed of the applicable constitutional principles in this case. In the first place, while the instruction that was given to the jury is—as just discussed—perhaps susceptible to interpretation as a permissive inference, taken as a whole it is at best ambiguous. The instruction did not inform the jury that if it found the basic facts it could, but was not required to, infer guilty knowledge, but instead told the jury that upon finding the basic facts, it "shall presume" such knowledge unless it had a reasonable doubt. As the Supreme Court noted in *Sandstrom*, "the common definition of 'presume' [is] 'to suppose to be true without proof,' Webster's New Collegiate Dictionary 911 (1974)" and because the jury was given no legal definition of the term, we cannot assume that the jury understood the instruction as doing no more than informing it that it was free either to infer, or not to infer, guilty knowledge from proof of the basic facts.

Second, the ambiguity in the instruction was exacerbated by the trial court's explanation of the operation of the presumption in response to the jury's request for clarification. As noted above, at that point the court reviewed the four basic facts that had to be found to bring the presumption into play and then stated: "The presumption is that the defendants bought such property knowing it to have been stolen * * *. There are two kinds of presumptions. One is a conclusive presumption that if you have the presumption, that's it, you don't go any further. This isn't that kind of presumption. It's what's called a rebuttable presumption, because you have the presumption, presume to know that the property was stolen, but they can go forward and raise a reasonable doubt that they actually knew that. So you still do have that question. Basically, it boils down to are you satisfied that they acquired the property or retained the property knowing it was stolen, or do you have a reasonable doubt."

The Attorney General's brief, relying on the last sentence of the above quote, insists that the jury must have understood the court's comments to mean that the presumption would have no effect on the prosecution's burden of proof. But that reading ignores the court's statement—two sentences earlier—that once the presumption comes into play "they [i.e., the defendants] can go forward and raise a reasonable doubt that they actually knew that." The jury could certainly have understood that comment to mean that once the prosecution proved the basic facts, the burden shifted to the defense to raise a reasonable doubt as to the ultimate fact; conversely, if the defense raised no such doubt, the prosecution's case on the issue of knowledge was deemed established as a matter of law on the basis of circumstantial evidence which, as a matter of common sense, allowed, but by no means compelled, a finding of the ultimate fact. If that was the jury's understanding, the presumption would not have operated merely as a permissive inference.

Accordingly, we conclude that from the instructions given in this case the jury could reasonably have interpreted the presumption of section 496 as relieving the prosecution of its burden of proving every element of the offense beyond a reasonable doubt. As *Ulster County* and *Sandstrom* establish, this was constitutional error.

One question remains: What should the trial court do with section 496's presumption on retrial? (4) As discussed above, section 496 as currently worded prescribes a mandatory presumption, which—under *Ulster County* and *Sandstrom* —is clearly unconstitutional. The Attorney General contends, however, that the presumption of section 496, to save its constitutionality, should be construed as a legislatively prescribed permissive inference, on which a jury should be instructed in an appropriate case. In addition to the familiar authorities which teach that statutes should be interpreted to preserve their constitutionality whenever possible the Attorney General relies on Evidence Code section 501 which provides that "[i]nsofar as any statute * * * assigns the burden of proof in a criminal case, such statute is subject to Penal Code section 1096," California's statutory embodiment of the rule that the prosecution bears the burden of proving guilt beyond a reasonable doubt. [W]e believe that the proposal is basically sound. Under Evidence Code section 501, any statute which assigns the burden of proof in a criminal case is made subject to the overriding rule that the prosecution bears the burden of proving guilt beyond a reasonable doubt. [In light of *Ulster County* and *Sandstrom*,] it appears more in keeping with the overall legislative intent for courts to pare down existing statutory presumptions to constitutionally permissible limits, rather than to abrogate them altogether.

With respect to section 496, the transformation of the statutory rebuttable presumption into a permissible inference appears quite reasonable and feasible. From the point of view of the defendant, a carefully drafted instruction which places the inference in context and does no more than inform the jury that upon the prosecution's proof of the four basic facts it is permitted—but not required—to infer guilty knowledge is fairly innocuous, for even without such an instruction a jury could, of course, reasonably infer that a secondhand dealer who fails to make reasonable inquiry when obtaining stolen property under suspicious circumstances knew that the property was stolen. As a number of commentators have pointed out, a trial court's instruction on such a permissive inference with reference to the specific facts of the case is comparable to a restrained form of judicial comment on the evidence. The common law has long recognized the propriety of instructing the jury in receiving stolen property cases that it may—but is not required to—similarly infer a defendant's guilty knowledge from his unexplained possession of recently stolen property, and both this court and the United States Supreme Court have confirmed the constitutionality of instructing the jury as to this permissive inference.

From the state's point of view, there is considerable benefit in retaining the "secondhand dealer" provision of section 496 in revised form as a permissive inference, even if it cannot survive as a mandatory presumption. First, preservation of the statutory provisions in a restrained form will still enable the court to inform the jury of an inference which the Legislature—drawing on its general experience— has concluded can often reasonably be drawn from proof of the basic facts; elimination of the device would deprive the jury of any legislative guidance in circumstances in which direct evidence of actual guilty knowledge will rarely be available. Second, even as a permissive inference, the statutory provision will serve an important substantive function in regulating the conduct of secondhand dealers, inducing such dealers to make reasonable inquiry when they are offered property that may be stolen. The state has a strong interest in encouraging dealers to conduct their business in this fashion in order to make it more difficult for thieves to dispose of their wares, and it appears appropriate to interpret section 496 to preserve this interest insofar as is constitutionally permissible.

Accordingly, we conclude that pursuant to Evidence Code section 501, section 496 should be construed as authorizing only a permissive inference, not a mandatory presumption. On remand, the trial court should fashion an appropriate instruction, which informs the jury of the permissive inference but at the same time makes clear that the prosecution retains the burden of proving every element of the offense beyond a reasonable doubt.

The conviction of receiving stolen property is reversed.

————

See Federal Rules of Evidence 301–302; California Evidence Code § 646.

Hypotheticals

(1) A sues X Insurance Company for $8000 damages for breach of a liability insurance policy. A had rear-ended B's car, injuring B. B sued A and got a judgment for $8000. X refused to defend A in B's lawsuit on the ground that the policy had been canceled before the accident occurred. At A's trial against X, it is admitted that A paid a year's premium on the policy when it was issued six months before the accident. X's defense is that the policy had been canceled two months before the accident under a policy provision for ten days' notice to the insured and a return of the unused premium. X calls C, a clerk for X, who identifies a copy of a letter from X to A canceling the policy 15 days from the date of the letter, which was two months prior to the A–B accident. C also testifies that she personally mailed the original to A, properly addressed and stamped, and that she enclosed X's check to A for the unused premium. A calls Y who testifies that she and C lived together and that on the date C claims to have mailed the letter to A, C was home sick in bed and didn't go to work that day, the day before, or the day after. X requests the court to instruct the jury that if the jury finds that X's letter to A was correctly addressed and properly mailed, the jury must find that A received the letter in the ordinary course of mail. Should the court grant X's requested instruction?

(2) Assume the same facts as in Illustration (1). In addition to presenting Y's testimony, A testifies that she has lived continuously at the same address to which the canceling notice was allegedly mailed, but has never received any letter from X Insurance Company; that she had no other insurance on her car than the policy issued by X Insurance Company; and that she had driven continuously for five years preceding the accident and has always carried liability insurance coverage. X requests the court to instruct the jury that a letter correctly addressed and properly mailed is presumed to have been received in the ordinary course of mail. What result?

Chapter XIII

OPINION, EXPERTISE AND EXPERTS; SCIENTIFIC AND DEMONSTRATIVE EVIDENCE

PART A. OPINION, EXPERTISE AND EXPERTS

MAGUIRE, EVIDENCE: COMMON SENSE AND COMMON LAW
23–27 (1947).[*]

OPINION

Another kind of evidence toward which courts manifest hostility is described as opinion. Indications are not lacking that wiser members of bench and bar have come to consider this hostility rather overdone in the past. But, even when shrunk to diminished proportions by the best of common sense, the opinion rule is important enough to merit description as our second working tool.

In a way, all human assertions are opinions. It may have seemed pedantic to write, a few pages back, the phrase "manifestations of people's belief about * * * matters of fact" instead of merely saying "statements", but the wording was advisedly chosen. Our whole conscious life is a process of forming working beliefs or opinions from the evidence of our senses, few of them exactly accurate, most of them near enough correct for practical use, some of them seriously erroneous. Every assertion involves the expression of one or more of these opinions. A rule of evidence which called for the exclusion of opinion in this broad sense would therefore make trials quite impossible.

There certainly *is*, though, an exclusionary opinion rule. We can get a fair idea of its general scope by splitting opinions two different ways—first, into the categories of impulsive and deliberate opinions; second, into the categories of commonplace and expert opinions. When Professor Gray said in his teaching notes: "A witness may give his opinion when it is of a kind which a normal man forms justly and correctly but on reasoning which is unconscious or difficult of analysis," he was using both these kinds of classification at once. The complement of his statement, phrased in broad terms without any attempt at meticulous exactitude, would be: "A non-expert witness may not give an opinion as to matters calling for expertness, nor may any witness give a deliberate opinion as to commonplace matters which can be

752

analyzed or broken down into rudimental factors." While we shall
have to say something more about expert testimony to round out the
topic, this latter complementary statement contains the meat of the
exclusionary opinion doctrine.

One great trouble with this doctrine is obviously difficulty in
determining when its prohibition does, and when it does not, apply.
But before taking up practical application and consequences, let us try
to phrase the underlying concepts. It is, of course, plain good sense to
refuse to let a non-expert purport to give evidence about matters he
does not understand. He is more likely to mislead than to afford sound
guidance. The trier of fact is equally capable of forming his own
conclusions. By expanding this last statement we shall get a phrasing
of the practice under which courts have tended to exclude testimony
consciously cast in terms of opinion and referring to commonplace
matters, whenever they believe this testimony can be broken down into
its rudiments—that is, normally, into statements of perception from
which the relevant opinion or conclusion is to be derived. It is
fundamental to our method of litigating factual issues that the trier of
fact, whether judge or juror, shall so far as his capacities and the
nature of the issues permit draw for himself all the conclusions which
build themselves into his determination. Witnesses are to state their
perceptions of fact, the triers to appraise credibility, make findings of
fundamental fact, and draw the inferences necessary to decision.

It scarcely needs illustration to show that restriction of layman's
opinion testimony to the limits indicated by Gray can be the cause of
endless difficulty. Indeed, this possibility has been painfully realized in
practice. Great play has been made of distinction between "opinion"
and "shorthand rendition of fact". Much dispute has arisen as to what
matters are, and what are not, "difficult of analysis". In tort cases
where plaintiffs have been hurt by falling down stairs, off platforms,
into areas, along theatre aisles, and so forth, there is constant bickering
as to whether witnesses may characterize the place or structure or
condition as dangerous, or must confine themselves to attempted recital
of its physical characteristics. So foreign to ordinary human communication has the latter method of expression proved in many of these
trials as almost to tongue-tie the witnesses.

Some judges refuse to worry much about this difficulty of thought
and statement. They have an easy practical solution based on the
belief that a little superfluous opinion evidence in matters of this kind
is not likely to do any great harm. What really counts is full presentation to the jury or judge of the evidence about rudimental facts, with
free rein to draw the correct conclusions. If perchance some needless
and maybe unserviceable expressions of opinion are mixed in by the
fact witnesses, nothing worse than slight loss of time has been suffered;
even in these terms, the lost minutes will probably be fewer than those
resulting from frequent wrangles over admissibility. Rule 401 of the
Model Code of Evidence is deliberately very liberal in this respect.

The emphasis just thrown upon the rudimental facts suggests an
interesting parallel between opinion evidence and hearsay. Often a

bare opinion, without exposition of its premises, and a bare hearsay assertion, without exposition of the declarant's power, opportunity, and inclination to perceive, remember, and narrate truly, are equally and for the same reason worthless as items of proof. The old Bible metaphor of the house built upon sand cannot safely be put out of mind until sound, solid rock foundation is shown. Indeed, the present author has asserted, and not altogether jocosely, that the hearsay rule is nothing more than a specialized manifestation of the opinion rule. Hearsay About Hearsay, 8 Univ.Chi.L.Rev. 621 (1941). The reasoning ventured is that hearsay is customarily offered without any adequate effort to demonstrate its value by evidence as to the reliability of the declarant; that an attempt to supply this defect by testimony of non-expert witnesses concerning his reliability would fail because on such an issue such witnesses are not deemed capable of giving effective evidence; but that an attempt to supply the defect by the testimony of a witness who could qualify as an expert on human credibility in general, and had adequate personal knowledge of the very declarant, might raise a meritorious contention.

COMMONWEALTH v. HOLDEN

Supreme Court of Pennsylvania, 1957.
390 Pa. 221, 134 A.2d 868.

[Prosecution for first degree murder. The court affirmed the judgment of conviction, holding the evidence sufficient. The court gave no attention to the point discussed in the following dissenting opinion—Ed.]

MUSMANNO, Justice (dissenting). The Majority Opinion fails to discuss a very important matter raised by the defendant Charles Holden in his appeal to this Court for a new trial.

On December 31, 1955, between 5:15 and 6:40 a.m., Cora Smith was killed in her home as the result of being struck over the head. The defendant, Charles Holden, was accused, tried, and convicted of her murder. He maintained in his defense that he was innocent since he was not in the victim's home at the time of the brutal attack.

At the time of Holden's arrest, he was taken by the police to the home of a Ralph Jones who had been with Holden for several hours prior to the killing. In Holden's presence, Jones was questioned by the police. The matter of this questioning became a subject for inquiry at the later trial. The assistant district attorney representing the Commonwealth asked Jones if, at the time he was being quizzed by the police in Holden's presence, Holden did anything that was unusual. Jones replied:

> "Well, during the period of time that the detectives were questioning me in his presence, I believe one of them noticed him to sort of wink or something."

The assistant district attorney then asked Jones what Holden meant, and Jones replied:

> "I didn't rightfully know whether it was a wink or something that was in his eye."

The prosecuting attorney's question was a flagrant violation of the rules of evidence and should not have been permitted. What Jones may have thought that Holden meant by the wink, if it was a wink, was entirely speculative. The prosecuting attorney might just as well have asked: "What was Holden thinking of at the time?" In fact, the question imported that very type of query because obviously the eye, no matter how eloquent it is supposed to be in the minds of poets, novelists, and dreamers, is still not capable, by a blink, to telegraph complicated messages, unless, of course, the blinker and the blinkee have previously agreed upon a code.

When Jones replied that he did not know whether Holden had actually winked or had been troubled by a foreign substance in his eye, the Commonwealth's attorney asked him about a statement he had made to the police some time following the winking incident. On January 11th, a few days after the blinking affair, Captain Flynn of the City Detective Bureau asked Jones: "What did you take this wink to be?" and Jones replied:

> "I think he was trying to get me to make an alibi for him
> to cover up some of his actions and I don't know nothing about
> any of his actions."

Commonwealth's counsel sought to introduce this statement at the trial and defense counsel properly objected, explaining:

> "We object to that. Whatever it was, it wasn't made in
> the presence of the defendant, Charles Holden."

The objection was overruled and the jury was thus informed that the defendant endeavored to have Jones frame an alibi for him. On what evidence was this information based? On a wink.

And what did the wink say? I repeat:

> "I think he was trying to get me to make an alibi for him
> to cover up some of his actions and I don't know nothing about
> any of his actions."

It will be noted that the stupendous and compendious wink not only solicited the fabrication of a spurious alibi but specified that it was "to cover up some of his actions." One movement of the eyelid conveyed a message of 21 words. Not even the most abbreviated Morse code could say so much with such little expenditure of muscular and mechanical power.

Although the statement of the interpretation of the wink is preposterous on its face, I can see how it could be made to seem very informative and convincing to the jury, since it was given to the jury with the Court's approval. If Holden had actually spoken to Jones the words which Jones related in his interpretation of the wink, no more effective admission of guilty knowledge could be imagined. Jones and Holden had been together prior to the killing. Holden tells Jones to make up an alibi so that Jones can extend their companionship of the evening to an hour including and beyond the time of the killing. And then Jones not only refuses to do what Holden asks him to do, but relates the criminal attempt on the part of Holden to suborn perjury.

But the fact of the matter is that Holden did not ask Jones to fabricate an alibi. He did not ask him to "cover up some of his actions." All that Holden did was to wink. No one knows whether he was trying to convey a message, whether he was attempting to shut out a strong ray of light, or whether a bit of dust troubled him at the moment. The Court, however, allowed the jury to believe that the wink was a semaphoric signal to Jones to commit perjury.

Was ever more ridiculous evidence presented in a murder trial? What is to happen to our rules of evidence in criminal trials if they can be breached so glaringly, without reproof or criticism by this Court? Holden was convicted and sentenced to life imprisonment. He might have been sentenced to death. On a wink.

And the Majority does not consider the matter of sufficient importance even to mention it.

If a witness is to be allowed to state what he believes a wink said, why should he not be allowed to interpret a cough? Or a sneeze? Or a grunt? Or a hiccough? Why should he indeed not be empowered to testify as to what is passing through an accused's brain? Why not permit mind readers to read a defendant's mind, and thus eliminate the jury system completely because who knows better than the defendant himself whether or not he committed the crime of which he stands accused?

The refusal of this Court to grant a new trial, with so momentous a violation of the defendant's rights, duly noted and excepted to on the record, would suggest that here the law has not only winked but closed both eyes.

WALTZ, INTRODUCTION TO CRIMINAL EVIDENCE
305–25 (1991).*

OPINION, EXPERTISE, AND EXPERTS

A.

The Opinion Rule

Opinion Testimony by a Layman. The law of evidence includes a well-known general rule against testimony by laymen in the form of an *opinion* or *conclusion.* (In lawyer series on television one is forever hearing counsel say, "Object, Your Honor, calls for a conclusion!") Generally speaking, it is true that a layman, called to the stand to give testimony, must restrict himself to describing material facts about which he has firsthand knowledge. He cannot ordinarily unburden himself of opinions and conclusions which he has drawn from his firsthand observations. This is true for one of two reasons: either the lay witness is technically unqualified, for lack of some essential skill, training, or experience, to draw such a conclusion; or the jurors themselves are fully capable of drawing the right conclusion from the recited facts—and if they are, the witness's opinion testimony would invade the rightful province of the jury.

* Copyright, 1991, by Jon R. Waltz.

Not all jurisdictions enforce the opinion rule with equal force. Judges will be quick to exclude opinions on ultimate issues—for example, "In my opinion the defendant is guilty of this crime"—but may be slower to react to conclusory statements that do not go to the very heart of the case.

Furthermore, there are numerous realistic exceptions to the rule against opinion testimony. Most of them involve lay "shorthand" testimony where it is next to impossible to express the matter in any other way.

Examples:

    a. *Matters of taste and smell*—"It smelled like gunpowder."

    b. *Another's emotions*—"He seemed nervous."

    c. *Vehicular speed*—"He was going very, very fast."

    d. *Voice identification*—"I've known Clyde Bushmat for fifteen years and I'd recognize his voice anywhere. It was Bushmat's voice on the telephone."

    e. *A witness's own intent, where relevant*—"I was planning on crossing the street."

    f. *Genuineness of another's handwriting*—"That's my husband's signature."

    g. *Another's irrational conduct*—"He was acting like a crazy man."

    h. *Intoxication*—"The man was drunk."

Reasoning Behind the Rule Against Lay Opinion Testimony. A fundamental aspect of the reasoning underlying the opinion rule is that factual conclusions that are within the grasp or comprehension of the average layman should be left to the jury, which supposedly is made up of just such average laymen. If a juror can just as well arrive at his own conclusions by adding together the factual components provided by the witnesses, there is no need for the witnesses to inject their own conclusions.

Example a.:

    In State v. Thorp, 72 N.C. 186 (1875), the defendant was charged with drowning her son Robert. The prosecution offered a witness who had known Robert. He testified that he was too far away from the defendant and the child she was holding to be certain that the child was Robert. He did testify, however, that it was "his best impression" that the child was Robert. The defendant's conviction was overturned on appeal because the witness had given prohibited opinion testimony.

Example b.:

    In Commonwealth v. Holden, 134 A.2d 868 (1957), the accused was convicted of murder. While he was in custody he gave the police an alibi to the effect that he had been with one Ralph Jones at the crucial time. Jones, questioned by the police, denied this. During the questioning of Jones, the accused, who was present, had winked at him. At trial Jones testified about the wink and stated that he interpreted it as a signal to him to supply the defendant with an alibi. Although the accused's conviction was affirmed without consideration of the opinion rule problem in any detail, one justice of the Pennsylvania Supreme Court noted that Jones's testimony reflected an opinion.

Example c.:

In United States v. Schneiderman, 106 F.Supp. 892 (S.D. Cal.1952), the defendants were charged with Smith Act violations. The Government offered the testimony of former members of the Communist party that the defendants, by their actions, appeared to be members of the party. The trial court held that this was permissible since there was no other way the witnesses could convey to the jury what they had observed. (This was a questionable ruling, made during the era of Senator Joseph R. McCarthy.)

The Federal Approach. Rule 701 of the Federal Rules of Evidence takes a practical approach: "If the witness is not testifying as an expert, his testimony in the form of opinions or inferences is limited to those opinions or inferences which are (a) rationally based on the perception of the witness and (b) helpful to a clear understanding of his testimony or the determination of a fact in issue."

B.

Experts and Expertise

An Exception to the Opinion Rule. Opinion testimony by expert witnesses comes in through an important exception to the general rule against opinion testimony.

The Definition of "Expert." There are those who have the mistaken notion that the title of "expert" can properly be bestowed only on a few members of professional groups who have a cluster of postgraduate degrees after their names. Some people think that only a scientist of one sort or another and perhaps a few engineers can rightly be called experts. But the term "expert," at least in the law and in common sense, is far broader in meaning than this. Anyone who has ever tried to repair his own automobile or television set knows that some people are experts at these kinds of work and some are not. The proficient garage mechanic is an expert in his field even though a Ph.D. may be the last thing he ever hoped to acquire; the trained and experienced television repairman is just as surely an expert as the most renowned neurosurgeon. The same sort of thing can be said of the brick mason, the sheet metal worker, the plumber, the carpenter, and the electrician, just to name a few more genuine experts.

Getting closer to the immediate point, the label "expert" applies to the firearms identification technician and those who are proficient at fingerprint or handwriting comparison. And it applies to the policeman who knows how to use, interpret, and explain special equipment, such as radar vehicular speed measuring devices and equipment for measuring blood-alcohol ratios. Thus a basic law dictionary, Black's, sweepingly defines experts as "men of science educated in the art, or persons possessing special or peculiar knowledge *acquired from practical experience*" (italics added).

The Four Basic Conditions of Expert Testimony. An expert witness, such as a pathologist or ballistics technician, can testify to an opinion, inference, or conclusion if four basic conditions are met:

(1) The opinions, inferences, or conclusions depend on special knowledge, skill, or training not within the ordinary experience of lay jurors;

(2) The witness must be shown to be qualified as a true expert in the particular field of expertise;

(3) The witness must testify to a reasonable degree of certainty (probability) regarding his opinion, inference, or conclusion; and

(4) Although this fourth condition is currently in the process of modification, at least in times past it has generally been true that an expert witness must first describe the data (facts) on which his opinion, inference, or conclusion is based or, in the alternative, he must testify in response to a hypothetical question that sets forth the underlying data.

Rationale Behind the Expert Witness Exception to the Rule Against Opinion Testimony. The reasoning behind letting expert witnesses give testimony in the form of opinions or conclusions is that experts have special training, knowledge, and skill in drawing conclusions from certain sorts of data that lay jurors do not have. Expert witnesses and their opinions are permissible only in areas in which lay jurors cannot draw conclusions unassisted.

* * *

Qualifying the Witness as an Expert. From what has been said thus far it follows that the exception for expert testimony is available only when the witness is shown to be a true expert in the field that is involved. Before a witness can testify to an expert opinion, examining counsel must lay the necessary foundation by bringing out the witness's training, experience, and special skills. Trial lawyers call this process "qualifying the witness."

At the conclusion of the direct questions aimed at qualifying the witness as an expert, and before examining counsel gets into the meat of the witness's testimony, opposing counsel is entitled to interrupt and engage in cross-examination as to the witness's expertise. This examination will be limited strictly to probing the witness's credentials as an expert.

Example a.:

BY THE PROSECUTING ATTORNEY: Give your full name if you would please.

A. Fred Stitz.

Q. Where do you live, Mr. Stitz?   1

A. In Chicago, Illinois. 373 West Pavon Street.   2

Q. What is your occupation or profession?   3
                                                                4

A. I'm an examiner of questioned documents.   5

Q. What does your work consist of?   6

A. I examine disputed documents and make reports as to 7
their genuineness. I examine typewriting and matters of 8
disputed interlineations, erasures, and deal with matters of 9
papers, pens, and inks.   10

Q. How long have you had this profession?   11
                                                                12

A. I have been doing this work since 1940.   13

Q. Do you devote all of your time to this work?   14

A. Yes, I do.   15
                                                                16

Q. Have you ever testified before in a court regarding 17
questioned documents?   18

A. I have testified in forty-two of the states and in Cana- 19
da.   20

Q. Have you had any special study to prepare yourself to 21
be an examiner of questioned documents?   22
                                                                  23

A. Oh, yes. I have read all of the texts on the subject of 24
questioned documents and on the related subjects that I men- 25
tioned. I have studied microscopy, inks and their manufac- 26
ture, paper and paper manufacturing, and photography. I 27
have all the necessary equipment. I have an office and a 28
laboratory for my work and I exchange ideas constantly with 29
other experts in this field.   30

Q. Where is your office and lab?   31

A. 662 North Pennell Street, Chicago.   32

Q. You are able, I take it, to compare handwriting of 33
known origin with handwriting of unknown origin and form a 34
conclusion or opinion as to whether they were written by the 35
same person?   36
                                                                  37

A. That's right.   38

Q. Then I will show you what has been marked Prosecu- 39
tion Exhibit Number 3 for Identification.   40

BY DEFENSE COUNSEL: Just a moment, if you please. 41
May I ask this witness a few questions, Your Honor?   42
                                                                     43

THE COURT: With respect to his qualifications?   44

BY DEFENSE COUNSEL: Yes.   45

THE COURT: You may proceed.   46

BY DEFENSE COUNSEL: Mr. Stitz, have you attended 47
any special schools that teach one how to become a handwrit- 48
ing expert?   49
                                                                  50

A. No, I don't think there are any.   51

Q. So you have no special degrees or certificates that reflect special study in a college or university?

A. No, I do not.

Q. Your supposed expertise is simply based on your own experience in examining documents, is that it?

A. That's right, and my reading and so on.

BY DEFENSE COUNSEL: Well, we have no strong objection to this witness testifying, Your Honor.

THE COURT: If that is supposed to be some kind of objection, counsel, it is overruled.

Example b.:

Q. What is your name, sir?

A. John V. DeMarco.

Q. Where do you live?

A. At the Belmont Hotel here in the city.

Q. What is your occupation or profession, sir?

A. I am a physician and toxicologist.

Q. Of what medical school are you a graduate, Doctor?

A. The Northwestern University Medical School in Chicago.

Q. When did you graduate?

A. In 1930.

Q. What was your undergraduate school?

A. The University of Michigan.

Q. What was your major field of study at Michigan?

A. Chemistry.

Q. After your graduation from medical school, what did you do?

A. I was with the Health Department in Chicago for three years and then in 1933 I became the toxicologist for the Coroner's Office in Chicago.

Q. Do you hold that position today?

A. Yes, I have held it continuously since 1933, with time off for military service during World War II.

Q. What have your duties been as a toxicologist?

A. My duties involve the examination of organs for the presence of poisons and research concerning poisons. I have conducted many post mortems.

Q. About how many since 1933?

A. Probably around ten thousand. And I examined the organs of many people on whom I did not do a post mortem.

Q. Do you hold any teaching positions at the present time?

A. Yes, I am Professor of Toxicology at Rush Medical College in Chicago.

Q. How long have you had this professorship, Doctor DeMarco?

A. Since 1947.

Q. Have you ever written anything on the subject of toxicology?

A. Yes, I've written a number of articles on poisons and their detection. I have written chapters that were included in texts on toxicology, and I have delivered papers at professional seminars.

Q. Would you describe toxicology for us, Doctor?

A. It is the science that deals with toxic substances, poisons, their origin, and their detection by chemical or other means.

Q. When you speak of a poison, what precisely do you mean?

THE COURT: Just a moment, counsel. Are you now going to get into this witness's substantive testimony?

BY EXAMINING COUNSEL: That was my intention, Your Honor.

THE COURT: Let me inquire of opposing counsel whether he desires at this point to examine further into the witness's qualifications.

BY OPPOSING COUNSEL: We reserve the right to cross-examine Doctor DeMarco on the substance of his testimony, Your Honor, but we do not dispute his qualifications as an expert in the field of toxicology.

THE COURT: Very well. You may proceed, counsel.

BY EXAMINING COUNSEL: What is it that you mean when you talk of a poison, Doctor?

A. A poison is a substance which, when taken into the system, is capable of seriously affecting health adversely or of causing death, and that's its principal action.

Stipulating to the Witness's Expertise. Sometimes counsel, realizing that the opposing side's witness has impressive credentials that will probably awe the jurors, will try to prevent the jury from hearing them described. Counsel does this by offering to stipulate (agree) that the witness is qualified to testify as an expert, thereby magnanimously saving opposing counsel from having to elicit the witness's full catalogue of credentials through the questioning process. This gambit is not usually successful. Opposing counsel is not obligated to accept an offered stipulation unless it gives him everything that he would be entitled to prove with evidence. And counsel is entitled to prove his expert witness's qualifications in some detail; a mere stipulation that he is qualified to testify does not give the side offering him anything to which it is entitled. Experienced counsel will know that it is important to show the details of his expert's training and experience in any case in which there is to be a battle of experts. This is so because the jurors must decide what weight to attach to the testimony of each side's experts. They can rationally apportion evidentiary weight only if they are in a position to compare the witnesses' relative qualifications.

Example:

Q. Doctor, will you give the jury your full name?

A. Jeffrey Eddy.

Q. Where do you reside?

A. 820 West Addison Street, Chicago, Illinois.

Q. What is your profession?

A. Physician and surgeon.

Q. What specialty, if any, have you made in your medical practice?

A. I specialize in neurosurgery.

Q. We'll come back to that, Doctor Eddy. How long have you practiced medicine?

A. Thirteen years this coming April.

Q. Of what medical school are you a graduate?

A. Northwestern University Medical School in Chicago.

Q. Have you done any postgraduate work?

BY OPPOSING COUNSEL: Pardon me just a moment. We would be willing to stipulate that Doctor Eddy is a qualified neurosurgeon and can testify here.

BY EXAMINING COUNSEL: We would rather make our proof on this, Your Honor. The jurors are entitled to hear his training and his experience in medicine and neurosurgery. They have to decide what weight to give his testimony, possibly in comparison with the testimony of an expert called by the other side, and they can't very well make that decision without hearing his qualifications.

THE COURT: It might speed things up a little if you accepted the stipulation, counsel, but I can't force you to do so. You may proceed to establish the witness's qualifications. Just don't get into the most minute details.

BY EXAMINING COUNSEL: Very well, Your Honor. We'll limit ourselves to the most important things. Doctor Eddy, have you had some postgraduate training?

BY OPPOSING COUNSEL: In view of our offer to stipulate, we object to counsel's going into this, Your Honor.

THE COURT: Overruled.

Sources of the Expert Witness's Data. Four sources of information are open to the expert witness in the formation of his or her opinions.

(1) The expert witness can express an opinion or conclusion based on facts personally observed by him, as occurs in the case of a medical

examiner who renders a conclusion concerning cause of death on the basis of data clinically observed. (Such an expert can take into account facts communicated to him by another expert. For example, the medical examiner can base his opinion in part on the report of an X-ray technician. If the data upon which the expert bases his opinion or inference are of a type reasonably relied on by experts in the field when forming opinions or inferences on the subject in question, the data need not themselves be admissible in evidence through the expert.)

(2) An expert witness who has been present in the courtroom can base an opinion on the evidence adduced if that evidence is not in conflict. (An expert will not be permitted to weigh conflicting evidence since, unbeknownst to anyone, he might accord it a weight different from that given it by the jurors.)

(3) In some jurisdictions, notably the federal and those state jurisdictions that have adopted Rule 703 of the Federal Rules of Evidence, an expert witness can base his or her opinion on data made known to him/her in *advance* of the trial or hearing. Furthermore, the data thus conveyed to the expert need not itself be received in evidence and, even beyond that, need not necessarily be legally admissible. All that is required under rules such as Federal Rule of Evidence 703 is that the inadmissible evidence relied on by the expert have been of "a type reasonably relied upon by experts in the particular field in forming opinions or inferences upon the subject." * * *

(4) An expert witness can base an opinion on data conveyed to him by means of a hypothetical question that is drawn from the evidence introduced during the trial. * * *

Efforts to Eliminate the Hypothetical Question. Obviously, the hypothetical question is often awkward and hypertechnical. It is fraught with possibilities of reversible error. Hypothetical questions can be extremely time-consuming and they are frequently confusing to jurors. More often than not they are used by counsel to make an extra summation in the middle of the case. Although counsel may think there is some advantage in getting this opportunity to summarize the evidence far in advance of closing arguments, it is more likely that he is putting the jurors to sleep. Still, there are lawyers who believe that the hypothetical question represents the best method yet devised for extracting helpful opinions from an expert witness who is not directly familiar with the facts of the case.

Efforts are occasionally made to do away with the necessity for using hypothetical questions. For example, Rule 705 of the RCP Federal Rules of Evidence would provide that an expert can testify in terms of opinion "without prior disclosure of the underlying facts or data." The major change intended to be accomplished by this language is the elimination of the necessity for the hypothetical question in eliciting expert testimony. Under Rule 705 examining counsel does not have to disclose underlying facts to his or her expert witness by means of a hypothetical question posed in open court as a preliminary to his or her opinion. The necessary data can be conveyed to the expert prior to his direct examination and it need not be disclosed during that examination. Of course, opposing counsel can cross-examine the expert about the data on which his opinion testimony is based.

* * *

Court-Appointed Experts. Ever since 1946 there has been a comprehensive federal procedure for court-appointed experts and many states have similar procedures. A federal trial judge can order the accused or the Government, or both, to show cause why expert witnesses should not be appointed and can request the parties to submit the names of possible witnesses. The judge can either appoint experts agreed upon by the parties or can appoint experts of his own selection. A court-appointed expert is informed of his or her duties by the judge, either in writing or at a conference at which the parties have an opportunity to take part. A court-appointed expert will inform the parties of his or her findings and can thereafter be called to the stand by the trial judge or any party to give testimony. Court-appointed experts are subject to full cross-examination by all parties.

Experts appointed by the trial court are most commonly encountered in cases in which it is suggested either that the accused was legally insane at the time of the offense charged or that the accused is presently incompetent to stand trial because of his inability to comprehend the proceedings and cooperate with his defense counsel. In such situations the trial court may appoint one or more psychiatrists to examine the accused and report.

The use of court-appointed experts occasionally avoids the frustrating phenomenon known as the battle of experts. Both sides in criminal and civil cases alike will shop for experts who are receptive to the position being taken by the side retaining them. Furthermore, some experts are in fact venal; one often hears remarks about "the best expert witness money can buy." And many reputable experts are unwilling to involve themselves in litigation. So, although the suggestion is occasionally made that court-appointed experts take on an aura of infallibility which they may not deserve, the trend is increasingly to provide for their use. The very availability of this appointment procedure reduces the need for resorting to it. This is because the mere possibility that the trial judge *might* appoint an objective, disinterested expert in a given case exerts a sobering influence on a party's expert and on the lawyer who is making use of his services.

Impeachment of Expert Witnesses. Aside from attacking his qualifications and disinterestedness or the thoroughness and competence of his investigation, there are two commonly encountered methods of attacking or impeaching an expert witness's opinion. They involve (1) contradictory material in authoritative publications in the field and (2) alteration of the facts of a hypothetical question put to the witness during his direct examination.

1. An expert witness can be confronted, on cross-examination, with contradictory material from authoritative published works in the pertinent field of expertise. In most jurisdictions it is not essential that the witness have relied on the particular treatise or other items of

literature in forming the conclusions given in his direct examination, although this was once a common requirement.

Example:

BY THE PROSECUTING ATTORNEY: Dr. Faust, you insisted in your direct testimony earlier this afternoon that a person who is a manic depressive may have a propensity for committing murder or assault to murder, didn't you?

A.   Well, "insist" is a pretty strong word but that's what I said.

Q.   And you believe your statement to be correct?   You think it is medically and physically sound?

A.   Certainly I do.

Q.   Dr. Faust, at any given time a manic depressive can be in either the manic or exhilarated phase or the depressive, the subdued or depressed phase of the psychosis, can he not?

A.   That's true.

Q.   Would your statement about a propensity to commit violent acts be as true of a person in the depressive state as it would be of a person who was in a manic state?

A.   I think so, yes.

Q.   Do other psychiatrists agree with your position in this respect?

A.   I don't know specifically but I would presume so.   My position is the correct one.

Q.   I see.   Do you know Dr. Carl S. Milcher's work entitled *The Murderer's Mind?*

A.   I know of it.   Everyone does.

Q.   Is Dr. Milcher a recognized authority on the psychotic condition of persons who have committed murder?

A.   I would say so.   He is a distinguished psychiatrist.

Q.   And has done a great deal of work in this area?

A.   Yes.

Q.   Did you in any way rely on Dr. Milcher's work in forming your opinions regarding the accused in this case? [This question, although not required in a number of jurisdictions, is usually asked anyway.]

A.   I may have unconsciously.   His work is a part of the fund of knowledge that I carry around in my head.

Q.   Dr. Faust, I hand you a copy of Dr. Milcher's book, to page 492.   On that page Dr. Milcher is discussing the manic depressive state, is he not?   Take your time and look at it, Dr. Faust, and then you can answer.

A.   Yes, he describes the state here.

Q. He mentions there that a person in the manic phase may have a propensity for murder or assault to murder, doesn't he?

A. Yes, he does.

Q. And Dr. Milcher is a widely recognized expert, is he not?

A. I said so.

Q. Yes, you did. Now look at the last full sentence on page 492 of Dr. Milcher's book. I want you to read that sentence to the court and jury. You can read it over to yourself first, if you want to, but then read it to the members of the jury, loud and clear.

A. [Reading.] "The depressive aspect of the illness manifests itself more commonly in suicide."

BY THE PROSECUTING ATTORNEY: Thank you, sir. That will be all.

2. Examining counsel will frequently omit certain facts from a hypothetical question put to his expert witness on direct examination. It is entirely permissible for opposing counsel to inquire whether consideration of the omitted facts would have an impact on the witness's opinion.

Example:

BY THE PROSECUTING ATTORNEY: Doctor Faust, if you were requested to assume these additional facts, which were not mentioned by defense counsel in his hypothetical question to you, namely [the omitted facts are recounted], would your opinion remain the same?

A. No, it wouldn't.

Q. What would your opinion be if we include those facts, Doctor?

A. [The witness gives his revised opinion.]

Sometimes facts included in a hypothetical question are later disproved by the evidence. In this situation the expert witness will be asked on cross-examination whether his conclusion would remain the same if those facts were eliminated from the hypothetical question.

Example:

BY THE PROSECUTING ATTORNEY: Doctor Faust, would your response to the hypothetical question have been different if in putting the question to you defense counsel had left out of consideration the statement that the blood found under the left shoulder was clotted?

A. My answer would have been different, yes.

* * *

WALTZ & INBAU, MEDICAL JURISPRUDENCE
54–56 (1971).*
[Footnotes omitted.]

THE REQUIREMENT OF EXPERT TESTIMONY

The plaintiff in a medical malpractice action is ordinarily required to produce, in support of his claim, the testimony of qualified medical experts. This is true, as we have earlier said, because the technical aspects of his claim will ordinarily be far beyond the competence of the lay jurors whose duty it is to assess the defendant doctor's conduct. The plaintiff, himself a layman in most instances, is not free simply to enter the courtroom, announce under oath that the defendant surgeon amputated his leg instead of saving it, and then request the jury to find the surgeon negligent.

The jurors, possessing no special expertise in the relevant field, are incapable of judging whether the facts described by the plaintiff, even assuming an accurate narration by him, add up to negligent conduct. And the plaintiff himself is incompetent to supply guidance; he, too, lacks the training and experience that would qualify him to characterize the defendant's conduct. Unless the facts in our hypothetical amputation case spoke for themselves and unmistakably pointed to malpractice (the defendant, although operating in a fully equipped hospital, unaccountably removed plaintiff's leg with a dull ax), the judge would direct a verdict in defendant's favor immediately after the plaintiff's presentation of evidence. The judge would say that there had been a failure of proof on the issue of negligence, as to which the plaintiff had the burden of proof. Since the mere filing of a lawsuit, unsupported at trial by any probative evidence, does not entitle one to the payment of damages, the plaintiff here must lose. The plaintiff could hope to prevail only if he came to court backed by one or more qualified expert witnesses.

There is nothing unique about the requirement of expert testimony in medical malpractice cases. All sorts of lawsuits involve technical issues that exceed the competence of lay witnesses and lay jurors. A successful criminal prosecution may depend on the testimony of a firearms identification expert, a fingerprint expert, a handwriting expert, a pathologist, and a couple of psychiatrists. Many types of civil suits other than malpractice cases may call forth an array of essential experts: mechanical or aeronautical engineers and metallurgists in a case involving an airplane that allegedly crashed as a consequence of metal fatigue in the wing structure; pathologists in a product liability case against a food processor (was the corn borer that slipped into defendant's canned corn truly toxic?); handwriting experts in a will contest; accountants, entomologists, civil engineers—the catalog of potentially vital expert witnesses in civil cases goes on and on. It is so lengthy a list because lawsuits so often involve esoteric issues which a jury, unaided, could not possibly resolve on any basis other than guesswork. To the extent that it can, the Anglo-American system of justice prohibits verdicts having baseless speculation as their only support. The requirement of expert testimony on technical issues is one designed to avoid guesswork verdicts.

In short, lay jurors have a reasonable basis in their own life experience for deciding that it is negligent—that it poses an unreasonable risk of harm to others—to drive an automobile down the wrong side of the highway at ninety miles an hour; on the other hand, their life experience gives them no basis for assessing, for example, a delicate and difficult surgical procedure.

In our hypothetical malpractice case involving the defendant's amputation of plaintiff's leg, then, the plaintiff would be required to produce qualified medical experts who were prepared (1) to explain the accepted medical procedures and considerations applicable to plaintiff's condition and (2) to express an opinion, based on the proved facts, that the defendant surgeon had unjustifiably failed to follow those procedures or had followed them incompetently. In a less obvious case the plaintiff's experts would have to provide an answer to a third question—that is, whether the defendant's improper conduct probably was the cause of the plaintiff's injury. Indeed, in a less clear case than one involving an amputation it might even be essential that medical experts establish that the plaintiff had in fact suffered injury.

To recapitulate in sequence, in a typical medical malpractice lawsuit the plaintiff must put qualified medical experts on the witness stand to testify (1) that plaintiff suffered an injury that produced the disability and other ill effects claimed by him; (2) that the cause of this injury, or at least a significant contributing cause of it, was the professional services rendered by the defendant doctor; (3) that the standard methods, procedures, and treatments in cases such as plaintiff's were such-and-so; and (4) that defendant's professional conduct toward plaintiff fell below or otherwise unjustifiably departed from the described standard. In steps 1 and 2 the plaintiff's experts are used to establish damage and the causal connection with that damage of defendant's conduct. These two steps are common to every type of personal injury action, whether it be an automobile collision case or a medical malpractice case. Steps 3 and 4 are peculiar to professional negligence cases for they impart content and meaning to the generalized standard of care uniquely applicable to such cases.

STATE v. ODOM

Supreme Court of New Jersey, 1989.
116 N.J. 65, 560 A.2d 1198.

HANDLER, J.

In this criminal appeal, the defendant was convicted of the possession of controlled dangerous substances with the intention to distribute. In the course of the trial, a police officer was qualified as an expert and permitted to testify that in his opinion the facts and circumstances surrounding the possession of the controlled dangerous substance indicated that they were possessed by the defendant not for personal use but with an intent to distribute them. A divided panel of the Appellate Division reversed the conviction. * * *

I.

At approximately 11:30 a.m. on January 31, 1986, Detective Timothy Jordan of the Paterson Police Department executed a search warrant at premises on North Main Street. Detective Jordan, along with Detectives Humphrey and Vaio, entered the attic apartment where they found defendant, Ernest Odom, and C.W., a juvenile. Defendant and C.W. were informed that the detectives were executing a search warrant. In the ensuing search, Detective Humphrey found a clear plastic bag containing eighteen vials of cocaine in crack form in the pillowcase on the bed. No other drugs or drug paraphernalia were found. The defendant was subsequently charged with possession of a controlled dangerous substance, cocaine, and possession of the same drug with intent to distribute.

At trial, the State offered Detective Sergeant Ronald Tierney as an expert in illegal narcotics. Defense counsel objected to the detective testifying, claiming the detective was unqualified because his experience was based on hearsay and his testimony would not assist the jury.

Detective Tierney had been a member of the Paterson Police force for sixteen and one-half years and had served with the narcotics squad for nine and one-half years. He had participated in over 8,000 investigations and had made approximately 4,000 narcotics arrests. The detective had also been involved in over 400 crack investigations and had spoken with crack dealers on over fifty occasions. He had arrested over 100 individuals distributing crack and had executed twenty search warrants where crack and crack paraphernalia were seized. In the past he had been qualified 1,000 times as an expert in trials involving narcotics distribution. The trial court found Detective Tierney qualified to testify as an expert.

The detective then testified about the packaging of crack, its street value, characteristics, and use. He was asked to assume the following facts, as adduced at trial, to be true: that a search warrant was executed, that eighteen vials of crack were found in a pillowcase in a bed in which defendant was found sleeping, that $24.00 was found in the apartment and that no other drug paraphernalia was found. He was asked based on his experiences and such facts if he had an opinion "whether Ernest Odom possessed 18 vials of crack for his own use or possessed them with the intent to distribute them." Defense counsel objected that the detective was incompetent to testify regarding state of mind. The court overruled the objection and the detective was again asked, "Do you have an opinion whether those 18 vials of crack were possessed for personal use or for the purpose of distributing them?" Detective Tierney stated that it was his opinion that the drugs were possessed with an intent to distribute them.

He then explained the basis for his opinion. He detailed the procedures for crack processing and packaging, the estimated value of a vial of crack, and the addictive impact of the drug. The detective also stated that the lack of paraphernalia relating to personal drug use was another factor considered in forming his opinion, noting that the distribution of crack required no paraphernalia.

Subsequently, defendant testified that he was a crack addict. He claimed he purchased all eighteen vials the night before for his personal use. According to defendant, he usually smoked the crack, using two pipes, which he kept in the closet but which were not found when the police searched the apartment. Thereafter, defendant was found guilty as charged.

As noted, the Appellate Division, in a reported decision, reversed defendant's conviction for possession of cocaine with intent to distribute and remanded the matter for a new trial. State v. Odom, 225 N.J. Super. 564, 543 A.2d 88 (1988). The majority found that the detective's opinion regarding defendant's purpose in possessing the drugs was not only unhelpful to the jury but that its probative value was outweighed by its potential for prejudice. The majority concluded that while expert testimony regarding the "use of and traffic in controlled dangerous substances" was permissible, an expert was precluded from expressing an opinion whether the circumstances of a particular case established an intent to distribute because that constituted a determination of the truth of the charge. The dissent, on the other hand, concluded that expert testimony in this area would be helpful to jurors and that a hypothetical question concerning intent was permissible.

II.

We have stated recently that the opinion of a duly-qualified expert may be presented to a jury if it will genuinely assist the jury in comprehending the evidence and determining issues of fact. The admissibility of expert testimony turns not on

> whether the subject matter is common or uncommon or whether many persons or few have knowledge of the matter, but [on] whether the witnesses offered as experts have peculiar knowledge or experience not common to the world which renders their opinions founded on such knowledge or experience any aid to the court or jury in determining the questions at issue.

Thus, the opinion of an expert can be admitted in evidence if it relates to a relevant subject that is beyond the understanding of the average person of ordinary experience, education, and knowledge. If the expert's testimony on such a subject would help the jury understand the evidence presented and determine the facts, it may be used as evidence. The witness offered as an expert must, of course, be suitably qualified and possessed of sufficient specialized knowledge to be able to express such an opinion and to explain the basis of that opinion. Once it is determined that this testimony will genuinely aid the jury, it can be admitted. Our Rules of Evidence codify these principles. Evid.R. 56(2).
* * *

The defendant stresses that the expert's testimony in this case relating to certain underlying facts, such as the quality and quantity of the drugs, their packaging, their estimated value, and addictive characteristics, would have been sufficient to enable the jury to draw its own conclusions concerning the significance of defendant's possession. * * * It simply does not follow, however, that once the expert has revealed his knowledge and given such an explanation of underlying facts, average persons with ordinary backgrounds would then be able to appreciate whether possession of those drugs would be for personal use or for distribution. As stated in *State v. Perez*, "it is unreasonable to assume that the average lay person called to serve as a juror would necessarily know what a person who possessed [a certain quantity of drugs in certain circumstances] was going to do with it." 218 N.J. Super. at 485, 528 A.2d 56. The jury, though enlightened by the expert's explanation of the significance of surrounding facts, does not thereby become expert in the field. Thus, under these circumstances, the subject of intent or purpose in connection with the possession of unlawful drugs is a matter of specialized knowledge of experts. In this case, we are satisfied that the testimony of the expert covered a subject beyond the understanding of average persons and was genuinely helpful to the jury in understanding the evidence presented and determining important issues of fact.

The further criticism of the expert's testimony that was expressed by the majority below is that the opinion presented a view of the criminal guilt of the defendant, and, for that reason, should have been withheld from the jury.

We have repeatedly and consistently recognized that a jury's determination of criminal guilt or innocence is its exclusive responsibility. A jury's verdict of ultimate criminal liability can never be equated simply with its determination of underlying facts; the determination of guilt or innocence transcends the facts on which it is based, no matter how compelling or inexorable those facts may be. The determination of facts that serve to establish guilt or innocence is a function reserved exclusively to the jury. Hence, an expert's testimony that expresses a direct opinion that defendant is guilty of the crime charged is wholly improper. See, e.g., State v. Landeros, 20 N.J. 69, 74, 118 A.2d 521 (1955) (improper for expert, when asked if the defendant was guilty, to reply, "He is as guilty as Mrs. Murphy's pet pig."); see also Shutka v. Pennsylvania R.R. Co., 74 N.J.Super. 381, 401–02, 181 A.2d 400 (App. Div.1962) (court allowed expert opinion regarding the ultimate issue, noting, however, that expert testimony that expressed "his belief as to how the case should be decided" would be improper).

In this case, Detective Tierney did not express an opinion that defendant was guilty of the crime charged. Defendant contends, however, that the opinion went too far because it expressed the view that defendant possessed the drugs with the intent to distribute. The majority agreed that this opinion was improper because it embraced an ultimate issue bearing so directly on guilt that it must be reserved exclusively for the jury.

Perez suggests that an opinion does not go too far as long as it does not express the view that defendant is guilty of the crime charged. The court in *Perez* said that "nowhere do we find the record to indicate that [the expert] stated defendant was guilty of the charges against him." 218 N.J.Super. at 485, 528 A.2d 56. It pointed out that Evidence Rule 56(2) and (3) allows an expert to testify about areas of specialized knowledge if that testimony "will assist the trier of fact to understand the evidence or determine a fact in issue," even if that opinion embraces an ultimate issue to be determined by the jury. ＊ ＊ ＊

We are satisfied in this case that the detective's opinion was based exclusively on the surrounding facts relating to the quantity and packaging of the drugs and their addictive quality, as well as the absence of drug-use paraphernalia; his explanation of these facts was clearly founded on his experience and specialized knowledge as an expert. The conclusion he drew—that possession of these drugs was for the purpose of distribution—was similarly derived from his expertise. We therefore conclude that as long as the expert does not express his opinion of defendant's guilt but simply characterizes defendant's conduct based on the facts in evidence in light of his specialized knowledge, the opinion is not objectionable even though it embraces ultimate issues that the jury must decide.

Moreover, such an opinion is permissible although it is expressed in terms that parallel the language of the statutory offense when that language also constitutes the ordinary parlance or expression of persons in everyday life. See, e.g., State v. Morton, supra, 74 N.J.Super. at 531–32, 181 A.2d 785 (police officer in drunk-driving case allowed to testify that defendant was under the influence of alcohol); State v. Rucker, 46 N.J.Super 162, 166, 134 A.2d 409 (App.Div.) (police experts in gambling prosecution allowed to testify as experts that certain papers were for use in a lottery), certif. denied, 25 N.J. 102 (1987); State v. Smith, 21 N.J. 326, 334, 121 A.2d 729 (1956) (same); State v. Arthur, 70 N.J.L. 425, 57 A. 156 (Sup.Ct.1904) (same). ＊ ＊ ＊

It may be that an expert's opinion is expressed in such a way as to emphasize that the expert believes the defendant is guilty of the crime charged under the statute. This would be impermissible. Thus, in United States v. Scop, 846 F.2d 135, rev'd in part on rehearing, 856 F.2d 5 (2d Cir.1988), the court observed:

> None of our prior cases, however, has allowed testimony similar to [the expert's] repeated use of statutory and regulatory language indicating guilt. For example, telling the jury that a defendant acted as a "steerer" or participated in a narcotics transaction differs from opining that the defendant "possessed narcotics, to wit, heroin, with intent to sell," or "aided and abetted the possession of heroin with intent to sell," the functional equivalent of [the expert's] testimony in a drug case. [Id. at 142.]

Here, an expert in the use and distribution of unlawful drugs can assist the jury by offering his opinion based on special knowledge and experience about the characteristics that serve to identify drugs that are being held for sale or distribution. Further, an expert opinion that the drugs were held for distribution, even though expressed in words that are similar to the statutory definition of the offense, does not rise to the level of an assertion that the defendant committed the crime charged or is guilty of the statutory offense.

In sum, we are satisfied that the expert's opinion in this case was properly admitted. It covered a subject that was within the specialized knowledge of the expert, and thus beyond the understanding of persons

of average knowledge, education, and experience; therefore, it was
reasonably required to assist the jury in understanding the evidence
and determining the facts. Further, although expressed in terms of
ultimate issues of fact, namely, whether drugs were possessed with the
intent to distribute, the expert's opinion did not impermissibly constitute the expression of a view that defendant was guilty of the crime
charged.

III.

This does not mean that the question posed and answered by the
expert in this case was proper. As demonstrated, the opinion was not
objectionable on the grounds that it expressed a view on a subject that
did not require expertise or a view that defendant was guilty of the
crime charged. Nevertheless, there are aspects of the proposed testimony that are problematic. It is therefore important that trial courts and
trial attorneys clearly understand the standards governing such expert
testimony and that juries be carefully instructed on how to consider
and use such testimony in their deliberations.

The majority below in part described such standards. It pointed
out that in proffering the opinion of an expert in this kind of case, the
hypothetical question should be carefully phrased to refer only to the
testimony and evidence adduced

> about the manner of packaging and processing for use or
> distribution, the significance of various quantities and concen-
> trations of narcotics, the roles of various drug paraphernalia,
> characteristics of the drugs themselves, the import of circum-
> stances surrounding possession, the conduct of the possessor
> and the manner in which drugs may be secreted or otherwise
> possessed for personal use or distribution.

[225 N.J.Super. at 573, 543 A.2d 88.]

Once this foundation has been laid, the expert should then be presented
with a hypothetical question through which he or she can advise the
jury of the significance of these facts on the issue of possession. Having
set forth this information in the form of a hypothetical, the expert may
be asked if, based on these assumed facts, he or she has an opinion
whether the drugs were possessed for personal use or for the purpose of
distribution.

It is also essential that the jury be advised, following the presentation of the expert's opinion, of the basis for that opinion. The hypothetical question should clearly indicate that it is the witness' opinion that
is being sought and that that opinion was formed assuming the facts
and circumstances adduced only at trial. It is important that the
witness, and the jury, understand that the opinion cannot be based on
facts that are not in evidence.

In addition, to the extent possible, the expert's answer should avoid
the precise terminology of the statute defining the criminal offense and
its necessary elements. While ordinary expression and plain language
should not be distorted, statutory language should be paraphrased.
Further, the defendant's name should not be used.

Finally, the trial court should carefully instruct the jury on the weight to be accorded to and the assessment of expert opinion testimony. It should be emphasized that the determination of ultimate guilt or innocence is to be made only by the jury.

In this case, the opinion of the expert was expressed in the ordinary language of average persons in everyday life. There was no undue repetition of the language of the statutory offense or references to the statutory offense. One aspect of the question, however, incorporated defendant's name in the hypothetical. Under the circumstances, however, the error is harmless. The jury was aware of defendant's admitted possession of the drugs.

The judgment below is reversed.

UNITED STATES v. SCOP

United States Court of Appeals, Second Circuit, 1988.
846 F.2d 135.

WINTER, Circuit Judge:

In 1980 and 1981, appellants Alan Scop, Raphael Bloom, Herbert Stone and Jack Ringer were variously involved in the initial offering and subsequent trading of the stock of an automobile dealership. Each was indicted for mail fraud in violation of 18 U.S.C. § 1341 (1982), securities fraud in violation of Section 10(b) of the Securities Exchange Act of 1934, 15 U.S.C. § 78j(b) (1982), and conspiracy to commit those offenses in violation of 18 U.S.C. § 371 (1982).[1] Appellants Bloom and Stone were also charged with making false declarations before a grand jury in violation of 18 U.S.C. § 1623 (1982). After a jury trial before Judge Pollack, appellants were convicted on all counts.

Several investors in the dealership's stock testified at trial, but the government's case was based primarily upon the testimony of a co-conspirator who testified pursuant to a plea agreement and upon that of a government investigator who testified as an expert witness. On appeal, appellants argue inter alia that their mail fraud, securities fraud and conspiracy convictions are time-barred and that the government's expert witness was wrongly allowed to give opinions that embodied legal conclusions and were based upon his assessment of the credibility of the testimony of other witnesses.

Because we believe that the expert witness's opinions were inadmissible, we reverse all but the false-declaration convictions. * * *

[Defendants were investors and traders in the stock of European Auto Classics (EAC). The prosecution's evidence indicated that they became involved in a scheme with one Sarcinelli to inflate the price of the stock. Sarcinelli eventually turned against the defendants and

1. The mail fraud statute, 18 U.S.C. § 1341, prohibits the use of the mails for the purpose of executing "any scheme or artifice to defraud." Section 10(b), 15 U.S.C. § 78j(b), outlaws the use of "any manipulative or deceptive device or contrivance in contravention" of rules promulgated by the Securities and Exchange Commission in connection with the purchase and sale of securities. The relevant SEC rule is Rule 10b–5, 17 C.F.R. § 240.10b–5 (1987), which makes unlawful the use of "manipulative and deceptive devices" in connection with the purchase and sale of any securities. * * *

became a government witness. Part of the scheme was described in his testimony as follows:]

Sarcinelli and his associates soon began bringing in customers for the stock and setting up "matched orders" or "matched trades" to be executed by Scop, Stone and Bloom. These "matched orders" involved Sarcinelli covering "both sides" of a transaction by providing the buyer, seller and price. Nevertheless, the stock price did not move as he had expected, reaching a price of no more than six cents per share. By late August or early September, Sarcinelli began to suspect that one of his partners was "back dooring" him by selling the stock on the open market, thereby undermining the scheme to control the stock's price. Sarcinelli severed all involvement in the scheme in November 1980.

After Sarcinelli withdrew, attempts to inflate the price of the stock appear to have ceased, and the stock generally declined, eventually becoming worthless. * * *

Whitten's Expert Testimony

The government called Stanley Whitten, the chief investigator for the SEC regional office in Chicago, as its final witness. Whitten had been a stockbroker for eight years prior to joining the SEC as an investigator in its Enforcement Division in 1974. He had spent over one thousand hours during four years of working on the present case and had interviewed approximately seventy witnesses. He had also assisted in the preparation of the indictment.

Whitten did not testify at trial as a witness with personal knowledge of relevant events. Claiming to be an expert in securities trading practices, he purported to base his testimony not on information obtained from his four-year investigation, but solely on the testimony and documentary evidence introduced at trial.

Whitten was allowed to answer over defense objections a question concerning his opinion as to whether there was a scheme to defraud investors in EAC stock from 1979 to 1982. He answered, "It is my opinion that the stock of European Auto Classics was manipulated and that certain individuals were active participants and material participants in the manipulation of that stock. And that these individuals engaged in a manipulative and fraudulent scheme in furtherance of that manipulation." Whitten consciously used the same formulation throughout his testimony. For example, when asked to name the "participants" in the scheme and the roles that they played, he corrected himself in mid-sentence to include the same elements in his answer: "I believe that the role at the inception, in terms of the participants and the manipulation—excuse me, the fraudulent manipulative practices that were engaged in. . . ." He also repeatedly described the defendants as "active participants" and "material participants" in the manipulation of EAC stock. On cross-examination Whitten acknowledged that his positive assessment of the testimony of the government's witnesses, including Sarcinelli, was a basis for his opinions. * * *

We agree with defendants that Whitten's repeated statements embodying legal conclusions exceeded the permissible scope of opinion testimony under the Federal Rules of Evidence. It is true that Fed.R. Evid. 704 states that "testimony in the form of an opinion or inference

otherwise admissible is not objectionable because it embraces an ultimate issue to be decided by the trier of fact."   However, Rule 704 was
not intended to allow experts to offer opinions embodying legal conclusions. [Here the court set forth the Advisory Committee's Note to Rule
704. See Appendix B.]

Had Whitten merely testified that controlled buying and selling of
the kind alleged here can create artificial price levels to lure outside
investors, no sustainable objection could have been made.   Instead,
however, Whitten made no attempt to couch the opinion testimony at
issue in even conclusory factual statements but drew directly upon the
language of the statute and accompanying regulations concerning "manipulation" and "fraud". See supra note 1. In essence, his opinions
were legal conclusions that were highly prejudicial and went well
beyond his province as an expert in securities trading.   Moreover,
because his opinions were calculated to "invade the province of the
court to determine the applicable law and to instruct the jury as to that
law," FAA v. Landy, 705 F.2d 624, 632 (2d Cir.), cert. denied, 464 U.S.
895, 104 S.Ct. 243, 78 L.Ed.2d 232 (1983), they could not have been
helpful to the jury in carrying out its legitimate functions.   "The
admission of such testimony would give the appearance that the court
was shifting to witnesses the responsibility to decide the case."   Marx &
Co. v. Diners' Club, Inc., 550 F.2d 505, 510 (2d Cir.) (citation omitted),
cert. denied, 434 U.S. 861, 98 S.Ct. 188, 54 L.Ed.2d 134 (1977).   "It is not
for witnesses to instruct the jury as to applicable principles of law, but
for the judge." Id. at 509–10; see also Torres v. County of Oakland, 758
F.2d 147, 150 (6th Cir.1985) ("The problem with testimony containing a
legal conclusion is in conveying the witness' unexpressed, and perhaps
erroneous, legal standards to the jury.").

"Manipulation," "scheme to defraud," and "fraud" are not self-
defining terms but rather have been the subject of diverse judicial
interpretations. *   *   *

The government argues, however, that Whitten's testimony was
proper under three of our recent decisions upholding opinion testimony
by government investigators. *   *   *

None of our prior cases, however, has allowed testimony similar to
Whitten's repeated use of statutory and regulatory language indicating
guilt.   For example, telling the jury that a defendant acted as a
"steerer" or participated in a narcotics transaction differs from opining
that the defendant "possessed narcotics, to wit, heroin, with the intent
to sell," or "aided and abetted the possession of heroin with intent to
sell," the functional equivalent of Whitten's testimony in a drug case.
It is precisely this distinction, between ultimate factual conclusions
that are dispositive of particular issues if believed, e.g., medical causation, and "inadequately explored legal criteria," that is drawn by the
Advisory Committee's Note.

We turn now to a second fatal objection to Whitten's opinion
testimony. On cross-examination, defense counsel brought out that
Whitten's opinions were based on his positive assessment of the trustworthiness and accuracy of the testimony of the government's witnesses, in particular that of Sarcinelli. We believe that expert witnesses

may not offer opinions on relevant events based on their personal assessment of the credibility of another witness's testimony. The credibility of witnesses is exclusively for the determination by the jury, and witnesses may not opine as to the credibility of the testimony of other witnesses at the trial. Even apart from the gross invasion of the province of the jury that Whitten's testimony represented, his only claim to expertise was limited to securities trading and did not encompass the evaluation of testimony. Moreover, even expert witnesses possessed of medical knowledge and skills that relate directly to credibility may not state an opinion as to whether another witness is credible, United States v. Azure, 801 F.2d 336, 340–41 (8th Cir.1986), although such witnesses may be permitted to testify to relevant physical or mental conditions.

It is true that Rule 705 allows an expert to state an opinion without disclosing the basis for it, and that a cross-examiner thus may elect not to probe into whether an expert witness's personal assessment of other witnesses' credibility is, a basis of the opinion. In a sense, therefore, defendants caused Whitten's credibility opinions to be exposed to the jury. Our objection to testimony on credibility is not limited, however, to the prejudicial effect such testimony may have on the jury. Rather, we believe that such testimony not only should be excluded as overly prejudicial but also renders inadmissible any secondary opinion based upon it. Our holding, therefore, is that witness A may not offer an opinion as to relevant facts based on A 's assessment of the trustworthiness or accuracy of witness B where B 's credibility is an issue to be determined by the trier of fact. Were we to rule otherwise, triers of fact would be called upon either to evaluate opinion testimony in ignorance of an important foundation for that opinion or to hear testimony that is otherwise inadmissible and highly prejudicial.

The present case exemplifies this dilemma. On the one hand, the jury could not accurately evaluate Whitten's testimony in ignorance of the fact that it was based in large part on his opinion that Sarcinelli was telling the truth. That judgment went well beyond the witness's purported expertise and vitiated whatever value his testimony had. On the other hand, testimony by one witness concerning the credibility of other testimony is objectionable in light of the presumption that the trier of fact is the best evaluator of credibility. Such testimony is thus not helpful to the trier of fact and is likely to be prejudicial.

Indeed, Whitten's offering of such an opinion was particularly objectionable. He had spent years investigating this case and had reached a conclusion well before trial as to the credibility of the various witnesses and parties. We believe it to be virtually impossible for an investigator so deeply involved in a case to put aside previous judgments regarding the credibility of witnesses and to render de novo judgments on their credibility after listening to the trial. Even if Whitten had such a sharply compartmentalized mind as to allow segregation of his various credibility analyses, such testimony by an investigator and opinions based thereon are clearly prejudicial when offered to a jury. * * * Certainly, the risk of a jury believing that an opinion offered as to credibility by an agent such as Whitten was based on his investigation as a whole rather than solely on evidence adduced at trial is particularly great.

We find nothing in Rule 703 inconsistent with our ruling. That Rule permits inadmissible evidence to be the basis of an expert's opinion where it is of "a type reasonably relied upon by experts in the particular field." As the Advisory Committee's Note makes plain in its illustration of decisions by physicians, the purpose of the rule is to align the law with the extrajudicial "practice of experts" who may base their opinions on technically inadmissible evidence, such as unauthenticated x-rays and oral reports by nurses. The Rule in no way purports to allow witnesses to assess the trustworthiness or accuracy of *testimony given in the same case* or to offer opinions based on such an assessment.

Our ruling thus does not preclude use of an expert such as Whitten to testify to methods by which share prices may be artificially inflated. Simple hypotheticals based on assumptions about testimony in the record can also be posed to the witness in a way that allows his or her opinions to be given but leaves the credibility issues to the jury. Our ruling thus also does not conflict with Rule 703's provision that the "facts or data in the particular case upon which an expert bases an opinion or inference may be thus . . . made known to the expert at . . . the hearing." Fed.R.Evid. 703; see also Fed.R.Evid. 703 Advisory Committee's Note ("expert [may] attend trial and hear the testimony establishing the facts"). Where such facts or data are based on the trial testimony of a witness whose credibility is not in dispute, the expert need not make a judgment about credibility. Where the credibility of the witness is an issue, the expert may assume the truth of his or her trial testimony and thereafter offer an opinion based on the substance of the testimony. There is thus no need for an expert to make, much less state to the jury, an assessment of credibility when offering an opinion based on trial testimony.

[The court concluded that the trial judge's treatment of Whitten's expert testimony was reversible error.]

PIERCE, Circuit Judge, concurring:

I concur in all of Judge Winter's thorough opinion except for the portion discussing the "second fatal objection" to Whitten's expert testimony. A question remains in my mind as to whether Judge Winter's conclusion that "expert witnesses may not offer opinions on relevant events based on their personal assessment of the credibility of another witness's testimony" is consistent with Rules 703 and 705 of the Federal Rules of Evidence and the Advisory Committee Notes. As I understand it, the expert's reliance on the testimony of a witness whose credibility is in question may be brought out on cross-examination and may not affect the foundation for admission of the opinion itself. * * *

INGRAM v. McCUISTON
Supreme Court of North Carolina, 1964.
261 N.C. 392, 134 S.E.2d 705.

Plaintiff instituted this action to recover for personal injuries which she alleges she sustained on March 16, 1961 when the automo-

bile of the defendant collided with the rear of her vehicle on South
Tryon Street in the City of Charlotte. In broad outline the facts are
these:

About 5:00 p.m. plaintiff, operating a Volkswagen, made a left turn
from Woodlawn Road onto Tryon Street, a two-lane roadway at that
point. At the same time, the defendant Linda Lee McCuiston was
approaching this intersection from the north on Tryon Street in a
Dodge automobile owned by her mother, the other defendant. The
distance of the Dodge from the intersection at the time of plaintiff's
entrance is a matter of dispute between the parties. After plaintiff had
proceeded south on Tryon Street in front of the defendant for about two
hundred and sixty feet, she stopped three to four feet behind the last
car in a long line of traffic which was waiting on a red traffic signal at
the Yorkmont Road intersection approximately five hundred and twenty feet ahead. The defendant's Dodge then collided with the rear of
plaintiff's Volkswagen causing it to strike the car immediately in front.
Again the evidence is conflicting. Plaintiff contends she came to a
gradual stop; defendant contends she stopped suddenly. In the two
impacts plaintiff sustained an injury to her neck and back which, in the
opinion of Dr. Robert E. Miller, the orthopedic specialist who treated
her, resulted in a five percent permanent disability to her neck and
thoracic spine. Plaintiff was "a nervous type individual," and at the
time of the collision she was three months pregnant. She contends
that her nervous condition was so aggravated by the collision that in
May 1962 she required psychiatric treatment. Plaintiff's psychiatrist,
Dr. Thomas A. Wright, Jr., discharged her in August 1962 as much
improved. In his opinion the emotional condition he observed in
plaintiff at the time she was referred to him could have been produced
by the automobile accident.

The pleadings and evidence raised issues of negligence, contributory negligence, and damages. The jury answered each in favor of the
plaintiff and awarded her substantial damages. From judgment entered on the verdict the defendants appealed.

SHARP, Justice. To establish the cause of plaintiff's injuries her
counsel propounded to Dr. Miller a hypothetical question which covers
six pages in the record. The defendants' objections to this question,
and to another which incorporated it by reference, were overruled.
The defendants assign these rulings as error and contend that they
were prejudicial because: (1) The question was based on assumed facts
of which there was no evidence; (2) it was based in part on the opinion
of another expert as to the plaintiff's condition; (3) it included assumed
facts totally unnecessary to enable the doctor to form a satisfactory
medical opinion; and (4) it was argumentative and unduly colored the
evidence in plaintiff's favor.

We have concluded that in order to discuss appellants' contentions
intelligibly we are forced to reproduce the hypothetical question here.
Therefore, it follows:

> (1) Q. "Now, Dr. Miller, for the purpose of this hypothetical
> question, assuming that the jury finds the facts to be, from the

evidence, and by its greater weight, that on March 16, 1961, and prior thereto, plaintiff Betty Pat Ingram was in excellent physical, emotional and psychological health, and suffering from no disability whatsoever, being an extremely active person from birth, having been brought up on a farm and actually worked in the fields, having held down a full-time job and being gainfully employed as of March 16, 1961; and that on March 16, 1961, at approximately 4:50 P.M., plaintiff Betty Pat Ingram was operating her husband's car, a 1960 Volkswagen, two-door sedan automobile, proceeding in a westerly direction on Woodlawn Road just inside the city limits of Charlotte, Mecklenburg County, North Carolina, and approaching the intersection of Woodlawn Road and South Tryon Street.

(2) "That the plaintiff *safely* brought her car to a complete stop on Woodlawn Road, in *lawful* obedience to a stop sign erected on said Woodlawn Road, directing traffic to stop completely before entering South Tryon Street, turning either left or right; and

(3) "That the plaintiff, after first having observed that no traffic was approaching on South Tryon Street close enough or in such a manner as to interfere with her safely entering South Tryon Street, and thus after first observing that her actions would not affect the movement of any other vehicle, and having given a *proper signal* of her intention to turn to her left, did then *lawfully* make a left turn, entering South Tryon Street and thereafter proceeding south along South Tryon St., in the right-hand or westerly lane.

(4) "Assuming, further, that the jury should find from the evidence and by its greater weight, that minor defendant Linda Lee McCuiston was operating her mother's 1950 Dodge and traveling in a southerly direction on South Tryon Street, here in Charlotte, also, approaching the intersection of South Tryon Street and Woodlawn Road, at approximately 4:57 P.M.; and

(5) "Further, that at the time mentioned herein, traffic was *extremely heavy* and practically bumper to bumper from the intersection of South Tryon Street and Woodlawn Road all the way down to the intersection of South Tryon Street or York Road and Yorkmont Road, and at which intersection there was located a red traffic light; and

(6) "That, as plaintiff Betty Pat Ingram started her left turn and started proceeding into South Tryon Street, *she saw, and anyone who was properly observant could and should have seen,* that the traffic south of Betty Pat Ingram's vehicle was just barely moving and obviously preparing to make a stop, in obedience to the traffic control device aforementioned; and

(7) "That, after the plaintiff had driven a very few feet south on South Tryon Street, she saw all of the cars, numbering between 15 and 20, south of her from a certain bridge on South Tryon Street all the way to the traffic signal aforementioned come to a complete stop, at which time the plaintiff also began

slowing down and preparing to stop behind the long line of traffic;

(8) "Assuming, further, that the jury should find from the evidence and by its greater weight that when the plaintiff started slowing down and preparing to stop, as aforementioned, the minor defendant, Linda Lee McCuiston, was directly behind the plaintiff's vehicle, some two or three or more car-lengths north, traveling exactly the same direction in the same traffic lane; and

(9) "That the plaintiff had no difficulty in stopping her car and did stop her car three or four feet behind another vehicle operated by a Mr. Guy V. Soule, at a point near the center of the bridge on South Tryon Street, at which time the plaintiff was sitting with the brake pedal on her car completely and fully depressed; and

(10) "That a very short time after the plaintiff stopped her vehicle, *in obedience to the traffic control device and because of the traffic stopped ahead of her,* she observed the minor defendant approaching at a rapid rate of speed, but did not have time to brace herself properly before her car was struck, *and actually had no place to go in her car anyhow;* and that the minor defendant struck the rear of the 1960 Volkswagen with the front of her larger 1950 Dodge, with such force as to drive the plaintiff's automobile forward *and ram the same* into the rear of the vehicle in front of her, despite the locked brakes on the car; and

(11) "Assuming that the jury further finds from the evidence and by its greater weight that at the moment of the first impact, *when the defendant rammed the front of her car into the rear of the car the plaintiff was driving, the* car was suddenly thrown forward, with the result that the body of the plaintiff was thrown back, snapping and whipping her neck and upper portion of her body; and that at the time of the second impact when the front of the plaintiff's car was driven by the force of the defendant's car into the rear of the vehicle operated by Mr. Guy V. Soule, that that impact caused the plaintiff's body to be *sharply* thrown forward, again snapping her neck in the manner of a whip and, likewise, throwing her suddenly and *with great force* forward, at which time her abdomen sustained, a *severe impact* with the steering wheel of the car the plaintiff was driving; and

(12) "Further, assuming the jury should find from the evidence and by its greater weight that the accident and the two impacts aforementioned subjected the plaintiff to a *severe jolt and strain,* the force of the two said impacts producing immediately excruciating pain *and agony,* in the plaintiff's neck, back, shoulder and arms; and

(13) "That at the time of the collision on March 16, 1961, the plaintiff had been pregnant for approximately three and a half months; and

(14) "Assuming, further, that the jury should find from the evidence and by its greater weight, that whereas plaintiff had not suffered any substantial emotional difficulty or disability prior to the accident, that the collision and the separate impact, coupled with the pregnant condition of the plaintiff, proximately caused the plaintiff from the date of the accident through the entire remainder of her pregnancy, up until the child was born on September 2, 1961, or for a period of more than five months, *constant mental anguish and shock,* caused by the *reasonable fear* that her serious personal injuries and the blow to her abdomen might cause her to sustain a miscarriage; and

(15) "Assuming, further, that the jury should find from the evidence and by its greater weight that the impact and the collision aforementioned subjected the plaintiff to *an extremely severe nervous and mental shock,* which permanently, to some extent, injured her nervous and mental systems, causing extensive and *permanent dislocation, psychoneurosis, nervous shock, nervousness, and traumatic neurosis or anxiety neurosis,* with the result that whereas plaintiff had never suffered such prior to the date of the accident, from the date of the accident and even for a considerable period of time after the birth of the plaintiff's baby, on September 2, 1961, the plaintiff suffered extremely from nightmares, worry and constant fear, and became in such a condition, as the result of the impact and the collision aforementioned, that she cried easily, became depressed and subject to suicidal tendencies; and

(16) "That her emotional condition became such that her orthopedic specialist, Dr. Robert E. Miller, referred her to a duly accredited psychiatrist, Dr. Thomas H. Wright, Jr., which psychiatrist diagnosed her condition as being an extremely depressive reaction, with nervous tension and depression greatly intensified since the date of the accident on March 16, 1961; and

(17) "That at the time the psychiatrist first examined the plaintiff in June of 1962, he found the plaintiff to have lost interest in life, being unable to concentrate and at times even not wishing to live; and

(18) "Assuming, further, that the jury finds from the evidence and by its greater weight that the plaintiff is still suffering emotional damage as the proximate result of the collision and the pain and suffering she endured, as above set out; and

(19) "Assuming, further, that from the time of the accident on March 16, 1961, despite extreme pain suffered in the neck, shoulder, back and other portions of the body, it was unsafe and impossible, safely, to take X-rays of the plaintiff, due to

her pregnant condition, which in turn increased her anxiety and mental anguish; and

(20) "Assuming, further, that the jury should find from the evidence and by its greater weight that the plaintiff suffered from an extremely severe sprain of the cervical spine, thoracic spine, and the lumbar spine, and further, that the plaintiff presently is permanently partially disabled to the extent of 5% disability of said cervical spine, thoracic spine and lumbar spine; and

(21) "That the plaintiff, as a proximate result of the accident and the injuries sustained in the accident, has incurred medical expenses to date in the sum of approximately $600.00, including the cost of drugs and prescriptions, the charges to the Miller Clinic, the charges of the psychiatrist, the charges of the Presbyterian [Hospital] and the charges of the x-ray specialist, the charges for a special corrective girdle and for a cervical collar prescribed by the Miller Clinic; and

(22) "That the plaintiff would be likely to incur additional future medical expenses, directly attributable to her condition caused by the injuries; then

(23) "Assuming that the jury finds the above facts to be true, from the evidence and by its greater weight, then do you have an opinion satisfactory to yourself, as to whether or not the accident in which the plaintiff was involved on March 16, 1961, when the plaintiff was stopped in her husband's automobile on South Tryon Street, sitting with her foot on the brake, when the defendant *crashed* into the rear of the plaintiff's vehicle, *with tremendous force* and at a rapid rate of speed, driving the vehicle forward, and actually knocking the front of the plaintiff's vehicle into the rear of another vehicle, with the two separate impacts first knocking the plaintiff's body to the rear and then throwing the plaintiff's body to the front, *striking her abdomen, with a severe blow,* she being then and there three and a half months' pregnant, could or might have produced the severe nervous and mental shock, which injured her nervous and mental system, and further, could or might have produced the extensive and permanent psychoneurosis, nervous shock, nervous and traumatic neurosis, and further, could or might have caused the plaintiff to suffer from the nightmares, worry and constant fear, the depression and being subject to crying easily, and without reason and being subject to suicidal tendencies, and further, could or might have produced the 5% permanent partial disability to the cervical spine, the thoracic spine and the lumbar spine." (Italics ours).

The doctor answered that in his opinion the collision could or might have produced the conditions described.

The next question was:

"Q. Dr. Miller, assuming that the jury finds the facts to be from the evidence and by its greater weight, as set out in the hypothetical question that was just put to you, do you have an opinion satisfactory to yourself as to whether or not the plaintiff has sustained any permanent injury, mentally or emotionally, or whether she presently is still partially disabled from the standpoint of her mental health?

"A. Well, you have got an expert sitting back there in the Court. He can answer that question better than I can. * * * Yes, I have an opinion. The question is, of course, in two parts. One is whether she has permanent partial disability from the emotional status and I think she does. The other is as to the permanent anxiety, and there is some permanency."

Under our system the jury finds the facts and draws the inferences therefrom. The use of the hypothetical question is required if it is to have the benefit of expert opinions upon factual situations of which the experts have no personal knowledge. However, under the adversary method of trial, the hypothetical question has been so abused that criticism of it is now widespread and noted by every authority on evidence. E.g., Stansbury, N.C. Evidence, s. 137 (2d ed. 1963); McCormick on Evidence, s. 16; Ladd, Expert Testimony, 5 Vand.L.Rev. 414, 427. Wigmore has urged that the hypothetical question be abolished: "Its abuses have become so obstructive and nauseous that no remedy short of extirpation will suffice. It is a logical necessity, but a practical incubus; and logic must here be sacrificed. After all, Law (in Mr. Justice Holmes' phrase) is much more than Logic. It is a strange irony that the hypothetical question, which is one of the few truly scientific features of the rules of Evidence, should have become that feature which does most to disgust men of science with the law of Evidence." II Wigmore, Evidence, s. 686 (3d ed. 1940). The comment contained in 2 Jones, Evidence, s. 422 (5th ed. 1958) might well have been directed at the hypothetical question involved in this appeal.

"The most meritorious of the criticisms are that the questions are often slanted for partisan advantage and are often so long and involved as to confuse rather than assist the jury, and, like some appellate court opinions, contain detailed recitals of factual surplusage not essential to support the conclusion reached."

To be competent, a hypothetical question may include only facts which are already in evidence or those which the jury might logically infer therefrom. Jackson v. Stancil, 253 N.C. 291, 116 S.E.2d 817; Stansbury, N.C. Evidence, s. 137 (2d ed. 1963) and cases therein cited. After a careful examination of the record, we find no evidence to support the following facts which were assumed in the hypothetical question involved on this appeal: (Figures in parentheses refer to correspondingly numbered paragraphs of the question.)

1. That the plaintiff "was in excellent physical, emotional, and psychological health," (1). All the evidence indicates that plaintiff had "always had some nervousness." Indeed, she told Dr. Miller that she was "an extremely apprehensive type individual."

2. That as a result of the collision plaintiff "became depressed and subject to suicidal tendencies," (15). There was ample evidence that plaintiff was abnormally depressed after the accident and during her entire pregnancy. However, there is no evidence either that she developed suicidal tendencies or that she lost the desire to live, as paragraph (17) of the question assumes the psychiatrist "found." Depression and suicidal tendencies are not necessarily synonymous.

3. "That the plaintiff presently is permanently partially disabled to the extent of 5% disability of said cervical spine, thoracic spine and lumbar spine," (20), (23). The evidence of such disability related only to the neck and thoracic spine. The doctor testified to no such disability in the lumbar spine.

Defendants' objection that the hypothetical question asked Dr. Miller, an orthopedic surgeon, was based in part upon the opinion of Dr. Wright, a psychiatrist, must also be sustained. Paragraphs (16) and (17) of the question reveal its reference to Dr. Wright's diagnosis of the plaintiff's condition "as being an extremely depressive reaction, with nervous tension and depression greatly intensified since the date of the accident on March 16, 1961." The question does not assume that plaintiff was actually suffering from an extreme depressive reaction; it merely states that Dr. Wright made this diagnosis. The inclusion of such a statement violates the rule in this jurisdiction that the opinion of an expert witness may not be predicated in whole or in part upon the opinions, inferences, or conclusions of other witnesses, whether they be expert or lay, unless their testimony is put to him hypothetically as an assumed fact. State v. David, 222 N.C. 242, 22 S.E.2d 633. When the hypothetical question is properly asked the jury can determine whether the assumed facts have been proven and weigh the opinion of the expert accordingly. An excellent statement of this rule appears in Quimby v. Greenhawk, 166 Md. 335, 340, 171 A. 59, 61:

> "Although a medical expert may base his opinion upon the facts testified to by another expert, the witness may not have submitted to him, as a part of the facts to be considered in the formation of his inference and conclusion, the opinion of such other expert on all or some of the facts to be considered by the witness from whom the answer is sought. To do so would destroy the premises of fact upon which an expert, by reason of his own peculiar technical skill and knowledge, is permitted to give in evidence his own inference and opinion."

The purpose of the first hypothetical question asked Dr. Miller was to elicit his opinion whether the collision on March 16, 1961 could have produced the five percent permanent disability which he found in plaintiff's neck and thoracic spine. The references therein to plaintiff's mental health had no bearing on the query whether the collision might have caused the injury to her neck and thoracic spine.

The purpose of the second question, which incorporated the first, was to find out whether, in his opinion, the plaintiff had sustained any permanent mental or emotional injury. As Dr. Miller himself told counsel, that question might have been more properly addressed to Dr.

Wright, the psychiatrist. Furthermore, when paragraph (15) of the question stated that the collision on March 16, 1961 did proximately cause some "permanent dislocation, psychoneurosis, nervous shock, nervousness, and traumatic neurosis or anxiety neurosis," it assumed the very fact which plaintiff's counsel sought to establish by the doctor's opinion.

The references in the question to plaintiff's childhood on the farm, the route and manner of driving which brought her to Tryon Street immediately before the collision, her consultations with Dr. Wright and his diagnosis of her condition, the fact that her lumbar spine could not be X-rayed because of her pregnancy, and the cost of medical bills in the past and in the future were totally irrelevant to the question of causation. An examination of paragraphs (2), (3), (4), (5), (6), (16), (17), (18), (19), (21), and (22) discloses the validity of defendants' objection to the question on grounds that it contained an assumption of irrelevant facts. Each of the other paragraphs in question contain one or more references to facts which, more succinctly phrased, might be included in a properly stated question.

The italicized words in paragraphs (3), (6), (11), (12), (14), and (23) are examples of the repetitious, slanted, and argumentative words and phrases of which the defendants properly complain. It was no part of the legitimate purpose of the hypothetical question under consideration to establish defendants' negligence; nor are six pages required to state a proper hypothetical question based on the relevant evidence in this case. A shorter question should be no more difficult to frame and it will be easier for the court to rule upon and the jury to understand.

Defendants' assignments of error based on their objections to the hypothetical questions must be sustained. Since the case goes back for a new trial, it is not necessary to consider the other assignments involving questions which may not arise thereon.

New trial.

WALTZ, THE NEW FEDERAL RULES OF EVIDENCE: AN ANALYSIS

112–113 (2d ed. 1975).*

Rule 705 is important and, rightly or wrongly, somewhat controversial. It provides that an expert can testify in terms of opinion "without prior disclosure of the underlying facts or data."

* * *

Rule 705 does not do away with the hypothetical question absolutely; it simply does away with any absolute requirement that a hypothetical be used by counsel. The use of the hypothetical question sometimes has its advantages and it remains to be seen whether trial lawyers will accept with any frequency this Rule's invitation to forego its use.

In any event, Rule 705 probably forecloses successful assignments of error based on a claim that opposing counsel's hypothetical question was incomplete, i.e., did not include all of the "underlying facts or data." In effect, the new rule places on the cross-examiner the burden of eliciting any missing data. Thus Rule 705 should serve to make examining counsel less nervous about the use of hypotheticals; no longer will it be essential to include each and every scrap of arguably pertinent data on pain of a successful objection or reversal.

MAYER v. BAISIER

Appellate Court of Illinois, Fourth District, 1986.
147 Ill.App.3d 150, 100 Ill.Dec. 649, 497 N.E.2d 827.

Justice SPITZ delivered the opinion of the court:

As administrator of the estate of Emil J. Mayer, Dorothy B. Mayer brought this wrongful death action in the circuit court of Sangamon County against defendants, Walter Baisier, Raymond Pearson, and St. John's Hospital (hospital), alleging medical malpractice. During a trial before a jury, defendant Pearson was dismissed following his testimony, on motion by the plaintiff. At the close of plaintiff's case in chief, the remaining two defendants moved for directed verdicts. After hearing arguments on the motions, the trial court directed verdicts in favor of defendant Baisier and defendant hospital. Plaintiff now appeals from the judgment of the circuit court directing a verdict in favor of defendant Baisier, contending that she established a *prima facie* case of medical malpractice against Baisier and, therefore, the trial court's judgment should be reversed. For the following reasons, we affirm the judgment of the trial court.

On October 14, 1977, Emil J. Mayer, the decedent, was admitted to St. John's Hospital in Springfield in order to undergo a "total left hip replacement" operation. On October 18, 1977, Walter Baisier, an orthopedic surgeon, performed the hip-replacement operation on decedent. On December 31, 1977, approximately 10 weeks after his surgery, decedent died as a result of massive sepsis or an overwhelming infection.

Thereafter, on December 31, 1979, plaintiff Dorothy Mayer, as administrator of the decedent's estate, brought a wrongful death action against decedent's internist, Raymond Pearson, his orthopedic surgeon, Walter Baisier, and the hospital for alleged medical malpractice. * * * A jury trial commenced on October 2, 1985. During trial, plaintiff introduced the testimony of six members of the decedent's family and three physicians. Two of the physicians who testified were defendant Pearson, decedent's first internist, and Dr. Victor Lary, the pathologist who performed the decedent's autopsy. * * *

Plaintiff also introduced the deposition testimony of Dr. Theodore Massell, taken May 20, 1982. Dr. Massell, board certified in general surgery, testified as plaintiff's expert witness. His testimony was based exclusively upon his review of decedent's hospital records and autopsy report, which were not offered into evidence.

In Massell's opinion, decedent's first internist, Dr. Pearson, improperly prescribed an anticoagulant medication known as Coumadin, which led to a tremendous hemorrhage into the area of the operation. The hemorrhage then caused a hematoma, or large collection of blood, which led to an abscess or infection at the operative site. He believed that this infection "contributed significantly" to decedent's death. From the records, he determined that Dr. Pearson also prescribed certain antibiotics, thought to possibly produce an infection of the colon known as pseudomembranous enterocolitis. This, he believed, could have contributed to decedent's death.

With respect to defendant Baisier, the orthopedic surgeon, Massell testified that the notations in the hospital records indicated:

> "Dr. Daisier [sic] apparently did not see Mr. Mayer but on one occasion from the 18th of October to his death on the 31st of December. I consider that very definitely and strongly a deviation below the accepted standard of care."

In his opinion, due to Dr. Baisier's "lack of seeing the patient," he failed to discontinue the anticoagulant Coumadin at the proper time. Massell also believed that Dr. Baisier allowed a hemovac, or drainage tube, to be removed from the operative site prematurely, pursuant to pretyped standing orders. Finally, Massell testified that decedent died of an overwhelming infection but that there were "differences in interpretation" as to the origin of the infection. * * *

Dr. Massell's expert testimony, based exclusively upon the decedent's hospital records and autopsy report, was allowed under Federal Rule 703. Through this testimony, plaintiff sought to establish that (1) because the hospital records contained only two notations by Baisier and his nurse following the surgery, then Baisier could have seen the decedent on no other occasions, thereby abandoning decedent; (2) according to the hospital records, Baisier improperly allowed decedent to receive the drug Coumadin and permitted a drainage tube to be removed from the operative site; and (3) assuming these facts to be true, such conduct constituted a deviation from the standard of proper post-operative care and treatment. The trial court ruled that although Massell's testimony regarding the contents of the hospital records was admissible as opinion testimony under Rule 703, it was not substantive evidence of Baisier's negligence.

Plaintiff first contends on appeal that because Massell's testimony as to the contents of the records is "clearly admissible," it should, therefore, be considered substantive evidence, sufficient to establish a *prima facie* case of negligence, pursuant to the holding in Wilson v. Clark (1981), 84 Ill.2d 186, 49 Ill.Dec. 308, 417 N.E.2d 1322. It is plaintiff's position that *Wilson* not only permits an expert to discuss hearsay data in explaining the basis for his opinion, but that *Wilson* also allows this testimony to convert the underlying hearsay data into substantive evidence.

Plaintiff's argument misapprehends the *Wilson* holding. The *Wilson* court held that due to the high degree of reliability of hospital records, an expert may render an opinion based on facts contained in those records, even if the records themselves are not in evidence. In so holding, the *Wilson* court expressly adopted Rule 703 of the Federal Rules of Evidence. The rule states:

> "The facts or data in the particular case upon which an expert bases an opinion or inference may be those perceived by or made known to him at or before the hearing. If of a type reasonably relied upon by experts in the particular field in forming opinions or inferences upon the subject, the facts or data need not be admissible in evidence."

The rationale of the supreme court in adopting Rule 703 was essentially one of promotion of judicial efficiency within the bounds of fairness to the respective parties. The court pointed out the extreme inefficiency of a system requiring an attorney to produce and examine all the authenticating witnesses.

Contrary to plaintiff's assertions, however, the *Wilson* decision "deals with testimony of experts based upon medical records, not with the admission of the records themselves * * *." (Thompson v. Lietz (1981), 95 Ill.App.3d 384, 391, 50 Ill.Dec. 915, 920, 420 N.E.2d 232, 237.) A review of the decisions interpreting *Wilson* reveals that the trial court properly permitted Massell to testify that he relied upon decedent's hospital records in formulating his opinion. Further, the trial court was correct in allowing Massell to testify to the contents of those records in explaining the basis of his opinion. These records, however, compiled by other nontestifying individuals, remained inadmissible hearsay. As one commentator has said, "[t]here is a clear distinction between data that is trustworthy enough to qualify as an exception to the hearsay rule, and data that is inadmissible but usable by experts in arriving at an opinion because it is relied upon by experts in the field." (Spector, People v. Ward: Toward a Reconstruction of Expert Testimony in Illinois, 26 DePaul L.Rev. 284, 291 (1977).) Thus, Massell's reliance upon and testimony regarding certain contents of the hospital records was permissible. Contrary to plaintiff's assertions, however, Massell's testimony did not transform the hospital records, either in whole or in part, into substantively admissible evidence. * * *

Massell's testimony regarding the contents of the hospital records was admissible only for the limited purpose of explaining the basis for his opinion. His testimony did not establish the truth of that hearsay data and did not convert that data into substantive evidence. Accordingly, Massell's testimony cannot be considered substantive proof of Baisier's alleged negligent conduct, and, therefore, is insufficient to establish a *prima facie* case for negligence. * * *

DEPARTMENT OF YOUTH SERVICES v. A JUVENILE

Supreme Judicial Court of Massachusetts, 1986.
398 Mass. 516, 499 N.E.2d 812.

ABRAMS, Justice.

The juvenile is in a secure facility (Butler Center) run by the Department of Youth Services (department). Although he is over eighteen, he is in the department's custody because a jury of six determined that if discharged from the department he "would be physically dangerous to the public because of his mental disorder or abnormality." See G.L. c. 120, §§ 16–20 (1984 ed.). The juvenile appeals, alleging that the statutory provisions under which he is held are unconstitutional; that the judge erred in permitting a psychiatrist to testify because he (the juvenile) was not warned that his statements to the psychiatrist could be used to extend his commitment to the department; that it was error to admit the doctor's opinion because his opinion was based on hearsay reports and conversations and not facts and data admitted in evidence; and that the judge erred in two other rulings. We granted direct appellate review on our own motion. For the reasons stated herein, we conclude there must be a new trial. We therefore reverse and remand for a new trial. * * *

[The court determined that the trial judge committed reversible error in admitting the testimony of a psychiatrist who had interviewed the juvenile. It held that the interview results were inadmissible because the psychiatrist had failed to warn the juvenile that the interview was not confidential and that what he said could be used against him. The court then turned to issues likely to recur at a new trial, including the following:]

During the trial the Commonwealth's expert said that he reviewed the records at the Butler Center which included "family history, psy-chology . . . testing, medical and neurological histories as well as interviews . . . conducted by the [department's] case workers with [the juvenile's] mother." The expert relied on these reports as well as his own interviews with the juvenile. None of the reports was offered in evidence. On appeal, the juvenile asserts that the judge should not have permitted the expert to state his opinion because the expert relied on facts not in evidence.

The settled and traditional rule in Massachusetts is that "[t]he competency of an expert witness to testify to his opinion rests upon unusual knowledge and extraordinary experience, superior to that of ordinary persons. The witness, being qualified in this particular, then may base his opinion upon facts observed by himself or within his own knowledge and testified to by himself or upon facts assumed in the questions put to him and supported either by admitted facts or by the testimony of other witnesses already given or to be given at the trial, or upon facts derived partly from one source and partly from the other." The Commonwealth cites to Proposed Mass.R.Evid. 703 as enlarging the basis for expert opinion. Because there is to be a new trial, we turn to consideration of Proposed Mass.R.Evid. 703.

Proposed Mass.R.Evid. 703 provides: "BASES OF OPINION TES-TIMONY BY EXPERTS The facts or data in the particular case upon which an expert bases an opinion or inference may be those perceived by or made known to him at or before the hearing. If of a type reasonably relied upon by experts in the particular field in forming opinions or inferences upon the subject, the facts or data need not be admissible in evidence." The proposed rule was taken verbatim from Fed.Rule 703.

The first sentence of Proposed Rule 703 tracks our current practice. The second sentence, however, which provides that an expert may base an opinion on facts or data *not admissible in evidence* "[i]f [the evidence is] of a type reasonably relied on by experts in the particular field" radically departs from our current practice. The Federal Advisory Committee states: "[T]he rule is designed to broaden the basis for expert opinions beyond that current in many jurisdictions and to bring the judicial practice into line with the practice of the experts themselves when not in court. Thus a physician in his own practice bases his diagnosis on information from numerous sources and of considerable variety, including statements by patients and relatives, reports and opinions from nurses, technicians and other doctors, hospital records, and X rays. Most of them are admissible in evidence, but only with the expenditure of substantial time in producing and examining various authenticating witnesses. The physician makes life-and-death decisions in reliance upon them. His validation, expertly performed and subject to cross-examination, ought to suffice for judicial purposes." See Advisory Committee's Note to Fed.R.Evid. 703, 28 U.S.C.App. 711 (1982 ed.).

"The proper inquiry is not what the court deems reliable, but what experts in the relevant discipline deem it to be." In re Japanese Elec. Prods., 723 F.2d 238, 277 (3d Cir.1983), cert. granted on other grounds, 471 U.S. 1002, 105 S.Ct. 1863, 85 L.Ed.2d 157 (1985), reversed and remanded sub nom., Matsushita Elec. Indus. Co., Ltd. v. Zenith Radio Corp., ___ U.S. ___, 106 S.Ct. 1348, 89 L.Ed.2d 538 (1986). The rule has been construed broadly by the Federal courts. See, e.g., United States v. Baca, 687 F.2d 1356, 1361 (10th Cir.1982) (expert could give opinion as to defendant's competence based on another doctor's evaluations); United States v. Lawson, 653 F.2d 299, 301–302 (7th Cir.1981) (psychiatrist could base his opinion on staff reports, defendant's interviews with other physicians, information received from United States Marine Corps, reports from the F.B.I. and " 'a large amount of information' furnished by the United States Attorney's Office"); Mannino v. International Mfg. Co., 650 F.2d 846, 853 (6th Cir.1981) (expert in biomechanical engineering could testify on improper design based on literature and information furnished by plaintiff's attorney); United States v. Bilson, 648 F.2d 1238, 1239 (9th Cir.1981) (psychiatrist could base his opinion of defendant's sanity on psychological tests administered by unlicensed psychologist); Bauman v. Centex Corp., 611 F.2d 1115, 1120 (5th Cir.1980) (expert could rely in part on research done in university library); O'Gee v. Dobbs Houses, Inc., 570 F.2d 1084, 1089 (2d Cir.1978) (physician as expert allowed to testify to patient's version of other doctors' opinions, court noted that expert also had reports by two of the other doctors as well as a hospital report). American Universal Ins. Co. v. Falzone, 644 F.2d 65, 66 (1st Cir.1981) (no error to permit expert to consider "contemporaneous and on-the-scene opinions of other investigators on his team . . . as to [their] portion of the investigation"). "The way to combat such evidence is by cross-examination, not claiming foul." Knightsbridge Mktg. Servs., Inc. v. Promociones Y Proyectos, 728 F.2d 572, 576 (1st Cir.1984). The various opinions construing rule 703 also may reflect the fact that in the

Federal courts some of the evidence would be admissible under the residual exceptions for hearsay. See Fed.R.Evid. 803(24) and 804(b)(5).

Federal Rule 703 has been described as raising a "serious potential for abuse." 1983 A.B.A. Sect.Litig., Emerging Problems Under the Federal Rules of Evidence 204, 210. "[B]y permitting experts to base opinions on data not admissible in evidence, Rule 703 encourages litigators to look for experts who will base their opinions, at least in part, on evidence that is otherwise inadmissible, but which the proponents of the experts would like the juries to hear. Whether or not using Rule 703 in this manner is an abuse, it is an increasingly common tactic." Arnolds, Federal Rule of Evidence 703; The Back Door Is Wide Open, 20 Forum 1, 18 (1984). "Rule 703 allows the expert to give a courtroom opinion based on facts or data which may be, although need not be, admissible evidence. The broad language of Rule 703 has, however, created uncertainty concerning the admissibility of material relied upon by the expert. The uncertainty focuses on whether the evidence is received as substantive proof, as a new exception to the hearsay rule, or whether the material may be mentioned only for the limited purpose of demonstrating what data the expert relied upon. This controversy has continued to plague the courts." (Footnotes omitted.) Carlson, Collision Course In Expert Testimony: Limitations On Affirmative Introduction of Underlying Data, 36 U.Fla.L.Rev. 234, 243 (1984). "Rule 703 is an undesignated thirtieth exception to the prohibition against hearsay. It authorizes trial judges to permit an expert witness to base his (or her) opinion testimony on inadmissible data conveyed to the witness outside the courtroom. And some of the cases go a long step farther and allow the expert, on his direct examination, to describe this inadmissible data to the factfinder. That is what is known as a back door and no matter how many limiting instructions you may have, it is an ominously large door." Waltz, Evidence is Dead, Wigmore Obsolescent: Long Live Judicial Discretion.[16] The rule "permits the jury to hear information that would normally be considered improper evidence." Rossi, Modern Evidence and the Expert Witness, 12 Litigation No. 1, 18, 24 (1985).

Because of the problems now arising under rule 703, we are not persuaded we should accept the principles of the proposed rule. We believe, however, that we should take a modest step by permitting an expert to base an opinion on facts or data not in evidence if the facts or data are independently admissible and are a permissible basis for an expert to consider in formulating an opinion. Such a change will eliminate the necessity of producing exhibits and witnesses whose sole function is to construct a proper foundation for the expert's opinion.

If a party believes that an expert is basing an opinion on inadmissible facts or data, the party may request a voir dire to determine the basis of the expert opinion. If the facts or data are admissible and of the sort that experts in that specialty reasonably rely on in forming

---

16. Remarks Delivered to Northwestern University, 23rd Annual Alumni-Faculty Luncheon (September 29, 1983), quoted in Arnolds, Federal Rule of Evidence 703: The Back Door is Wide Open, 20 Forum 1, 5 (1984).

their opinions, then the expert may state that opinion without the facts or data being admitted in evidence. ＊ ＊ ＊

MINNESOTA RULES OF EVIDENCE
As amended effective January 1, 1990.

RULE 703. BASES OF OPINION TESTIMONY BY EXPERTS

(a) The facts or data in the particular case upon which an expert bases an opinion or inference may be those perceived by or made known to the expert at or before the hearing. If of a type reasonably relied upon by experts in the particular field in forming opinions or inferences upon the subject, the facts or data need not be admissible in evidence.

(b) Underlying expert data must be independently admissible in order to be received upon direct examination; provided that when good cause is shown in civil cases and the underlying data is particularly trustworthy, the court may admit the data under this rule for the limited purpose of showing the basis for the expert's opinion. Nothing in this rule restricts admissibility of underlying expert data when inquired into on cross-examination.

UNITED STATES v. KRISTIANSEN
United States Court of Appeals, Eighth Circuit, 1990.
901 F.2d 1463.

HEANEY, Senior Circuit Judge.

Kolby Kristiansen appeals from his conviction for escape from a halfway house facility. He raises two challenges to the conduct of the trial. First, the district court improperly excluded defense questions to an expert under Rule 704(b) while allowing prosecution questions that should have been excluded under the same rule. Second, the prosecution's closing argument was improper. We affirm.

I.

Kolby Kristiansen was transferred to a halfway house on April 18, 1988, prior to an anticipated release from confinement. On June 1, 1988, Kristiansen called the halfway house and informed them that he was sick and unable to return that night. He was told to keep them informed. He called again each of the next two days indicating that he was still ill. He was told to come back in and the authorities would help him get treatment. He failed to do so. On June 6, he was arrested by United States marshals outside his wife's residence. He was charged with escaping from custody. 18 U.S.C.A. § 751(a) (Supp. 1990).

The defense's theory at trial was that Kristiansen was not guilty because he lacked, by reason of mental disease or defect, the willful intent to escape. The defense expert, Dr. Knowles, diagnosed Kristiansen as a cocaine addict and testified that Kristiansen had indicated that he was under the influence of cocaine at the time he failed to return.

Dr. Knowles also testified that Kristiansen was suffering from psychosis, which can cause an individual to fail to appreciate the wrongfulness of their actions.

The prosecution called several witnesses to refute the defense theory. Kristiansen's counselor at the halfway house and a marshal who arrested him testified that they detected no evidence of alcohol or drug use in their encounters with Kristiansen. A second marshal testified that Kristiansen said that "he could have really stayed hidden out or on the run a lot longer if he didn't care for his family." Two expert witnesses for the government testified that Kristiansen had a history of drug abuse but both concluded that he was not delusional. The jury found Kristiansen guilty of escape.

II.

Federal Rule of Evidence 704(b) prohibits mental health experts from offering an opinion as to whether the defendant possessed the required mental state at the time of their crime. During direct examination, the defense attempted to ask Dr. Knowles: "Now, would an individual—would this severe mental disease or defect, which you've testified Mr. Kristiansen has, if an individual has that, affect the individual's ability to appreciate the nature and quality of the wrongfulness of his acts?" The court sustained the prosecution's objection because it felt that including the word "would" in the question asked for an answer that reached the ultimate issue. The defense also wanted to ask Dr. Knowles: "Dr. Knowles, do you have an opinion whether at the time of the commission of the alleged offense in this case, the defendant's judgment was so severely impaired as to render him incapable of appreciating the nature, quality and wrongfulness of his act?" [Trial transcript] at 94–95 (offer of proof). The court did not allow this question. The defense was allowed to ask, however, "Doctor, could the severe mental disease or defect that you have testified with regard to, could that affect the ability of an individual to appreciate the nature or the quality or the wrongfulness of his acts?"

Dr. Knowles also testified that Kristiansen exhibited antisocial behavior. The prosecution asked on cross-examination of Dr. Knowles what antisocial behavior involved. Dr. Knowles indicated that it consisted of a lack of conscience and added, without being prompted:

> Because they are under no compunction to do right or to choose not to do wrong because they don't have that monitoring system that we all possess. So society treats them as being responsible for their behavior because they fail the test that the law has, they don't constitute the type of insanity or psychosis that constitutes a defense but they lack a very significant element of a normal functioning mind, so a sociopath will go through life leaving a path of waste and devastation behind him and yet he is [sic] wholly accountable because he lacks that single element of conscience that saves us from the same tragic consequences.

The prosecution followed up by asking: "So he is legally accountable for his acts as a sociopath?" A. "He is." Defense counsel did not object. During redirect, counsel asked the court if Knowles could be asked the previously disallowed defense questions in light of the cross-examination testimony. He argued that the door had been opened, but the court denied the request without explanation.

We review evidentiary rulings under the abuse of discretion standard. We have interpreted Rule 704(b) to exclude testimony that "specifically comments on the presence or absence of an element of the crime charged, . . . too conclusory to be helpful to the jury." United States v. Gipson, 862 F.2d 714, 716 (8th Cir.1988). We concluded that the trial court in Gipson properly excluded the question, " 'did [Gipson] have the requisite mental state to have willfully or intentionally attempted to escape,' " because it asked "for a mere legal conclusion." We approved asking the expert whether the defendant was suffering from a mental disease or defect at the time the crime was committed. Similarly, in United States v. Dubray, 854 F.2d 1099 (8th Cir.1988), we permitted a doctor to testify that the defendant was not suffering from psychosis at the time of the offense. We reasoned that this testimony related to the defendant's mental state which "has definite implications for the determination of Dubray's legal sanity," but that it did not state a legal conclusion "and did not state an opinion whether Dubray was able to appreciate the wrongfulness of his actions."

Under Gipson and Dubray, the defense clearly could ask whether Kristiansen was suffering from a mental disease or defect at the time of the offense. Just as clearly, the defense could not ask whether Kristiansen was unable to appreciate the nature and quality of his actions. The question the defense asked in its offer of proof was thus properly excluded. The more difficult question is whether the court erred in not permitting the defense to ask whether the mental disease or defect of the type that Kristiansen allegedly had would affect a person's ability to appreciate their actions.

We conclude that the defense should have been permitted to ask this question because it relates to the symptoms and qualities of the disease itself and does not call for an answer that describes Kristiansen's culpability at the time of the crime. Rule 704(b) was not meant to prohibit testimony that describes the qualities of a mental disease. "Under this proposal, expert psychiatric testimony would be limited to presenting and explaining their diagnoses, such as whether the defendant had a severe mental disease or defect and what the characteristics of such a disease or defect, if any, may have been." Comprehensive Crime Control Act of 1984, S.Rep. No. 225, 98th Cong., 2d Sess. 230 (1984). The fact that part of the wording of a question may track the legal test by asking if the disease prevents one suffering from the disease from understanding the nature and quality of an act does not violate the rule. The jury is left to ultimately decide whether the disease was so strongly present that the defendant himself suffered the effect of being unable to appreciate the quality of his act.

The court's error, however, was not prejudicial. The defense was permitted to ask if the mental condition Kristiansen allegedly suffered from "could" cause him to fail to appreciate the nature and quality of his actions. This question is sufficiently close in effect to a question substituting the word "would" that the court's error plainly did not affect the jury's decision. The defense was allowed to elicit testimony that Kristiansen suffered from a mental disease or defect and that the same type of disease or defect could affect his cognitive abilities.

The prosecution's questioning of Dr. Knowles presents a different problem. Asking the doctor if Kristiansen is legally accountable is clearly prohibited by Rule 704(b). Because the defense counsel did not object to this question or to his own witness' voluntary discourse on legal conclusions, we must decide only if it was error for the court not to overrule its previous decision preceding the defense's offer of proof and to allow the defense also to ask a question in violation of Rule 704(b). We hold that it was not error.

The defense counsel made a strategic choice to forego objecting to the prosecution's question and to his witness' testimony in the hopes that the court would allow him the same latitude. Counsel erred. The purpose of Rule 704(b) is to prevent a jury adjudicating an insanity claim from becoming thoroughly confused by medical experts' testimony about the ultimate legal issues. Senate Report at 223, 231. The proper course for the defense was to object to the prosecution's question rather than trying to use it as grounds for further violations of the rule. The district court has an obligation to minimize violations of the rules and was not required to even the playing field where no objection was made. The trial court could properly conclude that granting the request by the defense would be more prejudicial than helpful. Cf. Fed. R.Evid. 403. * * *

EXPANDED USE OF EXPERT WITNESSES
POSES NEW PROBLEMS FOR COUNSEL
The National Law Journal, Dec. 31, 1979.

Recent years have seen a quantum jump in the use of economic and other expert witnesses in complex commercial litigation in the federal courts. Forbes magazine recently commented upon this dramatic growth, and perhaps inferentially conjectured on the reason, observing "if prostitution is the oldest profession, economics may well be the newest." [1]

An example of the Dickensian proportions of this phenomenon is the trial in United States v. IBM Corp. before Chief Judge David Edelstein of the U.S. District Court for Southern District of New York. It began in May 1975 and its end is not yet in sight. The government, which ended its direct case in April 1978, utilized the testimony of four different expert witnesses. IBM is expected to use at least that many, if neither the pending settlement negotiations nor the proceedings to disqualify Chief Judge Edelstein interfere with the progress of the case.

1. Cheerful Days In The Dismal Science, Forbes, Jan. 8, 1979, p. 35.

Three of the government's expert witnesses were economists and the fourth was a computer industry consultant. These witnesses testified for a total period well over three months and comprised about 25 percent of the government's case. The government's principal economist testified for 78 days.

While the IBM case is not typical, other cases before judges, juries and administrative law judges present analogous problems of preparation and cross-examination.

The extensive growth in the use of expert witnesses is due in some considerable part to the liberal treatment afforded expert testimony under the Federal Rules of Evidence and particularly Rule 702.[2] The definition of an expert is broadly defined to include any witness qualified by special "knowledge, skill, experience, training or education," clearly going beyond traditional or restricted definitions of the term. The distinction between "expert" and "skilled" witnesses has been blurred or eliminated.

Unlike some state rules which permit an expert to testify only when such testimony is "necessary" to aid the trier of fact, Rule 702 broadens the ability to utilize such testimony by merely requiring that the testimony of the expert be "helpful" or "assist" the trier of fact in arriving at the truth. Once these rather modest qualifications are met, the expert may well be free to answer hypothetical questions and give a wide range of opinions so long as these statements are within his or her purported area of competence. Rule 704 [3] also removes another arguable limitation by specifically providing that an expert may give opinions on so-called "ultimate issues."

The Federal Rules also present a change from past practice with respect to the predicate or foundation for expert testimony. Under Rule 703 expert testimony need not necessarily be based on personal knowledge of the expert or evidence in the record. So long as there is suitable "indicia of trustworthiness" or "reasonable basis of reliability," an expert is permitted wide latitude as to the materials on which he may base his testimony.

Not surprisingly many practitioners have made wide and effective use of this broad latitude by resorting broadly to phrased "expert opinions" on ultimate issues, often based on little support in a record, to provide essential elements of a case for which little direct proof was available. Conjectural theories of liability or damages may thus assume the dignity of proof when asserted by an expert. Able advocates have, however, been able to respond to these tactics by effective use of

2. Federal Rule of Evidence 702:

If scientific, technical, or other specialized knowledge will assist the trier of fact to understand the evidence or to determine a fact in issue, a witness qualified as an expert by knowledge, skill, experience, training, or education, may testify thereto in the form of an opinion or otherwise.

3. Federal Rule of Evidence 704:

Testimony in the form of an opinion or inference otherwise admissible is not objectionable because it embraces an ultimate issue to be decided by the trier of fact.

discovery and cross-examination to the point where it may well be that the dangers of extensive use of experts can outweigh the advantages.

* * * The discovery devices available to the party confronted with an opponent's expert witness include principally: (1) F.R.Civ.P. Rule 26(b)(4), which generally provides for further discovery of experts as ordered by the court upon motion, and has been widely employed to authorize depositions of experts; (2) Rule 705 of the Federal Rules of Evidence which broadly defines the scope of cross-examination of an expert; and (3) Rule 612 of the Federal Rules of Evidence, which has, in some instances, provided for broad discovery of materials used by an expert to "refresh his memory."

Depositions and production of documents will generally not be granted until such interrogatories have been served. Rule 26(b)(4)(A) does not provide for the production of documents indicating that they can be obtained only upon court order, a matter within the broad discretion of the trial judge.

While the full scope of these discovery devices remains to be developed, it is already clear that Rule 612 will be a valuable tool for counsel who are confronted with an expert. More ominously, Rule 612 represents a frequently unexpected and extreme risk to the party employing the expert. The most important caveat is the danger of an inadvertent waiver of otherwise available privilege or immunity from discovery which is assumed to attach to preliminary factual or legal position papers or summaries.

For example, in preparing a case an attorney will generally find it valuable to work in close association with an expert. Counsel will seek to design a case with an eye toward economic or other theoretical concepts. Legal and economic thesis should be co-ordinated and each can be used to test the other. Because the attorney's work product and the experts analysis can easily become "so interrelated as to become a composite work of both," the attorney, working in such close proximity with the expert who is being prepared to testify runs the risk of losing the protection that present discovery rules generally afford "work product."

A recent series of cases have highlighted the questions as to the scope of Rule 612 [4] and its role in the disclosure of materials related to expert testimony.

A critical aspect of the controversy concerns whether Rule 612 allows for the broad discovery of records and documents that were used by an expert in preparation of testimony at a disposition or trial, or is limited to the discovery of materials actually referred to while testifying.

---

4. Rule provides in part: "* * * if a witness uses a writing to refresh his memory for the purpose of testifying, either (1) while testifying, or (2) before testifying, if the court in its discretion determines it is necessary in the interest of justice, an adverse party is entitled to have the writing produced at the hearing, to inspect it, to cross-examine the witness thereon, and to introduce in evidence those portions which relate to the testimony of the witness * * *."

The literal terms of the rule provide for mandatory disclosure on request of documents actually used to refresh a witness' recollection while testifying. Disclosure of materials consulted before testifying can become available upon application to the court. The scope of the term "before testifying" has been the basis for much of the expansion and uncertainty attendant to the rule. Read broadly it gives the court discretion to require disclosure of all sources of information that the expert used in forming his evaluation. These sources often include documents prepared by, or for, an attorney, that otherwise would probably be immune from disclosure. It then threatens to be the basis of an embarrassing, and substantively damaging, finding of waiver.

Bailey v. Meister Brau, Inc. was an early case dealing with this question. The defendants sought to gain access to documents used by plaintiff's expert at his deposition, which were claimed to be protected by attorney-client privilege. The court held that (a) "counsel is entitled to inspect any writing used by a witness to refresh his recollection," and (b) that any claim of privilege was waived by the manner of use of the otherwise privileged documents. The court concluded that to deny discovery would provide an unfair advantage to the attorney who used the documents to prepare a witness by handicapping the opponent who sought to cross examine the same witness.

Some later cases have limited *Bailey* and the reach of Rule 612 to materials or documents used to refresh recollection *while* testifying. However, a recent line of cases has rather explicitly sought to alert the bar that that Rule 612 can be construed to allow broad access to information and materials seen or used by experts, not necessarily with a direct nexus to testimony, notwithstanding the fact that it might otherwise be exempt from discovery.

In Berkey Photo, Inc. v. Eastman Kodak Co., plaintiff sought, at a deposition ordered by a magistrate under Rule 26, production of all documents used by the defendant's expert, including attorney notebooks which were claimed to be protected as work product. The notebooks had been prepared by counsel for his own use and were made available to aid the expert in his efforts to become familiar with the case. Defense counsel claimed they revealed intimate details of his strategy and efforts.

After an in camera review of the notebooks, and deciding that prior law did not give a clear enough warning of the dangers of waivers of the privilege, District Judge Marvin E. Frankel did not require production of the notebooks. Judge Frankel did indicate that Rule 612 is broad enough and designed to permit "access to those writings which may fairly be said to have an impact upon the testimony of the witness" and counsel working with an expert will henceforth have "powerful reason" to limit what the expert may review. He ruled that in subsequent cases a demand for documents reviewed by an expert should be honored so long as it seeks to "promote the search of credibility and memory" and that attorneys should expect this result when sharing their efforts with the testifying expert.

In Wheeling-Pittsburgh Steel Corp. v. Underwriters Laboratories, the court addressed these same issues and permitted the inspection of an attorney's file labeled "communications with clients" which was taken for review by plaintiff's metallurgical engineer several months earlier and returned the day before his testimony was to be given.

While the court cited *Bailey* and attempted to limit the scope of Rule 612, the decision was clearly premised upon the notion that any "writings which may fairly be said to have an impact upon" the testimony of the witness are discoverable.   The fact that the documents were used to refresh the witness' recollection prior to his testimony rather than during his testimony was deemed to be of no moment.   In addressing the question of privilege, the court held that such use of once privileged material constituted a waiver.

A device which has been employed to avoid some of these pitfalls in complex commercial litigation involves the use of so-called non-testimonial expert witnesses.   Under Rule 26(b)(4)(B) of the Federal Rules of Civil Procedure, discovery of facts known or opinions held by an expert who is not expected to be called as a witness is limited to showings of "exceptional circumstances.[5] "   This test seeks to minimize unfair advantage and to prevent unwarranted free rides on discovery when similar information is sufficiently obtainable.

Therefore, absent "exceptional circumstances," an attorney may generally retain a non-testimonial expert to help him gain an adequate understanding of the complexities of a particular area without running the same risk of disclosure as is involved in the use of testimonial experts.   Bryan v. John Beam Division of FMC Corp. indicates that when an expert testifies as to subject matter also addressed by a non-testimonial expert, a court may impose considerable limitations on the extent to which the particulars of the non-testimonial expert's research or preparation may be uncovered.

In *Bryan,* the court held that reports of non-testifying experts, examined and relied on by a testifying expert but inconsistent with his own * * * testimony, were not admissible even as impeachment evidence "unless the testifying expert based his opinion on the opinion in the examined report or testified directly from the report."   This result obtained, even though the testifying expert relied on data set forth in the reports.   The law and practice in this area await further development.

In sum, * * * practitioners are urged to think long and hard about whether you really want a long and important case to turn on whether a single expert witness can stand up on cross-examination.

Hypotheticals

(1) X is prosecuted for possession of marijuana.   X makes a motion to suppress the marijuana found in his possession on the ground of unreasonable search and seizure.   At the hearing, A, a police officer, testifies that he saw a water pipe through an open window of X's home and then went into the home without a search warrant and made the arrest and seizure.   On direct examina-

5. See FRCP 26(b)(4)(B) at Note 8.

tion A testifies that he was a high school graduate, that he had received police-academy training, that he had taken several academic courses at a college, that he had read numerous textbooks on narcotics, that he had worked with various officers on narcotic cases, that he had testified in narcotic violation cases, that he had seen narcotics used and demonstrated, that he had been working on the narcotics squad for two years; and that the pipe he saw in X's window was similar to a pipe he had seen in connection with other marijuana cases. The prosecutor then asked A for his opinion as to what use was made of the water pipe he observed in X's home. X requests permission to question A on voir dire on the ground that the witness lacks the qualification of an expert witness to testify to an opinion on the use of the water pipe. How should the court rule?

(2) H sues D, a builder, for damages for wrongful death and property loss. H's wife, W, was drowned and H's home was destroyed in a flood. H and W had bought the home, built by D at the foot of a canyon. H's claim of liability of D is that D should have guarded against the danger of flooding by constructing a wall or building the house on a higher foundation. H calls ME, a mechanical engineer, and qualifies ME as an expert by eliciting that he had been trained in hydraulics and hydrology; that he was familiar with the characteristics of flooding in hillside areas; that he had observed construction of several hundred residential developments in hillside areas such as that involved in H's case. On voir dire examination of ME by D, ME testifies that he has had no close involvement in the construction of homes and is unfamiliar with building practices of home builders. H then asks ME to state his opinion as to whether a reasonably prudent builder in the area, taking into account the topography of the area and the location of the house, would have utilized a retaining wall as a portion of the design for the structure. D makes a lack-of-qualification objection to H's question. The trial judge sustains D's objection. Is this correct?

(3) P was injured by using a power rotary lawn mower manufactured by D Mfg. Company. P sues D for damages, claiming that the lawn mower was defectively designed. P calls E, an expert on lawn mowers, to testify that the lawn mower was defectively designed. E states that his opinion is based on (1) articles published in Reader's Digest, Today's Health and consumer-bulletin magazines discussing the great number of injuries occurring from the use of rotary power lawn mowers, and (2) statistical surveys on the same subject in a book entitled, "Accidental Injuries Associated with Rotary Lawn Mowers," published by a department of the federal government. D moves to strike E's testimony on the ground that it is based on improper hearsay matter. The trial judge denies D's motion. Is this a proper ruling?

PART B. SCIENTIFIC AND DEMONSTRATIVE EVIDENCE

GIANNELLI, THE ADMISSIBILITY OF NOVEL SCIENTIFIC EVIDENCE: FRYE v. UNITED STATES, A HALF–CENTURY LATER

80 Colum.L.Rev. 1197, 1203–04 (1980).*

Courts have relied principally on two alternative tests to determine the admissibility of innovative scientific evidence. One approach, often associated with Professor McCormick, treats the validity of the underlying principle and the validity of the technique as aspects of relevancy. If, for example, everyone's voice is not unique, the results of voiceprint analysis will not tend to establish the identity of a speaker. Or, if fear of detection does not produce certain physiological reactions, the results of polygraph examinations will not tend to establish whether the subject of the examination was being deceptive. Similarly, if the principles underlying polygraph examinations and voiceprint identifications are valid but the techniques applying those principles are not valid, evidence derived from those techniques will be irrelevant. Under the relevancy approach, novel scientific evidence is treated the same as other kinds of evidence. Thus, if an expert testifies that an innovative technique is valid, a court could find that evidence derived from that technique is probative. Admissibility, however, would not be automatic. As with all relevant evidence, a court would have discretion to exclude the evidence if the probative value were outweighed by considerations of undue prejudice, misleading the jury, and undue consumption of time.

The admissibility of evidence derived from novel scientific techniques has not always been analyzed according to the relevancy approach. Indeed, at a rather early stage in the use of scientific evidence most courts adopted the standard proposed by *Frye v. United States*, a 1923 decision of the United States Court of Appeals for the D.C. Circuit.

In *Frye* the D.C. Circuit considered the admissibility of polygraph evidence as a case of first impression. In an oft-quoted passage, the court commented:

> Just when a scientific principle or discovery crosses the line between the experimental and demonstrable stages is difficult to define. Somewhere in this twilight zone the evidential force of the principle must be recognized, and while the courts will go a long way in admitting expert testimony deduced from a well-recognized scientific principle or discovery, the thing from which the deduction is made must be sufficiently established to have gained general acceptance in the particular field in which it belongs.

The court went on to hold that the polygraph had "not yet gained such standing and scientific recognition among physiological and psychological authorities."

In effect, *Frye* envisions an evolutionary process leading to the admissibility of scientific evidence. A novel technique must pass through an "experimental" stage in which it is scrutinized by the scientific community. Only after the technique has been tested successfully in this stage and has passed into the "demonstrable" stage will it receive judicial recognition. What is unique about the *Frye* opinion is the standard it establishes for distinguishing between the experimental and demonstrable stages. In contrast to the relevancy approach, it is not enough that a qualified expert, or even several experts, believes that a particular technique has entered the demonstrable stage; *Frye* imposes a special burden—the technique must be *generally accepted by the relevant scientific community*.

UNITED STATES v. PICCINONNA

United States Court of Appeals, Eleventh Circuit (en banc), 1989.
885 F.2d 1529.

FAY, Circuit Judge:

In this case, we revisit the issue of the admissibility at trial of polygraph expert testimony and examination evidence. Julio Piccinonna appeals his conviction on two counts of knowingly making false material statements to a Grand Jury in violation of Title IV of the Organized Crime Control Act of 1970. 18 U.S.C. 1623 (1982). Piccinonna argues that the trial judge erred in refusing to admit the testimony of his polygraph expert and the examination results. Because of the significant progress made in the field of polygraph testing over the past forty years and its increasingly widespread use, we reexamine our per se rule of exclusion and fashion new principles to govern the admissibility of polygraph evidence. Accordingly, we remand the case to the trial court to reconsider the admissibility of Piccinonna's polygraph test results in light of the principles we espouse today.

I. Background

Julio Piccinonna has been in the waste disposal business in South Florida for over twenty-five years. In 1983, a Grand Jury conducted hearings to investigate antitrust violations in the garbage business. The government believed that South Florida firms in the waste disposal business had agreed not to compete for each other's accounts, and to compensate one another when one firm did not adhere to the agreement and took an account from another firm.

Piccinonna was compelled to testify before the Grand Jury pursuant to a grant of immunity. The immunity, however, did not protect Piccinonna from prosecution for perjury committed during his testimony. Piccinonna testified that he had not heard of the agreement between garbage companies to refrain from soliciting each other's accounts and to compensate each other for taking accounts. The Grand Jury, however, also heard testimony from several witnesses involved in the disposal industry who implicated Piccinonna in the garbage industry agreement. On August 1, 1985, Piccinonna was indicted on four counts of perjury.

Prior to trial, Piccinonna requested that the Government stipulate to the admission into evidence of the results of a polygraph test which would be administered subsequently. The Government refused to stipulate to the admission of any testimony regarding the polygraph test or its results. Despite the Government's refusal, George B. Slattery, a licensed polygraph examiner, tested Piccinonna on November 25, 1985. Piccinonna asserted that the expert's report left no doubt that he did not lie when he testified before the Grand Jury. On November 27, 1985, Piccinonna filed a motion with the district court requesting a hearing on the admission of the polygraph testimony. On January 6, 1986, the district court held a hearing on the defendant's motions. Due to the per se rule, which holds polygraph evidence inadmissible in this circuit, the trial judge refused to admit the evidence. * * *

Piccinonna was convicted on two counts of making false material declarations concerning a matter the Grand Jury was investigating. * * * On appeal, Piccinonna urges us to modify our per se rule excluding polygraph evidence to permit its admission in certain circumstances.

II. The Per Se Rule

In federal courts, the admissibility of expert testimony concerning scientific tests or findings is governed by Rule 702 of the Federal Rules of Evidence. Rule 702 provides:

> If scientific, technical, or other specialized knowledge will assist the trier of fact to understand the evidence or to determine a fact in issue, a witness qualified as an expert by knowledge, skill, experience, training or education, may testify thereto in the form of an opinion or otherwise.

Fed.R.Evid. 702. Under this rule, to admit expert testimony the trial judge must determine that the expert testimony will be relevant and will be helpful to the trier of fact. In addition, courts require the proponent of the testimony to show that the principle or technique is generally accepted in the scientific community.

The general acceptance requirement originated in the 1923 case of *Frye v. United States*, 293 F. 1013 (D.C.Cir.1923). *Frye* involved a murder prosecution in which the trial court refused to admit results from a systolic blood pressure test, the precursor of the polygraph. The defendant appealed, arguing that the admissibility of the scientific test results should turn only on the traditional rules of relevancy and helpfulness to the trier of fact. The court of appeals disagreed and imposed the requirement that the area of specialty in which the court receives evidence must have achieved general acceptance in the scientific community. The court stated that "while courts will go a long way in admitting expert testimony deduced from a well-recognized scientific principle or discovery, the thing from which the deduction is made must be sufficiently established to have gained general acceptance in the particular field in which it belongs." The court concluded that the systolic blood pressure test lacked the requisite "standing and scientific recognition among physiological and psychological authorities."

Courts have applied the *Frye* standard to various types of scientific tests, including the polygraph. However, the *Frye* standard has historically been invoked only selectively to other types of expert testimony, and has been applied consistently only in cases where the admissibility of polygraph evidence was at issue. Most courts had little difficulty with the desirability of excluding polygraph evidence and thus, applied the *Frye* standard with little comment. This circuit also has consistently reaffirmed, with little discussion, the inadmissibility of polygraph evidence.

Recently, the application of the *Frye* standard to exclude polygraph evidence has been subject to growing criticism. Since the *Frye* decision,

tremendous advances have been made in polygraph instrumentation
and technique.   Better equipment is being used by more adequately
trained polygraph administrators.   Further, polygraph tests are used
extensively by government agencies.   Field investigative agencies such
as the FBI, the Secret Service, military intelligence and law enforcement agencies use the polygraph.   Thus, even under a strict adherence
to the traditional *Frye* standard, we believe it is no longer accurate to
state categorically that polygraph testing lacks general acceptance for
use in all circumstances.   For this reason, we find it appropriate to
reexamine the per se exclusionary rule and institute a rule more in
keeping with the progress made in the polygraph field.

III.   Differing Approaches to Polygraph Admissibility

Courts excluding polygraph evidence typically rely on three
grounds: 1) the unreliability of the polygraph test, 2) the lack of
standardization of polygraph procedure, and 3) undue impact on the
jury.   Proponents of admitting polygraph evidence have attempted to
rebut these concerns.   With regard to unreliability, proponents stress
the significant advances made in the field of polygraphy.   *   *   *
Further, proponents argue that the lack of standardization is being
addressed and will progressively be resolved as the polygraph establishes itself as a valid scientific test.   Finally, proponents argue that
there is no evidence that jurors are unduly influenced by polygraph
evidence.   In fact, several studies refute the proposition that jurors are
likely to give disproportionate weight to polygraph evidence.

In the wake of new empirical evidence and scholarly opinion which
have undercut many of the traditional arguments against admission of
polygraph evidence, a substantial number of courts have revisited the
admissibility question.   Three roughly identifiable approaches to the
problem have emerged.   First, the traditional approach holds polygraph
evidence inadmissible when offered by either party, either as substantive evidence or as relating to the credibility of a witness.   Second, a
significant number of jurisdictions permit the trial court, in its discretion, to receive polygraph evidence if the parties stipulate to the
evidence's admissibility before the administration of the test and if
certain other conditions are met.   Finally, some courts permit the trial
judge to admit polygraph evidence even in the absence of a stipulation,
but only when special circumstances exist.   In these jurisdictions, the
issue is within the sound discretion of the trial judge.   *   *   *

IV.   Principles for Admissibility

*   *   *

[W]e believe the best approach in this area is one which balances
the need to admit all relevant and reliable evidence against the danger
that the admission of the evidence for a given purpose will be unfairly
prejudicial.   Accordingly we outline two instances where polygraph
evidence may be admitted at trial, which we believe achieve the
necessary balance.

A. *Stipulation*

The first rule governing admissibility of polygraph evidence is one easily applied. Polygraph expert testimony will be admissible in this circuit when both parties stipulate in advance as to the circumstances of the test and as to the scope of its admissibility. The stipulation as to circumstances must indicate that the parties agree on material matters such as the manner in which the test is conducted, the nature of the questions asked, and the identity of the examiner administering the test. The stipulation as to scope of admissibility must indicate the purpose or purposes for which the evidence will be introduced. Where the parties agree to both of these conditions in advance of the polygraph test, evidence of the test results is admissible.

B. *Impeachment or Corroboration*

The second situation in which polygraph evidence may be admitted is when used to impeach or corroborate the testimony of a witness at trial. Admission of polygraph evidence for these purposes is subject to three preliminary conditions. First, the party planning to use the evidence at trial must provide adequate notice to the opposing party that the expert testimony will be offered. Second, polygraph expert testimony by a party will be admissible only if the opposing party was given reasonable opportunity to have its own polygraph expert administer a test covering substantially the same questions. Failure to provide adequate notice or reasonable opportunity for the opposing side to administer its own test is proper grounds for exclusion of the evidence.

Finally, whether used to corroborate or impeach, the admissibility of the polygraph administrator's testimony will be governed by the Federal Rules of Evidence for the admissibility of corroboration or impeachment testimony. For example, Rule 608 limits the use of opinion or reputation evidence to establish the credibility of a witness in the following way: "[E]vidence of truthful character is admissible only after the character of the witness for truthfulness has been attacked by opinion or reputation evidence or otherwise." Thus, evidence that a witness passed a polygraph examination, used to corroborate that witness's in-court testimony, would not be admissible under Rule 608 unless or until the credibility of that witness were first attacked. Even where the above three conditions are met, admission of polygraph evidence for impeachment or corroboration purposes is left entirely to the discretion of the trial judge.

Neither of these two modifications to the per se exclusionary rule should be construed to preempt or limit in any way the trial court's discretion to exclude polygraph expert testimony on other grounds under the Federal Rules of Evidence. Our holding states merely that in the limited circumstances delineated above, the *Frye* general acceptance test does not act as a bar to admission of polygraph evidence as a matter of law. * * * Thus, we agree with the Ninth Circuit "that polygraph evidence should not be admitted, even for limited purposes, unless the trial court has determined that 'the probative value of the polygraph evidence outweighs the potential prejudice and time consumption involved in presenting such evidence.' "

Thus under the Federal Rules of Evidence governing the admissibility of expert testimony, the trial court may exclude polygraph expert testimony because 1) the polygraph examiner's qualifications are unacceptable; 2) the test procedure was unfairly prejudicial or the test was poorly administered; or 3) the questions were irrelevant or improper. The trial judge has wide discretion in this area, and rulings on admissibility will not be reversed unless a clear abuse of discretion is shown.

V. Conclusion

We neither expect nor hope that today's holding will be the final word within our circuit on this increasingly important issue. The advent of new and developing technologies calls for flexibility within the legal system so that the ultimate ends of justice may be served. It is unwise to hold fast to a familiar rule when the basis for that rule ceases to be persuasive. We believe that the science of polygraphy has progressed to a level of acceptance sufficient to allow the use of polygraph evidence in limited circumstances where the danger of unfair prejudice is minimized. We proceed with caution in this area because the reliability of polygraph testing remains a subject of intense scholarly debate. As the field of polygraph testing continues to progress, it may become necessary to reexamine the rules regarding the admissibility of polygraph evidence.

The judgment of conviction is VACATED and the case is REMANDED to the district court for further proceedings consistent with this opinion.

JOHNSON, Circuit Judge, concurring in part and dissenting in part, in which RONEY, Chief Judge, HILL and CLARK, Circuit Judges, join:

I concur with the Court's holding that polygraph evidence should be admissible in this Circuit when both parties stipulate in advance to the circumstances of the test and to the scope of its admissibility, subject to the understanding that such stipulations may be accepted or rejected by the trial judge at his discretion. I dissent, however, from the Court's finding that the polygraph has gained acceptance in the scientific community as a reliable instrument for detecting lies, and from the Court's holding that polygraph evidence is admissible under Fed.R.Evid. 608.

I. POLYGRAPH THEORY

A. *Introduction*

The Court's reasoning begins with the proposition that polygraph technology has reached the point where its accuracy is generally accepted by the scientific community. In fact, the scientific community remains sharply divided on the reliability of the polygraph. U.S. Congress, Office of Technology Assessment, *Scientific Validity of Polygraph Testing: A Research Review and Evaluation—A Technical Memorandum* 43 (1983) [hereinafter *OTA Memorandum*]. Many theorists question the basic assumptions underlying the polygraph: that telling lies is stressful, and that this stress manifests itself in physiological responses which can be recorded on a polygraph.

The polygraph device records the subject's physiological activities (e.g., heart rate, blood pressure, respiration, and perspiration) as he is questioned by a polygraph examiner. Bull, What is the Lie Detection Test? in The Polygraph Test 11–12. There are two major types of polygraph examinations: the "control question test" and the "concealed information test." The control question test is used most frequently in investigating specific incidents. The examiner compares the data corresponding to (a) questions relevant to the crime (b) "control" questions designed to upset the subject but not directly relevant to the crime, and (c) neutral questions. If the subject reacts more strongly to the relevant questions than to the control and neutral questions, then the examiner infers that the subject is lying. There is much debate about the accuracy of control question tests in specific-incident investigations. Raskin, Does Science Support Polygraph Testing, in The Polygraph Test 98–99.

The concealed information test focuses on the fact that only the person involved in the crime could know the answers to certain questions. The examiner presents a series of multiple choice questions concerning the crime while the polygraph machine records the subject's physiological activities. If the subject has relatively strong physiological reactions to the correct alternatives, then the examiner infers that the subject is attempting to conceal information about the crime. The concealed information test assumes that information about the crime is protected, but in fact police often inform all suspects and even the media about the crime.

B. *The Polygraph Is Based On Questionable Assumptions*

Lie detection is based on four assumptions: (1) that individuals cannot control their physiologies and behavior, (2) that specific emotions can be triggered by specific stimuli, (3) that there are specific relationships between the different aspects of behavior (such as what people say, how they behave, and how they respond physiologically), and (4) that there are no differences among people, so that most people will respond similarly.

The assumption that individuals cannot control their physiologies is subject to serious debate. Some theorists argue that individuals can learn to control their physiological responses and that by producing physiological responses at opportune times during the polygraph test these people could portray themselves as truthful when they are not. Ney, Expressing Emotions and Controlling Feelings at 67 ("Jet-fighter pilots learn to control their emotions (and therefore their physiology) in order to operate with maximum efficiency under extreme physical and psychological stress.") These techniques for fooling the polygraph are called countermeasures. Gudjonsson, How to Defeat the Polygraph Tests in The Polygraph Test 126. Little research has been done on the effectiveness of countermeasures in reducing detection of lies, but the results of research that has been done, while conflicting, indicate that countermeasures can be effective. OTA Memorandum at 100–01;

Gudjonsson, How to Defeat the Polygraph Tests at 135 (concluding that use of physical countermeasures (e.g., pressing toes to floor) is effective when the subject has been trained in countermeasures).

Another assumption underlying the polygraph is that specific emotions will be triggered by the act of lying. Some theorists, however, do not believe that emotions are automatically triggered by the presence of such specific stimuli. These theorists see a more indirect causal chain between stimuli and emotion: a person is presented with stimuli, then appraises it, and only then reacts with an emotion, which is based on the person's cognitive appraisal of the stimuli. According to this theory, people can adjust their thinking to "reappraise" the stressful stimuli and create a different emotional reaction than one might expect. Ney, Expressing Emotions and Controlling Feelings 68 ("tell the truth and think of something painful and the truth may appear on the polygraph as a lie"). Of course, there would be no way for an examiner to determine how the subject is appraising the stimuli in his mind.

The third assumption underlying the polygraph is that there are set patterns of physiological responses that reflect dishonesty: changed blood pressure, heart rate, respiration, and perspiration. There is controversy over this proposition in the scientific community. Id. at 70; H.R. Hearing at 51 (statement of John F. Beary, III, M.D.) ("there is no Pinocchio response. If you lie your nose does not grow a half inch longer or some other unique bodily response.")

The fourth assumption underlying the lie detector is that people can be expected to respond to similar stimuli in similar ways. Some researchers maintain, however, that individuals do not respond to stress similarly and that no one index can be used to measure emotions in different individuals. Ney, Expressing Emotions and Controlling Feelings at 71–72; Gudjonsson, How to Defeat the Polygraph Tests 135.

C. *Appellant's Statistics Are Misleading*

Piccinonna claims that "the relevant scientific community" estimates the accuracy of the polygraph to be in the upper-eighty to mid-ninety percent range. This figure is misleading and subject to serious dispute. The polygraph must do two things: correctly identify liars and correctly identify those who are telling the truth.[7] No single figure, therefore, can fully express the accuracy of the polygraph. The Office of Technology Assessment compiled the results of six prior reviews of polygraph research, ten field studies, and fourteen analog studies that the Office of Technology Assessment determined met minimum scientific standards. All of the studies used the control question technique in specific-incident criminal investigation settings. The results were as follows:

Six prior reviews of field studies:

—average accuracy ranged from 64 to 98 percent.

---

7. For example, a polygraph examiner who accused every subject of lying would be 100% accurate at detecting liars. His accuracy at detecting those who are truthful, however, would be unacceptably low.

Ten individual field studies:

—correct guilty detections ranged from 70.6 to 98.6 percent and averaged 86.3 percent;

—correct innocent detections ranged from 12.5 to 94.1 percent and averaged 76 percent;

—false positive rate (innocent persons found deceptive) ranged from 0 to 75 percent and averaged 19.1 percent; and

—false negative rate (guilty persons found nondeceptive) ranged from 0 to 29.4 percent and averaged 10.2 percent.

Fourteen individual analog studies:

—correct guilty detections ranged from 35.4 to 100 percent and averaged 63.7 percent;

—correct innocent detections ranged from 32 to 91 percent and averaged 57.9 percent;

—false positives ranged from 2 to 50.7 percent and averaged 14.1 percent; and

—false negatives ranged from 0 to 28.7 percent and averaged 10.4 percent.

OTA Memorandum at 97. Note that because the question "Is the subject lying?" is a yes or no question, a random method of answering the question (e.g., a coin toss) would be correct 50% of the time. The Memorandum concluded,

> The wide variability of results from both prior research reviews and [The Office of Technology Assessment's] own review of individual studies makes it impossible to determine a specific overall quantitative measure of polygraph validity. The preponderance of research evidence does indicate that, when the control question technique is used in specific-incident criminal investigation, the polygraph detects deception at a rate better than chance, but with error rates that could be considered significant.

D. *Extrinsic Factors Affect Accuracy*

A number of extrinsic factors affect polygraph validity. Most important, because the examiner must formulate the questions, supplement the data with his own impression of the subject during the exam, and infer lies from a combination of the data and his impressions, the level of skill and training of the examiner will affect the reliability of the results. Unfortunately, there are no uniform standards for the training of polygraph examiners in this country.

A quality control system that reviews the examiners' conclusions also affects the validity of polygraph results. The results of most federally administered polygraph exams are checked by quality control officers, who call for reexaminations if the data does not indicate that the examiner's conclusion was correct. Barland, The Polygraph in the USA and Elsewhere 87. Few police examiners work within such a system, and almost no private examiners have quality control.

The length of a polygraph exam will also affect the validity of the results. One advocate of the polygraph has stated that an expert polygraph exam would take a minimum of several hours to complete. Senate Report at 43, 1988 U.S.Code Cong. and Admin.News at 730–31.

II. POLYGRAPH TESTS SHOULD BE EXCLUDED UNDER THE FEDERAL RULES OF EVIDENCE

Under Federal Rule of Evidence 702, expert testimony is proper if the testimony would assist the trier of fact in analyzing the evidence. Fed.R.Evid. 702 advisory committee's note (West 1989). Because the polygraph can predict whether a person is lying with accuracy that is only slightly greater than chance, it will be of little help to the trier of fact. * * * Because polygraph evidence is of little help to the trier of fact, and has great potential for prejudicing the trier of fact, confusing the issues and wasting time, it should be excluded under Federal Rule of Evidence 403.

The danger of prejudice, confusion of the issues and wasting time should also prevent courts from admitting polygraph evidence under Rule 608 for purposes of impeaching a witness. * * *

III. CONCLUSION

The scientific community remains sharply divided over the issue of the validity of polygraph exams. Although presented as a rigorously "scientific" procedure, the polygraph test in fact relies upon a highly subjective, inexact correlation of physiological factors having only a debatable relationship to dishonesty as such. The device detects lies at a rate only somewhat better than chance. Polygraph evidence, therefore, should not be admissible under Rule 702 or under Rule 608 to impeach a witness.

In this case, the government did not stipulate to the admissibility of the defendant's polygraph evidence and did not participate in selection of the examiner or the determination of the circumstances of the test. I would therefore AFFIRM the judgment below.

[Editors' note: As elsewhere, citations to authority have been eliminated without specific indication. The full opinions in United States v. Piccinonna contain extensive references to scientific and legal authority.]

LONGMORE v. MERRELL DOW PHARMACEUTICALS, INC.

United States District Court, District of Idaho, 1990.
737 F.Supp. 1117.

CALLISTER, Senior District Judge.

The Court has before it defendants' motions for summary judgment. The Court has heard oral argument and the motions have been fully briefed. The Court must determine if there are any genuine issues of material fact. See Fed.R.Civ.P. 56(c).

In this product liability action, the plaintiffs claim that their child's birth defects were caused by the mother's use of Bendectin during her pregnancy. She took the drug to combat the nauseous effects of morning sickness. The child, David Ronald Longmore, was born with Poland's Syndrome, a condition that leaves him without a chest muscle on the right side and with a shortening and webbing of his fingers on his right hand. David's mother and father filed this action individually and on behalf of David, claiming that the Bendectin caused David's birth defects.

The defendants have filed motions for summary judgment pointing to more than thirty-five human epidemiological studies finding no causal connection between Bendectin and birth defects. In response, the plaintiffs' experts will criticize these studies and use chemical analysis along with various types of animal studies to conclude that Bendectin could cause birth defects. Resolution of the summary judgment motions appears simple: the battling experts make summary judgment inappropriate. But the matter is complicated by three circuit courts that have found the plaintiffs' causation evidence insufficient as a matter of law in similar Bendectin litigation. Ealy v. Richardson–Merrell, Inc., 897 F.2d 1159 (D.C.Cir.1990); Brock v. Merrell–Dow Pharmaceuticals, Inc., 874 F.2d 307 (5th Cir.), modified 884 F.2d 166 (5th Cir.), reh'g denied, 884 F.2d 167 (en banc), cert. denied ___ U.S. ___, 110 S.Ct. 1511, 108 L.Ed.2d 646 (1990); Lynch v. Merrell–National Laboratories, Inc., 830 F.2d 1190 (1st Cir.).

The *Ealy* decision is representative and the most recent decision of these three cases. There, the D.C. Circuit, relying on the earlier case of Richardson v. Richardson–Merrell, Inc., 857 F.2d 823 (D.C.Cir.), cert. denied, ___ U.S. ___, 110 S.Ct. 218, 107 L.Ed.2d 171 (1989), held that testimony of the plaintiffs' experts concerning three types of scientific studies was inadmissible under Federal Rule of Evidence 703:

> These three types of studies then—chemical, in vitro [test tube], and in vivo [animal]—cannot furnish a sufficient foundation for a conclusion that Bendectin caused the birth defects at issue in this case. Studies of this kind, singly or in combination, are not capable of proving causation in human beings *in the face of the overwhelming body of contradictory epidemiological evidence.* Perhaps mindful of this, the last type of evidence considered by Dr. Done consisted of the epidemiological studies. *When such studies are available and relevant, and particularly when they are numerous and span a significant period of time,* they assume a very important role in determinations of questions of causation.

897 F.2d at 1161 (emphasis added) (quoting from Richardson v. Richardson–Merrell, Inc., supra at 830).

> The *Ealy* court then went on to hold that [t]herefore, under Rule 703, an opinion refuting this scientific consensus [the epidemiological studies] is inadmissible for lack of an adequate foundation, in the absence of other substantial probative evidence on which to base this opinion. It is this uncontroversial rule of evidence that is that ratio decidendi of Richardson and this case.

In the other two cases cited above, *Lynch* and *Brock,* the First and Fifth Circuits reached similar decisions. No Ninth Circuit case has yet come down addressing these issues. The Court is therefore faced with persuasive but not binding precedent. The three circuit decisions placed considerable emphasis on the epidemiological evidence, and the Court will begin its inquiry there.

For obvious reasons, scientists do not investigate the potential toxic effects of a drug by performing tests on human beings. Instead, scientific investigators must use an indirect route and extrapolate their results. Animal studies, epidemiology, chemical analysis, clinical studies, and other analytical tools are all part of the investigative process. The three circuit decisions were particularly impressed with epidemiology which is the statistical study of disease in human populations. Dore, A Commentary on the Use of Epidemiological Evidence in Demonstrating Cause–In–Fact, 7 Harv.Envtl.L.Rev. 429 (1983). By studying large groups of people, epidemiologists can determine the association between exposure to a chemical and disease. For example, epidemiological studies have concluded that exposure to vinyl chloride in the workplace is associated with an increased incidence of cancer in rubber workers. Hall & Silbergeld, Reappraising Epidemiology: A Response to Mr. Dore, 7 Harv.Envtl.L.Rev. 441 (1983). As another example, prenatal exposure to seed treated with methyl mercury is associated with birth defects in children. Id.

As these examples show, epidemiological studies "are general in that they deal with sources of diseases and groups of people rather than particular individuals." Dore, supra at 436. In the context of a civil trial, epidemiological studies could be used to show that a defendant's conduct increased the plaintiff's risk of injury but "could not answer the critical question whether the defendant's conduct actually injured the plaintiff." Dore, supra at 436.

It is also important that an epidemiological association usually requires a 95% level of confidence.[1] To explain this using a hypothetical example, assume an epidemiologist observed an increased incidence of Poland's Syndrome among babies born to mothers who had ingested Bendectin during pregnancy. Using a 95% confidence level, the epidemiologist will conclude that ingestion of Bendectin during pregnancy is associated with an increased incidence of Poland's Syndrome only where the probability is one in twenty—or less—that the observation of association resulted from random chance. If the probability is one in nineteen that the events occurred by chance, the association will be deemed "statistically insignificant." Thus, an epidemiologist would find the correlation between Poland's Syndrome and Bendectin ingestion "insignificant" even though the probability is 94.73% (eighteen out of nineteen) that the observed relationship is not related to random chance. It is therefore apparent that the scientific standard for determining causation is much stricter than the standard employed in this Court. While the epidemiologist may conclude that the observed asso-

---

1. In the study of epidemiology, confidence levels of 95%, 90%, "or occasionally 80% are most commonly used." Rothman, Modern Epidemiology at p. 119 (1986).

ciation is insignificant, the "certainty that the observed increase is related to its hypothetical cause rather than mere chance is still far more likely than not." Allen v. United States, 588 F.Supp. 247 (D.Utah 1984), rev'd on other grounds 816 F.2d 1417 (10th Cir.1987). As the Eleventh Circuit has recognized, "a distinction exists between legal sufficiency and scientific certainty." Wells v. Ortho Pharmaceutical Corp., 788 F.2d 741, 745 (11th Cir.1986). That distinction is vitally important in this case, as the following discussion will show. * * *

With regard to the factual question of causation, the plaintiff need only prove that it is more probably true than not that the mother's ingestion of Bendectin caused David's Poland's Syndrome. This certainly does not require a confidence level of 95%, 90% or even 80%. A cause-and-effect relationship may be deemed insignificant under stringent scientific standards, but nevertheless establish causation under legal standards. * * *

This Court does not mean to imply that epidemiological studies are without worth in proving causation. Certainly they play an important role. Hall & Silbergeld, supra. A jury might find the studies conclusive. But this Court cannot—at this stage of the case—find the epidemiological evidence "overwhelming." The studies are not designed to definitively prove individual causation, and they could label a cause "insignificant" that the legal system would find significant. As the Ninth Circuit has recognized, epidemiological studies are subject to error. Asarco, Inc. v. Occupational Safety & Health Admin., 746 F.2d 483, 493, n. 19 (9th Cir.1984). These factors combine to dilute the power of the studies in this summary judgment proceeding.

The *Ealy* case used Federal Rule of Evidence 703 to preclude the plaintiffs' experts from discussing animal or chemical studies because of the "overwhelming" nature of the epidemiological evidence. Rule 703 requires that the grounds relied on by an expert be of "a type reasonably relied upon by experts in the particular field in forming opinions or inferences on the subject." In this case, there is no attack in the pending motions on the qualifications of plaintiffs' experts. The defendants simply want to use the overwhelming nature of the epidemiological studies to bulldoze aside the plaintiffs' experts. Once the epidemiological evidence is stripped of its "overwhelming" label, does Rule 703 still preclude plaintiffs' expert testimony? Only if animal studies and chemical analysis are not reasonably relied upon by experts who attempt to investigate the connection between drugs and birth defects. And the Court cannot make such a finding on the basis of the record before it. As stated by Federal District Court Judge Louis H. Pollak in Villari v. Terminix Intern., Inc., 692 F.Supp. 568, 570 (E.D.Pa. 1988):

> While it may be true that the defendant can offer tests and experiments that do not support the findings of plaintiffs' experts, the defendant cannot deny that animal studies are routinely relied upon by the scientific community in assessing the carcinogenic effects of chemicals on humans. Even the defendant's own expert acknowledges that animal experiment

studies are based on "prudent presumptions," although he concludes that they should not be admitted. * * *

There are certainly many valid criticisms of the use of animal studies. The Court is not precluding the defendants from challenging during trial the admissibility of any particular animal studies. But such specific questions are not before the Court at this time. Animal studies are generally relied upon by experts determining the link between a drug and birth defects and the same is true for chemical analysis. While the Court will leave open the question of the admissibility of particular studies during the trial of this matter, the Court cannot now preclude all such studies under Rule 703.

There has been a great deal of general discussion that the plaintiffs' experts will mislead the jury. Rule 703 is subject to a Rule 403 analysis balancing probative value against the dangers of prejudice and confusion. The Court will certainly take a hard look at the expert testimony during trial. But as a general matter, the Court cannot state at this point that the expert testimony is precluded under Rule 403. In other Bendectin cases where the plaintiffs have used these very same experts, the juries—including an Idaho jury—have ruled that no causation exists between Bendectin and birth defects. Obviously, the experts are not achieving complete success in bamboozling juries, even assuming that is their goal.

To the extent that the decisions of the three circuit courts discussed earlier can be interpreted to require summary judgment in this case, such would be extraordinary and unprecedented. This Court cannot find at this stage of the proceedings that no causation exists as a matter of law: The experts have lined up on both sides; there are many questions concerning the scientific studies proffered by both parties; and the Idaho law provides that summary judgment on causation is normally inappropriate. * * *

When the three circuit decisions are read carefully, they evidence a profound frustration with hired-gun experts. This Court shares those frustrations. The Court will examine very carefully the expert testimony that is proffered in this case by both sides. Nothing in this opinion is to be construed to preclude either side from making specific challenges to evidentiary matters. The Court is simply holding that it cannot at this stage of the proceedings adopt a general rule precluding all testimony of plaintiffs' experts. The Court shall therefore deny the motions for summary judgment filed by defendants.

THE CASE AGAINST EXPERT WITNESSES

by Walter Olson
Fortune, September 25, 1989, 135–36, 138.*

Within the thriving business of suing people—what you might call the disservice sector of the American economy—expert witnesses occupy a fast-growing and controversial niche. Hardly a liability suit goes forward without an engineer or a doctor swearing that the product was misdesigned, or the injury devastating, or the hospital negligent. The other side then calls its expert to say the exact opposite. Both get paid handsomely.

Courts have always relied on expertise in one form or other. But sweeping changes in federal rules of evidence in the mid–1970s vastly widened the definition of an expert—and what that person can talk about. Says Jack Weinstein, a federal judge in Brooklyn: "An expert can be found to testify to the truth of almost any theory, no matter how frivolous." Unlike other witnesses, experts freely give opinions and can speak in the language of legal conclusions: "In my professional opinion, this was a clear case of malpractice." They are allowed to base their comments on evidence that for other witnesses would be inadmissible as hearsay. And they often make a big hit with juries.

No field is out of the experts' reach. Going through a nasty divorce? A forensic accountant will sketch a dazzlingly prosperous future for your spouse's business. Caught skimming the till? A hired psychologist will arouse sympathy with the jury by calling you a hapless victim of compulsive gambling syndrome. Your son was dropped from his college basketball team because of poor grades? A self-styled sportsologist can swear that if not for this unfairness Kevin could have earned $1 million a year with the pros.

A lively business has sprung up to bring lawyers and experts together. One of the biggest referral firms, Medical–Legal Consulting Service Inc. of Bethesda, Maryland, says it has 600 experts on call. If the first doctor it refers doesn't agree with your lawyer's theory on the case, the company promises to send over a second one free. Another firm, Medical Quality Foundation of Herndon, Virginia, has offered seminars on how lawyers can increase the size of jury awards. The referral services, and individual experts, put out colorful brochures listing the areas in which they can testify.

Exuberant ads in the back of *Trial* magazine, which is published by the Association of Trial Lawyers of America, tell the tale. One, headed "Heavyweight Malpractice Experts," features a photo of a man in a white clinical coat wearing boxing gloves. Other experts specialize in mishaps involving utility poles and so-called sport surfaces. Some ex-cops are eager to help in the growing area of "negligent security"—suits against the supermarket in whose parking lot you were assaulted, or the bank at whose automated cash machine you were robbed. "The more measured and impartial an expert is, the less likely he is to be used by either side," writes Professor John Langbein of the University of Chicago law school, who has himself testified. If the conscientious outsider resists the subtle pressure to get on the team by shading his opinions, he may not be called back. There seem to be plenty of willing replacements.

Experts in most demand are those with the surface polish that comes from previous trial combat. The more you appear in court, the more chances you get to appear again, picking up what you might call frequent-testifier bonus points. Counting in fees for strategy sessions, out-of-court appearances, and the like, just a few big cases may bring

more to a professor than he normally makes in a year. If he or his
consulting firm can swing a contingency deal—getting a share of the
jury's award—the pay can be huge.

Hence the rise of the professional witness. "You see the same
experts again and again around the country," says Arvin Maskin, a
New York lawyer who helped defend the Agent Orange case for the
U.S. government. Howard Balensweig, a semiretired Manhattan physician who spends much of his time as an expert in injury cases, says he
averages $3,500 for a day in court and $2,500 for half a day.

Lawyers for Merrell Dow Pharmaceuticals have grown quite familiar with Dr. Alan K. Done, a Salt Lake City physician and toxicologist
who travels around the country testifying that Bendectin, the company's anti-morning sickness drug, has caused or contributed to birth
defects. Merrell Dow sends in mainstream experts of its own by the
vanload, and usually wins. The Food and Drug Administration has
approved Bendectin, stating specifically that it does not increase the
risk of birth defects. The World Health Organization, which acts only
in an advisory capacity to member countries, basically supports the
FDA conclusion.

But when the occasional jury goes along with Dr. Done, the
damages can be huge, $95 million in the case of one child. The judge
rejected $75 million of that award. Other judgments against Merrell
Dow keep getting thrown out by judges at trial or on appeal; federal
judge Thomas Penfield Jackson cited the "now nearly universal scientific consensus" on the drug's safety. Still, because of the expense of
litigation, Merrell Dow has stopped selling it.

The expert needn't convince; he does well to confuse. If even the
pros can't seem to agree, the side with the weaker factual case at least
manages to stay in the game. When a bewildered jury decides that the
chemistry or geology or economics of the case must be just a matter of
opinion, it will often follow its other instincts—especially the natural
impulse to compensate a hardluck litigant at the expense of someone
with money.

Among the claims that arouse the most sympathy in jurors are
those of illness caused by pollution. In a typical pattern, neighbors of
some chemical or nuclear facility come to court complaining that the
plant has caused various ailments. Establishing a direct link between
low-level toxins and specific illnesses has been difficult if not impossible. So the litigants, backed by their lawyers and a growing group of
experts-for-hire, have developed a marvelously elastic theory: Pollution
can suppress the immune system. Thus, it can be blamed for a wide
range of common ailments from diabetes to learning problems, gall-
stones to hearing loss, depression to measles.

The experts—who call themselves clinical ecologists, practitioners
of environmental medicine, or immunologists—aver that even minute
exposures to man-made chemicals or radiation can alter the immune
system. The American Academy of Allergy and Immunology has
repudiated the theory, as has the California Medical Association. Still,

it plays well with juries. Yale law professor E. Donald Elliott says it has "dramatically changed the strategic balance in toxic tort cases."

A judge ordered Velsicol Chemical Co. to pay $22 million to a group of Toone, Tennessee, residents who claimed to have been harmed by leaks from a company landfill. Dr. Alan Levin, a San Francisco physician who treats AIDS patients, said of the plaintiffs: "In my opinion, their immune systems will never recover." (An appeals court later reversed part of the award and Velsicol settled the case, along with some other damage claims, for about $10 million.)

In a case brought by a group of Sedalia, Missouri, residents against Alcolac Inc., Arthur C. Zahalsky, who has a Ph.D. in microbiology and teaches immunology at Southern Illinois University, said several of the residents were suffering from "chemically induced AIDS," a dramatic malady unrecognized by mainstream science. The jury awarded $49 million in damages. The judge later set aside the ruling and ordered a new trial to recalculate damages. But the verdict of liability against Alcolac was allowed to stand by the Missouri Supreme Court. The company has asked the U.S. Supreme Court to review the case.

According to a court document, Zahalsky has no graduate credits in immunology, but he points out that such courses were not given when he went to school in the 1960s. He says he later audited courses in immunology at Washington University in St. Louis.

Questionable science used to be excluded on principle from the courtroom. Under the so-called Frye rule, named for a 1923 case, expert testimony could be admitted only if the scientific methods behind its conclusions would pass muster with most of those active in a particular field. The problem: What was a field, and who was active? Also, the courts in their caution tended to lag behind developments in forensic science.

Criticism intensified in the 1960s. Wasn't it elitist to insist on paper credentials before letting someone testify? What if the witness wanting to speak his piece, whose training had come in the school of hard knocks, turned out to be the next Galileo? Why waste time on what one court later dismissed as "scientific nose-counting"?

In 1975 Congress enacted new liberalized rules of evidence, and most states followed suit. Now all it takes to be an expert in many courts is a call from a lawyer. Trials filled with self-described accidentologists with coffeepot-to-railroad-car expertise, human factor engineers, measurers and calibrators of workplace emotional trauma and post-one-thing-and-another-syndrome, and more. By no means are all these folks charlatans; many say perfectly commonsensical things in court. But in so doing they can add an aura of scientific authority to propositions ("It hurts to get fired") that juries could grasp on their own.

The let-it-all-in trend may have peaked in 1984 when the federal appeals court in Washington suggested that as long as a scientific proposition with very thin support had not been palpably disproved, it might be best to send it to a jury for a vote. But a reaction was already afoot. A federal judge in Kansas threw out a radiation claim based on testimony he felt the experts "would not dare report in a peer-reviewed format." Then Judge Weinstein in Brooklyn dismissed the remainder of the Agent Orange cases, saying the expert affidavits claiming to prove connections between various illnesses and use of the herbicide were just too flimsy. (Cold comfort for seven chemical companies that had already agreed to spring for $180 million to settle claims with a more or less identical basis.)

An even clearer call to action came in 1986 from federal appeals judge Patrick Higginbotham of Dallas, often mentioned as a future Supreme Court nominee. A Pan Am flight had crashed in New Orleans and lawyers were having the inevitable, ghoulish argument over what each passenger's death was worth. An economist hired by a bereaved family declared that a young man's struggling business had been headed for tremendous success: His after-inflation income would have climbed year after year in an unbroken line for the next 40 years, yet he would have found ways to keep his tax rate down to a thrifty 5%. And so members of his family lost $1,778,873 as their hypothetical inheritance (they were already on their way to an initial award from Pan Am of $3 million for other kinds of damages). Higginbotham called the economist's figures "completely airborne" and called for a new trial. "It is time," he said, "to take hold of expert testimony in federal trials."

More and more of his colleagues on the bench seem to agree. Two appeals decisions have recently backed the dismissal of Bendectin verdicts on scientific grounds; one was written by Judge Spottswood Robinson III, a Lyndon Johnson appointee from the D.C. circuit's liberal wing. In overturning the immune damage award against Velsicol based largely on Dr. Levin's testimony, another appeals court noted that leading professional societies "have rejected clinical ecology as an unproven methodology lacking any scientific base in either fact or theory." What Georgetown law professor Paul Rothstein calls the strict scrutiny faction among judges is fast gaining ground.

Plaintiffs' lawyers object to this know-it-when-I-see-it judicial approach to bad science. They also oppose tighter laws of evidence or some kind of modern Frye rule. They argue that thorough cross-examination is protection enough against the roving jack-of-all-testimony. New York lawyer Paul Rheingold ruefully recalls what happened when he brought in an all-purpose expert to opine on the supposedly defective design of a motorcycle. The defendant's attorney rose and asked: Didn't the witness also testify in auto cases? Yes. And ladder cases? On the attorney went, ticking off specialties from the expert's promotional brochure—glass, fires, TVs, explosions? Yes, yes, yes, yes—by which point the jury might not have believed the expert if he had told them the time of day.

The lawyers have a point: Cross-examination can be a good defense. The American Corporate Counsel Institute has begun keeping a database of hostile expert testimony so defendants can better expose weaknesses as cases accumulate.

Broader reform is clearly needed. Imperfect though it is, some sort of peer review is the ultimate answer. Juries deserve to know whether what they are being told would get a witness laughed out of an ordinary lab or hospital. To rely on judges' instincts about the validity of expert testimony is both not enough and too much. Courts may not be ready to return to the discipline symbolized by the Frye rule, but there are alternatives. Elliott of Yale suggests that dubious testimony could be countered by a court-appointed expert who would explain what mainstream practitioners of that particular branch of science might think of the witness's theories.

Since junk science has made companies so vulnerable to all kinds of claims, American business has everything to gain by ousting it from the courtroom. And the public at large could begin to regain some of its former confidence in the justice system. Cynical lawyers call their experts saxophones because they can be played with such virtuosity. Let's hope the brassier ones are muted before long.

LANGBEIN, THE GERMAN ADVANTAGE IN CIVIL PROCEDURE

52 U.Chi.L.Rev. 823, 835–36 (1985).*

The European jurist who visits the United States and becomes acquainted with our civil procedure typically expresses amazement at our witness practice. His amazement turns to something bordering on disbelief when he discovers that we extend the sphere of partisan control to the selection and preparation of experts. In the Continental tradition experts are selected and commissioned by the court, although with great attention to safeguarding party interests. In the German system, experts are not even called witnesses. They are thought of as "judges' aides."

Perverse incentives. At the American trial bar, those of us who serve as expert witnesses are known as "saxophones." This is a revealing term, as slang often is. The idea is that the lawyer plays the tune, manipulating the expert as though the expert were a musical instrument on which the lawyer sounds the desired notes. I sometimes serve as an expert in trust and pension cases, and I have experienced the subtle pressures to join the team—to shade one's views, to conceal doubt, to overstate nuance, to downplay weak aspects of the case that one has been hired to bolster. Nobody likes to disappoint a patron; and beyond this psychological pressure is the financial inducement. Money changes hands upon the rendering of expertise, but the expert can run his meter only so long as his patron litigator likes the tune. Opposing counsel undertakes a similar exercise, hiring and schooling another expert to parrot the contrary position. The result is our familiar battle of opposing experts. The more measured and impartial an expert is, the less likely he is to be used by either side.

At trial, the battle of experts tends to baffle the trier, especially in jury courts. If the experts do not cancel each other out, the advantage

is likely to be with the expert whose forensic skills are the more
enticing. The system invites abusive cross-examination. Since each
expert is party-selected and party-paid, he is vulnerable to attack on
credibility regardless of the merits of his testimony. A defense lawyer
recently bragged about his technique of cross-examining plaintiffs'
experts in tort cases. Notice that nothing in his strategy varies with
the truthfulness of the expert testimony he tries to discredit:

> A mode of attack ripe with potential is to pursue a line of
> questions which, by their form and the jury's studied observa-
> tion of the witness in response, will tend to cast the expert as a
> "professional witness." By proceeding in this way, the cross-
> examiner will reap the benefit of a community attitude, cer-
> tain to be present among several of the jurors, that bias can be
> purchased, almost like a commodity.

Thus, the systematic incentive in our procedure to distort expertise
leads to a systematic distrust and devaluation of expertise. Short of
forbidding the use of experts altogether, we probably could not have
designed a procedure better suited to minimize the influence of expertise.

STATE v. CHAPPLE

Supreme Court of Arizona, En Banc, 1983.
135 Ariz. 281, 660 P.2d 1208.

FELDMAN, Justice.

Dolan Chapple was convicted on three counts of first degree murder * * *

FACTS

The instigator of this bizarre drama was Mel Coley, a drug dealer
who resided in Washington, D.C., but who was also connected with
dealers in Kansas City. Coley had a history of dealing with a supplier
named Bill Varnes, who lived near Phoenix.

Coley had made a large number of drug deals through Malcolm
Scott, a "middleman" who lived near Phoenix. Scott was also well
acquainted with Varnes * * *.

Coley telephoned in early December 1977 and told Scott that he
was interested in purchasing approximately 300 pounds of marijuana.
He asked Scott to act as middleman in the transaction. Scott was to
get $700 for his efforts. Scott testified that he called one or two of the
Arizona suppliers with whom he was acquainted and found they could
not supply the necessary quantity. He then called his sister, Pamela
Buck, who was a "good friend" of Varnes and had worked with him in
some drug deals. Scott asked Buck to contact her friend Varnes and
see whether he could handle the sale. Buck talked to Varnes and
reported to her brother that Varnes could supply the necessary amount
of marijuana at an agreed upon price.

On the evening of December 10 or the early morning of December
11, 1977, Coley arrived at the Phoenix airport from Washington, D.C.

Scott met him at the airport and found that Coley was accompanied by two strangers who were introduced as "Dee" and "Eric." Scott drove the three men to a trailer located at his parents' farm near Higley in Pinal County, Arizona. Scott had used this trailer in the past as a meeting place to consummate drug transactions. This meeting place was part of the service which Scott provided for his "finder's fee."

Coley, Dee and Eric spent the night at the trailer, while Scott returned to his residence in Mesa. The next morning Scott returned to the farm and took Coley to the airport where they picked up a brown leather bag. Back at the trailer, Scott observed Coley, Eric and Dee take four guns from the bag and clean them. Scott examined and handled one of the guns. Buck had also arrived at the trailer in Higley, and she and Dee were dispatched to Varnes' trailer in order to purchase a sample of the marijuana.

Later that morning the conversation between Coley, Eric and Dee indicated that it was likely there would be a "rip-off" of the marijuana and that Coley did not intend to pay for the goods. When Buck expressed to her brother the fear that Varnes would seek revenge if his goods were stolen, Scott told her not to worry because Varnes might never be seen again.

That evening, Scott and his sister met at the trailer with Coley, Eric and Dee. Varnes arrived with two companions, Eduardo Ortiz and Carlos Elsy. Ortiz and Elsy began to unload the marijuana and put it in the trailer.

After Ortiz and Elsy had finished unloading the marijuana and stacking it in the living room of the trailer, Dee suggested to Varnes that they go in the bedroom and "count the money." They started toward the bedroom and Buck went into the bathroom. A few moments later, Buck heard several shots, opened the bathroom door and ran out. Scott heard the shots while he was on the porch and saw a door of the trailer open. Elsy ran out, pursued by either Eric or Dee. After seeing Buck run out of the door at the other end of the trailer, Scott went back to the trailer and found Varnes dead in the bedroom of a gunshot wound to the head and Ortiz in the living room dead of a gunshot wound to the body. Subsequent ballistic tests showed they had been shot with different weapons. Elsy was outside, dead from a blow to the back of the head.

Dee and Eric then removed the marijuana from the trailer and loaded it into a car which Coley had directed Scott to buy the previous day.[1] Scott, Eric and Dee loaded the three bodies into the trunk of Varnes' car. That car was driven out to the desert, doused with gasoline and set afire. The trailer was cleaned to remove evidence of the crime and the carpet in the trailer was burned. The parties then left the scene of the crime and returned to Scott's house in Mesa. Eric and Dee asked for directions regarding the route to Kansas City and then left in the car containing the marijuana. Coley gave Scott and Buck $500 each. He then called the airport and reserved a seat to

---

1. Coley had given Scott $1,200 to buy a car. Scott got the car from "Harry the repo man" for $800, pocketing the difference.

leave for Washington, D.C. under the name of "James Logan." Scott returned to the trailer and completed the cleanup. Fear or remorse, or both, drove Scott to seek the aid of a lawyer, who succeeded in negotiating an immunity deal for Scott and in getting him to surrender to the sheriff.

Defendant does not contest any of the foregoing facts. Defendant is accused of being "Dee." He denies this. At his extradition hearing in Illinois, seven witnesses placed him in Cairo, Illinois during the entire month of December 1977, three of them testifying specifically to his presence in that town on December 11, the day of the crime. The same witnesses testified for him in the trial at which he was convicted. No direct or circumstantial evidence of any kind connects defendant to the crime,[2] other than the testimony of Malcolm Scott and Pamela Buck, neither of whom had ever met the defendant before the crime and neither of whom saw him after the crime except at the trial. Defendant was apprehended and tried only because Malcolm Scott and Pamela Buck picked his photograph out of a lineup more than one year after the date of the crime; he was convicted because they later identified both the photographs and defendant himself at trial.

* * *

Defendant argued at trial, and urges here, that even if Scott and Buck are not lying, their identification was a case of mistaken identity. The argument is that Scott and Buck picked the wrong picture out of the photographic lineup and that their subsequent photographic and in-court identifications were part of the "feedback phenomenon" and are simply continuations or repetitions of the same mistake. To support this contention of mistaken identification, defendant offered expert testimony regarding the various factors that affect the reliability of identification evidence. For the most part, that testimony was rejected by the trial court as not being within the proper sphere of expert testimony.

* * *

EXPERT TESTIMONY REGARDING EYEWITNESS IDENTIFICATION

On learning of Mel Coley's participation in the crime, the sheriff's office quickly procured photographs of Coley, which were shown to Scott and Buck in a photographic lineup on December 16, 1977. Both of them identified Coley, thus providing law enforcement with the first step in its efforts to apprehend Dee and Eric. The detectives then showed Scott and Buck various photographs and lineups containing pictures of known acquaintances of Mel Coley. At this same session, Scott pointed to a picture of James Logan and stated that it resembled Dee, though he could not be sure. So far as the record shows, no follow-up was made of this tentative identification. One of the photographic lineups displayed to Scott, but not to Buck, contained a picture of the defendant, Dolan Chapple, but Scott did not identify him as Dee.

---

2. Neither Coley, Eric nor Dee wore gloves during the events described. Latent fingerprints were found in the trailer and the vehicle containing the bodies, but did not match defendant's fingerprints.

The police continued to show the witnesses photographic lineups in an attempt to obtain an identification of Dee. Police efforts were successful on January 27, 1979, when Scott was shown a nine-picture photo lineup. For the first time, this lineup included photos of both Eric Perry, who had already been tentatively identified by Scott and Buck, and of the defendant; however, James Logan's photo was not included. Upon seeing this lineup, Scott immediately recognized Eric's picture again. About ten minutes later, Scott identified defendant's picture as Dee. Scott was then shown the picture of defendant he had failed to identify at a previous session and asked to explain why he had not previously identified it. He stated that he had no recollection of having seen it before. After Scott had identified Dee and before he could talk to his sister, the police showed Buck the same lineup. Buck identified the defendant as Dee.

Defendant argues that the jury could have found the in-court identification unreliable for a variety of reasons. The defendant argues that the identification of Dee from photographic lineups in this case was unreliable because of the time interval which passed between the occurrence of the event and the lineup and because of the anxiety and tension inherent in the situation surrounding the entire identification process.[3] The defendant also argues that since Scott and Buck had smoked marijuana on the days of the crime, their perception would have been affected, making their identification through photographs less reliable. Further, defendant claims the January 27, 1979 identification of Dee by Scott and Buck from the photographic lineup was the product of an unconscious transfer. Defendant claims that Scott picked the picture of Dolan Chapple and identified it as Dee because he remembered that picture from the previous lineup (when he had not been able to identify defendant's picture). Defendant urges that the in-court identifications were merely reinforcements of the initial error. Further, defendant claims that the identification was made on the basis of subsequently acquired information which affected memory. Finally, defendant argues that the confidence and certainty which Scott and Buck displayed in making their in-court identification at trial had no relation whatsoever to the accuracy of that identification and was, instead, the product of other factors.

It is against this complicated background, with identification the one issue on which the guilt or innocence of defendant hinged, that defense counsel offered the testimony of an expert on eyewitness identification in order to rebut the testimony of Malcolm Scott and his sister, Pamela Buck. The witness called by the defense was Dr. Elizabeth Loftus, a professor of psychology at the University of Washington. Dr. Loftus specializes in an area of experimental and clinical psychology dealing with perception, memory retention and recall. Her qualifications are unquestioned, and it may fairly be said that she "wrote the book" on the subject. The trial court granted the State's motion to suppress Dr. Loftus' testimony. Acknowledging that rulings

3. Buck and Scott both said they were frightened for their lives during the events. Since they are the only witnesses, one might assume they were also frightened and apprehensive during the time period when Eric and Dee were both at liberty.

on admissibility of expert testimony are within the discretion of the
trial court, defendant contends that the court erred and abused its
discretion in granting the motion to suppress Dr. Loftus' testimony.

The admissibility of expert testimony is governed by Rule 702, Ariz.
R. of Evid.   That rule states:

> If scientific, technical, or other specialized knowledge will
> assist the trier of fact to understand the evidence or to deter-
> mine a fact in issue, a witness qualified as an expert by
> knowledge, skill, experience, training, or education, may testify
> thereto in the form of an opinion or otherwise.

In what is probably the leading case on the subject, the Ninth
Circuit affirmed the trial court's preclusion of expert evidence on
eyewitness identification in United States v. Amaral.   In its analysis,
however, the court set out four criteria which should be applied in
order to determine the admissibility of such testimony.   These are: (1)
qualified expert; (2) proper subject; (3) conformity to a generally
accepted explanatory theory; and (4) probative value compared to
prejudicial effect.   Id. at 1153.   We approve this test and find that the
case at bar meets these criteria.

We recognize that the cases that have considered the subject have
uniformly affirmed trial court rulings denying admission of this type of
testimony.   However, a careful reading of these cases reveals that
many of them contain fact situations which fail to meet the *Amaral*
criteria or are decided on legal principles which differ from those we
follow in Arizona.   * * *

Applying the *Amaral* test to the case at bench, we find from the
record that the State has conceded that the expert was qualified and
that the question of conformity to generally accepted explanatory
theory is not raised and appears not to be a question in this case.   The
two criteria which must therefore be considered are (1) determination
of whether the probative value of the testimony outweighs its possible
prejudicial effect and (2) determination of whether the testimony was a
proper subject.

(1) PROBATIVE VALUE *vs.* PREJUDICE

The State argues that there would have been little probative value
to the witness' testimony and great danger of unfair prejudice.   The
latter problem is claimed to arise from the fact that Loftus' qualifications were so impressive that the jury might have given improper
weight to her testimony.   We do not believe that this raises the issue of
unfair prejudice.   The contention of lack of probative value is based on
the premise that the offer of proof showed that the witness would
testify to general factors which were applicable to this case and affect
the reliability of identification, but would not express any opinion with
regard to the accuracy of the specific identification made by Scott and
Buck and would not express an opinion regarding the accuracy percentage of eyewitness identification in general.

We believe that the "generality" of the testimony is a factor which favors admission. Witnesses are permitted to express opinions on ultimate issues but are not required to testify to an opinion on the precise questions before the trier of fact.

> Most of the literature assumes that experts testify only in the form of opinions. The assumption is logically unfounded. [Rule 702] accordingly recognizes that an expert on the stand may give a dissertation or exposition of scientific or other principles relevant to the case, leaving the trier of fact to apply them to the facts. Since much of the criticism of expert testimony has centered upon the hypothetical question, it seems wise to recognize that opinions are not indispensable and to encourage the use of expert testimony in non-opinion form when counsel believes the trier can itself draw the requisite inference.

Fed.R. of Evid. 702 advisory committee note.

(2) PROPER SUBJECT

The remaining criterion at issue is whether the offered evidence was a proper subject for expert testimony. Ariz.R. of Evid. 702 allows expert testimony if it "will assist the trier of fact to understand the evidence or to determine a fact in issue." Put conversely, the test "is whether the subject of inquiry is one of such common knowledge that people of ordinary education could reach a conclusion as intelligently as the witness * * *." Furthermore, the test is not whether the jury could reach some conclusion in the absence of the expert evidence, but whether the jury is qualified without such testimony "to determine intelligently and to the best possible degree the particular issue without enlightenment from those having a specialized understanding of the subject. * * *" Fed.R.Evid. 702 advisory committee note (quoting Ladd, Expert Testimony, 5 Vand.L.Rev. 414, 418 (1952)).

In excluding the evidence in the case at bench, the trial judge stated:

> I don't find anything that's been presented in the extensive discussions that I have read in your memorandum with regard to the fact that this expert is going to testify to anything that isn't within the common experience of the people on the jury, that couldn't really be covered in cross-examination of the witnesses who made the identification, and probably will be excessively argued in closing arguments to the jury.

This basis for the view that eyewitness identification is not a proper subject for expert testimony is the same as that adopted in United States v. Amaral, supra, and in the great majority of cases which have routinely followed *Amaral.*

However, after a careful review of these cases and the record before us, we have concluded that although the reasons cited by the trial judge would correctly permit preclusion of such testimony in the great majority of cases, it was error to refuse the testimony in the case at bench. In reaching this conclusion, we have carefully considered the offer of proof made by the defense in light of the basic concept of "proper subject" underlying Rule 702.

We note at the outset that the law has long recognized the inherent danger in eyewitness testimony.[4] Of course, it is difficult to tell whether the ordinary juror shares the law's inherent caution of eyewitness identification. Experimental data indicates that many jurors "may reach intuitive conclusions about the reliability of [such] testimony that psychological research would show are misguided." Note, Did Your Eyes Deceive You? Expert Psychological Testimony on the Unreliability of Eyewitness Identification, 29 Stan.L.Rev. 969, 1017 (1977).

Even assuming that jurors of ordinary education need no expert testimony to enlighten them to the danger of eyewitness identification, the offer of proof[5] indicated that Dr. Loftus' testimony would have informed the jury that there are many specific variables which affect the accuracy of identification and which apply to the facts of this case. For instance, while most jurors would no doubt realize that memory dims as time passes, Dr. Loftus presented data from experiments which showed that the "forgetting curve" is not uniform. Forgetting occurs very rapidly and then tends to level out; immediate identification is much more trustworthy than long-delayed identification. Thus, Scott's recognition of Logan's features as similar to those of Dee when Logan's picture was shown at the inception of the investigation is probably a more reliable identification than Scott's identification of Chapple's photograph in the photographic lineup thirteen months later. By the same token, Scott's failure to identify Chapple's photograph when it was first shown to him on March 26, 1978 (four months after the crime) and when Scott's ability to identify would have been far greater, is of key importance.

Another variable in the case is the effect of stress upon perception. Dr. Loftus indicated that research shows that most laymen believe that stressful events cause people to remember "better" so that what is seen in periods of stress is more accurately related later. However, experimental evidence indicates that stress causes inaccuracy of perception with subsequent distortion of recall.

Dr. Loftus would also have testified about the problems of "unconscious transfer," a phenomenon which occurs when the witness confuses a person seen in one situation with the person seen in a different situation. Dr. Loftus would have pointed out that a witness who takes part in a photo identification session without identifying any of the photographs and who then later sees a photograph of one of those persons may relate his or her familiarity with the picture to the crime rather than to the previous identification session.

4. "The vagaries of eye-witness identification are well know: the annals of criminal law are rife with instances of mistaken identification. * * * 'What is the worth of identification testimony even when uncontradicted? The identification of strangers is proverbially untrustworthy. The hazards of such testimony are established by a formidable number of instances in the records of English and American trials.'"

5. The offer of proof was taken with Dr. Loftus on the stand and the jury excluded from the courtroom.

Another variable involves assimilation of post-event information. Experimental evidence, shown by Dr. Loftus, confirms that witnesses frequently incorporate into their identifications inaccurate information gained subsequent to the event and confused with the event. An additional problem is the "feedback factor." We deal here with two witnesses who were related and who, according to Loftus' interview, engaged in discussions with each other about the identification of Dee. Dr. Loftus, who interviewed them, emphasized that their independent descriptions of Dee at times utilized identical language. Dr. Loftus would have explained that through such discussions identification witnesses can reinforce their individual identifications. Such reinforcement will often tend to heighten the certainty of identification. The same may be said of the continual sessions that each witness had with the police in poring over large groups of photographs.[6]

The last variable in this case concerns the question of confidence and its relationship to accuracy. Dr. Loftus' testimony and some experimental data indicate that there is no relationship between the confidence which a witness has in his or her identification and the actual accuracy of that identification. Again, this factor was specifically tied to the evidence in the case before us since both Scott and Buck indicated in their testimony that they were absolutely sure of their identification. Evidently their demeanor on the witness stand showed absolute confidence.[7]

We cannot assume that the average juror would be aware of the variables concerning identification and memory about which Dr. Loftus was qualified to testify.

> Depriving [the] jurors of the benefit of scientific research on eyewitness testimony force[d] them to search for the truth without full knowledge and opportunity to evaluate the strength of the evidence. In short, this deprivation prevent[ed] [the] jurors from having "the best possible degree" of "understanding the subject" toward which the law of evidence strives.

Note, supra, 29 Stan.L.Rev. at 1017–18. Thus, considering the standard of Rule 702, supra,—whether the expert testimony will assist the jury in determining an issue before them—and the unusual facts in this case, we believe that Dr. Loftus' offered evidence was a proper subject for expert testimony and should have been admitted.

Of course, the test is not whether we believe that under these facts the evidence was admissible, but whether the trial court abused its discretion in reaching the contrary conclusion. Our review of the record leads us to the following conclusions regarding the various

---

6. We do not suggest that the police attempted to prejudice the identification procedure. The facts show that the police were careful to avoid the possibility of prejudice. However, as Dr. Loftus pointed out, it is not possible to discuss identification of photographs with witnesses on seven different occasions, comprising a total of over 200 pictures, without giving the witness some "feedback" with respect to what the officers anticipate or expect the witness to find.

7. We base this conclusion on statements the prosecutor made in closing argument and in defense counsel's attempts to argue that the jurors should not be misled by the confidence which the witnesses displayed in their identification testimony.

factors which support admission or preclusion here. Among the factors considered are the following:

1.   The facts were close and one of the key factual disputes to be resolved involved the accuracy of the eyewitness identification. The preclusion ruling undercut the entire evidentiary basis for defendant's arguments on this issue.

2.   The testimony offered was carefully limited to an exposition of the factors affecting reliability, with experimental data supporting the witness' testimony and no attempt was made to have the witness render opinions on the actual credibility or accuracy of the identification witnesses. Issues of ultimate fact may be the subject of expert testimony, but witnesses are not "permitted as experts on how juries should decide cases." Ariz.R. of Evid. 704 comment.

3.   On the other hand, we see no significant prejudice to the State in permitting the testimony; the problem of time is not present in this case, since time spent on the crucial issue of the case can not be considered as "undue" loss of time. No other significant factor weighing against admission of the evidence seems present.

4.   No question exists with regard to three of the four criteria listed in United States v. Amaral, supra, being fulfilled by the factual situation present in this case.

5.   The key issue here pertained to the fourth criterion—the question of whether Loftus' evidence was a "proper subject" for expert testimony.

As indicated above, the key to this issue is whether the testimony might assist the jury to resolve the issues raised by the facts. In making this determination, the trial court must first consider those contentions of ultimate fact raised by the party offering the evidence and supported by evidentiary facts in the record. It must then determine whether the expert testimony will assist in resolving the issues.

In our view, the record clearly shows that Dr. Loftus' testimony would have been of considerable assistance in resolving some of the factual contentions raised by the parties in this case. Examples follow:

First, the photographs in evidence show that there is a resemblance between Logan and Chapple. Scott told the police that Logan's photograph resembled Dee. Scott then failed to identify Chapple's photograph when it was first shown to him. Considering these facts, might Scott's comments regarding the Logan photographs be considered an identification? Should it be considered more accurate than his identification of Chapple from the photographic lineup almost one year later? Loftus' testimony regarding the forgetting curve would have assisted the jury in deciding this issue.

Second, assuming the jury disregarded, as was its right, Scott's and Buck's denial of having discussed Dee's description prior to the identification of January 27, 1979, did the feedback/after-acquired information phenomena play a part in Buck's identification of defendant on the cropped-hair lineup? We cannot assume that ordinary jurors would necessarily be aware of the impact of these factors.

Third. Logan and Chapple bear some resemblance. Logan's picture had been the object of some comment between Scott and the sheriff's deputies shortly after the killing. Although he professed to have no memory of it, Scott had seen a picture of the defendant within a few months of the shooting. Was Scott's identification of defendant on the January 27, 1979 lineup therefore influenced by an unconscious transfer of memory? Since Dee evidently looked like Logan and Chapple, was this transfer phenomenon with regard to their photographs more pronounced than it was with regard to other photographs which were shown to Scott on more than one occasion?

Fourth. Since a cropped-hair picture of Logan, who bore a resemblance to defendant and was tentatively identified by Scott soon after the killing, was not included in the lineup of January 1979, were Scott and Buck given a reasonable choice with respect to the photos which they examined on the occasion on which they identified Chapple?

Fifth. The opportunity for perception by the witnesses in this case was great. Most of us would assume that where the opportunity for perception has been significantly greater than the usual case, the recall of the witness and the subsequent identification must be correspondingly more accurate than in most cases. The expert testimony may well have led to the opposite conclusion, though Dr. Loftus admitted that none of her experiments had been based upon situations where the opportunity for perception had been similar to that of the case at bench. Nevertheless, it is implicit in Loftus' testimony that even in cases such as this, the other factors described by her can have a significant impact on the accuracy of later identification.

Sixth, did the witnesses' absolute confidence in the identification bear any relationship to the accuracy of that identification? Again, contrary to Dr. Loftus' opinion, most people might assume that it would.

Each of the factual issues described above is raised by evidentiary facts in the record or reasonable inferences from those facts. In effect, the trial judge ruled that all of the information necessary to resolve the conflicting factual contentions on these issues was within the common experience of the jurors and could be covered in cross-examination of the identification witnesses and argued to the jury.

It is difficult to support this conclusion. For instance, while jurors are aware that lapse of time may make identification less reliable, they are almost certainly unaware of the forgetting curve phenomenon and the resultant inference that a prompt tentative identification may be much more accurate than later positive identification. Similarly, cross-examination is unlikely to establish any evidentiary support for argument that eyewitnesses who have given similar nonfactual descriptions of the criminal may have been affected by the feedback phenomenon. Again, experimental data provides evidentiary support to arguments which might otherwise be unpersuasive because they seem contrary to common "wisdom." [8]

8. This problem is apparent on review of final argument. One example is that counsel for the State continually emphasized the degree of certainty of the witness-

The phrase "within the discretion of the trial court" is often used but the reason for that phrase being applied to certain issues is seldom examined. One of the primary reasons an issue is considered discretionary is that its resolution is based on factors which vary from case to case and which involve the balance of conflicting facts and equitable considerations. Walsh v. Centeio, 692 F.2d 1239, 1242 (9th Cir.1982). Thus, the phrase "within the discretion of the trial court" does not mean that the court is free to reach any conclusion it wishes. It does mean that where there are opposing equitable or factual considerations, we will not substitute our judgment for that of the trial court.

Thus, while we have no problem with the usual discretionary ruling that the trier of facts needs no assistance from expert testimony on the question of reliability of identification, the unusual facts of this case compel the contrary conclusion. The preclusion ruling here was based upon a determination that the jury would not be assisted by expert testimony because the subjects embraced by that testimony could be elicited on cross-examination and argued without the evidentiary foundation. Preclusion here was not predicated upon a balancing of conflicting factual contentions or equitable considerations; it was based upon the court's own conclusion that scientific theory regarding the working of human memory could be developed on cross-examination and effectively argued without evidentiary foundation. The examples listed above demonstrate that under the facts here this conclusion was incorrect; there were a number of substantive issues of ultimate fact on which the expert's testimony would have been of significant assistance. Accordingly, we hold that the order precluding the testimony was legally incorrect and was unsupported by the record. It was, therefore, an abuse of discretion. Grant v. Public Service Company, 133 Ariz. 434, 652 P.2d 507 (1982).

In reaching this conclusion, we do not intend to "open the gates" to a flood of expert evidence on the subject. We reach the conclusion that Dr. Loftus should have been permitted to testify on the peculiar facts of this case and have no quarrel with the result reached in the vast majority of cases which we have cited above. The rule in Arizona will continue to be that in the usual case we will support the trial court's discretionary ruling on admissibility of expert testimony on eyewitness identification. Nor do we invite opinion testimony in even the most extraordinary case on the likelihood that a particular witness is correct or mistaken in identification or that eyewitness identification in general has a certain percentage of accuracy or inaccuracy.

* * *

HAYS, Justice, dissenting:

I cannot agree with the majority's position that the trial court abused its discretion in excluding the testimony of an expert witness on

es and argued the consequent accuracy of the identification. Defense counsel asked the jury not to be misled by the certainty of the witnesses and argued that even people who are wrong are sometimes certain of their identification. No doubt the jury could understand that idea without having heard expert testimony, but we think it fair to say that experimental evidence showing the lack of correlation between certainty and reliability of even truthful witnesses might have given the argument some persuasive force.

eyewitness identification. With a view to preserving the integrity of the jury as finders of fact, I dissent in part. * * *

* * *

I also disagree with the majority's conclusion that the average juror does not know that immediate identification is much more trustworthy than long-delayed identification. The average juror may not know the technical terms for this phenomenon, but that is not relevant to his ability to assess a witness' credibility.

My concern here goes beyond the borders of this case. Once we have opened the door to this sort of impeaching testimony, what is to prevent experts from attacking any real or supposed deficiency in every other mental faculty? The peculiar risk of expert testimony with its scientific aura of trustworthiness and the possibility of undue prejudice should be respected. I have great reluctance to permit academia to take over the fact-finding function of the jury. Although clothed in other guise, that will be the practical effect. With little to distinguish this case from the general rule against admitting expert testimony on eyewitness identification, we are left with no guidelines to decide the deluge of similar issues which are sure to result.

I dissent.

UNITED STATES v. SMITH

United States Court of Appeals, Seventh Circuit, 1989.
869 F.2d 348.

KANNE, Circuit Judge. Defendant Tamara Jo Smith was charged in the Northern District of Illinois with conspiracy to commit bank and wire fraud, and substantive counts of bank, credit card and wire fraud. She was convicted of 31 of the 37 counts with which she was charged. Smith challenges the use of a spectrographic voice identification expert at trial. We affirm.

I.   Facts

Tanya and Tamara Smith are identical twins who are commonly mistaken for one another. Some of their friends, however, could distinguish them by a small scar on Tanya's forehead.

In their scheme, the two women posed as bank employees and telephoned banks authorizing them to make fictitious wire transfers of nonexistent funds. They then arranged for various individuals to pick up the money at transferee banks or at Western Union. These persons would keep a small portion for themselves and turn the bulk over to the twins.

The two women were indicted and tried together. Because identity was a core dispute at trial, the government called a spectrographic voice identification expert to testify. The original voice identification expert, who prepared the spectrograms at issue here, was unable to testify at the last minute. The expert who testified was a substitute who was called in for the trial. Tamara challenges this expert testimony. She protests the use of spectrographic voice identification testimony in general, alleging that it is not generally accepted by the scientific community. She also contends that admission of the substitute expert's testimony violated her rights under the Confrontation Clause. If the person who actually prepared the spectrograms had been present to testify, Smith argues, she would have been able to discredit his qualifications and to establish that several trials in which his mentors had testified had been reversed because of the voice identification testimony.

II. Voice Identification Expert Testimony

Dr. Hirotaka Nakasone testified as an expert witness and voice examiner. He compared the recorded voices of Tanya and Tamara Smith to the recorded voice of the person who called the Harris Bank on November 23, 1984 and falsely identified herself as a bank employee attempting to arrange a wire transfer. He concluded that it was highly probable that this was Tanya Smith and highly probable that it was not Tamara Smith. He found that it was probable that Tanya, not Tamara, telephoned Northern Trust Bank on May 21 and 22, 1985. Dr. Nakasone found that it was probably Tamara, and probably not Tanya, who called the American National Bank regarding a separate wire, and probably Tanya, and probably not Tamara, who made another call to a New Jersey bank.

Smith challenges the district court's admission of this evidence against her on two grounds: the lack of general acceptance of spectrograms by the scientific community, and the fact that she had no opportunity to cross-examine the police detective who prepared the spectrograms used at trial. The government disputes these contentions.

In discussing the admissibility of this evidence in general, both parties cite Frye v. United States, 293 F. 1013 (D.C.Cir.1923) in which the court stated that:

> "Just when a scientific principle or discovery crosses a line between experimental and demonstrable stages is difficult to define. Somewhere in this twilight zone the evidential forces of a principle must be recognized, and while courts will go a long way in admitting expert testimony deduced from a well-recognized scientific principle or discovery, the thing from which the deduction must be made must be sufficiently established to have gained general acceptance in a particular field in which it belongs."

Id. at 1014.

Although the validity of the judge-made rule in Frye has been criticized by some courts and commentators for numerous reasons, this circuit has continued to affirm (and to apply) the Frye standard. Under the Frye test, several other circuits have held expert testimony concerning spectrographic voice identification admissible. See, e.g., United States v. Williams, 583 F.2d 1194, 1198–1201 (2d Cir.1978). We join these circuits today, and hold that expert testimony concerning spectrographic voice analysis is admissible in cases where the proponent of this testimony has established a proper foundation.

A. General Considerations

With respect to admission of expert testimony in general, Federal Rule of Evidence 702 provides:

> "If scientific, technical, or other specialized knowledge will assist the trier of fact to understand the evidence or to determine a fact in issue, a witness qualified as an expert by knowledge, skill, experience, training, or education, may testify thereto in the form of an opinion or otherwise."

Under this rule, trial courts have broad discretion to admit or exclude evidence, and their rulings will not be reversed absent an abuse of that discretion. In Lundy, this court summed up many of the predicates for admission of expert testimony when it said:

> "Because experts are given special latitude to testify based on hearsay and third-hand observations and to give opinions, see Fed.R.Evid. 702, courts have cautioned that an expert must be qualified as an expert, provide testimony that will assist the jury and rely only on evidence on which a reasonable expert in the field would rely * * *. Courts agree that it is improper to permit an expert to testify regarding facts that people of common understanding can easily comprehend."

809 F.2d at 395 (citations omitted).

In discussing whether expert testimony concerning spectrographic voice identification in particular is admissible under Frye, other circuits seem to have focused upon whether the technique is (a) reliable and (b) likely to mislead the jury. Williams, 583 F.2d at 1198–1200.

Regarding the reliability of such evidence, we make the observation made by other circuits that:

> "[N]either newness nor lack of absolute certainty in a test suffices to render it inadmissible in court. Every useful new development must have its first day in court. And court records are full of the conflicting opinions of doctors, engineers and accountants * * *."

United States v. Stifel, 433 F.2d 431, 437 (6th Cir.1970), cert. denied, 401 U.S. 994 (1971). Unanimity of opinion is not necessary among the scientific community to deem evidence reliable. The technique, moreover, need not be infallible to be reliable.

In Williams, the court noted several indicia of reliability of a given scientific technique. They include the potential rate of error, the existence and maintenance of standards, the care and concern with which a scientific technique has been employed (and whether it appears to lend itself to abuse), and its analogous relationship with other types of scientific techniques. A final factor is the presence of "fail-safe" characteristics: characteristics the variability of which will lead to different, rather than similar, results. The court in Williams opined that these indicia were present with regard to spectrograms.

The tendency of testimony on scientific techniques to mislead the jury relates to the fact that, because of the apparent objectivity of opinions with a scientific basis, the jury may cloak such evidence in an "aura of mystic infallibility." Williams, 583 F.2d at 1199; Baller, 519 F.2d at 466. In other words, the jury may give this testimony more weight than it is due. The tendency of such evidence to mislead the jury is reduced, however, by factors such as the comprehensibility of the technique, the ability of the jury to make the same comparisons as the expert, and the instruction of the jury by the trial judge as to their responsibility to discredit such evidence if they find it unconvincing. The weight of such testimony can be attacked, moreover, by cross-examination and refutation.

B. Admissibility in This Case

Smith's principal argument is that spectrographic voice identification has not received sufficient general acceptance in the scientific community to be admissible under Frye. She contends that in cases where courts have admitted voice identification testimony, these courts have too narrowly defined the relevant scientific community to include only those scientists who use the technique, and not those who oppose its use. The relevant scientific community includes not only those who utilize spectrographic voice identification techniques, but linguists, psychologists and engineers as well.

Smith also cites a 1979 report of the National Research Council, On the Theory and Practice of Voice Identification, saying that there is a wide disparity in this field between the development of the theories behind voice identification and its practice, the latter being more developed than the former. She also criticizes the fact that Nakasone, who never before had been qualified as a voice identification expert in a court of law, was allowed to testify. Smith also seizes on the fact that Nakasone admitted in his testimony that the field itself was controversial and that some studies had found high error rates. She acknowledges Williams and Stifel, discussed above, which advocate a flexible approach to applying the Frye test, but urges that "it is equally true that a scientific procedure must be accepted and proved reliable before it is brought into a courtroom lest the integrity of the judicial process succumb to charlatans and quacks."

As the government points out in its brief, Smith misconceives the manner in which the Frye test is to be applied. Under her view, it would seem, if there is any disagreement at all as to the reliability or validity of a scientific technique, the disputed evidence should not come in. This court has not applied the Frye test in such a manner. Polygraph (lie detector) test results long have been admissible in this circuit under the sound discretion of the trial judge, provided that this discretion is not abused. Polygraph tests are still of disputed reliability.

Turning finally to the instant case, we hold that the district judge did not abuse his discretion in admitting the testimony. Sufficient evidence of the reliability of this technique was adduced at trial.

Moreover, this technique is not, under the proper circumstances, likely to mislead the jury. We hold that such circumstances existed here.

The government presented ample evidence of the reliability of spectrographic voice identification at trial. In addition to describing the principles behind and the technique used to make spectrograms, Dr. Nakasone testified as to their reliability. He himself had performed spectrographic analysis and produced his own opinion thereon in 150 instances, even though he never before had testified as a voice identification expert in a court of law. In none of these cases had he been informed that he had made a misidentification.

Nakasone also testified as to studies performed in the field. He first discussed a study performed by Professor Oscar Tosi of Michigan State University in conjunction with the Michigan State Police from 1968 to 1970. Of the 35,000 comparisons made in this study, the error rate for false identifications was 2.4% and the error rate for false eliminations was about 6%. This study previously has been cited as authoritative by other federal courts of appeal. See, e.g., Williams, 583 F.2d at 1198; Baller, 519 F.2d at 465. A follow-up to that study conducted by Dr. Tosi involving only actual cases examined by trained voice examiners found no errors whatsoever.[10]

Nakasone also discussed a more recent report published by the FBI in June, 1987 in the Journal of the Acoustical Society of America. The cases in that report which were submitted to actual determinations yielded a .31% rate of false identifications and a .53% rate of false eliminations. Finally, Nakasone testified that variations, such as use of tapes not recorded under laboratory conditions and attempts by the speaker to disguise her voice, will increase the error rate of false eliminations. That is, instead of resulting in more false identifications, these variations will result in more false eliminations.

On cross-examination as to his qualifications, Dr. Nakasone readily admitted that no one's voice is one-hundred percent unique, and that the field of voice identification is not one-hundred percent reliable. He also indicated his awareness of other studies, the Campbell study and the Hazzen study. These studies had higher error rates than those cited by him, purportedly of 62.7 percent and 83.33 percent respectively. Nakasone also mentioned that no studies involving black females, which both of the defendants are, had been performed.

During subsequent cross-examination, Nakasone answered questions regarding the study performed by the National Research Council cited to by Smith in her brief. He also testified extensively as to intraspeaker and interspeaker variation. Nakasone agreed that no one says the same word exactly the same way twice and that it is currently only an assumption that interspeaker variation is sufficiently greater than intraspeaker variation for spectrographic analysis to be able to distinguish one person's voice from that of another.

10. Smith is correct that the National Research Council study, to which she cites in her brief, was performed after the Tosi study. She does not demonstrate, however, how this makes the first study per se unreliable.

We conclude that the district judge did not abuse his discretion in admitting Nakasone's testimony into evidence. This testimony contained many of the indicia of reliability discussed by the Second Circuit in Williams, supra. A thorough examination of the record reveals both that this technique is not one-hundred percent infallible and that the entire scientific community does not support it. As we discuss above, however, neither infallibility nor unanimity is a precondition for general acceptance of scientific evidence under Frye. We also note, as the government points out in its brief, that spectrographic identification is similar to lay identification of voices, which is admissible in this circuit.

Since sufficient indicia of reliability were present in this case, it was proper for the district judge to let this evidence go to the jury, in order for it to make the ultimate determination as to the credibility of Nakasone's testimony.

This testimony, moreover, was not likely to mislead the jury. The jury had the opportunity in this case to hear both the voice exemplars and the recorded conversations, and to see the spectrograms. Although the district judge did not give a specific instruction on Nakasone's testimony, he properly instructed the jury as to their sole prerogative to judge credibility of the witnesses and the weight of their testimony, and as to their right to reject expert testimony. Dr. Nakasone, moreover, was very candid at trial about the limitations of spectrography. He also was subject to rigorous cross-examination. As we discuss, below, it was not necessary that Smrkovski, who prepared the spectrograms, be cross-examined. We thus conclude that this testimony was admissible.

WALTZ, INTRODUCTION TO CRIMINAL EVIDENCE

385–389 (3d ed.).*

DNA Profiling

On August 26, 1988, a sleeping University of Illinois student was sexually assaulted in her darkened apartment. She could not identify her attacker because she was not wearing her contact lenses and the intruder had placed a pillow over her face.

On February 16, 1990, it took a jury only 75 minutes to convict Vincent Lipscomb on two counts of aggravated criminal sexual assault. The only identification evidence in the case against him was a so-called DNA test demonstrating that genetic material taken from a sample of the defendant's blood matched samples of semen taken from the victim. One of the prosecution's expert witnesses had testified that the odds against the occurrence of two identical DNA patterns were 1 in 6.8 billion. Since the world's population is only about 5 billion, the jury obviously thought it was on firm ground in finding Lipscomb guilty after hearing two weeks of expert testimony about deoxyribonucleic acid, non-polymorphous probes, band sizings, and autoradiograms. The jury based its verdict on the results of a new procedure that, in the years to come, is likely to revolutionize criminal investigation and proof. And yet it is disturbing to see a conviction for serious crime that is based entirely on the result of a testing methodology that in some respects is still in its infancy. Courts are rushing to accept DNA matching despite warnings from some segments of the scientific community that standards ensuring reliability are sorely lacking.

DNA profiling is a laboratory identification process. The term DNA profiling is a generic one, referring to two versions of what is known as Restriction Fragment Length Polymorphism (RFLP), which is a technique for analyzing the chromosomes forming the strand of the DNA molecule found in virtually every human cell. As a method of identifying perpetrators of violent crimes, DNA profiling will revolutionize law enforcement.

In a 1989 interview, Kenneth Nemmich, special agent in the FBI's Laboratory Division, said, "We're now doing DNA profiling routinely. It's the biological equivalent of fingerprinting, the closest to a positive personal identification." Agent Nimmich was referring to one of the most recent scientific techniques to come to the aid of law enforcement.

Prior to 1990, DNA profiling had been used in only a small number of cases and involved the work of a few private laboratories, although it had been used in Great Britain for a number of years. In late 1988, following a year of testing, the FBI initiated widespread American implementation of the technique. The process is now available not only to the FBI's own agents but also to any local police department. Under proper circumstances, DNA profiling permits positive identification of a suspect as the crime perpetrator, or excludes that person from further suspicion, based on the unique genetic material in a small specimen of blood, semen, or other body fluids or tissues. It is especially helpful in connection with sex crimes, historically the most difficult to solve. (On the civil side, the DNA technique is likely to become dispositive in most paternity actions, replacing blood typing; see, e.g., Matter of Adoption of "Baby Girl S," 532 N.Y.S.2d 634 (N.Y.1988).)

DNA testing reconstructs a descriptive physical profile, including eye and hair color, by unlocking the genetic codes that can be extracted from specimens as small as a hair, a drop of blood (even when drawn from a dead body), a skin scraping, or a dime-size spot of semen. Any description of this genetic "marking" process is likely to be mind-boggling to anyone who is not a molecular biologist; it is an extremely complicated and tedious process.

A sense of the technique can be conveyed simply by observing that DNA, which is short for deoxyribonucleic acid, is found in every human cell. It forms the genes and carries the code for heredity. And that genetic code is different in every person, with the exception of identical twins. Through a laborious testing process, the laboratory scientist, using specimens of the sort mentioned above that have been forwarded by criminal investigators or defense counsel, can extract this code and render it graphic. There follows a simplified but nonetheless formidable description of the process.

The original test, known in the United States by the trade name DNA Fingerprinting, was developed in England in the early 1980s at the University of Leicester by geneticist Alex Jeffreys. His technique

involves subjecting the DNA molecule to an enzyme that cuts the
molecule into fragments. These fragments are then propelled through
a gel by means of an electrical charge in a process called electrophoresis. The fragments will be of varying lengths. Since short fragments
will be propelled through the gel more rapidly than long ones, the
electrophoresis process sorts them by length, creating a pattern. To
"fix" (stabilize) this pattern so that it can be analyzed, radioactive
probes are introduced into the sample. These probes bind to a sequence of points or bases on the DNA fragments. The sample is then
blotted on photographic film, which is exposed by the radioactivity. A
pattern of bands emerges, looking very much like the bar code on
supermarket items.

Because every person's DNA pattern is unique (except, as mentioned, for those of identical twins), the pattern created by the sorted
fragments is unique to the test subject's DNA. Cellmark Diagnostics,
which markets DNA Fingerprinting in this country, represents that the
technique is 99.9 percent accurate. Jeffreys puts it as a statistical
proposition: he says that there is only a 1 in 1 quadrillion chance that
two unrelated persons will exhibit the same DNA "fingerprint." His
assertion is supported by a computerized database that tracks the
occurrence of gene frequencies within specific ethnic groups. This
database draws on blood samples that have been obtained, in the main,
from blood banks. (California is considering the establishment of a
statewide database, to be created from blood and saliva samples extracted from persons convicted of murder, assault, rape, and other
sexual offenses.) Another private testing laboratory, Lifecodes Corporation, performs what it calls DNA–Print. Its process is substantially
similar to Cellmark's. Cetus Corporation uses a variant of the RFLP
technique. It is less specific but can work with smaller samples.

With the entry of the FBI into DNA profiling, these private
laboratories will be used primarily by private individuals such as
criminal defendants. The fees charged by the private laboratories may
be prohibitive in some cases (perpetrators of violent crimes tend to be
poor people), which will give yet another advantage to the prosecution.
(As of 1990, for example, Cellmark Diagnostics charged between $1,500
and $2,000 per DNA test and between $750 and $1,000 a day for an
expert witness.)

As is often true of scientific techniques, the problem may be not so
much with methodology as with its human implementation. Standards
will have to be developed; the FBI has already gone a long way toward
generating them. For example, the proper preservation of evidence
samples is crucial and this poses some difficulties. One of these
difficulties is traceable to the fear of AIDS. Those who treat rape
victims are concerned that the victim may contract AIDS from her
attacker if potentially AIDS-contaminated bodily fluids are not quickly
removed. Thus the victim will immediately be cleansed of semen and
blood, resulting in the loss of critical evidence. The FBI has recommended that rape victims first be swabbed with a sterile tissue in order
to preserve DNA samples. At an even more basic level, there must be

assurances that the preserved sample is neither contaminated nor too degraded to be useful.

Another problem is that DNA patterns, if not handled with great care, can stretch or shift, making them difficult or impossible to interpret. A relatively recent Supreme Court decision—one that has been widely criticized—may also pose a threat. Arizona v. Youngblood, 488 U.S. 51, 109 S.Ct. 333 (1988), was a child molesting case involving the sodomizing of a boy who had been abducted from a carnival. A standard sexual assault kit was used to test the victim. Thereafter, the boy identified Youngblood as his assailant. At trial, in 1985, the defendant claimed mistaken identity. The police had permitted the semen samples to become degraded; they could no longer be tested to confirm or exclude Youngblood as possessing the assailant's blood type. The Arizona Court of Appeals reversed Youngblood's conviction, holding that due process is violated when identity is at issue and the police have permitted the destruction of evidence that could exclude the accused as the perpetrator.

The U.S. Supreme Court reversed the state court, saying "We . . . hold that unless a criminal defendant can show bad faith on the part of the police, failure to preserve potential useful evidence does not constitute a denial of due process of law." The threat posed by this ruling was addressed, in dissent, by Justice Blackmun: "As technology develops, the potential for this type of evidence to provide conclusive results on any number of questions will increase." Referring specifically to DNA testing, the Justice continued, "Current genetic testing measures . . . are already extraordinarily precise. . . . The importance of these types of evidence is indisputable, and requiring police to recognize their importance is not unreasonable."

By mid–1989 the FBI laboratory at Quantico, Virginia, had received over 200 specimens from its agents and from various police departments. Final reports in the first 80 of these cases demonstrate the efficacy of the DNA technique in identifying the innocent along with the guilty. In 50 cases the DNA profile positively tied the suspect to the crime under investigation, which was usually either rape or murder. In 20 cases the profiling process exonerated the original suspect. (In 10 cases the biological specimen was too tiny or too decayed to be testable.)

By mid–1989 the DNA testing technique had been involved in some 80 reported court cases. Its reliability went virtually unchallenged, the only question being (a) whether the test was properly conducted (b) on an appropriate biological specimen. As the DNA technique's utilization becomes increasingly widespread its impact on the disposition of criminal cases is likely to be dramatic, particularly in view of the fact that biological evidence—blood, hair, skin, semen—is much more commonly found at crime scenes than are usable fingerprints. The impact of DNA profiling will undoubtedly be most evident at the plea-bargaining stage of the criminal justice process. Lifecodes has reported that a majority of the criminal defendants tested by its laboratory changed their plea to "Guilty" after receiving adverse test results.

HOUTS, PHOTOGRAPHIC MISREPRESENTATION

Matthew Bender & Co.; San Francisco; 1964, pp. 5–46 to 5–49.

[8]—Lens Performance: Position of Automobiles

* * *

Figures 54 & 55 are taken from the same camera position behind the convertible automobile. A short focal length lens is used in *Figure 54*. This makes it appear that there is a substantial distance between the two vehicles and that perhaps the driver of the convertible would have had ample time to stop when the other car pulled out in front of him. *Figure 55* was taken with a long focal length lens which "pulls" the two vehicles together, making it appear that the driver of the convertible would not have had time to stop. * * *

WALTZ, INTRODUCTION TO CRIMINAL EVIDENCE

417–423 (1991).*

DEMONSTRATIVE EVIDENCE

A.

Historical Background

It is pointed out in [an earlier chapter] that demonstrative evidence is to be distinguished from real evidence in that demonstrative evidence consists of tangible materials that are used for illustrative or explanatory purposes only and do not purport to be "the real thing"—the murder weapon, the burglary tools actually used by the accused, the heroin seized by the narcotics agents when they arrested the defendant. It

Figure 54

Figure 55

was also mentioned in [an earlier chapter] that there are two basic types of demonstrative evidence: (1) *selected* demonstrative evidence, such as handwriting exemplars, and (2) *prepared* or *reproduced* demonstrative evidence, such as a sketch or diagram * * *. In this chapter we go into somewhat greater depth in describing types of demonstrative evidence and the range of possible objections to its use.

There has been a resurgence of interest in the imaginative use of demonstrative evidence, after a lengthy period during which trial lawyers were reluctant to rely on it for fear of causing an adverse reaction by jurors who might draw the implication that an essentially weak case was being overproved by means of unsubstantial gimmickry. Unquestionably, the use of demonstrative evidence has had its ups and downs, as the following commentary—made almost a hundred years ago—attests:

> In the early and rude ages there was a strong leaning toward the adoption of demonstrative and practical tests upon disputed questions. Doubting Thomases demanded the satisfaction of their senses. * * * As society grew civilized and refined, it seemed disposed to despise these demonstrative methods, and inclined more to the preference of a narration, at second-hand, by eye and ear witnesses. But in this busy century there seems to have been a relapse toward the earlier experimental spirit, and a disposition to make assurance doubly sure by any practical method addressed to the senses. (Browne, Practical Tests in Evidence, 4 Green Bag 510 (1892).)

Of course, there is nothing inherently wrong with evidence which is addressed to some sense other than that of hearing. One character in the musical My Fair Lady may have unwittingly summed up the attitude of many jury members when she said, "Words, words, words—

I'm sick of words. Is that all you [lawyers] can do? *Show me!"* (Italics added.)

For a number of years now, trial lawyers have paid increasing attention to demonstrative evidence as a means of *showing* the elements of a case to the fact-finder.

Perhaps the earliest reported use of demonstrative evidence was in the Case of *James Watson, the elder, Surgeon, on an Indictment charging him with High Treason,* 32 Howard State Trials 1 (1817). There was offered into evidence in that case a sketch of a flag that allegedly had been used to whip up a "treasonous assemblage" in England. Defense counsel objected, arguing that the flag "was a matter of verbal description not of description by drawing." The trial judge sneered and overruled the objection: "Can there be any objection to the production of a drawing, or a model, as illustrative of evidence? Surely there is nothing in the objection."

Another leading case, this time arising in America but not many years after the Watson trial, is Commonwealth v. Webster, 5 Cush. 295 (Sup.Jud.Ct.Mass.1850). Professor Webster had been charged with murdering Doctor Parkman and burning his body in a furnace. A mold of Doctor Parkman's jaw, made several years previously when he had been fitted for dentures, taken together with some teeth that had survived the furnace fire, was credited with securing Webster's conviction.

Today the propriety, in fact the wisdom, of using demonstrative evidence to help jurors follow the trial evidence goes pretty much without question in many cases, both criminal and civil. Objections to demonstrative evidence are frequently voiced, however.

B.

Bases for Objection to Demonstrative Evidence

Misguided Objections. Some objections to demonstrative evidence are misguided and will be swiftly overruled. Occasionally a lawyer will become confused about the proper application of the best evidence rule, discussed [earlier], and contend that the "original," and not "a mere example," must be produced in court. Thus one hears about the Texas judge who prohibited the use of a skeletal model because it did not consist of the very bones of the complaining witness (who was not dead). This judge had forgotten, if he ever knew, that the best evidence rule applies only to written documents.

Then, too, one sometimes encounters a misguided hearsay objection to demonstrative evidence. Defense counsel leaps up to object to the prosecution's offer of a witness's freehand sketch of a crime scene, asking, "How can we cross-examine a sketch, Your Honor?" What this objection misses, of course, is the fact that the sketch is being offered as a part of the testimony of a witness on the stand who is fully subject to confrontation and cross-examination.

Objections Grounded on Lack of Verity or Accuracy. As was suggested in [an earlier chapter], dealing with the perfecting of the trial record, a proper foundation or predicate must be laid before an item of demonstrative evidence can successfully be offered. The witness who is in a position to "sponsor" (authenticate) the exhibit must identify it and verify, the accuracy of whatever it portrays. This does not mean that the sponsoring witness must be the person who took the photograph or prepared the drawing, chart, or map.

Example:

BY THE PROSECUTING ATTORNEY: Officer Ham, you have testified that you were present, in your investigative capacity, at the scene of the murders, isn't that correct?

A. That's right, I was in the room for maybe three hours.

Q. And you have testified to its general layout and appearance, have you not?

A. I have.

Q. To your knowledge, were photographs of the room taken while you were there?

A. Yes, our photographer took a number of shots of the place.

Q. Officer Ham, I now hand you what previously has been marked Prosecution Exhibit 12 for Identification, being a photographic print, and ask you whether or not it is a fair and accurate representation of the room at 421 Melrose Street on the day in question?

A. Yes, sir, it is. That's exactly the way it looked.

BY THE PROSECUTING ATTORNEY: Your Honor, we offer prosecution's 12 into evidence.

BY DEFENSE COUNSEL: We have no objection.

THE COURT: The exhibit will be received.

There can be no stronger an objection to demonstrative evidence than that it is not a fair representation of what it supposedly depicts. If, for example, a photograph or map significantly distorts relevant aspects of the scene depicted, it will be subject to successful objection, or at least to an instruction that the jury is to disregard the distorted parts.

Occasionally photographs can be obtained only after autopsy procedures have in a sense distorted the picture of a deceased: the head has been shaved; large incisions have been made; sutures may be visible. Still, the tendency is to admit such photographs if they add to the case anything of real probative value. Thus in Young v. State, the court, commenting on the receipt in evidence of post-autopsy photographs, said, "[T]he fact that the ghastly appearance of the wounds, even though such appearance was heightened by the shaving of the head and the use of mercurochrome * * * did not make [the photographs] inadmissible."

So long as the color has not been artificially and misleadingly heightened, there is a trend toward preferring natural color to black-and-white photographs. Some years ago Professor Conrad, an authority on photographic evidence, wrote, "[W]e have used black and white photographs for so long that we accept them as the real thing. Actually, black and white photography is considered an abstract medium and does not represent reality as such. * * * The inherent realism of color photography has been urged [as preferable to black and white]. * * *" (Conrad, Evidential Aspects of Color Photography, 4 Jour. of Forensic Science 176, 178 (1959).)

The fact that a photograph or other item of demonstrative evidence has been retouched or marked will not, in and of itself, result in inadmissibility. For example, in State v. Weston, plaster casts of a body containing gunshot wounds had been prepared prior to autopsy. Many small blue dots had been placed on the casts by a witness who compared the casts with the body in order to distinguish the bullet wounds from air bubbles in the plaster casts. When the casts were offered in evidence to exemplify the location of the bullet wounds, defense counsel objected that "after the blue dots which indicate the wounds had been placed upon the cast it was no longer * * * a true representation of deceased's forearm and hand." The Oregon Supreme Court laid down the applicable principles:

> The jury was amply informed that the sole purpose of the blue dots was to indicate the presence of the wounds. Since the jurors could rightfully look at the indications of the wounds, we cannot understand how the help which these small dots gave them in locating the wounds would have prejudiced any interest properly claimed by the defendant. * * *
>
> [W]e deduce the rule that maps, photographs et cetera, containing markings, are not inadmissible if they are otherwise relevant and if the individual who made the mark or wrote the legend was familiar with the facts and so testifies, or if some other witness, familiar with the facts, adopts the mark or legend as his own. (See also Busch, Photographic Evidence, 4 DePaul Law Rev. 195 (1955).)

Models are sometimes rejected by trial courts because they may be misleading or confusing due to difference in scale.

Example A:

> San Mateo County v. Christian, ("While models may frequently be of great assistance to a court and jury, it is common knowledge that, even when constructed to scale, they may frequently, because of the great disparity in size between the model and the original, also be very misleading. * * *").

Example B:

> Martindale v. City of Mountain View, (in assault and battery case, testimony was that victim had been beaten with 2′ stick; offer in evidence of axe handle 3′ long rejected).

Courts are suspicious of filmed reenactments and posed photographs, lest they be misleading. A leading case, Richardson v. Missouri-K.T.R. Co. of Texas, arose on the civil side. To establish that the plaintiff himself had been negligent, the defendant introduced a color film showing plaintiff's shop foreman demonstrating how plaintiff's hand *"could* be caught and run through the blades" of a shaping machine (italics added). The foreman testified that "he did not know how the fingers of [plaintiff] were caught in the machine and therefore his experiments did not undertake to show how [plaintiff] was operating it at the time."

The Texas court brushed aside the plaintiff's objections to this filmed reenactment. "In the final analysis," the court said, "the increased danger of fraud peculiar to posed photographs must be weighed against their communicative value. Only the additional danger of fraud or suggestion separates this question from that of the admissibility of ordinary photographs."

In line with the Richardson decision, posed and photographed reenactments of a crime are sometimes admitted in evidence after a careful foundation, which manifests the accuracy of the reenactment, has been laid by the prosecuting attorney.

Gruesome Films and Photographs. As was intimated earlier, another prime basis of objections to demonstrative evidence is that the motion picture or still photograph is gruesome and inflammatory; in other words, that its potential for prejudice to the accused's right to a fair trial outweighs whatever probative worth it may have. An objection of this sort is directed to the trial judge's discretion.

A photograph or motion picture is not inadmissible simply because it is gruesome. That has been understood ever since the opinion in Franklin v. State involving some gruesome photographs:

> The throat of the deceased was cut; the character of the wound was important * * *; the man was killed and buried * * *; we cannot conceive of a more impartial and truthful witness than the sun, as its light stamps and seals the similitude of the wound on the photograph put before the jury; it would be more accurate than the memory of witnesses, and as the object of all evidence is to show the truth, why should not this dumb [in the sense of mute] witness show it?

Ever since *Franklin* it has been the rule that photographs and films are not rendered inadmissible simply because they depict in a graphic way the details of a shocking or revolting crime. They will be deemed inadmissible only if they are irrelevant to the issues in the case or where their probative worth is outweighed by their potential for unfair prejudice.

Example a:

> Johnson v. Commonwealth (hideous photographs showing mangled body in morgue, *held*, admissible to support autopsy surgeon's explanatory testimony).

Example b:

> Henninger v. State (three gruesome photographs showing knife wounds in back, partially severed head, and pantyhose wrapped around neck, *held*, admissible to establish identity of accused, cause of death, and to rebut claim of self-defense).

Appellate courts will conclude that it was an abuse of judicial discretion to receive gruesome photographs only when they were unnecessary, cumulative to the narrative testimony of witnesses, or where, although of minimal evidentiary value, they have been overemphasized to the jury. Thus it may be error to admit gruesome photographs when the testimony of an available pathologist would do just as well. In an early California case, Thrall v. Smiley, the court rejected drawings of the defendant's damaged teeth, noting that the sketches were not "necessary to illustrate the fact asserted [since] the extent of the injury could be as well understood from the statement of the dentist who repaired them." And projecting color slides of the deceased's wounds for a full half day during a four and one-half day trial has led to reversal. Some additional examples are given below:

Example A:

Commonwealth v. Dankel (where only factual dispute was whether accused aided in burglary during which a homicide occurred, introduction by prosecution of four gruesome photographs of victim, showing face eroded by ammonia burns, was reversible error).

Example B:

Terry v. State (where bruises and other injuries sustained by infant homicide victim had already been shown with pre-autopsy photographs, it was prejudicial error to receive four post-autopsy photographs depicting massive mutilation to child caused by autopsy procedures).

Example B:

Beagles v. State (where defense in first degree murder case admitted victim's death, the cause of death, and her identity, the admission of numerous gruesome color photographs of the victim was error: "Photographs should be received in evidence with great caution and photographs which show nothing more than a gory or gruesome portrayal should not be admitted.").

Trial judges will protect an accused against the use of demonstrative evidence the primary purpose of which is to whip jurors into a vindictive mood. But demonstrative evidence has a firmly settled place in criminal litigation. If it is used sparingly, with scrupulous accuracy, and only when it holds out genuine promise of making the case more readily understandable by judge and jurors, courts can be expected to be liberal in their rulings on the admissibility question.

APPENDIX A

FEDERAL RULES OF EVID
UNITED STATES COUR
MAGISTRATES

As amended to December 1

Table of Rules

Article I. General Provisions

Article II. Judicial Notice

Article III. Presumptions in Civil Actions and Proceedings

Article IV. Relevancy and Its Limits

1
2
3
4
5
6
7
8
9
10
11
12
13
14
15
16
17
18
19
20
21
22
23
24
25
26
27
28
29
30
31
32
33
34
35
36
37
38
39
40
41
42
43
44
45
46
47
48
49

ARTICLE I. GENERAL PROVISIONS

RULE 101. SCOPE

These rules govern proceedings in the courts of the United States and before United States bankruptcy judges and United States magistrates, to the extent and with the exceptions stated in rule 1101.

RULE 102. PURPOSE AND CONSTRUCTION

These rules shall be construed to secure fairness in administration, elimination of unjustifiable expense and delay, and promotion of growth and development of the law of evidence to the end that the truth may be ascertained and proceedings justly determined.

RULE 103. RULINGS ON EVIDENCE

(a) Effect of Erroneous Ruling. Error may not be predicated upon a ruling which admits or excludes evidence unless a substantial right of the party is affected, and

(1) *Objection.* In case the ruling is one admitting evidence, a timely objection or motion to strike appears of record, stating the specific ground of objection, if the specific ground was not apparent from the context; or

(2) *Offer of Proof.* In case the ruling is one excluding evidence, the substance of the evidence was made known to the court by offer or was apparent from the context within which questions were asked.

(b) Record of Offer and Ruling. The court may add any other or further statement which shows the character of the evidence, the form in which it was offered, the objection made, and the ruling thereon. It may direct the making of an offer in question and answer form.

(c) Hearing of Jury. In jury cases, proceedings shall be conducted, to the extent practicable, so as to prevent inadmissible evidence from being suggested to the jury by any means, such as making statements or offers of proof or asking questions in the hearing of the jury.

(d) Plain Error. Nothing in this rule precludes taking notice of plain errors affecting substantial rights although they were not brought to the attention of the court.

RULE 104. PRELIMINARY QUESTIONS

(a) Questions of Admissibility Generally. Preliminary questions concerning the qualification of a person to be a witness, the existence of a privilege, or the admissibility of evidence shall be determined by the court, subject to the provisions of subdivision (b). In making its determination it is not bound by the rules of evidence except those with respect to privileges.

(b) Relevancy Conditioned on Fact. When the relevancy of evidence depends upon the fulfillment of a condition of fact, the court shall admit it upon, or subject to, the introduction of evidence sufficient to support a finding of the fulfillment of the condition.

(c) Hearing of Jury. Hearings on the admissibility of confessions shall in all cases be conducted out of the hearing of the jury. Hearings on other preliminary matters shall be so conducted when the interests of justice require, or when an accused is a witness and so requests.

(d) Testimony by Accused. The accused does not, by testifying upon a preliminary matter, become subject to cross-examination as to other issues in the case.

(e) Weight and Credibility. This rule does not limit the right of a party to introduce before the jury evidence relevant to weight or credibility.

[Amended effective October 1, 1987.]

RULE 105. LIMITED ADMISSIBILITY

When evidence which is admissible as to one party or for one purpose but not admissible as to another party or for another purpose is admitted, the court, upon request, shall restrict the evidence to its proper scope and instruct the jury accordingly.

RULE 106. REMAINDER OF OR RELATED WRITINGS OR RECORDED STATEMENTS

When a writing or recorded statement or part thereof is introduced by a party, an adverse party may require the introduction at that time of any other part or any other writing or recorded statement which ought in fairness to be considered contemporaneously with it.

ARTICLE II. JUDICIAL NOTICE

RULE 201. JUDICIAL NOTICE OF ADJUDICATIVE FACTS

(a) **Scope of Rule.** This rule governs only judicial notice of adjudicative facts.

(b) **Kinds of Facts.** A judicially noticed fact must be one not subject to reasonable dispute in that it is either (1) generally known within the territorial jurisdiction of the trial court or (2) capable of accurate and ready determination by resort to sources whose accuracy cannot reasonably be questioned.

(c) **When Discretionary.** A court may take judicial notice, whether requested or not.

(d) **When Mandatory.** A court shall take judicial notice if requested by a party and supplied with the necessary information.

(e) **Opportunity to Be Heard.** A party is entitled upon timely request to an opportunity to be heard as to the propriety of taking judicial notice and the tenor of the matter noticed. In the absence of prior notification, the request may be made after judicial notice has been taken.

(f) **Time of Taking Notice.** Judicial notice may be taken at any stage of the proceeding.

(g) **Instructing Jury.** In a civil action or proceeding, the court shall instruct the jury to accept as conclusive any fact judicially noticed. In a criminal case, the court shall instruct the jury that it may, but is not required to, accept as conclusive any fact judicially noticed.

ARTICLE III. PRESUMPTIONS IN CIVIL ACTIONS AND PROCEEDINGS

RULE 301. PRESUMPTIONS IN GENERAL IN CIVIL ACTIONS AND PROCEEDINGS

In all civil actions and proceedings not otherwise provided for by Act of Congress or by these rules, a presumption imposes on the party against whom it is directed the burden of going forward with evidence to rebut or meet the presumption, but does not shift to such party the burden of proof in the sense of the risk of nonpersuasion, which remains throughout the trial upon the party on whom it was originally cast.

RULE 302. APPLICABILITY OF STATE LAW IN CIVIL ACTIONS AND PROCEEDINGS

In civil actions and proceedings, the effect of a presumption respecting a fact which is an element of a claim or defense as to which

State law supplies the rule of decision is determined in accordance with
State law.

ARTICLE IV. RELEVANCY AND ITS LIMITS

RULE 401. DEFINITION OF "RELEVANT EVIDENCE"

"Relevant evidence" means evidence having any tendency to make
the existence of any fact that is of consequence to the determination of
the action more probable or less probable than it would be without the
evidence.

RULE 402. RELEVANT EVIDENCE GENERALLY ADMISSIBLE; IRRELEVANT EVIDENCE INADMISSIBLE

All relevant evidence is admissible, except as otherwise provided by
the Constitution of the United States, by Act of Congress, by these
rules, or by other rules prescribed by the Supreme Court pursuant to
statutory authority. Evidence which is not relevant is not admissible.

RULE 403. EXCLUSION OF RELEVANT EVIDENCE ON GROUNDS OF PREJUDICE, CONFUSION, OR WASTE OF TIME

Although relevant, evidence may be excluded if its probative value
is substantially outweighed by the danger of unfair prejudice, confusion
of the issues, or misleading the jury, or by considerations of undue
delay, waste of time, or needless presentation of cumulative evidence.

RULE 404. CHARACTER EVIDENCE NOT ADMISSIBLE TO PROVE CONDUCT; EXCEPTIONS; OTHER CRIMES

(a) Character Evidence Generally. Evidence of a person's character or a trait of character is not admissible for the purpose of proving
action in conformity therewith on a particular occasion, except:

(1) *Character of Accused.* Evidence of a pertinent trait of character offered by an accused, or by the prosecution to rebut the same;

(2) *Character of Victim.* Evidence of a pertinent trait of character
of the victim of the crime offered by an accused, or by the prosecution
to rebut the same, or evidence of a character trait of peacefulness of the
victim offered by the prosecution in a homicide case to rebut evidence
that the victim was the first aggressor;

(3) *Character of Witness.* Evidence of the character of a witness, as
provided in rules 607, 608, and 609.

(b) Other crimes, wrongs, or acts. Evidence of other crimes,
wrongs, or acts is not admissible to prove the character of a person in
order to show action in conformity therewith. It may, however, be
admissible for other purposes, such as proof of motive, opportunity,
intent, preparation, plan, knowledge, identity, or absence of mistake or
accident, provided that upon request by the accused, the prosecution in
a criminal case shall provide reasonable notice in advance of trial, or

during trial if the court excuses pretrial notice on good cause shown, of the general nature of any such evidence it intends to introduce at trial.

RULE 405. METHODS OF PROVING CHARACTER

(a) **Reputation or Opinion.** In all cases in which evidence of character or a trait of character of a person is admissible, proof may be made by testimony as to reputation or by testimony in the form of an opinion. On cross-examination inquiry is allowable into relevant specific instances of conduct.

(b) **Specific Instances of Conduct.** In cases in which character or a trait of character of a person is an essential element of a charge, claim, or defense, proof may also be made of specific instances of that person's conduct.

RULE 406. HABIT; ROUTINE PRACTICE

Evidence of the habit of a person or of the routine practice of an organization, whether corroborated or not and regardless of the presence of eyewitnesses, is relevant to prove that the conduct of the person or organization on a particular occasion was in conformity with the habit or routine practice.

RULE 407. SUBSEQUENT REMEDIAL MEASURES

When, after an event, measures are taken which, if taken previously, would have made the event less likely to occur, evidence of the subsequent measures is not admissible to prove negligence or culpable conduct in connection with the event. This rule does not require the exclusion of evidence of subsequent measures when offered for another purpose, such as proving ownership, control, or feasibility of precautionary measures, if controverted, or impeachment.

RULE 408. COMPROMISE AND OFFERS TO COMPROMISE

Evidence of (1) furnishing or offering or promising to furnish, or (2) accepting or offering or promising to accept, a valuable consideration in compromising or attempting to compromise a claim which was disputed as to either validity or amount, is not admissible to prove liability for or invalidity of the claim or its amount. Evidence of conduct or statements made in compromise negotiations is likewise not admissible. This rule does not require the exclusion of any evidence otherwise discoverable merely because it is presented in the course of compromise negotiations. This rule also does not require exclusion when the evidence is offered for another purpose, such as proving bias or prejudice of a witness, negativing a contention of undue delay, or proving an effort to obstruct a criminal investigation or prosecution.

RULE 409. PAYMENT OF MEDICAL AND SIMILAR EXPENSES

Evidence of furnishing or offering or promising to pay medical, hospital, or similar expenses occasioned by an injury is not admissible to prove liability for the injury.

RULE 410. INADMISSIBILITY OF PLEAS, PLEA DISCUSSIONS, AND RELATED STATEMENTS

Except as otherwise provided in this rule, evidence of the following is not, in any civil or criminal proceeding, admissible against the defendant who made the plea or was a participant in the plea discussions:

(1) a plea of guilty which was later withdrawn;

(2) a plea of nolo contendere;

(3) any statement made in the course of any proceedings under Rule 11 of the Federal Rules of Criminal Procedure or comparable state procedure regarding either of the foregoing pleas; or

(4) any statement made in the course of plea discussions with an attorney for the prosecuting authority which do not result in a plea of guilty or which result in a plea of guilty later withdrawn.

However, such a statement is admissible (i) in any proceeding wherein another statement made in the course of the same plea or plea discussions has been introduced and the statement ought in fairness be considered contemporaneously with it, or (ii) in a criminal proceeding for perjury or false statement if the statement was made by the defendant under oath, on the record and in the presence of counsel.

RULE 411. LIABILITY INSURANCE

Evidence that a person was or was not insured against liability is not admissible upon the issue whether the person acted negligently or otherwise wrongfully. This rule does not require the exclusion of evidence of insurance against liability when offered for another purpose, such as proof of agency, ownership, or control, or bias or prejudice of a witness.

RULE 412. SEX OFFENSE CASES; RELEVANCE OF VICTIM'S PAST BEHAVIOR

(a) Notwithstanding any other provision of law, in a criminal case in which a person is accused of an offense under chapter 109A of title 18, United States Code, reputation or opinion evidence of the past sexual behavior of an alleged victim of such offense is not admissible.

(b) Notwithstanding any other provision of law, in a criminal case in which a person is accused of an offense under chapter 109A of title

18, United States Code, evidence of a victim's past sexual behavior other than reputation or opinion evidence is also not admissible, unless such evidence other than reputation or opinion evidence is—

(1) admitted in accordance with subdivisions (c)(1) and (c) (2) and is constitutionally required to be admitted; or

(2) admitted in accordance with subdivision (c) and is evidence of—

(A) past sexual behavior with persons other than the accused, offered by the accused upon the issue of whether the accused was or was not, with respect to the alleged victim, the source of semen or injury; or

(B) past sexual behavior with the accused and is offered by the accused upon the issue of whether the alleged victim consented to the sexual behavior with respect to which such offense is alleged.

(c)(1) If the person accused of committing an offense under chapter 109A of title 18, United States Code intends to offer under subdivision (b) evidence of specific instances of the alleged victim's past sexual behavior, the accused shall make a written motion to offer such evidence not later than fifteen days before the date on which the trial in which such evidence is to be offered is scheduled to begin, except that the court may allow the motion to be made at a later date, including during trial, if the court determines either that the evidence is newly discovered and could not have been obtained earlier through the exercise of due diligence or that the issue to which such evidence relates has newly arisen in the case. Any motion made under this paragraph shall be served on all other parties and on the alleged victim.

(2) The motion described in paragraph (1) shall be accompanied by a written offer of proof. If the court determines that the offer of proof contains evidence described in subdivision (b), the court shall order a hearing in chambers to determine if such evidence is admissible. At such hearing the parties may call witnesses, including the alleged victim, and offer relevant evidence. Notwithstanding subdivision (b) of rule 104, if the relevancy of the evidence which the accused seeks to offer in the trial depends upon the fulfillment of a condition of fact, the court, at the hearing in chambers or at a subsequent hearing in chambers scheduled for such purpose, shall accept evidence on the issue of whether such condition of fact is fulfilled and shall determine such issue.

(3) If the court determines on the basis of the hearing described in paragraph (2) that the evidence which the accused seeks to offer is relevant and that the probative value of such evidence outweighs the danger of unfair prejudice, such evidence shall be admissible in the trial to the extent an order made by the court specifies evidence which may be offered and

areas with respect to which the alleged victim may be examined or cross-examined.

(d) For purposes of this rule, the term "past sexual behavior" means sexual behavior other than the sexual behavior with respect to which an offense under chapter 109A of title 18, United States Code is alleged.

ARTICLE V. PRIVILEGES

RULE 501. GENERAL RULE

Except as otherwise required by the Constitution of the United States or provided by Act of Congress or in rules prescribed by the Supreme Court pursuant to statutory authority, the privilege of a witness, person, government, State, or political subdivision thereof shall be governed by the principles of the common law as they may be interpreted by the courts of the United States in the light of reason and experience. However, in civil actions and proceedings, with respect to an element of a claim or defense as to which State law supplies the rule of decision, the privilege of a witness, person, government, State, or political subdivision thereof shall be determined in accordance with State law.

ARTICLE VI. WITNESSES

RULE 601. GENERAL RULE OF COMPETENCY

Every person is competent to be a witness except as otherwise provided in these rules. However, in civil actions and proceedings, with respect to an element of a claim or defense as to which State law supplies the rule of decision, the competency of a witness shall be determined in accordance with State law.

RULE 602. LACK OF PERSONAL KNOWLEDGE

A witness may not testify to a matter unless evidence is introduced sufficient to support a finding that the witness has personal knowledge of the matter. Evidence to prove personal knowledge may, but need not, consist of the witness' own testimony. This rule is subject to the provisions of rule 703, relating to opinion testimony by expert witnesses.

RULE 603. OATH OR AFFIRMATION

Before testifying, every witness shall be required to declare that the witness will testify truthfully, by oath or affirmation administered in a form calculated to awaken the witness' conscience and impress the witness' mind with the duty to do so.

RULE 604. INTERPRETERS

An interpreter is subject to the provisions of these rules relating to qualification as an expert and the administration of an oath or affirmation to make a true translation.

RULE 605. COMPETENCY OF JUDGE AS WITNESS

The judge presiding at the trial may not testify in that trial as a witness. No objection need be made in order to preserve the point.

RULE 606. COMPETENCY OF JUROR AS WITNESS

(a) **At the Trial.** A member of the jury may not testify as a witness before that jury in the trial of the case in which the juror is sitting. If the juror is called so to testify, the opposing party shall be afforded an opportunity to object out of the presence of the jury.

(b) **Inquiry into Validity of Verdict or Indictment.** Upon an inquiry into the validity of a verdict or indictment, a juror may not testify as to any matter or statement occurring during the course of the jury's deliberations or to the effect of anything upon that or any other juror's mind or emotions as influencing the juror to assent to or dissent from the verdict or indictment or concerning the juror's mental processes in connection therewith, except that a juror may testify on the question whether extraneous prejudicial information was improperly brought to the jury's attention or whether any outside influence was improperly brought to bear upon any juror. Nor may a juror's affidavit or evidence of any statement by the juror concerning a matter about which the juror would be precluded from testifying be received for these purposes.

RULE 607. WHO MAY IMPEACH

The credibility of a witness may be attacked by any party, including the party calling the witness.

RULE 608. EVIDENCE OF CHARACTER AND CONDUCT OF WITNESS

(a) **Opinion and Reputation Evidence of Character.** The credibility of a witness may be attacked or supported by evidence in the form of opinion or reputation, but subject to these limitations: (1) the evidence may refer only to character for truthfulness or untruthfulness, and (2) evidence of truthful character is admissible only after the character of the witness for truthfulness has been attacked by opinion or reputation evidence or otherwise.

(b) **Specific Instances of Conduct.** Specific instances of the conduct of a witness, for the purpose of attacking or supporting the witness' credibility, other than conviction of crime as provided in rule 609, may not be proved by extrinsic evidence. They may, however, in the discretion of the court, if probative of truthfulness or untruthfulness, be inquired into on cross-examination of the witness (1) concerning the witness' character for truthfulness or untruthfulness, or (2) concerning the character for truthfulness or untruthfulness of another witness as to which character the witness being cross-examined has testified.

The giving of testimony, whether by an accused or by any other witness, does not operate as a waiver of the accused's or the witness' privilege against self-incrimination when examined with respect to matters which relate only to credibility.

RULE 609. IMPEACHMENT BY EVIDENCE OF CONVICTION OF CRIME

(a) **General Rule.** For the purpose of attacking the credibility of a witness,

(1) evidence that a witness other than an accused has been convicted of a crime shall be admitted, subject to Rule 403, if the crime was punishable by death or imprisonment in excess of one year under the law under which the witness was convicted, and evidence that an accused has been convicted of such a crime shall be admitted if the court determines that the probative value of admitting this evidence outweighs its prejudicial effect to the accused; and

(2) evidence that any witness has been convicted of a crime shall be admitted if it involved dishonesty or false statement, regardless of the punishment.

(b) **Time Limit.** Evidence of a conviction under this rule is not admissible if a period of more than ten years has elapsed since the date of the conviction or of the release of the witness from the confinement imposed for that conviction, whichever is the later date, unless the court determines, in the interests of justice, that the probative value of the conviction supported by specific facts and circumstances substantially outweighs its prejudicial effect. However, evidence of a conviction more than 10 years old as calculated herein, is not admissible unless the proponent gives to the adverse party sufficient advance written notice of intent to use such evidence to provide the adverse party with a fair opportunity to contest the use of such evidence.

(c) **Effect of Pardon, Annulment, or Certificate of Rehabilitation.** Evidence of a conviction is not admissible under this rule if (1) the conviction has been the subject of a pardon, annulment, certificate of rehabilitation, or other equivalent procedure based on a finding of the rehabilitation of the person convicted, and that person has not been convicted of a subsequent crime which was punishable by death or imprisonment in excess of one year, or (2) the conviction has been the subject of a pardon, annulment, or other equivalent procedure based on a finding of innocence.

(d) **Juvenile Adjudications.** Evidence of juvenile adjudications is generally not admissible under this rule. The court may, however, in a criminal case allow evidence of a juvenile adjudication of a witness other than the accused if conviction of the offense would be admissible to attack the credibility of an adult and the court is satisfied that admission in evidence is necessary for a fair determination of the issue of guilt or innocence.

(e) Pendency of Appeal. The pendency of an appeal therefrom does not render evidence of a conviction inadmissible. Evidence of the pendency of an appeal is admissible.

RULE 610. RELIGIOUS BELIEFS OR OPINIONS

Evidence of the beliefs or opinions of a witness on matters of religion is not admissible for the purpose of showing that by reason of their nature the witness' credibility is impaired or enhanced.

RULE 611. MODE AND ORDER OF INTERROGATION AND PRESENTATION

(a) Control by Court. The court shall exercise reasonable control over the mode and order of interrogating witnesses and presenting evidence so as to (1) make the interrogation and presentation effective for the ascertainment of the truth, (2) avoid needless consumption of time, and (3) protect witnesses from harassment or undue embarrassment.

(b) Scope of Cross–Examination. Cross-examination should be limited to the subject matter of the direct examination and matters affecting the credibility of the witness. The court may, in the exercise of discretion, permit inquiry into additional matters as if on direct examination.

(c) Leading Questions. Leading questions should not be used on the direct examination of a witness except as may be necessary to develop the witness' testimony. Ordinarily leading questions should be permitted on cross-examination. When a party calls a hostile witness, an adverse party, or a witness identified with an adverse party, interrogation may be by leading questions.

RULE 612. WRITING USED TO REFRESH MEMORY

Except as otherwise provided in criminal proceedings by section 3500 of title 18, United States Code, if a witness uses a writing to refresh memory for the purpose of testifying, either—

(1) while testifying, or

(2) before testifying, if the court in its discretion determines it is necessary in the interests of justice,

an adverse party is entitled to have the writing produced at the hearing, to inspect it, to cross-examine the witness thereon, and to introduce in evidence those portions which relate to the testimony of the witness. If it is claimed that the writing contains matters not related to the subject matter of the testimony the court shall examine the writing in camera, excise any portions not so related, and order

delivery of the remainder to the party entitled thereto. Any portion
withheld over objections shall be preserved and made available to the
appellate court in the event of an appeal. If a writing is not produced
or delivered pursuant to order under this rule, the court shall make
any order justice requires, except that in criminal cases when the
prosecution elects not to comply, the order shall be one striking the
testimony or, if the court in its discretion determines that the interests
of justice so require, declaring a mistrial.

RULE 613. PRIOR STATEMENTS OF WITNESSES

(a) **Examining Witness Concerning Prior Statement.** In examining a witness concerning a prior statement made by the witness,
whether written or not, the statement need not be shown nor its
contents disclosed to the witness at that time, but on request the same
shall be shown or disclosed to opposing counsel.

(b) **Extrinsic Evidence of Prior Inconsistent Statement of Witness.** Extrinsic evidence of a prior inconsistent statement by a witness
is not admissible unless the witness is afforded an opportunity to
explain or deny the same and the opposite party is afforded an opportunity to interrogate the witness thereon, or the interests of justice
otherwise require. This provision does not apply to admissions of a
party-opponent as defined in rule 801(d)(2).

RULE 614. CALLING AND INTERROGATION OF WITNESSES BY COURT

(a) **Calling by Court.** The court may, on its own motion or at the
suggestion of a party, call witnesses, and all parties are entitled to
cross-examine witnesses thus called.

(b) **Interrogation by Court.** The court may interrogate witnesses, whether called by itself or by a party.

(c) **Objections.** Objections to the calling of witnesses by the court
or to interrogation by it may be made at the time or at the next
available opportunity when the jury is not present.

RULE 615. EXCLUSION OF WITNESSES

At the request of a party the court shall order witnesses excluded
so that they cannot hear the testimony of other witnesses, and it may
make the order of its own motion. This rule does not authorize
exclusion of (1) a party who is a natural person, or (2) an officer or
employee of a party which is not a natural person designated as its
representative by its attorney, or (3) a person whose presence is shown
by a party to be essential to the presentation of the party's cause.

ARTICLE VII. OPINIONS AND EXPERT TESTIMONY

RULE 701. OPINION TESTIMONY BY LAY WITNESSES

If the witness is not testifying as an expert, the witness' testimony in the form of opinions or inferences is limited to those opinions or inferences which are (a) rationally based on the perception of the witness and (b) helpful to a clear understanding of the witness' testimony or the determination of a fact in issue.

RULE 702. TESTIMONY BY EXPERTS

If scientific, technical, or other specialized knowledge will assist the trier of fact to understand the evidence or to determine a fact in issue, a witness qualified as an expert by knowledge, skill, experience, training, or education, may testify thereto in the form of an opinion or otherwise.

RULE 703. BASES OF OPINION TESTIMONY BY EXPERTS

The facts or data in the particular case upon which an expert bases an opinion or inference may be those perceived by or made known to the expert at or before the hearing. If of a type reasonably relied upon by experts in the particular field in forming opinions or inferences upon the subject, the facts or data need not be admissible in evidence.

RULE 704. OPINION ON ULTIMATE ISSUE

(a) Except as provided in subdivision (b), testimony in the form of an opinion or inference otherwise admissible is not objectionable because it embraces an ultimate issue to be decided by the trier of fact.

(b) No expert witness testifying with respect to the mental state or condition of a defendant in a criminal case may state an opinion or inference as to whether the defendant did or did not have the mental state or condition constituting an element of the crime charged or of a defense thereto. Such ultimate issues are matters for the trier of fact alone.

RULE 705. DISCLOSURE OF FACTS OR DATA UNDERLYING EXPERT OPINION

The expert may testify in terms of opinion or inference and gives reasons therefor without prior disclosure of the underlying facts or data, unless the court requires otherwise. The expert may in any event be required to disclose the underlying facts or data on cross-examination.

RULE 706. COURT APPOINTED EXPERTS

(a) **Appointment.** The court may on its own motion or on the motion of any party enter an order to show cause why expert witnesses

should not be appointed, and may request the parties to submit nomina-
tions. The court may appoint any expert witnesses agreed upon by the
parties, and may appoint expert witnesses of its own selection. An
expert witness shall not be appointed by the court unless the witness
consents to act. A witness so appointed shall be informed of the
witness' duties by the court in writing, a copy of which shall be filed
with the clerk, or at a conference in which the parties shall have
opportunity to participate. A witness so appointed shall advise the
parties of the witness' findings, if any; the witness' deposition may be
taken by any party; and the witness may be called to testify by the
court or any party. The witness shall be subject to cross-examination
by each party, including a party calling the witness.

(b) **Compensation.** Expert witnesses so appointed are entitled to
reasonable compensation in whatever sum the court may allow. The
compensation thus fixed is payable from funds which may be provided
by law in criminal cases and civil actions and proceedings involving just
compensation under the fifth amendment. In other civil actions and
proceedings the compensation shall be paid by the parties in such
proportion and at such time as the court directs, and thereafter charged
in like manner as other costs.

(c) **Disclosure of Appointment.** In the exercise of its discretion,
the court may authorize disclosure to the jury of the fact that the court
appointed the expert witness.

(d) **Parties' Experts of Own Selection.** Nothing in this rule
limits the parties in calling expert witnesses of their own selection.

ARTICLE VIII. HEARSAY

RULE 801. DEFINITIONS

The following definitions apply under this article:

(a) **Statement.** A "statement" is (1) an oral or written assertion
or (2) nonverbal conduct of a person, if it is intended by the person as
an assertion.

(b) **Declarant.** A "declarant" is a person who makes a statement.

(c) **Hearsay.** "Hearsay" is a statement, other than one made by
the declarant while testifying at the trial or hearing, offered in evidence to prove the truth of the matter asserted.

(d) **Statements Which Are Not Hearsay.** A statement is not
hearsay if—

(1) *Prior Statement by Witness.* The declarant testifies at the trial
or hearing and is subject to cross-examination concerning the statement, and the statement is (A) inconsistent with the declarant's testimony, and was given under oath subject to the penalty of perjury at a
trial, hearing, or other proceeding, or in a deposition, or (B) consistent
with the declarant's testimony and is offered to rebut an express or
implied charge against the declarant of recent fabrication or improper

influence or motive, or (C) one of identification of a person made after perceiving the person; or

(2) *Admission by Party–Opponent.* The statement is offered against a party and is (A) the party's own statement in either an individual or a representative capacity or (B) a statement of which the party has manifested an adoption or belief in its truth, or (C) a statement by a person authorized by the party to make a statement concerning the subject, or (D) a statement by the party's agent or servant concerning a matter within the scope of the agency or employment, made during the existence of the relationship, or (E) a statement by a coconspirator of a party during the course and in furtherance of the conspiracy.

RULE 802. HEARSAY RULE

Hearsay is not admissible except as provided by these rules or by other rules prescribed by the Supreme Court pursuant to statutory authority or by Act of Congress.

RULE 803. HEARSAY EXCEPTIONS; AVAILABILITY OF DECLARANT IMMATERIAL

The following are not excluded by the hearsay rule, even though the declarant is available as a witness:

(1) Present Sense Impression. A statement describing or explaining an event or condition made while the declarant was perceiving the event or condition, or immediately thereafter.

(2) Excited Utterance. A statement relating to a startling event or condition made while the declarant was under the stress of excitement caused by the event or condition.

(3) Then Existing Mental, Emotional, or Physical Condition. A statement of the declarant's then existing state of mind, emotion, sensation, or physical condition (such as intent, plan, motive, design, mental feeling, pain, and bodily health), but not including a statement of memory or belief to prove the fact remembered or believed unless it relates to the execution, revocation, identification, or terms of declarant's will.

(4) Statements for Purposes of Medical Diagnosis or Treatment. Statements made for purposes of medical diagnosis or treatment and describing medical history, or past or present symptoms, pain, or sensations, or the inception or general character of the cause or external source thereof insofar as reasonably pertinent to diagnosis or treatment.

(5) Recorded Recollection. A memorandum or record concerning a matter about which a witness once had knowledge but now has insufficient recollection to enable the witness to testify fully and accurately, shown to have been made or adopted by the witness when the matter was fresh in the witness' memory and to reflect that knowledge correctly. If admitted, the memorandum or record may be

read into evidence but may not itself be received as an exhibit unless
offered by an adverse party.

(6) Records of Regularly Conducted Activity. A memorandum,
report, record, or data compilation, in any form, of acts, events, conditions, opinions, or diagnoses, made at or near the time by, or from
information transmitted by, a person with knowledge, if kept in the
course of a regularly conducted business activity, and if it was the
regular practice of that business activity to make the memorandum,
report, record, or data compilation, all as shown by the testimony of the
custodian or other qualified witness, unless the source of information or
the method or circumstances of preparation indicate lack of trustworthiness. The term "business" as used in this paragraph includes
business, institution, association, profession, occupation, and calling of
every kind, whether or not conducted for profit.

**(7) Absence of Entry in Records Kept in Accordance With the
Provisions of Paragraph (6).** Evidence that a matter is not included
in the memoranda reports, records, or data compilations, in any form,
kept in accordance with the provisions of paragraph (6), to prove the
nonoccurrence or nonexistence of the matter, if the matter was of a
kind of which a memorandum, report, record, or data compilation was
regularly made and preserved, unless the sources of information or
other circumstances indicate lack of trustworthiness.

(8) Public Records and Reports. Records, reports, statements,
or data compilations, in any form, of public offices or agencies, setting
forth (A) the activities of the office or agency, or (B) matters observed
pursuant to duty imposed by law as to which matters there was a duty
to report, excluding, however, in criminal cases matters observed by
police officers and other law enforcement personnel, or (C) in civil
actions and proceedings and against the Government in criminal cases,
factual findings resulting from an investigation made pursuant to
authority granted by law, unless the sources of information or other
circumstances indicate lack of trustworthiness.

(9) Records of Vital Statistics. Records or data compilations, in
any form, of births, fetal deaths, deaths, or marriages, if the report
thereof was made to a public office pursuant to requirements of law.

(10) Absence of Public Record or Entry. To prove the absence
of a record, report, statement, or data compilation, in any form, or the
nonoccurrence or nonexistence of a matter of which a record, report,
statement, or data compilation, in any form, was regularly made and
preserved by a public office or agency, evidence in the form of a
certification in accordance with rule 902, or testimony, that diligent
search failed to disclose the record, report, statement, or data compilation, or entry.

(11) Records of Religious Organizations. Statements of births,
marriages, divorces, deaths, legitimacy, ancestry, relationship by blood
or marriage, or other similar facts of personal or family history,
contained in a regularly kept record of a religious organization.

(12) Marriage, Baptismal, and Similar Certificates. Statements of fact contained in a certificate that the maker performed a marriage or other ceremony or administered a sacrament, made by a clergyman, public official, or other person authorized by the rules or practices of a religious organization or by law to perform the act certified, and purporting to have been issued at the time of the act or within a reasonable time thereafter.

(13) Family Records. Statements of fact concerning personal or family history contained in family Bibles, genealogies, charts, engravings on rings, inscriptions on family portraits, engravings on urns, crypts, or tombstones, or the like.

(14) Records of Documents Affecting an Interest in Property. The record of a document purporting to establish or affect an interest in property, as proof of the content of the original recorded document and its execution and delivery by each person by whom it purports to have been executed, if the record is a record of a public office and an applicable statute authorizes the recording of documents of that kind in that office.

(15) Statements in Documents Affecting an Interest in Property. A statement contained in a document purporting to establish or affect an interest in property if the matter stated was relevant to the purpose of the document, unless dealings with the property since the document was made have been inconsistent with the truth of the statement or the purport of the document.

(16) Statements in Ancient Documents. Statements in a document in existence twenty years or more the authenticity of which is established.

(17) Market Reports, Commercial Publications. Market quotations, tabulations, lists, directories, or other published compilations, generally used and relied upon by the public or by persons in particular occupations.

(18) Learned Treatises. To the extent called to the attention of an expert witness upon cross-examination or relied upon by the expert witness in direct examination, statements contained in published treatises, periodicals, or pamphlets on a subject of history, medicine, or other science or art, established as a reliable authority by the testimony or admission of the witness or by other expert testimony or by judicial notice. If admitted, the statements may be read into evidence but may not be received as exhibits.

(19) Reputation Concerning Personal or Family History. Reputation among members of a person's family by blood, adoption, or marriage, or among a person's associates, or in the community, concerning a person's birth, adoption, marriage, divorce, death, legitimacy, relationship by blood, adoption, or marriage, ancestry, or other similar fact of personal or family history.

(20) Reputation Concerning Boundaries or General History. Reputation in a community, arising before the controversy, as to boundaries of or customs affecting lands in the community, and reputation as to events of general history important to the community or State or nation in which located.

(21) Reputation as to Character. Reputation of a person's character among associates or in the community.

(22) Judgment of Previous Conviction. Evidence of a final judgment, entered after a trial or upon a plea of guilty (but not upon a plea of nolo contendere), adjudging a person guilty of a crime punishable by death or imprisonment in excess of one year, to prove any fact essential to sustain the judgment, but not including, when offered by the Government in a criminal prosecution for purposes other than impeachment, judgments against persons other than the accused. The pendency of an appeal may be shown but does not affect admissibility.

(23) Judgment as to Personal, Family, or General History, or Boundaries. Judgments as proof of matters of personal, family or general history, or boundaries, essential to the judgment, if the same would be provable by evidence of reputation.

(24) Other Exceptions. A statement not specifically covered by any of the foregoing exceptions but having equivalent circumstantial guarantees of trustworthiness, if the court determines that (A) the statement is offered as evidence of a material fact; (B) the statement is more probative on the point for which it is offered than any other evidence which the proponent can procure through reasonable efforts; and (C) the general purposes of these rules and the interests of justice will best be served by admission of the statement into evidence. However, a statement may not be admitted under this exception unless the proponent of it makes known to the adverse party sufficiently in advance of the trial or hearing to provide the adverse party with a fair opportunity to prepare to meet it, the proponent's intention to offer the statement and the particulars of it, including the name and address of the declarant.

RULE 804. HEARSAY EXCEPTIONS; DECLARANT UNAVAILABLE

(a) Definition of Unavailability. "Unavailability as a witness" includes situations in which the declarant—

(1) is exempted by ruling of the court on the ground of privilege from testifying concerning the subject matter of the declarant's statement; or

(2) persists in refusing to testify concerning the subject matter of the declarant's statement despite an order of the court to do so; or

(3) testifies to a lack of memory of the subject matter of the declarant's statement; or

(4) is unable to be present or to testify at the hearing because of death or then existing physical or mental illness or infirmity; or

(5) is absent from the hearing and the proponent of a statement has been unable to procure the declarant's attendance (or in the case of a hearsay exception under subdivision (b)(2), (3), or (4), the declarant's attendance or testimony) by process or other reasonable means.

A declarant is not unavailable as a witness if exemption, refusal, claim of lack of memory, inability, or absence is due to the procurement or wrongdoing of the proponent of a statement for the purpose of preventing the witness from attending or testifying.

(b) Hearsay Exceptions. The following are not excluded by the hearsay rule if the declarant is unavailable as a witness:

(1) *Former Testimony.* Testimony given as a witness at another hearing of the same or a different proceeding, or in a deposition taken in compliance with law in the course of the same or another proceeding, if the party against whom the testimony is now offered, or, in a civil action or proceeding, a predecessor in interest, had an opportunity and similar motive to develop the testimony by direct, cross, or redirect examination.

(2) *Statement Under Belief of Impending Death.* In a prosecution for homicide or in a civil action or proceeding, a statement made by a declarant while believing that the declarant's death was imminent, concerning the cause or circumstances of what the declarant believed to be impending death.

(3) *Statement Against Interest.* A statement which was at the time of its making so far contrary to the declarant's pecuniary or proprietary interest, or so far tended to subject the declarant to civil or criminal liability, or to render invalid a claim by the declarant against another, that a reasonable person in the declarant's position would not have made the statement unless believing it to be true. A statement tending to expose the declarant to criminal liability and offered to exculpate the accused is not admissible unless corroborating circumstances clearly indicate the trustworthiness of the statement.

(4) *Statement of Personal or Family History.* (A) A statement concerning the declarant's own birth, adoption, marriage, divorce, legitimacy, relationship by blood, adoption, or marriage, ancestry, or other similar fact of personal or family history, even though declarant had no means of acquiring personal knowledge of the matter stated; or (B) a statement concerning the foregoing matters, and death also, of another person, if the declarant was related to the other by blood, adoption, or marriage or was so intimately associated with the other's family as to be likely to have accurate information concerning the matter declared.

(5) *Other Exceptions.* A statement not specifically covered by any of the foregoing exceptions but having equivalent circumstantial guarantees of trustworthiness, if the court determines that (A) the statement is offered as evidence of a material fact; (B) the statement is more probative on the point for which it is offered than any other evidence which the proponent can procure through reasonable efforts; and (C) the general purposes of these rules and the interests of justice will best

be served by admission of the statement into evidence. However, a
statement may not be admitted under this exception unless the proponent of it makes known to the adverse party sufficiently in advance of
the trial or hearing to provide the adverse party with a fair opportunity
to prepare to meet it, the proponent's intention to offer the statement
and the particulars of it, including the name and address of the
declarant.

RULE 805. HEARSAY WITHIN HEARSAY

Hearsay included within hearsay is not excluded under the hearsay
rule if each part of the combined statements conforms with an exception to the hearsay rule provided in these rules.

RULE 806. ATTACKING AND SUPPORTING CREDIBILITY OF DECLARANT

When a hearsay statement, or a statement defined in Rule 801(d)(2)
(C), (D), or (E), has been admitted in evidence, the credibility of the
declarant may be attacked, and if attacked may be supported, by any
evidence which would be admissible for those purposes if declarant had
testified as a witness. Evidence of a statement or conduct by the
declarant at any time, inconsistent with the declarant's hearsay statement, is not subject to any requirement that the declarant may have
been afforded an opportunity to deny or explain. If the party against
whom a hearsay statement has been admitted calls the declarant as a
witness, the party is entitled to examine the declarant on the statement
as if under cross-examination.

ARTICLE IX. AUTHENTICATION AND IDENTIFICATION

RULE 901. REQUIREMENT OF AUTHENTICATION OR IDENTIFICATION

(a) General Provision. The requirement of authentication or
identification as a condition precedent to admissibility is satisfied by
evidence sufficient to support a finding that the matter in question is
what its proponent claims.

(b) Illustrations. By way of illustration only, and not by way of
limitation, the following are examples of authentication or identification conforming with the requirements of this rule:

(1) *Testimony of Witness With Knowledge.* Testimony that a matter is what it is claimed to be.

(2) *Nonexpert Opinion on Handwriting.* Nonexpert opinion as to
the genuineness of handwriting, based upon familiarity not acquired for
purposes of the litigation.

(3) *Comparison by Trier or Expert Witness.* Comparison by the
trier of fact or by expert witnesses with specimens which have been
authenticated.

(4) *Distinctive Characteristics and the Like.* Appearance, contents, substance, internal patterns, or other distinctive characteristics, taken in conjunction with circumstances.

(5) *Voice Identification.* Identification of a voice, whether heard firsthand or through mechanical or electronic transmission or recording, by opinion based upon hearing the voice at any time under circumstances connecting it with the alleged speaker.

(6) *Telephone Conversations.* Telephone conversations, by evidence that a call was made to the number assigned at the time by the telephone company to a particular person or business, if (A) in the case of a person, circumstances, including self-identification, show the person answering to be the one called, or (B) in the case of a business, the call was made to a place of business and the conversation related to business reasonably transacted over the telephone.

(7) *Public Records or Reports.* Evidence that a writing authorized by law to be recorded or filed and in fact recorded or filed in a public office, or a purported public record, report, statement, or data compilation, in any form, is from the public office where items of this nature are kept.

(8) *Ancient Documents or Data Compilation.* Evidence that a document or data compilation, in any form, (A) is in such condition as to create no suspicion concerning its authenticity, (B) was in a place where it, if authentic, would likely be, and (C) has been in existence 20 years or more at the time it is offered.

(9) *Process or System.* Evidence describing a process or system used to produce a result and showing that the process or system produces an accurate result.

(10) *Methods Provided by Statute or Rule.* Any method of authentication or identification provided by Act of Congress or by other rules prescribed by the Supreme Court pursuant to statutory authority.

RULE 902. SELF–AUTHENTICATION

Extrinsic evidence of authenticity as a condition precedent to admissibility is not required with respect to the following:

(1) Domestic Public Documents Under Seal. A document bearing a seal purporting to be that of the United States, or of any State, district, Commonwealth, territory, or insular possession thereof, or the Panama Canal Zone, or the Trust Territory of the Pacific Islands, or of a political subdivision, department, officer, or agency thereof, and a signature purporting to be an attestation or execution.

(2) Domestic Public Documents Not Under Seal. A document purporting to bear the signature in the official capacity of an officer or employee of any entity included in paragraph (1) hereof, having no seal, if a public officer having a seal and having official duties in the district or political subdivision of the officer or employee certifies under seal that the signer has the official capacity and that the signature is genuine.

(3) Foreign Public Documents.　A document purporting to be executed or attested in an official capacity by a person authorized by the laws of a foreign country to make the execution or attestation, and accompanied by a final certification as to the genuineness of the signature and official position (A) of the executing or attesting person, or (B) of any foreign official whose certificate of genuineness of signature and official position relates to the execution or attestation or is in a chain of certificates of genuineness of signature and official position relating to the execution or attestation.　A final certification may be made by a secretary of embassy or legation, consul general, consul, vice consul, or consular agent of the United States, or a diplomatic or consular official of the foreign country assigned or accredited to the United States.　If reasonable opportunity has been given to all parties to investigate the authenticity and accuracy of official documents, the court may, for good cause shown, order that they be treated as presumptively authentic without final certification or permit them to be evidenced by an attested summary with or without final certification.

(4) Certified Copies of Public Records.　A copy of an official record or report or entry therein, or of a document authorized by law to be recorded or filed and actually recorded or filed in a public office, including data compilations in any form, certified as correct by the custodian or other person authorized to make the certification, by certificate complying with paragraph (1), (2), or (3) of this rule or complying with any Act of Congress or rule prescribed by the Supreme Court pursuant to statutory authority.

(5) Official Publications.　Books, pamphlets, or other publications purporting to be issued by public authority.

(6) Newspapers and Periodicals.　Printed materials purporting to be newspapers or periodicals.

(7) Trade Inscriptions and the Like.　Inscriptions, signs, tags, or labels purporting to have been affixed in the course of business and indicating ownership, control, or origin.

(8) Acknowledged Documents.　Documents accompanied by a certificate of acknowledgment executed in the manner provided by law by a notary public or other officer authorized by law to take acknowledgments.

(9) Commercial Paper and Related Documents.　Commercial paper, signatures thereon, and documents relating thereto to the extent provided by general commercial law.

(10) Presumptions Under Acts of Congress.　Any signature, document, or other matter declared by Act of Congress to be presumptively or prima facie genuine or authentic.

RULE 903. SUBSCRIBING WITNESS' TESTIMONY UNNECESSARY

The testimony of a subscribing witness is not necessary to authenticate a writing unless required by the laws of the jurisdiction whose laws govern the validity of the writing.

ARTICLE X. CONTENTS OF WRITINGS, RECORDINGS, AND PHOTOGRAPHS

RULE 1001. DEFINITIONS

For purposes of this article the following definitions are applicable:

(1) Writings and Recordings. "Writings" and "recordings" consist of letters, words, or numbers, or their equivalent, set down by handwriting, typewriting, printing, photostating, photographing, magnetic impulse, mechanical or electronic recording, or other form of data compilation.

(2) Photographs. "Photographs" include still photographs, X-ray films, video tapes, and motion pictures.

(3) Original. An "original" of a writing or recording is the writing or recording itself or any counterpart intended to have the same effect by a person executing or issuing it. An "original" of a photograph includes the negative or any print therefrom. If data are stored in a computer or similar device, any printout or other output readable by sight, shown to reflect the data accurately, is an "original".

(4) Duplicate. A "duplicate" is a counterpart produced by the same impression as the original, or from the same matrix, or by means of photography, including enlargements and miniatures, or by mechanical or electronic re-recording, or by chemical reproduction, or by other equivalent techniques which accurately reproduces the original.

RULE 1002. REQUIREMENT OF ORIGINAL

To prove the content of a writing, recording, or photograph, the original writing, recording, or photograph is required, except as otherwise provided in these rules or by Act of Congress.

RULE 1003. ADMISSIBILITY OF DUPLICATES

A duplicate is admissible to the same extent as an original unless (1) a genuine question is raised as to the authenticity of the original or (2) in the circumstances it would be unfair to admit the duplicate in lieu of the original.

RULE 1004. ADMISSIBILITY OF OTHER EVIDENCE OF CONTENTS

The original is not required, and other evidence of the contents of a writing, recording, or photograph is admissible if—

(1) Originals Lost or Destroyed. All originals are lost or have been destroyed, unless the proponent lost or destroyed them in bad faith; or

(2) Original Not Obtainable. No original can be obtained by any available judicial process or procedure; or

(3) Original in Possession of Opponent. At a time when an original was under the control of the party against whom offered, that party was put on notice, by the pleadings or otherwise, that the contents would be a subject of proof at the hearing, and that party does not produce the original at the hearing; or

(4) Collateral Matters. The writing, recording, or photograph is not closely related to a controlling issue.

RULE 1005. PUBLIC RECORDS

The contents of an official record, or of a document authorized to be recorded or filed and actually recorded or filed, including data compilations in any form, if otherwise admissible, may be proved by copy, certified as correct in accordance with rule 902 or testified to be correct by a witness who has compared it with the original. If a copy which complies with the foregoing cannot be obtained by the exercise of reasonable diligence, then other evidence of the contents may be given.

RULE 1006. SUMMARIES

The contents of voluminous writings, records, or photographs which cannot conveniently be examined in court may be presented in the form of a chart, summary, or calculation. The originals, or duplicates, shall be made available for examination or copying, or both, by other parties at a reasonable time and place. The court may order that they be produced in court.

RULE 1007. TESTIMONY OR WRITTEN ADMISSION OF PARTY

Contents of writings, recordings, or photographs may be proved by the testimony or deposition of the party against whom offered or by that party's written admission, without accounting for the nonproduction of the original.

RULE 1008. FUNCTIONS OF COURT AND JURY

When the admissibility of other evidence of contents of writings, recordings, or photographs under these rules depends upon the fulfillment of a condition of fact, the question whether the condition has been fulfilled is ordinarily for the court to determine in accordance with the provisions of rule 104. However, when an issue is raised (a) whether the asserted writing ever existed, or (b) whether another writing, recording, or photograph produced at the trial is the original, or (c) whether other evidence of contents correctly reflects the contents, the

1
2
3
4
5
6
7
8
9
10
11
12
13
14
15
16
17
18
19
20
21
22
23
24
25
26
27
28
29
30
31
32
33
34
35
36
37
38
39
40
41
42
43
44
45
46
47
48
49
50

issue is for the trier of fact to determine as in the case of other issues of fact.

ARTICLE XI. MISCELLANEOUS RULES

RULE 1101. APPLICABILITY OF RULES

(a) **Courts and Magistrates.** These rules apply to the United States district courts, the District Court of Guam, the District Court of the Virgin Islands, the District Court for the Northern Mariana Islands, the United States courts of appeals, the United States Claims Court, and to United States bankruptcy judges and United States magistrates, in the actions, cases, and proceedings and to the extent hereinafter set forth. The terms "judge" and "court" in these Rules include United States bankruptcy judges and United States magistrates.

(b) **Proceedings Generally.** These rules apply generally to civil actions and proceedings, including admiralty and maritime cases, to criminal cases and proceedings, to contempt proceedings except those in which the court may act summarily, and to proceedings and cases under title 11, United States Code.

(c) **Rule of Privilege.** The rule with respect to privileges applies at all stages of all actions, cases, and proceedings.

(d) **Rules Inapplicable.** The rules (other than with respect to privileges) do not apply in the following situations:

(1) *Preliminary Questions of Fact.* The determination of questions of fact preliminary to admissibility of evidence when the issue is to be determined by the court under rule 104.

(2) *Grand Jury.* Proceedings before grand juries.

(3) *Miscellaneous Proceedings.* Proceedings for extradition or rendition; preliminary examinations in criminal cases; sentencing, or granting or revoking probation; issuance of warrants for arrest, criminal summonses, and search warrants; and proceedings with respect to release on bail or otherwise.

(e) **Rules Applicable in Part.** In the following proceedings these rules apply to the extent that matters of evidence are not provided for in the statutes which govern procedure therein or in other rules prescribed by the Supreme Court pursuant to statutory authority: the trial of minor and petty offenses by United States magistrates; review of agency actions when the facts are subject to trial de novo under section 706(2)(F) of title 5, United States Code; review of orders of the Secretary of Agriculture under section 2 of the Act entitled "An Act to authorize association of producers of agricultural products" approved February 18, 1922 (7 U.S.C. 292), and under sections 6 and 7(c) of the Perishable Agricultural Commodities Act, 1930 (7 U.S.C. 499f, 499g(c)); naturalization and revocation of naturalization under sections 310–318 of the Immigration and Nationality Act (8 U.S.C. 1421–1429); prize proceedings in admiralty under sections 7651–7681 of title 10, United

States Code; review of orders of the Secretary of the Interior under
section 2 of the Act entitled "An Act authorizing associations of
producers of aquatic products" approved June 25, 1934 (15 U.S.C. 522);
review of orders of petroleum control boards under section 5 of the Act
entitled "An Act to regulate interstate and foreign commerce in petroleum and its products by prohibiting the shipment in such commerce of
petroleum and its products produced in violation of State law, and for
other purposes", approved February 22, 1935 (15 U.S.C. 715d); actions
for fines, penalties, or forfeitures under part V of title IV of the Tariff
Act of 1930 (19 U.S.C. 1581–1624), or under the Anti–Smuggling Act (19
U.S.C. 1701–1711); criminal libel for condemnation, exclusion of imports, or other proceedings under the Federal Food, Drug, and Cosmetic
Act (21 U.S.C. 301–392); disputes between seamen under sections 4079,
4080, and 4081 of the Revised Statutes (22 U.S.C. 256–258); habeas
corpus under sections 2241–2254 of title 28, United States Code; motions to vacate, set aside or correct sentence under section 2255 of title
28, United States Code; actions for penalties for refusal to transport
destitute seamen under section 4578 of the Revised Statutes (46 U.S.C.
679); actions against the United States under the Act entitled "An Act
authorizing suits against the United States in admiralty for damage
caused by and salvage service rendered to public vessels belonging to
the United States, and for other purposes", approved March 3, 1925 (46
U.S.C. 781–790), as implemented by section 7730 of title 10, United
States Code.

RULE 1102. AMENDMENTS

Amendments to the Federal Rules of Evidence may be made as
provided in section 2072 of title 28 of the United States Code.

RULE 1103. TITLE

These rules may be known and cited as the Federal Rules of
Evidence.

APPENDIX B

COMMENTS TO THE FEDERAL RULES OF EVIDENCE FOR UNITED STATES COURTS AND MAGISTRATES

Rule 101

Note by Federal Judicial Center

The rule enacted by the Congress is the rule prescribed by the Supreme Court without change.

Advisory Committee's Note

Rule 1101 specifies in detail the courts, proceedings, questions, and stages of proceedings to which the rules apply in whole or in part.

Rule 102

Note by Federal Judicial Center

The rule enacted by the Congress is the rule prescribed by the Supreme Court without change.

Advisory Committee's Note

For similar provisions see Rule 2 of the Federal Rules of Criminal Procedure, Rule 1 of the Federal Rules of Civil Procedure, California Evidence Code § 2, and New Jersey Evidence Rule 5.

Rule 103

Note by Federal Judicial Center

The rule enacted by the Congress is the rule prescribed by the Supreme Court, amended by substituting "court" in place of "judge," with appropriate pronominal change.

Advisory Committee's Note

Subdivision (a) states the law as generally accepted today. Rulings on evidence cannot be assigned as error unless (1) a substantial right is affected, and (2) the nature of the error was called to the attention of the judge, so as to alert him to the proper course of action and enable opposing counsel to take proper corrective measures. The objection and the offer of proof are the techniques for accomplishing these objectives. For similar provisions see Uniform Rules 4 and 5; California Evidence Code §§ 353 and 354; Kansas Code of Civil Procedure §§ 60–404 and 60–405. The rule does not purport to change the law with respect to harmless error. See 28 USC § 2111, F.R.Civ.P. 61, F.R. Crim.P. 52, and decisions construing them. The status of constitutional error as harmless or not is treated in Chapman v. California, 386 U.S. 18, 87 S.Ct. 824, 17 L.Ed.2d 705 (1967), reh. denied id. 987, 87 S.Ct. 1283, 18 L.Ed.2d 241.

Subdivision (b). The first sentence is the third sentence of Rule 43(c) of the Federal Rules of Civil Procedure [1] virtually verbatim. Its purpose is to reproduce for an appellate court, insofar as possible, a true reflection of what occurred in the trial court. The second sentence is in part derived from the final sentence of Rule 43(c).[1] It is designed to resolve doubts as to what testimony the witness would have in fact given, and, in nonjury cases, to provide the appellate court with material for a possible final disposition of the case in the event of reversal of a ruling which excluded evidence. See 5 Moore's Federal Practice § 43.11 (2d ed. 1968). Application is made discretionary in view of the practical impossibility of formulating a satisfactory rule in mandatory terms.

Subdivision (c). This subdivision proceeds on the supposition that a ruling which excludes evidence in a jury case is likely to be a pointless procedure if the excluded evidence nevertheless comes to the attention of the jury. Bruton v. United States, 389 U.S. 818, 88 S.Ct. 126, 19 L.Ed.2d 70 (1968). Rule 43(c) of the Federal Rules of Civil Procedure [1] provides: "The court may require the offer to be made out of the hearing of the jury." In re McConnell, 370 U.S. 230, 82 S.Ct. 1288, 8 L.Ed.2d 434 (1962), left some doubt whether questions on which an offer is based must first be asked in the presence of the jury. The subdivision answers in the negative. The judge can foreclose a particular line of testimony and counsel can protect his record without a series of questions before the jury, designed at best to waste time and at worst "to waft into the jury box" the very matter sought to be excluded.

Subdivision (d). This wording of the plain error principle is from Rule 52(b) of the Federal Rules of Criminal Procedure. While judicial unwillingness to be constricted by mechanical breakdowns of the adversary system has been more pronounced in criminal cases, there is no scarcity of decisions to the same affect in civil cases. In general, see Campbell, Extent to Which Courts of Review Will Consider Questions Not Properly Raised and Preserved, 7 Wis.L. Rev. 91, 160 (1932); Vestal, Sua Sponte Consideration in Appellate Review, 27 Fordham L.Rev. 477 (1958–59); 64 Harv.L.Rev. 652 (1951). In the nature of things the application of the plain error rule will be more likely with respect to the admission of evidence than to exclusion, since failure to comply with normal requirements of offers of proof is likely to produce a record which simply does not disclose the error.

Rule 104

Note by Federal Judicial Center

The rule enacted by the Congress is the rule prescribed by the Supreme Court, amended by substituting "court" in place of "judge," with appropriate pronominal change, and by adding to subdivision (c) the concluding phrase, "or when an accused is a witness, if he so requests."[1]

1. Rule 43(c) of the Federal Rules of Civil Procedure was deleted by order of the Supreme Court entered on November 20, 1972, 93 S.Ct. 3073, 3075, 3076, 3077, 34 L.Ed.2d lxv, ccv, ccviii, which action was affirmed by the Congress in P.L. 93–595 § 3 (January 2, 1975).

1. The effect of the amendment was to restore language included in the 1971 Revised Draft of the Proposed Rules but deleted before the rules were presented to and prescribed by the Supreme Court.

Advisory Committee's Note

Subdivision (a). The applicability of a particular rule of evidence often depends upon the existence of a condition. Is the alleged expert a qualified physician? Is a witness whose former testimony is offered unavailable? Was a stranger present during a conversation between attorney and client? In each instance the admissibility of evidence will turn upon the answer to the question of the existence of the condition. Accepted practice, incorporated in the rule, places on the judge the responsibility for these determinations. McCormick § 53; Morgan, Basic Problems of Evidence 45–50 (1962).

To the extent that these inquiries are factual, the judge acts as a trier of fact. Often, however, rulings on evidence call for an evaluation in terms of a legally set standard. Thus when a hearsay statement is offered as a declaration against interest, a decision must be made whether it possesses the required against-interest characteristics. These decisions, too, are made by the judge.

In view of these considerations, this subdivision refers to preliminary requirements generally by the broad term "questions," without attempt at specification.

This subdivision is of general application. It must, however, be read as subject to the special provisions for "conditional relevancy" in subdivision (b) and those for confessions in subdivision (c).

If the question is factual in nature, the judge will of necessity receive evidence pro and con on the issue. The rule provides that the rules of evidence in general do not apply to this process. McCormick § 53, p. 123, n. 8, points out that the authorities are "scattered and inconclusive," and observes:

"Should the exclusionary law of evidence, 'the child of the jury system' in Thayer's phrase, be applied to this hearing before the judge? Sound sense backs the view that it should not, and that the judge should be empowered to hear any relevant evidence, such as affidavits or other reliable hearsay."

This view is reinforced by practical necessity in certain situations. An item, offered and objected to, may itself be considered in ruling on admissibility, though not yet admitted in evidence. Thus the content of an asserted declaration against interest must be considered in ruling whether it is against interest. Again, common practice calls for considering the testimony of a witness, particularly a child, in determining competency. Another example is the requirement of Rule 602 dealing with personal knowledge. In the case of hearsay, it is enough, if the declarant "so far as appears [has] had an opportunity to observe the fact declared." McCormick, § 10, p. 19.

If concern is felt over the use of affidavits by the judge in preliminary hearings on admissibility, attention is directed to the many important judicial determinations made on the basis of affidavits. Rule 47 of the Federal Rules of Criminal Procedure provides:

"An application to the court for an order shall be by motion. ＊ ＊ ＊ It may be supported by affidavit."

The Rules of Civil Procedure are more detailed. Rule 43(e), dealing with motions generally, provides:

"When a motion is based on facts not appearing of record the court may hear the matter on affidavits presented by the respective parties, but the court may direct that the matter be heard wholly or partly on oral testimony or depositions."

Rule 4(g) provides for proof of service by affidavit. Rule 56 provides in detail for the entry of summary judgment based on affidavits. Affidavits may supply the foundation for temporary restraining orders under Rule 65(b).

The study made for the California Law Revision Commission recommended an amendment to Uniform Rule 2 as follows:

"In the determination of the issue aforesaid [preliminary determination], exclusionary rules shall not apply, subject, however, to Rule 45 and any valid claim of privilege." Tentative Recommendation and a Study Relating to the Uniform Rules of Evidence (Article VIII, Hearsay), Cal.Law Revision Comm'n, Rep., Rec. & Studies, 470 (1962). The proposal was not adopted in the California Evidence Code. The Uniform Rules are likewise silent on the subject. However, New Jersey Evidence Rule 8(1), dealing with preliminary inquiry by the judge, provides:

"In his determination the rules of evidence shall not apply except for Rule 4 [exclusion on grounds of confusion, etc.] or a valid claim of privilege."

Subdivision (b). In some situations, the relevancy of an item of evidence, in the large sense, depends upon the existence of a particular preliminary fact. Thus when a spoken statement is relied upon to prove notice to X, it is without probative value unless X heard it. Or if a letter purporting to be from Y is relied upon to establish an admission by him, it has no probative value unless Y wrote or authorized it. Relevance in this sense has been labelled "conditional relevancy." Morgan, Basic Problems of Evidence 45–46 (1962). Problems arising in connection with it are to be distinguished from problems of logical relevancy, e.g. evidence in a murder case that accused on the day before purchased a weapon of the kind used in the killing, treated in Rule 401.

If preliminary questions of conditional relevancy were determined solely by the judge, as provided in subdivision (a), the functioning of the jury as a trier of fact would be greatly restricted and in some cases virtually destroyed. These are appropriate questions for juries. Accepted treatment, as provided in the rule, is consistent with that given fact questions generally. The judge makes a preliminary determination whether the foundation evidence is sufficient to support a finding of fulfillment of the condition. If so, the item is admitted. If after all the evidence on the issue is in, pro and con, the jury could reasonably conclude that fulfillment of the condition is not established, the issue is for them. If the evidence is not such as to allow a finding, the judge withdraws the matter from their consideration. Morgan, *supra;* California Evidence Code § 403; New Jersey Rule 8(2). See also Uniform Rules 19 and 67.

The order of proof here, as generally, is subject to the control of the judge.

Subdivision (c). Preliminary hearings on the admissibility of confessions must be conducted outside the hearing of the jury. See Jackson v. Denno, 378 U.S. 368, 84 S.Ct. 1774, 12 L.Ed.2d 908 (1964).[2] Otherwise, detailed treatment of when preliminary matters should be heard outside the hearing of the jury is not feasible. The procedure is time consuming. Not infrequently the same evidence which is relevant to the issue of establishment of fulfillment of a condition precedent to admissibility is also relevant to weight or credibility, and time is saved by taking foundation proof in the presence of the jury. Much evidence on preliminary questions, though not relevant to jury issues, may be

---

2. At this point the Advisory Committee's Note to the 1971 Revised Draft contained the sentence, "Also, due regard for the right of an accused not to testify generally in the case requires that he be given an option to testify out of the presence of the jury upon preliminary matters." The statement was deleted in view of the deletion from the rule, mentioned in the preceding footnote.

heard by the jury with no adverse effect. A great deal must be left to the discretion of the judge who will act as the interests of justice require.

Report of the House Committee on the Judiciary

Rule 104(c) as submitted to the Congress provided that hearings on the admissibility of confessions shall be conducted outside the presence of the jury and hearings on all other preliminary matters should be so conducted when the interests of justice require. The Committee amended the Rule to provide that where an accused is a witness as to a preliminary matter, he has the right, upon his request, to be heard outside the jury's presence. Although recognizing that in some cases duplication of evidence would occur and that the procedure could be subject to abuse, the Committee believed that a proper regard for the right of an accused not to testify generally in the case dictates that he be given an option to testify out of the presence of the jury on preliminary matters.

The Committee construes the second sentence of subdivision (c) as applying to civil actions and proceedings as well as to criminal cases, and on this assumption has left the sentence unamended.

Advisory Committee's Note

Subdivision (d). The limitation upon cross-examination is designed to encourage participation by the accused in the determination of preliminary matters. He may testify concerning them without exposing himself to cross-examination generally. The provision is necessary because of the breadth of cross-examination [possible] under Rule 611(b).

The rule does not address itself to questions of the subsequent use of testimony given by an accused at a hearing on a preliminary matter. See Walder v. United States, 347 U.S. 62 (1954); Simmons v. United States, 390 U.S. 377 (1968); Harris v. New York, 401 U.S. 222 (1971).

Report of Senate Committee on the Judiciary

Under rule 104(c) the hearing on a preliminary matter may at times be conducted in front of the jury. Should an accused testify in such a hearing, waiving his privilege against self-incrimination as to the preliminary issue, rule 104(d) provides that he will not generally be subject to cross-examination as to any other issue. This rule is not, however, intended to immunize the accused from cross-examination where, in testifying about a preliminary issue, he injects other issues into the hearing. If he could not be cross-examined about any issues gratuitously raised by him beyond the scope of the preliminary matters, injustice might result. Accordingly, in order to prevent any such unjust result, the committee intends the rule to be construed to provide that the accused may subject himself to cross-examination as to issues raised by his own testimony upon a preliminary matter before a jury.

Advisory Committee's Note

Subdivision (e). For similar provisions see Uniform Rule 8; California Evidence Code § 406; Kansas Code of Civil Procedure § 60–408; New Jersey Evidence Rule 8(1).

Rule 105

Note by Federal Judicial Center

The rule enacted by the Congress is the rule prescribed by the Supreme Court as Rule 106, amended by substituting "court" in place of "judge." Rule 105 as prescribed by the Court, which was deleted from the rules enacted by the Congress, is set forth in the Appendix hereto, together with a statement of the reasons for the deletion.

Advisory Committee's Note

A close relationship exists between this rule and Rule 403, which * * * [provides for] exclusion when "probative value is substantially outweighed by the danger of unfair prejudice, confusion of the issues, or misleading the jury." The present rule recognizes the practice of admitting evidence for a limited purpose and instructing the jury accordingly. The availability and effectiveness of this practice must be taken into consideration in reaching a decision whether to exclude for unfair prejudice under Rule 403. In Bruton v. United States, 389 U.S. 818, 88 S.Ct. 126, 19 L.Ed.2d 70 (1968), the Court ruled that a limiting instruction did not effectively protect the accused against the prejudicial effect of admitting in evidence the confession of a codefendant which implicated him. The decision does not, however, bar the use of limited admissibility with an instruction where the risk of prejudice is less serious.

Similar provisions are found in Uniform Rule 6; California Evidence Code § 355; Kansas Code of Civil Procedure § 60–406; New Jersey Evidence Rule 6. The wording of the present rule differs, however, in repelling any implication that limiting or curative instructions are sufficient in all situations.

Report of House Committee on the Judiciary

Rule 106 as submitted by the Supreme Court (now Rule 105 in the bill) dealt with the subject of evidence which is admissible as to one party or for one purpose but is not admissible against another party or for another purpose. The Committee adopted this Rule without change on the understanding that it does not affect the authority of a court to order a severance in a multi-defendant case.

Rule 106

Note by Federal Judicial Center

The rule enacted by the Congress is the rule prescribed by the Supreme Court as Rule 107 without change.

Advisory Committee's Note

The rule is an expression of the rule of completeness. McCormick § 56. It is manifested as to depositions in Rule 32(a)(4) of the Federal Rules of Civil Procedure, of which the proposed rule is substantially a restatement.

The rule is based on two considerations. The first is the misleading impression created by taking matters out of context. The second is the inadequacy of repair work when delayed to a point later in the trial. See McCormick § 56; California Evidence Code § 356. The rule does not in any way circumscribe the right of the adversary to develop the matter on cross-examination or as part of his own case.

For practical reasons, the rule is limited to writings and recorded statements and does not apply to conversations.

Rule 201

Note by Federal Judicial Center

The rule enacted by the Congress is the rule prescribed by the Supreme Court with the following changes:

In subdivisions (c) and (d) the words "judge or" before "court" were deleted.

Subdivision (g) as it is shown was substituted in place of, "The judge shall instruct the jury to accept as established any facts judicially noticed." The substituted language is from the 1969 Preliminary Draft. 46 F.R.D. 161, 195.

Advisory Committee's Note

Subdivision (a). This is the only evidence rule on the subject of judicial notice. It deals only with judicial notice of "adjudicative" facts. No rule deals with judicial notice of "legislative" facts. Judicial notice of matters of foreign law is treated in Rule 44.1 of the Federal Rules of Civil Procedure and Rule 26.1 of the Federal Rules of Criminal Procedure.

The omission of any treatment of legislative facts results from fundamental differences between adjudicative facts and legislative facts. Adjudicative facts are simply the facts of the particular case. Legislative facts, on the other hand, are those which have relevance to legal reasoning and the lawmaking process, whether in the formulation of a legal principle or ruling by a judge or court or in the enactment of a legislative body. The terminology was coined by Professor Kenneth Davis in his article An Approach to Problems of Evidence in the Administrative Process, 55 Harv.L.Rev. 364, 404–407 (1942). The following discussion draws extensively upon his writings. In addition, see the same author's Judicial Notice, 55 Colum.L.Rev. 945 (1955); Administrative Law Treatise, ch. 15 (1958); A System of Judicial Notice Based on Fairness and Convenience, in Perspectives of Law 69 (1964).

The usual method of establishing adjudicative facts is through the introduction of evidence, ordinarily consisting of the testimony of witnesses. If particular facts are outside the area of reasonable controversy, this process is dispensed with as unnecessary. A high degree of indisputability is the essential prerequisite.

Legislative facts are quite different. As Professor Davis says:

"My opinion is that judge-made law would stop growing if judges, in thinking about questions of law and policy, were forbidden to take into account the facts they believe, as distinguished from facts which are 'clearly * * * within the domain of the indisputable.' Facts most needed in thinking about difficult problems of law and policy have a way of being outside the domain of the clearly indisputable." A System of Judicial Notice Based on Fairness and Convenience, supra, at 82.

An illustration is Hawkins v. United States, 358 U.S. 74, 79 S.Ct. 136, 3 L.Ed.2d 125 (1958), in which the Court refused to discard the common law rule that one spouse could not testify against the other, saying, "Adverse testimony given in criminal proceedings would, we think, be likely to destroy almost any marriage." This conclusion has a large intermixture of fact, but the factual aspect is scarcely "indisputable." See Hutchins and Slesinger, Some Observations on the Law of Evidence—Family Relations, 13 Minn.L.Rev. 675 (1929). If the destructive effect of the giving of adverse testimony by a spouse is not indisputable, should the Court have refrained from considering it in the absence of supporting evidence?

"If the Model Code or the Uniform Rules had been applicable, the Court would have been barred from thinking about the essential factual ingredient of the problems before it, and such a result would be obviously intolerable. What the law needs at its growing points is more, not less, judicial thinking about the factual ingredients of problems of what the law ought to be, and the needed facts are seldom 'clearly' indisputable." Davis, supra, at 83.

Professor Morgan gave the following description of the methodology of determining domestic law:

"In determining the content or applicability of a rule of domestic law, the judge is unrestricted in his investigation and conclusion. He may reject the propositions of either party or of both parties. He may consult the sources of pertinent data to which they refer, or he may refuse to do so. He may make an independent search for persuasive data or rest content with what he has or what the parties present. * * * [T]he parties do no more than to assist; they control no part of the process." Morgan, Judicial Notice, 57 Harv.L.Rev. 269, 270–271 (1944).

This is the view which should govern judicial access to legislative facts. It renders inappropriate any limitation in the form of indisputability, any formal requirements of notice other than those already inherent in affording opportunity to hear and be heard and exchanging briefs, and any requirement of formal findings at any level. It should, however, leave open the possibility of introducing evidence through regular channels in appropriate situations. See Borden's Farm Products Co. v. Baldwin, 293 U.S. 194, 55 S.Ct. 187, 79 L.Ed. 281 (1934), where the cause was remanded for the taking of evidence as to the economic conditions and trade practices underlying the New York Milk Control Law.

Similar considerations govern the judicial use of non-adjudicative facts in ways other than formulating laws and rules. Thayer described them as a part of the judicial reasoning process.

"In conducting a process of judicial reasoning, as of other reasoning, not a step can be taken without assuming something which has not been proved; and the capacity to do this with competent judgment and efficiency, is imputed to judges and juries as part of their necessary mental outfit." Thayer, Preliminary Treatise on Evidence 279–280 (1898).

As Professor Davis points out, A System of Judicial Notice Based on Fairness and Convenience, in Perspectives of Law 69, 73 (1964), every case involves the use of hundreds or thousands of non-evidence facts. When a witness in an automobile accident case says "car," everyone, judge and jury included, furnishes, from non-evidence sources within himself, the supplementing information that the "car" is an automobile, not a railroad car, that it is self-propelled, probably by an internal combustion engine, that it may be assumed to have four wheels with pneumatic rubber tires, and so on. The judicial process cannot construct every case from scratch, like Descartes creating a world based on the postulate *Cogito, ergo sum.* These items could not possibly be introduced into evidence, and no one suggests that they be. Nor are they appropriate subjects for any formalized treatment of judicial notice of facts. See Levin and Levy, Persuading the Jury with Facts Not in Evidence: The Fiction-Science Spectrum, 105 U.Pa.L.Rev. 139 (1956).

Another aspect of what Thayer had in mind is the use of non-evidence facts to appraise or assess the adjudicative facts of the case. Pairs of cases from two jurisdictions illustrate this use and also the difference between non-evidence facts thus used and adjudicative facts. In People v. Strook, 347 Ill. 460, 179 N.E. 821 (1932), venue in Cook County had been held not established by testimony that the crime was committed at 7956 South Chicago Avenue, since judicial notice would not be taken that the address was in Chicago. However, the same court subsequently ruled that venue in Cook County was established by testimony that a crime occurred at 8900 South Anthony Avenue, since notice would be taken of the common practice of omitting the name of the city when speaking of local addresses, and the witness was testifying in Chicago. People v. Pride, 16 Ill.2d 82, 156 N.E.2d 551 (1951). And in Hughes v. Vestal, 264 N.C. 500, 142 S.E.2d 361 (1965), the Supreme Court of North Carolina disapproved the trial judge's admission in evidence of a state-published table of automobile stopping distances on the basis of judicial notice, though the court itself had referred to the same table in an earlier case in a "rhetorical and illustrative" way in determining that the defendant could not have stopped her car in time to avoid striking a child who suddenly appeared in the highway and that a nonsuit was properly granted. Ennis v. Dupree, 262 N.C. 224, 136 S.E.2d 702 (1964). See also Brown v. Hale, 263 N.C. 176, 139 S.E.2d 210 (1964); Clayton v. Rimmer, 262 N.C. 302, 136 S.E.2d 562 (1964). It is apparent that this use of non-evidence facts in evaluating the adjudicative facts of the case is not an appropriate subject for a formalized judicial notice treatment.

In view of these considerations, the regulation of judicial notice of facts by the present rule extends only to adjudicative facts.

What, then, are "adjudicative" facts? Davis refers to them as those "which relate to the parties," or more fully:

"When a court or an agency finds facts concerning the immediate parties— who did what, where, when, how, and with what motive or intent—the court or agency is performing an adjudicative function, and the facts are conveniently called adjudicative facts. ∗ ∗ ∗

"Stated in other terms, the adjudicative facts are those to which the law is applied in the process of adjudication. They are the facts that normally go to the jury in a jury case. They relate to the parties, their activities, their properties, their businesses." 2 Administrative Law Treatise 353.

Subdivision (b). With respect to judicial notice of adjudicative facts the tradition has been one of caution in requiring that the matter be beyond reasonable controversy. This tradition of circumspection appears to be soundly based, and no reason to depart from it is apparent. As Professor Davis says:

"The reason we use trial-type procedure, I think, is that we make the practical judgment, on the basis of experience, that taking evidence, subject to cross-examination and rebuttal, is the best way to resolve controversies involving disputes of adjudicative facts, that is, facts pertaining to the parties. The reason we require a determination on the record is that we think fair procedure in resolving disputes of adjudicative facts calls for giving each party a chance to meet in the appropriate fashion the facts that come to the tribunal's attention, and the appropriate fashion for meeting disputed adjudicative facts includes rebuttal evidence, cross-examination, usually confrontation, and argument (either written or oral or both). The key to a fair trial is opportunity to use the appropriate weapons (rebuttal evidence, cross-examination, and argument) to

meet adverse materials that come to the tribunal's attention." A System of
Judicial Notice Based on Fairness and Convenience, in Perspectives of Law 69,
93 (1964).

The rule proceeds upon the theory that these considerations call for dispensing
with traditional methods of proof only in clear cases. Compare Professor Davis'
conclusion that judicial notice should be a matter of convenience, subject to
requirements of procedural fairness. Id., 94.

This rule is consistent with Uniform Rule 9(1) and (2) which limit judicial
notice of facts to those "so universally known that they cannot reasonably be
the subject of dispute," those "so generally known or of such common notoriety
within the territorial jurisdiction of the court that they cannot reasonably be
the subject of dispute," and those "capable of immediate and accurate determination by resort to easily accessible sources of indisputable accuracy." The
traditional textbook treatment has included these general categories (matters of
common knowledge, facts capable of verification), McCormick §§ 324, 325, and
then has passed on into detailed treatment of such specific topics as facts
relating to the personnel and records of the court, id. § 327, and other
governmental facts, id. § 328. The California draftsmen, with a background of
detailed statutory regulation of judicial notice, followed a somewhat similar
pattern. California Evidence Code §§ 451, 452. The Uniform Rules, however,
were drafted on the theory that these particular matters are included within
the general categories and need no specific mention. This approach is followed
in the present rule.

The phrase "propositions of generalized knowledge," found in Uniform
Rule 9(1) and (2) is not included in the present rule. It was, it is believed,
originally included in Model Code Rules 801 and 802 primarily in order to
afford some minimum recognition to the right of the judge in his "legislative"
capacity (not acting as the trier of fact) to take judicial notice of very limited
categories of generalized knowledge. The limitations thus imposed have been
discarded herein as undesirable, unworkable, and contrary to existing practice.
What is left, then, to be considered, is the status of a "proposition of generalized
knowledge" as an "adjudicative" fact to be noticed judicially and communicated
by the judge to the jury. Thus viewed, it is considered to be lacking practical
significance. While judges use judicial notice of "prospositions of generalized
knowledge" in a variety of situations: determining the validity and meaning of
statutes, formulating common law rules, deciding whether evidence should be
admitted, assessing the sufficiency and effect of evidence, all are essentially
nonadjudicative in nature. When judicial notice is seen as a significant vehicle
for progress in the law, these are the areas involved, particularly in developing
fields of scientific knowledge. See McCormick 712. It is not believed that
judges now instruct juries as to "propositions of generalized knowledge" derived
from encyclopedias or other sources, or that they are likely to do so, or, indeed,
that it is desirable that they do so. There is a vast difference between ruling on
the basis of judicial notice that radar evidence of speed is admissible and
explaining to the jury its principles and degree of accuracy, or between using a
table of stopping distances of automobiles at various speeds in a judicial
evaluation of testimony and telling the jury its precise application in the case.
For cases raising doubt as to the propriety of the use of medical texts by lay
triers of fact in passing on disability claims in administrative proceedings, see
Sayers v. Gardner, 380 F.2d 940 (6th Cir. 1967); Ross v. Gardner, 365 F.2d 554
(6th Cir. 1966); Sosna v. Celebrezze, 234 F.Supp. 289 (E.D.Pa.1964); Glendenning v. Ribicoff, 213 F.Supp. 301 (W.D.Mo.1962).

Subdivisions (c) and (d). Under subdivision (c) the judge has a discretionary authority to take judicial notice, regardless of whether he is so requested by a party. The taking of judicial notice is mandatory, under subdivision (d), only when a party requests it and the necessary information is supplied. This scheme is believed to reflect existing practice. It is simple and workable. It avoids troublesome distinctions in the many situations in which the process of taking judicial notice is not recognized as such.

Compare Uniform Rule 9 making judicial notice of facts universally known mandatory without request, and making judicial notice of facts generally known in the jurisdiction or capable of determination by resort to accurate sources discretionary in the absence of request but mandatory if request is made and the information furnished. But see Uniform Rule 10(3), which directs the judge to decline to take judicial notice if available information fails to convince him that the matter falls clearly within Uniform Rule 9 or is insufficient to enable him to notice it judicially. Substantially the same approach is found in California Evidence Code §§ 451–453 and in New Jersey Evidence Rule 9. In contrast, the present rule treats alike all adjudicative facts which are subject to judicial notice.

Subdivision (e). Basic considerations of procedural fairness demand an opportunity to be heard on the propriety of taking judicial notice and the tenor of the matter noticed. The rule requires the granting of that opportunity upon request. No formal scheme of giving notice is provided. An adversely affected party may learn in advance that judicial notice is in contemplation, either by virtue of being served with a copy of a request by another party under subdivision (d) that judicial notice be taken, or through an advance indication by the judge. Or he may have no advance notice at all. The likelihood of the latter is enhanced by the frequent failure to recognize judicial notice as such. And in the absence of advance notice, a request made after the fact could not in fairness be considered untimely. See the provision for hearing on timely request in the Administrative Procedure Act, 5 U.S.C. § 556(e). See also Revised Model State Administrative Procedure Act (1961), 9C U.L.A. § 10(4) (Supp.1967).

Subdivision (f). In accord with the usual view, judicial notice may be taken at any stage of the proceedings, whether in the trial court or on appeal. Uniform Rule 12; California Evidence Code § 459; Kansas Rules of Evidence § 60–412; New Jersey Evidence Rule 12; McCormick § 330, p. 712.

Subdivision (g). Much of the controversy about judicial notice has centered upon the question whether evidence should be admitted in disproof of facts of which judicial notice is taken.

The writers have been divided. Favoring admissibility are Thayer, Preliminary Treatise on Evidence 308 (1898); 9 Wigmore § 2567; Davis, A System of Judicial Notice Based on Fairness and Convenience, in Perspectives of Law, 69, 76–77 (1964). Opposing admissibility are Keeffe, Landis and Shaad, Sense and Nonsense about Judicial Notice, 2 Stan.L.Rev. 664, 668 (1950); McNaughton, Judicial Notice—Excerpts Relating to the Morgan-Whitmore Controversy, 14 Vand.L.Rev. 779 (1961); Morgan, Judicial Notice, 57 Harv.L.Rev. 269, 279 (1944); McCormick 710–711. The Model Code and the Uniform Rules are predicated upon indisputability of judicially noticed facts.

The proponents of admitting evidence in disproof have concentrated largely upon legislative facts. Since the present rule deals only with judicial notice of adjudicative facts, arguments directed to legislative facts lose their relevancy.

Report of House Committee on the Judiciary

Rule 201(g) as received from the Supreme Court provided that when judicial notice of a fact is taken, the court shall instruct the jury to accept that fact as established. Being of the view that mandatory instruction to a jury in a criminal case to accept as conclusive any fact judicially noticed is inappropriate because contrary to the spirit of the Sixth Amendment right to a jury trial, the Committee adopted the 1969 Advisory Committee draft of this subsection, allowing a mandatory instruction in civil actions and proceedings and a discretionary instruction in criminal cases.

Advisory Committee's Note (Continued)

[The following portion of the Advisory Committee's Note is from the 1969 Preliminary Draft, 46 F.R.D. 161, 204.]

Within its relatively narrow area of adjudicative facts, the rule contemplates there is to be no evidence before the jury in disproof in civil cases. The judge instructs the jury to take judicially noticed facts as conclusive. This position is justified by the undesirable effects of the opposite rule in limiting the rebutting party, though not his opponent, to admissible evidence, in defeating the reasons for judicial notice, and in affecting the substantive law to an extent and in ways largely unforeseeable. Ample protection and flexibility are afforded by the broad provision for opportunity to be heard on request set forth in subdivision (e).

Criminal cases are treated somewhat differently in the rule. While matters falling within the common fund of information supposed to be possessed by jurors need not be proved, State v. Dunn, 221 Mo. 530, 120 S.W. 1179 (1909), these are not, properly speaking, adjudicative facts but an aspect of legal reasoning. The considerations which underlie the general rule that a verdict cannot be directed against the accused in a criminal case seem to foreclose the judge's directing the jury on the basis of judicial notice to accept as conclusive any adjudicative facts in the case. State v. Main, 91 R.I. 338, 180 A.2d 814 (1962); State v. Lawrence, 120 Utah 323, 234 P.2d 600 (1951). Cf. People v. Mayes, 113 Cal. 618, 45 P. 860 (1896); Ross v. United States, 374 F.2d 97 (8th Cir. 1967). However, this view presents no obstacle to the judge's advising the jury as to a matter judicially noticed, if he instructs them that it need not be taken as conclusive.

Note on Judicial Notice of Law (by the Advisory Committee)

By rules effective July 1, 1966, the method of invoking the law of a foreign country is covered elsewhere. Rule 44.1 of the Federal Rules of Civil Procedure; Rule 26.1 of the Federal Rules of Criminal Procedure. These two new admirably designed rules are founded upon the assumption that the manner in which law is fed into the judicial process is never a proper concern of the rules of evidence but rather of the rules of procedure. The Advisory Committee on Evidence, believing that this assumption is entirely correct, proposes no evidence rule with respect to judicial notice of law, and suggests that those matters of law which, in addition to foreign-country law, have traditionally been treated as requiring pleading and proof and more recently as the subject of judicial notice be left to the Rules of Civil and Criminal Procedure.

ARTICLE III.   PRESUMPTIONS IN CIVIL ACTIONS AND PROCEEDINGS

Rule 301

Note by Federal Judicial Center

The bill passed by the House substituted a substantially different rule in place of that prescribed by the Supreme Court. The Senate bill substituted yet a further version, which was accepted by the House, was enacted by the Congress, and is the rule shown above. The earlier versions are set forth in the Appendix hereto.

Report of Senate Committee on the Judiciary

This rule governs presumptions in civil cases generally. Rule 302 provides for presumptions in cases controlled by State law.

As submitted by the Supreme Court, presumptions governed by this rule were given the effect of placing upon the opposing party the burden of establishing the nonexistence of the presumed fact, once the party invoking the presumption established the basic facts giving rise to it.

Instead of imposing a burden of persuasion on the party against whom the presumption is directed, the House adopted a provision which shifted the burden of going forward with the evidence. They further provided that "even though met with contradicting evidence, a presumption is sufficient evidence of the fact presumed, to be considered by the trier of fact." The effect of the amendment is that presumptions are to be treated as evidence.

The committee feels the House amendment is ill-advised. As the joint committees (the Standing Committee on Practice and Procedure of the Judicial Conference and the Advisory Committee on the Rules of Evidence) stated: "Presumptions are not evidence, but ways of dealing with evidence."[1] This treatment requires juries to perform the task of considering "as evidence" facts upon which they have no direct evidence and which may confuse them in performance of their duties. California had a rule much like that contained in the House amendment. It was sharply criticized by Justice Traynor in Speck v. Sarver[2] and was repealed after 93 troublesome years.[3]

Professor McCormick gives a concise and compelling critique of the presumption as evidence rule:

* * *

Another solution, formerly more popular than now, is to instruct the jury that the presumption is 'evidence', to be weighed and considered with the testimony in the case. This avoids the danger that the jury may infer that the presumption is conclusive, but it probably means little to the jury, and certainly runs counter to accepted theories of the nature of evidence.[4]

1. Hearings Before the Committee on the Judiciary, United States Senate, H.R. 5463, p. 56.

2. 20 Cal.2d 585, 594, 128 P.2d 16, 21 (1942).

3. Cal.Ev.Code 1965 § 600.

4. McCormick, Evidence, 669 (1954); id. 825 (2d ed. 1972).

For these reasons the committee has deleted that provision of the House-passed rule that treats presumptions as evidence. The effect of the rule as adopted by the committee is to make clear that while evidence of facts giving rise to a presumption shifts the burden of coming forward with evidence to rebut or meet the presumption, it does not shift the burden of persuasion on the existence of the presumed facts. The burden of persuasion remains on the party to whom it is allocated under the rules governing the allocation in the first instance.

The court may instruct the jury that they may infer the existence of the presumed fact from proof of the basic facts giving rise to the presumption. However, it would be inappropriate under this rule to instruct the jury that the inference they are to draw is conclusive.

Conference Report

The House bill provides that a presumption in civil actions and proceedings shifts to the party against whom it is directed the burden of going forward with evidence to meet or rebut it. Even though evidence contradicting the presumption is offered, a presumption is considered sufficient evidence of the presumed fact to be considered by the jury. The Senate amendment provides that a presumption shifts to the party against whom it is directed the burden of going forward with evidence to meet or rebut the presumption, but it does not shift to that party the burden of persuasion on the existence of the presumed fact.

Under the Senate amendment, a presumption is sufficient to get a party past an adverse party's motion to dismiss made at the end of his case-in-chief. If the adverse party offers no evidence contradicting the presumed fact, the court will instruct the jury that if it finds the basic facts, it may presume the existence of the presumed fact. If the adverse party does offer evidence contradicting the presumed fact, the court cannot instruct the jury that it may *presume* the existence of the presumed fact from proof of the basic facts. The court may however, instruct the jury that it may infer the existence of the presumed fact from proof of the basic facts.

The Conference adopts the Senate amendment.

Rule 302

Note by Federal Judicial Center

The rule enacted by the Congress is the rule prescribed by the Supreme Court, amended by adding "and proceedings" after "actions."

Advisory Committee's Note

A series of Supreme Court decisions in diversity cases leaves no doubt of the relevance of Erie Railroad Co. v. Tompkins, 304 U.S. 64, 58 S.Ct. 817, 82 L.Ed. 1188 (1938), to questions of burden of proof. These decisions are Cities Service Oil Co. v. Dunlap, 308 U.S. 208, 60 S.Ct. 201, 84 L.Ed. 196 (1939), Palmer v. Hoffman, 318 U.S. 109, 63 S.Ct. 477, 87 L.Ed. 645 (1943), and Dick v. New York Life Ins. Co., 359 U.S. 437, 79 S.Ct. 921, 3 L.Ed.2d 935 (1959). They involved burden of proof, respectively, as to status as bona fide purchaser, contributory negligence, and nonaccidental death (suicide) of an insured. In each instance the state rule was held to be applicable. It does not follow, however, that all presumptions in diversity cases are governed by state law. In each case cited, the burden of proof question had to do with a substantive element of the claim or defense. Application of the state law is called for only when the presumption operates upon such an element. Accordingly the rule does not apply state law when the presumption operates upon a lesser aspect of the case, i.e. "tactical" presumptions.

The situations in which the state law is applied have been tagged for convenience in the preceding discussion as "diversity cases." The designation is not a completely accurate one since *Erie* applies to any claim or issue having its source in state law, regardless of the basis of federal jurisdiction, and does not apply to a federal claim or issue, even though jurisdiction is based on diversity. Vestal, Erie R. R. v. Tompkins: A Projection, 48 Iowa L.Rev. 248, 257 (1963); Hart and Wechsler, The Federal Courts and the Federal System, 697 (1953); 1A Moore, Federal Practice ¶ 0.305[3] (2d ed. 1965); Wright, Federal Courts, 217–218 (1963). Hence the rule employs, as appropriately descriptive, the phrase "as to which state law supplies the rule of decision." See A.L.I. Study of the Division of Jurisdiction Between State and Federal Courts, § 2344(c), p. 40, P.F.D. No. 1 (1965).

Presumptions in Criminal Cases

Note by Federal Judicial Center

The rules prescribed by the Supreme Court included Rule 303, Presumptions in Criminal Cases. The rule was not included in the rules enacted by the Congress. The rule, Advisory Committee's Note, and reasons given by the House of Representatives for excluding the rule are set forth in the Appendix hereto.

ARTICLE IV. RELEVANCY AND ITS LIMITS

Rule 401

Note by Federal Judicial Center

The rule enacted by the Congress is the rule prescribed by the Supreme Court without change.

Advisory Committee's Note

Problems of relevancy call for an answer to the question whether an item of evidence, when tested by the processes of legal reasoning, possesses sufficient probative value to justify receiving it in evidence. Thus, assessment of the probative value of evidence that a person purchased a revolver shortly prior to a fatal shooting with which he is charged is a matter of analysis and reasoning.

The variety of relevancy problems is coextensive with the ingenuity of counsel in using circumstantial evidence as a means of proof. An enormous number of cases fall in no set pattern, and this rule is designed as a guide for handling them. On the other hand, some situations recur with sufficient frequency to create patterns susceptible of treatment by specific rules. Rule 404 and those following it are of that variety; they also serve as illustrations of the application of the present rule as limited by the exclusionary principles of Rule 403.

Passing mention should be made of so-called "conditional" relevancy. Morgan, Basic Problems of Evidence 45–46 (1962). In this situation, probative value depends not only upon satisfying the basic requirement of relevancy as described above but also upon the existence of some matter of fact. For example, if evidence of a spoken statement is relied upon to prove notice, probative value is lacking unless the person sought to be charged heard the statement. The problem is one of fact, and the only rules needed are for the purpose of determining the respective functions of judge and jury. See Rules 104(b) and 901. The discussion which follows in the present note is concerned with relevancy generally, not with any particular problem of conditional relevancy.

Relevancy is not an inherent characteristic of any item of evidence but exists only as a relation between an item of evidence and a matter properly provable in the case. Does the item of evidence tend to prove the matter sought to be proved? Whether the relationship exists depends upon principles evolved by experience or science, applied logically to the situation at hand. James, Relevancy, Probability and the Law, 29 Calif.L.Rev. 689, 696, n. 15 (1941), in Selected Writings on Evidence and Trial 610, 615, n. 15 (Fryer ed. 1957). The rule summarizes this relationship as a "tendency to make the existence" of the fact to be proved "more probable or less probable." Compare Uniform Rule 1(2) which states the crux of relevancy as "a tendency in reason," thus perhaps emphasizing unduly the logical process and ignoring the need to draw upon experience or science to validate the general principle upon which relevancy in a particular situation depends.

The standard of probability under the rule is "more * * * probable than it would be without the evidence." Any more stringent requirement is unworkable and unrealistic. As McCormick § 152, p. 317, says, "A brick is not a wall," or, as Falknor, Extrinsic Policies Affecting Admissibility, 10 Rutgers L.Rev. 574, 576 (1956), quotes Professor McBaine, "* * * [I]t is not to be supposed that every witness can make a home run." Dealing with probability in the language of the rule has the added virtue of avoiding confusion between questions of admissibility and questions of the sufficiency of the evidence.

The rule uses the phrase "fact that is of consequence to the determination of the action" to describe the kind of fact to which proof may properly be directed. The language is that of California Evidence Code § 210; it has the advantage of avoiding the loosely used and ambiguous word "material." Tentative Recommendation and a Study Relating to the Uniform Rules of Evidence (Art. I. General Provisions), Cal. Law Revision Comm'n, Rep., Rec. & Studies, 10–11 (1964). The fact to be proved may be ultimate, intermediate, or evidentiary; it matters not, so long as it is of consequence in the determination of the action. Cf. Uniform Rule 1(2) which requires that the evidence relate to a "material" fact.

The fact to which the evidence is directed need not be in dispute. While situations will arise which call for the exclusion of evidence offered to prove a point conceded by the opponent, the ruling should be made on the basis of such considerations as waste of time and undue prejudice (see Rule 403), rather than under any general requirement that evidence is admissible only if directed to matters in dispute. Evidence which is essentially background in nature can scarcely be said to involve disputed matter, yet it is universally offered and admitted as an aid to understanding. Charts, photographs, views of real estate, murder weapons, and many other items of evidence fall in this category. A rule limiting admissibility to evidence directed to a controversial point would invite the exclusion of this helpful evidence, or at least the raising of endless questions over its admission. Cf. California Evidence Code § 210, defining relevant evidence in terms of tendency to prove a disputed fact.

Rule 402

Note by Federal Judicial Center

The rule enacted by the Congress is the rule prescribed by the Supreme Court, with the first sentence amended by substituting "prescribed" in place of "adopted", and by adding at the end thereof the phrase "pursuant to statutory authority."

Advisory Committee's Note

The provisions that all relevant evidence is admissible, with certain exceptions, and that evidence which is not relevant is not admissible are "a presupposition involved in the very conception of a rational system of evidence." Thayer, Preliminary Treatise on Evidence 264 (1898). They constitute the foundation upon which the structure of admission and exclusion rests. For similar provisions see California Evidence Code §§ 350, 351. Provisions that all relevant evidence is admissible are found in Uniform Rule 7(f); Kansas Code of Civil Procedure § 60–407(f); and New Jersey Evidence Rule 7(f); but the exclusion of evidence which is not relevant is left to implication.

Not all relevant evidence is admissible. The exclusion of relevant evidence occurs in a variety of situations and may be called for by these rules, by the Rules of Civil and Criminal Procedure, by Bankruptcy Rules, by Act of Congress, or by constitutional considerations.

Succeeding rules in the present article, in response to the demands of particular policies, require the exclusion of evidence despite its relevancy. In addition, Article V recognizes a number of privileges; Article VI imposes limitations upon witnesses and the manner of dealing with them; Article VII specifies requirements with respect to opinions and expert testimony; Article VIII excludes hearsay not falling within an exception; Article IX spells out the handling of authentication and identification; and Article X restricts the manner of proving the contents of writings and recordings.

The Rules of Civil and Criminal Procedure in some instances require the exclusion of relevant evidence. For example, Rules 30(b) and 32(a)(3) of the Rules of Civil Procedure, by imposing requirements of notice and unavailability of the deponent, place limits on the use of relevant depositions. Similarly, Rule 15 of the Rules of Criminal Procedure restricts the use of depositions in criminal cases, even though relevant. And the effective enforcement of the command, originally statutory and now found in Rule 5(a) of the Rules of Criminal Procedure, that an arrested person be taken without unnecessary delay before a commissioner or other similar officer is held to require the exclusion of statements elicited during detention in violation thereof. Mallory v. United States, 354 U.S. 449, 77 S.Ct. 1356, 1 L.Ed.2d 1479 (1957); 18 U.S.C. § 3501(c).

While congressional enactments in the field of evidence have generally tended to expand admissibility beyond the scope of the common law rules, in some particular situations they have restricted the admissibility of relevant evidence. Most of this legislation has consisted of the formulation of a privilege or of a prohibition against disclosure. 8 U.S.C. § 1202(f), records of refusal of visas or permits to enter United States confidential, subject to discretion of

Secretary of State to make available to court upon certification of need; 10
U.S.C. § 3693, replacement certificate of honorable discharge from Army not
admissible in evidence; 10 U.S.C. § 8693, same as to Air Force; 11 U.S.C.
§ 25(a)(10), testimony given by bankrupt on his examination not admissible in
criminal proceedings against him, except that given in hearing upon objection
to discharge; 11 U.S.C. § 205(a), railroad reorganization petition, if dismissed,
not admissible in evidence; 11 U.S.C. § 403(a), list of creditors filed with
municipal composition plan not an admission; 13 U.S.C. § 9(a), census information confidential, retained copies of reports privileged; 47 U.S.C. § 605, interception and divulgence of wire or radio communications prohibited unless
authorized by sender. These statutory provisions would remain undisturbed by
the rules.

The rule recognizes but makes no attempt to spell out the constitutional
considerations which impose basic limitations upon the admissibility of relevant
evidence. Examples are evidence obtained by unlawful search and seizure,
Weeks v. United States, 232 U.S. 383, 34 S.Ct. 341, 58 L.Ed. 652 (1914); Katz v.
United States, 389 U.S. 347, 88 S.Ct. 507, 19 L.Ed.2d 576 (1967); incriminating
statement elicited from an accused in violation of right to counsel, Massiah v.
United States, 377 U.S. 201, 84 S.Ct. 1199, 12 L.Ed.2d 246 (1964).

Report of House Committee on the Judiciary

Rule 402 as submitted to the Congress contained the phrase "or by other
rules adopted by the Supreme Court". To accommodate the view that the
Congress should not appear to acquiesce in the Court's judgment that it has
authority under the existing Rules Enabling Acts to promulgate Rules of
Evidence, the Committee amended the above phrase to read "or by other rules
prescribed by the Supreme Court pursuant to statutory authority" in this and
other Rules where the reference appears.

Rule 403

Note by Federal Judicial Center

The rule enacted by the Congress is the rule prescribed by the Supreme
Court without change.

Advisory Committee's Note

The case law recognizes that certain circumstances call for the exclusion of
evidence which is of unquestioned relevance. These circumstances entail risks
which range all the way from inducing decision on a purely emotional basis, at
one extreme, to nothing more harmful than merely wasting time, at the other
extreme. Situations in this area call for balancing the probative value of and
need for the evidence against the harm likely to result from its admission.
Slough, Relevancy Unraveled, 5 Kan.L.Rev. 1, 12–15 (1956); Trautman, Logical
or Legal Relevancy—A Conflict in Theory, 5 Van.L.Rev. 385, 392 (1952);
McCormick § 152, pp. 319–321. The rules which follow in this Article are
concrete applications evolved for particular situations. However, they reflect
the policies underlying the present rule, which is designed as a guide for the
handling of situations for which no specific rules have been formulated.

Exclusion for risk of unfair prejudice, confusion of issues, misleading the
jury, or waste of time, all find ample support in the authorities. "Unfair
prejudice" within its context means an undue tendency to suggest decision on
an improper basis, commonly, though not necessarily, an emotional one.

The rule does not enumerate surprise as a ground for exclusion, in this respect following Wigmore's view of the common law. 6 Wigmore § 1849. Cf. McCormick § 152, p. 320, n. 29, listing unfair surprise as a ground for exclusion but stating that it is usually "coupled with the danger of prejudice and confusion of issues." While Uniform Rule 45 incorporates surprise as a ground and is followed in Kansas Code of Civil Procedure § 60–445, surprise is not included in California Evidence Code § 352 or New Jersey Rule 4, though both the latter otherwise substantially embody Uniform Rule 45. While it can scarcely be doubted that claims of unfair surprise may still be justified despite procedural requirements of notice and instrumentalities of discovery, the granting of a continuance is a more appropriate remedy than exclusion of the evidence. Tentative Recommendation and a Study Relating to the Uniform Rules of Evidence (Art. VI. Extrinsic Policies Affecting Admissibility), Cal. Law Revision Comm'n, Rep., Rec. & Studies, 612 (1964). Moreover, the impact of a rule excluding evidence on the ground of surprise would be difficult to estimate.

In reaching a decision whether to exclude on grounds of unfair prejudice, consideration should be given to the probable effectiveness or lack of effectiveness of a limiting instruction. See Rule 106[105] and Advisory Committee's Note thereunder. The availability of other means of proof may also be an appropriate factor.

Rule 404

Note by Federal Judicial Center

The rule enacted by the Congress is the rule prescribed by the Supreme Court, with the second sentence of subdivision (b) amended by substituting "It may, however, be admissible" in place of "This subdivision does not exclude the evidence when offered."

Advisory Committee's Note

Subdivision (a). This subdivision deals with the basic question whether character evidence should be admitted. Once the admissibility of character evidence in some form is established under this rule, reference must then be made to Rule 405, which follows, in order to determine the appropriate method of proof. If the character is that of a witness, see Rules 608 and 609 for methods of proof.

Character questions arise in two fundamentally different ways. (1) Character may itself be an element of a crime, claim, or defense. A situation of this kind is commonly referred to as "character in issue." Illustrations are: the chastity of the victim under a statute specifying her chastity as an element of the crime of seduction, or the competency of the driver in an action for negligently entrusting a motor vehicle to an incompetent driver. No problem of the general relevancy of character evidence is involved, and the present rule therefore has no provision on the subject. The only question relates to allowable methods of proof, as to which see Rule 405, immediately following. (2) Character evidence is susceptible of being used for the purpose of suggesting an inference that the person acted on the occasion in question consistently with his character. This use of character is often described as "circumstantial." Illustrations are: evidence of a violent disposition to prove that the person was the aggressor in an affray, or evidence of honesty in disproof of a charge of theft. This circumstantial use of character evidence raises questions of relevancy as well as questions of allowable methods of proof.

In most jurisdictions today, the circumstantial use of character is rejected but with important exceptions: (1) an accused may introduce pertinent evidence of good character (often misleadingly described as "putting his character in issue"), in which event the prosecution may rebut with evidence of bad character; (2) an accused may introduce pertinent evidence of the character of the victim, as in support of a claim of self-defense to a charge of homicide or consent in a case of rape, and the prosecution may introduce similar evidence in rebuttal of the character evidence, or, in a homicide case, to rebut a claim that deceased was the first aggressor, however proved; and (3) the character of a witness may be gone into as bearing on his credibility. McCormick §§ 155–161. This pattern is incorporated in the rule. While its basis lies more in history and experience than in logic an underlying justification can fairly be found in terms of the relative presence and absence of prejudice in the various situations. Falknor, Extrinsic Policies Affecting Admissibility, 10 Rutgers L.Rev. 574, 584 (1956); McCormick § 157. In any event, the criminal rule is so deeply imbedded in our jurisprudence as to assume almost constitutional proportions and to override doubts of the basic relevancy of the evidence.

The limitation to pertinent traits of character, rather than character generally, in paragraphs (1) and (2) is in accordance with the prevailing view. McCormick § 158, p. 334. A similar provision in Rule 608, to which reference is made in paragraph (3), limits character evidence respecting witnesses to the trait of truthfulness or untruthfulness.

The argument is made that circumstantial use of character ought to be allowed in civil cases to the same extent as in criminal cases, i.e. evidence of good (nonprejudicial) character would be admissible in the first instance, subject to rebuttal by evidence of bad character. Falknor, Extrinsic Policies Affecting Admissibility, 10 Rutgers L.Rev. 574, 581–583 (1956); Tentative Recommendation and a Study Relating to the Uniform Rules of Evidence (Art. VI. Extrinsic Policies Affecting Admissibility), Cal. Law Revision Comm'n, Rep., Rec. & Studies, 657–658 (1964). Uniform Rule 47 goes farther, in that it assumes that character evidence in general satisfies the conditions of relevancy, except as provided in Uniform Rule 48. The difficulty with expanding the use of character evidence in civil cases is set forth by the California Law Revision Commission in its ultimate rejection of Uniform Rule 47, id., 615:

"Character evidence is of slight probative value and may be very prejudicial. It tends to distract the trier of fact from the main question of what actually happened on the particular occasion. It subtly permits the trier of fact to reward the good man and to punish the bad man because of their respective characters despite what the evidence in the case shows actually happened."

Much of the force of the position of those favoring greater use of character evidence in civil cases is dissipated by their support of Uniform Rule 48 which excludes the evidence in negligence cases, where it could be expected to achieve its maximum usefulness. Moreover, expanding concepts of "character," which seem of necessity to extend into such areas as psychiatric evaluation and psychological testing, coupled with expanded admissibility, would open up such vistas of mental examinations as caused the Court concern in Schlagenhauf v. Holder, 379 U.S. 104, 85 S.Ct. 234, 13 L.Ed.2d 152 (1964). It is believed that those espousing change have not met the burden of persuasion.

Subdivision (b) deals with a specialized but important application of the general rule excluding circumstantial use of character evidence. Consistently with that rule, evidence of other crimes, wrongs, or acts is not admissible to prove character as a basis for suggesting the inference that conduct on a particular occasion was in conformity with it. However, the evidence may be offered for another purpose, such as proof of motive, opportunity, and so on, which does not fall within the prohibition. In this situation the rule does not require that the evidence be excluded. No mechanical solution is offered. The determination must be made whether the danger of undue prejudice outweighs the probative value of the evidence in view of the availability of other means of proof and other factors appropriate for making decisions of this kind under Rule 403. Slough and Knightly, Other Vices, Other Crimes, 41 Iowa L.Rev. 325 (1956).

Report of House Committee on the Judiciary

The second sentence of Rule 404(b) as submitted to the Congress began with the words "This subdivision does not exclude the evidence when offered". The Committee amended this language to read "It may, however, be admissible", the words used in the 1971 Advisory Committee draft, on the ground that this formulation properly placed greater emphasis on admissibility than did the final Court version.

Report of Senate Committee on the Judiciary

This rule provides that evidence of other crimes, wrongs, or acts is not admissible to prove character but may be admissible for other specified purposes such as proof of motive.

Although your committee sees no necessity in amending the rule itself, it anticipates that the use of the discretionary word "may" with respect to the admissibility of evidence of crimes, wrongs, or acts is not intended to confer any arbitrary discretion on the trial judge. Rather, it is anticipated that with respect to permissible uses for such evidence, the trial judge may exclude it only on the basis of those considerations set forth in Rule 403, i.e. prejudice, confusion or waste of time.

Advisory Committee's Note to 1991 Amendment

Rule 404(b) has emerged as one of the most cited Rules in the Rules of Evidence. And in many criminal cases evidence of an accused's extrinsic acts is viewed as an important asset in the prosecution's case against an accused. Although there are a few reported decisions on use of such evidence by the defense, see, e.g., United States v. McClure, 546 F.2d 670 (5th Cir.1990) (acts of informant offered in entrapment defense), the overwhelming number of cases involve introduction of that evidence by the prosecution.

The amendment to Rule 404(b) adds a pretrial notice requirement in criminal cases and is intended to reduce surprise and promote early resolution on the issue of admissibility. The notice requirement thus places Rule 404(b) in the mainstream with notice and disclosure provisions in other rules of evidence. See, e.g., Rule 412 (written motion of intent to offer evidence under rule), Rule 609 (written notice of intent to offer conviction older than 10 years), Rule 803(24) and 804(b)(5) (notice of intent to use residual hearsay exceptions).

The Rule expects that counsel for both the defense and the prosecution will submit the necessary request and information in a reasonable and timely fashion. Other than requiring pretrial notice, no specific time limits are stated in recognition that what constitutes a reasonable request or disclosure will depend largely on the circumstances of each case. Compare Fla.Stat.Ann

§ 90.404(2)(b) (notice must be given at least 10 days before trial) *with* Tex.R. Evid. 404(b) (no time limit).

Likewise, no specific form of notice is required. The Committee considered and rejected a requirement that the notice satisfy the particularity requirements normally required of language used in a charging instrument. Cf. Fla. Stat.Ann. § 90.404(2)(b) (written disclosure must describe uncharged misconduct with particularity required of an indictment or information). Instead, the Committee opted for a generalized notice provision which requires the prosecution to apprise the defense of the general nature of the evidence of extrinsic acts. The Committee does not intend that the amendment will supercede other rules of admissibility or disclosure, such as the Jencks Act, 18 U.S.C. § 3500, et. seq. nor require the prosecution to disclose directly or indirectly the names and addresses of its witnesses, something it is currently not required to do under Federal Rule of Criminal Procedure 16.

The amendment requires the prosecution to provide notice, regardless of how it intends to use the extrinsic act evidence at trial, i.e., during its case-in-chief, for impeachment, or for possible rebuttal. The court in its discretion may, under the facts, decide that the particular request or notice was not reasonable, either because of the lack of timeliness or completeness. Because the notice requirement serves as condition precedent to admissibility of 404(b) evidence, the offered evidence is inadmissible if the court decides that the notice requirement has not been met.

Nothing in the amendment precludes the court from requiring the government to provide it with an opportunity to rule *in limine* on 404(b) evidence before it is offered or even mentioned during trial. When ruling *in limine*, the court may require the government to disclose to it the specifics of such evidence which the court must consider in determining admissibility.

The amendment does not extend to evidence of acts which are "intrinsic" to the charged offense, see United States v. Williams, 900 F.2d 823 (5th Cir. 1990) (noting distinction between 404(b) evidence and intrinsic offense evidence). Nor is the amendment intended to redefine what evidence would otherwise be admissible under Rule 404(b). Finally, the Committee does not intend through the amendment to affect the role of the court and the jury in considering such evidence. See United States v. Huddleston, —— U.S. ——, 108 S.Ct. 1496 (1988).

Rule 405

Note by Federal Judicial Center

The rule enacted by the Congress is the rule prescribed by the Supreme Court without change. The bill reported by the House Committee on the Judiciary deleted the provision in subdivision (a) for making proof by testimony in the form of an opinion, but the provision was reinstated on the floor of the House. See Congressional Record, February 6, 1974 (daily ed. pp. H546–H549).

Advisory Committee's Note

The rule deals only with allowable methods of proving character, not with the admissibility of character evidence, which is covered in Rule 404.

Of the three methods of proving character provided by the rule, evidence of specific instances of conduct is the most convincing. At the same time it possesses the greatest capacity to arouse prejudice, to confuse, to surprise, and to consume time. Consequently the rule confines the use of evidence of this kind to cases in which character is, in the strict sense, in issue and hence deserving of a searching inquiry. When character is used circumstantially and hence occupies a lesser status in the case, proof may be only by reputation and opinion. These latter methods are also available when character is in issue. This treatment is, with respect to specific instances of conduct and reputation, conventional contemporary common law doctrine. McCormick § 153.

In recognizing opinion as a means of proving character, the rule departs from usual contemporary practice in favor of that of an earlier day. See 7 Wigmore § 1986, pointing out that the earlier practice permitted opinion and arguing strongly for evidence based on personal knowledge and belief as contrasted with "the secondhand, irresponsible product of multiplied guesses and gossip which we term 'reputation'." It seems likely that the persistence of reputation evidence is due to its largely being opinion in disguise. Traditionally character has been regarded primarily in moral overtones of good and bad: chaste, peaceable, truthful, honest. Nevertheless, on occasion nonmoral considerations crop up, as in the case of the incompetent driver, and this seems bound to happen increasingly. If character is defined as the kind of person one is, then account must be taken of varying ways of arriving at the estimate. These may range from the opinion of the employer who has found the man honest to the opinion of the psychiatrist based upon examination and testing. No effective dividing line exists between character and mental capacity, and the latter traditionally has been provable by opinion.

According to the great majority of cases, on cross-examination inquiry is allowable as to whether the reputation witness has heard of particular instances of conduct pertinent to the trait in question. Michelson v. United States, 335 U.S. 469, 69 S.Ct. 213, 93 L.Ed. 168 (1948); Annot., 47 A.L.R.2d 1258. The theory is that, since the reputation witness relates what he has heard, the inquiry tends to shed light on the accuracy of his hearing and reporting. Accordingly, the opinion witness would be asked whether he knew, as well as whether he had heard. The fact, is, of course, that these distinctions are of slight if any practical significance, and the second sentence of subdivision (a) eliminates them as a factor in formulating questions. This recognition of the propriety of inquiring into specific instances of conduct does not circumscribe inquiry otherwise into the bases of opinion and reputation testimony.

The express allowance of inquiry into specific instances of conduct on cross-examination in subdivision (a) and the express allowance of it as part of a case in chief when character is actually in issue in subdivision (b) contemplate that testimony of specific instances is not generally permissible on the direct examination of an ordinary opinion witness to character. Similarly as to witnesses to the character of witnesses under Rule 608(b). Opinion testimony on direct in these situations ought in general to correspond to reputation testimony as now given, i.e., be confined to the nature and extent of observation and acquaintance upon which the opinion is based. See Rule 701.

Rule 406

Note by Federal Judicial Center

The rule enacted by the Congress is subdivision (a) of the rule prescribed by the Supreme Court. Subdivision (b) of the Court's rule was deleted for reasons stated in the Report of the House Committee on the Judiciary set forth below. The subdivision is included in the Appendix.

Advisory Committee's Note

Subdivision (a). An oft-quoted paragraph, McCormick, § 162, p. 340, describes habit in terms effectively contrasting it with character:

"Character and habit are close akin. Character is a generalized description of one's disposition, or of one's disposition in respect to a general trait, such as honesty, temperance, or peacefulness. 'Habit,' in modern usage, both lay and psychological, is more specific. It describes one's regular response to a repeated specific situation. If we speak of character for care, we think of the person's tendency to act prudently in all the varying situations of life, in business, family life, in handling automobiles and in walking across the street. A habit, on the other hand, is the person's regular practice of meeting a particular kind of situation with a specific type of conduct, such as the habit of going down a particular stairway two stairs at a time, or of giving the hand-signal for a left turn, or of alighting from railway cars while they are moving. The doing of the habitual acts may become semi-automatic."

Equivalent behavior on the part of a group is designated "routine practice of an organization" in the rule.

Agreement is general that habit evidence is highly persuasive as proof of conduct on a particular occasion. Again quoting McCormick § 162, p. 341:

"Character may be thought of as the sum of one's habits though doubtless it is more than this. But unquestionably the uniformity of one's response to habit is far greater than the consistency with which one's conduct conforms to character or disposition. Even though character comes in only exceptionally as evidence of an act, surely any sensible man in investigating whether X did a particular act would be greatly helped in his inquiry by evidence as to whether he was in the habit of doing it."

When disagreement has appeared, its focus has been upon the question what constitutes habit, and the reason for this is readily apparent. The extent to which instances must be multiplied and consistency of behavior maintained in order to rise to the status of habit inevitably gives rise to differences of opinion. Lewan, Rationale of Habit Evidence, 16 Syracuse L.Rev. 39, 49 (1964). While adequacy of sampling and uniformity of response are key factors, precise standards for measuring their sufficiency for evidence purposes cannot be formulated.

The rule is consistent with prevailing views. Much evidence is excluded simply because of failure to achieve the status of habit. Thus, evidence of intemperate "habits" is generally excluded when offered as proof of drunkenness in accident cases, Annot., 46 A.L.R.2d 103, and evidence of other assaults is inadmissible to prove the instant one in a civil assault action, Annot., 66 A.L.R.2d 806. In Levin v. United States, 119 U.S.App.D.C. 156, 338 F.2d 265 (1964), testimony as to the religious "habits" of the accused, offered as tending to prove that he was at home observing the Sabbath rather than out obtaining money through larceny by trick, was held properly excluded:

"It seems apparent to us that an individual's religious practices would not be the type of activities which would lend themselves to the characterization of 'invariable regularity.' [1 Wigmore 520.] Certainly the very volitional basis of the activity raises serious questions as to its invariable nature, and hence its probative value." Id. at 272.

These rulings are not inconsistent with the trend towards admitting evidence of business transactions between one of the parties and a third person as tending to prove that he made the same bargain or proposal in the litigated situation. Slough, Relevancy Unraveled, 6 Kan.L.Rev. 38–41 (1957). Nor are they inconsistent with such cases a Whittemore v. Lockheed Aircraft Corp., 65 Cal.App.2d 737, 151 P.2d 670 (1944), upholding the admission of evidence that plaintiff's intestate had on four other occasions flown planes from defendant's factory for delivery to his employer airline, offered to prove that he was piloting rather than a guest on a plane which crashed and killed all on board while en route for delivery.

A considerable body of authority has required that evidence of the routine practice of an organization be corroborated as a condition precedent to its admission in evidence. Slough, Relevancy Unraveled, 5 Kan.L.Rev. 404, 449 (1957). This requirement is specifically rejected by the rule on the ground that it relates to the sufficiency of the evidence rather than admissibility. A similar position is taken in New Jersey Rule 49. The rule also rejects the requirement of the absence of eyewitnesses, sometimes encountered with respect to admitting habit evidence to prove freedom from contributory negligence in wrongful death cases. For comment critical of the requirements see Frank J., in Cereste v. New York, N. H. & H. R. Co., 231 F.2d 50 (2d Cir. 1956), cert. denied 351 U.S. 951, 76 S.Ct. 848, 100 L.Ed. 1475, 10 Vand.L.Rev. 447 (1957); McCormick § 162, p. 342. The omission of the requirement from the California Evidence Code is said to have effected its elimination. Comment, Cal.Ev.Code § 1105.

Report of House Committee on the Judiciary

Rule 406 as submitted to Congress contained a subdivision (b) providing that the method of proof of habit or routine practice could be "in the form of an opinion or by specific instances of conduct sufficient in number to warrant a finding that the habit existed or that the practice was routine." The Committee deleted this subdivision believing that the method of proof of habit and routine practice should be left to the courts to deal with on a case-by-case basis. At the same time, the Committee does not intend that its action be construed as sanctioning a general authorization of opinion evidence in this area.

Rule 407

Note by Federal Judicial Center

The rule enacted by the Congress is the rule prescribed by the Supreme Court without change.

Advisory Committee's Note

The rule incorporates conventional doctrine which excludes evidence of subsequent remedial measures as proof of an admission of fault. The rule rests on two grounds. (1) The conduct is not in fact an admission, since the conduct is equally consistent with injury by mere accident or through contributory negligence. Or, as Baron Bramwell put it, the rule rejects the notion that "because the world gets wiser as it gets older, therefore it was foolish before." Hart v. Lancashire & Yorkshire Ry. Co., 21 L.T.R. N.S. 261, 263 (1869). Under a liberal theory of relevancy this ground alone would not support exclusion as the inference is still a possible one. (2) The other, and more impressive, ground for exclusion rests on a social policy of encouraging people to take, or at least not discouraging them from taking, steps in furtherance of added safety. The courts have applied this principle to exclude evidence of subsequent repairs, installation of safety devices, changes in company rules, and discharge of employees, and the language of the present rule is broad enough to encompass all of them. See Falknor, Extrinsic Policies Affecting Admissibility, 10 Rutgers L.Rev. 574, 590 (1956).

The second sentence of the rule directs attention to the limitations of the rule. Exclusion is called for only when the evidence of subsequent remedial measures is offered as proof of negligence or culpable conduct. In effect it rejects the suggested inference that fault is admitted. Other purposes are, however, allowable, including ownership or control, existence of duty, and feasibility of precautionary measures, if controverted, and impeachment. 2 Wigmore § 283; Annot., 64 A.L.R.2d 1296. Two recent federal cases are illustrative. Boeing Airplane Co. v. Brown, 291 F.2d 310 (9th Cir. 1961), an action against an airplane manufacturer for using an allegedly defectively designed alternator shaft which caused a plane crash, upheld the admission of evidence of subsequent design modification for the purpose of showing that design changes and safeguards were feasible. And Powers v. J. B. Michael & Co., 329 F.2d 674 (6th Cir. 1964), an action against a road contractor for negligent failure to put out warning signs, sustained the admission of evidence that defendant subsequently put out signs to show that the portion of the road in question was under defendant's control. The requirement that the other purpose be controverted calls for a automatic exclusion unless a genuine issue be present and allows the opposing party to lay the groundwork for exclusion by making an admission. Otherwise the factors of undue prejudice, confusion of issues, misleading the jury, and waste of time remain for consideration under Rule 403.

For comparable rules, see Uniform Rule 51; California Evidence Code § 1151; Kansas Code of Civil Procedure § 60–451; New Jersey Evidence Rule 51.

Rule 408

Note by Federal Judicial Center

The rule enacted by the Congress is the rule prescribed by the Supreme Court, amended by the insertion of the third sentence. Other amendments, proposed by the House bill, were not enacted, for reasons stated in the Report of the Senate Committee on the Judiciary and in the Conference Report, set forth below.

Advisory Committee's Note

As a matter of general agreement, evidence of an offer to compromise a claim is not receivable in evidence as an admission of, as the case may be, the validity or invalidity of the claim. As with evidence of subsequent remedial measures, dealt with in Rule 407, exclusion may be based on two grounds. (1) The evidence is irrelevant, since the offer may be motivated by a desire for peace rather than from any concession of weakness of position. The validity of this position will vary as the amount of the offer varies in relation to the size of the claim and may also be influenced by other circumstances. (2) A more consistently impressive ground is promotion of the public policy favoring the compromise and settlement of disputes. McCormick §§ 76, 251. While the rule is ordinarily phrased in terms of offers of compromise, it is apparent that a similar attitude must be taken with respect to completed compromises when offered against a party thereto. This latter situation will not, of course, ordinarily occur except when a party to the present litigation has compromised with a third person.

The same policy underlies the provision of Rule 68 of the Federal Rules of Civil Procedure that evidence of an unaccepted offer of judgment is not admissible except in a proceeding to determine costs.

The practical value of the common law rule has been greatly diminished by its inapplicability to admissions of fact, even though made in the course of compromise negotiations, unless hypothetical, stated to be "without prejudice," or so connected with the offer as to be inseparable from it. McCormick § 251, pp. 540–541. An inevitable effect is to inhibit freedom of communication with respect to compromise, even among lawyers. Another effect is the generation of controversy over whether a given statement falls within or without the protected area. These considerations account for the expansion of the rule herewith to include evidence of conduct or statements made in compromise negotiations, as well as the offer or completed compromise itself. For similar provisions see California Evidence Code §§ 1152, 1154.

The policy considerations which underlie the rule do not come into play when the effort is to induce a creditor to settle an admittedly due amount for a lesser sum. McCormick § 251, p. 540. Hence the rule requires that the claim be disputed as to either validity or amount.

The final sentence of the rule serves to point out some limitations upon its applicability. Since the rule excludes only when the purpose is proving the validity or invalidity of the claim or its amount, an offer for another purpose is not within the rule. The illustrative situations mentioned in the rule are supported by the authorities. As to proving bias or prejudice of a witness, see Annot., 161 A.L.R. 395, contra, Fenberg v. Rosenthal, 348 Ill.App. 510, 109 N.E.2d 402 (1952), and negativing a contention of lack of due diligence in presenting a claim, 4 Wigmore § 1061. An effort to "buy off" the prosecution or a prosecuting witness in a criminal case is not within the policy of the rule of exclusion. McCormick § 251, p. 542.

For other rules of similar import, see Uniform Rules 52 and 53; California Evidence Code §§ 1152, 1154; Kansas Code of Civil Procedure §§ 60–452, 60–453; New Jersey Evidence Rules 52 and 53.

Report of House Committee on the Judiciary

Under existing federal law evidence of conduct and statements made in compromise negotiations is admissible in subsequent litigation between the parties. The second sentence of Rule 408 as submitted by the Supreme Court proposed to reverse that doctrine in the interest of further promoting non-judicial settlement of disputes. Some agencies of government expressed the view that the Court formulation was likely to impede rather than assist efforts to achieve settlement of disputes. For one thing, it is not always easy to tell when compromise negotiations begin, and informal dealings end. Also, parties dealing with government agencies would be reluctant to furnish factual information at preliminary meetings; they would wait until "compromise negotiations" began and thus hopefully effect an immunity for themselves with respect to the evidence supplied. In light of these considerations the Committee recast the Rule so that admissions of liability or opinions given during compromise negotiations continue inadmissible, but evidence of unqualified factual assertions is admissible. The latter aspect of the Rule is drafted, however, so as to preserve other possible objections to the introduction of such evidence. The Committee intends no modification of current law whereby a party may protect himself from future use of his statements by couching them in hypothetical conditional form.

Report of Senate Committee on the Judiciary

This rule as reported makes evidence of settlement or attempted settlement of a disputed claim inadmissible when offered as an admission of liability or the amount of liability. The purpose of this rule is to encourage settlements which would be discouraged if such evidence were admissible.

Under present law, in most jurisdictions, statements of fact made during settlement negotiations, however, are excepted from this ban and are admissible. The only escape from admissibility of statements of fact made in a settlement negotiation is if the declarant or his representative expressly states that the statement is hypothetical in nature or is made without prejudice. Rule 408, as submitted by the Court reversed the traditional rule. It would have brought statements of fact within the ban and made them, as well as an offer of settlement, inadmissible.

The House amended the rule and would continue to make evidence of facts disclosed during compromise negotiations admissible. It thus reverted to the traditional rule. The House committee report states that the committee intends to preserve current law under which a party may protect himself by couching his statements in hypothetical form.[1] The real impact of this amendment, however, is to deprive the rule of much of its salutary effect. The exception for factual admissions was believed by the Advisory Committee to hamper free communication between parties and thus to constitute an unjustifiable restraint upon efforts to negotiate settlements—the encouragement of which is the purpose of the rule. Further, by protecting hypothetically phrased statements, it constituted a preference for the sophisticated, and a trap for the unwary.

Three States which had adopted rules of evidence patterned after the proposed rules prescribed by the Supreme Court opted for versions of rule 408 identical with the Supreme Court draft with respect to the inadmissibility of conduct or statements made in compromise negotiations.[2]

For those reasons, the committee has deleted the House amendment and restored the rule to the version submitted by the Supreme Court with one additional amendment. This amendment adds a sentence to insure that evidence, such as documents, is not rendered inadmissible merely because it is presented in the course of compromise negotiations if the evidence is otherwise discoverable. A party should not be able to immunize from admissibility documents otherwise discoverable merely by offering them in a compromise negotiation.

Conference Report

The House bill provides that evidence of admissions of liability or opinions given during compromise negotiations is not admissible, but that evidence of facts disclosed during compromise negotiations is not inadmissible by virtue of having been first disclosed in the compromise negotiations. The Senate amendment provides that evidence of conduct or statements made in compromise

1. See Report No. 93–650, dated November 15, 1973.

2. Nev.Rev.Stats. § 48.105; N.Mex. Stats.Anno. (1973 Supp.) § 20–4–408;

West's Wis.Stats.Anno. (1973 Supp.) § 904.08.

negotiations is not admissible. The Senate amendment also provides that the rule does not require the exclusion of any evidence otherwise discoverable merely because it is presented in the course of compromise negotiations.

The House bill was drafted to meet the objection of executive agencies that under the rule as proposed by the Supreme Court, a party could present a fact during compromise negotiations and thereby prevent an opposing party from offering evidence of that fact at trial even though such evidence was obtained from independent sources. The Senate amendment expressly precludes this result.

The Conference adopts the Senate amendment.

Rule 409

Note by Federal Judicial Center

The rule enacted by the Congress is the rule prescribed by the Supreme Court without change.

Advisory Committee's Note

The considerations underlying this rule parallel those underlying Rules 407 and 408, which deal respectively with subsequent remedial measures and offers of compromise. As stated in Annot., 20 A.L.R.2d 291, 293:

"[G]enerally, evidence of payment of medical, hospital, or similar expenses of an injured party by the opposing party, is not admissible, the reason often given being that such payment or offer is usually made from humane impulses and not from an admission of liability, and that to hold otherwise would tend to discourage assistance to the injured person."

Contrary to Rule 408, dealing with offers of compromise, the present rule does not extend to conduct or statements not a part of the act of furnishing or offering or promising to pay. This difference in treatment arises from fundamental differences in nature. Communication is essential if compromises are to be effected, and consequently broad protection of statements is needed. This is not so in cases of payments or offers or promises to pay medical expenses, where factual statements may be expected to be incidental in nature.

For rules on the same subject, but phrased in terms of "humanitarian motives," see Uniform Rule 52; California Evidence Code § 1152; Kansas Code of Civil Procedure § 60–452; New Jersey Evidence Rule 52.

Rule 410

Note by Federal Judicial Center

The rule prescribed by the Supreme Court consisted only of the first sentence of the rule enacted by the Congress, exclusive of the introductory phrase, "Except as otherwise provided by Act of Congress". Reasons for the amendments are stated in the Report of the House Committee on the Judiciary, Senate Committee on the Judiciary, and Conference, set forth below. See also the explanation by Chairman Hungate in the Congressional Record, December 18, 1974, H12253.

Advisory Committee's Note

Withdrawn pleas of guilty were held inadmissible in federal prosecutions in Kercheval v. United States, 274 U.S. 220, 47 S.Ct. 582, 71 L.Ed. 1009 (1927).

The Court pointed out that to admit the withdrawn plea would effectively set at naught the allowance of withdrawal and place the accused in a dilemma utterly inconsistent with the decision to award him a trial. The New York Court of Appeals, in People v. Spitaleri, 9 N.Y.2d 168, 212 N.Y.S.2d 53, 173 N.E.2d 35 (1961), reexamined and overturned its earlier decisions which had allowed admission. In addition to the reasons set forth in Kercheval, which was quoted at length, the court pointed out that the effect of admitting the plea was to compel defendant to take the stand by way of explanation and to open the way for the prosecution to call the lawyer who had represented him at the time of entering the plea. State court decisions for and against admissibility are collected in Annot., 86 A.L.R.2d 326.

Pleas of *nolo contendere* are recognized by Rule 11 of the Rules of Criminal Procedure, although the law of numerous States is to the contrary. The present rule gives effect to the principal traditional characteristic of the *nolo* plea, i.e. avoiding the admission of guilt which is inherent in pleas of guilty. This position is consistent with the construction of Section 5 of the Clayton Act, 15 U.S.C. § 16(a), recognizing the inconclusive and compromise nature of judgments based on *nolo* pleas. General Electric Co. v. City of San Antonio, 334 F.2d 480 (5th Cir. 1964); Commonwealth Edison Co. v. Allis-Chalmers Mfg. Co., 323 F.2d 412 (7th Cir. 1963), cert. denied 376 U.S. 939, 84 S.Ct. 794, 11 L.Ed. 2d 659; Armco Steel Corp. v. North Dakota, 376 F.2d 206 (8th Cir. 1967); City of Burbank v. General Electric Co., 329 F.2d 825 (9th Cir. 1964). See also state court decisions in Annot., 18 A.L.R.2d 1287, 1314.

Exclusion of offers to plead guilty or *nolo* has as its purpose the promotion of disposition of criminal cases by compromise. As pointed out in McCormick § 251, p. 543.

"Effective criminal law administration in many localities would hardly be possible if a large proportion of the charges were not disposed of by such compromises."

See also People v. Hamilton, 60 Cal.2d 105, 32 Cal.Rptr. 4, 383 P.2d 412 (1963), discussing legislation designed to achieve this result. As with compromise offers generally, Rule 408, free communication is needed, and security against having an offer of compromise or related statement admitted in evidence effectively encourages it.[1]

Limiting the exclusionary rule to use against the accused is consistent with the purpose of the rule, since the possibility of use for or against other persons will not impair the effectiveness of withdrawing pleas or the freedom of discussion which the rule is designed to foster. See A.B.A. Standards Relating to Pleas of Guilty § 2.2 (1968). See also the narrower provisions of New Jersey Evidence Rule 52(2) and the unlimited exclusion provided in California Evidence Code § 1153.

Report of House Committee on the Judiciary

The Committee added the phrase "Except as otherwise provided by Act of Congress" to Rule 410 as submitted by the Court in order to preserve particular congressional policy judgments as to the effect of a plea of guilty or of nolo contendere. See 15 U.S.C. 16(a). The Committee intends that its amendment refers to both present statutes and statutes subsequently enacted.

---

1. The rule as enacted, it should be noted, allows use of the statements for impeachment or in a subsequent prosecution for perjury or false statement.

Report of Senate Committee on the Judiciary

As adopted by the House, rule 410 would make inadmissible pleas of guilty or nolo contendere subsequently withdrawn as well as offers to make such pleas. Such a rule is clearly justified as a means of encouraging pleading. However, the House rule would then go on to render inadmissible for any purpose statements made in connection with these pleas or offers as well.

The committee finds this aspect of the House rule unjustified. Of course, in certain circumstances such statements should be excluded. If, for example, a plea is vitiated because of coercion, statements made in connection with the plea may also have been coerced and should be inadmissible on that basis. In other cases, however, voluntary statements of an accused made in court on the record, in connection with a plea, and determined by a court to be reliable should be admissible even though the plea is subsequently withdrawn. This is particularly true in those cases where, if the House rule were in effect, a defendant would be able to contradict his previous statements and thereby lie with impunity.[2] To prevent such an injustice, the rule has been modified to permit the use of such statements for the limited purposes of impeachment and in subsequent perjury or false statement prosecutions.

Conference Report

The House bill provides that evidence of a guilty or nolo contendere plea, of an offer of either plea, or of statements made in connection with such pleas or offers of such pleas, is inadmissible in any civil or criminal action, case or proceeding against the person making such plea or offer. The Senate amendment makes the rule inapplicable to a voluntary and reliable statement made in court on the record where the statement is offered in a subsequent prosecution of the declarant for perjury or false statement.

The issues raised by Rule 410 are also raised by proposed Rule 11(e)(6) of the Federal Rules of Criminal Procedure presently pending before Congress. This proposed rule, which deals with the admissibility of pleas of guilty or nolo contendere, offers to make such pleas, and statements made in connection with such pleas, was promulgated by the Supreme Court on April 22, 1974, and in the absence of congressional action will become effective on August 1, 1975. The conferees intend to make no change in the presently-existing case law until that date, leaving the courts free to develop rules in this area on a case-by-case basis.

The Conferees further determined that the issues presented by the use of guilty and nolo contendere pleas, offers of such pleas, and statements made in connection with such pleas or offers, can be explored in greater detail during Congressional consideration of Rule 11(e)(6) of the Federal Rules of Criminal Procedure. The Conferees believe, therefore, that it is best to defer its effective date until August 1, 1975. The Conferees intend that Rule 410 would be superseded by any subsequent Federal Rule of Criminal Procedure or Act of Congress with which it is inconsistent, if the Federal Rule of Criminal Procedure or Act of Congress takes effect or becomes law after the date of the enactment of the act establishing the rules of evidence.

The conference adopts the Senate amendment with an amendment that expresses the above intentions.

2. See Harris v. New York, 401 U.S. 222 (1971).

Rule 411

Note by Federal Judicial Center

The rule enacted by the Congress is the rule prescribed by the Supreme Court without change.

Advisory Committee's Note

The courts have with substantial unanimity rejected evidence of liability insurance for the purpose of proving fault, and absence of liability insurance as proof of lack of fault. At best the inference of fault from the fact of insurance coverage is a tenuous one, as is its converse. More important, no doubt, has been the feeling that knowledge of the presence or absence of liability insurance would induce juries to decide cases on improper grounds. McCormick § 168; Annot., 4 A.L.R.2d 761. The rule is drafted in broad terms so as to include contributory negligence or other fault of a plaintiff as well as fault of a defendant.

The second sentence points out the limits of the rule, using well established illustrations. Id.

For similar rules see Uniform Rule 54; California Evidence Code § 1155; Kansas Code of Civil Procedure § 60–454; New Jersey Evidence Rule 54.

Rule 412

ARTICLE V. PRIVILEGES

Rule 501

Note by Federal Judicial Center

The rules enacted by the Congress substituted the single Rule 501 in place of the 13 rules dealing with privilege prescribed by the Supreme Court as Article V. The 13 superseded rules, with Advisory Committee's Notes, are included in the Appendix. The reasons given in support of the congressional action are stated in the Report of the House Committee on the Judiciary, the Report of the Senate Committee on the Judiciary, and Conference Report, set forth below.

Report of House Committee on the Judiciary

Article V as submitted to Congress contained thirteen Rules. Nine of those Rules defined specific non-constitutional privileges which the federal courts must recognize (i.e. required reports, lawyer-client, psychotherapist-patient, husband-wife, communications to clergymen, political vote, trade secrets, secrets of state and other official information, and identity of informer). Another Rule provided that only those privileges set forth in Article V or in some other Act of Congress could be recognized by the federal courts. The three remaining Rules addressed collateral problems as to waiver of privilege by voluntary disclosure, privileged matter disclosed under compulsion or without opportunity to claim privilege, comment upon or inference from a claim of privilege, and jury instruction with regard thereto.

The Committee amended Article V to eliminate all of the Court's specific Rules on privileges. Instead, the Committee, through a single Rule, 501, left the law of privileges in its present state and further provided that privileges shall continue to be developed by the courts of the United States under a uniform standard applicable both in civil and criminal cases. That standard, derived from Rule 26 of the Federal Rules of Criminal Procedure, mandates the application of the principles of the common law as interpreted by the courts of the United States in the light of reason and experience. The words "person, government, State, or political subdivision thereof" were added by the Committee to the lone term "witnesses" used in Rule 26 to make clear that, as under present law, not only witnesses may have privileges. The Committee also included in its amendment a proviso modeled after Rule 302 and similar to language added by the Committee to Rule 601 relating to the competency of witnesses. The proviso is designed to require the application of State privilege law in civil actions and proceedings governed by Erie R. Co. v. Tompkins, 304 U.S. 64 (1938), a result in accord with current federal court decisions. See Republic Gear Co. v. Borg-Warner Corp., 381 F.2d 551, 555–556 n. 2 (2nd Cir. 1967). The Committee deemed the proviso to be necessary in the light of the Advisory Committee's view (see its note to Court Rule 501) that this result is not mandated under *Erie.*

The rationale underlying the proviso is that federal law should not supersede that of the States in substantive areas such as privilege absent a compelling reason. The Committee believes that in civil cases in the federal courts where an element of a claim or defense is not grounded upon a federal question, there is no federal interest strong enough to justify departure from State policy. In addition, the Committee considered that the Court's proposed Article V would have promoted forum shopping in some civil actions, depending upon differences in the privilege law applied as among the State and federal courts. The Committee's proviso, on the other hand, under which the federal courts are bound to apply the State's privilege law in actions founded upon a State-created right or defense, removes the incentive to "shop".

Report of Senate Committee on the Judiciary

Article V as submitted to Congress contained 13 rules. Nine of those rules defined specific nonconstitutional privileges which the Federal courts must recognize (i.e., required reports, lawyer-client, psychotherapist-patient, husband-wife, communications to clergymen, political vote, trade secrets, secrets of state and other official information, and identity of informer). Many of these rules contained controversial modifications or restrictions upon common law privileges. As noted supra, the House amended article V to eliminate all of the Court's specific rules on privileges. Through a single rule, 501, the House provided that privileges shall be governed by the principles of the common law as interpreted by the courts of the United States in the light of reason and experience (a standard derived from rule 26 of the Federal Rules of Criminal Procedure) except in the case of an element of a civil claim or defense as to which State law supplies the rule of decision, in which event state privilege law was to govern.

The committee agrees with the main thrust of the House amendment: that a federally developed common law based on modern reason and experience shall apply except where the State nature of the issues renders deference to State privilege law the wiser course, as in the usual diversity case. The committee understands that thrust of the House amendment to require that

State privilege law be applied in "diversity" cases (actions on questions of State law between citizens of different States arising under 28 U.S.C. § 1332). The language of the House amendment, however, goes beyond this in some respects, and falls short of it in others: State privilege law applies even in nondiversity, Federal question civil cases, where an issue governed by State substantive law is the object of the evidence (such issues do sometimes arise in such cases); and, in all instances where State privilege law is to be applied, e.g., on proof of a State issue in a diversity case, a close reading reveals that State privilege law is not to be applied unless the matter to be proved is an element of that state claim or defense, as distinguished from a step along the way in the proof of it.

The committee is concerned that the language used in the House amendment could be difficult to apply. It provides that "in civil actions * * * with respect to an element of a claim or defense as to which State law supplies the rule of decision," State law on privilege applies. The question of what is an element of a claim or defense is likely to engender considerable litigation. If the matter in question constitutes an element of a claim, State law supplies the privilege rule; whereas if it is a mere item of proof with respect to a claim, then, even though State law might supply the rule of decision, Federal law on the privilege would apply. Further, disputes will arise as to how the rule should be applied in an antitrust action or in a tax case where the Federal statute is silent as to a particular aspect of the substantive law in question, but Federal cases had incorporated State law by reference to State law.[1] Is a claim (or defense) based on such a reference a claim or defense as to which federal or State law supplies the rule of decision?

Another problem not entirely avoidable is the complexity or difficulty the rule introduces into the trial of a Federal case containing a combination of Federal and State claims and defenses, e.g. an action involving Federal antitrust and State unfair competition claims. Two different bodies of privilege law would need to be consulted. It may even develop that the same witness-testimony might be relevant on both counts and privileged as to one but not the other.[2]

The formulation adopted by the House is pregnant with litigious mischief. The committee has, therefore, adopted what we believe will be a clearer and more practical guideline for determining when courts should respect State rules of privilege. Basically, it provides that in criminal and Federal question civil cases, federally evolved rules on privilege should apply since it is Federal policy which is being enforced.[3] Conversely, in diversity cases where the litigation in question turns on a substantive question of State law, and is brought in the Federal courts because the parties reside in different States, the committee believes it is clear that State rules of privilege should apply unless the proof is directed at a claim or defense for which Federal law supplies the rule of decision (a situation which would not commonly arise.)[4] It is intended that the

1. For a discussion of reference to State substantive law, see note on Federal Incorporation by Reference of State Law, Hart & Wechsler, The Federal Courts and the Federal System, pp. 491–94 (2d ed. 1973).

2. The problems with the House formulation are discussed in Rothstein. The Proposed Amendments to the Federal Rules of Evidence, 62 Georgetown University Law Journal 125 (1973) at notes 25, 26 and 70–74 and accompanying text.

3. It is also intended that the Federal law of privileges should be applied with respect to pendant State law claims when they arise in a Federal question case.

4. While such a situation might require use of two bodies of privilege law, federal and state, in the same case, nevertheless the occasions on which this would be required are considerably reduced as compared with the House version, and confined to situations where the Federal and

State rules of privilege should apply equally in original diversity actions and diversity actions removed under 28 U.S.C. § 1441(b).

Two other comments on the privilege rule should be made. The committee has received a considerable volume of correspondence from psychiatric organizations and psychiatrists concerning the deletion of rule 504 of the rule submitted by the Supreme Court. It should be clearly understood that, in approving this general rule as to privileges, the action of Congress should not be understood as disapproving any recognition of a psychiatrist-patient, or husband-wife, or any other of the enumerated privileges contained in the Supreme Court rules. Rather, our action should be understood as reflecting the view that the recognition of a privilege based on a confidential relationship and other privileges should be determined on a case-by-case basis.

Further, we would understand that the prohibition against spouses testifying against each other is considered a rule of privilege and covered by this rule and not by rule 601 of the competency of witnesses.

Conference Report

Rule 501 deals with the privilege of a witness not to testify. Both the House and Senate bills provide that federal privilege law applies in criminal cases. In civil actions and proceedings, the House bill provides that state privilege law applies "to an element of a claim or defense as to which State law supplies the rule of decision." The Senate bill provides that "in civil actions and proceedings arising under 28 U.S.C. § 1332 or 28 U.S.C. § 1335, or between citizens of different States and removed under 28 U.S.C. § 1441(b) the privilege of a witness, person, government, State or political subdivision thereof is determined in accordance with State law, unless with respect to the particular claim or defense, Federal law supplies the rule of decision."

The wording of the House and Senate bills differs in the treatment of civil actions and proceedings. The rule in the House bill applies to evidence that relates to "an element of a claim or defense." If an item of proof tends to support or defeat a claim or defense, or an element of a claim or defense, and if state law supplies the rule of decision for that claim or defense, then state privilege law applies to that item of proof.

Under the provision in the House bill, therefore, state privilege law will usually apply in diversity cases. There may be diversity cases, however, where a claim or defense is based upon federal law. In such instances, federal privilege law will apply to evidence relevant to the federal claim or defense. See Sola Electric Co. v. Jefferson Electric Co., 317 U.S. 173 (1942).

In nondiversity jurisdiction civil cases, federal privilege law will generally apply. In those situations where a federal court adopts or incorporates state law to fill interstices or gaps in federal statutory phrases, the court generally will apply federal privilege law. As Justice Jackson has said:

> A federal court sitting in a non-diversity case such as this does not sit as a local tribunal. In some cases it may see fit for special reasons

State interests are such as to justify application of neither privilege law to the case as a whole. If the rule proposed here results in two conflicting bodies of privilege law applying to the same piece of evidence in the same case, it is contemplated that the rule favoring reception of the evidence should be applied. This policy is based on the present rule 43(a) of the Federal Rules of Civil Procedure which provides: In any case, the statute or rule which favors the reception of the evidence governs and the evidence shall be presented according to the most convenient method prescribed in any of the statutes or rules to which reference is herein made.

to give the law of a particular state highly persuasive or even controlling effect, but in the last analysis its decision turns upon the law of
the United States, not that of any state.

D'Oench, Duhme & Co. v. Federal Deposit Insurance Corp., 315 U.S. 447, 471
(1942) (Jackson, J., concurring). When a federal court chooses to absorb state
law, it is applying the state law as a matter of federal common law. Thus, state
law does not supply the rule of decision (even though the federal court may
apply a rule derived from state decisions), and state privilege law would not
apply. See C.A. Wright, Federal Courts 251–252 (2d ed. 1970); Holmberg v.
Armbrecht, 327 U.S. 392 (1946); DeSylva v. Ballentine, 351 U.S. 570, 581 (1956);
9 Wright & Miller, Federal Rules and Procedure § 2408.

In civil actions and proceedings, where the rule of decision as to a claim or
defense or as to an element of a claim or defense is supplied by state law, the
House provision requires that state privilege law apply.

The Conference adopts the House provision.

ARTICLE VI. WITNESSES

Rule 601

Note by Federal Judicial Center

The first sentence of the rule enacted by the Congress is the entire rule
prescribed by the Supreme Court, without change. The second sentence was
added by congressional action.

Advisory Committee's Note

This general ground-clearing eliminates all grounds of incompetency not
specifically recognized in the succeeding rules of this Article. Included among
the grounds thus abolished are religious belief, conviction of crime, and connection with the litigation as a party or interested person or spouse of a party or
interested person. With the exception of the so-called Dead Man's Acts,
American jurisdictions generally have ceased to recognize these grounds.

The Dead Man's Acts are surviving traces of the common law disqualification of parties and interested persons. They exist in variety too great to convey
conviction of their wisdom and effectiveness. These rules contain no provision
of this kind. * * *

No mental or moral qualifications for testifying as a witness are specified.
Standards of mental capacity have proved elusive in actual application. A
leading commentator observes that few witnesses are disqualified on that
ground. Weihofen, Testimonial Competence and Credibility, 34 Geo.Wash.L.
Rev. 53 (1965). Discretion is regularly exercised in favor of allowing the
testimony. A witness wholly without capacity is difficult to imagine. The
question is one particularly suited to the jury as one of weight and credibility,
subject to judicial authority to review the sufficiency of the evidence. 2
Wigmore §§ 501, 509. Standards of moral qualification in practice consist
essentially of evaluating a person's truthfulness in terms of his own answers
about it. Their principal utility is in affording an opportunity on voir dire
examination to impress upon the witness his moral duty. This result may,
however, be accomplished more directly, and without haggling in terms of legal
standards, by the manner of administering the oath or affirmation under Rule
603.

Admissibility of religious belief as a ground of impeachment is treated in Rule 610. Conviction of crime as a ground of impeachment is the subject of Rule 609. Marital relationship is the basis for privilege under Rule 505. Interest in the outcome of litigation and mental capacity are, of course, highly relevant to credibility and require no special treatment to render them admissible along with other matters bearing upon the perception, memory, and narration of witnesses.

Report of House Committee on the Judiciary

Rule 601 as submitted to the Congress provided that "Every person is competent to be a witness except as otherwise provided in these rules." One effect of the Rule as proposed would have been to abolish age, mental capacity, and other grounds recognized in some State jurisdictions as making a person incompetent as a witness. The greatest controversy centered around the Rule's rendering inapplicable in the federal courts the so-called Dead Man's Statutes which exist in some States. Acknowledging that there is substantial disagreement as to the merit of Dead Man's Statutes, the Committee nevertheless believed that where such statutes have been enacted they represent State policy which should not be overturned in the absence of a compelling federal interest. The Committee therefore amended the Rule to make competency in civil actions determinable in accordance with State law with respect to elements of claims or defenses as to which State law supplies the rule of decision. Cf. Courtland v. Walston & Co., Inc., 340 F.Supp. 1076, 1087–1092 (S.D.N.Y.1972).

Report of Senate Committee on the Judiciary

The amendment to rule 601 parallels the treatment accorded rule 501 discussed immediately above.

Conference Report

Rule 601 deals with competency of witnesses. Both the House and Senate bills provide that federal competency law applies in criminal cases. In civil actions and proceedings, the House bill provides that state competency law applies "to an element of a claim or defense as to which State law supplies the rule of decision." The Senate bill provides that "in civil actions and proceedings arising under 28 U.S.C. § 1332 or 28 U.S.C. § 1335, or between citizens of different States and removed under 28 U.S.C. § 1441(b) the competency of a witness, person, government, State or political subdivision thereof is determined in accordance with State law, unless with respect to the particular claim or defense, Federal law supplies the rule of decision."

The wording of the House and Senate bills differs in the treatment of civil actions and proceedings. The rule in the House bill applies to evidence that relates to "an element of a claim or defense." If an item of proof tends to support or defeat a claim or defense, or an element of a claim or defense, and if state law supplies the rule of decision for that claim or defense, then state competency law applies to that item of proof.

For reasons similar to those underlying its action on Rule 501, the Conference adopts the House provision.

Rule 602

Note by Federal Judicial Center

The rule enacted by the Congress is the rule prescribed by the Supreme Court without change.

Advisory Committee's Note

" * * * [T]he rule requiring that a witness who testifies to a fact which can be perceived by the senses must have had an opportunity to observe, and must have actually observed the fact" is a "most pervasive manifestation" of the common law insistence upon "the most reliable sources of information." McCormick § 10, p. 19. These foundation requirements may, of course, be furnished by the testimony of the witness himself; hence personal knowledge is not an absolute but may consist of what the witness thinks he knows from personal perception. 2 Wigmore § 650. It will be observed that the rule is in fact a specialized application of the provisions of Rule 104(b) on conditional relevancy.

This rule does not govern the situation of a witness who testifies to a hearsay statement as such, if he has personal knowledge of the making of the statement. Rules 801 and 805 would be applicable. This rule would, however, prevent him from testifying to the subject matter of the hearsay statement, as he has no personal knowledge of it.

The reference to Rule 703 is designed to avoid any question of conflict between the present rule and the provisions of that rule allowing an expert to express opinions based on facts of which he does not have personal knowledge.

Rule 603

Note by Federal Judicial Center

The rule enacted by the Congress is the rule prescribed by the Supreme Court without change.

Advisory Committee's Note

The rule is designed to afford the flexibility required in dealing with religious adults, atheists, conscientious objectors, mental defectives, and children. Affirmation is simply a solemn undertaking to tell the truth; no special verbal formula is required. As is true generally, affirmation is recognized by federal law. "Oath" includes affirmation, 1 U.S.C. § 1; judges and clerks may administer oaths and affirmations, 28 U.S.C. §§ 459, 953; and affirmations are acceptable in lieu of oaths under Rule 43(d) of the Federal Rules of Civil Procedure. Perjury by a witness is a crime, 18 U.S.C. § 1621.

Rule 604

Note by Federal Judicial Center

The rule enacted by the Congress is the rule prescribed by the Supreme Court without change.

Advisory Committee's Note

The rule implements Rule 43(f) of the Federal Rules of Civil Procedure and Rule 28(b) of the Federal Rules of Criminal Procedure, both of which contain provisions for the appointment and compensation of interpreters.

Rule 605

Note by Federal Judicial Center

The rule enacted by the Congress is the rule prescribed by the Supreme Court without change.

Advisory Committee's Note

In view of the mandate of 28 U.S.C. § 455 that a judge disqualify himself in "any case in which he * * * is or has been a material witness," the likelihood that the presiding judge in a federal court might be called to testify in the trial over which he is presiding is slight. Nevertheless the possibility is not totally eliminated.

The solution here presented is a broad rule of incompetency, rather than such alternatives as incompetency only as to material matters, leaving the matter to the discretion of the judge, or recognizing no incompetency. The choice is the result of inability to evolve satisfactory answers to questions which arise when the judge abandons the bench for the witness stand. Who rules on objections? Who compels him to answer? Can he rule impartially on the weight and admissibility of his own testimony? Can he be impeached or cross-examined effectively? Can he, in a jury trial, avoid conferring his seal of approval on one side in the eyes of the jury? Can he, in a bench trial, avoid an involvement destructive of impartiality? The rule of general incompetency has substantial support. See Report of the Special Committee on the Propriety of Judges Appearing as Witnesses, 36 A.B.A.J. 630 (1950); cases collected in Annot. 157 A.L.R. 311; McCormick § 68, p. 147; Uniform Rule 42; California Evidence Code § 703; Kansas Code of Civil Procedure § 60–442; New Jersey Evidence Rule 42. Cf. 6 Wigmore § 1909, which advocates leaving the matter to the discretion of the judge, and statutes to that effect collected in Annot. 157 A.L.R. 311.

The rule provides an "automatic" objection. To require an actual objection would confront the opponent with a choice between not objecting, with the result of allowing the testimony, and objecting, with the probable result of excluding the testimony but at the price of continuing the trial before a judge likely to feel that his integrity had been attacked by the objector.

Rule 606

Note by Federal Judicial Center

The rule enacted by the Congress is the rule prescribed by the Supreme Court, amended only by the addition of the concluding phrase "for these purposes." The bill originally passed by the House did not contain in the first sentence the prohibition as to matters or statements during the deliberations or the clause beginning "except."

Advisory Committee's Note

Subdivision (a). The considerations which bear upon the permissibility of testimony by a juror in the trial in which he is sitting as juror bear an obvious similarity to those evoked when the judge is called as a witness. See Advisory Committee's Note to Rule 605. The judge is not, however in this instance so involved as to call for departure from usual principles requiring objection to be made; hence the only provision on objection is that opportunity be afforded for its making out of the presence of the jury. Compare Rule 605.

Subdivision (b). Whether testimony, affidavits, or statements of jurors should be received for the purpose of invalidating or supporting a verdict or indictment, and if so, under what circumstances, has given rise to substantial differences of opinion. The familiar rubric that a juror may not impeach his own verdict, dating from Lord Mansfield's time, is a gross oversimplification. The values sought to be promoted by excluding the evidence include freedom of deliberation, stability and finality of verdicts, and protection of jurors against annoyance and embarrassment. McDonald v. Pless, 238 U.S. 264, 35 S.Ct. 785, 59 L.Ed. 1300 (1915). On the other hand, simply putting verdicts beyond effective reach can only promote irregularity and injustice. The rule offers an accommodation between these competing considerations.

The mental operations and emotional reactions of jurors in arriving at a given result would, if allowed as a subject of inquiry, place every verdict at the mercy of jurors and invite tampering and harassment. See Grenz v. Werre, 129 N.W.2d 681 (N.D.1964). The authorities are in virtually complete accord in excluding the evidence. Fryer, Note on Disqualification of Witnesses, Selected Writings on Evidence and Trial 345, 347 (Fryer ed. 1957); Maguire, Weinstein, et al., Cases on Evidence 887 (5th ed. 1965); 8 Wigmore § 2349 (McNaughton Rev.1961). As to matters other than mental operations and emotional reactions of jurors, substantial authority refuses to allow a juror to disclose irregularities which occur in the jury room, but allows his testimony as to irregularities occurring outside and allows outsiders to testify as to occurrences both inside and out. 8 Wigmore § 2354 (McNaughton Rev.1961). However, the door of the jury room is not necessarily a satisfactory dividing point, and the Supreme Court has refused to accept it for every situation. Mattox v. United States, 146 U.S. 140, 13 S.Ct. 50, 36 L.Ed. 917 (1892).

Under the federal decisions the central focus has been upon insulation of the manner in which the jury reached its verdict, and this protection extends to each of the components of deliberation, including arguments, statements, discussions, mental and emotional reactions, votes, and any other feature of the process. Thus testimony or affidavits of jurors have been held incompetent to show a compromise verdict, Hyde v. United States, 225 U.S. 347, 382 (1912); a quotient verdict, McDonald v. Pless, 238 U.S. 264 (1915); speculation as to insurance coverage, Holden v. Porter, 405 F.2d 878 (10th Cir.1969), Farmers Coop. Elev. Ass'n v. Strand, 382 F.2d 224, 230 (8th Cir.1967), cert. denied 389 U.S. 1014; misinterpretation of instructions, Farmers Coop. Elev. Ass'n v. Strand, supra; mistake in returning verdict, United States v. Chereton, 309 F.2d 197 (6th Cir.1962); interpretation of guilty plea by one defendant as implicating others, United States v. Crosby, 294 F.2d 928, 949 (2d Cir.1961). The policy does not, however, foreclose testimony by jurors as to prejudicial extraneous information or influences injected into or brought to bear upon the deliberative process. Thus a juror is recognized as competent to testify to statements by the bailiff or the introduction of a prejudicial newspaper account into the jury room, Mattox v. United States, 146 U.S. 140 (1892). See also Parker v. Gladden, 385 U.S. 363 (1966).

This rule does not purport to specify the substantive grounds for setting aside verdicts for irregularity; it deals only with the competency of jurors to testify concerning those grounds.

See also Rule 6(e) of the Federal Rules of Criminal Procedure and 18 U.S.C. § 3500, governing the secrecy of grand jury proceedings. The present rule does not relate to secrecy and disclosure but to the competency of certain witnesses and evidence.

Report of House Judiciary Committee

As proposed by the Court, Rule 606(b) limited testimony by a juror in the course of an inquiry into the validity of a verdict or indictment. He could testify as to the influence of extraneous prejudicial information brought to the jury's attention (e.g. a radio newscast or a newspaper account) or an outside influence which improperly had been brought to bear upon a juror (e.g. a threat to the safety of a member of his family), but he could not testify as to other irregularities which occurred in the jury room. Under this formulation a quotient verdict could not be attacked through the testimony of a juror, nor could a juror testify to the drunken condition of a fellow juror which so disabled him that he could not participate in the jury's deliberations.

The 1969 and 1971 Advisory Committee drafts would have permitted a member of the jury to testify concerning these kinds of irregularities in the jury room. The Advisory Committee note in the 1971 draft stated that " * * * the door of the jury room is not a satisfactory dividing point, and the Supreme Court has refused to accept it." The Advisory Committee further commented that—

> The trend has been to draw the dividing line between testimony as to mental processes, on the one hand, and as to the existence of conditions or occurrences of events calculated improperly to influence the verdict, on the other hand, without regard to whether the happening is within or without the jury room. * * * The jurors are the persons who know what really happened. Allowing them to testify as to matters other than their own reactions involves no particular hazard to the values sought to be protected. The rule is based upon this conclusion. It makes no attempt to specify the substantive grounds for setting aside verdicts for irregularity.

Objective jury misconduct may be testified to in California, Florida, Iowa, Kansas, Nebraska, New Jersey, North Dakota, Ohio, Oregon, Tennessee, Texas, and Washington.

Persuaded that the better practice is that provided for in the earlier drafts, the Committee amended subdivision (b) to read in the text of those drafts.

Report of Senate Judiciary Committee

As adopted by the House, this rule would permit the impeachment of verdicts by inquiry into, not the mental processes of the jurors, but what happened in terms of conduct in the jury room. This extension of the ability to impeach a verdict is felt to be unwarranted and ill-advised.

The rule passed by the House embodies a suggestion by the Advisory Committee of the Judicial Conference that is considerably broader than the final version adopted by the Supreme Court, which embodied long-accepted Federal law. Although forbidding the impeachment of verdicts by inquiry into the jurors' mental processes, it deletes from the Supreme Court version the proscription against testimony "as to any matter or statement occurring during the course of the jury's deliberations." This deletion would have the effect of opening verdicts up to challenge on the basis of what happened during the jury's internal deliberations, for example, where a juror alleged that the jury refused to follow the trial judge's instructions or that some of the jurors did not take part in deliberations.

Permitting an individual to attack a jury verdict based upon the jury's internal deliberations has long been recognized as unwise by the Supreme Court. In McDonald v. Pless, the Court stated:

* * *

[L]et it once be established that verdicts solemnly made and publicly returned into court can be attacked and set aside on the testimony of those who took part in their publication and all verdicts could be, and many would be, followed by an inquiry in the hope of discovering something which might invalidate the finding. Jurors would be harassed and beset by the defeated party in an effort to secure from them evidence of facts which might establish misconduct sufficient to set aside a verdict. If evidence thus secured could be thus used, the result would be to make what was intended to be a private deliberation, the constant subject of public investigation—to the destruction of all frankness and freedom of discussion and conference.[2]

* * *

As it stands then, the rule would permit the harassment of former jurors by losing parties as well as the possible exploitation of disgruntled or otherwise badly-motivated ex-jurors.

Public policy requires a finality to litigation. And common fairness requires that absolute privacy be preserved for jurors to engage in the full and free debate necessary to the attainment of just verdicts. Jurors will not be able to function effectively if their deliberations are to be scrutinized in post-trial litigation. In the interest of protecting the jury system and the citizens who make it work, rule 606 should not permit any inquiry into the internal deliberations of the jurors.

Conference Report

Rule 606(b) deals with juror testimony in an inquiry into the validity of a verdict or indictment. The House bill provides that a juror cannot testify about his mental processes or about the effect of anything upon his or another juror's mind as influencing him to assent to or dissent from a verdict or indictment. Thus, the House bill allows a juror to testify about objective matters occurring during the jury's deliberation, such as the misconduct of another juror or the reaching of a quotient verdict. The Senate bill does not permit juror testimony about any matter or statement occurring during the course of the jury's deliberations. The Senate bill does provide, however, that a juror may testify on the question whether extraneous prejudicial information was improperly brought to the jury's attention and on the question whether any outside influence was improperly brought to bear on any juror.

The Conference adopts the Senate amendment. The Conferees believe that jurors should be encouraged to be conscientious in promptly reporting to the court misconduct that occurs during jury deliberations.

2. 238 U.S. 264, at 267 (1914).

Rule 607

Note by Federal Judicial Center

The rule enacted by the Congress is the rule prescribed by the Supreme Court without change.

Advisory Committee's Note

The traditional rule against impeaching one's own witness is abandoned as based on false premises. A party does not hold out his witnesses as worthy of belief, since he rarely has a free choice in selecting them. Denial of the right leaves the party at the mercy of the witness and the adversary. If the impeachment is by a prior statement, it is free from hearsay dangers and is excluded from the category of hearsay under Rule 801(d)(1). Ladd, Impeachment of One's Own Witness—New Developments, 4 U.Chi.L.Rev. 69 (1936); McCormick § 38; 3 Wigmore §§ 896–918. The substantial inroads into the old rule made over the years by decisions, rules, and statutes are evidence of doubts as to its basic soundness and workability. Cases are collected in 3 Wigmore § 905. Revised Rule 32(a)(1) of the Federal Rules of Civil Procedure allows any party to impeach a witness by means of his deposition, and Rule 43(b) has allowed the calling and impeachment of an adverse party or person identified with him. Illustrative statutes allowing a party to impeach his own witness under varying circumstances are Ill.Rev.Stats.1967, c. 110, § 60; Mass.Laws Annot.1959, c. 233 § 23; 20 N.M.Stats.Annot.1953, § 20–2–4; N.Y. CPLR § 4514 (McKinney 1963); 12 Vt.Stats.Annot.1959, §§ 1641a, 1642. Complete judicial rejection of the old rule is found in United States v. Freeman, 302 F.2d 347 (2d Cir.1962). The same result is reached in Uniform Rule 20; California Evidence Code § 785; Kansas Code of Civil Procedure § 60–420. See also New Jersey Evidence Rule 20.

Rule 608

Note by Federal Judicial Center

The rule enacted by the Congress is the rule prescribed by the Supreme Court, changed only by amending the second sentence of subdivision (b). The sentence as prescribed by the Court read: "They may, however, if probative of truthfulness or untruthfulness and not remote in time, be inquired into on cross-examination of the witness himself or on cross-examination of a witness who testifies to his character for truthfulness or untruthfulness." The effect of the amendments was to delete the phrase "and not remote in time," to add the phrase "in the discretion of the court," and otherwise only to clarify the meaning of the sentence. The reasons for the amendments are stated in the Report of the House Committee on the Judiciary, set forth below. See also Note to Rule 405(a) by Federal Judicial Center, supra.

Advisory Committee's Note

Subdivision (a). In Rule 404(a) the general position is taken that character evidence is not admissible for the purpose of proving that the person acted in conformity therewith, subject, however, to several exceptions, one of which is character evidence of a witness as bearing upon his credibility. The present rule develops that exception.

In accordance with the bulk of judicial authority, the inquiry is strictly limited to character for veracity, rather than allowing evidence as to character generally. The result is to sharpen relevancy, to reduce surprise, waste of time, and confusion, and to make the lot of the witness somewhat less unattractive. McCormick § 44.

The use of opinion and reputation evidence as means of proving the character of witnesses is consistent with Rule 405(a). While the modern practice has purported to exclude opinion, witnesses who testify to reputation seem in fact often to be giving their opinions, disguised somewhat misleadingly as reputation. See McCormick § 44. And even under the modern practice, a common relaxation has allowed inquiry as to whether the witnesses would believe the principal witness under oath. United States v. Walker, 313 F.2d 236 (6th Cir.1963), and cases cited therein; McCormick § 44, pp. 94–95, n. 3.

Character evidence in support of credibility is admissible under the rule only after the witness' character has first been attacked, as has been the case at common law. Maguire, Weinstein, et al., Cases on Evidence 295 (5th ed. 1965); McCormick § 49, p. 105; 4 Wigmore § 1104. The enormous needless consumption of time which a contrary practice would entail justifies the limitation. Opinion or reputation that the witness is untruthful specifically qualifies as an attack under the rule, and evidence of misconduct, including conviction of crime, and of corruption also fall within this category. Evidence of bias or interest does not. McCormick § 49; 4 Wigmore §§ 1106, 1107. Whether evidence in the form of contradiction is an attack upon the character of the witness must depend upon the circumstances. McCormick § 49. Cf. 4 Wigmore §§ 1108, 1109.

As to the use of specific instances on direct by an opinion witness, see the Advisory Committee's Note to Rule 405, supra.

Subdivision (b). In conformity with Rule 405, which forecloses use of evidence of specific incidents as proof in chief of character unless character is an issue in the case, the present rule generally bars evidence of specific instances of conduct of a witness for the purpose of attacking or supporting his credibility. There are, however, two exceptions: (1) specific instances are provable when they have been the subject of criminal conviction, and (2) specific instances may be inquired into on cross-examination of the principal witness or of a witness giving an opinion of his character for truthfulness.

(1) Conviction of crime as a technique of impeachment is treated in detail in Rule 609, and here is merely recognized as an exception to the general rule excluding evidence of specific incidents for impeachment purposes.

(2) Particular instances of conduct, though not the subject of criminal conviction, may be inquired into on cross-examination of the principal witness himself or of a witness who testifies concerning his character for truthfulness. Effective cross-examination demands that some allowance be made for going into matters of this kind, but the possibilities of abuse are substantial. Consequently safeguards are erected in the form of specific requirements that the instances inquired into be probative of truthfulness or its opposite * * *. Also, the overriding protection of Rule 403 requires that probative value not be outweighed by danger of unfair prejudice, confusion of issues, or misleading the jury, and that of Rule 611 bars harassment and undue embarrassment.

The final sentence constitutes a rejection of the doctrine of such cases as People v. Sorge, 301 N.Y. 198, 93 N.E.2d 637 (1950), that any past criminal act relevant to credibility may be inquired into on cross-examination, in apparent disregard of the privilege against self-incrimination. While it is clear that an ordinary witness cannot make a partial disclosure of incriminating matter and then invoke the privilege on cross-examination, no tenable contention can be made that merely by testifying he waives his right to foreclose inquiry on cross-examination into criminal activities for the purpose of attacking his credibility. So to hold would reduce the privilege to a nullity. While it is true that an accused, unlike an ordinary witness, has an option whether to testify, if the option can be exercised only at the price of opening up inquiry as to any and all criminal acts committed during his lifetime, the right to testify could scarcely be said to possess much vitality. In Griffin v. California, 380 U.S. 609, 85 S.Ct. 1229, 14 L.Ed.2d 106 (1965), the Court held that allowing comment on the election of an accused not to testify exacted a constitutionally impermissible price, and so here. While no specific provision in terms confers constitutional status on the right of an accused to take the stand in his own defense, the existence of the right is so completely recognized that a denial of it or substantial infringement upon it would surely be of due process dimensions. See Ferguson v. Georgia, 365 U.S. 570, 81 S.Ct. 756, 5 L.Ed.2d 783 (1961); McCormick § 131; 8 Wigmore § 2276 (McNaughton Rev.1961). In any event, wholly aside from constitutional considerations, the provision represents a sound policy.

Report of House Committee on the Judiciary

The second sentence of Rule 608(b) as submitted by the Court permitted specific instances of misconduct of a witness to be inquired into on cross-examination for the purpose of attacking his credibility, if probative of truthfulness or untruthfulness, "and not remote in time." Such cross-examination could be of the witness himself or of another witness who testifies as to "his" character for truthfulness or untruthfulness.

The Committee amended the Rule to emphasize the discretionary power of the court in permitting such testimony and deleted the reference to remoteness in time as being unnecessary and confusing (remoteness from time of trial or remoteness from the incident involved?). As recast, the Committee amendment also makes clear the antecedent of "his" in the original Court proposal.

Rule 609

Note by Federal Judicial Center

Subdivision (a) of the rule prescribed by the Supreme Court was revised successively in the House, in the Senate, and in the Conference. The nature of the rule prescribed by the Court, the various amendments, and the reasons therefor are stated in the Report of the House Committee on the Judiciary, the Report of the Senate Committee on the Judiciary, and the Conference Report, set forth below.

Subdivision (b) of the rule prescribed by the Supreme Court was also revised successively in the House, in the Senate, and in the Conference. The nature of the rule prescribed by the Court, those amendments, and the reasons therefor are likewise stated in the Report of the House Committee on the Judiciary, the Report of the Senate Committee on the Judiciary, and the Conference Report, set forth below.

Subdivision (c) enacted by the Congress is the subdivision prescribed by the Supreme Court, with amendments and reasons therefor stated in the Report of the House Committee on the Judiciary, set forth below.

Subdivision (d) enacted by the Congress is the subdivision prescribed by the Supreme Court, amended in the second sentence by substituting "court" in place of "judge" and by adding the phrase "in a criminal case."

Subdivision (e) enacted by the Congress is the subdivision prescribed by the Supreme Court without change.

Advisory Committee's Note to 1990 Amendment

The amendment to Rule 609(a) makes two changes in the rule. The first change removes from the rule the limitation that the conviction may only be elicited during cross-examination, a limitation that virtually every circuit has found to be inapplicable. It is common for witnesses to reveal on direct examination their convictions to "remove the sting" of the impeachment. See e.g., United States v. Bad Cob, 560 F.2d 877 (8th Cir.1977). The amendment does not contemplate that a court will necessarily permit proof of prior convictions through testimony, which might be time-consuming and more prejudicial than proof through a written record. Rules 403 and 611(a) provide sufficient authority for the court to protect against unfair or disruptive methods of proof.

The second change effected by the amendment resolves an ambiguity as to the relationship of Rules 609 and 403 with respect to impeachment of witnesses other than the criminal defendant. See, Green v. Bock Laundry Machine Co., 109 S.Ct. 1981, 490 U.S. 504 (1989). The amendment does not disturb the special balancing test for the criminal defendant who chooses to testify. Thus, the rule recognizes that, in virtually every case in which prior convictions are used to impeach the testifying defendant, the defendant faces a unique risk of prejudice—i.e., the danger that convictions that would be excluded under Fed.R. Evid. 404 will be misused by a jury as propensity evidence despite their introduction solely for impeachment purposes. Although the rule does not forbid all use of convictions to impeach a defendant, it requires that the government show that the probative value of convictions as impeachment evidence outweighs their prejudicial effect.

Prior to the amendment, the rule appeared to give the defendant the benefit of the special balancing test when defense witnesses other than the defendant were called to testify. In practice, however, the concern about unfairness to the defendant is most acute when the defendant's own convictions are offered as evidence. Almost all of the decided cases concern this type of impeachment, and the amendment does not deprive the defendant of any meaningful protection, since Rule 403 now clearly protects against unfair impeachment of any defense witness other than the defendant. There are cases in which a defendant might be prejudiced when a defense witness is impeached. Such cases may arise, for example, when the witness bears a special relationship to the defendant such that the defendant is likely to suffer some spill-over effect from impeachment of the witness.

The amendment also protects other litigants from unfair impeachment of their witnesses. The danger of prejudice from the use of prior convictions is not confined to criminal defendants. Although the danger that prior convictions will be misused as character evidence is particularly acute when the defendant is impeached, the danger exists in other situations as well. The amendment reflects the view that it is desirable to protect all litigants from the unfair use of prior convictions, and that the ordinary balancing test of Rule 403, which provides that evidence shall not be excluded unless its prejudicial effect substantially outweighs its probative value, is appropriate for assessing the admissibility of prior convictions for impeachment of any witness other than a criminal defendant.

The amendment reflects a judgment that decisions interpreting Rule 609(a) as requiring a trial court to admit convictions in civil cases that have little, if anything, to do with credibility reach undesirable results. See, e.g., Diggs v. Lyons, 741 F.2d 577 (3d Cir.1984), cert. denied, 105 S.Ct. 2157 (1985). The amendment provides the same protection against unfair prejudice arising from prior convictions used for impeachment purposes as the rules provide for other evidence. The amendment finds support in decided cases. See, e.g., Petty v. Ideco, 761 F.2d 1146 (5th Cir.1985); Czajka v. Hickman, 703 F.2d 317 (8th Cir. 1983).

Fewer decided cases address the question whether Rule 609(a) provides any protection against unduly prejudicial prior convictions used to impeach government witnesses. Some courts have read Rule 609(a) as giving the government no protection for its witnesses. See, e.g., United States v. Thorne, 547 F.2d 56 (8th Cir.1976); United States v. Nevitt, 563 F.2d 406 (9th Cir.1977), cert. denied, 444 U.S. 847 (1979). This approach also is rejected by the amendment. There are cases in which impeachment of government witnesses with prior convictions that have little, if anything, to do with credibility may result in unfair prejudice to the government's interest in a fair trial and unnecessary embarrassment to a witness. Fed.R.Evid. 412 already recognizes this and excluded certain evidence of past sexual behavior in the context of prosecutions for sexual assaults.

The amendment applies the general balancing test of Rule 403 to protect all litigants against unfair impeachment of witnesses. The balancing test protects civil litigants, the government in criminal cases, and the defendant in a criminal case who calls other witnesses. The amendment addresses prior convictions offered under Rule 609, not for other purposes, and does not run afoul, therefore, of Davis v. Alaska, 415 U.S. 308 (1974). Davis involved the use of a prior juvenile adjudication not to prove a past law violation, but to prove bias. The defendant in a criminal case has the right to demonstrate the bias of a witness and to be assured a fair trial, but not to unduly prejudice a trier of fact. See generally Rule 412. In any case in which the trial court believes that confrontation rights require admission of impeachment evidence, obviously the Constitution would take precedence over the rule.

The probability that prior convictions of an ordinary government witness will be unduly prejudicial is low in most criminal cases. Since the behavior of the witness is not the issue in dispute in most cases, there is little chance that the trier of fact will misuse the convictions offered as impeachment evidence as propensity evidence. Thus, trial courts will be skeptical when the government objects to impeachment of its witnesses with prior convictions. Only when the government is able to point to a real danger of prejudice that is sufficient to outweigh substantially the probative value of the conviction for impeachment purposes will the conviction be excluded.

The amendment continues to divide subdivision (a) into subsections (1) and (2) thus facilitating retrieval under current computerized research programs which distinguish the two provisions. The Committee recommended no substantive change in subdivision (a)(2), even though some cases raise a concern about the proper interpretation of the words "dishonesty or false statement." These words were used but not explained in the original Advisory Committee Note accompanying Rule 609. Congress extensively debated the rule, and the Report of the House and Senate Conference Committee states that "[b]y the phrase 'dishonesty and false statement,' the Conference means crimes such as perjury, subornation of perjury, false statement, criminal fraud, embezzlement, or false pretense, or any other offense in the nature of crimen falsi, commission of which involves some element of deceit, untruthfulness, or falsification bearing on the accused's propensity to testify truthfully." The Advisory Committee concluded that the Conference Report provides sufficient guidance to trial courts and that no amendment is necessary, notwithstanding some decisions that take an unduly broad view of "dishonesty," admitting convictions such as for bank robbery or bank larceny. Subsection (a)(2) continues to apply to any witness, including a criminal defendant.

Finally, the Committee determined that it was unnecessary to add to the rule language stating that, when a prior conviction is offered under Rule 609, the trial court is to consider the probative value of the prior conviction for impeachment, not for other purposes. The Committee concluded that the title of the rule, its first sentence, and its placement among the impeachment rules clearly establish that evidence offered under Rule 609 is offered only for purposes of impeachment.

Advisory Committee's Note

As a means of impeachment, evidence of conviction of crime is significant only because it stands as proof of the commission of the underlying criminal act. There is little dissent from the general proposition that at least some crimes are relevant to credibility but much disagreement among the cases and commentators about which crimes are usable for this purpose. See McCormick § 43; 2 Wright, Federal Practice and Procedure: Criminal § 416 (1969). The weight of traditional authority has been to allow use of felonies generally, without regard to the nature of the particular offense, and of *crimen falsi* without regard to the grade of the offense. This is the view accepted by Congress in the 1970 amendment of § 14–305 of the District of Columbia Code, P.L. 91–358, 84 Stat. 473. Uniform Rule 21 and Model Code Rule 106 permit only crimes involving "dishonesty or false statement." Others have thought that the trial judge should have discretion to exclude convictions if the probative value of the evidence of the crime is substantially outweighed by the danger of unfair prejudice. Luck v. United States, 121 U.S.App.D.C. 151, 348 F.2d 763 (1965); McGowan, Impeachment of Criminal Defendants by Prior Convictions, 1970 Law & Soc. Order 1. * * *

The proposed rule incorporates certain basic safeguards, in terms applicable to all witnesses but of particular significance to an accused who elects to testify. These protections include the imposition of definite time limitations, giving effect to demonstrated rehabilitation, and generally excluding juvenile adjudications.

Subdivision (a). For purposes of impeachment, crimes are divided into two categories by the rule: (1) those of what is generally regarded as felony grade, without particular regard to the nature of the offense, and (2) those involving dishonesty or false statement, without regard to the grade of the offense. Provable convictions are not limited to violations of federal law. By reason of our constitutional structure, the federal catalog of crimes is far from being a complete one, and resort must be had to the laws of the states for the specification of many crimes. For example, simple theft as compared with theft from interstate commerce. Other instances of borrowing are the Assimilative Crimes Act, making the state law of crimes applicable to the special territorial and maritime jurisdiction of the United States, 18 U.S.C. § 13, and the provision of the Judicial Code disqualifying persons as jurors on the grounds of state as well as federal convictions, 28 U.S.C. § 1865. For evaluation of the crime in terms of seriousness, reference is made to the congressional measurement of felony (subject to imprisonment in excess of one year) rather than adopting state definitions which vary considerably. See 28 U.S.C. § 1865, supra, disqualifying jurors for conviction in state or federal court of crime punishable by imprisonment for more than one year.

Report of the House Committee on the Judiciary

Rule 609(a) as submitted by the Court was modeled after Section 133(a) of Public Law 91–358, 14 D.C.Code 305(b)(1), enacted in 1970. The Rule provided that:

> For the purpose of attacking the credibility of a witness, evidence that he has been convicted of a crime is admissible but only if the crime (1) was punishable by death or imprisonment in excess of one year under the law under which he was convicted or (2) involved dishonesty or false statement regardless of the punishment.

As reported to the Committee by the Subcommittee, Rule 609(a) was amended to read as follows:

> For the purpose of attacking the credibility of a witness, evidence that he has been convicted of a crime is admissible only if the crime (1) was punishable by death or imprisonment in excess of one year, unless the court determines that the danger of unfair prejudice outweighs the probative value of the evidence of the conviction, or (2) involved dishonesty or false statement.

In full committee, the provision was amended to permit attack upon the credibility of a witness by prior conviction only if the prior crime involved dishonesty or false statement. While recognizing that the prevailing doctrine in the federal courts and in most States allows a witness to be impeached by evidence of prior felony convictions without restriction as to type, the Committee was of the view that, because of the danger of unfair prejudice in such practice and the deterrent effect upon an accused who might wish to testify, and even upon a witness who was not the accused, cross-examination by evidence of prior conviction should be limited to those kinds of convictions bearing directly on credibility, i.e., crimes involving dishonesty or false statement.

Report of the Senate Committee on the Judiciary

As proposed by the Supreme Court, the rule would allow the use of prior convictions to impeach if the crime was a felony or a misdemeanor if the misdemeanor involved dishonesty or false statement. As modified by the House, the rule would admit prior convictions for impeachment purposes only if the offense, whether felony or misdemeanor, involved dishonesty or false statement.

The committee has adopted a modified version of the House-passed rule. In your committee's view, the danger of unfair prejudice is far greater when the accused, as opposed to other witnesses, testifies, because the jury may be prejudiced not merely on the question of credibility but also on the ultimate question of guilt or innocence. Therefore, with respect to defendants, the committee agreed with the House limitation that only offenses involving false statement or dishonesty may be used. By that phrase, the committee means

crimes such as perjury or subornation of perjury, false statement, criminal
fraud, embezzlement or false pretense, or any other offense, in the nature of
crimen falsi the commission of which involves some element of untruthfulness,
deceit or falsification bearing on the accused's propensity to testify truthfully.

With respect to other witnesses, in addition to any prior conviction involving false statement or dishonesty, any other felony may be used to impeach if,
and only if, the court finds that the probative value of such evidence outweighs
its prejudicial effect against the party offering that witness.

Notwithstanding this provision, proof of any prior offense otherwise admissible under rule 404 could still be offered for the purposes sanctioned by that
rule. Furthermore, the committee intends that notwithstanding this rule, a
defendant's misrepresentation regarding the existence or nature of prior convictions may be met by rebuttal evidence, including the record of such prior
convictions. Similarly, such records may be offered to rebut representations
made by the defendant regarding his attitude toward or willingness to commit a
general category of offense, although denials or other representations by the
defendant regarding the specific conduct which forms the basis of the charge
against him shall not make prior convictions admissible to rebut such statement.

In regard to either type of representation, of course, prior convictions may
be offered in rebuttal only if the defendant's statement is made in response to
defense counsel's questions or is made gratuitously in the course of cross-
examination. Prior convictions may not be offered as rebuttal evidence if the
prosecution has sought to circumvent the purpose of this rule by asking
questions which elicit such representations from the defendant.

One other clarifying amendment has been added to this subsection, that is,
to provide that the admissibility of evidence of a prior conviction is permitted
only upon cross-examination of a witness. It is not admissible if a person does
not testify. It is to be understood, however, that a court record of a prior
conviction is admissible to prove that conviction if the witness has forgotten or
denies its existence.

Conference Report

The House bill provides that the credibility of a witness can be attacked by
proof of prior conviction of a crime only if the crime involves dishonesty or false
statement. The Senate amendment provides that a witness' credibility may be
attacked if the crime (1) was punishable by death or imprisonment in excess of
one year under the law under which he was convicted or (2) involves dishonesty
or false statement, regardless of the punishment.

The Conference adopts the Senate amendment with an amendment. The
Conference amendment provides that the credibility of a witness, whether a
defendant or someone else, may be attacked by proof of a prior conviction but
only if the crime: (1) was punishable by death or imprisonment in excess of one
year under the law under which he was convicted and the court determines
that the probative value of the conviction outweighs its prejudicial effect to the
defendant; or (2) involved dishonesty or false statement regardless of the
punishment.

By the phrase "dishonesty and false statement" the Conference means
crimes such as perjury or subornation of perjury, false statement, criminal
fraud, embezzlement, or false pretense, or any other offense in the nature of

crimen falsi, the commission of which involves some element of deceit, untruth-fulness, or falsification bearing on the accused's propensity to testify truthfully.

The admission of prior convictions involving dishonesty and false statement is not within the discretion of the Court. Such convictions are peculiarly probative of credibility and, under this rule, are always to be admitted. Thus, judicial discretion granted with respect to the admissibility of other prior convictions is not applicable to those involving dishonesty or false statement.

With regard to the discretionary standard established by paragraph (1) of rule 609(a), the Conference determined that the prejudicial effect to be weighed against the probative value of the conviction is specifically the prejudicial effect *to the defendant.* The danger of prejudice to a witness other than the defendant (such as injury to the witness' reputation in his community) was considered and rejected by the Conference as an element to be weighed in determining admissibility. It was the judgment of the Conference that the danger of prejudice to a nondefendant witness is outweighed by the need for the trier of fact to have as much relevant evidence on the issue of credibility as possible. Such evidence should only be excluded where it presents a danger of improperly influencing the outcome of the trial by persuading the trier of fact to convict the defendant on the basis of his prior criminal record.

Advisory Committee's Note

Subdivision (b). Few statutes recognize a time limit on impeachment by evidence of conviction. However, practical considerations of fairness and relevancy demand that some boundary be recognized. See Ladd, Credibility Tests—Current Trends, 89 U.Pa.L.Rev. 166, 176–177 (1940). This portion of the rule is derived from the proposal advanced in Recommendation Proposing in Evidence Code, § 788(5), p. 142, Cal.Law Rev.Comm'n (1965), though not adopt-ed. See California Evidence Code § 788.

Report of the House Committee on the Judiciary

Rule 609(b) as submitted by the Court was modeled after Section 133(a) of Public Law 91–358, 14 D.C.Code 305(b)(2)(B), enacted in 1970. The Rule provided:

> Evidence of a conviction under this rule is not admissible if a period of more than ten years has elapsed since the date of the release of the witness from confinement imposed for his most recent convic-tion, or the expiration of the period of his parole, probation, or sentence granted or imposed with respect to his most recent conviction, whichever is the later date.

Under this formulation, a witness' entire past record of criminal convictions could be used for impeachment (provided the conviction met the standard of subdivision (a)), if the witness had been most recently released from confine-ment, or the period of his parole or probation had expired, within ten years of the conviction.

The Committee amended the Rule to read in the text of the 1971 Advisory Committee version to provide that upon the expiration of ten years from the date of a conviction of a witness, or of his release from confinement for that offense, that conviction may no longer be used for impeachment. The Commit-tee was of the view that after ten years following a person's release from confinement (or from the date of his conviction) the probative value of the conviction with respect to that person's credibility diminished to a point where it should no longer be admissible.

Report of the Senate Committee on the Judiciary

Although convictions over ten years old generally do not have much probative value, there may be exceptional circumstances under which the conviction substantially bears on the credibility of the witness. Rather than exclude all convictions over 10 years old, the committee adopted an amendment in the form of a final clause to the section granting the court discretion to admit convictions over 10 years old, but only upon a determination by the court that the probative value of the conviction supported by specific facts and circumstances, substantially outweighs its prejudicial effect.

It is intended that convictions over 10 years old will be admitted very rarely and only in exceptional circumstances. The rules provide that the decision be supported by specific facts and circumstances thus requiring the court to make specific findings on the record as to the particular facts and circumstances it has considered in determining that the probative value of the conviction substantially outweighs its prejudicial impact. It is expected that, in fairness, the court will give the party against whom the conviction is introduced a full and adequate opportunity to contest its admission.

Conference Report

The House bill provides in subsection (b) that evidence of conviction of a crime may not be used for impeachment purposes under subsection (a) if more than ten years have elapsed since the date of the conviction or the date the witness was released from confinement imposed for the conviction, whichever is later. The Senate amendment permits the use of convictions older than ten years, if the court determines, in the interests of justice, that the probative value of the conviction, supported by specific facts and circumstances, substantially outweighs its prejudicial effect.

The Conference adopts the Senate amendment with an amendment requiring notice by a party that he intends to request that the court allow him to use a conviction older than ten years. The Conferees anticipate that a written notice, in order to give the adversary a fair opportunity to contest the use of the evidence, will ordinarily include such information as the date of the conviction, the jurisdiction, and the offense or statute involved. In order to eliminate the possibility that the flexibility of this provision may impair the ability of a party-opponent to prepare for trial, the Conferees intend that the notice provision operate to avoid surprise.

Advisory Committee's Note

Subdivision (c). A pardon or its equivalent granted solely for the purpose of restoring civil rights lost by virtue of a conviction has no relevance to an inquiry into character. If, however, the pardon or other proceeding is hinged upon a showing of rehabilitation the situation is otherwise. The result under the rule is to render the conviction inadmissible. The alternative of allowing in evidence both the conviction and the rehabilitation has not been adopted for reasons of policy, economy of time, and difficulties of evaluation.

A similar provision is contained in California Evidence Code § 788. Cf. A.L.I. Model Penal Code, Proposed Official Draft § 306.6(3)(e) (1962), and discussion in A.L.I. Proceedings 310 (1961).

Pardons based on innocence have the effect, of course, of nullifying the conviction *ab initio.*

Report of House Committee on the Judiciary

Rule 609(c) as submitted by the Court provided in part that evidence of a witness' prior conviction is not admissible to attack his credibility if the conviction was the subject of a pardon, annulment, or other equivalent procedure, based on a showing of rehabilitation, and the witness has not been convicted of a subsequent crime. The Committee amended the Rule to provide that the "subsequent crime" must have been "punishable by death or imprisonment in excess of one year", on the ground that a subsequent conviction of an offense not a felony is insufficient to rebut the finding that the witness has been rehabilitated. The Committee also intends that the words "based on a finding of the rehabilitation of the person convicted" apply not only to "certificate of rehabilitation, or other equivalent procedure", but also to "pardon" and "annulment."

Advisory Committee's Note

Subdivision (d). The prevailing view has been that a juvenile adjudication is not usable for impeachment. Thomas v. United States, 74 App.D.C. 167, 121 F.2d 905 (1941); Cotton v. United States, 355 F.2d 480 (10th Cir.1966). This conclusion was based upon a variety of circumstances. By virtue of its informality, frequently diminished quantum of required proof, and other departures from accepted standards for criminal trials under the theory of *parens patriae,* the juvenile adjudication was considered to lack the precision and general probative value of the criminal conviction. While In re Gault, 387 U.S. 1, 87 S.Ct. 1428, 18 L.Ed.2d 527 (1967), no doubt eliminates these characteristics insofar as objectionable, other obstacles remain. Practical problems of administration are raised by the common provisions in juvenile legislation that records be kept confidential and that they be destroyed after a short time. While *Gault* was skeptical as to the realities of confidentiality of juvenile records, it also saw no constitutional obstacles to improvement. 387 U.S. at 25, 87 S.Ct. 1428. See also Note, Rights and Rehabilitation in the Juvenile Courts, 67 Colum.L.Rev. 281, 289 (1967). In addition, policy considerations much akin to those which dictate exclusion of adult convictions after rehabilitation has been established strongly suggest a rule of excluding juvenile adjudications. Admittedly, however, the rehabilitative process may in a given case be a demonstrated failure, or the strategic importance of a given witness may be so great as to require the overriding of general policy in the interests of particular justice. See Giles v. Maryland, 386 U.S. 66, 87 S.Ct. 793, 17 L.Ed.2d 737 (1967). Wigmore was outspoken in his condemnation of the disallowance of juvenile adjudications to impeach, especially when the witness is the complainant in a case of molesting a minor. 1 Wigmore § 196; 3 id. §§ 924a, 980. The rule recognizes discretion in the judge to effect an accommodation among these various factors by departing from the general principle of exclusion. In deference to the general pattern and policy of juvenile statutes, however, no discretion is accorded when the witness is the accused in a criminal case.

Subdivision (e). The presumption of correctness which ought to attend judicial proceedings supports the position that pendency of an appeal does not preclude use of a conviction for impeachment. United States v. Empire Packing Co., 174 F.2d 16 (17th Cir.1949), cert. denied 337 U.S. 959, 69 S.Ct. 1534, 93 L.Ed. 1758; Bloch v. United States, 226 F.2d 185 (9th Cir.1955), cert.

denied 350 U.S. 948, 76 S.Ct. 323, 100 L.Ed. 826 and 353 U.S. 959, 77 S.Ct. 868, 1 L.Ed.2d 910; and see Newman v. United States, 331 F.2d 968 (8th Cir.1964). Contra, Campbell v. United States, 85 U.S.App.D.C. 133, 176 F.2d 45 (1949). The pendency of an appeal is, however, a qualifying circumstance properly considerable.

Rule 610

Note by Federal Judicial Center

The rule enacted by the Congress is the rule prescribed by the Supreme Court without change.

Advisory Committee's Note

While the rule forecloses inquiry into the religious beliefs or opinions of a witness for the purpose of showing that his character for truthfulness is affected by their nature, an inquiry for the purpose of showing interest or bias because of them is not within the prohibition. Thus disclosure of affiliation with a church which is a party to the litigation would be allowable under the rule. Cf. Tucker v. Reil, 51 Ariz. 357, 77 P.2d 203 (1938). To the same effect, though less specifically worded, is California Evidence Code § 789. See 3 Wigmore § 936.

Rule 611

Note by Federal Judicial Center

Subdivision (a) of the rule enacted by the Congress is the subdivision prescribed by the Supreme Court, amended only by substituting "court" in place of "judge."

Subdivision (b) of the rule enacted by the Congress is substantially different from the subdivision prescribed by the Supreme Court. The nature of the changes and the reasons therefor are stated in the Report of the House Committee on the Judiciary, set forth below.

The first two sentences of subdivision (c) of the rule enacted by the Congress are the same as prescribed by the Supreme Court. The third sentence has been amended in the manner and for the reasons stated in the Report of the House Committee on the Judiciary, set forth below.

Advisory Committee's Note

Subdivision (a). Spelling out detailed rules to govern the mode and order of interrogating witnesses and presenting evidence is neither desirable nor feasible. The ultimate responsibility for the effective working of the adversary system rests with the judge. The rule sets forth the objectives which he should seek to attain.

Item (1) restates in broad terms the power and obligation of the judge as developed under common law principles. It covers such concerns as whether testimony shall be in the form of a free narrative or responses to specific questions, McCormick § 5, the order of calling witnesses and presenting evidence, 6 Wigmore § 1867, the use of demonstrative evidence, McCormick § 179, and the many other questions arising during the course of a trial which can be solved only by the judge's common sense and fairness in view of the particular circumstances.

Item (2) is addressed to avoidance of needless consumption of time, a matter of daily concern in the disposition of cases. A companion piece is found in the discretion vested in the judge to exclude evidence as a waste of time in Rule 403(b).

Item (3) calls for a judgment under the particular circumstances whether interrogation tactics entail harassment or undue embarrassment. Pertinent circumstances include the importance of the testimony, the nature of the inquiry, its relevance to credibility, waste of time, and confusion. McCormick § 42. In Alford v. United States, 282 U.S. 687, 694, 51 S.Ct. 218, 75 L.Ed. 624 (1931), the Court pointed out that, while the trial judge should protect the witness from questions which "go beyond the bounds of proper cross-examination merely to harass, annoy or humiliate," this protection by no means forecloses efforts to discredit the witness. Reference to the transcript of the prosecutor's cross-examination in Berger v. United States, 295 U.S. 78, 55 S.Ct. 629, 79 L.Ed. 1314 (1935), serves to lay at rest any doubts as to the need for judicial control in this area.

The inquiry into specific instances of conduct of a witness allowed under Rule 608(b) is, of course, subject to this rule.

Subdivision (b) *. The tradition in the federal courts and in numerous state courts has been to limit the scope of cross-examination to matters testified to on direct, plus matters bearing upon the credibility of the witness. Various reasons have been advanced to justify the rule of limited cross-examination. (1) A party vouches for his own witness but only to the extent of matters elicited on direct. Resurrection Gold Mining Co. v. Fortune Gold Mining Co., 129 Fed. 668, 675 (8th Cir.1904), quoted in Maguire, Weinstein, et al., Cases on Evidence 277 n. 38 (5th ed. 1965). But the concept of vouching is discredited, and Rule 6–07[607] rejects it. (2) A party cannot ask his own witness leading questions. This is a problem properly solved in terms of what is necessary for a proper development of the testimony rather than by a mechanistic formula similar to the vouching concept. See discussion under subdivision (c). (3) A practice of limited cross-examination promotes orderly presentation of the case. Finch v. Weiner, 109 Conn. 616, 145 Atl. 31 (1929). In the opinion of the Advisory Committee this latter reason has merit. It is apparent, however, that the rule of limited cross-examination thus viewed becomes an aspect of the judge's general control over the mode and order of interrogating witnesses and presenting evidence, to be administered as such. The matter is not one in which involvement at the appellate level is likely to prove fruitful. See, for example, Moyer v. Aetna Life Ins. Co., 126 F.2d 141 (3rd Cir.1942); Butler v. New York Central R. Co., 253 F.2d 281 (7th Cir.1958); United States v. Johnson, 285 F.2d 35 (9th Cir.1960); Union Automobile Indemnity Ass'n v. Capitol Indemnity Ins. Co., 310 F.2d 318 (7th Cir.1962). In view of these considerations, the rule is phrased in terms of a suggestion rather than a mandate to the trial judge.

The qualification "as if on direct examination," applicable when inquiry into additional matters is allowed is designed to terminate at that point the asking of leading questions as a matter of right and to bring into operation subdivision (c) of the rule.

The rule does not purport to determine the extent to which an accused who elects to testify thereby waives his privilege against self-incrimination. The question is a constitutional one, rather than a mere matter of administering the

* The Advisory Committee's Note to subdivision (b) is from the 1969 Preliminary Draft. 46 F.R.D. 161, 304.

trial. Under United States v. Simmons, 390 U.S. 377 (1968), no general waiver occurs when the accused testifies on such preliminary matters as the validity of a search and seizure or the admissibility of a confession. Rule 1–04(d) [104(d)], supra. When he testifies on the merits, however, can he foreclose inquiry into an aspect or element of the crime by avoiding it on direct? The affirmative answer given in Tucker v. United States, 5 F.2d 818 (8th Cir.1925), is inconsistent with the description of the waiver as extending to "all other relevant facts" in Johnson v. United States, 318 U.S. 189, 195 (1943). See also Brown v. United States, 356 U.S. 148 (1958). The situation of an accused who desires to testify on some but not all counts of a multiple-count indictment is one to be approached, in the first instance at least, as a problem of severance under Rule 14 of the Federal Rules of Criminal Procedure. Cross v. United States, 335 F.2d 987 (D.C.Cir.1964). Cf. United States v. Baker, 262 F.Supp. 657, 686 (D.D.C.1966). In all events, the extent of the waiver of the privilege against self-incrimination ought not to be determined as a by-product of a rule on scope of cross-examination.

Report of House Committee on the Judiciary

As submitted by the Court, Rule 611(b) provided:

> A witness may be cross-examined on any matter relevant to any issue in the case, including credibility. In the interests of justice, the judge may limit cross-examination with respect to matters not testified to on direct examination.

The Committee amended this provision to return to the rule which prevails in the federal courts and thirty-nine State jurisdictions. As amended, the Rule is in the text of the 1969 Advisory Committee draft. It limits cross-examination to credibility and to matters testified to on direct examination, unless the judge permits more, in which event the cross-examiner must proceed as if on direct examination. This traditional rule facilitates orderly presentation by each party at trial. Further, in light of existing discovery procedures, there appears to be no need to abandon the traditional rule.

Report of Senate Committee on the Judiciary

Rule 611(b) as submitted by the Supreme Court permitted a broad scope of cross-examination: "cross-examination on any matter relevant to any issue in the case" unless the judge, in the interests of justice, limited the scope of cross-examination.

The House narrowed the Rule to the more traditional practice of limiting cross-examination to the subject matter of direct examination (and credibility), but with discretion in the judge to permit inquiry into additional matters in situations where that would aid in the development of the evidence or otherwise facilitate the conduct of the trial.

The committee agrees with the House amendment. Although there are good arguments in support of broad cross-examination from prospectives of developing all relevant evidence, we believe the factors of insuring an orderly and predictable development of the evidence weigh in favor of the narrower rule, especially when discretion is given to the trial judge to permit inquiry into additional matters. The committee expressly approves this discretion and believes it will permit sufficient flexibility allowing a broader scope of cross-examination whenever appropriate.

The House amendment providing broader discretionary cross-examination permitted inquiry into additional matters only as if on direct examination. As a general rule, we concur with this limitation, however, we would understand that this limitation would not preclude the utilization of leading questions if the conditions of subsection (c) of this rule were met, bearing in mind the judge's discretion in any case to limit the scope of cross-examination.[1]

Further, the committee has received correspondence from Federal judges commenting on the applicability of this rule to section 1407 of title 28. It is the committee's judgment that this rule as reported by the House is flexible enough to provide sufficiently broad cross-examination in appropriate situations in multidistrict litigation.

Advisory Committee's Note

Subdivision (c). The rule continues the traditional view that the suggestive powers of the leading question are as a general proposition undesirable. Within this tradition, however, numerous exceptions have achieved recognition: The witness who is hostile, unwilling, or biased; the child witness or the adult with communication problems; the witness whose recollection is exhausted; and undisputed preliminary matters. 3 Wigmore §§ 774–778. An almost total unwillingness to reverse for infractions has been manifested by appellate courts. See cases cited in 3 Wigmore § 770. The matter clearly falls within the area of control by the judge over the mode and order of interrogation and presentation and accordingly is phrased in words of suggestion rather than command.

The rule also conforms to tradition in making the use of leading questions on cross-examination a matter of right. The purpose of the qualification "ordinarily" is to furnish a basis for denying the use of leading questions when the cross-examination is cross-examination in form only and not in fact, as for example the "cross-examination" of a party by his own counsel after being called by the opponent (savoring more of re-direct) or of an insured defendant who proves to be friendly to the plaintiff.

The final sentence deals with categories of witnesses automatically regarded and treated as hostile. Rule 43(b) of the Federal Rules of Civil Procedure has included only "an adverse party or an officer, director, or managing agent of a public or private corporation or of a partnership or association which is an adverse party." This limitation virtually to persons whose statements would stand as admissions is believed to be an unduly narrow concept of those who may safely be regarded as hostile without further demonstration. See, for example, Maryland Casualty Co. v. Kador, 225 F.2d 120 (5th Cir.1955), and Degelos v. Fidelity and Casualty Co., 313 F.2d 809 (5th Cir.1963), holding despite the language of Rule 43(b) that an insured fell within it, though not a party in an action under the Louisiana direct action statute. The phrase of the rule, "witness identified with" an adverse party, is designed to enlarge the category of persons thus callable.

Report of House Committee on the Judiciary

The third sentence of Rule 611(c) as submitted by the Court provided that:

> In civil cases, a party is entitled to call an adverse party or witness identified with him and interrogate by leading questions.

1. See McCormick on Evidence, §§ 24–26 (especially 24) (2d ed. 1972).

The Committee amended this Rule to permit leading questions to be used with respect to any hostile witness, not only an adverse party or person identified with such adverse party. The Committee also substituted the word "When" for the phrase "In civil cases" to reflect the possibility that in criminal cases a defendant may be entitled to call witnesses identified with the government, in which event the Committee believed the defendant should be permitted to inquire with leading questions.

Report of Senate Committee on the Judiciary

As submitted by the Supreme Court, the rule provided: "In civil cases, a party is entitled to call an adverse party or witness identified with him and interrogate by leading questions."

The final sentence of subsection (c) was amended by the House for the purpose of clarifying the fact that a "hostile witness"—that is a witness who is hostile in fact—could be subject to interrogation by leading questions. The rule as submitted by the Supreme Court declared certain witnesses hostile as a matter of law and thus subject to interrogation by leading questions without any showing of hostility in fact. These were adverse parties or witnesses identified with adverse parties. However, the wording of the first sentence of subsection (c) while generally prohibiting the use of leading questions on direct examination, also provides "except as may be necessary to develop his testimony." Further, the first paragraph of the Advisory Committee note explaining the subsection makes clear that they intended that leading questions could be asked of a hostile witness or a witness who was unwilling or biased and even though that witness was not associated with an adverse party. Thus, we question whether the House amendment was necessary.

However, concluding that it was not intended to affect the meaning of the first sentence of the subsection and was intended solely to clarify the fact that leading questions are permissible in the interrogation of a witness, who is hostile in fact, the committee accepts that House amendment.

The final sentence of this subsection was also amended by the House to cover criminal as well as civil cases. The committee accepts this amendment, but notes that it may be difficult in criminal cases to determine when a witness is "identified with an adverse party," and thus the rule should be applied with caution.

Rule 612

Note by Federal Judicial Center

The rule enacted by the Congress is the rule prescribed by the Supreme Court, amended by substituting "court" in place of "judge," with appropriate pronominal change, and in the first sentence, by substituting "the writing" in place of "it" before "produced," and by substituting the phrase "(1) while testifying, or (2) before testifying if the court in its discretion determines it is necessary in the interests of justice" in place of "before or while testifying." The reasons for the latter amendment are stated in the Report of the House Committee on the Judiciary, set forth below.

Advisory Committee's Note

The treatment of writings used to refresh recollection while on the stand is in accord with settled doctrine. McCormick § 9, p. 15. The bulk of the case law has, however, denied the existence of any right to access by the opponent when the writing is used prior to taking the stand, though the judge may have discretion in the matter. Goldman v. United States, 316 U.S. 129, 62 S.Ct. 993, 86 L.Ed. 1322 (1942); Needelman v. United States, 261 F.2d 802 (5th Cir.1958), cert. dismissed 362 U.S. 600, 80 S.Ct. 960, 4 L.Ed.2d 980, rehearing denied 363 U.S. 858, 80 S.Ct. 1606, 4 L.Ed.2d 1739, Annot., 82 A.L.R.2d 473, 562 and 7 A.L.R.3d 181, 247. An increasing group of cases has repudiated the distinction, People v. Scott, 29 Ill.2d 97, 193 N.E.2d 814 (1963); State v. Mucci, 25 N.J. 423, 136 A.2d 761 (1957); State v. Hunt, 25 N.J. 514, 138 A.2d 1 (1958); State v. Deslovers, 40 R.I. 89, 100 A. 64 (1917), and this position is believed to be correct. As Wigmore put it, "the risk of imposition and the need of safeguard is just as great" in both situations. 3 Wigmore § 762, p. 111. To the same effect is McCormick § 9, p. 17.

The purpose of the phrase "for the purpose of testifying" is to safeguard against using the rule as a pretext for wholesale exploration of an opposing party's files and to insure that access is limited only to those writings which may fairly be said in fact to have an impact upon the testimony of the witness.

The purpose of the rule is the same as that of the *Jencks* statute, 18 U.S.C. § 3500: to promote the search of credibility and memory. The same sensitivity to disclosure of government files may be involved; hence the rule is expressly made subject to the statute, subdivision (a) of which provides: "In any criminal prosecution brought by the United States, no statement or report in the possession of the United States which was made by a Government witness or prospective Government witness (other than the defendant) shall be the subject of subpena, discovery, or inspection until said witness has testified on direct examination in the trial of the case." Items falling within the purview of the statute are producible only as provided by its terms, Palermo v. United States, 360 U.S. 343, 351 (1959), and disclosure under the rule is limited similarly by the statutory conditions. With this limitation in mind, some differences of application may be noted. The *Jencks* statute applies only to statements of witnesses; the rule is not so limited. The statute applies only to criminal cases; the rule applies to all cases. The statute applies only to government witnesses; the rule applies to all witnesses. The statute contains no requirement that the statement be consulted for purposes of refreshment before or while testifying; the rule so requires. Since many writings would qualify under either statute or rule, a substantial overlap exists, but the identity of procedures makes this of no importance.

The consequences of nonproduction by the government in a criminal case are those of the *Jencks* statute, striking the testimony or in exceptional cases a mistrial. 18 U.S.C. § 3500(d). In other cases these alternatives are unduly limited, and such possibilities as contempt, dismissal, finding issues against the offender, and the like are available. See Rule 16(g) of the Federal Rules of Criminal Procedure and Rule 37(b) of the Federal Rules of Civil Procedure for appropriate sanctions.

Report of House Committee on the Judiciary

As submitted to Congress, Rule 612 provided that except as set forth in 18 U.S.C. 3500, if a witness uses a writing to refresh his memory for the purpose of testifying, "either before or while testifying," an adverse party is entitled to have the writing produced at the hearing, to inspect it, to cross-examine the witness on it, and to introduce in evidence those portions relating to the witness' testimony. The Committee amended the Rule so as still to require the

production of writings used by a witness while testifying, but to render the
production of writings used by a witness to refresh his memory before testifying
discretionary with the court in the interests of justice, as is the case under
existing federal law. See Goldman v. United States, 316 U.S. 129 (1942). The
Committee considered that permitting an adverse party to require the production of writings used before testifying could result in fishing expeditions among
a multitude of papers which a witness may have used in preparing for trial.

The Committee intends that nothing in the Rule be construed as barring
the assertion of a privilege with respect to writings used by a witness to refresh
his memory.

Rule 613

Note by Federal Judicial Center

The rule enacted by the Congress is the rule prescribed by the Supreme
Court, amended only by substituting "nor" in place of "or" in subdivision (a).

Advisory Committee's Note

Subdivision (a). The Queen's Case, 2 Br. & B. 284, 129 Eng.Rep. 976
(1820), laid down the requirement that a cross-examiner, prior to questioning
the witness about his own prior statement in writing, must first show it to the
witness. Abolished by statute in the country of its origin, the requirement
nevertheless gained currency in the United States. The rule abolishes this
useless impediment, to cross-examination. Ladd, Some Observations on Credibility: Impeachment of Witnesses, 52 Cornell L.Q. 239, 246–247 (1967); McCormick § 28; 4 Wigmore §§ 1259–1260. Both oral and written statements are
included.

The provision for disclosure to counsel is designed to protect against
unwarranted insinuations that a statement has been made when the fact is to
the contrary.

The rule does not defeat the application of Rule 1002 relating to production
of the original when the contents of a writing are sought to be proved. Nor
does it defeat the application of Rule 26(b)(3) of the Rules of Civil Procedure, as
revised, entitling a person on request to a copy of his own statement, though
the operation of the latter may be suspended temporarily.

Subdivision (b). The familiar foundation requirement that an impeaching statement first be shown to the witness before it can be proved by extrinsic
evidence is preserved but with some modifications. See Ladd, Some Observations on Credibility: Impeachment of Witnesses, 52 Cornell L.Q. 239, 247 (1967).
The traditional insistence that the attention of the witness be directed to the
statement on cross-examination is relaxed in favor of simply providing the
witness an opportunity to explain and the opposite party an opportunity to
examine on the statement, with no specification of any particular time or
sequence. Under this procedure, several collusive witnesses can be examined
before disclosure of a joint prior inconsistent statement. See Comment to
California Evidence Code § 770. Also, dangers of oversight are reduced. See
McCormick § 37, p. 68.

In order to allow for such eventualities as the witness becoming unavailable by the time the statement is discovered, a measure of discretion is conferred
upon the judge. Similar provisions are found in California Evidence Code
§ 770 and New Jersey Evidence Rule 22(b).

Under principles of *expression unius* the rule does not apply to impeachment by evidence of prior inconsistent conduct. The use of inconsistent statements to impeach a hearsay declaration is treated in Rule 806.

Rule 614

Note by Federal Judicial Center

The rule enacted by the Congress is the rule prescribed by the Supreme Court, amended only by substituting "court" in place of "judge," with conforming pronominal changes.

Advisory Committee's Note

Subdivision (a). While exercised more frequently in criminal than in civil cases, the authority of the judge to call witnesses is well established. McCormick § 8, p. 14; Maguire, Weinstein, et al., Cases on Evidence 303–304 (5th ed. 1965); 9 Wigmore § 2484. One reason for the practice, the old rule against impeaching one's own witness, no longer exists by virtue of Rule 607, supra. Other reasons remain, however, to justify the continuation of the practice of calling court's witnesses. The right to cross-examine, with all it implies, is assured. The tendency of juries to associate a witness with the party calling him, regardless of technical aspects of vouching, is avoided. And the judge is not imprisoned within the case as made by the parties.

Subdivision (b). The authority of the judge to question witnesses is also well established. McCormick § 8, pp. 12–13; Maguire, Weinstein, et al., Cases on Evidence 737–739 (5th ed. 1965); 3 Wigmore § 784. The authority is, of course, abused when the judge abandons his proper role and assumes that of advocate, but the manner in which interrogation should be conducted and the proper extent of its exercise are not susceptible of formulation in a rule. The omission in no sense precludes courts of review from continuing to reverse for abuse.

Subdivision (c). The provision relating to objections is designed to relieve counsel of the embarrassment attendant upon objecting to questions by the judge in the presence of the jury, while at the same time assuring that objections are made in apt time to afford the opportunity to take possible corrective measures. Compare the "automatic" objection feature of Rule 605 when the judge is called as a witness.

Rule 615

Note by Federal Judicial Center

The rule enacted by the Congress is the rule prescribed by the Supreme Court, amended only by substituting "court," in place of "judge," with conforming pronominal changes.

Advisory Committee's Note

The efficacy of excluding or sequestering witnesses has long been recognized as a means of discouraging and exposing fabrication, inaccuracy, and collusion. 6 Wigmore §§ 1837–1838. The authority of the judge is admitted, the only question being whether the matter is committed to his discretion or one of right. The rule takes the latter position. No time is specified for making the request.

Several categories of persons are excepted. (1) Exclusion of persons who are parties would raise serious problems of confrontation and due process. Under accepted practice they are not subject to exclusion. 6 Wigmore § 1841. (2) As the equivalent of the right of a natural-person party to be present, a party which is not a natural person is entitled to have a representative present. Most of the cases have involved allowing a police officer who has been in charge of an investigation to remain in court despite the fact that he will be a witness. United States v. Infanzon, 235 F.2d 318 (2d Cir.1956); Portomene v. United States, 221 F.2d 582 (5th Cir.1955); Powell v. United States, 208 F.2d 618 (6th Cir.1953); Jones v. United States, 252 F.Supp. 781 (W.D.Okl.1966). Designation of the representative by the attorney rather than by the client may at first glance appear to be an inversion of the attorney-client relationship, but it may be assumed that the attorney will follow the wishes of the client, and the solution is simple and workable. See California Evidence Code § 777. (3) The category contemplates such persons as an agent who handled the transaction being litigated or an expert needed to advise counsel in the management of the litigation. See 6 Wigmore § 1841, n. 4.

Report of Senate Committee on the Judiciary

Many district courts permit government counsel to have an investigative agent at counsel table throughout the trial although the agent is or may be a witness. The practice is permitted as an exception to the rule of exclusion and compares with the situation defense counsel finds himself in—he always has the client with him to consult during the trial. The investigative agent's presence may be extremely important to government counsel, especially when the case is complex or involves some specialized subject matter. The agent, too, having lived with the case for a long time, may be able to assist in meeting trial surprises where the best-prepared counsel would otherwise have difficulty. Yet, it would not seem the Government could often meet the burden under rule 615 of showing that the agent's presence is essential. Furthermore, it could be dangerous to use the agent as a witness as early in the case as possible, so that he might then help counsel as a nonwitness, since the agent's testimony could be needed in rebuttal. Using another, nonwitness agent from the same investigative agency would not generally meet government counsel's needs.

This problem is solved if it is clear that investigative agents are within the group specified under the second exception made in the rule, for "an officer or employee of a party which is not a natural person designated as its representative by its attorney." It is our understanding that this was the intention of the House committee. It is certainly this committee's construction of the rule.

ARTICLE VII. OPINIONS AND EXPERT TESTIMONY

Rule 701

Note by Federal Judicial Center

The rule enacted by the Congress is the rule prescribed by the Supreme Court without change.

Advisory Committee's Note

The rule retains the traditional objective of putting the trier of fact in possession of an accurate reproduction of the event.

Limitation (a) is the familiar requirement of first-hand knowledge or observation.

Limitation (b) is phrased in terms of requiring testimony to be helpful in resolving issues. Witnesses often find difficulty in expressing themselves in language which is not that of an opinion or conclusion. While the courts have made concessions in certain recurring situations, necessity as a standard for permitting opinions and conclusions has proved too elusive and too unadaptable to particular situations for purposes of satisfactory judicial administration. McCormick § 11. Moreover, the practical impossibility of determining by rule what is a "fact," demonstrated by a century of litigation of the question of what is a fact for purposes of pleading under the Field Code, extends into evidence also. 7 Wigmore § 1919. The rule assumes that the natural characteristics of the adversary system will generally lead to an acceptable result, since the detailed account carries more conviction than the broad assertion, and a lawyer can be expected to display his witness to the best advantage. If he fails to do so, cross-examination and argument will point up the weakness. See Ladd, Expert Testimony, 5 Vand.L.Rev. 414, 415–417 (1952). If, despite these considerations, attempts are made to introduce meaningless assertions which amount to little more than choosing up sides, exclusion for lack of helpfulness is called for by the rule.

The language of the rule is substantially that of Uniform Rule 56(1). Similar provisions are California Evidence Code § 800; Kansas Code of Civil Procedure § 60–456(a); New Jersey Evidence Rule 56(1).

Rule 702

Note by Federal Judicial Center

The rule enacted by the Congress is the rule prescribed by the Supreme Court without change.

Advisory Committee's Note

An intelligent evaluation of facts is often difficult or impossible without the application of some scientific, technical, or other specialized knowledge. The most common source of this knowledge is the expert witness, although there are other techniques for supplying it.

Most of the literature assumes that experts testify only in the form of opinions. The assumption is logically unfounded. The rule accordingly recognizes that an expert on the stand may give a dissertation or exposition of scientific or other principles relevant to the case, leaving the trier of fact to apply them to the facts. Since much of the criticism of expert testimony has centered upon the hypothetical question, it seems wise to recognize that opinions are not indispensable and to encourage the use of expert testimony in non-opinion form when counsel believes the trier can itself draw the requisite inference. The use of opinions is not abolished by the rule, however. It will continue to be permissible for the expert to take the further step of suggesting the inference which should be drawn from applying the specialized knowledge to the facts. See Rules 703 to 705.

Whether the situation is a proper one for the use of expert testimony is to be determined on the basis of assisting the trier. "There is no more certain test for determining when experts may be used than the common sense inquiry whether the untrained layman would be qualified to determine intelligently and to the best possible degree the particular issue without enlightenment from those having a specialized understanding of the subject involved in the dispute." Ladd, Expert Testimony, 5 Vand.L.Rev. 414, 418 (1952). When opinions are excluded, it is because they are unhelpful and therefore superfluous and a waste of time. 7 Wigmore § 1918.

The rule is broadly phrased. The fields of knowledge which may be drawn upon are not limited merely to the "scientific" and "technical" but extend to all "specialized" knowledge. Similarly, the expert is viewed, not in a narrow sense, but as a person qualified by "knowledge, skill, experience, training or education." Thus within the scope of the rule are not only experts in the strictest sense of the word, e.g. physicians, physicists, and architects, but also the large group sometimes called "skilled" witnesses, such as bankers or landowners testifying to land values.

Rule 703

Note by Federal Judicial Center

The rule enacted by the Congress is the rule prescribed by the Supreme Court without change.

Advisory Committee's Note

Facts or data upon which expert opinions are based may, under the rule, be derived from three possible sources. The first is the firsthand observation of the witness, with opinions based thereon traditionally allowed. A treating physician affords an example. Rheingold, The Basis of Medical Testimony, 15 Vand.L.Rev. 473, 489 (1962). Whether he must first relate his observations is treated in Rule 705. The second source, presentation at the trial, also reflects existing practice. The technique may be the familiar hypothetical question or having the expert attend the trial and hear the testimony establishing the facts. Problems of determining what testimony the expert relied upon, when the latter technique is employed and the testimony is in conflict, may be resolved by resort to Rule 705. The third source contemplated by the rule consists of presentation of data to the expert outside of court and other than by his own perception. In this respect the rule is designed to broaden the basis for expert opinions beyond that current in many jurisdictions and to bring the judicial practice into line with the practice of the experts themselves when not in court. Thus a physician in his own practice bases his diagnosis on information from numerous sources and of considerable variety, including statements by patients and relatives, reports and opinions from nurses, technicians and other doctors, hospital records, and X rays. Most of them are admissible in evidence, but only with the expenditure of substantial time in producing and examining various authenticating witnesses. The physician makes life-and-death decisions in reliance upon them. His validation, expertly performed and subject to cross-examination, ought to suffice for judicial purposes. Rheingold, supra, at 531; McCormick § 15. A similar provision is California Evidence Code § 801(b).

The rule also offers a more satisfactory basis for ruling upon the admissibility of public opinion poll evidence. Attention is directed to the validity of the techniques employed rather than to relatively fruitless inquiries whether hearsay is involved. See Judge Feinberg's careful analysis in Zippo Mfg. Co. v. Rogers Imports, Inc., 216 F.Supp. 670 (S.D.N.Y.1963). See also Blum et al., The Art of Opinion Research: A Lawyer's Appraisal of an Emerging Service, 24 U.Chi.L.Rev. 1 (1956); Bonynge, Trademark Surveys and Techniques and Their Use in Litigation, 48 A.B.A.J. 329 (1962); Zeisel, The Uniqueness of Survey Evidence, 45 Cornell L.Q. 322 (1960); Annot., 76 A.L.R.2d 919.

If it be feared that enlargement of permissible data may tend to break down the rules of exclusion unduly, notice should be taken that the rule requires that the facts or data "be of a type reasonably relied upon by experts in the particular field." The language would not warrant admitting in evidence the opinion of an "accidentologist" as to the point of impact in an automobile collision based on statements of bystanders, since this requirement is not satisfied. See Comment, Cal.Law Rev.Comm'n, Recommendation Proposing an Evidence Code 148–150 (1965).

Rule 704

Note by Federal Judicial Center

The rule [initially] enacted by the Congress is the rule prescribed by the Supreme Court without change. [Rule 704(b) was added by Congress in 1984.]

Advisory Committee's Note

Subdivision (a). The basic approach to opinions, lay and expert, in these rules is to admit them when helpful to the trier of fact. In order to render this approach fully effective and to allay any doubt on the subject, the so-called "ultimate issue" rule is specifically abolished by the instant rule.

The older cases often contained strictures against allowing witnesses to express opinions upon ultimate issues, as a particular aspect of the rule against opinions. The rule was unduly restrictive, difficult of application, and generally served only to deprive the trier of fact of useful information. 7 Wigmore §§ 1920, 1921; McCormick § 12. The basis usually assigned for the rule, to prevent the witness from "usurping the province of the jury," is aptly characterized as "empty rhetoric." 7 Wigmore § 1920, p. 17. Efforts to meet the felt needs of particular situations led to odd verbal circumlocutions which were said not to violate the rule. Thus a witness could express his estimate of the criminal responsibility of an accused in terms of sanity or insanity, but not in terms of ability to tell right from wrong or other more modern standard. And in cases of medical causation, witnesses were sometimes required to couch their opinions in cautious phrases of "might or could," rather than "did," though the result was to deprive many opinions of the positiveness to which they were entitled, accompanied by the hazard of a ruling of insufficiency to support a verdict. In other instances the rule was simply disregarded, and, as concessions to need, opinions were allowed upon such matters as intoxication, speed, handwriting, and value, although more precise coincidence with an ultimate issue would scarcely be possible.

Many modern decisions illustrate the trend to abandon the rule completely. People v. Wilson, 25 Cal.2d 341, 153 P.2d 720 (1944), whether abortion necessary to save life of patient; Clifford-Jacobs Forging Co. v. Industrial Comm., 19 Ill.2d 236, 166 N.E.2d 582 (1960), medical causation; Dowling v. L.H. Shattuck, Inc., 91 N.H. 234, 17 A.2d 529 (1941), proper method of shoring ditch; Schweig-

er v. Solbeck, 191 Or. 454, 230 P.2d 195 (1951), cause of landslide. In each
instance the opinion was allowed.

The abolition of the ultimate issue rule does not lower the bars so as to
admit all opinions. Under Rules 701 and 702, opinions must be helpful to the
trier of fact, and Rule 403 provides for exclusion of evidence which wastes time.
These provisions afford ample assurances against the admission of opinions
which would merely tell the jury what result to reach, somewhat in the manner
of the oath-helpers of an earlier day. They also stand ready to exclude opinions
phrased in terms of inadequately explored legal criteria. Thus the question,
"Did T have capacity to make a will?" would be excluded, while the question,
"Did T have sufficient mental capacity to know the nature and extent of his
property and the natural objects of his bounty and to formulate a rational
scheme of distribution?" would be allowed. McCormick § 12.

For similar provisions see Uniform Rule 56(4); California Evidence Code
§ 805; Kansas Code of Civil Procedure § 60–456(d); New Jersey Evidence Rule
56(3).

Rule 704(b)

Report of the Senate Committee on the Judiciary (1984)

The purpose of this amendment is to eliminate the confusing spectacle of
competing expert witnesses testifying to directly contradictory conclusions as to
the ultimate legal issue to be found by the trier of fact. Under this proposal,
expert psychiatric testimony would be limited to presenting and explaining
their diagnoses, such as whether the defendant had a severe mental disease or
defect and what the characteristics of such a disease or defect, if any, may have
been. The basis for this limitation on expert testimony in insanity cases is ably
stated by the American Psychiatric Association:

> [I]t is clear that psychiatrists are experts in medicine, not the law.
> As such, it is clear that the psychiatrist's first obligation and expertise
> in the courtroom is to "do psychiatry," i.e., to present medical informa-
> tion and opinion about the defendant's mental state and motivation
> and to explain in detail the reason for his medical-psychiatric conclu-
> sions. When, however, "ultimate issue" questions are formulated by
> the law and put to the expert witness who must then say "yea" or
> "nay," then the expert witness is required to make a leap in logic. He
> no longer addresses himself to medical concepts but instead must infer
> or intuit what is in fact unspeakable, namely, the probable relationship
> between medical concepts and legal or moral constructs such as free
> will. These impermissible leaps in logic made by expert witnesses
> confuse the jury. [Footnote omitted.] Juries thus find themselves
> listening to conclusory and seemingly contradictory psychiatric testi-
> mony that defendants are either "sane" or "insane" or that they do or
> do not meet the relevant legal test for insanity. This state of affairs
> does considerable injustice to psychiatry and, we believe, possibly to
> criminal defendants. In fact, in many criminal insanity trials both
> prosecution and defense psychiatrists do agree about the nature and
> even the extent of mental disorder exhibited by the defendant at the
> time of the act.
>
> Psychiatrists, of course, must be permitted to testify fully about
> the defendant's diagnosis, mental state and motivation (in clinical and
> common sense terms) at the time of the alleged act so as to permit the

jury or judge to reach the ultimate conclusion about which they and only they are expert. Determining whether a criminal defendant was legally insane is a matter for legal fact-finders, not for experts.

Moreover, the rationale for precluding ultimate opinion psychiatric testimony extends beyond the insanity defense to any ultimate mental state of the defendant that is relevant to the legal conclusion sought to be proven. The Committee has fashioned its Rule 704 provision to reach all such "ultimate" issues, e.g., premeditation in a homicide case, or lack of predisposition in entrapment.

Rule 705

Note by Federal Judicial Center

The rule enacted by the Congress is the rule prescribed by the Supreme Court, amended only by substituting "court" in place of "judge."

Advisory Committee's Note

The hypothetical question has been the target of a great deal of criticism as encouraging partisan bias, affording an opportunity for summing up in the middle of the case, and as complex and time consuming. Ladd, Expert Testimony, 5 Vand.L.Rev. 414, 426–427 (1952). While the rule allows counsel to make disclosure of the underlying facts or data as a preliminary to the giving of an expert opinion, if he chooses, the instances in which he is required to do so are reduced. This is true whether the expert bases his opinion on data furnished him at secondhand or observed by him at firsthand.

The elimination of the requirement of preliminary disclosure at the trial of underlying facts or data has a long background of support. In 1937 the Commissioners on Uniform State Laws incorporated a provision to this effect in their Model Expert Testimony Act, which furnished the basis for Uniform Rules 57 and 58. Rule 4515, N.Y. CPLR (McKinney 1963), provides:

"Unless the court orders otherwise, questions calling for the opinion of an expert witness need not be hypothetical in form, and the witness may state his opinion and reasons without first specifying the data upon which it is based. Upon cross-examination, he may be required to specify the data * * *."

See also California Evidence Code § 802; Kansas Code of Civil Procedure §§ 60–456, 60–457; New Jersey Evidence Rules 57, 58.

If the objection is made that leaving it to the cross-examiner to bring out the supporting data is essentially unfair, the answer is that he is under no compulsion to bring out any facts or data except those unfavorable to the opinion. The answer assumes that the cross-examiner has the advance knowledge which is essential for effective cross-examination. This advance knowledge has been afforded, though imperfectly, by the traditional foundation requirement. Rule 26(b)(4) of the Rules of Civil Procedure, as revised, provides for substantial discovery in this area, obviating in large measure the obstacles which have been raised in some instances to discovery of findings, underlying data, and even the identity of the experts. Friedenthal, Discovery and Use of an Adverse Party's Expert Information, 14 Stan.L.Rev. 455 (1962).

These safeguards are reinforced by the discretionary power of the judge to require preliminary disclosure in any event.

Rule 706

Note by Federal Judicial Center

The rule enacted by the Congress is the rule prescribed by the Supreme Court, amended by substituting "court" in place of "judge," with conforming pronominal changes, and, in subdivision (b), by substituting the phrase "and civil actions and proceedings" in place of "and cases" before "involving" in the second sentence.

Advisory Committee's Note

The practice of shopping for experts, the venality of some experts, and the reluctance of many reputable experts to involve themselves in litigation, have been matters of deep concern. Though the contention is made that court appointed experts acquire an aura of infallibility to which they are not entitled, Levy, Impartial Medical Testimony—Revisited, 34 Temple L.Q. 416 (1961), the trend is increasingly to provide for their use. While experience indicates that actual appointment is a relatively infrequent occurrence, the assumption may be made that the availability of the procedure in itself decreases the need for resorting to it. The ever-present possibility that the judge *may* appoint an expert in a given case must inevitably exert a sobering effect on the expert witness of a party and upon the person utilizing his services.

The inherent power of a trial judge to appoint an expert of his own choosing is virtually unquestioned. Scott v. Spanjer Bros., Inc., 298 F.2d 928 (2d Cir.1962); Danville Tobacco Assn. v. Bryant-Buckner Associates, Inc., 333 F.2d 202 (4th Cir.1964); Sink, The Unused Power of a Federal Judge to Call His Own Expert Witnesses, 29 S.Cal.L.Rev. 195 (1956); 2 Wigmore § 563, 9 id. § 2484; Annot., 95 A.L.R.2d 383. Hence the problem becomes largely one of detail.

The New York plan is well known and is described in Report by Special Committee of the Association of the Bar of the City of New York: Impartial Medical Testimony (1956). On recommendation of the Section of Judicial Administration, local adoption of an impartial medical plan was endorsed by the American Bar Association. 82 A.B.A.Rep. 184–185 (1957). Descriptions and analyses of plans in effect in various parts of the country are found in Van Dusen, A United States District Judge's View of the Impartial Medical Expert System, 32 F.R.D. 498 (1963); Wick and Kightlinger, Impartial Medical Testimony Under the Federal Civil Rules: A Tale of Three Doctors, 34 Ins. Counsel J. 115 (1967); and numerous articles collected in Klein, Judicial Administration and the Legal Profession 393 (1963). Statutes and rules include California Evidence Code §§ 730–733; Illinois Supreme Court Rule 215(d), Ill.Rev.Stat. 1969, c. 110A, § 215(d); Burns Indiana Stats.1956, § 9–1702; Wisconsin Stats. Annot.1958, § 957.27.

In the federal practice, a comprehensive scheme for court appointed experts was initiated with the adoption of Rule 28 of the Federal Rules of Criminal Procedure in 1946. The Judicial Conference of the United States in 1953 considered court appointed experts in civil cases, but only with respect to whether they should be compensated from public funds, a proposal which was rejected. Report of the Judicial Conference of the United States 23 (1953). The present rule expands the practice to include civil cases.

Subdivision (a) is based on Rule 28 of the Federal Rules of Criminal Procedure, with a few changes, mainly in the interest of clarity. Language has been added to provide specifically for the appointment either on motion of a party or on the judge's own motion. A provision subjecting the court appointed expert to deposition procedures has been incorporated. The rule has been revised to make definite the right of any party, including the party calling him, to cross-examine.

Subdivision (b) combines the present provision for compensation in criminal cases with what seems to be a fair and feasible handling of civil cases, originally found in the Model Act and carried from there into Uniform Rule 60. See also California Evidence Code §§ 730–731. The special provision for Fifth Amendment compensation cases is designed to guard against reducing constitutionally guaranteed just compensation by requiring the recipient to pay costs. See Rule 71A(*l*) of the Rules of Civil Procedure.

Subdivision (c) seems to be essential if the use of court appointed experts is to be fully effective. Uniform Rule 61 so provides.

Subdivision (d) is in essence the last sentence of Rule 28(a) of the Federal Rules of Criminal Procedure.

Advisory Committee's Note

Introductory Note: The Hearsay Problem

The factors to be considered in evaluating the testimony of a witness are perception, memory, and narration. Morgan, Hearsay Dangers and the Application of the Hearsay Concept, 62 Harv.L.Rev. 177 (1948), Selected Writings on Evidence and Trial 764, 765 (Fryer ed. 1957); Shientag, Cross-Examination—A Judge's Viewpoint, 3 Record 12 (1948); Strahorn, A Reconsideration of the Hearsay Rule and Admissions, 85 U.Pa.L.Rev. 484, 485 (1937), Selected Writings, supra, 756, 757; Weinstein, Probative Force of Hearsay, 46 Iowa L.Rev. 331 (1961). Sometimes a fourth is added, sincerity, but in fact it seems merely to be an aspect of the three already mentioned.

In order to encourage the witness to do his best with respect to each of these factors, and to expose any inaccuracies which may enter in, the Anglo-American tradition has evolved three conditions under which witnesses will ideally be required to testify: (1) under oath, (2) in the personal presence of the trier of fact, (3) subject to cross-examination.

(1) Standard procedure calls for the swearing of witnesses. While the practice is perhaps less effective than in an earlier time, no disposition to relax the requirement is apparent, other than to allow affirmation by persons with scruples against taking oaths.

(2) The demeanor of the witness traditionally has been believed to furnish trier and opponent with valuable clues. Universal Camera Corp. v. N.L.R.B., 340 U.S. 474, 495–496, 71 S.Ct. 456, 95 L.Ed. 456 (1951); Sahm, Demeanor Evidence: Elusive and Intangible Imponderables, 47 A.B.A.J. 580 (1961), quoting numerous authorities. The witness himself will probably be impressed with the solemnity of the occasion and the possibility of public disgrace. Willingness to falsify may reasonably become more difficult in the presence of the person against whom directed. Rules 26 and 43(a) of the Federal Rules of Criminal and Civil Procedure, respectively, include the general requirement that testimony be taken orally in open court. The Sixth Amendment right of confrontation is a manifestation of these beliefs and attitudes.

(3) Emphasis on the basis of the hearsay rule today tends to center upon the condition of cross-examination. All may not agree with Wigmore that

cross-examination is "beyond doubt the greatest legal engine ever invented for the discovery of truth," but all will agree with his statement that it has become a "vital feature" of the Anglo-American system. 5 Wigmore § 1367, p. 29. The belief, or perhaps hope, that cross-examination is effective in exposing imperfections of perception, memory, and narration is fundamental. Morgan, Foreword to Model Code of Evidence 37 (1942).

The logic of the preceding discussion might suggest that no testimony be received unless in full compliance with the three ideal conditions. No one advocates this position. Common sense tells that much evidence which is not given under the three conditions may be inherently superior to much that is. Moreover, when the choice is between evidence which is less than best and no evidence at all, only clear folly would dictate an across-the-board policy of doing without. The problem thus resolves itself into effecting a sensible accommodation between these considerations and the desirability of giving testimony under the ideal conditions.

The solution evolved by the common law has been a general rule excluding hearsay but subject to numerous exceptions under circumstances supposed to furnish guarantees of trustworthiness. Criticisms of this scheme are that it is bulky and complex, fails to screen good from bad hearsay realistically, and inhibits the growth of the law of evidence.

Since no one advocates excluding all hearsay, three possible solutions may be considered: (1) abolish the rule against hearsay and admit all hearsay; (2) admit hearsay possessing sufficient probative force, but with procedural safeguards; (3) revise the present system of class exceptions.

(1) Abolition of the hearsay rule would be the simplest solution. The effect would not be automatically to abolish the giving of testimony under ideal conditions. If the declarant were available, compliance with the ideal conditions would be optional with either party. Thus the proponent could call the declarant as a witness as a form of presentation more impressive than his hearsay statement. Or the opponent could call the declarant to be cross-examined upon his statement. This is the tenor of Uniform Rule 63(1), admitting the hearsay declaration of a person "who is present at the hearing and available for cross-examination." Compare the treatment of declarations of available declarants in Rule 801(d)(1) of the instant rules. If the declarant were unavailable, a rule of free admissibility would make no distinctions in terms of degrees of noncompliance with the ideal conditions and would exact no quid pro quo in the form of assurances of trustworthiness. Rule 503 of the Model Code did exactly that, providing for the admissibility of any hearsay declaration by an unavailable declarant, finding support in the Massachusetts act of 1898, enacted at the instance of Thayer, Mass.Gen.L.1932, c. 233 § 65, and in the English act of 1938, St.1938, c. 28, Evidence. Both are limited to civil cases. The draftsmen of the Uniform Rules chose a less advanced and more conventional position. Comment, Uniform Rule 63. The present Advisory Committee has been unconvinced of the wisdom of abandoning the traditional requirement of some particular assurance of credibility as a condition precedent to admitting the hearsay declaration of an unavailable declarant.

In criminal cases, the Sixth Amendment requirement of confrontation would no doubt move into a large part of the area presently occupied by the hearsay rule in the event of the abolition of the latter. The resultant split between civil and criminal evidence is regarded as an undesirable development.

(2) Abandonment of the system of class exceptions in favor of individual treatment in the setting of the particular case, accompanied by procedural

safeguards, has been impressively advocated. Weinstein, The Probative Force of Hearsay, 46 Iowa L.Rev. 331 (1961). Admissibility would be determined by weighing the probative force of the evidence against the possibility of prejudice, waste of time, and the availability of more satisfactory evidence. The bases of the traditional hearsay exceptions would be helpful in assessing probative force. Ladd, The Relationship of the Principles of Exclusionary Rules of Evidence to the Problem of Proof, 18 Minn.L.Rev. 506 (1934). Procedural safeguards would consist of notice of intention to use hearsay, free comment by the judge on the weight of the evidence, and a greater measure of authority in both trial and appellate judges to deal with evidence on the basis of weight. The Advisory Committee has rejected this approach to hearsay as involving too great a measure of judicial discretion, minimizing the predictability of rulings, enhancing the difficulties of preparation for trial, adding a further element to the already over-complicated congeries of pretrial procedures, and requiring substantially different rules for civil and criminal cases. The only way in which the probative force of hearsay differs from the probative force of other testimony is in the absence of oath, demeanor, and cross-examination as aids in determining credibility. For a judge to exclude evidence because he does not believe it has been described as "altogether atypical, extraordinary. * * *" Chadbourn, Bentham and the Hearsay Rule—A Benthamic View of Rule 63(4) (c) of the Uniform Rules of Evidence, 75 Harv.L.Rev. 932, 947 (1962).

(3) The approach to hearsay in these rules is that of the common law, i.e., a general rule excluding hearsay, with exceptions under which evidence is not required to be excluded even though hearsay. The traditional hearsay exceptions are drawn upon for the exceptions, collected under two rules, one dealing with situations where availability of the declarant is regarded as immaterial and the other with those where unavailability is made a condition to the admission of the hearsay statement. Each of the two rules concludes with a provision for hearsay statements not within one of the specified exceptions "but having comparable [equivalent] circumstantial guarantees of trustworthiness." Rules 803(24) and 804(b)(6)[5]. This plan is submitted as calculated to encourage growth and development in this area of the law, while conserving the values and experience of the past as a guide to the future.

Confrontation and Due Process

Until very recently, decisions invoking the confrontation clause of the Sixth Amendment were surprisingly few, a fact probably explainable by the former inapplicability of the clause to the states and by the hearsay rule's occupancy of much the same ground. The pattern which emerges from the earlier cases invoking the clause is substantially that of the hearsay rule, applied to criminal cases: an accused is entitled to have the witnesses against him testify under oath, in the presence of himself and trier, subject to cross-examination; yet considerations of public policy and necessity require the recognition of such exceptions as dying declarations and former testimony of unavailable witnesses. Mattox v. United States, 156 U.S. 237, 15 S.Ct. 337, 39 L.Ed. 409 (1895); Motes v. United States, 178 U.S. 458, 20 S.Ct. 993, 44 L.Ed. 1150 (1900); Delaney v. United States, 263 U.S. 586, 44 S.Ct. 206, 68 L.Ed. 462 (1924). Beginning with Snyder v. Massachusetts, 291 U.S. 97, 54 S.Ct. 330, 78 L.Ed. 674 (1934), the Court began to speak of confrontation as an aspect of procedural due process, thus extending its applicability to state cases and to federal cases other than criminal. The language of *Snyder* was that of an elastic concept of hearsay. The deportation case of Bridges v. Wixon, 326 U.S. 135, 65 S.Ct. 1443, 89 L.Ed. 2103 (1945), may be read broadly as imposing a

strictly construed right of confrontation in all kinds of cases or narrowly as the
product of a failure of the Immigration and Naturalization Service to follow its
own rules. In re Oliver, 333 U.S. 257, 68 S.Ct. 499, 92 L.Ed. 682 (1948), ruled
that cross-examination was essential to due process in a state contempt proceeding, but in United States v. Nugent, 346 U.S. 1, 73 S.Ct. 991, 97 L.Ed. 1417
(1953), the court held that it was not an essential aspect of a "hearing" for a
conscientious objector under the Selective Service Act. Stein v. New York, 346
U.S. 156, 196, 73 S.Ct. 1077, 97 L.Ed. 1522 (1953), disclaimed any purpose to
read the hearsay rule into the Fourteenth Amendment, but in Greene v.
McElroy, 360 U.S. 474, 79 S.Ct. 1400, 3 L.Ed.2d 1377 (1959), revocation of
security clearance without confrontation and cross-examination was held unauthorized, and a similar result was reached in Willner v. Committee on Character, 373 U.S. 96, 83 S.Ct. 1175, 10 L.Ed.2d 224 (1963). Ascertaining the
constitutional dimensions of the confrontation-hearsay aggregate against the
background of these cases is a matter of some difficulty, yet the general pattern
is at least not inconsistent with that of the hearsay rule.

In 1965 the confrontation clause was held applicable to the states. Pointer
v. Texas, 380 U.S. 400, 85 S.Ct. 1065, 13 L.Ed.2d 923 (1965). Prosecution use of
former testimony given at a preliminary hearing where petitioner was not
represented by counsel was a violation of the clause. The same result would
have followed under conventional hearsay doctrine read in the light of a
constitutional right to counsel, and nothing in the opinion suggests any difference in essential outline between the hearsay rule and the right of confrontation. In the companion case of Douglas v. Alabama, 380 U.S. 415, 85 S.Ct. 1074,
13 L.Ed.2d 934 (1965), however, the result reached by applying the confrontation clause is one reached less readily via the hearsay rule. A confession
implicating petitioner was put before the jury by reading it to the witness in
portions and asking if he made that statement. The witness refused to answer
on grounds of self-incrimination. The result, said the Court, was to deny cross-
examination, and hence confrontation. True, it could broadly be said that the
confession was a hearsay statement which for all practical purposes was put in
evidence. Yet a more easily accepted explanation of the opinion is that its real
thrust was in the direction of curbing undesirable prosecutorial behavior,
rather than merely applying rules of exclusion, and that the confrontation
clause was the means selected to achieve this end. Comparable facts and a like
result appeared in Brookhart v. Janis, 384 U.S. 1, 86 S.Ct. 1245, 16 L.Ed.2d 314
(1966).

The pattern suggested in *Douglas* was developed further and more distinct-
ly in a pair of cases at the end of the 1966 term. United States v. Wade, 388
U.S. 218, 87 S.Ct. 1926, 18 L.Ed.2d 1149 (1967), and Gilbert v. California, 388
U.S. 263, 87 S.Ct. 1951, 18 L.Ed.2d 1178 (1967), hinged upon practices followed
in identifying accused persons before trial. This pretrial identification was said
to be so decisive an aspect of the case that accused was entitled to have counsel
present; a pretrial identification made in the absence of counsel was not itself
receivable in evidence and, in addition, might fatally infect a courtroom
identification. The presence of counsel at the earlier identification was described as a necessary prerequisite for "a meaningful confrontation at trial."
United States v. Wade, supra, 388 U.S. at p. 236, 87 S.Ct. at p. 1937. *Wade*
involved no evidence of the fact of a prior identification and hence was not
susceptible of being decided on hearsay grounds. In *Gilbert,* witnesses did
testify to an earlier identification, readily classifiable as hearsay under a fairly
strict view of what constitutes hearsay. The Court, however, carefully avoided
basing the decision on the hearsay ground, choosing confrontation instead. 388

U.S. 263, 272, n. 3, 87 S.Ct. 1951. See also Parker v. Gladden, 385 U.S. 363, 87 S.Ct. 468, 17 L.Ed.2d 420 (1966), holding that the right of confrontation was violated when the bailiff made prejudicial statements to jurors, and Note, 75 Yale L.J. 1434 (1966).

Under the earlier cases, the confrontation clause may have been little more than a constitutional embodiment of the hearsay rule, even including traditional exceptions but with some room for expanding them along similar lines. But under the recent cases the impact of the clause clearly extends beyond the confines of the hearsay rule. These considerations have led the Advisory Committee to conclude that a hearsay rule can function usefully as an adjunct to the confrontation right in constitutional areas and independently in nonconstitutional areas. In recognition of the separateness of the confrontation clause and the hearsay rule, and to avoid inviting collisions between them or between the hearsay rule and other exclusionary principles, the exceptions set forth in Rules 803 and 804 are stated in terms of exemption from the general exclusionary mandate of the hearsay rule, rather than in positive terms of admissibility. See Uniform Rule 63(1) to (31) and California Evidence Code §§ 1200–1340.

ARTICLE VIII. HEARSAY

Rule 801

Note by Federal Judicial Center

The rule enacted by the Congress is the rule prescribed by the Supreme Court, with two amendments to subdivision (d)(1). The first of these amendments inserted in item (A), after "testimony," the phrase "and was given under oath subject to the penalty of perjury at a trial, hearing, or other proceeding, or in a deposition." The other amendment consisted of the deletion of item (C), which dealt with prior statements of identification. The reasons for these amendments are stated in the Report of the House Committee on the Judiciary, the Report of the Senate Committee on the Judiciary, and the Conference Report, set forth below.

Advisory Committee's Note

Subdivision (a). The definition of "statement" assumes importance because the term is used in the definition of hearsay in subdivision (c). The effect of the definition of "statement" is to exclude from the operation of the hearsay rule all evidence of conduct, verbal or nonverbal, not intended as an assertion. The key to the definition is that nothing is an assertion unless intended to be one.

It can scarcely be doubted that an assertion made in words is intended by the declarant to be an assertion. Hence verbal assertions readily fall into the category of "statement." Whether nonverbal conduct should be regarded as a statement for purposes of defining hearsay requires further consideration. Some nonverbal conduct, such as the act of pointing to identify a suspect in a lineup, is clearly the equivalent of words, assertive in nature, and to be regarded as a statement. Other nonverbal conduct, however, may be offered as evidence that the person acted as he did because of his belief in the existence of the condition sought to be proved, from which belief the existence of the condition may be inferred. This sequence is, arguably, in effect an assertion of the existence of the condition and hence properly includable within the hearsay concept. See Morgan, Hearsay Dangers and the Application of the Hearsay Concept, 62 Harv.L.Rev. 177, 214, 217 (1948), and the elaboration in Finman, Implied Assertions as Hearsay: Some Criticisms of the Uniform Rules of Evidence, 14 Stan.L.Rev. 682 (1962). Admittedly evidence of this character is untested with respect to the perception, memory, and narration (or their equivalents) of the actor, but the Advisory Committee is of the view that these dangers are minimal in the absence of an intent to assert and do not justify the loss of the evidence on hearsay grounds. No class of evidence is free of the possibility of fabrication, but the likelihood is less with nonverbal than with assertive verbal conduct. The situations giving rise to the nonverbal conduct are such as virtually to eliminate questions of sincerity. Motivation, the nature of the conduct, and the presence or absence of reliance will bear heavily upon the weight to be given the evidence. Falknor, The "Hear-Say" Rule as a "See-Do" Rule: Evidence of Conduct, 33 Rocky Mt.L.Rev. 133 (1961). Similar considerations govern nonassertive verbal conduct and verbal conduct which is assertive but offered as a basis for inferring something other than the matter asserted, also excluded from the definition of hearsay by the language of subdivision (c).

When evidence of conduct is offered on the theory that it is not a statement, and hence not hearsay, a preliminary determination will be required to determine whether an assertion is intended. The rule is so worded as to place the burden upon the party claiming that the intention existed; ambiguous and doubtful cases will be resolved against him and in favor of admissibility. The determination involves no greater difficulty than many other preliminary questions of fact. Maguire, The Hearsay System: Around and Through the Thicket, 14 Vand.L.Rev. 741, 765–767 (1961).

For similar approaches, see Uniform Rule 62(1); California Evidence Code §§ 225, 1200; Kansas Code of Civil Procedure § 60–459(a); New Jersey Evidence Rule 62(1).

Subdivision (c). The definition follows along familiar lines in including only statements offered to prove the truth of the matter asserted. McCormick § 225; 5 Wigmore § 1361, 6 id. § 1766. If the significance of an offered statement lies solely in the fact that it was made, no issue is raised as to the truth of anything asserted, and the statement is not hearsay. Emich Motors Corp. v. General Motors Corp., 181 F.2d 70 (7th Cir.1950), rev'd on other grounds 340 U.S. 558, 71 S.Ct. 408, 95 L.Ed. 534, letters of complaint from customers offered as a reason for cancellation of dealer's franchise, to rebut contention that franchise was revoked for refusal to finance sales through affiliated finance company. The effect is to exclude from hearsay the entire category of "verbal acts" and "verbal parts of an act," in which the statement itself affects the legal rights of the parties or is a circumstance bearing on conduct affecting their rights.

The definition of hearsay must, of course, be read with reference to the definition of statement set forth in subdivision (a).

Testimony given by a witness in the course of court proceedings is excluded since there is compliance with all the ideal conditions for testifying.

Subdivision (d). Several types of statements which would otherwise literally fall within the definition are expressly excluded from it:

(1) *Prior statement by witness.* Considerable controversy has attended the question whether a prior out-of-court statement by a person now available for cross-examination concerning it, under oath and in the presence of the trier of

fact, should be classed as hearsay. If the witness admits on the stand that he made the statement and that it was true, he adopts the statement and there is no hearsay problem. The hearsay problem arises when the witness on the stand denies having made the statement or admits having made it but denies its truth. The argument in favor of treating these latter statements as hearsay is based upon the ground that the conditions of oath, cross-examination, and demeanor observation did not prevail at the time the statement was made and cannot adequately be supplied by the later examination. The logic of the situation is troublesome. So far as concerns the oath, its mere presence has never been regarded as sufficient to remove a statement from the hearsay category, and it receives much less emphasis than cross-examination as a truth-compelling device. While strong expressions are found to the effect that no conviction can be had or important right taken away on the basis of statements not made under fear of prosecution for perjury, Bridges v. Wixon, 326 U.S. 135, 65 S.Ct. 1443, 89 L.Ed. 2103 (1945), the fact is that, of the many common law exceptions to the hearsay rule, only that for reported testimony has required the statement to have been made under oath.

[It should be noted, however, that rule 801(d)(1)(A), as enacted by the Congress, requires that a prior inconsistent statement have been made under oath.] Nor is it satisfactorily explained why cross-examination cannot be conducted subsequently with success. The decisions contending most vigorously for its inadequacy in fact demonstrate quite thorough exploration of the weaknesses and doubts attending the earlier statement. State v. Saporen, 205 Minn. 358, 285 N.W. 898 (1939); Ruhala v. Roby, 379 Mich. 102, 150 N.W.2d 146 (1967); People v. Johnson, 68 Cal.2d 646, 68 Cal.Rptr. 599, 441 P.2d 111 (1968). In respect to demeanor, as Judge Learned Hand observed in Di Carlo v. United States, 6 F.2d 364 (2d Cir.1925), when the jury decides that the truth is not what the witness says now, but what he said before, they are still deciding from what they see and hear in court. The bulk of the case law nevertheless has been against allowing prior statements of witnesses to be used generally as substantive evidence. Most of the writers and Uniform Rule 63(1) have taken the opposite position.

The position taken by the Advisory Committee in formulating this part of the rule is founded upon an unwillingness to countenance the general use of prior prepared statements as substantive evidence, but with a recognition that particular circumstances call for a contrary result. The judgment is one more of experience than of logic. The rule requires in each instance, as a general safeguard, that the declarant actually testify as a witness, and it then enumerates three situations in which the statement is excepted from the category of hearsay. Compare Uniform Rule 63(1) which allows any out-of-court statement of a declarant who is present at the trial and available for cross-examination.

(A) Prior inconsistent statements traditionally have been admissible to impeach but not as substantive evidence. Under the rule they are substantive evidence. As has been said by the California Law Revision Commission with respect to a similar provision:

"Section 1235 admits inconsistent statements of witnesses because the dangers against which the hearsay rule is designed to protect are largely nonexistent. The declarant is in court and may be examined and cross-examined in regard to his statements and their subject matter. In many cases the inconsistent statement is more likely to be true than the testimony of the witness at the trial because it was made nearer in time to the matter to which it relates and is less likely to be influenced by the controversy that gave rise to the litigation. The trier of fact has the declarant before it and can observe his demeanor and the nature of his testimony as he denies or tries to explain away the inconsistency. Hence, it is in as good a position to determine the truth or falsity of the prior statement as it is to determine the truth or falsity of the inconsistent testimony given in court. Moreover, Section 1235 will provide a party with desirable protection against the 'turncoat' witness who changes his story on the stand and deprives the party calling him of evidence essential to his case." Comment, California Evidence Code § 1235. See also McCormick § 39. The Advisory Committee finds these views more convincing than those expressed in People v. Johnson, 68 Cal.2d 646, 68 Cal.Rptr. 599, 441 P.2d 111 (1968). The constitutionality of the Advisory Committee's view was upheld in California v. Green, 399 U.S. 149, 90 S.Ct. 1930, 26 L.Ed.2d 489 (1970). Moreover, the requirement that the statement be inconsistent with the testimony given assures a thorough exploration of both versions while the witness is on the stand and bars any general and indiscriminate use of previously prepared statements.

[It should be noted that the rule as enacted by the Congress also requires that the prior inconsistent statements have been made under oath.]

Report of House Committee on the Judiciary

Present federal law, except in the Second Circuit, permits the use of prior inconsistent statements of a witness for impeachment only. Rule 801(d)(1) as proposed by the Court would have permitted all such statements to be admissible as substantive evidence, an approach followed by a small but growing number of State jurisdictions and recently held constitutional in California v. Green, 399 U.S. 149 (1970). Although there was some support expressed for the Court Rule, based largely on the need to counteract the effect of witness intimidation in criminal cases, the Committee decided to adopt a compromise version of the Rule similar to the position of the Second Circuit. The Rule as amended draws a distinction between types of prior inconsistent statements (other than statements of identification of a person made after perceiving him which are currently admissible, see United States v. Anderson, 406 F.2d 719, 720 (4th Cir.), cert. denied, 395 U.S. 967 (1969)) and allows only those made while the declarant was subject to cross-examination at a trail [trial] or hearing or in a deposition, to be admissible for their truth. Compare United States v. DeSisto, 329 F.2d 929 (2nd Cir.), cert. denied, 377 U.S. 979 (1964); United States v. Cunningham, 446 F.2d 194 (2nd Cir.1971) (restricting the admissibility of prior inconsistent statements as substantive evidence to those made under oath in a formal proceeding, but not requiring that there have been an opportunity for cross-examination). The rationale for the Committee's decision is that (1) unlike in most other situations involving unsworn or oral statements, there can be no dispute as to whether the prior statement was made; and (2) the context of a formal proceeding, an oath, and the opportunity for cross-examination provide firm additional assurances of the reliability of the prior statement.

Report of Senate Committee on the Judiciary

Rule 801 defines what is and what is not hearsay for the purpose of admitting a prior statement as substantive evidence. A prior statement of a witness at a trial or hearing which is inconsistent with his testimony is, of course, always admissible for the purpose of impeaching the witness' credibility.

As submitted by the Supreme Court, subdivision (d)(1)(A) made admissible as substantive evidence the prior statement of a witness inconsistent with his present testimony.

The House severely limited the admissibility of prior inconsistent statements by adding a requirement that the prior statement must have been subject to cross-examination, thus precluding even the use of grand jury statements. The requirement that the prior statement must have been subject to cross-examination appears unnecessary since this rule comes into play only when the witness testifies in the present trial. At that time, he is on the stand and can explain an earlier position and be cross-examined as to both.

The requirement that the statement be under oath also appears unnecessary. Notwithstanding the absence of an oath contemporaneous with the statement, the witness, when on the stand, qualifying or denying the prior statement, is under oath. In any event, of all the many recognized exceptions to the hearsay rule, only one (former testimony) requires that the out-of-court statement have been made under oath. With respect to the lack of evidence of the demeanor of the witness at the time of the prior statement, it would be difficult to improve upon Judge Learned Hand's observation that when the jury decides that the truth is not what the witness says now but what he said before, they are still deciding from what they see and hear in court.[1]

The rule as submitted by the Court has positive advantages. The prior statement was made nearer in time to the events, when memory was fresher and intervening influences had not been brought into play. A realistic method is provided for dealing with the turncoat witness who changes his story on the stand.[2]

New Jersey, California, and Utah have adopted a rule similar to this one; and Nevada, New Mexico, and Wisconsin have adopted the identical Federal rule.

For all of these reasons, we think the House amendment should be rejected and the rule as submitted by the Supreme Court reinstated.[3]

Conference Report

The House bill provides that a statement is not hearsay if the declarant testifies and is subject to cross-examination concerning the statement and if the statement is inconsistent with his testimony and was given under oath subject to cross-examination and subject to the penalty of perjury at a trial or hearing or in a deposition. The Senate amendment drops the requirement that the prior statement be given under oath subject to cross-examination and subject to the penalty of perjury at a trial or hearing or in a deposition.

The Conference adopts the Senate amendment with an amendment, so that the rule now requires that the prior inconsistent statement be given under oath subject to the penalty of perjury at a trial, hearing, or other proceeding, or in a deposition. The rule as adopted covers statements before a grand jury. Prior

1. Di Carlo v. United States, 6 F.2d 364 (2d Cir.1925).

2. See Comment, California Evidence Code § 1235; McCormick, Evidence, § 38 (2nd ed. 1972).

3. It would appear that some of the opposition to this Rule is based on a concern that a person could be convicted solely upon evidence admissible under this Rule. The Rule, however, is not addressed to the question of the sufficiency of evidence to send a case to the jury, but merely as to its admissibility. Factual circumstances could well arise where, if this were the sole evidence, dismissal would be appropriate.

inconsistent statements may, of course, be used for impeaching the credibility
of a witness.   When the prior inconsistent statement is one made by a
defendant in a criminal case, it is covered by Rule 801(d)(2).

Advisory Committee's Note

(B) Prior consistent statements traditionally have been admissible to rebut
charges of recent fabrication or improper influence or motive but not as
substantive evidence. Under the rule they are substantive evidence. The prior
statement is consistent with the testimony given on the stand, and, if the
opposite party wishes to open the door for its admission in evidence, no sound
reason is apparent why it should not be received generally.

Report of Senate Committee on the Judiciary

As submitted by the Supreme Court and as passed by the House, subdivision (d)(1)(c)[C] of rule 801 made admissible the prior statement identifying a
person made after perceiving him. The committee decided to delete this
provision because of the concern that a person could be convicted solely upon
evidence admissible under this subdivision.

Conference Report

The House bill provides that a statement is not hearsay if the declarant
testifies and is subject to cross-examination concerning the statement and the
statement is one of identification of a person made after perceiving him. The
Senate amendment eliminated this provision.

The Conference adopts the Senate amendment.

Editorial Note

Subdivision (d)(1)(C) was included in the rule as prescribed by the Supreme
Court but was deleted by the Congress in enacting the rules, as indicated in the
Conference Report above. However, the subdivision was restored by Act
effective Oct. 31, 1975. Therefore the Advisory Committee's Note to the
subdivision is now reprinted below.

Advisory Committee's Note

(C) The admission of evidence of identification finds substantial support,
although it falls beyond a doubt in the category of prior out-of-court statements.
Illustrative are People v. Gould, 54 Cal.2d 621, 7 Cal.Rptr. 273, 354 P.2d 865
(1960); Judy v. State, 218 Md. 168, 146 A.2d 29 (1958); State v. Simmons, 63
Wash.2d 17, 385 P.2d 389 (1963); California Evidence Code § 1238; New Jersey
Evidence Rule 63(1)(c); N.Y.Code of Criminal Procedure § 393–b. Further
cases are found in 4 Wigmore § 1130. The basis is the generally unsatisfactory
and inconclusive nature of courtroom identifications as compared with those
made at an earlier time under less suggestive conditions. The Supreme Court
considered the admissibility of evidence of prior identification in Gilbert v.
California, 388 U.S. 263, 87 S.Ct. 1951, 18 L.Ed.2d 1178 (1967). Exclusion of
lineup identification was held to be required because the accused did not then
have the assistance of counsel. Significantly, the Court carefully refrained
from placing its decision on the ground that testimony as to the making of a
prior out-of-court identification ("That's the man") violated either the hearsay
rule or the right of confrontation because not made under oath, subject to

immediate cross-examination, in the presence of the trier. Instead the Court observed:

"There is a split among the States concerning the admissibility of prior extra-judicial identifications, as independent evidence of identity, both by the witness and third parties present at the prior identification. See 71 A.L.R.2d 449. It has been held that the prior identification is hearsay, and, when admitted through the testimony of the identifier, is merely a prior consistent statement. The recent trend, however, is to admit the prior identification under the exception that admits as substantive evidence a prior communication by a witness who is available for cross-examination at the trial. See 5 A.L.R.2d Later Case Service 1225–1228. * * *" 388 U.S. at 272, n. 3, 87 S.Ct. at 1956.

(2) *Admissions.* Admissions by a party-opponent are excluded from the category of hearsay on the theory that their admissibility in evidence is the result of the adversary system rather than satisfaction of the conditions of the hearsay rule. Strahorn, A Reconsideration of the Hearsay Rule and Admissions, 85 U.Pa.L.Rev. 484, 564 (1937); Morgan, Basic Problems of Evidence 265 (1962); 4 Wigmore § 1048. No guarantee of trustworthiness is required in the case of an admission. The freedom which admissions have enjoyed from technical demands of searching for an assurance of trustworthiness in some against-interest circumstance, and from the restrictive influences of the opinion rule and the rule requiring firsthand knowledge, when taken with the apparently prevalent satisfaction with the results, calls for generous treatment of this avenue to admissibility.

The rule specifies five categories of statements for which the responsibility of a party is considered sufficient to justify reception in evidence against him:

(A) A party's own statement is the classic example of an admission. If he has a representative capacity and the statement is offered against him in that capacity, no inquiry whether he was acting in the representative capacity in making the statement is required; the statement need only be relevant to representative affairs. To the same effect is California Evidence Code § 1220. Compare Uniform Rule 63(7), requiring a statement to be made in a representative capacity to be admissible against a party in a representative capacity.

(B) Under established principles an admission may be made by adopting or acquiescing in the statement of another. While knowledge of contents would ordinarily be essential, this it not inevitably so: "X is a reliable person and knows what he is talking about." See McCormick § 246, p. 527, n. 15. Adoption or acquiescence may be manifested in any appropriate manner. When silence is relied upon, the theory is that the person would, under the circumstances, protest the statement made in his presence, if untrue. The decision in each case calls for an evaluation in terms of probable human behavior. In civil cases, the results have generally been satisfactory. In criminal cases, however, troublesome questions have been raised by decisions holding that failure to deny is an admission: the inference is a fairly weak one, to begin with; silence may be motivated by advice of counsel or realization that "anything you say may be used against you"; unusual opportunity is afforded to manufacture evidence; and encroachment upon the privilege against self-incrimination seems inescapably to be involved. However, recent decisions of the Supreme Court relating to custodial interrogation and the right to counsel appear to resolve these difficulties. Hence the rule contains no special provisions concerning failure to deny in criminal cases.

(C) No authority is required for the general proposition that a statement authorized by a party to be made should have the status of an admission by the party. However, the question arises whether only statements to third persons should be so regarded, to the exclusion of statements by the agent to the principal. The rule is phrased broadly so as to encompass both. While it may be argued that the agent authorized to make statements to his principal does not speak for him, Morgan, Basic Problems of Evidence 273 (1962), communication to an outsider has not generally been thought to be an essential characteristic of an admission. Thus a party's books or records are usable against him, without regard to any intent to disclose to third persons. 5 Wigmore § 1557. See also McCormick § 78, pp. 159–161. In accord is New Jersey Evidence Rule 63(8)(a). Cf. Uniform Rule 63(8)(a) and California Evidence Code § 1222 which limit status as an admission in this regard to statements authorized by the party to be made "for" him, which is perhaps an ambiguous limitation to statements to third persons. Falknor, Vicarious Admissions and the Uniform Rules, 14 Vand.L.Rev. 855, 860–861 (1961).

(D) The tradition has been to test the admissibility of statements by agents, as admissions, by applying the usual test of agency. Was the admission made by the agent acting in the scope of his employment? Since few principals employ agents for the purpose of making damaging statements, the usual result was exclusion of the statement. Dissatisfaction with this loss of valuable and helpful evidence has been increasing. A substantial trend favors admitting statements related to a matter within the scope of the agency or employment. Grayson v. Williams, 256 F.2d 61 (10th Cir.1958); Koninklijke Luchtvaart Maatschappij N.V. KLM Royal Dutch Airlines v. Tuller, 110 U.S.App.D.C. 282, 292 F.2d 775, 784 (1961); Martin v. Savage Truck Lines, Inc., 121 F.Supp. 417 (D.D.C.1954), and numerous state court decisions collected in 4 Wigmore, 1964 Supp., pp. 66–73, with comments by the editor that the statements should have been excluded as not within scope of agency. For the traditional view see Northern Oil Co. v. Socony Mobil Oil Co., 347 F.2d 81, 85 (2d Cir.1965) and cases cited therein. Similar provisions are found in Uniform Rule 63(9)(a), Kansas Code of Civil Procedure § 60–460(i)(1), and New Jersey Evidence Rule 63(9)(a).

(E) The limitation upon the admissibility of statements of co-conspirators to those made "during the course and in furtherance of the conspiracy" is in the accepted pattern. While the broadened view of agency taken in item (iv) might suggest wider admissibility of statements of co-conspirators, the agency theory of conspiracy is at best a fiction and ought not to serve as a basis for admissibility beyond that already established. See Levie, Hearsay and Conspiracy, 52 Mich.L.Rev. 1159 (1954); Comment, 25 U.Chi.L.Rev. 530 (1958). The rule is consistent with the position of the Supreme Court in denying admissibility to statements made after the objectives of the conspiracy have either failed or been achieved. Krulewitch v. United States, 336 U.S. 440, 69 S.Ct. 716, 93 L.Ed. 790 (1949); Wong Sun v. United States, 371 U.S. 471, 490, 83 S.Ct. 407, 9 L.Ed.2d 441 (1963). For similarly limited provisions see California Evidence Code § 1223 and New Jersey Rule 63(9)(b). Cf. Uniform Rule 63(9)(b).

Report of Senate Committee on the Judiciary

The House approved the long-accepted rule that "a statement by a coconspirator of a party during the course and in furtherance of the conspiracy" is not hearsay as it was submitted by the Supreme Court. While the rule refers to a coconspirator, it is this committee's understanding that the rule is meant to carry forward the universally accepted doctrine that a joint venturer is considered as a coconspirator for the purposes of this rule even though no conspiracy has been charged. United States v. Rinaldi, 393 F.2d 97, 99 (2d Cir.), cert. denied 393 U.S. 913 (1968); United States v. Spencer, 415 F.2d 1301, 1304 (7th Cir.1969).

Rule 802

Note by Federal Judicial Center

The rule enacted by the Congress is the rule prescribed by the Supreme Court, amended by substituting "prescribed" in place of "adopted" and by inserting the phrase "pursuant to statutory authority."

Advisory Committee's Note

The provision excepting from the operation of the rule hearsay which is made admissible by other rules adopted by the Supreme Court or by Act of Congress continues the admissibility thereunder of hearsay which would not qualify under these Evidence Rules. The following examples illustrate the working of the exception:

Federal Rules of Civil Procedure

Rule 4(g): proof of service by affidavit.

Rule 32: admissibility of depositions.

Rule 43(e): affidavits when motion based on facts not appearing of record.

Rule 56: affidavits in summary judgment proceedings.

Rule 65(b): showing by affidavit for temporary restraining order.

Federal Rules of Criminal Procedure

Rule 4(a): affidavits to show grounds for issuing warrants.

Rule 12(b)(4): affidavits to determine issues of fact in connection with motions.

Acts of Congress

10 U.S.C. § 7730: affidavits of unavailable witnesses in actions for damages caused by vessel in naval service, or towage or salvage of same, when taking of testimony or bringing of action delayed or stayed on security grounds.

29 U.S.C. § 161(4): affidavit as proof of service in NLRB proceedings.

38 U.S.C. § 5206: affidavit as proof of posting notice of sale of unclaimed property by Veterans Administration.

Rule 803

Note by Federal Judicial Center

The rule enacted by the Congress retains the 24 exceptions set forth in the rule prescribed by the Supreme Court. Three of the exceptions, numbered (6), (8), and (24) have been amended in respects that may fairly be described as substantial. Others, numbered (5), (7), (14), and (16), have been amended in lesser ways. The remaining 17 are unchanged. The amendments are, in numerical order, as follows.

Exception (5) as prescribed by the Supreme Court was amended by inserting after "made" the phrase "or adopted by the witness."

Exception (6) as prescribed by the Supreme Court was amended by substituting the phrase, "if kept in the course of a regularly conducted business activity, and if it was the regular practice of that business activity to make the memorandum, report, record, or data compilation, all," in place of "all in the course of a regularly conducted activity"; by substituting "source" in place of "sources"; by substituting the phrase, "the method or circumstances of preparation," in place of "other circumstances"; and by adding the second sentence.

Exception (7) as prescribed by the Supreme Court was amended by substituting the phrase, "kept in accordance with the provisions of paragraph (6)," in place of "of a regularly conducted activity." The exception prescribed by the Supreme Court included a comma after "memoranda," while the congressional enactment does not.

Exception (8) as prescribed by the Supreme Court was amended by inserting in item (B) after "law" the phrase, "as to which matters there was a duty to report, excluding, however, in criminal cases matters observed by police officers and other law enforcement personnel," and by substituting in item (C) the phrase "civil actions and proceedings," in place of "civil cases."

Exception (14) as prescribed by the Supreme Court was amended by substituting "authorizes" in place of "authorized."

Exception (16) as prescribed by the Supreme Court was amended by substituting the phrase, "the authenticity of which," in place of "whose authenticity."

Exception (24) as prescribed by the Supreme Court was amended by substituting "equivalent" in place of "comparable," and adding all that appears after "trustworthiness" in the exception as enacted by the Congress.

Advisory Committee's Note

The exceptions are phrased in terms of nonapplication of the hearsay rule, rather than in positive terms of admissibility, in order to repel any implication that other possible grounds for exclusion are eliminated from consideration.

The present rule proceeds upon the theory that under appropriate circumstances a hearsay statement may possess circumstantial guarantees of trustworthiness sufficient to justify nonproduction of the declarant in person at the trial even though he may be available. The theory finds vast support in the many exceptions to the hearsay rule developed by the common law in which unavailability of the declarant is not a relevant factor. The present rule is a synthesis of them, with revision where modern developments and conditions are believed to make that course appropriate.

In a hearsay situation, the declarant is, of course, a witness, and neither this rule nor Rule 804 dispenses with the requirement of firsthand knowledge. It may appear from his statement or be inferable from circumstances. See Rule 602.

Exceptions (1) and (2). In considerable measure these two examples overlap, though based on somewhat different theories. The most significant practical difference will lie in the time lapse allowable between event and statement.

The underlying theory of Exception (1) is that substantial contemporaneity of event and statement negative the likelihood of deliberate or conscious misrepresentation. Moreover, if the witness is the declarant, he may be examined on the statement. If the witness is not the declarant, he may be examined as to the circumstances as an aid in evaluating the statement. Morgan, Basic Problems of Evidence 340–341 (1962).

The theory of Exception (2) is simply that circumstances may produce a condition of excitement which temporarily stills the capacity of reflection and produces utterances free of conscious fabrication. 6 Wigmore § 1747, p. 135. Spontaneity is the key factor in each instance, though arrived at by somewhat different routes. Both are needed in order to avoid needless niggling.

While the theory of Exception (2) has been criticized on the ground that excitement impairs accuracy of observation as well as eliminating conscious fabrication, Hitchins and Slesinger, Some Observations on the Law of Evidence: Spontaneous Exclamations, 28 Colum.L.Rev. 432 (1928), it finds support in cases without number. See cases in 6 Wigmore § 1750; Annot. 53 A.L.R.2d 1245 (statements as to cause of or responsibility for motor vehicle accident); Annot., 4 A.L.R.3d 149 (accusatory statements by homicide victims). Since unexciting events are less likely to evoke comment, decisions involving Exception (1) are far less numerous. Illustrative are Tampa Elec. Co. v. Getrost, 151 Fla. 558, 10 So.2d 83 (1942); Houston Oxygen Co. v. Davis, 139 Tex. 1, 161 S.W.2d 474 (1942); and cases cited in McCormick § 273, p. 585, n. 4.

With respect to the *time element,* Exception (1) recognizes that in many, if not most, instances precise contemporaneity is not possible, and hence a slight lapse is allowable. Under Exception (2) the standard of measurement is the duration of the state of excitement. "How long can excitement prevail? Obviously there are no pat answers and the character of the transaction or event will largely determine the significance of the time factor." Slough, Spontaneous Statements and State of Mind, 46 Iowa L.Rev. 224, 243 (1961); McCormick § 272, p. 580.

Participation by the declarant is not required: a non-participant may be moved to describe what he perceives, and one may be startled by an event in which he is not an actor. Slough, supra; McCormick, supra; 6 Wigmore § 1755; Annot., 78 A.L.R.2d 300.

Whether *proof of the startling event* may be made by the statement itself is largely an academic question, since in most cases there is present at least circumstantial evidence that something of a startling nature must have occurred. For cases in which the evidence consists of the condition of the declarant (injuries, state of shock), see Insurance Co. v. Mosely, 75 U.S. (8 Wall.) 397, 19 L.Ed. 437 (1869); Wheeler v. United States, 93 U.S.App.D.C. 159, 211 F.2d 19 (1953), cert. denied 347 U.S. 1019, 74 S.Ct. 876, 98 L.Ed. 1140; Wetherbee v. Safety Casualty Co., 219 F.2d 274 (5th Cir.1955); Lampe v. United States, 97 U.S.App.D.C. 160, 229 F.2d 43 (1956). Nevertheless, on occasion the only evidence may be the content of the statement itself, and rulings that it may be sufficient are described as "increasing," Slough, supra at 246, and as the "prevailing practice," McCormick § 272, p. 579. Illustrative are Armour & Co. v. Industrial Commission, 78 Colo. 569, 243 P. 546 (1926); Young v. Stewart, 191 N.C. 297, 131 S.E. 735 (1926). Moreover, under Rule 104(a) the judge is not limited by the hearsay rule in passing upon preliminary questions of fact.

Proof of declarant's perception by his statement presents similar considerations when declarant is identified. People v. Poland, 22 Ill.2d 175, 174 N.E.2d 804 (1961). However, when declarant is an unidentified bystander, the cases indicate hesitancy in upholding the statement alone as sufficient, Garrett v. Howden, 73 N.M. 307, 387 P.2d 874 (1963); Beck v. Dye, 200 Wash. 1, 92 P.2d

1113 (1939), a result which would under appropriate circumstances be consistent with the rule.

Permissible *subject matter* of the statement is limited under Exception (1) to description or explanation of the event or condition, the assumption being that spontaneity, in the absence of a startling event, may extend no farther. In Exception (2), however, the statement need only "relate" to the startling event or condition, thus affording a broader scope of subject matter coverage. 6 Wigmore §§ 1750, 1754. See Sanitary Grocery Co. v. Snead, 67 App.D.C. 129, 90 F.2d 374 (1937), slip-and-fall case sustaining admissibility of clerk's statement, "That has been on the floor for a couple of hours," and Murphy Auto Parts Co., Inc. v. Ball, 101 U.S.App.D.C. 416, 249 F.2d 508 (1957), upholding admission, on issue of driver's agency, of his statement that he had to call on a customer and was in a hurry to get home. Quick, Hearsay, Excitement, Necessity and the Uniform Rules: A Reappraisal of Rule 63(4), 6 Wayne L.Rev. 204, 206–209 (1960).

Similar provisions are found in Uniform Rule 63(4)(a) and (b); California Evidence Code § 1240 (as to Exception (2) only); Kansas Code of Civil Procedure § 60–460(d)(1) and (2); New Jersey Evidence Rule 63(4).

Exception (3) is essentially a specialized application of Exception (1), presented separately to enhance its usefulness and accessibility. See McCormick §§ 265, 268.

The exclusion of "statements of memory or belief to prove the fact remembered or believed" is necessary to avoid the virtual destruction of the hearsay rule which would otherwise result from allowing state of mind, provable by a hearsay statement, to serve as the basis for an inference of the happening of the event which produced the state of mind. Shepard v. United States, 290 U.S. 96, 54 S.Ct. 22, 78 L.Ed. 196 (1933); Maguire, The Hillmon Case—Thirty-three Years After, 38 Harv.L.Rev. 709, 719–731 (1925); Hinton, States of Mind and the Hearsay Rule, 1 U.Chi.L.Rev. 394, 421–423 (1934). The rule of Mutual Life Ins. Co. v. Hillmon, 145 U.S. 285, 12 S.Ct. 909, 36 L.Ed. 706 (1892), allowing evidence of intention as tending to prove the doing of the act intended, is, of course, left undisturbed.

The carving out, from the exclusion mentioned in the preceding paragraph, of declarations relating to the execution, revocation, identification, or terms of declarant's will represents an *ad hoc* judgment which finds ample reinforcement in the decisions, resting on practical grounds of necessity and expediency rather than logic. McCormick § 271, pp. 577–578; Annot., 34 A.L.R.2d 588, 62 A.L.R.2d 855. A similar recognition of the need for and practical value of this kind of evidence is found in California Evidence Code § 1260.

Report of House Committee on the Judiciary

Rule 803(3) was approved in the form submitted by the Court to Congress. However, the Committee intends that the Rule be construed to limit the doctrine of Mutual Life Insurance Co. v. Hillmon, 145 U.S. 285, 295–300 (1892), so as to render statements of intent by a declarant admissible only to prove his future conduct, not the future conduct of another person.

Advisory Committee's Note

Exception (4). Even those few jurisdictions which have shied away from generally admitting statements of present condition have allowed them if made to a physician for purposes of diagnosis and treatment in view of the patient's strong motivation to be truthful. McCormick § 266, p. 563. The same guarantee of trustworthiness extends to statements of past conditions and medical history, made for purposes of diagnosis or treatment. It also extends to statements as to causation, reasonably pertinent to the same purposes, in accord with the current trend, Shell Oil Co. v. Industrial Commission, 2 Ill.2d 590, 119 N.E.2d 224 (1954); McCormick § 266, p. 564; New Jersey Evidence Rule 63(12)(c). Statements as to fault would not ordinarily qualify under this latter language. Thus a patient's statement that he was struck by an automobile would qualify but not his statement that the car was driven through a red light. Under the exception the statement need not have been made to a physician. Statements to hospital attendants, ambulance drivers, or even members of the family might be included.

Conventional doctrine has excluded from the hearsay exception, as not within its guarantee of truthfulness, statements to a physician consulted only for the purpose of enabling him to testify. While these statements were not admissible as substantive evidence, the expert was allowed to state the basis of his opinion, including statements of this kind. The distinction thus called for was one most unlikely to be made by juries. The rule accordingly rejects the limitation. This position is consistent with the provision of Rule 703 that the facts on which expert testimony is based need not be admissible in evidence if of a kind ordinarily relied upon by experts in the field.

Report of House Committee on the Judiciary

After giving particular attention to the question of physical examination made solely to enable a physician to testify, the Committee approved Rule 803(4) as submitted to Congress, with the understanding that it is not intended in any way to adversely affect present privilege rules or those subsequently adopted.

Report of Senate Committee on the Judiciary

The House approved this rule as it was submitted by the Supreme Court "with the understanding that it is not intended in any way to adversely affect present privilege rules." We also approve this rule, and we would point out with respect to the question of its relation to privileges, it must be read in conjunction with rule 35 of the Federal Rules of Civil Procedure which provides that whenever the physical or mental condition of a party (plaintiff or defendant) is in controversy, the court may require him to submit to an examination by a physician. It is these examinations which will normally be admitted under this exception.

Advisory Committee's Note

Exception (5). A hearsay exception for recorded recollection is generally recognized and has been described as having "long been favored by the federal and practically all the state courts that have had occasion to decide the question." United States v. Kelly, 349 F.2d 720, 770 (2d Cir.1965), citing numerous cases and sustaining the exception against a claimed denial of the right of confrontation. Many additional cases are cited in Annot., 82 A.L.R.2d 473, 520. The guarantee of trustworthiness is found in the reliability inherent in a record made while events were still fresh in mind and accurately reflecting them. Owens v. State, 67 Md. 307, 316, 10 A. 210, 212 (1887).

The principal controversy attending the exception has centered, not upon the propriety of the exception itself, but upon the question whether a preliminary requirement of impaired memory on the part of the witness should be imposed. The authorities are divided. If regard be had only to the accuracy of the evidence, admittedly impairment of the memory of the witness adds nothing to it and should not be required. McCormick § 277, p. 593; 3 Wigmore § 738, p. 76; Jordan v. People, 151 Colo. 133, 376 P.2d 699 (1962), cert. denied 373 U.S. 944, 83 S.Ct. 1553, 10 L.Ed.2d 699; Hall v. State, 223 Md. 158, 162 A.2d 751 (1960); State v. Bindhammer, 44 N.J. 372, 209 A.2d 124 (1965). Nevertheless, the absence of the requirement, it is believed, would encourage the use of statements carefully prepared for purposes of litigation under the supervision of attorneys, investigators, or claim adjusters. Hence the example includes a requirement that the witness not have "sufficient recollection to enable him to testify fully and accurately." To the same effect are California Evidence Code § 1237 and New Jersey Rule 63(1)(b), and this has been the position of the federal courts. Vicksburg & Meridian R.R. v. O'Brien, 119 U.S. 99, 7 S.Ct. 118, 30 L.Ed. 299 (1886); Ahern v. Webb, 268 F.2d 45 (10th Cir.1959); and see N.L.R.B. v. Hudson Pulp and Paper Corp., 273 F.2d 660, 665 (5th Cir.1960); N.L.R.B. v. Federal Dairy Co., 297 F.2d 487 (1st Cir.1962). But cf. United States v. Adams, 385 F.2d 548 (2d Cir.1967).

No attempt is made in the exception to spell out the method of establishing the initial knowledge or the contemporaneity and accuracy of the record, leaving them to be dealt with as the circumstances of the particular case might indicate. Multiple person involvement in the process of observing and recording, as in Rathbun v. Brancatella, 93 N.J.L. 222, 107 A. 279 (1919), is entirely consistent with the exception.

Locating the exception at this place in the scheme of the rules is a matter of choice. There were two other possibilities. The first was to regard the statement as one of the group of prior statements of a testifying witness which are excluded entirely from the category of hearsay by Rule 801(d)(1). That category, however, requires that declarant be "subject to cross-examination," as to which the impaired memory aspect of the exception raises doubts. The other possibility was to include the exception among those covered by Rule 804. Since unavailability is required by that rule and lack of memory is listed as a species of unavailability by the definition of the term in Rule 804(a)(3), that treatment at first impression would seem appropriate. The fact is, however, that the unavailability requirement of the exception is of a limited and peculiar nature. Accordingly, the exception is located at this point rather than in the context of a rule where unavailability is conceived of more broadly.

Report of House Committee on the Judiciary

Rule 803(5) as submitted by the Court permitted the reading into evidence of a memorandum or record concerning a matter about which a witness once had knowledge but now has insufficient recollection to enable him to testify accurately and fully, "shown to have been made when the matter was fresh in his memory and to reflect that knowledge correctly." The Committee amended this Rule to add the words "or adopted by the witness" after the phrase "shown to have been made", a treatment consistent with the definition of "statement" in the Jencks Act, 18 U.S.C. 3500. Moreover, it is the Committee's understanding that a memorandum or report, although barred under this Rule, would nonetheless be admissible if it came within another hearsay exception. This last stated principle is deemed applicable to all the hearsay rules.

Report of Senate Committee on the Judiciary

Rule 803(5) as submitted by the Court permitted the reading into evidence of a memorandum or record concerning a matter about which a witness once had knowledge but now has insufficient recollection to enable him to testify accurately and fully, "shown to have been made when the matter was fresh in his memory and to reflect that knowledge correctly." The House amended the rule to add the words "or adopted by the witness" after the phrase "shown to have been made," language parallel to the Jencks Act.[1]

The committee accepts the House amendment with the understanding and belief that it was not intended to narrow the scope of applicability of the rule. In fact, we understand it to clarify the rule's applicability to a memorandum adopted by the witness as well as one made by him. While the rule as submitted by the Court was silent on the question of who made the memorandum, we view the House amendment as a helpful clarification, noting, however, that the Advisory Committee's note to this rule suggests that the important thing is the accuracy of the memorandum rather than who made it.

The committee does not view the House amendment as precluding admissibility in situations in which multiple participants were involved.

When the verifying witness has not prepared the report, but merely examined it and found it accurate, he has adopted the report, and it is therefore admissible. The rule should also be interpreted to cover other situations involving multiple participants, e.g., employer dictating to secretary, secretary making memorandum at direction of employer, or information being passed along a chain of persons, as in Curtis v. Bradley.[2]

The committee also accepts the understanding of the House that a memorandum or report, although barred under this rule, would nonetheless be admissible if it came within another hearsay exception. We consider this principle to be applicable to all the hearsay rules.

Advisory Committee's Note

Exception (6) represents an area which has received much attention from those seeking to improve the law of evidence. The Commonwealth Fund Act was the result of a study completed in 1927 by a distinguished committee under the chairmanship of Professor Morgan. Morgan et al., The Law of Evidence: Some Proposals for its Reform 63 (1927). With changes too minor to mention, it was adopted by Congress in 1936 as the rule for federal courts. 28 U.S.C. § 1732. A number of states took similar action. The Commissioners on Uniform State Laws in 1936 promulgated the Uniform Business Records as Evidence Act, 9A U.L.A. 506, which has acquired a substantial following in the states. Model Code Rule 514 and Uniform Rule 63(13) also deal with the subject. Difference of varying degrees of importance exist among these various treatments.

These reform efforts were largely within the context of business and commercial records, as the kind usually encountered, and concentrated considerable attention upon relaxing the requirement of producing as witnesses, or accounting for the nonproduction of, all participants in the process of gathering, transmitting, and recording information which the common law had

1. 18 U.S.C. § 3500.

2. 65 Conn. 99, 31 Atl. 591 (1894). See also, Rathbun v. Brancatella, 93 N.J.L. 222, 107 Atl. 279 (1919); see also McCormick on Evidence, § 303 (2d ed. 1972).

evolved as a burdensome and crippling aspect of using records of this type. In their areas of primary emphasis on witnesses to be called and the general admissibility of ordinary business and commercial records, the Commonwealth Fund Act and the Uniform Act appear to have worked well. The exception seeks to preserve their advantages.

On the subject of what witnesses must be called, the Commonwealth Fund Act eliminated the common law requirement of calling or accounting for all participants by failing to mention it. United States v. Mortimer, 118 F.2d 266 (2d Cir.1941); La Porte v. United States, 300 F.2d 878 (9th Cir.1962); McCormick § 290, p. 608. Model Code Rule 514 and Uniform Rule 63(13) did likewise. The Uniform Act, however, abolished the common law requirement in express terms, providing that the requisite foundation testimony might be furnished by "the custodian or other qualified witness." Uniform Business Records as Evidence Act, § 2; 9A U.L.A. 506. The exception follows the Uniform Act in this respect.

The element of unusual reliability of business records is said variously to be supplied by systematic checking, by regularity and continuity which produce habits of precision, by actual experience of business in relying upon them, or by a duty to make an accurate record as part of a continuing job or occupation. McCormick §§ 281, 286, 287; Laughlin, Business Entries and the Like, 46 Iowa L.Rev. 276 (1961). The model statutes and rules have sought to capture these factors and to extend their impact by employing the phrase "regular course of business," in conjunction with a definition of "business" far broader than its ordinarily accepted meaning. The result is a tendency unduly to emphasize a requirement of routineness and repetitiveness and an insistence that other types of records be squeezed into the fact patterns which give rise to traditional business records. * * *

Amplification of the kinds of activities producing admissible records has given rise to problems which conventional business records by their nature avoid. They are problems of the source of the recorded information, of entries in opinion form, of motivation, and of involvement as participant in the matters recorded.

Sources of information presented no substantial problem with ordinary business records. All participants, including the observer or participant furnishing the information to be recorded, were acting routinely, under a duty of accuracy, with employer reliance on the result, or in short "in the regular course of business." If, however, the supplier of the information does not act in the regular course, an essential link is broken; the assurance of accuracy does not extend to the information itself, and the fact that it may be recorded with scrupulous accuracy is of no avail. An illustration is the police report incorporating information obtained from a bystander: the officer qualifies as acting in the regular course but the informant does not. The leading case, Johnson v. Lutz, 253 N.Y. 124, 170 N.E. 517 (1930), held that a report thus prepared was inadmissible. Most of the authorities have agreed with the decision. Gencarella v. Fyfe, 171 F.2d 419 (1st Cir.1948); Gordon v. Robinson, 210 F.2d 192 (3d Cir. 1954); Standard Oil Co. of California v. Moore, 251 F.2d 188, 214 (9th Cir.1957), cert. denied 356 U.S. 975, 78 S.Ct. 1139, 2 L.Ed.2d 1148; Yates v. Bair Transport, Inc., 249 F.Supp. 681 (S.D.N.Y.1965); Annot., 69 A.L.R.2d 1148. Cf. Hawkins v. Gorea Motor Express, Inc., 360 F.2d 933 (2d Cir.1966). Contra, 5 Wigmore § 1530a, n. 1, pp. 391–392. The point is not dealt with specifically in the Commonwealth Fund Act, the Uniform Act, or Uniform Rule 63(13). However, Model Code Rule 514 contains the requirement "that it was the regular course of that business for one with personal knowledge * * * to make such a memorandum or record or to transmit information thereof to be included in such a memorandum or record * * *." The rule follows this lead in requiring an informant with knowledge acting in the course of the regularly conducted activity.

Entries in the form of opinions were not encountered in traditional business records in view of the purely factual nature of the items recorded, but they are now commonly encountered with respect to medical diagnoses, prognoses, and test results, as well as occasionally in other areas. The Commonwealth Fund Act provided only for records of an "act, transaction, occurrence, or event," while the Uniform Act, Model Code Rule 514, and Uniform Rule 63(13) merely added the ambiguous term "condition." The limited phrasing of the Commonwealth Fund Act, 28 U.S.C. § 1732, may account for the reluctance of some federal decisions to admit diagnostic entries. New York Life Ins. Co. v. Taylor, 79 U.S.App.D.C. 66, 147 F.2d 297 (1945); Lyles v. United States, 103 U.S.App.D.C. 22, 254 F.2d 725 (1957), cert. denied 356 U.S. 961, 78 S.Ct. 997, 2 L.Ed.2d 1067; England v. United States, 174 F.2d 466 (5th Cir.1949); Skogen v. Dow Chemical Co., 375 F.2d 692 (8th Cir.1967). Other federal decisions, however, experienced no difficulty in freely admitting diagnostic entries. Reed v. Order of United Commercial Travelers, 123 F.2d 252 (2d Cir.1941); Buckminster's Estate v. Commissioner of Internal Revenue, 147 F.2d 331 (2d Cir.1944); Medina v. Erickson, 226 F.2d 475 (9th Cir.1955); Thomas v. Hogan, 308 F.2d 355 (4th Cir.1962); Glawe v. Rulon, 284 F.2d 495 (8th Cir.1960). In the state courts, the trend favors admissibility. Borucki v. MacKenzie Bros. Co., 125 Conn. 92, 3 A.2d 224 (1938); Allen v. St. Louis Public Service Co., 365 Mo. 677, 285 S.W.2d 663, 55 A.L.R.2d 1022 (1956); People v. Kohlmeyer, 284 N.Y. 366, 31 N.E.2d 490 (1940); Weis v. Weis, 147 Ohio St. 416, 72 N.E.2d 245 (1947). In order to make clear its adherence to the latter position the rule specifically includes both diagnoses and opinions, in addition to acts, events, and conditions, as proper subjects of admissible entries.

Problems of the motivation of the informant have been a source of difficulty and disagreement. In Palmer v. Hoffman, 318 U.S. 109, 63 S.Ct. 477, 87 L.Ed. 645 (1943), exclusion of an accident report made by the since deceased engineer, offered by defendant railroad trustees in a grade crossing collision case, was upheld. The report was not "in the regular course of business," not a record of the systematic conduct of the business as a business, said the Court. The report was prepared for use in litigating, not railroading. While the opinion mentions the motivation of the engineer only obliquely, the emphasis on records of routine operations is significant only by virtue of impact on motivation to be accurate. Absence of routineness raises lack of motivation to be accurate. The opinion of the Court of Appeals had gone beyond mere lack of motive to be accurate: the engineer's statement was "dripping with motivations to misrepresent." Hoffman v. Palmer, 129 F.2d 976, 991 (2d Cir.1942). The direct introduction of motivation is a disturbing factor, since absence of motive to misrepresent has not traditionally been a requirement of the rule; that records might be self-serving has not been a ground for exclusion. Laughlin, Business Records and the Like, 46 Iowa L.Rev. 276, 285 (1961). As Judge Clark said in his dissent, "I submit that there is hardly a grocer's account book which could not be excluded on that basis." 129 F.2d at 1002. A physician's evaluation report of a personal injury litigant would appear to be in the routine of his business. If the report is offered by the party at whose instance it was made, however, it has been held inadmissible, Yates v. Bair Transport, Inc., 249 F.Supp. 681 (S.D.N.Y.1965), otherwise if offered by the opposite party, Korte v. New York, N.H. & H.R. Co., 191 F.2d 86 (2d Cir.1951), cert. denied 342 U.S. 868, 72 S.Ct. 108, 96 L.Ed. 652.

The decisions hinge on motivation and which party is entitled to be concerned about it. Professor McCormick believed that the doctor's report or the accident report were sufficiently routine to justify admissibility. McCormick § 287, p. 604. Yet hesitation must be experienced in admitting everything which is observed and recorded in the course of a regularly conducted activity. Efforts to set a limit are illustrated by Hartzog v. United States, 217 F.2d 706 (4th Cir.1954), error to admit worksheets made by since deceased deputy collector in preparation for the instant income tax evasion prosecution, and United States v. Ware, 247 F.2d 698 (7th Cir.1957), error to admit narcotics agents' records of purchases. See also Exception (8), infra, as to the public record aspects of records of this nature. Some decisions have been satisfied as to motivation of an accident report if made pursuant to statutory duty, United States v. New York Foreign Trade Zone Operators, 304 F.2d 792 (2d Cir.1962); Taylor v. Baltimore & O.R. Co., 344 F.2d 281 (2d Cir.1965), since the report was oriented in a direction other than the litigation which ensued. Cf. Matthews v. United States, 217 F.2d 409 (5th Cir.1954). The formulation of specific terms which would assure satisfactory results in all cases is not possible. Consequently the rule proceeds from the base that records made in the course of a regularly conducted activity will be taken as admissible but subject to authority to exclude if "the sources of information or other circumstances indicate lack of trustworthiness."

Occasional decisions have reached for enhanced accuracy by requiring involvement as a participant in matters reported. Clainos v. United States, 82 U.S.App.D.C. 278, 163 F.2d 593 (1947), error to admit police records of convictions; Standard Oil Co. of California v. Moore, 251 F.2d 188 (9th Cir.1957), cert. denied 356 U.S. 975, 78 S.Ct. 1139, 2 L.Ed.2d 1148, error to admit employees' records of observed business practices of others. The rule includes no requirement of this nature. Wholly acceptable records may involve matters merely observed, e.g. the weather.

The form which the "record" may assume under the rule is described broadly as a "memorandum, report, record, or data compilation, in any form." The expression "data compilation" is used as broadly descriptive of any means of storing information other than the conventional words and figures in written or documentary form. It includes, but is by no means limited to, electronic computer storage. The term is borrowed from revised Rule 34(a) of the Rules of Civil Procedure.

Report of House Committee on the Judiciary

Rule 803(6) as submitted by the Court permitted a record made "in the course of a regularly conducted activity" to be admissible in certain circumstances. The Committee believed there were insufficient guarantees of reliability in records made in the course of activities falling outside the scope of "business" activities as that term is broadly defined in 28 U.S.C. 1732. Moreover, the Committee concluded that the additional requirement of Section 1732 that it must have been the regular practice of a business to make the record is a necessary further assurance of its trustworthiness. The Committee accordingly amended the Rule to incorporate these limitations.

Report of Senate Committee on the Judiciary

Rule 803(6) as submitted by the Supreme Court permitted a record made in the course of a regularly conducted activity to be admissible in certain circumstances. This rule constituted a broadening of the traditional business records hearsay exception which has been long advocated by scholars and judges active in the law of evidence.

The House felt there were insufficient guarantees of reliability of records not within a broadly defined business records exception. We disagree. Even under the House definition of "business" including profession, occupation, and "calling of every kind," the records of many regularly conducted activities will, or may be, excluded from evidence. Under the principle of ejusdem generis, the intent of "calling of every kind" would seem to be related to work-related endeavors—e.g., butcher, baker, artist, etc.

Thus, it appears that the records of many institutions or groups might not be admissible under the House amendments. For example, schools, churches, and hospitals will not normally be considered businesses within the definition. Yet, these are groups which keep financial and other records on a regular basis in a manner similar to business enterprises. We believe these records are of equivalent trustworthiness and should be admitted into evidence.

Three states, which have recently codified their evidence rules, have adopted the Supreme Court version of rule 803(6), providing for admission of memoranda of a "regularly conducted activity." None adopted the words "business activity" used in the House amendment.[3]

Therefore, the committee deleted the word "business" as it appears before the word "activity". The last sentence then is unnecessary and was also deleted.

It is the understanding of the committee that the use of the phrase "person with knowledge" is not intended to imply that the party seeking to introduce the memorandum, report, record, or data compilation must be able to produce, or even identify, the specific individual upon whose first-hand knowledge the memorandum, report, record or data compilation was based. A sufficient foundation for the introduction of such evidence will be laid if the party seeking to introduce the evidence is able to show that it was the regular practice of the activity to base such memorandums, reports, records, or data compilations upon a transmission from a person with knowledge, e.g., in the case of a content of a shipment of goods, upon a report from the company's receiving agent or in the case of a computer printout, upon a report from the company's computer programmer or one who has knowledge of the particular record system. In short, the scope of the phrase "person with knowledge" is meant to be coterminous with the custodian of the evidence or other qualified witness. The committee believes this represents the desired rule in light of the complex nature of modern business organizations.

Conference Report

The House bill provides in subsection (6) that records of a regularly conducted "business" activity qualify for admission into evidence as an exception to the hearsay rule. "Business" is defined as including "business, profession, occupation and calling of every kind." The Senate amendment drops the requirement that the records be those of a "business" activity and eliminates the definition of "business." The Senate amendment provides that records are admissible if they are records of a regularly conducted "activity."

3. See Nev.Rev.Stats. § 15.135; N.Mex. Stats. (1973 Supp.) § 20–4–803(6); West's Wis.Stats.Anno. (1973 Supp.) § 908.03(6).

The Conference adopts the House provision that the records must be those of a regularly conducted "business" activity. The Conferees changed the definition of "business" contained in the House provision in order to make it clear that the records of institutions and associations like schools, churches and hospitals are admissible under this provision. The records of public schools and hospitals are also covered by Rule 803(8), which deals with public records and reports.

Advisory Committee's Note

Exception (7). Failure of a record to mention a matter which would ordinarily be mentioned is satisfactory evidence of its nonexistence. Uniform Rule 63(14), Comment. While probably not hearsay as defined in Rule 801, supra, decisions may be found which class the evidence not only as hearsay but also as not within any exception. In order to set the question at rest in favor of admissibility, it is specifically treated here. McCormick § 289, p. 609; Morgan, Basic Problems of Evidence 314 (1962); 5 Wigmore § 1531; Uniform Rule 63(14); California Evidence Code § 1272; Kansas Code of Civil Procedure § 60–460(n); New Jersey Evidence Rule 63(14).

Report of House Committee on the Judiciary

Rule 803(7) as submitted by the Court concerned the *absence* of entry in the records of a "regularly conducted activity." The Committee amended this Rule to conform with its action with respect to Rule 803(6).

Advisory Committee's Note

Exception (8). Public records are a recognized hearsay exception at common law and have been the subject of statutes without number. McCormick § 291. See, for example, 28 U.S.C. § 1733, the relative narrowness of which is illustrated by its nonapplicability to nonfederal public agencies, thus necessitating resort to the less appropriate business record exception to the hearsay rule. Kay v. United States, 255 F.2d 476 (4th Cir.1958). The rule makes no distinction between federal and nonfederal offices and agencies.

Justification for the exception is the assumption that a public official will perform his duty properly and the unlikelihood that he will remember details independently of the record. Wong Wing Foo v. McGrath, 196 F.2d 120 (9th Cir.1952), and see Chesapeake & Delaware Canal Co. v. United States, 250 U.S. 123, 39 S.Ct. 407, 63 L.Ed. 889 (1919). As to items (A) and (B), further support is found in the reliability factors underlying records of regularly conducted activities generally. See Exception (6), supra.

(A) Cases illustrating the admissibility of records of the office's or agency's own activities are numerous. Chesapeake & Delaware Canal Co. v. United States, 250 U.S. 123, 39 S.Ct. 407, 63 L.Ed. 889 (1919), Treasury records of miscellaneous receipts and disbursements; Howard v. Perrin, 200 U.S. 71, 26 S.Ct. 195, 50 L.Ed. 374 (1906), General Land Office records; Ballew v. United States, 160 U.S. 187, 16 S.Ct. 263, 40 L.Ed. 388 (1895), Pension Office records.

(B) Cases sustaining admissibility of records of matters observed are also numerous. United States v. Van Hook, 284 F.2d 489 (7th Cir.1960), remanded for resentencing 365 U.S. 609, 81 S.Ct. 823, 5 L.Ed.2d 821, letter from induction officer to District Attorney, pursuant to army regulations, stating fact and circumstances of refusal to be inducted; T'Kach v. United States, 242 F.2d 937 (5th Cir.1957), affidavit of White House personnel officer that search of records showed no employment of accused, charged with fraudulently representing himself as an envoy of the President; Minnehaha County v. Kelley, 150 F.2d 356 (8th Cir.1945); Weather Bureau records of rainfall; United States v. Meyer, 113 F.2d 387 (7th Cir.1940), cert. denied 311 U.S. 706, 61 S.Ct. 174, 85 L.Ed. 459, map prepared by government engineer from information furnished by men working under his supervision.

(C) The more controversial area of public records is that of the so-called "evaluative" report. The disagreement among the decisions has been due in part, no doubt, to the variety of situations encountered, as well as to differences in principle. Sustaining admissibility are such cases as United States v. Dumas, 149 U.S. 278, 13 S.Ct. 872, 37 L.Ed. 734 (1893), statement of account certified by Postmaster General in action against postmaster; McCarty v. United States, 185 F.2d 520 (5th Cir.1950), reh. denied 187 F.2d 234, Certificate of Settlement of General Accounting Office showing indebtedness and letter from Army official stating Government had performed, in action on contract to purchase and remove waste food from Army camp; Moran v. Pittsburgh-Des Moines Steel Co., 183 F.2d 467 (3d Cir.1950), report of Bureau of Mines as to cause of gas tank explosion; Petition of W—, 164 F.Supp. 659 (E.D.Pa.1958), report by Immigration and Naturalization Service investigator that petitioner was known in community as wife of man to whom she was not married. To the opposite effect and denying admissibility are Franklin v. Skelly Oil Co., 141 F.2d 568 (10th Cir.1944), State Fire Marshal's report of cause of gas explosion; Lomax Transp. Co. v. United States, 183 F.2d 331 (9th Cir.1950), Certificate of Settlement from General Accounting Office in action for naval supplies lost in warehouse fire; Yung Jin Teung v. Dulles, 229 F.2d 244 (2d Cir.1956), "Status Reports" offered to justify delay in processing passport applications. * * * Various kinds of evaluative reports are admissible under federal statutes: 7 U.S.C. § 78, findings of Secretary of Agriculture prima facie evidence of true grade of grain; 7 U.S.C. § 210(f), findings of Secretary of Agriculture prima facie evidence in action for damages against stockyard owner; 7 U.S.C. § 292, order by Secretary of Agriculture prima facie evidence in judicial enforcement proceedings against producers association monopoly; 7 U.S.C. § 1622(h), Department of Agriculture inspection certificates of products shipped in interstate commerce prima facie evidence; 8 U.S.C. § 1440(c), separation of alien from military service on conditions other than honorable provable by certificate from department in proceedings to revoke citizenship; 18 U.S.C. § 4245, certificate of Director of Prisons that convicted person has been examined and found probably incompetent at time of trial prima facie evidence in court hearing on competency; 42 U.S.C. § 269(b), bill of health by appropriate official prima facie evidence of vessel's sanitary history and condition and compliance with regulations; 46 U.S.C. § 679, certificate of consul presumptive evidence of refusal of master to transport destitute seamen to United States. While these statutory exceptions to the hearsay rule are left undisturbed, Rule 802, the willingness of Congress to recognize a substantial measure of admissibility for evaluative reports is a helpful guide.

Factors which may be of assistance in passing upon the admissibility of evaluative reports include: (1) the timeliness of the investigation, McCormick, Can the Courts Make Wider Use of Reports of Official Investigations? 42 Iowa L.Rev. 363 (1957); (2) the special skill or experience of the official, id., (3) whether a hearing was held and the level at which conducted, Franklin v. Skelly Oil Co., 141 F.2d 568 (10th Cir.1944); (4) possible motivation problems suggested by Palmer v. Hoffman, 318 U.S. 109, 63 S.Ct. 477, 87 L.Ed. 645 (1943). Others no doubt could be added.

The formulation of an approach which would give appropriate weight to all possible factors in every situation is an obvious impossibility. Hence the rule, as in Exception (6), assumes admissibility in the first instance but with ample provision for escape if sufficient negative factors are present. In one respect, however, the rule with respect to evaluative reports under item (C) is very specific: they are admissible only in civil cases and against the government in criminal cases in view of the almost certain collision with confrontation rights which would result from their use against the accused in a criminal case.

Report of House Committee on the Judiciary

The Committee approved Rule 803(8) without substantive change from the form in which it was submitted by the Court. The Committee intends that the phrase "factual findings" be strictly construed and that evaluations or opinions contained in public reports shall not be admissible under this Rule.

CONGRESSIONAL RECORD—HOUSE

Feb. 6, 1974, pp. H563–565

Amendment offered by Ms. Holtzman

Ms. HOLTZMAN. Mr. Chairman, I offer an amendment.

The Clerk read as follows:

Amendment offered by Ms. Holtzman: On page 94, line 11, after the word "law" and before the comma, insert the following: "as to which matters there was a duty to report".

Ms. HOLTZMAN. Mr. Chairman, I will try to be very brief, because it is late in the day.

My amendment is offered to clarify and narrow a provision on the hearsay rule (Rule 803(8)(B)). This rule now provides that if any Government employee in the course of his duty observes something—in fact, anything—and makes a report of that observation, that report can be entered into evidence at a trial whether criminal or civil, without the opportunity to cross-examine the author of the report.

While I respect Government employees, I think we would all concede that they are fallible, exactly like every other human. We do not provide such broad exceptions to the hearsay rule for ordinary mortals.

My amendment makes it crystal clear that random observations by a Government employee cannot be introduced as an exception to the hearsay rule and be insulated from cross-examination. My amendment would allow reports of "matters observed" by a public official only if he had a duty to report about such matters. One operating under such a duty is far more likely to observe and report accurately.

I urge adoption of this amendment in order to narrow and restrict the broad exception to the hearsay rule in the bill.

Mr. HUNGATE. Mr. Chairman, I rise in opposition to the amendment.

This is a matter that was considered in the subcommittee, and we decided to stay with the language as presented to the House here, which states as follows:

Records, reports, statements, or data compilations, in any form, of public offices or agencies, setting forth (A) the activities of the office or

1   agency, or (B) matters observed pursuant to duty imposed by law.

2   * * *

3   Mr. Chairman, this is where the point of disagreement occurred. We
4 stayed with that version of the bill, and I would recommend that version to the
5 Committee of the Whole House.

6   Mr. DANIELSON. Mr. Chairman, I rise in support of the amendment
7 offered by the gentlewoman from New York (Ms. Holtzman).

8   I think if we leave this language in the proposed bill, we are opening the
9 door to a host of problems, the like of which we have probably never seen in a
10 trial court.

11   I think the proper approach, in order to eliminate this, is simply to adopt
12 the gentlewoman's amendment, and eliminate this provision, simply because
13 there is absolutely no restriction on the sort of material which could come in
14 under the language as proposed.

15   I urge the adoption of the gentlewoman's amendment.

16   Mr. DENNIS. Mr. Chairman, I rise in support of the gentlewoman's
17 amendment.

18   So that the committee will know what we are talking about here, this
19 permits the introduction in evidence as an exception to the hearsay rule of
20 public records and reports, statements, or data compilations in any form of
21 matters observed pursuant to duty imposed by law. The gentlewoman would
22 add "as to which matters there was a duty to report."

23   Again it is a matter of judgment, but the difference would be this:
24 Supposing you had a divorce case and you tried to put in a report of a social
25 worker, rather than putting the social worker on the stand; under the commit-
26 tee's language anything she said in the report which would be observed by her
27 pursuant to her general duties would be admissible. Under the amendment,
28 only those things as to which she had some duty to make a report would be
29 admissible.

30   If the law required her to observe and report certain things about a
31 condition in the home, that could come in, but if she put in a lot of other stuff
32 there, she could not put that in without calling her as a witness and giving the
33 opposition a chance to cross examine her.

34   On the whole I think the amendment improves the bill, and I support it.

35   The CHAIRMAN. The question is on the amendment offered by the
36 gentlewoman from New York (Ms. Holtzman).

37   The amendment was agreed to.

38
39   Amendment offered by Mr. Dennis

40   Mr. DENNIS. Mr. Chairman, I offer an amendment.

41   The Clerk read as follows:

42   Amendment offered by Mr. Dennis: On page 94, line 11 of the bill,
43   after the word "law", insert the words "excluding, however, in criminal
44   cases matters observed by police officers and other law enforcement
45   personnel".

46   Mr. DENNIS. Mr. Chairman, this goes to the same subject matter as the
47 last amendment. It deals with official statements and reports.

48   What I am saying here is that in a criminal case, only, we should not be
49 able to put in the police report to prove your case without calling the
50

policeman. I think in a criminal case you ought to have to call the policeman
on the beat and give the defendant the chance to cross examine him, rather
than just reading the report into evidence. That is the purpose of this
amendment.

Ms. HOLTZMAN. Mr. Chairman, I rise in support of the amendment.

I will be very brief again.

I commend my colleague for raising this point. Again his purpose is to
restrict the possible abuse of hearsay evidence.

I think the gentleman's amendment is very valuable and reaffirms the
right of cross examination to the accused. It also permits those engaged in civil
trials the right of cross examination. Cross-examination guarantees of due
process of law and a fair trial.

(Ms. HOLTZMAN asked and was given permission to revise and extend her
remarks.)

Mr. SMITH of New York. Mr. Chairman, I rise in opposition to the
amendment.

Mr. Chairman, in reading this amendment it seems to me that the effect of
the gentleman's amendment is to treat police officers and other law enforcement officers as second-class citizens, because we have already agreed that we
are going to allow in as exceptions to the hearsay rule matters observed
pursuant to duty imposed by law. The gentleman from Indiana would exclude
from that as follows: "Excluding however, in criminal cases, matters observed
by police officers and other law enforcement personnel." This would be so even
though they were matters observed pursuant to a duty imposed by law.

I just think we are treading in an area the impact of which will be very
unfortunate and the effect of which is to make police officers and law enforcement officers second-class citizens and persons less trustworthy than social
workers or garbage collectors.

Mr. DENNIS. Mr. Chairman, will the gentleman yield?

Mr. SMITH of New York. I will be glad to yield to the gentleman from
Indiana.

Mr. DENNIS. Mr. Chairman, I would like to say on that point that of
course that is not my idea. I think the point is that we are dealing here with
criminal cases, and in a criminal case the defendant should be confronted with
the accuser to give him the chance to cross examine. This is not any reflection
on the police officer, but in a criminal case that is the type of report with
which, in fact, one is going to be concerned.

Mr. JOHNSON of Colorado. Mr. Chairman, will the gentleman yield?

Mr. SMITH of New York. I yield to the gentleman from Colorado.

Mr. JOHNSON of Colorado. Mr. Chairman, as an ex-prosecutor I cannot
imagine that the gentleman would be advocating that a policeman's report
could come in to help convict a man, and not have the policeman himself
subject to cross-examination.

Is that what the gentleman is advocating?

Mr. SMITH of New York. That is what I am advocating in that the
policeman's report, if he is not available, should be admissible when it is made
pursuant to a duty imposed on that law enforcement officer by law. This is the
amendment we have just adopted, and for other public officers these police
reports ought to be admissible, whatever their probative value might be.

Mr. JOHNSON of Colorado. Mr. Chairman, if the gentleman will yield further, as I said, I was a prosecutor in a State court, and there were so many cases where good cross-examination indicated a lack of investigative ability on the part of the man who made the report that I became more and more convinced that good cross-examination was one of the principal elements in any criminal trial. If the officer who made the investigation is not available for cross-examination, then you cannot have a fair trial.

I cannot believe the gentleman would be saying that we should be able to convict people where the police officer's statement is not subject to cross-examination.

Mr. SMITH of New York. All I am saying to the gentleman from Colorado is that—and I will concede that the gentleman has probably had greater experience in this field than I have had—all I am saying is that it seems to me that it should be allowed for the jury to consider such a report, together with all of the other aspects of the case, if this report was made by a police officer pursuant to a duty imposed upon that police officer by law.

I will have to admit to the gentleman from Colorado that it is not the best evidence.

Mr. JOHNSON of Colorado. If the gentleman will yield still further, I will have to say that in my opinion the Supreme Court would have to ultimately declare that kind of a rule unconstitutional if we did pass it, and that the present amendment is one that would have to be passed if we are going to preserve the rights and traditions of individuals that have been in existence since 1066—I think that is when it started.

Mr. BRASCO. Mr. Chairman, I move to strike the requisite number of words.

(Mr. BRASCO asked and was given permission to revise and extend his remarks.)

Mr. BRASCO. Mr. Chairman, I would like to ask the author of the amendment, the gentleman from Indiana (Mr. Dennis) a question. I am deeply disturbed and troubled about these rules that have been brought out today.

It seems to me that many critical areas have been overlooked.

One of the basic tenets of our law is that one should be confronted by one's accuser and be able to cross-examine the accuser.

There are many, many exceptions to the hearsay rule here.

As I understand it the gentleman from New York (Mr. Smith) is advocating, in opposition to the amendment offered by the gentleman from Indiana (Mr. Dennis) that if a police officer made a report that he saw Mr. X with a gun on such and such an occasion, and then thereafter that police officer is unavailable that that statement could be used in a criminal trial against Mr. X without the defense attorney having the opportunity to cross examine the officer with respect to his position with relation to Mr. X, the time of the day, whether he was under a light, or whether there was no light, how much time did he have in which to see the gun, and all other observations relevant to the case.

Mr. DENNIS. Mr. Chairman, I would say in answer to the question raised by the gentleman from New York (Mr. Brasco) that if the statements of the police officer in his report would, in the language of this bill, be "matters observed pursuant to a duty imposed by law, and as to which he was under a duty to make a report," and I rather think they might be, that then what the gentleman says is true, and would be true.

I am trying to remove that possibility, by saying that the rule will not apply in the case the gentleman is talking about.

Mr. BRASCO. I support the gentleman. I am just standing up talking, because I cannot believe that we would for one moment entertain any other rule. I would hope we would do it with all cases of hearsay.

Mr. HUNT. Mr. Chairman, will the gentleman yield?

Mr. BRASCO. I will be glad to yield to the gentleman from New Jersey if the gentleman wishes me to yield to him.

Mr. HUNT. I had no intention of getting into this argument, but when the gentleman brings in the word "investigator," then I have to get in.

Mr. BRASCO. I did not say it.

Mr. HUNT. I know the gentleman from New York did not, but it was discussed. The only time I can recall in my 34 years of law enforcement that a report of an investigator was admissible in court was to test the credibility of an officer. We would never permit a report to come in unchallenged. We would never even think about bringing in a report in lieu of the officer being there to have that officer cross-examined; but reports were admitted as evidentiary fact for the purpose of testing the officer's credibility and perhaps to refresh his memory. That has always been the rule of law in the State of New Jersey, and I hope it will always remain that way—and even the Federal canons.

Mr. BRASCO. I do not think that the gentleman's amendment interferes with that at all. I think what he is talking about is that the prosecution could use this to prove its case in chief with the possibility of no other evidence being presented.

Mr. HUNT. He is talking about bringing the report in in lieu of an officer, and that certainly is not the case.

Mr. DENNIS. Mr. Chairman, will the gentleman yield?

Mr. BRASCO. I yield to the gentleman from Indiana.

Mr. DENNIS. I thank the gentleman for yielding. I certainly agree this amendment has nothing to do with what my friend, the gentleman from New Jersey, is talking about. This applies only to a hearsay exception, where it would be attempted to bring this report in instead of the officer to prove one's case in chief, which one could do if we do not pass this amendment; but we could still use the report to contradict him and cross-examine him.

Mr. HUNT. Certainly, but the gentleman is speaking of the best evidence available then in lieu of the direct evidence.

Mr. DENNIS. I say we should bring in the man who saw it and put him on the stand.

Mr. HUNT. Certainly, the gentleman is right.

The CHAIRMAN. The question is on the amendment offered by the gentleman from Indiana (Mr. Dennis).

The amendment was agreed to.

Report of Senate Committee on the Judiciary

The House approved rule 803(8), as submitted by the Supreme Court, with one substantive change. It excluded from the hearsay exception reports containing matters observed by police officers and other law enforcement personnel in criminal cases. Ostensibly, the reason for this exclusion is that observations by police officers at the scene of the crime or the apprehension of the defendant are not as reliable as observations by public officials in other cases because of the adversarial nature of the confrontation between the police and the defendant in criminal cases.

The committee accepts the House's decision to exclude such recorded observations where the police officer is available to testify in court about his observation. However, where he is unavailable as unavailability is defined in rule 804(a)(4) and (a)(5), the report should be admitted as the best available evidence. Accordingly, the committee has amended rule 803(8) to refer to the provision of rule 804(b)(5), which allows the admission of such reports, records or other statements where the police officer or other law enforcement officer is unavailable because of death, then existing physical or mental illness or infirmity, or not being successfully subject to legal process. [This version of rule 804(b)(5) was not included in the rules as enacted.]

The House Judiciary Committee report contained a statement of intent that "the phrase 'factual findings' in subdivision (c) be strictly construed and that evaluations or opinions contained in public reports shall not be admissible under this rule." The committee takes strong exception to this limiting understanding of the application of the rule. We do not think it reflects an understanding of the intended operation of the rule as explained in the Advisory Committee notes to this subsection. The Advisory Committee notes on subsection (c) of this subdivision point out that various kinds of evaluative reports are now admissible under Federal statutes. 7 U.S.C. § 78, findings of Secretary of Agriculture prima facie evidence of true grade of grain; 42 U.S.C. § 269(b), bill of health by appropriate official prima facie evidence of vessel's sanitary history and condition and compliance with regulations. These statutory exceptions to the hearsay rule are preserved. Rule 802. The willingness of Congress to recognize these and other such evaluative reports provides a helpful guide in determining the kind of reports which are intended to be admissible under this rule. We think the restrictive interpretation of the House overlooks the fact that while the Advisory Committee assumes admissibility in the first instance of evaluative reports, they are not admissible if, as the rule states, "the sources of information or other circumstances indicate lack of trustworthiness."

The Advisory Committee explains the factors to be considered:

* * *

Factors which may be of assistance in passing upon the admissibility of evaluative reports include: (1) the timeliness of the investigation, McCormick, Can the Courts Make Wider Use of Reports of Official Investigations? 42 Iowa L.Rev. 363 (1957); (2) the special skill or experience of the official, id.; (3) whether a hearing was held and the level at which conducted, Franklin v. Skelly Oil Co., 141 F.2d 568 (19th Cir.1944): (4) possible motivation problems suggested by Palmer v.

Hoffman, 318 U.S. 109, 63 S.Ct. 477, 87 L.Ed. 645 (1943). Others no doubt could be added.[4]

* * *

The committee concludes that the language of the rule together with the explanation provided by the Advisory Committee furnish sufficient guidance on the admissibility of evaluative reports.

Conference Report

The Senate amendment adds language, not contained in the House bill, that refers to another rule that was added by the Senate in another amendment (Rule 804(b)(5)—Criminal law enforcement records and reports).

In view of its action on Rule 804(b)(5) (Criminal law enforcement records and reports), the Conference does not adopt the Senate amendment and restores the bill to the House version.

Advisory Committee's Note

Exception (9). Records of vital statistics are commonly the subject of particular statutes making them admissible in evidence, Uniform Vital Statistics Act, 9C U.L.A. 350 (1957). The rule is in principle narrower than Uniform Rule 63(16) which includes reports required of persons performing functions authorized by statute, yet in practical effect the two are substantially the same. Comment Uniform Rule 63(16). The exception as drafted is in the pattern of California Evidence Code § 1281.

Exception (10). The principle of proving nonoccurrence of an event by evidence of the absence of a record which would regularly be made of its occurrence, developed in Exception (7) with respect to regularly conducted [business] activities, is here extended to public records of the kind mentioned in Exceptions (8) and (9). 5 Wigmore § 1633(6), p. 519. Some harmless duplication no doubt exists with Exception (7). For instances of federal statutes recognizing this method of proof, see 8 U.S.C. § 1284(b), proof of absence of alien crewman's name from outgoing manifest prima facie evidence of failure to detain or deport, and 42 U.S.C. § 405(c)(3), (4)(B), (4)(C), absence of HEW record prima facie evidence of no wages or self-employment income.

The rule includes situations in which absence of a record may itself be the ultimate focal point of inquiry, e.g. People v. Love, 310 Ill. 558, 142 N.E. 204 (1923), certificate of Secretary of State admitted to show failure to file documents required by Securities Law, as well as cases where the absence of a record is offered as proof of the nonoccurrence of an event ordinarily recorded.

The refusal of the common law to allow proof by certificate of the lack of a record or entry, has no apparent justification, 5 Wigmore § 1678(7), p. 752. The rule takes the opposite position, as do Uniform Rule 63(17); California Evidence Code § 1284; Kansas Code of Civil Procedure § 60–460(c); New Jersey Evidence Rule 63(17). Congress has recognized certification as evidence of the lack of a record. 8 U.S.C. § 1360(d), certificate of Attorney General or other designated officer that no record of Immigration and Naturalization Service of specified nature or entry therein is found, admissible in alien cases.

Exception (11). Records of activities of religious organizations are currently recognized as admissible at least to the extent of the business records exception to the hearsay rule, 5 Wigmore § 1523, p. 371, and Exception (6)

---

4. Advisory Committee's notes, to rule 803(8)(c).

would be applicable. However, both the business record doctrine and Exception (6) require that the person furnishing the information be one in the business or activity. The result is such decisions as Daily v. Grand Lodge, 311 Ill. 184, 142 N.E. 478 (1924), holding a church record admissible to prove fact, date, and place of baptism, but not age of child except that he had at least been born at the time. In view of the unlikelihood that false information would be furnished on occasions of this kind, the rule contains no requirement that the informant be in the course of the activity. See California Evidence Code § 1315 and Comment.

Exception (12). The principle of proof by certification is recognized as to public officials in Exceptions (8) and (10), and with respect to authentication in Rule 902. The present exception is a duplication to the extent that it deals with a certificate by a public official, as in the case of a judge who performs a marriage ceremony. The area covered by the rule is, however, substantially larger and extends the certification procedure to clergymen and the like who perform marriages and other ceremonies or administer sacraments. Thus certificates of such matters as baptism or confirmation, as well as marriage, are included. In principle they are as acceptable evidence as certificates of public officers. See 5 Wigmore § 1645, as to marriage certificates. When the person executing the certificate is not a public official, the self-authenticating character of documents purporting to emanate from public officials, see Rule 902, is lacking and proof is required that the person was authorized and did make the certificate. The time element, however, may safely be taken as supplied by the certificate, once authority and authenticity are established, particularly in view of the presumption that a document was executed on the date it bears.

For similar rules, some limited to certificates of marriage, with variations in foundation requirements, see Uniform Rule 63(18); California Evidence Code § 1316; Kansas Code of Civil Procedure § 60–460(p); New Jersey Evidence Rule 63(18).

Exception (13). Records of family history kept in family Bibles have by long tradition been received in evidence. 5 Wigmore §§ 1495, 1496, citing numerous statutes and decisions. See also Regulations, Social Security Administration, 20 C.F.R. § 404.703(c), recognizing family Bible entries as proof of age in the absence of public or church records. Opinions in the area also include inscriptions on tombstones, publicly displayed pedigrees, and engravings on rings. Wigmore, supra. The rule is substantially identical in coverage with California Evidence Code § 1312.

Report of House Committee on the Judiciary

The Committee approved this Rule in the form submitted by the Court, intending that the phrase "Statements of fact concerning personal or family history" be read to include the specific types of such statements enumerated in Rule 803(11).

Advisory Committee's Note

Exception (14). The recording of title documents is a purely statutory development. Under any theory of the admissibility of public records, the records would be receivable as evidence of the contents of the recorded document, else the recording process would be reduced to a nullity. When, however, the record is offered for the further purpose of proving execution and delivery, a problem of lack of firsthand knowledge by the recorder, not present as to contents, is presented. This problem is solved, seemingly in all jurisdictions, by qualifying for recording only those documents shown by a specified procedure, either acknowledgement or a form of probate, to have been executed and delivered. 5 Wigmore §§ 1647–1651. Thus what may appear in the rule, at first glance, as endowing the record with an effect independently of local law and inviting difficulties of an *Erie* nature under Cities Service Oil Co. v. Dunlap, 308 U.S. 208, 60 S.Ct. 201, 84 L.Ed. 196 (1939), is not present, since the local law in fact governs under the example.

Exception (15). Dispositive documents often contain recitals of fact. Thus a deed purporting to have been executed by an attorney in fact may recite the existence of the power of attorney, or a deed may recite that the grantors are all the heirs of the last record owner. Under the rule, these recitals are exempted from the hearsay rule. The circumstances under which dispositive documents are executed and the requirement that the recital be germane to the purpose of the document are believed to be adequate guarantees of trustworthiness, particularly in view of the nonapplicability of the rule if dealings with the property have been inconsistent with the document. The age of the document is of no significance, though in practical application the document will most often be an ancient one. See Uniform Rule 63(29), Comment.

Similar provisions are contained in Uniform Rule 63(29); California Evidence Code § 1330; Kansas Code of Civil Procedure § 60–460(aa); New Jersey Evidence Rule 63(29).

Exception (16). Authenticating a document as ancient, essentially in the pattern of the common law, as provided in Rule 901(b)(8), leaves open as a separate question the admissibility of assertive statements contained therein as against a hearsay objection. 7 Wigmore § 2145a. Wigmore further states that the ancient document technique of authentication is universally conceded to apply to all sorts of documents, including letters, records, contracts, maps, and certificates, in addition to title documents, citing numerous decisions. Id. § 2145. Since most of these items are significant evidentially only insofar as they are assertive, their admission in evidence must be as a hearsay exception. But see 5 id. § 1573, p. 429, referring to recitals in ancient deeds as a "limited" hearsay exception. The former position is believed to be the correct one in reason and authority. As pointed out in McCormick § 298, danger of mistake is minimized by authentication requirements, and age affords assurance that the writing antedates the present controversy. See Dallas County v. Commercial Union Assurance Co., 286 F.2d 388 (5th Cir.1961), upholding admissibility of 58-year-old newspaper story. Cf. Morgan, Basic Problems of Evidence 364 (1962), but see id. 254.

For a similar provision, but with the added requirement that "the statement has since generally been acted upon as true by persons having an interest in the matter," see California Evidence Code § 1331.

Exception (17). Ample authority at common law supported the admission in evidence of items falling in this category. While Wigmore's text is narrowly oriented to lists, etc., prepared for the use of a trade or profession, 6 Wigmore § 1702, authorities are cited which include other kinds of publications, for example, newspaper market reports, telephone directories, and city directories. Id. §§ 1702–1706. The basis of trustworthiness is general reliance by the public or by a particular segment of it, and the motivation of the compiler to foster reliance by being accurate.

For similar provisions, see Uniform Rule 63(30); California Evidence Code § 1340; Kansas Code of Civil Procedure § 60–460(bb); New Jersey Evidence Rule 63(30). Uniform Commercial Code § 2–724 provides for admissibility in evidence of "reports in official publications or trade journals or in newspapers or periodicals of general circulation published as the reports of such [established commodity] market."

Exception (18). The writers have generally favored the admissibility of learned treatises, McCormick § 296, p. 621; Morgan, Basic Problems of Evidence 366 (1962); 6 Wigmore § 1692, with the support of occasional decisions and rules, City of Dothan v. Hardy, 237 Ala. 603, 188 So. 264 (1939); Lewandowski v. Preferred Risk Mut. Ins. Co., 33 Wis.2d 69, 146 N.W.2d 505 (1966), 66 Mich.L.Rev. 183 (1967); Uniform Rule 63(31); Kansas Code of Civil Procedure § 60–460(cc), but the great weight of authority has been that learned treatises are not admissible as substantive evidence though usable in the cross-examination of experts. The foundation of the minority view is that the hearsay objection must be regarded as unimpressive when directed against treatises since a high standard of accuracy is engendered by various factors: the treatise is written primarily and impartially for professionals, subject to scrutiny and exposure for inaccuracy, with the reputation of the writer at stake. 6 Wigmore § 1692. Sound as this position may be with respect to trustworthiness, there is, nevertheless, an additional difficulty in the likelihood that the treatise will be misunderstood and misapplied without expert assistance and supervision. This difficulty is recognized in the cases demonstrating unwillingness to sustain findings relative to disability on the basis of judicially noticed medical texts. Ross v. Gardner, 365 F.2d 554 (6th Cir.1966); Sayers v. Gardner, 380 F.2d 940 (6th Cir.1967); Colwell v. Gardner, 386 F.2d 56 (6th Cir.1967); Glendenning v. Ribicoff, 213 F.Supp. 301 (W.D.Mo.1962); Cook v. Celebrezze, 217 F.Supp. 366 (W.D.Mo.1963); Sosna v. Celebrezze, 234 F.Supp. 289 (E.D.Pa.1964); and see McDaniel v. Celebrezze, 331 F.2d 426 (4th Cir.1964). The rule avoids the danger of misunderstanding and misapplication by limiting the use of treatises as substantive evidence to situations in which an expert is on the stand and available to explain and assist in the application of the treatise if desired. The limitation upon receiving the publication itself physically in evidence, contained in the last sentence, is designed to further this policy.

The relevance of the use of treatises on cross-examination is evident. This use of treatises has been the subject of varied views. The most restrictive position is that the witness must have stated expressly on direct his reliance upon the treatise. A slightly more liberal approach still insists upon reliance but allows it to be developed on cross-examination. Further relaxation dispenses with reliance but requires recognition as an authority by the witness, developable on cross-examination. The greatest liberality is found in decisions allowing use of the treatise on cross-examination when its status as an authority is established by any means. Annot., 60 A.L.R.2d 77. The exception is hinged upon this last position, which is that of the Supreme Court, Reilly v. Pinkus, 338 U.S. 269, 70 S.Ct. 110, 94 L.Ed. 63 (1949), and of recent well considered state court decisions, City of St. Petersburg v. Ferguson, 193 So.2d 648 (Fla.App.1967), cert. denied Fla., 201 So.2d 556; Darling v. Charleston Memorial Community Hospital, 33 Ill.2d 326, 211 N.E.2d 253 (1965); Dabroe v. Rhodes Co., 64 Wash.2d 431, 392 P.2d 317 (1964).

In Reilly v. Pinkus, supra, the Court pointed out that testing of professional knowledge was incomplete without exploration of the witness' knowledge of and attitude toward established treatises in the field. The process works equally well in reverse and furnishes the basis of the rule.

The rule does not require that the witness rely upon or recognize the treatise as authoritative, thus avoiding the possibility that the expert may at the outset block cross-examination by refusing to concede reliance or authoritativeness. Dabroe v. Rhodes Co., supra. Moreover, the rule avoids the unreality of admitting evidence for the purpose of impeachment only, with an instruction to the jury not to consider it otherwise. The parallel to the treatment of prior inconsistent statements will be apparent. See Rules 613(b) and 801(d)(1).

Exceptions (19), (20), and (21). Trustworthiness in reputation evidence is found "when the topic is such that the facts are likely to have been inquired about and that persons having personal knowledge have disclosed facts which have thus been discussed in the community; and thus the community's conclusion, if any has been formed, is likely to be a trustworthy one." 5 Wigmore § 1580, p. 444, and see also § 1583. On this common foundation, reputation as to land boundaries, customs, general history, character, and marriage have come to be regarded as admissible. The breadth of the underlying principle suggests the formulation of an equally broad exception, but tradition has in fact been much narrower and more particularized, and this is the pattern of these exceptions in the rule.

Exception (19) is concerned with matters of personal and family history. Marriage is universally conceded to be a proper subject of proof by evidence of reputation in the community. 5 Wigmore § 1602. As to such items as legitimacy, relationship, adoption, birth, and death, the decisions are divided. Id. § 1605. All seem to be susceptible to being the subject of well founded repute. The "world" in which the reputation may exist may be family, associates, or community. This world has proved capable of expanding with changing times from the single uncomplicated neighborhood, in which all activities take place, to the multiple and unrelated worlds of work, religious affiliation, and social activity, in each of which a reputation may be generated. People v. Reeves, 360 Ill. 55, 195 N.E. 443 (1935); State v. Axilrod, 248 Minn. 204, 79 N.W.2d 677 (1956); Mass.Stat.1947, c. 410, M.G.L.A. c. 233 § 21A; 5 Wigmore § 1616. The family has often served as the point of beginning for allowing community reputation. 5 Wigmore § 1488. For comparable provisions see Uniform Rule 63(26), (27)(c); California Evidence Code §§ 1313, 1314; Kansas Code of Civil Procedure § 60–460(x), (y)(3); New Jersey Evidence Rule 63(26), (27)(c).

The first portion of Exception (20) is based upon the general admissibility of evidence of reputation as to land boundaries and land customs, expanded in this country to include private as well as public boundaries. McCormick § 299, p. 625. The reputation is required to antedate the controversy, though not to be ancient. The second portion is likewise supported by authority, id., and is designed to facilitate proof of events when judicial notice is not available. The historical character of the subject matter dispenses with any need that the reputation antedate the controversy with respect to which it is offered. For similar provisions see Uniform Rule 63(27)(a), (b); California Evidence Code §§ 1320–1322; Kansas Code of Civil Procedure § 60–460(y), (1), (2); New Jersey Evidence Rule 63(27)(a), (b).

Exception (21) recognizes the traditional acceptance of reputation evidence as a means of proving human character. McCormick §§ 44, 158. The exception deals only with the hearsay aspect of this kind of evidence. Limitations upon admissibility based on other grounds will be found in Rules 404, relevancy of character evidence generally, and 608, character of witness. The exception is in effect a reiteration, in the context of hearsay, of Rule 405(a). Similar provisions are contained in Uniform Rule 63(28); California Evidence Code

§ 1324; Kansas Code of Civil Procedure § 60–460(z); New Jersey Evidence Rule 63(28).

Exception (22). When the status of a former judgment is under consideration in subsequent litigation, three possibilities must be noted: (1) the former judgment is conclusive under the doctrine of res judicata, either as a bar or a collateral estoppel; or (2) it is admissible in evidence for what it is worth; or (3) it may be of no effect at all. The first situation does not involve any problem of evidence except in the way that principles of substantive law generally bear upon the relevancy and materiality of evidence. The rule does not deal with the substantive effect of the judgment as a bar or collateral estoppel. When, however, the doctrine of res judicata does not apply to make the judgment either a bar or a collateral estoppel, a choice is presented between the second and third alternatives. The rule adopts the second for judgments of criminal conviction of felony grade. This is the direction of the decisions, Annot., 18 A.L.R.2d 1287, 1299, which manifest an increasing reluctance to reject *in toto* the validity of the law's factfinding processes outside the confines of res judicata and collateral estoppel. While this may leave a jury with the evidence of conviction but without means to evaluate it, as suggested by Judge Hinton, Note 27 Ill.L.Rev. 195 (1932), it seems safe to assume that the jury will give it substantial effect unless defendant offers a satisfactory explanation, a possibility not foreclosed by the provision. But see North River Ins. Co. v. Militello, 104 Colo. 28, 88 P.2d 567 (1939), in which the jury found for plaintiff on a fire policy despite the introduction of his conviction for arson. For supporting federal decisions see Clark, J., in New York & Cuba Mail S.S. Co. v. Continental Cas. Co., 117 F.2d 404, 411 (2d Cir.1941); Connecticut Fire Ins. Co. v. Farrara, 277 F.2d 388 (8th Cir.1960).

Practical considerations require exclusion of convictions of minor offenses, not because the administration of justice in its lower echelons must be inferior, but because motivation to defend at this level is often minimal or nonexistent. Cope v. Goble, 39 Cal.App.2d 448, 103 P.2d 598 (1940); Jones v. Talbot, 87 Idaho 498, 394 P.2d 316 (1964); Warren v. Marsh, 215 Minn. 615, 11 N.W.2d 528 (1943); Annot., 18 A.L.R.2d 1287, 1295–1297; 16 Brooklyn L.Rev. 286 (1950); 50 Colum.L.Rev. 529 (1950); 35 Cornell L.Q. 872 (1950). Hence the rule includes only convictions of felony grade, measured by federal standards.

Judgments of conviction based upon pleas of *nolo contendere* are not included. This position is consistent with the treatment of *nolo* pleas in Rule 410 and the authorities cited in the Advisory Committee's Note in support thereof.

While these rules do not in general purport to resolve constitutional issues, they have in general been drafted with a view to avoiding collision with constitutional principles. Consequently the exception does not include evidence of the conviction of a third person, offered against the accused in a criminal prosecution to prove any fact essential to sustain the judgment of conviction. A contrary position would seem clearly to violate the right of confrontation. Kirby v. United States, 174 U.S. 47, 19 S.Ct. 574, 43 L.Ed. 890 (1899), error to convict of possessing stolen postage stamps with the only evidence of theft being the record of conviction of the thieves. The situation is to be distinguished from cases in which conviction of another person is an element of the crime, e.g. 15 U.S.C. § 902(d), interstate shipment of firearms to a known convicted felon, and, as specifically provided, from impeachment.

For comparable provisions see Uniform Rule 63(20); California Evidence Code § 1300; Kansas Code of Civil Procedure § 60–460(r); New Jersey Evidence Rule 63(20).

Exception (23). A hearsay exception in this area was originally justified on the ground that verdicts were evidence of reputation. As trial by jury graduated from the category of neighborhood inquests, this theory lost its validity. It was never valid as to chancery decrees. Nevertheless the rule persisted, though the judges and writers shifted ground and began saying that the judgment or decree was as good evidence as reputation. See City of London v. Clerke, Carth. 181, 90 Eng.Rep. 710 (K.B. 1691); Neill v. Duke of Devonshire, 8 App.Cas. 135 (1882). The shift appears to be correct, since the process of inquiry, sifting, and scrutiny which is relied upon to render reputation reliable is present in perhaps greater measure in the process of litigation. While this might suggest a broader area of application, the affinity to reputation is strong, and paragraph (23) goes no further, not even including character.

The leading case in the United States, Patterson v. Gaines, 47 U.S. (6 How.) 550, 599, 12 L.Ed. 553 (1847), follows in the pattern of the English decisions, mentioning as illustrative matters thus provable: manorial rights, public rights of way, immemorial custom, disputed boundary, and pedigree. More recent recognition of the principle is found in Grant Bros. Construction Co. v. United States, 232 U.S. 647, 34 S.Ct. 452, 58 L.Ed. 776 (1914), in action for penalties under Alien Contract Labor Law, decision of board of inquiry of Immigration Service admissible to prove alienage of laborers, as a matter of pedigree; United States v. Mid-Continent Petroleum Corp., 67 F.2d 37 (10th Cir.1933), records of commission enrolling Indians admissible on pedigree; Jung Yen Loy v. Cahill, 81 F.2d 809 (9th Cir.1936), board decisions as to citizenship of plaintiff's father admissible in proceeding for declaration of citizenship. Contra, In re Estate of Cunha, 49 Haw. 273, 414 P.2d 925 (1966).

Exception (24). The preceding 23 exceptions of Rule 803 and the first five [four] exceptions of Rule 804(b), infra, are designed to take full advantage of the accumulated wisdom and experience of the past in dealing with hearsay. It would, however, be presumptuous to assume that all possible desirable exceptions to the hearsay rule have been catalogued and to pass the hearsay rule to oncoming generations as a closed system. Exception (24) and its companion provision in Rule 804(b)(6)[5] are accordingly included. They do not contemplate an unfettered exercise of judicial discretion, but they do provide for treating new and presently unanticipated situations which demonstrate a trustworthiness within the spirit of the specifically stated exceptions. Within this framework, room is left for growth and development of the law of evidence in the hearsay area, consistently with the broad purposes expressed in Rule 102. See Dallas County v. Commercial Union Assur. Co., 286 F.2d 388 (5th Cir. 1961).

Report of House Committee on the Judiciary

The proposed Rules of Evidence submitted to Congress contained identical provisions in Rules 803 and 804 (which set forth the various hearsay exceptions), to the effect that the federal courts could admit any hearsay statement not specifically covered by any of the stated exceptions, if the hearsay statement was found to have "comparable circumstantial guarantees of trustworthiness."

The Committee deleted these provisions (proposed rules 803(24) and 804(b) (6)) as injecting too much uncertainty into the law of evidence and impairing the ability of practitioners to prepare for trial. It was noted that Rule 102 directs the courts to construe the Rules of Evidence so as to promote "growth and development." The Committee believed that if additional hearsay exceptions are to be created, they should be by amendments to the Rules, not on a case-by-case basis.

Report of Senate Committee on the Judiciary

The proposed Rules of Evidence submitted to Congress contained identical provisions in rules 803 and 804 (which set forth the various hearsay exceptions), admitting any hearsay statement not specifically covered by any of the stated exceptions, if the hearsay statement was found to have "comparable circumstantial guarantees of trustworthiness." The House deleted these provisions (proposed rules 803(24) and 804(b)(6)) as injecting "too much uncertainty" into the law of evidence and impairing the ability of practitioners to prepare for trial. The House felt that rule 102, which directs the courts to construe the Rules of Evidence so as to promote growth and development, would permit sufficient flexibility to admit hearsay evidence in appropriate cases under various factual situations that might arise.

We disagree with the total rejection of a residual hearsay exception. While we view rule 102 as being intended to provide for a broader construction and interpretation of these rules, we feel that, without a separate residual provision, the specifically enumerated exceptions could become tortured beyond any reasonable circumstances which they were intended to include (even if broadly construed). Moreover, these exceptions, while they reflect the most typical and well recognized exceptions to the hearsay rule, may not encompass every situation in which the reliability and appropriateness of a particular piece of hearsay evidence make clear that it should be heard and considered by the trier of fact.

The committee believes that there are certain exceptional circumstances where evidence which is found by a court to have guarantees of trustworthiness equivalent to or exceeding the guarantees reflected by the presently listed exceptions, and to have a high degree of probativeness and necessity could properly be admissible.

The case of Dallas County v. Commercial Union Assoc. Co., Ltd., 286 F.2d 388 (5th Cir.1961) illustrates the point. The issue in that case was whether the tower of the county courthouse collapsed because it was struck by lightning (covered by insurance) or because of structural weakness and deterioration of the structure (not covered). Investigation of the structure revealed the presence of charcoal and charred timbers. In order to show that lightning may not have been the cause of the charring, the insurer offered a copy of a local newspaper published over 50 years earlier containing an unsigned article describing a fire in the courthouse while it was under construction. The Court found that the newspaper did not qualify for admission as a business record or an ancient document and did not fit within any other recognized hearsay exception. The court concluded, however, that the article was trustworthy because it was inconceivable that a newspaper reporter in a small town would report a fire in the courthouse if none had occurred. See also United States v. Barbati, 284 F.Supp. 409 (E.D.N.Y.1968).

Because exceptional cases like the *Dallas County* case may arise in the future, the committee has decided to reinstate a residual exception for rules 803 and 804(b).

The committee, however, also agrees with those supporters of the House version who felt that an overly broad residual hearsay exception could emasculate the hearsay rule and the recognized exceptions or vitiate the rationale behind codification of the rules.

Therefore, the committee has adopted a residual exception for rules 803 and 804(b) of much narrower scope and applicability than the Supreme Court version. In order to qualify for admission, a hearsay statement not falling within one of the recognized exceptions would have to satisfy at least four conditions. First, it must have "equivalent circumstantial guarantees of trustworthiness." Second, it must be offered as evidence of a material fact. Third, the court must determine that the statement "is more probative on the point for which it is offered than any other evidence which the proponent can procure through reasonable efforts." This requirement is intended to insure that only statements which have high probative value and necessity may qualify for admission under the residual exceptions. Fourth, the court must determine that "the general purposes of these rules and the interests of justice will best be served by admission of the statement into evidence."

It is intended that the residual hearsay exceptions will be used very rarely, and only in exceptional circumstances. The committee does not intend to establish a broad license for trial judges to admit hearsay statements that do not fall within one of the other exceptions contained in rules 803 and 804(b). The residual exceptions are not meant to authorize major judicial revisions of the hearsay rule, including its present exceptions. Such major revisions are best accomplished by legislative action. It is intended that in any case in which evidence is sought to be admitted under these subsections, the trial judge will exercise no less care, reflection and caution than the courts did under the common law in establishing the now-recognized exceptions to the hearsay rule.

In order to establish a well-defined jurisprudence, the special facts and circumstances which, in the court's judgment, indicates that the statement has a sufficiently high degree of trustworthiness and necessity to justify its admission should be stated on the record. It is expected that the court will give the opposing party a full and adequate opportunity to contest the admission of any statement sought to be introduced under these subsections.

Conference Report

The Senate amendment adds a new subsection, (24), which makes admissible a hearsay statement not specifically covered by any of the previous twenty-three subsections, if the statement has equivalent circumstantial guarantees of trustworthiness and if the court determines that (A) the statement is offered as evidence of a material fact; (B) the statement is more probative on the point for which it is offered than any other evidence the proponent can procure through reasonable efforts; and (C) the general purposes of these rules and the interests of justice will best be served by admission of the statement into evidence.

The House bill eliminated a similar, but broader, provision because of the conviction that such a provision injected too much uncertainty into the law of evidence regarding hearsay and impaired the ability of a litigant to prepare adequately for trial.

The Conference adopts the Senate amendment with an amendment that provides that a party intending to request the court to use a statement under this provision must notify any adverse party of this intention as well as of the particulars of the statement, including the name and address of the declarant. This notice must be given sufficiently in advance of the trial or hearing to provide any adverse party with a fair opportunity to prepare to contest the use of the statement.

Rule 804

Note by Federal Judicial Center

The rule prescribed by the Supreme Court was amended by the Congress in a number of respects as follows:

Subdivision (a). Paragraphs (1) and (2) were amended by substituting "court" in place of "judge," and paragraph (5) was amended by inserting "(or in the case of a hearsay exception under subdivision (b)(2), (3), or (4), his attendance or testimony)".

Subdivision (b). Exception (1) was amended by inserting "the same or" after "course of," and by substituting the phrase "if the party against whom the testimony is now offered, or, in a civil action or proceeding, a predecessor in interest, had an opportunity and similar motive to develop the testimony by direct, cross, or redirect examination" in place of "at the instance of or against a party with an opportunity to develop the testimony by direct, cross, or redirect examination, with motive and interest similar to those of the party against whom now offered."

Exception (2) as prescribed by the Supreme Court, dealing with statements of recent perception, was deleted by the Congress. It is included in the Appendix hereto as an aid to interpretation. Exception (2) as enacted by the Congress is Exception (3) prescribed by the Supreme Court, amended by inserting at the beginning, "In a prosecution for homicide or in a civil action or proceeding".

Exception (3) as enacted by the Congress is Exception (4) prescribed by the Supreme Court, amended in the first sentence by deleting, after "another," the phrase "or to make him an object of hatred ridicule, or disgrace," and amended in the second sentence by substituting, after "unless," the phrase, "corroborating circumstances clearly indicate the trustworthiness of the statement," in place of "corroborated."

Exception (4) as enacted by the Congress is Exception (5) prescribed by the Supreme Court without change.

Exception (5) as enacted by the Congress is Exception (6) prescribed by the Supreme Court, amended by substituting "equivalent" in place of "comparable" and by adding all after "trustworthiness."

Advisory Committee's Note

As to firsthand knowledge on the part of hearsay declarants, see the introductory portion of the Advisory Committee's Note to Rule 803.

Subdivision (a). The definition of unavailability implements the division of hearsay exceptions into two categories by Rules 803 and 804(b).

At common law the unavailability requirement was evolved in connection with particular hearsay exceptions rather than along general lines. For example, see the separate explications of unavailability in relation to former testimony, declarations against interest, and statements of pedigree, separately developed in McCormick §§ 234, 257, and 297. However, no reason is apparent for making distinctions as to what satisfies unavailability for the different exceptions. The treatment in the rule is therefore uniform although differences in the range of process for witnesses between civil and criminal cases will

lead to a less exacting requirement under item (5). See Rule 45(e) of the
Federal Rules of Civil Procedure and Rule 17(e) of the Federal Rules of
Criminal Procedure.

Five instances of unavailability are specified:

(1) Substantial authority supports the position that exercise of a claim of
privilege by the declarant satisfies the requirement of unavailability (usually in
connection with former testimony). Wyatt v. State, 35 Ala.App. 147, 46 So.2d
837 (1950); State v. Stewart, 85 Kan. 404, 116 P. 489 (1911); Annot., 45
A.L.R.2d 1354; Uniform Rule 62(7)(a); California Evidence Code § 240(a)(1);
Kansas Code of Civil Procedure § 60–459(g)(1). A ruling by the judge is
required, which clearly implies that an actual claim of privilege must be made.

(2) A witness is rendered unavailable if he simply refuses to testify concerning the subject matter of his statement despite judicial pressures to do so, a
position supported by similar considerations of practicality. Johnson v. People,
152 Colo. 586, 384 P.2d 454 (1963); People v. Pickett, 339 Mich. 294, 63 N.W.2d
681, 45 A.L.R.2d 1341 (1954). Contra, Pleau v. State, 255 Wis. 362, 38 N.W.2d
496 (1949).

(3) The position that a claimed lack of memory by the witness of the
subject matter of his statement constitutes unavailability likewise finds support
in the cases, though not without dissent. McCormick § 234, p. 494. If the
claim is successful, the practical effect is to put the testimony beyond reach, as
in the other instances. In this instance, however, it will be noted that the lack
of memory must be established by the testimony of the witness himself, which
clearly contemplates his production and subjection to cross-examination.

Report of House Committee on the Judiciary

Rule 804(a)(3) was approved in the form submitted by the Court. However,
the Committee intends no change in existing federal law under which the court
may choose to disbelieve the declarant's testimony as to his lack of memory.
See United States v. Insana, 423 F.2d 1165, 1169–1170 (2nd Cir.), cert. denied,
400 U.S. 841 (1970).

Advisory Committee's Note

(4) Death and infirmity find general recognition as grounds. McCormick
§§ 234, 257, 297; Uniform Rule 62(7)(c); California Evidence Code § 240(a)(3);
Kansas Code of Civil Procedure § 60–459(g)(3); New Jersey Evidence Rule 62(6)
(c). See also the provisions on use of depositions in Rule 32(a)(3) of the Federal
Rules of Civil Procedure and Rule 15(e) of the Federal Rules of Criminal
Procedure.

(5) Absence from the hearing coupled with inability to compel attendance
by process or other reasonable means also satisfies the requirement. McCormick § 234; Uniform Rule 62(7)(d) and (e); California Evidence Code § 240(a)(4)
and (5); Kansas Code of Civil Procedure § 60–459(g)(4) and (5); New Jersey
Rule 62(6)(b) and (d). See the discussion of procuring attendance of witnesses
who are nonresidents or in custody in Barber v. Page, 390 U.S. 719, 88 S.Ct.
1318, 20 L.Ed.2d 255 (1968).

If the conditions otherwise constituting unavailability result from the
procurement or wrongdoing of the proponent of the statement, the requirement
is not satisfied. * * *

1
2
3
4
5
6
7
8
9
10
11
12
13
14
15
16
17
18
19
20
21
22
23
24
25
26
27
28
29
30
31
32
33
34
35
36
37
38
39
40
41
42
43
44
45
46
47
48
49
50

Report of House Committee on the Judiciary

Rule 804(a)(5) as submitted to the Congress provided, as one type of situation in which a declarant would be deemed "unavailable", that he be "absent from the hearing and the proponent of his statement has been unable to procure his attendance by process or other reasonable means." The Committee amended the Rule to insert after the word "attendance" the parenthetical expression "(or, in the case of a hearsay exception under subdivision (b)(2), (3), or (4), his attendance or testimony)". The amendment is designed primarily to require that an attempt be made to depose a witness (as well as to seek his attendance) as a precondition to the witness being deemed unavailable. The Committee, however, recognized the propriety of an exception to this additional requirement when it is the declarant's former testimony that is sought to be admitted under subdivision (b)(1).

Report of Senate Committee on the Judiciary

Subdivision (a) of rule 804 as submitted by the Supreme Court defined the conditions under which a witness was considered to be unavailable. It was amended in the House.

The purpose of the amendment, according to the report of the House Committee on the Judiciary, is "primarily to require that an attempt be made to depose a witness (as well as to seek his attendance) as a precondition to the witness being unavailable."[1]

Under the House amendment, before a witness is declared unavailable, a party must try to depose a witness (declarant) with respect to dying declarations, declarations against interest, and declarations of pedigree. None of these situations would seem to warrant this needless, impractical and highly restrictive complication. A good case can be made for eliminating the unavailability requirement entirely for declarations against interest cases.[2]

In dying declaration cases, the declarant will usually, though not necessarily, be deceased at the time of trial. Pedigree statements which are admittedly and necessarily based largely on word of mouth are not greatly fortified by a deposition requirement.

Depositions are expensive and time-consuming. In any event, deposition procedures are available to those who wish to resort to them. Moreover, the deposition procedures of the Civil Rules and Criminal Rules are only imperfectly adapted to implementing the amendment. No purpose is served unless the deposition, if taken, may be used in evidence. Under Civil Rule (a)(3) and Criminal Rule 15(e), a deposition, though taken, may not be admissible, and under Criminal Rule 15(a) substantial obstacles exist in the way of even taking a deposition.

For these reasons, the committee deleted the House amendment.

The committee understands that the rule as to unavailability, as explained by the Advisory Committee "contains no requirement that an attempt be made to take the deposition of a declarant." In reflecting the committee's judgment, the statement is accurate insofar as it goes. Where, however, the proponent of the statement, with knowledge of the existence of the statement, fails to

1. H.Rept. 93–650, at p. 15.

2. Uniform rule 63(10); Kan.Stat.Anno. 60–460(j); 2A N.J.Stats.Anno. 84–63(10).

confront the declarant with the statement at the taking of the deposition, then 1
the proponent should not, in fairness, be permitted to treat the declarant as 2
"unavailable" simply because the declarant was not amenable to process 3
compelling his attendance at trial. The committee does not consider it neces- 4
sary to amend the rule to this effect because such a situation abuses, not 5
conforms to, the rule. Fairness would preclude a person from introducing a 6
hearsay statement on a particular issue if the person taking the deposition was 7
aware of the issue at the time of the deposition but failed to depose the 8
unavailable witness on that issue. 9

Conference Report 10

Subsection (a) defines the term "unavailability as a witness". The House 11
bill provides in subsection (a)(5) that the party who desires to use the statement 12
must be unable to procure the declarant's attendance by process or other 13
reasonable means. In the case of dying declarations, statements against 14
interest and statements of personal or family history, the House bill requires 15
that the proponent must also be unable to procure the declarant's *testimony* 16
(such as by deposition or interrogatories) by process or other reasonable means. 17
The Senate amendment eliminates this latter provision. 18

The Conference adopts the provision contained in the House bill. 19
20

Advisory Committee's Note 21

Subdivision (b). Rule 803, supra, is based upon the assumption that a 22
hearsay statement falling within one of its exceptions possesses qualities which 23
justify the conclusion that whether the declarant is available or unavailable is 24
not a relevant factor in determining admissibility. The instant rule proceeds 25
upon a different theory: hearsay which admittedly is not equal in quality to 26
testimony of the declarant on the stand may nevertheless be admitted if the 27
declarant is unavailable and if his statement meets a specified standard. The 28
rule expresses preferences: testimony given on the stand in person is preferred 29
over hearsay, and hearsay, if of the specified quality, is preferred over complete 30
loss of the evidence of the declarant. The exceptions evolved at common law 31
with respect to declarations of unavailable declarants furnish the basis for the 32
exceptions enumerated in the proposal. The term "unavailable" is defined in 33
subdivision (a). 34

Exception (1). Former testimony does not rely upon some set of circum- 35
stances to substitute for oath and cross-examination, since both oath and 36
opportunity to cross-examine were present in fact. The only missing one of the 37
ideal conditions for the giving of testimony is the presence of trier and 38
opponent ("demeanor evidence"). This is lacking with all hearsay exceptions. 39
Hence it may be argued that former testimony is the strongest hearsay and 40
should be included under Rule 803, supra. However, opportunity to observe 41
demeanor is what in a large measure confers depth and meaning upon oath and 42
cross-examination. Thus in cases under Rule 803 demeanor lacks the signifi- 43
cance which it possesses with respect to testimony. In any event, the tradition, 44
founded in experience, uniformly favors production of the witness if he is 45
available. The exception indicates continuation of the policy. This preference 46
for the presence of the witness is apparent also in rules and statutes on the use 47
of depositions, which deal with substantially the same problem. 48

Under the exception, the testimony may be offered (1) against the party 49
against whom it was previously offered or (2) against the party *by* whom it was 50
previously offered. In each instance the question resolves itself into whether

fairness allows imposing, upon the party against whom now offered, the handling of the witness on the earlier occasion. (1) If the party against whom now offered is the one against whom the testimony was offered previously, no unfairness is apparent in requiring him to accept his own prior conduct of cross-examination or decision not to cross-examine. Only demeanor has been lost, and that is inherent in the situation. (2) If the party against whom now offered is the one *by* whom the testimony was offered previously, a satisfactory answer becomes somewhat more difficult. One possibility is to proceed somewhat along the line of an adoptive admission, i.e. by offering the testimony proponent in effect adopts it. However, this theory savors of discarded concepts of witnesses' belonging to a party, of litigants' ability to pick and choose witnesses, and of vouching for one's own witnesses. Cf. McCormick § 246, pp. 526–527; 4 Wigmore § 1075. A more direct and acceptable approach is simply to recognize direct and redirect examination of one's own witness as the equivalent of cross-examining an opponent's witness. Falknor, Former Testimony and the Uniform Rules: A Comment, 38 N.Y.U.L.Rev. 651, n. 1 (1963); McCormick § 231, p. 483. See also 5 Wigmore § 1389. Allowable techniques for dealing with hostile, double-crossing, forgetful, and mentally deficient witnesses leave no substance to a claim that one could not adequately develop his own witness at the former hearing. An even less appealing argument is presented when failure to develop fully was the result of a deliberate choice.

The common law did not limit the admissibility of former testimony to that given in an earlier trial of the same case, although it did require identity of issues as a means of insuring that the former handling of the witness was the equivalent of what would now be done if the opportunity were presented. Modern decisions reduce the requirement to "substantial" identity. McCormick § 233. Since identity of issues is significant only in that it bears on motive and interest in developing fully the testimony of the witness, expressing the matter in the latter terms is preferable. Id. Testimony given at a preliminary hearing was held in California v. Green, 399 U.S. 149, 90 S.Ct. 1930, 26 L.Ed.2d 489 (1970), to satisfy confrontation requirements in this respect.

As a further assurance of fairness in thrusting upon a party the prior handling of the witness, the common law also insisted upon identity of parties, deviating only to the extent of allowing substitution of successors in a narrowly construed privity. Mutuality as an aspect of identity is now generally discredited, and the requirement of identity of the offering party disappears except as it might affect motive to develop the testimony. Falknor, supra, at 652; McCormick § 232, pp. 487–488. The question remains whether strict identity, or privity, should continue as a requirement with respect to the party against whom offered. * * *

Report of House Committee on the Judiciary

Rule 804(b)(1) as submitted by the Court allowed prior testimony of an unavailable witness to be admissible if the party against whom it is offered or a person "with motive and interest similar" to his had an opportunity to examine the witness. The Committee considered that it is generally unfair to impose upon the party against whom the hearsay evidence is being offered responsibility for the manner in which the witness was previously handled by another party. The sole exception to this, in the Committee's view, is when a party's predecessor in interest in a civil action or proceeding had an opportunity and similar motive to examine the witness. The Committee amended the Rule to reflect these policy determinations.

Advisory Committee's Note

Exception (3). The exception is the familiar dying declaration of the common law, expanded somewhat beyond its traditionally narrow limits. While the original religious justification for the exception may have lost its conviction for some persons over the years, it can scarcely be doubted that powerful psychological pressures are present. See 5 Wigmore § 1443 and the classic statement of Chief Baron Eyre in Rex v. Woodcock, 1 Leach 500, 502, 168 Eng.Rep. 352, 353 (K.B.1789).

The common law required that the statement be that of the victim, offered in a prosecution for criminal homicide. Thus declarations by victims in prosecutions for other crimes, e.g. a declaration by a rape victim who dies in childbirth, and all declarations in civil cases were outside the scope of the exception. An occasional statute has removed these restrictions, as in Colo.R.S. § 52–1–20, or has expanded the area of offenses to include abortions, 5 Wigmore § 1432, p. 224, n. 4. Kansas by decision extended the exception to civil cases. Thurston v. Fritz, 91 Kan. 468, 138 P. 625 (1914). While the common law exception no doubt originated as a result of the exceptional need for the evidence in homicide cases, the theory of admissibility applies equally in civil cases * * *. The same considerations suggest abandonment of the limitation to circumstances attending the event in question, yet when the statement deals with matters other than the supposed death, its influence is believed to be sufficiently attenuated to justify the limitation. Unavailability is not limited to death. See subdivision (a) of this rule. Any problem as to declarations phrased in terms of opinion is laid at rest by Rule 701, and continuation of a requirement of first-hand knowledge is assured by Rule 602.

Comparable provisions are found in Uniform Rule 63(5); California Evidence Code § 1242; Kansas Code of Civil Procedure § 60–460(e); New Jersey Evidence Rule 63(5).

Report of House Committee on the Judiciary

Rule 804(b)(3) as submitted by the Court (now Rule 804(b)(2) in the bill) proposed to expand the traditional scope of the dying declaration exception (i.e. a statement of the victim in a homicide case as to the cause or circumstances of his believed imminent death) to allow such statements in all criminal and civil cases. The Committee did not consider dying declarations as among the most reliable forms of hearsay. Consequently, it amended the provision to limit their admissibility in criminal cases to homicide prosecutions, where exceptional need for the evidence is present. This is existing law. At the same time, the Committee approved the expansion to civil actions and proceedings where the stakes do not involve possible imprisonment, although noting that this could lead to forum shopping in some instances.

Advisory Committee's Note

Exception (4). The circumstantial guaranty of reliability for declarations against interest is the assumption that persons do not make statements which are damaging to themselves unless satisfied for good reason that they are true. Hileman v. Northwest Engineering Co., 346 F.2d 668 (6th Cir.1965). If the statement is that of a party, offered by his opponent, it comes in as an admission, Rule 803(d)(2), and there is no occasion to inquire whether it is against interest, this not being a condition precedent to admissibility of admissions by opponents.

The common law required that the interest declared against be pecuniary or proprietary but within this limitation demonstrated striking ingenuity in discovering an against-interest aspect. Higham v. Ridgway, 10 East 109, 103 Eng.Rep. 717 (K.B.1808); Reg. v. Overseers of Birmingham, 1 B. & S. 763, 121 Eng.Rep. 897 (Q.B.1861); McCormick, § 256, p. 551 nn. 2 and 3.

The exception discards the common law limitation and expands to the full logical limit. One result is to remove doubt as to the admissibility of declarations tending to establish a tort liability against the declarant or to extinguish one which might be asserted by him, in accordance with the trend of the decisions in this country. McCormick, § 254, pp. 548–549. * * * And finally, exposure to criminal liability satisfies the against-interest requirement. The refusal of the common law to concede the adequacy of a penal interest was no doubt indefensible in logic, see the dissent of Mr. Justice Holmes in Donnelly v. United States, 228 U.S. 243, 33 S.Ct. 449, 57 L.Ed. 820 (1913), but one senses in the decisions a distrust of evidence of confessions by third persons offered to exculpate the accused arising from suspicions of fabrication either of the fact of the making of the confession or in its contents, enhanced in either instance by the required unavailability of the declarant. Nevertheless, an increasing amount of decisional law recognizes exposure to punishment for crime as a sufficient stake. People v. Spriggs, 60 Cal.2d 868, 36 Cal.Rptr. 841, 389 P.2d 377 (1964); Sutter v. Easterly, 354 Mo. 282, 189 S.W.2d 284 (1945); Band's Refuse Removal, Inc. v. Fairlawn Borough, 62 N.J.Super. 522, 163 A.2d 465 (1960); Newberry v. Commonwealth, 191 Va. 445, 61 S.E.2d 318 (1950); Annot., 162 A.L.R. 446. The requirement of corroboration is included in the rule in order to effect an accommodation between these competing considerations. When the statement is offered by the accused by way of exculpation, the resulting situation is not adapted to control by rulings as to the weight of the evidence, and hence the provision is cast in terms of a requirement preliminary to admissibility. Cf. Rule 406(a). The requirement of corroboration should be construed in such a manner as to effectuate its purpose of circumventing fabrication.

Ordinarily the third-party confession is thought of in terms of exculpating the accused, but this is by no means always or necessarily the case: it may include statements implicating him, and under the general theory of declarations against interest they would be admissible as related statements. Douglas v. Alabama, 380 U.S. 415, 85 S.Ct. 1074, 13 L.Ed.2d 934 (1965), and Bruton v. United States, 389 U.S. 818, 88 S.Ct. 126, 19 L.Ed.2d 70 (1968), both involved confessions by codefendants which implicated the accused. While the confession was not actually offered in evidence in *Douglas,* the procedure followed effectively put it before the jury, which the Court ruled to be error. Whether the confession might have been admissible as a declaration against penal interest was not considered or discussed. *Bruton* assumed the inadmissibility, as against the accused, of the implicating confession of his codefendant, and centered upon the question of the effectiveness of a limiting instruction. These decisions, however, by no means require that all statements implicating another person be excluded from the category of declarations against interest. Whether a statement is in fact against interest must be determined from the circumstances of each case. Thus a statement admitting guilt and implicating another person, made while in custody, may well be motivated by a desire to curry favor with the authorities and hence fail to qualify as against interest.

See the dissenting opinion of Mr. Justice White in *Bruton*. On the other hand, the same words spoken under different circumstances, e.g., to an acquaintance, would have no difficulty in qualifying. The rule does not purport to deal with questions of the right of confrontation.

The balancing of self-serving against disserving aspects of a declaration is discussed in McCormick § 256.

For comparable provisions, see Uniform Rule 63(10); California Evidence Code § 1230; Kansas Code of Civil Procedure § 60–460(j); New Jersey Evidence Rule 63(10).

Report of House Committee on the Judiciary

Rule 804(b)(4) as submitted by the Court (now Rule 804(b)(3) in the bill) provided as follows:

> *Statement against interest.*—A statement which was at the time of its making so far contrary to the declarant's pecuniary or proprietary interest or so far tended to subject him to civil or criminal liability or to render invalid a claim by him against another or to make him an object of hatred, ridicule, or disgrace, that a reasonable man in his position would not have made the statement unless he believed it to be true. A statement tending to exculpate the accused is not admissible unless corroborated.

The Committee determined to retain the traditional hearsay exception for statements against pecuniary or proprietary interest. However, it deemed the Court's additional references to statements tending to subject a declarant to civil liability or to render invalid a claim by him against another to be redundant as included within the scope of the reference to statements against pecuniary or proprietary interest. See Gichner v. Antonio Triano Tile and Marble Co., 410 F.2d 238 (D.C.Cir.1968). Those additional references were accordingly deleted.

The Court's Rule also proposed to expand the hearsay limitation from its present federal limitation to include statements subjecting the declarant to criminal liability and statements tending to make him an object of hatred, ridicule, or disgrace. The Committee eliminated the latter category from the subdivision as lacking sufficient guarantees of reliability. See United States v. Dovico, 380 F.2d 325, 327 nn. 2, 4 (2nd Cir.), cert. denied, 389 U.S. 944 (1967). As for statements against penal interest, the Committee shared the view of the Court that some such statements do possess adequate assurances of reliability and should be admissible. It believed, however, as did the Court, that statements of this type tending to exculpate the accused are more suspect and so should have their admissibility conditioned upon some further provision insuring trustworthiness. The proposal in the Court Rule to add a requirement of simple corroboration was, however, deemed ineffective to accomplish this purpose since the accused's own testimony might suffice while not necessarily increasing the reliability of the hearsay statement. The Committee settled upon the language "unless corroborating circumstances clearly indicate the trustworthiness of the statement" as affording a proper standard and degree of discretion. It was contemplated that the result in such cases as Donnelly v. United States, 228 U.S. 243 (1912), where the circumstances plainly indicated reliability, would be changed. The Committee also added to the Rule the final sentence from the 1971 Advisory Committee draft, designed to codify the doctrine of Bruton v. United States, 391 U.S. 123 (1968). The Committee does not intend to affect the existing exception to the *Bruton* principle where the codefendant takes the stand and is subject to cross-examination, but believed there was no need to make specific provision for this situation in the Rule, since in that event the declarant would not be "unavailable".

Report of Senate Committee on the Judiciary

The rule defines those statements which are considered to be against interest and thus of sufficient trustworthiness to be admissible even though hearsay. With regard to the type of interest declared against, the version submitted by the Supreme Court included inter alia, statements tending to subject a declarant to civil liability or to invalidate a claim by him against another. The House struck these provisions as redundant. In view of the conflicting case law construing pecuniary or proprietary interests narrowly so as to exclude, e.g., tort cases, this deletion could be misconstrued.

Three States which have recently codified their rules of evidence have followed the Supreme Court's version of this rule, i.e., that a statement is against interest if it tends to subject a declarant to civil liability.[3]

The committee believes that the reference to statements tending to subject a person to civil liability constitutes a desirable clarification of the scope of the rule. Therefore, we have reinstated the Supreme Court language on this matter.

The Court rule also proposed to expand the hearsay limitation from its present federal limitation to include statements subjecting the declarant to statements tending to make him an object of hatred, ridicule, or disgrace. The House eliminated the latter category from the subdivision as lacking sufficient guarantees of reliability. Although there is considerable support for the admissibility of such statements (all three of the State rules referred to supra, would admit such statements), we accept the deletion by the House.

The House amended this exception to add a sentence making inadmissible a statement or confession offered against the accused in a criminal case, made by a codefendant or other person implicating both himself and the accused. The sentence was added to codify the constitutional principle announced in Bruton v. United States, 391 U.S. 123 (1968). *Bruton* held that the admission of the extrajudicial hearsay statement of one codefendant inculpating a second codefendant violated the confrontation clause of the sixth amendment.

The committee decided to delete this provision because the basic approach of the rules is to avoid codifying, or attempting to codify, constitutional evidentiary principles, such as the fifth amendment's right against self-incrimination and, here, the sixth amendment's right of confrontation. Codification of a constitutional principle is unnecessary and, where the principle is under development, often unwise. Furthermore, the House provision does not appear to recognize the exceptions to the *Bruton* rule, e.g. where the codefendant takes the stand and is subject to cross examination; where the accused confessed, see United States v. Mancusi, 404 F.2d 296 (2d Cir.1968), cert. denied 397 U.S. 942 (1907); where the accused was placed at the scene of the crime, see United States v. Zelker, 452 F.2d 1009 (2d Cir.1971). For these reasons, the committee decided to delete this provision.

3. Nev.Rev.Stats. § 51.345; N.Mex. Wis.Stats.Anno. (1973 Supp.) § 908.-
Stats. (1973 Supp.) § 20–4–804(4); West's 045(4).

The Senate amendment to subsection (b)(3) provides that a statement is against interest and not excluded by the hearsay rule when the declarant is unavailable as a witness, if the statement tends to subject a person to civil or criminal liability or renders invalid a claim by him against another. The House bill did not refer specifically to civil liability and to rendering invalid a claim against another. The Senate amendment also deletes from the House bill the provision that subsection (b)(3) does not apply to a statement or confession, made by a codefendant or another, which implicates the accused and the person who made the statement, when that statement or confession is offered against the accused in a criminal case.

The Conference adopts the Senate amendment. The Conferees intend to include within the purview of this rule, statements subjecting a person to civil liability and statements rendering claims invalid. The Conferees agree to delete the provision regarding statements by a codefendant, thereby reflecting the general approach in the Rules of Evidence to avoid attempting to codify constitutional evidentiary principles.

Advisory Committee's Note

Exception (5). The general common law requirement that a declaration in this area must have been made *ante litem motam* has been dropped, as bearing more appropriately on weight than admissibility. See 5 Wigmore § 1483. Item (i) specifically disclaims any need of firsthand knowledge respecting declarant's own personal history. In some instances it is self-evident (marriage) and in others impossible and traditionally not required (date of birth). Item (ii) deals with declarations concerning the history of another person. As at common law, declarant is qualified if related by blood or marriage. 5 Wigmore § 1489. In addition, and contrary to the common law, declarant qualifies by virtue of intimate association with the family. Id., § 1487. The requirement sometimes encountered that when the subject of the statement is the relationship between two other persons the declarant must qualify as to both is omitted. Relationship is reciprocal. Id., § 1491.

For comparable provisions, see Uniform Rule 63(23), (24), (25); California Evidence Code §§ 1310, 1311; Kansas Code of Civil Procedure § 60–460(u), (v), (w); New Jersey Evidence Rules 63(23), 63(24), 63(25).

Exception (6). In language and purpose, this exception is identical with Rule 803(24). See the Advisory Committee's Note to that provision.

Reports of House and Senate Committees on the Judiciary

[This exception and its companion exception in Rule 803(24) are discussed together in the congressional committee reports. The reports are set forth under rule 803(24), supra.]

Conference Report

The Senate amendment adds a new subsection, (b)(6)[5], which makes admissible a hearsay statement not specifically covered by any of the five previous subsections, if the statement has equivalent circumstantial guarantees of trustworthiness and if the court determines that (A) the statement is offered as evidence of a material fact; (B) the statement is more probative on the point for which it is offered than any other evidence the proponent can procure through reasonable efforts; and (C) the general purposes of these rules and the interests of justice will best be served by admission of the statement into evidence.

The House bill eliminated a similar, but broader, provision because of the conviction that such a provision injected too much uncertainty into the law of evidence regarding hearsay and impaired the ability of a litigant to prepare adequately for trial.

The Conference adopts the Senate amendment with an amendment that renumbers this subsection and provides that a party intending to request the court to use a statement under this provision must notify any adverse party of this intention as well as of the particulars of the statement, including the name and address of the declarant. This notice must be given sufficiently in advance of the trial or hearing to provide any adverse party with a fair opportunity to prepare to contest the use of the statement.

Conference Report

Senate Provision Deleted

The Senate amendment adds a new hearsay exception [804(b)(5)], not contained in the House bill, which provides that certain law enforcement records are admissible if the officer-declarant is unavailable to testify or be present because of (1) death or physical or mental illness or infirmity or (2) absence from the proceeding and the proponent of the statement has been unable to procure his attendance by process or other reasonable means.

The Conference does not adopt the Senate amendment, preferring instead to leave the bill in the House version, which contained no such provision.

Rule 805

Note by Federal Judicial Center

The rule enacted by the Congress is the rule prescribed by the Supreme Court without change.

Advisory Committee's Note

On principle it scarcely seems open to doubt that the hearsay rule should not call for exclusion of a hearsay statement which includes a further hearsay statement when both conform to the requirements of a hearsay exception. Thus a hospital record might contain an entry of the patient's age based on information furnished by his wife. The hospital record would qualify as a regular entry except that the person who furnished the information was not acting in the routine of the business. However, her statement independently qualifies as a statement of pedigree (if she is unavailable) or as a statement made for purposes of diagnosis or treatment, and hence each link in the chain falls under sufficient assurances. Or, further to illustrate, a dying declaration may incorporate a declaration against interest by another declarant. See McCormick § 290, p. 611.

Rule 806

Note by Federal Judicial Center

The rule enacted by the Congress is the rule prescribed by the Supreme Court, amended by inserting the phrase "or a statement defined in Rule 801(d) (2), (C), (D), or (E)."

Advisory Committee's Note

The declarant of a hearsay statement which is admitted in evidence is in effect a witness. His credibility should in fairness be subject to impeachment and support as though he had in fact testified. See Rules 608 and 609. There are however, some special aspects of the impeaching of a hearsay declarant which require consideration. These special aspects center upon impeachment by inconsistent statement, arise from factual differences which exist between the use of hearsay and an actual witness and also between various kinds of hearsay, and involve the question of applying to declarants the general rule disallowing evidence of an inconsistent statement to impeach a witness unless he is afforded an opportunity to deny or explain. See Rule 613(b).

The principal difference between using hearsay and an actual witness is that the inconsistent statement will in the case of the witness almost inevitably of necessity in the nature of things be a *prior* statement, which it is entirely possible and feasible to call to his attention, while in the case of hearsay the inconsistent statement may well be a *subsequent* one, which practically precludes calling it to the attention of the declarant. The result of insisting upon observation of this impossible requirement in the hearsay situation is to deny the opponent, already barred from cross-examination, any benefit of this important technique of impeachment. The writers favor allowing the subsequent statement. McCormick § 37, p. 69; 3 Wigmore § 1033. The cases, however, are divided. Cases allowing the impeachment include People v. Collup, 27 Cal.2d 829, 167 P.2d 714 (1946); People v. Rosoto, 58 Cal.2d 304, 23 Cal.Rptr. 779, 373 P.2d 867 (1962); Carver v. United States, 164 U.S. 694, 17 S.Ct. 228, 41 L.Ed. 602 (1897). Contra, Mattox v. United States, 156 U.S. 237, 15 S.Ct. 337, 39 L.Ed. 409 (1895); People v. Hines, 284 N.Y. 93, 29 N.E.2d 483 (1940). The force of *Mattox,* where the hearsay was the former testimony of a deceased witness and the denial of use of a subsequent inconsistent statement was upheld, is much diminished by *Carver,* where the hearsay was a dying declaration and denial of use of a subsequent inconsistent statement resulted in reversal. The difference in the particular brand of hearsay seems unimportant when the inconsistent statement is a *subsequent* one. True, the opponent is not totally deprived of cross-examination when the hearsay is former testimony or a deposition but he is deprived of cross-examining on the statement or along lines suggested by it. Mr. Justice Shiras, with two justices joining him, dissented vigorously in *Mattox.*

When the impeaching statement was made *prior* to the hearsay statement, differences in the kinds of hearsay appear which arguably may justify differences in treatment. If the hearsay consisted of a simple statement by the witness, e.g. a dying declaration or a declaration against interest, the feasibility of affording him an opportunity to deny or explain encounters the same practical impossibility as where the statement is a subsequent one, just discussed, although here the impossibility arises from the total absence of anything resembling a hearing at which the matter could be put to him. The courts by a large majority have ruled in favor of allowing the statement to be used under these circumstances. McCormick § 37, p. 69; 3 Wigmore § 1033. If, however, the hearsay consists of former testimony or a deposition, the possibility of calling the prior statement to the attention of the witness or deponent is not ruled out, since the opportunity to cross-examine was available. It might thus be concluded that with former testimony or depositions the conventional foundation should be insisted upon. Most of the cases involve depositions, and Wigmore describes them as divided. 3 Wigmore § 1031. Deposition procedures at best are cumbersome and expensive, and to require the laying of the foundation may impose an undue burden. Under the federal practice, there is no way of knowing with certainty at the time of taking a deposition whether it is merely for discovery or will ultimately end up in evidence. With respect to both former testimony and depositions the possibility exists that knowledge of the statement might not be acquired until after the time of the cross-examination. Moreover, the expanded admissibility of former testimony and depositions under Rule 804(b)(1) calls for a correspondingly expanded approach to impeachment. The rule dispenses with the requirement in all hearsay situations, which is readily administered and best calculated to lead to fair results.

Notice should be taken that Rule 26(f) of the Federal Rules of Civil Procedure, as originally submitted by the Advisory Committee, ended with the following:

"* * * and, without having first called them to the deponent's attention, may show statements contradictory thereto made at any time by the deponent."

This language did not appear in the rule as promulgated in December, 1937. See 4 Moore's Federal Practice ¶¶ 26.01[9], 26.35 (2d ed.1967). In 1951, Nebraska adopted a provision strongly resembling the one stricken from the federal rule:

"Any party may impeach any adverse deponent by self-contradiction without having laid foundation for such impeachment at the time such deposition was taken." R.S.Neb. § 25–1267.07.

For similar provisions, see Uniform Rule 65; California Evidence Code § 1202; Kansas Code of Civil Procedure § 60–462; New Jersey Evidence Rule 65.

The provision for cross-examination of a declarant upon his hearsay statement is a corollary of general principles of cross-examination. A similar provision is found in California Evidence Code § 1203.

Report of Senate Committee on the Judiciary

Rule 906[806], as passed by the House and as proposed by the Supreme Court provides that whenever a hearsay statement is admitted, the credibility of the declarant of the statement may be attacked, and if attacked may be supported, by any evidence which would be admissible for those purposes if the declarant had testified as a witness. Rule 801 defines what is a hearsay statement. While statements by a person authorized by a party-opponent to make a statement concerning the subject, by the party-opponent's agent or by a coconspirator of a party—see rule 801(d)(2)(C), (D) and (E)—are traditionally defined as exceptions to the hearsay rule, rule 801 defines such admission by a party-opponent as statements which are not hearsay. Consequently, rule 806 by referring exclusively to the admission of hearsay statements, does not appear to allow the credibility of the declarant to be attacked when the declarant is a coconspirator, agent or authorized spokesman. The committee is of the view that such statements should open the declarant to attacks on his credibility. Indeed, the reason such statements are excluded from the operation of rule 806 is likely attributable to the drafting technique used to codify the hearsay rule, viz. some statements, instead of being referred to as exceptions to the hearsay rule, are defined as statements which are not hearsay. The phrase "or a statement defined in rule 801(d)(2)(C), (D) and (E)" is added to the rule in order to subject the declarant of such statements, like the declarant of hearsay statements, to attacks on his credibility.[1]

Conference Report

The Senate amendment permits an attack upon the credibility of the declarant of a statement if the statement is one by a person authorized by a party-opponent to make a statement concerning the subject, only by an agent of a party-opponent, or one by a coconspirator of the party-opponent, as these statements are defined in Rules 801(d)(2)(C), (D) and (E). The House bill has no such provision.

The Conference adopts the Senate amendment. The Senate amendment conforms the rule to present practice.

ARTICLE IX.   AUTHENTICATION AND IDENTIFICATION

Rule 901

Note by Federal Judicial Center

The rule enacted by the Congress is the rule prescribed by the Supreme Court, amended in subdivision (b)(10) by substituting "prescribed" in place of "adopted," and by adding "pursuant to statutory authority."

Advisory Committee's Note

Subdivision (a). Authentication and identification represent a special aspect of relevancy. Michael and Adler, Real Proof, 5 Vand.L.Rev. 344, 362 (1952); McCormick §§ 179, 185; Morgan, Basic Problems of Evidence 378 (1962). Thus a telephone conversation may be irrelevant because on an unrelated topic or because the speaker is not identified. The latter aspect is the one here involved. Wigmore describes the need for authentication as "an inherent logical necessity." 7 Wigmore § 2129, p. 564.

This requirement of showing authenticity or identity falls in the category of relevancy dependent upon fulfillment of a condition of fact and is governed by the procedure set forth in Rule 104(b).

The common law approach to authentication of documents has been criticized as an "attitude of agnosticism," McCormick, Cases on Evidence 388, n. 4 (3rd ed. 1956), as one which "departs sharply from men's customs in ordinary affairs," and as presenting only a slight obstacle to the introduction of forgeries in comparison to the time and expense devoted to proving genuine writings which correctly show their origin on their face, McCormick § 185, pp. 395, 396.

---

1. The committee considered it unnecessary to include statements contained in rule 801(d)(2)(A) and (B)—the statement by the party-opponent himself or the statement of which he has manifested his adoption—because the credibility of the party-opponent is always subject to an attack on his credibility.

Today, such available procedures as requests to admit and pretrial conference afford the means of eliminating much of the need for authentication or identification. Also, significant inroads upon the traditional insistence on authentication and identification have been made by accepting as at least prima facie genuine items of the kind treated in Rule 902, infra. However, the need for suitable methods of proof still remains, since criminal cases pose their own obstacles to the use of preliminary procedures, unforeseen contingencies may arise, and cases of genuine controversy will still occur.

Subdivision (b). The treatment of authentication and identification draws largely upon the experience embodied in the common law and in statutes to furnish illustrative applications of the general principle set forth in subdivision (a). The examples are not intended as an exclusive enumeration of allowable methods but are meant to guide and suggest, leaving room for growth and development in this area of the law.

The examples relate for the most part to documents, with some attention given to voice communications and computer print-outs. As Wigmore noted, no special rules have been developed for authenticating chattels. Wigmore, Code of Evidence § 2086 (3rd ed.1942).

It should be observed that compliance with requirements of authentication or identification by no means assures admission of an item into evidence, as other bars, hearsay for example, may remain.

Example (1) contemplates a broad spectrum ranging from testimony of a witness who was present at the signing of a document to testimony establishing narcotics as taken from an accused and accounting for custody through the period until trial, including laboratory analysis. See California Evidence Code § 1413, eyewitness to signing.

Example (2) states conventional doctrine as to lay identification of handwriting, which recognizes that a sufficient familiarity with the handwriting of another person may be acquired by seeing him write, by exchanging correspondence, or by other means, to afford a basis for identifying it on subsequent occasions. McCormick § 189. See also California Evidence Code § 1416. Testimony based upon familiarity acquired for purposes of the litigation is reserved to the expert under the example which follows.

Example (3). The history of common law restrictions upon the technique of proving or disproving the genuineness of a disputed specimen of handwriting through comparison with a genuine specimen, by either the testimony of expert witnesses or direct viewing by the triers themselves, is detailed in 7 Wigmore §§ 1991–1994. In breaking away, the English Common Law Procedure Act of 1854, 17 and 18 Vict., c. 125, § 27, cautiously allowed expert or trier to use exemplars "proved to the satisfaction of the judge to be genuine" for purposes of comparison. The language found its way into numerous statutes in this country, e.g., California Evidence Code §§ 1417, 1418. While explainable as a measure of prudence in the process of breaking with precedent in the handwriting situation, the reservation to the judge of the question of the genuineness of exemplars and the imposition of an unusually high standard of persuasion are at variance with the general treatment of relevancy which depends upon fulfillment of a condition of fact. Rule 104(b). No similar attitude is found in other comparison situations, e.g., ballistics comparison by jury, as in Evans v. Commonwealth, 230 Ky. 411, 19 S.W.2d 1091 (1929), or by experts, Annot., 26 A.L.R.2d 892, and no reason appears for its continued existence in handwriting cases. Consequently Example (3) sets no higher standard for handwriting specimens and treats all comparison situations alike, to be governed by Rule

104(b). This approach is consistent with 28 U.S.C. § 1731: "The admitted or proved handwriting of any person shall be admissible, for purposes of comparison, to determine genuineness of other handwriting attributed to such person."

Precedent supports the acceptance of visual comparison as sufficiently satisfying preliminary authentication requirements for admission in evidence. Brandon v. Collins, 267 F.2d 731 (2d Cir.1959); Wausau Sulphate Fibre Co. v. Commissioner of Internal Revenue, 61 F.2d 879 (7th Cir.1932); Desimone v. United States, 227 F.2d 864 (9th Cir.1955).

Example (4). The characteristics of the offered item itself, considered in the light of circumstances, afford authentication techniques in great variety. Thus a document or telephone conversation may be shown to have emanated from a particular person by virtue of its disclosing knowledge of facts known peculiarly to him; Globe Automatic Sprinkler Co. v. Braniff, 89 Okl. 105, 214 P. 127 (1923); California Evidence Code § 1421; similarly, a letter may be authenticated by content and circumstances indicating it was in reply to a duly authenticated one. McCormick § 192; California Evidence Code § 1420. Language patterns may indicate authenticity or its opposite. Magnuson v. State, 187 Wis. 122, 203 N.W. 749 (1925); Arens and Meadow, Psycholinguistics and the Confession Dilemma, 56 Colum.L.Rev. 19 (1956).

Example (5). Since aural voice identification is not a subject of expert testimony, the requisite familiarity may be acquired either before or after the particular speaking which is the subject of the identification, in this respect resembling visual identification of a person rather than identification of handwriting. Cf. Example (2), supra, People v. Nichols, 378 Ill. 487, 38 N.E.2d 766 (1942); McGuire v. State, 200 Md. 601, 92 A.2d 582 (1952); State v. McGee, 336 Mo. 1082, 83 S.W.2d 98 (1935).

Example (6). The cases are in agreement that a mere assertion of his identity by a person talking on the telephone is not sufficient evidence of the authenticity of the conversation and that additional evidence of his identity is required. The additional evidence need not fall in any set pattern. Thus the content of his statements or the reply technique, under Example (4), supra, or voice identification under Example (5), may furnish the necessary foundation. Outgoing calls made by the witness involve additional factors bearing upon authenticity. The calling of a number assigned by the telephone company reasonably supports the assumption that the listing is correct and that the number is the one reached. If the number is that of a place of business, the mass of authority allows an ensuing conversation if it relates to business reasonably transacted over the telephone, on the theory that the maintenance of the telephone connection is an invitation to do business without further identification. Matton v. Hoover Co., 350 Mo. 506, 166 S.W.2d 557 (1942); City of Pawhuska v. Crutchfield, 147 Okl. 4, 293 P. 1095 (1930); Zurich General Acc. & Liability Ins. Co. v. Baum, 159 Va. 404, 165 S.E. 518 (1932). Otherwise, some additional circumstance of identification of the speaker is required. The authorities divide on the question whether the self-identifying statement of the person answering suffices. Example (6) answers in the affirmative on the assumption that usual conduct respecting telephone calls furnish adequate assurances of regularity, bearing in mind that the entire matter is open to exploration before the trier of fact. In general, see McCormick § 193; 7 Wigmore § 2155; Annot., 71 A.L.R. 5, 105 id. 326.

Example (7). Public records are regularly authenticated by proof of custody, without more. McCormick § 191; 7 Wigmore §§ 2158, 2159. The example extends the principle to include data stored in computers and similar methods, of which increasing use in the public records area may be expected. See California Evidence Code §§ 1532, 1600.

Example (8). The familiar ancient document rule of the common law is extended to include data stored electronically or by other similar means. Since the importance of appearance diminishes in this situation, the importance of custody or place where found increases correspondingly. This expansion is necessary in view of the widespread use of methods of storing data in forms other than conventional written records.

Any time period selected is bound to be arbitrary. The common law period of 30 years is here reduced to 20 years, with some shift of emphasis from the probable unavailability of witnesses to the unlikeliness of a still viable fraud after the lapse of time. The shorter period is specified in the English Evidence Act of 1938, 1 & 2 Geo. 6, c. 28, and in Oregon R.S.1963, § 41.360(34). See also the numerous statutes prescribing periods of less than 30 years in the case of recorded documents. 7 Wigmore § 2143.

The application of Example (8) is not subject to any limitation to title documents or to any requirement that possession, in the case of a title document, has been consistent with the document. See McCormick § 190.

Example (9) is designed for situations in which the accuracy of a result is dependent upon a process or system which produces it. X rays afford a familiar instance. Among more recent developments is the computer, as to which see Transport Indemnity Co. v. Seib, 178 Neb. 253, 132 N.W.2d 871 (1965); State v. Veres, 7 Ariz.App. 117, 436 P.2d 629 (1968); Merrick v. United States Rubber Co., 7 Ariz.App. 433, 440 P.2d 314 (1968); Freed, Computer Print-Outs as Evidence, 16 Am.Jur.Proof of Facts 273; Symposium, Law and Computers in the Mid-Sixties, ALI–ABA (1966); 37 Albany L.Rev. 61 (1967). Example (9) does not, of course, foreclose taking judicial notice of the accuracy of the process or system.

Example (10). The example makes clear that methods of authentication provided by Act of Congress and by the Rules of Civil and Criminal Procedure or by Bankruptcy Rules are not intended to be superseded. Illustrative are the provisions for authentication of official records in Civil Procedure Rule 44 and Criminal Procedure Rule 27, for authentication of records of proceedings by court reporters in 28 U.S.C. § 753(b) and Civil Procedure Rule 80(c), and for authentication of depositions in Civil Procedure Rule 30(f).

Rule 902

Note by Federal Judicial Center

The rule enacted by the Congress is the rule prescribed by the Supreme Court, amended as follows:

Paragraph (4) was amended by substituting "prescribed" in place of "adopted," and by adding "pursuant to statutory authority."

Paragraph (8) was amended by substituting "in the manner provided by law by" in place of "under the hand and seal of."

Advisory Committee's Note

Case law and statutes have, over the years, developed a substantial body of instances in which authenticity is taken as sufficiently established for purposes of admissibility without extrinsic evidence to that effect, sometimes for reasons of policy but perhaps more often because practical considerations reduce the possibility of unauthenticity to a very small dimension. The present rule collects and incorporates these situations, in some instances expanding them to occupy a larger area which their underlying considerations justify. In no instance is the opposite party foreclosed from disputing authenticity.

Paragraph (1). The acceptance of documents bearing a public seal and signature, most often encountered in practice in the form of acknowledgments or certificates authenticating copies of public records, is actually of broad application. Whether theoretically based in whole or in part upon judicial notice, the practical underlying considerations are that forgery is a crime and detection is fairly easy and certain. 7 Wigmore § 2161, p. 638; California Evidence Code § 1452. More than 50 provisions for judicial notice of official seals are contained in the United States Code.

Paragraph (2). While statutes are found which raise a presumption of genuineness of purported official signatures in the absence of an official seal, 7 Wigmore § 2167; California Evidence Code § 1453, the greater ease of effecting a forgery under these circumstances is apparent. Hence this paragraph of the rule calls for authentication by an officer who has a seal. Notarial acts by members of the armed forces and other special situations are covered in paragraph (10).

Paragraph (3) provides a method for extending the presumption of authenticity to foreign official documents by a procedure of certification. It is derived from Rule 44(a)(2) of the Rules of Civil Procedure but is broader in applying to public documents rather than being limited to public records.

Paragraph (4). The common law and innumerable statutes have recognized the procedure of authenticating copies of public records by certificate. The certificate qualifies as a public document, receivable as authentic when in conformity with paragraph (1), (2), or (3). Rule 44(a) of the Rules of Civil Procedure and Rule 27 of the Rules of Criminal Procedure have provided authentication procedures of this nature for both domestic and foreign public records. It will be observed that the certification procedure here provided extends only to public records, reports, and recorded documents, all including data compilations, and does not apply to public documents generally. Hence documents provable when presented in original form under paragraphs (1), (2), or (3) may not be provable by certified copy under paragraph (4).

Paragraph (5). Dispensing with preliminary proof of the genuineness of purportedly official publications, most commonly encountered in connection with statutes, court reports, rules, and regulations, has been greatly enlarged by statutes and decisions. 5 Wigmore § 1684. Paragraph (5), it will be noted, does not confer admissibility upon all official publications; it merely provides a means whereby their authenticity may be taken as established for purposes of admissibility. Rule 44(a) of the Rules of Civil Procedure has been to the same effect.

Paragraph (6). The likelihood of forgery of newspapers or periodicals is slight indeed. Hence no danger is apparent in receiving them. Establishing the authenticity of the publication may, of course, leave still open questions of authority and responsibility for items therein contained. See 7 Wigmore § 2150. Cf. 39 U.S.C. § 4005(b), public advertisement prima facie evidence of agency of person named, in postal fraud order proceeding; Canadian Uniform Evidence Act, Draft of 1936, printed copy of newspaper prima facie evidence that notices or advertisements were authorized.

Paragraph (7). Several factors justify dispensing with preliminary proof of genuineness of commercial and mercantile labels and the like. The risk of forgery is minimal. Trademark infringement involves serious penalties. Great efforts are devoted to inducing the public to buy in reliance on brand names, and substantial protection is given them. Hence the fairness of this treatment finds recognition in the cases. Curtiss Candy Co. v. Johnson, 163 Miss. 426, 141 So. 762 (1932), Baby Ruth candy bar; Doyle v. Continental Baking Co., 262 Mass. 516, 160 N.E. 325 (1928), loaf of bread; Weiner v. Mager & Throne, Inc., 167 Misc. 338, 3 N.Y.S.2d 918 (1938), same. And see W.Va.Code 1966, § 47–3–5, trade-mark on bottle prima facie evidence of ownership. Contra, Keegan v. Green Giant Co., 150 Me. 283, 110 A.2d 599 (1954); Murphy v. Campbell Soup Co., 62 F.2d 564 (1st Cir. 1933). Cattle brands have received similar acceptance in the western states. Rev.Code Mont. 1947, § 46–606; State v. Wolfley, 75 Kan. 406, 89 P. 1046 (1907); Annot., 11 L.R.A.(N.S.) 87. Inscriptions on trains and vehicles are held to be prima facie evidence of ownership or control. Pittsburgh, Ft. W. & C. Ry. v. Callaghan, 157 Ill. 406, 41 N.E. 909 (1895); 9 Wigmore § 2510a. See also the provision of 19 U.S.C. § 1615(2) that marks, labels, brands, or stamps indicating foreign origin are prima facie evidence of foreign origin of merchandise.

Paragraph (8). In virtually every state, acknowledged title documents are receivable in evidence without further proof. Statutes are collected in 5 Wigmore § 1676. If this authentication suffices for documents of the importance of those affecting titles, logic scarcely permits denying this method when other kinds of documents are involved. Instances of broadly inclusive statutes are California Evidence Code § 1451 and N.Y.CPLR 4538, McKinney's Consol. Laws 1963.

Report of House Committee on the Judiciary

Rule 902(8) as submitted by the Court referred to certificates of acknowledgment "under the hand and seal of" a notary public or other officer authorized by law to take acknowledgments. The Committee amended the Rule to eliminate the requirement, believed to be inconsistent with the law in some States, that a notary public must affix a seal to a document acknowledged before him. As amended the Rule merely requires that the document be executed in the manner prescribed by State law.

Advisory Committee's Note

Paragraph (9). Issues of the authenticity of commercial paper in federal courts will usually arise in diversity cases, will involve an element of a cause of action or defense, and with respect to presumptions and burden of proof will be controlled by Erie Railroad Co. v. Tompkins, 304 U.S. 64, 58 S.Ct. 817, 82 L.Ed. 1188 (1938). Rule 302, supra. There may, however, be questions of authenticity involving lesser segments of a case or the case may be one governed by federal common law. Clearfield Trust Co. v. United States, 318 U.S. 363, 63 S.Ct. 573, 87 L.Ed. 838 (1943). Cf. United States v. Yazell, 382 U.S. 341, 86 S.Ct. 500, 15 L.Ed.2d 404 (1966). In these situations, resort to the useful authentication provisions of the Uniform Commercial Code is provided for. While the phrasing is in terms of "general commercial law," in order to avoid the potential complications inherent in borrowing local statutes, today one would have difficulty in determining the general commercial law without referring to the Code. See Williams v. Walker-Thomas Furniture Co., 121 U.S.App.D.C. 315, 350 F.2d 445 (1965). Pertinent Code provisions are sections 1–202, 3–307, and 3–510, dealing with third-party documents, signatures on negotiable instruments, protests, and statements of dishonor.

Report of House Committee on the Judiciary

The Committee approved Rule 902(9) as submitted by the Court. With respect to the meaning of the phrase "general commercial law", the Committee intends that the Uniform Commercial Code, which has been adopted in virtually every State, will be followed generally, but that federal commercial law will apply where federal commercial paper is involved. See Clearfield Trust Co. v. United States, 318 U.S. 363 (1943). Further, in those instances in which the issues are governed by Erie R. Co. v. Tompkins, 304 U.S. 64 (1938), State law will apply irrespective of whether it is the Uniform Commercial Code.

Advisory Committee's Note

Paragraph (10). The paragraph continues in effect dispensations with preliminary proof of genuineness provided in various Acts of Congress. See, for example, 10 U.S.C. § 936, signature, without seal, together with title, prima facie evidence of authenticity of acts of certain military personnel who are given notarial powers; 15 U.S.C. § 77f(a), signature on SEC registration presumed genuine; 26 U.S.C. § 6064, signature to tax return prima facie genuine.

Rule 903

Note by Federal Judicial Center

The rule enacted by the Congress is the rule prescribed by the Supreme Court without change.

Advisory Committee's Note

The common law required that attesting witnesses be produced or accounted for. Today the requirement has generally been abolished except with respect to documents which must be attested to be valid, e.g. wills in some states. McCormick § 188. Uniform Rule 71; California Evidence Code § 1411; Kansas Code of Civil Procedure § 60–468; New Jersey Evidence Rule 71; New York CPLR Rule 4537.

ARTICLE X. CONTENTS OF WRITINGS, RECORDINGS, AND PHOTOGRAPHS

———

Rule 1001

Note by Federal Judicial Center

The rule enacted by the Congress is the rule prescribed by the Supreme Court, amended in paragraph (2) by inserting "video tapes."

Advisory Committee's Note

In an earlier day, when discovery and other related procedures were strictly limited, the misleading named "best evidence rule" afforded substantial guarantees against inaccuracies and fraud by its insistence upon production of original documents. The great enlargement of the scope of discovery and related procedures in recent times has measurably reduced the need for the rule. Nevertheless important areas of usefulness persist: discovery of documents outside the jurisdiction may require substantial outlay of time and money; the unanticipated document may not practically be discoverable; criminal cases have built-in limitations on discovery. Cleary and Strong, The Best Evidence Rule: An Evaluation in Context, 51 Iowa L.Rev. 825 (1966).

Paragraph (1). Traditionally the rule requiring the original centered upon accumulations of data and expressions affecting legal relations set forth in words and figures. This meant that the rule was one essentially related to writings. Present day techniques have expanded methods of storing data, yet the essential form which the information ultimately assumes for usable purposes is words and figures. Hence the considerations underlying the rule dictate its expansion to include computers, photographic systems, and other modern developments.

Report of House Committee on the Judiciary

The Committee amended this Rule expressly to include "video tapes" in the definition of "photographs."

Advisory Committee's Note

Paragraph (3). In most instances, what is an original will be self-evident and further refinement will be unnecessary. However, in some instances particularized definition is required. A carbon copy of a contract executed in duplicate becomes an original, as does a sales ticket carbon copy given to a customer. While strictly speaking the original of a photograph might be thought to be only the negative, practicality and common usage require that any print from the negative be regarded as an original. Similarly, practicality and usage confer the status of original upon any computer printout. Transport Indemnity Co. v. Seib, 178 Neb. 253, 132 N.W.2d 871 (1965).

Paragraph (4). The definition describes "copies" produced by methods possessing an accuracy which virtually eliminates the possibility of error. Copies thus produced are given the status of originals in large measure by Rule 1003, infra. Copies subsequently produced manually, whether handwritten or typed, are not within the definition. It should be noted that what is an original for some purposes may be a duplicate for others. Thus a bank's microfilm record of checks cleared is the original as a record. However, a print offered as a copy of a check whose contents are in controversy is a duplicate. This result is substantially consistent with 28 U.S.C. § 1732(b). Compare 26 U.S.C. § 7513(c), giving full status as originals to photographic reproductions of tax returns and other documents, made by authority of the Secretary of the Treasury, and 44 U.S.C. § 399(a), giving original status to photographic copies in the National Archives.

Rule 1002

Note by Federal Judicial Center

The rule enacted by the Congress is the rule prescribed by the Supreme Court without change.

Advisory Committee's Note

The rule is the familiar one requiring production of the original of a document to prove its contents, expanded to include writings, recordings, and photographs, as defined in Rule 1001(1) and (2), supra.

Application of the rule requires a resolution of the question whether contents are sought to be proved. Thus an event may be proved by nondocumentary evidence, even though a written record of it was made. If, however, the event is sought to be proved by the written record, the rule applies. For example, payment may be proved without producing the written receipt which was given. Earnings may be proved without producing books of account in which they are entered. McCormick § 198; 4 Wigmore § 1245. Nor does the rule apply to testimony that books or records have been examined and found not to contain any reference to a designated matter.

The assumption should not be made that the rule will come into operation on every occasion when use is made of a photograph in evidence. On the contrary, the rule will seldom apply to ordinary photographs. In most instances a party *wishes* to introduce the item and the question raised is the propriety of receiving it in evidence. Cases in which an offer is made of the testimony of a witness as to what he saw in a photograph or motion picture, without producing the same, are most unusual. The usual course is for a witness on the stand to identify the photograph or motion picture as a correct representation of events which he saw or of a scene with which he is familiar. In fact he adopts the picture as his testimony, or, in common parlance, uses the picture to illustrate his testimony. Under these circumstances, no effort is made to prove the contents of the picture, and the rule is inapplicable. Paradis, The Celluloid Witness, 37 U.Colo.L.Rev. 235, 249–251 (1965).

On occasion, however, situations arise in which contents are sought to be proved. Copyright, defamation, and invasion of privacy by photograph or motion picture falls in this category. Similarly as to situations in which the picture is offered as having independent probative value, e.g. automatic photograph of bank robber. See People v. Doggett, 83 Cal.App.2d 405, 188 P.2d 792 (1948), photograph of defendants engaged in indecent act; Mouser and Philbin, Photographic Evidence—Is There a Recognized Basis for Admissibility? 8 Hastings L.J. 310 (1957). The most commonly encountered of this latter group is of course, the X ray, with substantial authority calling for production of the original. Daniels v. Iowa City, 191 Iowa 811, 183 N.W. 415 (1921); Cellamare v. Third Ave. Transit Corp., 273 App.Div. 260, 77 N.Y.S.2d 91 (1948); Patrick & Tilman v. Matkin, 154 Okl. 232, 7 P.2d 414 (1932); Mendoza v. Rivera, 78 P.R.R. 569 (1955).

It should be noted, however, that Rule 703, supra, allows an expert to give an opinion based on matters not in evidence, and the present rule must be read as being limited accordingly in its application. Hospital records which may be admitted as business records under Rule 803(6) commonly contain reports interpreting X rays by the staff radiologist, who qualifies as an expert, and these reports need not be excluded from the records by the instant rule.

The reference to Acts of Congress is made in view of such statutory provisions as 26 U.S.C. § 7513, photographic reproductions of tax returns and documents, made by authority of the Secretary of the Treasury, treated as originals, and 44 U.S.C. § 399(a), photographic copies in National Archives treated as originals.

Rule 1003

Note by Federal Judicial Center

The rule enacted by the Congress is the rule prescribed by the Supreme Court without change.

Advisory Committee's Note

When the only concern is with getting the words or other contents before the court with accuracy and precision, then a counterpart serves equally as well as the original, if the counterpart is the product of a method which insures accuracy and genuineness. By definition in Rule 1001(4), supra, a "duplicate" possesses this character.

Therefore, if no genuine issue exists as to authenticity and no other reason exists for requiring the original, a duplicate is admissible under the rule. This position finds support in the decisions, Myrick v. United States, 332 F.2d 279 (5th Cir. 1964), no error in admitting photostatic copies of checks instead of original microfilm in absence of suggestion to trial judge that photostats were incorrect; Johns v. United States, 323 F.2d 421 (5th Cir. 1963), not error to admit concededly accurate tape recording made from original wire recording; Sauget v. Johnston, 315 F.2d 816 (9th Cir.1963), not error to admit copy of agreement when opponent had original and did not on appeal claim any discrepancy. Other reasons for requiring the original may be present when only a part of the original is reproduced and the remainder is needed for cross-examination or may disclose matters qualifying the part offered or otherwise useful to the opposing party. United States v. Alexander, 326 F.2d 736 (4th Cir. 1964). And see Toho Bussan Kaisha, Ltd. v. American President Lines, Ltd., 265 F.2d 418, 76 A.L.R.2d 1344 (2d Cir.1959).

Report of House Committee on the Judiciary

The Committee approved this Rule in the form submitted by the Court, with the expectation that the courts would be liberal in deciding that a "genuine question is raised as to the authenticity of the original."

Rule 1004

Note by Federal Judicial Center

The rule enacted by the Congress is the rule prescribed by the Supreme Court without change.

Advisory Committee's Note

Basically the rule requiring the production of the original as proof of contents has developed as a rule of preference: if failure to produce the original is satisfactorily explained, secondary evidence is admissible. The instant rule specifies the circumstances under which production of the original is excused.

The rule recognizes no "degrees" of secondary evidence. While strict logic might call for extending the principle of preference beyond simply preferring the original, the formulation of a hierarchy of preferences and a procedure for making it effective is believed to involve unwarranted complexities. Most, if not all, that would be accomplished by an extended scheme of preferences will, in any event, be achieved through the normal motivation of a party to present the most convincing evidence possible and the arguments and procedures available to his opponent if he does not. Compare McCormick § 207.

Paragraph (1). Loss or destruction of the original, unless due to bad faith of the proponent, is a satisfactory explanation of nonproduction. McCormick § 201.

Report of House Committee on the Judiciary

The Committee approved Rule 1004(1) in the form submitted to Congress. However, the Committee intends that loss or destruction of an original by another person at the instigation of the proponent should be considered as tantamount to loss or destruction in bad faith by the proponent himself.

Advisory Committee's Note

Paragraph (2). When the original is in the possession of a third person, inability to procure it from him by resort to process or other judicial procedure is a sufficient explanation of nonproduction. Judicial procedure includes subpoena duces tecum as an incident to the taking of a deposition in another jurisdiction. No further showing is required. See McCormick § 202.

Paragraph (3). A party who has an original in his control has no need for the protection of the rule if put on notice that proof of contents will be made. He can ward off secondary evidence by offering the original. The notice procedure here provided is not to be confused with orders to produce or other discovery procedures, as the purpose of the procedure under this rule is to afford the opposite party an opportunity to produce the original, not to compel him to do so. McCormick § 203.

Paragraph (4). While difficult to define with precision, situations arise in which no good purpose is served by production of the original. Examples are the newspaper in an action for the price of publishing defendant's advertisement, Foster-Holcomb Investment Co. v. Little Rock Publishing Co., 151 Ark. 449, 236 S.W. 597 (1922), and the streetcar transfer of plaintiff claiming status as a passenger, Chicago City Ry. Co. v. Carroll, 206 Ill. 318, 68 N.E. 1087 (1903). Numerous cases are collected in McCormick § 200, p. 412, n. 1.

Rule 1005

Note by Federal Judicial Center

The rule enacted by the Congress is the rule prescribed by the Supreme Court without change.

Advisory Committee's Note

Public records call for somewhat different treatment. Removing them from their usual place of keeping would be attended by serious inconvenience to the public and to the custodian. As a consequence judicial decisions and statutes commonly hold that no explanation need be given for failure to produce the original of a public record. McCormick § 204; 4 Wigmore §§ 1215–1228. This blanket dispensation from producing or accounting for the original would open the door to the introduction of every kind of secondary evidence of contents of public records were it not for the preference given certified or compared copies. Recognition of degrees of secondary evidence in this situation is an appropriate *quid pro quo* for not applying the requirement of producing the original.

The provisions of 28 U.S.C. § 1733(b) apply only to departments or agencies of the United States. The rule, however, applies to public records generally and is comparable in scope in this respect to Rule 44(a) of the Rules of Civil Procedure.

Rule 1006

Note by Federal Judicial Center

The rule enacted by the Congress is the rule prescribed by the Supreme Court without change.

Advisory Committee's Note

The admission of summaries of voluminous books, records, or documents offers the only practicable means of making their contents available to judge and jury. The rule recognizes this practice, with appropriate safeguards. 4 Wigmore § 1230.

Rule 1007

Note by Federal Judicial Center

The rule enacted by the Congress is the rule prescribed by the Supreme Court without change.

Advisory Committee's Note

While the parent case, Slatterie v. Pooley, 6 M. & W. 664, 151 Eng.Rep. 579 (Exch. 1840), allows proof of contents by evidence of an oral admission by the party against whom offered, without accounting for nonproduction of the original, the risk of inaccuracy is substantial and the decision is at odds with the purpose of the rule giving preference to the original. See 4 Wigmore § 1255. The instant rule follows Professor McCormick's suggestion of limiting this use of admissions to those made in the course of giving testimony or in writing. McCormick § 208, p. 424. The limitation of course, does not call for excluding evidence of an oral admission when nonproduction of the original has been accounted for and secondary evidence generally has become admissible. Rule 1004, supra.

A similar provision is contained in New Jersey Evidence Rule 70(1) (h).

Rule 1008

Note by Federal Judicial Center

The rule enacted by the Congress is the rule prescribed by the Supreme Court, amended by substituting "court" in place of "judge," and by adding at the end of the first sentence the phrase "in accordance with the provisions of rule 104."

Advisory Committee's Note

Most preliminary questions of fact in connection with applying the rule preferring the original as evidence of contents are for the judge, under the general principles announced in Rule 104, supra. Thus, the question whether the loss of the originals has been established, or of the fulfillment of other conditions specified in Rule 1004, supra, is for the judge. However, questions may arise which go beyond the mere administration of the rule preferring the original and into the merits of the controversy. For example, plaintiff offers secondary evidence of the contents of an alleged contract, after first introducing evidence of loss of the original, and defendant counters with evidence that no such contract was ever executed. If the judge decides that the contract was never executed and excludes the secondary evidence, the case is at an end without ever going to the jury on a central issue. Levin, Authentication and Content of Writings, 10 Rutgers L.Rev. 632, 644 (1956). The latter portion of the instant rule is designed to insure treatment of these situations as raising jury questions. The decision is not one for uncontrolled discretion of the jury but is subject to the control exercised generally by the judge over jury determinations. See Rule 104(b), supra.

For similar provisions, see Uniform Rule 70(2); Kansas Code of Civil Procedure § 60–467(b); New Jersey Evidence Rule 70(2), (3).

ARTICLE XI. MISCELLANEOUS RULES

Rule 1101

Note by Federal Judicial Center

The rule enacted by the Congress is the rule prescribed by the Supreme Court, amended as follows:

Subdivision (a) was amended in the first sentence by inserting "the Court of Claims" and by inserting "actions, cases, and." It was amended in the second sentence by substituting "terms" in place of "word," by inserting the phrase "and 'court'," and by adding "commissioners of the Court of Claims."

Subdivision (b) was amended by substituting "civil actions and proceedings" in place of "civil actions," and by substituting "criminal cases and proceedings" in place of "criminal proceedings."

Subdivision (c) was amended by substituting "rule" in place of "rules" and by changing the verb to the singular.

Subdivision (d) was amended by deleting "those" after "other than" and by substituting "Rule 104" in place of "Rule 104(a)."

Subdivision (e) was amended by substituting "prescribed" in place of "adopted" and by adding "pursuant to statutory authority." The form of the statutory citations was also changed.

Advisory Committee's Note

Subdivision (a). [This portion of the Advisory Committee's Note discussed the courts for which the various enabling acts granted the Supreme Court power to prescribe rules. Congressional enactment of the rules has rendered the discussion moot. The enabling acts did not include the Court of Claims.]

Report of House Committee on the Judiciary

Subdivision (a) as submitted to the Congress, in stating the courts and judges to which the Rules of Evidence apply, omitted the Court of Claims and commissioners of that Court. At the request of the Court of Claims, the Committee amended the Rule to include the Court and its commissioners within the purview of the Rules.

Advisory Committee's Note

Subdivision (b) is a combination of the language of the enabling acts, supra, with respect to the kinds of proceedings in which the making of rules is authorized. It is subject to the qualifications expressed in the subdivisions which follow.

Subdivision (c), singling out the rules of privilege for special treatment, is made necessary by the limited applicability of the remaining rules.

Subdivision (d). The rule is not intended as an expression as to when due process or other constitutional provisions may require an evidentiary hearing. Paragraph (1) restates, for convenience, the provisions of the second sentence of Rule 104(a), supra. See Advisory Committee's Note to that rule.

(2) While some states have statutory requirements that indictments be based on "legal evidence," and there is some case law to the effect that the rules of evidence apply to grand jury proceedings, 1 Wigmore § 4(5), the Supreme Court has not accepted this view. In Costello v. United States, 350 U.S. 359, 76 S.Ct. 406, 100 L.Ed. 397 (1965), the Court refused to allow an indictment to be attacked, for either constitutional or policy reasons, on the ground that only hearsay evidence was presented.

"It would run counter to the whole history of the grand jury institution, in which laymen conduct their inquiries unfettered by technical rules. Neither justice nor the concept of a fair trial requires such a change." Id. at 364.

The rule as drafted does not deal with the evidence required to support an indictment.

(3) The rule exempts preliminary examinations in criminal cases. Authority as to the applicability of the rules of evidence to preliminary examinations has been meagre and conflicting. Goldstein, The State and the Accused: Balance of Advantage in Criminal Procedure, 69 Yale L.J. 1149, 1168, n. 53 (1960); Comment, Preliminary Hearings on Indictable Offenses in Philadelphia, 106 U. of Pa.L.Rev. 589, 592–593 (1958). Hearsay testimony is, however, customarily received in such examinations. Thus in a Dyer Act case, for example, an affidavit may properly be used in a preliminary examination to prove ownership of the stolen vehicle, thus saving the victim of the crime the hardship of having to travel twice to a distant district for the sole purpose of testifying as to ownership. It is believed that the extent of the applicability of the Rules of Evidence to preliminary examinations should be appropriately dealt with by the Federal Rules of Criminal Procedure which regulate those proceedings.

Extradition and rendition proceedings are governed in detail by statute. 18 U.S.C. §§ 3181–3195. They are essentially administrative in character. Traditionally the rules of evidence have not applied. 1 Wigmore § 4(6). Extradition proceedings are accepted from the operation of the Rules of Criminal Procedure. Rule 54(b)(5) of Federal Rules of Criminal Procedure.

The rules of evidence have not been regarded as applicable to sentencing or probation proceedings, where great reliance is placed upon the presentence investigation and report. Rule 32(c) of the Federal Rules of Criminal Procedure requires a presentence investigation and report in every case unless the court otherwise directs. In Williams v. New York, 337 U.S. 241, 69 S.Ct. 1079, 93 L.Ed. 1337 (1949), in which the judge overruled a jury recommendation of life imprisonment and imposed a death sentence, the Court said that due process does not require confrontation or cross-examination in sentencing or passing on probation, and that the judge has broad discretion as to the sources and types of information relied upon. Compare the recommendation that the substance of all derogatory information be disclosed to the defendant, in A.B.A. Project on Minimum Standards for Criminal Justice, Sentencing Alternatives and Procedures § 4.4, Tentative Draft (1967, Sobeloff, Chm.). Williams was adhered to in Specht v. Patterson, 386 U.S. 605, 87 S.Ct. 1209, 18 L.Ed.2d 326 (1967), but not extended to a proceeding under the Colorado Sex Offenders Act, which was said to be a new charge leading in effect to punishment, more like the recidivist statutes where opportunity must be given to be heard on the habitual criminal issue.

Warrants for arrest, criminal summonses, and search warrants are issued upon complaint or affidavit showing probable cause. Rules 4(a) and 41(c) of the Federal Rules of Criminal Procedure. The nature of the proceedings makes application of the formal rules of evidence inappropriate and impracticable.

Criminal contempts are punishable summarily if the judge certifies that he saw or heard the contempt and that it was committed in the presence of the court. Rule 42(a) of the Federal Rules of Criminal Procedure. The circumstances which preclude application of the rules of evidence in this situation are not present, however, in other cases of criminal contempt.

Proceedings with respect to release on bail or otherwise do not call for application of the rules of evidence. The governing statute specifically provides:

"Information stated in, or offered in connection with, any order entered pursuant to this section need not conform to the rules pertaining to the admissibility of evidence in a court of law." 18 U.S.C.A. § 3146(f).

This provision is consistent with the type of inquiry contemplated in A.B.A. Project on Minimum Standards for Criminal Justice, Standards Relating to Pretrial Release, § 4.5(b), (c), p. 16 (1968). The references to the weight of the evidence against the accused, in Rule 46(a) (1), (c) of the Federal Rules of Criminal Procedure and in 18 U.S.C.A. § 3146(b), as a factor to be considered, clearly do not have in view evidence introduced at a hearing under the rules of evidence.

The rule does not exempt habeas corpus proceedings. The Supreme Court held in Walker v. Johnston, 312 U.S. 275, 61 S.Ct. 574, 85 L.Ed. 830 (1941), that the practice of disposing of matters of fact on affidavit, which prevailed in some circuits, did not "satisfy the command of the statute that the judge shall proceed 'to determine the facts of the case, by hearing the testimony and arguments.'" This view accords with the emphasis in Townsend v. Sain, 372 U.S. 293, 83 S.Ct. 745, 9 L.Ed.2d 770 (1963), upon trial-type proceedings, id. 311, 83 S.Ct. 745, with demeanor evidence as a significant factor, id. 322, 83 S.Ct. 745, in applications by state prisoners aggrieved by unconstitutional detentions. Hence subdivision (e) applies the rules to habeas corpus proceedings to the extent not inconsistent with the statute.

Subdivision (e). In a substantial number of special proceedings, *ad hoc* evaluation has resulted in the promulgation of particularized evidentiary provisions, by Act of Congress or by rule adopted by the Supreme Court. Well adapted to the particular proceedings, though not apt candidates for inclusion in a set of general rules, they are left undisturbed. Otherwise, however, the rules of evidence are applicable to the proceedings enumerated in the subdivision.

Report of House Committee on the Judiciary

Subdivision (b) [E] was amended merely to substitute positive law citations for those which were not.

Rule 1102

Note by Federal Judicial Center

This rule was not included among those prescribed by the Supreme Court. The rule prescribed by the Court as 1102 now appears as 1103.

Rule 1103

Note by Federal Judicial Center

The rule enacted by the Congress is the rule prescribed by the Supreme Court as Rule 1102 without change.

Sec. 2.   (a) Title 28 of the United States Code is amended—

(1) by inserting immediately after section 2075 the following new section:

"§ 2076.   Rules of evidence

"The Supreme Court of the United States shall have the power to prescribe amendments to the Federal Rules of Evidence.   Such amendments shall not take effect until they have been reported to Congress by the Chief Justice at or after the beginning of a regular session of Congress but not later than the first day of May, and until the expiration of one hundred and eighty days after they have been so reported; but if either House of Congress within that time shall by resolution disapprove any amendment so reported it shall not take effect.   The effective date of any amendment so reported may be deferred by either House of Congress to a later date or until approved by Act of Congress.   Any rule whether proposed or in force may be amended by Act of Congress.   Any provision of law in force at the expiration of such time and in conflict with any such amendment not disapproved shall be of no further force or effect after such amendment has taken effect.   Any such amendment creating, abolishing, or modifying a privilege shall have no force or effect unless it shall be approved by act of Congress"; and

(2) by adding at the end of the table of sections of chapter 131 the following new item:

"2076.   Rules of evidence."

(b) Section 1732 of title 28 of the United States Code is amended by striking out subsection (a), and by striking out "(b)".

(c) Section 1733 of title 28 of the United States Code is amended by adding at the end thereof the following new subsection:

"(c) This section does not apply to cases, actions, and proceedings to which the Federal Rules of Evidence apply."

Sec. 3. The Congress expressly approves the amendments to the Federal Rules of Civil Procedure, and the amendments to the Federal Rules of Criminal Procedure, which are embraced by the orders entered by the Supreme Court of the United States on November 20, 1972, and December 18, 1972, and such amendments shall take effect on the one hundred and eightieth day beginning after the date of the enactment of this Act.

Approved Jan. 2, 1975.

APPENDIX C

APPENDIX OF DELETED AND SUPERSEDED MATERIALS WITH NOTES

[Rules originally prescribed by the Supreme Court but deleted from the rules enacted by Congress in 1975]

Table of Rules

Rule 105

SUMMING UP AND COMMENT BY JUDGE

[Not enacted.]

After the close of the evidence and arguments of counsel, the judge may fairly and impartially sum up the evidence and comment to the jury upon the weight of the evidence and the credibility of the witnesses, if he also instructs the jury that they are to determine for themselves the weight of the evidence and the credit to be given to the witnesses and that they are not bound by the judge's summation or comment.

Note by Federal Judicial Center

The foregoing rule prescribed by the Supreme Court was deleted from the rules enacted by the Congress.

Advisory Committee's Note

The rule states the present rule in the federal courts. Capital Traction Co. v. Hof, 174 U.S. 1, 13–14, 19 S.Ct. 580, 43 L.Ed. 873 (1899). The judge must, of course, confine his remarks to what is disclosed by the evidence. He cannot convey to the jury his purely personal reaction to credibility or to the merits of the case; he can be neither argumentative nor an advocate. Quercia v. United States, 289 U.S. 466, 469, 53 S.Ct. 698, 77 L.Ed. 1321 (1933); Billeci v. United States, 87 U.S.App.D.C. 274, 184 F.2d 394, 402, 24 A.L.R.2d 881 (1950). For further discussion see the series of articles by Wright, The Invasion of Jury: Temperature of the War, 27 Temp.L.Q. 137 (1953), Instructions to the Jury: Summary Without Comment, 1954 Wash.U.L.Q. 177, Adequacy of Instructions to the Jury, 53 Mich.L.Rev. 505, 813 (1955); A.L.I. Model Code of Evidence, Comment to Rule 8; Maguire, Weinstein, et al., Cases and Materials on Evidence 737–740 (5th ed. 1965); Vanderbilt, Minimum Standards of Judicial Administration 224–229 (1949).

Report of the House Committee on the Judiciary

Rule 105 as submitted by the Supreme Court concerned the issue of summing up and comment by the judge. It provided that after the close of the evidence and the arguments of counsel, the presiding judge could fairly and impartially sum up the evidence and comment to the jury upon its weight and the credibility of the witnesses, if he also instructed the jury that it was not bound thereby and must make its own determination of those matters. The Committee recognized that the Rule as submitted is consistent with long standing and current federal practice. However, the aspect of the Rule dealing with the authority of a judge to comment on the weight of the evidence and the credibility of witnesses—an authority not granted to judges in most State courts—was highly controversial. After much debate the Committee determined to delete the entire Rule, intending that its action be understood as reflecting no conclusion as to the merits of the proposed Rule and that the subject should be left for separate consideration at another time.

Report of Senate Committee on the Judiciary

This rule as submitted by the Supreme Court permitted the judge to sum up and comment on the evidence. The House struck the rule.

The committee accepts the House action with the understanding that the present Federal practice, taken from the common law, of the trial judge's discretionary authority to comment on and summarize the evidence is left undisturbed.

Rule 301

PRESUMPTIONS IN GENERAL

[As prescribed by Supreme Court]

In all cases not otherwise provided for by Act of Congress or by these rules a presumption imposes on the party against whom it is directed the burden of proving that the nonexistence of the presumed fact is more probable than its existence.

Rule 301

PRESUMPTIONS IN GENERAL IN CIVIL ACTIONS AND PROCEEDINGS

[As passed by House of Representatives]

In all civil actions and proceedings not otherwise provided for by Act of Congress or by these rules, a presumption imposes on the party against whom it is directed the burden of going forward with the evidence, and, even though met with contradicting evidence, a presumption is sufficient evidence of the fact presumed, to be considered by the trier of the facts.

Note by Federal Judicial Center

Neither of the above versions of Rule 301 was enacted.

This rule governs presumptions generally. See Rule 302 for presumptions controlled by state law and Rule 303 for those against an accused in a criminal case.

Presumptions governed by this rule are given the effect of placing upon the opposing party the burden of establishing the nonexistence of the presumed fact, once the party invoking the presumption establishes the basic facts giving rise to it. The same considerations of fairness, policy, and probability which dictate the allocation of the burden of the various elements of a case as between the prima facie case of a plaintiff and affirmative defenses also underlie the creation of presumptions. These considerations are not satisfied by giving a lesser effect to presumptions. Morgan and Maguire, Looking Backward and Forward at Evidence, 50 Harv.L.Rev. 909, 913 (1937); Morgan, Instructing the Jury upon Presumptions and Burden of Proof, 47 Harv.L.Rev. 59, 82 (1933); Cleary, Presuming and Pleading: An Essay on Juristic Immaturity, 12 Stan.L. Rev. 5 (1959).

The so-called "bursting bubble" theory, under which a presumption vanishes upon the introduction of evidence which would support a finding of the nonexistence of the presumed fact, even though not believed, is rejected as according presumptions too "slight and evanescent" an effect. Morgan and Maguire, supra, at p. 913.

In the opinion of the Advisory Committee, no constitutional infirmity attends this view of presumptions. In Mobile, J. & K. C. R. Co. v. Turnipseed, 219 U.S. 35, 31 S.Ct. 136, 55 L.Ed. 78 (1910), the Court upheld a Mississippi statute which provided that in actions against railroads proof of injury inflicted by the running of trains should be prima facie evidence of negligence by the railroad. The injury in the case had resulted from a derailment. The opinion made the points (1) that the only effect of the statute was to impose on the railroad the duty of producing some evidence to the contrary, (2) that an inference may be supplied by law if there is a rational connection between the fact proved and the fact presumed, as long as the opposite party is not precluded from presenting his evidence to the contrary, and (3) that considerations of public policy arising from the character of the business justified the application in question. Nineteen years later, in Western & Atlantic R. Co. v. Henderson, 279 U.S. 639, 49 S.Ct. 445, 73 L.Ed. 884 (1929), the Court overturned a Georgia statute making railroads liable for damages done by trains, unless the railroad made it appear that reasonable care had been used, the presumption being against the railroad. The declaration alleged the death of plaintiff's husband from a grade crossing collision, due to specified acts of negligence by defendant. The jury were instructed that proof of the injury raised a presumption of negligence; the burden shifted to the railroad to prove ordinary care; and unless it did so, they should find for plaintiff. The instruction was held erroneous in an opinion stating (1) that there was no rational connection between the mere fact of collision and negligence on the part of anyone, and (2) that the statute was different from that in *Turnipseed* in imposing a burden upon the railroad. The reader is left in a state of some confusion. Is the difference between a derailment and a grade crossing collision of no significance? Would the *Turnipseed* presumption have been bad if it had imposed a burden of persuasion on defendant, although that would in nowise have impaired its "rational connection"? If *Henderson* forbids imposing a burden of persuasion on defendants, what happens to affirmative defenses?

Two factors serve to explain *Henderson.* The first was that it was common ground that negligence was indispensable to liability. Plaintiff thought so, drafted her complaint accordingly, and relied upon the presumption. But how in logic could the same presumption establish her alternative grounds of negligence that the engineer was so blind he could not see decedent's truck and that he failed to stop after he saw it? Second, take away the basic assumption of no liability without fault, as *Turnipseed* intimated might be done ("considerations of public policy arising out of the character of the business"), and the structure of the decision in *Henderson* fails. No question of logic would have arisen if the statute had simply said: a prima facie case of liability is made by proof of injury by a train; lack of negligence is an affirmative defense, to be pleaded and proved as other affirmative defenses. The problem would be one of economic due process only. While it seems likely that the Supreme Court of 1929 would have voted that due process was denied, that result today would be unlikely. See, for example, the shift in the direction of absolute liability in the consumer cases. Prosser, The Assault upon the Citadel (Strict Liability to the Consumer), 69 Yale L.J. 1099 (1960).

Any doubt as to the constitutional permissibility of a presumption imposing a burden of persuasion of the nonexistence of the presumed fact in civil cases is laid at rest by Dick v. New York Life Ins. Co., 359 U.S. 437, 79 S.Ct. 921, 3 L.Ed. 2d 935 (1959). The Court unhesitatingly applied the North Dakota rule that the presumption against suicide imposed on defendant the burden of proving that the death of insured, under an accidental death clause, was due to suicide.

"Proof of coverage and of death by gunshot wound shifts the burden to the insurer to establish that the death of the insured was due to his suicide." 359 U.S. at 443, 79 S.Ct. at 925.

"In a case like this one, North Dakota presumes that death was accidental and places on the insurer the burden of proving that death resulted from suicide." Id. at 446, 79 S.Ct. at 927.

The rational connection requirement survives in criminal cases, Tot v. United States, 319 U.S. 463, 63 S.Ct. 1241, 87 L.Ed. 1519 (1943), because the Court has been unwilling to extend into that area the greater-includes-the-lesser theory of Ferry v. Ramsey, 277 U.S. 88, 48 S.Ct. 443, 72 L.Ed. 796 (1928). In that case the Court sustained a Kansas statute under which bank directors were personally liable for deposits made with their assent and with knowledge of insolvency, and the fact of insolvency was prima facie evidence of assent and knowledge of insolvency. Mr. Justice Holmes pointed out that the state legislature could have made the directors personally liable to depositors in every case. Since the statute imposed a less stringent liability, "the thing to be considered is the result reached, not the possibly inartificial or clumsy way of reaching it." Id. at 94, 48 S.Ct. at 444. Mr. Justice Sutherland dissented: though the state could have created an absolute liability, it did not purport to do so; a rational connection was necessary, but lacking, between the liability created and the prima facie evidence of it; the result might be different if the basis of the presumption were being open for business.

The Sutherland view has prevailed in criminal cases by virtue of the higher standard of notice there required. The fiction that everyone is presumed to know the law is applied to the substantive law of crimes as an alternative to complete unenforceability. But the need does not extend to criminal evidence and procedure, and the fiction does not encompass them. "Rational connection" is not fictional or artificial, and so it is reasonable to suppose that Gainey should have known that his presence at the site of an illicit still could convict him of being connected with (carrying on) the business, United States v. Gainey, 380 U.S. 63, 85 S.Ct. 754, 13 L.Ed.2d 658 (1965), but not that Romano should have known that his presence at a still could convict him of possessing it, United States v. Romano, 382 U.S. 136, 86 S.Ct. 279, 15 L.Ed.2d 210 (1965).

In his dissent in Gainey, Mr. Justice Black put it more artistically:

"It might be argued, although the Court does not so argue or hold, that Congress if it wished could make presence at a still a crime in itself, and so Congress should be free to create crimes which are called 'possession' and 'carrying on an illegal distillery business' but which are defined in such a way that unexplained presence is sufficient and indisputable evidence in all cases to support conviction for those offenses. See Ferry v. Ramsey, 277 U.S. 88, 48 S.Ct. 443, 72 L.Ed. 796. Assuming for the sake of argument that Congress could make unexplained presence a criminal act, and ignoring also the refusal of this Court in other cases to uphold a statutory presumption on such a theory, see Heiner v. Donnan, 285 U.S. 312, 52 S.Ct. 358, 76 L.Ed. 772, there is no indication here that Congress intended to adopt such a misleading method of draftsmanship, nor in my judgment could the statutory provisions if so construed escape condemnation for vagueness, under the principles applied in Lanzetta v. New Jersey, 306 U.S. 451, 59 S.Ct. 618, 83 L.Ed. 888, and many other cases." 380 U.S. at 84, n. 12, 85 S.Ct. at 766.

And the majority opinion in *Romano* agreed with him:

"It may be, of course, that Congress has the power to make presence at an illegal still a punishable crime, but we find no clear indication that it intended to so exercise this power. The crime remains possession, not presence, and with all due deference to the judgment of Congress, the former may not constitutionally be inferred from the latter." 382 U.S. at 144, 86 S.Ct. at 284.

The rule does not spell out the procedural aspects of its application. Questions as to when the evidence warrants submission of a presumption and what instructions are proper under varying states of fact are believed to present no particular difficulties.

Report of House Committee on the Judiciary

Rule 301 as submitted by the Supreme Court provided that in all cases a presumption imposes on the party against whom it is directed the burden of proving that the nonexistence of the presumed fact is more probable than its existence. The Committee limited the scope of Rule 301 to "civil actions and proceedings" to effectuate its decision not to deal with the question of presumptions in criminal cases. (See note on Rule 303 in discussion of Rules deleted). With respect to the weight to be given a presumption in a civil case, the Committee agreed with the judgment implicit in the Court's version that the so-called "bursting bubble" theory of presumptions, whereby a presumption vanishes upon the appearance of any contradicting evidence by the other party, gives to presumptions too slight an effect. On the other hand, the Committee believed that the Rule proposed by the Court, whereby a presumption permanently alters the burden of persuasion, no matter how much contradicting evidence is introduced—a view shared by only a few courts—lends too great a force to presumptions. Accordingly, the Committee amended the Rule to adopt an intermediate position under which a presumption does not vanish upon the introduction of contradicting evidence, and does not change the burden of persuasion; instead it is merely deemed sufficient evidence of the fact presumed, to be considered by the jury or other finder of fact.

Rule 303

PRESUMPTIONS IN CRIMINAL CASES

[Not enacted.]

(a) Scope. Except as otherwise provided by Act of Congress, in criminal cases, presumptions against an accused, recognized at common law or created by statute, including statutory provisions that certain facts are prima facie evidence of other facts or of guilt, are governed by this rule.

(b) Submission to jury. The judge is not authorized to direct the jury to find a presumed fact against the accused. When the presumed fact establishes guilt or is an element of the offense or negatives a defense, the judge may submit the question of guilt or of the existence of the presumed fact to the jury, if, but only if, a reasonable juror on the evidence as a whole, including the evidence of the basic facts, could find guilt or the presumed fact beyond a reasonable doubt. When the presumed fact has a lesser effect, its existence may be submitted to the jury if the basic facts are supported by substantial evidence, or are otherwise established, unless the evidence as a whole negatives the existence of the presumed fact.

(c) Instructing the jury. Whenever the existence of a presumed fact against the accused is submitted to the jury, the judge shall give an instruction that the law declares that the jury may regard the basic facts as sufficient evidence of the presumed fact but does not require it to do so. In addition, if the presumed fact establishes guilt or is an element of the offense or negatives a defense, the judge shall instruct the jury that its existence must, on all the evidence, be proved beyond a reasonable doubt.

Note by Federal Judicial Center

The foregoing rule prescribed by the Supreme Court was deleted from the rules enacted by the Congress.

Advisory Committee's Note

Subdivision (a). This rule is based largely upon A.L.I. Model Penal Code § 1.12(5) P.O.D. (1962) and United States v. Gainey, 380 U.S. 63, 85 S.Ct. 754, 13 L.Ed.2d 658 (1965). While the rule, unlike the Model Penal Code provision, spells out the effect of common law presumptions as well as those created by statute, cases involving the later are no doubt of more frequent occurrence. Congress has enacted numerous provisions to lessen the burden of the prosecution, principally though not exclusively in the fields of narcotics control and taxation of liquor. Occasionally, in the pattern of the usual common law treatment of such matters as insanity, they take the form of assigning to the defense the responsibility of raising specified matters as affirmative defenses, which are not within the scope of these rules. See Comment, A.L.I. Model Penal Code § 1.13, T.D. No. 4 (1955). In other instances they assume a variety of forms which are the concern of this rule. The provision may be that proof of a specified fact (possession or presence) is sufficient to authorize conviction. 26

U.S.C. § 4704(a), unlawful to buy or sell opium except from original stamped package—absence of stamps from package prima facie evidence of violation by person in possession; 26 U.S.C. § 4724(c), unlawful for person who has not registered and paid special tax to possess narcotics—possession presumptive evidence of violation. Sometimes the qualification is added, "unless the defendant explains the possession [presence] to the satisfaction of the jury." 18 U.S.C. § 545, possession of unlawfully imported goods sufficient for conviction of smuggling, unless explained; 21 U.S.C. § 174, possession sufficient for conviction of buying or selling narcotics known to have been imported unlawfully, unless explained. See also 26 U.S.C. § 5601(a)(1), (a)(4), (a)(8), (b)(1), (b)(2), (b)(4), relating to distilling operations. Another somewhat different pattern makes possession evidence of a particular element of the crime. 21 U.S.C. § 176b, crime to furnish unlawfully imported heroin to juveniles—possession sufficient proof of unlawful importation, unless explained; 50 U.S.C.A.App. § 462(b), unlawful to possess draft card not lawfully issued to holder, with intent to use for purposes of false identification—possession sufficient evidence of intent, unless explained. See also 15 U.S.C. § 902(f), (i).

Differences between the permissible operation of presumptions against the accused in criminal cases and in other situations prevent the formulation of a comprehensive definition of the term "presumption," and none is attempted. Nor do these rules purport to deal with problems of the validity of presumptions except insofar as they may be found reflected in the formulation of permissible procedures.

The presumption of innocence is outside the scope of the rule and unaffected by it.

Subdivisions (b) and (c). It is axiomatic that a verdict cannot be directed against the accused in a criminal case, 9 Wigmore § 2495, p. 312, with the corollary that the judge is without authority to direct the jury to find against the accused as to any element of the crime, A.L.I. Model Penal Code § 1.12(1) P.O.D. (1962). Although arguably the judge could direct the jury to find against the accused as to a lesser fact, the tradition is against it, and this rule makes no use of presumptions to remove any matters from final determination by the jury.

The only distinction made among presumptions under this rule is with respect to the measure of proof required in order to justify submission to the jury. If the effect of the presumption is to establish guilt or an element of the crime or to negative a defense, the measure of proof is the one widely accepted by the Courts of Appeals as the standard for measuring the sufficiency of the evidence in passing on motions for directed verdict (now judgment of acquittal): an acquittal should be directed when reasonable jurymen must have a reasonable doubt. Curley v. United States, 81 U.S.App.D.C. 389, 160 F.2d 229 (1947), cert. denied 331 U.S. 837, 67 S.Ct. 1511, 91 L.Ed. 1850; United States v. Honeycutt, 311 F.2d 660 (4th Cir. 1962); Stephens v. United States, 354 F.2d 999 (5th Cir. 1965); Lambert v. United States, 261 F.2d 799 (5th Cir. 1958); United States v. Leggett, 292 F.2d 423 (6th Cir. 1961); Cape v. United States, 283 F.2d 430 (9th Cir. 1960); Cartwright v. United States, 335 F.2d 919 (10th Cir. 1964). Cf. United States v. Gonzales Castro, 228 F.2d 807 (2d Cir. 1956); United States v. Masiello, 235 F.2d 279 (2d Cir. 1956), cert. denied Stickel v. United States, 352 U.S. 882, 77 S.Ct. 100, 1 L.Ed.2d 79; United States v. Feinberg, 140 F.2d 592 (2d Cir. 1944). But cf. United States v. Arcuri, 282 F.Supp. 347 (E.D.N.Y.1968), aff'd. 405 F.2d 691, cert. denied 395 U.S. 913; United States v. Melillo, 275 F.Supp. 314 (E.D.N.Y.1968). If the presumption operates upon a lesser aspect of the case than the issue of guilt itself or an element of the crime or negativing a defense, the required measure of proof is the less stringent one of substantial evidence, consistently with the attitude usually taken with respect to particular items of evidence. 9 Wigmore § 2497, p. 324.

The treatment of presumptions in the rule is consistent with United States v. Gainey, 380 U.S. 63, 85 S.Ct. 754, 13 L.Ed.2d 658 (1965), where the matter was considered in depth. After sustaining the validity of the provision of 26 U.S.C. § 5601(b)(2) that presence at the site is sufficient to convict of the offense of carrying on the business of distiller without giving bond, unless the presence is explained to the satisfaction of the jury, the Court turned to procedural considerations and reached several conclusions. The power of the judge to withdraw a case from the jury for insufficiency of evidence is left unimpaired; he may submit the case on the basis of presence alone, but he is not required to do so. Nor is he precluded from rendering judgment notwithstanding the verdict. It is proper to tell the jury about the "statutory inference," if they are told it is not conclusive. The jury may still acquit, even if it finds defendant present and his presence is unexplained. [Compare the mandatory character of the instruction condemned in Bollenbach v. United States, 326 U.S. 607, 66 S.Ct. 402, 90 L.Ed. 350 (1945).] To avoid any implication that the statutory language relative to explanation be taken as directing attention to failure of the accused to testify, the better practice, said the Court, would be to instruct the jury that they may draw the inference unless the evidence provides a satisfactory explanation of defendant's presence, omitting any explicit reference to the statute.

The Final Report of the National Commission on Reform of Federal Criminal Laws § 103(4) and (5) (1971) contains a careful formulation of the consequences of a statutory presumption with an alternative formulation set forth in the Comment thereto, and also of the effect of a prima facie case. In the criminal code there proposed, the terms "presumption" and "prima facie case" are used with precision and with reference to these meanings. In the federal criminal law as it stands today, these terms are not used with precision. Moreover, common law presumptions continue. Hence it is believed that the rule here proposed is better adapted to the present situation until such time as the Congress enacts legislation covering the subject, which the rule takes into account. If the subject of common law presumptions is not covered by legislation, the need for the rule in that regard will continue.

Report of House Committee on the Judiciary

Rule 303, as submitted by the Supreme Court was directed to the issues of when, in criminal cases, a court may submit a presumption to a jury and the type of instruction it should give. The Committee deleted this Rule since the subject of presumptions in criminal cases is addressed in detail in bills now pending before the Committee to revise the federal criminal code. The Committee determined to consider this question in the course of its study of these proposals.

Rule 406

HABIT; ROUTINE PRACTICE

[Subdivision (b) not enacted.]

(b) Method of proof. Habit or routine practice may be proved by testimony in the form of an opinion or by specific instances of conduct sufficient in number to warrant a finding that the habit existed or that the practice was routine.

Advisory Committee's Note

* * *

Subdivision (b). Permissible methods of proving habit or routine conduct include opinion and specific instances sufficient in number to warrant a finding that the habit or routine practice in fact existed. Opinion evidence must be "rationally based on the perception of the witness" and helpful, under the provisions of Rule 701. Proof by specific instances may be controlled by the overriding provisions of Rule 403 for exclusion on grounds of prejudice, confusion, misleading the jury, or waste of time. Thus the illustrations following A.L.I. Model Code of Evidence Rule 307 suggests the possibility of admitting testimony by W that on numerous occasions he had been with X when X crossed a railroad track and that on each occasion X had first stopped and looked in both directions, but discretion to exclude offers of 10 witnesses, each testifying to a different occasion.

Similar provisions for proof by opinion or specific instances are found in Uniform Rule 50 and Kansas Code of Civil Procedure § 60–450. New Jersey Rule 50 provides for proof by specific instances but is silent as to opinion. The California Evidence Code is silent as to methods of proving habit, presumably proceeding on the theory that any method is relevant and all relevant evidence is admissible unless otherwise provided. Tentative Recommendation and a Study Relating to the Uniform Rules of Evidence (Art. VI. Extrinsic Policies Affecting Admissibility), Rep., Rec. & Study, Cal. Law Rev. Comm'n 620 (1964).

Report of House Committee on the Judiciary

[Reasons for deleting subdivision (b) are stated in the report, which is set forth in the main text under rule 406, supra.]

ARTICLE V.   PRIVILEGES

Note by Federal Judicial Center

The 13 rules numbered 501–513 prescribed by the Supreme Court as Article V were replaced by a single rule 501 in the rules enacted by the Congress. The rules are included here for informational purposes only.

Rule 501

PRIVILEGES RECOGNIZED ONLY AS PROVIDED

[Not enacted.]

Except as otherwise required by the Constitution of the United States or provided by Act of Congress, and except as provided in these rules or in other rules adopted by the Supreme Court, no person has a privilege to:

(1) Refuse to be a witness; or

(2) Refuse to disclose any matter; or

(3) Refuse to produce any object or writing; or

(4) Prevent another from being a witness or disclosing any matter or producing any object or writing.

Advisory Committee's Note

No attempt is made in these rules to incorporate the constitutional provisions which relate to the admission and exclusion of evidence, whether denominated as privileges or not. The grand design of these provisions does not readily lend itself to codification. The final reference must be the provisions themselves and the decisions construing them. Nor is formulating a rule an appropriate means of settling unresolved constitutional questions.

Similarly, privileges created by act of Congress are not within the scope of these rules. These privileges do not assume the form of broad principles; they are the product of resolving particular problems in particular terms. Among them are included such provisions as 13 U.S.C. § 9, generally prohibiting official disclosure of census information and conferring a privileged status on retained copies of census reports; 42 U.S.C. § 2000e–5(a), making inadmissible in evidence anything said or done during Equal Employment Opportunity conciliation proceeding; 42 U.S.C. § 2240, making required reports of incidents by nuclear facility licensees inadmissible in actions for damages; 45 U.S.C. §§ 33, 41, similarly as to reports of accidents by railroads; 49 U.S.C. § 1441(e), declaring C.A.B. accident investigation reports inadmissible in actions for damages. The rule leaves them undisturbed.

The reference to other rules adopted by the Supreme Court makes clear that provisions relating to privilege in those rules will continue in operation. See, for example, the "work product" immunity against discovery spelled out under the Rules of Civil Procedure in Hickman v. Taylor, 329 U.S. 495, 67 S.Ct. 385, 91 L.Ed. 451 (1947), now formalized in revised Rule 26(b) (3) of the Rules of Civil Procedure, and the secrecy of grand jury proceedings provided by Criminal Rule 6.

With respect to privileges created by state law, these rules in some instances grant them greater status than has heretofore been the case by according them recognition in federal criminal proceedings, bankruptcy, and federal question litigation. See Rules 502 and 510. There is, however, no provision generally adopting state-created privileges.

In federal criminal prosecutions the primacy of federal law as to both substance and procedure has been undoubted. See, for example, United States v. Krol, 374 F.2d 776 (7th Cir. 1967), sustaining the admission in a federal prosecution of evidence obtained by electronic eavesdropping, despite a state statute declaring the use of these devices unlawful and evidence obtained therefrom inadmissible. This primacy includes matters of privilege. As stated in 4 Barron, Federal Practice and Procedure § 2151, p. 175 (1951):

"The determination of the question whether a matter is privileged is governed by federal decisions and the state statutes or rules of evidence have no application."

In Funk v. United States, 290 U.S. 371, 54 S.Ct. 212, 78 L.Ed. 369 (1933), the Court had considered the competency of a wife to testify for her husband and concluded that, absent congressional action or direction, the federal courts were to follow the common law as they saw it "in accordance with present day standards of wisdom and justice." And in Wolfle v. United States, 291 U.S. 7, 54 S.Ct. 279, 78 L.Ed. 617 (1934), the Court said with respect to the standard appropriate in determining a claim of privilege for an alleged confidential communication between spouses in a federal criminal prosecution:

"So our decision here, in the absence of Congressional legislation on the subject, is to be controlled by common law principles, not by local statute." Id., 13, 54 S.Ct. at 280.

On the basis of *Funk* and *Wolfle*, the Advisory Committee on Rules of Criminal Procedure formulated Rule 26, which was adopted by the Court. The pertinent part of the rule provided:

"The ∗ ∗ ∗ privileges of witnesses shall be governed, except when an act of Congress or these rules otherwise provide, by the principles of the common law as they may be interpreted ∗ ∗ ∗ in the light of reason and experience."

As regards bankruptcy, section 21(a) of the Bankruptcy Act provides for examination of the bankrupt and his spouse concerning the acts, conduct, or property of the bankrupt. The Act limits examination of the spouse to business transacted by her or to which she is a party but provides "That the spouse may be so examined, any law of the United States or of any State to the contrary notwithstanding." 11 U.S.C. § 44(a). The effect of the quoted language is clearly to override any conflicting state rule of incompetency or privilege against spousal testimony. A fair reading would also indicate an overriding of any contrary state rule of privileged confidential spousal communications. Its validity has never been questioned and seems most unlikely to be. As to other privileges, the suggestion has been made that state law applies, though with little citation of authority, 2 Moore's Collier on Bankruptcy ¶ 21.13, p. 297 (14th ed. 1961). This position seems to be contrary to the expression of the Court in McCarthy v. Arndstein, 266 U.S. 34, 39, 45 S.Ct. 16, 69 L.Ed. 158 (1924), which speaks in the pattern of Rule 26 of the Federal Rules of Criminal Procedure:

"There is no provision [in the Bankruptcy Act] prescribing the rules by which the examination is to be governed. These are, impliedly, the general rules governing the admissibility of evidence and the competency and compellability of witnesses."

With respect to federal question litigation, the supremacy of federal law may be less clear, yet indications that state privileges are inapplicable preponderate in the circuits. In re Albert Lindley Lee Memorial Hospital, 209 F.2d 122 (2d Cir. 1953), cert. denied Cincotta v. United States, 347 U.S. 960, 74 S.Ct. 709, 98 L.Ed. 1104; Colton v. United States, 306 F.2d 633 (2d Cir. 1962); Falsone v. United States, 205 F.2d 734 (5th Cir. 1953); Fraser v. United States, 145 F.2d 139 (6th Cir. 1944), cert. denied 324 U.S. 849, 65 S.Ct. 684, 89 L.Ed. 1409; United States v. Brunner, 200 F.2d 276 (6th Cir. 1952). Contra, Baird v. Koerner, 279 F.2d 623 (9th Cir. 1960). Additional decisions of district courts are collected in Annot., 95 A.L.R.2d 320, 336. While a number of the cases arise from administrative income tax investigations, they nevertheless support the broad proposition of the inapplicability of state privileges in federal proceedings.

In view of these considerations, it is apparent that, to the extent that they accord state privileges standing in federal criminal cases, bankruptcy, and federal question cases, the rules go beyond what previously has been thought necessary or proper.

On the other hand, in diversity cases, or perhaps more accurately cases in which state law furnishes the rule of decision, the rules avoid giving state privileges the affect which substantial authority has thought necessary and proper. Regardless of what might once have been thought to be the command of Erie R. Co. v. Tompkins, 304 U.S. 64, 58 S.Ct. 817, 82 L.Ed. 1188 (1938), as to observance of state created privileges in diversity cases, Hanna v. Plumer, 380 U.S. 460, 85 S.Ct. 1136, 14 L.Ed.2d 8 (1965), is believed to locate the problem in the area of choice rather than necessity. Wright, Procedural Reform: Its Limitations and Its Future, 1 Ga.L.Rev. 563, 572–573 (1967). Contra, Republic Gear Co. v. Borg-Warner Corp., 381 F.2d 551, 555, n. 2 (2d Cir. 1967), and see authorities there cited. Hence all significant policy factors need to be considered in order that the choice may be a wise one.

The arguments advanced in favor of recognizing state privileges are: a state privilege is an essential characteristic of a relationship or status created by state law and thus is substantive in the *Erie* sense; state policy ought not to be frustrated by the accident of diversity; the allowance or denial of a privilege is so likely to affect the outcome of litigation as to encourage forum selection on that basis, not a proper function of diversity jurisdiction. There are persuasive answers to these arguments.

(1) As to the question of "substance," it is true that a privilege commonly represents an aspect of a relationship created and defined by a State. For example, a confidential communications privilege is often an incident of marriage. However, in litigation involving the relationship itself, the privilege is not ordinarily one of the issues. In fact, statutes frequently make the communication privilege inapplicable in cases of divorce. McCormick § 88, p. 177. The same is true with respect to the attorney-client privilege when the parties to the relationship have a falling out. The reality of the matter is that privilege is called into operation, not when the relation giving rise to the privilege is being litigated, but when the litigation involves something substantively devoid of relation to the privilege. The appearance of privilege in the case is quite by accident, and its effect is to block off the tribunal from a source of information. Thus its real impact is on the method of proof in the case, and in comparison any substantive aspect appears tenuous.

(2) By most standards, criminal prosecutions are attended by more serious consequences than civil litigation, and it must be evident that the criminal area has the greatest sensitivity where privilege is concerned. Nevertheless, as previously noted, state privileges traditionally have given way in federal criminal prosecutions. If a privilege is denied in the area of greatest sensitivity, it tends to become illusory as a significant aspect of the relationship out of which it arises. For example, in a state having by statute an accountant's privilege, only the most imperceptible added force would be given the privilege by putting the accountant in a position to assure his client that, while he could not block disclosure in a federal criminal prosecution, he could do so in diversity cases as well as in state court proceedings. Thus viewed, state interest in privilege appears less substantial than at first glance might seem to be the case.

Moreover, federal interest is not lacking. It can scarcely be contended that once diversity is invoked the federal government no longer has a legitimate concern in the quality of judicial administration conducted under its aegis.

The demise of conformity and the adoption of the Federal Rules of Civil Procedure stand as witness to the contrary.

(3) A large measure of forum shopping is recognized as legitimate in the American judicial system. Subject to the limitations of jurisdiction and the relatively modest controls imposed by venue provisions and the doctrine of forum non conveniens, plaintiffs are allowed in general a free choice of forum. Diversity jurisdiction has as its basic purpose the giving of a choice, not only to plaintiffs but, in removal situations, also to defendants. In principle, the basis of the choice is the supposed need to escape from local prejudice. If the choice were tightly confined to that basis, then complete conformity to local procedure as well as substantive law would be required. This, of course, is not the case, and the choice may in fact be influenced by a wide range of factors. As Dean Ladd has pointed out, a litigant may select the federal court "because of the federal procedural rules, the liberal discovery provisions, the quality of jurors expected in the federal court, the respect held for federal judges, the control of federal judges over a trial, the summation and comment upon the weight of evidence by the judge, or the authority to grant a new trial if the judge regards the verdict against the weight of the evidence." Ladd, Privileges, 1969 Ariz.St. L.J. 555, 564. Present Rule 43(a) of the Civil Rules specifies a broader range of admissibility in federal than in state courts and makes no exception for diversity cases. Note should also be taken that Rule 26(b) (2) of the Rules of Civil Procedure, as revised, allows discovery to be had of liability insurance, without regard to local state law upon the subject.

When attention is directed to the practical dimensions of the problem, they are found not to be great. The privileges affected are few in number. Most states provide a physician-patient privilege; the proposed rules limit the privilege to a psychotherapist-patient relationship. See Advisory Committee's Note to Rule 504. The area of marital privilege under the proposed rules is narrower than in most states. See Rule 505. Some states recognize privileges for journalists and accountants; the proposed rules do not.

Physician-patient is the most widely recognized privilege not found in the proposed rules. As a practical matter it was largely eliminated in diversity cases when Rule 35 of the Rules of Civil Procedure became effective in 1938. Under that rule, a party physically examined pursuant to court order, by requesting and obtaining a copy of the report or by taking the deposition of the examiner, waives any privilege regarding the testimony of every other person who has examined him in respect of the same condition. While waiver may be avoided by neither requesting the report nor taking the examiner's deposition, the price is one which most litigant-patients are probably not prepared to pay.

Rule 502

REQUIRED REPORTS PRIVILEGED BY STATUTE

[Not enacted.]

A person, corporation, association, or other organization or entity, either public or private, making a return or report required by law to be made has a privilege to refuse to disclose and to prevent any other person from disclosing the return or report, if the law requiring it to be made so provides. A public officer or agency to whom a return or report is required by law to be made has a privilege to refuse to disclose the return or report if the law requiring it to be made so provides. No privilege exists under this rule in actions involving perjury, false statements, fraud in the return or report, or other failure to comply with the law in question.

Advisory Committee's Note

Statutes which require the making of returns or reports sometimes confer on the reporting party a privilege against disclosure, commonly coupled with a prohibition against disclosure by the officer to whom the report is made. Some of the federal statutes of this kind are mentioned in the Advisory Committee's Note to Rule 501, supra. See also the Note to Rule 402, supra. A provision against disclosure may be included in a statute for a variety of reasons, the chief of which are probably assuring the validity of the statute against claims of self-incrimination, honoring the privilege against self-incrimination, and encouraging the furnishing of the required information by assuring privacy.

These statutes, both state and federal, may generally be assumed to embody policies of significant dimension. Rule 501 insulates the federal provisions against disturbance by these rules; the present rule reiterates a result commonly specified in federal statutes and extends its application to state statutes of similar character. Illustrations of the kinds of returns and reports contemplated by the rule appear in the cases, in which a reluctance to compel disclosure is manifested. In re Reid, 155 F. 933 (E.D.Mich.1906), assessor not compelled to produce bankrupt's property tax return in view of statute forbidding disclosure; In re Valecia Condensed Milk Co., 240 F. 310 (7th Cir. 1917), secretary of state tax commission not compelled to produce bankrupt's income tax returns in violation of statute; Herman Bros. Pet Supply, Inc. v. N.L.R.B., 360 F.2d 176 (6th Cir. 1966), subpoena denied for production of reports to state employment security commission prohibited by statute, in proceeding for back wages. And see the discussion of motor vehicle accident reports in Krizak v. W.C. Brooks & Sons, Inc., 320 F.2d 37, 42–43 (4th Cir. 1963). Cf. In re Hines, 69 F.2d 52 (2d Cir. 1934).

Rule 503

LAWYER–CLIENT PRIVILEGE

[Not enacted.]

(a) **Definitions.** As used in this rule:

(1) A "client" is a person, public officer, or corporation, association, or other organization or entity, either public or private, who is rendered professional legal services by a lawyer, or who consults a lawyer with a view to obtaining professional legal services from him.

(2) A "lawyer" is a person authorized, or reasonably believed by the client to be authorized, to practice law in any state or nation.

(3) A "representative of the lawyer" is one employed to assist the lawyer in the rendition of professional legal services.

(4) A communication is "confidential" if not intended to be disclosed to third persons other than those to whom disclosure is in furtherance of the rendition of professional legal services to the client or those reasonably necessary for the transmission of the communication.

(b) **General rule of privilege.** A client has a privilege to refuse   1
to disclose and to prevent any other person from disclosing confidential   2
communications made for the purpose of facilitating the rendition of   3
professional legal services to the client, (1) between himself or his   4
representative and his lawyer or his lawyer's representative, or (2)   5
between his lawyer and the lawyer's representative, or (3) by him or his   6
lawyer to a lawyer representing another in a matter of common   7
interest, or (4) between representatives of the client or between the   8
client and a representative of the client, or (5) between lawyers repre-   9
senting the client.   10

(c) **Who may claim the privilege.** The privilege may be claimed   11
by the client, his guardian or conservator, the personal representative   12
of a deceased client, or the successor, trustee, or similar representative   13
of a corporation, association, or other organization, whether or not in   14
existence. The person who was the lawyer at the time of the communi-   15
cation may claim the privilege but only on behalf of the client. His   16
authority to do so is presumed in the absence of evidence to the   17
contrary.   18

(d) **Exceptions.** There is no privilege under this rule: 19
                                                                    20

(1) Furtherance of crime or fraud. If the services of the lawyer   21
were sought or obtained to enable or aid anyone to commit or plan to   22
commit what the client knew or reasonably should have known to be a   23
crime or fraud; or   24

(2) Claimants through same deceased client. As to a communica-   25
tion relevant to an issue between parties who claim through the same   26
deceased client, regardless of whether the claims are by testate or   27
intestate succession or by *inter vivos* transaction; or   28

(3) Breach of duty by lawyer or client. As to a communication   29
relevant to an issue of breach of duty by the lawyer to his client or by   30
the client to his lawyer; or   31

(4) Document attested by lawyer. As to a communication relevant   32
to an issue concerning an attested document to which the lawyer is an   33
attesting witness; or   34
                                                                    35

(5) Joint clients. As to a communication relevant to a matter of   36
common interest between two or more clients if the communication was   37
made by any of them to a lawyer retained or consulted in common,   38
when offered in an action between any of the clients.   39
                                                                    40

Advisory Committee's Note   41

Subdivision (a). (1) The definition of "client" includes governmental   42
bodies, Connecticut Mutual Life Ins. Co. v. Shields, 18 F.R.D. 448 (S.D.N.Y.   43
1955); People ex rel. Department of Public Works v. Glen Arms Estate, Inc.,   44
230 Cal.App.2d 841, 41 Cal.Rptr. 303 (1965); Rowley v. Ferguson, 48 N.E.2d 243   45
(Ohio App. 1942); and corporations, Radiant Burners, Inc. v. American Gas   46
Assn., 320 F.2d 314 (7th Cir. 1963). Contra, Gardner, A Personal Privilege for   47
Communications of Corporate Clients—Paradox or Public Policy, 40 U.Det.L.J.   48
299, 323, 376 (1963). The definition also extends the status of client to one   49
consulting a lawyer preliminarily with a view to retaining him, even though   50

actual employment does not result. McCormick, § 92, p. 184. The client need not be involved in litigation; the rendition of legal service or advice under any circumstances suffices. 8 Wigmore § 2294 (McNaughton Rev. 1961). The services must be professional legal services; purely business or personal matters do not qualify. McCormick § 92, p. 184.

The rule contains no definition of "representative of the client." In the opinion of the Advisory Committee, the matter is better left to resolution by decision on a case-by-case basis. The most restricted position is the "control group" test, limiting the category to persons with authority to seek and act upon legal advice for the client. See *e.g.*, City of Philadelphia v. Westinghouse Electric Corp., 210 F.Supp. 483 (E.D.Pa. 1962), mandamus and prohibition denied sub nom. General Electric Co. v. Kirkpatrick, 312 F.2d 742 (3d Cir.), cert. denied 372 U.S. 943; Garrison v. General Motors Corp., 213 F.Supp. 515 (S.D.Cal. 1963); Hogan v. Zletz, 43 F.R.D. 308 (N.D.Okla. 1967), aff'd sub nom. Natta v. Hogan, 392 F.2d 686 (10th Cir. 1968); Day v. Illinois Power Co., 50 Ill. App.2d 52, 199 N.E.2d 802 (1964). Broader formulations are found in other decisions. See, e.g., United States v. United Shoe Machinery Corp., 89 F.Supp. 357 (D.Mass. 1950); Zenith Radio Corp. v. Radio Corp. of America, 121 F.Supp. 792 (D.Del. 1954); Harper & Row Publishers, Inc. v. Decker, 423 F.2d 487 (7th Cir. 1970), aff'd without opinion by equally divided court 400 U.S. 955 (1971), reh. denied 401 U.S. 950; D.I. Chadbourne, Inc. v. Superior Court, 60 Cal.2d 723, 36 Cal.Rptr. 468, 388 P.2d 700 (1964). Cf. Rucker v. Wabash R. Co., 418 F.2d 146 (7th Cir. 1969). See generally, Simon, The Attorney-Client Privilege as Applied to Corporations, 65 Yale L.J. 953, 956–966 (1956); Note, Attorney-Client Privilege for Corporate Clients: The Control Group Test, 84 Harv.L.Rev. 424 (1970).

The status of employees who are used in the process of communicating, as distinguished from those who are parties to the communication, is treated in paragraph (4) of subdivision (a) of the rule.

(2) A "lawyer" is a person licensed to practice law in any state or nation. There is no requirement that the licensing state or nation recognize the attorney-client privilege, thus avoiding excursions into conflict of laws questions. "Lawyer" also includes a person reasonably believed to be a lawyer. For similar provisions, see California Evidence Code § 950.

(3) The definition of "representative of the lawyer" recognizes that the lawyer may, in rendering legal services, utilize the services of assistants in addition to those employed in the process of communicating. Thus the definition includes an expert employed to assist in rendering legal advice. United States v. Kovel, 296 F.2d 918 (2d Cir. 1961) (accountant). Cf. Himmelfarb v. United States, 175 F.2d 924 (9th Cir. 1949). It also includes an expert employed to assist in the planning and conduct of litigation, though not one employed to testify as a witness. Lalance & Grosjean Mfg. Co. v. Haberman Mfg. Co., 87 F. 563 (S.D.N.Y.1898), and see revised Civil Rule 26(b) (4). The definition does not, however, limit "representative of the lawyer" to experts. Whether his compensation is derived immediately from the lawyer or the client is not material.

(4) The requisite confidentiality of communication is defined in terms of intent. A communication made in public or meant to be relayed to outsiders or which is divulged by the client to third persons can scarcely be considered confidential. McCormick § 95. The intent is inferable from the circumstances. Unless intent to disclose is apparent, the attorney-client communication is confidential. Taking or failing to take precautions may be considered as bearing on intent.

Practicality requires that some disclosure be allowed beyond the immediate circle of lawyer-client and their representatives without impairing confidentiality. Hence the definition allows disclosure to persons "to whom disclosure is in furtherance of the rendition of professional legal services to the client," contemplating those in such relation to the client as "spouse, parent, business associate, or joint client." Comment, California Evidence Code § 952.

Disclosure may also be made to persons "reasonably necessary for the transmission of the communication," without loss of confidentiality.

Subdivision (b) sets forth the privilege, using the previously defined terms: client, lawyer, representative of the lawyer, and confidential communication.

Substantial authority has in the past allowed the eavesdropper to testify to overheard privileged conversations and has admitted intercepted privileged letters. Today, the evolution of more sophisticated techniques of eavesdropping and interception calls for abandonment of this position. The rule accordingly adopts a policy of protection against these kinds of invasion of the privilege.

The privilege extends to communications (1) between client or his representative and lawyer or his representative, (2) between lawyer and lawyer's representative, (3) by client or his lawyer to a lawyer representing another in a matter of common interest, (4) between representatives of the client or the client and a representative of the client, and (5) between lawyers representing the client. All these communications must be specifically for the purpose of obtaining legal services for the client; otherwise the privilege does not attach.

The third type of communication occurs in the "joint defense" or "pooled information" situation, where different lawyers represent clients who have some interests in common. In Chahoon v. Commonwealth, 62 Va. 822 (1871), the court said that the various clients might have retained one attorney to represent all; hence everything said at a joint conference was privileged, and one of the clients could prevent another from disclosing what the other had himself said. The result seems to be incorrect in overlooking a frequent reason for retaining different attorneys by the various clients, namely actually or potentially conflicting interests in addition to the common interest which brings them together. The needs of these cases seem better to be met by allowing each client a privilege as to his own statements. Thus if all resist disclosure, none will occur. Continental Oil Co. v. United States, 330 F.2d 347 (9th Cir. 1964). But, if for reasons of his own, a client wishes to disclose his own statements made at the joint conference, he should be permitted to do so, and the rule is to that effect. The rule does not apply to situations where there is no common interest to be promoted by a joint consultation, and the parties meet on a purely adversary basis. Vance v. State, 190 Tenn. 521, 230 S.W.2d 987 (1950), cert. denied 339 U.S. 988, 70 S.Ct. 1010, 94 L.Ed. 1389. Ct. Hunydee v. United States, 355 F.2d 183 (9th Cir. 1965).

Subdivision (c). The privilege is, of course, that of the client, to be claimed by him or by his personal representative. The successor of a dissolved corporate client may claim the privilege. California Evidence Code § 953; New Jersey Evidence Rule 26(1). Contra, Uniform Rule 26(1).

The lawyer may not claim the privilege on his own behalf. However, he may claim it on behalf of the client. It is assumed that the ethics of the profession will require him to do so except under most unusual circumstances. American Bar Association, Canons of Professional Ethics, Canon 37. His authority to make the claim is presumed unless there is evidence to the contrary, as would be the case if the client were now a party to litigation in which the question arose and were represented by other counsel. Ex parte Lipscomb, 111 Tex. 409, 239 S.W. 1101 (1922).

Subdivision (d) in general incorporates well established exceptions.

(1) The privilege does not extend to advice in aid of future wrongdoing. 8 Wigmore § 2298 (McNaughton Rev. 1961). The wrongdoing need not be that of the client. The provision that the client knew or reasonably should have known of the criminal or fraudulent nature of the act is designed to protect the client who is erroneously advised that the proposed action is within the law. No preliminary finding that sufficient evidence aside from the communication has been introduced to warrant a finding that the services were sought to enable the commission of a wrong is required. Cf. Clark v. United States, 289 U.S. 1, 15–16, 53 S.Ct. 465, 77 L.Ed. 993 (1933); Uniform Rule 26(2)(a). While any general exploration of what transpired between attorney and client would, of course, be inappropriate, it is wholly feasible, either at the discovery stage or during trial, so to focus the inquiry by specific questions as to avoid any broad inquiry into attorney-client communications. Numerous cases reflect this approach.

(2) Normally the privilege survives the death of the client and may be asserted by his representative. Subdivision (c), supra. When, however, the identity of the person who steps into the client's shoes is in issue, as in a will contest, the identity of the person entitled to claim the privilege remains undetermined until the conclusion of the litigation. The choice is thus between allowing both sides or neither to assert the privilege, with authority and reason favoring the latter view. McCormick § 98; Uniform Rule 26(2)(b); California Evidence Code § 957; Kansas Code of Civil Procedure § 60–426(b)(2); New Jersey Evidence Rule 26(2)(b).

(3) The exception is required by considerations of fairness and policy when questions arise out of dealings between attorney and client, as in cases of controversy over attorney's fees, claims of inadequacy of representation, or charges of professional misconduct. McCormick § 95; Uniform Rule 26(2)(c); California Evidence Code § 958; Kansas Code of Civil Procedure § 60–426(b)(3); New Jersey Evidence Rule 26(2)(c).

(4) When the lawyer acts as attesting witness, the approval of the client to his so doing may safely be assumed, and waiver of the privilege as to any relevant lawyer-client communications is a proper result. McCormick § 92, p. 184; Uniform Rule 26(2)(d); California Evidence Code § 959; Kansas Code of Civil Procedure § 60–426(b)(d) [*sic*].

(5) The subdivision states existing law. McCormick § 95, pp. 192–193. For similar provisions, see Uniform Rule 26(2)(e); California Evidence Code § 962; Kansas Code of Civil Procedure § 60–426(b)(4); New Jersey Evidence Rule 26(2). The situation with which this provision deals is to be distinguished from the case of clients with a common interest who retain different lawyers. See subdivision (b)(3) of this rule, supra.

Rule 504

PSYCHOTHERAPIST-PATIENT PRIVILEGE

[Not enacted]

(a) Definitions.

(1) A "patient" is a person who consults or is examined or interviewed by a psychotherapist.

(2) A "psychotherapist" is (A) a person authorized to practice medicine in any state or nation, or reasonably believed by the patient so to be, while engaged in the diagnosis or treatment of a mental or emotional condition, including drug addiction, or (B) a person licensed or certified as a psychologist under the laws of any state or nation, while similarly engaged.

(3) A communication is "confidential" if not intended to be disclosed to third persons other than those present to further the interest of the patient in the consultation, examination, or interview, or persons reasonably necessary for the transmission of the communication, or persons who are participating in the diagnosis and treatment under the direction of the psychotherapist, including members of the patient's family.

(b) General rule of privilege. A patient has a privilege to refuse to disclose and to prevent any other person from disclosing confidential communications, made for the purposes of diagnosis or treatment of his mental or emotional condition, including drug addiction, among himself, his psychotherapist, or persons who are participating in the diagnosis or treatment under the direction of the psychotherapist, including members of the patient's family.

(c) Who may claim the privilege. The privilege may be claimed by the patient, by his guardian or conservator, or by the personal representative of a deceased patient. The person who was the psychotherapist may claim the privilege but only on behalf of the patient. His authority so to do is presumed in the absence of evidence to the contrary.

(d) Exceptions.

(1) Proceedings for hospitalization. There is no privilege under this rule for communications relevant to an issue in proceedings to hospitalize the patient for mental illness, if the psychotherapist in the course of diagnosis or treatment has determined that the patient is in need of hospitalization.

(2) Examination by order of judge. If the judge orders an examination of the mental or emotional condition of the patient, communications made in the course thereof are not privileged under this rule with respect to the particular purpose for which the examination is ordered unless the judge orders otherwise.

(3) Condition an element of claim or defense. There is no privilege under this rule as to communications relevant to an issue of the mental or emotional condition of the patient in any proceeding in which he relies upon the condition as an element of his claim or defense, or, after the patient's death, in any proceeding in which any party relies upon the condition as an element of his claim or defense.

Advisory Committee's Note

The rules contain no provision for a general physician-patient privilege. While many states have by statute created the privilege, the exceptions which have been found necessary in order to obtain information required by the public interest or to avoid fraud are so numerous as to leave little if any basis for the privilege. Among the exclusions from the statutory privilege, the following may be enumerated; communications not made for purposes of diagnosis and treatment; commitment and restoration proceedings; issues as to wills or otherwise between parties claiming by succession from the patient; actions on insurance policies; required reports (venereal diseases, gunshot wounds, child abuse); communications in furtherance of crime or fraud; mental or physical condition put in issue by patient (personal injury cases); malpractice actions; and some or all criminal prosecutions. California, for example, excepts cases in which the patient puts his condition in issue, all criminal proceedings, will and similar contests, malpractice cases, and disciplinary proceedings, as well as certain other situations, thus leaving virtually nothing covered by the privilege. California Evidence Code §§ 990–1007. For other illustrative statutes see Ill.Rev.Stat.1967, c. 51, § 5.1; N.Y.C.P.L.R. § 4504; N.C.Gen.Stat.1953, § 8–53. Moreover, the possibility of compelling gratuitous disclosure by the physician is foreclosed by his standing to raise the question of relevancy. See Note on "Official Information" Privilege following Rule 509, infra.

The doubts attendant upon the general physician-patient privilege are not present when the relationship is that of psychotherapist and patient. While the common law recognized no general physician-patient privilege, it had indicated a disposition to recognize a psychotherapist-patient privilege, Note, Confidential Communications to a Psychotherapist: A New Testimonial Privilege, 47 Nw.U.L.Rev. 384 (1952), when legislatures began moving into the field.

The case for the privilege is convincingly stated in Report No. 45, Group for the Advancement of Psychiatry 92 (1960):

"Among physicians, the psychiatrist has a special need to maintain confidentiality. His capacity to help his patients is completely dependent upon their willingness and ability to talk freely. This makes it difficult if not impossible for him to function without being able to assure his patients of confidentiality and, indeed, privileged communication. Where there may be exceptions to this general rule * * *, there is wide agreement that confidentiality is a *sine qua non* for successful psychiatric treatment. The relationship may well be likened to that of the priest-penitent or the lawyer-client. Psychiatrists not only explore the very depths of their patients' conscious, but their unconscious feelings and attitudes as well. Therapeutic effectiveness necessitates going beyond a patient's awareness and, in order to do this, it must be possible to communicate freely. A threat to secrecy blocks successful treatment."

A much more extended exposition of the case for the privilege is made in Slovenko, Psychiatry and a Second Look at the Medical Privilege, 6 Wayne

L.Rev. 175, 184 (1960), quoted extensively in the careful Tentative Recommendation and Study Relating to the Uniform Rules of Evidence (Article V.
Privileges), Cal.Law Rev. Comm'n, 417 (1964). The conclusion is reached that
Wigmore's four conditions needed to justify the existence of a privilege are
amply satisfied.

Illustrative statutes are Cal.Evidence Code §§ 1010–1026; Ga.Code § 38–
418 (1961 Supp.); Conn.Gen.Stat., § 52–146a (1966 Supp.); Ill.Rev.Stat.1967, c.
51, § 5.2.

While many of the statutes simply place the communications on the same
basis as those between attorney and client, 8 Wigmore § 2286, n. 23 (McNaughton Rev.1961), basic differences between the two relationships forbid resorting
to attorney-client save as a helpful point of departure. Goldstein and Katz,
Psychiatrist-Patient Privilege: The GAP Proposal and the Connecticut Statute,
36 Conn.B.J. 175, 182 (1962).

Subdivision (a). (1) The definition of patient does not include a person
submitting to examination for scientific purposes. Cf. Cal.Evidence Code
§ 1101. Attention is directed to 42 U.S.C. 242(a)(2), as amended by the Drug
Abuse and Control Act of 1970, P.L. 91–513, authorizing the Secretary of
Health, Education, and Welfare to withhold the identity of persons who are the
subjects of research on the use and effect of drugs. The rule would leave this
provision in full force. See Rule 501.

(2) The definition of psychotherapist embraces a medical doctor while
engaged in the diagnosis or treatment of mental or emotional conditions,
including drug addiction, in order not to exclude the general practitioner and to
avoid the making of needless refined distinctions concerning what is and what
is not the practice of psychiatry. The requirement that the psychologist be in
fact licensed, and not merely be believed to be so, is believed to be justified by
the number of persons, other than psychiatrists, purporting to render psychotherapeutic aid and the variety of their theories. Cal.Law Rev. Comm'n, supra,
at pp. 434–437.

The clarification of mental or emotional condition as including drug addition is consistent with current approaches to drug abuse problems. See, e.g.,
the definition of "drug dependent person" in 42 U.S.C. 201(q), added by the
Drug Abuse Prevention and Control Act of 1970, P.L. 91–513.

(3) Confidential communication is defined in terms conformable with those
of the lawyer-client privilege, Rule 503(a)(4), supra, with changes appropriate to
the difference in circumstance.

Subdivisions (b) and (c). The lawyer-client rule is drawn upon for the
phrasing of the general rule of privilege and the determination of those who
may claim it. See Rule 503(b) and (c).

The specific inclusion of communications made for the diagnosis and
treatment of drug addiction recognizes the continuing contemporary concern
with rehabilitation of drug dependent persons and is designed to implement
that policy by encouraging persons in need thereof to seek assistance. The
provision is in harmony with Congressional actions in this area. See 42 U.S.C.
§ 260, providing for voluntary hospitalization of addicts or persons with drug
dependence problems and prohibiting use of evidence of admission or treatment
in any proceeding against him, and 42 U.S.C. § 3419 providing that in voluntary or involuntary commitment of addicts the results of any hearing, examination, test, or procedure used to determine addiction shall not be used against
the patient in any criminal proceeding.

Subdivision (d). The exceptions differ substantially from those of the attorney-client privilege, as a result of the basic differences in the relationships. While it has been argued convincingly that the nature of the psychotherapist-patient relationship demands complete security against legally coerced disclosure in all circumstances, Louisell, The Psychologist in Today's Legal World: Part II, 41 Minn.L.Rev. 731, 746 (1957), the committee of psychiatrists and lawyers who drafted the Connecticut statute concluded that in three instances the need for disclosure was sufficiently great to justify the risk of possible impairment of the relationship. Goldstein and Katz, Psychiatrist-Patient Privilege: The GAP Proposal and the Connecticut Statute, 36 Conn.B.J. 175 (1962). These three exceptions are incorporated in the present rule.

(1) The interests of both patient and public call for a departure from confidentiality in commitment proceedings. Since disclosure is authorized only when the psychotherapist determines that hospitalization is needed, control over disclosure is placed largely in the hands of a person in whom the patient has already manifested confidence. Hence damage to the relationship is unlikely.

(2) In a court ordered examination, the relationship is likely to be an arm's length one, though not necessarily so. In any event, an exception is necessary for the effective utilization of this important and growing procedure. The exception, it will be observed, deals with a court ordered examination rather than with a court appointed psychotherapist. Also, the exception is effective only with respect to the particular purpose for which the examination is ordered. The rule thus conforms with the provisions of 18 U.S.C. § 4244 that no statement made by the accused in the course of an examination into competency to stand trial is admissible on the issue of guilt and of 42 U.S.C. § 3420 that a physician conducting an examination in a drug addiction commitment proceeding is a competent and compellable witness.

(3) By injecting his condition into litigation, the patient must be said to waive the privilege, in fairness and to avoid abuses. Similar considerations prevail after the patient's death.

Rule 505

HUSBAND–WIFE PRIVILEGE

[Not enacted.]

(a) General rule of privilege. An accused in a criminal proceeding has a privilege to prevent his spouse from testifying against him.

(b) Who may claim the privilege. The privilege may be claimed by the accused or by the spouse on his behalf. The authority of the spouse to do so is presumed in the absence of evidence to the contrary.

(c) Exceptions. There is no privilege under this rule (1) in proceedings in which one spouse is charged with a crime against the person or property of the other or of a child of either, or with a crime against the person or property of a third person committed in the course of committing a crime against the other, or (2) as to matters occurring prior to the marriage, or (3) in proceedings in which a spouse is charged with importing an alien for prostitution or other immoral purpose in violation of 8 U.S.C. § 1328, with transporting a female in

interstate commerce for immoral purposes or other offense in violation 1
of 18 U.S.C. §§ 2421–2424, or with violation of other similar statutes. 2

3

Advisory Committee's Note   4

Subdivision (a). Rules of evidence have evolved around the marriage 5
relationship in four respects: (1) incompetency of one spouse to testify for the 6
other; (2) privilege of one spouse not to testify against the other; (3) privilege of 7
one spouse not to have the other testify against him; and (4) privilege against 8
disclosure of confidential communications between spouses, sometimes extend- 9
ed to information learned by virtue of the existence of the relationship. Today 10
these matters are largely governed by statutes. 11

With the disappearance of the disqualification of parties and interested 12
persons, the basis for spousal incompetency no longer existed, and it, too, 13
virtually disappeared in both civil and criminal actions. Usually reached by 14
statute, this result was reached for federal courts by the process of decision. 15
Funk v. United States, 290 U.S. 371, 54 S.Ct. 212, 78 L.Ed. 369 (1933). These 16
rules contain no recognition of incompetency of one spouse to testify for the 17
other. 18

While some 10 jurisdictions recognize a privilege not to testify against one's 19
spouse in a criminal case, and a much smaller number do so in civil cases, the 20
great majority recognizes no privilege on the part of the testifying spouse, and 21
this is the position taken by the rule. Compare Wyatt v. United States, 362 22
U.S. 525, 80 S.Ct. 901, 4 L.Ed.2d 931 (1960), a Mann Act prosecution in which 23
the wife was the victim. The majority opinion held that she could not claim 24
privilege and was compellable to testify. The holding was narrowly based: The 25
Mann Act presupposed that the women with whom it dealt had no independent 26
wills of their own, and this legislative judgment precluded allowing a victim- 27
wife an option whether to testify, lest the policy of the statute be defeated. A 28
vigorous dissent took the view that nothing in the Mann Act required depar- 29
ture from usual doctrine, which was conceived to be one of allowing the injured 30
party to claim or waive privilege.

About 30 jurisdictions recognize a privilege of an accused in a criminal case 31
to prevent his or her spouse from testifying. It is believed to represent the one 32
aspect of marital privilege the continuation of which is warranted. In Hawkins 33
v. United States, 358 U.S. 74, 79 S.Ct. 136, 3 L.Ed.2d 125 (1958) it was sustained. 34
Cf. McCormick § 66; 8 Wigmore § 2228 (McNaughton Rev.1961): Comment, 35
Uniform Rule 23(2).

36
The rule recognizes no privilege for confidential communications. The 37
traditional justifications for privileges not to testify against a spouse and not to 38
be testified against by one's spouse have been the prevention of marital 39
dissension and the repugnancy of requiring a person to condemn or be con- 40
demned by his spouse. 8 Wigmore §§ 2228, 2241 (McNaughton Rev.1961). 41
These considerations bear no relevancy to marital communications. Nor can it 42
be assumed that marital conduct will be affected by a privilege for confidential 43
communications of whose existence the parties in all likelihood are unaware. 44
The other communication privileges, by way of contrast, have as one party a 45
professional person who can be expected to inform the other of the existence of 46
the privilege. Moreover, the relationships from which those privileges arise are 47
essentially and almost exclusively verbal in nature, quite unlike marriage. See 48
Hutchins and Slesinger, Some Observations on the Law of Evidence: Family 49
Relations, 13 Minn.L.Rev. 675 (1929). Cf. McCormick § 90; 8 Wigmore § 2337 50
(McNaughton Rev.1961).

The parties are not spouses if the marriage was a sham, Lutwak v. United States, 344 U.S. 604 (1953), or they have been divorced, Barsky v. United States, 339 F.2d 180 (9th Cir.1964), and therefore the privilege is not applicable.

Subdivision (b). This provision is a counterpart of Rules 503(c), 504(c), and 506(c). Its purpose is to provide a procedure for preventing the taking of the spouse's testimony notably in grand jury proceedings, when the accused is absent and does not know that a situation appropriate for a claim of privilege is presented. If the privilege is not claimed by the spouse, the protection of Rule 512 is available.

Subdivision (c) contains three exceptions to the privilege against spousal testimony in criminal cases.

(1) The need of limitation upon the privilege in order to avoid grave injustice in cases of offenses against the other spouse or a child of either can scarcely be denied. Wigmore § 2239 (McNaughton Rev.1961). The rule therefore disallows any privilege against spousal testimony in these cases and in this respect is in accord with the result reached in Wyatt v. United States, 362 U.S. 525, 80 S.Ct. 901, 4 L.Ed.2d 931 (1960), a Mann Act prosecution, denying the accused the privilege of excluding his wife's testimony, since she was the woman who was transported for immoral purposes.

(2) The second exception renders the privilege inapplicable as to matters occurring prior to the marriage. This provision eliminates the possibility of suppressing testimony by marrying the witness.

(3) The third exception continues and expands established Congressional policy. In prosecutions for importing aliens for immoral purposes, Congress has specifically denied the accused any privilege not to have his spouse testify against him. 8 U.S.C. § 1328. No provision of this nature is included in the Mann Act, and in Hawkins v. United States, 358 U.S. 74, 79 S.Ct. 136, 3 L.Ed.2d 125 (1958), the conclusion was reached that the common law privilege continued. Consistency requires similar results in the two situations. The rule adopts the Congressional approach, as based upon a more realistic appraisal of the marriage relationship in cases of this kind, in preference to the specific result in *Hawkins*. Note the common law treatment of pimping and sexual offenses with third persons as exceptions to marital privilege. 8 Wigmore § 2239 (McNaughton Rev.1961).

With respect to bankruptcy proceedings, the smallness of the area of spousal privilege under the rule and the general inapplicability of privileges created by state law render unnecessary any special provision for examination of the spouse of the bankrupt, such as that now contained in section 21(a) of the Bankruptcy Act. 11 U.S.C. § 44(a).

For recent statutes and rules dealing with husband-wife privileges, see California Evidence Code §§ 970–973, 980–987; Kansas Code of Civil Procedure §§ 60–423(b), 60–428; New Jersey Evidence Rules 23(2), 28.

Rule 506

COMMUNICATIONS TO CLERGYMEN

[Not enacted.]

(a) Definitions. As used in this rule:

(1) A "clergyman" is a minister, priest, rabbi, or other similar functionary of a religious organization, or an individual reasonably believed so to be by the person consulting him.

(2) A communication is "confidential" if made privately and not intended for further disclosure except to other persons present in furtherance of the purpose of the communication.

(b) General rule of privilege. A person has a privilege to refuse to disclose and to prevent another from disclosing a confidential communication by the person to a clergyman in his professional character as spiritual adviser.

(c) Who may claim the privilege. The privilege may be claimed by the person, by his guardian or conservator, or by his personal representative if he is deceased. The clergyman may claim the privilege on behalf of the person His authority so to do is presumed in the absence of evidence to the contrary.

Advisory Committee's Note

The considerations which dictate the recognition of privileges generally seem strongly to favor a privilege for confidential communications to clergymen. During the period when most of the common law privileges were taking shape, no clear-cut privilege for communications between priest and penitent emerged. 8 Wigmore § 2394 (McNaughton Rev.1961). The English political climate of the time may well furnish the explanation. In this country, however, the privilege has been recognized by statute in about two-thirds of the states and occasionally by the common law process of decision. Id., § 2395; Mullen v. United States, 105 U.S.App.D.C. 25, 263 F.2d 275 (1959).

Subdivision (a). Paragraph (1) defines a clergyman as a "minister, priest, rabbi, or other similar functionary of a religious organization." The concept is necessarily broader than that inherent in the ministerial exemption for purposes of Selective Service. See United States v. Jackson, 369 F.2d 936 (4th Cir. 1966). However, it is not so broad as to include all self-denominated "ministers." A fair construction of the language requires that the person to whom the status is sought to be attached be regularly engaged in activities conforming at least in a general way with those of a Catholic priest, Jewish rabbi, or minister of an established Protestant denomination, though not necessarily on a full-time basis. No further specification seems possible in view of the lack of licensing and certification procedures for clergymen. However, this lack seems to have occasioned no particular difficulties in connection with the solemnization of marriages, which suggests that none may be anticipated here. For similar definitions of "clergyman" see California Evidence Code § 1030; New Jersey Evidence Rule 29.

The "reasonable belief" provision finds support in similar provisions for lawyer-client in Rule 503 and for psychotherapist-patient in Rule 504. A parallel is also found in the recognition of the validity of marriages performed by unauthorized persons if the parties reasonably believed them legally qualified. Harper and Skolnick, Problems of the Family 153 (Rev.Ed.1962).

(2) The definition of "confidential" communication is consistent with the use of the term in Rule 503(a)(5) for lawyer-client and in Rule 504(a)(3) for psychotherapist-patient, suitably adapted to communications to clergymen.

Subdivision (b). The choice between a privilege narrowly restricted to doctrinally required confessions and a privilege broadly applicable to all confidential communications with a clergyman in his professional character as spiritual adviser has been exercised in favor of the latter. Many clergymen now receive training in marriage counseling and the handling of personality problems. Matters of this kind fall readily into the realm of the spirit. The same considerations which underlie the psychotherapist-patient privilege of Rule 504 suggest a broad application of the privilege for communications to clergymen.

State statutes and rules fall in both the narrow and the broad categories. A typical narrow statute proscribes disclosure of "a confession ＊ ＊ ＊ made ＊ ＊ ＊ in the course of discipline enjoined by the church to which he belongs." Ariz.Rev.Stats.Ann.1956, § 12–2233. See also California Evidence Code § 1032; Uniform Rule 29. Illustrative of the broader privilege are statutes applying to "information communicated to him in a confidential manner, properly entrusted to him in his professional capacity, and necessary to enable him to discharge the functions of his office according to the usual course of his practice or discipline, wherein such person so communicating ＊ ＊ ＊ is seeking spiritual counsel and advice," Fla.Stats.Ann.1960, § 90.241, or to any "confidential communication properly entrusted to him in his professional capacity, and necessary and proper to enable him to discharge the functions of his office according to the usual course of practice or discipline," Iowa Code Ann.1950, § 622.10. See also Ill.Rev.Stats.1967, c. 51, § 48.1; Minn.Stats.Ann.1945, § 595.02(3); New Jersey Evidence Rule 29.

Under the privilege as phrased, the communicating person is entitled to prevent disclosure not only by himself but also by the clergyman and by eavesdroppers. For discussion see Advisory Committee's Note under lawyer-client privilege, Rule 503(b).

The nature of what may reasonably be considered spiritual advice makes it unnecessary to include in the rule a specific exception for communications in furtherance of crime or fraud, as in Rule 503(d)(1).

Subdivision (c) makes clear that the privilege belongs to the communicating person. However, a prima facie authority on the part of the clergyman to claim the privilege on behalf of the person is recognized. The discipline of the particular church and the discreetness of the clergyman are believed to constitute sufficient safeguards for the absent communicating person. See Advisory Committee's Note to the similar provision with respect to attorney-client in Rule 503(c).

Rule 507

POLITICAL VOTE

[Not enacted.]

Every person has a privilege to refuse to disclose the tenor of his vote at a political election conducted by secret ballot unless the vote was cast illegally.

Advisory Committee's Note

Secrecy in voting is an essential aspect of effective democratic government, insuring free exercise of the franchise and fairness in elections. Secrecy after the ballot has been cast is as essential as secrecy in the act of voting. Nutting,

Freedom of Silence: Constitutional Protection Against Governmental Intrusion in Political Affairs, 47 Mich.L.Rev. 181, 191 (1948). Consequently a privilege has long been recognized on the part of a voter to decline to disclose how he voted. Required disclosure would be the exercise of "a kind of inquisitorial power unknown to the principles of our government and constitution, and might be highly injurious to the suffrages of a free people, as well as tending to create cabals and disturbances between contending parties in popular elections." Johnston v. Charleston, 1 Bay 441, 442 (S.C.1795).

The exception for illegally cast votes is a common one under both statutes and case law, Nutting, supra, at p. 192; 8 Wigmore § 2214, p. 163 (McNaughton Rev.1961). The policy considerations which underlie the privilege are not applicable to the illegal voter. However, nothing in the exception purports to foreclose an illegal voter from invoking the privilege against self-incrimination under appropriate circumstances.

For similar provisions, see Uniform Rule 31; California Evidence Code § 1050; Kansas Code of Civil Procedure § 60–431; New Jersey Evidence Rule 31.

Rule 508

TRADE SECRETS

[Not enacted.]

A person has a privilege, which may be claimed by him or his agent or employee, to refuse to disclose and to prevent other persons from disclosing a trade secret owned by him, if the allowance of the privilege will not tend to conceal fraud or otherwise work injustice. When disclosure is directed, the judge shall take such protective measure as the interests of the holder of the privilege and of the parties and the furtherance of justice may require.

Advisory Committee's Note

While sometimes said not to be a true privilege, a qualified right to protection against disclosure of trade secrets has found ample recognition, and, indeed, a denial of it would be difficult to defend. 8 Wigmore § 2212(3) (McNaughton Rev.1961). And see 4 Moore's Federal Practice ¶¶ 30.12 and 34.15 (2nd ed. 1963 and Supp.1965) and 2A Barron and Holtzoff, Federal Practice and Procedure § 715.1 (Wright ed. 1961). Congressional policy is reflected in the Securities Exchange Act of 1934, 15 U.S.C. § 78x, and the Public Utility Holding Company Act of 1933, id. § 79v, which deny the Securities and Exchange Commission authority to require disclosure of trade secrets or processes in applications and reports. See also Rule 26(c)(7) of the Rules of Civil Procedure, as revised, mentioned further hereinafter.

Illustrative cases raising trade-secret problems are: E.I. Du Pont de Nemours Powder Co. v. Masland, 244 U.S. 100, 37 S.Ct. 575, 61 L.Ed. 1016 (1917), suit to enjoin former employee from using plaintiff's secret processes, countered by defense that many of the processes were well known to the trade; Segal Lock & Hardware Co. v. FTC, 143 F.2d 935 (2d Cir.1944), question whether expert locksmiths employed by FTC should be required to disclose methods used by them in picking petitioner's "pick-proof" locks; Dobson v. Graham, 49 F. 17 (E.D.Pa.1889), patent infringement suit in which plaintiff sought to elicit from former employees now in the hire of defendant the respects in which defendant's machinery differed from plaintiff's patented machinery; Putney v. Du Bois Co., 240 Mo.App. 1075, 226 S.W.2d 737 (1950), action for injuries allegedly sustained from using defendant's secret formula dishwashing compound. See 8 Wigmore § 2212(3) (McNaughton Rev.1961); Annot., 17 A.L.R.2d 383; 49 Mich.L.Rev. 133 (1950). The need for accommodation between protecting trade secrets, on the one hand, and eliciting facts required for full and fair presentation of a case, on the other hand, is apparent. Whether disclosure should be required depends upon a weighing of the competing interests involved against the background of the total situation, including consideration of such factors as the dangers of abuse, good faith, adequacy of protective measures, and the availability of other means of proof.

The cases furnish examples of the bringing of judicial ingenuity to bear upon the problem of evolving protective measures which achieve a degree of control over disclosure. Perhaps the most common is simply to take testimony *in camera.* Annot., 62 A.L.R.2d 509. Other possibilities include making disclosure to opposing counsel but not to his client, E.I. Du Pont de Nemours Powder Co. v. Masland, 244 U.S. 100, 37 S.Ct. 575, 61 L.Ed. 1016 (1917); making disclosure only to the judge (hearing examiner), Segal Lock & Hardware Co. v. FTC, 143 F.2d 935 (2d Cir.1944); and placing those present under oath not to make disclosure, Paul v. Sinnott, 217 F.Supp. 84 (W.D.Pa.1963).

Rule 26(c) of the Rules of Civil Procedure, as revised, provides that the judge may make "any order which justice requires to protect a party or person from annoyance, embarrassment, oppression, or undue burden or expense, including one or more of the following: * * * (7) that a trade secret or other confidential research, development, or commercial information not be disclosed or be disclosed only in a designated way * * *." While the instant evidence rule extends this underlying policy into the trial, the difference in circumstances between discovery stage and trial may well be such as to require a different ruling at the trial.

For other rules recognizing privilege for trade secrets, see Uniform Rule 32; California Evidence Code § 1060; Kansas Code of Civil Procedure § 60–432; New Jersey Evidence Rule 32.

Rule 509

SECRETS OF STATE AND OTHER OFFICIAL INFORMATION

[Not enacted.]

(a) Definitions.

(1) Secret of state. A "secret of state" is a governmental secret relating to the national defense or the international relations of the United States.

(2) Official information. "Official information" is information within the custody or control of a department or agency of the government the disclosure of which is shown to be contrary to the public interest and which consists of: (A) intragovernmental opinions or recommendations submitted for consideration in the performance of decisional or policymaking functions, or (B) subject to the provisions of 18 U.S.C. § 3500, investigatory files compiled for law enforcement purposes and not otherwise available, or (C) information within the

custody or control of a governmental department or agency whether
initiated within the department or agency or acquired by it in its
exercise of its official responsibilities and not otherwise available to the
public pursuant to 5 U.S.C. § 552.

(b) General rule of privilege. The government has a privilege to
refuse to give evidence and to prevent any person from giving evidence
upon a showing of reasonable likelihood of danger that the evidence
will disclose a secret of state or official information, as defined in this
rule.

(c) Procedures. The privilege for secrets of state may be claimed
only by the chief officer of the government agency or department
administering the subject matter which the secret information sought
concerns, but the privilege for official information may be asserted by
any attorney representing the government. The required showing may
be made in whole or in part in the form of a written statement. The
judge may hear the matter in chambers, but all counsel are entitled to
inspect the claim and showing and to be heard thereon, except that, in
the case of secrets of state, the judge upon motion of the government,
may permit the government to make the required showing in the above
form *in camera.* If the judge sustains the privilege upon a showing *in
camera,* the entire text of the government's statements shall be sealed
and preserved in the court's records in the event of appeal. In the case
of privilege claimed for official information the court may require
examination *in camera* of the information itself. The judge may take
any protective measure which the interests of the government and the
furtherance of justice may require.

(d) Notice to government. If the circumstances of the case
indicate a substantial possibility that a claim of privilege would be
appropriate but has not been made because of oversight or lack of
knowledge, the judge shall give or cause notice to be given to the officer
entitled to claim the privilege and shall stay further proceedings a
reasonable time to afford opportunity to assert a claim of privilege.

(e) Effect of sustaining claim. If a claim of privilege is sustained
in a proceeding to which the government is a party and it appears that
another party is thereby deprived of material evidence, the judge shall
make any further orders which the interests of justice require, including striking the testimony of a witness, declaring a mistrial, finding
against the government upon an issue as to which the evidence is
relevant, or dismissing the action.

Advisory Committee's Note

Subdivision (a). (1) The rule embodies the privilege protecting military
and state secrets described as "well established in the law of evidence," United
States v. Reynolds, 345 U.S. 1, 6, 73 S.Ct. 528, 97 L.Ed. 727 (1953), and as one
"the existence of which has never been doubted," 8 Wigmore § 2378, p. 794
(McNaughton Rev.1961).

The use of the term "national defense," without attempt at further elucida-
tion, finds support in the similar usage in statutory provisions relating to the

crimes of gathering, transmitting, or losing defense information, and gathering or delivering defense information to aid a foreign government. 18 U.S.C. §§ 793, 794. See also 5 U.S.C. § 1002; 50 U.S.C.App. § 2152(d). In determining whether military or state secrets are involved, due regard will, of course, be given to classification pursuant to executive order.

(2) The rule also recognizes a privilege for specified types of official information and in this respect is designed primarily to resolve questions of the availability to litigants of data in the files of governmental departments and agencies. In view of the lesser danger to the public interest than in cases of military and state secrets, the official information privilege is subject to a generally overriding requirement that disclosure would be contrary to the public interest. It is applicable to three categories of information.

(A) Intergovernmental opinions or recommendations submitted for consideration in the performance of decisional or policy making functions. The policy basis of this aspect of the privilege is found in the desirability of encouraging candor in the exchange of views within the government. Kaiser Aluminum & Chemical Corp. v. United States, 141 Ct.Cl. 38, 157 F.Supp. 939 (1958); Davis v. Braswell Motor Freight Lines, Inc., 363 F.2d 600 (5th Cir.1966); Ackerly v. Ley, 420 F.2d 1336 (D.C.Cir.1969). A privilege of this character is consistent with the Freedom of Information Act, 5 U.S.C. § 552(b)(5), and with the standing of the agency to raise questions of relevancy, though not a party, recognized in such decisions as Boeing Airplane Co. v. Coggeshall, 108 U.S.App.D.C. 106, 280 F.2d 654, 659 (1960) (Renegotiation Board) and Freeman v. Seligson, 132 U.S. App.D.C. 56, 405 F.2d 1326, 1334 (1968) (Secretary of Agriculture).

(B) Investigatory files compiled for law enforcement purposes. This category is expressly made subject to the provisions of the Jencks Act, 18 U.S.C. § 3500, which insulates prior statements or reports of government witnesses in criminal cases against subpoena, discovery, or inspection until the witness has testified on direct examination at the trial but then entitles the defense to its production. Rarely will documents of this nature be relevant until the author has testified and thus placed his credibility in issue. Further protection against discovery of government files in criminal cases is found in Criminal Procedure Rule 16(a) and (b). The breadth of discovery in civil cases, however, goes beyond ordinary bounds of relevancy and raises problems calling for the exercise of judicial control, and in making provision for it the rule implements the Freedom of Information Act, 18 U.S.C. § 552(b)(7).

(C) Information exempted from disclosure under the Freedom of Information Act, 5 U.S.C. § 552. In 1958 the old "housekeeping" statute which had been relied upon as a foundation for departmental regulations curtailing disclosure was amended by adding a provision that it did not authorize withholding information from the public. In 1966 the Congress enacted the Freedom of Information Act for the purpose of making information in the files of departments and agencies, subject to certain specified exceptions, available to the mass media and to the public generally. 5 U.S.C. § 552. These enactments are significant expressions of Congressional policy. The exceptions in the Act are not framed in terms of evidentiary privilege, thus recognizing by clear implication that the needs of litigants may stand on somewhat different footing from those of the public generally. Nevertheless, the exceptions are based on values obviously entitled to weighty consideration in formulating rules of evidentiary privilege. In some instances in these rules, exceptions in the Act have been made the subject of specific privileges, e.g., military and state secrets in the present rule and trade secrets in Rule 508. The purpose of the present

provision is to incorporate the remaining exceptions of the Act into the
qualified privilege here created, thus subjecting disclosure of the information to
judicial determination with respect to the effect of disclosure on the public
interest. This approach appears to afford a satisfactory resolution of the
problems which may arise.

Subdivision (b). The rule vests the privileges in the government where
they properly belong rather than a party or witness. See United States v.
Reynolds, supra, p. 7, 73 S.Ct. 528. The showing required as a condition
precedent to claiming the privilege represents a compromise between complete
judicial control and accepting as final the decision of a departmental officer.
See Machin v. Zuckert, 114 U.S.App.D.C. 335, 316 F.2d 336 (1963), rejecting in
part a claim of privilege by the Secretary of the Air Force and ordering the
furnishing of information for use in private litigation. This approach is
consistent with *Reynolds.*

Subdivision (c). In requiring the claim of privilege for state secrets to be
made by the chief departmental officer, the rule again follows *Reynolds,*
insuring consideration by a high-level officer. This provision is justified by the
lesser participation by the judge in cases of state secrets. The full participation
by the judge in official information cases, on the contrary, warrants allowing
the claim of privilege to be made by a government attorney.

Subdivision (d) spells out and emphasizes a power and responsibility on
the part of the trial judge. An analogous provision is found in the requirement
that the court certify to the Attorney General when the constitutionality of an
act of Congress is in question in an action to which the government is not a
party. 28 U.S.C. § 2403.

Subdivision (e). If privilege is successfully claimed by the government in
litigation to which it is not a party, the effect is simply to make the evidence
unavailable, as though a witness had died or claimed the privilege against self-
incrimination, and no specification of the consequences is necessary. The rule
therefore deals only with the effect of a successful claim of privilege by the
government in proceedings to which it is a party. Reference to other types of
cases serves to illustrate the variety of situations which may arise and the
impossibility of evolving a single formula to be applied automatically to all of
them. The privileged materials may be the statement of government witness,
as under the *Jencks* statute, which provides that, if the government elects not
to produce the statement, the judge is to strike the testimony of the witness, or
that he may declare a mistrial if the interests of justice so require. 18 U.S.C.
§ 3500(d). Or the privileged materials may disclose a possible basis for applying pressure upon witnesses. United States v. Beekman, 155 F.2d 580 (2d Cir.
1946). Or they may bear directly upon a substantive element of a criminal
case, requiring dismissal in the event of a successful claim of privilege. United
States v. Andolschek, 142 F.2d 503 (2d Cir.1944); and see United States v.
Reynolds, 345 U.S. 1, 73 S.Ct. 528, 97 L.Ed. 727 (1953). Or they may relate to
an element of a plaintiff's claim against the government, with the decisions
indicating unwillingness to allow the government's claim of privilege for secrets
of state to be used as an offensive weapon against it. United States v.
Reynolds, supra; Republic of China v. National Union Fire Ins. Co., 142 F.Supp.
551 (D.Md.1956).

Rule 510

IDENTITY OF INFORMER

[Not enacted.]

(a) **Rule of privilege.** The government or a state or subdivision thereof has a privilege to refuse to disclose the identity of a person who has furnished information relating to or assisting in an investigation of a possible violation of law to a law enforcement officer or member of a legislative committee or its staff conducting an investigation.

(b) **Who may claim.** The privilege may be claimed by an appropriate representative of the government, regardless of whether the information was furnished to an officer of the government or of a state or subdivision thereof. The privilege may be claimed by an appropriate representative of a state or subdivision if the information was furnished to an officer thereof, except that in criminal cases the privilege shall not be allowed if the government objects.

(c) **Exceptions.**

(1) Voluntary disclosure; informer a witness. No privilege exists under this rule if the identity of the informer or his interest in the subject matter of his communication has been disclosed to those who would have cause to resent the communication by a holder of the privilege or by the informer's own action or if the informer appears as a witness for the government.

(2) Testimony on merits. If it appears from the evidence in the case or from other showing by a party that an informer may be able to give testimony necessary to a fair determination of the issue of guilt or innocence in a criminal case or a material issue on the merits in a civil case to which the government is a party, and the government invokes the privilege, the judge shall give the government an opportunity to show *in camera* facts relevant to determining whether the informer can, in fact, supply that testimony. The showing will ordinarily be in the form of affidavits, but the judge may direct that testimony be taken if he finds that the matter cannot be resolved satisfactorily upon affidavit. If the judge finds that there is a reasonable probability that the informer can give the testimony, and the government elects not to disclose his identity, the judge on motion of the defendant in a criminal case shall dismiss the charges to which the testimony would relate, and the judge may do so on his own motion. In civil cases, he may make any order that justice requires. Evidence submitted to the judge shall be sealed and preserved to be made available to the appellate court in the event of an appeal, and the contents shall not otherwise be revealed without consent of the government. All counsel and parties shall be permitted to be present at every stage of proceedings under this subdivision except a showing *in camera,* at which no counsel or party shall be permitted to be present.

(3) Legality of obtaining evidence. If information from an informer
is relied upon to establish the legality of the means by which evidence
was obtained and the judge is not satisfied that the information was
received from an informer reasonably believed to be reliable or credible,
he may require the identity of the informer to be disclosed. The judge
shall, on request of the government, direct that the disclosure be made
in camera. All counsel and parties concerned with the issue of legality
shall be permitted to be present at every stage of proceedings under
this subdivision except a disclosure *in camera,* at which no counsel or
party shall be permitted to be present. If disclosure of the identity of
the informer is made *in camera,* the record thereof shall be sealed and
preserved to be made available to the appellate court in the event of an
appeal, and the contents shall not otherwise be revealed without
consent of the government.

Advisory Committee's Note

The rule recognizes the use of informers as an important aspect of law
enforcement, whether the informer is a citizen who steps forward with information or a paid undercover agent. In either event, the basic importance of
anonymity in the effective use of informers is apparent, Bocchicchio v. Curtis
Publishing Co., 203 F.Supp. 403 (E.D.Pa.1962), and the privilege of withholding
their identity was well established at common law. Roviaro v. United States,
353 U.S. 53, 59, 77 S.Ct. 623, 1 L.Ed.2d 639 (1957); McCormick § 148; 8
Wigmore § 2374 (McNaughton Rev.1961).

Subdivision (a). The public interest in law enforcement requires that the
privilege be that of the government, state, or political subdivision, rather than
that of the witness. The rule blankets in as an informer anyone who tells a
law enforcement officer about a violation of law without regard to whether the
officer is one charged with enforcing the particular law. The rule also applies
to disclosures to legislative investigating committees and their staffs, and is
sufficiently broad to include continuing investigations.

Although the tradition of protecting the identity of informers has evolved
in an essentially criminal setting, noncriminal law enforcement situations
involving possibilities of reprisal against informers fall within the purview of
the considerations out of which the privilege originated. In Mitchell v. Roma,
265 F.2d 633 (3d Cir.1959), the privilege was given effect with respect to persons
informing as to violations of the Fair Labor Standards Act, and in Wirtz v.
Continental Finance & Loan Co., 326 F.2d 561 (5th Cir.1964), a similar case, the
privilege was recognized, although the basis of decision was lack of relevancy to
the issues in the case.

Only identity is privileged; communications are not included except to the
extent that disclosure would operate also to disclose the informer's identity.
The common law was to the same effect. 8 Wigmore § 2374, at p. 765
(McNaughton Rev.1961). See also Roviaro v. United States, supra, 353 U.S. at
p. 60, 77 S.Ct. 623; Bowman Dairy Co. v. United States, 341 U.S. 214, 221, 71
S.Ct. 675, 95 L.Ed. 879 (1951).

The rule does not deal with the question whether presentence reports made
under Criminal Procedure Rule 32(c) should be made available to an accused.

Subdivision (b). Normally the "appropriate representative" to make the
claim will be counsel. However, it is possible that disclosure of the informer's

identity will be sought in proceedings to which the government, state, or subdivision, as the case may be, is not a party. Under these circumstances effective implementation of the privilege requires that other representatives be considered "appropriate." See, for example, Bocchicchio v. Curtis Publishing Co., 203 F.Supp. 403 (E.D.Pa.1962), a civil action for libel, in which a local police officer not represented by counsel successfully claimed the informer privilege.

The privilege may be claimed by a state or subdivision of a state if the information was given to its officer, except that in criminal cases it may not be allowed if the government objects.

Subdivision (c) deals with situations in which the informer privilege either does not apply or is curtailed.

(1) If the identity of the informer is disclosed, nothing further is to be gained from efforts to suppress it. Disclosure may be direct, or the same practical effect may result from action revealing the informer's interest in the subject matter. See, for example, Westinghouse Electric Corp. v. City of Burlington, 122 U.S.App.D.C. 65, 351 F.2d 762 (1965), on remand City of Burlington v. Westinghouse Electric Corp., 246 F.Supp. 839 (D.D.C.1965), which held that the filing of civil antitrust actions destroyed as to plaintiffs the informer privilege claimed by the Attorney General with respect to complaints of criminal antitrust violations. While allowing the privilege in effect to be waived by one not its holder, i.e. the informer himself, is something of a novelty in the law of privilege, if the informer chooses to reveal his identity, further efforts to suppress it are scarcely feasible.

The exception is limited to disclosure to "those who would have cause to resent the communication," in the language of Roviaro v. United States, 353 U.S. 53, 60, 77 S.Ct. 623, 1 L.Ed.2d 639 (1957), since disclosure otherwise, e.g., to another law enforcing agency, is not calculated to undercut the objects of the privilege.

If the informer becomes a witness for the government, the interests of justice in disclosing his status as a source of bias or possible support are believed to outweigh any remnant of interest in nondisclosure which then remains. See Harris v. United States, 371 F.2d 365 (9th Cir.1967), in which the trial judge permitted detailed inquiry into the relationship between the witness and the government. Cf. Attorney General v. Briant, 15 M. & W. 169, 153 Eng. Rep. 808 (Exch.1846). The purpose of the limitation to witnesses for the government is to avoid the possibility of calling persons as witnesses as a means of discovery whether they are informers.

(2) The informer privilege, it was held by the leading case, may not be used in a criminal prosecution to suppress the identity of a witness when the public interest in protecting the flow of information is outweighed by the individual's right to prepare his defense. Roviaro v. United States, supra. The rule extends this balancing to include civil as well as criminal cases and phrases it in terms of "a reasonable probability that the informer may be able to give testimony necessary to a fair determination of the issue of guilt or innocence in a criminal case or of a material issue on the merits in a civil case." Once the privilege is invoked a procedure is provided for determining whether the informer can in fact supply testimony of such nature as to require disclosure of his identity, thus avoiding a "judicial guessing game" on the question. United States v. Day, 384 F.2d 464, 470 (3d Cir.1967). An investigation *in camera* is calculated to accommodate the conflicting interests involved. The rule also spells out specifically the consequences of a successful claim of the privilege in

a criminal case; the wider range of possibilities in civil cases demands more flexibility in treatment. See Advisory Committee's Note to Rule 509(e), supra.

(3) One of the acute conflicts between the interest of the public in nondisclosure and the avoidance of unfairness to the accused as a result of nondisclosure arises when information from an informer is relied upon to legitimate a search and seizure by furnishing probable cause for an arrest without a warrant or for the issuance of a warrant for arrest or search. McCray v. Illinois, 386 U.S. 300, 87 S.Ct. 1056, 18 L.Ed.2d 62 (1967), rehearing denied 386 U.S. 1042. A hearing *in camera* provides an accommodation of these conflicting interests. United States v. Jackson, 384 F.2d 825 (3d Cir.1967). The limited disclosure to the judge avoids any significant impairment of secrecy, while affording the accused a substantial measure of protection against arbitrary police action. The procedure is consistent with McCray and the decisions there discussed.

Rule 511

WAIVER OF PRIVILEGE BY VOLUNTARY DISCLOSURE

[Not enacted.]

A person upon whom these rules confer a privilege against disclosure of the confidential matter or communication waives the privilege if he or his predecessor while holder of the privilege voluntarily discloses or consents to disclosure of any significant part of the matter or communication. This rule does not apply if the disclosure is itself a privileged communication.

Advisory Committee's Note

The central purpose of most privileges is the promotion of some interest or relationship by endowing it with a supporting secrecy or confidentiality. It is evident that the privilege should terminate when the holder by his own act destroys this confidentiality. McCormick §§ 87, 97, 106; 8 Wigmore §§ 2242, 2327–2329, 2374, 2389–2390 (McNaughton Rev.1961).

The rule is designed to be read with a view to what it is that the particular privilege protects. For example, the lawyer-client privilege covers only communications, and the fact that a client has discussed a matter with his lawyer does not insulate the client against disclosure of the subject matter discussed, although he is privileged not to disclose the discussion itself. See McCormick § 93. The waiver here provided for is similarly restricted. Therefore a client, merely by disclosing a subject which he had discussed with his attorney, would not waive the applicable privilege; he would have to make disclosure of the communication itself in order to effect a waiver.

By traditional doctrine, waiver is the intentional relinquishment of a known right. Johnson v. Zerbst, 304 U.S. 458, 464, 58 S.Ct. 1019, 82 L.Ed. 1461 (1938). However, in the confidential privilege situations, once confidentiality is destroyed through voluntary disclosure, no subsequent claim of privilege can restore it, and knowledge or lack of knowledge of the existence of the privilege appears to be irrelevant. California Evidence Code § 912; 8 Wigmore § 2327 (McNaughton Rev.1961).

Rule 512

PRIVILEGED MATTER DISCLOSED UNDER COMPULSION OR WITHOUT OPPORTUNITY TO CLAIM PRIVILEGE

[Not enacted.]

Evidence of a statement or other disclosure of privileged matter is not admissible against the holder of the privilege if the disclosure was (a) compelled erroneously or (b) made without opportunity to claim the privilege.

Advisory Committee's Note

Ordinarily a privilege is invoked in order to forestall disclosure. However, under some circumstances consideration must be given to the status and effect of a disclosure already made. Rule 511, immediately preceding, gives voluntary disclosure the effect of a waiver, while the present rule covers the effect of disclosure made under compulsion or without opportunity to claim the privilege.

Confidentiality, once destroyed, is not susceptible of restoration, yet some measure of repair may be accomplished by preventing use of the evidence against the holder of the privilege. The remedy of exclusion is therefore made available when the earlier disclosure was compelled erroneously or without opportunity to claim the privilege.

With respect to erroneously compelled disclosure, the argument may be made that the holder should be required in the first instance to assert the privilege, stand his ground, refuse to answer, perhaps incur a judgment of contempt, and exhaust all legal recourse, in order to sustain his privilege. See Fraser v. United States, 145 F.2d 139 (6th Cir.1944), cert. denied 324 U.S. 849, 65 S.Ct. 684, 89 L.Ed. 1409; United States v. Johnson, 76 F.Supp. 538 (M.D.Pa. 1947), aff'd 165 F.2d 42 (3d Cir.1947), cert. denied 332 U.S. 852, 68 S.Ct. 355, 92 L.Ed. 422, reh. denied 333 U.S. 834, 68 S.Ct. 457, 92 L.Ed. 1118. However, this exacts of the holder greater fortitude in the face of authority than ordinary individuals are likely to possess, and assumes unrealistically that a judicial remedy is always available. In self-incrimination cases, the writers agree that erroneously compelled disclosures are inadmissible in a subsequent criminal prosecution of the holder, Maguire, Evidence of Guilt 66 (1959); McCormick § 127; 8 Wigmore § 2270 (McNaughton Rev.1961), and the principle is equally sound when applied to other privileges. The modest departure from usual principles of res judicata which occurs when the compulsion is judicial is justified by the advantage of having one simple rule, assuring at least one opportunity for judicial supervision in every case.

The second circumstance stated as a basis for exclusion is disclosure made without opportunity to the holder to assert his privilege. Illustrative possibilities are disclosure by an eavesdropper, by a person used in the transmission of a privileged communication, by a family member participating in psychotherapy, or privileged data improperly made available from a computer bank.

Rule 513

COMMENT UPON OR INFERENCE FROM CLAIM OF PRIVILEGE; INSTRUCTION

[Not enacted.]

(a) **Comment or inference not permitted.** The claim of a privilege, whether in the present proceeding or upon a prior occasion, is not a proper subject of comment by judge or counsel. No inference may be drawn therefrom.

(b) **Claiming privilege without knowledge of jury.** In jury cases, proceedings shall be conducted, to the extent practicable, so as to facilitate the making of claims of privilege without the knowledge of the jury.

(c) **Jury instruction.** Upon request, any party against whom the jury might drawn an adverse inference from a claim of privilege is entitled to an instruction that no inference may be drawn therefrom.

Advisory Committee's Note

Subdivision (a). In Griffin v. California, 380 U.S. 609, 614, 85 S.Ct. 1229, 14 L.Ed.2d 106 (1965), the Court pointed out that allowing comment upon the claim of a privilege "cuts down on the privilege by making its assertion costly." Consequently it was held that comment upon the election of the accused not to take the stand infringed upon his privilege against self-incrimination so substantially as to constitute a constitutional violation. While the privileges governed by these rules are not constitutionally based, they are nevertheless founded upon important policies and are entitled to maximum effect. Hence the present subdivision forbids comment upon the exercise of a privilege, in accord with the weight of authority. Courtney v. United States, 390 F.2d 521 (9th Cir.1968); 8 Wigmore §§ 2243, 2322, 2386; Barnhart, Privilege in the Uniform Rules of Evidence, 24 Ohio St.L.J. 131, 137–138 (1963). Cf. McCormick § 80.

Subdivision (b). The value of a privilege may be greatly depreciated by means other than expressly commenting to a jury upon the fact that it was exercised. Thus, the calling of a witness in the presence of the jury and subsequently excusing him after a sidebar conference may effectively convey to the jury the fact that a privilege has been claimed, even though the actual claim has not been made in their hearing. Whether a privilege will be claimed is usually ascertainable in advance and the handling of the entire matter outside the presence of the jury is feasible. Destruction of the privilege by innuendo can and should be avoided. Tallo v. United States, 344 F.2d 467 (1st Cir.1965); United States v. Tomaiolo, 249 F.2d 683 (2d Cir.1957); San Fratello v. United States, 343 F.2d 711 (5th Cir.1965); Courtney v. United States, 390 F.2d 521 (9th Cir.1968); 6 Wigmore § 1808, pp. 275–276; 6 U.C.L.A.L.Rev. 455 (1959). This position is in accord with the general agreement of the authorities that an accused cannot be forced to make his election not to testify in the presence of the jury. 8 Wigmore § 2268, p. 407 (McNaughton Rev.1961).

Unanticipated situations are, of course, bound to arise, and much must be left to the discretion of the judge and the professional responsibility of counsel.

Subdivision (c). Opinions will differ as to the effectiveness of a jury instruction not to draw an adverse inference from the making of a claim of privilege. See Bruton v. United States, 389 U.S. 818, 88 S.Ct. 126, 19 L.Ed.2d 70 (1968). Whether an instruction shall be given is left to the sound judgment of counsel for the party against whom the adverse inference may be drawn. The instruction is a matter of right, if requested. This is the result reached in Bruno v. United States, 308 U.S. 287, 60 S.Ct. 198, 84 L.Ed. 257 (1939), holding that an accused is entitled to an instruction under the statute (now 18 U.S.C. § 3481) providing that his failure to testify creates no presumption against him.

The right to the instruction is not impaired by the fact that the claim of privilege is by a witness, rather than by a party, provided an adverse inference against the party may result.

Rule 804

HEARSAY EXCEPTIONS: DECLARANT UNAVAILABLE

[Subdivision (b)(2) not enacted.]

* * *

(b) Hearsay exceptions. The following are not excluded by the hearsay rule if the declarant is unavailable as a witness:

* * *

(2) *Statement of recent perception.* A statement, not in response to the instigation of a person engaged in investigating, litigating, or settling a claim, which narrates, describes, or explains an event or condition recently perceived by the declarant, made in good faith, not in contemplation of pending or anticipated litigation in which he was interested, and while his recollection was clear.

Note by Federal Judicial Center

Hearsay exception (b)(2) is set forth above as prescribed by the Supreme Court. It was not included in the rules enacted by the Congress but is reproduced here for such value as it may have for purposes of interpretation.

Advisory Committee's Note

Exception (2). The rule finds support in several directions. The well known Massachusetts Act of 1898 allows in evidence the declaration of any deceased person made in good faith before the commencement of the action and upon personal knowledge. Mass.G.L., c. 233, § 65. To the same effect is R.I. G.L. § 9–19–11. Under other statutes, a decedent's statement is admissible on behalf of his estate in actions against it, to offset the presumed inequality resulting from allowing a surviving opponent to testify. California Evidence Code § 1261; Conn.G.S., § 52–172; and statutes collected in 5 Wigmore § 1576. See also Va.Code § 8–286, allowing statements made when capable by a party now incapable of testifying.

In 1938 the Committee on Improvements in the Law of Evidence of the American Bar Association recommended adoption of a statute similar to that of Massachusetts but with the concept of unavailability expanded to include, in addition to death, cases of insanity or inability to produce a witness or take his deposition. 63 A.B.A. Reports 570, 584, 600 (1938). The same year saw enactment of the English Evidence Act of 1938, allowing written statements made on personal knowledge, if declarant is deceased or otherwise unavailable or if the court is satisfied that undue delay or expense would otherwise be caused, unless declarant was an interested person in pending or anticipated relevant proceedings.   Evidence Act of 1938, 1 & 2 Geo. 6, c. 28; Cross on Evidence 482 (3rd ed. 1967).

Model Code Rule 503(a) provided broadly for admission of any hearsay declaration of an unavailable declarant.   No circumstantial guarantees of trustworthiness were required.   Debate upon the floor of the American Law Institute did not seriously question the propriety of the rule but centered upon what should constitute unavailability.   18 A.L.I. Proceedings 90–134 (1941).

The Uniform Rules draftsman took a less advanced position, more in the pattern of the Massachusetts statute, and invoked several assurances of accuracy: recency of perception, clarity of recollection, good faith, and antecedence to the commencement of the action.   Uniform Rule 63(4)(c).

Opposition developed to the Uniform Rule because of its countenancing of the use of statements carefully prepared under the tutelage of lawyers, claim adjusters, or investigators with a view to pending or prospective litigation. Tentative Recommendation and a Study Relating to the Uniform Rules of Evidence (Art. VIII. Hearsay Evidence), Cal.Law Rev.Comm'n, 318 (1962); Quick, Excitement, Necessity and the Uniform Rules: A Reappraisal of Rule 63(4), 6 Wayne L.Rev. 204, 219–224 (1960).   To meet this objection, the rule excludes statements made at the instigation of a person engaged in investigating, litigating, or settling a claim.   It also incorporates as safeguards the good faith and clarity of recollection required by the Uniform Rule and the exclusion of a statement by a person interested in the litigation provided by the English act.

With respect to the question whether the introduction of a statement under this exception against the accused in a criminal case would violate his right of confrontation, reference is made to the last paragraph of the Advisory Committee's Note under Exception (1), supra.

Report of House Committee on the Judiciary

Rule 804(b)(2), a hearsay exception submitted by the Court, titled "Statement of recent perception", read as follows:

> A statement, not in response to the instigation of a person engaged in investigating, litigating, or settling a claim, which narrates, describes, or explains an event or condition recently perceived by the declarant, made in good faith, not in contemplation of pending or anticipated litigation in which he was interested, and while his recollection was clear.

The Committee eliminated this Rule as creating a new and unwarranted hearsay exception of great potential breadth.   The Committee did not believe that statements of the type referred to bore sufficient guarantees of trustworthiness to justify admissibility.

APPENDIX D

THE EVIDENCE CODE OF THE STATE OF CALIFORNIA

The people of the State of California do enact as follows:

Division 1

PRELIMINARY PROVISIONS AND CONSTRUCTION

§ 1. Short title

This code shall be known as the Evidence Code.

§ 2. Common law rule construing code abrogated

The rule of the common law, that statutes in derogation thereof are to be strictly construed, has no application to this code. This code establishes the law of this state respecting the subject to which it relates, and its provisions are to be liberally construed with a view to effecting its objects and promoting justice.

§ 3. Constitutionality

If any provision or clause of this code or application thereof to any person or circumstances is held invalid, such invalidity shall not affect other provisions or applications of the code which can be given effect without the invalid provision or application, and to this end the provisions of this code are declared to be severable.

§ 4. Construction of code

Unless the provision or context otherwise requires, these preliminary provisions and rules of construction shall govern the construction of this code.

§ 5. Effect of headings

Division, chapter, article, and section headings do not in any manner affect the scope, meaning, or intent of the provisions of this code.

§ 6. References to statutes

Whenever any reference is made to any portion of this code or of any other statute, such reference shall apply to all amendments and additions heretofore or hereafter made.

§ 7. "Division," "chapter," "article," "section," "subdivision," and "paragraph"

Unless otherwise expressly stated:

(a) "Division" means a division of this code.

(b) "Chapter" means a chapter of the division in which that term occurs.

(c) "Article" means an article of the chapter in which that term occurs.

(d) "Section" means a section of this code.

(e) "Subdivision" means a subdivision of the section in which that term occurs.

(f) "Paragraph" means a paragraph of the subdivision in which that term occurs.

§ 8. Construction of tenses

The present tense includes the past and future tenses; and the future, the present.

§ 9. Construction of genders

The masculine gender includes the feminine and neuter.

§ 10. Construction of singular and plural

The singular number includes the plural; and the plural, the singular.

§ 11. "Shall" and "may"

"Shall" is mandatory and "may" is permissive.

§ 12. Code becomes operative January 1, 1967; effect on pending proceedings

(a) This code shall become operative on January 1, 1967, and shall govern proceedings in actions brought on or after that date and, except as provided in subdivision (b), further proceedings in actions pending on that date.

(b) Subject to subdivision (c), a trial commenced before January 1, 1967, shall not be governed by this code. For the purpose of this subdivision:

(1) A trial is commenced when the first witness is sworn or the first exhibit is admitted into evidence and is terminated when the issue upon which such evidence is received is submitted to the trier of fact. A new trial, or a separate trial of a different issue, commenced on or after January 1, 1967, shall be governed by this code.

(2) If an appeal is taken from a ruling made at a trial commenced before January 1, 1967, the appellate court shall apply the law applicable at the time of the commencement of the trial.

(c) The provisions of Division 8 (commencing with Section 900) relating to privileges shall govern any claim of privilege made after December 31, 1966.

Division 2

WORDS AND PHRASES DEFINED

§ 100. Application of definitions

Unless the provision or context otherwise requires, these definitions govern the construction of this code.

§ 105. "Action"

"Action" includes a civil action and a criminal action.

§ 110. "Burden of producing evidence"

"Burden of producing evidence" means the obligation of a party to introduce evidence sufficient to avoid a ruling against him on the issue.

§ 115. "Burden of proof"

"Burden of proof" means the obligation of a party to establish by evidence a requisite degree of belief concerning a fact in the mind of the trier of fact or the court. The burden of proof may require a party to raise a reasonable doubt concerning the existence or nonexistence of a fact or that he establish the existence or nonexistence of a fact by a preponderance of the evidence, by clear and convincing proof, or by proof beyond a reasonable doubt.

Except as otherwise provided by law, the burden of proof requires proof by a preponderance of the evidence.

§ 120. "Civil action"

"Civil action" includes civil proceedings.

§ 125. "Conduct"

"Conduct" includes all active and passive behavior, both verbal and nonverbal.

§ 130. "Criminal action"

"Criminal action" includes criminal proceedings.

§ 135. "Declarant"

"Declarant" is a person who makes a statement.

§ 140. "Evidence"

"Evidence" means testimony, writings, material objects, or other things presented to the senses that are offered to prove the existence or nonexistence of a fact.

§ 145. "The hearing"

"The hearing" means the hearing at which a question under this code arises, and not some earlier or later hearing.

§ 150. "Hearsay evidence"

"Hearsay evidence" is defined in Section 1200.

§ 160. "Law"

"Law" includes constitutional, statutory, and decisional law.

§ 165. "Oath"

"Oath" includes affirmation or declaration under penalty of perjury.

§ 170. "Perceive"

"Perceive" means to acquire knowledge through one's senses.

§ 175. "Person"

"Person" includes a natural person, firm, association, organization, partnership, business trust, corporation, or public entity.

§ 180. "Personal property"

"Personal property" includes money, goods, chattels, things in action, and evidences of debt.

§ 185. "Property"

"Property" includes both real and personal property.

§ 190. "Proof"

"Proof" is the establishment by evidence of a requisite degree of belief concerning a fact in the mind of the trier of fact or the court.

§ 195. "Public employee"

"Public employee" means an officer, agent, or employee of a public entity.

§ 200. "Public entity"

"Public entity" includes a nation, state, county, city and county, city, district, public authority, public agency, or any other political subdivision or public corporation, whether foreign or domestic.

§ 205. "Real property"

"Real property" includes lands, tenements, and hereditaments.

§ 210. "Relevant evidence"

"Relevant evidence" means evidence, including evidence relevant to the credibility of a witness or hearsay declarant, having any tendency in reason to prove or disprove any disputed fact that is of consequence to the determination of the action.

§ 220. "State"

"State" means the State of California, unless applied to the different parts of the United States. In the latter case, it includes any state, district, commonwealth, territory, or insular possession of the United States.

§ 225. "Statement"

"Statement" means (a) oral or written verbal expression or (b) nonverbal conduct of a person intended by him as a substitute for oral or written verbal expression.

§ 230. "Statute"

"Statute" includes a treaty and a constitutional provision.

§ 235. "Trier of fact"

"Trier of fact" includes (a) the jury and (b) the court when the court is trying an issue of fact other than one relating to the admissibility of evidence.

§ 240. "Unavailable as a witness"

(a) Except as otherwise provided in subdivision (b), "unavailable as a witness" means that the declarant is any of the following:

(1) Exempted or precluded on the ground of privilege from testifying concerning the matter to which his or her statement is relevant.

(2) Disqualified from testifying to the matter.

(3) Dead or unable to attend or to testify at the hearing because of then existing physical or mental illness or infirmity.

(4) Absent from the hearing and the court is unable to compel his or her attendance by its process.

(5) Absent from the hearing and the proponent of his or her statement has exercised reasonable diligence but has been unable to procure his or her attendance by the court's process.

(b) A declarant is not unavailable as a witness if the exemption, preclusion, disqualification, death, inability, or absence of the declarant was brought about by the procurement or wrongdoing of the proponent of his or her statement for the purpose of preventing the declarant from attending or testifying.

(c) Expert testimony which establishes that physical or mental trauma resulting from an alleged crime has caused harm to a witness of sufficient severity that the witness is physically unable to testify or is unable to testify without suffering substantial trauma may constitute a sufficient showing of unavailability pursuant to paragraph (3) of subdivision (a). As used in this section, the term "expert" means a physician and surgeon, including a psychiatrist, or any person described by subdivision (b), (c), or (e) of Section 1010.

The introduction of evidence to establish the unavailability of a witness under this subdivision shall not be deemed procurement of unavailability, in absence of proof to the contrary.

§ 250. "Writing"

"Writing" means handwriting, typewriting, printing, photostating, photographing, and every other means of recording upon any tangible thing any form of communication or representation, including letters, words, pictures, sounds, or symbols, or combinations thereof.

§ 255. "Original"

"Original" means the writing itself or any counterpart intended to have the same effect by a person executing or issuing it. An "original" of a photograph includes the negative or any print therefrom. If data are stored in a computer or similar device, any printout or other output readable by sight, shown to reflect the data accurately, is an "original."

§ 260. "Duplicate"

A "duplicate" is a counterpart produced by the same impression as the original, or from the same matrix, or by means of photography, including enlargements and miniatures, or by mechanical or electronic rerecording, or by chemical reproduction, or by other equivalent technique which accurately reproduces the original.

Division 3

GENERAL PROVISIONS

CHAPTER 1. APPLICABILITY OF CODE

§ 300. Applicability of code

Except as otherwise provided by statute, this code applies in every action before the Supreme Court or a court of appeal, superior court, municipal court, or justice court, including proceedings in such actions conducted by a referee, court commissioner, or similar officer, but does not apply in grand jury proceedings.

CHAPTER 2. PROVINCE OF COURT AND JURY

§ 310. Questions of law for court

(a) All questions of law (including but not limited to questions concerning the construction of statutes and other writings, the admissibility of evidence, and other rules of evidence) are to be decided by the court. Determination of issues of fact preliminary to the admission of evidence are to be decided by the court as provided in Article 2 (commencing with Section 400) of Chapter 4.

(b) Determination of the law of an organization of nations or of the law of a foreign nation or a public entity in a foreign nation is a question of law to be determined in the manner provided in Division 4 (commencing with Section 450).

§ 311. Procedure when foreign or sister-state law cannot be determined

If the law of an organization of nations, a foreign nation or a state other than this state, or a public entity in a foreign nation or a state other than this state, is applicable and such law cannot be determined, the court may, as the ends of justice require, either:

(a) Apply the law of this state if the court can do so consistently with the Constitution of the United States and the Constitution of this state; or

(b) Dismiss the action without prejudice or, in the case of a reviewing court, remand the case to the trial court with directions to dismiss the action without prejudice.

§ 312. Jury as trier of fact

Except as otherwise provided by law, where the trial is by jury:

(a) All questions of fact are to be decided by the jury.

(b) Subject to the control of the court, the jury is to determine the effect and value of the evidence addressed to it, including the credibility of witnesses and hearsay declarants.

CHAPTER 3. ORDER OF PROOF

§ 320. Power of court to regulate order of proof

Except as otherwise provided by law, the court in its discretion shall regulate the order of proof.

CHAPTER 4. ADMITTING AND EXCLUDING EVIDENCE

ARTICLE 1. GENERAL PROVISIONS

§ 350. Only relevant evidence admissible

No evidence is admissible except relevant evidence.

§ 351.1 Polygraph examinations; results, opinion of examiner or reference; exclusion

(a) Notwithstanding any other provision of law, the results of a polygraph examination, the opinion of a polygraph examiner, or any reference to an offer to take, failure to take, or taking of a polygraph examination, shall not be admitted into evidence in any criminal proceeding, including pretrial and post conviction motions and hearings, or in any trial or hearing of a juvenile for a criminal offense, whether heard in juvenile or adult court, unless all parties stipulate to the admission of such results.

(b) Nothing in this section is intended to exclude from evidence statements made during a polygraph examination which are otherwise admissible.

§ 352. Discretion of court to exclude evidence

The court in its discretion may exclude evidence if its probative value is substantially outweighed by the probability that its admission will (a) necessitate undue consumption of time or (b) create substantial danger of undue prejudice, of confusing the issues, or of misleading the jury.

§ 352.1. Criminal sex acts; victim's address and telephone number

In any criminal proceeding under Section 261, Section 264.1, subdivision (d) of Section 286, or subdivision (d) of Section 288a of the Penal Code, or in any criminal proceeding under subdivision (c) of Section 286 or subdivision (c) of Section 288a of the Penal Code in which the defendant is alleged to have compelled the participation of the victim by force, violence, duress, menace, or threat of great bodily harm, the district attorney may, upon written motion with notice to the defendant or the defendant's attorney, if he or she is represented by an attorney, within a reasonable time prior to any hearing, move to exclude from evidence the current address and telephone number of any victim at such hearing.

The court may order that evidence of the victim's current address and telephone number be excluded from any hearings conducted pursuant to such criminal proceeding if the court finds that the probative value of such evidence is outweighed by the creation of substantial danger to the victim.

Nothing in this section shall abridge or limit the defendant's right to discover or investigate such information.

§ 353. Effect of erroneous admission of evidence

A verdict or finding shall not be set aside, nor shall the judgment or decision based thereon be reversed, by reason of the erroneous admission of evidence unless:

(a) There appears of record an objection to or a motion to exclude or to strike the evidence that was timely made and so stated as to make clear the specific ground of the objection or motion; and

(b) The court which passes upon the effect of the error or errors is of the opinion that the admitted evidence should have been excluded on the ground stated and that the error or errors complained of resulted in a miscarriage of justice.

§ 354. Effect of erroneous exclusion of evidence

A verdict or finding shall not be set aside, nor shall the judgment or decision based thereon be reversed, by reason of the erroneous exclusion of evidence unless the court which passes upon the effect of the error or errors is of the opinion that the error or errors complained of resulted in a miscarriage of justice and it appears of record that:

(a) The substance, purpose, and relevance of the excluded evidence was made known to the court by the questions asked, an offer of proof, or by any other means;

(b) The rulings of the court made compliance with subdivision (a) futile; or

(c) The evidence was sought by questions asked during cross-examination or recross-examination.

§ 355. Limited admissibility

When evidence is admissible as to one party or for one purpose and is inadmissible as to another party or for another purpose, the court upon request shall restrict the evidence to its proper scope and instruct the jury accordingly.

§ 356. Entire act, declaration, conversation, or writing may be brought out to elucidate part offered

Where part of an act, declaration, conversation, or writing is given in evidence by one party, the whole on the same subject may be inquired into by an adverse party; when a letter is read, the answer may be given; and when a detached act, declaration, conversation, or writing is given in evidence, any other act, declaration, conversation, or writing which is necessary to make it understood may also be given in evidence.

ARTICLE 2. PRELIMINARY DETERMINATIONS ON ADMISSIBILITY OF EVIDENCE

§ 400. "Preliminary fact"

As used in this article, "preliminary fact" means a fact upon the existence or nonexistence of which depends the admissibility or inad-

missibility of evidence. The phrase "the admissibility or inadmissibility of evidence" includes the qualification or disqualification of a person
to be a witness and the existence or nonexistence of a privilege.

§ 401. "Proffered evidence"

As used in this article, "proffered evidence" means evidence, the
admissibility or inadmissibility of which is dependent upon the existence or nonexistence of a preliminary fact.

§ 402. Procedure for determining foundational and other preliminary facts

(a) When the existence of a preliminary fact is disputed, its existence or nonexistence shall be determined as provided in this article.

(b) The court may hear and determine the question of the admissibility of evidence out of the presence or hearing of the jury; but in a
criminal action, the court shall hear and determine the question of the
admissibility of a confession or admission of the defendant out of the
presence and hearing of the jury if any party so requests.

(c) A ruling on the admissibility of evidence implies whatever
finding of fact is prerequisite thereto; a separate or formal finding is
unnecessary unless required by statute.

§ 403. Determination of foundational and other preliminary facts where relevancy, personal knowledge, or authenticity is disputed

(a) The proponent of the proffered evidence has the burden of
producing evidence as to the existence of the preliminary fact, and the
proffered evidence is inadmissible unless the court finds that there is
evidence sufficient to sustain a finding of the existence of the preliminary fact, when:

(1) The relevance of the proffered evidence depends on the existence of the preliminary fact;

(2) The preliminary fact is the personal knowledge of a witness
concerning the subject matter of his testimony;

(3) The preliminary fact is the authenticity of a writing; or

(4) The proffered evidence is of a statement or other conduct of a
particular person and the preliminary fact is whether that person made
the statement or so conducted himself.

(b) Subject to Section 702, the court may admit conditionally the
proffered evidence under this section, subject to evidence of the preliminary fact being supplied later in the course of the trial.

(c) If the court admits the proffered evidence under this section,
the court:

(1) May, and on request shall, instruct the jury to determine
whether the preliminary fact exists and to disregard the proffered
evidence unless the jury finds that the preliminary fact does exist.

(2) Shall instruct the jury to disregard the proffered evidence if the court subsequently determines that a jury could not reasonably find that the preliminary fact exists.

§ 404. Determination of whether proffered evidence is incriminatory

Whenever the proffered evidence is claimed to be privileged under Section 940, the person claiming the privilege has the burden of showing that the proffered evidence might tend to incriminate him; and the proffered evidence is inadmissible unless it clearly appears to the court that the proffered evidence cannot possibly have a tendency to incriminate the person claiming the privilege.

§ 405. Determination of foundational and other preliminary facts in other cases

With respect to preliminary fact determinations not governed by Section 403 or 404:

(a) When the existence of a preliminary fact is disputed, the court shall indicate which party has the burden of producing evidence and the burden of proof on the issue as implied by the rule of law under which the question arises. The court shall determine the existence or nonexistence of the preliminary fact and shall admit or exclude the proffered evidence as required by the rule of law under which the question arises.

(b) If a preliminary fact is also a fact in issue in the action:

(1) The jury shall not be informed of the court's determination as to the existence or nonexistence of the preliminary fact.

(2) If the proffered evidence is admitted, the jury shall not be instructed to disregard the evidence if its determination of the fact differs from the court's determination of the preliminary fact.

§ 406. Evidence affecting weight or credibility

This article does not limit the right of a party to introduce before the trier of fact evidence relevant to weight or credibility.

CHAPTER 5. WEIGHT OF EVIDENCE GENERALLY

§ 410. "Direct evidence"

As used in this chapter, "direct evidence" means evidence that directly proves a fact, without an inference or presumption, and which in itself, if true conclusively establishes that fact.

§ 411. Direct evidence of one witness sufficient

Except where additional evidence is required by statute, the direct evidence of one witness who is entitled to full credit is sufficient for proof of any fact.

§ 412. Party having power to produce better evidence

If weaker and less satisfactory evidence is offered when it was within the power of the party to produce stronger and more satisfactory evidence, the evidence offered should be viewed with distrust.

§ 413. Party's failure to explain or deny evidence

In determining what inferences to draw from the evidence or facts in the case against a party, the trier of fact may consider, among other things, the party's failure to explain or to deny by his testimony such evidence or facts in the case against him, or his willful suppression of evidence relating thereto, if such be the case.

Division 4

JUDICIAL NOTICE

§ 450. Judicial notice may be taken only as authorized by law

Judicial notice may not be taken of any matter unless authorized or required by law.

§ 451. Matters which must be judicially noticed

Judicial notice shall be taken of the following:

(a) The decisional, constitutional, and public statutory law of this state and of the United States, and the provisions of any charter described in Section 3, 4, or 5 of Article XI of the California Constitution.

(b) Any matter made a subject of judicial notice by Section 11343.6, 11344.6, or 18576 of the Government Code or by Section 1507 of Title 44 of the United States Code.[1]

(c) Rules of professional conduct for members of the bar adopted pursuant to Section 6076 of the Business and Professions Code and rules of practice and procedure for the courts of this state adopted by the Judicial Council.

(d) Rules of pleading, practice, and procedure prescribed by the United States Supreme Court, such as the Rules of the United States Supreme Court, the Federal Rules of Civil Procedure, the Federal Rules of Criminal Procedure, the Admiralty Rules, the Rules of the Court of Claims, the Rules of the Customs Court, and the General Orders and Forms in Bankruptcy.

(e) The true signification of all English words and phrases and of all legal expressions.

(f) Facts and propositions of generalized knowledge that are so universally known that they cannot reasonably be the subject of dispute.

§ 452. Matters which may be judicially noticed

Judicial notice may be taken of the following matters to the extent that they are not embraced within Section 451:

(a) The decisional, constitutional, and statutory law of any state of the United States and the resolutions and private acts of the Congress of the United States and of the Legislature of this state.

(b) Regulations and legislative enactments issued by or under the authority of the United States or any public entity in the United States.

(c) Official acts of the legislative, executive, and judicial departments of the United States and of any state of the United States.

(d) Records of (1) any court of this state or (2) any court of record of the United States or of any state of the United States.

(e) Rules of court of (1) any court of this state or (2) any court of record of the United States or of any state of the United States.

(f) The law of an organization of nations and of foreign nations and public entities in foreign nations.

(g) Facts and propositions that are of such common knowledge within the territorial jurisdiction of the court that they cannot reasonably be the subject of dispute.

(h) Facts and propositions that are not reasonably subject to dispute and are capable of immediate and accurate determination by resort to sources of reasonably indisputable accuracy.

§ 453. Compulsory judicial notice upon request

The trial court shall take judicial notice of any matter specified in Section 452 if a party requests it and:

(a) Gives each adverse party sufficient notice of the request, through the pleadings or otherwise, to enable such adverse party to prepare to meet the request; and

(b) Furnishes the court with sufficient information to enable it to take judicial notice of the matter.

§ 454. Information that may be used in taking judicial notice

(a) In determining the propriety of taking judicial notice of a matter, or the tenor thereof:

(1) Any source of pertinent information, including the advice of persons learned in the subject matter, may be consulted or used, whether or not furnished by a party.

(2) Exclusionary rules of evidence do not apply except for Section 352 and the rules of privilege.

(b) Where the subject of judicial notice is the law of an organization of nations, a foreign nation, or a public entity in a foreign nation and the court resorts to the advice of persons learned in the subject matter, such advice, if not received in open court, shall be in writing.

§ 455. Opportunity to present information to court

With respect to any matter specified in Section 452 or in subdivision (f) of Section 451 that is of substantial consequence to the determination of the action:

(a) If the trial court has been requested to take or has taken or proposes to take judicial notice of such matter, the court shall afford each party reasonable opportunity, before the jury is instructed or before the cause is submitted for decision by the court, to present to the court information relevant to (1) the propriety of taking judicial notice of the matter and (2) the tenor of the matter to be noticed.

(b) If the trial court resorts to any source of information not received in open court, including the advice of persons learned in the subject matter, such information and its source shall be made a part of the record in the action and the court shall afford each party reasonable opportunity to meet such information before judicial notice of the matter may be taken.

§ 456. Noting for record denial of request to take judicial notice

If the trial court denies a request to take judicial notice of any matter, the court shall at the earliest practicable time so advise the parties and indicate for the record that it has denied the request.

§ 457. Instructing jury on matter judicially noticed

If a matter judicially noticed is a matter which would otherwise have been for determination by the jury, the trial court may, and upon request shall, instruct the jury to accept as a fact the matter so noticed.

§ 458. Judicial notice by trial court in subsequent proceedings

The failure or refusal of the trial court to take judicial notice of a matter, or to instruct the jury with respect to the matter, does not preclude the trial court in subsequent proceedings in the action from taking judicial notice of the matter in accordance with the procedure specified in this division.

§ 459. Judicial notice by reviewing court

(a) The reviewing court shall take judicial notice of (1) each matter properly noticed by the trial court and (2) each matter that the trial court was required to notice under Section 451 or 453. The reviewing court may take judicial notice of any matter specified in Section 452. The reviewing court may take judicial notice of a matter in a tenor different from that noticed by the trial court.

(b) In determining the propriety of taking judicial notice of a matter, or the tenor thereof the reviewing court has the same power as the trial court under Section 454.

(c) When taking judicial notice under this section of a matter specified in Section 452 or in subdivision (f) of Section 451 that is of substantial consequence to the determination of the action, the reviewing court shall comply with the provisions of subdivision (a) of Section 455 if the matter was not theretofore judicially noticed in the action.

(d) In determining the propriety of taking judicial notice of a matter specified in Section 452 or in subdivision (f) of Section 451 that is of substantial consequence to the determination of the action, or the

1
2
3
4
5
6
7
8
9
10
11
12
13
14
15
16
17
18
19
20
21
22
23
24
25
26
27
28
29
30
31
32
33
34
35
36
37
38
39
40
41
42
43
44
45
46
47
48
49
50

tenor thereof, if the reviewing court resorts to any source of information not received in open court or not included in the record of the action, including the advice of persons learned in the subject matter, the reviewing court shall afford each party reasonable opportunity to meet such information before judicial notice of the matter may be taken.

§ 460. Appointment of expert by court

Where the advice of persons learned in the subject matter is required in order to enable the court to take judicial notice of a matter, the court on its own motion or on motion of any party may appoint one or more such persons to provide such advice. If the court determines to appoint such a person, he shall be appointed and compensated in the manner provided in Article 2 (commencing with Section 730) of Chapter 3 of Division 6.

Division 5

BURDEN OF PROOF; BURDEN OF PRODUCING EVIDENCE; PRESUMPTIONS AND INFERENCES

CHAPTER 1. BURDEN OF PROOF

ARTICLE 1. GENERAL

§ 500. Party who has the burden of proof

Except as otherwise provided by law, a party has the burden of proof as to each fact the existence or nonexistence of which is essential to the claim for relief or defense that he is asserting.

§ 501. Burden of proof in criminal action generally

Insofar as any statute, except Section 522, assigns the burden of proof in a criminal action, such statute is subject to Penal Code Section 1096.

§ 502. Instructions on burden of proof

The court on all proper occasions shall instruct the jury as to which party bears the burden of proof on each issue and as to whether that burden requires that a party raise a reasonable doubt concerning the

existence or nonexistence of a fact or that he establish the existence or
nonexistence of a fact by a preponderance of the evidence, by clear and
convincing proof, or by proof beyond a reasonable doubt.

ARTICLE 2. BURDEN OF PROOF ON SPECIFIC ISSUES

§ 520. Claim that person guilty of crime or wrongdoing

The party claiming that a person is guilty of crime or wrongdoing
has the burden of proof on that issue.

§ 521. Claim that person did not exercise care

The party claiming that a person did not exercise a requisite degree
of care has the burden of proof on that issue.

§ 522. Claim that person is or was insane

The party claiming that any person, including himself, is or was
insane has the burden of proof on that issue.

CHAPTER 2. BURDEN OF PRODUCING EVIDENCE

§ 550. Party who has the burden of producing evidence

(a) The burden of producing evidence as to a particular fact is on
the party against whom a finding on that fact would be required in the
absence of further evidence.

(b) The burden of producing evidence as to particular fact is
initially on the party with the burden of proof as to that fact.

CHAPTER 3. PRESUMPTIONS AND INFERENCES

ARTICLE 1. GENERAL

§ 600. Presumption and inference defined

(a) A presumption is an assumption of fact that the law requires to
be made from another fact or group of facts found or otherwise
established in the action. A presumption is not evidence.

(b) An inference is a deduction of fact that may logically and
reasonably be drawn from another fact or group of facts found or
otherwise established in the action.

§ 601. Classification of presumptions

A presumption is either conclusive or rebuttable. Every rebuttable
presumption is either (a) a presumption affecting the burden of producing evidence or (b) a presumption affecting the burden of proof.

§ 602. Statute making one fact prima facie evidence of another fact

A statute providing that a fact or group of facts is prima facie evidence of another fact establishes a rebuttable presumption.

§ 603. Presumption affecting the burden of producing evidence defined

A presumption affecting the burden of producing evidence is a presumption established to implement no public policy other than to facilitate the determination of the particular action in which the presumption is applied.

§ 604. Effect of presumption affecting burden of producing evidence

The effect of a presumption affecting the burden of producing evidence is to require the trier of fact to assume the existence of the presumed fact unless and until evidence is introduced which would support a finding of its nonexistence, in which case the trier of fact shall determine the existence or nonexistence of the presumed fact from the evidence and without regard to the presumption. Nothing in this section shall be construed to prevent the drawing of any inference that may be appropriate.

§ 605. Presumption affecting the burden of proof defined

A presumption affecting the burden of proof is a presumption established to implement some public policy other than to facilitate the determination of the particular action in which the presumption is applied, such as the policy in favor of establishment of a parent and child relationship, the validity of marriage, the stability of titles to property, or the security of those who entrust themselves or their property to the administration of others.

§ 606. Effect of presumption affecting burden of proof

The effect of a presumption affecting the burden of proof is to impose upon the party against whom it operates the burden of proof as to the nonexistence of the presumed fact.

§ 607. Effect of certain presumptions in a criminal action

When a presumption affecting the burden of proof operates in a criminal action to establish presumptively any fact that is essential to the defendant's guilt, the presumption operates only if the facts that give rise to the presumption have been found or otherwise established beyond a reasonable doubt, and, in such case, the defendant need only raise a reasonable doubt as to the existence of the presumed fact.

ARTICLE 2. CONCLUSIVE PRESUMPTIONS

§ 620. Conclusive presumptions

The presumptions established by this article, and all other presumptions declared by law to be conclusive, are conclusive presumptions.

§ 621. Child of the marriage; notice of motion for blood tests

(a) Except as provided in subdivision (b), the issue of a wife cohabiting with her husband, who is not impotent or sterile, is conclusively presumed to be a child of the marriage.

(b) Notwithstanding the provisions of subdivision (a), if the court finds that the conclusions of all the experts, as disclosed by the evidence based upon blood tests performed pursuant to Chapter 2 (commencing with Section 890) of Division 7 are that the husband is not the father of the child, the question of paternity of the husband shall be resolved accordingly.

(c) The notice of motion for blood tests under subdivision (b) may be filed not later than two years from the child's date of birth by the husband, or for purposes of establishing paternity by the presumed father or the child through or by the child's guardian ad litem.

(d) The notice of motion for blood tests under subdivision (b) may be filed by the mother of the child not later than two years from the child's date of birth if the child's biological father has filed an affidavit with the court acknowledging paternity of the child.

(e) Subdivision (b) shall not apply to any case coming within Section 7005 of the Civil Code, or to any case in which the wife, with the consent of the husband, conceived by means of a surgical procedure.

(f) The notice of motion for the blood tests pursuant to subdivision (b) shall be supported by a declaration under oath submitted by the moving party stating the factual basis for placing the issue of paternity before the court. This requirement shall not apply to any case pending before the court on September 30, 1980.

(g) Subdivision (b) shall not apply to any case which has reached final judgment of paternity on September 30, 1980.

(h) As used in this section "presumed father" has the meaning given in Section 7004 of the Civil Code.

§ 622. Facts recited in written instrument

The facts recited in a written instrument are conclusively presumed to be true as between the parties thereto, or their successors in interest; but this rule does not apply to the recital of a consideration.

§ 623. Estoppel by own statement or conduct

Whenever a party has, by his own statement or conduct, intentionally and deliberately led another to believe a particular thing true and to act upon such belief, he is not, in any litigation arising out of such statement or conduct, permitted to contradict it.

§ 624. Estoppel of tenant to deny title of landlord

A tenant is not permitted to deny the title of his landlord at the time of the commencement of the relation.

ARTICLE 3. PRESUMPTIONS AFFECTING THE BURDEN OF PRODUCING EVIDENCE

§ 630. Presumptions affecting the burden of producing evidence

The presumptions established by this article, and all other rebuttable presumptions established by law that fall within the criteria of Section 603, are presumptions affecting the burden of producing evidence.

§ 631. Money delivered by one to another

Money delivered by one to another is presumed to have been due to the latter.

§ 632. Thing delivered by one to another

A thing delivered by one to another is presumed to have belonged to the latter.

§ 633. Obligation delivered up to the debtor

An obligation delivered up to the debtor is presumed to have been paid.

§ 634. Person in possession of order on himself

A person in possession of an order on himself for the payment of money, or delivery of a thing, is presumed to have paid the money or delivered the thing accordingly.

§ 635. Obligation possessed by creditor

An obligation possessed by the creditor is presumed not to have been paid.

§ 636. Payment of earlier rent or installments

The payment of earlier rent or installments is presumed from a receipt for later rent or installments.

§ 637. Ownership of things possessed

The things which a person possesses are presumed to be owned by him.

§ 638. Ownership of property by person who exercises acts of ownership

A person who exercises acts of ownership over property is presumed to be the owner of it.

§ 639. Judgment correctly determines rights of parties

A judgment, when not conclusive, is presumed to correctly determine or set forth the rights of the parties, but there is no presumption that the facts essential to the judgment have been correctly determined.

§ 640. Writing truly dated

A writing is presumed to have been truly dated.

§ 641. Letter received in ordinary course of mail

A letter correctly addressed and properly mailed is presumed to have been received in the ordinary course of mail.

§ 642. Conveyance by person having duty to convey real property

A trustee or other person, whose duty it was to convey real property to a particular person, is presumed to have actually conveyed to him when such presumption is necessary to perfect title of such person or his successor in interest.

§ 643. Authenticity of ancient document

A deed or will or other writing purporting to create, terminate, or affect an interest in real or personal property is presumed to be authentic if it:

(a) Is at least 30 years old;

(b) Is in such condition as to create no suspicion concerning its authenticity;

(c) Was kept, or if found was found, in a place where such writing, if authentic, would be likely to be kept or found; and

(d) Has been generally acted upon as authentic by persons having an interest in the matter.

§ 644. Book purporting to be published by public authority

A book, purporting to be printed or published by public authority, is presumed to have been so printed or published.

§ 645. Book purporting to contain reports of cases

A book, purporting to contain reports of cases adjudged in the tribunals of the state or nation where the book is published, is presumed to contain correct reports of such cases.

§ 645.1 Printed materials purporting to be particular newspaper or periodical

Printed materials, purporting to be a particular newspaper or periodical, are presumed to be that newspaper or periodical if regularly issued at average intervals not exceeding three months.

§ 646. Res ipsa loquitur; instruction

(a) As used in this section, "defendant" includes any party against whom the res ipsa loquitur presumption operates.

(b) The judicial doctrine of res ipsa loquitur is a presumption affecting the burden of producing evidence.

(c) If the evidence, or facts otherwise established, would support a res ipsa loquitur presumption and the defendant has introduced evi-

1
2
3
4
5
6
7
8
9
10
11
12
13
14
15
16
17
18
19
20
21
22
23
24
25
26
27
28
29
30
31
32
33
34
35
36
37
38
39
40
41
42
43
44
45
46
47
48
49
50

dence which would support a finding that he was not negligent or that any negligence on his part was not a proximate cause of the occurrence, the court may, and upon request shall, instruct the jury to the effect that:

(1) If the facts which would give rise to a res ipsa loquitur presumption are found or otherwise established, the jury may draw the inference from such facts that a proximate cause of the occurrence was some negligent conduct on the part of the defendant; and

(2) The jury shall not find that a proximate cause of the occurrence was some negligent conduct on the part of the defendant unless the jury believes, after weighing all the evidence in the case and drawing such inferences therefrom as the jury believes are warranted, and it is more probable than not that the occurrence was caused by some negligent conduct on the part of the defendant.

§ 647. Return of process served by registered process server

The return of a process server registered pursuant to Chapter 16 (commencing with Section 22350) of Division 8 of the Business and Professions Code upon process or notice establishes a presumption, affecting the burden of producing evidence, of the facts stated in the return.

ARTICLE 4. PRESUMPTIONS AFFECTING THE BURDEN OF PROOF

§ 660. Presumptions affecting the burden of proof

The presumptions established by this article, and all other rebuttable presumptions established by law that fall within the criteria of Section 605, are presumptions affecting the burden of proof.

§ 662. Owner of legal title to property is owner of beneficial title

The owner of the legal title to property is presumed to be the owner of the full beneficial title. This presumption may be rebutted only by clear and convincing proof.

§ 663. Ceremonial marriage

A ceremonial marriage is presumed to be valid.

§ 664. Official duty regularly performed

It is presumed that official duty has been regularly performed. This presumption does not apply on an issue as to the lawfulness of an arrest if it is found or otherwise established that the arrest was made without a warrant.

§ 665. Ordinary consequences of voluntary act

A person is presumed to intend the ordinary consequences of his voluntary act. This presumption is inapplicable in a criminal action to establish the specific intent of the defendant where specific intent is an element of the crime charged.

§ 666. Judicial action lawful exercise of jurisdiction

Any court of this state or the United States, or any court of general jurisdiction in any other state or nation, or any judge of such a court, acting as such, is presumed to have acted in the lawful exercise of its jurisdiction. This presumption applies only when the act of the court or judge is under collateral attack.

§ 667. Death of person not heard from in five years

A person not heard from in five years is presumed to be dead.

§ 668. Unlawful intent

An unlawful intent is presumed from the doing of an unlawful act. This presumption is inapplicable in a criminal action to establish the specific intent of the defendant where specific intent is an element of the crime charged.

§ 669. Failure to exercise due care

(a) The failure of a person to exercise due care is presumed if:

(1) He violated a statute, ordinance, or regulation of a public entity;

(2) The violation proximately caused death or injury to person or property;

(3) The death or injury resulted from an occurrence of the nature which the statute, ordinance, or regulation was designed to prevent; and

(4) The person suffering the death or the injury to his person or property was one of the class of persons for whose protection the statute, ordinance, or regulation was adopted.

(b) This presumption may be rebutted by proof that:

(1) The person violating the statute, ordinance, or regulation did what might reasonably be expected of a person of ordinary prudence, acting under similar circumstances, who desired to comply with the law; or

(2) The person violating the statute, ordinance, or regulation was a child and exercised the degree of care ordinarily exercised by persons of his maturity, intelligence, and capacity under similar circumstances, but the presumption may not be rebutted by such proof if the violation occurred in the course of an activity normally engaged in only by adults and requiring adult qualifications.

§ 669.1 Local standards of conduct for peace officers; presumption of failure to exercise due care

A local rule, regulation, or guideline setting forth standards of conduct for peace officers in the use of deadly force shall not be considered a statute, ordinance, or regulation of a public entity within the meaning of Section 669.

This section affects only the application of the presumption set forth in Section 669; it does not affect what evidence is admissible in a civil action.

The provisions of this section shall be applicable to any cause of action arising out of facts occurring on or after January 1, 1984, but before January 1, 1989, regardless of the date the action is commenced or tried.

This section shall remain in effect until January 1, 1989, and on that date is repealed unless a later enacted statute, which is chaptered before that date, deletes or extends that date.

§ 669.5   Ordinances limiting building permits or development of buildable lots for residential purposes; impact on supply of residential units; actions challenging validity

(a) Any ordinance enacted by the governing body of a city, county, or city and county which (1) directly limits, by number, the building permits that may be issued for residential construction or the buildable lots which may be developed for residential purposes, or (2) changes the standards of residential development on vacant land so that the governing body's zoning is rendered in violation of Section 65913.1 of the Government Code is presumed to have an impact on the supply of residential units available in an area which includes territory outside the jurisdiction of the city, county, or city and county.

(b) With respect to any action which challenges the validity of an ordinance specified in subdivision (a) the city, county, or city and county enacting the ordinance shall bear the burden of proof that the ordinance is necessary for the protection of the public health, safety, or welfare of the population of the city, county, or city and county.

(c) This section does not apply to state and federal building code requirements or local ordinances which (1) impose a moratorium, to protect the public health and safety, on residential construction for a specified period of time, if, under the terms of the ordinance, the moratorium will cease when the public health or safety is no longer jeopardized by the construction (2) create agricultural preserves under Chapter 7 (commencing with Section 51200) of Part 1 of Division 1 of Title 5 of the Government Code, or (3) restrict the number of buildable parcels or designate lands within a zone for nonresidential uses in order to protect agricultural uses as defined in subdivision (b) of Section 51201 of the Government Code or open-space land as defined in subdivision (b) of Section 65560 of the Government Code.

(d) This section shall not apply to a voter approved ordinance adopted by referendum or initiative prior to the effective date of this section which (1) requires the city, county, or city and county to establish a population growth limit which represents its fair share of each year's statewide population growth, or (2) which sets a growth rate of no more than the average population growth rate experienced by the state as a whole. Paragraph (2) of subdivision (a) does not apply to a voter-approved ordinance adopted by referendum or initiative which

exempts housing affordable to persons and families of low or moderate
income, as defined in Section 50093 of the Health and Safety Code, or
which otherwise provides low- and moderate-income housing sites
equivalent to such an exemption.

Division 6

WITNESSES

CHAPTER 1. COMPETENCY

§ 700. General rule as to competency

Except as otherwise provided by statute, every person, irrespective
of age, is qualified to be a witness and no person is disqualified to
testify to any matter.

§ 701. Disqualification of witness

(a) A person is disqualified to be a witness if he or she is:

(1) Incapable of expressing himself or herself concerning the matter so as to be understood, either directly or through interpretation by
one who can understand him; or

(2) Incapable of understanding the duty of a witness to tell the
truth.

(b) In any proceeding held outside the presence of a jury, the court
may reserve challenges to the competency of a witness until the
conclusion of the direct examination of that witness.

§ 702. Personal knowledge of witness

(a) Subject to Section 801, the testimony of a witness concerning a
particular matter is inadmissible unless he has personal knowledge of
the matter. Against the objection of a party, such personal knowledge
must be shown before the witness may testify concerning the matter.

(b) A witness' personal knowledge of a matter may be shown by
any otherwise admissible evidence, including his own testimony.

§ 703. Judge as witness

(a) Before the judge presiding at the trial of an action may be
called to testify in that trial as a witness, he shall, in proceedings held
out of the presence and hearing of the jury, inform the parties of the

information he has concerning any fact or matter about which he will be called to testify.

(b) Against the objection of a party, the judge residing at the trial of an action may not testify in that trial as a witness. Upon such objection, the judge shall declare a mistrial and order the action assigned for trial before another judge.

(c) The calling of the judge presiding at a trial to testify in that trial as a witness shall be deemed a consent to the granting of a motion for mistrial, and an objection to such calling of a judge shall be deemed a motion for mistrial.

(d) In the absence of objection by a party, the judge presiding at the trial of an action may testify in that trial as a witness.

§ 703.5 Judge or arbitrator as witness; subsequent civil proceeding; exceptions

No person presiding at any judicial or quasi-judicial proceeding shall be competent to testify, in any subsequent civil proceeding, as to any statement or conduct occurring at the prior proceeding, except as to a statement or conduct that could (a) give rise to civil or criminal contempt, (b) constitute a crime, (c) be the subject of investigation by the State Bar or Commission on Judicial Performance, or (d) give rise to disqualification proceedings under paragraph (a) or (b) subdivision (a) of Section 170.1 of the Code of Civil Procedure.

§ 704. Juror as witness

(a) Before a juror sworn and impaneled in the trial of an action may be called to testify before the jury in that trial as a witness, he shall, in proceedings conducted by the court out of the presence and hearing of the remaining jurors, inform the parties of the information he has concerning any fact or matter about which he will be called to testify.

(b) Against the objection of a party, a juror sworn and impaneled in the trial of an action may not testify before the jury in that trial as a witness. Upon such objection, the court shall declare a mistrial and order the action assigned for trial before another jury.

(c) The calling of a juror to testify before the jury as a witness shall be deemed a consent to the granting of a motion for mistrial, and an objection to such calling of a juror shall be deemed a motion for mistrial.

(d) In the absence of objection by a party, a juror sworn and impaneled in the trial of an action may be compelled to testify in that trial as a witness.

CHAPTER 2. OATH AND CONFRONTATION

§ 710. Oath required

Every witness before testifying shall take an oath or make an affirmation or declaration in the form provided by law except that a child under the age of 10, in the court's discretion, may be required only to promise to tell the truth.

§ 711. Confrontation

At the trial of an action, a witness can be heard only in the presence and subject to the examination of all the parties to the action, if they choose to attend and examine.

§ 712. Blood samples; technique in taking; affidavits in criminal actions; service; objections

Notwithstanding Sections 711 and 1200, at the trial of a criminal action, evidence of the technique used in taking blood samples may be given by a registered nurse, licensed vocational nurse, or licensed clinical laboratory technologist or clinical laboratory bioanalyst, by means of an affidavit. The affidavit shall be admissible, provided the party offering the affidavit as evidence has served all other parties to the action, or their counsel, with a copy of the affidavit no less than 10 days prior to trial. Nothing in this section shall preclude any party or his counsel from objecting to the introduction of the affidavit at any time, and requiring the attendance of the affiant, or compelling attendance by subpoena.

CHAPTER 3. EXPERT WITNESSES

ARTICLE 1. EXPERT WITNESSES GENERALLY

§ 720. Qualification as an expert witness

(a) A person is qualified to testify as an expert if he has special knowledge, skill, experience, training, or education sufficient to qualify him as an expert on the subject to which his testimony relates. Against the objection of a party, such special knowledge, skill, experience, training, or education must be shown before the witness may testify as an expert.

(b) A witness' special knowledge, skill, experience, training, or education may be shown by any otherwise admissible evidence, including his own testimony.

§ 721. Cross-examination of expert witness

(a) Subject to subdivision (b), a witness testifying as an expert may be cross-examined to the same extent as any other witness and, in addition, may be fully cross-examined as to (1) his qualifications, (2) the subject to which his expert testimony relates, and (3) the matter upon which his opinion is based and the reasons for his opinion.

(b) If a witness testifying as an expert testifies in the form of an opinion, he may not be cross-examined in regard to the content or tenor of any scientific, technical, or professional text, treatise, journal, or similar publication unless:

(1) The witness referred to, considered, or relied upon such publication in arriving at or forming his opinion; or

(2) Such publication has been admitted in evidence.

§ 722. Credibility of expert witness

(a) The fact of the appointment of an expert witness by the court may be revealed to the trier of fact.

(b) The compensation and expenses paid or to be paid to an expert witness by the party calling him is a proper subject of inquiry by any adverse party as relevant to the credibility of the witness and the weight of his testimony.

§ 723. Limit on number of expert witnesses

The court may, at any time before or during the trial of an action, limit the number of expert witnesses to be called by any party.

ARTICLE 2. APPOINTMENT OF EXPERT WITNESS BY COURT

§ 730. Appointment of expert by court

When it appears to the court, at any time before or during the trial of an action, that expert evidence is or may be required by the court or by any party to the action, the court on its own motion or on motion of any party may appoint one or more experts to investigate, to render a report as may be ordered by the court, and to testify as an expert at the trial of the action relative to the fact or matter as to which the expert evidence is or may be required. The court may fix the compensation for these services, if any, rendered by any person appointed under this section, in addition to any service as a witness, at the amount as seems reasonable to the court.

Nothing in this section shall be construed to permit a person to perform any act for which a license is required unless the person holds the appropriate license to lawfully perform that act.

§ 731. Payment of court-appointed expert

(a) In all criminal actions and juvenile court proceedings, the compensation fixed under Section 730 shall be a charge against the county in which such action or proceeding is pending and shall be paid out of the treasury of such county on order of the court.

(b) In any county in which the board of supervisors so provides, the compensation fixed under Section 730 for medical experts in civil actions in such county shall be a charge against and paid out of the treasury of such county on order of the court.

(c) Except as otherwise provided in this section, in all civil actions, the compensation fixed under Section 730 shall, in the first instance, be apportioned and charged to the several parties in such proportion as the court may determine and may thereafter be taxed and allowed in like manner as other costs.

§ 732. Calling and examining court-appointed expert

Any expert appointed by the court under Section 730 may be called and examined by the court or by any party to the action. When such witness is called and examined by the court, the parties have the same right as is expressed in Section 775 to cross-examine the witness and to object to the questions asked and the evidence adduced.

§ 733. Right to produce other expert evidence

Nothing contained in this article shall be deemed or construed to prevent any party to any action from producing other expert evidence on the same fact or matter mentioned in Section 730; but, where other expert witnesses are called by a party to the action, their fees shall be paid by the party calling them and only ordinary witness fees shall be taxed as costs in the action.

CHAPTER 4. INTERPRETERS AND TRANSLATORS

§ 750. Rules relating to witnesses apply to interpreters and translators

A person who serves as an interpreter or translator in any action is subject to all the rules of law relating to witnesses.

§ 751. Oath required of interpreters and translators

(a) An interpreter shall take an oath that he or she will make a true interpretation to the witness in a language that the witness understands and that he or she will make a true interpretation of the witness' answers to questions to counsel, court, or jury, in the English language, with his or her best skill and judgment.

(b) In any proceeding in which a deaf or hard-of-hearing person is testifying under oath the interpreter certified pursuant to subdivision (f) of Section 754 shall advise the court whenever he or she is unable to comply with his or her oath taken pursuant to subdivision (a).

(c) A translator shall take an oath that he or she will make a true translation in the English language of any writing he or she is to decipher or translate.

(d) An interpreter or translator regularly employed by the court and certified in accordance with Article 4 (commencing with Section 68560) of Chapter 2 of Title 8 of the Government Code, may file an oath as prescribed by this section with the clerk of the court. The filed oath shall serve for all subsequent court proceedings until the appointment is revoked by the court.

§ 752. Interpreters for witnesses

(a) When a witness is incapable of understanding the English language or is incapable of expressing himself or herself in the English language so as to be understood directly by counsel, court, and jury, an interpreter whom he or she can understand and who can understand him or her shall be sworn to interpret for him or her.

(b) The record shall identify the interpreter who may be appointed and compensated as provided in Article 2 (commencing with Section 730) of Chapter 3.

§ 753. Translators of writings

(a) When the written characters in a writing offered in evidence are incapable of being deciphered or understood directly, a translator who can decipher the characters or understand the language shall be sworn to decipher or translate the writing.

(b) The record shall identify the translator who may be appointed and compensated as provided in Article 2 (commencing with Section 730) of Chapter 3.

§ 754. Deaf or hard-of-hearing persons; interpreter in civil or criminal action; qualifications; intermediary interpreters; compensation; rosters; use of statement against person in criminal or quasi-criminal investigation or proceeding

(a) As used in this section, "deaf or hard-of-hearing person" means a person with a hearing loss so great as to prevent his or her understanding language spoken in a normal tone, but does not include a hard-of-hearing person provided with, and able to fully participate in the proceedings through the use of, an assistive listening system or computer-aided transcription equipment provided pursuant to Section 54.8 of the Civil Code.

(b) In any civil or criminal action, including any action involving a traffic or other infraction or any juvenile court proceeding, or any proceeding to determine the mental competency of a person, or any administrative hearing, where a party or witness is a deaf or hard-of-hearing person and the deaf or hard-of-hearing person is present and participating, the proceedings shall be interpreted in a language that the deaf or hard-of-hearing person understands by a qualified interpreter appointed by the court, tribunal, hearing officer, or other appropriate authority, or as agreed upon by the parties.

(c) For purposes of this section, "appointing authority" means a court, department, board, commission, agency, licensing or legislative body, or other body for proceedings requiring a qualified interpreter.

(d) For the purposes of this section, "interpreter" includes, but is not limited to, an oral interpreter, a sign language interpreter, or a deaf-blind interpreter, depending upon the needs of the deaf or hard-of-hearing person.

(e) For purposes of this section, "intermediary interpreter" means a deaf, hard-of-hearing, or hearing person who is able to assist in providing an accurate interpretation between spoken English and sign language or between variants of sign language or between American Sign Language and other foreign languages by acting as an intermediary between the deaf person and the qualified interpreter.

(f) For purposes of this section, "qualified interpreter" means an interpreter who has been certified as competent to interpret court proceedings by a testing organization, agency, or educational institution approved by the Judicial Council as qualified to administer tests to court interpreters for the deaf or hard-of-hearing.

(g) In the event that the appointed interpreter is not familiar with the deaf or hard-of-hearing person's use of particular signs or his or her particular variant of sign language, the court or other appointing authority shall, in consultation with the deaf or hard-of-hearing person or his or her representative, appoint an intermediary interpreter.

(h) Prior to January 1, 1992, the Judicial Council shall conduct a study to establish the guidelines pursuant to which it shall determine which testing organizations, agencies, or educational institutions will be approved to administer tests for certification of court interpreters for the deaf and hard-of-hearing. It is the intent of the Legislature that the study obtain the widest possible input from the public, including, but not limited to, educational institutions, the judiciary, linguists, members of the State Bar, court interpreters, members of professional interpreting organizations, and members of the deaf and hard-of-hearing communities. After obtaining public comment and completing its study, the Judicial Council shall publish these guidelines and shall approve one or more entities to administer testing for court interpreters for the deaf and hard-of-hearing. Initial approval of testing entities by the Judicial Council shall occur prior to January 1, 1992.

Commencing January 1, 1992, court interpreters for the deaf or hard-of-hearing shall meet the qualifications specified in subdivision (f).

(i) Persons appointed to serve as interpreters under this section shall be paid, in addition to actual travel costs, the prevailing rate paid to persons employed by the court to provide other interpreter services unless such service is considered to be a part of the person's regular duties as an employee of the state, county, or other political subdivision of the state. Payment of the interpreter's fee shall be a charge against the county, or other political subdivision of the state, in which such action is pending. Payment of the interpreter's fee in administrative proceedings shall be a charge against the appointing board, agency, commission, or licensing authority.

(j) No statement, written or oral, made by a person who is deaf or hard-of-hearing in reply to a question of a peace officer, or any other person having a prosecutorial function in any criminal or quasi-criminal investigation or proceeding, may be used against that deaf or hard-of-hearing person unless the statement was made knowingly, voluntarily, and intelligently and was accurately interpreted, or the court makes a special finding that the statement was made knowingly, voluntarily, and intelligently.

(k) In obtaining services of an interpreter for the purpose of obtaining a statement subject to subdivision (j), priority shall be given to first obtaining a qualified interpreter.

(*l*) Nothing in subdivision (j) or (k) shall be deemed to supersede the requirement of subdivision (b) for use of a qualified interpreter for deaf or hard-of-hearing persons participating as parties or witnesses in a trial or hearing.

(m) In any action or proceeding in which a deaf or hard-of-hearing person is a participant, the court or administrative authority shall not commence proceedings until the appointed interpreter is in full view of and spatially situated to assure proper communication with the deaf or hard-of-hearing person or persons involved as participants.

(n) Each superior court shall maintain a current roster of qualified interpreters certified pursuant to subdivision (f).

§ 754.5 Privilege of communication between deaf or hard-of-hearing person and another person if interpreter was used

Whenever an otherwise valid privilege exists between a deaf or hard-of-hearing person and another person, that privilege is not waived merely because an interpreter was used to facilitate their communication.

CHAPTER 5. METHOD AND SCOPE OF EXAMINATION

ARTICLE 1. DEFINITIONS

§ 760. "Direct examination"

"Direct examination" is the first examination of a witness upon a matter that is not within the scope of a previous examination of the witness.

§ 761. 'Cross-examination"

"Cross-examination" is the examination of a witness by a party other than the direct examiner upon a matter that is within the scope of the direct examination of the witness.

§ 762. "Redirect examination"

"Redirect examination" is an examination of a witness by the direct examiner subsequent to the cross-examination of the witness.

§ 763. "Recross-examination"

"Recross-examination" is an examination of a witness by a cross-examiner subsequent to a redirect examination of the witness.

§ 764. "Leading question"

A "leading question" is a question that suggests to the witness the answer that the examining party desires.

ARTICLE 2.   EXAMINATION OF WITNESSES

§ 765. Court to control mode of interrogation

(a) The court shall exercise reasonable control over the mode of interrogation of a witness so as to make such interrogation as rapid, as distinct, and as effective for the ascertainment of the truth, as may be, and to protect the witness from undue harassment or embarrassment.

(b) With a witness under the age of 14, the court shall take special care to protect him or her from undue harassment or embarrassment, and to restrict the unnecessary repetition of questions. The court shall also take special care to insure that questions are stated in a form which is appropriate to the age of the witness. The court may in the interests of justice, on objection by a party, forbid the asking of a question which is in a form that is not reasonably likely to be understood by a person of the age of the witness.

§ 766. Responsive answers

A witness must give responsive answers to questions, and answers that are not responsive shall be stricken on motion of any party.

§ 767. Leading questions

(a) Except under special circumstances where the interests of justice otherwise require:

(1) A leading question may not be asked of a witness on direct or redirect examination.

(2) A leading question may be asked of a witness on cross-examination or recross-examination.

(b) The court may in the interests of justice permit a leading question to be asked of a child under 10 years of age in a case involving a prosecution under Section 273a, 273d, or 288 of the Penal Code.

§ 768. Writings

(a) In examining a witness concerning a writing, it is not necessary to show, read, or disclose to him any part of the writing.

(b) If a writing is shown to a witness, all parties to the action must be given an opportunity to inspect it before any question concerning it may be asked of the witness.

§ 769. Inconsistent statement or conduct

In examining a witness concerning a statement or other conduct by him that is inconsistent with any part of his testimony at the hearing, it is not necessary to disclose to him any information concerning the statement or other conduct.

§ 770. Evidence of inconsistent statement of witness

Unless the interests of justice otherwise require, extrinsic evidence of a statement made by a witness that is inconsistent with any part of his testimony at the hearing shall be excluded unless:

(a) The witness was so examined while testifying as to give him an opportunity to explain or to deny the statement; or

(b) The witness has not been excused from giving further testimony in the action.

§ 771. Production of writing used to refresh memory

(a) Subject to subdivision (c), if a witness, either while testifying or prior thereto, uses a writing to refresh his memory with respect to any matter about which he testifies, such writing must be produced at the hearing at the request of an adverse party and, unless the writing is so produced, the testimony of the witness concerning such matter shall be stricken.

(b) If the writing is produced at the hearing, the adverse party may, if he chooses, inspect the writing, cross-examine the witness concerning it, and introduce in evidence such portion of it as may be pertinent to the testimony of the witness.

(c) Production of the writing is excused, and the testimony of the witness shall not be stricken, if the writing:

(1) Is not in the possession or control of the witness or the party who produced his testimony concerning the matter; and

(2) Was not reasonably procurable by such party through the use of the court's process or other available means.

§ 772. Order of examination

(a) The examination of a witness shall proceed in the following phases: direct examination, cross-examination, redirect examination, recross-examination, and continuing thereafter by redirect and recross-examination.

(b) Unless for good cause the court otherwise directs, each phase of the examination of a witness must be concluded before the succeeding phase begins.

(c) Subject to subdivision (d), a party may, in the discretion of the court, interrupt his cross-examination, redirect examination, or recross-examination of a witness, in order to examine the witness upon a matter not within the scope of a previous examination of the witness.

(d) If the witness is the defendant in a criminal action, the witness may not, without his consent, be examined under direct examination by another party.

§ 773. Cross-examination

(a) A witness examined by one party may be cross-examined upon any matter within the scope of the direct examination by each other party to the action in such order as the court directs.

(b) The cross-examination of a witness by any party whose interest is not adverse to the party calling him is subject to the same rules that are applicable to the direct examination.

§ 774. Re-examination

A witness once examined cannot be reexamined as to the same matter without leave of the court, but he may be reexamined as to any new matter upon which he has been examined by another party to the action. Leave may be granted or withheld in the court's discretion.

§ 775. Court may call witnesses

The court, on its own motion or on the motion of any party, may call witnesses and interrogate them the same as if they had been produced by a party to the action, and the parties may object to the questions asked and the evidence adduced the same as if such witnesses were called and examined by an adverse party. Such witnesses may be cross-examined by all parties to the action in such order as the court directs.

§ 776. Examination of adverse party or witness

(a) A party to the record of any civil action, or a person identified with such a party, may be called and examined as if under cross-examination by any adverse party at any time during the presentation of evidence by the party calling the witness.

(b) A witness examined by a party under this section may be cross-examined by all other parties to the action in such order as the court directs; but, subject to subdivision (e), the witness may be examined only as if under redirect examination by:

(1) In the case of a witness who is a party, his own counsel and counsel for a party who is not adverse to the witness.

(2) In the case of a witness who is not a party, counsel for the party with whom the witness is identified and counsel for a party who is not adverse to the party with whom the witness is identified.

(c) For the purpose of this section, parties represented by the same counsel are deemed to be a single party.

(d) For the purpose of this section, a person is identified with a party if he is:

(1) A person for whose immediate benefit the action is prosecuted or defended by the party.

1
2
3
4
5
6
7
8
9
10
11
12
13
14
15
16
17
18
19
20
21
22
23
24
25
26
27
28
29
30
31
32
33
34
35
36
37
38
39
40
41
42
43
44
45
46
47
48
49
50

(2) A director, officer, superintendent, member, agent, employee, or managing agent of the party or of a person specified in paragraph (1), or any public employee of a public entity when such public entity is the party.

(3) A person who was in any of the relationships specified in paragraph (2) at the time of the act or omission giving rise to the cause of action.

(4) A person who was in any of the relationships specified in paragraph (2) at the time he obtained knowledge of the matter concerning which he is sought to be examined under this section.

(e) Paragraph (2) of subdivision (b) does not require counsel for the party with whom the witness is identified and counsel for a party who is not adverse to the party with whom the witness is identified to examine the witness as if under redirect examination if the party who called the witness for examination under this section:

(1) Is also a person identified with the same party with whom the witness is identified.

(2) Is the personal representative, heir, successor, or assignee of a person identified with the same party with whom the witness is identified.

§ 777. Exclusion of witness

(a) Subject to subdivisions (b) and (c), the court may exclude from the courtroom any witness not at the time under examination so that such witness cannot hear the testimony of other witnesses.

(b) A party to the action cannot be excluded under this section.

(c) If a person other than a natural person is a party to the action, an officer or employee designated by its attorney is entitled to be present.

§ 778. Recall of witness

After a witness has been excused from giving further testimony in the action, he cannot be recalled without leave of the court. Leave may be granted or withheld in the court's discretion.

CHAPTER 6. CREDIBILITY OF WITNESSES

ARTICLE I. GENERALLY

§ 780. General rule as to credibility

Except as otherwise provided by statute, the court or jury may consider in determining the credibility of a witness any matter that has any tendency in reason to prove or disprove the truthfulness of this testimony at the hearing, including but not limited to any of the following:

(a) His demeanor while testifying and the manner in which he testifies.

(b) The character of his testimony.

(c) The extent of his capacity to perceive, to recollect, or to communicate any matter about which he testifies.

(d) The extent of his opportunity to perceive any matter about which he testifies.

(e) His character for honesty or veracity or their opposites.

(f) The existence or nonexistence of a bias, interest, or other motive.

(g) A statement previously made by him that is consistent with his testimony at the hearing.

(h) A statement made by him that is inconsistent with any part of his testimony at the hearing.

(i) The existence or nonexistence of any fact testified to by him.

(j) His attitude toward the action in which he testifies or toward the giving of testimony.

(k) His admission of untruthfulness.

§ 782. Sexual offenses; evidence of sexual conduct of complaining witness; procedure for admissibility

(a) In any prosecution under Section 261, 264.1, 286, 288, 288a, 288.5, or 289 of the Penal Code, or for assault with intent to commit, attempt to commit, or conspiracy to commit any crime defined in any * * * of those sections, except where the crime is alleged to have occurred in a local detention facility, as defined in Section 6031.4, or in a state prison, as defined in Section 4504, if evidence of sexual conduct of the complaining witness is offered to attack the credibility of the complaining witness under Section 780, the following procedure shall be followed:

(1) A written motion shall be made by the defendant to the court and prosecutor stating that the defense has an offer of proof of the relevancy of evidence of the sexual conduct of the complaining witness proposed to be presented and its relevancy in attacking the credibility of the complaining witness.

(2) The written motion shall be accompanied by an affidavit in which the offer of proof shall be stated.

(3) If the court finds that the offer of proof is sufficient, the court shall order a hearing out of the presence of the jury, if any, and at such hearing allow the questioning of the complaining witness regarding the offer of proof made by the defendant.

(4) At the conclusion of the hearing, if the court finds that evidence proposed to be offered by the defendant regarding the sexual conduct of

the complaining witness is relevant pursuant to Section 780, and is not inadmissible pursuant to Section 352 of this code, the court may make an order stating what evidence may be introduced by the defendant, and the nature of the questions to be permitted. The defendant may then offer evidence pursuant to the order of the court.

(b) As used in this section, "complaining witness" means the alleged victim of the crime charged, the prosecution of which is subject to this section.

§ 783. **Sexual harassment, sexual assault, or sexual battery cases; admissibility of evidence of plaintiff's sexual conduct; procedure**

In any civil action alleging conduct which constitutes sexual harassment, sexual assault, or sexual battery, if evidence of sexual conduct of the plaintiff is offered to attack credibility of the plaintiff under Section 780, the following procedures shall be followed:

(a) A written motion shall be made by the defendant to the court and the plaintiff's attorney stating that the defense has an offer of proof of the relevancy of evidence of the sexual conduct of the plaintiff proposed to be presented.

(b) The written motion shall be accompanied by an affidavit in which the offer of proof shall be stated.

(c) If the court finds that the offer of proof is sufficient, the court shall order a hearing out of the presence of the jury, if any, and at the hearing allow the questioning of the plaintiff regarding the offer of proof made by the defendant.

(d) At the conclusion of the hearing, if the court finds that evidence proposed to be offered by the defendant regarding the sexual conduct of the plaintiff is relevant pursuant to Section 780, and is not inadmissible pursuant to Section 352, the court may make an order stating what evidence may be introduced by the defendant, and the nature of the questions to be permitted. The defendant may then offer evidence pursuant to the order of the court.

ARTICLE 2. ATTACKING OR SUPPORTING CREDIBILITY

§ 785. **Parties may attack or support credibility**

The credibility of a witness may be attacked or supported by any party, including the party calling him.

§ 786. **Character evidence generally**

Evidence of traits of his character other than honesty or veracity, or their opposites, is inadmissible to attack or support the credibility of a witness.

§ 787. **Specific instances of conduct**

Subject to Section 788, evidence of specific instances of his conduct relevant only as tending to prove a trait of his character is inadmissible to attack or support the credibility of a witness.

§ 788. Prior felony conviction

For the purpose of attacking the credibility of a witness, it may be shown by the examination of the witness or by the record of the judgment that he has been convicted of a felony unless:

(a) A pardon based on his innocence has been granted to the witness by the jurisdiction in which he was convicted.

(b) A certificate of rehabilitation and pardon has been granted to the witness under the provisions of Chapter 3.5 (commencing with Section 4852.01) of Title 6 of Part 3 of the Penal Code.

(c) The accusatory pleading against the witness has been dismissed under the provisions of Penal Code Section 1203.4, but this exception does not apply to any criminal trial where the witness is being prosecuted for a subsequent offense.

(d) The conviction was under the laws of another jurisdiction and the witness has been relieved of the penalties and disabilities arising from the conviction pursuant to a procedure substantially equivalent to that referred to in subdivision (b) or (c).

§ 789. Religious belief

Evidence of his religious belief or lack thereof is inadmissible to attack or support the credibility of a witness.

§ 790. Good character of witness

Evidence of the good character of a witness is inadmissible to support his credibility unless evidence of his bad character has been admitted for the purpose of attacking his credibility.

§ 791. Prior consistent statement of witness

Evidence of a statement previously made by a witness that is consistent with his testimony at the hearing is inadmissible to support his credibility unless it is offered after:

(a) Evidence of a statement made by him that is inconsistent with any part of his testimony at the hearing has been admitted for the purpose of attacking his credibility, and the statement was made before the alleged inconsistent statement; or

(b) An express or implied charge has been made that his testimony at the hearing is recently fabricated or is influenced by bias or other improper motive, and the statement was made before the bias, motive for fabrication, or other improper motive is alleged to have arisen.

CHAPTER 7. HYPNOSIS OF WITNESSES

§ 795. Testimony of hypnosis subject; admissibility; conditions

(a) The testimony of a witness is not inadmissible in a criminal proceeding by reason of the fact that the witness has previously undergone hypnosis for the purpose of recalling events which are the subject of the witness' testimony, if all of the following conditions are met:

(1) The testimony is limited to those matters which the witness recalled and related prior to the hypnosis.

(2) The substance of the prehypnotic memory was preserved in written, audiotape, or videotape form prior to the hypnosis.

(3) The hypnosis was conducted in accordance with all of the following procedures:

(A) A written record was made prior to hypnosis documenting the subject's description of the event, and information which was provided to the hypnotist concerning the subject matter of the hypnosis.

(B) The subject gave informed consent to the hypnosis.

(C) The hypnosis session, including the pre- and post-hypnosis interviews, was videotape recorded for subsequent review.

(D) The hypnosis was performed by a licensed medical doctor, psychologist, or licensed clinical social worker experienced in the use of hypnosis or a licensed marriage, family and child counselor certified in hypnosis by the Board of Behavioral Science Examiners and independent of and not in the presence of law enforcement, the prosecution, or the defense.

(4) Prior to admission of the testimony, the court holds a hearing pursuant to Section 402 of the Evidence Code at which the proponent of the evidence proves by clear and convincing evidence that the hypnosis did not so affect the witness as to render the witness' prehypnosis recollection unreliable or to substantially impair the ability to cross-examine the witness concerning the witness' prehypnosis recollection. At the hearing, each side shall have the right to present expert testimony and to cross-examine witnesses.

(b) Nothing in this section shall be construed to limit the ability of a party to attack the credibility of a witness who has undergone hypnosis, or to limit other legal grounds to admit or exclude the testimony of that witness.

Division 7

OPINION TESTIMONY AND SCIENTIFIC EVIDENCE

CHAPTER 1. EXPERT AND OTHER OPINION TESTIMONY

ARTICLE 1. EXPERT AND OTHER OPINION TESTIMONY GENERALLY

§ 800. Opinion testimony by lay witness

If a witness is not testifying as an expert, his testimony in the form of an opinion is limited to such an opinion as is permitted by law, including but not limited to an opinion that is:

(a) Rationally based on the perception of the witness; and

(b) Helpful to a clear understanding of his testimony.

§ 801. Opinion testimony by expert witness

If a witness is testifying as an expert, his testimony in the form of an opinion is limited to such an opinion as is:

(a) Related to a subject that is sufficiently beyond common experience that the opinion of an expert would assist the trier of fact; and

(b) Based on matter (including his special knowledge, skill, experience, training, and education) perceived by or personally known to the witness or made known to him at or before the hearing, whether or not admissible, that is of a type that reasonably may be relied upon by an expert in forming an opinion upon the subject to which his testimony relates, unless an expert is precluded by law from using such matter as a basis for his opinion.

§ 802. Statement of basis of opinion

A witness testifying in the form of an opinion may state on direct examination the reasons for his opinion and the matter (including, in the case of an expert, his special knowledge, skill, experience, training, and education) upon which it is based, unless he is precluded by law from using such reasons or matters as a basis for his opinion. The court in its discretion may require that a witness before testifying in the form of an opinion be first examined concerning the matter upon which his opinion is based.

§ 803. Opinion based on improper matter

The court may, and upon objection shall, exclude testimony in the form of an opinion that is based in whole or in significant part on matter that is not a proper basis for such an opinion. In such case, the witness may, if there remains a proper basis for his opinion, then state his opinion after excluding from consideration the matter determined to be improper.

§ 804. Opinion based on opinion or statement of another

(a) If a witness testifying as an expert testifies that his opinion is based in whole or in part upon the opinion or statement of another person, such other person may be called and examined by any adverse party as if under cross-examination concerning the opinion or statement.

(b) This section is not applicable if the person upon whose opinion or statement the expert witness has relied is (1) a party, (2) a person identified with a party within the meaning of subdivision (d) of Section 776, or (3) a witness who has testified in the action concerning the subject matter of the opinion or statement upon which the expert witness has relied.

(c) Nothing in this section makes admissible an expert opinion that is inadmissible because it is based in whole or in part on the opinion or statement of another person.

(d) An expert opinion otherwise admissible is not made inadmissible by this section because it is based on the opinion or statement of a person who is unavailable for examination pursuant to this section.

§ 805. Opinion on ultimate issue

Testimony in the form of an opinion that is otherwise admissible is not objectionable because it embraces the ultimate issue to be decided by the trier of fact.

ARTICLE 2. EVIDENCE OF MARKET VALUE OF PROPERTY

§ 810. Application of article

(a) Except where another rule is provided by statute, this article provides special rules of evidence applicable to any action in which the value of property is to be ascertained.

(b) This article does not govern ad valorem property tax assessment or equalization proceedings.

§ 811. Value of property

As used in this article, "value of property" means market value of any of the following:

(a) Real property or any interest therein.

(b) Real property or any interest therein and tangible personal property valued as a unit.

§ 812. Market value; interpretation of meaning

This article is not intended to alter or change the existing substantive law, whether statutory or decisional, interpreting the meaning of "market value," whether denominated "fair market value" or otherwise.

§ 813. Value of property; authorized opinions; view of property; admissible evidence

(a) The value of property may be shown only by the opinions of any of the following:

(1) Witnesses qualified to express such opinions.

(2) The owner or the spouse of the owner of the property or property interest being valued.

(3) An officer, regular employee, or partner designated by a corporation, partnership, or unincorporated association that is the owner of the property or property interest being valued, if the designee is knowledgeable as to the value of the property or property interest.

(b) Nothing in this section prohibits a view of the property being valued or the admission of any other admissible evidence (including but not limited to evidence as to the nature and condition of the property and, in an eminent domain proceeding, the character of the improvement proposed to be constructed by the plaintiff) for the limited purpose of enabling the court, jury, or referee to understand and weigh the testimony given under subdivision (a); and such evidence, except evidence of the character of the improvement proposed to be constructed by the plaintiff in an eminent domain proceeding, is subject to impeachment and rebuttal.

(c) For the purposes of subdivision (a), "owner of the property or property interest being valued" includes, but is not limited to, the following persons:

(1) A person entitled to possession of the property.

(2) Either party in an action or proceeding to determine the ownership of the property between the parties if the court determines that it would not be in the interest of efficient administration of justice to determine the issue of ownership prior to the admission of the opinion of the party.

§ 814. Matter upon which opinion must be based

The opinion of a witness as to the value of property is limited to such an opinion as is based on matter perceived by or personally known to the witness or made known to the witness at or before the hearing, whether or not admissible, that is of a type that reasonably may be relied upon by an expert in forming an opinion as to the value of property, including but not limited to the matters listed in Sections 815 to 821, inclusive, unless a witness is precluded by law from using such matter as a basis for an opinion.

§ 815. Sales of subject property

When relevant to the determination of the value of property, a witness may take into account as a basis for an opinion the price and other terms and circumstances of any sale or contract to sell and purchase which included the property or property interest being valued or any part thereof if the sale or contract was freely made in good faith within a reasonable time before or after the date of valuation, except that in an eminent domain proceeding where the sale or contract to sell and purchase includes only the property or property interest being taken or a part thereof, such sale or contract to sell and purchase may not be taken into account if it occurs after the filing of the lis pendens.

§ 816. Comparable sales

When relevant to the determination of the value of property, a witness may take into account as a basis for his opinion the price and other terms and circumstances of any sale or contract to sell and purchase comparable property if the sale or contract was freely made in good faith within a reasonable time before or after the date of valuation. In order to be considered comparable, the sale or contract must have been made sufficiently near in time to the date of valuation, and the property sold must be located sufficiently near the property being valued, and must be sufficiently alike in respect to character, size, situation, usability, and improvements, to make it clear that the property sold and the property being valued are comparable in value and that the price realized for the property sold may fairly be considered as shedding light on the value of the property being valued.

§ 817. Leases of subject property

(a) Subject to subdivision (b), when relevant to the determination of the value of property, a witness may take into account as a basis for an opinion the rent reserved and other terms and circumstances of any lease which included the property or property interest being valued or any part thereof which was in effect within a reasonable time before or after the date of valuation, except that in an eminent domain proceeding where the lease includes only the property or property interest being taken or a part thereof, such lease may not be taken into account in the determination of the value of property if it is entered into after the filing of the lis pendens.

(b) A witness may take into account a lease providing for a rental fixed by a percentage or other measurable portion of gross sales or gross income from a business conducted on the leased property only for the purpose of arriving at an opinion as to the reasonable net rental value attributable to the property or property interest being valued as provided in Section 819 or determining the value of a leasehold interest.

§ 818. Comparable leases

For the purpose of determining the capitalized value of the reasonable net rental value attributable to the property or property interest being valued as provided in Section 819 or determining the value of a leasehold interest, a witness may take into account as a basis for his opinion the rent reserved and other terms and circumstances of any lease of comparable property if the lease was freely made in good faith within a reasonable time before or after the date of valuation.

§ 819. Capitalization of income

When relevant to the determination of the value of property, a witness may take into account as a basis for his opinion the capitalized value of the reasonable net rental value attributable to the land and existing improvements thereon (as distinguished from the capitalized value of the income or profits attributable to the business conducted thereon).

§ 820. Reproduction cost

When relevant to the determination of the value of property, a witness may take into account as a basis for his opinion the value of the property or property interest being valued as indicated by the value of the land together with the cost of replacing or reproducing the existing improvements thereon, if the improvements enhance the value of the property or property interest for its highest and best use, less whatever depreciation or obsolescence the improvements have suffered.

§ 821. Conditions in general vicinity of subject property

When relevant to the determination of the value of property, a witness may take into account as a basis for his opinion the nature of the improvements on properties in the general vicinity of the property or property interest being valued and the character of the existing uses being made of such properties.

§ 822. Matter upon which opinion may not be based

(a) In an eminent domain or inverse condemnation proceeding, notwithstanding the provisions of Sections 814 to 821, inclusive, the following matter is inadmissible as evidence and shall not be taken into account as a basis for an opinion as to the value of property:

(1) The price or other terms and circumstances of an acquisition of property or a property interest if the acquisition was for a public use for which the property could have been taken by eminent domain, except that the price or other terms and circumstances of an acquisition of property appropriated to a public use or a property interest so appropriated shall not be excluded under this section if the acquisition was for the same public use for which the property could have been taken by eminent domain.

(2) The price at which an offer or option to purchase or lease the property or property interest being valued or any other property was made, or the price at which such property or interest was optioned, offered, or listed for sale or lease, except that an option, offer, or listing may be introduced by a party as an admission of another party to the proceeding; but nothing in this subdivision permits an admission to be used as direct evidence upon any matter that may be shown only by opinion evidence under Section 813.

(3) The value of any property or property interest as assessed for taxation purposes or the amount of taxes which may be due on the property, but nothing in this subdivision prohibits the consideration of actual or estimated taxes for the purpose of determining the reasonable net rental value attributable to the property or property interest being valued.

(4) An opinion as to the value of any property or property interest other than that being valued.

(5) The influence upon the value of the property or property interest being valued of any noncompensable items of value, damage, or injury.

(6) The capitalized value of the income or rental from any property or property interest other than that being valued.

(b) In an action other than an eminent domain or inverse condemnation proceeding, the matters listed in subdivision (a) are not admissible as evidence, and may not be taken into account as a basis for an opinion as to the value of property, except to the extent permitted under the rules of law otherwise applicable.

(c) The amendments made to this section during the 1987 portion of the 1987–88 Regular Session of the Legislature shall not apply to or affect any petition filed pursuant to this section before January 1, 1988.

§ 823. **No relevant market for property**

Notwithstanding any other provision of this article, the value of property for which there is no relevant market may be determined by any method of valuation that is just and equitable.

ARTICLE 3. OPINION TESTIMONY ON PARTICULAR SUBJECTS

§ 870. **Opinion as to sanity**

A witness may state his opinion as to the sanity of a person when:

(a) The witness is an intimate acquaintance of the person whose sanity is in question;

(b) The witness was a subscribing witness to a writing, the validity of which is in dispute, signed by the person whose sanity is in question and the opinion relates to the sanity of such person at the time the writing was signed; or

(c) The witness is qualified under Section 800 or 801 to testify in the form of an opinion.

CHAPTER 2. BLOOD TESTS TO DETERMINE PATERNITY

§ 890. **Short title**

This chapter may be cited as the Uniform Act on Blood Tests to Determine Paternity.

§ 891. **Interpretation**

This act shall be so interpreted and construed as to effectuate its general purpose to make uniform the law of those states which enact it.

§ 892. **Order for blood tests in civil actions involving paternity**

In a civil action in which paternity is a relevant fact, the court may upon its own initiative or upon suggestion made by or on behalf of any person whose blood is involved, and shall upon motion of any party to the action made at a time so as not to delay the proceedings unduly, order the mother, child, and alleged father to submit to blood tests. If any party refuses to submit to such tests, the court may resolve the question of paternity against such party or enforce its order if the rights of others and the interests of justice so require. Any party's refusal to submit to such tests shall be admissible in evidence in any proceeding to determine paternity.

§ 893. Tests made by experts

The tests shall be made by experts qualified as examiners of blood types who shall be appointed by the court. The experts shall be called by the court as witnesses to testify to their findings and shall be subject to cross-examination by the parties. Any party or person at whose suggestion the tests have been ordered may demand that other experts, qualified as examiners of blood types, perform independent tests under order of the court, the results of which may be offered in evidence. The number and qualifications of such experts shall be determined by the court.

§ 894. Compensation of experts

The compensation of each expert witness appointed by the court shall be fixed at a reasonable amount. It shall be paid as the court shall order. The court may order that it be paid by the parties in such proportions and at such times as it shall prescribe, or that the proportion of any party be paid by the county, and that, after payment by the parties or the county or both, all or part or none of it be taxed as costs in the action.

§ 895. Determination of paternity

If the court finds that the conclusions of all the experts, as disclosed by the evidence based upon the tests, are that the alleged father is not the father of the child, the question of paternity shall be resolved accordingly. If the experts disagree in their findings or conclusions, or if the tests show the probability of the alleged father's paternity, the question, subject to the provisions of Section 352, shall be submitted upon all the evidence, including evidence based upon the tests.

§ 895.5 Rebuttable presumption of paternity; paternity index of 100 or more

(a) There is a rebuttable presumption, affecting the burden of proof, of paternity, if the court finds that the paternity index, as calculated by the experts qualified as examiners of genetic markers, is 100 or greater. This presumption may only be rebutted by a preponderance of the evidence.

(b) As used in this section:

(1) "Genetic markers" mean separate identifiable genes or complexes of genes generally isolated as a result of blood typing, at least seven of which are normally tested in a paternity determination.

(2) "Paternity index" means the commonly accepted indicator used for denoting the existence of paternity. It represents the mathematically computed probability that the putative father is the true father of the child, as opposed to any other man of similar ethnic background. The paternity index, computed using results of various paternity tests following accepted statistical principles for the computation of probability, shall be in accordance with the method of expression accepted at the International Conference on Parentage Testing at Airlie House, Virginia, May 1982, sponsored by the American Association of Blood Banks.

§ 896. Limitation on application in criminal matters

This chapter applies to criminal actions subject to the following limitations and provisions:

(a) An order for the tests shall be made only upon application of a party or on the court's initiative.

(b) The compensation of the experts shall be paid by the county under order of court.

(c) The court may direct a verdict of acquittal upon the conclusions of all the experts under the provisions of Section 895; otherwise, the case shall be submitted for determination upon all the evidence.

§ 897. Right to produce other expert evidence

Nothing contained in this chapter shall be deemed or construed to prevent any party to any action from producing other expert evidence on the matter covered by this chapter; but where other expert witnesses are called by a party to the action, their fees shall be paid by the party calling them and only ordinary witness fees shall be taxed as costs in the action.

Division 8

PRIVILEGES

CHAPTER 1. DEFINITIONS

§ 900. Application of definitions

Unless the provision or context otherwise requires, the definitions in this chapter govern the construction of this division. They do not govern the construction of any other division.

§ 901. "Proceeding"   1

"Proceeding" means any action, hearing, investigation, inquest, or   2
inquiry (whether conducted by a court, administrative agency, hearing 3
officer, arbitrator, legislative body, or any other person authorized by 4
law) in which, pursuant to law, testimony can be compelled to be given. 5
                                                                         6
§ 902. "Civil proceeding"   7

"Civil proceeding" means any proceeding except a criminal pro-   8
ceeding.   9
                                                                        10
§ 903. "Criminal proceeding"   11

"Criminal proceeding" means: 12
                                                                        13
(a) A criminal action; and   14

(b) A proceeding pursuant to Article 3 (commencing with Section   15
3060) of Chapter 7 of Division 4 of Title 1 of the Government Code to 16
determine whether a public officer should be removed from office for 17
willful or corrupt misconduct in office.   18
                                                                        19
§ 904. Blank   20
§ 905. "Presiding officer"   21

"Presiding officer" means the person authorized to rule on a claim 22
of privilege in the proceeding in which the claim is made.   23
                                                                        24

CHAPTER 2. APPLICABILITY OF DIVISION   25
                                                                        26
§ 910. Applicability of division   27

Except as otherwise provided by statute, the provisions of this   28
division apply in all proceedings. The provisions of any statute making 29
rules of evidence inapplicable in particular proceedings, or limiting the 30
applicability of rules of evidence in particular proceedings, do not make 31
this division inapplicable to such proceedings.   32
                                                                        33

CHAPTER 3. GENERAL PROVISIONS   34
RELATING TO PRIVILEGES   35
                                                                        36
§ 911. General rule as to privileges   37

Except as otherwise provided by statute: 38

(a) No person has a privilege to refuse to be a witness.   39

(b) No person has a privilege to refuse to disclose any matter or to 40
refuse to produce any writing, object, or other thing.   41

(c) No person has a privilege that another shall not be a witness or 42
shall not disclose any matter or shall not produce any writing, object, or 43
other thing.   44
                                                                        45
§ 912. Waiver of privilege   46

(a) Except as otherwise provided in this section, the right of any 47
person to claim a privilege provided by Section 954 (lawyer-client 48
privilege), 980 (privilege for confidential marital communications), 994 49
                                                                        50

1 (physician-patient privilege), 1014 (psychotherapist-patient privilege),
2 1033 (privilege of penitent), 1034 (privilege of clergyman), or 1035.8
3 (sexual assault victim-counselor privilege) is waived with respect to a
4 communication protected by such privilege if any holder of the privi-
5 lege, without coercion, has disclosed a significant part of the communi-
6 cation or has consented to such disclosure made by anyone. Consent to
7 disclosure is manifested by any statement or other conduct of the
8 holder of the privilege indicating consent to the disclosure, including
9 failure to claim the privilege in any proceeding in which the holder has
10 the legal standing and opportunity to claim the privilege.

11 (b) Where two or more persons are joint holders of a privilege
12 provided by Section 954 (lawyer-client privilege), 994 (physician-patient
13 privilege), 1014 (psychotherapist-patient privilege), or 1035.8 (sexual
14 assault victim-counselor privilege), a waiver of the right of a particular
15 joint holder of the privilege to claim the privilege does not affect the
16 right of another joint holder to claim the privilege. In the case of the
17 privilege provided by Section 980 (privilege for confidential marital
18 communications), a waiver of the right of one spouse to claim the
19 privilege does not affect the right of the other spouse to claim the
20 privilege.

21 (c) A disclosure that is itself privileged is not a waiver of any
22 privilege.
23

24 (d) A disclosure in confidence of a communication that is protected
25 by a privilege provided by Section 954 (lawyer-client privilege), 994
26 (physician-patient privilege), 1014 (psychotherapist-patient privilege), or
27 1035.8 (sexual assault victim-counselor privilege), when such disclosure
28 is reasonably necessary for the accomplishment of the purpose for
29 which the lawyer, physician, psychotherapist, or sexual assault counsel-
30 or was consulted, is not a waiver of the privilege.

31
32 **§ 913. Comment on, and inferences from, exercise of privilege**

33 (a) If in the instant proceeding or on a prior occasion a privilege is
34 or was exercised not to testify with respect to any matter, or to refuse
35 to disclose or to prevent another from disclosing any matter, neither
36 the presiding officer nor counsel may comment thereon, no presump-
37 tion shall arise because of the exercise of the privilege, and the trier of
38 fact may not draw any inference therefrom as to the credibility of the
39 witness or as to any matter at issue in the proceeding.

40 (b) The court, at the request of a party who may be adversely
41 affected because an unfavorable inference may be drawn by the jury
42 because a privilege has been exercised, shall instruct the jury that no
43 presumption arises because of the exercise of the privilege and that the
44 jury may not draw any inference therefrom as to the credibility of the
45 witness or as to any matter at issue in the proceeding.

§ 914. Determination of claim of privilege; limitation on punishment for contempt

(a) The presiding officer shall determine a claim of privilege in any proceeding in the same manner as a court determines such a claim under Article 2 (commencing with Section 400) of Chapter 4 of Division 3.

(b) No person may be held in contempt for failure to disclose information claimed to be privileged unless he has failed to comply with an order of a court that he disclose such information. This subdivision does not apply to any governmental agency that has constitutional contempt power, nor does it apply to hearings and investigations of the Industrial Accident Commission, nor does it impliedly repeal Chapter 4 (commencing with Section 9400) of Part 1 of Division 2 of Title 2 of the Government Code. If no other statutory procedure is applicable, the procedure prescribed by Section 1991 of the Code of Civil Procedure shall be followed in seeking an order of a court that the person disclose the information claimed to be privileged.

§ 915. Disclosure of privileged information in ruling on claim of privilege

(a) Subject to subdivision (b), the presiding officer may not require disclosure of information claimed to be privileged under this division in order to rule on the claim of privilege; provided, however, that in any hearing conducted pursuant to subdivision (c) of Section 1524 of the Penal Code in which a claim of privilege is made and the court determines that there is no other feasible means to rule on the validity of such claim other than to require disclosure, the court shall proceed in accordance with subdivision (b).

(b) When a court is ruling on a claim of privilege under Article 9 (commencing with Section 1040) of Chapter 4 (official information and identity of informer) or under Section 1060 (trade secret) and is unable to do so without requiring disclosure of the information claimed to be privileged, the court may require the person from whom disclosure is sought or the person authorized to claim the privilege, or both, to disclose the information in chambers out of the presence and hearing of all persons except the person authorized to claim the privilege and such other persons as the person authorized to claim the privilege is willing to have present. If the judge determines that the information is privileged, neither he nor any other person may ever disclose, without the consent of a person authorized to permit disclosure, what was disclosed in the course of the proceedings in chambers.

§ 916. Exclusion of privileged information where persons authorized to claim privilege are not present

(a) The presiding officer, on his own motion or on the motion of any party, shall exclude information that is subject to a claim of privilege under this division if:

(1) The person from whom the information is sought is not a person authorized to claim the privilege; and

(2) There is no party to the proceeding who is a person authorized to claim the privilege.

(b) The presiding officer may not exclude information under this section if:

(1) He is otherwise instructed by a person authorized to permit disclosure; or

(2) The proponent of the evidence establishes that there is no person authorized to claim the privilege in existence.

§ 917. Presumption that certain communications are confidential

Whenever a privilege is claimed on the ground that the matter sought to be disclosed is a communication made in confidence in the course of the lawyer-client, physician-patient, psychotherapist-patient, clergy-man-penitent, or husband-wife relationship, the communication is presumed to have been made in confidence and the opponent of the claim of privilege has the burden of proof to establish that the communication was not confidential.

§ 918. Effect of error in overruling claim of privilege

A party may predicate error on a ruling disallowing a claim of privilege only if he is the holder of the privilege, except that a party may predicate error on a ruling disallowing a claim of privilege by his spouse under Section 970 or 971.

§ 919. Admissibility where disclosure erroneously compelled; claim of privilege coercion

(a) Evidence of a statement or other disclosure of privileged information is inadmissible against a holder of the privilege if:

(1) A person authorized to claim the privilege claimed it but nevertheless disclosure erroneously was required to be made; or

(2) The presiding officer did not exclude the privileged information as required by Section 916.

(b) If a person authorized to claim the privilege claimed it, whether in the same or a prior proceeding, but nevertheless disclosure erroneously was required by the presiding officer to be made, neither the failure to refuse to disclose nor the failure to seek review of the order of the presiding officer requiring disclosure indicates consent to the disclosure or constitutes a waiver and, under these circumstances, the disclosure is one made under coercion.

§ 920. No implied repeal

Nothing in this division shall be construed to repeal by implication any other statute relating to privileges.

CHAPTER 4.　PARTICULAR PRIVILEGES

ARTICLE 1.　PRIVILEGE OF DEFENDANT IN CRIMINAL CASE

§ 930.　Privilege not to be called as a witness and not to testify

To the extent that such privilege exists under the Constitution of the United States or the State of California, a defendant in a criminal case has a privilege not to be called as a witness and not to testify.

ARTICLE 2.　PRIVILEGE AGAINST SELF–INCRIMINATION

§ 940.　Privilege against self-incrimination

To the extent that such privilege exists under the Constitution of the United States or the State of California, a person has a privilege to refuse to disclose any matter that may tend to incriminate him.

ARTICLE 3.　LAWYER–CLIENT PRIVILEGE

§ 950.　"Lawyer"

As used in this article, "lawyer" means a person authorized, or reasonably believed by the client to be authorized, to practice law in any state or nation.

§ 951.　"Client"

As used in this article, "client" means a person who, directly or through an authorized representative, consults a lawyer for the purpose of retaining the lawyer or securing legal service or advice from him in his professional capacity, and includes an incompetent (a) who himself so consults the lawyer or (b) whose guardian or conservator so consults the lawyer in behalf of the incompetent.

§ 952.　"Confidential communication between client and lawyer"

As used in this article, "confidential communication between client and lawyer" means information transmitted between a client and his lawyer in the course of that relationship and in confidence by a means which, so far as the client is aware, discloses the information to no third persons other than those who are present to further the interest of the client in the consultation or those to whom disclosure is reasonably necessary for the transmission of the information or the accomplishment of the purpose for which the lawyer is consulted, and includes a legal opinion formed and the advice given by the lawyer in the course of that relationship.

§ 953. "Holder of the privilege"

As used in this article, "holder of the privilege" means:

(a) The client when he has no guardian or conservator.

(b) A guardian or conservator of the client when the client has a guardian or conservator.

(c) The personal representative of the client if the client is dead.

(d) A successor, assign, trustee in dissolution, or any similar representative of a firm, association, organization, partnership, business trust, corporation, or public entity that is no longer in existence.

§ 954. Lawyer-client privilege

Subject to Section 912 and except as otherwise provided in this article, the client, whether or not a party, has a privilege to refuse to disclose, and to prevent another from disclosing, a confidential communication between client and lawyer if the privilege is claimed by:

(a) The holder of the privilege;

(b) A person who is authorized to claim the privilege by the holder of the privilege; or

(c) The person who was the lawyer at the time of the confidential communication, but such person may not claim the privilege if there is no holder of the privilege in existence or if he is otherwise instructed by a person authorized to permit disclosure.

The relationship of attorney and client shall exist between a law corporation as defined in Article 10 (commencing with Section 6160) of Chapter 4 of Division 3 of the Business and Professions Code and the persons to whom it renders professional services, as well as between such persons and members of the State Bar employed by such corporation to render services to such persons. The word "persons" as used in this subdivision includes partnerships, corporations, associations and other groups and entities.

§ 955. When lawyer required to claim privilege

The lawyer who received or made a communication subject to the privilege under this article shall claim the privilege whenever he is present when the communication is sought to be disclosed and is authorized to claim the privilege under subdivision (c) of Section 954.

§ 956. Exception: Crime or fraud

There is no privilege under this article if the services of the lawyer were sought or obtained to enable or aid anyone to commit or plan to commit a crime or a fraud.

§ 957. Exception: Parties claiming through deceased client

There is no privilege under this article as to a communication relevant to an issue between parties all of whom claim through a deceased client, regardless of whether the claims are by testate or intestate succession or by inter vivos transaction.

§ 958. Exception: Breach of duty arising out of lawyer-client relationship

There is no privilege under this article as to a communication relevant to an issue of breach, by the lawyer or by the client, of a duty arising out of the lawyer-client relationship.

§ 959. Exception: Lawyer as attesting witness

There is no privilege under this article as to a communication relevant to an issue concerning the intention or competence of a client executing an attested document of which the lawyer is an attesting witness, or concerning the execution or attestation of such a document.

§ 960. Exception: Intention of deceased client concerning writing affecting property interest

There is no privilege under this article as to a communication relevant to an issue concerning the intention of a client, now deceased, with respect to a deed of conveyance, will, or other writing, executed by the client, purporting to affect an interest in property.

§ 961. Exception: Validity of writing affecting property interest

There is no privilege under this article as to a communication relevant to an issue concerning the validity of a deed of conveyance, will, or other writing, executed by a client, now deceased, purporting to affect an interest in property.

§ 962. Exception: Joint clients

Where two or more clients have retained or consulted a lawyer upon a matter of common interest, none of them, nor the successor in interest of any of them, may claim a privilege under this article as to a communication made in the course of that relationship when such communication is offered in a civil proceeding between one of such clients (or his successor in interest) and another of such clients (or his successor in interest).

ARTICLE 4. PRIVILEGE NOT TO TESTIFY AGAINST SPOUSE

§ 970. Privilege not to testify against spouse

Except as otherwise provided by statute, a married person has a privilege not to testify against his spouse in any proceeding.

§ 971. Privilege not to be called as a witness against spouse

Except as otherwise provided by statute, a married person whose spouse is a party to a proceeding has a privilege not to be called as a witness by an adverse party to that proceeding without the prior express consent of the spouse having the privilege under this section unless the party calling the spouse does so in good faith without knowledge of the marital relationship.

§ 972. When privilege not applicable

A married person does not have a privilege under this article in:

(a) A proceeding brought by or on behalf of one spouse against the other spouse.

(b) A proceeding to commit or otherwise place his or her spouse or his or her spouse's property, or both, under the control of another because of the spouse's alleged mental or physical condition.

(c) A proceeding brought by or on behalf of a spouse to establish his or her competence.

(d) A proceeding under the Juvenile Court Law, Chapter 2 (commencing with Section 200) of Part 1 of Division 2 of the Welfare and Institutions Code.

(e) A criminal proceeding in which one spouse is charged with:

(1) A crime against the person or property of the other spouse or of a child, parent, relative, or cohabitant of either, whether committed before or during marriage.

(2) A crime against the person or property of a third person committed in the course of committing a crime against the person or property of the other spouse, whether committed before or during marriage.

(3) Bigamy.

(4) A crime defined by Section 270 or 270a of the Penal Code.

(f) A proceeding resulting from a criminal act which occurred prior to legal marriage of the spouses to each other regarding knowledge acquired prior to that marriage if prior to the legal marriage the witness spouse was aware that his or her spouse had been arrested for or had been formally charged with the crime or crimes about which the spouse is called to testify.

(g) A proceeding brought against the spouse by a former spouse so long as the property and debts of the marriage have not been adjudicated, or in order to establish, modify, or enforce a child, family or spousal

support obligation arising from the marriage to the former spouse; in a
proceeding brought against a spouse by the other parent in order to
establish, modify, or enforce a child support obligation for a child of a
nonmarital relationship of the spouse; or in a proceeding brought
against a spouse by the guardian of a child of that spouse in order to
establish, modify, or enforce a child support obligation of the spouse.
The married person does not have a privilege under this subdivision to
refuse to provide information relating to the issues of income, expenses,
assets, debts, and employment of either spouse, but may assert the
privilege as otherwise provided in this article if other information is
requested by the former spouse, guardian, or other parent of the child.

Any person demanding the otherwise privileged information made
available by this subdivision, who also has an obligation to support the
child for whom an order to establish, modify, or enforce child support is
sought, waives his or her marital privilege to the same extent as the
spouse as provided in this subdivision.

§ 973. Waiver of privilege

(a) Unless erroneously compelled to do so, a married person who
testifies in a proceeding to which his spouse is a party, or who testifies
against his spouse in any proceeding, does not have a privilege under
this article in the proceeding in which such testimony is given.

(b) There is no privilege under this article in a civil proceeding
brought or defended by a married person for the immediate benefit of
his spouse or of himself and his spouse.

ARTICLE 5. PRIVILEGE FOR CONFIDENTIAL MARITAL COMMUNICATIONS

§ 980. Privilege for confidential marital communications

Subject to Section 912 and except as otherwise provided in this
article, a spouse (or his guardian or conservator when he has a guardian or conservator), whether or not a party, has a privilege during the
marital relationship and afterwards to refuse to disclose, and to prevent
another from disclosing, a communication if he claims the privilege and
the communication was made in confidence between him and the other
spouse while they were husband and wife.

§ 981. Exception: Crime or fraud

There is no privilege under this article if the communication was
made, in whole or in part, to enable or aid anyone to commit or plan to
commit a crime or a fraud.

§ 982. Exception: Commitment or similar proceeding

There is no privilege under this article in a proceeding to commit
either spouse or otherwise place him or his property, or both, under the
control of another because of his alleged mental or physical condition.

§ **983. Exception: Proceeding to establish competence**

There is no privilege under this article in a proceeding brought by or on behalf of either spouse to establish his competence.

§ **984. Exception: Proceeding between spouses**

There is no privilege under this article in:

(a) A proceeding brought by or on behalf of one spouse against the other spouse.

(b) A proceeding between a surviving spouse and a person who claims through the deceased spouse, regardless of whether such claim is by testate or intestate succession or by inter vivos transaction.

§ **985. Exception: Certain criminal proceedings**

There is no privilege under this article in a criminal proceeding in which one spouse is charged with:

(a) A crime committed at any time against the person or property of the other spouse or of a child of either.

(b) A crime committed at any time against the person or property of a third person committed in the course of committing a crime against the person or property of the other spouse.

(c) Bigamy.

(d) A crime defined by Section 270 or 270a of the Penal Code.

§ **986. Exception: Juvenile court proceedings**

There is no privilege under this article in a proceeding under the Juvenile Court Law, Chapter 2 (commencing with Section 200) of Part 1 of Division 2 of the Welfare and Institutions Code.

§ **987. Exception: Communication offered by spouse who is criminal defendant**

There is no privilege under this article in a criminal proceeding in which the communication is offered in evidence by a defendant who is one of the spouses between whom the communication was made.

ARTICLE 6.   PHYSICIAN–PATIENT PRIVILEGE

§ **990. "Physician"**

As used in this article, "physician" means a person authorized, or reasonably believed by the patient to be authorized, to practice medicine in any state or nation.

§ **991. "Patient"**

As used in this article, "patient" means a person who consults a physician or submits to an examination by a physician for the purpose of securing a diagnosis or preventive palliative, or curative treatment of his physical or mental or emotional condition.

§ 992. "Confidential communication between patient and physician"

As used in this article, "confidential communication between patient and physician" means information, including information obtained by an examination of the patient, transmitted between a patient and his physician in the course of that relationship and in confidence by a means which, so far as the patient is aware, discloses the information to no third persons other than those who are present to further the interest of the patient in the consultation or those to whom disclosure is reasonably necessary for the transmission of the information or the accomplishment of the purpose for which the physician is consulted, and includes a diagnosis made and the advice given by the physician in the course of that relationship.

§ 993. "Holder of the privilege"

As used in this article, "holder of the privilege" means:

(a) The patient when he has no guardian or conservator.

(b) A guardian or conservator of the patient when the patient has a guardian or conservator.

(c) The personal representative of the patient if the patient is dead.

§ 994. Physician-patient privilege

Subject to Section 912 and except as otherwise provided in this article, the patient, whether or not a party, has a privilege to refuse to disclose, and to prevent another from disclosing, a confidential communication between patient and physician if the privilege is claimed by:

(a) The holder of the privilege;

(b) A person who is authorized to claim the privilege by the holder of the privilege; or

(c) The person who was the physician at the time of the confidential communication, but such person may not claim the privilege if there is no holder of the privilege in existence or if he is otherwise instructed by a person authorized to permit disclosure.

The relationship of a physician and patient shall exist between a medical or podiatry corporation as defined in the Medical Practice Act and the patient to whom it renders professional services, as well as between such patients and licensed physicians and surgeons employed by such corporation to render services to such patients. The word "persons" as used in this subdivision includes partnerships, corporations, associations, and other groups and entities.

§ 995. When physician required to claim privilege

The physician who received or made a communication subject to the privilege under this article shall claim the privilege whenever he is present when the communication is sought to be disclosed and is authorized to claim the privilege under subdivision (c) of Section 994.

§ 996. Exception: Patient-litigant exception

There is no privilege under this article as to a communication relevant to an issue concerning the condition of the patient if such issue has been tendered by:

(a) The patient;

(b) Any party claiming through or under the patient;

(c) Any party claiming as a beneficiary of the patient through a contract to which the patient is or was a party; or

(d) The plaintiff in an action brought under Section 376 or 377 of the Code of Civil Procedure for damages for the injury or death of the patient.

§ 997. Exception: Crime or tort

There is no privilege under this article if the services of the physician were sought or obtained to enable or aid anyone to commit or plan to commit a crime or a tort or to escape detection or apprehension after the commission of a crime or a tort.

§ 998. Exception: Criminal proceeding

There is no privilege under this article in a criminal proceeding.

§ 999. Exception: Communication relating to patient condition in proceeding to recover damages; good cause

There is no privilege under this article as to a communication relevant to an issue concerning the condition of the patient in a proceeding to recover damages on account of the conduct of the patient if good cause for disclosure of the communication is shown.

§ 1000. Exception: Parties claiming through deceased patient

There is no privilege under this article as to communication relevant to an issue between parties all of whom claim through a deceased patient, regardless of whether the claims are by testate or intestate succession or by inter vivos transaction.

§ 1001. Exception: Breach of duty arising out of physician-patient relationship

There is no privilege under this article as to a communication relevant to an issue of breach, by the physician or by the patient, of a duty arising out of the physician-patient relationship.

§ 1002. Exception: Intention of deceased patient concerning writing affecting property interest

There is no privilege under this article as to a communication relevant to an issue concerning the intention of a patient, now deceased, with respect to a deed of conveyance, will, or other writing, executed by the patient, purporting to affect an interest in property.

§ 1003. Exception: Validity of writing affecting property interest

There is no privilege under this article as to a communication relevant to an issue concerning the validity of a deed of conveyance, will, or other writing, executed by a patient, now deceased, purporting to affect an interest in property.

§ 1004. Exception: Commitment or similar proceeding

There is no privilege under this article in a proceeding to commit the patient or otherwise place him or his property, or both, under the control of another because of his alleged mental or physical condition.

§ 1005. Exception: Proceeding to establish competence

There is no privilege under this article in a proceeding brought by or on behalf of the patient to establish his competence.

§ 1006. Exception: Required report

There is no privilege under this article as to information that the physician or the patient is required to report to a public employee, or as to information required to be recorded in a public office, if such report or record is open to public inspection.

§ 1007. Exception: Proceeding to terminate right, license or privilege

There is no privilege under this article in a proceeding brought by a public entity to determine whether a right, authority, license, or privilege (including the right or privilege to be employed by the public entity or to hold a public office) should be revoked, suspended, terminated, limited, or conditioned.

ARTICLE 7. PSYCHOTHERAPIST–PATIENT PRIVILEGE

§ 1010. "Psychotherapist"

As used in this article, "psychotherapist" means:

(a) A person authorized, or reasonably believed by the patient to be authorized, to practice medicine in any state or nation who devotes, or is reasonably believed by the patient to devote, a substantial portion of his or her time to the practice of psychiatry;

(b) A person licensed as a psychologist under Chapter 6.6 (commencing with Section 2900) of Division 2 of the Business and Professions Code;

(c) A person licensed as a clinical social worker under Article 4 (commencing with Section 9040) of Chapter 17 of Division 3 of the Business and Professions Code, when he or she is engaged in applied psychotherapy of a nonmedical nature.

(d) A person who is serving as a school psychologist and holds a credential authorizing such service issued by the state.

(e) A person licensed as a marriage, family and child counselor under Chapter 13 (commencing with Section 4980) of Division 2 of the Business and Professions Code.

(f) A person registered as a psychological assistant who is under the supervision of a licensed psychologist or board certified psychiatrist as required by Section 2913 of the Business and Professions Code, or a person registered as a marriage, family, and child counselor intern who is under the supervision of a licensed marriage, family, and child counselor, a licensed clinical social worker, a licensed psychologist, or a licensed physician certified in psychiatry, as specified in Section 4980.44 of the Business and Professions Code.

(g) A person registered as an associate clinical social worker who is under the supervision of a licensed clinical social worker, a licensed psychologist, or a board certified psychiatrist as required by Section 4996.20 of the Business and Professions Code.

(h) A person exempt from the Psychology Licensing Law pursuant to subdivision (d) of Section 2909 of the Business and Professions Code who is under the supervision of a licensed psychologist or board certified psychiatrist.

(i) A psychological intern as defined in Section 2911 of the Business and Professions Code who is under the supervision of a licensed psychologist or board certified psychiatrist.

(j) A trainee, as defined in subdivision (c) of Section 4980.03 of the Business and Professions Code, who is fulfilling his or her supervised practicum required by subdivision (b) of Section 4980.40 of the Business and Professions Code and is supervised by a licensed psychologist, board certified psychiatrist, a licensed clinical social worker, or a licensed marriage, family, and child counselor.

§ 1010.5 **Privileged communication between patient and educational psychologist**

A communication between a patient and an educational psychologist, licensed under Article 5 (commencing with Section 4986) of Chapter 13 of Division 2 of the Business and Professions Code, shall be privileged to the same extent, and subject to the same limitations, as a communication between a patient and a psychotherapist described in subdivisions (c), (d), and (e) of Section 1010.

§ 1011. **"Patient"**

As used in this article, "patient" means a person who consults a psychotherapist or submits to an examination by a psychotherapist for the purpose of securing a diagnosis or preventive, palliative, or curative treatment of his mental or emotional condition or who submits to an examination of his mental or emotional condition for the purpose of scientific research on mental or emotional problems.

§ 1012. **"Confidential communication between patient and psychotherapist"**

As used in this article, "confidential communication between patient and psychotherapist" means information, including information obtained by an examination of the patient, transmitted between a

patient and his psychotherapist in the course of that relationship and
in confidence by a means which, so far as the patient is aware, discloses
the information to no third persons other than those who are present to
further the interest of the patient in the consultation, or those to whom
disclosure is reasonably necessary for the transmission of the information or the accomplishment of the purpose for which the psychotherapist is consulted, and includes a diagnosis made and the advice given by
the psychotherapist in the course of that relationship.

§ 1013. "Holder of the privilege"

As used in this article, "holder of the privilege" means:

(a) The patient when he has no guardian or conservator.

(b) A guardian or conservator of the patient when the patient has a
guardian or conservator.

(c) The personal representative of the patient if the patient is dead.

§ 1014. Psychotherapist-patient privilege; application to individuals and entities

Subject to Section 912 and except as otherwise provided in this
article, the patient, whether or not a party, has a privilege to refuse to
disclose, and to prevent another from disclosing, a confidential communication between patient and psychotherapist if the privilege is claimed
by:

(a) The holder of the privilege;

(b) A person who is authorized to claim the privilege by the holder
of the privilege; or

(c) The person who was the psychotherapist at the time of the
confidential communication, but such person may not claim the privilege if there is no holder of the privilege in existence or if he is
otherwise instructed by a person authorized to permit disclosure.

The relationship of a psychotherapist and patient shall exist between a psychological corporation as defined in Article 9 (commencing
with Section 2995) of Chapter 6.6 of Division 2 of the Business and
Professions Code a marriage, family, and child counseling corporation
as defined in Article 6 (commencing with Section 4987.5) of Chapter 13
of Division 2 of the Business and Professions Code, or a licensed clinical
social workers corporation as defined in Article 5 (commencing with
Section 9070) of Chapter 17 of Division 3 of the Business and Professions Code, and the patient to whom it renders professional services, as
well as between such patients and psychotherapists employed by such
corporations to render services to such patients. The word "persons"
as used in this subdivision includes partnerships, corporations, associations and other groups and entities.

§ 1014.5 Minor under mental health treatment or counseling

Notwithstanding any other provision of law, with respect to situations in which a minor has requested and been given mental health

treatment or counseling pursuant to Section 25.9 of the Civil Code, the professional person rendering such mental health treatment or counseling has the psychotherapist-patient privilege.

§ 1015. When psychotherapist required to claim privilege

The psychotherapist who received or made a communication subject to the privilege under this article shall claim the privilege whenever he is present when the communication is sought to be disclosed and is authorized to claim the privilege under subdivision (c) of Section 1014.

§ 1016. Exception: Patient-litigant exception

There is no privilege under this article as to a communication relevant to an issue concerning the mental or emotional condition of the patient if such issue has been tendered by:

(a) The patient;

(b) Any party claiming through or under the patient;

(c) Any party claiming as a beneficiary of the patient through a contract to which the patient is or was a party; or

(d) The plaintiff in an action brought under Section 376 or 377 of the Code of Civil Procedure for damages for the injury or death of the patient.

§ 1017. Exception: Court-appointed psychotherapist

(a) There is no privilege under this article if the psychotherapist is appointed by order of a court to examine the patient, but this exception does not apply where the psychotherapist is appointed by order of the court upon the request of the lawyer for the defendant in a criminal proceeding in order to provide the lawyer with information needed so that he may advise the defendant whether to enter or withdraw a plea based on insanity or to present a defense based on his mental or emotional condition.

(b) There is no privilege under this article if the psychotherapist is appointed by the Board of Prison Terms to examine a patient pursuant to the provisions of Article 4 (commencing with Section 2960) of Chapter 7 of Title 1 of Part 3 of the Penal Code.

§ 1018. Exception: Crime or tort

There is no privilege under this article if the services of the psychotherapist were sought or obtained to enable or aid anyone to commit or plan to commit a crime or a tort or to escape detection or apprehension after the commission of a crime or a tort.

§ 1019. Exception: Parties claiming through deceased patient

There is no privilege under this article as to a communication relevant to an issue between parties all of whom claim through a deceased patient, regardless of whether the claims are by testate or intestate succession or by inter vivos transaction.

§ 1020. Exception: Breach of duty arising out of psychotherapist-patient relationship

There is no privilege under this article as to a communication relevant to an issue of breach, by the psychotherapist or by the patient, of a duty arising out of the psychotherapist-patient relationship.

§ 1021. Exception: Intention of deceased patient concerning writing affecting property interest

There is no privilege under this article as to a communication relevant to an issue concerning the intention of a patient, now deceased, with respect to a deed of conveyance, will, or other writing, executed by the patient, purporting to affect an interest in property.

§ 1022. Exception: Validity of writing affecting property interest

There is no privilege under this article as to a communication relevant to an issue concerning the validity of a deed of conveyance, will, or other writing, executed by a patient, now deceased, purporting to affect an interest in property.

§ 1023. Exception: Proceeding to determine sanity of criminal defendant

There is no privilege under this article in a proceeding under Chapter 6 (commencing with Section 1367) of Title 10 of Part 2 of the Penal Code initiated at the request of the defendant in a criminal action to determine his sanity.

§ 1024. Exception: Patient dangerous to himself or others

There is no privilege under this article if the psychotherapist has reasonable cause to believe that the patient is in such mental or emotional condition as to be dangerous to himself or to the person or property of another and that disclosure of the communication is necessary to prevent the threatened danger.

§ 1025. Exception: Proceeding to establish competence

There is no privilege under this article in a proceeding brought by or on behalf of the patient to establish his competence.

§ 1026. Exception: Required report

There is no privilege under this article as to information that the psychotherapist or the patient is required to report to a public employee or as to information required to be recorded in a public office, if such report or record is open to public inspection.

§ 1027. Exception: Child under 16 victim of crime

There is no privilege under this article if all of the following circumstances exist:

(a) The patient is a child under the age of 16.

(b) The psychotherapist has reasonable cause to believe that the patient has been the victim of a crime and that disclosure of the communication is in the best interest of the child.

ARTICLE 8.   CLERGYMAN–PENITENT PRIVILEGES

§ 1030.   "Clergyman"

As used in this article, "clergyman" means a priest, minister, religious practitioner, or similar functionary of a church or of a religious denomination or religious organization.

§ 1031.   "Penitent"

As used in this article, "penitent" means a person who has made a penitential communication to a clergyman.

§ 1032.   "Penitential communication"

As used in this article, "penitential communication" means a communication made in confidence, in the presence of no third person so far as the penitent is aware, to a clergyman who, in the course of the discipline or practice of his church, denomination, or organization, is authorized or accustomed to hear such communications and, under the discipline or tenets of his church, denomination, or organization, has a duty to keep such communications secret.

§ 1033.   Privilege of penitent

Subject to Section 912, a penitent, whether or not a party, has a privilege to refuse to disclose, and to prevent another from disclosing, a penitential communication if he claims the privilege.

§ 1034.   Privilege of clergyman

Subject to Section 912, a clergyman, whether or not a party, has a privilege to refuse to disclose a penitential communication if he claims the privilege.

ARTICLE 8.5   SEXUAL ASSAULT VICTIM– COUNSELOR PRIVILEGE

§ 1035.   Victim

As used in this article, "victim" means a person who consults a sexual assault victim counselor for the purpose of securing advice or assistance concerning a mental, physical, or emotional condition caused by a sexual assault.

§ 1035.2   Sexual assault victim counselor

As used in this article, "sexual assault victim counselor" means any of the following:

(a) A person who is engaged in any office, hospital, institution, or center commonly known as a rape crisis center, whose primary purpose is the rendering of advice or assistance to victims of sexual assault and

who has received a certificate evidencing completion of a training
program in the counseling of sexual assault victims issued by a counseling center that meets the criteria for the award of a grant established
pursuant to Section 13837 of the Penal Code and who meets one of the
following requirements:

(1) Is a psychotherapist as defined in Section 1010; has a master's
degree in counseling or a related field; or has one year of counseling
experience, at least six months of which is in rape crisis counseling.

(2) Has 40 hours of training as described below and is supervised
by an individual who qualifies as a counselor under paragraph (1). The
training, supervised by a person qualified under paragraph (1), shall
include, but not be limited to, the following areas: law, medicine,
societal attitudes, crisis intervention and counseling techniques, role
playing, referral services, and sexuality.

(b) A person who is employed by any organization providing the
programs specified in Section 13835.2 of the Penal Code, whether
financially compensated or not, for the purpose of counseling and
assisting sexual assault victims, and who meets one of the following
requirements:

(1) Is a psychotherapist as defined in Section 1010; has a master's
degree in counseling or a related field; or has one year of counseling
experience, at least six months of which is in rape assault counseling.

(2) Has the minimum training for sexual assault counseling required by guidelines established by the employing agency pursuant to
subdivision (c) of Section 13835.10 of the Penal Code, and is supervised
by an individual who qualifies as a counselor under paragraph (1). The
training, supervised by a person qualified under paragraph (1), shall
include, but not be limited to, the following areas: law, victimology,
counseling techniques, client and system advocacy, and referral services.

§ 1035.4. Confidential communication between the sexual assault coun-
selor and the victim; disclosure

As used in this article, "confidential communication between the
sexual assault counselor and the victim" means information transmitted between the victim and the sexual assault counselor in the course of
their relationship and in confidence by a means which, so far as the
victim is aware, discloses the information to no third persons other
than those who are present to further the interests of the victim in the
consultation or those to whom disclosures are reasonably necessary for
the transmission of the information or an accomplishment of the
purposes for which the sexual assault counselor is consulted. The term
includes all information regarding the facts and circumstances involving the alleged sexual assault and also includes all information regarding the victim's prior or subsequent sexual conduct, and opinions
regarding the victim's sexual conduct or reputation in sexual matters.

The court may compel disclosure of information received by the
sexual assault counselor which constitutes relevant evidence of the

facts and circumstances involving an alleged sexual assault about which the victim is complaining and which is the subject of a criminal proceeding if the court determines that the probative value outweighs the effect on the victim, the treatment relationship, and the treatment services if disclosure is compelled. The court may also compel disclosure in proceedings related to child abuse if the court determines the probative value outweighs the effect on the victim, the treatment relationship, and the treatment services if disclosure is compelled.

When a court is ruling on a claim of privilege under this article, the court may require the person from whom disclosure is sought or the person authorized to claim the privilege, or both, to disclose the information in chambers out of the presence and hearing of all persons except the person authorized to claim the privilege and such other persons as the person authorized to claim the privilege is willing to have present. If the judge determines that the information is privileged and must not be disclosed, neither he or she nor any other person may ever disclose, without the consent of a person authorized to permit disclosure, what was disclosed in the course of the proceedings in chambers.

If the court determines certain information shall be disclosed, the court shall so order and inform the defendant. If the court finds there is a reasonable likelihood that particular information is subject to disclosure pursuant to the balancing test provided in this section, the following procedure shall be followed:

(1) The court shall inform the defendant of the nature of the information which may be subject to disclosure.

(2) The court shall order a hearing out of the presence of the jury, if any, and at the hearing allow the questioning of the sexual assault counselor regarding the information which the court has determined may be subject to disclosure.

(3) At the conclusion of the hearing, the court shall rule which items of information, if any, shall be disclosed. The court may make an order stating what evidence may be introduced by the defendant and the nature of questions to be permitted. The defendant may then offer evidence pursuant to the order of the court. Admission of evidence concerning the sexual conduct of the complaining witness is subject to Sections 352, 782, and 1103.

§ **1035.6 Holder of the privilege**

As used in this article, "holder of the privilege" means:

(a) The victim when such person has no guardian or conservator.

(b) A guardian or conservator of the victim when the victim has a guardian or conservator.

(c) The personal representative of the victim if the victim is dead.

§ 1035.8 Refusal and prevention of disclosure by victim

A victim of a sexual assault, whether or not a party, has a privilege to refuse to disclose, and to prevent another from disclosing, a confidential communication between the victim and a sexual assault victim counselor if the privilege is claimed by:

(a) The holder of the privilege;

(b) A person who is authorized to claim the privilege by the holder of the privilege; or

(c) The person who was the sexual assault victim counselor at the time of the confidential communication, but such person may not claim the privilege if there is no holder of the privilege in existence or if he is otherwise instructed by a person authorized to permit disclosure.

§ 1036. Claim of privilege by sexual assault victim counselor

The sexual assault victim counselor who received or made a communication subject to the privilege under this article shall claim the privilege whenever he is present when the communication is sought to be disclosed and is authorized to claim the privilege under subdivision (c) of Section 1035.8.

§ 1036.2 Sexual assault

As used in this article, "sexual assault" includes:

(a) Rape, as defined in Section 261 of the Penal Code;

(b) Unlawful sexual intercourse, as defined in Section 261.5 of the Penal Code;

(c) Rape in concert with force and violence, as defined in Section 264.1 of the Penal Code;

(d) Rape of a spouse, as defined in Section 262 of the Penal Code.

(e) Sodomy, as defined in Section 286 of the Penal Code, except a violation of subdivision (e) of that section.

(f) A violation of Section 288 of the Penal Code.

(g) Oral copulation, as defined in Section 288a of the Penal Code, except a violation of subdivision (e) of that section.

(h) Penetration of the genital or anal openings of another person with a foreign object, substance, instrument, or device, as specified in Section 289 of the Penal Code.

(i) Annoying or molesting a child under 18, as defined in Section 647a of the Penal Code.

(j) Any attempt to commit any of the above acts.

ARTICLE 8.7 DOMESTIC VIOLENCE VICTIM–COUNSELOR PRIVILEGE

§ 1037. Victim

As used in this article, "victim" means any person who suffers domestic violence, as defined in Section 1037.7.

§ 1037.1 Domestic violence counselor; qualifications

As used in this article "domestic violence counselor" means any of the following:

(a) A person who is employed by any organization providing the programs specified in Section 18294 of the Welfare and Institutions Code, whether financially compensated or not, for the purpose of rendering advice or assistance to victims of domestic violence, who has received specialized training in the counseling of domestic violence victims, and who meets one of the following requirements:

(1) Has a master's degree in counseling or a related field; or has one year of counseling experience, at least six months of which is in the counseling of domestic violence victims.

(2) Has at least 40 hours of training as specified in this paragraph and is supervised by an individual who qualifies as a counselor under paragraph (1); or is a psychotherapist, as defined in Section 1010. The training, supervised by a person qualified under paragraph (1), shall include, but need not be limited to, the following areas: history of domestic violence, civil and criminal law as it relates to domestic violence, societal attitudes towards domestic violence, peer counseling techniques, housing, public assistance and other financial resources available to meet the financial needs of domestic violence victims, and referral services available to domestic violence victims.

(b) A person who is employed by any organization providing the programs specified in Section 13835.2 of the Penal Code, whether financially compensated or not, for the purpose of counseling and assisting victims of domestic violence, and who meets one of the following requirements:

(1) Is a psychotherapist as defined in Section 1010; has a master's degree in counseling or a related field; or has one year of counseling experience, at least six months of which is in counseling victims of domestic violence.

(2) Has the minimum training for counseling victims of domestic violence required by guidelines established by the employing agency pursuant to subdivision (c) of Section 13835.10 of the Penal Code, and is supervised by an individual who qualifies as a counselor under paragraph (1). The training, supervised by a person qualified under paragraph (1), shall include, but not be limited to, the following areas: law, victimology, counseling techniques, client and system advocacy, and referral services.

§ 1037.2 Confidential communication; compulsion of disclosure by court; claim of privilege

As used in this article, "confidential communication" means information transmitted between the victim and the counselor in the course of their relationship and in confidence by a means which, so far as the victim is aware, discloses the information to no third persons other than those who are present to further the interests of the victim in the

consultation or those to whom disclosures are reasonably necessary for
the transmission of the information or an accomplishment of the
purposes for which the domestic violence counselor is consulted. It
includes all information regarding the facts and circumstances involving all incidences of domestic violence, as well as all information about
the children of the victim or abuser and the relationship of the victim
with the abuser.

The court may compel disclosure of information received by a
domestic violence counselor which constitutes relevant evidence of the
facts and circumstances involving a crime allegedly perpetrated against
the victim or another household member and which is the subject of a
criminal proceeding, if the court determines that the probative value of
the information outweighs the effect of disclosure of the information on
the victim, the counseling relationship, and the counseling services.
The court may compel disclosure if the victim is either dead or not the
complaining witness in a criminal action against the perpetrator. The
court may also compel disclosure in proceedings related to child abuse
if the court determines that the probative value of the evidence outweighs the effect of the disclosure on the victim, the counseling relationship, and the counseling services.

When a court rules on a claim of privilege under this article, it
may require the person from whom disclosure is sought or the person
authorized to claim the privilege, or both, to disclose the information in
chambers out of the presence and hearing of all persons except the
person authorized to claim the privilege and such other persons as the
person authorized to claim the privilege consents to have present. If
the judge determines that the information is privileged and shall not be
disclosed, neither he nor she nor any other person may disclose,
without the consent of a person authorized to permit disclosure, any
information disclosed in the course of the proceedings in chambers.

If the court determines that information shall be disclosed, the
court shall so order and inform the defendant in the criminal action. If
the court finds there is a reasonable likelihood that any information is
subject to disclosure pursuant to the balancing test provided in this
section, the procedure specified in subdivisions (1), (2), and (3) of Section
1035.4 shall be followed.

§ 1037.3 Child abuse; reporting

Nothing in this article shall be construed to limit any obligation to
report instances of child abuse as required by Section 11166 of the
Penal Code.

§ 1037.4 Holder of the privilege

As used in this article, "holder of the privilege" means:

(a) The victim when he or she has no guardian or conservator.

(b) A guardian or conservator of the victim when the victim has a
guardian or conservator.

§ 1037.5 Privilege of refusal to disclose communication; claimants

A victim of domestic violence, whether or not a party to the action, has a privilege to refuse to disclose, and to prevent another from disclosing, a confidential communication between the victim and a domestic violence counselor if the privilege is claimed by any of the following persons:

(a) The holder of the privilege.

(b) A person who is authorized to claim the privilege by the holder of the privilege.

(c) The person who was the domestic violence counselor at the time of the confidential communication. However, that person may not claim the privilege if there is no holder of the privilege in existence or if he or she is otherwise instructed by a person authorized to permit disclosure.

§ 1037.6 Claim of privilege by counselor

The domestic violence counselor who received or made a communication subject to the privilege granted by this article shall claim the privilege whenever he or she is present when the communication is sought to be disclosed and he or she is authorized to claim the privilege under subdivision (c) of Section 1037.5.

§ 1037.7 Domestic violence; abuse; family or household member; other persons

(a) "Domestic violence" is abuse perpetrated against a family or household member, or against a person as provided in subdivisions (d) and (e).

(b) "Abuse" means intentionally or recklessly causing or attempting to cause bodily injury, or placing another person in reasonable apprehension of imminent serious bodily injury to herself, himself, or another.

(c) "Family or household member" means a spouse, former spouse, parent, child, any other adult person related by consanguinity or affinity within the second degree, or any other person who regularly resides in the household, or who within the last six months regularly resided in the household.

(d) A person who is the parent of a minor child where (1) there exists the presumption that the male parent is the father of any minor child of the female parent pursuant to the Uniform Parentage Act, Part 7 (commencing with Section 7000) of Division 4 of the Civil Code, and (2) one parent has perpetrated abuse as defined in subdivision (b) against the other parent.

(e) A person who is in, or has been in, a dating, courtship, or engagement relationship and abuse as defined in subdivision (b) has been perpetrated against that person by the person with whom they have had a dating, courtship, or engagement relationship.

ARTICLE 9.   OFFICIAL INFORMATION AND IDENTITY OF INFORMER

§ 1040.   Privilege for official information

(a) As used in this section, "official information" means information acquired in confidence by a public employee in the course of his or her duty and not open, or officially disclosed, to the public prior to the time the claim of privilege is made.

(b) A public entity has a privilege to refuse to disclose official information, and to prevent another from disclosing official information, if the privilege is claimed by a person authorized by the public entity to do so and:

(1) Disclosure is forbidden by an act of the Congress of the United States or a statute of this state; or

(2) Disclosure of the information is against the public interest because there is a necessity for preserving the confidentiality of the information that outweighs the necessity for disclosure in the interest of justice; but no privilege may be claimed under this paragraph if any person authorized to do so has consented that the information be disclosed in the proceeding. In determining whether disclosure of the information is against the public interest, the interest of the public entity as a party in the outcome of the proceeding may not be considered.

(c) Notwithstanding any other provision of law, the Employment Development Department shall disclose to law enforcement agencies, in accordance with the provisions of subdivision (k) of Section 1095 and subdivision (b) of Section 2714 of the Unemployment Insurance Code, information in its possession relating to any person if an arrest warrant has been issued for the person for commission of a felony.

§ 1041.   Privilege for identity of informer

(a) Except as provided in this section, a public entity has a privilege to refuse to disclose the identity of a person who has furnished information as provided in subdivision (b) purporting to disclose a violation of a law of the United States or of this state or of a public entity in this state, and to prevent another from disclosing such identity, if the privilege is claimed by a person authorized by the public entity to do so and:

(1) Disclosure is forbidden by an act of the Congress of the United States or a statute of this state; or

(2) Disclosure of the identity of the informer is against the public interest because there is a necessity for preserving the confidentiality of his identity that outweighs the necessity for disclosure in the interest of justice; but no privilege may be claimed under this paragraph if any person authorized to do so has consented that the identity of the informer be disclosed in the proceeding. In determining whether disclosure of the identity of the informer is against the public interest,

the interest of the public entity as a party in the outcome of the proceeding may not be considered.

(b) This section applies only if the information is furnished in confidence by the informer to:

(1) A law enforcement officer;

(2) A representative of an administrative agency charged with the administration or enforcement of the law alleged to be violated; or

(3) Any person for the purpose of transmittal to a person listed in paragraph (1) or (2).

(c) There is no privilege under this section to prevent the informer from disclosing his identity.

§ 1042. Adverse order or finding in certain cases

(a) Except where disclosure is forbidden by an act of the Congress of the United States, if a claim of privilege under this article by the state or a public entity in this state is sustained in a criminal proceeding, the presiding officer shall make such order or finding of fact adverse to the public entity bringing the proceeding as is required by law upon any issue in the proceeding to which the privileged information is material.

(b) Notwithstanding subdivision (a), where a search is made pursuant to a warrant valid on its face, the public entity bringing a criminal proceeding is not required to reveal to the defendant official information or the identity of an informer in order to establish the legality of the search or the admissibility of any evidence obtained as a result of it.

(c) Notwithstanding subdivision (a), in any preliminary hearing, criminal trial, or other criminal proceeding, any otherwise admissible evidence of information communicated to a peace officer by a confidential informant, who is not a material witness to the guilt or innocence of the accused of the offense charged, is admissible on the issue of reasonable cause to make an arrest or search without requiring that the name or identity of the informant be disclosed if the judge or magistrate is satisfied, based upon evidence produced in open court, out of the presence of the jury, that such information was received from a reliable informant and in his discretion does not require such disclosure.

(d) When, in any such criminal proceeding, a party demands disclosure of the identity of the informant on the ground the informant is a material witness on the issue of guilt, the court shall conduct a hearing at which all parties may present evidence on the issue of disclosure. Such hearing shall be conducted outside the presence of the jury, if any. During the hearing, if the privilege provided for in Section 1041 is claimed by a person authorized to do so or if a person who is authorized to claim such privilege refuses to answer any question on the ground that the answer would tend to disclose the identity of the informant, the prosecuting attorney may request that the court hold an in camera hearing. If such a request is made, the court shall hold such a hearing outside the presence of the defendant and his counsel. At the in camera hearing, the prosecution may offer evidence which would tend to disclose or which discloses the identity of the informant to aid the court in its determination whether there is a reasonable possibility that nondisclosure might deprive the defendant of a fair trial. A reporter shall be present at the in camera hearing. Any transcription of the proceedings at the in camera hearing, as well as any physical evidence presented at the hearing, shall be ordered sealed by the court, and only a court may have access to its contents. The court shall not order disclosure, nor strike the testimony of the witness who invokes the privilege, nor dismiss the criminal proceeding, if the party offering the witness refuses to disclose the identity of the informant, unless, based upon the evidence presented at the hearing held in the presence of the defendant and his counsel and the evidence presented at the in camera hearing, the court concludes that there is a reasonable possibility that nondisclosure might deprive the defendant of a fair trial.

§ 1043. Peace officer personnel records; discovery or disclosure; procedure

(a) In any case in which discovery or disclosure is sought of peace officer personnel records or records maintained pursuant to Section 832.5 of the Penal Code or information from the records, the party seeking the discovery or disclosure shall file a written motion with the appropriate court or administrative body upon 10 days' written notice to the governmental agency which has custody and control of the records. The written notice shall be given at the times prescribed by subdivision (b) of section 1005 of the Code of Civil Procedure. Upon receipt of the notice the governmental agency served shall immediately notify the individual whose records are sought.

(b) The motion shall include all of the following:

(1) Identification of the proceeding in which discovery or disclosure is sought, the party seeking discovery or disclosure, the peace officer whose records are sought, the governmental agency which has custody and control of the records, and the time and place at which the motion for discovery or disclosure shall be heard;

(2) A description of the type of records or information sought; and

(3) Affidavits showing good cause for the discovery or disclosure sought, setting forth the materiality thereof to the subject matter involved in the pending litigation and stating upon reasonable belief that the governmental agency identified has the records or information from the records.

(c) No hearing upon a motion for discovery or disclosure shall be held without full compliance with the notice provisions of this section except upon a showing by the moving party of good cause for noncompliance, or upon a waiver of such hearing by the governmental agency identified as having the records.

§ 1044. Medical or psychological history records; right of access

Nothing in this article shall be construed to affect the right of access to records of medical or psychological history where such access would otherwise be available under Section 996 or 1016.

§ 1045. Peace officers; access to records of complaints or discipline imposed; relevancy; protective orders

(a) Nothing in this article shall be construed to affect the right of access to records of complaints, or investigations of complaints, or discipline imposed as a result of such investigations, concerning an event or transaction in which the peace officer participated, or which he perceived, and pertaining to the manner in which he performed his duties, provided that such information is relevant to the subject matter involved in the pending litigation.

(b) In determining relevance the court shall examine the information in chambers in conformity with Section 915, and shall exclude from disclosure:

(1) Information consisting of complaints concerning conduct occurring more than five years before the event or transaction which is the subject of the litigation in aid of which discovery or disclosure is sought.

(2) In any criminal proceeding the conclusions of any officer investigating a complaint filed pursuant to Section 832.5 of the Penal Code.

(3) Facts sought to be disclosed which are so remote as to make disclosure of little or no practical benefit.

(c) In determining relevance where the issue in litigation concerns the policies or pattern of conduct of the employing agency, the court shall consider whether the information sought may be obtained from order records maintained by the employing agency in the regular course of agency business which would not necessitate the disclosure of individual personnel records.

(d) Upon motion seasonably made by the governmental agency which has custody or control of the records to be examined or by the officer whose records are sought, and upon good cause showing the necessity thereof, the court may make any order which justice requires to protect the officer or agency from unnecessary annoyance, embarrassment or oppression.

(e) The court shall, in any case or proceeding permitting the disclosure or discovery of any peace officer records requested pursuant to Section 1043, order that the records disclosed or discovered may not be used for any purpose other than a court proceeding pursuant to applicable law.

§ 1046. Allegation of excessive force by peace officer during arrest; police arrest report

In any case, otherwise authorized by law, in which the party seeking disclosure is alleging excessive force by a peace officer in connection with the arrest of that party, the motion shall include a copy of the police report setting forth the circumstances under which the party was stopped and arrested.

§ 1047. Arrests; records of peace officers; exemption from disclosure

Records of peace officers, including supervisorial peace officers, who either were not present during the arrest or had no contact with the party seeking disclosure from the time of the arrest until the time of booking, shall not be subject to disclosure.

ARTICLE 10. POLITICAL VOTE

§ 1050. Privilege to protect secrecy of vote

If he claims the privilege, a person has a privilege to refuse to disclose the tenor of his vote at a public election where the voting is by secret ballot unless he voted illegally or he previously made an unprivileged disclosure of the tenor of his vote. (Stats.1965, c. 299, § 2.)

ARTICLE 11. TRADE SECRET

§ 1060. Privilege to protect trade secret

If he or his agent or employee claims the privilege, the owner of a trade secret has a privilege to refuse to disclose the secret, and to prevent another from disclosing it, if the allowance of the privilege will not tend to conceal fraud or otherwise work injustice.

§ 1061. Procedure for assertion of trade secret privilege

(a) For purposes of this section, and Sections 1062 and 1063:

(1) "Trade secret" means "trade secret," as defined in subdivision (d) of Section 3426.1 of the Civil Code, or paragraph (9) of subdivision (a) of Section 499c of the Penal Code.

(2) "Article" means "article," as defined in paragraph (2) of subdivision (a) of Section 499c of the Penal Code.

(b) In addition to Section 1062, the following procedure shall apply whenever the owner of a trade secret wishes to assert his or her trade secret privilege, as provided in Section 1060, during a criminal proceeding:

(1) The owner of the trade secret shall file a motion for a protective order, or the People may file the motion on the owner's behalf and with the owner's permission. The motion shall include an affidavit based upon personal knowledge listing the affiant's qualifications to give an opinion concerning the trade secret at issue, identifying, without revealing, the alleged trade secret and articles which disclose the secret, and presenting evidence that the secret qualifies as a trade secret under either subdivision (d) of Section 3426.1 of the Civil Code or paragraph (9) of subdivision (a) of Section 499c of the Penal Code. The motion and affidavit shall be served on all parties in the proceeding.

(2) Any party in the proceeding may oppose the request for the protective order by submitting affidavits based upon the affiant's personal knowledge. The affidavits shall be filed under seal, but shall be provided to the owner of the trade secret and to all parties in the proceeding. Neither the owner of the trade secret nor any party in the

proceeding may disclose the affidavit to persons other than to counsel of record without prior court approval.

(3) The movant shall, by a preponderance of the evidence, show that the issuance of a protective order is proper. The court may rule on the request without holding an evidentiary hearing. However, in its discretion, the court may choose to hold an in camera evidentiary hearing concerning disputed articles with only the owner of the trade secret, the People's representative, the defendant, and defendant's counsel present. If the court holds such a hearing, the parties' right to examine witnesses shall not be used to obtain discovery, but shall be directed solely toward the question of whether the alleged trade secret qualifies for protection.

(4) If the court finds that a trade secret may be disclosed during any criminal proceeding unless a protective order is issued and that the issuance of a protective order would not conceal a fraud or work an injustice, the court shall issue a protective order limiting the use and dissemination of the trade secret, including, but not limited to, articles disclosing that secret. The protective order may, in the court's discretion, include the following provisions:

(A) That the trade secret may be disseminated only to counsel for the parties, including their associate attorneys, paralegals, and investigators, and to law enforcement officials or clerical officials.

(B) That the defendant may view the secret only in the presence of his or her counsel, or if not in the presence of his or her counsel, at counsel's offices.

(C) That any party seeking to show the trade secret, or articles containing the trade secret, to any person not designated by the protective order shall first obtain court approval to do so:

(i) The court may require that the person receiving the trade secret do so only in the presence of counsel for the party requesting approval.

(ii) The court may require the person receiving the trade secret to sign a copy of the protective order and to agree to be bound by its terms. The order may include a provision recognizing the owner of the trade secret to be a third-party beneficiary of that agreement.

(iii) The court may require a party seeking disclosure to an expert to provide that expert's name, employment history, and any other relevant information to the court for examination. The court shall accept that information under seal, and the information shall not be disclosed by any court except upon termination of the action and upon a showing of good cause to believe the secret has been disseminated by a court-approved expert. The court shall evaluate the expert and determine whether the expert poses a discernible risk of disclosure. The court shall withhold approval if the expert's economic interests place the expert in a competitive position with the victim, unless no other experts are available. The court may interview the expert in camera in aid of its ruling. If the court rejects the expert, it shall state its reasons for doing so on the record and a transcript of those reasons shall be prepared and sealed.

(D) That no articles disclosing the trade secret shall be filed or otherwise made a part of the court record available to the public without approval of the court and prior notice to the owner of the secret. The owner of the secret may give either party permission to accept the notice on the owner's behalf.

(E) Other orders as the court deems necessary to protect the integrity of the trade secret.

(c) A ruling granting or denying a motion for a protective order filed pursuant to subdivision (b) shall not be construed as a determination that the alleged trade secret is or is not a trade secret as defined by subdivision (d) of Section 3426.1 of the Civil Code or paragraph (9) of subdivision (a) of Section 499c of the Penal Code. Such a ruling shall not have any effect on any civil litigation.

(d) A protective order entered by a municipal court pursuant to this section shall remain in effect in a superior court unless that order is amended or vacated for good cause shown.

(e) This section shall have prospective effect only and shall not operate to invalidate previously entered protective orders.

§ 1062. Exclusion of public from criminal proceeding; motion; contents; hearing; determination

(a) Notwithstanding any other provision of law, in a criminal case, the court, upon motion of the owner of a trade secret, or upon motion by the People with the consent of the owner, may exclude the public from any portion of a criminal proceeding where the proponent of closure has demonstrated a substantial probability that the trade secret would otherwise be disclosed to the public during that proceeding and a substantial probability that the disclosure would cause serious harm to the owner of the secret, and where the court finds that there is no overriding public interest in an open proceeding. No evidence, however, shall be excluded during a criminal proceeding pursuant to this section if it would conceal a fraud, work an injustice, or deprive the People or the defendant of a fair trial.

(b) The motion made pursuant to subdivision (a) shall identify, without revealing, the trade secrets which would otherwise be disclosed to the public. A showing made pursuant to subdivision (a) shall be made during an in camera hearing with only the owner of the trade secret, the People's representative, the defendant, and defendant's counsel present. A court reporter shall be present during the hearing. Any transcription of the proceedings at the in camera hearing, as well as any articles presented at that hearing, shall be ordered sealed by the court and only a court may allow access to its contents upon a showing of good cause. The court, in ruling upon the motion made pursuant to subdivision (a), may consider testimony presented or affidavits filed in any proceeding held in that action.

(c) If, after the in camera hearing described in subdivision (b), the court determines that exclusion of trade secret information from the public is appropriate, the court shall close only that portion of the criminal proceeding necessary to prevent disclosure of the trade secret. Before granting the motion, however, the court shall find and state for the record that the moving party has met its burden pursuant to subdivision (b), and that the closure of that portion of the proceeding will not deprive the People or the defendant of a fair trial.

(d) The owner of the trade secret, the People, or the defendant may seek relief from a ruling denying or granting closure by petitioning a higher court for extraordinary relief.

(e) Whenever the court closes a portion of a criminal proceeding pursuant to this section, a transcript of that closed proceeding shall be made available to the public as soon as practicable. The court shall redact any information qualifying as a trade secret before making that transcript available.

(f) The court, subject to Section 867 of the Penal Code, may allow witnesses who are bound by a protective order entered in the criminal proceeding protecting trade secrets, pursuant to Section 1061, to remain within the courtroom during the closed portion of the proceeding.

§ 1063. Sealing of articles protected by protective order; procedures

The following provisions shall govern requests to seal articles which are protected by a protective order entered pursuant to Evidence Code Section 1060 or 1061:

(a) The People shall request sealing of articles reasonably expected to be filed or admitted into evidence as follows:

(1) No less than 10 court days before trial, and no less than five court days before any other criminal proceeding, the People shall file with the court a list of all articles which the People reasonably expect to file with the court, or admit into evidence, under seal at that proceeding. That list shall be available to the public. The People may be relieved from providing timely notice upon showing that exigent circumstances prevent that notice.

(2) The court shall not allow the listed articles to be filed, admitted into evidence, or in any way made a part of the court record otherwise open to the public before holding a hearing to consider any objections to the People's request to seal the articles. The court at that hearing shall allow those objecting to the sealing to state their objections.

(3) After hearing any objections to sealing, the court shall conduct an in camera hearing with only the owner of the trade secret contained within those articles, the People's representative, defendant, and defendant's counsel present. The court shall review the articles sought to be sealed, evaluate objections to sealing, and determine whether the People have satisfied the constitutional standards governing public access to articles which are part of the judicial record. The court may consider testimony presented or affidavits filed in any proceeding held in that

action. The People, defendant, and the owner of the trade secret may file
affidavits based on the affiant's personal knowledge to be considered at
that hearing. Those affidavits are to be sealed and not released to the
public, but shall be made available to the parties. The court may rule on
the request to seal without taking testimony. If the court takes testimony, examination of witnesses shall not be used to obtain discovery, but
shall be directed solely toward whether sealing is appropriate.

(4) If the court finds that the movant has satisfied appropriate
constitutional standards with respect to sealing particular articles, the
court shall seal those articles if and when they are filed, admitted into
evidence, or in any way made a part of the court record otherwise open
to the public. The articles shall not be unsealed absent an order of a
court upon a showing of good cause. Failure to examine the court file
for notice of a request to seal shall not constitute good cause to consider
objections to sealing.

(b) The following procedure shall apply to other articles made a
part of the court record:

(1) Where any articles protected by a protective order entered
pursuant to Section 1060 or 1061 are filed, admitted into evidence, or in
any way made a part of the court record in such a way as to be
otherwise open to the public, the People, a defendant, or the owner of a
trade secret contained within those articles may request the court to
seal those articles.

(2) The request to seal shall be made by noticed motion filed with
the court. It may also be made orally in court at the time the articles
are made a part of the court record. Where the request is made orally,
the movant must file within 24 hours a written description of that
request, including a list of the articles which are the subject of that
request. These motions and lists shall be available to the public.

(3) The court shall promptly conduct hearings as provided in
paragraphs (2), (3), and (4) of subdivision (a). The court shall, pending
the hearings, seal those articles which are the subject of the request.
Where a request to seal is made orally, the court may conduct hearings
at the time the articles are made a part of the court record, but shall
reconsider its ruling in light of additional objections made by objectors
within two court days after the written record of the request to seal is
made available to the public.

(4) Any articles sealed pursuant to these hearings shall not be
unsealed absent an order of a court upon a showing of good cause.
Failure to examine the court file for notice of a request to seal shall not
constitute good cause to consider objections to sealing.

CHAPTER 5. IMMUNITY OF NEWSMAN FROM CITATION FOR CONTEMPT

§ 1070. Newsmen's refusal to disclose news source

(a) A publisher, editor, reporter, or other person connected with or
employed upon a newspaper, magazine, or other periodical publication,

or by a press association or wire service, or any person who has been so connected or employed, cannot be adjudged in contempt by a judicial, legislative, administrative body, or any other body having the power to issue subpoenas, for refusing to disclose, in any proceeding as defined in Section 901, the source of any information procured while so connected or employed for publication in a newspaper, magazine or other periodical publication, or for refusing to disclose any unpublished information obtained or prepared in gathering, receiving or processing of information for communication to the public.

(b) Nor can a radio or television news reporter or other person connected with or employed by a radio or television station, or any person who has been so connected or employed, be so adjudged in contempt for refusing to disclose the source of any information procured while so connected or employed for news or news commentary purposes on radio or television, or for refusing to disclose any unpublished information obtained or prepared in gathering, receiving or processing of information for communication to the public.

(c) As used in this section, "unpublished information" includes information not disseminated to the public by the person from whom disclosure is sought, whether or not related information has been disseminated and includes, but is not limited to, all notes, outtakes, photographs, tapes or other data of whatever sort not itself disseminated to the public through a medium of communication, whether or not published information based upon or related to such material has been disseminated.

Division 9

EVIDENCE AFFECTED OR EXCLUDED BY EXTRINSIC POLICIES

CHAPTER 1. EVIDENCE OF CHARACTER, HABIT OR CUSTOM

§ 1100. **Manner of proof of character**

Except as otherwise provided by statute, any otherwise admissible evidence (including evidence in the form of an opinion, evidence of reputation, and evidence of specific instances of such person's conduct) is admissible to prove a person's character or a trait of his character.

§ 1101. **Evidence of character to prove conduct**

(a) Except as provided in this section and in Sections 1102 and 1103, evidence of a person's character or a trait of his or her character (whether in the form of an opinion, evidence of reputation, or evidence

of specific instances of his or her conduct) is <u>inadmissible when offered</u> 1
<u>to prove his or her conduct on a specified occasion.</u> 2

(b) Nothing in this section prohibits the admission of evidence that 3
a person committed a crime, civil wrong, or other act when relevant to 4
prove some fact (such as motive, opportunity, intent, preparation, plan, 5
knowledge, identity, absence of mistake or accident, or whether a 6
defendant in a prosecution for an unlawful sexual act or attempted 7
unlawful sexual act did not reasonably and in good faith believe that 8
the victim consented) other than his or her disposition to commit such 9
an act. 10

(c) Nothing in this section affects the admissibility of evidence 11
offered to support or attack the credibility of a witness. 12
13

§ 1102. **Opinion and reputation evidence of character of criminal defen-** 14
dant to prove conduct 15

In a criminal action, evidence of the defendant's character or a 16
trait of his character in the form of an opinion or evidence of his 17
reputation is not made inadmissible by Section 1101 if such evidence is: 18
19

(a) Offered by the defendant to prove his conduct in conformity 20
with such character or trait of character. 21

(b) Offered by the prosecution to rebut evidence adduced by the 22
defendant under subdivision (a). 23
24

§ 1103. **Evidence of character of victim of crime to prove conduct;** 25
evidence of complaining witness' sexual conduct in rape pros- 26
ecution 27

(a) In a criminal action, evidence of the character or a trait of 28
character (in the form of an opinion, evidence of reputation, or evidence 29
of specific instances of conduct) of the victim of the crime for which the 30
defendant is being prosecuted is not made inadmissible by Section 1101 31
if such evidence is: 32

(1) Offered by the defendant to prove conduct of the victim in 33
conformity with such character or trait of character. 34

(2) Offered by the prosecution to rebut evidence adduced by the 35
defendant under paragraph (1). 36
37

1103.   (a) In a criminal action, evidence of the character or a trait 38
of character (in the form of an opinion evidence of reputation, or 39
evidence of specific instances of conduct) of the victim of the crime for 40
which the defendant is being prosecuted is not made inadmissible by 41
Section 1101 if the evidence is: 42

(1) Offered by the defendant to prove conduct of the victim in 43
conformity with the character or trait of character. 44

(2) Offered by the prosecution to rebut evidence adduced by the 45
defendant under paragraph (1). 46

(b) In a criminal action, evidence of the defendant's character for 47
violence or trait of character for violence (in the form of an opinion, 48
evidence of reputation, or evidence of specific instances of conduct) is 49
50

not made inadmissible by Section 1101 if the evidence is offered by the prosecution to prove conduct of the defendant in conformity with the character or trait of character and is offered after evidence that the victim had a character for violence or a trait of character tending to show violence has been adduced by the defendant under paragraph (1) of subdivision (a).

(c)(1) Notwithstanding any other provision of this code to the contrary, and except as provided in this subdivision, in any prosecution under Section 261 or 264.1 of the Penal Code, or under Section 286, 288a, or 289 of the Penal Code, or for assault with intent to commit, attempt to commit, or conspiracy to commit a crime defined in any such section, except where the crime is alleged to have occurred in a local detention facility, as defined in Section 6031.4, or in a state prison, as defined in Section 4504, opinion evidence, reputation evidence, and evidence of specific instances of the complaining witness' sexual conduct, or any of such evidence, is not admissible by the defendant in order to prove consent by the complaining witness.

(2) Paragraph (1) shall not be applicable to evidence of the complaining witness' sexual conduct with the defendant.

(3) If the prosecutor introduces evidence, including testimony of a witness, or the complaining witness as a witness gives testimony, and that evidence or testimony relates to the complaining witness' sexual conduct, the defendant may cross-examine the witness who gives the testimony and offer relevant evidence limited specifically to the rebuttal of the evidence introduced by the prosecutor or given by the complaining witness.

(4) Nothing in this subdivision shall be construed to make inadmissible any evidence offered to attack the credibility of the complaining witness as provided in Section 782.

(5) As used in this section, "complaining witness" means the alleged victim of the crime charged, the prosecution of which is subject to this subdivision.

§ 1104. Character trait for care or skill

Except as provided in Sections 1102 and 1103, evidence of a trait of a person's character with respect to care or skill is inadmissible to prove the quality of his conduct on a specified occasion.

§ 1105. Habit or custom to prove specific behavior

Any otherwise admissible evidence of habit or custom is admissible to prove conduct on a specified occasion in conformity with the habit or custom.

§ 1106. Sexual harassment, sexual assault, or sexual battery cases; opinion or reputation evidence of plaintiff's sexual conduct; inadmissibility; exception; cross-examination

(a) In any civil action alleging conduct which constitutes sexual harassment, sexual assault, or sexual battery, opinion evidence, reputation evidence, and evidence of specific instances of plaintiff's sexual conduct, or any of such evidence, is not admissible by the defendant in order to prove consent by the plaintiff or the absence of injury to the plaintiff, unless the injury alleged by the plaintiff is in the nature of loss of consortium.

(b) Subdivision (a) shall not be applicable to evidence of the plaintiff's sexual conduct with the alleged perpetrator.

(c) If the plaintiff introduces evidence, including testimony of a witness, or the plaintiff as a witness gives testimony, and the evidence or testimony relates to the plaintiff's sexual conduct, the defendant may cross-examine the witness who gives the testimony and offer relevant evidence limited specifically to the rebuttal of the evidence introduced by the plaintiff or given by the plaintiff.

(d) Nothing in this section shall be construed to make inadmissible any evidence offered to attack the credibility of the plaintiff as provided in Section 783.

CHAPTER 2. OTHER EVIDENCE AFFECTED OR EXCLUDED BY EXTRINSIC POLICIES

§ 1150. Evidence to test a verdict

(a) Upon an inquiry as to the validity of a verdict, any otherwise admissible evidence may be received as to statements made, or conduct, conditions, or events occurring, either within or without the jury room, of such a character as is likely to have influenced the verdict improperly. No evidence is admissible to show the effect of such statement, conduct, condition, or event upon a juror either in influencing him to assent to or dissent from the verdict or concerning the mental processes by which it was determined.

(b) Nothing in this code affects the law relating to the competence of a juror to give evidence to impeach or support a verdict.

§ 1151. Subsequent remedial conduct

When, after the occurrence of an event, remedial or precautionary measures are taken, which, if taken previously, would have tended to make the event less likely to occur, evidence of such subsequent measures is inadmissible to prove negligence or culpable conduct in connection with the event.

§ 1152. Offer to compromise and the like

(a) Evidence that a person has, in compromise or from humanitarian motives, furnished or offered or promised to furnish money or any other thing, act, or service to another who has sustained or will sustain or claims that he has sustained or will sustain loss or damage, as well as any conduct or statements made in negotiation thereof, is inadmissible to prove his liability for the loss or damage or any part of it.

(b) In the event that evidence of an offer to compromise is admitted in an action for breach of the covenant of good faith and fair dealing or violation of subdivision (h) of Section 790.03 of the Insurance Code, then at the request of the party against whom the evidence is admitted, or at the request of the party who made the offer to compromise that was admitted, evidence relating to any other offer or counteroffer to compromise the same or substantially the same claimed loss or damage shall also be admissible for the same purpose as the initial evidence regarding settlement. Other than as may be admitted in an action for breach of the covenant of good faith and fair dealing or violation of subdivision (h) of Section 790.03 of the Insurance Code, evidence of settlement offers shall not be admitted in a motion for a new trial, in any proceeding involving an additur or remittitur, or on appeal.

(c) This section does not affect the admissibility of evidence of:

(1) Partial satisfaction of an asserted claim or demand without questioning its validity when such evidence is offered to prove the validity of the claim; or

(2) A debtor's payment or promise to pay all or a part of his preexisting debt when such evidence is offered to prove the creation of a new duty on his part or a revival of his preexisting duty.

§ 1152.5 Mediation

(a) Subject to the conditions and exceptions provided in this section, when persons agree to conduct and participate in a mediation for the purpose of compromising, settling, or resolving a dispute:

(1) Evidence of anything said or of any admission made in the course of the mediation is not admissible in evidence, and disclosure of any such evidence shall not be compelled, in any civil action in which, pursuant to law, testimony can be compelled to be given.

(2) Unless the document otherwise provides, no document prepared for the purpose of, or in the course of, or pursuant to, the mediation, or copy thereof, is admissible in evidence, and disclosure of any such document shall not be compelled, in any civil action in which, pursuant to law, testimony can be compelled to be given.

(b) Subdivision (a) does not limit the admissibility of evidence if all persons who conducted or otherwise participated in the mediation consent to its disclosure.

(c) This section does not apply unless, before the mediation begins, the persons who agree to conduct and participate in the mediation execute an agreement in writing that sets out the text of subdivisions (a) and (b) and states that the persons agree that this section shall apply to the mediation.

(d) This section does not apply where the admissibility of the evidence is governed by Section 4351.5 or 4607 of the Civil Code or by Section 1747 of the Code of Civil Procedure.

(e) Nothing in this section makes admissible evidence that is inadmissible under Section 1152 or any other statutory provision, including, but not limited to, the sections listed in subdivision (d). Nothing in this section limits the confidentiality provided pursuant to Section 65 of the Labor Code.

(f) Paragraph (2) of subdivision (a) does not limit either of the following:

(1) The admissibility of the agreement referred to in subdivision (c).

(2) The effect of an agreement not to take a default in a pending civil action.

§ 1153. Offer to plead guilty or withdraw plea of guilty by criminal defendant

Evidence of a plea of guilty, later withdrawn, or of an offer to plead guilty to the crime charged or to any other crime, made by the defendant in a criminal action is inadmissible in any action or in any proceeding of any nature, including proceedings before agencies, commissions, boards, and tribunals.

§ 1153.5 Offer for civil resolution of crimes against property

Evidence of an offer for civil resolution of a criminal matter pursuant to the provisions of Section 33 of the Code of Civil Procedure, or admissions made in the course of or negotiations for the offer shall not be admissible in any action.

§ 1154. Offer to discount a claim

Evidence that a person has accepted or offered or promised to accept a sum of money or any other thing, act, or service in satisfaction of a claim, as well as any conduct or statements made in negotiation thereof, is inadmissible to prove the invalidity of the claim or any part of it.

§ 1155. Liability insurance

Evidence that a person was, at the time a harm was suffered by another, insured wholly or partially against loss arising from liability for that harm is inadmissible to prove negligence or other wrongdoing.

§ 1156. Records of medical study of in-hospital staff committee

(a) In-hospital medical or medical-dental staff committees of a licensed hospital may engage in research and medical or dental study for the purpose of reducing morbidity or mortality, and may make findings and recommendations relating to such purpose. Except as provided in subdivision (b), the written records of interviews, reports, statements, or memoranda of such in-hospital medical or medical-dental staff committees relating to such medical or dental studies are subject to Sections 2016 to 2036, inclusive, of the Code of Civil Procedure (relating to discovery proceedings) but, subject to subdivisions (c) and (d), shall not be admitted as evidence in any action or before any administrative body, agency, or person.

(b) The disclosure, with or without the consent of the patient, of information concerning him to such in-hospital medical or medical-dental staff committee does not make unprivileged any information that would otherwise be privileged under Section 994 or 1014; but, notwithstanding Sections 994 and 1014, such information is subject to discovery under subdivision (a) except that the identity of any patient may not be discovered under subdivision (a) unless the patient consents to such disclosure.

(c) This section does not affect the admissibility in evidence of the original medical or dental records of any patient.

(d) This section does not exclude evidence which is relevant evidence in a criminal action.

§ 1156.1 Records of medical or psychiatric studies of quality assurance committees

(a) A committee established in compliance with Sections 4070 and 5624 of the Welfare and Institutions Code may engage in research and medical or psychiatric study for the purpose of reducing morbidity or mortality, and may make findings and recommendations to the county and state relating to such purpose. Except as provided in subdivision (b), the written records of interviews, reports, statements, or memoranda of such committees relating to such medical or psychiatric studies are subject to Sections 2016 to 2036, inclusive, of the Code of Civil Procedure but, subject to subdivisions (c) and (d), shall not be admitted as evidence in any action or before any administrative body, agency, or person.

(b) The disclosure, with or without the consent of the patient, of information concerning him or her to such committee does not make unprivileged any information that would otherwise be privileged under Section 994 or 1014. However, notwithstanding Sections 994 and 1014, such information is subject to discovery under subdivision (a) except that the identity of any patient may not be discovered under subdivision (a) unless the patient consents to such disclosure.

(c) This section does not affect the admissibility in evidence of the original medical or psychiatric records of any patient.

(d) This section does not exclude evidence which is relevant evidence in a criminal action.

§ 1157. Proceedings and records of organized committees having responsibility of evaluation and improvement of quality of care; exceptions

(a) Neither the proceedings nor the records of organized committees of medical, medical-dental, podiatric, registered dietitian, psychological, or veterinary staffs in hospitals, or of a peer review body, as defined in Section 805 of the Business and Professions Code, having the responsibility of evaluation and improvement of the quality of care rendered in the hospital, or for that peer review body, or medical or dental review or dental hygienist review or chiropractic review or podiatric review or registered dietitian review or veterinary review committees of local medical, dental, dental hygienist, podiatric, dietetic, veterinary, or chiropractic societies, or psychological review committees of state or local psychological associations or societies having the responsibility of evaluation and improvement of the quality of care, shall be subject to discovery.

(b) Except as hereinafter provided, no person in attendance at a meeting of any of those committees shall be required to testify as to what transpired at that meeting.

(c) The prohibition relating to discovery or testimony does not apply to the statements made by any person in attendance at a meeting of any of those committees who is a party to an action or proceeding the subject matter of which was reviewed at that meeting, or to any person requesting hospital staff privileges, or in any action against an insurance carrier alleging bad faith by the carrier in refusing to accept a settlement offer within the policy limits.

(d) The prohibitions in this section do not apply to medical, dental, dental hygienist, podiatric, dietetic, psychological, veterinary, or chiropractic society committees that exceed 10 percent of the membership of the society, nor to any of those committees if any person serves upon the committee when his or her own conduct or practice is being reviewed.

(e) The amendments made to this section by Chapter 1081 of the Statutes of 1983, or at the 1985 portion of the 1985–86 Regular Session of the Legislature, or at the 1990 portion of the 1989–90 Regular Session of the Legislature, do not exclude the discovery or use of relevant evidence in a criminal action.

§ 1157.5 Organized committee of nonprofit medical care foundation or professional standards review organization; proceedings and records

Except in actions involving a claim of a provider of health care services for payment for such services, the prohibition relating to discovery or testimony provided by Section 1157 shall be applicable to the proceedings or records of an organized committee of any nonprofit medical care foundation or professional standards review organization which is organized in a manner which makes available professional competence to review health care services with respect to medical necessity, quality of care, or economic justification of charges or level of care.

§ 1157.6 Proceedings and records of quality assurance committees for county health facilities

Neither the proceedings nor the records of a committee established in compliance with Sections 4070 and 5624 of the Welfare and Institutions Code having the responsibility of evaluation and improvement of the quality of mental health care rendered in county operated and contracted mental health facilities shall be subject to discovery. Except as provided in this section, no person in attendance at a meeting of any such committee shall be required to testify as to what transpired thereat. The prohibition relating to discovery or testimony shall not apply to the statements made by any person in attendance at such a meeting who is a party to an action or proceeding the subject matter of which was reviewed at such meeting, or to any person requesting facility staff privileges.

§ 1157.7 **Application of Section 1157 discovery or testimony prohibitions; application of public records and meetings provisions**

The prohibition relating to discovery or testimony provided in Section 1157 shall be applicable to proceedings and records of any committee established by a local governmental agency to monitor, evaluate, and report on the necessity, quality, and level of specialty health services, including, but not limited to, trauma care services, provided by a general acute care hospital which has been designated or recognized by that governmental agency as qualified to render specialty health care services. The provisions of Chapter 3.5 (commencing with Section 6250) of Division 7 of Title 1 of the Government Code and Chapter 9 (commencing with Section 54950) of Division 2 of Title 5 of the Government Code shall not be applicable to the committee records and proceedings.

§ 1158. **Presentation of authorization for inspection and copying of patient's records; failure to comply; costs**

Whenever, prior to the filing of any action or the appearance of a defendant in an action, an attorney at law or his or her representative presents a written authorization therefor signed by an adult patient, by the guardian or conservator of his person or estate, or, in the case of a minor, by a parent or guardian of the minor, or by the personal representative or an heir of a deceased patient, or a copy thereof, a physician and surgeon, dentist, registered nurse, dispensing optician, registered physical therapist, podiatrist, licensed psychologist, osteopath, chiropractor, clinical laboratory bioanalyst, clinical laboratory technologist, or pharmacist or pharmacy, duly licensed as such under the laws of the state, or a licensed hospital, shall make all of the patient's records under his, hers or its custody or control available for inspection and copying by such attorney at law or his, or her, representative, promptly upon the presentation of the written authorization.

No copying may be performed by any medical provider enumerated above, or by an agent thereof, when the requesting attorney has employed a professional photocopier or anyone identified in Section 22451 of the Business and Professions Code as his or her representative to obtain or review the records on his or her behalf. The presentation of the authorization by the agent on behalf of the attorney shall be sufficient proof that the agent is the attorney's representative.

Failure to make such records available, during business hours, within five days after the presentation of the written authorization, may subject the person or entity having custody or control of the records to liability for all reasonable expenses, including attorney's

fees, incurred in any proceeding to enforce the provisions of this
section.

All reasonable costs incurred by any person or entity enumerated
above in making patient records available pursuant to this section may
be charged against the person whose written authorization required the
availability of such records.

"Reasonable cost," as used in this section, shall include, but not be
limited to, the following specific costs: ten cents ($0.10) per page for
standard reproduction of documents of a size 8½ by 14 inches or less;
twenty cents ($0.20) per page for copying of documents from microfilm;
actual costs for the reproduction of oversize documents or the reproduction of documents requiring special processing which are made in
response to an authorization; reasonable clerical costs incurred in
locating and making the records available to be billed at the maximum
rate of sixteen dollars ($16) per hour per person, computed on the basis
of four dollars ($4) per quarter hour or fraction thereof; actual postage
charges; and actual costs, if any, charged to the witness by a third
person for the retrieval and return of records held by that third person.

Where the records are delivered to the attorney or the attorney's
representative for inspection or photocopying at the record custodian's
place of business, the only fee for complying with the authorization
shall not exceed fifteen dollars ($15), plus actual costs, if any, charged
to the record custodian by a third person for retrieval and return of
records held offsite by the third person.

Division 10

HEARSAY EVIDENCE

CHAPTER 1.   GENERAL PROVISIONS

§ 1200.   The hearsay rule

(a) "Hearsay evidence" is evidence of a statement that was made
other than by a witness while testifying at the hearing and that is
offered to prove the truth of the matter stated.

(b) Except as provided by law, hearsay evidence is inadmissible.

(c) This section shall be known and may be cited as the hearsay
rule.

§ 1201.   Multiple hearsay

A statement within the scope of an exception to the hearsay rule is
not inadmissible on the ground that the evidence of such statement is
hearsay evidence if such hearsay evidence consists of one or more

statements each of which meets the requirements of an exception to the hearsay rule.

§ 1202. Credibility of hearsay declarant

Evidence of a statement or other conduct by a declarant that is inconsistent with a statement by such declarant received in evidence as hearsay evidence is not inadmissible for the purpose of attacking the credibility of the declarant though he is not given and has not had an opportunity to explain or to deny such inconsistent statement or other conduct. Any other evidence offered to attack or support the credibility of the declarant is admissible if it would have been admissible had the declarant been a witness at the hearing. For the purposes of this section, the deponent of a deposition taken in the action in which it is offered shall be deemed to be a hearsay declarant.

§ 1203. Cross-examination of hearsay declarant

(a) The declarant of a statement that is admitted as hearsay evidence may be called and examined by any adverse party as if under cross-examination concerning the statement.

(b) This section is not applicable if the declarant is (1) a party, (2) a person identified with a party within the meaning of subdivision (d) of Section 776, or (3) a witness who has testified in the action concerning the subject matter of the statement.

(c) This section is not applicable if the statement is one described in Article 1 (commencing with Section 1220), Article 3 (commencing with Section 1235), or Article 10 (commencing with Section 1300) of Chapter 2 of this division.

(d) A statement that is otherwise admissible as hearsay evidence is not made inadmissible by this section because the declarant who made the statement is unavailable for examination pursuant to this section.

§ 1203.1. Hearsay offered at preliminary examination; inapplication of § 1203

Section 1203 is not applicable if the hearsay statement is offered at a preliminary examination, as provided in Section 872 of the Penal Code.

§ 1204. Hearsay statement offered against criminal defendant

A statement that is otherwise admissible as hearsay evidence is inadmissible against the defendant in a criminal action if the statement was made, either by the defendant or by another, under such circumstances that it is inadmissible against the defendant under the Constitution of the United States or the State of California.

§ 1205. No implied repeal

Nothing in this division shall be construed to repeal by implication any other statute relating to hearsay evidence.

CHAPTER 2. EXCEPTIONS TO THE HEARSAY RULE

ARTICLE 1. CONFESSIONS AND ADMISSIONS

§ 1220. Admission of party

Evidence of a statement is not made inadmissible by the hearsay rule when offered against the declarant in an action to which he is a party in either his individual or representative capacity, regardless of whether the statement was made in his individual or representative capacity.

§ 1221. Adoptive admission

Evidence of a statement offered against a party is not made inadmissible by the hearsay rule if the statement is one of which the party, with knowledge of the content thereof, has by words or other conduct manifested his adoption or his belief in its truth.

§ 1222. Authorized admission

Evidence of a statement offered against a party is not made inadmissible by the hearsay rule if:

(a) The statement was made by a person authorized by the party to make a statement or statements for him concerning the subject matter of the statement; and

(b) The evidence is offered either after admission of evidence sufficient to sustain a finding of such authority or, in the court's discretion as to the order of proof, subject to the admission of such evidence.

§ 1223. Admission of co-conspirator

Evidence of a statement offered against a party is not made inadmissible by the hearsay rule if:

(a) The statement was made by the declarant while participating in a conspiracy to commit a crime or civil wrong and in furtherance of the objective that conspiracy;

(b) The statement was made prior to or during the time that the party was participating in that conspiracy; and

(c) The evidence is offered either after admission of evidence sufficient to sustain a finding of the facts specified in subdivisions (a) and (b) or, in the court's discretion as to the order of proof, subject to the admission of such evidence.

§ 1224. Statement of declarant whose liability or breach of duty is in issue

When the liability, obligation, or duty of a party to a civil action is based in whole or in part upon the liability, obligation, or duty of the declarant, or when the claim or right asserted by a party to a civil action is barred or diminished by a breach of duty by the declarant, evidence of a statement made by the declarant is as admissible against the party as it would be if offered against the declarant in an action involving that liability, obligation, duty, or breach of duty.

§ 1225. Statement of declarant whose right or title is in issue

When a right, title, or interest in any property or claim asserted by a party to a civil action requires a determination that a right, title or interest exists or existed in the declarant, evidence of a statement made by the declarant during the time the party now claims the declarant was the holder of the right, title, or interest is as admissible against the party as it would be if offered against the declarant in an action involving that right, title, or interest.

§ 1226. Statement of minor child in parent's action for child's injury

Evidence of a statement by a minor child is not made inadmissible by the hearsay rule if offered against the plaintiff in an action brought under Section 376 of the Code of Civil Procedure for injury to such minor child.

§ 1227. Statement of declarant in action for his wrongful death

Evidence of a statement by the deceased is not made inadmissible by the hearsay rule if offered against the plaintiff in an action for wrongful death brought under Section 377 of the Code of Civil Procedure.

§ 1228. Admissibility of certain out-of-court statements of minors under the age of 12; establishing elements of certain sexually oriented crimes; notice to defendant

Notwithstanding any other provision of law, for the purpose of establishing the elements of the crime in order to admit as evidence the confession of a person accused of violating Section 261, 264.1, 285, 286, 288, 288a, 289, or 647a of the Penal Code, a court, in its discretion, may

determine that a statement of the complaining witness is not made
inadmissible by the hearsay rule if it finds all of the following:

(a) The statement was made by a minor child under the age of 12,
and the contents of the statement were included in a written report of a
law enforcement official or an employee of a county welfare department.

(b) The statement describes the minor child as a victim of sexual
abuse.

(c) The statement was made prior to the defendant's confession.
The court shall view with caution the testimony of a person recounting
hearsay where there is evidence of personal bias or prejudice.

(d) There are no circumstances, such as significant inconsistencies
between the confession and the statement concerning material facts
establishing any element of the crime or the identification of the
defendant, that would render the statement unreliable.

(e) The minor child is found to be unavailable pursuant to paragraph (2) or (3) of subdivision (a) of Section 240 or refuses to testify.

(f) The confession was memorialized in a trustworthy fashion by a
law enforcement official.

If the prosecution intends to offer a statement of the complaining
witness pursuant to this section, the prosecution shall serve a written
notice upon the defendant at least 10 days prior to the hearing or trial
at which the prosecution intends to offer the statement.

If the statement is offered during trial, the court's determination
shall be made out of the presence of the jury. If the statement is found
to be admissible pursuant to this section, it shall be admitted out of the
presence of the jury and solely for the purpose of determining the
admissibility of the confession of the defendant.

ARTICLE 2.   DECLARATIONS AGAINST INTEREST

§ 1230. Declarations against interest

Evidence of a statement by a declarant having sufficient knowledge
of the subject is not made inadmissible by the hearsay rule if the
declarant is unavailable as a witness and the statement, when made,
was so far contrary to the declarant's pecuniary or proprietary interest,
or so far subjected him to the risk of civil or criminal liability, or so far
tended to render invalid a claim by him against another, or created
such a risk of making him an object of hatred, ridicule, or social
disgrace in the community, that a reasonable man in his position would
not have made the statement unless he believed it to be true. (Stats.
1965, c. 299, § 2.)

ARTICLE 3. PRIOR STATEMENTS OF WITNESSES

§ 1235. Inconsistent statement

Evidence of a statement made by a witness is not made inadmissible by the hearsay rule if the statement is inconsistent with his testimony at the hearing and is offered in compliance with Section 770.

§ 1236. Prior consistent statement

Evidence of a statement previously made by a witness is not made inadmissible by the hearsay rule if the statement is consistent with his testimony at the hearing and is offered in compliance with Section 791.

§ 1237. Past recollection recorded

(a) Evidence of a statement previously made by a witness is not made inadmissible by the hearsay rule if the statement would have been admissible if made by him while testifying, the statement concerns a matter as to which the witness has insufficient present recollection to enable him to testify fully and accurately, and the statement is contained in a writing which:

(1) Was made at a time when the fact recorded in the writing actually occurred or was fresh in the witness' memory;

(2) Was made (i) by the witness himself or under his direction or (ii) by some other person for the purpose of recording the witness' statement at the time it was made;

(3) Is offered after the witness testifies that the statement he made was a true statement of such fact; and

(4) Is offered after the writing is authenticated as an accurate record of the statement.

(b) The writing may be read into evidence, but the writing itself may not be received in evidence unless offered by an adverse party.

§ 1238. Prior identification

Evidence of a statement previously made by a witness is not made inadmissible by the hearsay rule if the statement would have been admissible if made by him while testifying and:

(a) The statement is an identification of a party or another as a person who participated in a crime or other occurrence;

(b) The statement was made at a time when the crime or other occurrence was fresh in the witness' memory; and

(c) The evidence of the statement is offered after the witness testifies that he made the identification and that it was a true reflection of his opinion at that time.

ARTICLE 4. SPONTANEOUS, CONTEMPORANEOUS, AND DYING DECLARATIONS

§ 1240. Spontaneous statement

Evidence of a statement is not made inadmissible by the hearsay rule if the statement:

(a) Purports to narrate, describe, or explain an act, condition, or event perceived by the declarant; and

(b) Was made spontaneously while the declarant was under the stress of excitement caused by such perception.

§ 1241. Contemporaneous statement

Evidence of a statement is not made inadmissible by the hearsay rule if the statement:

(a) Is offered to explain, qualify, or make understandable conduct of the declarant; and

(b) Was made while the declarant was engaged in such conduct.

§ 1242. Dying declaration

Evidence of a statement made by a dying person respecting the cause and circumstances of his death is not made inadmissible by the hearsay rule if the statement was made upon his personal knowledge and under a sense of immediately impending death.

ARTICLE 5. STATEMENTS OF MENTAL OR PHYSICAL STATE

§ 1250. Statement of declarant's then existing mental or physical state

(a) Subject to Section 1252, evidence of a statement of the declarant's then existing state of mind, emotion, or physical sensation (including a statement of intent, plan, motive, design, mental feeling, pain, or bodily health) is not made inadmissible by the hearsay rule when:

(1) The evidence is offered to prove the declarant's state of mind, emotion, or physical sensation at that time or at any other time when it is itself an issue in the action; or

(2) The evidence is offered to prove or explain acts or conduct of the declarant.

(b) This section does not make admissible evidence of a statement of memory or belief to prove the fact remembered or believed.

§ 1251. Statement of declarant's previously existing mental or physical state

Subject to Section 1252, evidence of a statement of the declarant's state of mind, emotion, or physical sensation (including a statement of intent, plan, motive, design, mental feeling, pain, or bodily health) at a time prior to the statement is not made inadmissible by the hearsay rule if:

(a) The declarant is unavailable as a witness; and

(b) The evidence is offered to prove such prior state of mind, emotion, or physical sensation when it is itself an issue in the action and the evidence is not offered to prove any fact other than such state of mind, emotion or physical sensation.

§ 1252. Limitation on admissibility of statement of mental or physical state

Evidence of a statement is inadmissible under this article if the statement was made under circumstances such as to indicate its lack of trustworthiness.

ARTICLE 6. STATEMENTS RELATING TO WILLS AND TO CLAIMS AGAINST ESTATES

§ 1260. Statement concerning declarant's will

(a) Evidence of a statement made by a declarant who is unavailable as a witness that he has or has not made a will, or has or has not revoked his will, or that identifies his will, is not made inadmissible by the hearsay rule.

(b) Evidence of a statement is inadmissible under this section if the statement was made under circumstances such as to indicate its lack of trustworthiness.

§ 1261. Statement of decedent offered in action against his estate

(a) Evidence of a statement is not made inadmissible by the hearsay rule when offered in an action upon a claim or demand against the estate of the declarant if the statement was made upon the personal knowledge of the declarant at a time when the matter had been recently perceived by him and while his recollection was clear.

(b) Evidence of a statement is inadmissible under this section if the statement was made under circumstances such as to indicate its lack of trustworthiness.

ARTICLE 7. BUSINESS RECORDS

§ 1270. "A business"

As used in this article, "a business" includes every kind of business, governmental activity, profession, occupation, calling, or operation of institutions, whether carried on for profit or not.

§ 1271. Business record

Evidence of a writing made as a record of an act, condition, or event is not made inadmissible by the hearsay rule when offered to prove the act, condition, or event if:

(a) The writing was made in the regular course of a business;

(b) The writing was made at or near the time of the act, condition, or event;

(c) The custodian or other qualified witness testifies to its identity and the mode of its preparation; and

(d) The sources of information and method and time of preparation were such as to indicate its trustworthiness.

§ 1272. Absence of entry in business records

Evidence of the absence from the records of a business of a record of an asserted act, condition, or event is not made inadmissible by the hearsay rule when offered to prove the nonoccurrence of the act or event, or the nonexistence of the condition, if:

(a) It was the regular course of that business to make records of all such acts, conditions, or events at or near the time of the act, condition, or event and to preserve them; and

(b) The sources of information and method and time of preparation of the records of that business were such that the absence of a record of an act, condition, or event is a trustworthy indication that the act or event did not occur or the condition did not exist.

ARTICLE 8. OFFICIAL RECORDS AND OTHER OFFICIAL WRITINGS

§ 1280. Record by public employee

Evidence of a writing made as a record of an act, condition, or event is not made inadmissible by the hearsay rule when offered to prove the act, condition or event if:

(a) The writing was made by and within the scope of duty of a public employee;

(b) The writing was made at or near the time of the act, condition, or event; and

(c) The sources of information and method and time of preparation were such as to indicate its trustworthiness.

§ 1281. Record of vital statistic

Evidence of a writing made as a record of a birth, fetal death, death, or marriage is not made inadmissible by the hearsay rule if the maker was required by law to file the writing in a designated public office and the writing was made and filed as required by law.

§ 1282. Finding of presumed death by authorized federal employee

A written finding of presumed death made by an employee of the United States authorized to make such finding pursuant to the Federal Missing Persons Act (56 Stats. 143, 1092, and P.L. 408, Ch. 371, 2d Sess. 78th Cong.; 50 U.S.C. App. 1001–1016), as enacted or as heretofore or hereafter amended, shall be received in any court, office, or other place in this state as evidence of the death of the person therein found to be dead and of the date, circumstances, and place of his disappearance.

§ 1283. Record by federal employee that person is missing, captured, or the like

An official written report or record that a person is missing, missing in action, interned in a foreign country, captured by a hostile force, beleaguered by a hostile force, besieged by a hostile force, or detained in a foreign country against his will, or is dead or is alive, made by an employee of the United States authorized by any law of the United States to make such report or record shall be received in any court, office, or other place in this state as evidence that such person is missing, missing in action, interned in a foreign country, captured by a hostile force, beleaguered by a hostile force, besieged by a hostile force, or detained in a foreign country against his will, or is dead or is alive.

§ 1284. Statement of absence of public record

Evidence of a writing made by the public employee who is the official custodian of the records in a public office, reciting diligent search and failure to find a record, is not made inadmissible by the hearsay rule when offered to prove the absence of a record in that office.

ARTICLE 9. FORMER TESTIMONY

§ 1290. "Former testimony"

As used in this article, "former testimony" means testimony given under oath in:

(a) Another action or in a former hearing or trial of the same action;

(b) A proceeding to determine a controversy conducted by or under the supervision of an agency that has the power to determine such a controversy and is an agency of the United States or a public entity in the United States;

(c) A deposition taken in compliance with law in another action; or

(d) An arbitration proceeding if the evidence of such former testimony is a verbatim transcript thereof.

§ 1291. Former testimony offered against party to former proceeding

(a) Evidence of former testimony is not made inadmissible by the hearsay rule if the declarant is unavailable as a witness and:

(1) The former testimony is offered against a person who offered it in evidence in his own behalf on the former occasion or against the successor in interest of such person; or

(2) The party against whom the former testimony is offered was a party to the action or proceeding in which the testimony was given and had the right and opportunity to cross-examine the declarant with an interest and motive similar to that which he has at the hearing.

(b) The admissibility of former testimony under this section is subject to the same limitations and objections as though the declarant were testifying at the hearing, except that former testimony offered under this section is not subject to:

(1) Objections to the form of the question which were not made at the time the former testimony was given.

(2) Objections based on competency or privilege which did not exist at the time the former testimony was given.

§ 1292. Former testimony offered against person not a party to former proceeding

(a) Evidence of former testimony is not made inadmissible by the hearsay rule if:

(1) The declarant is unavailable as a witness;

(2) The former testimony is offered in a civil action; and

(3) The issue is such that the party to the action or proceeding in which the former testimony was given had the right and opportunity to cross-examine the declarant with an interest and motive similar to that which the party against whom the testimony is offered has at the hearing.

(b) The admissibility of former testimony under this section is subject to the same limitations and objections as though the declarant were testifying at the hearing, except that former testimony offered under this section is not subject to objections based on competency or privilege which did not exist at the time the former testimony was given.

§ 1293. Former testimony made at a preliminary examination by a minor child as a complaining witness; admissibility

(a) Evidence of former testimony made at a preliminary examination by a minor child who was the complaining witness is not made inadmissible by the hearsay rule if:

(1) The former testimony is offered in a proceeding to declare the minor a dependent child of the court pursuant to Section 300 of the Welfare and Institutions Code.

(2) The issues are such that a defendant in the preliminary examination in which the former testimony was given had the right and opportunity to cross-examine the minor child with an interest and motive similar to that which the parent or guardian against whom the testimony is offered has at the proceeding to declare the minor a dependent child of the court.

(b) The admissibility of former testimony under this section is subject to the same limitations and objections as though the minor child were testifying at the proceeding to declare him or her a dependent child of the court.

(c) The attorney for the parent or guardian against whom the former testimony is offered or, if none, the parent or guardian may make a motion to challenge the admissibility of the former testimony upon a showing that new substantially different issues are present in the proceeding to declare the minor a dependent child than were present in the preliminary examination.

(d) As used in this section, "complaining witness" means the alleged victim of the crime for which a preliminary examination was held.

(e) This section shall apply only to testimony made at a preliminary examination on and after January 1, 1990.

ARTICLE 10. JUDGMENTS

§ 1300. Judgment of conviction of crime punishable as felony

Evidence of a final judgment adjudging a person guilty of a crime punishable as a felony is not made inadmissible by the hearsay rule when offered in a civil action to prove any fact essential to the judgment whether or not the judgment was based on a plea of nolo contendere.

§ 1301. Judgment against person entitled to indemnity

Evidence of a final judgment is not made inadmissible by the hearsay rule when offered by the judgment debtor to prove any fact which was essential to the judgment in an action in which he seeks to:

(a) Recover partial or total indemnity or exoneration for money paid or liability incurred because of the judgment;

(b) Enforce a warranty to protect the judgment debtor against the liability determined by the judgment; or

(c) Recover damages for breach of warranty substantially the same as the warranty determined by the judgment to have been breached.

§ 1302. Judgment determining liability of third person

When the liability, obligation, or duty of a third person is in issue in a civil action, evidence of a final judgment against that person is not made inadmissible by the hearsay rule when offered to prove such liability, obligation, or duty.

ARTICLE 11. FAMILY HISTORY

§ 1310. Statement concerning declarant's own family history

(a) Subject to subdivision (b), evidence of a statement by a declarant who is unavailable as a witness concerning his own birth, marriage, divorce, a parent and child relationship, relationship by blood or marriage, race, ancestry, or other similar fact of his family history is not made inadmissible by the hearsay rule, even though the declarant had no means of acquiring personal knowledge of the matter declared.

(b) Evidence of a statement is inadmissible under this section if the statement was made under circumstances such as to indicate its lack of trustworthiness.

§ 1311. Statement concerning family history of another

(a) Subject to subdivision (b), evidence of a statement concerning the birth, marriage, divorce, death, parent and child relationship, race, ancestry, relationship by blood or marriage, or other similar fact of the family history of a person other than the declarant is not made inadmissible by the hearsay rule if the declarant is unavailable as a witness and:

(1) The declarant was related to the other by blood or marriage; or

(2) The declarant was otherwise so intimately associated with the other's family as to be likely to have had accurate information concerning the matter declared and made the statement (i) upon information received from the other or from a person related by blood or marriage to the other or (ii) upon repute in the other's family.

(b) Evidence of a statement is inadmissible under this section if the statement was made under circumstances such as to indicate its lack of trustworthiness.

§ 1312. Entries in family records and the like

Evidence of entries in family Bibles or other family books or charts, engravings on rings, family portraits, engravings on urns, crypts, or tombstones, and the like, is not made inadmissible by the hearsay rule when offered to prove the birth, marriage, divorce, death, parent and child relationship, race, ancestry, relationship by blood or marriage, or other similar fact of the family history of a member of the family by blood or marriage.

§ 1313. Reputation in family concerning family history

Evidence of reputation among members of a family is not made inadmissible by the hearsay rule if the reputation concerns the birth, marriage, divorce, death, parent and child relationship, race, ancestry, relationship by blood or marriage, or other similar fact of the family history of a member of the family by blood or marriage.

§ 1314. Reputation in community concerning family history

Evidence of reputation in a community concerning the date or fact of birth, marriage, divorce, or death of a person resident in the community at the time of the reputation is not made inadmissible by the hearsay rule.

§ 1315. Church records concerning family history

Evidence of a statement concerning a person's birth, marriage, divorce, death, parent and child relationship, race, ancestry, relationship by blood or marriage, or other similar fact of family history which is contained in a writing made as a record of a church, religious denomination, or religious society is not made inadmissible by the hearsay rule if:

(a) The statement is contained in a writing made as a record of an act, condition, or event that would be admissible as evidence of such act, condition, or event under Section 1271; and

(b) The statement is of a kind customarily recorded in connection with the act, condition, or event recorded in the writing.

§ 1316. Marriage, baptismal and similar certificates

Evidence of a statement concerning a person's birth, marriage, divorce, death, parent and child relationship, race, ancestry, relationship by blood or marriage, or other similar fact of family history is not made inadmissible by the hearsay rule if the statement is contained in a certificate that the maker thereof performed a marriage or other ceremony or administered a sacrament and:

(a) The maker was a clergyman, civil officer, or other person authorized to perform the acts reported in the certificate by law or by the rules, regulations, or requirements of a church, religious denomination, or religious society; and

(b) The certificate was issued by the maker at the time and place of the ceremony or sacrament or within a reasonable time thereafter.

ARTICLE 12. REPUTATION AND STATEMENTS CONCERNING COMMUNITY HISTORY, PROPERTY INTERESTS, AND CHARACTER

§ 1320. Reputation concerning community history

Evidence of reputation in a community is not made inadmissible by the hearsay rule if the reputation concerns an event of general history of the community or of the state or nation of which the community is a part and the event was of importance to the community.

§ 1321. Reputation concerning public interest in property

Evidence of reputation in a community is not made inadmissible by the hearsay rule if the reputation concerns the interest of the public in property in the community and the reputation arose before controversy.

§ 1322. Reputation concerning boundary or custom affecting land

Evidence of reputation in a community is not made inadmissible by the hearsay rule if the reputation concerns boundaries of, or customs affecting, land in the community and the reputation arose before controversy.

§ 1323. Statement concerning boundary

Evidence of a statement concerning the boundary of land is not made inadmissible by the hearsay rule if the declarant is unavailable as a witness and had sufficient knowledge of the subject, but evidence of a statement is not admissible under this section if the statement was made under circumstances such as to indicate its lack of trustworthiness.

§ 1324. Reputation concerning character

Evidence of a person's general reputation with reference to his character or a trait of his character at a relevant time in the community in which he then resided or in a group with which he then habitually associated is not made inadmissible by the hearsay rule.

ARTICLE 13. DISPOSITIVE INSTRUMENTS AND ANCIENT WRITINGS

§ 1330. Recitals in writings affecting property

Evidence of a statement contained in a deed of conveyance or a will or other writing purporting to affect an interest in real or personal property is not made inadmissible by the hearsay rule if:

(a) The matter stated was relevant to the purpose of the writing;

(b) The matter stated would be relevant to an issue as to an interest in the property; and

(c) The dealings with the property since the statement was made have not been inconsistent with the truth of the statement.

§ 1331. Recitals in ancient writings

Evidence of a statement is not made inadmissible by the hearsay rule if the statement is contained in a writing more than 30 years old and the statement has been since generally acted upon as true by persons having an interest in the matter.

ARTICLE 14. COMMERCIAL, SCIENTIFIC, AND SIMILAR PUBLICATIONS

§ 1340. Commercial lists and the like

Evidence of a statement, other than an opinion, contained in a tabulation, list, directory, register, or other published compilation is not made inadmissible by the hearsay rule if the compilation is generally used and relied upon as accurate in the course of a business as defined in Section 1270.

§ 1341. Publications concerning facts of general notoriety and interest

Historical works, books of science or art, and published maps or charts, made by persons indifferent between the parties, are not made inadmissible by the hearsay rule when offered to prove facts of general notoriety and interest.

ARTICLE 15. DECLARANT UNAVAILABLE AS WITNESS

§ 1350. Unavailable declarant; hearsay rule

(a) In a criminal proceeding charging a serious felony, evidence of a statement made by a declarant is not made inadmissible by the hearsay rule if the declarant is unavailable as a witness, and all of the following are true:

(1) There is clear and convincing evidence that the declarant's unavailability was knowingly caused by, aided by, or solicited by the party against whom the statement is offered for the purpose of preventing the arrest or prosecution of the party and is the result of the death by homicide or the kidnapping of the declarant.

(2) There is no evidence that the unavailability of the declarant was caused by, aided by, solicited by, or procured on behalf of, the party who is offering the statement.

(3) The statement has been memorialized in a tape recording made by a law enforcement official, or in a written statement prepared by a law enforcement official and signed by the declarant and notarized in the presence of the law enforcement official, prior to the death or kidnapping of the declarant.

(4) The statement was made under circumstances which indicate its trustworthiness and was not the result of promise, inducement, threat, or coercion.

(5) The statement is relevant to the issues to be tried.

(6) The statement is corroborated by other evidence which tends to connect the party against whom the statement is offered with the commission of the serious felony with which the party is charged. The corroboration is not sufficient if it merely shows the commission of the offense or the circumstances thereof.

(b) If the prosecution intends to offer a statement pursuant to this section, the prosecution shall serve a written notice upon the defendant at least 10 days prior to the hearing or trial at which the prosecution intends to offer the statement, unless the prosecution shows good cause for the failure to provide that notice. In the event that good cause is shown, the defendant shall be entitled to a reasonable continuance of the hearing or trial.

(c) If the statement is offered during trial, the court's determination shall be made out of the presence of the jury. If the defendant elects to testify at the hearing on a motion brought pursuant to this section, the court shall exclude from the examination every person except the clerk, the court reporter, the bailiff, the prosecutor, the investigating officer, the defendant and his or her counsel, an investigator for the defendant, and the officer having custody of the defendant. Notwithstanding any other provision of law, the defendant's testimony at the hearing shall not be admissible in any other proceeding except the hearing brought on the motion pursuant to this section. If a transcript is made of the defendant's testimony, it shall be sealed and transmitted to the clerk of the court in which the action is pending.

(d) As used in this section, "serious felony" means any of the felonies listed in subdivision (c) of Section 1192.7 of the Penal Code or any violation of Section 11351, 11352, 11378, or 11379 of the Health and Safety Code.

(e) If a statement to be admitted pursuant to this section includes hearsay statements made by anyone other than the declarant who is

unavailable pursuant to subdivision (a), those hearsay statements are
inadmissible unless they meet the requirements of an exception to the
hearsay rule.

Division 11

WRITINGS

CHAPTER 1. AUTHENTICATION AND PROOF OF WRITINGS

ARTICLE 1. REQUIREMENT OF AUTHENTICATION

§ 1400. Authentication defined

Authentication of a writing means (a) the introduction of evidence sufficient to sustain a finding that it is the writing that the proponent of the evidence claims it is or (b) the establishment of such facts by any other means provided by law.

§ 1401. Authentication required

(a) Authentication of a writing is required before it may be received in evidence.

(b) Authentication of a writing is required before secondary evidence of its content may be received in evidence.

§ 1402. Authentication of altered writing

The party producing a writing as genuine which has been altered, or appears to have been altered, after its execution, in a part material to the question in dispute, must account for the alteration or appearance thereof. He may show that the alteration was made by another, without his concurrence, or was made with the consent of the parties affected by it, or otherwise properly or innocently made, or that the alteration did not change the meaning or language of the instrument. If he does that, he may give the writing in evidence, but not otherwise.

ARTICLE 2. MEANS OF AUTHENTICATING AND PROVING WRITINGS

§ 1410. Article not exclusive

Nothing in this article shall be construed to limit the means by which a writing may be authenticated or proved.

§ 1410.5. Graffiti constitutes a writing; admissibility

(a) For purposes of this chapter, a writing shall include any graffiti consisting of written words, insignia, symbols, or any other markings which convey a particular meaning.

(b) Any writing described in subdivision (a), or any photograph thereof, may be admitted into evidence in an action for vandalism, for the purpose of proving that the writing was made by the defendant.

(c) The admissibility of any fact offered to prove that the writing was made by the defendant shall, upon motion of the defendant, be ruled upon outside the presence of the jury, and is subject to the requirements of Sections 1416, 1417, and 1418.

§ 1411. Subscribing witness' testimony unnecessary

Except as provided by statute, the testimony of a subscribing witness is not required to authenticate a writing.

§ 1412. Use of other evidence when subscribing witness' testimony required

If the testimony of a subscribing witness is required by statute to authenticate a writing and the subscribing witness denies or does not recollect the execution of the writing, the writing may be authenticated by other evidence.

§ 1413. Witness to the execution of a writing

A writing may be authenticated by anyone who saw the writing made or executed, including a subscribing witness.

§ 1414. Authentication by admission

A writing may be authenticated by evidence that:

(a) The party against whom it is offered has at any time admitted its authenticity; or

(b) The writing has been acted upon as authentic by the party against whom it is offered.

§ 1415. Authentication by handwriting evidence

A writing may be authenticated by evidence of the genuineness of the handwriting of the maker.

§ 1416. Proof of handwriting by person familiar therewith

A witness who is not otherwise qualified to testify as an expert may state his opinion whether a writing is in the handwriting of a supposed

writer if the court finds that he has personal knowledge of the handwriting of the supposed writer. Such personal knowledge may be
acquired from:

(a) Having seen the supposed writer write;

(b) Having seen a writing purporting to be in the handwriting of
the supposed writer and upon which the supposed writer has acted or
been charged;

(c) Having received letters in the due course of mail purporting to
be from the supposed writer in response to letters duly addressed and
mailed by him to the supposed writer; or

(d) Any other means of obtaining personal knowledge of the handwriting of the supposed writer.

§ 1417. Comparison of handwriting by trier of fact

The genuineness of handwriting, or the lack thereof, may be proved
by a comparison made by the trier of fact with handwriting (a) which
the court finds was admitted or treated as genuine by the party against
whom the evidence is offered or (b) otherwise proved to be genuine to
the satisfaction of the court.

§ 1418. Comparison of writing by expert witness

The genuineness of writing, or the lack thereof, may be proved by a
comparison made by an expert witness with writing (a) which the court
finds was admitted or treated as genuine by the party against whom
the evidence is offered or (b) otherwise proved to be genuine to the
satisfaction of the court.

§ 1419. Exemplars when writing is 30 years old

Where a writing whose genuineness is sought to be proved is more
than 30 years old, the comparison under Section 1417 or 1418 may be
made with writing purporting to be genuine, and generally respected
and acted upon as such, by persons having an interest in knowing
whether it is genuine.

§ 1420. Authentication by evidence of reply

A writing may be authenticated by evidence that the writing was
received in response to a communication sent to the person who is
claimed by the proponent of the evidence to be the author of the
writing.

§ 1421. Authentication by content

A writing may be authenticated by evidence that the writing refers
to or states matters that are unlikely to be known to anyone other than
the person who is claimed by the proponent of the evidence to be the
author of the writing.

ARTICLE 3. PRESUMPTIONS AFFECTING ACKNOWLEDGED WRITINGS AND OFFICIAL WRITINGS

§ 1450. Classification of presumptions in article

The presumptions established by this article are presumptions affecting the burden of producing evidence.

§ 1451. Acknowledged writings

A certificate of the acknowledgment of a writing other than a will, or a certificate of the proof of such a writing, is prima facie evidence of the facts recited in the certificate and the genuineness of the signature of each person by whom the writing purports to have been signed if the certificate meets the requirements of Article 3 (commencing with Section 1180) of Chapter 4, Title 4, Part 4, Division 2 of the Civil Code.

§ 1452. Official seals

A seal is presumed to be genuine and its use authorized if it purports to be the seal of:

(a) The United States or a department, agency, or public employee of the United States.

(b) A public entity in the United States or a department, agency, or public employee of such public entity.

(c) A nation recognized by the executive power of the United States or a department, agency, or officer of such nation.

(d) A public entity in a nation recognized by the executive power of the United States or a department, agency, or officer of such public entity.

(e) A court of admiralty or maritime jurisdiction.

(f) A notary public within any state of the United States.

§ 1453. Domestic official signatures

A signature is presumed to be genuine and authorized if it purports to be the signature, affixed in his official capacity, of:

(a) A public employee of the United States.

(b) A public employee of any public entity in the United States.

(c) A notary public within any state of the United States.

§ 1454. Foreign official signatures

A signature is presumed to be genuine and authorized if it purports to be the signature, affixed in his official capacity, of an officer, or deputy of an officer, of a nation or public entity in a nation recognized by the executive power of the United States and the writing to which the signature is affixed is accompanied by a final statement certifying the genuineness of the signature and the official position of (a) the person who executed the writing or (b) any foreign official who has certified either the genuineness of the signature and official position of

the person executing the writing or the genuineness of the signature
and official position of another foreign official who has executed a
similar certificate in a chain of such certificates beginning with a
certificate of the genuineness of the signature and official position of
the person executing the writing. The final statement may be made
only by a secretary of an embassy or legation, consul general, consul,
vice consul, consular agent, or other officer in the foreign service of the
United States stationed in the nation, authenticated by the seal of his
office.

CHAPTER 2. SECONDARY EVIDENCE OF WRITINGS

ARTICLE 1. BEST EVIDENCE RULE

§ 1500. The best evidence rule

Except as otherwise provided by statute, no evidence other than the
original of a writing is admissible to prove the content of a writing.
This section shall be known and may be cited as the best evidence rule.

§ 1500.5 Printed representation of computer information or computer program used by or stored on computer or computer readable storage media; admissibility of evidence; presumption; burden of proof

Notwithstanding the provisions of Section 1500, a printed representation of computer information or a computer program which is being
used by or stored on a computer or computer readable storage media
shall be admissible to prove the existence and content of the computer
information or computer program.

Computer recorded information or computer programs, or copies of
computer recorded information or computer programs, shall not be
rendered inadmissible by the best evidence rule. Printed representations of computer information and computer programs will be presumed to be accurate representations of the computer information or
computer programs that they purport to represent. This presumption,
however, will be a presumption affecting the burden of producing
evidence only. If any party to a judicial proceeding introduces evidence
that such a printed representation is inaccurate or unreliable, the party
introducing it into evidence will have the burden of proving, by a
preponderance of evidence, that the printed representation is the best
available evidence of the existence and content of the computer information or computer programs that it purports to represent.

§ 1501. Copy of lost or destroyed writing

A copy of a writing is not made inadmissible by the best evidence rule if the writing is lost or has been destroyed without fraudulent intent on the part of the proponent of the evidence.

§ 1502. Copy of unavailable writing

A copy of a writing is not made inadmissible by the best evidence rule if the writing was not reasonably procurable by the proponent by use of the court's process or by other available means.

§ 1503. Copy of writing under control of opponent

(a) A copy of a writing is not made inadmissible by the best evidence rule if, at a time when the writing was under the control of the opponent, the opponent was expressly or impliedly notified, by the pleadings or otherwise, that the writing would be needed at the hearing, and on request at the hearing the opponent has failed to produce the writing. In a criminal action, the request at the hearing to produce the writing may not be made in the presence of the jury.

(b) Though a writing requested by one party is produced by another, and is thereupon inspected by the party calling for it, the party calling for the writing is not obliged to introduce it as evidence in the action.

§ 1504. Copy of collateral writing

A copy of a writing is not made inadmissible by the best evidence rule if the writing is not closely related to the controlling issues and it would be inexpedient to require its production.

§ 1505. Other secondary evidence of writings described in Sections 1501 to 1504

If the proponent does not have in his possession or under his control a copy of a writing described in Section 1501, 1502, 1503, or 1504, other secondary evidence of the content of the writing is not made inadmissible by the best evidence rule. This section does not apply to a writing that is also described in Section 1506 or 1507.

§ 1506. Copy of public writing

A copy of a writing is not made inadmissible by the best evidence rule if the writing is a record or other writing that is in the custody of a public entity.

§ 1507. Copy of recorded writing

A copy of a writing is not made inadmissible by the best evidence rule if the writing has been recorded in the public records and the record or an attested or a certified copy thereof is made evidence of the writing by statute.

§ 1508. Other secondary evidence of writings described in Sections 1506 and 1507

If the proponent does not have in his possession a copy of a writing described in Section 1506 or 1507 and could not in the exercise of reasonable diligence have obtained a copy, other secondary evidence of the content of the writing is not made inadmissible by the best evidence rule.

§ 1509. Voluminous writings

Secondary evidence, whether written or oral, of the content of a writing is not made inadmissible by the best evidence rule if the writing consists of numerous accounts or other writings that cannot be examined in court without great loss of time, and the evidence sought from them is only the general result of the whole; but the court in its discretion may require that such accounts or other writings be produced for inspection by the adverse party.

§ 1510. Copy of writing produced at the hearing

A copy of a writing is not made inadmissible by the best evidence rule if the writing has been produced at the hearing and made available for inspection by the adverse party.

§ 1511. Duplicates; admissibility

A duplicate is admissible to the same extent as an original unless (a) a genuine question is raised as to the authenticity of the original or (b) in the circumstances it would be unfair to admit the duplicate in lieu of the original.

ARTICLE 2. OFFICIAL WRITINGS AND RECORDED WRITINGS

§ 1530. Copy of writing in official custody

(a) A purported copy of a writing in the custody of a public entity, or of an entry in such a writing, is prima facie evidence of the existence and content of such writing or entry if:

(1) The copy purports to be published by the authority of the nation or state, or public entity therein in which the writing is kept;

(2) The office in which the writing is kept is within the United States or within the Panama Canal Zone, the Trust Territory of the Pacific Islands, or the Ryukyu Islands, and the copy is attested or certified as a correct copy of the writing or entry by a public employee, or a deputy of a public employee, having the legal custody of the writing; or

(3) The office in which the writing is kept is not within the United States or any other place described in paragraph (2) and the copy is attested as a correct copy of the writing or entry by a person having authority to make attestation. The attestation must be accompanied by a final statement certifying the genuineness of the signature and the

official position of (i) the person who attested the copy as a correct copy or (ii) any foreign official who has certified either the genuineness of the signature and official position of the person attesting the copy or the genuineness of the signature and official position of another foreign official who has executed a similar certificate in a chain of such certificates beginning with a certificate of the genuineness of the signature and official position of the person attesting the copy. Except as provided in the next sentence, the final statement may be made only by a secretary of an embassy or legation, consul general, consul, vice consul, or consular agent of the United States, or a diplomatic or consular official of the foreign country assigned or accredited to the United States. Prior to January 1, 1971, the final statement may also be made by a secretary of an embassy or legation, consul general, consul, vice consul, consular agent, or other officer in the foreign service of the United States stationed in the nation in which the writing is kept, authenticated by the seal of his office. If reasonable opportunity has been given to all parties to investigate the authenticity and accuracy of the documents, the court may, for good cause shown, (i) admit an attested copy without the final statement or (ii) permit the writing or entry in foreign custody to be evidenced by an attested summary with or without a final statement.

(b) The presumptions established by this section are presumptions affecting the burden of producing evidence.

§ 1531. Certification of copy for evidence

For the purpose of evidence, whenever a copy of a writing is attested or certified, the attestation or certificate must state in substance that the copy is a correct copy of the original, or of a specified part thereof, as the case may be.

§ 1532. Official record of recorded writing

(a) The official record of a writing is prima facie evidence of the existence and content of the original recorded writing if:

(1) The record is in fact a record of an office of a public entity; and

(2) A statute authorized such a writing to be recorded in that office.

(b) The presumption established by this section is a presumption affecting the burden of producing evidence.

ARTICLE 3. PHOTOGRAPHIC COPIES OF WRITINGS

§ 1550. Photographic copies made as business records

A photostatic, microfilm, microcard, miniature photographic or other photographic copy or reproduction, or an enlargement thereof, of a writing is as admissible as the writing itself if such copy or reproduction was made and preserved as a part of the records of a business (as defined by Section 1270) in the regular course of such business. The introduction of such copy, reproduction, or enlargement does not preclude admission of the original writing if it is still in existence.

§ 1551. Photographic copies where original destroyed or lost

A print, whether enlarged or not, from a photographic film (including a photographic plate, microphotographic film, photostatic negative, or similar reproduction) of an original writing destroyed or lost after such film was taken or a reproduction from an electronic recording of video images on magnetic surfaces is admissible as the original writing itself if, at the time of the taking of such film or electronic recording, the person under whose direction and control it was taken attached thereto, or to the sealed container in which it was placed and has been kept, or incorporated in the film or electronic recording, a certification complying with the provisions of Section 1531 and stating the date on which, and the fact that, it was so taken under his direction and control.

ARTICLE 4.   PRODUCTION OF BUSINESS RECORDS

§ 1560.   Compliance with subpoena duces tecum for business records

(a) As used in this article:

(1) "Business" includes every kind of business described in Section 1270.

(2) "Record" includes every kind of record maintained by such a business.

(b) Except as provided in Section 1564, when a subpoena duces tecum is served upon the custodian of records or other qualified witness of a business in an action in which the business is neither a party nor the place where any cause of action is alleged to have arisen, and the subpoena requires the production of all or any part of the records of the business, it is sufficient compliance therewith if the custodian or other qualified witness, within five days after the receipt of the subpoena in any criminal action or within the time agreed upon by the party who served the subpoena and the custodian or other qualified witness, or within 15 days after the receipt of the subpoena in any civil action or within the time agreed upon by the party who served the subpoena and the custodian or other qualified witness, delivers by mail or otherwise a true, legible, and durable copy of all the records described in the subpoena to the clerk of court or to the judge if there be no clerk or to such other person as described in subdivision (a) of Section 2018 of the Code of Civil Procedure, together with the affidavit described in Section 1561.

(c) The copy of the records shall be separately enclosed in an inner envelope or wrapper, sealed, with the title and number of the action, name of witness, and date of subpoena clearly inscribed thereon; the sealed envelope or wrapper shall then be enclosed in an outer envelope or wrapper, sealed, and directed as follows:

(1) If the subpoena directs attendance in court, to the clerk of such court, or to the judge thereof if there be no clerk.

(2) If the subpoena directs attendance at a deposition, to the officer before whom the deposition is to be taken, at the place designated in

the subpoena for the taking of the deposition or at the officer's place of business.

(3) In other cases, to the officer, body, or tribunal conducting the hearing, at a like address.

(d) Unless the parties to the proceeding otherwise agree, or unless the sealed envelope or wrapper is returned to a witness who is to appear personally, the copy of the records shall remain sealed and shall be opened only at the time of trial, deposition, or other hearing, upon the direction of the judge, officer, body, or tribunal conducting the proceeding, in the presence of all parties who have appeared in person or by counsel at the trial, deposition, or hearing. Records which are original documents and which are not introduced in evidence or required as part of the record shall be returned to the person or entity from whom received. Records which are copies may be destroyed.

(e) As an alternative to the procedures described in subdivisions (b), (c), and (d), the subpoenaing party may direct the witness to make the records available for inspection or copying by the party's attorney or the attorney's representative at the witness' business address under reasonable conditions during normal business hours. It shall be the responsibility of the attorney's representative to deliver any copy of the records as directed in the subpoena.

§ 1561. Affidavit accompanying records

(a) The records shall be accompanied by the affidavit of the custodian or other qualified witness, stating in substance each of the following:

(1) The affiant is the duly authorized custodian of the records or other qualified witness and has authority to certify the records.

(2) The copy is a true copy of all the records described in the subpoena.

(3) The records were prepared by the personnel of the business in the ordinary course of business at or near the time of the act, condition, or event.

(4) The records described in the subpoena duces tecum were delivered to the attorney or his or her representative for copying at the custodian's or witness' place of business, pursuant to subdivision (e) of Section 1560 of the Evidence Code.

(b) If the business has none of the records described, or only part thereof, the custodian or other qualified witness shall so state in the affidavit, and deliver the affidavit and such records as are available in the manner provided in Section 1560.

(c) Where the records described in the subpoena were delivered to the attorney or his or her representative for copying at the custodian's or witness' place of business, in lieu of the affidavit required by subdivision (a), the records shall be accompanied by an affidavit by the attorney or his or her representative stating that the copy is a true copy of all the records delivered to the attorney or his or her representative for copying.

§ 1562. Admissibility of affidavit and copy of records

The copy of the records is admissible in evidence to the same extent as though the original thereof were offered and the custodian had been present and testified to the matters stated in the affidavit. The affidavit is admissible as evidence of the matters stated therein pursuant to Section 1561 and the matters so stated are presumed true. When more than one person has knowledge of the facts, more than one affidavit may be made. The presumption established by this section is a presumption affecting the burden of producing evidence.

§ 1563. One witness and mileage fee

[Omitted]

§ 1564. Personal attendance of custodian and production of original records

The personal attendance of the custodian or other qualified witness and the production of the original records is not required unless, at the discretion of the requesting party, the subpoena duces tecum contains a clause which reads:

"The personal attendance of the custodian or other qualified witness and the production of the original records are required by this subpoena. The procedure authorized pursuant to subdivision (b) of Section 1560, and Sections 1561 and 1562, of the Evidence Code will not be deemed sufficient compliance with this subpoena."

Original records produced pursuant to this section may be inspected or copied by the subpoenaing attorney or his or her representative at the address of the witness. The only fee for such copying shall be fifteen dollars ($15), except for the retrieval of records stored on microfilm which may be charged at the rate specified in paragraph (1) of subdivision (b) of Section 1563.

§ 1565. Service of more than one subpoena duces tecum

If more than one subpoena duces tecum is served upon the custodian of records or other qualified witness and the personal attendance of the custodian or other qualified witness is required pursuant to Section 1564, the witness shall be deemed to be the witness of the party serving the first such subpoena duces tecum.

§ 1566. Applicability of article

This article applies in any proceeding in which testimony can be compelled.

CHAPTER 3. OFFICIAL WRITINGS AFFECTING PROPERTY

§ 1600. Record of document affecting property interest

(a) The record of an instrument or other document purporting to establish or affect an interest in property is prima facie evidence of the existence and content of the original recorded document and its execution and delivery by each person by whom it purports to have been executed if:

(1) The record is in fact a record of an office of a public entity; and

(2) A statute authorized such a document to be recorded in that office.

(b) The presumption established by this section is a presumption affecting the burden of proof.

§ 1601. **Proof of content of lost official record affecting property**

(a) Subject to subdivisions (b) and (c), when in any action it is desired to prove the contents of the official record of any writing lost or destroyed by conflagration or other public calamity, after proof of such loss or destruction, the following may, without further proof, be admitted in evidence to prove the contents of such record:

(1) Any abstract of title made and issued and certified as correct prior to such loss or destruction, and purporting to have been prepared and made in the ordinary course of business by any person engaged in the business of preparing and making abstracts of title prior to such loss or destruction; or

(2) Any abstract of title, or of any instrument affecting title, made, issued, and certified as correct by any person engaged in the business of insuring titles or issuing abstracts of title to real estate, whether the same was made, issued, or certified before or after such loss or destruction and whether the same was made from the original records or from abstract and notes, or either, taken from such records in the preparation and upkeeping of its plant in the ordinary course of its business.

(b) No proof of the loss of the original writing is required other than the fact that the original is not known to the party desiring to prove its contents to be in existence.

(c) Any party desiring to use evidence admissible under this section shall give reasonable notice in writing to all other parties to the action who have appeared therein, of his intention to use such evidence at the trial of the action, and shall give all such other parties a reasonable opportunity to inspect the evidence, and also the abstracts, memoranda, or notes from which it was compiled, and to take copies thereof.

§ 1602. **Repealed by Stats.1967, c. 650, § 10**

§ 1603. **Deed by officer in pursuance of court process**

A deed of conveyance of real property, purporting to have been executed by a proper officer in pursuance of legal process of any of the courts of record of this state, acknowledged and recorded in the office of the recorder of the county wherein the real property therein described is situated, or the record of such deed, or a certified copy of such record, is prima facie evidence that the property or interest therein described was thereby conveyed to the grantee named in such deed. The presumption established by this section is a presumption affecting the burden of proof.

§ 1604. Certificate of purchase or of location of lands

A certificate of purchase, or of location, of any lands in this state, issued or made in pursuance of any law of the United States or of this state, is prima facie evidence that the holder or assignee of such certificate is the owner of the land described therein; but this evidence may be overcome by proof that, at the time of the location, or time of filing a preemption claim on which the certificate may have been issued, the land was in the adverse possession of the adverse party, or those under whom he claims, or that the adverse party is holding the land for mining purposes.

§ 1605. Authenticated Spanish title records

Duplicate copies and authenticated translations of original Spanish title papers relating to land claims in this state, derived from the Spanish or Mexican governments, prepared under the supervision of the Keeper of Archives, authenticated by the Surveyor-General or his successor and by the Keeper of Archives, and filed with a county recorder, in accordance with Chapter 281 of the Statutes of 1865–66, are admissible as evidence with like force and effect as the originals and without proving the execution of such originals.

INDEX

References are to Pages

[1]

†